THE COMPLETE BOOK OF ROD BUILDING AND TACKLE MAKING

C. BOYD PFEIFFER

Guilford, Connecticut
An imprint of Globe Pequot Press

TO BRENDA

Lyons Press is an imprint of Globe Pequot Press.

Project editor: David Legere
Text design: Sheryl P. Kober
Layout artist: Sue Murray

Library of Congress Cataloging-in-Publication data is available on file.

ISBN 978-0-7627-7347-3

Printed in the United States of America
10 9 8 7 6 5 4 3 2 1

CONTENTS

NOTE TO THE READER

I have made every effort to describe rod-building and lure-making methods that are easy and safe. Familiarity with tools is important in any craft, no less so in making fishing tackle. When making some tackle—such as molding lead sinkers, bucktails, tin squids, and soft plastic lures—improper techniques may prove to be dangerous. The methods of tackle building that I describe are safe when the directions are followed. When and where necessary, I warn readers of any possible dangers. **However, neither the author nor the publisher can assume responsibility for any damages or injuries that may result from the construction, molding, repair, building, creating, or formation of rods, lures, or other tackle described in this book, or from careless or improper procedures or use of products or tools.**

This book on rod building and lure making is as complete as I can make it. I have tried to include all the types of tackle that can easily be made in any home workshop. Obviously there may be some special methods of tackle making and even some special tackle items with which I am not familiar. While I am unable to enter into extensive correspondence with readers, I would be delighted to hear of new and different tackle items or tackle-making methods. Readers can contact me through the publisher.

ACKNOWLEDGMENTS

Books are only rarely the work of a single mind. This book—both the first edition, *Tackle Craft,* the subsequent edition, *Modern Tackle Craft* in hardback, *The Complete Book of Tackle Making* in soft cover, and this edition *The Complete Book of Rod Building and Tackle Making*—is no exception.

For more than sixty years I have been experimenting with making fishing tackle and at various times have made and used all the types of gear mentioned in this book.

However, along the way I have picked others' brains, and I have constantly learned of new methods, tricks, tips, and types of tackle that can be built by the home craftsman. Fortunately for the rod builder and lure maker, more and more information on these subjects is increasingly available. Magazine articles, the magazine *RodMaker,* books, pamphlets, booklets, other printed information, shows, The International Custom Rod Building Exposition (held in North Carolina, each February), films, DVDs, and tips on the television fishing shows have all been helpful. For this, a general debt of gratitude is owed and gratefully acknowledged.

Many companies, and individuals in those companies, have helped immensely in this, my previous tackle-making books, and other projects. Thus, many thanks go to the following:

Tom Kirkman, who has always made me feel welcome at his International Custom Rod Building Exposition. He has shared his knowledge, ideas, tips, and has been forthright with his magazine (*RodMaker*) and the many articles and information that abound within its six issues per year. He has also kindly loaned photographs of rod-making techniques for this book, all credited on the appropriate photos and pages. I am deeply appreciative of his help and friendship.

Al Jackson has been unstinting in his aid and help to me over the years. Without Al Jackson and his consistent and constant help, this book and previous efforts would have been far poorer. Al has been the man behind the rod design for many familiar companies, and he has been responsible for many of the designs, innovations, and efforts to make a better rod and a better blank in this and other countries. I owe a lot to Al for his friendship and his constant efforts to help me with this work and to educate me about rod building.

Thanks to Bill Stevens of Swampland Rods for his friendship, constant encouragement, help, and advice with various aspects of rod-building methods and techniques.

I'm grateful to Billy Vivona of North East Rod Builders for his tips and techniques for working with foam and adding trim rings, inlays, and other designs to EVA grip materials. Appreciation also goes to Billy for his critical read and feedback of the section in this book on his ideas on foam handle designs.

Thank you to Roger Seiders of Flex Coat for his inside information on rod wrap finishes (Flex Coat) and for his constant help with rod-building ideas. Appreciation also goes to Roger for his permission to use charts and material from his catalogs and publications, here credited in this book.

Kevin Knox helped me in my understanding of the application of abalone to rods, and provided photos.

Ken and Lana Preston shared with me their work in pushing the envelope by using colored beads as part of decorative designs on rod blanks, and have advanced my knowledge of this art form.

Vikki and Mike Pedersen of Riley Rods helped in my understanding of foam core grips with carbon skins to make shaped and various-sized handles for rods. I also appreciate their critical reading of the section on making foam core and carbon skin rod grips.

Thanks to Vic Cutter of PacBay for his help with PacBay products and for understanding tackle parts and guides in general.

I'm grateful to Jim Ising of Fuji for his help in learning more about guide ring design and Fuji products.

Much thanks is due to Mary Jane Williamson of the American Sportfishing Association for her help in updating and revising the section in appendix B "Sales of Tackle."

Jack Goellner, retired editor for Johns Hopkins University Press, has given me sage advice on editing, publishing, and the publishing business.

Thank you to Ande for the use of knot illustrations in the book, and to AFTCO Manufacturing Company and Bill Shedd for the loan of materials for photos.

B. D. Class Enterprises provided materials used for photos.

Bead Chain Tackle and Pete Renkert gave permission to use the size charts of their products.

Bellinger Reel Seats loaned materials for photos.

Berkley and Company and Mike Fine gave permission to use their line art on knots, snells, and terminal tackle.

DNY Marketing loaned materials and sizing charts for their products.

Do-It and Jerry Bond loaned materials and gave permission to use certain charts.

Stren Line allowed for the use of their charts on knots and snells.

Environmental Technology, Ed LaFley, and CEO David Fonsen provided information on their casting resins and epoxies for making offshore trolling lures, and for samples used for photography.

The Gaines Company and Tom Eggler provided for materials used for photos.

Gamakatsu provided sizing charts of their hooks.

Thank you to Gudebrod (Wel-Tec, LLC) and David LeGrande for materials for photos and permission to use size charts of their products.

Hilts Molds and Roy Hilts loaned materials and gave permission to use certain charts.

Lakeland gave permission to use size charts of their lure components.

Lamiglas provided information and blanks for photo purposes and guide-spacing charts.

Mason Tackle Company and Chip Powell gave materials and permission to use some sizing charts.

M-F Manufacturing and Bob Maserang provided materials used for photos.

Perfection Tip loaned materials and gave permission to use size charts of their products.

Mildrum Manufacturing Company and Ted Benson loaned guides used for some photos.

Thanks to O. Mustad and Son, USA, for hooks for photos and hook-size charts.

St. Croix and Jeff Schluter provided materials used for photos and permissions for guide-spacing charts for their rod blanks.

Sevenstrand Tackle Corporation and Bill Goodman gave permission to use artwork on the proper crimping of leader sleeves.

Thanks to Tri-Peek International for photo samples, information on their Easy Weld micro flame torch, and products for welding.

VMC provided sizing charts for their hooks.

Thank you to the Worth Company and David Worth for materials for photos and permission to use size charts of their lure components.

The Wright and McGill Company and Gene Wilson gave permission to use size charts of their hooks.

Special thanks must be singled out for the late Cam Clark, Roy Hilts, and Jerry Bond. Cam Clark, the editor of *RodCrafters,* the magazine of the organization started by Dale Clemens, was gracious in his cooperation, friendship, and help—providing me with photo models of the many decorative wraps and weaves that he has made on rods, and which served as samples for his courses on rod-building. For the 1993 edition of this book he also had my great appreciation. He was an early pioneer in the art of weaving.

Jerry Bond of Do-It and Roy Hilts of Hilts Molds rendered yeoman service by reading the chapter on molding bucktails. Both were generous in their kind comments and constructive criticism. I thank them for the time they took for this time-consuming task.

In addition, good friends have served for decades as sounding boards for my ideas and theories, sharing freely their ideas and constructive criticisms, suggestions, and comments. Thus, special thanks for the friendship and help over the years go to Chuck Edghill, Norm Bartlett, Lefty Kreh, Ed Russell, the late Joe Zimmer, Bill May, Jim Heim, and others. Joe Zimmer was particularly helpful with his ideas on rod design and building of big-game offshore rods, an area of his expertise and fishing interest. In addition, Tony Tochterman and his wife Dee of Tochterman's Tackle Shop, Baltimore, Maryland (410-327-6942) have always been extremely helpful in answering questions and giving me the straight skinny on tackle trends as they see them in their sales of fishing tackle and fishing tackle component parts.

My late wife Jackie deserves special mention. When *Tackle Craft* was completed (1974), she thought that she had seen the end of books from me and that her days of retyping my chicken scratches were over. It was five books and a lot of her typing and work later before we bought a computer, retiring her from her role as a typist of books, magazine articles, brochures, and from her other efforts—twenty-one years of making my bad-looking stuff look good. That she is not here to receive these thanks is unfortunate. She was both a critic and inspiration.

I met my present wife Brenda several years after I was widowed and she was divorced. With this book and with other books, articles, columns, and other writing, she has always served as a valued sounding board and constructive critic. Her thoughts on my writing and her comments have always been welcome. I always appreciate her thoughtful comments on ways that I can improve my work. I value her as a person, as my wife, and as a constructive critic of this and other writing efforts.

My thanks also to my deceased father and mother, who, while not anglers, instilled early in me a love for the outdoors and encouraged me to seek my own path in life.

For the original and 1993 edition, Nick Lyons and the staff at the Lyons Press deserve special thanks and recognition for taking on such a monumental task, sticking with it—and me—while I struggled to bring this monster into being. Currently, I thank Globe Pequot, editor Steve Culpepper, editor Allen Jones (especially Allen Jones!), and others on the staff for their help in dealing with the updated and totally revised edition—under a new name—that you hold in your hands. The manuscript and photo package—as that for the original version of the book—grew far larger than any of us anticipated, and far larger than *Tackle Craft* and the earlier 1993 versions *Modern Tackle Craft* and *The Complete Book of Tackle Making.* Some medical problems unnecessarily delayed earlier completion of this work and revision. For that I thank Allen Jones, Steve Culpepper, and others involved with the project for their forbearance and patience.

—C. Boyd Pfeiffer

INTRODUCTION

There are four good reasons for making your own tackle. It is a fun hobby, it can save you money over the cost of commercially available equipment, it allows you to make custom tackle that is unavailable elsewhere, and it helps you to become a better angler. That last reason deserves some explaining. I've found, as have others, that by making your own tackle you understand it better—understand what it takes to make an effective rod, lure, or tackle accessory. It also helps that you have spent only a fraction of the cost of equivalent commercial gear. Not counting the fun it is to make things, lures are cheaper, and rods are less expensive while also being designed for a specific purpose. As a result you begin to fish deeper, cast into more difficult structure, fish the "impossible" places. Yes, you do lose some of your homemade lures, but as a result of fishing where others won't, you also catch more and bigger fish and catch them more often.

Tackle crafting can be as comprehensive as you want; it can be very casual or involve only one type of lure or tackle part. It can be simple—with little outlay of money and minimal expenditure of time—or it can be as complex, expansive, and expensive as you wish.

And there never seems to be enough written on the subject—either in books or magazine articles. My books *Tackle Craft* (1974) and *Modern Tackle Craft* (1993) along with *The Complete Book of Tackle Making* (1999), of which this is an updated, expanded, and completely rewritten version, were the only ones at the time covering both lures and rods. A similar book of the same time period, *Fiberglass Rod Making* by Dale Clemens, addressed rod making but not any aspects of lure making or making tackle accessories such as nets or gaffs.

Many books on any of these crafts are out of date or out of print or deal only with rods or lures—not both. In contrast you can find a couple dozen books on fly tying for every book on some form of tackle building. Flies, bass bugs, and similar lures tied by means of standard fly-tying methods and using a fly-tying vise and tools will not be dealt with here. Excellent publications on these subjects (some of them mine, such as *Simple Flies, Tying Terrestrials, Bug Making, The Complete Photo Guide to Fly Tying, Shad Fishing, Tying Trout Flies,* and *Tying Warmwater Flies*) would make any such addition here superfluous.

Perhaps you have considered making your own lures and rods in the past but never actually tried it. Often those who have yet to try tackle making think it will take too much skill or too many tools or be too time-consuming.

Nothing is further from the truth. With only two pairs of pliers (which you may already have), you can make any of the standard spinner designs on the market, in addition to originating new designs. Without any tools at all, you can wrap a rod. The standard rod-wrapping support and thread-tension device is nice but not absolutely necessary. You can make a one-time-use rod-wrapping tool with a cardboard box, a teacup, and a telephone book.

And you can make any soft-plastic lure with only the molds required. If desired you can make molds for soft plastics from a worm model and plaster of Paris. Other simple tools found on any home workbench allow you to assemble spoons and make wire rigs and spreaders, wood plugs (carve them with a pocketknife), and spinnerbaits and buzzbaits. With the proper molds and melting pots, it is easy to make any type of sinker or bucktail.

Note that while several chapters in this book cover tools, each chapter also includes a listing of both the basic tool needs and additional tools that might be helpful.

Making tackle is fun. It is associated with fishing and allows all of us to remain active in our sport, even when seasons or conditions don't allow getting on the water. It is a great wintertime hobby that pays dividends once fishing season opens and you are back on the water.

The degree of skill required for making fishing tackle varies with the type of tackle being made and the degree of precision desired in the lure or rod. I've seen some rods and lures that are truly works of art and as fine examples of the craftsman's skill as can be found. I've also seen lures and rods that looked like rejects after the last day of a flea market. What both types have in common is that they catch fish. The slight flaw in the paint job on a wood plug, the molding error in a soft-plastic lure, the imperfect tail tied on a bucktail, or the badly wrapped guide on a rod might affect how you or others feel about the tackle; it won't likely affect the tackle's performance or the number of fish you catch.

This is not to endorse sloppy workmanship but only to suggest that while your skills and results in making tackle will improve over time, the first lure, rod, or tackle accessory you make will no doubt work well enough to help you catch fish.

Making tackle also saves you money. Just how much is difficult to say, but some ideas are suggested in each chapter. For example, if you mold sinkers from lead wheel weights that you get for free from a service station, the only cost is for the mold, which is quickly amortized. (*Note:* Pure lead is best, but alloyed wheel weights will work.) Carving wood plugs often allows you to make lures that are one-tenth or less the cost of store lures—the only expense is in the hardware and paint. Assembly is all that is required for making spinners and some types of spinnerbaits and buzzbaits. Expensive offshore lures are easy to make if you invest a little time and imagination to develop the right molds and inserts for these plastic cast or epoxy big-game lures.

Basic but highly sensitive and effective fishing rods can be built at a low cost compared to commercially equivalent models, and all tackle can be customized as you wish. You can design your own lures; try different plugs, spinners and spoons; and make rods designed with complex thread wraps or with different guide and handle arrangements.

One point about this book: It does not take each model, design, and shape of lure or rod in turn and give specific instructions and blueprints for making that particular size, design, and shape of lure or rod. It does provide extensive and detailed information on many methods of designing, making, and modifying lures and rods. Most chapters list variations of lures that can be made following the basic instructions outlined in that chapter. Methods of making some lure types that are not yet commercially available are also described. Thus this book is designed to expand your thinking, open your imagination, and teach you basic tackle-building skills.

This book has some purposeful repetition. For example, tools and how to make some tools are covered in the first two chapters. But each chapter on a specific lure or rod construction method also covers tools. Thus each chapter stands alone—or almost alone—to save you from repeatedly having to refer to other chapters for more information.

Although this book has a beginning, middle, and end, there is no end to tackle building. At one point in writing this book, I was talking to Dick French of Dale Clemens Custom Tackle and learned of a new computer program that allows you to preplan weaving thread in decorative rod wraps. You can draw the design on a computer screen and print it out, and the program will plan the thread wraps for the diameter of the rod, even adjusting as necessary if you decide to change thread size.

The craft company Aleene's has introduced a granular plastic material that can be heated in boiling water and then shaped into any design desired. It comes in many colors and is available at craft and hobby stores. To date, I haven't yet figured out how to use this for making lures, but something will occur to me, or to someone else. A similar product is available in sheet form, lending itself to the idea of making spoons or other impressed flat-lure shapes.

In recent years ways to use thin sheets of abalone, cut cork rings, mix colors of foam handle materials, marbleize reel seats, make shaped foam grips, and use beads in decorative wraps have all been figured out by creative rod builders. I am not advocating making lures or rods to sell, but this is a natural extension for some rod-building and lure-making fishermen. Tackle making should be fun, and the complexities of operating a successful tackle business are too extensive to cover here. If you're contemplating this, be sure to read appendix B. This appendix touches on the business, legal, and governmental aspects of turning a hobby into a small business.

This book is meant to increase your personal fishing and fishing-related pleasure. I hope you will get as much enjoyment out of reading and learning from *The Complete Book of Rod Building and Tackle Making* as I've had in preparing it. More important, I hope you have as much fun making and experimenting with your own fishing tackle as I have had in making mine.

1
Tools and Materials

Introduction • Safety Equipment • Bench or Worktable • Vise • Lighting • Hammers • Handsaws • Electric Saws • Drills • Drill Presses • Twist Drill Bits • Pliers • Leader-Crimping Pliers • Metal Snips • Files • Reamers • Soldering Iron • Pop-Style Riveter • Electric Grinder • Electric Sander • Lathe • Wire Formers • Dividers • Rule • Anvil • Gate Cutter • Fly-Tying Tools • Rod-Building Tools • Curing Motor • Handle Seater • Tapered Reamer • Tip-Top Gauge • Cork and Foam Cutters • Rod-Wrapping Tools • Thread Tension Devices • Burnisher • Torch • Alcohol Lamp • Scalpel • Diamond Wrap Tools • Masking Tape • Safety Equipment

INTRODUCTION

Proper tools are the secret to doing any job well. A repairman who comes to your house to fix a dishwasher, TV, oven, or hot water heater always has a well-equipped toolbox. A carpenter or cabinetmaker could not begin constructing anything without the proper woodworking tools. By the same token, the tackle tinkerer must have the proper tools to construct the many types of fishing tackle. Fortunately the basic tools needed for making most fishing tackle are not expensive or hard to get. In all likelihood you already have a number of the required tools or can improvise others.

Many can be made, as outlined in chapter 2. And it is important to realize early on that much tackle crafting requires a minimum of tools, materials, and skills.

It is not necessary to collect or buy all the tools listed before you begin making fishing tackle and lures. You may be interested only in two or three types of lures or accessories and will never need the tools required for making other lures. Each chapter lists both the minimally required tools and those tools that are not required but make the job easier—or perhaps are required for major jobs or larger scale operations.

If you plan to make all the tackle covered in this book, you will ultimately need or want most or all the *basic* tools listed. You may in time wish to get some of the optional or extra tools to make some tasks easier or less time-consuming. In all cases you *must* have and use the basic safety equipment listed for each type of tackle.

Otherwise look at the materials list at the beginning of each chapter for suggestions on required tools before heading to the tackle shop or hardware store. Try where possible to substitute the same or similar tools that you may already have on hand.

SAFETY EQUIPMENT

Minimal safety equipment is needed for most tackle-crafting tasks. Following are some items you should consider:

- *Goggles.* Even if you wear glasses (which provide some protection), goggles are always helpful. They are a must when doing tasks that could impact your eyes or face. For example, when cutting wire to make rigs and jigs for fishing, a cut end of wire can fly off wildly. Goggles are a must for this to prevent the possibility of eye injury. Good workshop goggles are available at any hardware store or from major suppliers such as Home Depot and Lowe's. Get a pair and wear them anytime there is a chance of eye injury.

- *Gloves.* Heavy workbench gloves come in handy when you're handling items that might injure your hands or might be too hot to hold. Gloves are good for working with wire, cutting out plug bodies, sawing glass or graphite rod blanks, or hammering out spoon and lure bodies from metal. They are also important when handling hot items—from ladles and pots of lead for making sinkers and lead lures to pans of melted plastic for making soft-plastic lures such as worms and crayfish.

- *Apron.* Wearing an apron helps prevent damage to your regular clothing from paint spills, accidental cuts and scrapes, or excessive wear from repeated tool use.

- *Face mask or breathing mask.* For chores such as sanding cork or grinding carbon materials, a breathing mask is a must. If you are dealing with paint or chemical fumes on a regular basis or at any time in an enclosed area, you will need an appropriate mask that protects against the intake of toxic fumes.

BENCH OR WORKTABLE

You will need a place to work and to hold tools, materials, and finished products. This can be as simple as a small TV tray to hold the parts and materials for making a few spinners. However, you will want a sturdy workshop bench for sawing out wood-plug bodies, making gaffs, and wrapping rods. When molding plastic lures (worms), lead sinkers, lead bucktails, jig heads, tin squids, and the like, you may have to work in the kitchen, where you will have access to heat for melting materials and to ventilation for dissipating any resulting fumes. In other cases you may want to work on a camp stove on an outdoor picnic table for the same purposes. A small square or rectangle of thin plywood, Masonite, scrap kitchen countertop material (laminate), aluminum sheeting, or large kitchen hot pad will be necessary to catch spilled metal or plastic, saving the kitchen counter or picnic table from possible scarring.

If your tackle-making efforts are unwelcome in the kitchen or at the picnic table, there are several other options. One is to use a propane torch or stove in your workshop. Another is to use a hot plate in your workshop to melt the soft plastic used in making worms and grubs. Or you might get a self-contained electric heater and melting pot for melting the lead for bucktail and sinker molding. A *sturdy* workplace is a must for melting lead. If you use a heavy furnace that must be bolted down for security and safety, you will not be able to work with a sheet of plywood over the kitchen counter.

I use several types of workbenches when making tackle. I have a long, sturdy workbench—8 feet by 3 feet—made from two-by-fours that are upended, through-bolted, and mounted with a heavy machine vise. For heavy work it is as sturdy as a bomb shelter and just about as heavy. Two similar but lighter weight workbenches of equal size flank this central bench. One contains a small, specialized rod-building lathe I use for turning rod handles, rod parts, butt caps, wood plugs, and some metal parts. The other is kept free for any overflow of work from the main bench. This third workbench is also ideal for mounting rod-wrapping tools, fly-tying vises, and similar temporary tools. I also have a completely separate fly-tying table and work area for tying flies. For lead molding I use a small, sturdy workbench where I can bolt down any furnaces and cover the wood top with sheet metal for easy cleanup.

I use yet another, smaller, square workbench as a repository for power tools. These are not all necessary for tackle crafting but are handy at times. They are all bolted down and include a grinder, sander, a small drill press, a small Dremel lathe for turning lures, and a small band saw. Bins underneath this bench hold hand power tools, such as several power drills, a saber saw, a circular saw, a belt sander, and a soldering iron. For some tackle work, such as the maintenance, modification, and repair of reels, I have a separate small workbench (about 6 × 2 feet) in my rod, reel, and lure tackle-storage room. I also have a fly-tying bench that sometimes doubles as a workbench for

A view of the middle section of the author's workbench. Note the perfboard on the back wall to hold tools and the drawers under the workbench for tools and materials. At the far right end of the bench is a small rod-building lathe for turning handles, etc.

making small lures such as spinners and is also used for tying tails on bucktails and jigs and for rigging trolling lures.

Over or near each workbench I mount perfboard (Pegboard is one brand name) for hanging tools, reels, special parts, small power tools, and so on. The variety of styles and lengths of hooks available for this board make it possible to hang almost any tool or part. Both ⅛- and ¼-inch-thick perfboard is available, with the ⅛-inch board sufficient for most tackle and small tool applications.

VISE

A vise is a necessity for holding wood securely in order to cut it to the right sizes and shapes for making plugs, holding sheet metal when making spoons, and clamping materials for similar drilling and cutting operations.

Woodworkers' vises are ideal for holding wood because they have special large, wood-faced jaws that prevent damage to the wood being held. Most mount below or flush with the workbench top. A machinist's vise mounts on top of the bench and has machined steel jaws. Most have a swivel base for turning the vise; others can also be turned at an angle to vertical. Permanently mounted vises are best, but some smaller vises that clamp (like a C-clamp) onto a table or workbench are quite adequate for most tackle crafting.

I like the machinist-style vise. It has more versatility of movement and plenty of clamping power. In most cases, even when working with wood, any scarring that the jaws might cause will be cut or sanded away as you finish a plug body, smooth a spoon-blade blank, or polish other materials. Also, it is easy to make jaw-covering faces of wood, composition material, aluminum, or copper. I like the soft-metal aluminum or copper faces; they can easily be cut and bent to shape and size to fit over the jaws and are easily replaced as desired.

LIGHTING

Proper lighting over any work area is essential. Without it, doing good work is impossible and in some cases even dangerous. If you can't see well, you can't cut or drill well or make good tackle. I like the double fluorescent "shop lights" sold in any hardware store or major outlets such as Walmart, Kmart, Sears, Home Depot, and

Lowe's in 2-, 4-, and 8-foot lengths. I use a bank of 4-foot-length lights.

Fluorescent lights come in a variety of different colors, from cool white to warm-spectrum light. Get the type of light you prefer. I find the cool white to be somewhat harsh, although the warm light may be too warm for some tastes. I like the soft white best. For uniformity of lighting, be sure to use bulbs of the same color tone.

For the best general lighting, mount the main lights over the front edge of the workbench. Use supplemental lighting such as incandescent-bulb swing-arm lights for spotlighting.

On small workshop projects, a small swing-arm or gooseneck lamp with a 60- or 75-watt bulb may be adequate. These corkscrew lights screw into the socket of any lamp base. Today most are fluorescent, and a 20- to 25-watt fluorescent bulb will give you the same light intensity as the 60- to 75-watt incandescent bulbs of the past. Small high-intensity lights are also good for getting a large amount of light into a small area.

HAMMERS

Hammers are not needed for much tackle-craft work. They are needed for hammering out metal to make spoon blades, for getting a hammered finish on a spoon, for any task where you have to use a drift (a punching tool), or for making some of the tools that will be suggested later.

Ball-peen hammers are best for most tackle-craft work; you do not need the claw (to pull nails) found on carpenter's hammers. You can pick a variety of sizes: Ball-peen hammers are rated by the weight of the head, from about 4-ounce through 6-, 8-, 10-, and 12-ounce and heavier sizes. Cross-peen hammers are also useful for making straight marks on metal lures, since they have a wedgelike (chisel) end opposite the hammer face.

If you have a carpenter's hammer, you can certainly make do in most cases. Other types of useful hammers are the soft-face hammers (either plastic or hard rubber or one end of each) and brass-head hammers that are soft enough not to scratch metal surfaces. Both styles are ideal for making spoon blades. A wood mallet also can be used for tackle crafting and can sometimes be used in place of other hammer types.

To maximize striking force when forging spoon blades (hammering them into a concave shape), consider dead-blow hammers. These hammers are made with lead shot in the hollow head to minimize rebound and maximize striking force. They are relatively expensive, however, so be sure you are serious about making your own metal spoons and spinner blades—and making enough of them to amortize the hammer cost—before purchasing one.

HANDSAWS

Although saws are not needed in most tackle crafting, there are some exceptions:

- Cutting wood for carving your own wood plugs. Use a regular crosscut saw (usually you will be cutting across the grain when sawing long lengths of square cross-section material into plug or lathe lengths). Coping saws and keyhole saws also work well.

- Cutting rod blanks when you want to chop a blank at the tip or butt to make a rod of a different action. Use a hacksaw with a very fine blade (32 teeth per inch is best). Often a regular hacksaw is too large and bulky. A small saw that consists only of a handle to hold the blade is best and is easy to handle. Jeweler's saws also work well, since they have very fine teeth and are designed for fine cutting of metal. They work equally well for cutting graphite rod blanks and minimizing splintering. These are more expensive than a regular coping or hacksaw, however, and will not be necessary unless you're doing a lot of metal cutting for lures and metal parts or chopping graphite blanks.

- Cutting metal to fashion spoons, squids, and other similar lures. Use a regular-style hacksaw (with frame) with a metal cutting blade (24 or

Different types of cutting blades used for tackle crafting. The three to the left are hacksaw blades; the one to the right is an X-Acto saw. Fine-tooth blades such as those with 50 teeth per inch (far right) or 32 teeth per inch (second from right) are required for cutting rod blanks.

32 teeth per inch). A jeweler's saw is also excellent for this job.

ELECTRIC SAWS

Electric saws are also helpful for tackle crafting, but unless you are into a large-scale operation, they are usually not worth buying just for making tackle. If you have one or more electric saws for other purposes and also use it for tackle crafting, so much the better. Some possibilities and their uses include:

- *Band saw.* Large band saws cost well into the hundreds of dollars, but smaller ones with 8-, 10-, or 12-inch throats (the distance between the blade and the edge of the tool equals the width of the material that can be handled) are ideal. Small benchtop styles are good and can usually be found in hardware stores and through mail-order outlets. Used ones sold through newspaper ads or in flea markets are also good bets. It is important to get one that has or uses a narrow blade of about ¼ inch, because blade width controls the radius of any cut that can be made. A thin blade makes it possible to make sharp-curve-radius cuts from square wood blanks.
- *Scroll saw.* Scroll saws will also cut the shape of a plug from a wood blank, but if you're making any but the smallest plugs, they are not best. Most scroll saws are designed to work with ⅜- to ½-inch-thick material, usually far thinner than the 1- to 1½-inch thickness of most plugs. They are okay for wood up to ¾-inch thick, but the thicker the wood the slower the work—and the greater the possibility of blade breakage, crooked cuts, and work chattering because the blade binds up.
- *Saber saw.* Saber saws have a reciprocating blade, like the scroll saw, but are heavy duty enough for general work. Often saber saws are used for light cutting in construction or home repairs. Because they usually have a large gap around the blade, they cannot be mounted upside down and used as a stationary saw. They are okay for general cutting and for sawing wood to length for use in a lathe or for carving.

DRILLS

An electric or a hand drill is useful for drilling holes in spoons or spinner parts, making pilot holes in wood or plastic plugs, and making molds. Although small single-speed nonreversible ¼-inch drills are often available very cheaply, variable-speed reversible ⅜-inch chuck drills are better. With these you can use the fastest speed for wood, moderate speeds for metal, and slow speeds for plastic (so that you do not burn or melt the material).

Rechargeable electric drills allow you to work without cords anywhere you want and are fine for tackle-crafting projects. So are Dremel or Dremel-type rotary tools, which are small high-speed tools with specialized chucks for holding small drill bits, sanding discs, router bits, sanding drums, and stones. These are particularly good for working on the small parts used in tackle building. Several models of Dremel tools and a wide range of accessories are available.

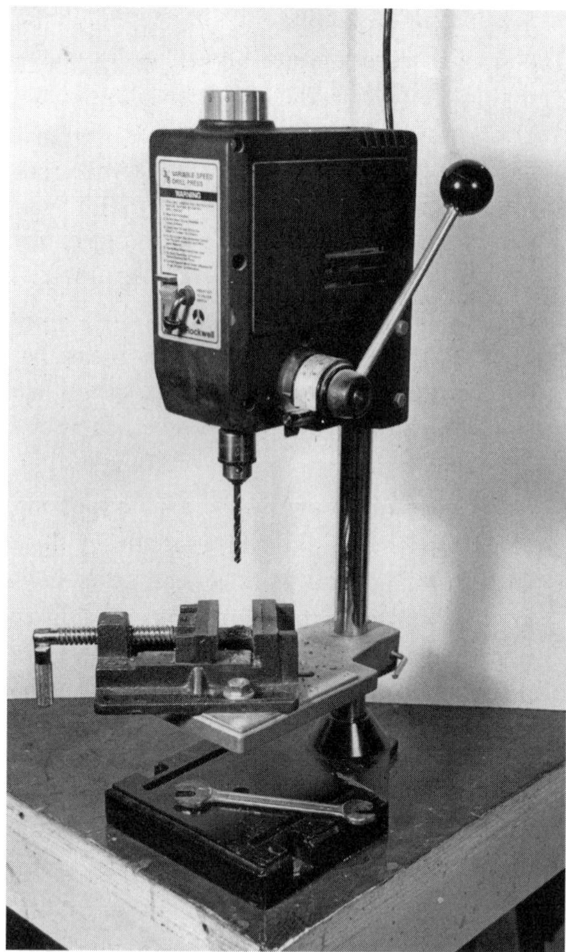

Example of small drill press useful for tackle crafting. This one has had a vise added to hold parts securely—a must for serious drill-press work.

DRILL PRESSES

Drill presses are stand-mounted drills. Most have a variety of speeds or different speed settings and come with a ⅜-inch or larger chuck. Many are expensive and mounted on floor stands, but smaller, inexpensive tabletop styles are ideal for tackle making.

As with band saws, the larger drill presses have a larger throat for taking larger chunks of material, but this is seldom a problem for the small-scale work of making lures. If you use a drill press, be sure to get a drill-press vise that will mount to the work base and hold the work as a bench vise does. Several types and sizes are available, some relatively inexpensive; some hold work at various angles.

There are also brackets designed to hold standard hand-operated electric drills. These are fine for simple tasks, but they are not as accurate or capable of repeat work as are true drill presses. Similarly there is a fine bracket that holds a Dremel tool, in effect making a miniature drill press out of it.

TWIST DRILL BITS

Twist drill bits are needed in small sizes for drilling pilot holes and through-drilling plugs for hook hangers for saltwater fishing.

Twist drills come in several sizes: Most come in fractional-inch sizes, ranging down to about 1/16 inch, sometimes to 1/64 inch. These are used by most home craftsmen, carpenters, and machinists. Letter sizes are used in the machine trades and are usually larger, ranging from A (small, 0.234 inch, or slightly smaller than ¼ inch) to Z (the largest at 0.413 inch, slightly less than ½ inch). Numbered drill bits, also used in the machine trades, range from 80 (the smallest, at 0.0135 inch, and smaller than 1/64 inch) to 1 (the largest at 0.228 inch, or slightly smaller than ¼ inch). The most useful for tackle crafters will be the fractional sizes, because the precise sizes used for machining are seldom if ever required in making rods, lures, or tackle. The most useful sizes are usually between 1/32 and ⅛ inch.

For making plugs with through-wire runs through the length of the plug, you will need longer drill bits. (Wood and especially balsa plugs need through-wire construction to prevent the loss of a strong or toothy fish if the fish shatters the plug. The through-wire construction, in which all hooks are attached to the same wire or plate as the line-tie, prevents fish loss. Most saltwater and muskie/pike plugs are made this way.) You will also need long drill bits for making or expanding holes in handle and grip materials for fitting grips and handles onto a rod blank. For these consider the 6- or 12-inch-long bits.

Long drill bits are often called aircraft or electrician's bits. Unlike standard bits, in which the drill length varies by the drill size (diameter), they

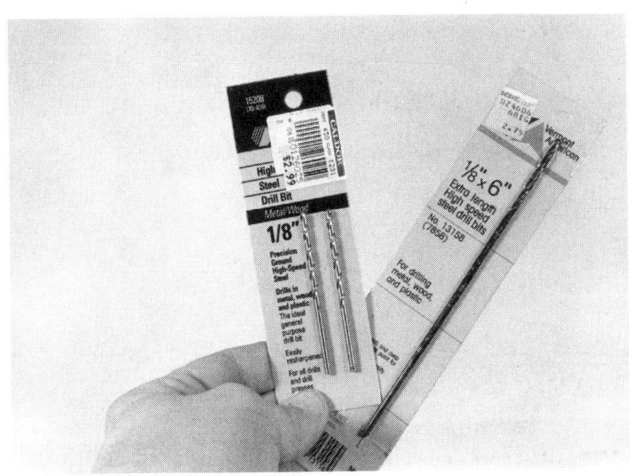

A longer drill bit (right) is compared to standard bits (left) of the same diameter. The longer bits, sometimes called aircraft or electrician's bits, are available in many diameters and in 6- and 12-inch lengths.

come in standard 6- and 12-inch lengths. In most cases the 6-inch length is adequate for drilling end to end through a plug. The longer drill bits can be used but are more difficult to stabilize. They are handy for making pilot holes and for drilling and sanding the center bore of rod handles.

PLIERS

Several types of pliers are needed, and these will be among your most useful tools. Large combination pliers (slip-joint or arc-joint pliers in which the pivot point is adjustable) can be used to hold lures during painting processes, while adding split rings and lips and hook hangers, and while drilling holes. Opened wide, large-jaw pliers can be used to hold hot jig and sinker molds. In general, smaller pliers are better for most tacklemaking jobs. Best is a pair of small round-nose pliers to form eyes in wire when making spinners, spinnerbaits, buzzbaits, some trolling rigs, and similar lures. These pliers come in various sizes, from about 4½ inches and larger, and have round, tapered jaws to allow any size eye to be formed in the wire.

Sets of pliers and wire cutters can be found in hardware, electronics, or hobby shops. Often these sets include four or five tools, such as tapered round-nose pliers, diagonal wire cutters, end-cutting wire cutters, long-nose pliers, and flat-nose pliers. All are very handy for the tackle tinkerer. If you do not get a set like this, you will still need a pair of wire cutters in addition to the round-nose pliers listed above. Some sets include different types of pliers and cutters, such as extra-long-nose pliers, bent-nose pliers, and wide-jaw pliers.

Of the cutters, diagonal wire cutters are best because they will cut closer to the spinner or lure body than will end-cutting cutters. Even with diagonal wire cutters, however, there are differences in the placement of the jaw's cutting edges. Some are shaped so that the edge of the jaw is flush with the pliers to minimize tag ends. Others are made so that the edges of the jaws are inset slightly. The best are those with flush cutting jaws. Wire cutters are good not only for cutting excess wire in making spinners but also for cutting lead (sprue) from molded jigs and sinkers.

Cheap long-nose pliers are helpful in painting. With these you can hold a lure by the lip, line-tie, or wire and paint it by dipping or spraying. The advantage, particularly with spraying, is that you will not get your hands covered with paint. Use cheap pliers for this; you are

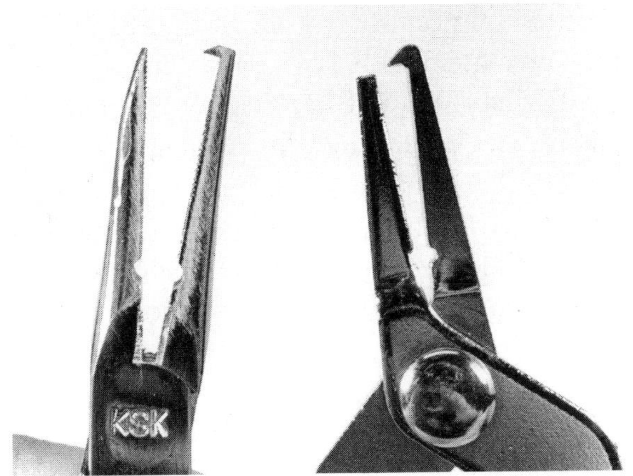

Split-ring pliers—to the left, precision pliers; to the right, an inexpensive pair. They have small teeth on one jaw to open the split ring for adding hooks and parts. The author modified the pair on the left by grinding down the nontoothed jaw to work with small split rings.

not concerned about precision or quality workmanship as long as the pliers hold well—and of course they will become covered with paint.

Compound-action parallel-closing pliers are useful for many purposes. Originally made under the Bernard Sportmate label, today many brands are available in several different sizes. They are ideal when holstered in a belt sheath for fishing (I would not be without a pair) but are also handy for tackle making. The parallel-acting jaws hold nuts securely, and all these pliers have very strong wire cutters to cut wire, screw eyes, or even hook shanks. Although they are most useful when fishing, I also particularly like the Donnmar stainless steel fisherman's pliers and the lightweight FF-1 pliers by Sports Tools for many tackle-crafting needs.

Vise grips or locking pliers are particularly good for tackle making. I like the Vise-Grip brand because they are sturdy and a number of different styles and sizes of pliers are available. Basically this type of pliers locks when closed, and the locking tension is adjustable by means of a screw. A simple lever unlocks the pliers to release the gripped object. For both fishing and tackle making, I particularly like small long-nose styles, which make it easy to grip small lures and parts.

Split-ring pliers are specialized pliers for opening split rings. They have a tapered flat jaw in combination with a second jaw that overlaps the first slightly and has a small tooth at the end by which split rings can be pried apart. The Worth Company makes these in an inexpensive flat model and two sizes of better quality pliers. They are ideal for adding hooks to hook hangers via split rings or for replacing hooks on any lure.

LEADER-CRIMPING PLIERS

These specialty pliers are used to close and crimp the leader sleeves used in rigging heavy leaders, big-game leaders, and similar rigs that require leader sleeves. Several types are available. One type is the cup-opposing-cup style, used for crimping oval sleeves. The point-opposing-cup style is designed for working with round sleeves only. Each style of crimping pliers *must* be used with the correct style of sleeve; otherwise the sleeves can be damaged and the crimp made poor and weak.

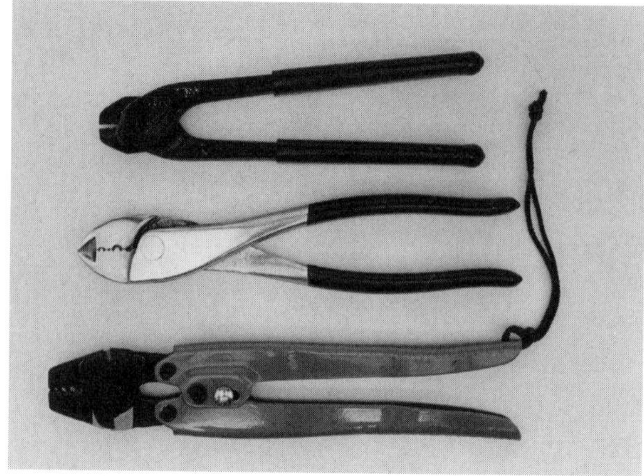

Pliers designed to crimp leader sleeves. At bottom is the cup-opposing-cup style; at center is an example of the point-opposing-cup style. Each takes a different type of sleeve.

These pliers come in a number of different styles, including small hand pliers for simple crimping operations and larger, compound-action pliers that are preset for a given force for a certain style of sleeve. This type is best when working with large sleeves such as those used for the heavy leaders and riggings for offshore big-game fishing. They are the type preferred for crimping and making 250- to 400-pound test leaders of wire or mono for billfish and other gamefish.

METAL SNIPS

You will need snips for metalworking only if you plan to make your own spoons from sheet metal or cut sheet metal for spinner blades or accessories (metal tackle boxes or lure boxes, for instance). If the metal you plan to work with is thin (under 20 gauge), regular duckbill snips will work fine. Several sizes are available, with the smallest usually the cheapest and easiest to use for making lures.

For cutting heavier gauge metal, for spoons and such, you will need the heavier leverage of aviation snips, sometimes called compound-leverage

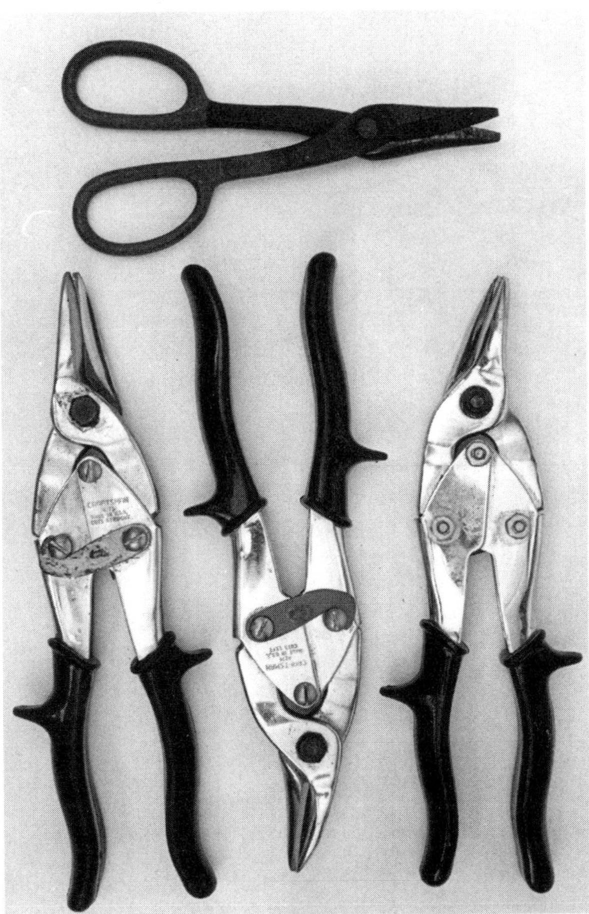
Sheet-metal snips. Top are duckbill snips. Below are three styles of aviation snips—right-cutting, left-cutting, and straight-cutting. Some snips incorporate all three cuts in one tool.

snips. These snips, which usually have about a 12:1 power ratio or leverage advantage over regular snips, are available in both inexpensive and high-quality tools. The inexpensive models are often designed as "all-in-one" tools, in which one snip will cut in any direction. The better quality snips are made with specifically designed jaws to cut in a certain direction. Therefore you will need three of the high-quality snips, or a complete set: one each to cut straight, left, and right. One of the inexpensive all-purpose snips will cost about a quarter of the price of one set of three better snips. As with the dead-blow hammers for forming spoon blades, high-quality snips are not really economical unless you plan on cutting a large number of spoon blades.

FILES

You will need several files for a variety of tackle-making operations. Coarse flat files are used for shaping spoons, roughing out wood plugs, filing points on gaffs, and similar tasks. Medium files give a smoother finish in these same operations and can also be used for the preliminary shaping of rod grips. Fine-tooth files are useful to remove the flash (excess lead) from molded jigs and bucktails, making and finishing molds, sharpening hooks, and filing down guide feet for a smooth fit on a rod blank. It also helps to have files in several configurations, including flat and half-round. The half-round files are perhaps the best because you get one flat side and one rounded side, which is good for shaping the concave parts of wood plugs and similar tasks.

Fine files are very handy for a variety of tackle tasks and often come in sets. I have a set of a dozen that includes flat, triangular, round, half-round, oval, knife, and other shapes. Often these are called needle-style or Swiss-style files. Some come with handles; others do not.

For making your own rods with cork handles, be sure to get a rat-tail file that can be used to ream out the holes in cork rings to exactly fit the rod you are building. (A reamer is a good substitute.)

Wood rasps are good for initial rough work on cork rod grips and wood-plug bodies. One rasp, usually a half-round, is sufficient for most jobs. The best length for most files, with the exception of the small set of fine files, is about 8 to 10 inches. Smaller files are difficult to work with, while larger ones just overpower the work and job.

If you plan to work extensively on tackle and to make your own lures and rods, you may want some special files and accessories. All-purpose files will do most jobs, but since they are not specifically designed for use on lead, aluminum, or brass, they tend to clog up quickly when used on these metals. Special open-tooth files are available that are designed to work with softer metals without clogging up.

Be sure to buy a file cleaner, often called a file card. These small, flat cleaners have very short, tempered metal bristles for cleaning particles from file teeth.

One additional file/rasp tool is used with an electric drill but serves the purpose of a rasp or file. When fitted onto the end of a bit extension, the rotary file and rasp allows you to rasp out holes in foam grips. The small rotary bit fits into the extension, which in turn fits into the drill.

REAMERS

Reamers are available from any hardware store and will usually ream holes from ⅛ to ½ inch. They are ideal for enlarging the holes in cork rings to fit onto rod blanks.

Special long reamers just for rods are available from many rod supply catalogs. Consider a set of rod-building reamers for extensive work on rod handles. These come in sets of three or four, each reamer a different diameter. They consist of tapered lengths with a spiral sanding strip wrapped around each of the tapered shafts (about 12 to 18 inches long) for reaming out a center hole in foam or a preformed cork grip to fit properly on a rod blank. When the sanding strip wears out, replacement strips are available to glue in place.

You can make your own reamers as outlined in chapter 2. I like reamers better than rat-tail files for rod work, since they are easier and quicker to use.

SOLDERING IRON

A soldering iron will be helpful in making spoons and some specialized lures that use spoon and spinner blades. An electric soldering iron with a small tip, the type used in radio and electronics work, is best. Often small soldering irons like this come in kits with several tips, or with optional tips for specific tasks.

With a soldering iron you can solder hooks to spoon blades, solder hooks to spinner blades to make small ice-fishing lures, and weight blades with solder to make a heavier lure or to change the action of a blade.

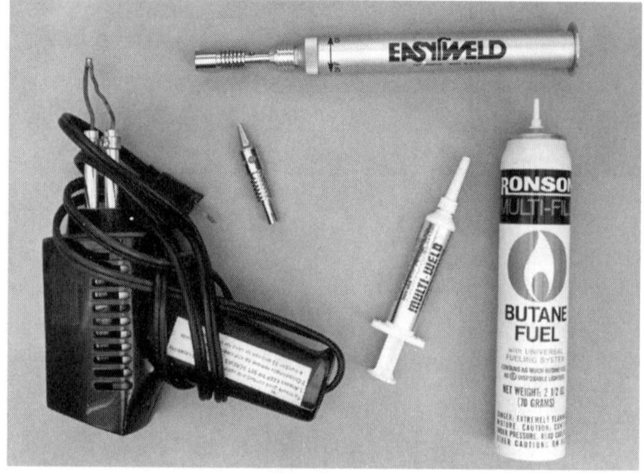

Examples of flame and gun soldering tools. The gun to the left has a fine tip for working with lures; the flame torch at top right fills with butane and provides a small flame for welding.

POP-STYLE RIVETER

Pop riveters, those that rivet from one side of a piece of material, are ideal for some tackle tasks. On larger spoons they allow you to rivet the eye of a hook into the hole drilled into a spoon to make a fixed-hook spoon. They can also be used for repairing reel seats in which the metal swaged hood becomes loose on the barrel or for fastening together triple-wing buzzbait blades of your own design. Those that take the smallest-size rivets, with ⅛-inch shanks, are most useful.

ELECTRIC GRINDER

Electric grinders are not required but can be used to smooth and polish spoon blades, sharpen tools, and accomplish similar tasks. Most useful are the small hobbyist-size grinders with two wheels of about a 5- or 6-inch diameter.

ELECTRIC SANDER

Electric sanders will do some of the same things electric grinders do. They will not easily sharpen many tools but can be used for polishing and fine-shaping spoon blades, sanding wood plug bodies, and removing flash from molded-lead sinkers and jig heads. There are a number of types of bench sanders (the type you will want if you get one), including belt and disc sanders. I like the belt sanders best because they allow sanding against the firm support of the flexible belt. Many of these hobby-type tools include both a belt and a disc sander.

LATHE

Even inexpensive machine lathes are priced high for the use you get from them in tackle building, but there are some specialized rod-building lathes on the market, along with small hobby-type woodworking lathes, that can be used for rod building and lure turning. A lathe is ideal for turning handles and grips for rod building and even for rod wrapping if it can be run at a very slow speed. Lathes are ideal for turning wood plugs for making lures. If you are considering a lathe for turning handles for rods, remember that you must turn the handle and *then* glue it onto the rod. Or get a lathe that has a through-center tail stock or a long enough bed to allow you to place the entire rod blank into the lathe. The through-center tail stock will allow you to run the rod blank above the handle, through rollers or a centering bearing, to support the rod and keep it from whipping around as the lathe turns the handle.

There are other lathe possibilities. A small Dremel Moto-Lathe, while not large enough for rod work, is ideal for turning wood plugs. Once widely available, this model has been taken off the market. Some might still be available through secondhand shops or at flea markets. The Dremel was available alone or in a kit with tools and accessories.

Small substitute lathes can also be helpful. One inexpensive possibility is a woodturning attachment that can be used with any hand electric drill. In essence it is a bench-mounted clamp that holds the drill upside down but horizontal by means of a special bracket and large hose-type clamp, with a small bed and tail stock for holding the work. You can find this attachment in hardware stores, catalog hardware houses, and stores such as Sears and JCPenney. One in a current Sears catalog will hold work up to 16 inches long and 4½ inches in diameter—ideal for turning handles separate from the rod and for turning any size wood plug. Flex Coat also sells the supports necessary to hold a hand drill and to support the rod for rod-building tasks.

Examples of two lathes for hobby and tackle-crafting work. The large lathe in the foreground was designed for rod work; the small Dremel lathe (discontinued by the company) is ideal for turning plug bodies.

Some aspects of rod making today require a lathe. A wood or metal lathe (usually either will work for the tasks required in rod building) is necessary for making the borehole in wood or acrylic grips, for some fancy wood handles, etc. Hobby-type lathes will work fine. These are available from most tool shops and from some mail-order woodworking supply houses. Note that you will only need a lathe like this for some rod handle work.

WIRE FORMERS

Several types of wire formers are available. Some are small, inexpensive tools that allow the forming of various types of eyes in most spinner and spinnerbait wires. They are great for the lure maker who has trouble using pliers to make eyes or who does not want to use pliers. One model looks like a screwless C-clamp and with a turn of the handle will make a variety of wire forms, eyes, and bends.

Larger, more-expensive wire formers are bench-mounted and come with attachments or have accessories available for making eyes and bends in different-size wire. Different collets are available for different wire-size ranges. One such tool available from several mail-order companies (Mud Hole, Cabela's) is made of sturdy cast iron and will clamp to any table or workbench up to 1¾ inches thick by means of screw clamps. With two handles working in opposite planes, it will make virtually any type of spinner or wire eye, bend, snell, or wire form. Collets available for this include those for wire from 0.018 through 0.025 inch, 0.026 through 0.029 inch, and 0.030 through 0.035 inch. Although relatively expensive, these tools are extremely versatile for any serious tackle maker of spinners, spinnerbaits, buzzbaits, and wire forms.

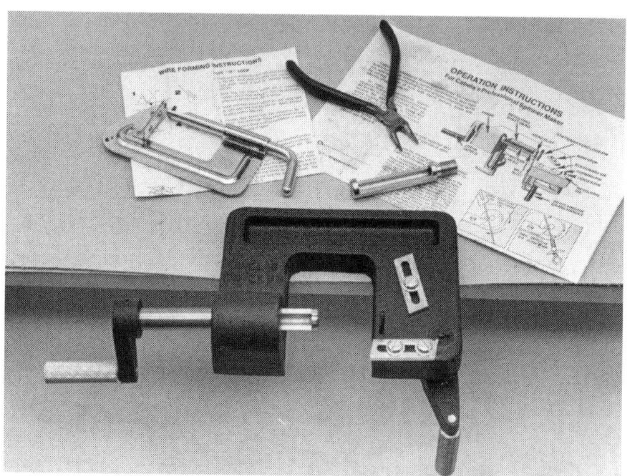

Several types of wire formers are available for making spinner and spinnerbait forms. The Cabela's tool in the foreground clamps to a workbench, is relatively expensive, and is designed for heavy, continuous work. An extra, revolving shaft head is also shown. The wire-forming tool (upper left) from the Worth Company does simple tasks on light wire. The round-nose pliers (upper right) are also useful for most tasks. The two wire-forming tools come with instructions.

DIVIDERS

Dividers as used by carpenters are useful to transfer dimensions from one part of a piece of work to another. They are ideal for checking the dimensions of both sides of a wood plug, the length of a guide wrap on both sides of a rod guide, or the length of wire in a spinner. Straight dividers are ideal and much better for most tasks than inside or outside calipers.

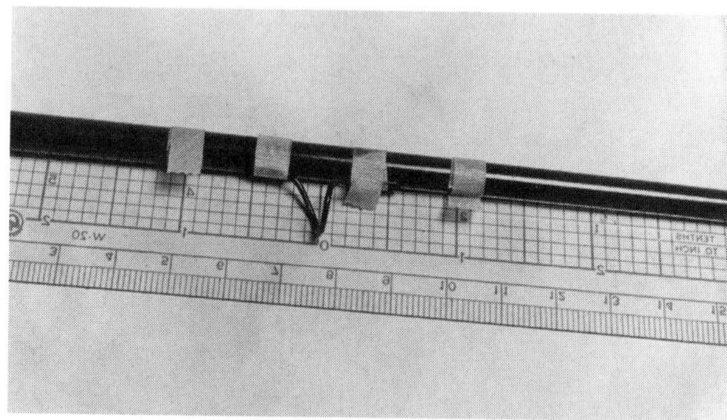

This type of rule is ideal for tackle building, since it has a center "0" that makes it easy to mark the center of the guide ring and to indicate identical marks for beginning wraps.

RULE

A rule, or ruler, as this tool is commonly called, is necessary for measuring parts in lure or rod building. The best ones are made of plastic or metal, with measurements in both inches and millimeters. Six-inch rules are ideal for measuring lure parts; 18- to

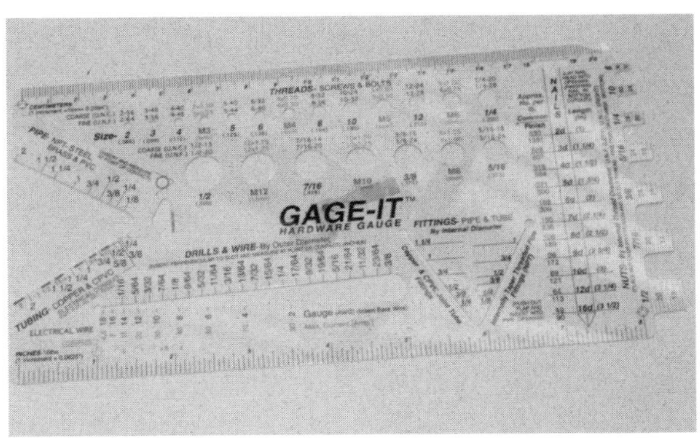

Some hardware gauges like this one are helpful in determining angles, lengths, and dimensions of parts for rod building and lure making.

24-inch rules are better for measuring handles and guide spacing on rods. One small rule that is ideal for rod work has a "0 center" mark and inches or millimeters measured out from this center point. These rules are made by the C-Thru Ruler Company and are ideal to mark the center position of a taped-down guide to assure that the guide wraps on both feet are of equal length. They are available at stationery and drafting-supply stores.

ANVIL

If you are planning to make a number of spoons from scratch, a small anvil will come in handy. Several sizes are available in hardware and hobby stores. Get one that has a horn at one end for working with odd shapes. Anvils can be either mounted to a workbench or used independently on a sturdy work surface.

Two types of small hobby anvils for swaging lures, hammering scale marks on spoons, etc.

GATE CUTTER

Although called a "gate cutter" by companies such as Do-It and Hilts Molds, these are really specialized cutters for stripping wire. As a gate cutter for removing the sprue from lead castings, they should be used only for lead or plastic and not for the heavy hard wire used in fishing.

FLY-TYING TOOLS

Special fly-tying tools are very useful for some aspects of tackle building. A fly-tying vise is a must for bucktails, other types of tied tails on spinnerbaits and buzzbaits (though these are an exception to the slip-on tails usually used), fur and feather tails tied on spinner hooks, and other tied tails for various lures. Other accessories used in fly tying are useful as well.

Fly-Tying Vise

Fly-tying vises are designed to hold a hook, upon which various materials are tied. Vises are commonly used in all aspects of fly tying but are also very useful for tying bucktails and dressed hooks for spinners and plugs. The cost of a vise ranges from very inexpensive to several hundred dollars. The simple inexpensive ones work fine for tackle building.

Be sure to get a vise with jaws that will open wide enough to hold the largest hook on which you wish to tie materials. Some vises have separate jaws for different hooks, while others advertise that they will securely hold any hook from a size 28 through a 5/0. Failure to use a vise with jaws that will hold the large-size hooks can result in sprung jaws, a broken vise, and insecure clamping of the hook. Remember that the hooks for lures on which you will be tying are far larger than the standard hooks used for most fly tying.

Most vises are available on either a pedestal base or with a clamp base. The pedestal bases are ideal if you are going to move around the house—tying bucktails on the basement workbench, on a TV table in the family room, on an office desk, or on any surface to which you cannot clamp the vise or do not wish to scar the surface.

Clamp-on vises are sturdier, and as a result of the adjustable clamp they allow up-and-down adjustment of the vise head for more comfortable tying.

Other Fly-Tying Accessories

An entire mini-industry has been built around the various types of fly-tying vises and other fly-tying tools and accessories. Although these are most useful for true fly tying and are less necessary for the more basic bucktails and hook tying, they are still handy to have. Some accessories to consider include:

Bobbin holders. These are small arms that are usually attached to the vise post and hold the thread on a bobbin out of the way. They are useful for holding the thread clear while winding hackle when tying dry flies or palmered-hackle bodies.

Bobbins. Any fly or bucktail can be tied using thread cut from a spool, but a bobbin that holds and guides the thread makes tying easier, allows more precise thread work, reduces thread waste, creates constant thread tension, and causes less fatigue. Many companies make bobbins in various styles (metal and no-grooving ceramic tips), in different sizes for different spools (Gudebrod makes two bobbin sizes), and in different tubing lengths. If you are serious about bobbins, it helps to have one for each thread color or thread size you use.

Bodkins. Bodkins are nothing more than a metal point on a handle and are used for picking out thread and adding head cement to a wrap to secure it. Easy to make, they are handy for many tackle tasks (see chapter 2).

Half-hitch tools. To finish off any wrap, you must use a half-hitch finish or a whip-finish. Special tools are available to make these tasks easier. Half-hitch tools are usually double-ended, with a different head on each end to fit different hooks. They can only be used on the heads of hooks in back of the eye and will not work on any wrap in which you have to bring the thread over part of the lure or jig, as with bucktail heads. For this you must use a freehand half-hitch finish or a whip-finish.

Whip-finisher. Whip-finishers are more complex to use and require some practice, but they allow a tier to finish a wrap with a whip-finish. As with half-hitch tools, most can only be used on a wrap that is finished on the hook shank just in back of the hook eye. Some do allow working to make the completed wrap over the lead head or other parts of the lure.

Hackle pliers. These are small, spring-operated clamps that hold hackle for winding around a hook shank. They are useful for wrapping hackle on some special jigs such as crappie flies (really jigs) and similar hackled jig heads. Several styles and sizes are available.

Details on all these tools can be found in the many books available on fly tying, and purchase is easy through any fly-fishing shop or through the many mail-order catalogs that cater to fly tiers. Some of the mail-order companies listed in appendix F include fly-tying tools and materials; other sources can be found through the various fly-fishing magazines.

There are also special tools made exclusively for rod building, which usually are only available from tackle shops or mail-order outlets.

ROD-BUILDING TOOLS

Calipers

Precision inside and outside measuring calipers are not absolutely required, but they can be useful. With these instruments that can measure in either millimeters or inches (thousandths), you can easily compare inside and outside ring sizes of guides and precisely check short lengths of short items and diameters.

Cork Handle Gluing Clamp

These clamps for gluing cork rings together to make a handle are available at some shops, but they are easy to make using scraps of wood and threaded rod. (See chapter 2 for instructions.)

By means of a thumb screw "chuck" to hold the rod, a commercial curing motor turns the rod at a slow speed to prevent the finish from sagging.

CURING MOTOR

Curing motors are a necessity for building rods today because all the best finishes are thick epoxy or polyurethane, which require constant slow rotation once applied to the blank to prevent the finish from sagging and dripping.

Curing motors come as either DC (either one or two D or C batteries) or AC operated. Motors typically range from about 4 to 10 rpm, although a slightly slower or faster speed also works. All include some form of chuck to hold the rod. Chuck variations include simple rubber butt caps that can be fitted onto the motor and adjusted to any rod, a simple three-jaw chuck of thumb screws, or self-centering chucks of rubber or aluminum (these are most like a lathe chuck). Some chucks are nothing more than a heavy rubber membrane stretched over a rotating cup, with the rod or rod blank mounted in a hole in the center of the membrane. This thick membrane, almost like an automobile tire tube, holds the rod securely enough for the slow rotation.

These tools usually come with, or have as an option, a support for the other end of the rod. The best are those that are AC operated. You can also make your own curing motor tool, as outlined in chapter 2.

HANDLE SEATER

Handle seaters are easy to make (see chapter 2), but they are also available from some tackle shops and component houses. In essence it is a board with one or more holes, by which a synthetic (Hypalon or EVA) grip can be pushed into place on a blank.

TAPERED REAMER

These are long reamers with a grit finish for tapering cork grips and rings. Most are about 18 inches long and come in several size grits. They are available from most mail-order houses dealing with rod components.

TIP-TOP GAUGE

Gauges are available from tackle shops and component-parts houses. Several major guide and tip-top companies make them now. Most are a small plastic rule or device that has holes into which you can size a rod tip and nubs to size a tip-top. They usually include sizes from 4⁄64 through 32⁄64 inch. In the sizes indicated, they can also measure metal ferrules.

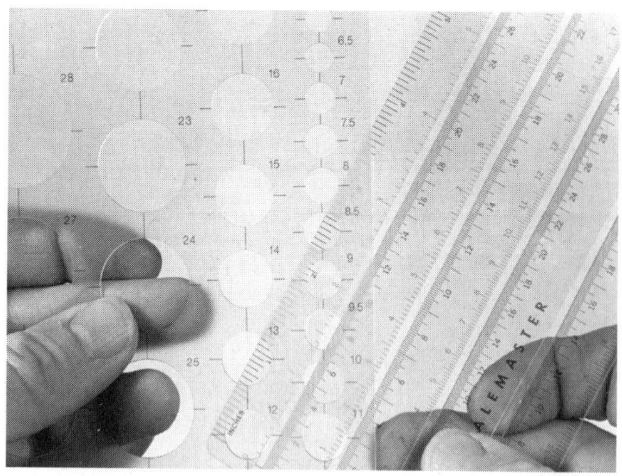

Various scales are available to make rod-wrapping thread designs easy. These are two scales used for lining up decorative butt wraps on rods. The circle template is used to line up decorative wraps on the rod; the straight scales are used to measure for those wraps.

CORK AND FOAM CUTTERS

Cutters to cut foam and cork rings and handle lengths into sections for making patterns and checkerboards are handy if you want this look on your rods. Mud Hole makes a cork cutter that will cut ½-inch-thick rings into the sections required for regluing and adding to a cork grip. North East Rod Builders has a similar (but differently working) cutter that will do the same thing with foam EVA sections so that you can make contrast colored rings and sections for rod grips.

ROD-WRAPPING TOOLS

These are available in both manual and electric models. The manual models range from simple wood racks with notches at each end to hold the rod and a thread tension device attached to the base, to more sophisticated tools of aluminum or with special attachments or features for wrapping or other rod-building tasks. Some locally made house brands are available from tackle shops and mail-order companies. Currently Jann's Netcraft, Renzetti, Flex Coat, Mud Hole, American Tackle, Pacific Bay (PacBay), and Merrick Tackle all offer rod-wrapping tools. These vary from simple clamp-on wrapping tools to motorized long-bed machines with several rod supports for holding parts of the rod blank and up to eight thread carriages to hold thread spools for complex wrapping.

Electric models usually include a power supply, a built-in chuck to hold the rod, and a base with one or several additional rod supports. Usually the device is controlled by a foot-pedal rheostat control for adjustment of thread-wrapping speed. Often the base is on a rack that will slide back and forth, enabling the rod builder to sit in one spot and wrap, sliding the rod and motor base along the rack as needed to wrap each guide.

Small rod-wrapping tools are available from many suppliers. This example—from Flex Coat—contains felt-protected V-blocks and sewing machine–style tension devices. An extension to support long blanks is also shown.

Although some simple manual rod winders are inexpensive, the variable-speed, aluminum-base, aluminum-chuck, roller-rod-support machines can be very expensive. Some of these come with optional slow-rpm curing motors. Details on any of these can be found in catalogs. You can also make your own simple machines, as noted in chapter 2.

In considering any of these tools, get as many catalogs as you can and examine features and prices to determine the features you want and what you can afford.

One important feature with manual machines is the ability to adjust the position of the thread tension device and one-end rod support. It also

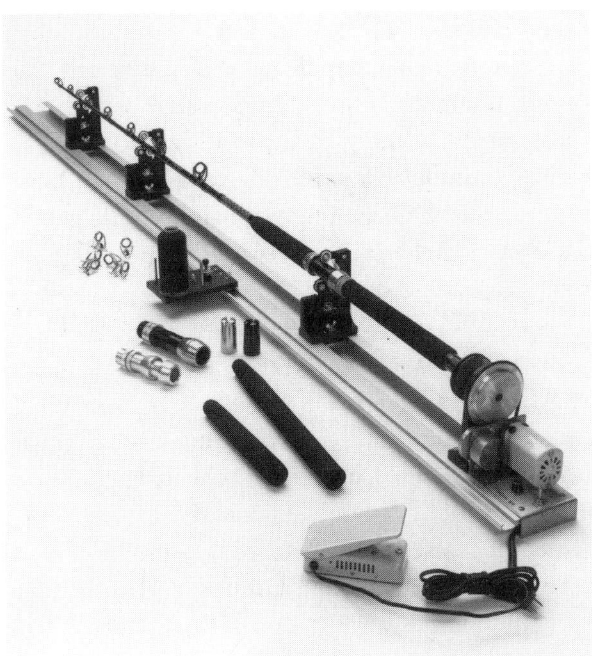

Many companies make power wrappers that are controlled by a foot pedal and turn a blank on rollers for fast, easy wrapping. This one is by Pacific Bay.

helps to be able to get an additional single rod support for working with long blanks or one-piece blanks. However, you can make your own additional support or jury-rig a support if necessary. These adjustments make it possible not only to wrap any guide but also to do the small decorative wrap on the end of a tip-top or the combination decorative/hoop-strength wrap required for self-ferrules.

For electric models, make sure the motor has a secure chuck, either a thumbscrew or a self-centering chuck, so that you can hold any rod. If working with complete rods in which the handle has been attached, there is an advantage to working with thumbscrews or a non-self-centering chuck. This will allow you to mount rods in the chuck that have an offset angle (some trigger-style rods), as well as any of the pistol-grip-handle rods. If working on long rods such as one-piece or long two-piece surf sticks, you may need extension base sections to hold the whole rod and to allow wrapping guides at one end. If this is a possibility, consider the length of the base when buying the machine, and explore the possibility of obtaining extra extensions if needed.

THREAD TENSION DEVICES

These are available as separate items from most parts outlets. They are usually the thread tension devices used in sewing machines, adapted for thread wrapping. These can be bought at sewing and fabric stores in addition to tackle and mail-order houses.

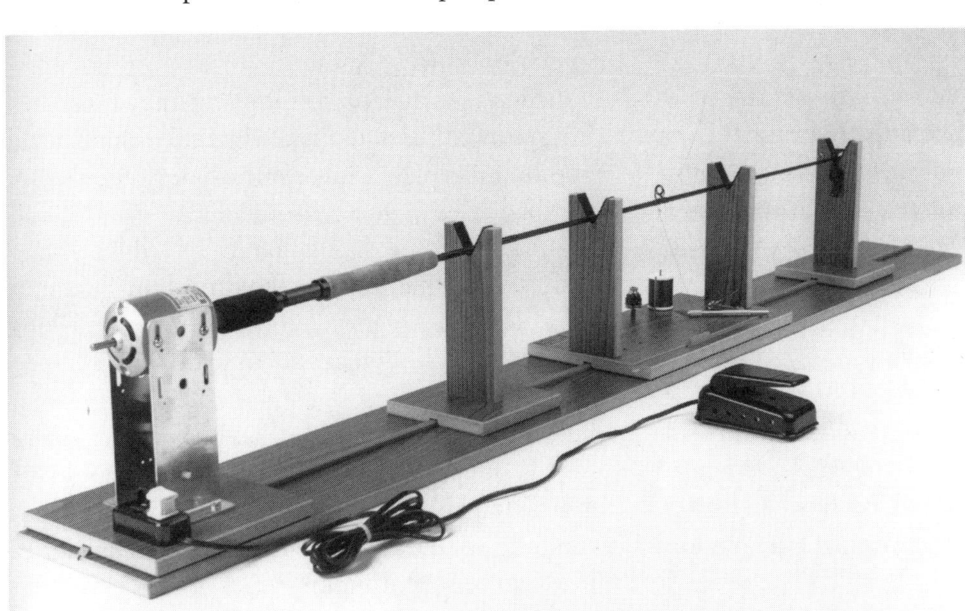

Another example of a power rod wrapper, with foot pedal. This one by Flex Coat has felt-covered V-blocks for the blank.

BURNISHER

This is a small tool, usually plastic, to help smooth guide wraps and to close or prevent any gaps in the thread wrap. Good substitutes include plastic-barrel ballpoint pens or similar devices.

TORCH

Small alcohol or butane torches are useful in removing bubbles from thread-wrap finishes by the application of quick heat. They are also helpful in removing and replacing tip-tops. In addition, small butane torches are available for welding and soldering operations, such as fastening hooks to small ice-fishing blades or larger spoons. Some of these torches, such as the butane Micro Flame Torch & Soldering Iron made by Tri-Peek International, Inc., are designed specifically for small-flame hobby work and are ideal for tackle-crafting purposes. The torch is easily filled from butane fuel injectors and comes with flame and soldering tips. Solder, as with the Tri-Peek Aluminum Weld and the company's Multi-Weld (for soldering everything but aluminum, magnesium, and pot metal) is available for these tools.

ALCOHOL LAMP

An alcohol lamp is very useful for wrapping rods. The side of the flame can be used for singing the thread wrap to remove any small fuzzy areas and to make finishing easier. These lamps are also useful to heat a tip-top before attaching it to a rod tip with a heat-set cement or one of the several ferrule cements made for this purpose.

SCALPEL

A scalpel, along with its disposable replacement blades, is ideal for cutting excess thread in rod wrapping. If you have a choice in blades, choose the #11, which is sharply pointed and has a flat cutting edge, ideal for tackle-craft and rod work.

DIAMOND WRAP TOOLS

These tools help in making and laying out diamond, chevron, and other decorative wraps. The tools consist of templates that allow the positioning of diamond or chevron marking points on four sides of a rod, along with right-angle gauges for checking the initial crossing threads after the first wrap is laid down.

MASKING TAPE

Masking tape in ⅛-, ¼-, ⅜-, and ½-inch thicknesses is available from some tackle parts catalogs, art stores, hobby shops, automotive supply shops (where it is used for pin-striping), and stationery stores. It is ideal for determining and laying out the guide spacing on rods and for masking fine parts of lures for painting. The ⅛-inch size is best for holding guides while rod wrapping; the ½-inch size is best for masking lures for painting.

SAFETY EQUIPMENT

Basic safety equipment is a must for safe tackle building, especially when power tools are used or when lead is molded. Drilling, sawing, grinding, sanding, and lathe operations frequently throw off small bits of wood and metal and dust. To prevent injury to your eyes, wear safety goggles during these and all other shop and tackle-making operations. This is especially important when cutting spinner wire; drilling, cutting, and making spinner blades and wire riggings; and making and hammering spoons blades. Safety goggles are inexpensive and good insurance.

A shop apron is also handy for all workshop tasks—from painting to molding lead bucktails to working with power tools. Pick a good long apron that will protect you and your clothes.

When molding bucktails and sinkers, wear heavy gloves to prevent burns. Either heavy work gloves or, preferably, welder's gloves should be worn. If you carefully follow the directions on molding with lead, you will seldom if ever have a problem or spill. In many years of tackle making and molding sinkers and bucktails, I have never

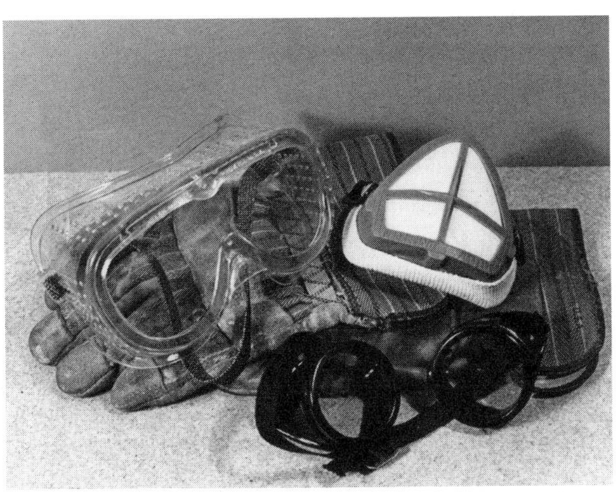

Safety equipment is very important in tackle crafting. The heavy gloves are useful for holding molds and ladles when pouring sinkers and bucktails, the facemask protects during painting, and the goggles provide eye protection for most shop and hobby operations.

had a serious spill. Even if such a spill occurred, it is unlikely that it would spill on your hands, but the added protection of gloves is definitely worthwhile. In addition, when working to make lots of lures, the ladles, pots, and molds will become hot. Gloves make handling these items easy and comfortable.

Since spray painting is used for finishing many lures, it is worthwhile to invest in a small breathing mask fitted with removable, replaceable filters. (Most of the excess spray paint can be trapped by using a "paint box," as outlined in chapter 15.) It is also handy to have some disposable rubber or plastic (latex or nitrile) gloves on hand. These make it easy to paint without having to clean up afterwards. The disposable gloves are sturdy enough for painting and can be thrown out after use.

It is also important to have adequate ventilation, preferably an exhaust fan. These precautions and suggestions concerning ventilation and the use of a breathing mask are just as important for molding lead lures and sinkers and molding soft plastics as they are for painting. See the chapters on these lures for specific suggestions.

The important thing is to use all available safety equipment. This means not only the above equipment but also any other you learn about. Equally important is common sense in using power tools. Basically this means removing any jewelry, wristwatches, ties, loose sweaters or jackets, and scarves; rolling up your sleeves; and wearing a work apron. This will prevent any jewelry or clothing from becoming caught in power tools with damaging, even tragic, results. When using a power tool, be sure to read, understand, and follow the directions and safety rules for that tool. The general suggestions and ideas on the use of power tools here and in subsequent chapters are in addition to—not in place of—the basic operations and safety information supplied by individual manufacturers, suppliers, and dealers.

Remember that you do not need all the equipment mentioned—or even most of it—to make much of your own tackle. (The one exception is safety equipment.) The discussion in this chapter is meant as a comprehensive overview of the tools you might want to consider using if you already have them on hand or buying if you get heavily into one type of tackle making where these tools can save time and, eventually, money.

There are substitutes for some of these tools that amount to almost no-cost replacements. These are covered in the next chapter, along with directions for the construction of some specialized tools for rod and tackle making that you might not be able to find.

2
Substitute Tools and Tools to Make

Introduction • Small Vise or Fly-Tying Vise • Wire Former • Pigtail Wire Former • Anvil • Metal Finishing Stamps • Bobbins • Rod Wrappers • Rod-Handle Gluing Clamp • Cork Handle Reamers • Curing Motor • Curing Motor Counterweight • Burnisher • Handle Seater • Decorative-Wrap Layout Tools • Decorative-Wrap-Alignment Checker • Loop Wrap Finisher • Tension Stabilizer • Rod Cutting Miter Box

INTRODUCTION

A friend, who was active in fly tying and teaching fly tying to kids, related the story of a small boy who wanted to learn to tie but did not have the money for a vise. In class he was all right because vises were provided, but at home he had a problem. His imaginative solution was to take two large washers, thread a large screw through them, and secure the screw into the edge of a scrap of wood. When fastened tightly the two washers would hold a fly-tying hook securely between the flat surfaces. When the screw was loosened with a screwdriver, the finished fly could be removed and a new hook added. Presto—a practical, no-frills fly-tying vise, one that could be used for fly tying or securing jig heads for tying on tail material.

While few of us have such limited means, there are ways to cut costs and make do without buying every tool in sight. Some suggestions follow.

SMALL VISE OR FLY-TYING VISE

One possibility for a simple vise is to use locking pliers (Vise-Grips) for holding jig heads for tying, spoons for drilling holes, and similar vise work. Clamp the pliers or Vise-Grips into a regular bench vise to secure them. In addition, there are locking pliers that have a C-clamp type of arrangement built into the handles so that the tool can be clamped onto a table or workbench and used to hold tackle parts.

WIRE FORMER

One way to make a wire former to form eyes of all types in wire of all sizes does not even require round-nose pliers. Hammer a nail or two into a block of wood and cut the head off of the nail with a hacksaw. File the cut smooth and remove any burrs. Removing the head of the nail allows you to remove the wire form or eye once you have made it by wrapping the wire about the nail shaft. Since the nail will determine the size of the eye, you can make different formers for different-size eyes, as needed. These allow you to place wire between the two nails and then bend the wire around one nail to make an eye. The excess wire can be used for wrapping around the wire shaft to secure the eye. You can also make such wire formers with several nails in several positions for specific wire-forming tasks.

The best method for making wire formers is to hammer two nails into a block of wood with only a space to accommodate the thickness of the wire separating them. That way the shafts of the two nails will hold the end of the wire in place while you wrap the wire around one of the nail shafts to form an eye.

To make this handy tool, choose a nail for the eye size you desire and hammer it into a block of wood. (Scraps of end-grain two-by-fours or two-by-sixes are ideal for this.) Saw off the head. Then place the wire next to the hammered-in nail and place another nail close to the wire so that the space between the two heads is just large enough for the chosen wire size.

Nails hammered in the end grain of a block of wood make for easy-to-construct wire formers for making sinker eyes, hook lears, bottom spreaders, and similar heavy-wire rigs. The nail heads are sawed off to allow removal of the wire once formed.

Hammer this second nail straight into the wood and remove its head. The second nail provides a leverage point for bending the wire around the main nail. When you are forming a wrapped eye, it allows you to make the shoulder bends that are necessary to form the eye on-center with the wire shaft.

This style of wire former is also ideal for making bends in larger wire, such as household or hobby copper or brass wire; through-wire hook hangers for use in saltwater or balsa plugs; hook lears for saltwater bottom rigs; and large eyes for sinkers and tin squids.

To make a wire former to form simple eyes with larger wire, you will need two nails hammered in side by side, as above. To make simple "omega"-shape wire eyes for molding into lead and tin squids and sinkers, you will need three nails hammered in a V shape so that the central nail can be used to form the eye and the two side nails used to form the flare that will hold the eye in the sinker/squid.

To make a longer figure-eight shape for sinkers or squids, you will need five or six nails hammered in a larger V for the additional bends in the wire. Spaced-out nails can be used to make similar bends in combination with other eyes on the wire, as in making the additional necessary eyes for hook lears in bottom rigs. (A hook lear is a wire or plastic form used to offset a snelled hook from the main line of a bottom rig so that it will not tangle and will present the bait better.)

As you make these wire formers, other combinations of bends and wire rigs will come to mind. In cutting off the nail heads, remember that shorter nail lengths are best because leverage that will weaken the nail positions will increase as the wire is bent higher above the wood base. Consider making some nails longer or shorter than others to facilitate working and bending the wire around the nails. Both common and finishing nails will work for this, although common nails are usually heavier (thicker) in a given length and size. Special nonbending hardened nails, such as are used for concrete work, are also good for this purpose, although most are not smooth (rough or fluted finishes are common), making it more difficult to remove the finished wire rigs and eyes. Because these nails are hardened, it is also more difficult to cut off the heads.

Sawing the nails off to complete the wire former: These are custom made for each type of wire form.

PIGTAIL WIRE FORMER

A pigtail swivel functions just like a snap swivel except that in place of the snap there is a pigtail wrapping of wire. Any attachment to it is made by threading along the pigtail—like an open spring—to hold the lure or hook or to place the swivel as a slide swivel on a line for a fish-finder rig.

The tool to make this is a simple one. You will need a wire former to make an eye in which the ends of the wire cross at right angles. Then one end of the wire is held straight while the other end is wrapped in an open-spring wrap. The tool for this consists of a steel or aluminum rod about ¼ to ⅜ inch in diameter, though you can make any size you wish. (You can even make it out of wood.) Drill a hole straight through the center of the rod and then cut out half of the rod about ¾ to 1 inch from one end. The result is a round rod, flat at one end, with a hole straight through it.

The pigtail end is then made in any wire rigging by sliding one end of the wire into the hole, holding the open eye flat on the flattened area of the rod and up against the shoulder, then wrapping the rest of the wire around the round portion of the rod to form the open pigtail. Remove the wire from the tool, cut off any excess, and finish by using a standard wire former to make a closed eye, adding a swivel (if desired) as you do so.

To make the pigtail former, the appropriate diameter of metal rod is center drilled and then sawed longitudinally in half, as shown here. One side of the rod is removed.

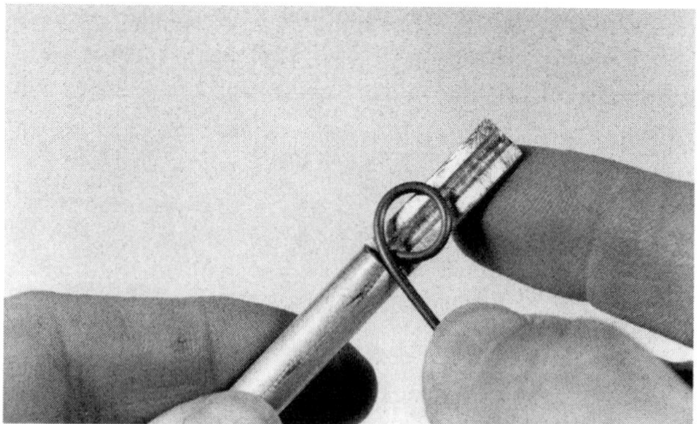

Once the eye is completed, the shaft is inserted into the hole through the pigtail former and the wire bent around the main part of the rod. This eye must be formed before any changes are made to the other end of the wire.

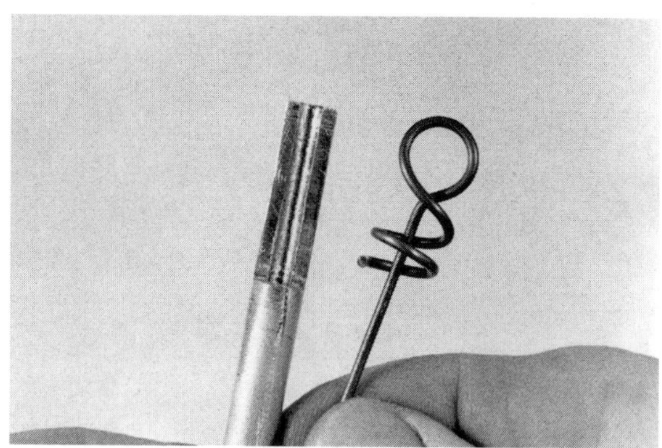

Pigtail wire former and the resultant eye (here shown in larger than normal size for clarity). The pigtail eye allows for addition or removal of rigs without opening and closing snaps.

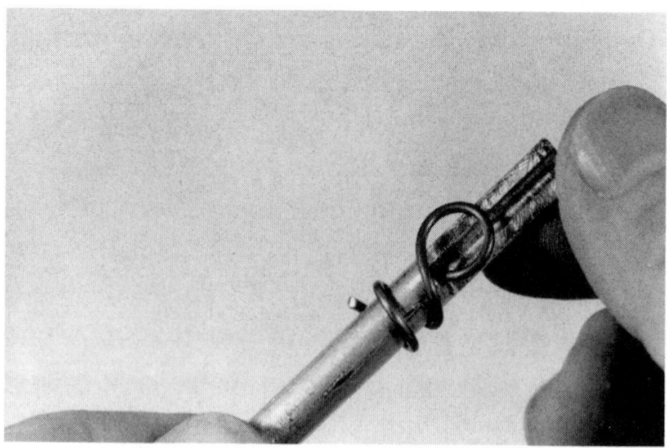

Completed pigtail wire before being removed from the wire former.

ANVIL

An anvil is helpful in forming spoon and spinner-blade blanks. Since anvils that are sold commercially seldom have the shapes you need to hammer into the spoon blade, you are often better off making your own shaping form from a wood block. Hardwood is best, although soft wood like pine will also work. (Soft wood will not last as long, however.) To make a wood form, first determine the shape you want in a spoon blade, and use a chisel or gouge to cut this shape into the block. Usually you will want to cut it slightly deeper than the curve you want, because the spoon metal will have some bounce to it. Once you get the rough shape, you may wish to smooth it using a router, ball-head stone, or file bit in a drill or Dremel Moto-Tool.

Using a grinding stone to cut depressions into a block of wood to serve as templates for hammering spoons.

If you don't have the tools for cutting out a round, smooth shape, you may be able to hammer it using a regular carpenter's or ball-peen hammer. Lacking this, you can use an old teaspoon or tablespoon, repeatedly heating it red hot and burning it into the wood to create a depression. Routers and rotary files for electric drills and drill presses also work well for this. You may wish to make several depressions for different spoon sizes and shapes.

To make hammered finishes on the convex side of a spoon blade, you need a raised area on which to hold the spoon while you work with a chisel or stamping device. Hammering stampings while holding the spoon on a flat surface or iron anvil would only tend to flatten it. To make a round end on which to hold a spoon for this (like a horn on an anvil), you can use several sizes of wood dowel: Round off the end with a grinder, sander, or wood rasp, and glue the dowel into a hole of the same size on your wood-block anvil. The dowel should only be raised about ½ to 1 inch above the flat surface of the block. An electric drill or brace and bit will drill these holes easily. One-half-, ¾-, 1-, and 1½-inch dowels are ideal sizes for this purpose.

Another possibility is to use a wooden darning egg (the kind used to darn socks and available at sewing supply stores). Cut the egg into several parts that can be glued onto the anvil or fitted on a short length of dowel that is glued to the anvil.

METAL FINISHING STAMPS

In addition to using the nail sets and various commercial punches described in chapter 8, you can make your own stamps to obtain certain finishes or markings. Use hardened nails or short lengths of steel rod in ⅛-, ¼-, and ⅜-inch diameters. File the ends into different shapes. These shapes can include sharp or blunt chisel ends, curves, or Vs (to simulate fish scales), dots, Xs, and +'s. First file the rod or nail to a flat blunt end, and then use a file or grinder to remove excess material to get the shape you want. The

Stamping tools can be made from nails and other steel rods. These allow stamping of markings into metal blades.

stamps are used exactly as are punches and nail sets (described in chapter 8) to make markings on metal.

BOBBINS

Bobbins are used to hold thread for fly tying and jig making, in the latter to tie tails onto the bucktail and jig heads. Both types of bobbins are really the same and are used for the same basic purpose. We'll consider the bobbin a tool in this section.

To make a bobbin from coat-hanger wire, cut the hook from the wire with wire cutters. (Compound-action wire cutters are best for this heavy wire.) Straighten the wire. Next make a right-angle bend about ½ inch from one end. Then make a second right-angle bend (to form a J shape) about 1½ to 2 inches from the first. Consider the width of the spool to be placed in the bobbin, and make a loop in the wire with pliers so that the loop centers on about one-half the width of the spool. Cut the end of the wire. To determine the spot to cut, measure the length of the wire from the center of the loop to the end of the wire at the bend. For example, if you make the first bend ½ inch from the end of the wire, the second bend 2 inches from the first bend, and there is ¾ inch of wire from the second bend to the loop, add these figures together to make the cut 3¼ inches from the loop.

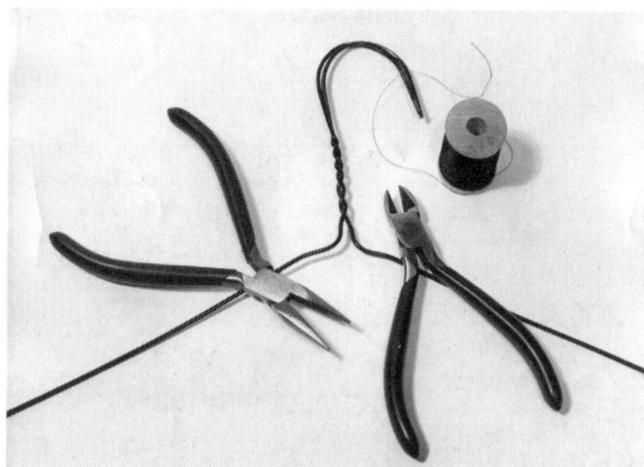
Tools and materials required for making a simple bobbin with which to wrap tail materials on bucktail bodies and treble hooks.

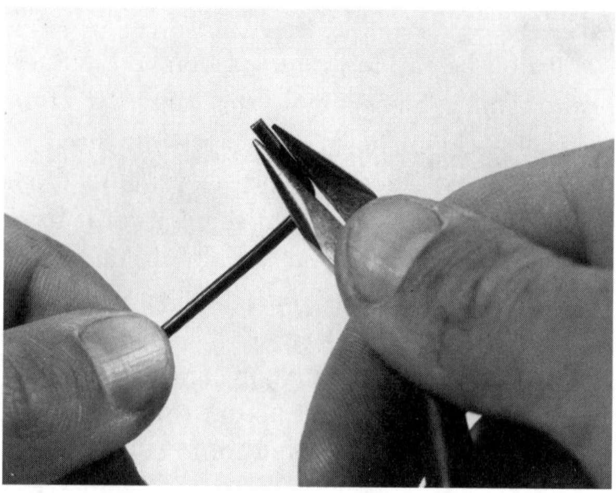
First bend made in coat-hanger wire.

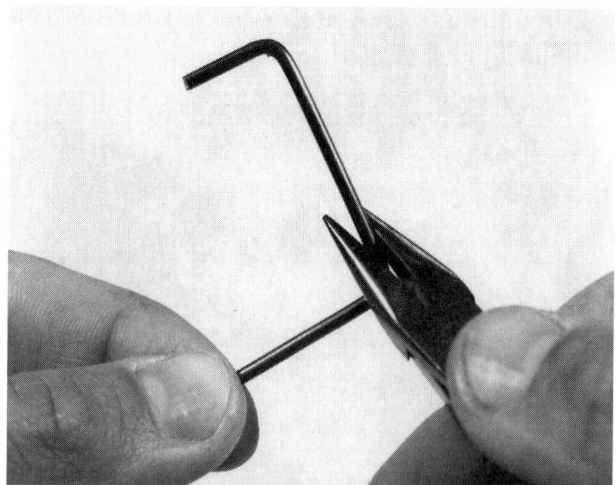
Second bend made in coat-hanger wire.

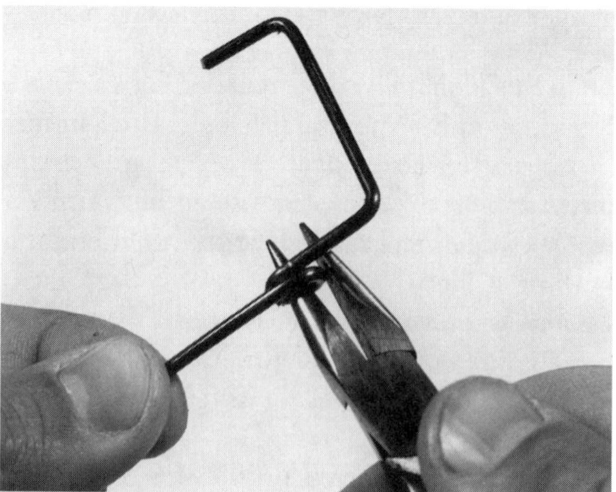
Loop in wire is made for the thread to run through while winding thread.

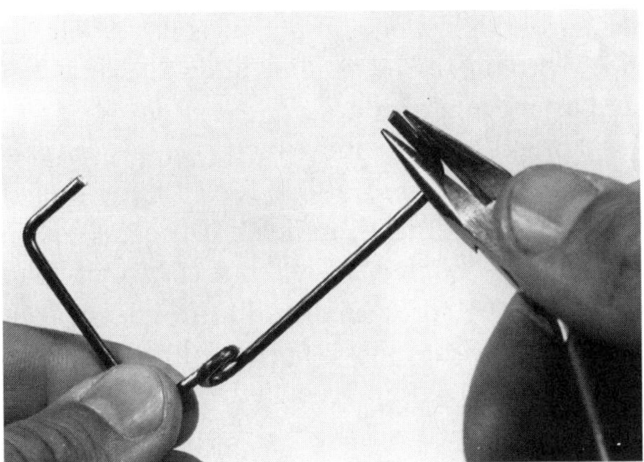

Third bend in wire.

Completed bobbin with thread through loop.

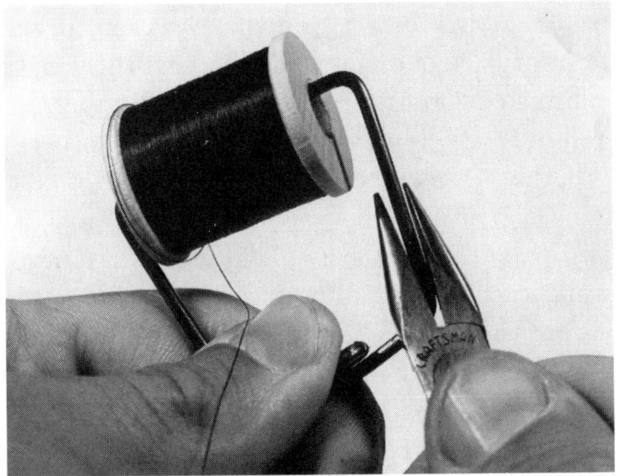

Fourth bend in the wire is made with the spool in place. The tension on the spool is adjusted by the degree of bend in the wire and wire pressure against the side of the spool.

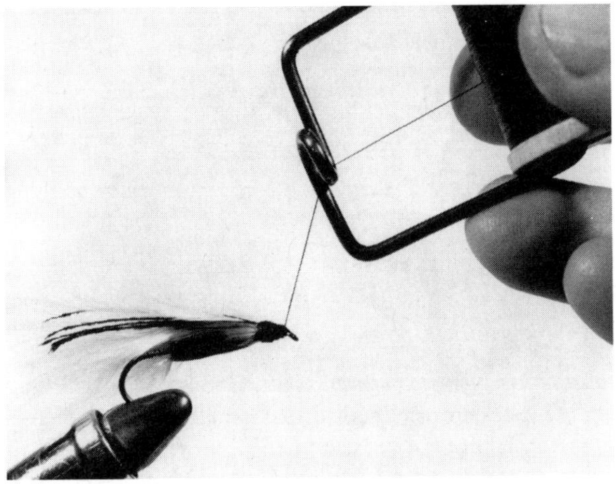

Completed bobbin being used to wrap thread.

To complete the bobbin, make a right-angle bend ½ inch from the end of the wire and a final bend 2 inches from the first. In completing this bend, place the spool of thread into the two open-end posts and sharply angle the final bend to create tension on the side of the spool. Tension can easily be adjusted in this way.

A modification of this can be done by making additional bends from the center point to make an extended loop arm for more control of the thread. These extended arms can be twisted to keep them from opening or left parallel so that a rubber band can be used to help control tension on the thread spool.

Another type of bobbin that is ideal for wrapping jigs and bucktails was developed by angler Keith Walters of Bozman, Maryland. Keith used lamp parts and strap iron to make a simple but effective bobbin. Keith suggests using the heavy strap iron made for hanging radios in cars and trucks. Bend the strap iron into a C shape, with the top and bottom of the C just wide enough to bracket the spool of thread. Midway between these two parallel straps, drill a hole that is large enough to accommodate a short length (3 to 5 inches) of the threaded tubing used for lamp fixtures. Fasten one end of the threaded tubing into the hole in the bracket, using a nut on one side of the bracket to hold the threaded rod, a pull-chain finial nut on the other. Add another pull-chain finial nut to the other end of the tubing. This smooth end, normally used for a pull-cord or chain in a lamp, protects the thread on both ends of the tubing. To hold the thread spool in place, use a bolt and nut or a wing nut.

ROD WRAPPERS

There are dozens of types and variations of tools for wrapping guides on rods. They range from the simple to the highly complex—and expensive. The simple methods and tools are best for those who will make just one or two rods or repair a guide or two. Good basic manual or electric rod wrappers are ideal for the serious rod builder, while those who are into custom rod building as a part-time business or for a tackle shop or fishing club can go with the expensive multipurpose wrappers. Some ideas follow:

One easy, no-cost way to wrap rods involves only a teacup, a telephone book or books, and two sheets of clean typing paper. Work at a kitchen or card table and place the rod-wrapping thread in the cup or a bowl. This will keep the thread from rolling around on the table or off onto the floor. Next run the thread through a phone book, using a sheet of clean typing paper over each of the opposing pages to prevent the thread from becoming soiled by the inks. Tension is controlled by how deeply the thread is run through the book or by how many additional books are placed on top of the phone book holding the thread. Hold the rod and wrap it by rotating it in your hands, pulling the thread through the book. The disadvantage of this method is that the thread is not easily visible where it begins to lay down on the rod, making gaps or errors more likely than with some other methods.

An alternative method is to locate a comfortable open-back chair, place the teacup behind the chair, run the wrapping thread between two sheets of typing paper on the chair seat, and sit on it. Wrap the rod by turning it in your hands, and control the thread tension by shifting your weight. Another alternative is to run the thread between clean sheets of paper placed in the center of a telephone book that is placed on the floor with the thread running under the chair legs and up in front of you.

For either of the above methods, it is possible to make a support for the rod so that you do not grow tired holding it in midair. There are several possibilities for this, all without cost. One is to obtain a long corrugated-cardboard box, cut out all of the top and most (but not all) of the front and back. Cut a deep V notch in each end or side. The notch will hold the rod while you turn it, and the open front allows room for your hands. If you are working from the teacup on a table, you will need a slot or gap in the back of the box for passage of the thread. Note that you can't cut the front or back out completely, because this would eliminate support for the ends holding the rod. You must also leave some support at the corners.

Another method is to use a length of coat hanger bent into a lowercase "h" shape and the two parallel arms bent to clamp tightly onto a workbench or table. The other end—the upper part of the h—can be curved or bent into a shallow V to hold the rod. You will need two of these tools—one on each side of you.

For a more permanent but still dirt-cheap rod-wrapping tool, use a scrap piece of wood shelving cut into three pieces: two short ones of the same length and one longer. Fasten the two short pieces

V cuts in the upright supports used to support a rod when wrapping on guides. Such supports, mounted on a base, can also support a rod when using a curing motor. The plastic strips prevent scratches in the rod blank.

to the long piece, which should be 18 to 24 inches long. Before nailing or screwing the ends on the base, cut a sharp V notch into the top end of each to hold the rod.

To keep the rough wood from scratching a fine blank, you must add a protective surface to these V cuts. One possibility is to use self-adhesive felt, available from craft and hobby stores, and cut it into strips to cover the Vs. I like using smooth plastic: Use any thin plastic from a flat food container (I use one-gallon milk containers, but other containers work just as well), cut strips the width of the Vs, and tack the strips in place. Make sure that the tacks are high on the V so that they will not touch the rod blank. These plastic strips are very smooth, and in years of using them, I have never scratched a blank. If you use felt, check periodically for wear, replacing when necessary.

A fancier alternative is to use rollers for the rod while wrapping on guides. You can use simple 2-inch-diameter casters, sometimes called tray casters. These come on a short post so that they can be easily mounted on top of any board or on a block that in turn can be mounted on a ⅜-inch aluminum rod (available from the do-it-yourself aluminum section of hardware stores) and then mounted in a standard clamp-on fly-tying base. This allows vertical adjustment of the rollers, and the rollers will turn to prevent scratching the rod. If the bases are mounted as closely as possible, most brands of casters will end up with about ⅛ inch of clearance between the two rollers. Since the rollers are plastic and are injection-molded with a seam line down the center, I like to sand the seam off with sandpaper and then cover the rollers with narrow (¼-inch) masking tape, available at art supply stores or some tackle parts mail-order houses. The masking tape provides a soft base and also some grip to keep the rollers turning as you turn the rod, at the same time protecting the rod from the hard-plastic seam line.

By their length, the wood bases only allow support of the rod at predetermined places, so you might have to wrap a guide in such a position that a previous guide will interfere with turning the rod because it will hit at the notch. (Clamp-type supports with the rollers can be positioned anywhere on a table edge.) There are many solutions to this. The first is to make one end movable with two ½-inch-long dowels glued into its bottom to fit into a series of matching holes drilled into the base at various positions.

Another option is to make a base with two strips of wood with a slot in between that will take an L-shaped wood end. A bolt and washer/wing nut through the base of the L will hold the end support at any desired position. Simpler but similar is a plain wood base with an L-shaped support end that can be clamped with a C-clamp to a workbench. Two of these will allow any type of rod and support positioning. With any of these systems, measurements have

Simple thread-tension devices and rod rollers are easy to make. Here, fly-tying clamps are used to support a ⅜-inch rod, which in turn holds short wood blocks into which are mounted plastic chair rollers. While not shown, it is best to wrap the rollers with two layers of masking tape to protect the rod and for grip for easy rolling. The thread-tension device is a standard commercial style that also clamps to the worktable.

to be adjusted so that both ends are level with the base. This allows wrapping on a horizontal plane. If one end is not adjusted properly, rods with a steep taper might be difficult to wrap. In all cases, only one end needs to be adjustable or movable.

There are several ways to make a tension device for this tool. One is to mount a screw eye into the central base and run thread on a bobbin through the eye. The screw eye will hold the thread in place, and the bobbin will create the tension. Another possibility is to acquire and mount a thread tension device made for sewing machines, available from sewing and fabric outlets. A third option is to mount a flat-head machine bolt from underneath the base (drill a hole) and mount the spool on the bolt, adjusting tension with a compression spring, available at hardware stores, between two washers and fastened securely with a wing nut or double locking nuts. The best fasteners are the lock nuts that have a small nub of plastic or rubber in the threads; these allow the nut to be turned but also lock it in place to prevent slight movements. Otherwise you may find periodic adjustment necessary to maintain tension, because the turning thread will tend to tighten or loosen the tension, depending upon the relation of the turning spool to the thread direction.

The homemade tension device that I like best, even though it requires mounting the tool over the edge of the table and clamping it in place, involves the use of two 3-inch small-eyebolts, two compression springs, two washers, two wing nuts, and one thin rod or 4-inch shoulder bolt and wing nut. To make this tool, drill two holes 3 inches apart in the center of a flat board. (This base need be nothing more than a piece of scrap wood that you can clamp to the table with C-clamps.) Make the holes about 1 inch from the front edge of the wood scrap. Run the eyebolts through these holes, and underneath the base mount one compression spring, washer, and wing nut on each eyebolt. Mount the thread on the thin rod or the long bolt that you have run between the two eyebolts. This way, tension can be adjusted from underneath and is never affected by turning the thread spool, as can happen if the spool is mounted on a bolt.

In making this device, try to get eyebolts (I use ¼-20 thread, but any size will work) with small eyes so that small spools of rod-wrapping thread can be used. Large eyebolts are often too large for this purpose. If you can't get small eyebolts, you can still use this system by fastening a small block of wood between the two eyebolts to elevate the thread and create tension. An alternative is to go with smaller-thread-diameter eyebolts, since smaller diameter wire has smaller eyes. Either 3/16- or ⅛-inch-diameter eyebolts will work. Because the spool will be turning on the edges of the eyebolts, use a small sheet of plastic (such as was cut from milk bottles for the rod holders) with punched holes for the eyebolts to hold it in place. This will also smooth the tension for effortless guide wrapping.

Electric rod wrappers can be made with jury-rigged parts from other tools, from sewing machine parts, and from parts available from

Homemade thread-tension device for wrapping rods. Made of extruded aluminum, this device will clamp to any table. The thread tension is adjusted from underneath using eyebolts, springs, and wing nuts. The device will hold any size thread spool. Similar devices can be made from wood shelving.

some catalogs. Basically they include a block to hold a simple three-jawed drill or lathe chuck; a motor controlled by a rheostat (speed control) floor pedal; and a bed, usually of rails, holding adjustable roller supports to support the rod and an adjustable-tension device. There are endless variations of these devices, some with the motor and bed riding on a separate bed of rails so that the whole rod-wrapping assembly can slide along the rails, eliminating the need for the rod builder to move to make each successive wrap.

ROD-HANDLE GLUING CLAMP

When you are making cork handles and grips, a rod-handle gluing clamp is a handy, inexpensive, easy-to-make, and easy-to-use tool. A gluing clamp makes it easy to clamp the cork rings of a handle together until the glue cures, prior to shaping, and to make sure there is a good, tight bond between each cork face.

There are two basic ways to make a gluing clamp. The first involves two 2 × 1 × 5-inch strips of wood, two ¼-20 treaded rods, six nuts, two wing nuts, and two washers to fit the threaded rods. The threaded rods can be other diameters if you like, and their length should be based on the length of the handles you are making. The threaded rod can be anything from 12 inches long (usually too short unless you are making handles separate from the rod and adding them later) to 36 inches long (necessary only for surf rods, where you will be gluing the grips directly onto the rod blank).

Drill a hole into the center of each of the wood strips to accommodate the rod blank. Make the size of the hole appropriate to the diameter of the blanks you are using. Drill two more holes—one on each side of the center hole—to fit the threaded rods. Attach one end of each of the threaded rods into the outer holes in one of the wood strips, using nuts and washers to lock them into place on each side of the wood strip.

Ream out the two outer holes in the other wood strip so that the threaded rods will slide easily through them. Slip the second wood strip onto the threaded rods, and fasten with washers and the wing nuts.

The cork rings are added and glued to the blank to build up the rod handle. Then the base of the gluing clamp is slipped over one end of the blank and the wood strip is seated against the cork rings at one end of the handle. Slip the other wood strip (at the opposite end of the gluing clamp) over the rod blank and onto the threaded rods, add the washers and wing nuts, and tighten the second wood strip to draw the cork rings together for curing.

One disadvantage of this tool is that if you are making a short handle with long threaded rods, you will have to turn the wing nuts a lot to get tension on the cork grips. A solution is to modify the tool as follows: Use two strips of wood as above, but on one of them cut slots

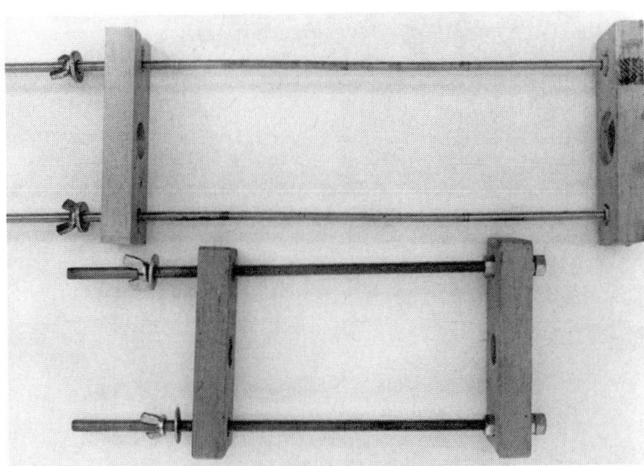

Two lengths of cork-handled clamps using threaded rod, scrap wood, nuts, and wing nuts.

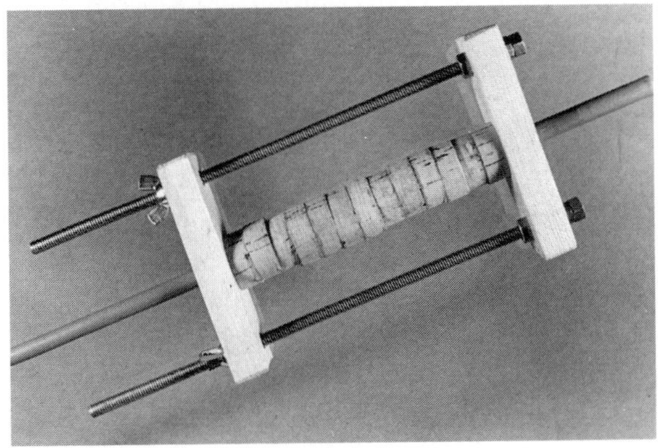

Cork grip clamped in homemade handle clamp.

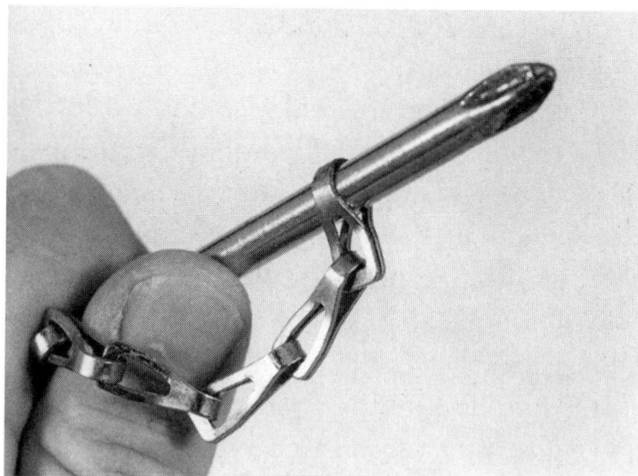
To make an adjustable cork clamp, first open up a chain link to fit onto an eyebolt.

completely through the wood from each end to the two side holes. Use a large saw blade to cut a groove into the top of this end over the top of each hole (center of the slot).

Instead of threaded rods, use two chains of any length desired. Any light chain will work well provided that it fits through the sawed slot. (I like safety or sash chains.) You will also need two 4-inch-long eyebolts (¼-20), two washers, and two wing nuts to fit them, along with two hitch-pin clips. Fasten the end of each chain to the eyebolts by opening the eyebolt and sliding a link in place before closing the bolt. Lightly ream out the holes at the one end so that the eyebolts will slide easily.

Open eyebolt to accept the chain link for the adjustable part of the cork clamp.

Fixed end of the cork clamp where the hitch-pin clips are placed in the chain to adjust for the length of the cork grip.

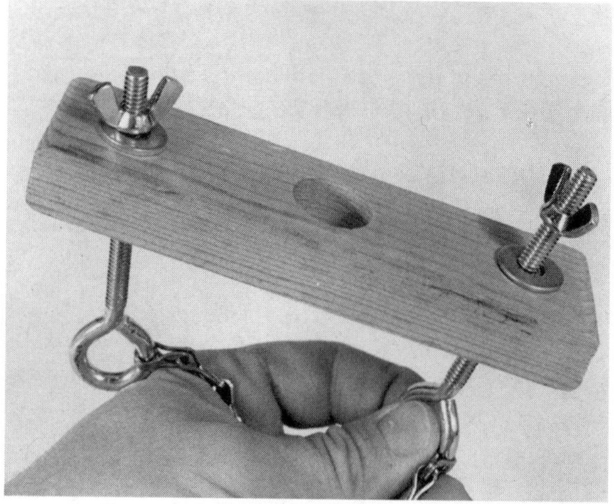
Adjustable part of the cork clamp: The rod blank can fit through the center hole, and the wing nuts adjust the pressure on the cork grip.

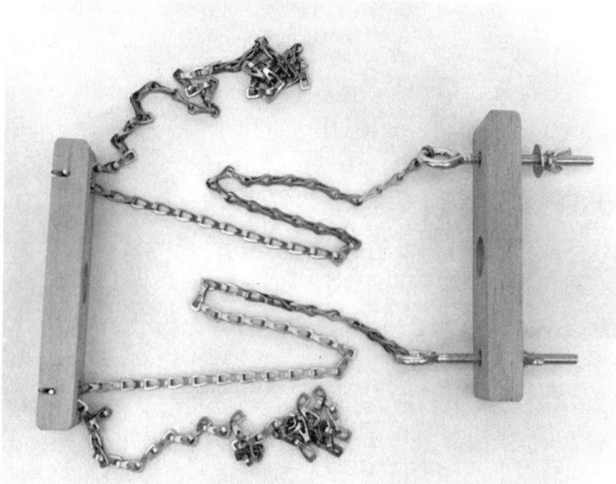
Completed cork clamp with chain, hitch-pin clips, and adjustable eyebolt.

To use the tool, run the wing nuts down to the end of the threaded eyebolts. Slip the hitch-pin clips through the chain links at the appropriate length for the rod grip you are making. Slip the rod blank into the center hole of each wood strip, slide the chain into the slot in one wood strip, and slip a hitch-pin clip into the chain and into the groove in the wood strip to hold the chain in place. Tighten the cork clamp by turning the wing nuts to draw the clamp together.

The advantage of this tool is that it is quick and easy to use. After clamping a short fly-rod grip of only 6 inches, it is easy to remove and readjust the tool by moving the hitch-pin clips to clamp a 24-inch-long surf handle. The only turning required is no more than the length of the threaded eyebolts. Of course you have to make and glue the handle before the reel seat is added or lengthen the gluing clamp so that the reel seat is included, drawing up the cork handle against one end only.

Another possibility is to use a modification of a carpenter's pipe clamp. These tools are sold in sets, with the sliding part of the clamp and the threaded adjustable part—you provide the pipe. The clamp can be made any length and is usually reserved for larger clamping jobs. If you have one (don't buy one just for clamping rod handles), you can use a small C-clamp to hold a wood yoke on each end. These yokes should be cut from short lengths of shelving, and a deep U should be cut into one end. Use the C-clamp to hold the wood yoke onto the existing clamp surface, and place the rod with the handle cork in between these yokes.

If you have a pipe clamp and want to make a permanent cork clamp, you can weld a similar-shaped yoke of steel onto the clamp faces. If you use flat steel for these additions, you can still use the pipe clamp for general carpentry tasks.

Take care to use only slight pressure, because these clamps are capable of great force. Too much pressure, regardless of the type of clamp used, will squeeze the glue out of the adjoining cork faces and may even deform the cork rings.

CORK HANDLE REAMERS

Standard, commercially available reamers are not long enough, nor do they have a gentle enough taper to ream out an entire cork handle. Long reamers are necessary for shaping the hole in a cork handle made on a threaded rod and then fitted to a rod blank, or when using commercially available preformed cork grips. Also, they must have a taper similar to that of most rod blanks at the handle end.

There are several ways to make these reamers. The best base for a reamer is a scrap piece of rod blank about 18 inches long. It is best to make several sizes, or diameters, for reaming out cork grips for different-size rods. One way is to cut thin strips (about ¼ to ½ inch wide) of coarse sandpaper from a sheet. Run these over the edge of a table to "break" the backing paper so that it will not crack or split when wrapped around the scrap rod blank. Coat the entire scrap blank with a thin coat of 24-hour epoxy glue. Then, starting at one end, spiral-wrap the sandpaper strips around the reamer blank to completely cover it.

An alternative method is to clamp down both ends of the sandpaper strips, backing side up, and then coat the sandpaper backing with epoxy glue. Spiral-wrap the strips around the reamer, covering it completely or leaving gaps between the strips where the blank will show. This is the better of the two methods, because it will leave spiral channels for cleaning out the cork dust as you work the reamer. If you were to coat the blank with glue and then spiral-wrap, leaving these spaces, you would fill up these channels with glue and reduce the effectiveness of the tool.

A third method of making a reamer is to coat abrasive grit directly onto a glue-coated rod blank. Some commercial-style hardware stores sell the type of grit used on sandpaper, but alternatives are plain sand (the kind found at fresh- or saltwater beaches or used to fill a child's sandbox) and sand-blasting sand. The problem with natural sand is that it will vary widely in

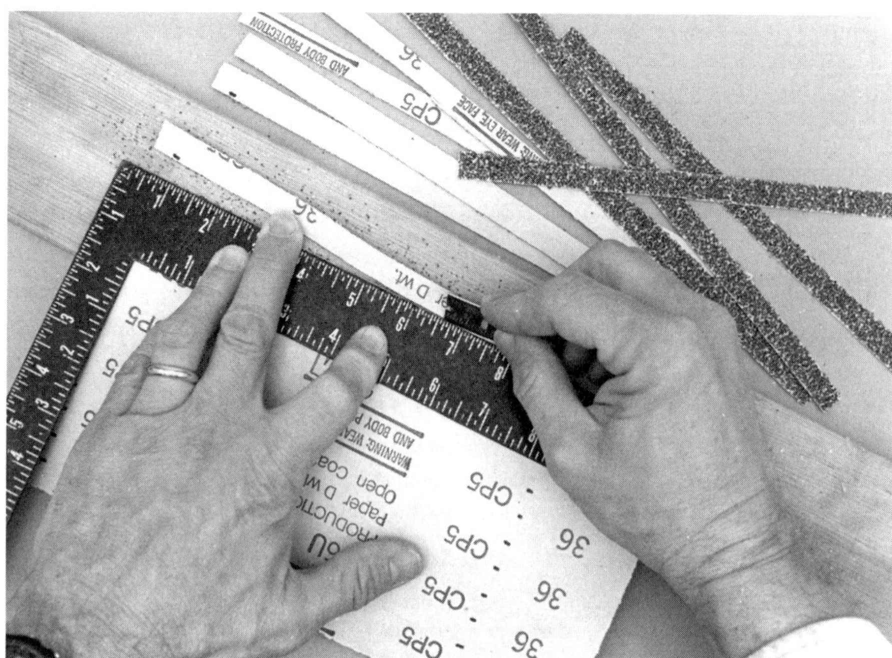

Cork reamers can be made from scraps of blank and strips of coarse sandpaper. Here, a ruler is used to cut strips of sandpaper from a sheet. The strips are then glued onto the tapered blank to make the reamer.

Two types of homemade reamer. The one on top has a solid wrapping of coarse strips of sandpaper; the one on the bottom has grooves between the sandpaper for clearing the cork dust while working.

size and sharpness. Many of the particles will be rounded and thus less effective for reaming. Sand-blasting sand is sharp and comes in various grades, but unfortunately it is only available in large quantities—like hundred-pound bags! Perhaps a call to a sand-blasting company could get you a pound or two.

To make a reamer this way, spread the grit out evenly on a sheet of wax paper. Then coat the scrap rod blank with epoxy glue. Make it a thin coating so that it does not run, or use some of the gel-type glues that are more viscous. You can coat the entire blank or use a spatula or craft stick to coat it in a spiral, leaving channels, or coat the blank in rings to leave segmented abrasive areas and channels. Once you have it coated, press the reamer down into the grit on the wax paper, lifting, turning, and pressing it back down in the grit to get complete coverage. Roll it lightly in the grit and then set it aside to cure overnight. Some grit will come off during initial use, but after this stage the reamer should be good for many handle shapings.

CURING MOTOR

Curing motors are required to properly cure the finish on rod wraps when modern epoxy and urethane finishes are applied. These finishes are thicker than the varnish used in the past and will sag and drip if the rod is not supported horizontally and turned for several hours until the finish cures. Commercial curing motors are available, but you can build your own.

You will need a slow-turning motor such as those used for barbecue rotisserie spits or slow-clock or timing motors. The best are those that

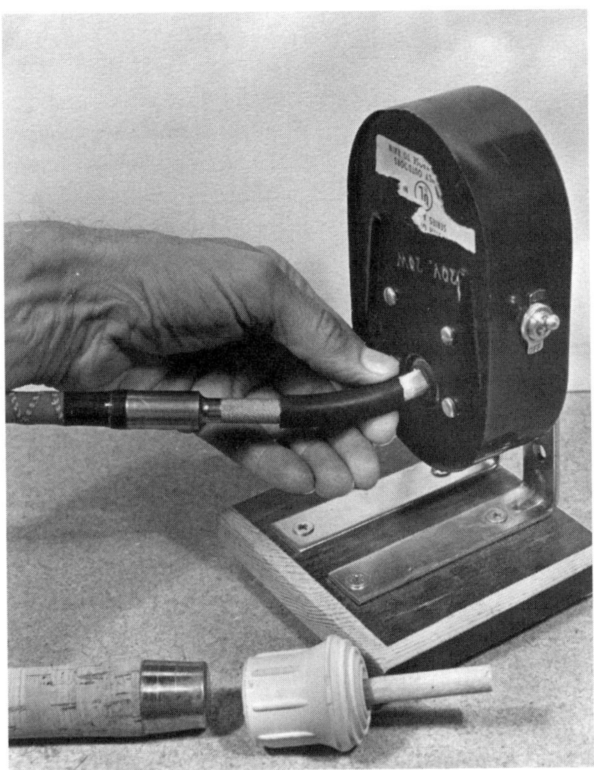

Curing motor made from a low-rpm rotisserie motor from a barbecue grill, with a wooden blind wedge in the square hole and rubber tubing to connect with the butt on a casting rod. Other types of attachment can be used, as shown by the crutch tip (to hold the rod blank or butt cap) mounted on a wooden dowel in the foreground.

have a turning speed of 1 to 20 rpm and are AC style, so that you do not have to continually buy batteries. They must have enough power or gearing to turn the heaviest rod that you might want to build. I like rotisserie motors. They are heavy duty, work well, and often can be purchased inexpensively at flea markets or acquired from neighbors who are throwing out an old grill. You will have to jury-rig a system for holding the butt end of the rod. How you do it will depend on the motor.

Rotisserie-style motors have a blind square hole for the spit, some motors have a short shaft, and others end in small gear wheels. For the blind square hole, you can cut down a dowel and blind-wedge it into the hole. (Place a wedge in the square hole so that forcing or driving the dowel into the hole will wedge it into place.)

For gears or shafts, the best system is usually to glue a rod-holding device onto the shaft or to fasten a rod-holding device onto a block of wood that in turn can be drilled to fit onto a gear or shaft. This can be done with a series of rubber butt caps fitted to different blocks of wood that can be force-fitted onto the shaft, or with a block permanently glued or fastened to the motor butt and fitted with a threaded rod and wing nut to hold butt caps punched with an appropriate-size hole.

You can also use a standard plastic 3-inch-diameter PVC end cap or similar metal cap and drill and tap for thumbscrews at three points placed equidistant around the perimeter. For this I like ¼-20 thumb screws. A 3⁄16-inch tap drill will work fine. Once the holes are drilled and tapped, add the thumbscrews. For use, adjust the thumbscrews to hold the finished rod.

Another alternative is to use a standard PVC end cap fitted onto the rotating motor and a hose clamp to hold a piece of slightly stretched inner tube or similar rubber. Before adding the rubber membrane, punch a hole in its middle through which the end of the rod can be inserted when the hole is stretched. This

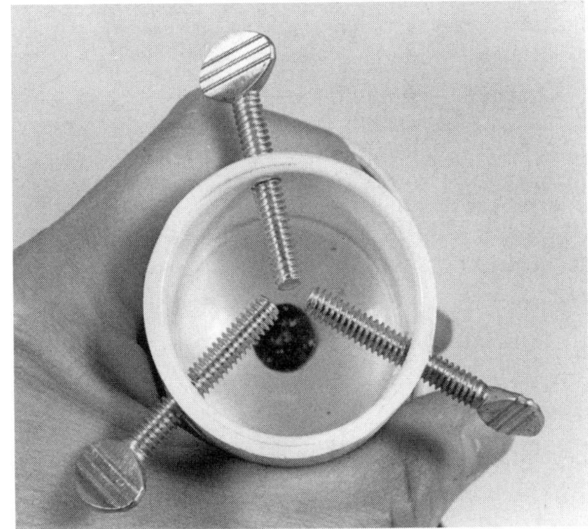

Thumbscrews in a PVC pipe end cap make an ideal holder for a rod-curing motor. The cap must be mounted onto a low-rpm motor for curing rods. The plastic is easy to drill and tap for these thumbscrews.

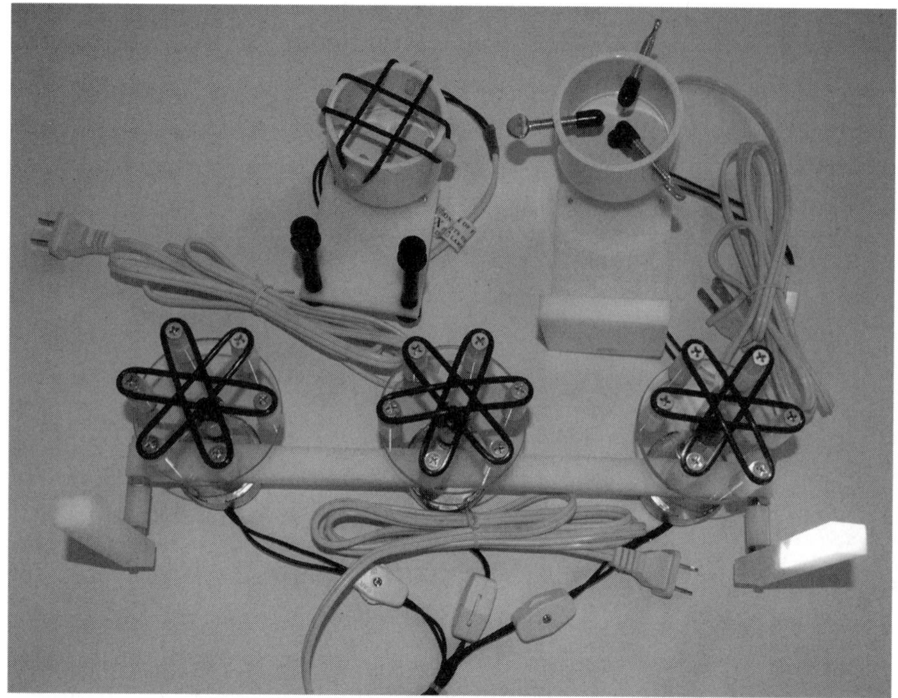

Examples of several types of rod curing motors for slow turning when curing an epoxy finish to prevent sagging. These are commercially manufactured, but similar designs can be made by any rod builder.

system is fine for light rods like fly rods but is not as good when heavy guides, such as found on offshore rods, might create enough torque to cause the rod to slip during rotation.

You could also measure around the outside of the plastic PVC end cap at four equidistant spots, drill a small pilot hole at each spot, and then insert a very short round or pan head screw. A ¼- or ⅜-inch screw is best. For this method buy two O-rings to fit over the opposite positioned screws. The result is that the two O-rings cross in the center of the end cap to make it possible to secure the end of a butt cap or a rod into the crossing O-rings. You can also do this with more pressure and for a slightly smaller butt cap (as with a fly rod) by marking and drilling at six positions equidistant around the perimeter of the cap so that three O-rings cross in the center.

CURING MOTOR COUNTERWEIGHT

If you're building large offshore rods, the roller guides added to many will add significant weight to the upper (reel) side of the rod. This can create a strain on the curing motor so that it will just barely rotate with the weight of the guides, or it may not rotate at all with this added weight to one side.

One way to adjust for this is to use a counterweight attached to the rod so that the weight is opposite (180 degrees) the guide positions. On most of these offshore rods, sets of five roller guides are used with the addition of a tip-top. The weight of the guide standing off from the rod blank can make a different in rotation. The tip-top, close to the axis of the rod blank, will make little difference. Guides vary in weight and the leverage factor involved; AFTCO guides are used here as a standard for determining a counterweight.

The weights for a five-guide set of different AFTCO rollers are as follows:

- Big Foot Super Heavy Duty roller guide set—for 80 to unlimited line class (Set 76)—8½ ounces
- Wind-On Roller Guides—for 30 to unlimited class wind-on leaders (Set 66)—7-plus ounces
- Heavy Duty Roller Guides—for 20 to 80 line class (Set 56)—2⅔ ounces
- Regular Roller Guides—for 16 to 50 line class (Set 16)—2⅓ ounces

Knowing these weights you can then calculate the counterweight you need to come close to the weight of the guides on the offshore trolling rods you're curing. You do not need to match these weights exactly—only try to come relatively close to reduce some of the torque of the small curing motor in turning the rod. I use wide fender washers for weight; by adding more or fewer washers you can adjust the weight as needed. Since I am using ¼-inch threaded bolts or rod to hold the weight, I like fender washers with ⅜-inch holes and a diameter of 1½ inches. Using these, I find that the weights necessary for the above four sets of roller guides are as follows:

- Set 16—0.145 pound
- Set 56—0.160 pound
- Set 66—0.445 pound
- Set 76—0.530 pound

To make the counterweight device, you will need two 1-by-2 strips of wood about 4 inches long each, two 4-inch-long ¼-20 eyebolts, one 4-inch length of a ¼-20 threaded rod (or cut the head off a bolt), and five ¼-20 wing nuts.

Drill 5⁄16-inch holes through the outer edges of the two strips of wood and a 7⁄32-inch hole (pilot hole) partway through the center of one strip. Opposite this center hole and also in the additional strip, cut a 90-degree angle V notch in each wood strip. The facing notches will fit onto the rod by means of the reel seat, ferrule, or even on the lower part of the rod blank itself if needed.

For additional ease of application, cut out the side of one hole on one of the wood strips. This allows you to swing the strip out of the way when adding the counterweight to the rod and then swing the strip back in place to tighten the threaded rods and secure the counterweight onto the rod. Fender washer counterweights can be added before or after this step.

BURNISHER

Burnishers are available commercially, but easy substitutes for smoothing thread wraps and closing thread gaps include plastic pens, used-up felt-tip markers, or other similar small, smooth implements. Be sure to use only the smooth skin of the tool to smooth the wraps—not the point.

HANDLE SEATER

Handle seaters are used to push synthetic grips into place on a rod. They can be made several ways. One way is to use a 1 × 2 × 15-inch board. Drill a 1-inch hole through the center, and to one side drill additional holes measuring ¾ inch and ⅜ inch. To the other side drill ½- and ¼-inch holes. Any of these holes can be used to push the grip into place. Pick the hole size that's just barely larger than the diameter of the rod at the top of the handle. To use, place the handle seater over the rod blank after the foam grip is placed on the blank. Use both hands to push the seater down, and slide the grip down the blank. Handle seaters are necessary because the diameter of any synthetic grip must be smaller than the diameter of the blank in order to hold the blank properly.

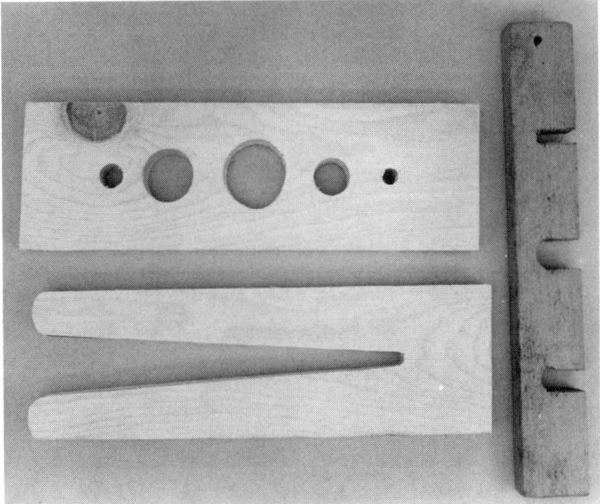

Three types of handle seaters that will work for foam or cork grips.

Another way to make the same basic tool is to use a board with a central hole of about 1 to 1½ inches and use this as a brace against another piece of wood that contains smaller holes of 1, ¾, ½, ⅜, and ¼ inch. I have even made seaters with a rotary wood "wheel," on which the holes are drilled. The wheel is screwed to the wood board so that the small holes are lined up with the larger hole in the board, and the tool is pushed down, wheel first, to move the handle into place.

DECORATIVE-WRAP LAYOUT TOOLS

Tools for laying out diamond, chevron, and similar wrap patterns can be purchased, though they are not made specifically for this purpose. For example, a circle template has a number of different circles, most with marks to indicate the four quadrants. By placing the circle template on the blank at the handle and selecting a circle of the same size as the blank, it is possible to lay out 180- or 90-degree marks for single or double diamonds, chevrons, and other wraps.

It is best to first wrap the blank above the handle with masking tape on which you'll make the quadrant marks. Then slide the template hole in place, making sure it is the right size hole with a snug fit. Line up one of the quadrant marks with the center of the reel seat, and mark the masking tape with the two or four quadrant marks as desired. Remove the template and wrap the blank again with masking tape just above where you want the decorative wrap to end.

Repeat the process at this spot (using a small template circle) and make two or four more marks, making sure they are completely aligned with the original marks.

An easy way to check this is to use a strong overhead light (fluorescent lights are good) that will make a streak or reflection of light running the length of the blank. Hold the rod and your head steady, and rotate the blank to line up the streak of light with the mark made at the handle. (I find that it helps to do this with one eye closed.) Then, without moving your head or the rod, run your eye to the upper wrap of masking tape and rotate the circle template to line up the quadrant mark with the streak of light. Check several times, and then mark the masking tape. Once these marks are made, it is simple to use a rule to line up the respective quadrant marks and to mark the blank, at which points the initial threads should cross.

You can buy special rulers (from stationery, drafting, and art supply stores) that have individual marks for various measured distances. These rulers have specific scales for measurements of 3/16, 5/16, and ⅝ inch, and so on, as well as the more common ¼-, ½-, and ¾-inch spacings. They make it easy to space out the decorative wrap without the calculations required when using regular rules.

DECORATIVE-WRAP-ALIGNMENT CHECKER

A decorative-wrap-alignment checker can easily be made from a right-angle piece of clear plastic. This tool is used to line up the initial crossing threads of decorative wraps. The clear plastic makes it possible to line up the crossing threads with the sharp bend. Commercially manufactured clear-plastic angles, used as wallpaper and paint outside-corner protectors for homes and offices, are available in several widths and lengths.

LOOP WRAP FINISHER

The standard method of finishing rod wraps is to loop the thread, wrap over the loop, cut the end of the thread, and place it through the loop, pulling the loop through to tuck the thread under the last wraps.

The problem is that making these turns after laying down a loop of thread often causes the loop to spiral and tangle around the blank and guides. You can prevent this by making a simple wrap finisher that consists of nothing more than short strips of hook-and-loop fastener (Velcro), a small eyelet or rivet, and a short length of

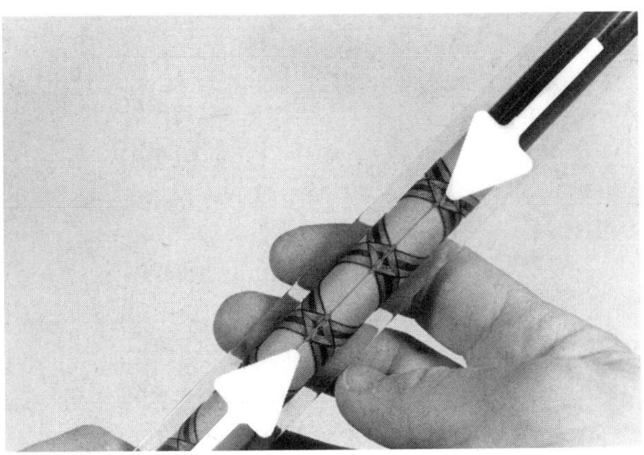

Clear corner edging used for checking decorative wraps. The optical line formed by the sharp bend in the clear plastic (arrows) makes it easy to check the wrap alignment.

monofilament. To make it, cut a length of hook-and-loop fastener about 3 to 4 inches long. Cut one end into a square and the other end into two opposing angles. Making these angle cuts will allow small tag ends to stick out for easy opening of the finisher.

Use an awl to poke a hole through both sides of the square-cut end, and insert and seat a small eyelet. These eyelets are sold in kits in sewing-supply stores. You also can use a rivet, sew the two parts, or even glue them. Through the eyelet, or attached to that end of the hook-and-loop material, add a small loop of monofilament fishing line. Place the knot at the eyelet or close to this position. Use a size of monofilament relative to the size of the thread used and the pressure used to wrap the guide in place. I find that ten- to twelve-pound test mono works well, but lighter or heavier line can be used if desired.

To use the finisher, first wrap to the point where the loop is wrapped down. At this point, open the hook-and-loop fastener and secure it around the rod blank with the loop end over the wraps. Then wrap over the monofilament for the desired number of turns. Cut the end of the thread, tuck it through the monofilament loop, and pull and loop through to pull the thread under the previous wraps. Remove the wrap finisher until it's needed on the next guide.

TENSION STABILIZER

A tension holder or stabilizer allows you to maintain tension on an incomplete thread wrap on a rod when you have to leave the wrapping bench. If you don't use something like this tool, or don't tape the thread down (a messier alternative), the thread wrap will lose tension.

A tension holder is nothing more than a piece of wire with a sharp bend in each end. One end must be covered with rubber or plastic tubing before bending. The tubing creates friction on the rod to prevent it from rotating back and losing thread tension. The hook on the other end holds a sinker of any type. Usually 2 to 4 ounces is a good weight, although you might want more for big rods where heavier thread and more tension are used. You can also

This simple tension holder maintains basic tension on the thread wrap while wrapping a rod should you have to leave the wrapping bench. The plastic-coated wire will not hurt the rod; the weight prevents the rod from turning and the tension from slipping.

bend this hook into an eye to permanently attach the weight.

I have made these from plastic-coated coat-hanger wire, stiff utility wire (or plain coat-hanger wire) with slip-on plastic or rubber tubing, and utility wire coated with the latex rubber dip sold and used for coating tool handles.

Keep a tension stabilizer on your wrapping table. To use, slip the sinker onto the hook and place the rubberized hook on the rod next to the wrapping thread. This will allow you to take coffee, telephone, and bathroom breaks.

ROD CUTTING MITER BOX

A miter box allows you to cut material at a right angle (90 degrees) or a specific angle (45 degrees or 60/30 degrees) as required. For cutting rod blanks, you will want a 90-degree angle cut when chopping blanks (chapter 26) or assuring a squared base for determining the spine of a rod.

You can easily make a miter box with some strips of 6-inch-wide shelving. Start by cutting a 1-foot-long section for the base. Then cut a 10-inch-long section and cut it in half lengthwise at a 45-degree angle. If necessary, sand or polish these two 45-degree cuts. Turn one of these over and glue (Elmer's Glue-All is good) and tack with brads to the base strip. The result will be a board with a center V, or channel. Use flathead screws to attach a right-angle brace to each side of the V-channel, making sure that the flat upright side of the brace is flush with the end of the V-channel. Then you can place a rod blank into the V-channel and hold it while using a fine-tooth saw blade at the brace (right-angle point) to cut through the blank. Make sure that you wrap the blank with several layers of masking tape to prevent any splintering as you cut.

3
Spinners

Introduction • Tools • Spinner Parts and Materials • Steps in Building a Typical Spinner • Correcting Problems • Variations in Spinner Design and Construction • Figuring Spinner Weights • Spinner Kits

Basic Safety Requirements

Goggles

A clean, clear place to work

Basic Tools

Needle-nose or round-nose pliers with side cutters

Helpful Tools

Small round-nose pliers

Diagonal wire cutters or compound-action pliers with wire cutters

Wire former (commercial or homemade)

Worth (or other brand) split-ring pliers

Compound-leverage fishing pliers

INTRODUCTION

Spinners are among the most popular and effective lures for a wide range of freshwater gamefish. That they are not used more widely in salt water is probably more a function of rust and corrosion than a lack in their ability to catch fish. Spinners predate many other types of lures. Some catalogs of the 1890s prominently displayed them. The Wilkinson Co., a distributor of the time, shows Pflueger's Success Luminous Spoon. Although called a spoon, this was really a spinner design with a straight shaft and fluted fish-head-pattern blade that revolved around the shaft on a clevis. The lure was equipped with a feather-dressed treble hook. Similar "spoons" are shown in earlier catalogs. In 1988 Mepps, makers of some of the best-known spinners, celebrated its fiftieth anniversary in the United States. Mepps began here in 1939, before the big influx of spinning in the late 1940s and early 1950s. It was probably the influx of spinning tackle that tremendously increased the popularity of these small, light lures, since spinning tackle made them easy to cast. Previously these lures were mostly trolled.

Today spinners retain their high popularity and effectiveness. In all their variety of colors, styles, sizes, shapes, and finishes, they are among the best lures for almost all types of freshwater gamefish and some saltwater gamefish as well. Unfortunately these small hunks of metal are also relatively expensive. And to be fished well, they must be fished deep. This means more fish, but it also means more lost lures, because the treble hooks of typical spinners catch easily on underwater snags.

By making your own spinners, you can reduce a substantial part of the cost of these lures—and as a result find yourself fishing more effectively as your concern over losing them lessens.

TOOLS

Many anglers avoid tinkering with spinners because of false notions about either the complexity of making them or the tools required. Many anglers think that a complex, expensive wire former is required to bend and form the eyes on the spinner shafts. Few of us can afford such expensive equipment to make only one type of lure. Although this tool (sold by Cabela's and other companies) is handy and will make wire-forming very easy, all you really need is a pair of round- or needle-nose pliers with built-in side cutters. (If your pliers lack this feature,

Commercial wire former making a wrap in a spinner wire. This tool is used for high-production spinner making. Interchangeable rotating shafts are available for different sizes of wire.

you'll also need a pair of diagonal wire cutters.) As noted in chapter 2, you can avoid this expense by making a simple wire former from nails and a block of wood, reducing the tool cost to zip.

The pros and cons of each type of tool you can use (*not* must have!) are as follows:

Production wire formers. The Tacklemaker, available from some tackle shops and a number of mail-order suppliers, clamps to the table, has bins to hold parts, and uses different collets or heads for working with different-size wires. Wire ranges, in fractions of an inch, for this are 0.018 to 0.025, 0.026 to 0.032, and 0.033 to 0.040. Two handles adjust to make different types of eyes and bends in wire. This tool is ideal but relatively expensive.

Wire formers. These smaller, relatively inexpensive wire formers are available from many shops and catalogs. They look like a C-clamp with an adjustable handle that can be turned to form simple wraps and bends, including wrapped eyes. They will not handle wire smaller than 0.020.

Tack-L-Tool. This wire former from Netcraft also has a handle for turning wrapped eyes and other bends and can be used freehand or mounted to a worktable. Like the small wire formers, it is inexpensive.

Separate handle on the commercial wire former makes various R- and Omega-type bends in wire, along with bends for snap-closure and coil-spring fasteners.

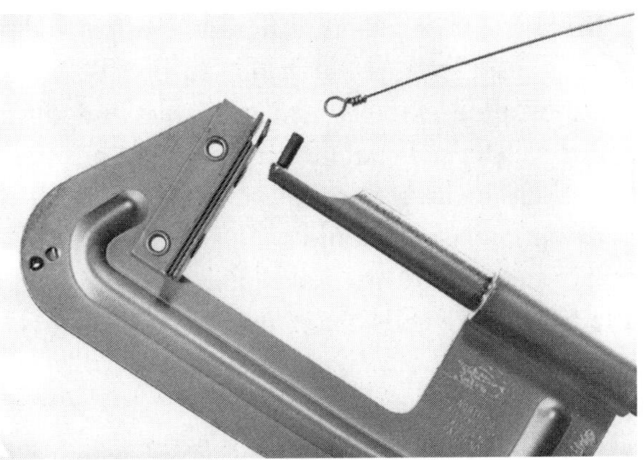

The Worth wire former can be used to make several different types of eyes and bends in spinner wire.

completely round and thus will make a perfectly round eye in any wire. In most cases these jaws are tapered so that, by using different parts of the jaws, different-size eyes can be formed.

Wire cutters. These are only necessary if you do not have wire cutters built into your pliers or wire formers. Some form of wire cutter (built-in or separate) is necessary to cut off excess wire after finishing a spinner. The best are those with flush diagonal cutters; the compound-leverage action of fishing pliers will cut easier, although not as close to the shaft.

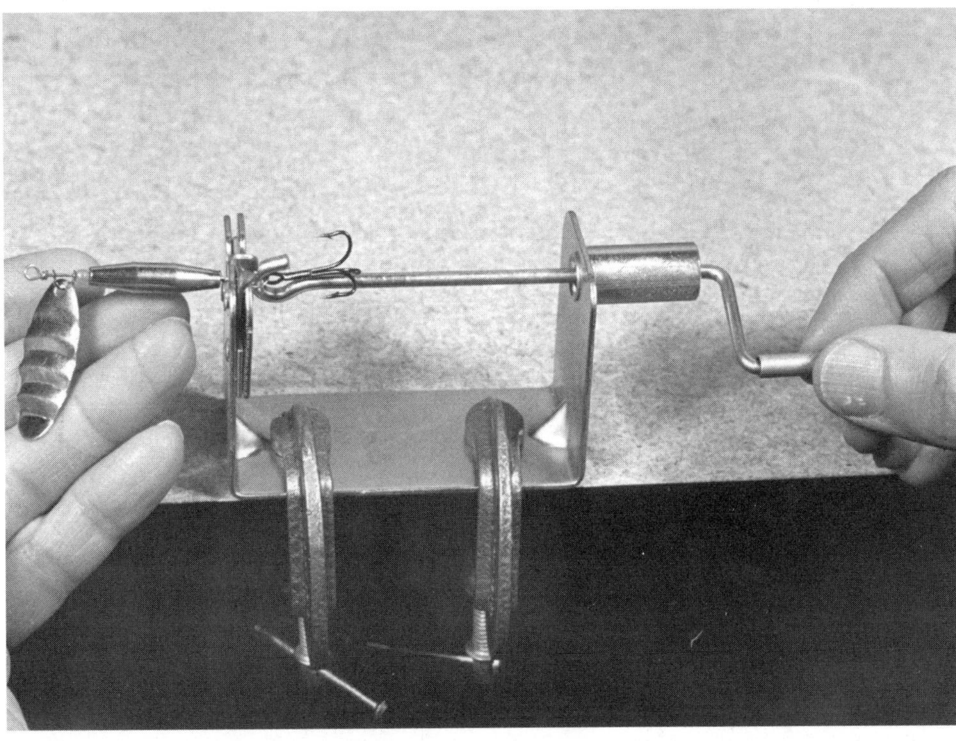

This Netcraft wire former clamps to a table, as shown, to make spinner making easy.

Needle-nose pliers. These are listed simply because they are more common in most shops than the preferred round-nose pliers. The singular disadvantage of these pliers is that the two jaws are not round but half-round, making it almost impossible to get a completely round eye in a spinner. They are okay to use if you have them, since any slight irregularity in the eye will not affect fishing performance or reduce the number of strikes possible.

Round-nose pliers. These are preferred over needle-nose pliers simply because both jaws are

Split-ring pliers. These are available through tackle shops and parts catalogs. Several styles are available from Worth, including an inexpensive pair and two sizes of precision pliers. All styles work the same way: They have a small tooth over the end of the tapered jaw, the tooth making it possible to pick up and open any size of split ring for adding to a wrapped eye or hook. I like to modify these pliers by slightly sharpening the tapered jaw and reducing the size of the tooth to make it easier to pick up the split rings.

SPINNER PARTS AND MATERIALS

Spinners generally consist of a shaft, clevis, spinner blade or blades, body or beads, hooks, and tail dressings. The shaft, with an eye at each end, holds the body or beads and the clevis, which in turn holds the rotating blade. A hook is attached to the lower eye. Specific parts and details follow.

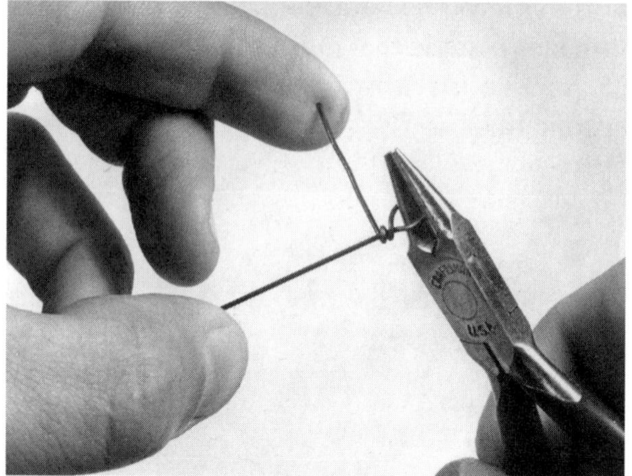

Most spinner-making tasks can be done with a pair of round-nose pliers, as shown, and wire cutters.

Spinner Shafts

These are usually made of straightened piano wire or stainless steel wire. If you plan to fish in salt or brackish water, get the stainless steel shafts. They cost a little more than tinned piano-wire shafts but are readily available. The slight cost difference is worth it.

For standard spinners, there are several types of eyes on the shafts. Shafts are available in several lengths, usually ranging from 3 inches to 8 inches. While wire sizes of 0.024 to 0.030 are typical of most shafts, some range up to 0.035 and larger.

Shafts are available in straight lengths, with a single (one end) wrapped eye, or with an open eye (closed with a spring and used to change hooks and parts), self-lock-snap shafts (in which the eye has a formed spring lock), and swivel shafts (which have a barrel swivel eye at one end built onto the shaft).

The straight lengths (no eye) must have both eyes (one at each end) formed. Use these only if you plan to form some different eyes to make some of the spinner variations to be discussed later. Straight wire is also available in longer lengths (usually about 18 inches) or in coils that are about 16 inches in diameter and sold on a per-pound basis. Stainless steel, tinned piano, and brass wire are often available this way. Usually the spring coils are tempered so that there is no curve or curl. Use caution if the coils are not spring-tempered, because it may be impossible to completely and properly straighten out these lengths.

The wrapped-eye shaft is the most useful for making most typical spinners because the eye can be used for the line-tie and the rest of the body and blade added to the shaft, with the hook added to an eye that is formed to complete the spinner.

The open-eye type, also called a spring-closure eye, has an eye with the end bent parallel to the main shaft and closed by means of a short (¼- to ½-inch-long) spring. These are ideal for those lures where you wish to change hooks, add lure dressing to hooks, add additional wire or second hooks for minnow or bait rigs, or add a spinner to the front of a lure or fly.

The self-lock-snap type (also called a self-clip or safety-lock-wire shaft) is similar to the open-eye but has a small right-angle hook on the end of the open eye so that the eye can be

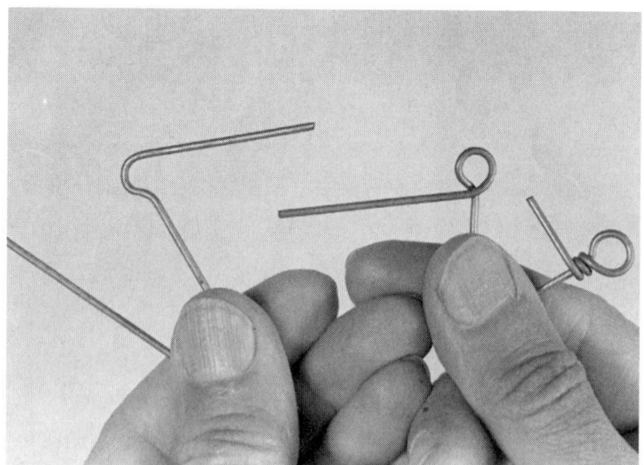

Method of making a simple wrapped eye: From left to right, beginning with straight shaft to first and second bend, completed eye, and wrapped eye. Eye must have excess wire trimmed after this final stage.

closed by snapping it on the shaft. It also allows changing parts, hooks, and riggings but does not require the spring closure.

Swivel shafts are rated by the size of the swivel, ranging from a number 10 (small) through a number 3 (large) swivel, and come in lengths from 3 to 5 inches. This swivel has a wrapped rotating eye coming from one end of the barrel; the shaft (usually brass) emerges from the other end.

With the exception of the brass swivel shafts, shafts are springy and are made of tinned or stainless steel. With diameters ranging from 0.026 to 0.040, you can make spinners with stiff shafts or light-wire shafts that will vibrate. All of this wire is strong, so go for the lightest wire to increase vibration. However, in some styles the light, bendable wire can sometimes cause turning parts to bind. This is particularly true of double-blade styles, to be discussed later. Tough fish will bend and sometimes ruin light-wire spinners.

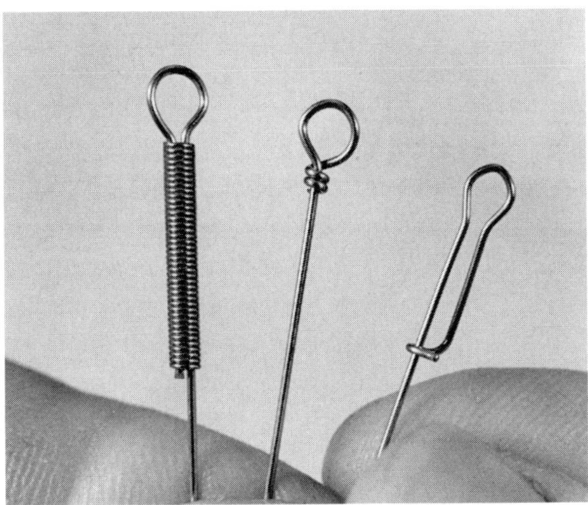

Types of wire eyes used for making spinners. Shafts are available with these eyes formed. Left to right: coil-spring closure, wrapped eye, and snap closure.

Order enough wire to make the lures you want, because quantity purchases will reduce cost. Also be sure to order wire not only with the best type of eye for your purposes but also of the proper length. Remember that you will need some wire to work with in making the eye. Usually 1 to 2 inches extra is sufficient. Thus, for a 1-inch-long spinner, get 3-inch-long wire; for a 2-inch spinner, 4-inch wire; and for a 3-inch-long spinner, 5-inch wire or longer. This gives you enough length to form the eye, make the wraps or closure type that you want, and cut off the excess.

The best way to buy all spinner shafts is in lots of one hundred or more, since this will give you the best pricing. To avoid getting a lot of different shafts, get spinner shafts in the longest length that is practical and useful, even if you will be making some short spinners. That way you can get a larger bundle (at a lower cost) of, say, 6-inch shafts rather than getting one hundred each of 3-, 5-, and 6-inch shafts, all for different-size spinners.

Clevises

These should also be bought in lots of one hundred each, although if you'll be working with different-size blades, you may wish to get two or more sizes. Clevises come in several styles, including folded, stamped-stirrup, wire-stirrup, and fast-change styles.

The folded type is made by stamping out sheet metal in an O shape and then folding it over into a U shape, with the holes formed by the fold of the metal in the upper part of the U. The shaft runs through these holes, and the bend of the U holds the spinner blade. I do not like the folded clevises for spinners; I feel the broader folded portion of metal might create more water resistance and thus slightly interfere with blade rotation. However, many manufacturers use folded clevises on their commercial spinners, so my fears are probably more fanciful than factual. The folded types are best on monofilament worm rigs, because the folded wire will wear less on the monofilament used in these rigs. (Worm rigs are covered in chapter 12, "Miscellaneous Lures.") Five sizes are available, in both nickel finish and polished brass.

Stamped clevises are made from an I-shaped piece of metal with a hole punched in each end. They are bent into a U shape so that the thin edge of metal cuts the water smoothly as the blade turns. The shaft runs through the two holes in the ends, which are parallel once bent into the U shape.

Wire clevises are similar but have a round wire, and the ends are forged flat and punched. Of the three types of clevises, these have the nicest appearance close up, although the fish probably won't care. Stamped and wire clevises usually are available in nickel finish and four sizes. Most sizes in all clevises run from 0 to 1 to 3 or 4; the larger the number, the larger the clevis.

Some clevises are a fast-change style to allow for changing spinner blades at will. One fast-change type is made of plastic in two sizes and several colors. It has a plastic collar through which the shaft runs and a tiny clip into which spinner blades can be fastened. There is also a fast-change wire clevis in a U shape, with a small open spring on each end. This spring allows for changing the clevis, but it works best on flexible cable or monofilament rather than the stiffer wire used in spinners.

In choosing any type of clevis, it is important to choose the proper size for the size of the spinner blade you will use. For rapid and easy spinning you want the smallest clevis possible, but too small a clevis may cause the blade to bind against the shaft. Unfortunately there is no easy way to check this. If you're in a store, temporarily assemble a sample clevis, blade, and shaft to check for binding.

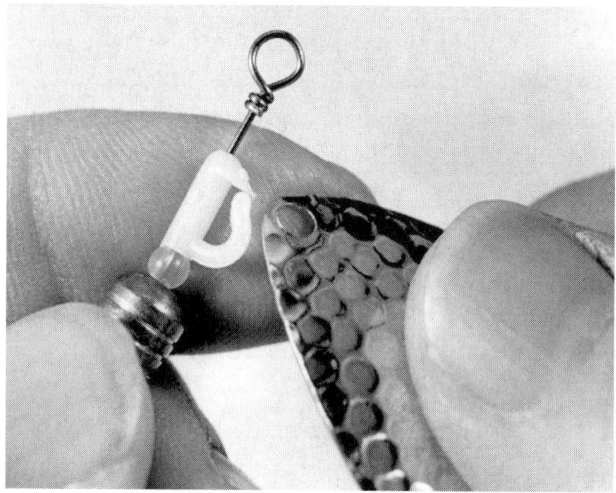

A quick-change clevis allows you to quickly change spinner blades while fishing.

You can make your own clevises, although most of these will be large. You will need safety chain (sometimes called sash chain), which has a fold-over oval link. By cutting these links out to make separate brass ovals, you can fold the ovals into a clevis.

The easiest way to do this is to cut a slot into a wood board, lay the link across it, and use a thin chisel, hacksaw blade, or similar device to form the oval link into a folded U. Place a nail of the size required to form a wire sleeve into the slot. Use flat-jaw pliers or clamp the rest of the folded oval in a vise to form a flattened U around the nail. Remove the nail to use the clevis.

Note that I said this was possible—not easy, fast, or economical. In fact, with the low cost of clevises, this is simply unnecessary work. The only real reason for making clevises is if you wish to use one on a larger diameter wire form or for a heavy-duty spinner made on thicker than normal wire, where normal clevises won't work.

Blades

Blades come in such a bewildering array of styles, sizes, colors, finishes, and shapes that an orderly description is all but impossible. Standard spinner blades used to include the Indiana, Colorado, and willowleaf styles. Today these are joined by badger styles, fluted trolling, regular trolling, Chopper (a fat, bowling-pin shape), in-line, French style, spin true, ripple, rotoblade, June Bug, bent-edge (the Presto from Netcraft), and swing styles. Following are some popular styles:

Colorado. This is a basic fat-style spinner blade found on many lures. As a result of its fat shape, it will spin at a pronounced angle from the shaft when on a spinner.

Indiana. This slightly thinner style of spinner blade still has a rounded end. It will also spin at an angle from the shaft, but not as much as in the Colorado.

Willowleaf. With its pointed end, this blade looks like a leaf from a willow tree. These spin very close to the shaft of a spinner when they rotate.

Serrated. These blades come in seven sizes and in brass, polished brass, and nickel finishes. They are available in both smooth and hex pattern finishes and look like a standard willowleaf blade with a scalloped or serrated outer edge for more action (water turbulence) and flash.

Whiptail. Whiptail blades come in five sizes and several finishes, looking in silhouette like a baitfish. Two of them in a tandem spinner can appear like a school of baitfish thrashing through the water.

Olympic. The nine sizes of these blades all look like a very wide, pointed-end willowleaf. They are very popular in the Pacific Northwest for salmon and trout. They are available in brass, polished brass, nickel, and gold finishes, both plain and hammered.

Badger. These blades are slightly thicker or fatter than the Indiana, but not nearly as fat as the Colorado. Some companies use this term for a thinner, lightweight blade in the Colorado and Indiana styles.

Regular trolling blades. These are like fat willowleaf blades but are designed for trolling rigs. They really belong in the chapter on miscellaneous lures but are included here because they can be used for spinners.

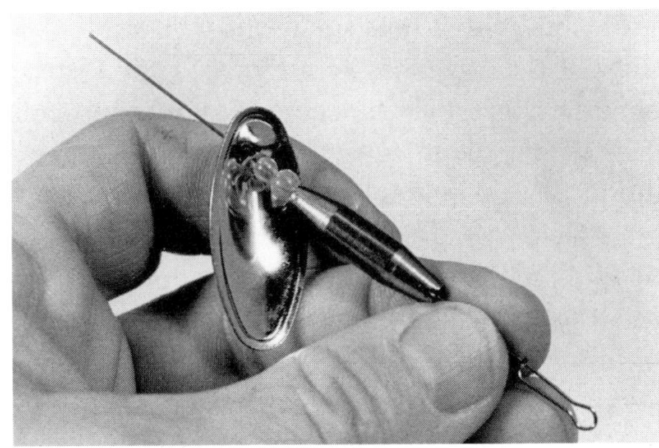

In-line spinner. These special blades do not use a clevis; the shaft goes through a hole partway down the blade. The blade still rotates rapidly.

Fluted trolling blades. These are like regular trolling blades but with a slightly scalloped edge.

Chopper blades. Used in a popular brand of spinnerbaits, these blades are made by one company and are available through tackle dealers in kit form. The blades have a figure-eight shape—a shape like a Shmoo if you remember *Li'l Abner* or like a Smurf if you don't.

In-line blades. These are relatively new to component parts, although a similar blade has been used for years on a popular spinner (Panther Martin). It consists of a fat, egg-shaped style of

Many different blades are available for making spinners and spinnerbaits.

blade, but with a hole about one-quarter to one-third of the way back from the head end instead of at the edge. A clevis is not used with this blade because the shaft runs through the hole. This unique style provides lots of vibration.

French style. These blades have a forged, raised bevel, similar to the blade used in a popular spinner. They are called Spem blades in some catalogs.

Spin-true blades. These, along with the Rotospins, have an angled blade and an additional bent extension arm that holds the blade at a specific angle. The shaft runs through the hole at the top end of the blade and the extension arm in order to achieve this fixed position and rotation.

Rotospin blades. These are like the spin-true blades but in a slightly fatter shape.

June Bug. These blades have a stamped-out extension arm (stamped from the middle of the blade) through which the shaft runs to hold the blade at a specific angle.

Bent-edge. Also called Presto blades, these have a slightly bent or cupped edge. This employs one of the tricks of the bass-fishing pros, who often bend the edges of their spinner blades to get more vibration, noise, and action from spinners and similar spinner-blade lures.

Swing blades. These blades are slim and uniform throughout, unlike the Colorado or Indiana blades that are tapered at the top like an egg. These are most like a willowleaf with the ends rounded off. They are a copy of a blade used on a well-known lure (the C. P. Swing).

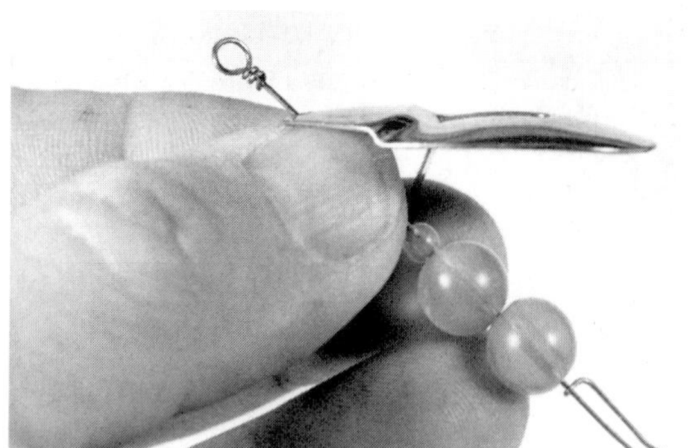

Example of June Bug spinner used often for baitfishing. The snap-closure shaft allows for adding a straight-eye, long-shank hook for holding worms, leeches, minnows, etc.

Ripple blades. These are like swing blades and about the same shape, but with horizontal ripples or bends in the blade for added flash and attraction.

All these blades require clevises except for the in-line style, in which the shaft runs through the hole in the blade, and the fixed-position blades such as the Rotospin and June Bug.

Sizes

Blades sizes range widely. Numbers are used to indicate size for each blade style, although the length of a #4 willowleaf (about 1⅞ inches) is not the same as a #4 Colorado (about 1¼ inches). Sizes range from small 00 and 000 designations that are about the size of a little fingernail, up to 6s, 7s, and 8s (the maximum size number varies with the blade style) that can be as long as 3⅞ inches. There are also occasionally half sizes, such as a 3½ or 4½. The size must be compatible with the total lure, clevis, and beads or body. The larger the blade, the larger the clevis needed to prevent binding. Also, larger bodies are usually used with large blades. Note that there are no industry standards, although most companies are close in their sizing. Worth Company, a major manufacturer of blades and parts for the lure business, has a chart of size comparison of their blades with similar or identical blades by two other competitors, Lakeland and Hagen's. This chart is reproduced, courtesy of the Worth Company, in appendix D of this book. Lakeland has a fat catalog showing all their spoon and spinner blade sizes.

Finishes and Colors

All spinner blades come in specific finishes, some in painted colors. Most are metallic, with a nickel finish the most popular. Other popular finishes include copper, brass, gold plate, and two-tone finishes, although nickel/copper is most popular. These are polished finishes, but the blades are also available in hammered and hex finishes.

Both hammered and smooth-polished blades are available in baked-on painted finishes. These include such colors as red, chartreuse, black, orange, green, blue, purple, and white. Combinations are available with one color on one side and a second on the other, or with a metallic finish on one side and paint on the other. Blades with painted spots, stripes, scale patterns, herringbone stripes, and other patterns are also commonly available.

Worth offers spinner blades in many colors and designs. Lakeland finishes for their spinner blades include plain, hammered, fluted, diamond, hex, scale, rib, prism, and ripple blade patterns. Some Lakeland spinner blades come in up to eight different finishes, including rainbow, blue firetiger, green firetiger, orange frog, green frog, blue horizon, watermelon, and red flame.

I have occasionally seen plastic blades in opaque- and translucent-colored finishes. The translucent-finish blades usually have some glitter in them for added flash. Because these blades are lighter, they throb far less in the water and have less of a strobelike flash from the reflective surface. They have a completely different action.

Plastic blades come in typical colors, such as chartreuse, hot pink, green, glitter chartreuse, glitter red, glitter blue, pearl, glitter purple, and glitter brown, and in standard shapes such as the Colorado and Indiana.

Pearl blades, once widely popular, are seen less often today. They are available for making your own spinners. They are cut from shell and drilled and shaped like other spoons. Usually limited sizes and shapes are available, with sizes 00 through 3 in the Indiana style most popular.

It is also possible to make your shell blades from natural freshwater or saltwater shells. First use a small pointed and tapered grinding bit (like that available with Dremel tools) to drill a hole through the blade. With the blade drilled for the spinner shaft, use a motorized grinder or sander to sand the edges of the shell to a blade shape. You want to work in this order because breakage most often occurs when drilling the shaft hole. It is better to have breakage before doing anything else than after you have shaped the blades. Blades are easily and quickly shaped after drilling a smooth and effective hole.

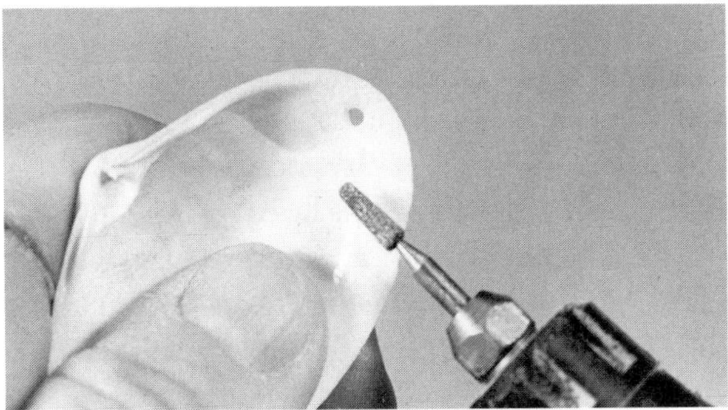

Spinner blades can be made out of shell, but it is not recommended because of the high percentage of breakage. Here the eye is formed using a small high-speed grinding tool bit.

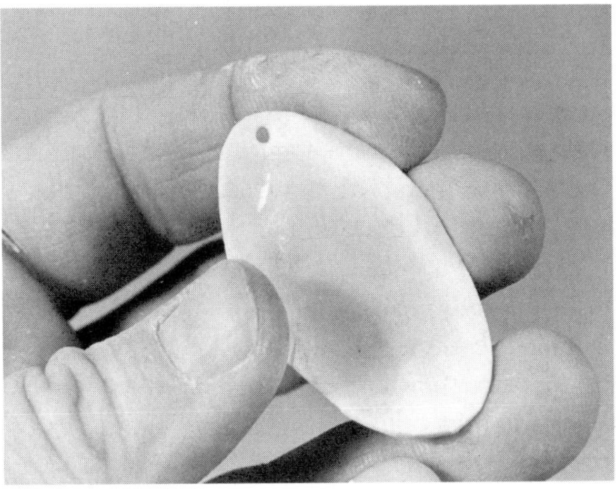

Completed spinner blade from natural shell. Grind the blade shape after drilling the hole, since breakage is most likely to occur when drilling.

You can make your own blades by cutting handles off lightweight teaspoons and tablespoons or hammering out blades from light metal using the techniques listed in chapter 8. To make blades from teaspoons, buy spoons in sets or individually from dollar stores or when on sale to get the cheapest price. You can use other items for blades as well. One option is the brightly colored plastic fingernails sold in cosmetic departments. They are usually too expensive for serious consideration, though, since so many metallic-finish and painted blades are available specifically for tackle making.

Beads

Beads are used to make up a wide variety of commercial spinners, and perhaps the most popular and well known of this style is the C. P. Swing. Brass beads are used in this lure.

Beads come in a wide variety of sizes, styles, colors, and materials, so the choices and combinations are really infinite. Examples of bead styles include:

Solid brass beads. These are just what the name says—solid brass, polished, and with a hole drilled through to allow slipping onto the spinner shaft. Typical hole sizes are about 0.052 to 0.063 inch, plenty large enough for any spinner shaft (usually 0.024 to 0.035) and often large enough for the larger diameter shafts (often 0.040) used for spinnerbaits, buzzbaits, and similar jig-spinner forms. Typical sizes range from ⅛ though $^{11}/_{32}$ inch, in $^{1}/_{32}$-inch increments. They are commonly available in both polished brass and nickel plate.

Hollow brass beads. These are hollow brass and thus lighter in weight. They come in both lacquered brass and nickel finishes, and because of the way they are made, they often have a slightly larger hole than the solid brass beads. The sizes are usually the same as those found in the brass beads.

Salmon red beads. These are translucent plastic beads in a salmon red or bright pink color and are widely popular for a number of spinners as the main beads to make up the body, as attractor beads added at one end of the spinner, or as a small bearing for the clevis in place of the "unies" made for this purpose.

Often these are called "fluorescent" or "fire" beads to indicate their color, although fluorescence can be found in many colors.

While all salmon beads are smooth and polished, several shapes are available, including round, oval, and pear. Unlike the brass beads, which all seem to be measured in fractional inches, these and most other beads are measured in millimeters. Round beads range in size from 2½ to 10 millimeters. Oval beads are listed by millimeters in two dimensions, with typical sizes being 3 × 6, 5 × 7, 6 × 8½, 7 × 10, and 8 × 11½. Pear beads also are measured in two dimensions—4 × 5½, 5½ × 8, 8 × 11½, 8 × 16, and 12 × 18. These are also called teardrop beads.

Translucent beads. These are like the salmon beads but come in yellow, light green, blue, and sometimes other colors. They are usually available only in round shapes but in the full range of sizes.

Faceted plastic beads. These are like the translucent beads but with cut sides or facets for added sparkle. They are only available in the round shape in all the typical sizes and in blue, red, yellow, purple, and gold colors.

Opaque beads. These are also usually available only in polished round shapes but come

Beads and bodies available for making spinners and other tackle. The top two rows are beads; the bottom two rows are various spinner bodies.

in opaque colors including black, dark green, blue, yellow, and red. Sizes usually range from 3 through 10 millimeters.

Luminous beads. These are not fluorescent but are glow-in-the-dark, also called luminous or phosphorescent. They are charged by light and will glow for some time after exposure, usually 3 or 4 hours. They are usually an off-shade, yellowish ivory or sick yellow. In the dark they glow yellow, although other colors are available. Sizes range from 3 to 10 millimeters.

Pearl beads. These plastic beads have a pearl finish and range in size from 3 to 10 millimeters.

Round glass beads. Translucent bright red, somewhat like the salmon beads, glass beads are not as widely used as they once were. Typical sizes are from 4 through 10 millimeters; prices, particularly in the smaller sizes, are much higher than for plastic beads.

Faceted glass beads. These are also red, but with cut sides for more flash and sparkle. In price and size they are about the same as the round glass beads.

Tee beads. Tee beads are made of plastic, usually in three colors: yellow, blue, and fluorescent red. The shape comes to a point like a thin six-sided pyramid, and the beads look a little like a shortened golf tee. Because they are larger than other beads, they are often used on larger spinners and sometimes on offshore trolling lures.

Plated plastic beads. Plated beads are plastic that is plated a gold or silver color. Sizes from 3 to 8 millimeters are available.

In addition to the beads described above, lots of variations can be found through art and craft stores and mail-order outlets. I have a craft store near me, and I find lots of additional parts for making spinners and other lures. Here are some of the beads I've discovered:

Tri-beads. These are triangle-shaped—somewhat like stubby propellers—with a center hole for threading on the shaft. They will stack up on the shaft and make for a neat body when used this way. Several sizes of these plastic beads are available, in a wide variety of opaque and translucent colors. In the larger sizes I like them not only for larger spinners but also for small or thin offshore trolling lures (see chapter 11). These are also beginning to show up in the tackle-component catalogs for larger spinners or as beads used as spacers for offshore skirted trolling lures.

Starflake beads. These look like stylized snowflakes with six "wings" or projections from the center hole. Most are large—the smallest I have seen was 12 millimeters, the largest 25 millimeters. The smaller sizes are fine for spinners; the larger are good for offshore trolling lures and other uses.

Floating beads. These are designed for adding to a snelled hook to float a lure or to make a "floating" jig head. These medium-size beads are available in a variety of colors, including luminous (glow-in-the-dark), purple, coral, green, black, and red. The two sizes available are ⅜ and ½ inch in diameter. They can be added to spinners when you want to reduce the total weight of the lure for casting on certain tackle or to help float a lure up off of the bottom to prevent snagging or loss.

Bodies. Although beads work fine to make up the body of a typical spinner, there are larger body forms that accomplish the same purpose. In some cases several are used, just as they are on commercially made spinners. They come in brass, lead, or plastic.

Brass bodies. These are solid brass but are available in a polished-brass or polished-nickel finish. There are no names for the many shapes available, but they are identical or similar to those used in standard commercial spinners. Torpedo shapes are the most popular and are available in about six sizes and weights. Little ones are about ⅝ inch long and weigh 5/64 ounce; the largest are about 1¼ inches and weigh 7/32 ounce.

There are various lengths and shapes that look like little bullets or lead-bullet castings; small, pointed, tapered bodies; those that resemble strung beads; and some odd shapes that defy description. Prices range widely, depending upon the number bought, the finish, and the size and complexity of the shape.

In general the nickel-finish bodies are more expensive than the solid brass. These bodies often have a small slot in one end so that the spinner wire can be bent to lock the body in place when making the lures in reverse (tail to line-tie) fashion.

Lead bodies. These are usually available both unpainted and painted, the latter in a wide variety of colors. Both come in 1-inch (0.1875 ounce) or 1⅛-inch (0.250 ounce) lengths. They have holes large enough for any size wire.

Plastic bodies. Plastic bodies are similar to the brass or lead bodies. Most common are those in a small tapered shape (like a cigar) that is about 1 inch to 1½ inches long. You can get similar small plastic "beads" from art-and-craft shops, sometimes sold as spaghetti beads. Those that I have used measure bout ¾ inch long and come in bright colors, as do the fishing-tackle plastic bodies. Any of these can be used as a single complete body on a spinner or in combination with beads, brass bodies, or other parts. Similar craft beads with a larger hole, called pony beads, are also available but in general are not as useful because the hole is too large. They will work better on offshore lures, though.

Hooks

Treble hooks are used on most typical spinners, but single or double hooks can also be used. Always use good hooks, such as those made by Mustad, Eagle Claw, VMC, Gamakatsu, Tiemco, or similar brands. Many variations in treble hooks are available, including shank length (standard, short, and long), finish (bronze, gold, japanned, nickel, tinned), and point style (curved, beaked, circle, or straight). Treble hooks come with fixed eyes or with sliced eyes in which the hook can be added to a fixed, permanent hook hanger and the hook eye closed with pliers. From a standpoint of tradition at least, most spinners use bronze-finish, standard-shank-length, straight- or curved-point trebles.

Dressed treble hooks, available from some companies, allow you to make dressed spinners without having to tie your own bucktail, fur, feathers, or synthetics onto bare trebles. These dressed trebles are more expensive than plain trebles, but they are time savers and avoid the need for a fly-tying vise or other tools required to tie dressed hooks.

The one main advantage of double hooks is that their construction allows them to be slid off the spinner eye and changed or replaced as required.

Single hooks require a straight eye, since a turned-up or turned-down eye will not allow the hook to hang straight in the current—it will kink to one side. Open-eye single hooks, Siwash style, will also work and can be closed onto a spinner eye with pliers.

Among the several advantages of single hooks on spinners (or any lure) are that they are easier to unhook from toothy fish (using the necessary pliers, it is easier and quicker to remove one hook than several) and that single hooks can usually be used in larger sizes than trebles without upsetting the balance of a lure. Also, larger single hooks with a thicker shaft diameter are usually stronger when fishing for large fish.

Other Parts

Depending on the style of spinner, there are other parts to consider. These include:

Unies. These are tiny metal (nickel or brass) beads that are made specifically to serve as a bearing for the rotating clevis. This does not mean you have to use these as a bearing, but for maximum reflection and action of the blades, you should use a small bead if not using a uni or two. Since these are small, only one size is available, and color is not important. Although plastic unies can be used, metal is usually best; with heavy fishing and constant wear, the plastic can become worn from the constantly turning clevis.

Coil springs. These are used as a closure and lock for the open-eye type of shaft. Several sizes are available and are used according to the shaft size chosen. The Worth Company lists their 0.045-inch diameter coils for wire from 0.020 to 0.022, the 0.051-inch coils for wire from 0.024 to 0.026, and their 0.064-inch coils for wire diameter from 0.028 to 0.032.

Coil lengths range from ¼ to 1 inch and come in tinned wire or stainless steel. The price is usually the same for either material.

Split rings. Split rings are used for a wide variety of purposes in making lures, primarily for attaching hooks to lures, as line-ties, to connect lure parts, and to add attractors such as spinner blades or plastic teasers. Split rings come in stainless steel, tinned wire, or brass; in small to large sizes (0 to 12); and in lightweight or heavyweight wire. The smallest (size 0) from one catalog are 0.165 inch (about ⅙ inch) in diameter, and the largest size (12) is about 0.740 inch (¾ inch) in diameter. Split rings are just like the familiar split-ring key rings—a double wrap of spring wire that can be twisted onto a hook or lure.

Tubing. Tubing in many colors is used as an attractor on spinners and can be found on many commercial brands. It is added by slipping small lengths over the hook shank to further attract fish into hitting the spinner.

Although red is most common, other colors, including white, yellow, green, pink, black, and blue, can be used. Most such tubing is vinyl plastic about ⅛ inch in diameter and is usually sold by the foot. Rubber tubing in small sizes and bright colors is also available for the same purpose.

Small pieces of tubing are cut (usually about ⅜ to ⅝ inch long) and slipped over the treble-hook shank before the spinner is completed. The colored tubing must be short enough to fit over the shank without binding the eye so that the hook will swing free. An exception to this is that some anglers will use a slightly longer length of tubing so that they can slide it up over the spinner-shaft eye and hook eye to bind the two together and keep the hook in line with the spinner shaft. (There are other ways to do this, which we'll explore later in this chapter.)

Lure flippers. These are small oval (usually) pieces of plastic placed onto the spinner-shaft eye along with the hook eye and used for dressing up the lure, as does the attractor tubing. There is some variety in shape but not in color of commercially available flippers. Most are translucent red with a hole punched at one end, and several small sizes in egg, oval, or fishtail shapes are available. They can be added to any lure using a split ring. Sometimes they are called "tail tags."

Skirts. Because of their large size, skirts are not usually used on spinners; they are usually reserved for the larger spinners used for pike, muskie, and similar large fish. They must be put on before the hook is permanently attached to the spinner shaft or else used with a snap-lock spinner shaft that allows removal of the hook for adding or removing skirts (or tubing or tail tags) at will.

STEPS IN BUILDING A TYPICAL SPINNER

Although the listing of all these spinner parts can sometimes be confusing, the construction of a spinner is simplicity itself. Take, for example, a standard spinner, such as one with a brass swing blade, body of brass beads, and treble hook.

First pick a shaft of the wrapped-eye type that is about 5 inches long, for ease of handling. The wrapped eye will be the "line eye," or line-tie end of the lure. Next take a stamped or wire clevis and put it through the hole in the end of the blade. (It is a good idea to use as small a clevis as possible in all spinners. The small clevis will spin better and start easier than will larger ones. However, make sure the clevis isn't so small that it allows the spinner blade to bind against it or the spinner shaft.)

Now hold the blade, with the clevis through the hole, and place the spinner shaft through the two holes in the clevis. Check now to be sure that the concave side of the blade is next to the spinner shaft when the blade hangs against the lower part of the shaft. If the blade is on backward, remove the shaft from the clevis and replace it correctly, with the concave side of the blade resting next to the shaft.

Next add the body parts to the shaft. You may first want to add a uni as a bearing for the blade clevis, as shown in the accompanying photos. You may also want to add a cone-shaped tapered end to the upper part before adding the beads. Since this typical lure is made up of brass beads, select the size and number of beads to go on the shaft. Depending on the blade size and the size of the beads chosen, you might use three, four, or five beads. In general all bodies should be about the length of the spinner blade as it hangs down against the shaft. You can vary from this of course, but it's a good general rule. Regardless of the size of the beads chosen, select a small brass bead to rest against the clevis and to serve as a bearing for easy rotation of the blade and clevis.

One alternative to this method is to first use one or two of the small brass or nickel unies that are designed as bearings for the clevis. Another alternative is to use a tiny red glass bead as a bearing. In the case of making a spinner with body parts or with large beads, you will have to use one of these options anyway (small brass bead, uni, or small glass bead) as a bearing for the clevis. This will provide a relatively frictionless surface, allowing the clevis to turn freely. (As described before, plastic beads may wear in time and are not recommended for this use.)

The rest of the body in our typical spinner is built of larger, then successively smaller, beads to give the body an overall cigar shape or taper. Of course you do not have to go with this shape and can use beads in any configuration or size arrangement you want—running from small to large, large to small, in an hourglass shape, or any other combination or variation. The total length should be such that the spinner blade and bottom bead will rest at about the same spot.

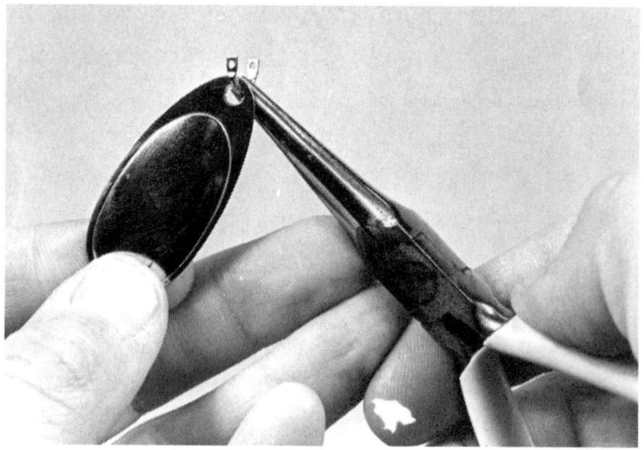

Making a spinner 1: Placing the blade on the clevis.

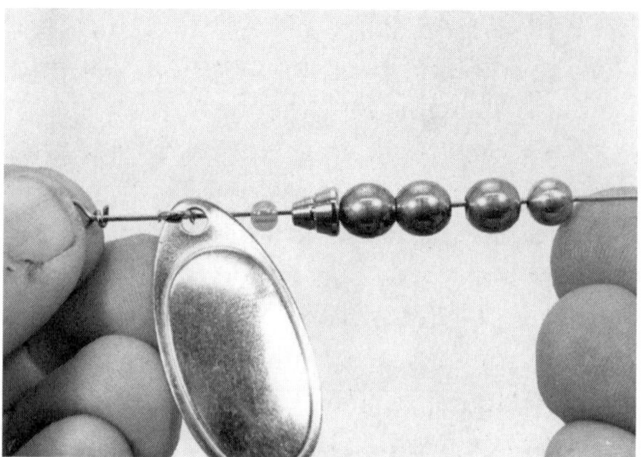

Making a spinner 2: Adding beads (and/or body) to the shaft.

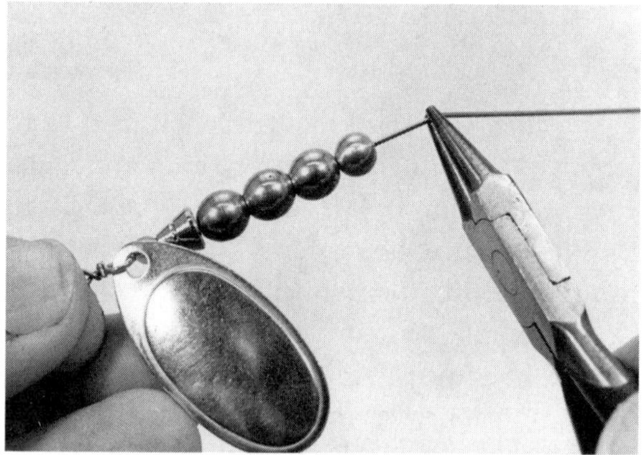

Making a spinner 3: Making the first bend in the wire to complete the spinner.

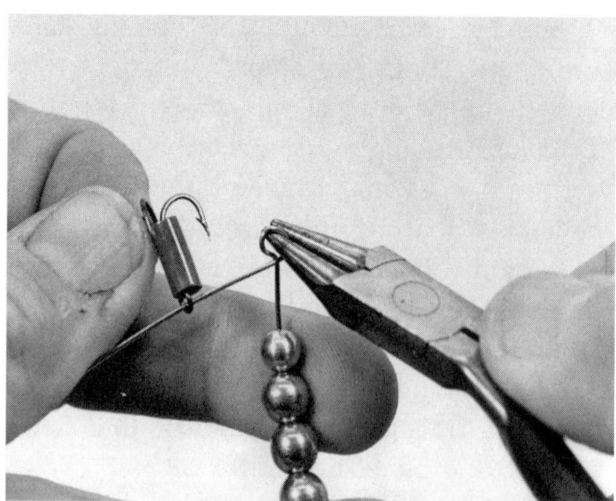

Making a spinner 4: Completed eye with a single wrap of the wire. The hook is still to be added, adding the hook onto which colored tubing has been added first.

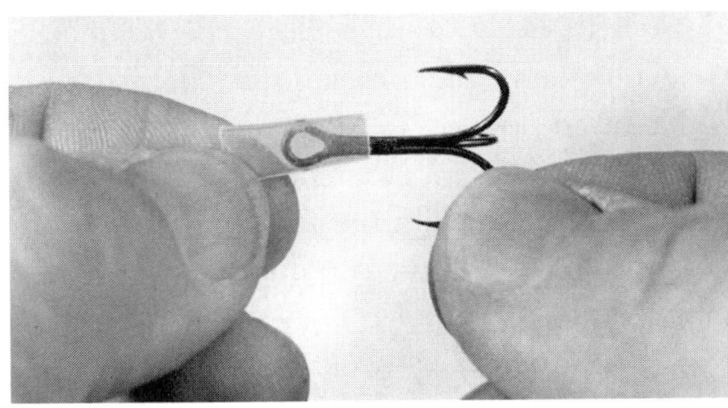

Making a spinner 5: Colored tubing can be used on any treble hook, as shown, to add to the attractiveness of the lure.

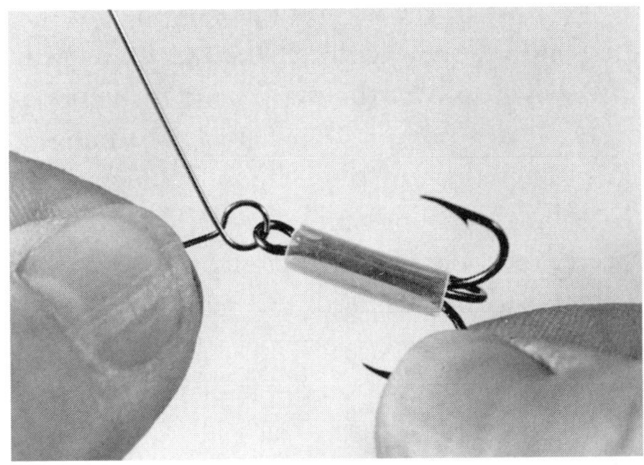

Making a spinner 6: Treble with colored tubing on the hook shank and the hook on the formed eye before the eye is wrapped.

Beneath the last bead, leave about ⅜ inch to ½ inch of clearance. This clearance is important, because without it parts of the spinner body and clevis may bind between the two shaft eyes once the spinner is completed and the lower hook eye is wrapped.

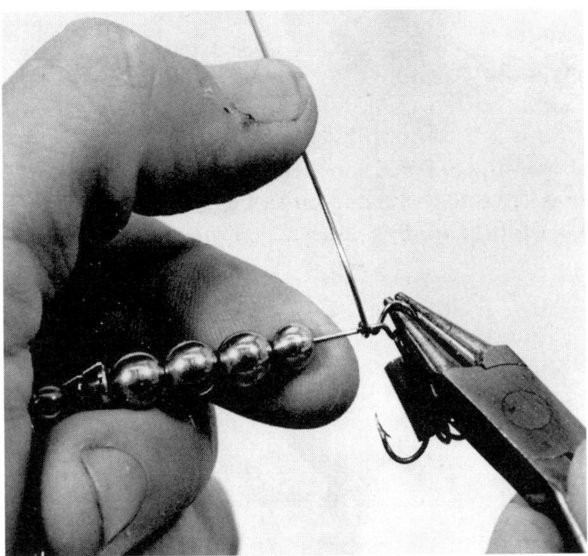

Making a spinner 7: Wrapping the eye. This binds the hook to the spinner.

Making a spinner 8: Completed spinner.

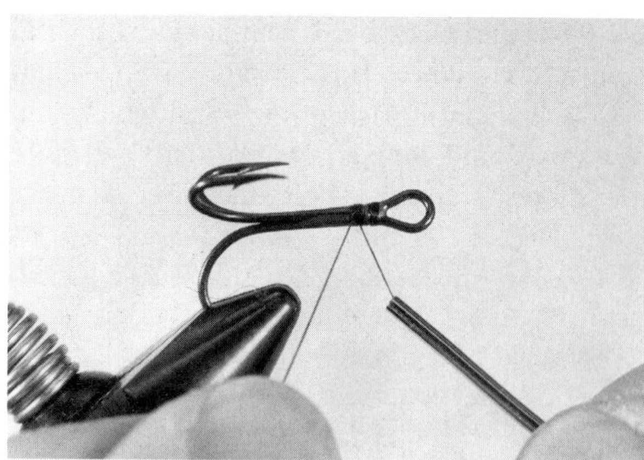

Other ways in which hooks can be decorated include dressing with a wrapped-on fur tail. Here, the treble hook is held in a fly-tying vise and wrapped with thread.

Overwrapping the fur to be added to the hook. Note that the fur completely surrounds the hook shank.

At this ⅜- to ½-inch clearance point, use your round-nose pliers to bend the shaft sharply. If the round-nose jaws are tapered, hold the wire by the end of the jaws to make a relatively sharp bend. Then reposition the jaws so that you are holding the wire higher up on the jaws (on the more rounded part of the jaws). Hold the free end of the wire just beneath the body parts. Bend the free end of the wire completely (360 degrees) around the one jaw. To do this you will first need to make an approximately 270-degree bend, at which point you will have to readjust the position of the wire in the jaws to continue the bend. When complete, the free end of the wire will cross over the sharp bend made previously. At this point add any attractor tubing or skirt material to the treble hook. To add attractor tubing, first measure the shank length of the treble hook exclusive of the eye and hook bends. Cut the tubing to this length with scissors, and slip it over the eye of the treble hook. If using a skirt, slip it on the same way. To dress a treble hook with fur or feathers, tie the materials on using fly-tying methods or the methods described for finishing a bucktail in chapter 4.

Using scissors to trim the excess fur forward of the hook shank and the tie-down point with thread.

Wrap the fur in place, and build up a solid protective layer of thread.

Finish the wrap with a series of half-hitches to tie down the thread. Alternatively, tie down with a whip-finish.

Complete the dressed hook with a coat of protective finish (nail polish, epoxy, or fly-head cement) on the wrap. Several coats are required.

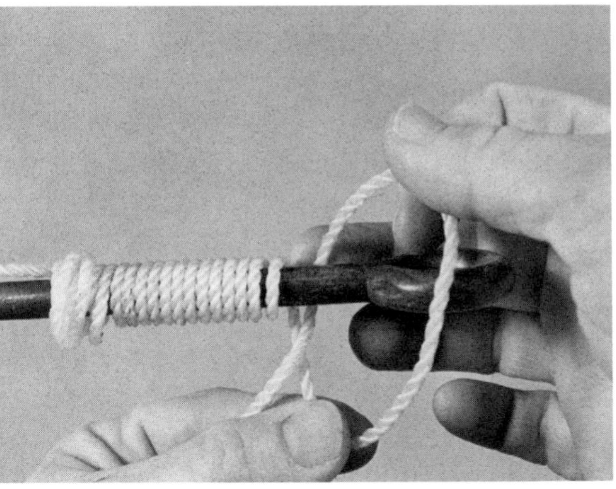

Details of completing thread wrap on dressed hooks, here on an oversize hook and heavy cord. Here a half-hitch is placed on the hook. Several of these are used to secure the thread.

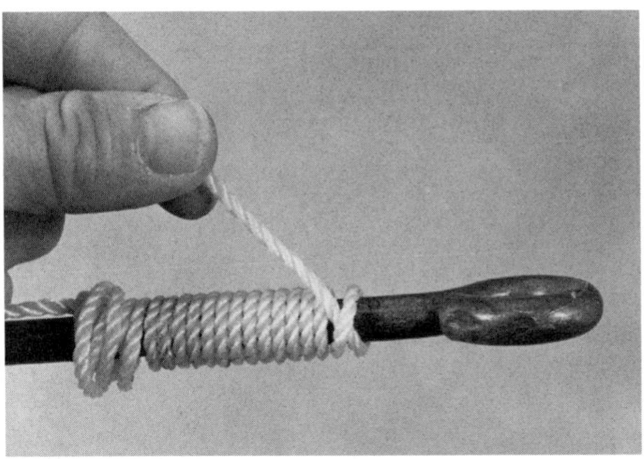

Half-hitch pulled up into place.

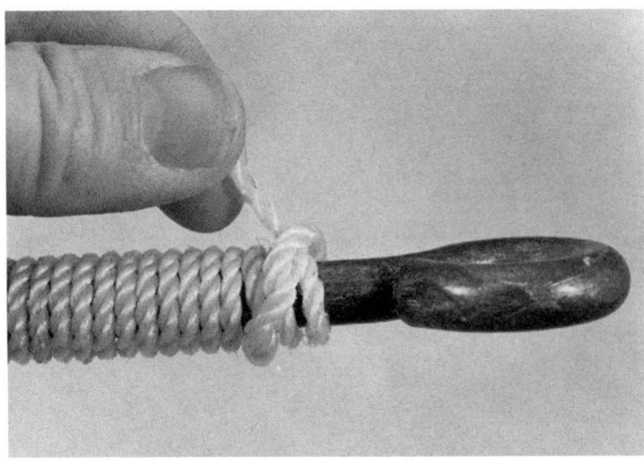

Several half-hitches in place to secure thread. (A large cord is used in these photos for clarity.)

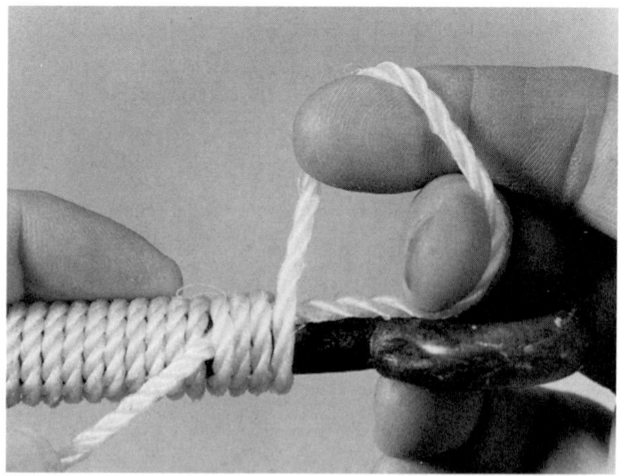
Make the whip-finish by wrapping around the thread and hook shank with a loop as shown here. Make four to five turns this way.

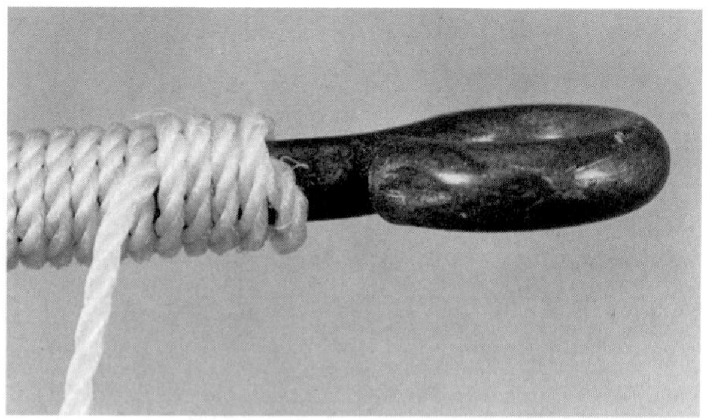
Whip-finish pulled up tight.

Next slip the eye of the hook onto the free end of the wire, and carefully push the hook eye past the previous wire bend and onto the formed eye for completion. If you plan to add a tail tag or lure flipper, add it at this time. Now hold the end of the shaft and the end of the hook (and lure flipper, if used) securely with pliers, and carefully (watch the hook points!) wrap the free end of the wire tightly around the shaft of the spinner. Make two turns. If the loose end of the wire is long enough, you can do this by hand; otherwise, another pair of pliers will help. To make sure the turns are tight, hold the wire (by hand or with pliers) as close to the spinner shaft as possible. After making the two turns, clip off the excess wire with wire cutters.

Caution: Be sure you are wearing your goggles when cutting off this surplus wire. Hold the spinner over a wastebasket and aim the end of the wire toward the bottom, because the cut portion will fly off. This can be dangerous unless you follow the above directions exactly. Another way to prevent this is to hold the spinner in your palm and use two fingers to hold the shaft to be cut as you use your other hand on the wire cutters.

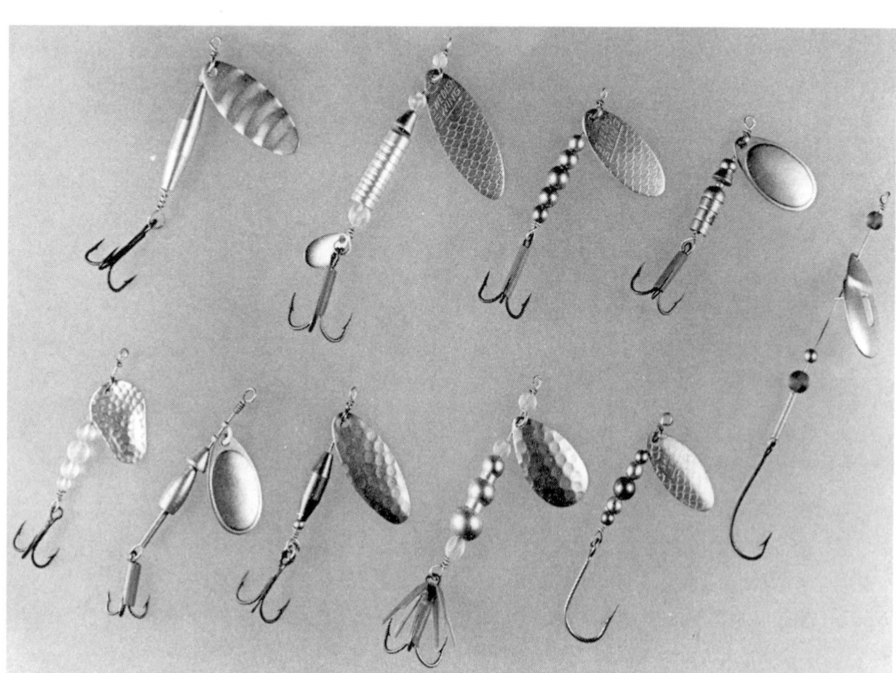
Examples of finished standard spinners using various blades and beads or bodies along with several hook styles.

When you've finished, you will have an imitation of a well-known spinner that is effective for trout, crappie, bass, pike, sunfish, perch, walleye, and other gamefish.

CORRECTING PROBLEMS

Sometimes after completing a spinner, you will find that the blade will not work or spin as expected. There can be several causes for this. You may not have allowed enough clearance on the shaft between the parts, so the clevis binds and does not turn. Another possibility, particularly for Colorado and similar fat blades that spin at a larger angle to the shaft, is that too small a clevis might cause the blade to bind on the shaft.

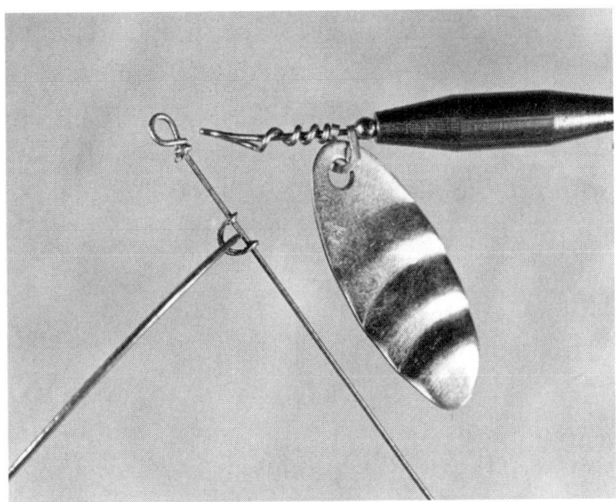

Problems in making spinners include eyes that aren't tightly wrapped, clevises bound against the body (both at right), and using too small a clevis on a blade so that the blade binds against the shaft (left).

It is best of course to check carefully before the eye is wrapped to prevent such problems. However, if the lure is complete, try lightly squeezing the clevis with pliers to give a tiny amount of additional play to the parts on the spinner shaft. This will also give the blade more play on the clevis. Generally the two ends of the clevis can be squeezed together about one-half of the normal spread without adversely affecting the clevis action. Squeeze too much and the clevis will bind on the shaft or blade and ruin the spinner. This procedure works best only with stamped or wire clevises—not the folded style, which are difficult to bend this way.

Another problem can occur if the bearing bead or uni has a small rough spot that prevents the blade from turning freely. Try to check this before bending the wire to complete the shaft. If the bearing bead is plastic, you might be able to remove the rough spot with a knife blade. Otherwise, the only solution is to cut the spinner shaft and salvage the usable parts for the next lure.

Sometimes the eyes will not end up in a straight line with the shaft of the spinner. Although this is more of a perceived than a real problem, you can correct it by adjusting the eye position. Place needle-nose pliers on the shaft next to the eye and a tapered round-nose pliers jaw in the spinner wire eye. Bend both slightly until they are properly lined up.

VARIATIONS IN SPINNER DESIGN AND CONSTRUCTION

While the previously described method can be used for making dozens of different spinners using different body, blade, shaft, and hook combinations, there are other ways to make spinners, as well as other spinner designs you can utilize. Some possibilities and variations follow.

Body Types

In addition to the bead construction noted, you can use lead, plastic, brass, or nickel bodies for the same purpose. In one sense this is even simpler, because many of these bodies are large enough to be used singly. In other cases you will want to combine several smaller body styles to make up the body on a spinner shaft. Many popular commercial lures are made this way.

Bodies can also be combined with beads, and different color combinations of bodies and beads can be used. Regardless of the type of body used, you will still need a small bearing bead or uni directly beneath the clevis and above the body for proper blade turning.

Propeller Spinners

These spinners use propeller blades in place of the clevis and a single blade. They are built the same way as outlined above but with the propeller blade taking the place of the spinner blade and clevis. These spinners are subject to spinning and line twist (as are almost all spinners—homemade and commercial). For proper turning you still need a uni or bearing bead under the propeller.

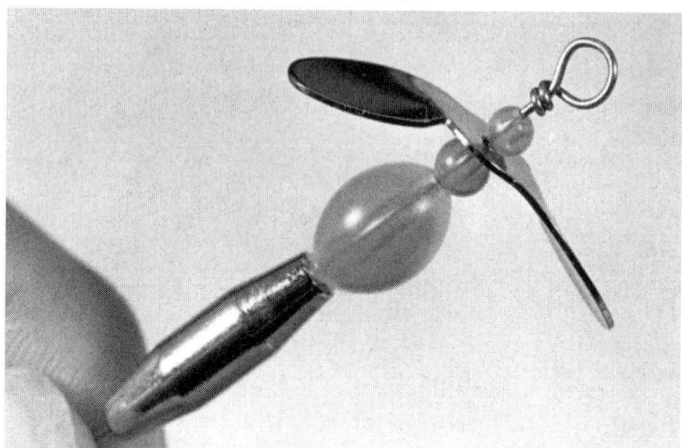

Example of propeller spinner in which simple propeller blade is used on shaft.

Keel Spinners

Spinners spin—and cause line twist. One way to prevent this is to use a body shaped like a keel. Unfortunately there are no keel-shaped spinner bodies that I know of. There are two solutions to this, however. One is to use a keel-sinker mold and modify it so that you can use an insert pin (more about this in chapter 5). This insert pin will run through the length of the mold cavity to make a sinker with a hole completely through its long axis rather than with an eye at each end. Painted a bright color over a base coat of white, this is ideal for use as a spinner body.

Another alternative is to use a regular keel sinker, paint it for use as a body, and use it in line with other parts to make up a unique spinner. The painted sinker will be the body, attached to a treble hook with a split ring at the tail eye. The forward eye will be attached by a split ring to a short shaft spinner holding the spinner blade, clevis, and a bearing bead or a uni or two. In essence this becomes an in-line-parts combination spinner, although in the water it will resemble a standard spinner. The keel reduces or prevents twisting, but the keel shape of the body might interfere with the blade on spinners where the blade spins close to the body axis. Check for this by trying a prototype in running water, or use a wide-spinning blade such as a Colorado or Indiana. Willowleaf blades usually spin too close to the shaft to be useful in this variation.

Another way to make a keeled spinner is to start to make a typical spinner, but don't clip the wire on completion. Instead, with the wire at a right angle bend to the wire of the spinner itself, add a small egg sinker to make the lure with a weighted keel. Make another right-angle bend in the wire to hold the small egg sinker in place. Alternatively, you can wrap the remaining wire around the main spinner shaft for a permanent lock. In doing either of these variations, be sure to start with long enough wire and to leave extra clearance for the extra space on the shaft required by the snap lock or wire wrap. As with the keel sinker, it is also important to leave room for blade clearance and turning.

Coping with Twist

A keel spinner or variation is one way to cope with line twist, but it's not the only way. You can also add a swivel to the upper end of the spinner. This will help but is best if it is a ball-bearing swivel, since this is the freest moving. It is also far more expensive than regular swivels. In using one, you will probably want to start with straight wire (no formed eyes or bends) to build the swivel right on the upper eye. Some ball-bearing swivels have a small split ring as an eye on each side. For these you can start with an eyed shaft, threading the split ring onto the spinner eye. An alternative, if you are making a spinner using a coil-spring (open) spinner shaft or one with a snap lock, is to build the spinner in reverse, starting with the hook end and ending up with the wrapped eye formed with the swivel in place. As has been mentioned, shafts with built-in swivels are available, but none have built-in ball-bearing swivels.

Another possibility is to make the spinner with a longer than normal wire shaft (about 1 to 1½ inches longer than normal). Thus you will have about 1 to 1½ inches of extra play on the shaft when the spinner is complete. Then use pliers to bend the upper part of the shaft at about a 60-degree angle to the main shaft. This offsets the center of pull on the turning of the blade—reducing if not completely eliminating spinner twist. You must have the wire offset for this to work. Within reason, the more offset the wire, the less possibility of line twist. In all cases, be sure to leave enough clearance in the main shaft for the blade to turn. If you wish to have a specific length of bent wire at the front of the spinner blade, make this bend first and then build the spinner normally.

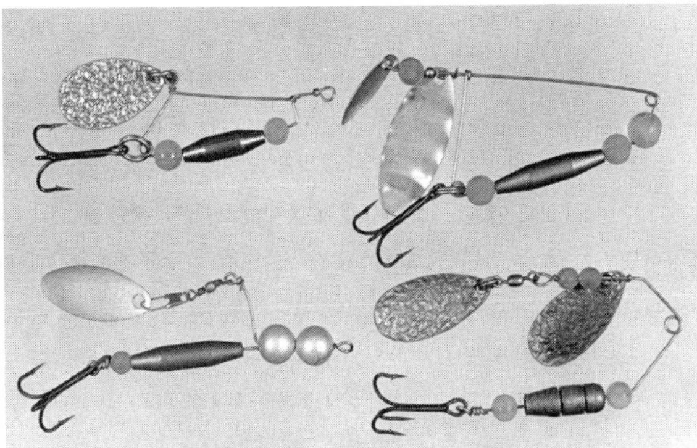

Keeled spinners are designed to reduce or eliminate line twist.

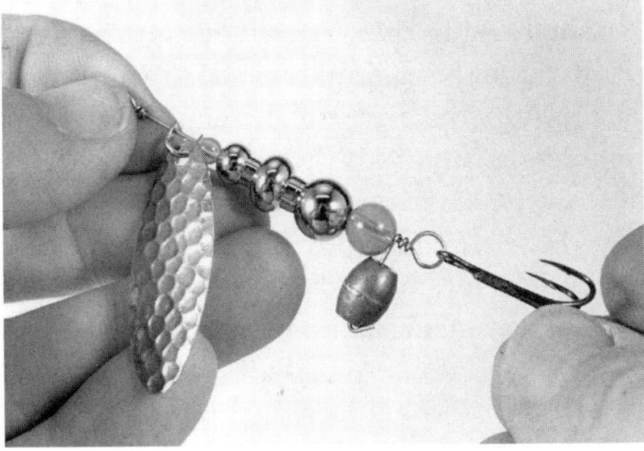

Here a keeled spinner has been made by using the end of the spinner wire to add a small egg sinker, which will serve as the keel.

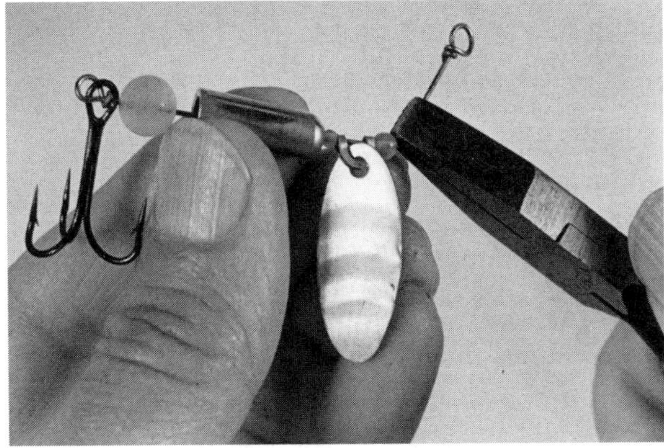

Using an extra length of wire to make a spinner in which the forward wire is bent to the side. This will also reduce or eliminate line twist.

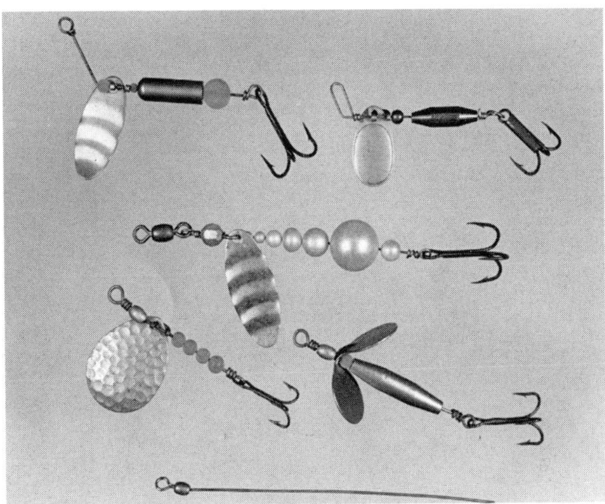

Spinner with bent shaft (top two) to prevent line twist and spinners made with swivel eyes (bottom of photo), also to reduce line twist.

Reverse-Built Spinners

The only reason to reverse-build a spinner is if it is simpler than building it from the head down—for example, if you are making spinners with the open loop (coil-spring closure) or snap lock for changing hooks and parts or adding the spinner in a combination with another lure. You could make the spinner from the top down and form the open or snap-lock ends with pliers, but the wrapped eye is simpler and just as easy to do at the upper end as at the hook end. You can buy spinner shafts with the open loop or spring-lock closure eye for the lower end. In fact, it is really easier to make them in reverse and wrap the upper eye, since in this method a hook is not attached or interfering with turning of the blade.

Another reason to make reverse-built spinners is to use the tapered brass bodies that have a slot in the end of the body. In this case you can build the lure from the tail up, beginning with an open-loop eye, adding a treble hook, and then slipping the tapered body over both wires. Take the short end of the wire and bend it sharply into the slot in the upper part of the body. Since these bodies are usually longer than the end of the wire on manufactured open-eye shafts, you may wish to make this eye from straight lengths of wire. However, there is no problem with making this type of spinner on the open-loop eye shafts, because the spinner will be plenty strong enough without the

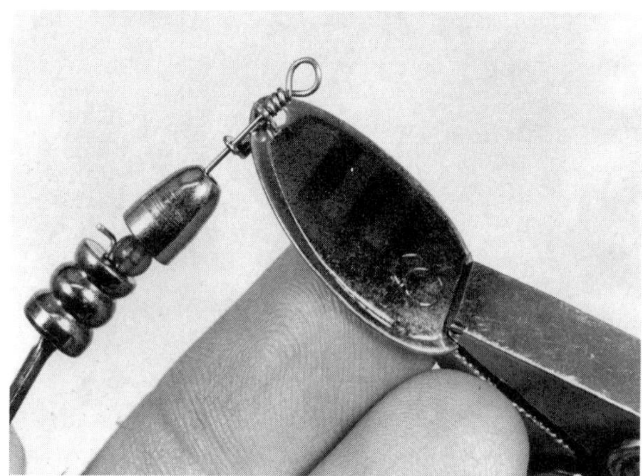

Example of reverse-built spinner in which the hook and body are added first and built up from the bottom and the blade/clevis added last, the wrapped eye completing the lure.

wire folded into the body slot. Once you've added the body and bent the wire, clip off the excess and then continue to add body parts, ending with a uni or bearing bead, the blade on a clevis, and finally wrapping a line-tie eye in the upper end of the shaft.

Even without a slotted body, you can build spinners this way. By the same token, the presence of a slot in a body does not mean that you *have* to build it this way. You can make them the same way as is described for the typical spinner.

Yet another reason for building in reverse is if you are making an odd-shape spinner that will be easier to build from the tail up than from the line-tie down. Three types of shafts with eyes are available. A close examination of any spinner style or design will suggest the best way to build it and the best type of shaft to use.

Forward-Weighted Spinners

Forward-weighted spinners have a weight ahead of the spinner blade to get the lure down deeper. This type of lure, whether called a spinner, forward-weighted spinner, weight-forward spinner, or forward-weighted spinnerbait, is often used to fish for walleye and other deep-water species.

Although commercial lures use special heads for the front of this kind of lure, you can make the same lures. Blanks with molded-in heads on a straight wire are sometimes available through tackle and mail-order shops. Some companies (Do-It, in particular) have molds with which you can mold your own heads. Do-It makes five different molds of Erie jig-spinners, keel spinners, and walleye spinners that have the lead head up front and the rest of the lure built on a 0.030-inch-diameter wire. A variety of lures can be made from these heads or molds. (Techniques for molding these can be found in chapter 4.)

Lacking blanks with heads, you can use an egg sinker that is threaded onto the wrapped-eye shaft, using the wrapped eye for the line-tie. Because the egg sinker pressing against the clevis will stop blade rotation, place a sharp right-angle bend into the wire. Using needle-nose pliers, make another right-angle bend so that the shaft ends up with a small step, or Z bend, in it right behind the egg sinker. This Z bend on the main shaft prevents the egg sinker from sliding down the shaft and interfering with the blade rotation. Then build the spinner normally, using blades, clevises, beads, or body parts, and ending with a single, double, or treble hook.

An alternative is to use a small drop of solder or epoxy glue on the main shaft just forward of the rear blade to prevent binding by the egg sinker.

A lot of these lures (especially for walleye) are fished with bait. To make a bait rig using a removable long-shank single hook, make the same lure in reverse, using an open, coil-spring, or snap-lock loop and leaving clearance for blade turning and so that the sharp bends will prevent the forward weight from binding the blade. If desired, paint the egg sinker or dress it up a bit by adding fore and aft colored beads. Another method is to use a small keel sinker with a modified mold and insert pin (as mentioned above for preventing twist) and slip this onto the shaft as a body. This is more typical of the shape found in these spinner bodies and will help keel the lure and prevent line twist.

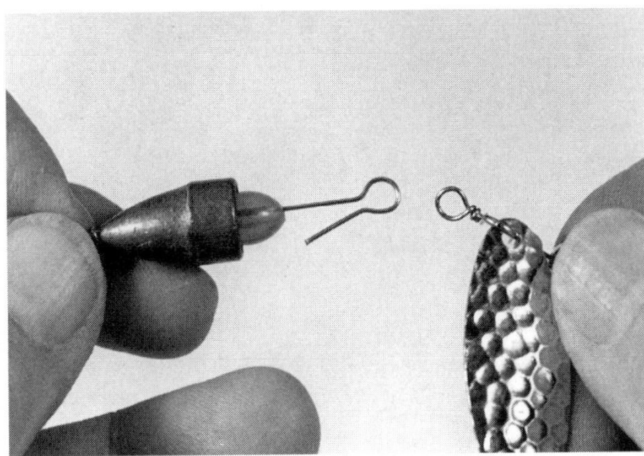

Making a forward-weighted jointed spinner. Here the forward weight is on one shaft, with the closure fixed with a red tapered bead instead of a coil spring. The blade-and-hook part (or a standard spinner) is added here.

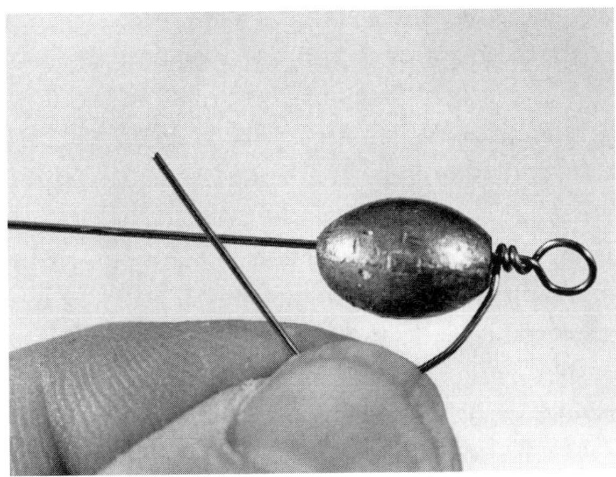

Making a forward-weighted spinner by adding an egg sinker to the spinner shaft first. Excess wire locks the sinker in place to prevent the blade from binding.

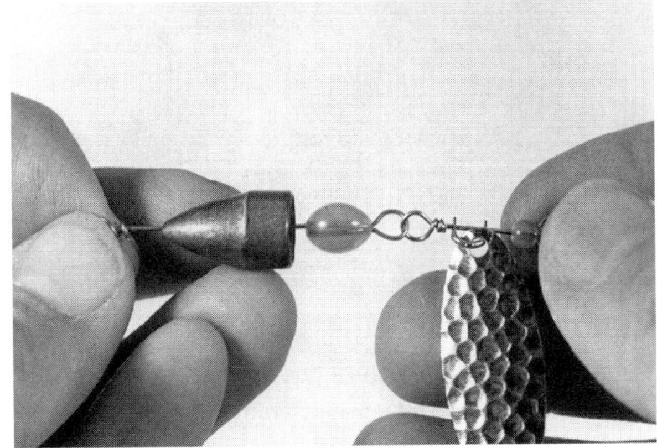

Completed spinner made into a forward-weighted style with the addition of the sinker section.

Example of completed forward-weighted spinner.

Some years ago, another type of weight-forward spinner appeared on the market. It looked like a standard spinner but with the addition of a long, skinny, dull black weight on the forward part. This part was not meant to attract fish; it was there to get the lure down deep. Spinners with different length forward

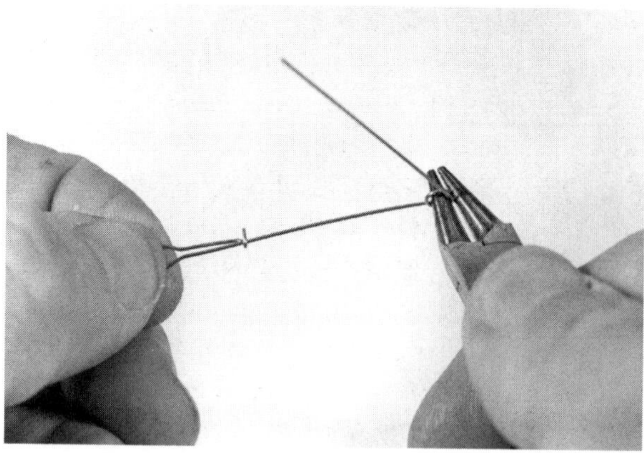

Making the safety-pin bend in a spinnerbait wire for adding to a jig.

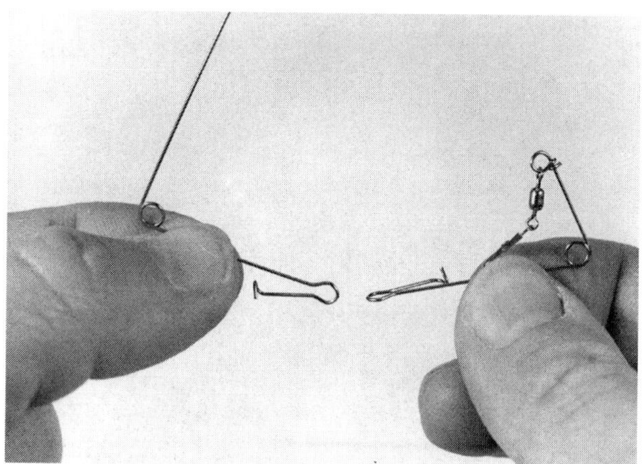

Partially completed spinner-jig form (left) and completed form (right), prior to blade being added.

weights were designed for different depths and types of fishing. You can do this too, using the same procedure described and substituting several small egg sinkers, hollow pencil lead (available for West Coast steelhead fishing or constructed with special sinker molds), several thin clinch-on sinkers, pinched-on split shot, or a series of brass beads. If you use beads, or if the sinkers are bright, paint them black or dark gray to reduce the apparent bulk and size of the lure. You will still have to make the right-angle bends in the wire between the forward part and the spinner parts to prevent blade binding.

You also can make two separate parts: (1) the slim sinker portion with two eyes and (2) the spinner. The two are joined at the eyes. Yet another possibility is to make the forward sinker portion with an eye at one end and a coil-spring open eye or snap-lock eye at the other. This way, any length or weight sinker can be placed on any spinner.

Spinnerbait Wires

These are a safety-pin style of spinnerbait wire that is made with a snap-lock or open-coil spring-wire shaft bent into a safety-pin shaft and ending with one or two spinner blades. With the easy-attach end, it is made to convert any jig into a spinnerbait. The central eye in the middle of the "safety pin" replaces the eye of the jig for line attachment.

To build one, add the coil spring to the shaft (if using one) and use round-nose pliers to make a complete circular eye in the middle of the wire. When this part is complete, the wire ends should be at about a 60- to 90-degree angle, although this can be adjusted as desired for your fishing. At the end of the wire, make a wrapped eye around a swivel. (The swivel allows the blade to turn freely and spin.) Use a split ring to attach a spinner blade to the swivel to complete this lure accessory. To add two spinner blades to the shaft, first thread on a blade and clevis, add a bead or two (again, these bearing surfaces are important for blade movement), and complete. Depending on the angle that the wire and lure come through the water, the forward blade (on the clevis/shaft) may not completely rotate but will flash and turn from the water resistance. These wires can be made any size to match any size jig.

Bait Spinners

Bait spinners are nothing more than spinners designed for use with worms, minnows, leeches, or similar long, swimming baits. Most are built with an open-coil spring or spring-lock closure and thus are made in reverse order from the typical spinner. They can be made working from the top down or the bottom up. They also usually use long-shank single hooks. Be sure to use a straight eye hook (not turned up or down) to prevent kinking. Some rigs use two single hooks: a smaller one to lip-hook a minnow or hold a piece of pork rind and a larger, longer-shank hook to body-hook the minnow or serve as a main trailer hook. Both are attached to the same spinner eye.

Double Spinners

These use two spinner blades, both on clevises and both on the same shaft. One is forward of the other, making for a longer spinner. To make one, begin with the wrapped eye and add the clevis and blade as for a typical spinner. Add some bearing beads or unies, make a right-angle bend, and then make a second bend close to the first using needle-nose pliers. The result is a small Z-shaped bend like that used for the weight-forward spinner described above. Then add the second spinner blade and clevis and the body to complete the lure. Remember that failure to add the slight crimp or bend to the shaft just ahead of the second blade will cause water pressure on the forward blade to bind the second blade. You also could bend a circle or eye into the main shaft as a

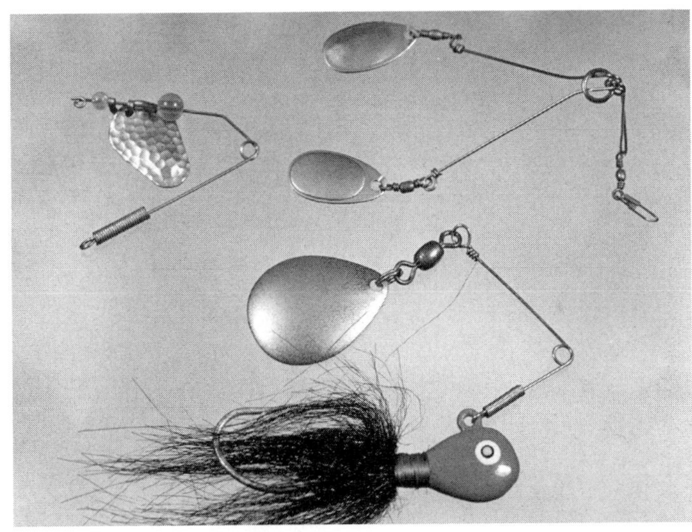

Examples of different spinner rigs to fit on a jig. Top left, blade on shaft with clevis; top right, twin blades with snap for jig attachment; bottom, single blade on swivel attached to jig with coil-spring fastener.

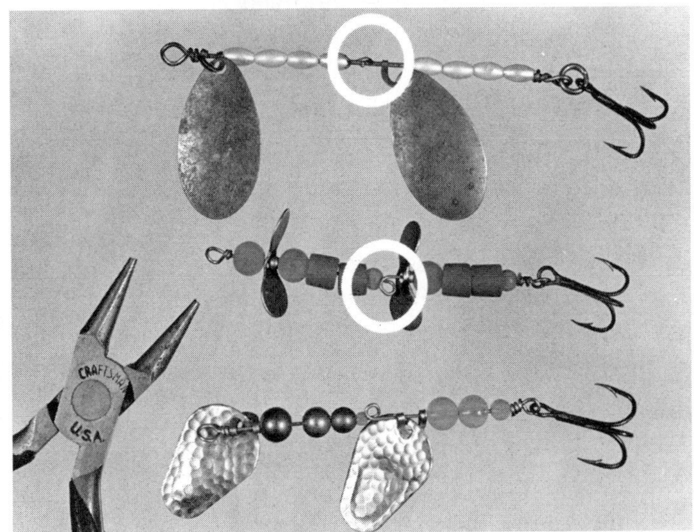

Making double spinners: Methods to prevent binding of the rear spinner blade by the forward components include a drop of solder on the shaft (top photo) and an eye wrapped in the center of the shaft (center). A sharp kink (two bends) in the wire will accomplish the same thing.

stop to prevent the first spinner components from sliding down on the second spinner and stopping the blade rotation.

An alternative to the sharp bends is to add a small drop of solder or epoxy glue to serve as a stop for the forward blade and beads. Spinners can be made like this with two blades and one body, two of each (almost like two spinners on one shaft), or even three blades, if desired. The variations are endless, but with each addition of a blade or body, the spinner gets longer.

Spinnerbait Spinners

In general, spinnerbaits (covered in chapter 6) are larger and formed by casting lead on a special hook/wire form. Paint, skirts, and spinner blades are added to the lead bodies. Tiny spinnerbaits, which I call "minibaits" or "minispinnies," are small variations of spinnerbaits that can be made by using spinner-making techniques and parts. This results in smaller lures for small-fish populations and spinnerbaits that can be cast on ultralight tackle.

These are made just like the spinnerbait wire that is added to jigs, except that you make them with a small body of spinner parts, usually bodies or brass beads for weight. Begin with a straight (no eyes or forms) shaft, and make a wrapped eye around a swivel. Use a split ring to add a spinner blade to the other eye of the swivel. Using as much shaft as you like (you can make short-arm or long-arm spinnerbaits, as you prefer) make a complete eye bend in the wire, with the free end about 60 to 90 degrees to the upper arm. Add the body parts or beads desired for the body of the minibait. Form the wrapped eye as described for the typical spinner, adding the treble, single, or double hook at the same time.

If you wish a straight, single, fixed hook in line with the minibait, there are several ways to do this. One is to use red attractor tubing to hold the free-swinging hook in line with the body. Another is to use the minibait wire, thread it through the eye of the single hook, and then wrap the wire around the shank of the hook. It helps to solder this in place. Make sure that the hook point is up (pointed toward the spinner blade) in all minibaits, just as in spinnerbaits.

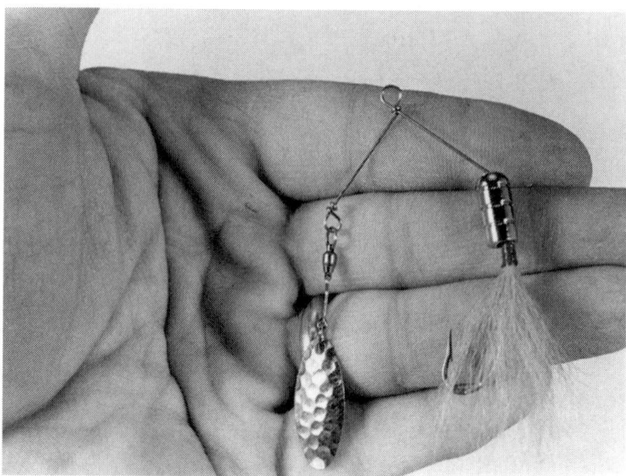

Mini-spinnerbait formed of spinner components on spinner wire.

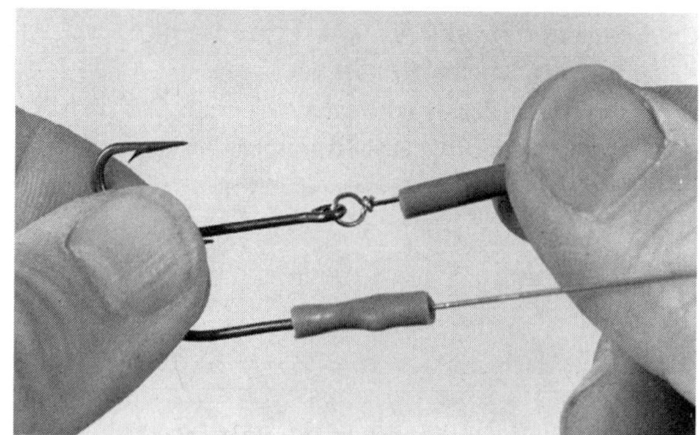

One way to keep a hook straight on a spinner wire is to use a small piece of rubber tubing slipped onto the spinner wire and then over the hook eye/spinner eye.

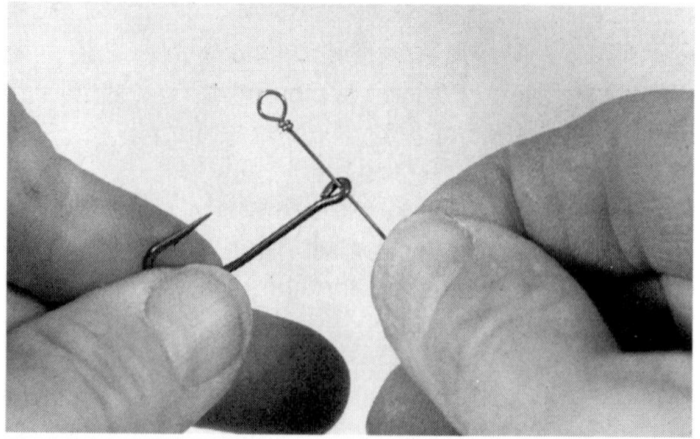

It is also possible to make a fixed solid connection between a spinner wire and hook. First slip the spinner wire through the hook eye in a downward direction as shown.

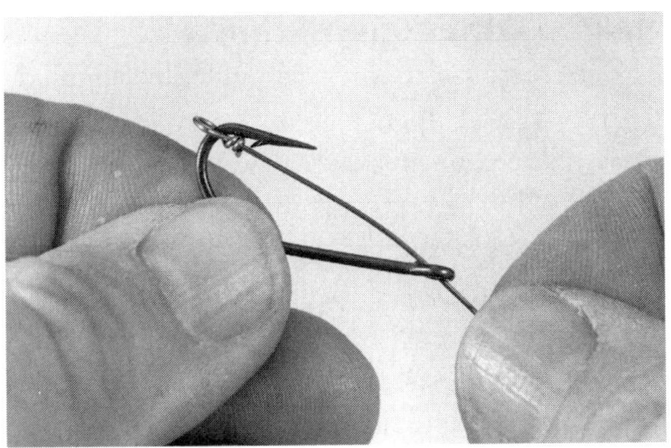

Next slip the wrapped wire eye over the hook point.

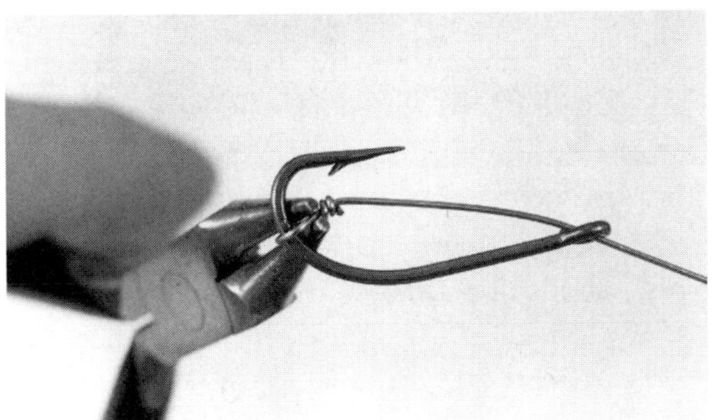

Continue, slightly bending the spinner wire eye as shown.

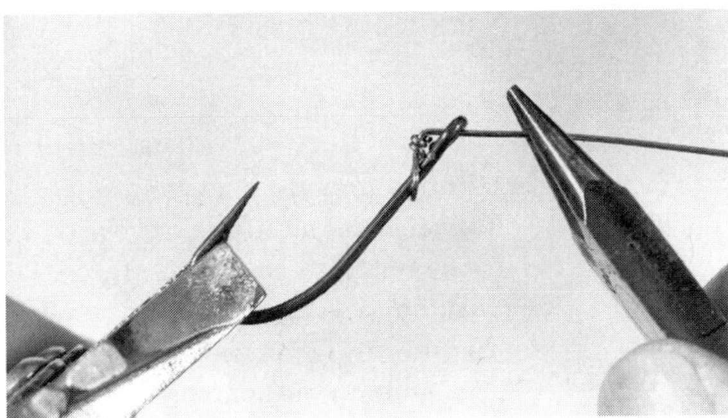

Force the two eyes close together (pull one with pliers with other in vise, or bend eye as shown) to make a fixed connection.

It is also possible to make two-blade minibaits by adding a second blade to the main shaft with a clevis and some bearing beads to help the blade rotate. Because the purpose is to make spinnerbaits smaller in size and weight than the ⅛-ounce minimum weight available commercially or from molding heads, use small lightweight beads and brass spinner bodies together with small blades in the 00 to 1 sizes.

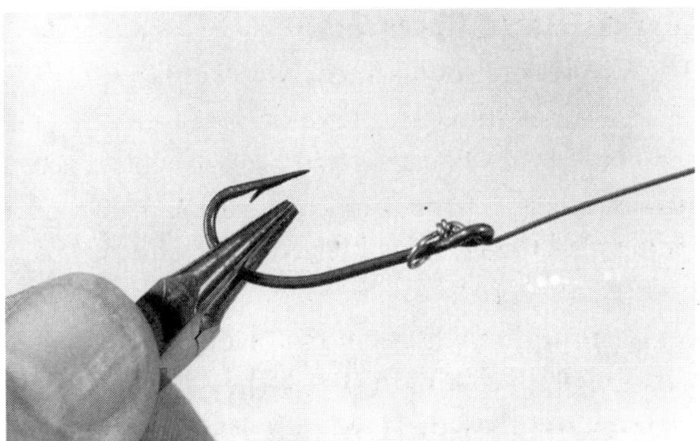

Bend the wire shaft up and parallel with the hook shank to complete.

Split-Ring Spinners

These do not have rotating spinner blades on a shaft. Instead the spinner blade is attached to a split ring, usually with a swivel in front and a treble hook in back. Usually, large split rings are used, and some of these have two blades, one on each side of the hook. Once widely used, split-ring spinners are not often seen now, but they will still catch fish.

As mentioned, it is possible to use this method to make keeled and other combination spinners. Attach the blade-and-hook combination to the rear of a painted keel sinker to make a variation of a weight-forward spinner or spinnerbait.

Two types of Colorado spinners: The one on the left has two swivels (standard construction), the one on the right only one.

Fixed-Blade Spinners

These spinners look much like regular spinners in the water, but they do not use a clevis, and the blade is always at a fixed angle. Typical fixed blades are the June Bug and various Rotospin blades. All have arms (Rotospin from the top, June Bug from the center blade) so that the shaft goes through two holes in the blade to hold it at a fixed angle to the main shaft. They all rotate well and are popular; the June Bug spinner is widely used for fishing bait on a hook attached to the open-coil spring eye at the rear.

Tail Spinners

These are nothing more than a variation of a standard spinner in which the blade is at the rear of the body. The body is built forward on the wire shaft, and the shaft is crimped or fixed with solder to provide clearance so that the rear blade (on a clevis) will spin. It is best to use fat blades (like the Colorado or badger) that will spin at an angle to the shaft so as not to hit the hook just behind the blade.

Making Other Shaft Forms

Although you can buy wires with wrapped, snap-lock, and open coil-spring eyes, you can also make your own. The wrapped eye was described in the typical spinner construction.

To make a snap-lock eye, first make sure you have enough wire. Begin by making a sharp bend in the wire with needle-nose pliers or the ends of tapered round-jaw pliers. Then use the larger diameter portion of the pliers jaw to form an eye, bending the wire 360 degrees. Hold the eye with the tips of the round-nose jaws or with the needle-nose pliers and make a sharp bend so that the end of the wire is almost parallel to the main shaft. At this point the wire will look like the outline of a keyhole. About ½ inch up from this point, use the finest tips of the round-nose pliers to make a tiny J shape in the wire. This J should be at right angles to the plane of the two wires, not in line with them. Then use the needle-nose or round-nose pliers to make a sharp bend so that the J can be snapped over the main shaft. At this point it will be easier to

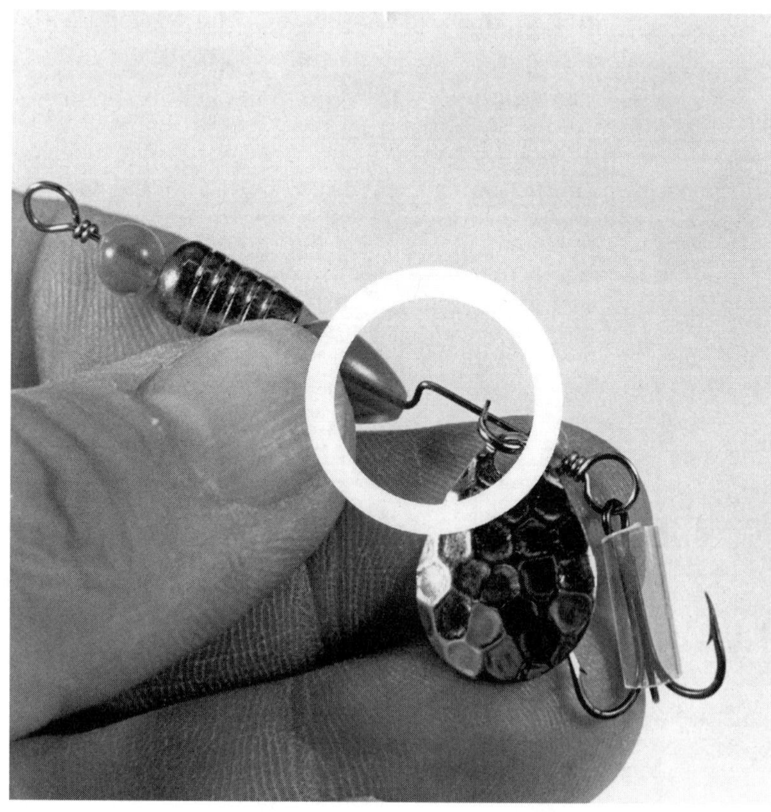

Another method of making a forward-weighted spinner using a spinner body on the shaft. First making two sharp bends as shown to prevent the blade from binding, then adding the spinner blade and finally the hook on a wrapped eye.

clip off the remaining wire, using proper safety precautions as described earlier.

To make an open coil-spring-eye form, follow the same procedure, but do not make the J shape at the end. Clip the wire to about a ½- to ⅝-inch length, measuring from the sharp bend above the eye. Use a coil spring on the main wire shaft to close it. (Often this coil spring must be added first, before making the bends. And enough clearance must be added to the main shaft so that the coil spring can be slid up the shaft to allow opening the shaft for adding or removing a hook.)

FIGURING SPINNER WEIGHTS

Because most spinners are light and cast well with light or ultralight spinning or spin-cast tackle, you may not need or be concerned with weights for your spinners. The component-parts companies may or may not list the weights of all parts, although they do sometimes list the weight of the brass beads and bodies in fractional ounces. If you are concerned about the weight of the total lure, there are several ways to determine it. One is to compare your finished spinner in size and style to an existing commercially made spinner for which you know or can determine the weight. This won't be exact, but it will usually be close enough for figuring tackle needs.

The second method involves weighing the parts in quantity. To do this, get a good postage scale and add parts to the scale until you reach a weight in ounces. Count the items and figure the fractional weight of each item. Do this with each item, and convert the resulting fractions to a common denominator to determine the total weight of the lure. For greater accuracy you can use a grain or powder scale. Using a small cup for measuring beads (reset the scale to zero when doing this) will keep them from rolling off the pan.

A third possibility is to make up a quantity of identical lures, add them to the scale until 1 ounce is reached, then count the number of lures to determine the fractional weight. This is usually the easiest way to figure lure weights.

SPINNER KITS

Kits for making lures are available from manufacturers such as the Worth Company or from individual suppliers that make their own house-brand kits. Different kits are often available, including kits for making spinners, spinnerbaits, and spoons. Spinner kits often include a simple wire former, paints for finishing bodies, and enough shafts, clevises, swivels, coil springs, snaps, blades, bodies, and hooks to make twenty-five or more lures. The paint and wire former, plus the excess parts, can be used for making spinners of varying design with additional parts.

Other companies have spinner kits available. Cabela's has two kits containing spinner blades and crane-snap swivels for quick-change convenience. These kits are primarily designed for spinnerbait blade changes but can be used for spinners as well. Some companies sell kits with tools and paints, others with parts only. Jann's Netcraft, Mud Hole, and others all carry spinner parts.

4
Bucktails and Jigs

Introduction • Types of Molds • Hooks • Sources of Lead • Heat Sources • Safety • Molding Techniques • Molding Steps • Finishing Molded Bucktails • Wrapping Tails on Lead Heads • Jig Components and Kits

Basic Safety Requirements

Goggles

Welder's or other heavy gloves for handling molds, pots, ladles

Respirator mask of appropriate design for lead fumes

Heavy apron

A clean, clear, sturdy countertop on which to work, preferably covered with sheet metal

Basic Tools

Old cooking pot

Cheap gravy ladle or large serving spoon

Bucktail molds

Fly-tying vise, machinist's vise, or C-clamp

Hot pads

File

(**Important!** The old cooking pot and gravy ladle/serving spoon are never to be used again in the kitchen or with foods.)

Helpful Tools

Plumber's melting pot

Plumber's ladle

Gate cutters or shears

Wire cutters

Ingot molds

Heavy pliers

Electric-element handheld melting pot

Electric bottom-feed furnace

Split-ring pliers

Compound-leverage fishing pliers

Spinner-making tools (may be useful for some assembly and modifications)

INTRODUCTION

If asked to choose one lure that's good for all types of fishing, many expert anglers would name the lead-headed jig, or bucktail. Time and experience have proven that this lure, in all its many variations of size, shape, tail, and modifications, can effectively imitate saltwater baitfish, eels, squid, crabs, and freshwater minnows, crayfish, hellgrammites, stone cats, and similar baits.

Commercial bucktails and jigs come in tiny 1⁄80-ounce sizes and giants that weigh up to 24 ounces. While all of these lures are basically lead heads molded on a hook, those used in salt water are generally called bucktails, while those used in fresh water are called bucktails or jigs. All are essentially the same: a lead head on a special hook with a skirt or tail. Some variations are manufactured (and possible when making your own) with lips, tail spinners, jointed bodies, and the like.

Skirts on these simple lures can include bucktail (hence the name), other furs, artificial furs (synthetic tail materials), craft fur (similar to artificial fur for the fly-tying trade and available from craft, fabric, and hobby shops), feathers, saddle hackle, frayed polypropylene rope, fine strands of nylon (SuperHair), Living Rubber, strands of dynel (similar to nylon), and marabou. Vinyl skirts, soft-plastic grubs, minnows, soft-plastic skirts, trailer tails, crawdad tails, plastic frogs, salamanders, eels, and shrimp are possible slip-ons for some types of jig heads. Most of these latter jigs and bucktails have special collars with one or more barbs designed to hold the soft-plastic addition in place.

Most jig or bucktail types have different names. Sometimes the same lure will have different names in different geographical areas. In addition, molds for the same type of head may have different names according to the manufacturer. Typical bucktails include:

Banjo-eye bucktails. With bulging eyes; for use in saltwater and striped bass fishing along the mid-Atlantic Coast. Often trolled and tied with a straight-fur (bucktail or similar artificial fur) tail. Often heavy; weight varies from ¼ ounce to 8 ounces.

Crappie killers. Small, usually with a round head; often tied with a chenille body or palmered (hackle-wrapped) chenille body and marabou tail for added action. Used for crappie; also used in a variety of sizes for many other gamefish. Often 1/80 to ⅜ ounce in size.

Shad darts. Small tapered, lead heads with sloping fronts; originally designed for American and hickory shad but used for a variety of panfish, sunfish, and crappie. Usually about 1/32 to ¾ ounce.

Bullet-head or bullet-nose bucktails. Molded with a bullet head for a long, streamlined look; usually used in salt water. Sizes from ¼ ounce to 4 ounces.

Glider or slider heads. Made with a flat horizontal head for slider fishing with a short worm or grub tail. Also used to make bonefish jigs for fishing shallow-water flats in salt water. Mostly small, about 1/16 to ¾ ounce.

Lima bean, Upperman-style, or flathead jigs. These have a slim vertical but round or egg shape when seen from the side. They are very popular for saltwater fishing because they sink rapidly and are easy to work.

Commercial bucktails range in price from a few cents for small simple styles to several dollars or more for the large, heavy, saltwater bucktails or those with glass-eye inserts, special tails, or similar features. These same lures can be home-molded and tied for a fraction of the commercial cost.

Molding bucktails takes only the proper mold, a few hooks, some lead, and an old file. To finish and tie up the bucktail takes only the tail material, thread, paint, and a vise of some sort for clamping the hook in place while tying on the tail materials. These supplies serve as a bare minimum. A ladle and special melting pot or handheld electric furnace are better for melting lead than are the old soup ladle and cooking pot sometimes used. Wire cutters are handy for removing the lead sprue that attaches to the head from the molten lead that was poured through the sprue hole or gate of the mold. Special gate cutters are available in two sizes from manufacturers such as Do-It and Hilts Molds. These are sometimes spring-loaded, have cushioned plastic grips, and will shear lead sprue close to the jig head. One important point: Do *not* use these for cutting wire.

TYPES OF MOLDS

Commercially molded jigs and bucktails are made in several ways. One is to use a round two-part mold (much like two pie plates but larger and made of special rubber) and a centrifugal molding machine to spin the molten lead from a central sprue hole out into all the cavities placed around the rim. The molded result, before the jigs are cut out, resembles a lead wagon wheel complete with spokes and with a large lead arbor. The molded jig heads make up the outer rim. This is not for the home craftsman; the machinery is designed for large-quantity production work, and the cost is very high. Commercial molders also use heavy-duty precision single-cavity aluminum molds fed by a bottom-feeding furnace. A number of molds are used in rotation so that a high commercial production output is possible.

Various types and brands of bucktail and sinker molds by Hilts Molds, Do-It Corp., and Li'l Mac.

For the home craftsman, the molds available commercially are usually two-piece, made of aluminum or aluminum alloy, and have one or more lure cavities. These cavities form the lure when the molten lead is poured into them through a tapered funnel-like opening called a sprue hole, gate, or down-gate.

At one time, molds for fishermen were different from those for the small commercial operation. Today that separation is disappearing as more and more fishermen are making their own tackle and using precision molds that produce high-quality lures. For example, molds from Do-It and Hilts Molds, both major manufacturers of molds for the home craftsman and small business, are well within the price range of any sportsman. Some tackle craftsmen have a dozen or more molds for making different bucktail heads. Do-It, Hilts Molds, Li'l Mac, and others also have molds that make multiple lures of the same weight that are better for those selling lures or needing only one size lead head for specialized fishing.

A typical mold from Do-It for making a round-head jig—model JNR-6-A—will make one each of 1/80-, 1/64-, 1/32-, 1/16-, 1/8-, and 1/4-ounce heads. The production molds make all heads of the same size, such as in the similar model 1249 mold, which makes seven 1/32-ounce round-head jigs. Other Do-It production molds, such as the 1250, 1251, and 1252, make seven 1/16-, 1/8-, and 1/4-ounce lures, respectively. The same applies to Hilts Molds—their model LMRH-M will make one each of 1/32-, 1/16-, 1/8-, 1/4-, 3/8-, and 1/2-ounce round-head collared and barbed jig heads. The LMRH-32-6 will make six each of the above heads, all in a 1/32-ounce size. Hilts Molds has similar multiple-cavity, single-size molds for other sizes, through 1/2 ounce. The difference is not really in the quality of the mold or of the jigs produced but in the variety of lures made. Most fishermen will want a variety of head sizes, and the standard molds allow this with the purchase of one mold in place of a half dozen.

All modern molds from companies such as Do-It and Hilts Molds are top quality and designed to produce lures without flash or fins. ("Flash" and "fins" are molder's terms for excess metal that leaks from the mold where the two mold halves join. When this occurs, the excess must be filed off or removed to make top-grade bucktails. This work is unacceptable for the commercial molder and a nuisance for the home craftsman. It is far more cost-efficient to buy only those molds that will produce top-quality, flash-free results.)

Molds come in several different designs. Pinned molds are the least expensive but also the most difficult to work with. They consist of two flat sides with a registration pin-and-socket arrangement to hold the two halves together and line them up properly for good registration. They must be clamped together with C-clamps, spring clamps, or otherwise held securely each time a lure is molded. They are made in two separate halves, usually with a pin on one side of each mold half that fits into a socket on the other half as the mold is closed. Pinned molds usually form very good lures with little flash.

Although these molds are somewhat inconvenient to use, they are inexpensive and mold lures just as well as any other type of mold. However, the clamping and unclamping of the mold is time-consuming and makes it difficult to turn out a number of lures quickly, particularly when the mold starts to get hot from repeated pourings. One way to speed up this operation when using pinned molds is to use a pair of woodworker's spring-loaded gluing clamps to hold the halves together. If using gluing clamps, be sure to remove the vinyl tip protectors or the hot molds may burn them.

Another type of mold has two clamps, one on each side of the mold, the clamps holding the two halves together for pouring. Otherwise they are just like the pinned molds and do have pins and sockets for proper registration of the two half-cavities. A variation of this is a design in which one side is hinged and the other spring clamped. Because of the hinge on these molds, registration pins may be absent. In most cases there is at least one pin and socket on the opposite side of the hinge to keep the parts aligned.

The most popular and widely available molds are those that are hinged and handled. These are my personal favorites because they are easy to work with and produce excellent results. The hinge holds the two halves in perfect alignment, and the two handles make it easy to hold the mold together for quick and efficient operation. Registration pins—usually on the handle side—also help to align the two halves for perfect lures. The only slight disadvantage is that the handles can quickly get uncomfortably hot. This is more theoretical than actual, because most molds have heavy wood or plastic handles. Wearing heavy gloves can prevent discomfort when handling molds with metal handles. All molds get hot in use and for the best results should be gently heated before use to prevent incomplete castings.

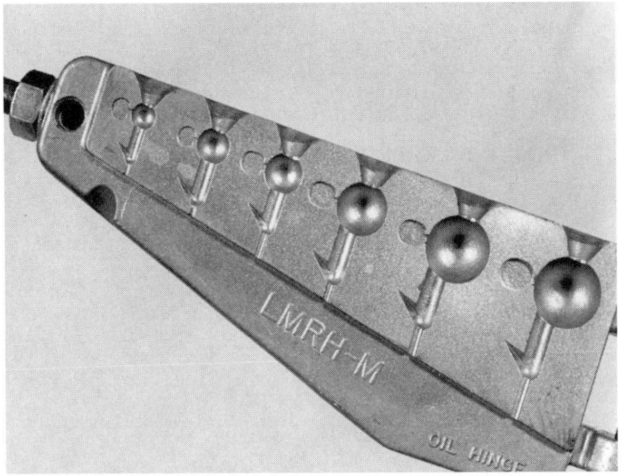

Another example from Hilts Molds showing a ball-head jig designed to take a grub tail. (The barb molded into the collar holds the grub in place.)

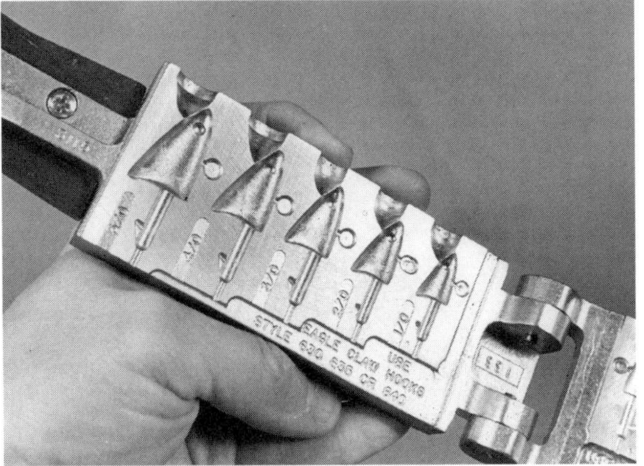

Example of arrowhead jig mold by Do-It Corp. Note that the hook style and different sizes of hooks are noted on the mold and that the mold produces different sizes of heads.

The number of cavities in a mold is often determined by the size of the mold blank. Thus a mold to make small jigs might contain as many as eight cavities. A mold for larger lures, such as one to make 3- and 4-ounce spearhead jigs from Do-It, might have only two cavities (one of each size), while the Hilts Molds Scampee Bullet Nose and Big Bullet Nose jig molds have only single cavities for these lures that range from 12 to 24 ounces each.

Molds also sometimes require pins, plates, or rods to make holes, slots, or cavities. Those requiring plates and rods are more typical of molds for sinkers, which require these parts to make a specific sinker. Plates to make a slot, for example, are required to make split-shot, rubber-core, and pinch-on (clinch-on) sinkers, while rods are required for the holes through egg sinkers, bullet-weights for worm-fishing, and similar type sinkers.

Pins are sometimes required in molds to make weedless jigs and bucktails because the pin produces a socket in the back of the head for gluing in a Y or nylon-fiber weed guard. Some molds allow you to mold Y or brush guards in place, eliminating the need to glue later.

Molds vary widely in the variety of heads they produce, even aside from the many sizes and various shapes. The simplest type will make one or more simple, plain bucktails. Molds are available that make similar simple heads that are modified with the addition of one or more barbs on the lead collar behind the head: The barbs help hold soft-plastic tails, minnows, grubs, and the like in place. Other molds have circular ribs around the collar or a small ball on the end of the collar to help in tying and holding bucktail or other tail materials in place. Some have sockets on the sides of the head for gluing on plastic or glass eyes for added attraction. Still others include the core pins for molding in weed guard sockets or for molding in the weed guards themselves.

Some jig and bucktail molds take inserts in addition to the hook. These inserts can include the aforementioned Y or nylon weed guards molded into the head of the lure. Usually these are made of materials that will not melt in the short contact with the hot lead, which makes it easy to mold weedless jigs. Some large molds require insert eyes, to which the line is tied. The large Hilts Molds Bullet Nose jigs require this in the 6- through 24-ounce sizes, since the hook sizes required (10/0 or 11/0) do not

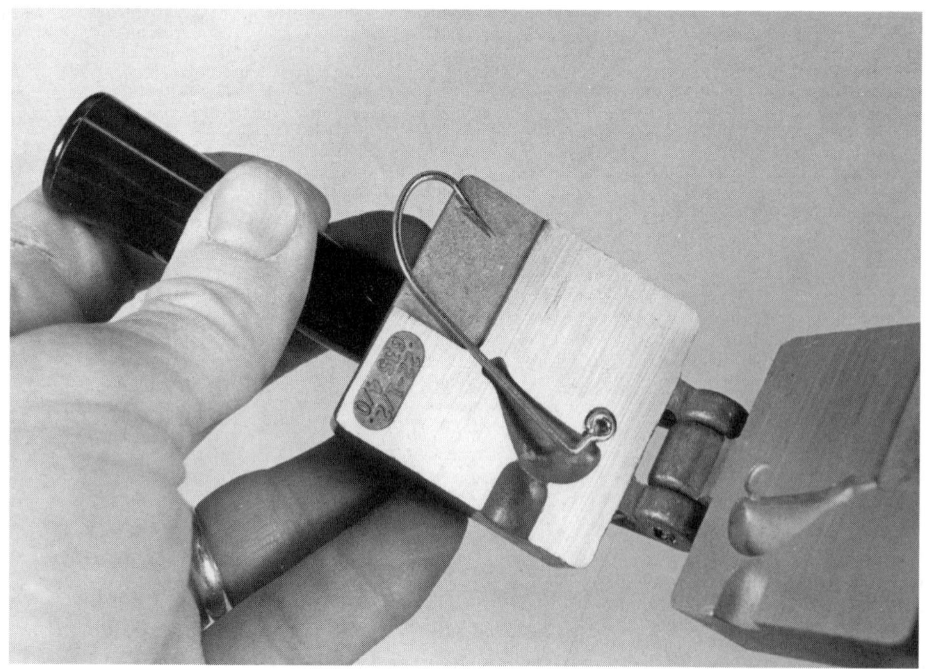

Another example from Li'l Mac, this with the hook in place.

come in the bent-shank bucktail style for this mold. Regular hooks are used with the insert eyes added for a line-tie.

Do-It has a bass spin jig (model ARK-3198FS) that uses not only the nylon weed guard or brass pin insert but also a length of multistrand wire for adding a spinner blade after finishing the jig. The spinner addition makes it more like a spinnerbait in construction, but the line-tie is still to the hook eye, and the finished lure is fished liked a jig.

Do-It also has a "blank" mold to allow home craftspeople to make their own head designs should a specialty head or size not be available from a manufacturer. The Do-It style is a completely blank mold (model 1155) in which the mold can be cut by a tool-and-die maker or machine shop to form the cavity area, hook-and-eye channels, and the gate and sprue. Because this type of work can be very expensive, get an estimate before ordering a blank mold. Do-It does not do any machine work for these projects.

Hilts Molds has a Perfect Replica mold (model PRMOLD) that is a blank mold with a recessed box and four sprues. It is used with the PRMR-1 kit, which consists of two pieces of silicone rubber that have a modeling-clay consistency to allow making a mold from an existing wood, plaster, lead, or similar material copy lure. The silicone is set by vulcanizing at 375 degrees Fahrenheit for 45 minutes in a regular oven. The frame can be reused, and extra silicone kits are available. (See chapter 17 for more details.)

A blank mold similar to the Do-It model is available from Li'l Mac (model A-3200-1).

In addition to the above assortment of molds, mold replacement parts are available. Do-It and Li'l Mac carry and sell replacement wood handles to fit any of their molds, Palmer can supply replacement plastic handles for their molds, and Hilts Molds offers replacement bolt-in plastic-covered steel handles for their molds.

I particularly like molds that have important information engraved or molded into the mold. Both Do-It and Hilts Molds do this, with the information usually including the hook sizes that will fit each cavity (this will vary with the cavity on most hobby molds), the hook style or styles that will fit (hook styles vary and are not universally interchangeable among different molds), the weight of the lure molded in each cavity, and so on. Some, such as Do-It, even have a notice on the mold suggesting oiling the hinges periodically! STP or other heavy oils are excellent for this.

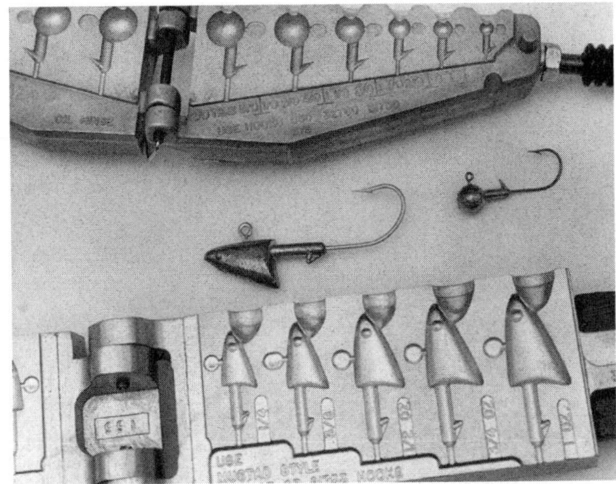

Examples of molds, and the jigs they produce, from Hilts Molds (top) and Do-It Corp. (bottom). Both companies have a wide variety of bucktail, lead lure, sinker, and similar molds.

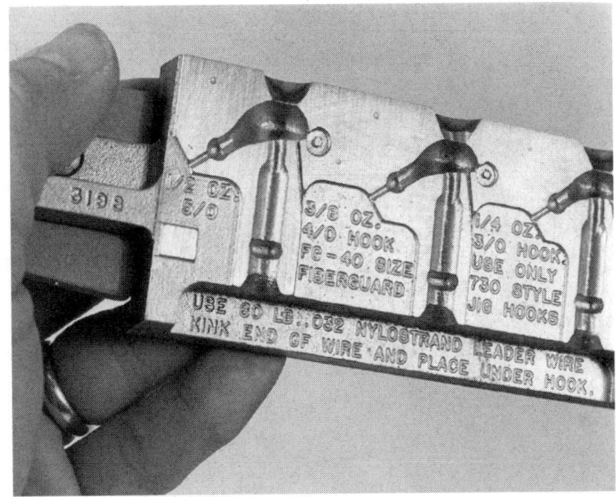

This jig mold from Hilts Molds will mold in the plastic weed guard and make four sizes of jigs. Note the weight, hook style, and hook weight imprinted on the mold for ready reference.

HOOKS

Special hooks are required in most molds for bucktails. Exceptions can be found in some lures, such as the very large bucktails for which the special bent hooks are not available and the specialized lead lures (not really bucktails) that have a lead body, molded-in wire form for the line-tie, and hooks and a tail spinner. These are often generically called tail spinners and are like the commercially available Little George and similar horse-head and pony-head lures.

Other examples of specialty lures include the slab spoon lure, vertical jigging spoons, structure spoons, and diamond jigs. All of these require wire forms or insert eyes for hook- and line-ties but usually use standard free-swinging treble hooks instead of the molded-in bucktail single hooks.

Standard bucktail hooks come in a wide variety of sizes and styles, but all have a bend in the shank near the eye of the hook. In most cases this bend is at a right angle to the rest of the hook shank, but some hooks (often the larger sizes) have a 45- or 60-degree bend to the shank. Examples of hooks with the right-angle bend include the Eagle Claw 630 series and the Mustad 32760. Those with a partial bend include the Eagle Claw 730 wide-throat flipping hooks and the Mustad 34195. The sizes of most manufacturers' jig hooks range from about 12 through 7/0.

In almost all cases, the hook eye is in line with the plane of the hook. (One exception is the style 1623, in which the eye is at right angles to the hook plane and the slight shank bend is near the hook. This is used in the stand-up jig from Do-It, in which the large "foot" of the head holds the hook point up and high.)

These hooks come in regular and extra-heavy wire, round and forged shanks, and various bends, including Aberdeen, Model Perfect, O'Shaughnessy, Sproat, and similar basic hook styles. Hook finishes include bronzed, gold, nickel, and tinned. Any of these platings will work in both fresh and salt water, although saltwater use might require a freshwater rinse for jigs molded on bronze or gold hooks. Tinned hooks are often best for salt water.

All these hooks are good and reliable, although their features vary. For example, light-wire hooks will bend under stress, something that is an advantage in some freshwater jig fishing where hooks are often snagged and must be pulled free. It is a disadvantage in other types of fishing, primarily in saltwater fishing, where long fights are typical and a light-wire hook can result in a lost fish.

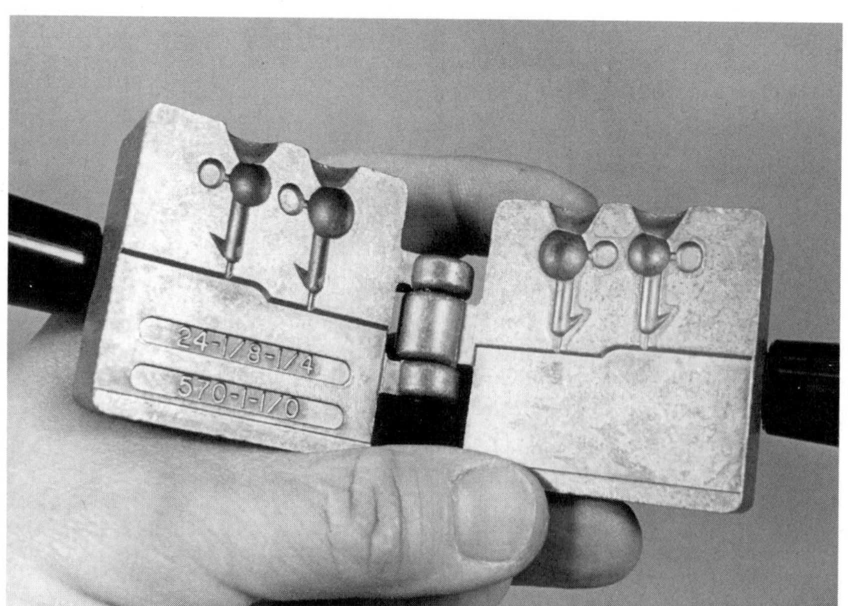

This mold from Li'l Mac is from the company's Midget Mold series, although larger molds for bucktails and sinkers are available.

In some cases standard-style hooks are used. This is usually only done with the very large jigs, such as the Hilts Molds Big Bullet Nose jig in all sizes from 6 through 24 ounces. These jigs take either 10/0 or 11/0 hooks; specialty jig hooks are not made in these sizes.

I cannot emphasize too strongly that you must use the right hook style for each mold. The eye must fit into a small round depression in the mold, and the hook's wire diameter and shape must fit the mold cavity exactly. The right size is also important. Using the right style but too small or too large a size will result in the hook fitting into the mold at a cocked angle. Any of these situations will result in the mold not closing properly or flash forming around the hook shank or the joint of the mold halves.

SOURCES OF LEAD

Lead and lead alloys are available in a variety of forms and mixes and from a number of sources. Pure lead is available from companies that manufacture molding supplies such as furnaces and molds. Pure lead is soft and as a result will pour and form easily. Plumbing-supply houses also sell pure lead, and it can be bought in better hardware stores.

All service stations that change tires or mount new tires have ample supplies of old lead in the tire weights that come off the wheels. Large stations often sell their weights, but some smaller stations are glad to have them taken off their hands. These weights have a steel bracket in them to clip the lead onto the wheel. In addition, they are often coated with road grease and oil. The impurities and metal clips on these wheel weights must be skimmed off the top of the molten metal as slag before the lead can be poured. The metal clip for rim attachment of the tire weight will also melt off and float on the surface of the lead to be skimmed off. These weights are not pure lead but an alloy, usually with some antimony and tin mixed in to make for a harder alloy. They also require a higher heating temperature than pure lead, and as a result will often pour easier. Antimony melts at 1,166 degrees Fahrenheit, lead at 621 degrees. A small percentage of antimony in lead will result in different alloys melting at different temperatures. As a result, lead alloy will handle a little differently during pouring and may not fill small-cavity molds as easily as will the softer pure lead. However, if you can get it free, the price is right and the result will be fine for larger jigs and large sinkers (see chapter 5).

Other sources of lead are junkyards, scrap-metal yards, lead sheathing, and lead from cable used in telephone and other underground wiring. Telephone-wiring sheathing is almost pure lead—about 98 percent pure—although the lead solder used to join sections of pipe or wiring is a lead alloy. Never, never, ever melt down batteries for lead, because all lead batteries contain acid and are extremely dangerous and hazardous to handle. In addition, the small batteries (sizes AAA through D) commonly used in toys, flashlights, and electric equipment may explode if heated over a flame. You may, however, be able to get "battery lead," which has been melted down from batteries by recovery companies and thus is safe to use.

Your choice of lead might be dictated by cost or availability. If these are not important to you, consider the following: Pure lead will melt most easily, will have the least amount of impurities and slag, and will pour most easily for the best filling of all molds, especially small mold cavities. However, because it is soft, it will dent more easily if it hits rocks during casting, resulting also in chipped paint. Harder lead alloys with a mix of antimony and tin will not pour as easily, nor will they fill small-cavity molds as well as pure lead, but they will be harder when molded for fewer paint chipping and denting problems when fished around hard structures. There is no right answer to this dilemma, and some commercial manufacturers of jigs, bucktails, and spinnerbaits use pure soft lead while others use harder lead alloys. I use all types of lead and lead alloys, but I try to keep them separate so as not to combine them any further.

The following handy reference to lead content in various materials is from Li'l Mac Molds:

Lead Type	Percentage Lead	Percentage Tin	Percentage Antimony
Pig Lead	99.6	---	---
Cable Sheathing	98.5	---	---
Battery Lead	90.0	---	10.0
Plumbers Solder	67.0	33.0	---
Wheel Weights	90.0	1.0	9.0
Type Metal	82.0	3.0	15.0

(Courtesy Li'l Mac Molds)

HEAT SOURCES

The actual process of molding lead-head lures is a simple one, but it must be carried out carefully and with forethought both for safety and to attain the best results.

While molding bucktails is fun, it must be done safely. Roy Hilts, former owner of Hilts Molds and in the business of manufacturing molds for almost forty years, says: "Never become so confident that you are not scared of it."

The first safety consideration is the place where the molding will be done. The kitchen stove is one possible place for melting lead and pouring lures, although Roy Hilts does not like it because of the possibility of lead spilling on countertops, the floor, and the sink. (Molten lead and water *never* mix, and water thrown on a spill can cause explosive splatters of molten lead.) But I like the kitchen area for several reasons.

First, there are several stove burners so that several pots of lead can be kept hot at once. This is important if you need a large quantity of lead. Second, kitchen stoves always have an exhaust fan nearby. This can be a typical above-stove hood-type exhaust fan or a fan that exhausts below. Since there can be trace elements of toxic substances in lead (even pure lead), and since lead itself is a toxic substance, a good high-volume exhaust fan is a must for any melting and molding operation. If your kitchen or work area does not have a fan or a properly working fan, do not work in the area. Proper exhaust when working around molten lead is crucial to your long-term health and that of your family. It might also help to open windows on the opposite side of the kitchen for cross-ventilation.

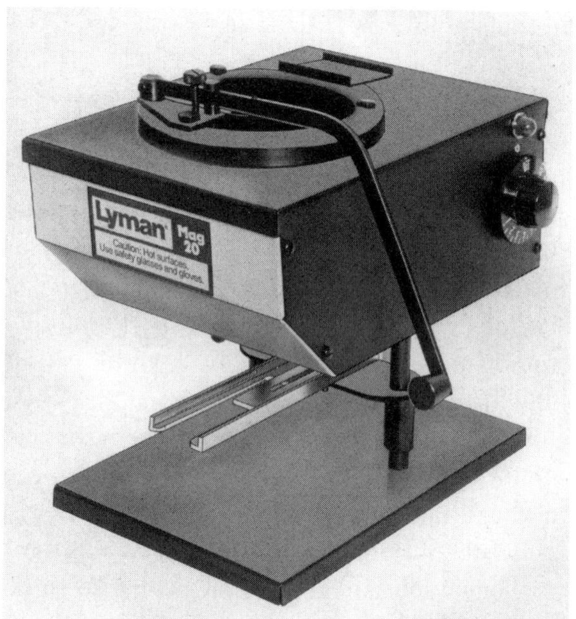

A sophisticated molding furnace. The tracks for holding molds and the lever for releasing lead through a bottom opening indicate a bottom feed. While designed mainly for bullet molding, these are used and usually easily adapted for bucktail and sinker casting. Photo courtesy of Lyman

A third advantage to using the kitchen area is that usually there is ample counter or table space for laying out molds, hooks, and the other tools and materials required. Of utmost importance in using the kitchen for this purpose—if you want to be allowed in the house again—is to cover all working surfaces with a protective layer of ¼-inch or thicker plywood, thick Masonite, thick wood paneling scraps, hot pads, or a similar sturdy, non-heat-conducting material. Do not use anything thin, plastic, or metal. (They will usually not protect adequately from the extremes of heat necessary to melt lead.) The best solution is complete coverage, first with ¼-inch plywood topped by large-size hot pads made of aluminum or stainless steel. Some hot pads and sheets are available in sizes up to an 18 × 24-inch rectangle. Several of these placed over the area immediately surrounding the stove will work fine.

Aluminum or stainless steel pads are better than scraps of wood, because they make for easier cleanup of any small spills of lead. Lead will stick to wood or similar materials (although it can be pried off them), but when cool it can be lifted easily from most metal surfaces. Completely cover the sink and any wet or moist areas. Also be sure to remove all exposed food and to completely clean all work areas after molding, after removing all the lead and tools, before exposing food to the area again. For your family's health, this is a must. *No exceptions!*

If you lack a suitable kitchen area in which to work, it is possible to use other heat sources outside (OUTSIDE ONLY!), such as liquid-fuel camping stoves, propane and butane stoves and torches, some electric hot plates, and outdoor charcoal and propane barbecue grills. Be sure to use them only where safe (outdoor stoves and heat sources are to be used outdoors only), and be sure that you have sufficient sturdy, steady tables or other level work surfaces that you can cover and protect as needed. As with the kitchen stove, these must be used with adequate ventilation and air exhaust. One advantage of a separate, special workplace is that you can bolt a furnace in place there. You can bolt a furnace to a section of shelving board and place this on a covered kitchen countertop, but make sure the result is sturdy and stable.

Electric lead-melting furnaces were used in the past primarily for molding lead bullets, but they are becoming more common for molding sinkers and bucktails. They eliminate the need for a local heat source because they can be plugged in anywhere, use regular 120-volt household electric service, and do not have an open flame as do some other heat sources. All these furnaces work with a heating element much like the small immersion heaters that are popular for heating water for tea, coffee, and soup.

Palmer, Hilts Molds, Lee, RCBS, and Lyman all make electric melt furnaces. (The latter three are made primarily for bullet molding.) They range from the small Palmer Hot Pot, which holds 4 pounds of lead, up to the giant Hilts Molds Ultimate Inferno, which will melt up to 35 pounds of lead at a time on household current. (It does require a heavy circuit—preferably at least 20 amps—because it uses 1,600 watts.)

The smaller units usually pour from the top as if from a ladle; you pour the lead from the heated container into the mold cavity through the sprue hole. Larger units either bottom-feed through a bottom nozzle or top-pour, but with the ladle supported and balanced for easy pouring. The Ultimate Inferno, for example, is capable of pouring through the top spout or through the bottom ⅛- and ¼-inch-diameter nozzles and bottom-pour plug. Most of the bottom-pour furnaces are best for smaller cavity molds, from 1/20-ounce up to about 2 ounces. Larger cavity molds have larger gates or sprue holes and can be filled easily either with handheld or frame-supported ladles. The 35-pound-capacity Ultimate Inferno from Hilts Molds can bottom-pour large quantities. Roy Hilts says he can completely fill a 5-pound rock-cod-sinker mold through the bottom spout of this furnace.

Many of these electric furnaces have options of top- or bottom-pour capabilities, and replacement elements are available should an electric element burn out over time. One option available for several of the furnaces is mold guides, which can be fitted to the bottom-feed furnace to properly position the mold for easy, accurate pouring. The guides are available primarily from the companies making bullet-molding furnaces, although some can be fitted onto different furnace brands.

Most of the better furnaces have a rheostat control to adjust the temperature between perhaps 500 and 800 degrees Fahrenheit. This allows proper heating of a variety of lead and lead alloys whose melting temperatures are within these ranges. The smaller, ladle-type electric heaters do not have this capability.

Some melting furnaces are simply electric pots that will melt lead but require a separate ladle to transfer molten lead from the pot to the mold.

One big advantage of a bottom-feed furnace is that any slag, dross, or impurities will stay on the molten lead's surface, making it less likely that these impurities will mix in with the lead used in the lead heads. Furnaces also provide greater flexibility in working area because you are not confined to the kitchen but can mold anywhere there is a sturdy work area and a proper electric outlet. Another advantage to furnaces is speed. When properly set up, and with skill and experience, production of up to 400 jigs per hour is possible. **Important:** These speeds are attainable only with experience. Casting lead heads is not a speed contest, and safety concerns must be paramount at all times.

Furnaces must be positioned on a firm, sturdy work surface with ample space for molds, hooks, and any other equipment or safety necessities. Ideally, furnaces should be bolted to the work surface or workbench top.

Many furnace models are available. Although some can be expensive, others, such as the Palmer Hot Pot, are relatively inexpensive. Take your time in considering such a purchase, and thoroughly examine all available furnaces to determine the one best suited to your purposes, budget, and production needs.

In addition to kitchen stoves and electric furnaces, other types of heat sources can be used for melting lead. Single- or two-burner camp stoves operating on liquid fuel (like the Coleman models) or small cylinders of propane or butane are also ideal for molding bucktails. They have the advantage of portability, something definitely not possible with a kitchen stove or when you are limited to a locality with the proper amperage outlet for an electric furnace. These stoves allow bucktail molding in an open garage, carport, breezeway, backyard, gazebo, or on a patio or deck. Be aware, however, that most parts of the house, even a workshop, will lack the ventilation of a kitchen or the outdoor areas, and ventilation is vital for your long-term health when molding lead.

If you use a camp stove, be sure to match it with a flat-bottom pot to hold the lead. The flat bottom is critical to prevent wobbling and possible spills of molten lead. Pots and matching ladles for melting lead are available from tackle shops, mail-order supply houses for lure-making parts, and hardware stores carrying plumbing supplies. If you use a large ladle in place of a pot, you will need a rack to support the ladle. These racks are made for gas stoves and are designed to allow a small pot to be used on a larger burner by concentrating the flame to the smaller pot bottom.

Plumber's pots will vary within a capacity of 5 to 20 pounds of lead; the ladles will hold from 4 to 16 ounces of lead. Bullet caster's ladles are smaller and more precise, often with two spouts (on opposite sides for both right- and left-hand pourers), and some have partitions at the spout to hold back slag. The bullet caster's ladles usually hold less lead, however—from 1 to 4 ounces—so are less effective when molding larger bucktails.

It is important to use a large enough ladle or pot. Most small pots that can be heated on stoves will hold about 6 to 10 pounds of lead. A ladle might hold 1 to 2 pounds. This sounds like a lot until you start to fill molds. For example, to make 4-ounce bucktails in a four-cavity mold, you will use 1 pound of lead in one pouring.

The ideal ladle for working from an open pot is the kind (often used by bullet casters) that has a vertical partition across the ladle near the spout. The partition has holes in the bottom so that lead will flow from one side of the partition to the other. This allows only pure lead into the mold, since the slag that floats to the top is kept back by the partition.

If necessary, you can get by with a soup ladle and a discarded cooking pot, but be careful. Make sure these do not have soldered or heat-sealed joints or handle fastenings that might loosen or weaken with the high heats used for melting lead. Make sure the pot and ladle are sturdy and will hold the weight of lead you will be using. If you are at all doubtful, do not use them. And once you do use them for melting lead, *never again* use them for food or drink.

SAFETY

Safety in handling lead must be paramount in any operation to make bucktails, jigs, and sinkers. The cautions presented in this chapter are equally important for chapter 5, "Sinkers and Tin Squids," and must be reviewed before you attempt to make sinkers, tin squids, or bucktails.

Safety in molding lead heads must be on several levels. Lead can be a dangerous, toxic substance. In addition, it often contains minute amounts of impurities such as tin, antimony, and arsenic, which are poisonous, and mercury, the vapor of which is highly poisonous.

Because it does not flush easily from the body, lead has an accumulative effect. Lead absorbed over time builds to higher levels, and too high a level is toxic. Examples of the danger are found when children eat lead paint chips (lead is no longer used in paints) and as a result experience mental impairment as well as other medical problems.

Lead is absorbed into the body when its fumes are inhaled (thus the need for proper venting or an outside location when melting lead). The fumes are deposited on the mucous membranes of the nose or mouth and subsequently swallowed, absorbed by ingestion (thus the need for proper hand-washing after handling lead and care around food), or by contact with oil-soluble lead that is absorbed directly into the skin, as in smoking while molding.

Certain safety procedures in handling and melting lead are necessary. These include making sure that you work in a properly vented area. This does not mean just a workspace in a large area, or one with passive ventilation, but one (as with the kitchen vent fan) that will actively pull the fumes from the work area and vent them outside. Lacking proper ventilation, work outside.

Do not smoke. Experts warn that smoking while molding is one of the principal ways lead can be ingested or absorbed. Lead is transferred to your hands, which in turn is transferred to the cigarette or cigar, which in turn is transferred to your mouth. Lead also could be deposited on the cigarette paper and then burned and inhaled as the cigarette is smoked.

Take your smokes before or after molding, and be sure to wash thoroughly as described after molding and before handling any smoking materials.

Do not eat or drink anything while melting lead or molding lead heads. This is a must—lead will be absorbed onto your hands and can be transferred to food and thus into your body. Be sure to wash your hands properly and thoroughly after each molding session and before doing anything else. Use *plenty* of soap. Best are the heavy-duty hand cleaners that are gritty (such as Lava), which will thoroughly clean your hands of oil-carried lead or other lead residue.

Wear protective clothing to prevent lead-to-skin contact. A long-sleeve shirt, a cap or hat, and gloves are helpful. Heavy insulated gloves are particularly good because they aid in safe handling of molds and ladles while minimizing contact with lead or lead-based oils or substances.

In addition to these main concerns over working with lead, there are also the safety concerns of working with the high heat necessary to melt lead. Whether using pure lead or lead alloys, or even pure tin (more on the subject of making tin squids in chapter 5), molten metal is dangerous if not handled carefully and systematically. Tin melts at 449 degrees Fahrenheit, pure lead at 621 degrees Fahrenheit. Although it may seem repetitive to you, follow these guidelines when preparing and working with any molten metal.

Note that these guidelines are in addition to those for safety. They *do not* replace them.

- Before beginning to mold bucktail heads or sinkers, make sure there is no competing activity in the house or area where you will be working. Do not mold when others, particularly children, are in your area or likely to interfere physically or by distraction. Molding requires all of your concentration. Put all pets in a secure place (basement, bathroom, inside if you are working outside, outside if you are working inside) for the duration of the molding session. Make sure others in the house know what you're doing so that they do not release pets or allow children to go into your work area.

- Make sure you have adequate ventilation if you are working at home. While this is important for safety, it is also important if you want to be allowed back in the house after the molding session is over. Many spouses are very unsympathetic to the fumes and odors of lead molding, but the main reason for proper ventilation is of course safety.

- Make sure you have a safe, sturdy workplace with a counter of ample size that is properly protected with large hot pads, sheets of plywood, or similar insulating sheets. Make sure that any lead that might spill will be contained so as not to ruin countertops, flooring, or other equipment.

- Use an adequate furnace or heating source. If working with a furnace, camp stove, torch, or barbecue grill not specifically made for melting metal, make sure it is sturdy—not at all wobbly—and will not slip or move as you work. Similarly, make sure that any pots used on such stoves are flat bottomed and stable. (Lee pots have a wide, flat bottom just for this purpose.) Lead is heavy, and a small pot can hold 10 or 20 pounds and be completely uncontrollable if the lead starts to spill. Make sure you have furnaces and melting pots bolted down properly.

- Work out a plan for your molding, pouring, and handling of hooks and molds. Use your steadier, stronger hand to control pouring the lead while the other hand holds the mold. If you are right-handed and working with a bottom-feed furnace, use your right hand for the furnace controls and hold the jig mold in your left hand to line it up under the furnace spout. If you work with a top-pouring electric furnace, it helps to use your right hand to control the lead and your left to hold the mold handles. If you work with a pot (electric or heated separately) and separate ladle, hold the ladle with your right hand and pour into the mold being held with your left hand. (The latter two suggestions assume you are right-handed. Reverse the directions if you are a southpaw.) Regardless of method, you will need a large working area to the left of the heat source to minimize the amount of movement you will need to make with a lead-filled ladle or to eliminate crossover where you would have to bring a mold across or in front of the molten lead supply. Again, reverse the directions if you are left-handed.

- *Never* cool a mold or lead by dipping it in water, and never have water anywhere near the molding operation. Moisture or water in the melting pot or ladle or dropped into the molten lead will cause the metal to explode violently, with dangerous and potentially disastrous results.

None of these guidelines are designed as scare tactics to keep you from molding your own lead heads. If you have molded lead heads or sinkers before, you already know and follow most or all of these cautions. And if you are new to molding lead heads, you'll recognize most of them as just plain common sense. But they are most important commonsense rules.

MOLDING TECHNIQUES

As just mentioned, it is important to have a basic game plan and working arrangement when handling lead. If you have not molded sinkers before, *before starting* the actual process, go through the motions of adding hooks to the mold, closing the mold, pouring the lead, opening the mold, removing the lead heads, cutting the sprue from the head, adding more hooks, and so on. In other words: Rehearse the full cycle of molding to make sure you have enough space, nothing is in the way, and the best arrangement for repeated molding has been prepared.

Plan on making a lot of molded heads at once—this will save time and money. I like to mold lures, but I do not like to prolong the process by molding only a few at a time on repeated days. It's a waste of both time and electricity or other fuel source every time the lead is remelted. Once the pot of lead is melted, it is easy to add more ingots to keep the operation going. It is far simpler, more time-efficient, and more economical to mold 50 to 200 lead heads of a favorite fishing lure at one time, even though that supply might last for several seasons.

There are no real tricks to molding, but here are two suggestions to maximize your time: Work with a partner or fishing buddy, and work with several molds. The reasons are simple. With a two-man operation, it is easy to separate the work as follows: One person is responsible for picking up the prepared molds and filling them with molten lead. The second person places the hooks in the molds, close the molds, leaves them on their sides and ready for pouring, and removes the lead heads from the cooled molds. In some cases it might even help to have two persons doing these latter tasks: one to place hooks in the molds, the other to remove the completed lead heads. Although none of these tasks are difficult, they do take care, especially when adding the hooks to hot molds and removing the still-hot lead heads from the molds. Using several molds allows for a rotation of this process and prevents one mold from getting too hot from repeated use.

If there is any trick to getting good lead heads, it is in having the lead hot and the mold warm. When the lead first melts, it will be a bright, glistening silvery color, almost the sheen of highly polished sterling silver or a brand-new silver-plated spoon. As more lead is added (or as lead ingots or excess sprue is added to replenish the molten lead), the temperature will drop and the lead will turn mushy. It will still be molten but will have a slushy appearance. To me it looks like silver oatmeal or mashed potatoes.

In part, the temperature range will vary with the type of alloy or lead used. Lead with a little (2.5 percent) tin will have only a short temperature range, 9 degrees, through this slushy stage until it reaches the liquid temperature. An alloy with 95 percent lead and 5 percent tin will have a broader temperature range, 75 degrees, between solid and liquid. A similar alloy of 91 percent lead, 2 percent tin, and 7 percent antimony will have a range of 62 degrees; an alloy of 94 percent tin and 6 percent antimony will have a 64-degree pasty or slushy temperature range.

The lead must be heated beyond this slushy stage to a molten liquid stage before you can work with it. It must be hot enough to pour smoothly and rapidly into the mold and to completely fill the cavity or cavities. One way to judge the proper temperature is to heat the lead until it becomes a purplish or golden color. Because this is at a higher temperature, it might bring to the surface some additional impurities, giving the surface a slightly scummy appearance. Too much of a purplish/blue/red hue in the surface sheen indicates that tin is drossing out of the lead (oxides are rising to the surface and separating); careful, slow stirring might be required.

These impurities may not matter unless the scum and slag are so excessive that they will interfere with filling the mold with pure lead. If they do not seem excessive, skim off any slag with an old tablespoon reserved for that purpose. Before that, however, try stirring to reintroduce the lighter metals into the alloy mixture.

Take care that you do not overheat the lead, particularly if working with alloys. Excessive heat will tend to separate the metals in the alloys (usually tin and antimony added to the lead) so that fluxing and stirring are necessary. Fluxing, a process used primarily by bullet-casters and involving adding tallow or candle wax to the lead, is smelly and creates excessive fumes. If you do have excessive drossing or scumming indicative of metal separation, fluxing can help you achieve a better-mixed alloy. One tip is to use plain candle wax or beeswax, about a ¼-inch-diameter chunk for 3 pounds of molten lead. Add it carefully to the melt, and immediately touch a match to it to burn off the black fumes that will otherwise result. Because of these fumes, avoid working in the kitchen. Also, try this first on a small scale to get a feel for the extent of the fumes and smoke that can occur.

Stirring will help mix the metals, which otherwise will tend to separate as a result of their different specific gravities. Lead that is too hot can overheat molds, increase the time it takes the lead heads to cool for removal from the mold, cause a frosty or crystalline appearance on the surface of the lead head, cause lead to run along the seam lines of the mold, and increase the possibility of flash on the completed head.

When molding bucktails you often don't know the type or percentage of the metals in lead alloys. In most cases you can get by with scrap lead (usually an alloy), but if problems occur, stick to pure lead. The additions of other metals to the lead will cause various effects—some good, some bad. Tin alloys easily with lead and is very ductile (thus ideal for the old-style tin squids). Tin is lighter than lead but adds strength. Antimony also adds strength to lead, along with hardness, and might be something to consider when molding lead heads that will be cast around and into rocks. Other substances, such as zinc, aluminum, arsenic (added to older car-battery lead), iron, copper, and nickel, sometimes found in lead alloys do not help in any way.

When using alloys, it is important to periodically stir the molten lead because the lighter metals will rise to the surface as dross; skimming them off may result in losing the positive characteristics the metals added to the alloy.

If you work from a bottom-pour furnace, you will have few problems other than adjusting the spout and feed of the furnace to the quantity of lead needed for the mold used. For this reason, it is best to use molds that fit any mold guides that come with the furnace or that you rig for this purpose and whose cavity sizes match the amount of lead released from the bottom-pour. In most cases you will be limited in the amount of lead you can pour. (There are exceptions, such as the Hilts Molds Ultimate Inferno, which will pour any amount of lead through the bottom spout.)

On most bottom-feed furnaces, you will not be able to use any molds that have wire or projections (such as spinnerbaits, walleye spinners, bottom-bounce/bottom-walker sinker molds, tail spinners, or molds using large hooks that project from the mold), because they will interfere with placing the nozzle tight to the mold sprue.

The melting pot (electric or stove-heated) provides a ready "stock" of melted lead to pour into the mold. However, unless the pot is designed specifically with a spout and tilting arm or lever, *never* pour from the pot—use a ladle. Unfortunately many beginners have problems in using a ladle to dip lead from the pot. The problems usually result from using a cold ladle or one that has been allowed to cool between pours. A cold ladle will rapidly cool the lead before you can begin to pour it into the mold. There are two solutions: (1) If you use a lightweight ladle, keep it in the pot so that the cup of the ladle is always at the temperature of the molten lead. (2) Use a second burner and rest the ladle on this burner (properly supported and secured) to heat it and keep the lead it picks up at the proper molten temperature. The hot ladle can easily be refilled from the larger pot. Keep the ladle hot and dry, and never put a cold ladle into molten lead.

Similarly, the mold must be kept warm. The mold will eventually become warm through repeated moldings, but you must heat the mold before you begin. The best way to do this is to pour lead into the mold cavities (without hooks or eyes or inserts) until complete, perfect heads are achieved. If you heat the mold on the stove, use only the lowest heat for a few minutes: Excessive heat will not allow the heads to cool easily and might even warp aluminum molds. Some furnaces, such as the 20-pound Lyman MAG 20 bottom-feeding furnace, have a "warming shelf" to keep molds hot.

Proper and easier molding is achieved by smoking the mold cavities with a flame. A candle flame works fine, as shown here. Molds should be resmoked when required, usually indicated by incomplete castings or casting with a ripple finish. The smaller the mold cavity, the more important it is to smoke the mold.

If you heat molds by casting heads, do so *without* hooks until perfect results are achieved. The early imperfect heads can be returned to the melting pot or furnace. Use care, because they might leak lead through the channels for the hooks and wire. This will occur where hooks are placed in the cavities for complete heads. I like molds to be just slightly too hot to touch, but experience with your individual molds will dictate the proper working temperature.

While a cold mold or cool lead from a cold ladle will cause imperfect castings, other casting problems can occur. Sometimes the sprue hole is not quite large enough to fill the mold cavity before cooling begins. I recall one of my molds that cast four bullet-shaped bucktails, all the same size. No matter what molten lead temperature I achieved, whether I used alloy or pure lead, how hot the mold or ladle was, or which sprue hole I filled first, one cavity always produced poor, incomplete results. I drilled out the sprue hole slightly to enlarge it, and since then the mold has worked fine.

If you find this necessary, be very careful that any drilling or reaming is confined to the sprue hole only and does not go deep enough to damage the mold cavity. The best solution is to hold the mold closed in a drill-press vise and drill straight down, using a stop on the bit or on the drill-press arm to prevent cavity damage. If you lack a drill or drill press, you can do this with a razor blade, X-Acto knife, or scalpel, carefully carving away the excess aluminum to enlarge and smooth the gate hole.

Sometimes large cast bucktails will have a rippled surface. One solution to this, and in fact something that should be done with every mold, is to smoke the mold with a candle flame. For some reason, candle flame smoke helps create smoother bucktails (and sinkers) and reduces molding problems. The theory behind this is that the smoke layer creates an insulation that allows the molten lead to flow freely without forming ripples.

Too hot a mold or lead also creates problems, since this might remove some metals of the alloy (changing the characteristics of the lead head) or create a frosty, crystalline surface and increase the

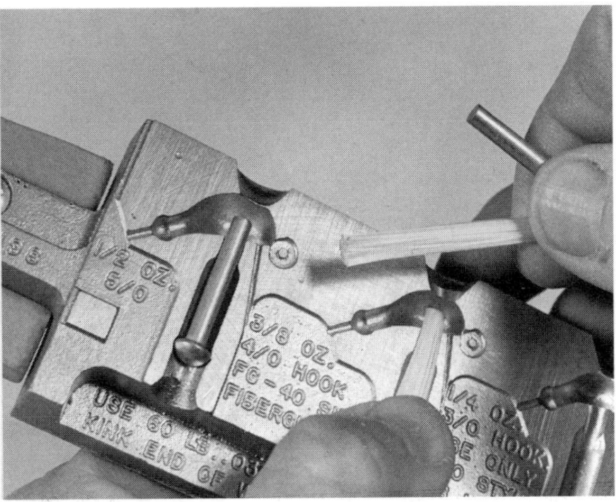

Insert pins and brush guards in place, also held separately.

possibility of flash or fins on the lure edges where the two mold haves come together. This can happen to a slight degree with any mold, but it is far less likely with the machined inner surfaces of today's high-quality molds. You must avoid this flash, because it requires time and effort to remove it for perfect results. Other causes of flash include the mold not closing completely, using the wrong size or style of hook, using of a dirty mold, and lead in the mold hinge from an overpour.

MOLDING STEPS

The actual steps of molding lead heads are simple. First place the special jig hooks in the mold, taking care that you use the right brand, style, and size for each cavity. After the hooks are properly positioned, close the mold carefully by bringing the second half over onto the first, which is kept level and horizontal. Hold or clamp the mold halves together securely. If you work in a team and use several or more molds, you may wish to use spring-style carpenter's clamps to hold the molds closed so that the hooks do not slip. If you do this, remove any plastic protective tips, which might burn.

If you use a bottom-feed furnace, adjust the spout lever or feed to the quantity of lead needed for each mold cavity. Slide or place the mold into the mold guides, and make sure the sprue hole is directly under and in close contact with the furnace spout. Pour the lead into each mold cavity, remove the mold from the furnace, and lay it down. Allow it to cool before attempting to remove the lead heads.

If you will be using a top-pour, trunnion-pivoted furnace, make sure the pot pours well and straight. If necessary, use sturdy blocks of wood as a base on which to support the mold, making sure the support is at the right height for proper pouring. (This support height might have to be changed with different molds.) This is always helpful but is especially important when using molds to make larger bucktails, because a multiple-cavity mold where each cavity makes a several-ounce lure can mean that more than a pound of lead will be necessary for one pour.

If you use a ladle, remove it from the pot or stove where it is kept to maintain proper heat for smooth pouring. Usually you can rest the lip of the ladle on the edge of the mold for support, but take care in doing this to prevent the ladle from slipping and spilling molten lead. Finish the pour, and set the mold aside.

If you work with large lures, you may have to keep the mold upright for a few moments for the lead to cool sufficiently before placing the mold on its side. This cooling can easily be seen by watching the lead in the sprue; it will change

Molding requires a high heat to melt lead. If not using an electric furnace or pot, one good source is the kitchen stove, provided that proper safety techniques are used (see text). Note the wood block to hold the ladle level and the board to the right of the stove to protect the kitchen countertop.

from a liquid shiny sheen to a more crystalline, slightly duller surface as it cools. Also, the lead will dip slightly in the center, since the cooling process will usually draw some liquid lead from the sprue area to adjust for the slight shrinkage that occurs when lead cools.

When pouring by any of these methods, make sure the lead does not spill outside the sprue area. If lead laps over the sides of the mold or into the hinge area, it will be difficult if not impossible to open the mold without first prying or cutting the excess lead free.

If working with a partner on a rotation method with several molds, you should have separate places for the filled molds and those that are ready to be poured. Once a filled mold is cool, open it carefully. The lead heads will still be hot, so lift them out of the mold with pliers (handling by the sprue only to avoid damaging the body) or with heavy gloves, and place the heads on a hot pad. If you have a mold where the lead heads will fall out, make sure the heads fall onto a soft surface, such as an old folded-up towel, to protect them from damage. This is particularly important with heavy heads when using pure (soft) lead. Once the lead heads are cooled, make sure you do not handle them with your bare hands. This will deposit oils onto the lead, which will interfere with painting the heads. If you use the heads bare, as for slider-fishing, worm-fishing, or grubs or minnow tails, this will not matter. Place more hooks into the mold, and you are ready to cast that mold again.

Cut away the excess lead that forms in the sprue hole of each cavity by using wire cutters or special lead-cutting gate cutters. Most of the mold-manufacturing companies sell these special cutters that are to be used only for lead or plastic (not for wire). The excess lead, sometimes called sprue for the entrance hole into the mold, can be added to the lead stockpot.

It is best to leave lead in the melting furnaces when you finish, because it will heat the additional lead more rapidly at the next session, saving electricity and lessening the possibility of damage to the heating coils. If you don't want to keep the leftover lead in the pot or ladle when you are finished molding, buy some ingot molds. Pour this lead into them to form small "pigs."

There is nothing wrong with leaving lead in the pot until the next pouring session. But you might still want ingot molds if you get lead in odd shapes and sizes and wish to melt it down into usable bars. If you are using different alloys and wish to keep them separate, work out a system of marking the pigs with a chisel, scratch awl, or felt-tip marker.

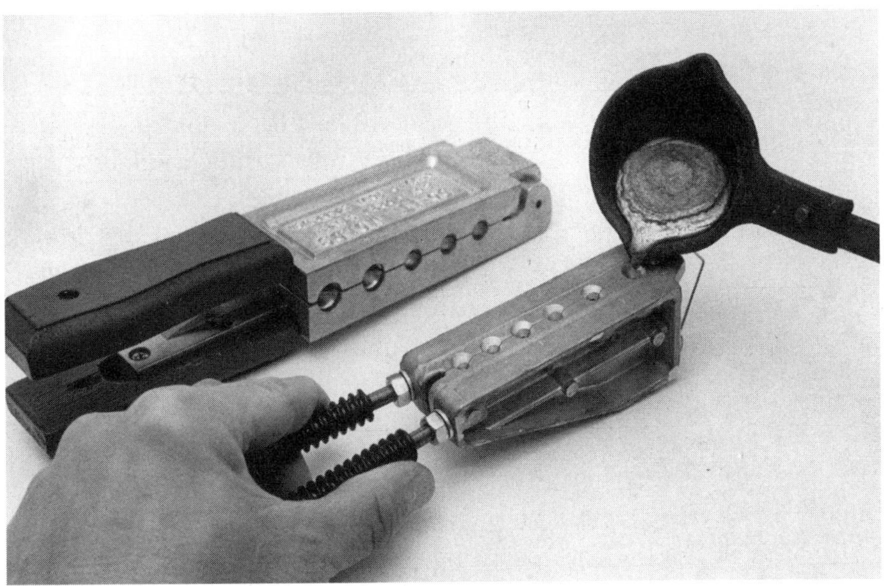

Pouring molds. Always use heavy gloves to hold the ladle, properly support the mold, and pour quickly but carefully. The Hilts mold is being poured; the Do-It mold has been filled with hooks and will be poured next. Working in a rotation system like this is more efficient.

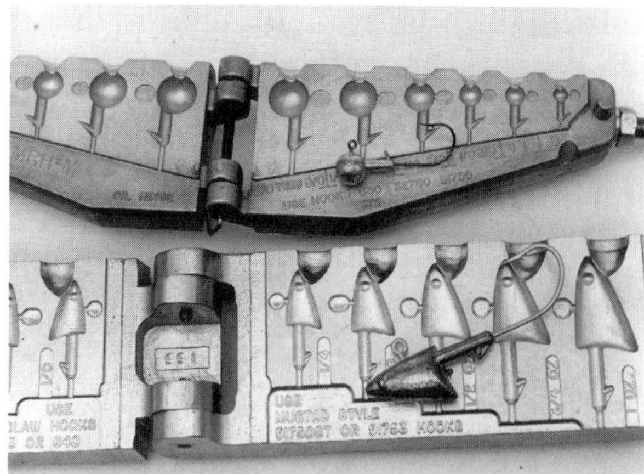

Example of jig heads from two different molds. Top, a Hilts mold; bottom, a Do-It mold.

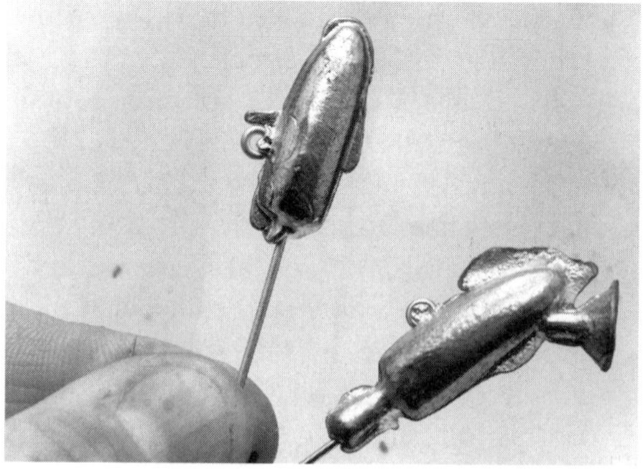

Examples of defective molded heads as a result of using the wrong hooks, not closing the mold properly, using a mold that is not hot enough, or not smoking the mold.

A large saltwater bucktail head, here removed from a single-cavity smoked mold.

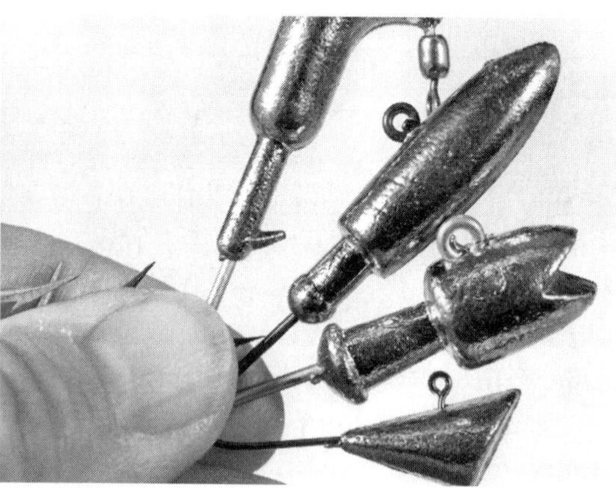

Examples of molded lead heads after being removed from the molds and the sprue cut off.

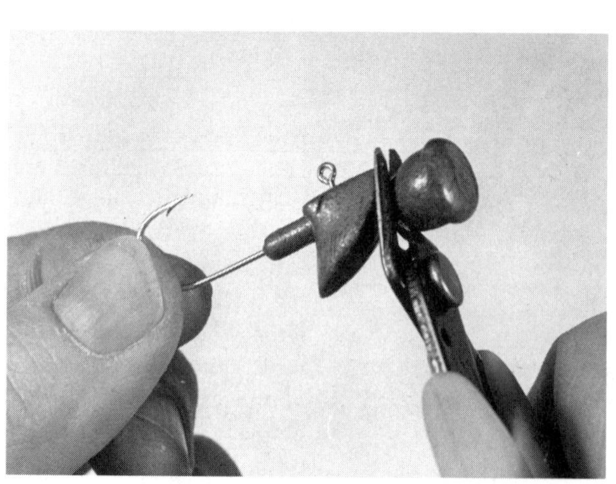

Using gate cutters (available from Hilts Molds, Do-It Corp., and other sources) to clip the sprue from a molded bucktail head.

FINISHING MOLDED BUCKTAILS

Once all the heads have been molded, make sure you handle them only with lightweight gloves. Rubber dishwashing gloves or cotton gardening gloves are fine for this. The gloves prevent the oils from your hands from coating the lead heads and interfering with paint adherence.

There is still work to do before the lure can be tied onto the end of a line. First check the head carefully, especially the hook eye and the seam line where the two mold halves met. If lead has deposited in the eye, there are several ways to remove it. One is to use a pair of side-cutting wire cutters; gently (do not cut through

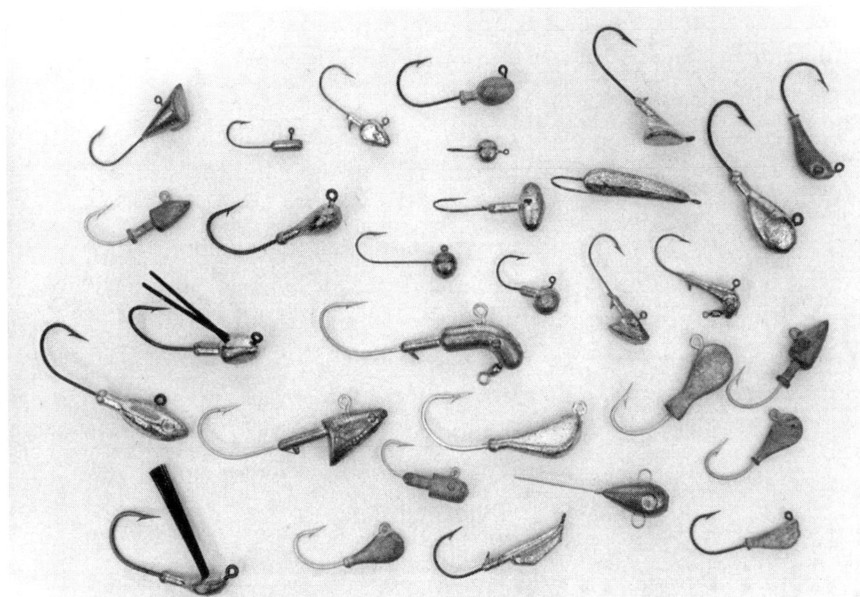

Various styles and sizes of jig heads and lures from several different manufacturers.

the hook wire) cut around the base of the eye, and twist free any excess lead. Another way is to use a small awl, ice pick, or similar pointed instrument to poke the lead out of the eye. I use an old small screwdriver that I ground down to a four-sided point (like a pyramid) that serves as a coarse reamer to remove lead. Punch-out tools are also made specifically for this task.

Ideally there should be no flash on the sides of the lure. If there is a small amount, it can be removed with a coarse file. Regular files are designed to be used with steel and other hard metals, and although they will work on lead, there are special files on the market designed for use with special metals that are more appropriate for this task. The designation of "lead," "brass," or "aluminum" indicates the material (lead in this case) on which the files are designed to work. Flat and half-round shapes are typically available. Prices are slightly higher than for similar files designed for iron and steel.

If you are turning out a quantity of bucktails and not tying them up immediately, it is still wise to give them a base coat of paint or primer shortly after molding. If the lead heads are not painted, they will slowly oxidize, making paint adherence more difficult. Any quality color paint will work well, although white is preferred because it provides a good base for any light or bright colors painted on later. Until the lead heads are painted, be sure to handle them with gloves to prevent skin oils from transferring to the lure.

The problem with any lead-head lure is that the paint will chip off if the lure hits a rock. This is true even with most commercially made bucktails. The pros and cons of various types of paint and the methods of using them to paint bucktails and jigs (as well as other lures) are covered in chapter 15.

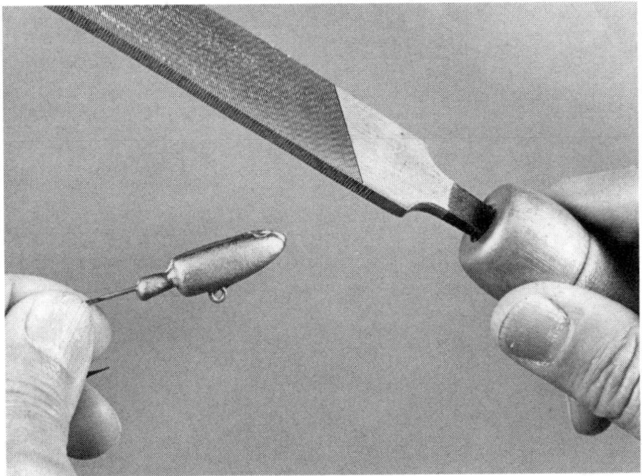

Using a file to smooth any flash from along the joint line of the two mold sides or cavity halves. If the mold is a good mold and if the right size and style hook is used, this is generally not necessary.

After the first coat of paint or primer to prevent oxidation is applied, the lead head can be left indefinitely without finishing. I usually keep a stock supply of different styles and sizes of lead heads on hand, all painted with primer or a base coat of white, to tie up at my leisure or as needed.

Another option is to use the powder paints in which the lead lure is heated slightly and then dipped in the powder paint to create a permanent durable paint coating. I'll have more on this in chapter 15.

WRAPPING TAILS ON LEAD HEADS

To finish a traditional bucktail lure, place the hook of the painted or unpainted lead head in a vise. A small fly-tying vise works best for this step, and most vises today have interchangeable jaws to adjust to different size hooks. Lacking that, any small vise or clamp will do in a pinch. Some possibilities here include Vise-Grips (which can be clamped in a larger vise or to a table with a C-clamp, although self-clamping styles are also available), a small clamp-on work vise, or hobby vises.

You will need thread and preferably a bobbin to hold the thread. Fly-tying or rod-wrapping thread will work fine. Do not use cotton sewing thread—it is too fuzzy to produce good results. The best thread sizes are 2/0 for small bucktails up to about ¾ ounce, size A for larger bucktails to about 4 ounces, and size D or E thread for anything larger. If making a very thick tail, you may wish to go to a slightly larger thread for the lure size to tie the material down tightly. While you can wrap by holding a spool of thread, it will be far easier to use a bobbin such as is used in fly tying.

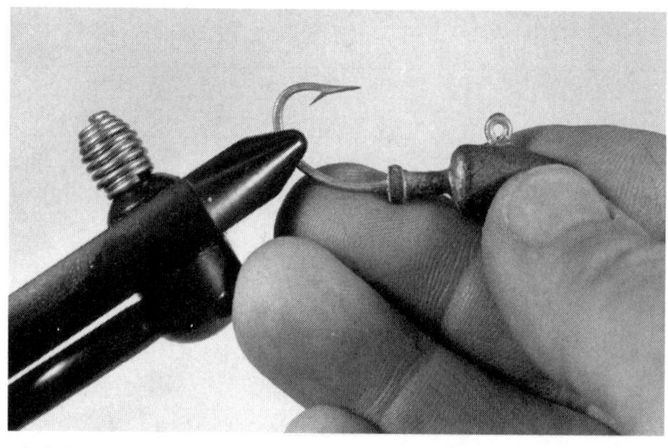

Finishing a jig head involves wrapping the collar with tail materials. The first step in this is to clamp the hook into a fly-tying vise or a simple vise substitute.

Typical tail materials include fur, bucktail, artificial fur, saddle hackles, crinkly nylon, polypropylene fibers (often unraveled from polypropylene rope), marabou, Mylar strips, or special materials such as SuperHair, Krystal Flash, and Sparkle Flash. These materials—and many more available today—can also be used in combination.

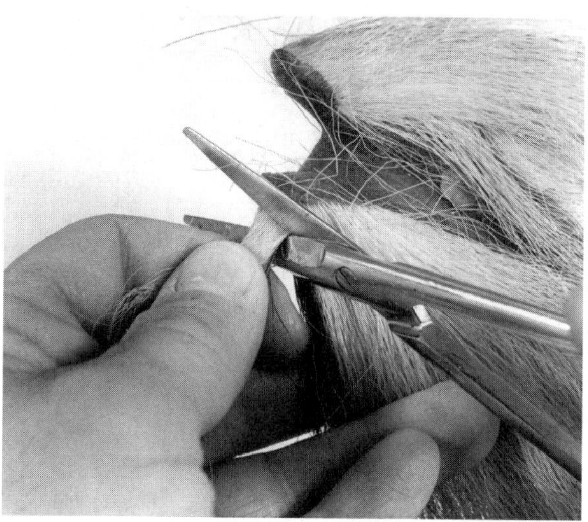

Deer tail fur is clipped from the skin for use as the tail material on a jig.

Bucktail heads will differ, some having a completely bare hook shank, some having a molded-in lead collar, and others with ridges to help hold the body and tail material or with a slight ball at the end to prevent the material and thread from slipping off.

Begin by wrapping the thread several times around the collar or hook shank. After several turns wrap the thread back over the previous wraps, in essence tying the thread down with the tension of the overwraps. Continue to wrap, and after several more turns cut off any excess thread. From this point on it will be necessary to maintain tension (though there is an exception at one step) to keep the thread or materials from loosening.

Choose the tail material, cut the proper amount close to the skin or the base (if synthetic), and measure it for length on the bucktail head. For best results the tail should extend past the hook bend. General guides are to make it about one and a half to one and three-quarters the length of the hook shank so that the tail extends well *past* the bend of the hook.

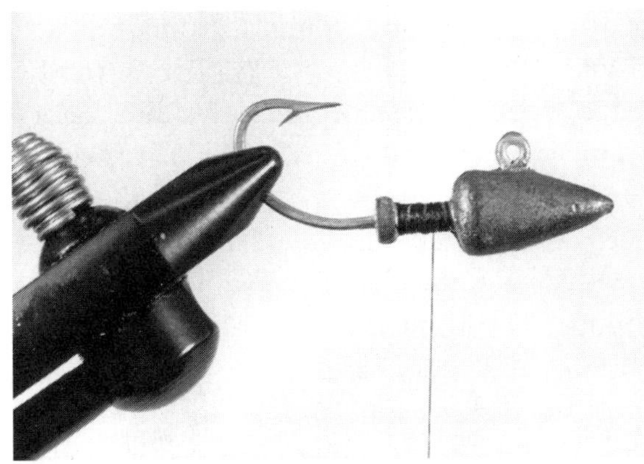

Using standard tying techniques, tie down the thread as shown and build up a base of thread on the jig collar.

There are two basic ways to add a fur or artificial-fur tail to the lure. One is to take the full bunch of fur and hold it in position on top of the hook shank or collar, spiral several slightly loose wraps of thread around the fur and hook, and pull the thread down tight, continuing to wrap as you do so. While doing this, spiral and push the fur uniformly around the hook so that it covers the entire hook shank or collar.

The second method is to use small bunches of the fur and tie each down tightly in place around the hook shank or collar. These small sections assure more complete, even coverage, particularly on larger heads. This method takes longer, but it usually produces better results for the beginner.

If you make very thick-tailed bucktails on larger heads, the thick fur is often difficult to cut off at the rear of the head (in front of the thread wrap). One solution is to cut the fur to

Begin by holding the fur over the top of the collar and wrapping the thread over it several times. Rotate the fur before pulling the thread tight to spread the fur uniformly around the collar.

Fur spread uniformly around the jig collar. Excess fur forward of the collar is clipped off with scissors.

Once the excess fur is clipped off, wrap the fur tail completely with thread as shown.

length before tying it down, and then tie the fur in place so that no subsequent cutting is necessary. Another way is to soak the butt end of the cut fur in hot water for a few minutes to soften it, which makes cutting the fur on the lure easier.

Some lures use only fur as a tail; others mix fur with saddle hackles, Mylar strips, Krystal Flash, synthetics, and/or other materials. In these cases it is usually best to wrap the fur in place before adding other materials. The reverse is also possible: adding the more fragile materials first and then protecting them with a wrapped layer of fur.

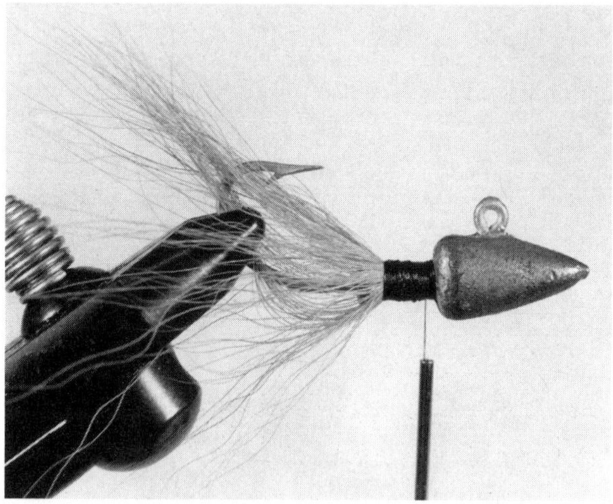

Completely wrapped tail on unpainted jig body.

You can make two-tone fur bodies by tying in two fur bundles—one on top of the hook shank or collar and one underneath. Typical color combinations are dark on top and light on the bottom (so-called countershading, simulating the colors in baitfish), including red-white, red-yellow, black-white, black-yellow, red-pink, blue-white, green-white; green-yellow for salt water; and all these combinations along with black-brown, black-red, and black-orange for fresh water.

Some bucktails and jigs require bodies on the hook shank or collar. These are of the "Doll Fly" type, also called crappie flies (really jigs with a lead head). For this almost any plain hook or plain collar (no barbs for soft plastics) can be used. The thread is tied down as above and then wound to the rear of the hook shank. The tail (often marabou) is tied into the rear of the hook shank, just forward of the bend. Once the tail is tied down, the body materials are tied down at the same spot. If a palmered hackle is to be used, it is tied in at this time. Typical body materials include hackle palmered over the body, chenille wrapped around the hook shank, or a combination of both to make a fly-like jig.

Once the body material or materials are tied down at the tail, wrap the thread forward and tie down about ¼ inch behind the ball head. Then the body materials—first the chenille and then the hackle—are wound forward and tied off with the thread. The body materials can be tied in separately or together. Other alternatives are to wrap the tail materials in place with a hackle wrapped in place right behind the head, much as the hackle in a cork bass bug is tied down. Variations of these ties can be used, following fly-tying methods and techniques, but most jigs and bucktails are pretty basic.

Some materials are more difficult to work with than others. Nylon tail material has a tendency to pull out unless it is tied down very tightly. It is a good idea to soak the butt ends of nylon material with clear fingernail polish or fly-tier's head cement while it is being wrapped on. This will help to hold the nylon in place. Polypropylene tails can be made from a piece of poly rope, the fibers frayed out from the rope and bunched to make a kinky tail. Another way to do this is to tie a short length of the rope in place on the hook shank, threading the hook through the end of the rope to make sure that the fibers are bunched uniformly. Then fray the ends after the rope is securely tied down. An awl, bodkin, needle, fine nail, or similar sharp tool is ideal for this. Fray a little at a time to prevent loosening the material. Bucktails using this material are highly popular and successful, particularly in the Gulf Coast area, where they are advertised and sold as being excellent for ling, the local name for cobia.

Once the tail or body materials are all tied in place, any excess material that laps over the bucktail head must be clipped off square. Do this with fine scissors, or use a razor blade. A razor blade works well to cut around the hook shank or collar, but be sure to avoid cutting thread. At this point the thread must be tied down and cemented to secure it. To do this you can finish the thread with half-hitches or with a whip-finish. To make a whip-finish, turn the thread so that you continually wrap over the original wraps, which are then pulled tight.

An easier way to finish the thread is with several half-hitches. Twist the thread to make a half-hitch, pull the knot snug against the body, and repeat several times to secure the thread. After the last one, clip the thread with scissors and the bucktail is almost finished. If the bucktail was painted completely, you can finish it by protecting the thread with a coat of clear fly-head cement, clear nail polish, or even the same paint used on the head of the jig. If you use anything other than the same paint to paint the lure, take care that you do not cause a reaction between two dissimilar coatings.

Another possibility is to coat a bright—such as red—wrapping thread with epoxy, since epoxy will generally not react with other substances. You can use the same finishing epoxies as are used for wrapping guide wraps, such as Flex Coat, U-40, and Gudebrod. You will have to turn the lure so that the epoxy does not sag or drip. The same companies that make slow-rpm rod-curing motors for this purpose also make similar slow-rpm curing motors for lures, or a rod-curing motor can be slightly modified for lures with the addition of a clip or firm foam wheel to hold the lure.

If you have not painted or completely painted the head, you can dip it in a liquid color at this point, covering and sealing the thread wrap and painting the body at the same time. A second dip may be required (after drying) to completely seal the head. Then you can finish the head by spraying, dipping the forward half of the head, or painting eyes. (Details on painting are covered in chapter 15.) Eyes can be added in a variety of ways, also detailed in chapter 15.

Another method of finishing the wrap is to wrap down a small triangular patch of plastic

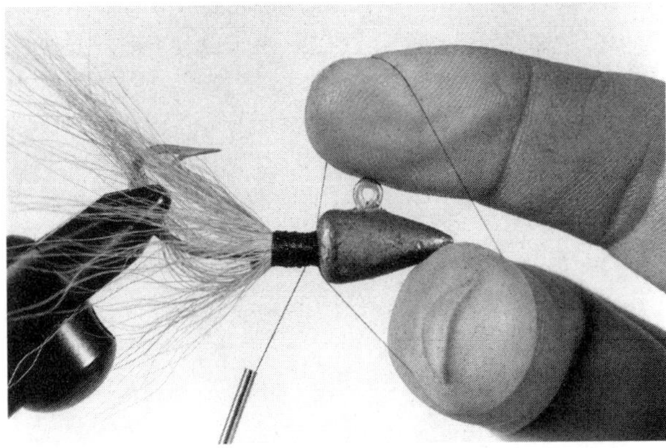

To finish the wrap, use a whip-finish or several half-hitches (shown here) to secure the thread. At this point the head can be painted, either by dipping or brushing. The thread wrap will thus be completely covered, making the wrap and head a uniform color as well as protecting the wrap from moisture.

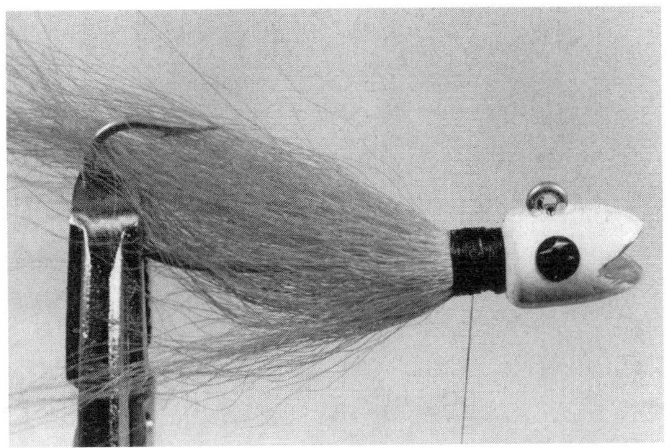

Another way to finish a wrap on a bucktail is to tie in a plastic collar to protect the thread wrap. To do this (here shown on a painted and finished bucktail head), continue the wrap as shown.

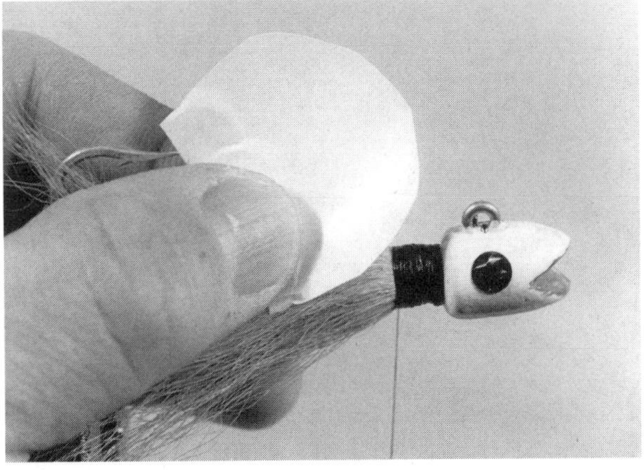

Cut a small piece of flexible vinyl or similar plastic for use as a collar around the wrap.

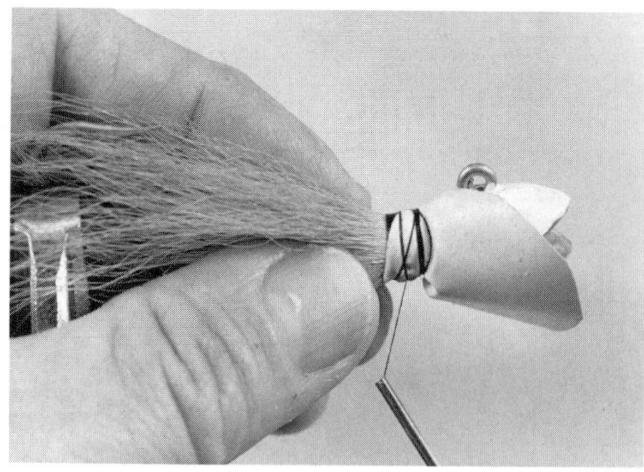

Wrap the collar in place in reverse so that when complete, the collar can be folded back over the thread wrap.

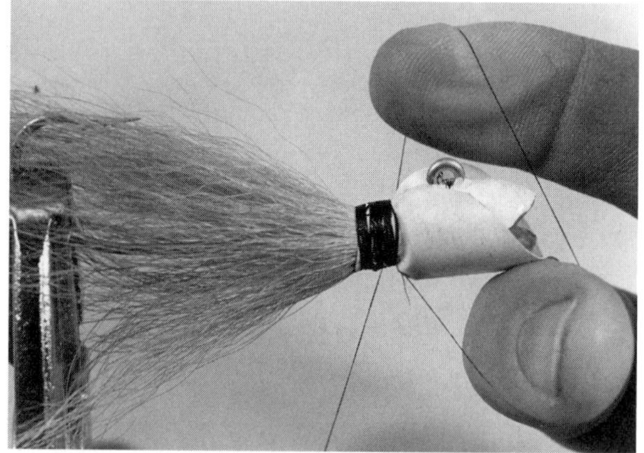

Once the collar is wrapped securely, finish the wrap with a whip-finish or series of half-hitches (shown).

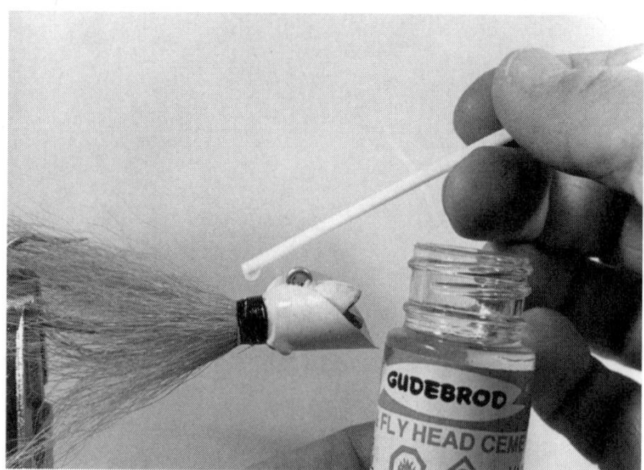

To protect the thread wraps, coat with fly-head cement, nail polish, paint, or a similar sealer.

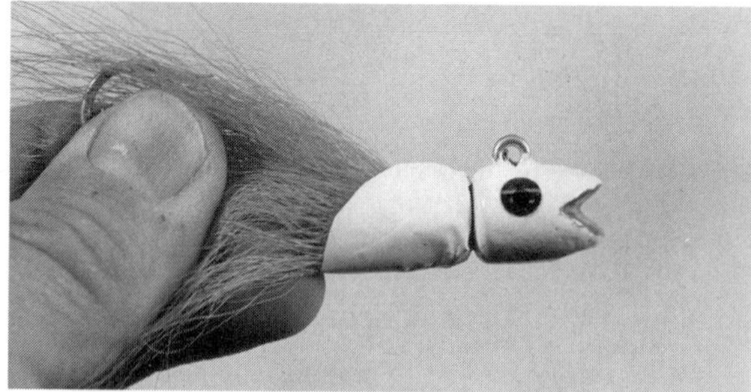

Completed bucktail with the vinyl collar folded back over the thread wrap to protect it and provide additional color to the lure.

sheeting, leaving the forward part of the triangle pointed forward and uncovered. Once the thread wrap is tied down, protect it with a clear sealer and fold the plastic sheeting back over it. This method is used for many commercial jigs, particularly saltwater models.

JIG COMPONENTS AND KITS

For those who do not wish to mold their own bodies, molded heads are available that can be tied into finished lures. They are available both bare and painted, in most of the sizes and styles available to the home molder using commercial molds.

Cabela's, Netcraft, Mud Hole, Merrick, Jann's Netcraft, Bass Pro Shops, Hagen's, and other companies sell jig heads this way. Most of those sold bare are used bare with soft plastic grubs, worms, teasers, and plastic minnows.

There is no rule stating you have to paint the jig head, even if you tie on a permanent tail. In fact, most fishermen can relate experiences of catching lots of fish on jigs that are beat up and missing most or all of their paint. Although I paint my jig heads, my feeling, and the feeling of many, is that it is the action and color of the tail or soft plastic that attracts the fish, not the paint on the lead head.

Jig kits are also available through tackle shops and mail-order companies, the most popular and widely known of which is the Worth kit, comprising twenty-four complete lures from prepainted heads. This is an ideal, safe way to get youngsters into lure making.

5
Sinkers and Tin Squids

Introduction • Sinker-Mold Types • Sinker Types and Sizes • Sinker Costs • Molding Techniques • Metal Squids • Lead Lures • Finishing Tin Squids and Lead Lures • Costs of Metal Lures

Basic Safety Requirements

Goggles

Welder's or other heavy gloves for handling molds, pots, and ladles

Respirator mask

Heavy apron

A clean, clear, sturdy countertop on which to work

Basic Tools

Old cooking pot

Cheap gravy ladle or large serving spoon

Sinker and/or tin squid molds

Hot pads

File

Helpful Tools

Plumber's melting pot

Plumber's ladle

Gate cutters or shears

Wire cutters

Ingot molds

Heavy pliers

Electric-element handheld ladle

Electric bottom-feed furnace

Worth split-ring pliers

Compound-leverage fishing pliers

Spinner-making tools (may be useful for some assembly and modifications)

INTRODUCTION

Sinkers can be molded just as easily as bucktail bodies. In one sense they are more satisfying for the beginner, because once a sinker is popped from the mold and the excess lead (left from pouring through the sprue hole) is removed, it is ready to use. No finishing, painting, or tying is required.

Sinker molds come in the same styles as bucktail molds: pinned, clamped, and hinged-handled models. As with bucktails, the hinged-handled models are the easiest to use and handle. There are some differences between bucktail and sinker molds, however. Not all sinker molds are made of aluminum, as are jig and bucktail molds. Some sinker molds and tin-squid molds have in the past been made of cast iron with machined molding surfaces. Because cast-iron molds can rust when not in use, they require more care and maintenance. Should you have or acquire one of these iron molds, one way to prevent rust is to soak it in a mixture of equal parts motor oil and kerosene and then stand it on edge to drain (preferably on newspaper) for a few days until it is dry. Make sure it is completely dry before using it.

SINKER-MOLD TYPES

Sinker molds can be separated into several different styles:

No-insert sinker molds. This is my term; by it I mean those molds that do not require any addition of brass eyelets, swivels, rings, wires, core rods, or plates to make holes or slots, as for egg sinkers and pinch-on sinkers. This type of sinker mold casts the eye in lead at the same time the sinker cavity is filled. Sinker styles include molds for bank sinkers, pyramid sinkers, walking sinkers, pencil sinkers, snagless sinkers, bell sinkers, dollar sinkers, and others.

The big advantage of these types of molds and sinkers is that they are very fast to use—there is nothing to add to the mold before pouring. The only requirements are a hot mold and pourable lead. With these molds sinkers can be turned out as rapidly as you can safely pour lead into the mold and pop it out again.

Sinker molds with core rods or insert pins. These sinkers also have no brass eyes, swivels, or line-tie inserts added, but they do require a core rod (often called a pull pin) or insert plate in the mold to properly form the sinker. Usually the brass pull pin has a handle and is infinitely reusable. It is placed into the closed mold, and the lead is poured into the cavity. It is pulled out immediately after pouring and will leave a hole in the sinker.

Similarly, sinker molds requiring insert plates leave a slot in the finished sinker. The insert plate is placed in the mold before it is closed and the lead is poured into the cavities. The plate is usually removed with the sinkers attached when the mold is opened, and the sinkers are slipped off the plate.

Examples of sinkers made with a hole using the pull pin include egg, worm bullet-weight, pencil, and commercial net sinkers. Sinkers requiring a slot from the insert plate include pinch-on, rubber-core, and split-shot sinkers.

These sinkers are almost as fast to mold as those without any inserts or additions, because the plate or pull pin is easily placed in the mold before or after closing and is the only item to go into the mold. The core rods or plates are supplied with accompanying molds, and replacements are available should the rods or plates be lost or broken.

Sinker molds requiring eyes. These sinker molds require eyes or an addition to each cavity. Usually these are line-ties and vary from simple figure-eight brass eyelets to swivels and special pins or wire forms. Sinkers made this way include bass-casting, cannonball, crescent, pencil, pyramid, river, round concave, round flat, in-line trolling, bead-chain trolling, keel trolling, storm, three-sided pyramid, bulldozer, claw, silver-dollar, cushion, spoon, banana, torpedo, and miniball sinkers; bell sinkers with brass eyelets; and cannonball weights for downrigger trolling.

Usually the brass eyelets, swivels, bead chain, wire forms, and similar inserts are available in bags of one hundred or one thousand of each size. Sometimes they are sold by the pound, with the number per pound varying by the size of the brass eyelet. Swivels are sold by the hundred or by the gross.

When molding some sinkers, such as straight torpedo or banana-shaped trolling sinkers, wire forms are needed. These wire forms are also available by the hundred. Some, such as the Do-It bottom-bouncing sinker, take a long wire form that extends from both ends of the lead and is designed to prevent snagging when fishing lures or bait along the bottom.

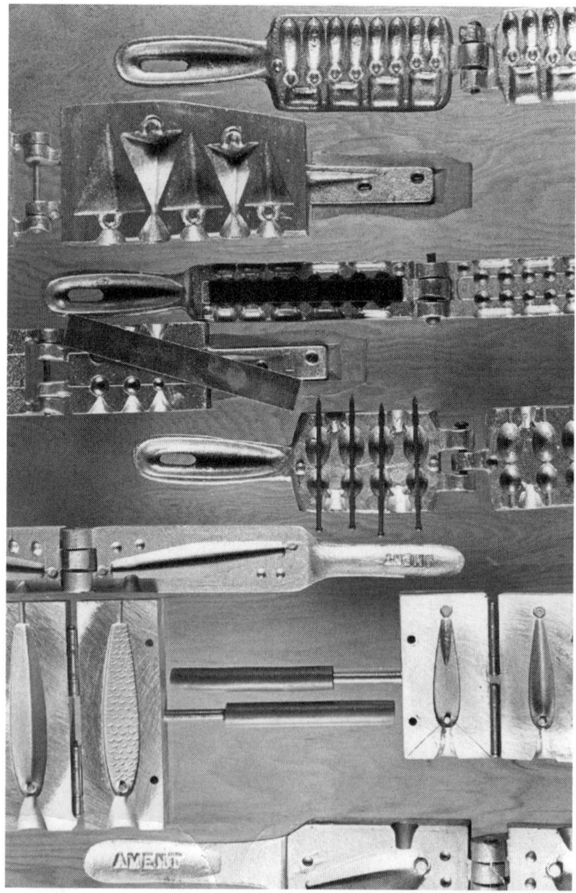

Typical sinker and tin-squid molds, including those for egg sinkers, split shot, pyramid sinkers, bank sinkers, and several types of tin squids.

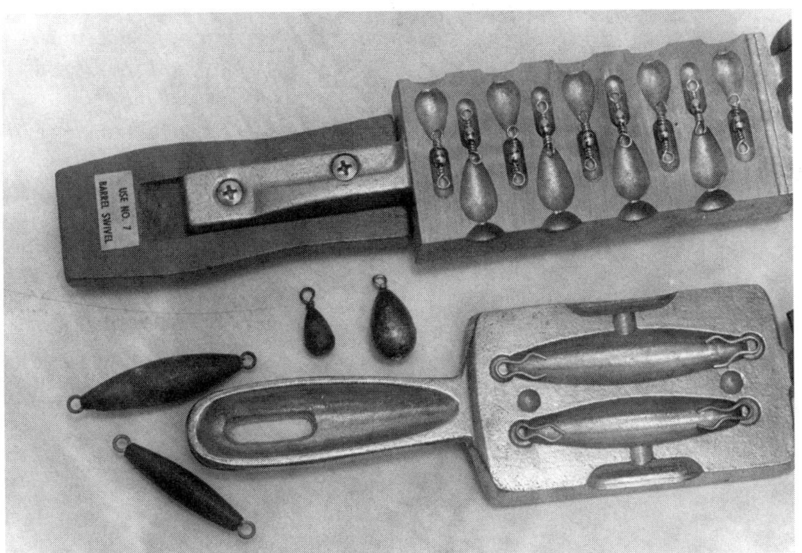

Some sinkers and tin-squid molds require eye forms in the mold. Here swivels are placed in the mold for molding casting sinkers in a Do-It mold; brass eyes are placed in a trolling-sinker mold.

It is also important to note that with some sinker molds, the sinkers can be cast with either a brass eye or a self-casting lead eye. These molds usually include pyramid, bass-casting, and some trolling styles. Use caution with this, because some lead eyes formed in molds designed for brass eyes will be weaker.

Most of the sinker molds in the larger sizes will also cast in the lead sinker the size of the sinker in ounces. This is almost always found in bank, pyramid, cannonball, egg, pinch-on, no-snag, walking, and various trolling sinkers. This information may be found on bass-casting, bell, and keel sinkers but is never found on the small sizes such as worm bullet-weights, split-shot, and small flat sinkers.

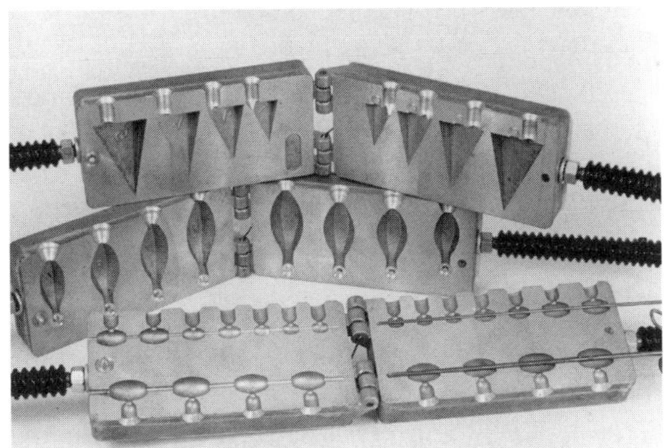

Sinker molds from Hilts Molds including, top to bottom, pyramid, bank, and egg sinker molds.

There are also simple molds for lures and other purposes. Spin jig heads for through-line lures (like a jig, but threaded on the line) and off-shore through-leader trolling heads use core rods to make the hole in the lures. Molds for cannon-ball downrigger weights to 12 pounds, slab-sided structure and casting spoons, duck decoy sinkers, and slingshot pellets are all available from the same companies that make sinker and bucktail molds.

SINKER TYPES AND SIZES

As with bucktail molds, sinker and lure molds come in production types in which all cavities make the same size of sinker or lure or in combination types with assorted or combination cavities that make a range of sizes of a given sinker. In most cases the molds that make an assortment of sizes are most useful, but if you need only one size of sinker, the production molds will make more of them quicker without wasting additional cavities.

Basic sinker types and the size ranges available in molds include:

Bank sinkers. These are ideal sinkers for much fresh- and saltwater fishing. Shaped like a tapered hourglass with a molded eye at the top, they are best when fishing around rocks because they tend to remain snag free. Sizes range from ⅛ ounce up to 20 ounces.

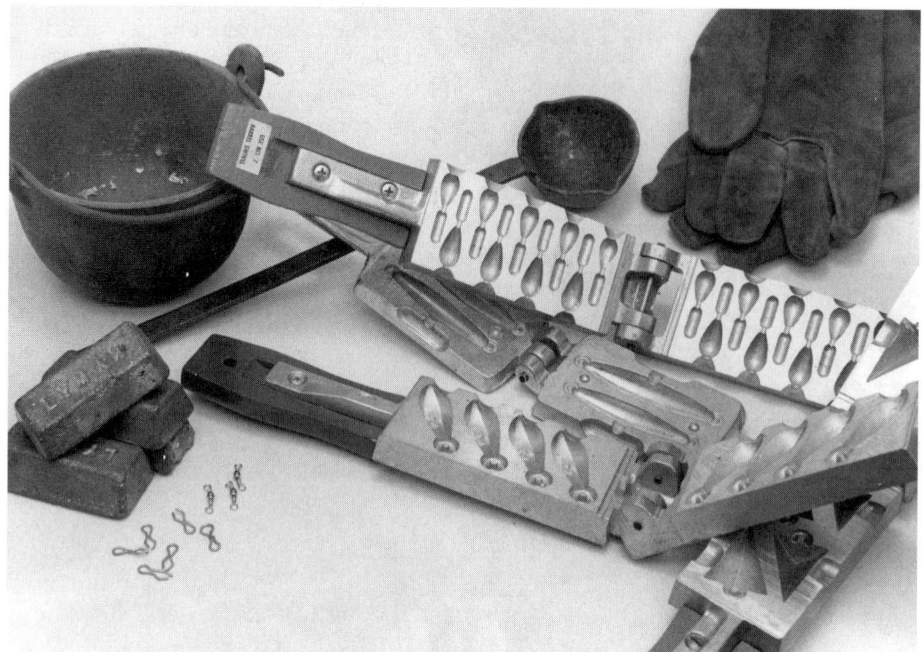

Examples of various sinker and squid molds, three of which are from Do-It, including molds for casting, bank, and pyramid sinkers. Also shown are the heavy gloves, pot, and ladle used when not molding with an electric pot or furnace.

Pyramid sinkers. Used for sandy-bottom fishing such as surf fishing, they are very popular on the Atlantic Coast. Both four- and three-sided pyramid-sinker molds are available. Sizes range from 1 ounce to 20 ounces.

Storm sinkers. These are just like pyramid sinkers but with a long, tapered, round point on the end. Sizes range from 2 to 8 ounces.

Bass-casting sinkers. These look like an inverted teardrop with a molded-on swivel. They are popular for much freshwater fishing and some saltwater use. Sizes range from 1/8 ounce to 8 ounces.

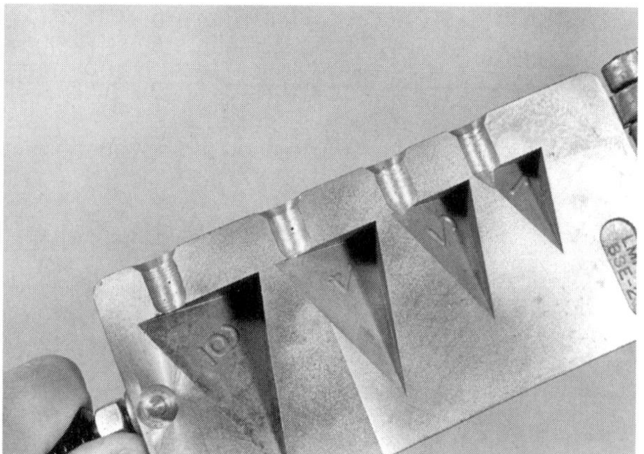

Mold cavities in a Hilts mold. The socket for the sinker eye is on the opposing half of the mold.

Bell sinkers. These are just like bass-casting sinkers in shape but have a lead molded eye or brass eyelet for a line-tie in place of the swivel. Sizes range from 1/8 ounce to 2 ounces.

Cannonball sinkers. A new design, copied from the heavier cannonball weights used in downrigger fishing, they are round balls with a brass eyelet. Sizes range from 1/2 ounce to 3 pounds.

Bottom-bounce sinkers. These are formed on a wire with a right-angle bend at one end; the wire is formed with two eyes (one at the bend and one at the free end) for fishing the bottom with lures or bait. They are very snagless for river and rocky-bottom fishing. Sizes range from 3/4 ounce to 1 3/4 ounces.

Bulldozer sinkers. These look like a miniature scoop or are shaped like a Y with the eyelet at the junction of the upper part of the arms. They are designed to hold in sand for surf fishing. Sizes range from 1 ounce to 5 ounces.

Claw sinkers. These too are designed for surf fishing on sandy bottoms and are shaped like a triangle with a projection on the bottom and an eyelet at the point. Sizes range from 1 ounce to 8 ounces. Similar sinkers with claw wires are also made in the shape of a bank sinker.

Crescent, banana, and kidney sinkers. These are designed for trolling, with a curved shape to prevent line twist. The curved crescent, banana, or kidney shape works like a keel on the line. Eyes are at both ends for tying the sinker between the line and leader. The degree of curve or bend in the sinker is usually relative to the weight and size. Sizes range from 1 ounce to 6 ounces.

In-line, trolling, and torpedo sinkers. These are all similar in that they are shaped like a small, tapered torpedo or cigar with an eye or bead chain on each end. They are designed as trolling sinkers to be placed on the line or between the line and leader. The eyes are centered on the weight so that there is no keel effect as with the crescent, kidney, or banana sinkers. Sizes range from 1 ounce to 24 ounces.

Egg sinkers. These are made with a large hole running through them and are designed so that the line will run freely to allow a bait-taking fish to run without dragging or feeling the weight of the sinker. As the name suggests, they are shaped like an egg. Sizes range from ⅛ ounce to 11 ounces.

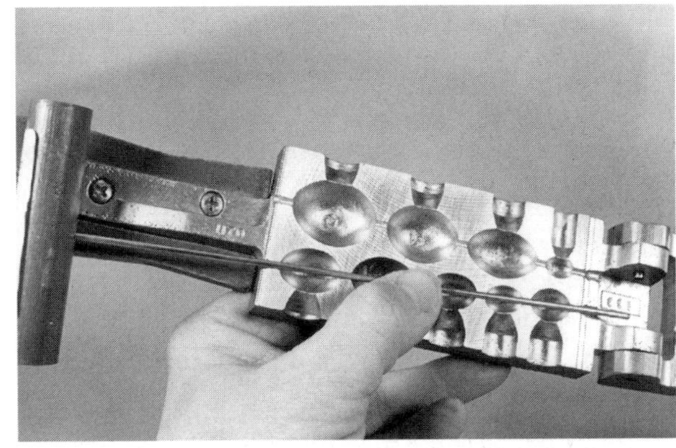

This egg-sinker mold from Do-It uses a handled pin that is placed in one side for pouring and then immediately pulled out and run into the core holes on the other side for molding the cavities on the other side of the mold.

Flat round, dollar, river, round concave, round flat, silver-dollar, and cushion sinkers. All of these are similar, although they will differ individually as to edge types, side shapes, and so on. All are flat like a silver dollar, for which one style is named. Sizes range from ¼ ounce to 10 ounces.

Split-shot, removable split-shot sinkers. All molds are similar, and most require an insert plate.

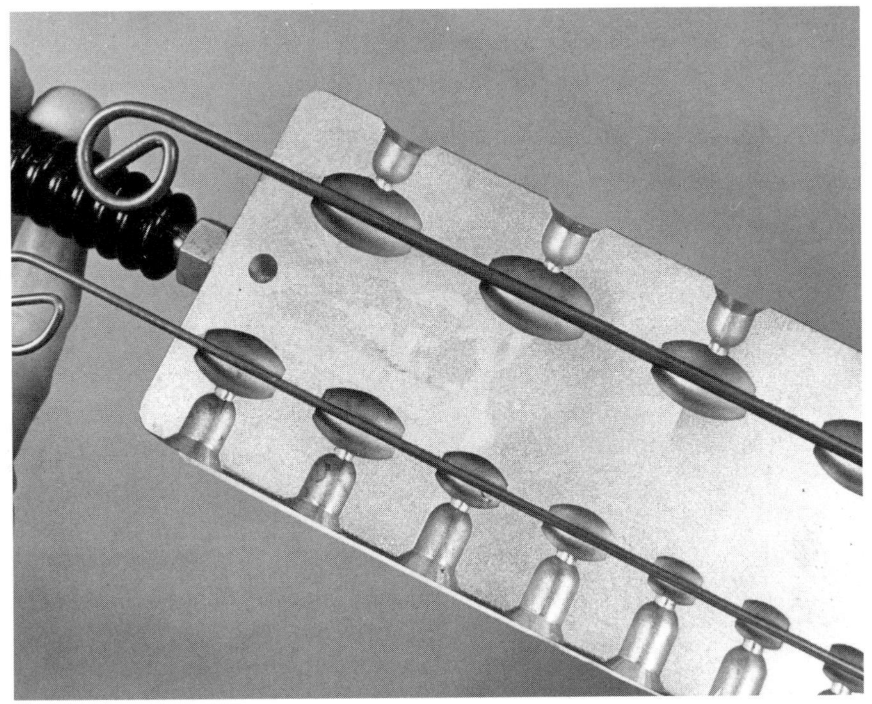

Example of egg-sinker mold from Hilts Molds. The two pins (of different sizes for the different sinkers molded) form the hole through the sinker and are pulled out immediately after molding. Note that to mold all cavities, the mold must be turned over after filling the cavities on one side.

They are round with a split or slot in one side to clamp onto the line or leader. Some have "ears" on the side opposite the slot to allow for opening and reuse. Sizes range from 1⁄64 to 1 ounce. For these or any type of sinker that is clamped onto the line, use only pure soft lead.

Pinch-on sinkers. These have small "ears" on each end on either side of a slot through which the line is run. The ears pinch onto the line to hold the sinker in position. Sizes include 1⁄16 ounce to 1½ ounces. These also require pure soft lead.

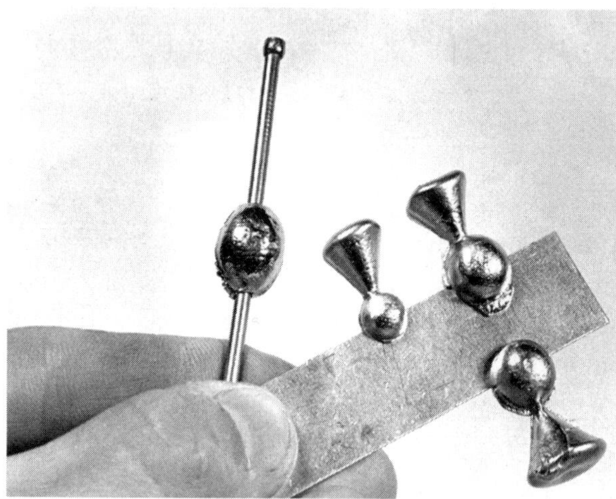

Egg sinker and split shot before the pins and insert sheets are removed (normally they would be removed as soon as the lead has solidified). These show how the holes and slots are formed in these sinkers.

Rubber-core sinkers. These are similar to the pinch-on sinkers in the tapered cigar shape but have a rubber slug in the center slot that is designed to be turned in order to hold the sinker in place on the line. Sizes range from 1⁄16 ounce through 1½ ounces. The rubber centers are available from mold manufacturers or from component-parts houses.

Pencil sinkers. These are available fashioned like a solid rod (designed to be slipped into rubber tubing for snagless bottom fishing) with eyes at both ends, with an eye at one end, or with a hole through the long axis for through-line threading. They are straight-sided and come in sizes from 1¼ to 4 ounces. Several diameters are available to fit different tubing. with the most popular being 3⁄16, ¼, and ⅜ inch.

Bullet weights, worm weights. Used for plastic-worm fishing, these are placed on the line in front of the worm. They are like a bullet or round spear point in shape. Sizes that can be molded include ⅛ through ½ ounce.

Walking, snagless, and spoon sinkers. The shapes of these vary slightly, but all are flat and wide and tapered, with a molded-in eye at the small end, and are designed for snagless fishing. Sizes range from ⅛ ounce to 4 ounces.

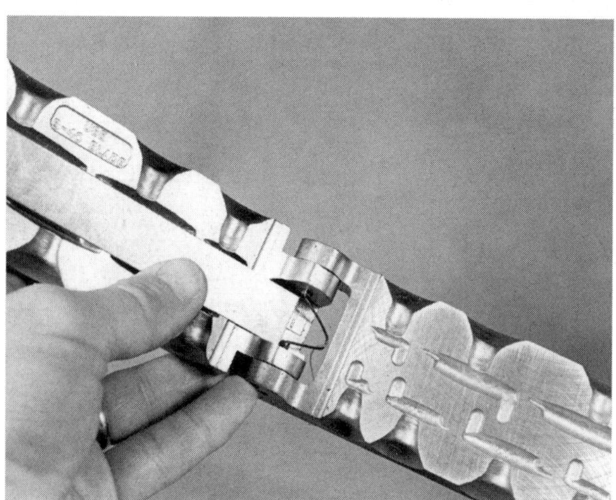

Insert sheet being placed in a Do-It pinch-on sinker mold, which works the same as a split-shot mold to form the slot and sinker "ears."

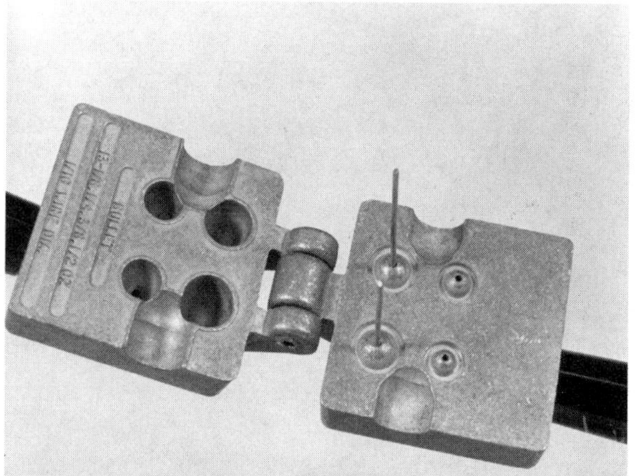

Bullet-weight mold from Li'l Mac, in which the core pins to form the hole in the worm bullet weights go through both halves of the mold rather than in the core hole between the two halves.

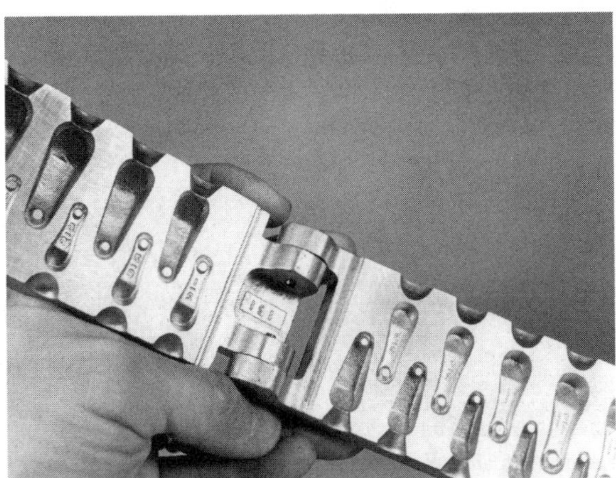

Example of a walking-sinker mold from Do-It. Note that the cavities or opposing sides differ.

Rock-cod sinkers. These look like a small brick with one rounded end and range in size from 1 pound to 5 pounds.

Snag weights. These are not lures, not bucktails, and not sinkers. They are really snatch hooks used to retrieve objects from the bottom and, where legal, to hook and catch fish by snagging. The weight is molded right onto the treble hook. Hook sizes range from 2/0 to 14/0 in trebles; weights are from ½ ounce to 8 ounces.

SINKER COSTS

Sinkers become almost free if you mold your own. If you can get lead or lead alloys free from scrap or wheel weights, then your only cost is for the molds and the ladle and furnace, if you use one. If you melt lead in old but sturdy pots and incur only the cost of the molds, the cost of your sinkers amortizes quickly. If you buy the electric pot, ladle, and gate cutters described in chapter 4, the only other cost is for a mold or molds. When free lead is available, the total cost per sinker will drop to only a few cents in time. If you forget the basic costs of the molding tools and can get lead for free, then there is no cost for the sinkers other than the cost for eyelets for those sinker types that require them.

Three factors will affect the cost of molding your own sinkers. One, if you mold bucktail heads, the cost of basic equipment such as furnaces and ladles is amortized over the cost of the lures and sinkers; it is not a separate cost. Two, if you mold sinkers requiring insert eyes or wire forms, this cost must be added. Three, if you want to make a lot of different sinker types, then you will need a lot of different molds. One solution to this is for friends to band together, each one buying different sinker (or bucktail) molds for the use of all. Fishing clubs can do the same thing, setting aside certain nights for sinker and bucktail molding or loaning out the molds as a membership service.

MOLDING TECHNIQUES

Be sure to read and review the section on safety and molding techniques in chapter 4. The same basic techniques of molding and the steps in working with molten lead and molds are basically identical for bucktails and sinkers, with only a few differences. Reading and understanding these basic steps as they were outlined earlier is a must before proceeding.

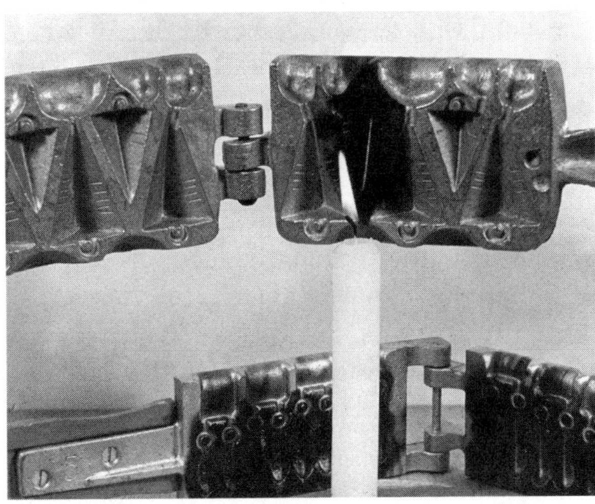

Smoking a mold with a candle flame.

Just as hooks are placed in bucktails molds, some sinkers require the placement of brass eyelets, swivels, or wire forms that are molded into the completed sinker, or of core rods or plates that are used to help form holes or slots.

Use care to support the mold when pouring, such as is done here when using a ladle to pour an egg-sinker mold.

Removing sinkers from sinker mold. Use pliers, as the sinkers (and bucktails when using bucktail molds) will be very hot. Heavy gloves provide additional protection.

Although brass eyes are standard for pyramid, bell, keel, and some trolling sinkers, it may be preferable to mold the sinker without them, forming a lead eye instead. (In some molds this is possible; in others it is not. On some molds the manufacturer may list these options; otherwise you will have to experiment. It will be quicker, easier, and less expensive if you do not have to use brass eyes or any forms.)

There is one additional advantage to a lead eye, along with one disadvantage. The advantage of the molded eye in fishing rocky or snaggy areas is that a hung sinker can sometimes be broken off when snagged. A molded-in brass eye will seldom break. If the lead eye of the sinker breaks, the loss is only an easily made, inexpensive sinker; if brass eyes are used, the line must be cut or broken, possibly resulting in the loss of lure, hook, bobber, or other terminal gear. Some molds are made with this "breakaway" feature in mind. Others have a mold cavity designed to take an eyelet or molded-in eye.

However, if the sinker is tied directly to the line and used continuously, there is some danger that the rough lead in the large molded eye will wear the line, causing it to break. This is not like the loss of a fish or lure, but a new sinker must be tied on when it happens. One way to avoid this is to tie the line to a large snap for the sinker or to retie the sinker to the line several times a

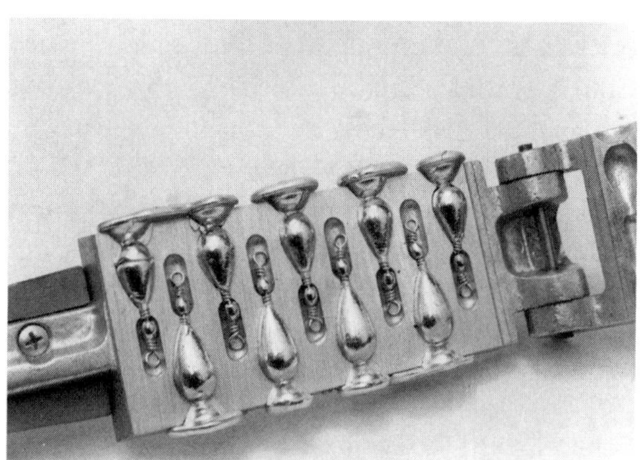

Do-It mold with casting sinkers in place after being molded and before being removed from the mold.

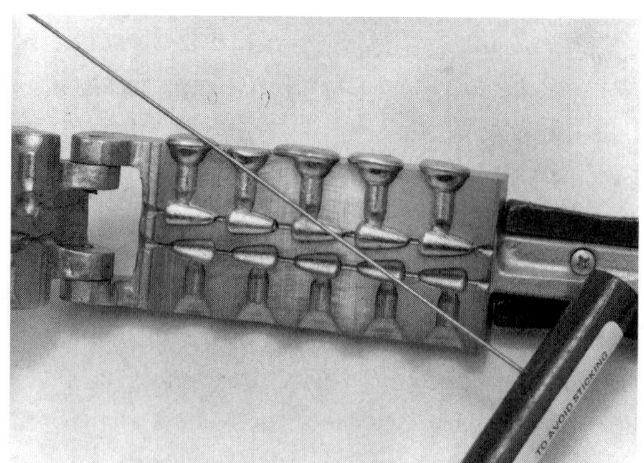

Do-It mold for making worm bullet weights; a pin forms the hole in the sinkers.

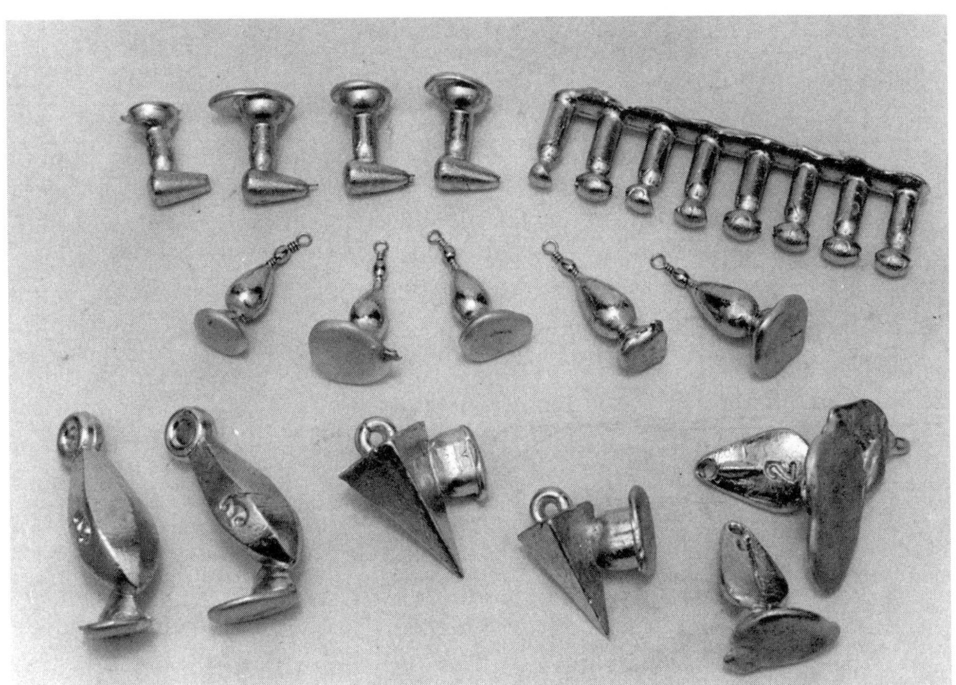

Various sinkers before the sprue (excess lead) is cut off. Wire cutters or special lead gate cutters are best for this. Since sinkers are not used as lures, no additional finishing is required.

day, checking for line damage and removing all abraded sections of line.

Generally the choice of lead or lead alloy for sinkers is even less of a consideration than for bucktails, since a dented or scrapped sinker can't affect fishing results as might a similarly damaged jig head. However, in the case of split-shot and pinch-on sinkers, you *must* use soft, or pure, lead. Any lead with antimony in it will be harder and will prevent the closing of split-shot or sinker ears, or they might break. Even worse, the hard lead alloy might damage the line, causing it to break with a fish on.

Since a sinker's appearance is not important, you can use several methods to remove the sprue. The gate cutters mentioned for bucktail molding are the best, but wire cutters, twisting the sprue off with pliers, or using any kind of snip will work.

When molding sinkers and metal lures, make sure you have enough lead on hand. Large molds will use lead fast, and some lead sinker molds will use lead at a rate of 2 to 10 ounces for many saltwater sinkers, with some sinkers even requiring 5 pounds of lead.

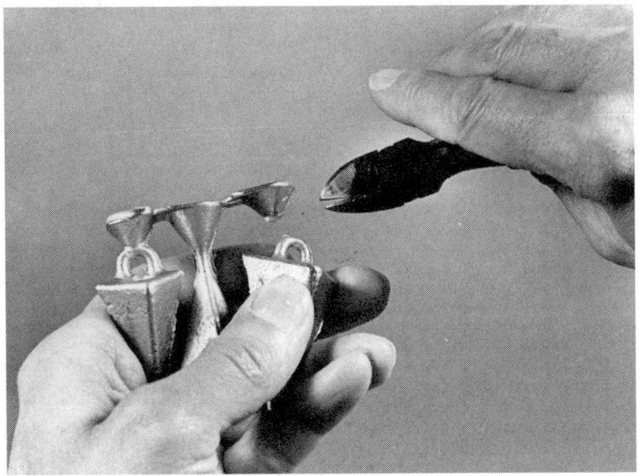

Removing the sprue from a sinker with wire cutters.

METAL SQUIDS

Metal squids are used by surf anglers and are widely regarded as one of the best lures for certain surf-fishing situations, either alone or rigged with pork rind, strip bait, or a skirt of some kind. You can also use metal squids or lures when inshore fishing from boats or from piers and jetties, both trolled and cast. Some have fixed hooks; others have free-swinging hooks, either plain or dressed with skirt material. Most that are sold commercially today are not cast but forged and are chrome- or nickel-plated.

Although the word "squid" is used, metal or tin squids can resemble any of a large number of small inshore baitfish that come in a variety of different shapes. As a result, tin or metal squids come in both broad, short models and long, thin lures. The short, broad ones imitate herring, killifish, menhaden, mullet, and anchovy; the longer thin ones can imitate sand eels, various saltwater minnows, silversides, spearing, and similar fish, including squid.

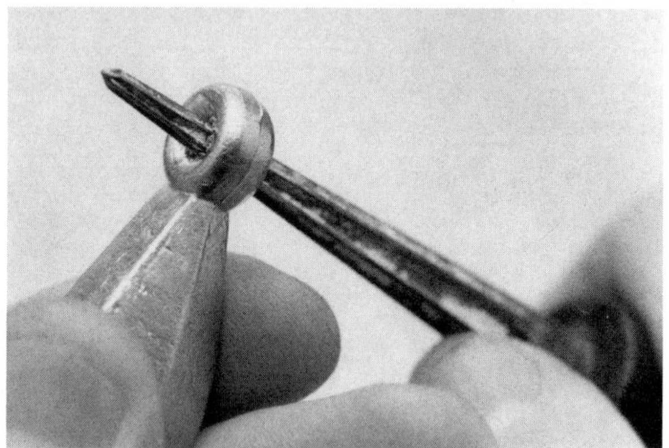

If flash tends to clog the molded-in eyes on some sinkers, a simple woodworking reamer will immediately remove excess lead and smooth the hole.

While these tin or, perhaps more correctly, metal squid lures can be made of lead or other metals, including zinc, tin squids are perhaps best known and most popular among surf fishermen. The tin used in these lures has the advantage of staying bright (lead dulls rapidly) and bendable, so an angler can bend the lure to a shape that provides action in the water. This is partly because tin weighs less than lead, so the lure will twist in the water when bent properly. (The difference in weight is about a 5:8 ratio, so a tin lure weighing 2½ ounces would weigh 4 ounces if it were made of lead. Of course this also means you get more lures from a pound of tin.)

If not using tin, there are some disadvantages in molding tin squids. For example, wheel weights and type metal alloys are harder and make it very difficult to bend a tin squid into a lure that has more action, as can be done with tin.

An advantage of tin-squid molding is that tin melts at a lower temperature (449 degrees Fahrenheit) than lead, so it will not take as long to heat or use as much fuel to stay at a molten temperature. As with larger trolling sinkers (which they resemble), tin squids require an eyelet on each end or a hook molded into one end of the lure. Those for swinging hooks require a second eyelet, and the hook is added later by means of a split ring or by an open-eye Siwash-style hook.

LEAD LURES

Metal lures can also be molded by using lead or other alloys, although they are usually painted or covered later with prism tape to brighten them, because lead is far duller in appearance than tin. Type metal, or linotype metal (a mixture of lead, tin, and antimony), will stay brighter than pure lead, though not as bright as tin.

Lead lures cannot usually be bent to shape for a swimming action, although some very thin, long lures of pure soft lead can be bent for better action in the water.

Lure molds for lead molding can include the thin tin-squid type, as well as vertical casting and jigging spoons, diamond lures (diamond in cross section and thin like a minnow), casting spoons that resemble the stainless steel jigging spoons, and other slab-sided lures. Some, such as the Hilts Slab Mold (model LM SLAB-W), are even made in a fish shape, complete with fins and tail features. This mold comes in ½- to 5-ounce sizes in both through-line and wire-form (eyelet) styles. Other similar lure molds include the Do-It jigging spoon mold (model JS-3-A) and several casting spoon molds.

Molds for making tin lures are not labeled as such, and any mold for making lead items can be used for molding tin. Thus metal lures of tin, lead, or other alloys (even zinc) can be made in any of the aluminum or cast molds from any of the major mold manufacturers.

One-piece molds for tin squids or lead-slab lures are not available commercially, but because these lures are usually flat or slab sided, one-piece or open-face molds can be made from plaster, silicone molding material, wood, or metal. (Directions for this are found in chapter 16.)

Using an open-face mold is easy, because there is no sprue hole through which the metal must be poured, no possibility of unfilled parts of the cavity, no possibility of air pockets, and no opening or closing of the mold. Any inserts must be placed in the mold for line and hook attachment, and the hook must be added for fixed-hook lures. The open mold and these inserts do require more careful pouring and special caution to prevent overpouring. Also, since the insert material is lighter than the lead, you might have to hold it in place with a metal carpenter's spring clamp until the lead cools.

Position the mold near the melting tin, pour rapidly, and allow the lead to cool. Open-face molds can be made with a small slot at one end to hold the hook in place. Or the hook can be slipped into the molten tin and held in place briefly until the metal solidifies. Wear heavy gloves or use pliers to hold the hook, because it will become hot.

If you do overpour slightly, you have two choices. One is to dump the mold contents back into the pot for remelting, removing the eyelets and any hooks as the lure melts. If you do this, use pliers to hold the hook point out of the molten metal, and remove the hook from the pot as soon as possible so as not to ruin the temper of the hook. If you suspect the temper has been affected, do not use the hook.

If the overflow is slight, the other solution is to use snips to remove excess flash. Because they have a compound action for cutting heavier metal, aviation snips are ideal for this, although regular sheet-metal snips will work if the metal is soft (pure lead or tin) and not too thick.

FINISHING TIN SQUIDS AND LEAD LURES

Completed slab lures may be used as is if the hook is molded in, or they may be finished with a swinging hook and any dressing. If the lure has two eyelets, then a free-swinging hook must be added. This can be a treble, double, or single hook, with single hooks used in most lures.

There are several ways to add a hook. Double hooks with separate double shanks can be slid onto the eyelet or, for more action, slipped onto a split ring added to the eyelet. Single hooks come in an open-eye style that can be attached to the eyelet or a separately added split ring. The hook eye is then closed to secure the hook. Treble hooks are made the same way, with open eyes that can be closed once added to a lure and a split shank for threading onto an eyelet, or they may be added by means of a split ring. If adding hooks using a split ring, add both the lure eyelet and the hook to the split ring at the same time to reduce any spreading of the split ring and to save time. To do this, use split-ring pliers to first open the ring, then slide the hook on, followed by the lure eyelet, and finally rotate the split ring while holding both parts to attach them. If you use a single or double hook in which you want the hook points aligned with one side of the lure, align this first before adding the parts.

If you make lures with a dressed hook, tie on the dressing *before* adding the hook to the lure. You can buy dressed hooks or dress them yourself using fly-tying methods or the methods outlined for tail attachment on bucktails. Basically, clamp the hook in a fly-tying or similar vise, and wrap the thread around the hook and over the previous wraps to hold the thread in place. Use size 2/0 thread for small hooks to size 2 or 4, size A thread for larger hooks to size 4/0 or 5/0, and size D or E (rod-wrapping) thread for larger hooks. Once the thread is tied down, wrap the tail materials of fur, artificial fur, saddle hackle, Mylar, nylon, or similar material onto the hook. Make several turns of thread to firmly secure the material, and then clip off any excess in front of the wrap.

Finish the wrap and tie it off with several half-hitches or a whip-finish. Protect the wrap with a touch of paint (red is always good), nylon-base nail polish (colored or clear—Sally Hansen Hard as Nails brand is good), or, if you're after toothy fish, epoxy finish.

You can also use rubber or plastic tubing in short lengths or with longer split tails on the hook, and this also must be added before the hook is placed on the lure. Soft-plastic tails such as grubs and worms can be added to the hook later. If you plan to do this, consider one of the barbed-shank hooks that are designed to hold bait or soft plastic.

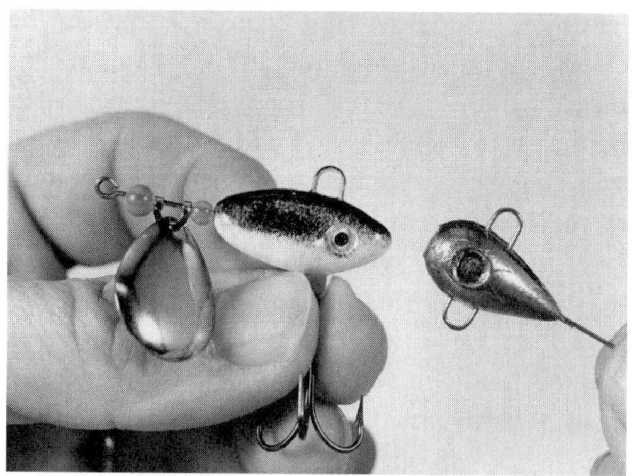

Tail-spinner lead lure complete (painted and hooks and blade attached) on the left; example of a bare molded lure (although a slightly different style) on the right.

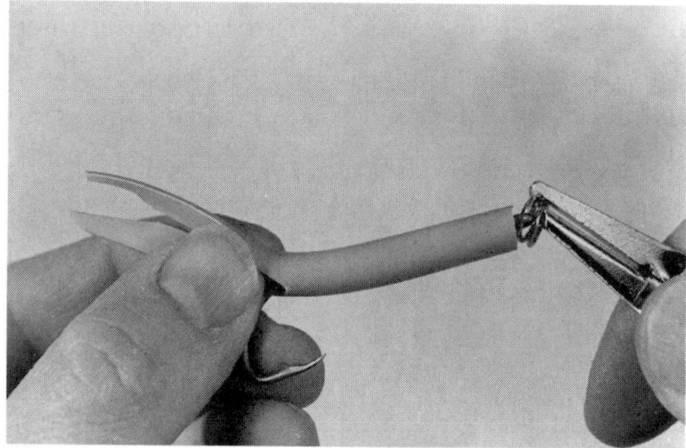

Finishing some lead lures or tin squids requires adding hooks and tail materials. Here a hook skirted with a split tail of surgical tubing will be added to a small slab lure.

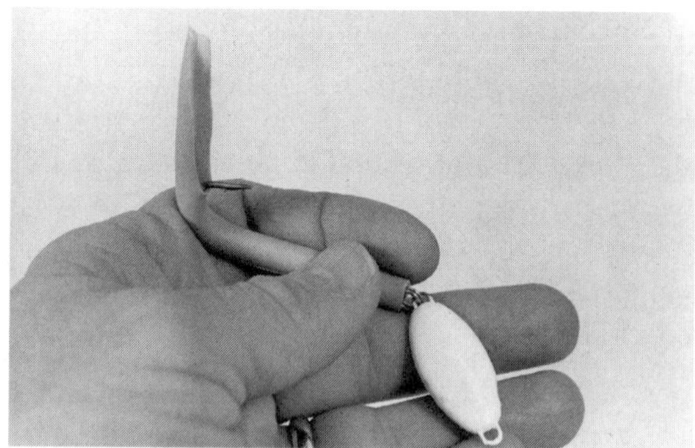

Small slab lead lure, painted, with the hook and surgical-tubing tail added.

COSTS OF METAL LURES

If the metal is free, as it often is in wheel weights, the cost of metal lures can be minimal. Most lure molds with one to four cavities sell for about the cost of a sinker or bucktail mold.

The technique of molding sinkers and tin squids is easy. With the cost of lead sinkers and metal lures constantly rising, molding your own not only makes sense but also saves cents. Starting with these easy-to-make tackle items is a natural for anyone who wants to cut the cost of angling while adding to the wintertime or off-season pleasure of tackle craft.

Once sinker or bucktail molding is complete, excess lead can be poured into ingot molds, available from most companies. If using a furnace or electric pot, you can leave excess lead in the pot for rapid heating next time. Check manufacturers' recommendations on this.

6

Spinnerbaits and Buzzbaits

Introduction • Tools • Parts • Molding Techniques • Finishing • Spinnerbait Assembly • Buzzbait Assembly • In-Line or Weight-Forward Spinner Assembly • Variations

Basic Safety Requirements for Molding

Welder's or other heavy gloves for handling molds, pots, ladles

Respirator mask

Heavy apron

A clean, clear place with a heavy countertop on which to work

Basic Tools for Molding

Old cooking pot

Cheap gravy ladle or large serving spoon

Bucktail, spinnerbait, and buzzbait molds

Fly-tying vise, machinist's vise, or C-clamp

Hot pads

File

Helpful Tools for Molding

Plumber's melting pot

Plumber's ladle

Gate cutters or shears

Wire cutters

Ingot molds

Heavy pliers

Electric-element handheld ladle

Electric bottom-feed furnace

Split-ring pliers

Compound-leverage fishing pliers

Spinner-making tools (may be useful for some assembly and modifications)

Basic Safety Requirements for Assembly

Goggles

A clean, clear place to work

Basic Tools for Assembly

Needle-nose or round-nose pliers with side cutters

Helpful Tools for Assembly

Small round-nose pliers

Diagonal wire cutters or compound-action pliers with wire cutters

Wire former (commercial or homemade)

Split-ring pliers

Compound-leverage fishing pliers

INTRODUCTION

Lures resembling spinnerbaits have been around a long time, but the lure as we know it has been popular and in the same general design since about the early 1900s. In 1917 and 1918 the Shannon Twinspinner, made by the Jamison Company, was an early precursor of the twin-spinnerbait style we know today. Even then there were about a dozen or more variations of this basic style, although the Twinspinner seems to be the most widely remembered today.

Buzzbaits are not that new, but some of the early Al Foss Wigglers from the same period were not unlike the in-line buzzbaits of today. Also similar were the early Fred Arbogast Hawaiian Wigglers, still sold by the Arbogast Company today. The typical J-shaped wire-form buzzbaits appeared about 1940. In-line buzzbaits appeared at about the same time.

Modern spinnerbaits come in small through large sizes; in single spin, tandem spin (blades in line with each other), and twin spin (two blades with each blade at the end of a separate upper arm); in stiff and flexible (cable) wire; and with a variety of modifications in skirts, blades, and head styles.

Another variation, usually under a separate subcategory, is the in-line or weight-forward spinner. These are designed for bottom fishing for walleye and are called spinners because they are of a straight-line construction on a weighted-head shaft, even though they have similarities to a spinnerbait. The straight-line construction resembles a standard spinner; the weighted head makes them perform like a spinnerbait. A good argument could be made for either description. They are included here because they require molding the head if you want to make them from scratch and thus require the same techniques used to make lead-head spinnerbaits and buzzbaits. All these variations, plus many more, can be built into any homemade spinnerbait.

Buzzbaits come in two basic styles. One is the older, less-common, in-line style in which a straight shaft holds the propeller or spinner blade, behind which are the weighted head and skirted hook. These are made with the same techniques used for in-line spinners. The more common buzzbaits are made on a bent-wire form that resembles a J lying on its side, with the longer end of the shaft holding the weighted head and skirted hook and the upper, or shorter, arm ending with the single or double delta or buzz propeller blades. Some variations include small "clicker" or "clacker" blades on the upright part of the arm that will click against the buzzbait to make a fish-attracting noise. Other unusual variations include side-by-side arms and blades and various head styles.

Spinnerbaits and buzzbaits are designed primarily for bass, although both work well for a host of other, primarily freshwater, gamefish, including walleye, muskie, pike, and crappie (in small-size lures). There is even a large commercially marketed buzzbait for saltwater big-game trolling.

All these lures are included in this chapter because they are all built on a wire shaft and have a lead head, a skirt, and one or more metal blades.

TOOLS

Tools for building buzzbaits and spinnerbaits are no different from those used for building spinners and molding bucktails, because buzzbaits and spinnerbaits are in essence a combination of spinner and bucktail parts and techniques. To build them from scratch by molding the bodies and assembling the blades and parts, you will need the basic tools listed at the beginning at this chapter. If you have already built jigs and spinners by following the instructions in chapters 3 and 4, you will have these tools. If you skipped to this chapter first, go back and read chapters 3 and 4 for ideas and details—and especially for the safety tips and instructions.

Required tools include basic molding tools such as furnace, pot, ladles, and safety equipment. For assembly you will need some wire-forming tools such as round-nose or needle-nose pliers, wire cutters, and split-ring pliers.

You do not have to mold your own bodies. You can buy painted or unpainted spinnerbait blanks in sizes from about ⅛ through ¾ ounces.

Parts for making spinnerbaits include wire forms, molded wire-form bodies, blades, hooks, skirts, split rings, swivels, beads, and clevises. In most cases only round-nose pliers will be needed for assembly.

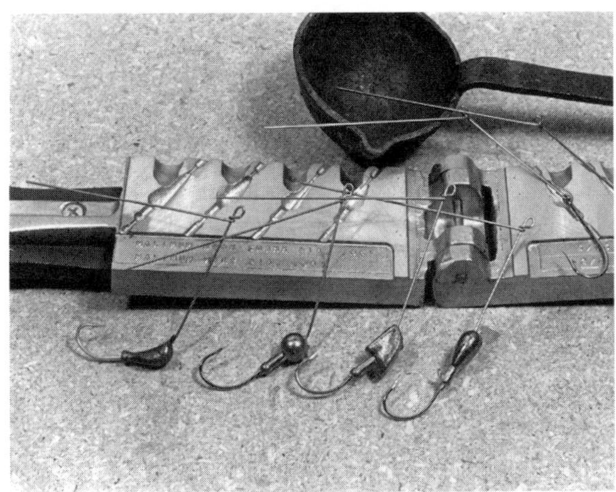

A mold and the spinnerbait forms necessary to produce spinnerbaits from various molds. The hooks and wires are joined (wire looped into the hook eye) to prevent pulling apart when fishing.

In these cases you will not need the tools used to mold the bodies or the other required parts. However, as will be discussed shortly, molding bodies for spinnerbaits is slightly different from molding jig and bucktail heads.

PARTS

Parts will vary with the type of spinnerbait or buzzbait to be made, and many of these parts are already listed in chapters 3 and 4. Be sure to check these chapters for full details and more information.

Some of the parts needed for making spinnerbaits and buzzbaits include:

Hooks. Hooks for molding spinnerbaits and buzzbaits are special. First, because these hooks are fastened to the spinnerbait or buzzbait wire by the hook eye, they must be straight eyed. They are also straight hooks, neither kirbed nor offset, and with a medium-length shank. Although many hooks will fill these basic requirements, special spinnerbait and buzzbait hooks have very small eyes. This is because the hook eye, along with the spinnerbait or buzzbait wire, is molded into a relatively small lead head. Hooks with large eyes (really normal size eyes for the size of the hook) are more likely to result in incomplete heads or heads with a void or flaw in the side. Typical hooks range in size from about #1 through 5/0.

Stinger hooks are similar but with a regular eye so that they can be slipped over the point and past the barb of the main spinnerbait hook. Usually a size close to that of the main hook is best.

Wires. You can purchase straight wire lengths or coils of wire for making spinnerbaits and buzzbaits. Straight wires with a small hook on one end to fasten into the hook eye are available in 0.029, 0.035, or 0.040-inch-diameter wire. Bent wire in the typical two-legged safety-pin form for spinnerbaits and the J-shaped form for buzzbaits is also readily available. Bent wire for spinnerbaits is usually lighter than that for standard buzzbaits, but some small-diameter wire for small-size buzzbaits is also available. Typical wire diameters in fractions of an inch for spinnerbaits from several manufacturers are 0.035 or 0.040 inch. Buzzbait wire is 0.035 inch for the small buzzbaits, 0.045, 0.051, or 0.052 inch for the larger forms.

In addition, wire forms come in several different styles. Spinnerbait wires are available in a long, twisted eye form, a long "R" eye form (an open eye preferred by some anglers), and an open R-style "short-arm" wire. All these forms have the small J-shaped bend at the end to attach the hook eye in the mold.

Lighter wires are available to make spinnerbaits and buzzbaits with some vibration. Wire of about 0.022 or 0.026 inch diameter will make lures that vibrate; the degree of vibration depends on the type and size of blade or blades used.

If you use straight wire, you will need round-nose pliers, needle-nose pliers, or a wire former capable of working with the wire size chosen to make the several bends necessary for these versatile lures. If there is a choice, stainless steel wire is best for lures because it won't rust, as may tinned wire. Most of the wire currently sold for spinnerbaits, spinners, and buzzbaits is stainless steel.

Spinnerbait and buzzbait blanks. To eliminate molding the bodies in which the hooks and wire are required, you can buy formed bodies. These usually have a tapered lead head and come in ⅛- through ¾-ounce sizes, with the hook and wire molded in place. They come unpainted (bare lead), painted in a white base coat, or painted in finished colors.

Blades, spinnerbaits. Blades for spinnerbaits are the same as those used for spinners, listed in chapter 3. The same colors, sizes, finishes, and styles are all suitable for spinnerbaits. Thus typical blades for spinnerbaits include the standard willowleaf, Indiana, Colorado, and swing blades, although deep-cut blades, ribbed blades, and fluted blades are getting more popular. The several exceptions generally not found on spinnerbaits might be the fixed-angle blades in which no clevis is used and in which the shaft runs straight through the two holes in the blade—the holes and arms designed to hold the blade at a specific angle—and the in-line blades in which the shaft runs through the hole in the single blade set somewhat back from the forward edge of the blade. Examples include the in-line spinner blade, June Bug blade, Rotospin blades, and similar types. This does not mean they cannot be used for spinnerbaits, only that they have seldom been commercially used in these lures.

In most cases, larger blades are used on single-spin spinnerbaits and smaller blades on the twin-spin style, while tandem in-line spinnerbaits usually use one larger blade on the back and a smaller one in front. In tandem spinnerbaits the blades can be the same style, finish, color, and size or completely different. In most cases they have an identical finish on both sides of the blade.

Blades, buzzbaits. Buzzbait blades are completely different from the spinner-type of blades on spinnerbaits. Spinner and spinnerbait blades have a tapered elliptical shape with a hole at one end for attachment to the lure. Those for buzzbaits come in several styles of propeller blade. The so-called delta blades are shaped like a big triangle or the letter "A," like the delta wing of a supersonic jet or like the wings of a skate or stingray.

The two outer wings of the blades are bent in opposing directions to make the blade spin in the water. Holes formed and stamped in the center keep the blade on the shaft. These blades are almost always used singly, although sometimes a small clicker or clacker blade is used to hit against the front of the delta wing. Different sizes of delta blades are available, with sizes ranging from 1 inch long by 1¼ inches wide to 1⅝ inches long by 1$^{15}/_{16}$ inches wide.

Smaller blades, sometimes called counter or counter-rotating blades, also have right-angle bends in the edges of the wings with holes

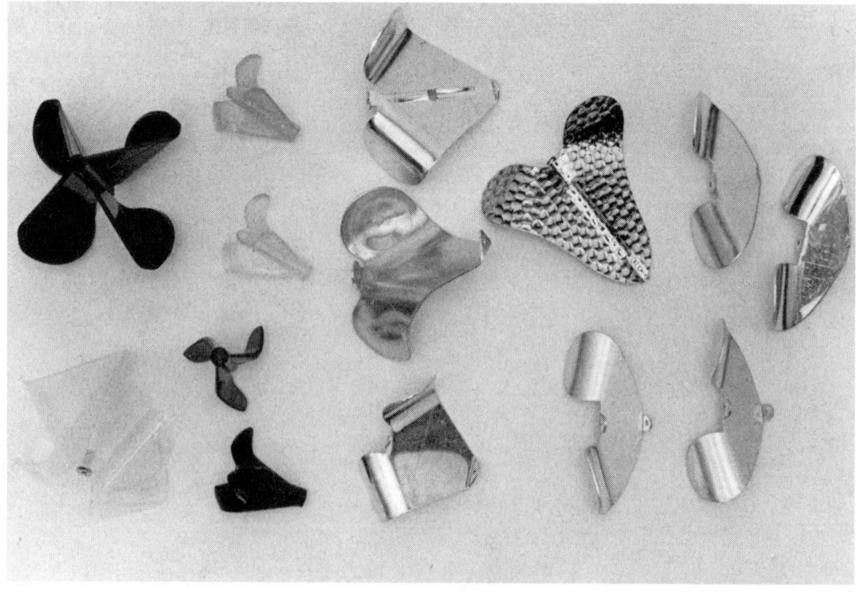

Buzzbait blades come in many styles, colors, finishes, and materials. Shown are four-blade, triple-blade, plastic, metal, delta-wing, cupped-wing, double counter-rotating, and other types of blades.

through the center for the shaft. As smaller blades are designed more and more to be used in sets of two, one turns clockwise and the other counterclockwise. The opposite-turning blades make a lot of fuss on the water and counter any tendency of the buzzbait to spin or rotate in one direction. This is particularly important on the straight-line or in-line buzzbaits, less so on those using the J-shaped arms. Although spinner blades are often stamped of brass and finished in nickel, copper, or brass or are painted, buzzbait blades are usually nickel-coated brass or aluminum. Most blades are sold individually or, in the case of the counter-rotating blades, in sets of two. More and more blades are being made available in molded plastic in many colors and also different blade (three or four) configurations.

A new innovation is the introduction of sets of two separate wings (blades) that are designed to slide together (back to back) on a shaft to make a clattering noise as the blade turns. They are separate to make a loose, clattering, four-blade or quad wing. They are usually aluminum and available in several sizes from 1⅟16 inches to 1¾ inches in width.

In addition to the metal buzzbait blades, plastic blades are available. These come in several sizes in triple and quad wings molded in each blade. They are usually of the larger delta shapes, designed for one blade per lure. Most have the metal (aluminum) pop-rivet blade collar molded into the rear of the blade, although some do not.

Many colors are available and will vary with the manufacturer. Clear, red, black, white, chartreuse, pink, yellow, and blue are common. The advantage of these blades is that the greater number of wings (three or four as opposed to two) will allow a slower retrieve for the same surface fuss.

Clicker or clacker blades are relatively new; they were first developed on commercially manufactured lures. These small blades look like a wing or a pennant, with holes for the shaft. They slide on the upright part of the arm and are designed to hit the blade with each revolution. As with the technique of the main blades lightly dinging the shaft on each rotation, these clacker or clicker blades give the lure more noise. Most are of aluminum, with ¾- and 1-inch lengths standard.

Blade collar. These are really pop-rivet collars used behind the buzzbait blades to create the squeaking sounds characteristic of these lures. Although you can use regular pop-rivet collars, popping out the metal shaft used to pull the rivet tight, it is far better and cheaper to buy these collars in bulk.

Cable. Cable is sometimes used for making spinnerbaits, in imitation of some of the commercially available styles that use flexible wire (cable) for either the entire wire form of the lure or for the upper arm. Stainless steel cable is best, in sizes from 0.030 to 0.040. If you use cable, you will also need crimping pliers and some leader sleeves to form loops in the wire. (Construction is covered later in this chapter.)

Swivels. Swivels allow spinnerbait blades to turn at the end of the arm. This is also possible with buzzbaits, though seldom done. There are several ways to use swivels, one of which is to attach a swivel to the end of an arm and then attach a blade to the swivel with a split ring. It is also possible to use a snap swivel with the swivel attached to the arm; the snap is used to attach the blade for instant changes of blade color, size, and shape.

Swivels can also be used, though they rarely are, as attachments to the line-tie eye for more action and also to prevent the line from wrapping around the arms of the spinnerbait during fishing.

Clevises. Clevises are used in two ways on spinnerbaits. As with spinners, they are used to hold a spinner blade on the upper-arm shaft on in-line tandem spinners. The smaller front blade will fit on a clevis on the shaft and will flap and wobble. It may not rotate around the shaft, as will a spinner blade on a spinner shaft, although this will depend upon the angle at which the upper arm rides in the water. The rear blade can be fixed the same way but is more likely to be fixed to a swivel attached to the end of the arm for free rotation and swinging.

Clevises can also be used on the front of the arm at the line-tie position. In this, straight wire must be used or the arm must be straightened so that a large clevis can be slipped in place on the shaft. The use of a clevis here reduces the possibility of the line getting tangled around the arm or blades on a cast or when flipping. Since the clevis can rotate completely around the shaft, such tangles are lessened. For free movement of the clevis, a single bead should be used both above and below it. Otherwise the clevis might bind on the wire bend to defeat its purpose.

Clevises are not used in buzzbaits, although a substitute for the clacker blade mentioned above is to use a small spinner blade on a clevis, attached to the upright arm: The spinner blade will be struck by the buzz blade on each rotation.

Beads. The same variety of beads used in spinners can be used in spinnerbaits and buzzbaits. Most beads are small, red, and used for bearings and to add a little color to the lure. They are used primarily on tandem spinnerbaits as bearings for the front blade that rotates around the shaft. For this, red glass and hard-plastic beads are used in small sizes of 2½ to 4 millimeters. Larger sizes and different colors can be used for special applications.

Unies. Unies, the small special beads used exclusively for bearings, also can be used for bearings on clevis-mounted blades in tandem spinnerbaits.

Snaps. Snaps and snap swivels allow for blade changes on spinnerbaits when they are added to the end of the arm. The snap swivel must be added by the swivel to the arm; the snap is used to hold the blade. Snap swivels incorporating regular snaps, interlock snaps, Duo-Lock snaps, or other snaps will work. The smallest possible snaps are best to reduce the bulk of the lure.

Split rings. Split rings have many applications in making spinnerbaits. They are used to connect snap swivels to upper arms, to the front of the lure line-tie for added action, or to attach blades to swivels. Sizes range from tiny (00) to large (8) but should be as small as possible for the purpose without causing binding or cramping of the parts joined. Polished brass, nickel-plated brass, nickel-plated steel, and zinc-plated steel split rings are all available; the nickel-plated styles are best for most freshwater applications.

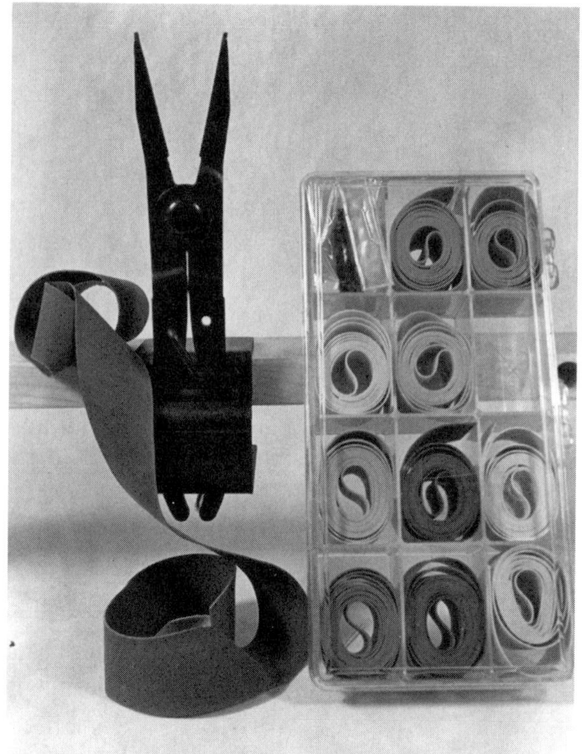

A skirt kit that includes the tool and materials for making rubber skirts for spinnerbaits and buzzbaits. A variety of colors are available.

Butt rings. These small rings, also sometimes called jump rings, are not as strong as a split ring and should *never* be used for a line-tie or hook attachment. (An exception would be if the rings are soldered shut for strength.) They are ideal for attaching a spinner blade to a swivel or for some similar nonstress task.

MOLDING TECHNIQUES

Molding spinnerbaits is similar to molding jigs and bucktails, but there's a difference. The difference is that in addition to placing a hook in the mold, you must also add the spinnerbait wire. Other than that, the molding is about the same.

For the best results, make sure the mold has been smoked as described in chapter 4. Preheat the mold as described for bucktail molds, making sure the mold is hot enough that lead fills the cavity evenly, but not so hot as to be dangerous or to warp the mold. The cold metal parts of the hook shank and spinnerbait wire will cool any molten lead rapidly.

Most molds, such as the excellent models by Do-It and Hilts Molds, specify not only the hook type and size required but also the wire size to be used. In most cases this wire is readily available. You usually can't use larger diameter wire, because the mold will not close securely and flash will result not only at the wire but also along the entire joint. You can use smaller diameter wire, but then you risk lead leakage—flash—around the wire. Any such flash formed will affect the appearance of the lure but not its function. If desired, the flash is easily removed.

The wire must be straight to fit into the mold properly, so any wire from coils must be checked and straightened if necessary.

Before using the wire you must make sure you have a small J-shaped bend in the end that fits into the mold cavity and that the J fits through the hook eye. As listed before, the hook eyes should be small to allow for complete coating of these parts by the lead.

Straight wire is best if you plan to make spinnerbaits or buzzbaits with any special additions, such as clacker blades on the upright arm of a buzzbait or a clevis as the line-tie on the arm of a spinnerbait or buzzbait. Both parts require a relatively straight wire to slide in place. If you use a formed wire, the wire must be opened or straightened, at least partly, to add these parts.

Similarly, cable can be used in place of wire, but the small J-shaped bend on the end is a must to hook the cable into the hook eye in the molded-lead head. It is really best to twist the wire around the eye some so that it is impossible for the cable wire to pull out. Another alternative is to use a leader sleeve to make a closed loop on the hook eye.

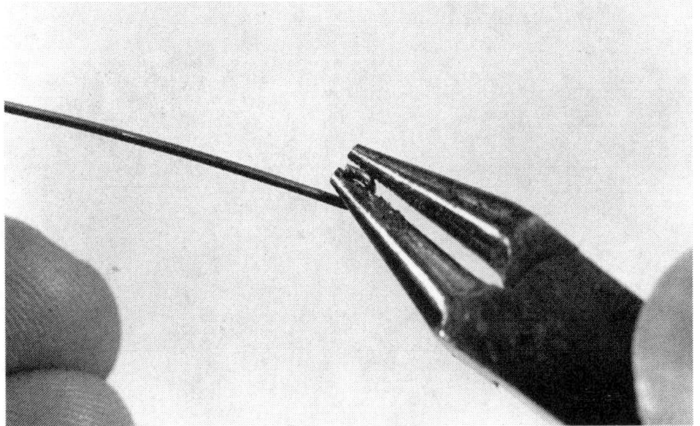

Bending the hook in the wire to mold a spinnerbait or buzzbait. The hook fits over the eye of the hook for a permanent attachment.

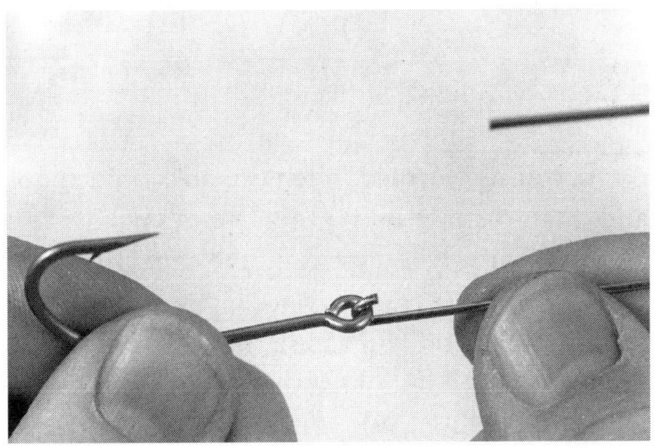

The hook of the wire on a buzzbait (shown here) or spinnerbait hooked onto the eye of the hook.

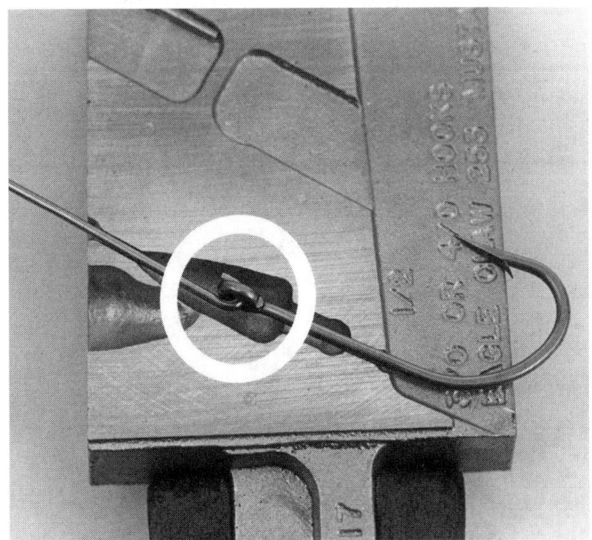

The wire and hook in the mold with the two hooked together. Circle is around the hook parts.

Molding spinnerbaits is a little different from molding jigs, as the wires or hooks will extend up into the molding area as shown. Use basic safe molding procedures for this step.

If you use formed wire (available from shops and mail-order stores), the line-tie bends and arms will already be formed in the wire. The small J-shaped bend may or may not be formed. Failure to form this bend will assure that the wire will at some point pull out of the lead body, resulting in a lost lure or fish. While remote, that same possibility exists if the J-shaped bend is not placed over the hook eye.

Place the wire and hooks into the mold properly, with the wires extending out one side of the mold. In some cases the hook points and bends may also extend out the other side, making these molds impossible to set down on a table once they are ready to be filled with lead. To provide a steady support for the mold during pouring, use a small block of wood to hold the hinge end of the mold while you hold the handles and pour. An alternative is to use a long block of wood and rest one side of the mold on it. The spinnerbait wires or hook bends will hang down alongside, and clearance must be provided to allow for this. Do not try to pour these molds or any mold without some kind of support. If the wires or hooks extend up (on the gate or sprue-hole side) you may not be able to use a bottom-feed furnace, because the bottom spout must contact the sprue hole. If this is a problem, use a ladle or top-pour furnace.

In some cases the bend of the hook may extend below the mold and thus make it difficult to get a solid support for the mold. To adjust for this use a small block of wood, as shown, and rest one side of the mold on this block while pouring lead.

Once the spinnerbait bodies are molded, following the directions in chapter 4, allow the mold to cool, place it on its side, and open it carefully. If you pry the lead heads out of the mold, do so carefully; do not try to lever them by using the lightweight spinner wire. Doing so risks bending the wire to the side of the lure, which can result in an unbalanced spinnerbait. If this does happen, it is easy to bend the wire back in line with the body and hook.

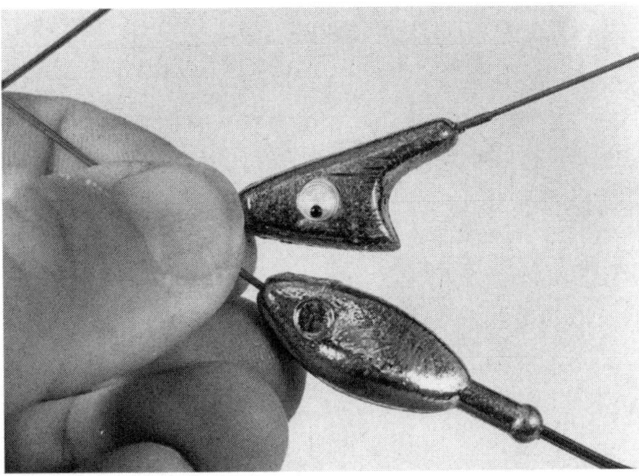

Some spinnerbaits and buzzbaits have molded-in sockets for painted or added eyes, as shown here. For illustrative purposes the upper example has had a doll eye added, although in normal operation this would only be done after assembling and painting the lure.

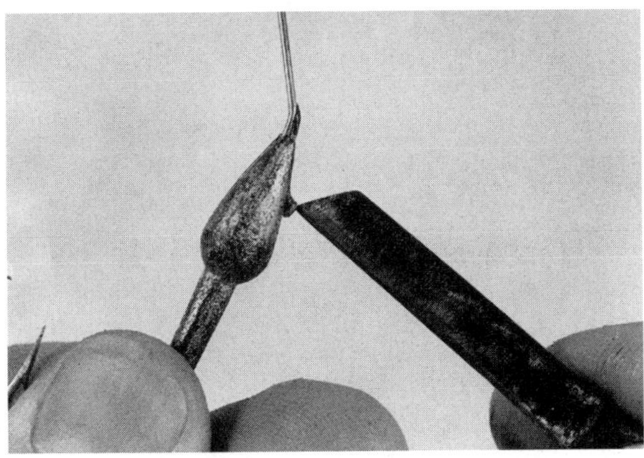

Some imperfections in the lead head might be noticeable after molding. These are easily removed with gate cutters or by filing.

Once the bodies are removed, cut off any excess lead using gate cutters or flush-cut wire cutters. Because spinnerbaits and buzzbaits are painted upon completion, do not touch these lead heads at all until they are at least painted with a base coat of white or primer. As with jigs, handle them with gloves or by the hook (or wire in this case) to keep your skin's oils off the lead. To prevent oxidation, paint or give the lure a primer coat within 24 hours of molding. After a primer coat, they are protected from oxidation and can be put aside to be painted at any time.

FINISHING

Finishing spinnerbaits and buzzbaits can be accomplished on several different levels, depending on how they were molded. If they were molded on straight wires, then the wire will have to be bent into shape for the finished lure and the lead lure heads painted. If preformed wires were used, then painting only is required, followed by assembly of the blades, beads, and other components. If you formed the lead heads on straight wires, you might want to paint the heads before forming the wires. This might make for easier painting, and the painted heads can be handled while you bend the wire, something that should not be done to unpainted lead heads without wearing gloves.

Painting is thoroughly covered in chapter 15, but some tips here are important. You should paint or at least put a base coat on the lead heads as soon as possible. Paint adherence on any metal is never good, but some factors make this even more difficult on lead. First, the oils from skin contact and handling will prevent good adherence; second, lead will oxidize, and this oxidation will further prevent good paint adherence.

Bending wire to form it is easy with round-nose pliers. Before doing so, however, decide if you will be adding anything to the wire. For example, if you want anything on the lower arm of a spinnerbait, you must add it before making any bends. The same applies to a buzzbait. If you add a clacker blade to a buzzbait, you will have to make the first line-tie bend and then add the bead, clacker blade, and another bead before making the second bend for the upper arm.

Assuming you are making the bends on a spinnerbait and beginning with straight wire, first decide on the type of line-tie you want. Measure the length of the lower arm and then make the desired bend. If you make an R-type bend in the wire, all the bending will be on the same plane as the angle of the spinnerbait. Grasp the wire with the pliers, and bend the wire through a three-quarter turn upward with the pliers. (By making the bend upward, the wire end will be bent back and toward the hook point.) Hold the wire bend with the pliers, take the end of the wire, and bend

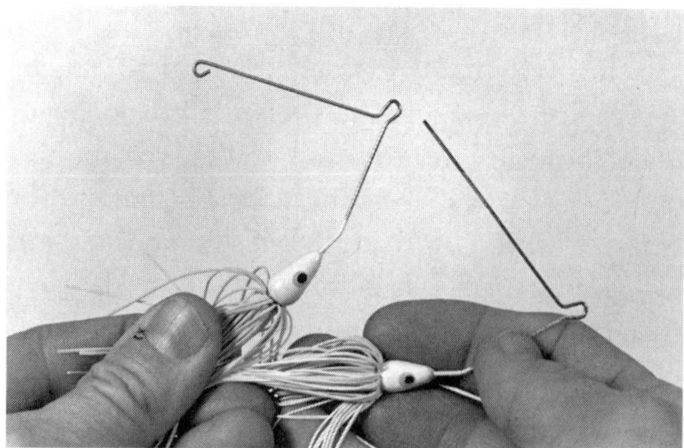

Examples of molded—unfinished and painted—spinnerbait heads.

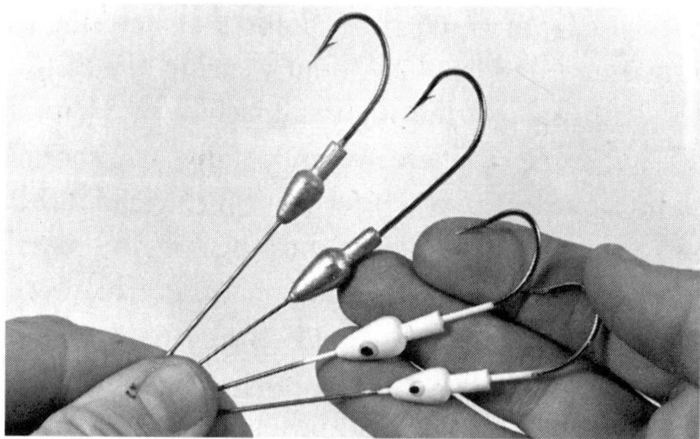

Unpainted and painted spinnerbait bodies with the wire molded into the body and through a J form in the wire, secured to the hook. These still require finishing the lure with the right-angle bend and the addition of blades and skirts.

it back up again to make the lower part of the R bend. The result is the R, or open-eye, bend.

To make a wrapped eye, measure the length of the wire for the lower arm and grasp the wire with round-nose pliers. Bend the wire *up* past a full turn (about 540 degrees) so that the two parts of the wire cross or touch. In essence, what you are doing is making one and a half complete turns with the eyes on the same plane as the spinnerbait, ending with the upper arm at about a 60- to 90-degree angle to the lower arm. This is the type of eye used on many commercial spinnerbaits.

Another way to make a wrapped eye is to measure the length of the wire for the lower arm and grasp the wire with the pliers. Bend the wire *down* through a 360-degree bend so that the end of the wire overlaps the lower arm. Hold the eye with the round-nose pliers, and wrap the end of the wire a full turn around the lower arm so that the end of the wire sticks straight up, in line with the hook and lower arm.

It is also possible to make a wrapped eye by bending the wire *up* a full 360 degrees, but this will end with the upper arm pointing down. To complete the wrap you then have a choice of making either an additional half-wrap or one and a half wraps of the wire around the lower arm. The one and a half wraps are more than required, and the half-wrap is not as sturdy as it should be. Thus the initial downward bend to allow for one complete wrap is best.

Another method is to bend the wire *down* a full 360 degrees around the round-nose pliers jaw, then continue bending on the same plane so that the upper wire is angled back over the hook point. There are no tight wraps around the lower wire.

Once the eye is complete and the upper arm is in the upward-angled position, the spinnerbait is ready for assembly. The upper and lower arm should form a 90- to 45-degree angle, but this can be adjusted when the lure is completed.

Buzzbaits are made in two different ways: in-line and bent-arm. If you make the in-line buzzbaits, start with the straight wire (not the wire forms), and keep the wire straight until you're ready to complete the assembly. Making the bent-arm buzzbaits requires using formed wire or bending the straight wire. Bending wire to complete buzzbait forms is very similar to the above instructions, with the R, or open eye, almost universally used. The wraps are made exactly as are the eyes for spinnerbaits, but you might find the wire slightly harder to work because buzzbait wire is usually thicker than spinnerbait wire.

When completing the buzzbait eye, make sure the upper arm is at a 90-degree angle to the straight lower arm. Once this bend is made, measure the spot where you will make the bend in the upright arm to form the upper arm that is parallel to the main arm and body.

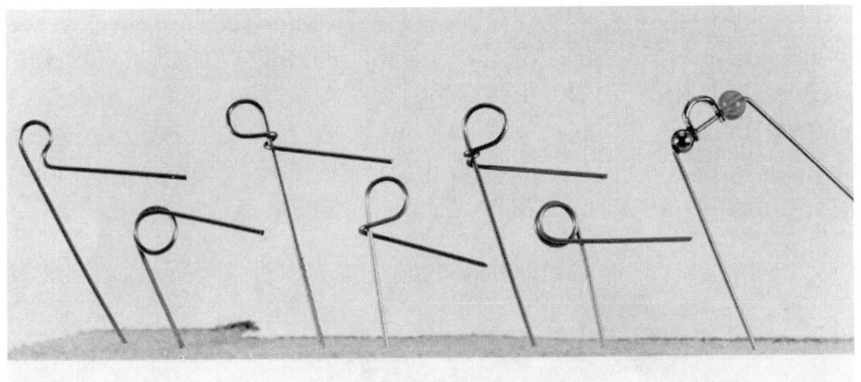

Examples of eyes used for spinnerbaits. The R, or open eye, is to the left; others are examples of various styles and types of wrapped eyes. The one to the right uses a clevis and beads to prevent the clevis from sliding up the arm. Normally identical beads would be used, but one metal and one red plastic bead are used here for illustrative purposes.

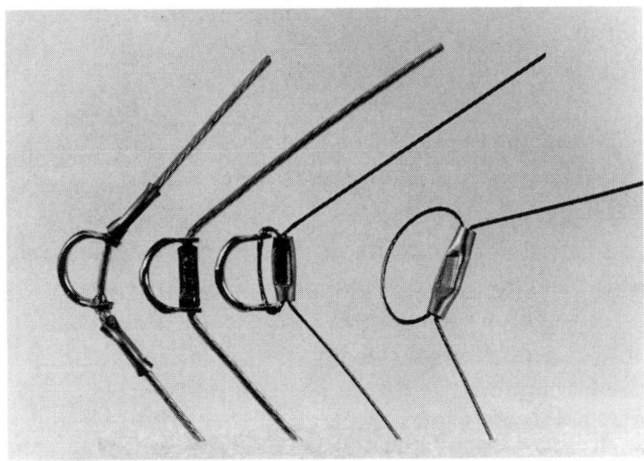

Examples of eyes (line-ties) that can be used when making spinnerbaits of cable. These all use leader sleeves in some way to prevent the line-tie or clevis from slipping.

This upper arm holds the buzz blade or blades and keeps them in line with the axis of the lure body. This bend can be critical—you need enough clearance for the blade to turn, yet the blade should turn close to the main shaft, particularly if you wish to turn the lure so that the blade lightly dings the wire with each revolution or hits a clacker blade.

To make the bend, use round- or square-jaw pliers and hold the wire securely, bending sharply at the premeasured and marked spot. When bending, make sure the wire is in plane with the hook bend so that the blade runs true with the lure body.

At this point the lure bodies are ready to assemble into lures.

SPINNERBAIT ASSEMBLY

Single-Blade Spinnerbaits

Single-blade spinnerbaits are easy to assemble because they only require adding a blade to the end of the upper-arm wire. First decide whether you wish a short-arm or long-arm spinnerbait. If you want a short-arm spinnerbait, cut the upper-arm wire accordingly. If you are unsure as to correct length, check some commercial short-arm spinnerbaits to get an idea. Cut for that length, but be sure to allow an additional ¼ to ⅜ inch for the eye bend to hold the blade.

Any type of blade in any finish and any size can be used, but in general single-spin spinnerbaits use larger blades than do twin- or tandem-spin spinnerbaits. In addition to the blade you will also need a split ring or butt ring and swivel. The split ring or butt ring connects the blade and swivel. If you use a butt or jump ring, you will need two pairs of pliers to spread the ring open, add the swivel and blade, and close the ring again. If you use a split ring, use the correct size. Split rings range from the small size 00 to the large size 8. The split ring must be large enough to prevent binding of the parts. Also, you should use split-ring pliers. These are available in small inexpensive models and in more-precise pliers. Both work well, and both have straight jaws with a small tooth on the end of one jaw, by which the split ring can be separated and opened. Open the split ring with the pliers, and add the blade and the swivel to the ring together. Once the blade and swivel are on one of the prongs of the split ring, rotate the split ring with the pliers' jaws while holding the blade and swivel until they both move freely on the ring. Once these parts are connected, use the round-nose pliers on the end of the wire, bending it into an almost complete circle. Leave enough room to add the swivel, and then close the wire eye with pliers.

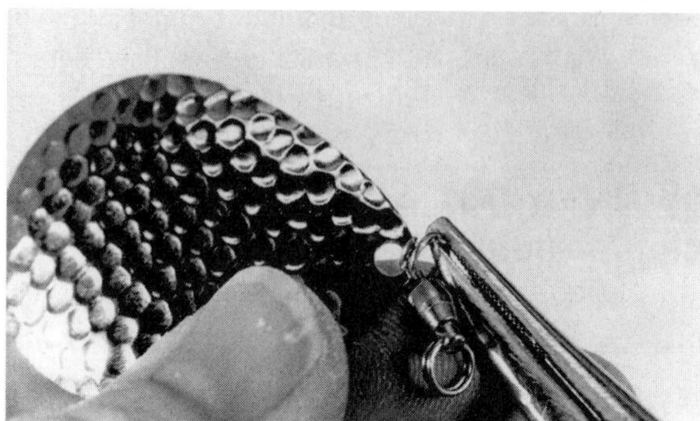
Adding a blade and swivel together with a split ring and split-ring pliers for attachment to a spinnerbait arm. Here a ball-bearing swivel is used.

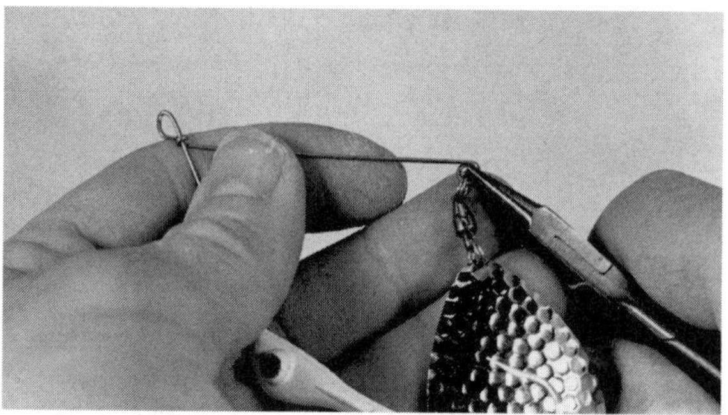
Completing the eye on the upper arm of a spinnerbait to hold the blade and swivel in place. This has been designed as a long-arm spinnerbait.

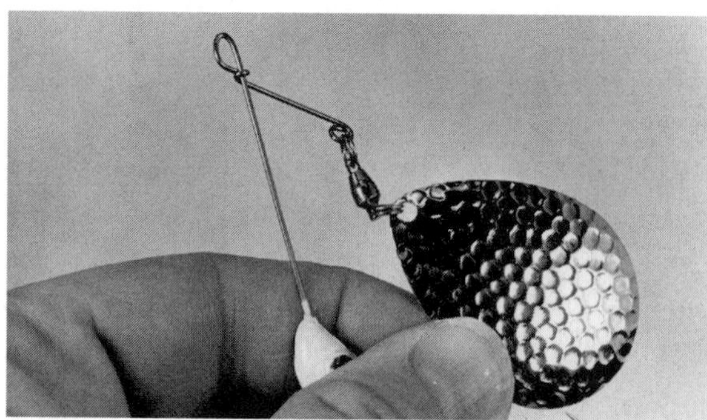
The same techniques can be used to make a short-arm spinnerbait. The spinnerbait shown here was modified by cutting back the upper arm and reattaching the blade.

An alternative is to add a snap swivel to the end of the wire by making a bend in the wire. This will allow you to add or change any type, size, style, or finish of blade you want, anytime you want. It is a simple modification, easily done, and allows for increased versatility of this lure.

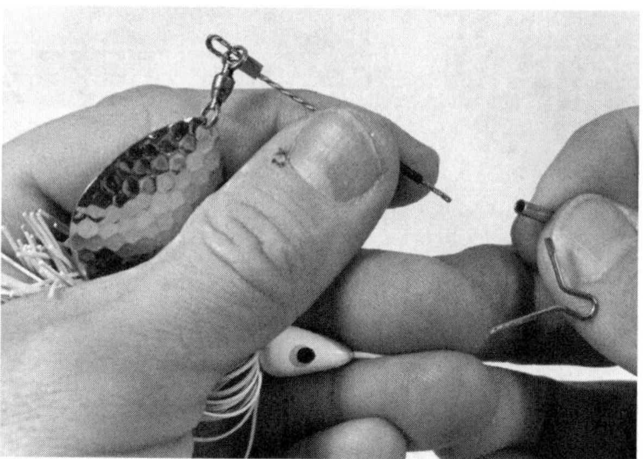
Some kits for making cable-arm spinnerbaits allow attachment of the two parts using leader sleeves, as shown. The sleeve slides onto the cable arm and is then crimped.

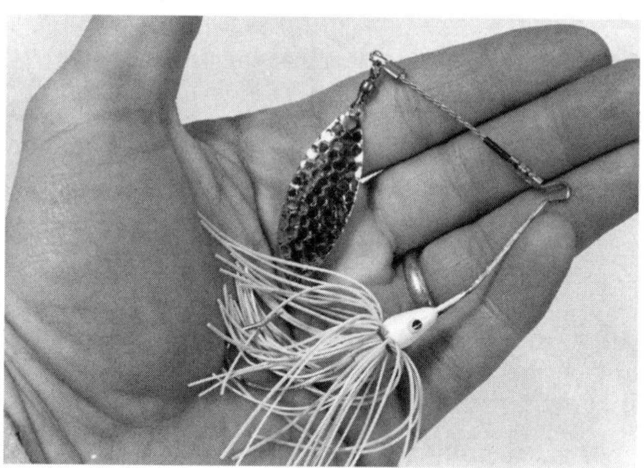
Completed cable-arm spinnerbait.

Tandem-Blade Spinnerbaits

Tandem-blade spinnerbaits have two blades on a single shaft. Usually the forward blade is smaller and may be a different style and finish than the larger rear blade. As a result, almost anything goes in two-blade spinnerbaits. The main difference in the two blades is that the forward blade is normally on a clevis and thus may rotate or just swing and flop around to create flash. (There are variations—you can use a swivel or snap swivel here; see directions later in this chapter.) The rear blade is on a swivel or snap swivel and does rotate. To construct these, first choose a clevis that will fit the forward blade and allow clearance for it to rotate or swing. Place the clevis through the hole in the blade. Add one or more small beads or unies to the shaft to serve both as color and also as spacers to prevent the clevis from flopping forward on a cast and jamming against the line-tie eye. These beads can be hollow metal, solid metal, red plastic, or anything you like, but they usually should be small. Do not add too many, or the water pressure on them might impede the movement of the forward blade and clevis. Next slide the clevis and blade onto the shaft, making sure the convex side of the blade faces forward when the blade hangs free.

Add two or three more small beads or unies on the shaft to serve as bearings; otherwise the clevis will bind against the eye in the wire. These beads may be the same color or of a different color and finish from those used to the rear of the clevis. Once these parts are added, finish as above, adding a swivel, split ring, and blade, or snap swivel and blade, to a small eye bent in the end of the wire.

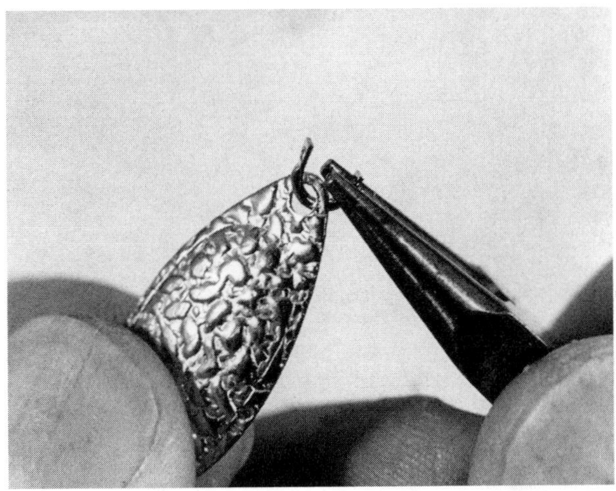

Attaching a clevis to a spinner blade for a spinnerbait. Either single- or double-blade (the second blade) spinnerbaits can be made this way, since the blade will still generally rotate completely around the upper arm of the lure.

Two blades on one arm are possible using several different techniques. Here the main blade is attached normally with a swivel and snap (the snap used for blade changes), while the smaller forward blade is attached to the shaft by a clevis. Beads separate the two blades.

In most cases the forward, smaller, blade rides close to the rear blade as a result of the few beads added that only provide marginal space between the two blades. This is fine and is how most commercial spinnerbaits are made, but you can space them out farther if you wish by moving the clevis of the smaller blade forward on the shaft. There are several ways to do this. One is to use more beads or unies on the shaft behind the clevis so that they separate the two blades. Another way is to use a small section of thin tubing on the shaft. Empty ballpoint-pen ink tubes, narrow fuel-line tubing for model airplanes (available at hobby shops), the thin spray tubing from cans of demoisturizers, and the thin straws used as coffee stirrers in fast-food places can all be used. Be sure to measure the length of tubing you will need before cutting, and add two or three beads forward of the tubing (between the tubing and the clevis) to serve as bearings for the free-swinging clevis.

Another way to accomplish this is to slide the forward beads, the clevis and blade, and the bearing beads onto the shaft and then make two sharp, close right-angle bends—like a

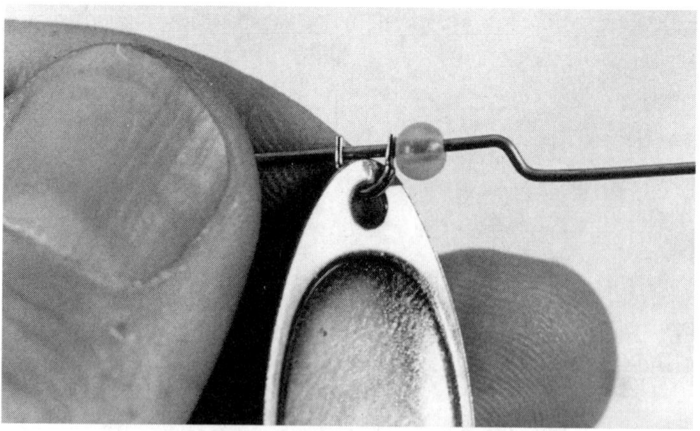

One way to separate several blades is to make two sharp bends in the upper arm as shown to keep the forward blade from sliding back. To do this, first add the blade on a clevis and at least one bearing bead as shown.

Bend in upper arm of spinnerbait, with circle around the bend and the blade/bead position.

modified Z—to keep the bearing beads from sliding along the shaft beyond this point. A drop of solder on the wire shaft at the appropriate point will also provide more spacing, but this is often more trouble to accomplish than the methods just described.

The skirt on a spinnerbait is added in one of several ways. First, any tail material or skirting can be tied on using the fly-tying techniques described fully in chapter 4. If you are tying on plastic or rubber skirts, you will have to use minimal tension, since too much tension can cut the material. Second, the living-rubber style of skirting can be added by using the special pliers to open the rubber O-rings: Hold the rubber in place with the pliers, slide the rubber and hook collar into place, and close the pliers to secure the skirt. Then the skirting—in sheet form until cut—is trimmed with scissors to form the living-rubber strands. This material can also be tied in place on spinnerbaits. Third, some skirts are available and sold with a rubber O-ring

Three ways of marking double- or multiple-blade spinnerbaits. Left to right: using a double bent shaft with a bead, using beads, and using thin tubing with beads as separators.

on them. These are simply threaded over the hook point and bend and up onto the skirt socket or positioning point on the end of the lead head. A final method is not to use any natural or artificial skirting but a grub tail or worms as a trailer attractant. Those with curved tails usually are best because of the rippling, lifelike action.

Adding skirts using a skirt tool. Small collars are placed on the thin end tips of the special "pliers" and the handle locked to hold this open position. The table clamp allows easy use of the tool.

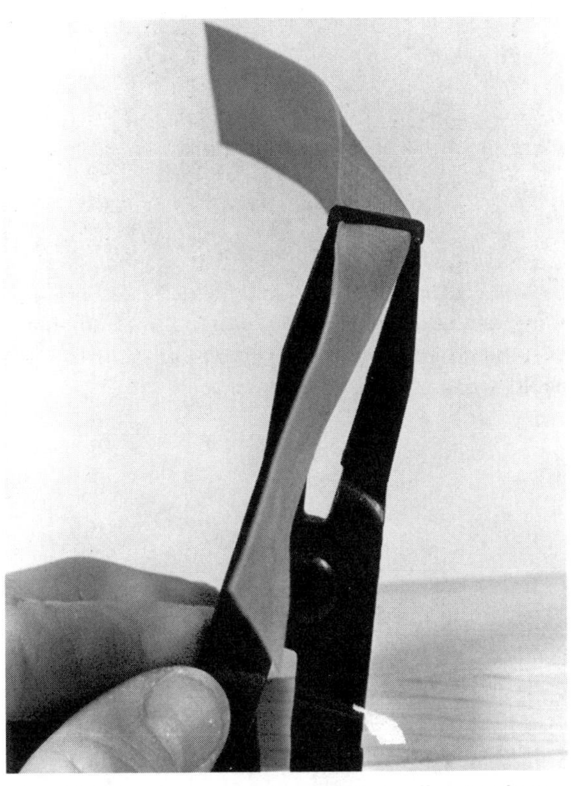

The skirt-sheet material through the collar, ready to be positioned and trimmed to form the skirt.

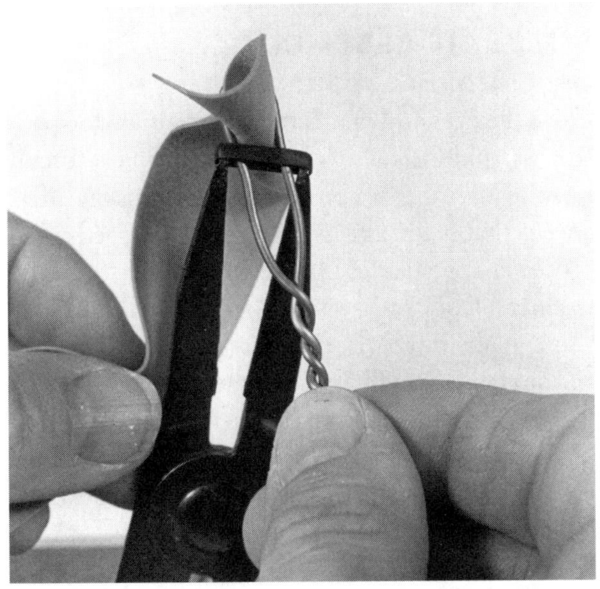

Using a small loop of wire (made by the author) makes it easy to bring a length of skirt-sheet material through the rubber collar.

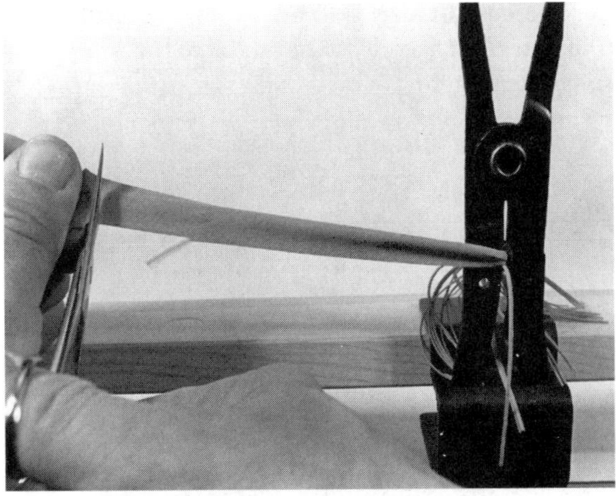

Here the skirt has been moved to a clamped position on the tool and secured in place with the table clamp. Pulling the sheet material as shown and then trimming separates the sections of the sheet to form the skirt.

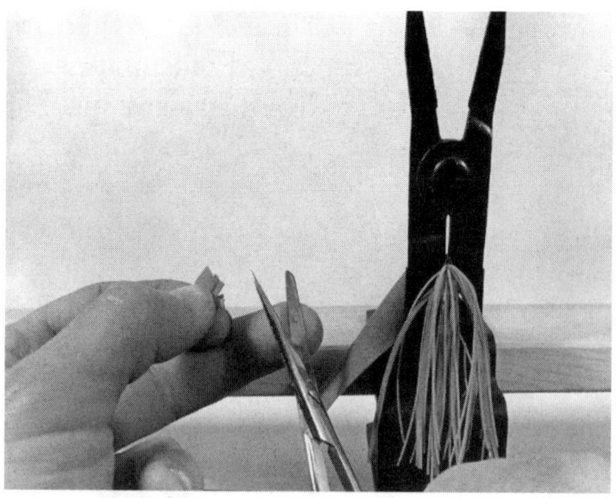

Completed skirt on one side, with the small amount of trimmed material. Trim as little as possible to avoid waste.

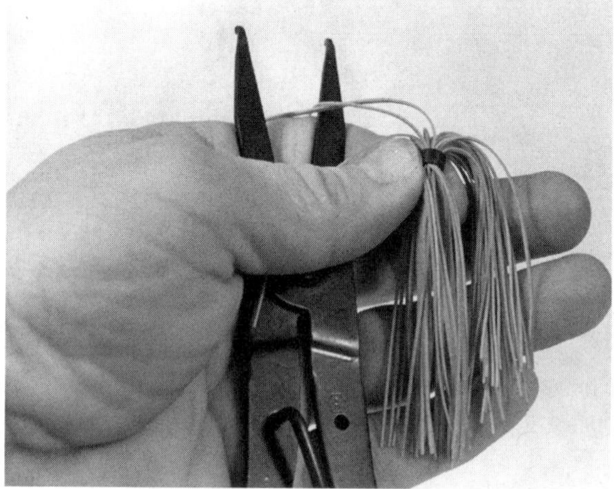

Completed skirt after the second side has been trimmed. Skirt is ready to be added to the spinnerbait or buzzbait.

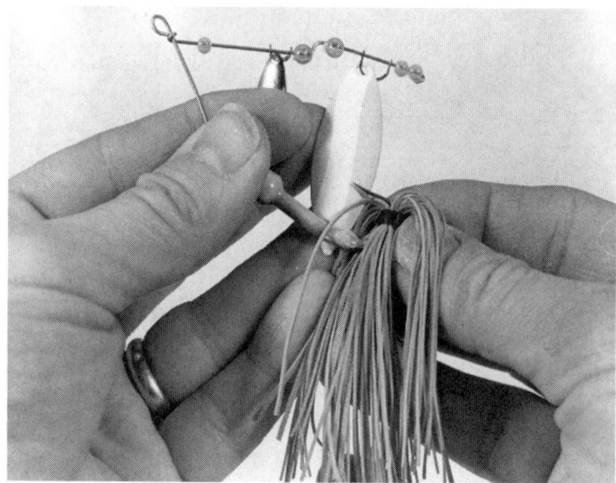

Adding completed skirt to spinnerbait. Rubber collar holds skirt in place and on hook shank.

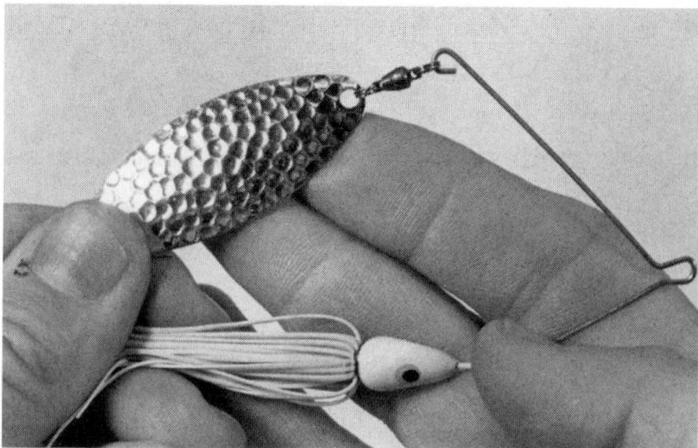

Single-blade spinnerbait with a standard rubber skirt. Skirt is on in reversed fashion, standard for most lures.

Silicone sparkle skirt with a stinger hook added to the lure.

BUZZBAIT ASSEMBLY

Bent-Arm Buzzbaits

Once the eyes and bends in a buzzbait are formed, the assembly is relatively simple and very much like the assembly of spinnerbaits. The main difference is that buzzbaits use one or two cupped-wing propeller-type blades on the shaft rather than the spinner blades on a swivel or clevis. To make a single-blade buzzbait, first thread a small bead on the shaft. This will prevent the blade from sliding forward and binding against the bend in the upper arm. Next thread the blade on the shaft. Finally add a small pop-rivet or blade collar both to serve as a bearing and to make the squeaking sound favored in buzzbaits. (Some plastic buzzbait blades come with a molded-in aluminum collar, thus eliminating this step.) Once the collar is in place, make a right-angle bend in the shaft after measuring and marking where you want the blade positioned on the shaft. Use compound-action cutting pliers to cut off any excess wire.

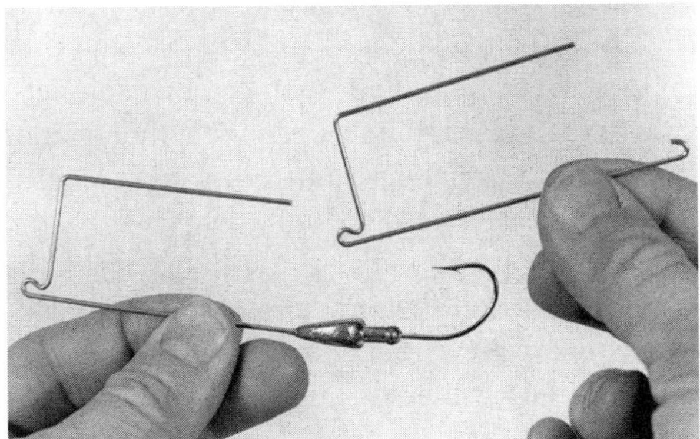

Buzzbaits can be bought molded with wires and hooks, or wire forms can be purchased for use in molds to make these bodies.

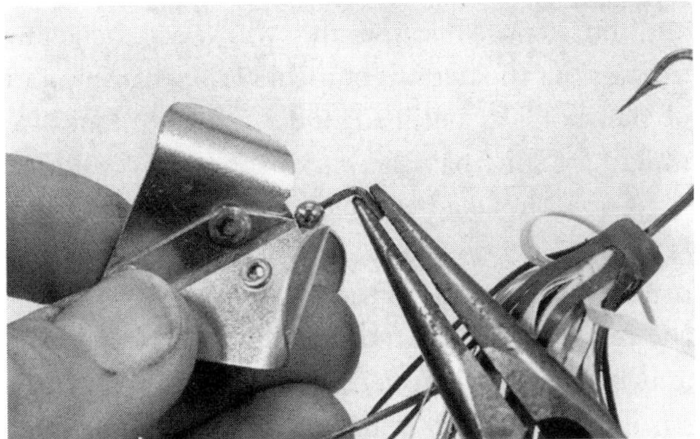

Adding a triple-wing delta blade to a buzzbait. A bearing bead is added in back of the blade and then the upper arm bent to hold the parts on the shaft.

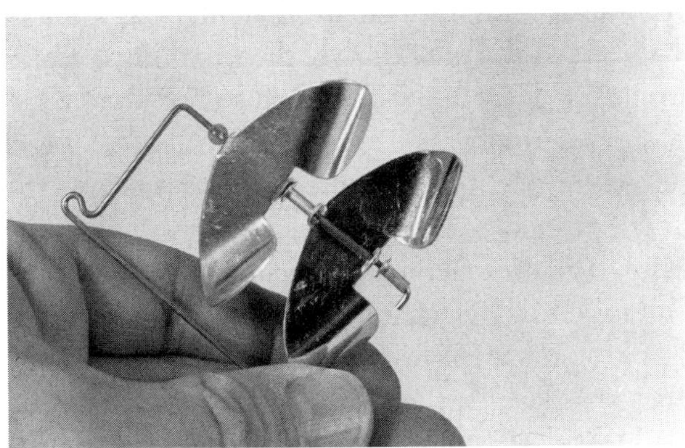

Double, counter-rotating blades on a buzzbait, separated by a sleeve.

Left, buzzbait with single large triple-wing blade; right, a double-wing buzzbait.

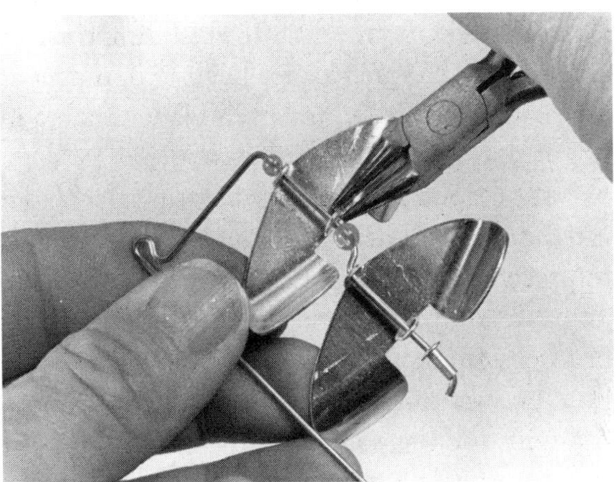

One way to separate the two blades on a double-blade buzzbait is to use the double-crimped bends in the arm, as shown here. If the blade binds slightly, sometimes bending the attached ear, as shown, will help to free it.

In-Line Buzzbaits

In-line buzzbaits work the same way on the surface of the water but are made somewhat differently than the bent-arm buzzers. Because these are built in a straight line with the hook shank and main shaft, the only bending is that of the eye for the line-tie when the lure assembly is completed. Since in-line buzzbaits will have a tendency to rotate, use only the tandem counter-rotating blades or a large delta blade with a counter-rotating blade in front. Assuming you are working with wire (the hook and wire molded in the lead body), first thread on a small bead as a bearing or spacer, then add a blade collar or pop-rivet speaker, and then follow with the large or rear blade. Add several more beads after the rear blade as spacers to make sure the two blades do not hit and bind. Add the second blade, a final bead, and then make a simple loop eye for a line-tie.

The pressure of the first blade against the beads serving as spacers will slightly slow the second or rear blade, but not enough to be noticeable. If you are concerned about this and wish to completely separate the two blades for totally free movement, there are two solutions. One is to make two small, closely spaced right-angle bends in the wire immediately forward of the rear blade to prevent it from sliding back. If you do this, be sure to use a bead or pop rivet as a bearing directly behind each blade. Then add the second blade and finish as above.

The second method of separating the blades is to add a small drop of solder to the wire shaft to prevent the forward blade from sliding back. You can add the solder as the lure is being built or after completion. If you do so after completion, be sure to allow enough space and play in the wire for the soldering operation. Also, be sure to provide a pop rivet or bead as a bearing behind each of the blades.

Skirts are added using the same materials and methods described for spinnerbaits: artificial fur, feather, or rubber or plastic skirting material tied in place; a rubber or plastic skirt slipped on; or a soft-plastic grub tail or worm slid onto the hook.

IN-LINE OR WEIGHT-FORWARD SPINNER ASSEMBLY

In-line or weight-forward spinners are really a compromise between spinnerbaits and spinners, but since they require a molded-in head, they are included here. Unlike spinners in which all the parts are threaded onto a bare shaft, these lures have molded heads; yet unlike spinnerbaits, they are built in line. The forward-weight design allows them to be fished on the bottom; as a result they are popular walleye lures. In essence they are really like an in-line buzzbait with the blades and body reversed in position and spinner blades used instead of buzzbait blades.

Different head designs are available, and they go by names like walleye spinners, Erie spinners, Erie rigs, and keel spinners. Unlike spinnerbait or buzzbait heads that have a wire and hook molded in, these lures are molded on a looped-eye wire, with the loop eye forming the line-tie and the wire then threaded with a spinner blade and ending with a clip eye that allows opening and closing. This clip eye holds a straight-eye hook that can be dressed or that more typically is used to hold bait. Typical baits for these rigs for walleye include minnows, night crawlers, and leeches.

These lures are molded using the same techniques used to mold jig heads, sinkers, spinnerbaits, and buzzbaits. Because the wire used generally extends out the bottom of the mold, special support of the mold, as outlined under the techniques for molding spinnerbait and buzzbait heads, is required.

Once the head is molded, the rest of the lure is ready to be assembled. For this, a bead or two is usually threaded onto the shaft that extends from the rear of the head. This is followed by a clevis and blade. Any spinner blade in any size or finish is possible, but walleye fishermen often favor French-style blades in nickel or copper finish. This is followed by two or more beads to serve as spacers and bearings for easy turning of the blade.

The clip is formed by first making a small J-shaped bend in the wire, then making a right-angle bend just above this bend so that the J bend is angled to the side. Finish with a wider bend about 1 inch up the wire, formed so that the J-shaped hook will catch on the main shaft of the wire. The arrangement allows opening and closing for adding or changing hooks.

Hooks should be straight-eyed, with a slightly long shank. Often Mustad 3366G hooks are used ("G" for the gold finish) because they have unusually large eyes that will swing freely on the end of the spinner and minimize tangling and twisting on both cast and retrieve.

The same methods described for adding skirts to standard spinnerbaits are used for in-line spinnerbaits, if and when skirts are used. Often live minnows or leeches are used in place of a skirt when fishing for walleye.

VARIATIONS

There are a number of possible variations of all these lures: Some can be done on only one type of lure, while others are applicable to any of them. In fact, some of the following variations are adapted from commercial lures of the present and past. You can apply your own imagination to any of these lures. You can try many variations, but plan the order of assembly or construction modification necessary to the lure before beginning.

Variations in Line-ties

The open R-eye or the wrapped eye is standard in most spinnerbaits and buzzbaits. Other possibilities include one that I call the "omega eye," which is really a variation of the R-eye with an additional bend in the vertical leg of the "R" to make it like the Greek letter omega (Ω). This is easily done by forming the eye at the proper position and then making a sharp bend away from it on each side to spread the legs of the lure. This is possible on any type of spinnerbait or bent-arm buzzbait.

It is also possible to place a free-swinging clevis on the wire shaft for the line-tie. To do this start with straight wire, add a small bead as a spacer, and then add a large stirrup-style clevis and a second bead. Make a bend below and one above these parts to keep them in place. For spinnerbaits these can be sharp-angle beads; on a bent-arm buzzbait the lower arm will have a sharp 90-degree bend, and the upper arm will have a slight bend to keep the clevis from sliding up.

Another variation on buzzbaits is to make a sharp right-angle bend to form the upright arm, add the beads and clevis, and then make two sharp, close-together right-angle bends (like Zs) to keep the clevis from sliding. An alternative is to add the beads and clevis and then add a short length (premeasured) of thin plastic or metal tubing to keep the clevis from sliding up the shaft. In making these you *must* use the stirrup-style clevis—the folded types have sharp edges that could cut the line.

A variation similar to the above is to add a swivel for a line-tie. A bead both above and below, as with the clevis, is necessary. Another method of doing this is to add a swivel (no beads) when making a wrapped eye. This is possible on both spinnerbaits and buzzbaits, although both variations are more practical on spinnerbaits. Both methods can be used when constructing spinnerbaits with cable, as will be described later in this chapter. The one variation when using cable is that you must use a crimped-on leader sleeve above and below the clevis or swivel bearing to keep it from sliding on the cable. Bends on flexible cable are not sufficiently permanent to keep a clevis or swivel in place.

Variations in Blade Position and Number

The instructions listed above are for generally accepted styles of spinnerbaits and buzzbaits. However, extra blades can be added to spinnerbaits and buzzbaits, and blades can be placed in other than standard positions. An example would be to include extra blades on the upper arm of spinnerbait, each separated by a few beads and spacers, and each on its own clevis to swing around on retrieve. Using this method it is possible to make three-, four-, and even five-bladed spinnerbaits, with one large blade on a swivel at the end of the arm and all others on clevises on the upper arm. These extra blades can be added to any spinnerbait constructed, whether you work with straight wire and mold the lure or buy unpainted or painted molded heads.

Similarly, it is possible to add small blades to the lower arm of the spinnerbait, although this must be done only with straight wires because the blades and clevises must be added before the wire is bent and the line-tie eye is formed.

You can also add a blade to the forward part of the upper arm, make a kink in the wire, and then continue as before to make a two- or three-blade style. Another way to separate blades in any two- or three-blade spinnerbait is to use bearing beads next to the clevis, separated by thin plastic or metal tubing.

One easy way to add extra blades to produce a spinnerbait with a wild action is to use a three-way swivel and add a blade (using a jump ring or split ring) to each of two eyes, adding the swivel to the arm with the third eye. The result will be blades that rotate at the same time they move around each other. The same or different sizes, styles, and finishes can be used in the choice of the two blades. Typically, different sizes, styles, and colors are used for maximum visual and vibration effects.

Another way to add spinner blades to a tandem spinnerbait is to use a swivel or snap swivel in place of the clevis. Thread a bead or two on the upper shaft, add a swivel or snap swivel, then another bead or two (or whatever you wish to used to produce the spacing desired), and then finally make the J bend in the wire to finish the spinnerbait with the larger tail blade. Add a small spinner blade to the snap swivel, or use a split ring to join a blade and the swivel eye to complete the lure.

Extra blades are not usually added to buzzbaits, with one exception. This is to add a single spinner blade to the end of the wire, as in making a single-blade spinnerbait. This is in addition to the single delta or double-counter blades on the typical bent-arm buzzbait, and does give the lure a little additional flash. Usually small blades are used, of any style or finish. A variation of this idea is to add two blades to two eyes of a three-way swivel, attaching the third eye to the end of the arm of the buzzbait. These blades are usually small but can be of matching or different styles or finishes for endless combinations. Since buzzbait wire is often heavier than spinnerbait wire, take care in forming the eye for these variations. You may have to use heavier round-nose pliers, or to form part of an eye, add the swivel, and then close the eye with flat-nose pliers. Another technique is to use a small torch to heat and soften the wire, then make the bends while the end of the wire is still hot.

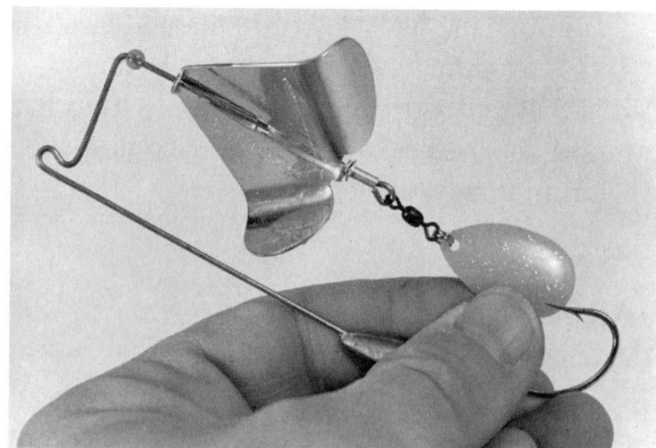

Variations in buzzbaits. Here a single spinner blade is attached by a swivel to the end of the buzzbait arm. A standard delta-wing blade is used.

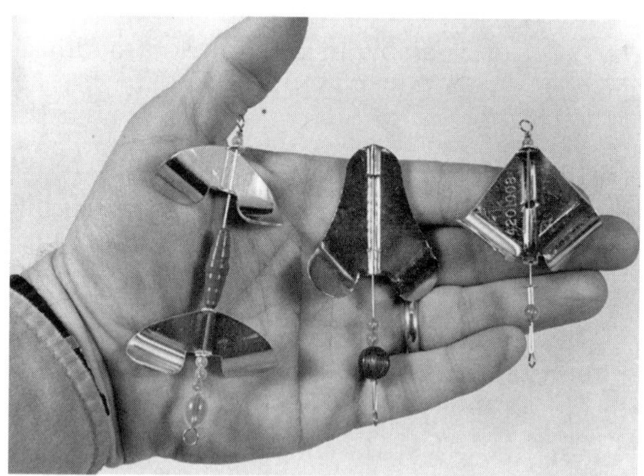

Three styles of separate buzzers that can be added in front of any lure, including spinners, spinnerbaits, spoons, and jigs. Left, double-wing counter-rotating blades with a red body in between; center and right, single delta blades. All make it easy to add lures through a snap or coil-spring fastener.

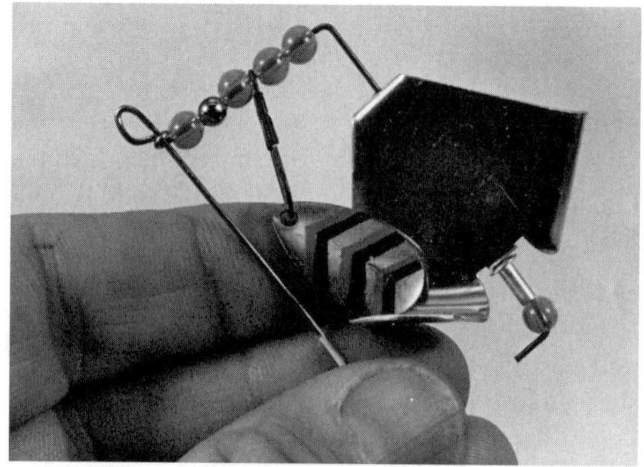

Delta-wing buzzbait with a homemade click blade added using a snap and standard spinner blade.

It is difficult to make blade additions to in-line buzzbaits, but one possibility is to thread a regular spinner blade on a clevis (with bearing beads fore and aft), make a slight kink in the wire to prevent pressure on these parts, and then add the single delta or double-counter blades to the shaft. The single spinner blade will rotate while the propeller-type delta or counter blades will spin on the shaft. This will make for a slightly larger, longer, and bulkier-looking lure, but one that's ideal for pike and muskie.

Weight-forward or walleye-style spinners typically have one spinner blade on the shaft behind the weighted head, but more can be added. Two blades on clevises are possible, separated by bead spacers, a tubing spacer, or a dot of solder on the shaft and between the two blades. It is also possible to use one or more small propeller blades or even small buzzbait blades, although this is seldom seen. Because these lures are fished on or close to the bottom, the spinner blades that hug close to the shaft are more practical than the broader propeller blades.

Spinner blades placed on the hook are a possibility for all of these lures. Usually small blades are best to add a little flash to the lure. These can be forced over the hook barb, or a folded clevis can be forced over the hook point and barb. Other attachments can include small red or other-colored plastic tags, chamois, or the Dri-Rind-type tails and split lengths of red or colored plastic tubing.

Protecting spinnerbait swivels from weeds and algae is easy by using discarded ballpoint pens. The tapered end cut from a ballpoint pen is used as shown to slide over the wire before the blade is added to the shaft. Make sure the cut-off pen end will only cover the swivel, not interfere with the blade rotation.

Variations in Blades

Although all the assembly instructions and examples so far have included the standard commercially available spinner blades in basic styles (mostly willowleaf, Colorado, and Indiana), it is possible to make blades by using the techniques outlined in chapter 8. Usually the cost of spinner blades makes this uneconomical.

It is also possible to make different blades such as those now beginning to be seen on some commercial lures. One of these involves a flat rectangular piece of sheet metal twisted into a spiral. The resultant spiral causes the blade to rotate when the spinnerbait is retrieved. A hole punched into the center of one end allows for attachment to a swivel or snap swivel.

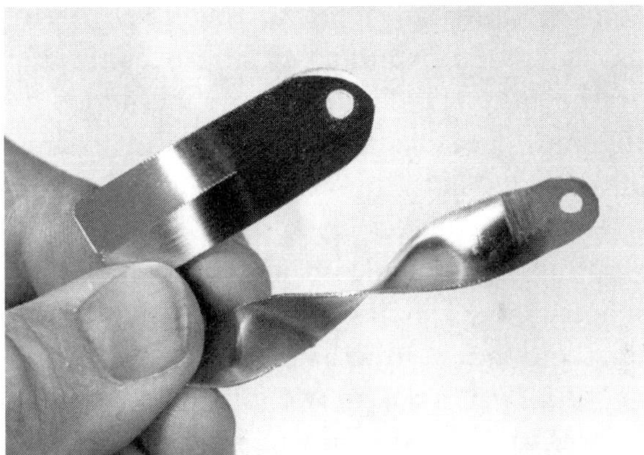

Different types of blades for spinnerbaits can be made using scrap sheet metal. These were made from scrap sheet metal. The one on the left has a split end to form two blades; the one on the right is twisted. Both rotate on their own axis when attached to the end of an arm with a swivel.

Another method involves using a similar flat rectangular sheet of metal and cutting it lengthwise halfway through the metal. Spreading these cut ends in opposite directions results in a propeller blade that will rotate through the water. Punch or drill a hole in the opposite uncut end to attach to the spinnerbait. Rectangles of metal about ½ inch by 2 inches are best for most of these blades, although any size rectangle can be used.

Variations in Wire Forms, Eyes, Arms

Arms on spinnerbaits and buzzbaits can be bent at various angles for optimal performance in the water. Often spinnerbait wire must be bent sharply at the junction with the lead head so that the hook is in line with the retrieve direction of the lure.

Double-arm spinnerbaits, in which one blade is at the end of each arm, can be molded, although this is not typical. One way to do this is to use two wires in the mold that are connected to the hook eye. These wires must be lighter than the wire that would normally be used, or they will not fit or allow the mold to be closed properly, thus causing flash on the lead head. Once these wires are molded in, it is easy to wrap an eye with them and then separate them so that they extend to each side of spinnerbait and over the top of the hook. Then blades can be added to the end of each arm as per the instructions of a single-blade spinnerbait. Though this is seldom seen, blades can also be added to the shaft, using the same lineup of bearing beads, spacers, and clevises as used for double- or tandem-blade spinnerbaits.

One way to add two blades on double arms is to add a jointed wire to the upper arm with a blade at each end of the wire. To do this cut back the upper arm, make a slight bend about ¾ inch from the end and a second bend about ¼ inch from the first. These bends will be the beginning of a triangle in the end of the wire. Before proceeding, form a tight coil spring in the center of a straight spinner or spinnerbait wire using a wire former or round-nose pliers. Slide this wire onto the straight length of the upper arm and then finish the bend on the upper arm with pliers. Cut any excess wire if necessary. Bend the two end wires at a slight backward angle, and add spinner blades to the ends.

Another way to do this is to mold or buy a standard single-wire spinnerbait wire form and use the upper arm to wrap a very tight multiple wrap (almost like a tension spring). This

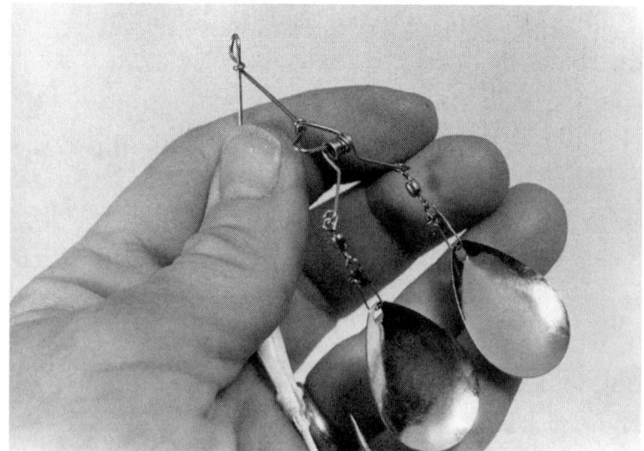

Another method of making a double-arm, double-blade spinnerbait by forming a "stirrup" in the end of a short wire and then adding a double-arm attachment, as shown. The coiled center is made in the same manner as making a spring with round-nose pliers; the other bends and arm lengths are easily made.

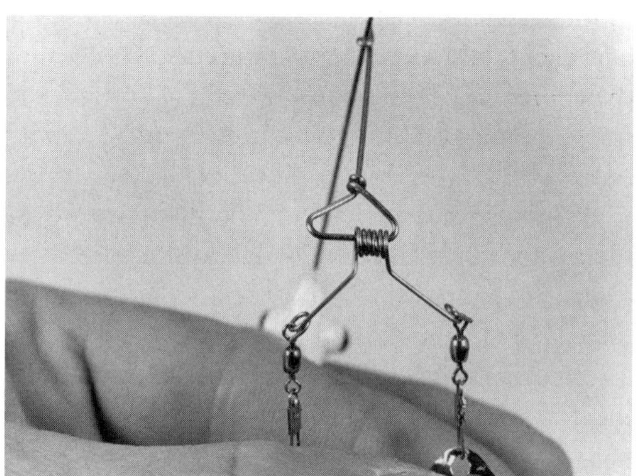

Details of above to show the various bends and wire forms.

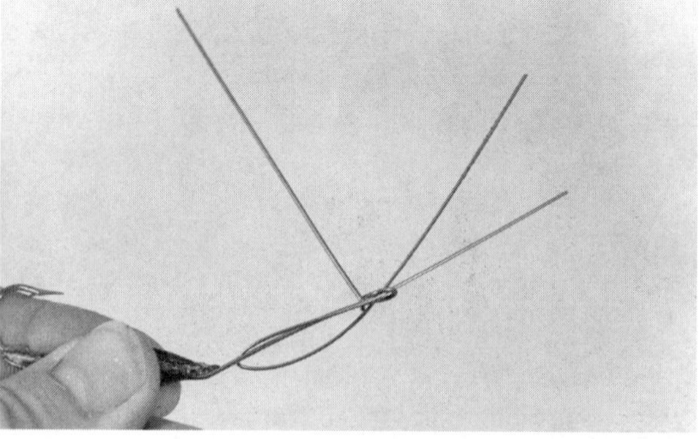

Making a triple-arm, triple-wing spinnerbait. Doubled spinnerbait wire is placed over the lower arm and up through the line-tie. For this it is best to have the line-tie in a horizontal plane instead of the standard vertical plane.

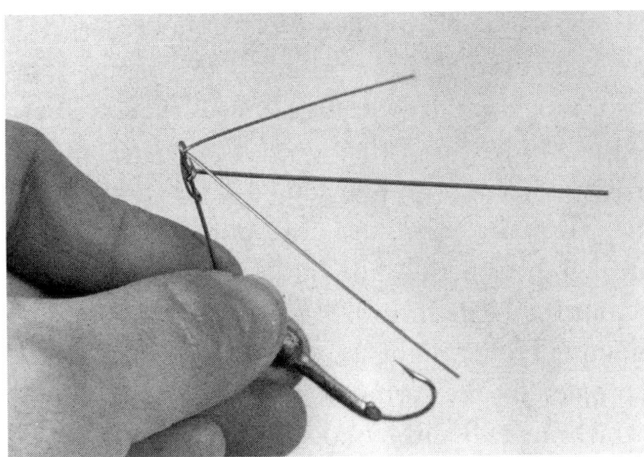

Completed three-arm spinnerbait body in which the two arms have been pulled tight and bent back and at an angle. Single or double blades can be attached to each arm.

wrap must be at right angles to the axis of the wire. Run a separate wire through this spring-like wrap, center it, and make a slight bend on each side of the wrap. Then the ends of this wire are used for blade attachment to make a free-swinging twin-blade spinnerbait. This method has been used successfully commercially.

You can make spinnerbaits with three arms—a technique just recently seen commercially. To do this use standard spinnerbait wire to make a typical spinnerbait bend in the wire with a typical looped eye. To add the two additional arms, use thinner, lighter wire and thread the wire through the eye, around the rear of the lower shaft wire, and then up through the eye going in the opposite direction of the original wire.

It often helps to make a sharp bend in the light wire so that the two ends are parallel and then run the two ends up through the eye in opposite directions so that the wires exit the eye in opposite directions. Bend these wires in the plane or direction you wish, and add single or double blades to them along with the main central wire.

Another way to do this is to make a wrapped eye but turn the eye at right angles to the plane of the spinnerbait and run the wires up through this eye or line-tie. The end result is the same in both cases.

You can make buzzbaits with free-swinging blades so that the buzzbait may be used as a surface lure that will sink and "helicopter" down into a hole. To do this, clip the upper arm of the buzzbait off short and make a simple loop or eye in the end. Then add the buzzbait blade or blades onto a separate wire shaft and form an eye in it that is attached to the loop in the upper wire arm. The result is a buzzbait that will track straight when used on the surface (like a normal buzzbait) but will swing up from water pressure to helicopter on the fall.

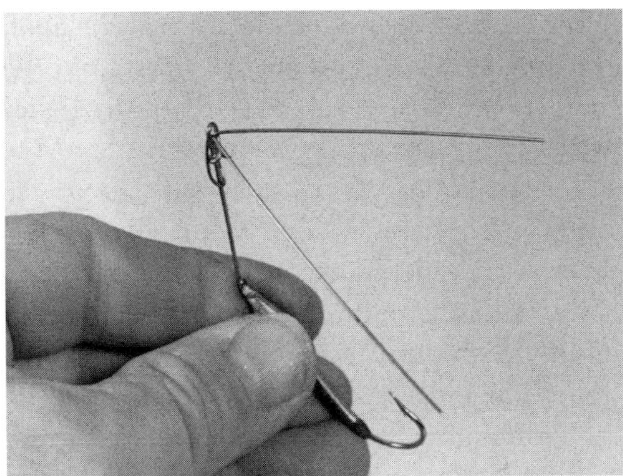

By clipping the center arm of the above arrangement, it is possible to make a double-arm spinnerbait.

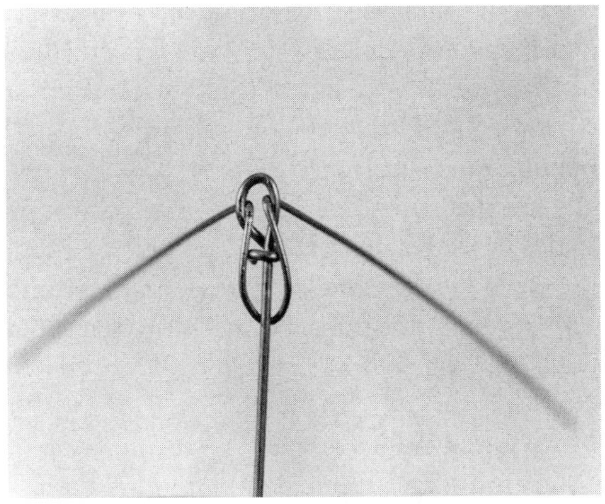

Detail of the double-arm arrangement to show the position of the two added wires. The same would be true for a triple-arm spinnerbait, by leaving the center arm long.

Cable Construction

Spinnerbaits can be made using cable in place of stiff wire. Any size cable can be used, although nylon-covered cable about twenty- to thirty-pound test is best. You will also need leader sleeves matched for the wire size. You can make an eye or loop on the hook and mold the wire into the lead head, or you can use a standard jig with the desired head shape and attach the cable to the external hook eye with leader sleeves. To do the first, make sure the cable is secure in the mold so that it will not pull out later. For the latter method, thread a leader sleeve on the end of the cable, thread the cable through the hook eye, and bend it sharply about ½ inch from the end. Thread this end back through the leader sleeve, and crimp the sleeve to secure.

To make an eye for a line-tie, there are several possibilities. One is to thread the wire through a leader sleeve once and then once again in the same direction to make a loop of cable. Crimp the leader sleeve to keep the cable from sliding. A variation of this is to thread the cable through a stirrup clevis or swivel before going through the leader sleeve the second time. Use a bearing bead above and below the clevis. Then the clevis or swivel may be used for the line-tie. Thread bearing beads, a spinner blade/clevis, and more bearing beads onto the cable, and then cut the cable where you wish the end of the wire to be. Make a leader-sleeve loop at the end, and at the same time secure the swivel holding the rear blade.

Another line-tie variation is to thread a leader sleeve on the cable, then a bearing bead, the clevis, a second bearing bead, and a second leader sleeve. Crimp the leader sleeves to hold the clevis in place on the cable.

Jig-Spinner Wires

You can use stiff spinnerbait wire to make jig-spinners that are in essence the wire end of a spinnerbait and are designed to be used with a standard jig to make up a flexible-head spinnerbait. These are available commercially, either as separate wires to use with any jig or as a complete jig-and-spinner wire. In most cases they are used in small sizes, primarily for crappie, panfish, sauger, and white bass. Since they are used with standard jigs, they do not have the smooth tapered heads found on standard spinnerbaits.

To make these, use any spinnerbait or spinner wire. Generally the lighter, springier wire of about 0.024 inch to 0.045 inch in diameter and designed for straight spinners is best, because the completed wire forms must have a catch for jig attachment. Begin by taking a short length (5 to 6 inches) of any light-spring stainless steel wire, and form an open or R-style eye, wrapped eye, or loop eye in the middle of the wire. For the jig attachment make a spring-closed open eye or clip eye at one end. To make the spring-closed open eye, first slide a coil-spring fastener onto the wire. This is used to lock the open eye in place, and the usual fastener inside diameter of 0.070 inch will fit any wire from 0.024 inch to 0.030 inch. One-half inch from the end of the wire, make a small kink using needle-nose pliers. Use the larger end of a pair of round-nose pliers to make a round eye in the wire, ending with a kink on the other side of the round eye so that the eye is centered on the wire shaft. The coil spring can then be slid down over both wires to lock the eye closed or slid up the wire to expose the open end for removal or the addition of a jig.

To make a clip eye, first bend one end of the wire in a sharp, small J shape. Make a sharp right-angle bend in this wire just above the J and then a second bend or open eye in the wire about ½ to ¾ inch from the J hook. Make sure this open eye is made so that, when it is complete, the J hook will clip onto the standing wire. This eye also allows the addition or removal of any jig head.

One or two blades and the appropriate hardware are added to the other end of the wire, using techniques already discussed for making one- or two-blade spinnerbaits.

It is also possible to make these spinnerbaits of cable by using cable techniques and a clevis for the line-tie. Since you cannot make a coil-spring open eye or clip eye on the end of the wire, you can use leader sleeves for a permanent attachment to the jig head or to attach a snap that in turn allows attachment and removal of the jig head.

Variations in Hooks

An unusual variation in spinnerbaits is to make them with a large blade and a lot of bearing spacers on the upper arm so that the blade is attached close to the center of the lure or at the fork of the two arms, with the hook attached to the upper arm to make a lure with two opposing hooks, almost like ice tongs. The hook can be soldered to the eye in the wire to keep it from flopping around and snagging on the lower hook. An easier way to do this is to use a short length of rubber or plastic tubing first threaded on the wire, then backed up over the wire/hook-eye joint to hold the hook straight and in place. This type of lure was manufactured some years ago, with only fair commercial success, but it can be fashioned by any tackle hobbyist.

Some hook variations are obvious. Stinger hooks on spinnerbaits and buzzbaits are well known, although some of the methods of placing them there are not. Any single hook can be placed on any spinnerbait or buzzbait, provided that the eye of the stinger hook is large enough to fit over the barb of the fixed hook. Even this can be adjusted either by slightly opening the eye of the stringer hook or bending down the barb of the fixed hook.

Once you bend down the barb of the fixed hook, you can open it again by prying with a knife blade. You can open the eye of a stinger hook by using wire cutters, using them as prying levers by placing the cutter jaws at the open end of the hook eye and gently squeezing to pry open the eye. Do this with care, because some brittle hook eyes may shatter. With this as with all tackle-making operations, use goggles for eye protection. Once it's on the fixed hook, the stinger-hook eye can be closed with pliers.

This method of attaching free-swinging stinger hooks does allow for tangling and snagging, so some means of stabilizing the hook is a must. There are several methods to do this. One is to use a paper or leather punch and punch plastic discs out of a coffee-can or similar plastic lid. These discs are then given a center hole with an awl and placed on the fixed hook both above and below the stinger hook. They will help stabilize the stinger hook on the bend of the fixed hook but will still allow it to swing from side to side. A better method is to use a small piece of rubber (preferably) or plastic tubing that will just fit over the eye of the stinger hook. Forcing the eye on the fixed hook with this tubing in place helps stabilize the hook in line with the lure. An even better method is to use a slightly longer piece of tubing (about 1½ inches) and thread the fixed hook through ¼ inch of the tubing. Thread the tubing partially onto the fixed hook, place the eye of the stinger hook in the opposite end of the tubing, and then impale this stinger hook on the fixed hook. Slide the tubing up on the shank of the fixed hook to keep the stinger hook in line with the lure at all times.

Some alternatives are to use a small scrap piece of plastic worm over the eye of the hook or a longer 1½-inch length threaded onto the fixed hook to stabilize the eye of the stinger hook, as with the tubing above. In any of these methods, the stinger hook can be point-up or point-down, although point-up is the standard method.

Other possibilities for hooks include using double hooks or treble hooks for stinger hooks or using these hooks on a short length of heavy leader (usually no longer than 2 or 3 inches) snelled to both the shank of the fixed hook and to the stinger hook.

It is also possible to make lures with free-swinging hooks. This is standard on in-line spinners and can be added when molding spinnerbaits and buzzbaits by molding the heads with a wire eyelet form (you will have to make these) in the head in place of a hook. Then use a split ring to attach a free-swinging single or double hook. An alternative to this is to use a long wire form and run the wire straight through the head cavity to make a long J-shaped eye in the end. To keep the lead head from sliding on the wire, bend a small kink at the spot that is in the center of the lead head. Then attach the hook to the exposed wire eye.

Skirts

Skirts for spinnerbaits and buzzbaits are typically slipped on following the assembly of the arms and blade components in the finished lure. These use the rubber or plastic-fringe skirts that will slip easily onto the collar of any spinnerbait or buzzbait. Exceptions include skirts that are tied permanently onto the lure, those that use the small rubber O-rings that are slid up or rolled onto the collar, and those that use filament rubber.

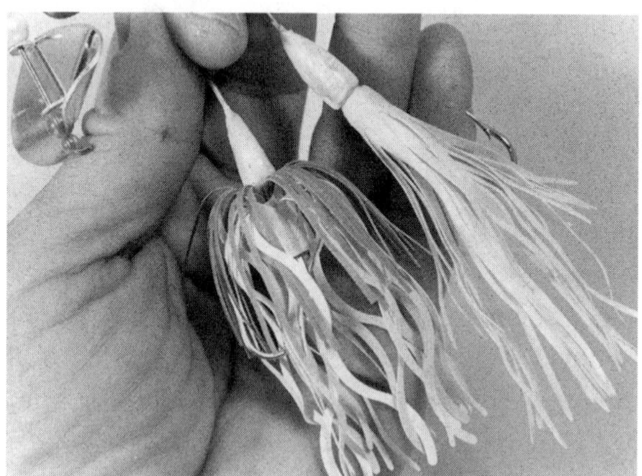

Two methods of adding skirts to spinnerbaits and buzzbaits. Left, reversed style for more bulk and flare; right, standard style that makes for a slimmer profile with less action.

To tie a skirt onto a spinnerbait or buzzbait, apply the same techniques used for tying on jig and bucktail skirts. Begin by wrapping the thread around the lead collar several times, and secure by wrapping over these previous wraps. Continue with several wraps to firmly secure the thread, and then tie in the skirt materials. Skirt materials of fur, artificial fur, saddle hackle, nylon, Mylar, or metalized fibers can all be used. Hold the skirt material over the collar, make several turns of thread around it, and do some adjusting to make sure it completely covers the lead collar. Clip off any excess material forward of the collar, wrap completely to cover the skirt material, and tie off with half-hitches. Once the skirt is tied off, finish with fly-tying head cement, clear or colored nylon-based fingernail polish, paint, or epoxy finish.

Filament rubber skirts are made with a special spreading-pliers tool, and when finished they are rolled or slid up onto the lure collar.

In-line buzzbaits can be made jointed (left) or on a single straight-through wire (right). Any standard buzzbait blade style can be used.

7
Soft-Plastic Lures

Introduction • Tools • Materials • Parts • General Molding Techniques • Steps in Molding Representative Plastic Lures • Lures with Two or More Colors • Molding Round Lures • Two-Piece and One-Piece Plaster Molds • Molding in Hooks and Leaders; Making Worm Rigs • Variations in Worms and Worm Rigs • Kits

Basic Tools

- Plastic or rubber one-piece molds
- Two-piece molds
- Injector for two-piece molds
- Melting pot
- Stirring sticks

Helpful Tools

- Hot plate or special melting stove
- Special plastic-melting furnace
- Gloves
- Cooling pan
- Pizza cutter
- Scissors
- Threading needle
- Electric heat-melt-cement gun

INTRODUCTION

Many anglers who buy soft-plastic worms, grubs, and minnows are not aware that worms just as soft, just as good, and in a variety of colors and sizes can be made at home for a few pennies each. And although worms and molds for making them are popular, it is also possible to

Some molds and materials, along with pots that are sold for the purpose of molding soft-plastic lures.

make a wide variety of soft freshwater and saltwater plastics that include worms of all lengths and styles—curved-tail worms, grubs, shrimp tails, minnows, eels, snakes, spinnerbait tails, frogs, salamanders, lizards, crayfish, egg sacks, and some larger saltwater soft plastics. In addition, you can make your own molds for lures for which commercial molds are unavailable.

Only a few tools and parts are needed, along with some easy-to-obtain molding plastic, colors, and scents. The procedure is simple and quite safe and makes it easy to produce quantities of soft plastics in any color and style desired.

TOOLS

The tools needed for making soft-plastic lures include molds, injectors, pots, and stirrers.

Molds. Molds for making soft-plastic lures used to be available only in one-piece styles where you poured the molten plastic into the open mold, filling it and making a worm or other lure with a half-body molded on one side but with a flat surface on the open side of the mold. These were (and still are) made in a shiny hard plastic, a more-flexible shiny plastic, and aluminum. These one-piece molds facilitate the direct pouring of molten plastic from the pot or ladle. These molds are available from the M-F and mail-order tackle companies that carry rod and lure components and parts. Two-piece molds to make round lures by using an injector are available from suppliers such as Jann's Netcraft, Mud Hole, and Hagen along with other companies that sell component parts for making lures and rods.

Open-face molds are just that—open on one side of the mold cavity. While most commercial worms today are injection-molded in round multiple-cavity two-part molds, originally they were made using the open-mold method. The results from one-piece molds are semiround worms, although the molds are designed to make a worm as close to round as possible.

Two-part molds are made with registration pins and locking plastic C-clamps to hold the two sides together. These molds will form a completely round worm. These are available from Jann's Netcraft and Hagen's as well as many tackle shops and mail-order companies. Most require an injector tool to squirt the soft plastic into the sprue or gate of the mold. Those that do not require a separate injector have a built-in reservoir on one side of the mold into which a fitted plunger inserts to inject the plastic. Some of these are fitted together with wing nuts to hold the two parts together. Those by Jann's and others have a built-in injector; the molten plastic is poured into the injector, a plunger is added (almost like a medical syringe), and then the plastic is injected into the mold without under- or overfilling.

Injectors. These are used only with two-piece molds to inject the soft plastic. They work like a simple medical syringe, with a cavity and a plunger that pushes the liquid plastic through a small spout and into the mold.

Plastic-melting stove. Some companies sell these stoves for melting plastic in pots. In most cases they are identical to small single-burner hot plates. Most have an adjustable rheostat temperature control and will plug into standard 120-volt outlets.

Pouring pan. Any type of small flat-bottom aluminum pan can be used for melting plastic. Inexpensive cookware pots are fine, but some companies offer similar or smaller pots for melting smaller quantities of plastic. It is important to have a flat bottom on these pans, as well as some form of lip for easy pouring. In some cases it helps to use pliers to further accentuate this spout for easy pouring and cleanup.

Stirring sticks. Stirring sticks can be anything from Popsicle sticks, tongue depressors, and plastic straws (although usually these are too weak for good stirring) to scraps of wood or short sections of round wood dowels. The main thing is to have a stick that will allow you to stir completely and thoroughly as the plastic is being heated. It also helps to have some long stirring sticks to stir the liquid plastic in its container before it is poured into the pan for melting.

Glue gun. Glue guns used for regular hot-melt cement are useful for molding plastic lures. With

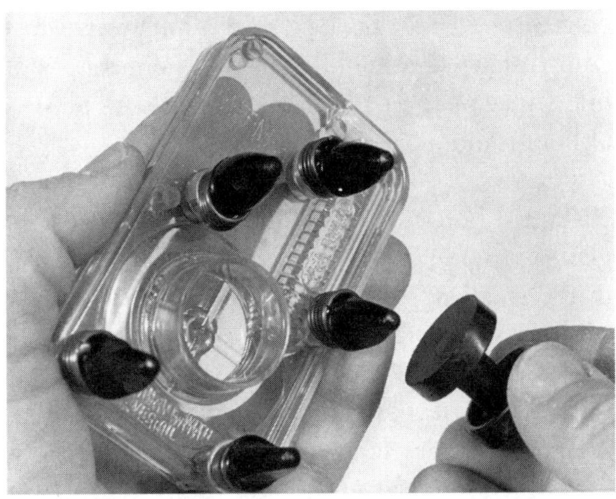

A two-piece mold from Hilts Molds for making round soft plastics. The black spring-loaded pins lock the two parts together; the plunger (right) is used to push molten plastic into the mold through an injection system.

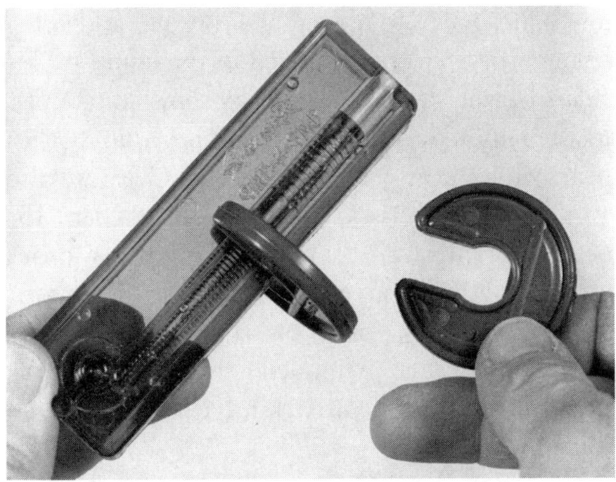

Another injection soft-plastic mold that uses a separate injection plunger system. The plastic C-clamps hold the two mold halves together.

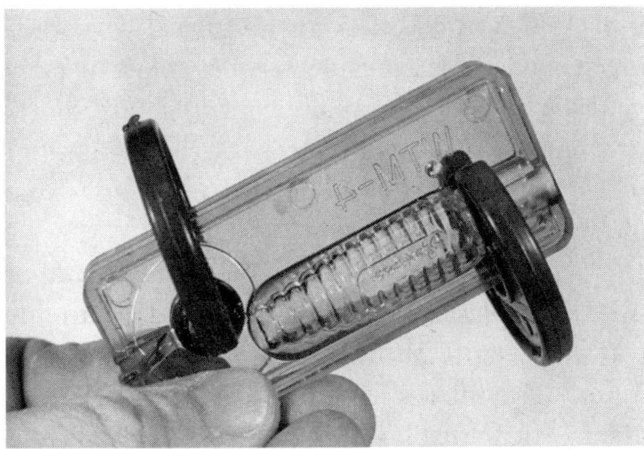

Soft-plastic mold with the two clamps in place.

a short "stick" of colored plastic inserted into the open end of the glue gun and with a follow-up "push stick," it is possible to dress up soft-plastic lures with spots and stripes of different colors using the heated gun to melt and deposit small amounts of the colored-plastic sticks in specific spots on the lure.

Repair tools. Fly tiers use cauterizers to sever and shape some products used in fly tying. Lure makers can use the same thing to modify or repair soft plastics. These small, battery-operated tools have a fine tip like that of an electronics soldering iron. It instantly becomes red hot when turned on to allow melting, sealing, and welding parts of soft-plastic lures to make them more useful or to repair them when damaged by a striking fish.

MATERIALS

Materials for making soft plastics include various types of plastic, along with additives.

Liquid plastic. Liquid plastic probably varies from manufacturer to manufacturer, but it is basically a milky-white liquid plastic or Plastisol with a petroleum base that turns clear and solid, though soft, when heated. When cooled it becomes the soft plastic that we know in soft-plastic lures. In most cases melting temperature is about 300 to 350 degrees Fahrenheit. It is usually sold in pint, quart, gallon, five-gallon, and fifty-five-gallon drum containers.

Unless you want clear lures, the plastic must have color added to it. It also can be mixed with additives containing hardener, softener, glitter, and various scents.

Some companies sell different formulas of liquid plastics, such as standard and super soft. The super-soft plastic will make the extra-soft worms popular today. You can make standard plastic soft by adding special softeners.

Biodegradable materials. Some companies such as Hagen's (through their Lorie Kay Bait Creations) have a molding material that is biodegradable, similar to some of the commercial brands of soft lures of a few years back. A quart of this material will make about ten batches of their lures with their lure molds, with each mold making ten to nineteen lures, depending on the type of lure being molded. Color and glitter can also be added to this material and to these molds to make a variety of lure types that will ultimately break down in the water.

Softeners. These are also sold in pint through five-gallon containers and are added to liquid plastic to make softer lures. Although there are no rules as to how much softener to add to liquid plastic, usually a mix of about one to two ounces of softener to a pint of plastic (a 1:8 or 1:16 ratio) is about right. More or less can be used as desired, or follow specific manufacturer's instructions.

As with liquid plastic, the softener is milky white. Naturally the softer the lure becomes the more fragile it is, and the more likely it is to tear and become abraded while fishing. Extra-soft lures are a must for some kinds of fishing, as in worm-fishing for bass.

Hardener. Also sold in pint through five-gallon containers, hardener is used to make harder, tougher lures. This is often a requirement for saltwater fishing, where durability is more important than softness and the fish are not as finicky as largemouth bass. The hardener is also a milky-white liquid, and it is best to begin with a ratio of 1 or 2 ounces of hardener to 1 pint of plastic. Hardener is usually added to the cold, raw liquid plastic before melting, but be sure to follow specific manufacturer's instructions.

Worm oil. This is not used for molding but in the packaging of worms to make them seem more slippery and lively. Too much will make the worms and the packaging seem slimy; none at all will make it difficult to remove the worms from a plastic bag. Worms can be soaked in the oil, or the oil can be added to the worms when they are packaged.

Colors. Although the liquid plastic is milky in color in the bottle, it becomes clear when melted. Therefore color must be added to the lure. Most available colors are highly concentrated, so a little bit goes a long way. Most companies recommend a starting point of about one ounce of color added to one gallon of plastic, although more or less can be used.

Colors are available in 1-, 2-, 4-, 16-, and 32-ounce bottles. Some companies sell colors in glass jars; others provide plastic squeeze bottles in the smaller sizes, with dropper spouts for easy application. Typical standard colors include black, blue, green, purple, red, yellow, white, strawberry, watermelon green, pink, brown, silver, orange, natural, avocado green, amber brown, golden yellow, lemon yellow, lime green, strawberry red, motor oil, violet, violet grape, grape, and black grape. Some companies supply colors in both opaque and translucent shades, although the opaque colors can be used in very small amounts to make translucent lures. Fluorescent colors are available in red, yellow, blue, green, pink, orange, purple, and other colors. These colors are added to the liquid plastic *before* heating (recommended by some companies, insisted upon by others). Standard pearl, along with pearl white, pearl yellow, and pearl silver, are also available to give plastic lures a pearl-like sheen. The pearl colors are available in liquid or powder forms, of which a small amount is added to the plastic or to other colors. Some companies recommend ¼ teaspoon to a small pan filled halfway with plastic. The dry pearl can be mixed into clear plastic for a different look.

Glow-in-the-dark pigment is also available to make lures that will glow for a while after exposure to light. The pigment is available in liquid or powder forms and can be added to paint or to liquid plastic. In addition to the typical yellowish-green shade, it is available in other colors, usually yellow and red. Phosphorescent lures are illegal in some areas—be sure to check the regulations where you'll be fishing before making lures that glow in the dark.

Glitter. Glitter is nothing more than metal or metalized plastic flake that can be added to any soft-plastic lure. The soft-plastic parts catalogs list a few colors such as silver, gold, blue, black, and green, but glitter is also available from craft and garment shops (it is used to decorate clothing) in other colors, including pink, yellow, bronze, brown, chartreuse, and purple, usually in ½- or 1-ounce bottles. It can be added to liquid plastic before or after heating. If using craft store glitter, try it on one or two lures before molding a whole batch to make sure it won't cause a reaction or other problems. Glitter sold by the tackle crafting companies is designed to work effectively with the soft-plastic and lure molds.

Glitter can imbue worms with a "salt-and-pepper" look if used in quantity or in larger size particles. Glitter also can be added to wet paint on lures or mixed with a clear sealer and added to plugs. More on these applications is found in chapter 15.

Scents. Scents can be added to liquid plastic before or after heating or to finished worms. Available scents include anise, strawberry, licorice, wild cherry, raspberry, cheddar cheese, and fish. Unless they specifically recommend or state that they will not harm plastic worms, do not use the spray or dip scents used in fishing. These in concentration may cause some worms to "melt." Adding scents to a liquid plastic formula or to a bag of worms after molding is counterproductive. Scent can, however, be sprayed onto a worm during fishing. The scents designed to be used with worms are usually sold in 1-, 2-, or 4-ounce bottles and are highly concentrated; only a few drops per pan of plastic are needed in most cases.

Salt. Standard table salt can be added to liquid plastic. Usually up to 30 percent salt by volume can be added to any soft-plastic lure. As with commercial salt worms, this is supposed to increase strikes.

PARTS

Although no parts as such are required for molding worms or soft-plastic lures, additional parts can be used in assembly or when making rigged lures. Examples include worm rigs that use molded-in hooks or incorporate blades and beads strung on mono on the rigged lure for added attraction. Most worms used to be made and sold this way, although now most worms sold for that purpose are designed for specific applications, such as walleye or "do-nothing" bass fishing.

The parts are no different from those used for making spinners. Complete descriptions of these parts can be found in chapter 3, but here are some generalities.

Monofilament. Monofilament line, usually about thirty-pound test, is used for the rigging and is molded into the worm. Any mono can be used, and you can choose heavier or lighter pound test as required.

Wire. Wire is seldom used for a worm rigging, but that doesn't mean you can't use it if you so desire. Usually twenty-pound cable, uncoated or nylon-coated, is used for this.

Beads. Beads of plastic, metal, and glass are commonly used for color, flash, and as bearings for blade clevises on worm rigs. A wide range of sizes and types can be found in any lure-parts component catalog. Floating beads are popular with some rigs, and these also are available in a variety of colors. One way to add beads to worm rings after the fact is with U.S. Tackle Speedo Beads, which can be added or removed at will. They float and come in two sizes.

Blades. Blades vary widely, although typical blades are generally small and of the same type as is commonly used for spinners. These include Colorado, Indiana, and willowleaf styles. Some worm rigs also use propeller blades. These are all small size and are usually the same blades used for propeller top-water plugs.

Clevises. Clevises for mono or wire rigs should be of the folded style. They have a wider bearing surface on the mono and thus are less likely to wear through it, as might occur with the thinner stirrup clevises. Several sizes are available, and the size must be chosen both to fit the mono or wire and to provide clearance without binding for the chosen blade.

GENERAL MOLDING TECHNIQUES

Because you will be working with a hot substance, it pays to use caution when molding soft-plastic lures. Use goggles, wear gloves when working with the hot pans used for melting the plastic, and wear an apron to protect against spills. You will also need a spacious work area. The same work areas recommended for molding bucktails and sinkers are fine—kitchen, basement, garage, deck or patio, carport, workshop. These should all have some ventilation (for this reason the kitchen is ideal) because there will be some smell and fumes with most soft-plastic molding.

The main work area should have a heat source, lots of counter space, and ventilation. Unlike with lead molding, a water source is desirable when working with plastics, since water is used in cooling the pans that hold the hot lures after they are removed from the mold.

The kitchen stove can be used for a heat source, but the key here is to keep the heat low and controlled. Unlike lead molding, where high heat will melt the lead quicker, too much heat when melting liquid plastic will scorch the plastic and ruin it—and fill the kitchen with fumes in the process.

If you mold in an area other than the kitchen, a variable-heat (rheostat) one- or two-burner hot plate is an ideal heater. It will allow heating to a controlled temperature, and you can work anywhere there is an electrical outlet. A one-burner hot plate is fine if you make only one color or finish molding in one color before starting another. If you make lures in which two colors are used in a single mold (such as a firetail worm), you will need a two-burner model because two pans of liquid color will have to be kept hot at the same time.

Take care in heating, because overheating will lead to noxious fumes and some smoke. Also, the plastic is flammable, so low heating over an electric burner is usually safer than using an open flame.

Because of the possibility of fumes, make sure you have adequate ventilation, using the vent fan in the kitchen or making similar arrangements for fans and open windows in any other part of the house where you might work. Molding outside on a hot plate or camp stove (be careful of the open flames though) is ideal on calm days in mild weather.

Safety is important, because the liquid plastic and any additives will melt in the range of 300 to 350 Fahrenheit. The plastic can burn, though not badly, and it does cool quickly. As with molding lead, consider wearing a breathing mask, goggles, and even gloves.

You will need a shallow pan or cold water to cool the worms or soft-plastic lures. A shallow baking pan or similar container with sides about 2 inches high is ideal. A large pan is best, because you want the cooling plastic lures to lie naturally in it. If they cool in bent or contorted positions, they will remain that way and cannot be used.

Always start with very little color and make a test run of a lure or two to check the color. The color always looks different in a mass of plastic in the pan than it does in a single lure. If you have too little color, you can always add more; you can even remelt the test lure if you wish. If you have too much color, you then have to add large quantities of liquid plastic to dilute it. It's easier to start with a little color and add more as necessary.

Just as you can remelt a test lure, you can also save and recycle scraps left over from molding, but you *must* keep colors separate. If you don't, you'll end up with a brownish, muddy color.

Lubricate your molds, pans, and injectors periodically, using only liquid vegetable oil.

If you overpour so that some plastic flows beyond the mold cavity with open-face molds, you can salvage it. First allow the lure to cool and cure properly in the water pan, then lay it open, cavity-side down, and use a pizza-cutter wheel to trim around the edges. This is the fastest method, although trimming also can be done with scissors.

One problem many plastic molders have is plastic dripping from the spout after pouring. A suggestion for solving this is to use a paper towel, cloth, or small block of cured plastic to mop up any excess. Another possibility is to use a small rubber spatula like the ones used in cake making to scrape batter out of the bowl. This allows you to scrape up all the plastic and return it to the melting pan. It also helps if you bend the pouring

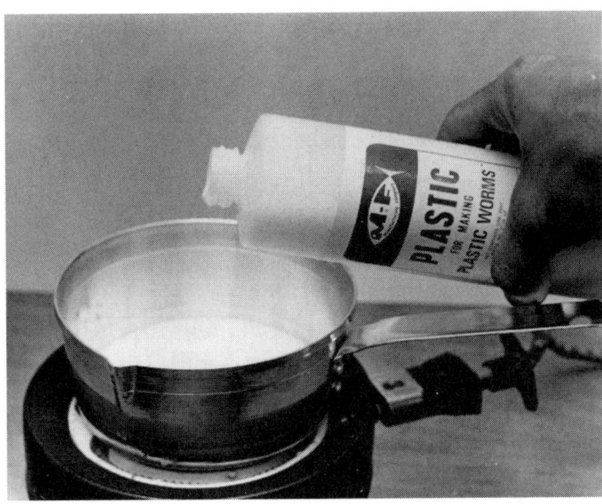

To mold, liquid plastic is poured into a pan, here heated on an electric hot plate. The liquid plastic is milky in color and consistency.

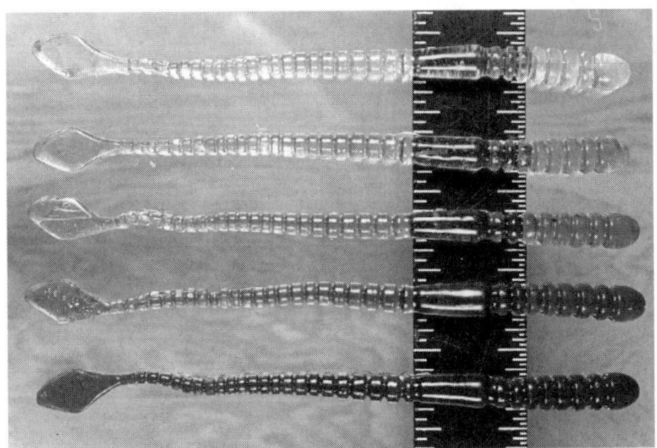

Different shades of worms can be made by using different quantities of color in the liquid plastic. Here the same worm is shown in five different shades.

spout to make it more pronounced to reduce or prevent dripping.

The secret of molding good lures is to make sure the liquid plastic is mixed and melted properly. The milklike (both in color and consistency) plastic is added to the pan, and the heat is started low and then gradually (very gradually) raised as the plastic melts. The plastic will go from a milky liquid to a thicker, somewhat lumpy consistency like that of warm tapioca pudding. Continue heating past this stage to bring the plastic to a smooth, syrupy consistency not unlike thick molasses or pancake syrup.

Add any desired hardener or softener at this time, followed by the color (although the fluorescent colors usually must be added before melting), which is mixed in thoroughly. Then add any scents, glitter, or other additives.

Note: While most scents, glitter, and color are added after the plastic has been melted, be sure to follow the manufacturer's directions. Plastics and additives may differ slightly according to manufacturer, and following directions is critical for good results.

Once the plastic contains the proper additives and you have tested a lure or two for color, you can begin molding. Some general tips for open-face molds follow.

- You may find that the larger size pans often used for melting plastic are too large to use easily for pouring, especially for small molds or fine details. Try using a small implement that you can dip into the main pan to get enough plastic to fill one mold cavity. Some possibilities here are gravy ladles, small aluminum measuring cups (¼- to ½-cup sizes are good), large spoons, and small tuna cans. In all cases, make a pronounced spout or reform the existing spout for good pouring. These smaller containers also allow you to pour closer to the mold, making for greater accuracy. Once you use these kitchen tools and pots or pans for molding plastic, do not ever again use them for food preparation. This is important for safety!

- Begin pouring at the tail end of the mold, particularly when making curved-tail worms, grubs, and similar lures. And when molding frogs, crayfish, and similar lures with fine or delicate parts, begin at the smallest parts of the mold cavity too. This is the preferred method because the liquid plastic will be at its hottest and most liquid when you begin the pour and will gradually cool as you continue to pour. This is particularly true if you pour from the smaller dipper ladles or pans. You want the hottest, most liquid plastic to fill small cavities. You can easily fill the main

To prevent burning and smells, use low heat to melt the plastic. The plastic will first turn thick and lumpy—like tapioca—then turn thin, clear, and smooth. Shown is the "tapioca" stage.

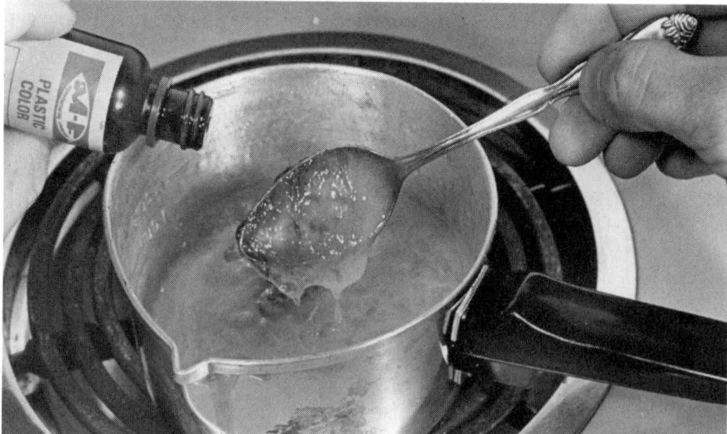

Checking the plastic again, this time heating on a stove. Heating on a stove does have some advantages, since the heat can be controlled more easily. Add any color at this stage.

Once the liquid plastic is smooth and the color mixed in, pour into any open-face molds by beginning at one end and working to the other.

cavity of the worm, grub, crayfish, or frog later.

- Don't mix and then store soft plastics of different colors together. The darker colors will stain or elute into the plastic lures of lighter shades or colors. Even if you mix colors of similar shade—red and orange, yellow and light green—the colors will still tend to mix and muddle slightly. One way to prevent this is to pour clear soft plastic and use glitter as the coloring agent. The Mylar, metallic, or plastic glitter is trapped in the plastic and cannot stain other lures. Thus glitter worms of green, blue, red, yellow, gold, and silver can be mixed and stored together, provided that the glitter was added to a clear plastic for pouring. Note that you usually have to use a lot more glitter to create a color than you would normally use in a light-colored or translucent soft plastic.

- Once lures are poured, allow the filled mold to cool for a few minutes. You can hasten this by placing the mold into the water pan, but this risks getting water into the mold. This is not dangerous, as it is with lead molding, but it will make for deformed lures if all the water is not removed from the mold before the next pour. Once the mold and lure are slightly cooled, you can remove the lure. To do this use your thumb or finger to roll the edge of the soft plastic lure up slightly, then grasp the lure carefully and slowly lift and pull it out. Do not use force, because this will stretch the final result. Immediately place the lure

Once the molds are completely filled, use a cloth or paper towel to wipe the lip to prevent spills and drips.

When working with curved-tail or detailed molds, begin filling at the tail or detail areas before filling the main body of the mold.

Once the molds are filled with liquid plastic, place them into a shallow pan of cold water to cure.

into the pan of water, and make sure it is lying horizontally and straight and is not in contact with other lures. Allow it to cure in the water until it can be handled without bending or deforming. This will take at least a few minutes. If you do get any deformed lures, once they are thoroughly dry you can put them back in the melting pot (same color of course) for remelting.

- For best results, use several molds on a rotation basis. This allows two or three molds and their contents to cure as you pour others, and you will not have to wait to remove a lure from a mold. One person in a team of two can do this, since there are no hooks added to the mold to slow down the loading and pouring process. (There are ways to mold in hooks, as will be covered shortly.)

- Because these are all open-face molds (there is no closed cavity, which would make a round lure) it helps to slightly overfill the cavity to make for a more rounded result. Although most commercial worms are made in two-part injection molds and come out round, the fact that your worms and grubs have a flat side will not affect your fishing. In fact, at one time all worms were made in exactly this way.

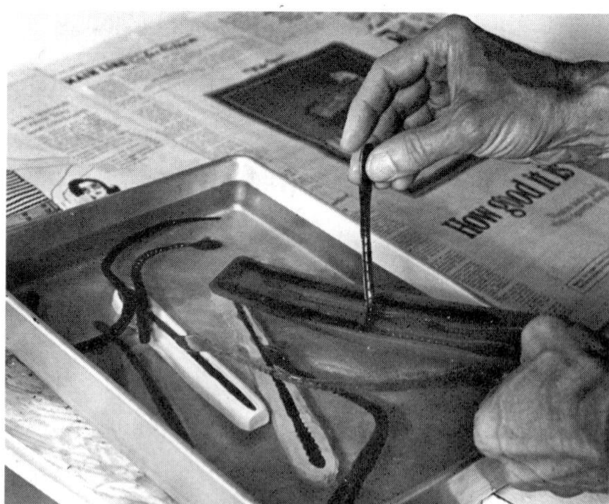

Once the soft-plastic lures are cool enough to remove, pull them out and put them in the water for additional cooling. The cool water also allows them to cool straight, preventing misshapen lures.

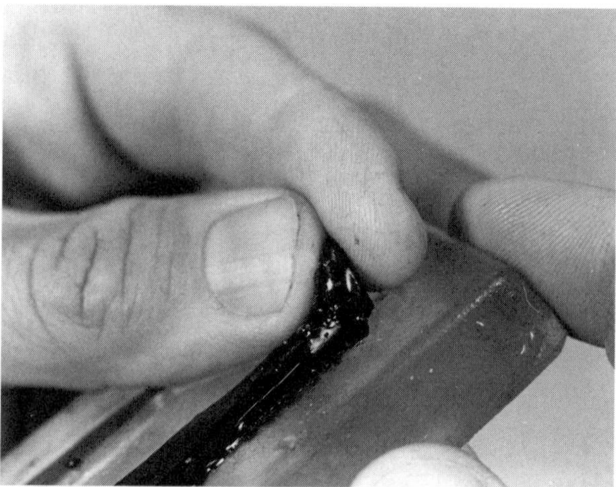

Begin to remove a soft-plastic lure from the mold by rolling one end of the lure out of the mold. Then grasp the lure and pull slowly and evenly to prevent stretching the soft plastic.

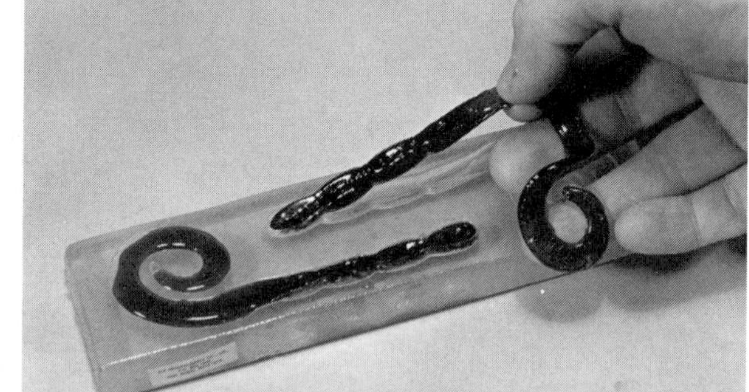

Lures being removed from the mold.

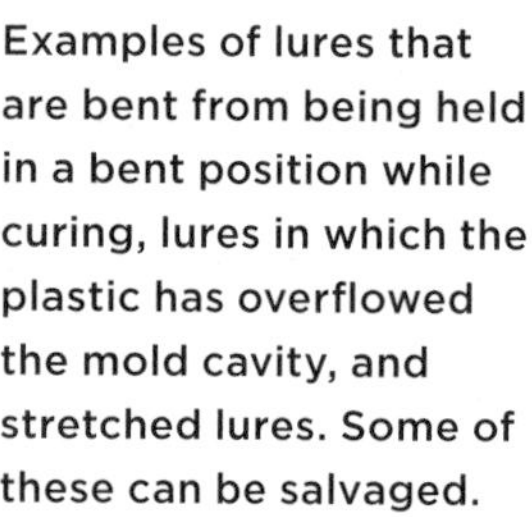

Examples of lures that are bent from being held in a bent position while curing, lures in which the plastic has overflowed the mold cavity, and stretched lures. Some of these can be salvaged.

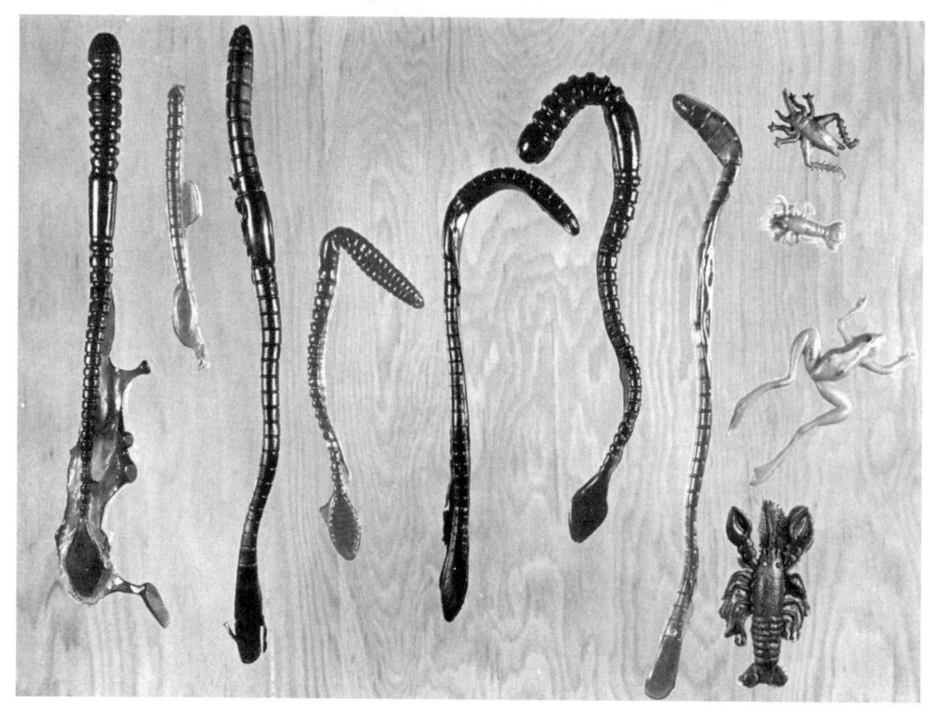

STEPS IN MOLDING REPRESENTATIVE PLASTIC LURES

The steps in molding soft plastics are simple. Use one of the heat sources outlined above to slowly heat the plastic to a syrupy consistency. Add color, glitter, scent, or other additives when required, usually after the plastic is melted. Use care in pouring, and pour first into the smallest parts of the mold cavity. Thus fill legs, antennae, tails on worms, or grub tails first, and then fill the body to slightly overflowing. Stop pouring, wipe the pan lip to prevent dripping, and place the mold in a large shallow pan of water to cool. Remove the mold from the pan, gently remove the lure, and place the lure horizontally in the same or another pan of water. Make sure the mold is clean and dry before preparing to pour another lure.

Another way to cool the mold with the lure without risking getting water in it is to place the mold on top of a tray of ice cubes or a block of ice. Once the lure is slightly cooled, it can be rolled out and floated in a pan of water.

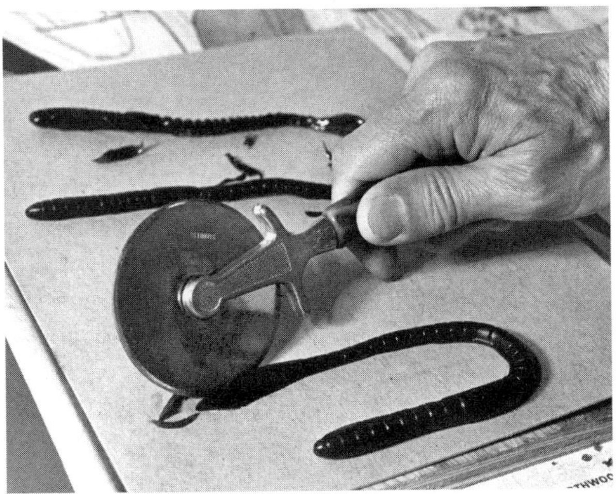

One way to salvage a lure in which the plastic has overflowed the mold is to use a pizza cutter to remove excess plastic.

LURES WITH TWO OR MORE COLORS

Lures can be made of two or more colors, with stripes and dots, or with different-color tails, as follows:

Blue worm with a red tail. For this you will need two pots of plastic, one red and one blue. First pour a small quantity of red plastic into the tail area, immediately place the red pan back on the heater, and fill the rest of the cavity with the blue plastic from the blue pan. The two colors of liquid plastic will meet and fuse.

You may wish to try this in reverse, pouring the blue body first, followed by the red tail. Depending on how your molds are made, you may find that pouring one way causes more "bleeding" or free-flowing into the other part of the mold cavity, thus not producing as good a result. Use the method that works best after trying both. If you do have to scrap some of these lures after a trial run or two, make sure you cut them exactly at the color joint to avoid contaminating one color with another when you remelt them.

This color technique works best with opaque or strong colors or at least an opaque or bright tail. Naturally, it can also be used to make two-color lures with the color joint at any point in the lure. Because some cavities fill from the bottom up, you may have to pour small quantities of each color several times to make for a sharp color separation.

Obviously this technique can be used with any color combination you desire.

Black worm with white stripe. Use two colors of plastic, white and black, and make them strong or opaque. Pour a thin band of white the whole length of the mold to make the white stripe, and replace the pan of white plastic on the stove. Allow the poured plastic to cool for a minute before pouring black into the mold, filling it to slightly overflowing as outlined earlier. Any combination of colors can be used.

Green frog with yellow legs and red eyes. You'll need three pots of colored liquid plastic for this lure, and like the two preceding lures, the colors should be opaque for the most striking results. First pour the yellow legs. Then use a toothpick or nail to remove enough plastic from the red pot to make red eyes in the mold at the proper spots. Allow the legs and eyes to cool slightly, and then fill the entire cavity with the green color. Similar methods can be used for molding different colors of fins, gill plates, and eyes on minnow molds and for various combinations of molds for salamanders, crayfish, jig tails, worms, grubs, and other shapes.

MOLDING ROUND LURES

It is possible to make completely round soft-plastic lures using a two-part mold and a simple method of injection molding. Such molds are available from Hilts (the same company that makes lead jig molds) under their Super Sport label. These molds are strong, clear polycarbonate in two parts, which are held together with simple plastic C-shaped clips that work like spring clamps. Older molds that use screws and wing nuts come with an open reservoir and plunger to inject plastic into the tail area of the mold cavity.

Holding the mold and the plunger, raise the mold to a vertical position and press the plunger firmly to fill the rest of the cavity with the plastic. The vertical maneuver is necessary because there are vent holds in the end of the mold (the upper end when the mold is in a vertical position), which must be filled with plastic. Stop pressing the plunger when the vent holes are full of plastic.

Allow the mold to cool completely in a vertical position before opening the mold cavity. Proper cooling will take about 2 minutes. There will be some shrinkage of the plastic in the vent holes, but this is normal.

Remove the wing nuts and open the mold. Use scissors or a razor blade to remove the excess plastic at the gate and the vent holes. Save this excess plastic and add it to the pan for remelting and reusing. Reassemble the mold for the next injection.

You can make two-color worms or lures with these molds as follows.

Open the mold and cut off the gate, the plastic at the vent holes, and also as much of the tail as you want to be a different color, without removing the molded lure. Use a razor blade, but cut carefully to keep from damaging the mold. It is best to cut on a slant to create more surface area for good adhesion with the next color. Close the mold, secure it with the wing nuts, add a small amount of a second color of plastic to the cup in the mold, and use the plunger to inject plastic into the tail area of the mold cavity. Then, holding the mold and the plunger, raise the mold to a vertical position and press the plunger firmly to fill the rest of the cavity with the plastic. Allow the plastic to cool, open the mold, and remove the lure.

The rest of the Hilts Super Sport molds use a separate injection system. This allows one injector to be used with a variety of molds to make a variety of lures. In addition, the injector is large enough to hold enough plastic to fill several mold cavities, speeding the operation, particularly if several different molds are used in rotation.

- **Prepare the liquid plastic.** Open the mold and spray the halves lightly with spray vegetable oil. (Do this only occasionally, as needed, to help ease removal of completed lures.) Close the mold and secure it with the C-clips provided. Spray the injector cavity and plunger with vegetable oil. Place the injector cavity on the table (the nozzle will be down) and fill it to within about ½ inch of the top with liquid plastic. Insert the plunger and turn the injector over so that the nozzle is up. (If some liquid plastic flows through the nozzle when it is down, remove the plastic carefully.)

- **Place the mold onto the nozzle tip.** (The mold will have one small hole designed to mate with the injector nozzle and one larger hole that is a vertical vent hole.) Place both hands on the mold and push it firmly and slowly down to compress the injector, which will fill the mold. Be sure to use both hands; trying this with one hand could cause you to tip the mold and spill the plastic. Continue pressing down until the vent hole is completely or partially filled.

Remove the mold from the injector and set it upright to cool for several minutes.

- **Use the same injector with more plastic on additional molds until you run out of plastic.** Once you are finished, allow the plastic in the injector to set up. Open the injector and remove the solid plastic with a thin bent wire. (A small wire with a hook on one end makes plastic removal easy.) Once the molds are cool, remove the C-clamps, open the mold, and remove the lure. If the mold is completely cool, cut off the excess plastic at the gate and vent holes. Add the excess to the remelting pan.

Two-colored worms and lures can be made with these molds with a procedure similar to that for the self-contained molds:

Open the mold and carefully (taking care not to damage the mold) cut off the tail or other part of the worm you wish to replace with a second color. Reassemble the mold and inject a second color into the mold. You can make three-color worms by repeating this step to produce a worm with a head, middle, and tail of three different colors.

You can make gradual color changes of two or more colors in one worm by injecting the mold halfway or one-third full with one color and then immediately following with another injector, previously prepared, with the second, and then even a third, color. You can create blood-line worms by filling a mold cavity to within 1 inch of the top with one color and immediately following with a second color, under pressure, to fill the worm with a contrasting-color centerline.

Some Hilts Super Sport molds have three injection gates. These are for three-tail trailers and salamanders. For these molds, first fill the side cavities with liquid plastic, and then inject plastic into the bottom gate to completely fill the mold. This allows you to make these lures with flippers and curved tails of a different color than used on the main body. Use the two-injector technique outlined above.

Hilts also makes a hinged aluminum two-part Scampee mold for making a saltwater twin-tail grub lure using harder plastic, which would be hard to inject without flash or leakage.

TWO-PIECE AND ONE-PIECE PLASTER MOLDS

You can make your own plaster molds for molding worms, grubs, and similar soft-plastic lures. Generally it is best to use commercial molds, because plaster molds will chip in time and produce less-than-perfect results. Using methods similar to those for making plaster bucktail molds, you can make two-piece molds using a commercial round-worm or two-sided lure as a model. (Complete details for making this kind of mold for worms and bucktails are described in chapter 16.)

Using such a mold is similar to the molding of bucktails, except that liquid plastic is used in place of lead. The soft plastic is prepared in the same fashion as for the one-piece molds. Clamp the two pieces of the plaster mold together with several rubber bands, and then stand the mold upright. Slowly and carefully pour the liquid plastic into it.

It is extremely important to have the liquid plastic properly prepared, with no lumps that might clog the mold before it is completely filled. A plastic lump may fill the sprue hole, preventing the passage of additional plastic and resulting in a defective, unusable lure.

If there is one trick to pouring, it is to pour the hot liquid plastic carefully down one *side* of the sprue hole and cavity. This allows the plastic to run all the way to the bottom of the mold cavity while also allowing air to escape through the sprue hole. If a lot of plastic is suddenly dumped into the sprue hole, it will clog the hole, preventing the escape of air and impeding the downward flow of the hot plastic. All too often the plastic will begin to cool and cure before the mold can be completely filled. You can drill or otherwise form a vent hole in the bottom of the mold; this sometimes lessens the problem, but the hole must be large. Otherwise the liquid plastic will not flow evenly to fill the mold cavity, or an air bubble will develop in the center of the worm.

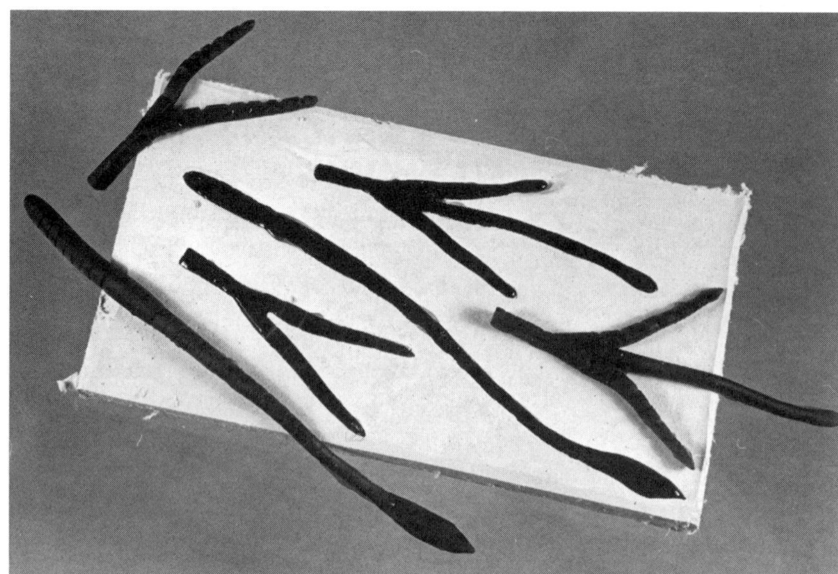

Plaster molds can be used (see chapter 16, "Making Molds for Lead and Soft-Plastic Lures"), but the cavity must be painted to avoid a matte finish on the worm body and leakage of the liquid plastic into the porous plaster. Parts of worms, as shown here, can be used to make "masters" for new types of worm molds. This is an open-face one-side mold.

If, after you follow the above instructions carefully, the mold cavity still does not fill with plastic, enlarge the sprue hole. (This operation is detailed in chapter 16.) I like the sprue hole in a two-piece plaster mold to be about the diameter of the head of the worm. It makes it easy to get perfect lures this way, and the excess plastic that accumulates is easy to cut off and reuse.

Plaster molds must cure in air—placing them into water to cool, as for plastic and rubber molds, would ruin them. Since the plaster molds are thicker, and since the two-part molds do not allow as much heat exchange, using them is slower than making plastic lures in commercial open-face molds. One solution, particularly since the two-piece molds are inexpensive to make, is to make a half dozen or so (of the same or different designs) so that you can mold in a rotation system so that the first mold will be cool and the lure cured enough for removal by the time you have poured the last mold. Another alternative is to use two-piece molds alternately with one-piece commercial molds.

Making one-piece plaster molds is also described in chapter 16. They are used in exactly the same way as rubber and plastic commercial molds except that they cannot be placed in water for cooling; they must be air-cooled and cured, as with the two-piece plaster molds.

These plaster molds can be used to make any type of soft-plastic lure, although they are probably best for making unusual lures for which molds are not available commercially.

MOLDING IN HOOKS AND LEADERS; MAKING WORM RIGS

All the soft-plastic lures described to this point are molded unrigged; that is, without the addition of hooks or snells. Most anglers prefer their lures this way, especially the worms, because it allows specific rigging for specific fishing situations or species sought.

Any soft-plastic lure can be molded in one-piece molds with hooks or snells in it. Complete worm rigs, with beads and blades, can be made up. Even without harness rings it is possible to mold in hooks or snells. The best way to do this is to buy rubber or plastic molds and slit each end of the mold to hold the leader in place during molding. You could also use a fine saw (like that from X-Acto) to cut a slit into the hard-plastic open-face molds for the same purpose.

To mold leaders or snells in place in a mold prepared this way, take an 18- to 24-inch length of fifteen- to thirty-pound-test monofilament (it should be stronger than the line used for fishing the lure) and snell a hook to the mono. Leave a

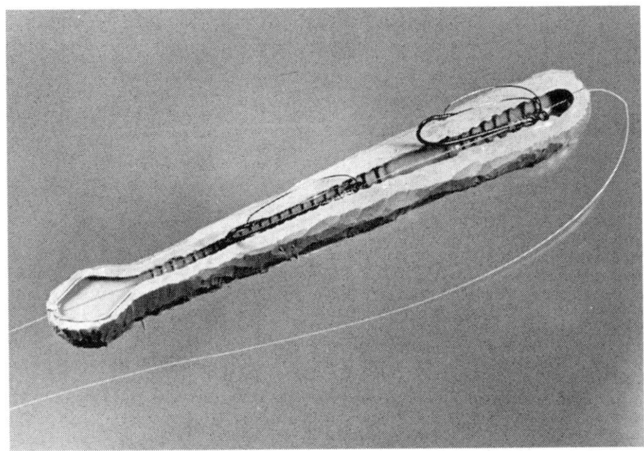

One way to make a rigged soft-plastic worm is to snell hooks with monofilament and place the mono straight in the mold cavity. Here a rubber mold allows small slits to be cut in each end to hold the mono securely.

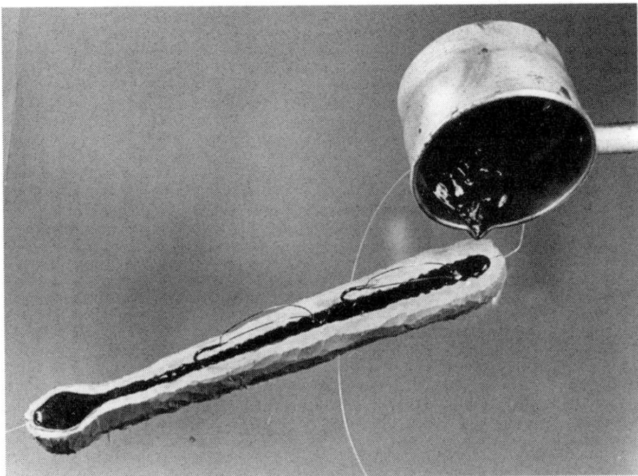

Filling the mold with liquid plastic, imbedding the hook shanks and mono in the plastic lure.

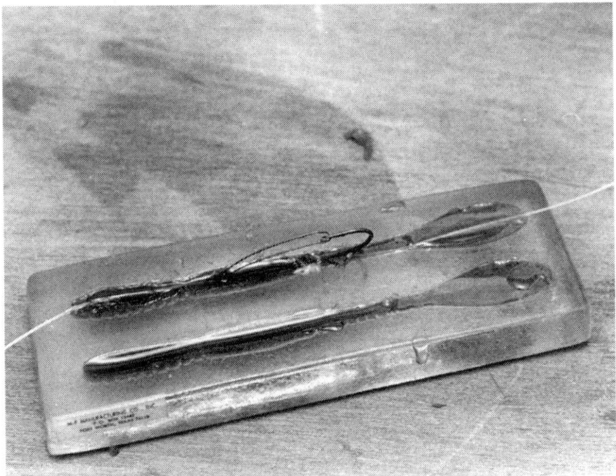

Another example of molding a mono-rigged hook, this time using a hard M-F mold.

long tail of mono that can be secured to the slit in the mold. One, two, or three hooks can be snelled to the hook, depending on the rig and the length of the worm. Slip the two ends of the mono into the slits at each end of the mold. Position the hooks in the mold cavity, and pour the plastic into the mold in the usual way. The result is a worm, minnow, or other lure with molded-in hooks and leader. This always makes for an exposed hook-point rig, but you can use plain hooks or those with wire weed guards. Once the lure is removed from the mold, clip the end of the mono at the tail.

To finish the lure, take the longer piece of mono (at the head of the worm or lure) and tie a loop knot or attach a combination of beads and blades. To make a complete rig, add several plastic beads and a propeller or spinner blade on a folded clevis. (The folded clevises will work better here than on spinner wire when making spinners.) You can rig these with any size, color, and type of beads and blades, although most are made with about a half dozen red plastic beads and a single spinner or propeller blade. Finish with a loop knot, using a figure eight, perfection loop, or surgeon's loop knot. An alternative is to tie on a barrel or ball bearing swivel using an improved clinch knot.

Another way to rig worms is after they are molded, using a tip from Bing McClellan, late president of Burke Lures. Bing developed and even sold for a while a worm rigger that consisted of a long needle, with the eye exposed, in a short wood-dowel handle. This tool can be made easily by pushing an upholstery needle or similar long large-eye needle (check a sewing supply store) into a wood dowel. It allows easy rigging of snelled hooks and Texas rigs placed in the rear of the worm.

To rig this way, run the needle into the worm from the rear, beginning at the point where you want the bend of the hook to be. Run the needle eye out through the head of the worm, thread the monofilament through the needle eye, and pull the needle *back* through the worm body with the mono. Pull the mono

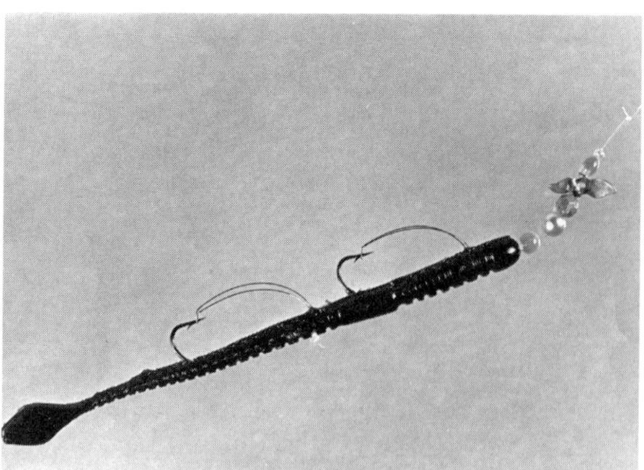

Finished worm with beads and spinner blade rigged on the mono, the mono finished with a loop knot.

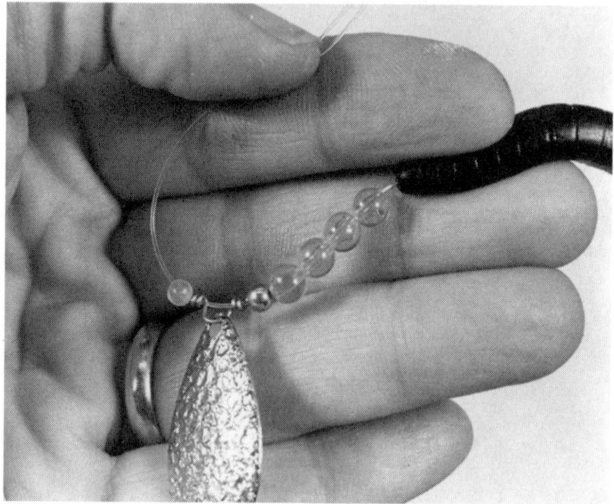

Another example of a spinner blade on a clevis on a worm rig. Beads serve as bearings for the blade on the clevis.

Once the worm rig is complete, any excess mono is clipped from the tail of the worm.

out, tie on or snell the hook, and then pull the mono through the worm to properly and carefully position the hook.

VARIATIONS IN WORMS AND WORM RIGS

Variations in molding and making worms and other soft-plastic lures are endless. The most common are variations in color, glitter, scent, and salt. Others include adding softener or hardener. Usually the bass angler will want a very soft lure, the saltwater angler a tougher, harder lure. Either is possible by the addition of the right liquid enhancer to the basic plastic.

Another variation is to use the same dumbbell lead eyes favored by fly tiers. You will have to choose the mold and/or eyes carefully to make sure the width of the eyes is equal to the width of the mold. Rubber molds are preferred for this, since they can be adjusted a little to accommodate a tight-fitting set of eyes. The eyes can be painted first and then molded into the lure and left as is, or the plastic "skin" that usually forms over the eye can be popped off to expose them.

These eyes in different weights can be added to other parts of the worm to add more weight for faster sinking in deep fishing. You can also use lead wire or lead-core trolling line (lead covered by a braided coating), held in place in the slits of the mold as mono would be, and mold the worm around it. This will also add weight for faster sinking but will affect the flexibility of the worm somewhat. Different sizes of lead wire (again used by fly tiers) are available for different sink rates. One way to partially control the loss in flexibility is to run the lead-core or lead wire through the front half or two-thirds of the worm only, leaving the tail free to wiggle.

Although they are usually added after the fact, it is easy to add one or more of the various plastic, metal, or glass worm rattles to molds for incorporation into the lure.

Other longitudinal fibers can be added for various purposes. In translucent worms, a long standard or strands of Krystal Flash, tinsel chenille, tinsel, Mylar tubing, or other material from fly-tying, craft, sewing, or hobby shops will add color and flash. The material is held in place in the worm mold in the same way that mono is and then clipped close once the worm is removed. Such fibers can be added to unrigged worms or to mono- and hook-rigged worms. If the fibers are strong enough, it is possible to use the long-shank worm-rigger (long needle with dowel handle previously described) to pull the fibers through the molded worm just as line is pulled through to rig hook a in the back of the head.

Another variation is the result of an innovation from one of the commercial worm companies. In 1989 Culprit Bait Company added a small patch of the "loop" portion of hook-and-loop-fastener material to their worms. The small patch, usually about 1½ inches long, catches in the tiny teeth of a largemouth bass to give the angler more time to set the hook and reduce the chances of the fish spitting out the worm. You can do the same thing with a small, thin strip or patch of this material added to the open side of an open-face worm before the liquid plastic has time to set up and cure. Such patches are easy to cut to size and add to the effectiveness of any plastic worm or lure.

KITS

Worm kits are available from a number of companies. There are worm-making kits that include special worm molds, 1 or 2 pints each of different plastic formulas, bottles of popular colors, a bottle of oil, and a pouring pan. M-F offers a basic worm kit that includes a double-cavity 7-inch curly-tail mold, black and purple color, liquid plastic, and instructions.

Hilts has five different worm-making kits, and each makes a different type of soft-plastic lure. The WTK-1 makes a 7-inch curved-tail worm; the WTK-2 kit makes a 3-inch double-curved-tail trailer; and the DIK-1 kit makes a 6-inch round worm and a 3-inch curved-tail worm. The DIK-2 makes a scorpion flat-tail worm and a 3-inch curved-tail worm; the DIK-3 makes a 3-inch curved-tail grub and a curved-tail scorpion worm. The first two kits have self-contained injector molds; the latter three have two molds each, with separate injectors. All five kits include liquid plastic and purple color; the DIK-1, DIK-2, and DIK-3 kits also contain fluorescent chartreuse color.

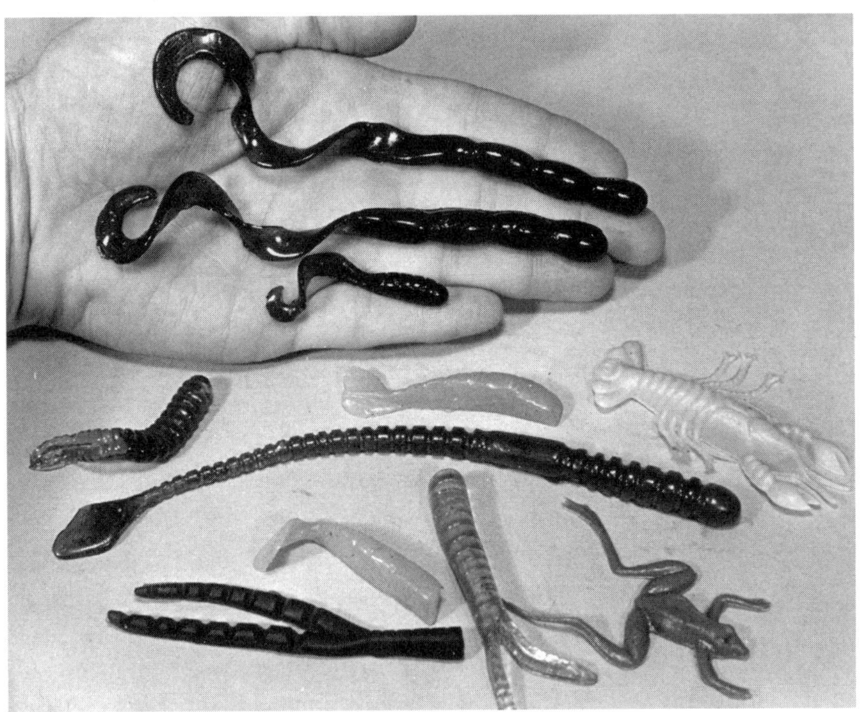

Examples of soft-plastic lures made from liquid plastic and simple molds.

8
Spoons

Introduction • Tools • Hardware • Spoon Construction and Assembly • Making Spoon Blades • Steps in Making Spoon Blades • Making Fixed-Hook Spoons • Variations in Making Spoons • Miscellaneous Spoons and Metal Lures • Spoon Kits

Basic Safety Requirements

- Goggles
- Gloves
- Apron

Basic Tools for Assembly

- Small round-nose pliers
- Split-ring pliers

Basic Tools for Cutting and Hammering Blades

- Tin snips or aviation snips
- Hacksaw
- Files
- Electric drill and bits
- Ball-peen hammer

Helpful Tools

- Jeweler's saw
- Small anvil
- Plastic and rubber hammers
- Metal chisels in various sizes
- Nail set
- Punch
- Soldering iron

INTRODUCTION

No special talents or tools are needed to construct spoons that are almost identical to those found in tackle stores—all it takes is a small pair of round-nose or split-ring pliers and the appropriate spoon components. With just this one tool, readily available spoon "blades," treble hooks, split rings, and swivels can be assembled into workable lures in just a few minutes. With the right tool and parts, you can probably turn out five to ten of the simplest swinging-hook-style spoons per minute.

TOOLS

Serious spoon makers should invest in a pair of split-ring pliers. Several brands of quality tools are available on the market. These pliers have thin, straight jaws with an overlapping "tooth" or hook on the end of one jaw that allows easy opening of a split ring to place it on a lure or add to a hook eye. The better quality pliers—available in several sizes—also have a notch farther back on the jaws for crimping leader sleeves and making wire leaders. The pointed end can be used to open split shot.

I like to modify these pliers slightly by grinding the lower (toothless) jaw to more of a point to allow me to easily pick up and work with the smallest sizes of split rings. You may wish to sharpen the point of the tooth slightly for the same purpose.

For those with original ideas on making different types of spoons or hard-core do-it-yourselfers, spoons can be made from raw materials. If this is the case, you'll find metal snips, aviation (compound-action cutting) snips, a jeweler's saw, several sizes and styles of files, an anvil, a ball-peen hammer, and a soldering iron either useful or necessary, depending on the lure and how it's made.

Standard metal snips or duckbill snips are fine for cutting spoon blades out of light metal; the compound-action aviation snips are better for cutting out heavier sheet metals. Compound-cutting snips come in straight-cutting, right-cutting, and left-cutting styles. Since few spoons require straight cuts, you may get by with either the right- or left-cutting style.

For very thick metals you will need a small jeweler's saw. In addition, you'll need files to polish and smooth the rough edges of the cut spoon blades. To shape the blades you will need various plastic and rubber hammers, ball-peen hammers, anvils, and wood blocks to form the curves that give the spoon action. Chisels and punches are also useful to give the spoon surface a hammered or scalelike finish.

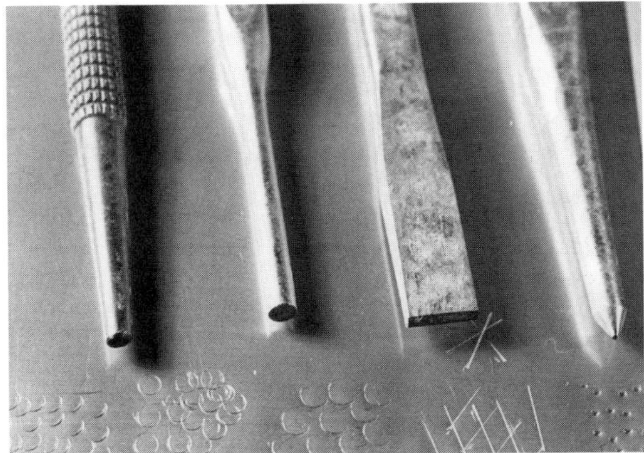

Nail sets, drifts, chisels, and punches can be used to make scale and other marks in the surface of spoons.

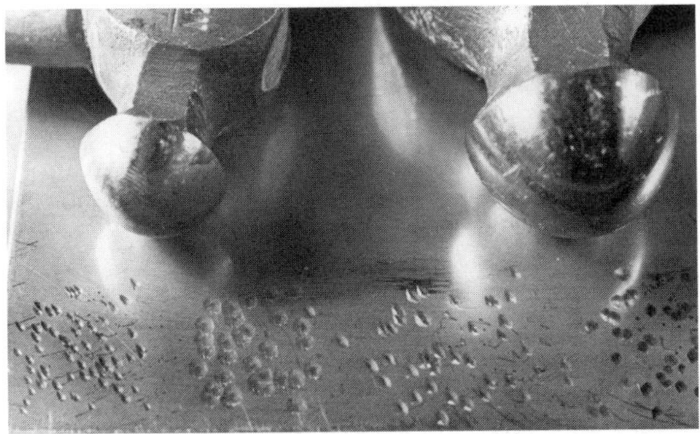

Ball-peen hammers hit on the ball, or on the side of the ball, can also make different marks in spoon surfaces.

An electric drill is necessary to drill holes through both ends of the blade for the line-tie split ring and the swinging hook or to make the holes for fastening a fixed hook. Small drill bits from about 1⁄16 to 1⁄8 inch in diameter are best for drilling these holes. A countersink is also helpful for polishing the hole after drilling.

A soldering iron with a small tip or a soldering torch with a small flame is handy for soldering hooks onto small spoon blades to make small spoons, jigging spoons, and ice-fishing lures for crappie, panfish, trout, and bass.

HARDWARE

The basic parts of any spoon with free-swinging hooks are the hook, blade, and split rings. For fixed-hook spoons you will also need a rivet, a small bolt, or other means to attach the hook to the spoon blade.

Many home craftsmen, and some commercial spoon manufacturers, make spoons without a ring, snap, or split ring at the line-tie. It is much better, however, to add a split ring, snap, snap swivel, or soldered jump ring to the line-tie hole. Without such an attachment, the spoon will not have the best movement or action, particularly when tied to heavy line or wire. Even more important, the rough edges of the drilled hole may cut the line while you're casting or playing a fish. To prevent this, be sure to add some type of attachment link to all spoons. If you use more-expensive ball-bearing swivels to prevent line twist, be sure to use them with snaps or split rings to attach to each spoon.

Spoon blades come in a wide variety of sizes and shapes for everything from panfish to muskie and saltwater gamefish. Blades as short as 1 inch and as long as 5 inches are readily available. As with spinner blades, they are available in a variety of finishes, including nickel, brass, gold, copper, and even painted, as with the popular red-and-white-striped pike spoon. Many standard and fluorescent colors and combinations are also sold. One recent catalog showed a variety of spoon blades in eleven different styles and forty-plus painted and/or plated finishes. However, not all finishes were available in all blade styles.

The cost of a spoon blade varies with its size, thickness, and finish. In almost all cases, though, they are about a third to an eighth the cost of a commercial lure. The cost of the hooks and split ring must be added to this, but the total is still small considering the quality you get from these ready-made and finished blades and the little bit of time required to assemble them.

In addition, you can use spinner blades for spoons by drilling a hole in the rear of the blade and rigging it as a swinging-hook lure. These provide greater variety because they are available in sizes of about ¾ inch long to about 3 inches long, in plain and hammered metal finishes, in single- and multiple-shade painted finishes, in fluorescent colors, and painted on one or both sides. These same blades in small sizes, soldered to a single hook and painted or left bright, make ideal fixed-hook spoons for ice and panfish fishing.

Split rings are necessary in all stages of spoon making for both line-ties and hook attachment. Split rings are not the only possibility, however. You can use jump rings; but because these are not as strong, they must be soldered. You sometimes see soldered jump rings on commercial spoons and lures.

Another possibility is a small snap of some type. The easiest to use are the Berkley Cross-Lok snaps or the Duo-Lock snaps. These can be opened at both ends, so you can add, remove, or replace them at will. Regular snaps and nickel interlock snaps are alternatives. For spoons that rotate and twist the line, snap swivels are the best choice, with the ball-bearing style the best of these.

Some form of swivel is a must for trolling, and in cases of severe line twist of fast-rotating lures, even ball-bearing swivels may not be enough. In these cases use ball-bearing swivels, but also consider in-line trolling rudders and sinkers between the line and leader to prevent twist.

Ball-bearing swivels are made by Sampo, Berkley, and other companies and are usually available in black and bright finishes in many sizes. Solid-ring swivels, split-ring and lock snaps, split rings and safety snaps, solid-ring and coast-lock snaps, and solid-ring Pompanette snaps are also manufactured in ball-bearing swivel styles. Swivels can be used alone, fastened as a line-tie to the spoon with a split ring. Some of the ball-bearing styles come with a split ring at each end to make this quick and easy.

The Bead Chain Tackle Company makes freely turning swivels as well as single-snap swivels, double-snap swivels, and lock-type snap swivels. These feature the multiple swiveling of the many links of bead chain and are particularly popular in saltwater applications.

Such swivels and fasteners as those from Bead Chain, Sampo, Berkley, and others will add to the cost of the finished lure but more than make up for the additional cost by reducing or eliminating line-twist and cut-line problems. If you make lots of spoons and don't want to add an expensive ball-bearing swivel to each, add the split ring to the spoon and use a ball-bearing snap swivel on the end of the line.

Spoons can be rigged with single, double, or treble hooks, with the single hooks used in swinging or fixed style. For the free-swinging hook, the treble is the most popular, although for some Western freshwater applications and for much saltwater fishing, heavy-wire single hooks are preferred.

All three types of hooks come in a full range of sizes and styles. Treble hooks range from the tiny #18 up through 5/0 or larger in regular-shank, short-shank, and extra-strong-wire styles. Bronze, cadmium, nickel, gold, tinned, and stainless steel hooks are all available. Standard treble hooks require a split ring in order to be attached to a spoon unless they are one of two styles designed to slip onto a spoon blade. One of these styles has an open eye that is closed with pliers once on the lure. The second type has an open split shank that allows sliding on, much as a double shank hook is slid in place.

Double hooks are formed from one piece of wire so that the hook can be slipped on or off at any time simply by spreading the two shanks apart to slip it onto a screw eye or split ring. They range in size from #14 through 5/0 and come in both 90-degree and 120-degree hook-spreads. Most of the finishes previously listed are available.

Single hooks come in hundreds of variations, many of which can be used for spoons. Generally spoon hooks must be straight-eye (not turned-up or turned-down), regular length or short, and can be straight or bent to one side (kerbed or offset). Sizes from #22 through 12/0 are available in most of the finishes listed. Siwash single hooks have an open eye that can be slipped onto a spoon blade or split ring and then closed with pliers.

I have changed my mind several times over the years on the use of stainless steel for bait hooks in salt water. I used them at first, and then I did not so that my hooks would more quickly rust out of a lost fish. Now I am using them again because recent research indicates that stainless steel is less damaging to fish and is expelled just as quickly. I still think stainless steel is best for lures, including spoons. Spoons aren't usually lost, and if they are lost in a fish, the fish is generally hooked in the lip, where the hook is more easily dislodged than is a deeply placed bait hook. The use of stainless steel hooks in saltwater applications also reduces the amount of time required for care and maintenance of lures or for replacing rusted and ruined hooks. If stainless steel is not available or is too costly, tinned hooks are a good substitute.

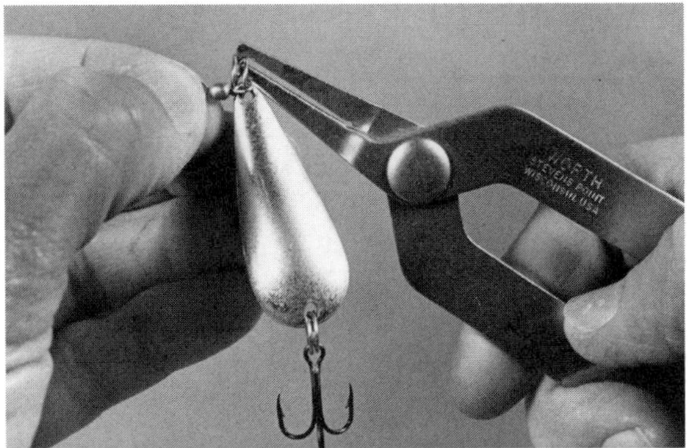

Assembly of spoons from commercially available blanks involves only a set of split-ring pliers to add hooks and line-ties.

SPOON CONSTRUCTION AND ASSEMBLY

Constructing a spoon from readily available parts is quite simple. Choose the spoon blade you want for your lure, choose a hook style and size to match it, and finally choose a split ring to match both parts. The split ring to connect the hook and spoon blade should not be overly large, but it must be strong enough that it won't pull apart during the strike or playing the fish. It should be large enough to provide clearance between the spoon eye and the hook eye without binding.

Use round-nose pliers or, better still, split-ring pliers. If you use round- or needle-nose pliers, pull one side of the split ring open and insert one jaw of the pliers into the gap to hold the ring open. Place the open ring on the spoon blade, followed immediately by the hook eye. Hold the two parts (spoon blade and hook), and use the pliers to rotate the split ring until both parts are completely on the ring and move freely. Turning the split ring through both parts at one time is quicker and allows you to complete the lure in less time. Also, opening the split ring a second time might deform and weaken it. Be sure to position the hook in the desired direction; the hook point can be positioned on the concave or convex side of the lure. Usually all swinging-hook lures are positioned with the hook on the concave side of the blade, causing them to ride up and be more weedless as the lure wobbles through the water. Using split-ring pliers makes the job easier because the tooth on one jaw allows easy opening of the split ring in order to slide it on the spoon blade and hook.

Assembly of a spoon from a cut and polished stainless steel teaspoon.

Once the split ring is one, turn it until all the parts move freely. Add a split ring or other line-tie to the other end of the spoon, and the assembly is completed. You can also add a swivel to the line-tie split ring at this point as desired or needed.

MAKING SPOON BLADES

Making spoon blanks, or blades, from sheet metal adds to the complexity of making spoons. Of course it also reduces cost. The advantage of making blades is that you can be as original as you want, using any type of metal in a wide variety of shapes, thicknesses, sizes, and finishes. The disadvantage is that it is time-consuming and does require some special tools.

Sheet metals that can be used in making spoon blades include copper, brass, steel, stainless steel, and aluminum, along with nickel-, gold-, and silver-plated metals. Other metals or plated finishes may be used, but these are generally too costly or difficult to obtain.

Most of the metals listed above are not difficult to obtain. Aluminum sheet and ⅛- and ¼-inch bar stock are available from hardware stores that stock these do-it-yourself metals. Copper sheeting is available from some hobby shops. Copper tubing, which can be hammered to shape, is available from hardware stores and plumbing-supply houses. Brass, steel, and stainless steel are sometimes available from hobby shops or hardware stores. Additional sources include craft stores, discount-lumber and home-supply shops, even junkyards. If you are searching for some special material, look in the Yellow Pages under "Metals" or "Scrap Metals." Often these suppliers deal only with large quantities, but you may get lucky and be able to buy a few pounds of what you need, especially if one of the suppliers is a fisherman.

Obviously a lure made of any of these metals will have different cutting, polishing, and finishing requirements, as well as different weight and action in the water, than a lure made of another metal. Even so, some generalities about spoon blanks are possible.

Thin sheet metals (nontempered, up to about 20 gauge) can be cut with regular tin or sheet-metal snips. (This will vary, because tin snips come with standard and duckbill cutting blades and in lengths from short to long. Those with long handles will have greater leverage in cutting and will thus cut easier than will short-handled models.)

Often these metals are too thin for most spoons, although they are fine for spinner blades and for the very thin dodgers used as attractors in front of a fly, lure, or bait in deep, Great Lakes–style trolling.

For thicker metal that cannot be cut with standard tin snips, you have two alternatives. One is to use aviation snips, often called compound-leverage cutters. These exert greater pressure than tin snips because they are designed for greater leverage in cutting. The disadvantage is that three snips are required for complete metalworking: one pair each for straight, right-, and left-handed cuts. If the spoon and spinner blades desired are simple shapes, you can often get by with one set of aviation snips, using them to rough out the metal and then finishing with a file, grinder, or sander. For making curves, choose left-cutting snips if you are right-handed and right-cutting snips if you are left-handed. The cuts will be easier to make this way.

One recent addition to the tool market is aviation snips designed so that one tool will cut left curves, right curves, and straight. While not quite as precise as the separate individual-purpose tools, they work fine for cutting out heavy metal spoon blades.

Even the aviation/compound-leverage snips have limits, however, based in part on the material being cut. Copper, aluminum, and brass, for example, are far easier to cut than stainless steel, so thicker sheets of these metals can be cut more easily than sheets of stainless. Heavy metals are often used for making thick spoons used for vertical jigging or structure fishing—the so-called structure spoons, jigging spoons, or slab spoons. In large sizes these are popular for surf fishing. (These can also be cast in tin or lead, as described in chapter 5, or made other ways, as described in chapter 12.)

Cutting the heavy metals used to make these spoons for Western, saltwater, and deep-lake fishing is beyond the limits of cutting tools. The best solution, and the second of the choices mentioned earlier, is a fine-blade hacksaw or fine-blade metal saw. One disadvantage of the hacksaw is that the thick blade only allows it to cut straight. The straight cuts require extensive recutting or filing to round off the edges. Small metal or jeweler's saws have narrower blades (¼ inch on a metal saw compared to ½ inch or more on a hacksaw blade) and thus can cut a circle of a smaller radius. Thin and wirelike blades are available to fit into a jeweler's saw or hacksaw, and these will cut in any direction to make any shape desired.

Hobbyists who have electric jigsaws with metal-cutting blades will find these a distinct advantage because they cut quickly and are easy to use. But they *are* expensive. If you already have one, use it. If you don't, think long and hard before buying on for the sole purpose of cutting out metal spoon blades.

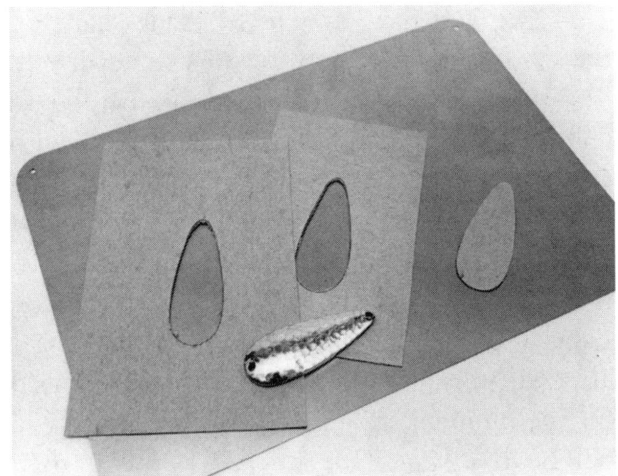

Templates of either the spoon or the spoon outline can be used to mark and shape spoons. These templates are of cardboard—you can make permanent ones of sheet steel or plastic sheeting.

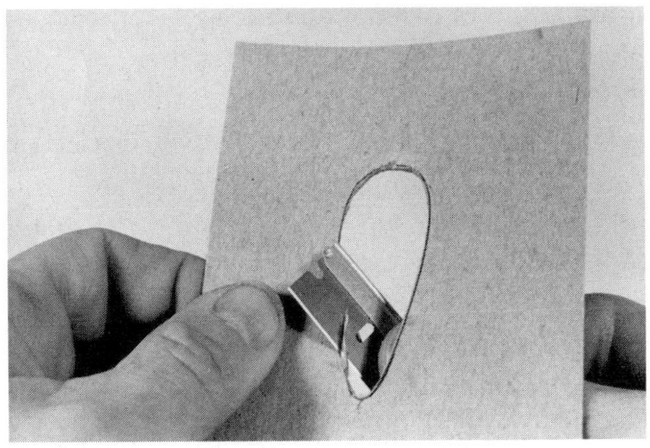

Cutting a sheet of cardboard that will be used as a template for outlining a spoon. This type of template, as opposed to one in the actual shape of the spoon, is easier to hold and use when the spoon is small.

STEPS IN MAKING SPOON BLADES

Shaping the Blade

The first step in making any spoon, spinner blade, or flat metal shape is to determine the shape and size of the blade you desire. To do this, draw spoon-blade outlines on paper until you are satisfied with one. You may want to trace some commercially made blades to get an idea of what you want. In fact, it helps to trace an existing blade lightly and then alter the shape in heavier strokes as desired. Copy the final shape onto heavier cardboard. (One way to do this is to fasten the paper on the cardboard and use a pin or awl to prick the outline every ¼ inch or so. Then use the pinpricks in a "connect-the-dot" exercise to draw the shape on the cardboard.)

If the blade is bilaterally symmetrical (exactly the same shape on both sides), an alternative method will make the final result better: Draw a centerline on the paper, trace or draw one side of the spoon blade, fold the paper along the centerline, and trace the second side from the first. That way, both sides will be absolutely identical. The finished drawing can then be traced on the cardboard.

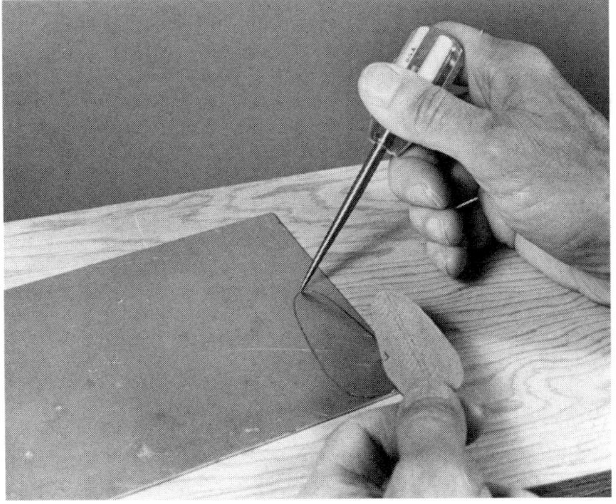

Using a template the shape of the spoon to mark sheet metal for cutting.

Once you have drawn the blade shape on the cardboard, use sharp scissors to cut it out. The best method is to discard the cardboard cutout piece and use the cardboard sheet with the blade outline as a template. The template can easily be held onto the metal for tracing.

Trace the blade shape into the edge of the metal sheet (to minimize waste) with an awl. Label the template and keep it for future use after you've traced all the blade shapes you need for the moment. Initially, and especially if you will be making a shape different from that used in commercial spoons, you may wish to make only a few blades and test them for action. If the shape performs as you expect, you can easily make more. If it doesn't you have only "wasted" a few pieces of metal (and probably learned a lot about spoon-shaping and construction).

Cut out the spoon blade using tin snips, aviation snips, a hacksaw, jeweler's saw, or electric saw. If you use snips, hold them in one hand and the metal in the other, turning the metal and the snips to fashion the curves and shape of the blade. If you use a saw, clamp the metal in a vise. With a metal vise use some scrap pieces of wood, plastic sheeting, or sheet metal to keep the scored jaws from damaging the spoon blade. Clamp as close as possible to the edge that is to be cut to prevent the metal from bending or chattering as you make the cut.

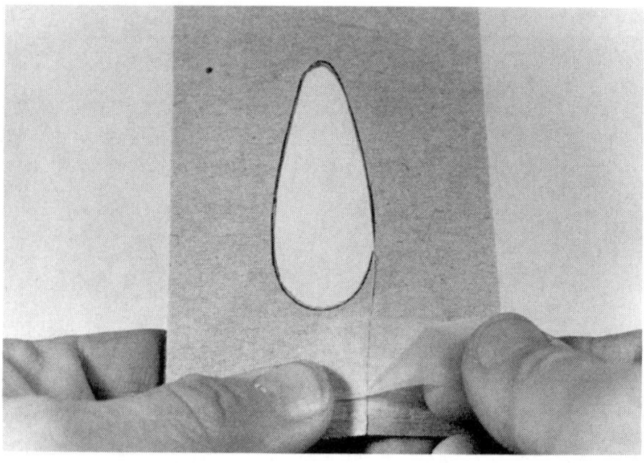

When making a template in which the spoon shape is removed, cut through the cardboard and along the edge with scissors to make a smooth shape. The cut made in the cardboard is taped before use as shown here.

Cut as closely as possible to, preferably right on, the drawn line. After the initial cut, smooth the spoon blade with a large quick-cutting file. You can work by holding the file and blade in your hands or clamp the blade in a vise as you file; you can even fasten the file in the vise (protect the teeth with wood scraps) and scrape the edge of the blank against it. This latter method is often best for rounded spoon edges. Use successively finer files to smooth the blade edges, ending with emery cloth or an old, inexpensive sharpening stone. (If you use a stone, use only an *old* one—smoothing the spoon edge this way will groove the stone and ruin it for tool- and knife-sharpening purposes.)

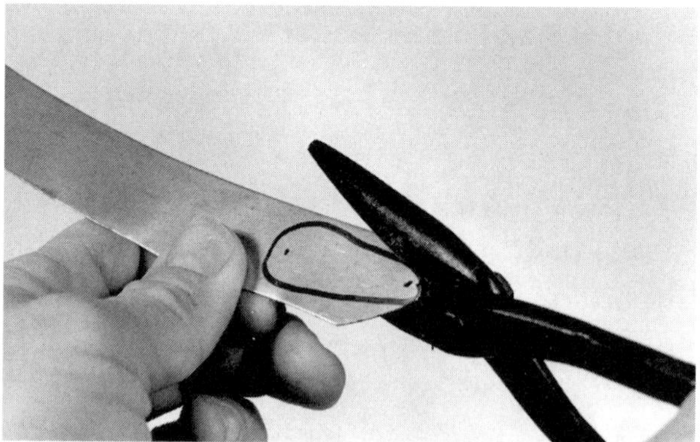

Using duckbill snips to cut thin metal to make a fluttering spoon.

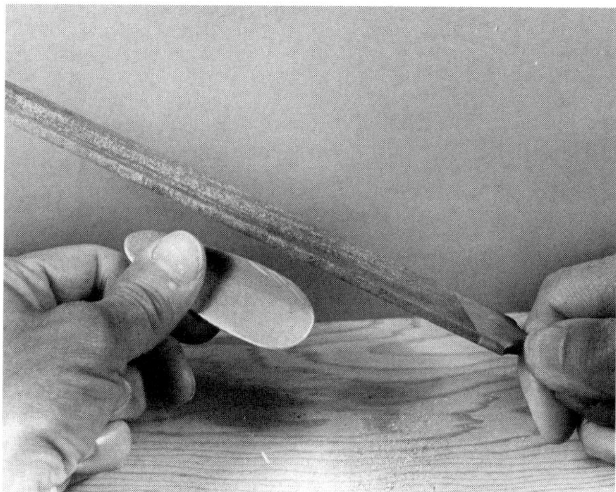

A file, electric sander, or grinder makes it easy to smooth the cut edges when making spoons or spinner blades. Here a file is used to smooth the blade edges.

Drilling the Holes

With regard to drilling and other steps, such as the following step of hammering the blade to shape, be sure to use appropriate care. Use safety devices along with such precautions as removing ties, rolling up sleeves, and removing jewelry and wristwatches.

Once the blade is shaped and smoothed, the next step is to drill a hole in each end, hammer it into the proper curvature, and finish, if desired, with a hammered, scaled, decaled, or painted finish. It is best to drill both holes in the blade while it is still flat, because it is always easier to work on flat than on rounded or curved metal. You can use a hand drill, although a portable electric drill is better; a drill press is best. In all cases, keep the drill bit at right angles to the blade. Support the blade on a wood scrap in a vise, or clamp or secure it to the drill-press table.

Use a small drill bit, one sized appropriately for the blade size. Usually this will be about 1⁄16 to 1⁄8 inch, but it can be varied if desired. Make sure the bits are hardened and designed for metal. (Before starting to drill, use a small punch, awl, or prick-punch to mark the drilling spot and prevent the drill bit from slipping or walking.) Use a slow speed to prevent the drill bit from "walking" on the metal and allow it to bite into the metal. This is especially important with harder metals such as steel and stainless steel, less so with soft metals such as copper, brass, and aluminum.

Control is easy with a drill press; with a handheld electric drill you will want one with a variable speed control. You can hold the trigger lightly for a slow speed. Make sure the hole you make is large enough for the split ring or hook eye and that it is close to the edge but not so close that it might pull out. If additional holes are desired for adding glass or plastic eyes, for action or water flow, or for attaching other parts such as small spinner blades, drill these holes now.

Using an electric drill held in a drill-press holder to drill out the hole on a spoon blade. As shown, it is easiest to drill before the spoon is bent to final shape.

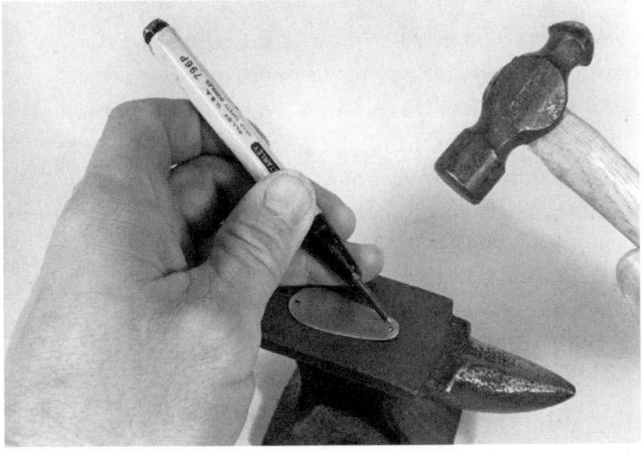

Mark the spot for drilling for the hook and line-tie attachments by using a punch on a small anvil. The punch makes a mark that will also prevent the bit from drifting or walking while drilling.

Take care to drill both holes exactly on the centerline of the spoon unless an erratic wobbling action is desired. You might experiment with off-center drilling, which can provide interesting results and fish-catching action. It is also possible to drill several holes for the line-tie at several points around the forward edge so that you have a choice when tying the lure and in the resulting action. Generally the farther the line-tie hole is from the centerline of the lure, the more erratic the action. You will have to add split rings to all these holes or else be sure to use a snap at the end of the line to prevent line damage or possible line cutting.

Hammering Blades to Shape

Once the blade is cut, polished, and drilled, the next steps are to add any finishing marks in the metal and to hammer the blade into the desired curve for the best action in the water. These operations can be completed in either order, but there are advantages and disadvantages to either choice.

Hammering the curve into the lure first makes it more difficult to add any finishing marks to the convex side of the lure later. It is easy to hammer finishing marks on the concave side of the lure; you can do it while hammering the spoon blade to shape or after it is shaped.

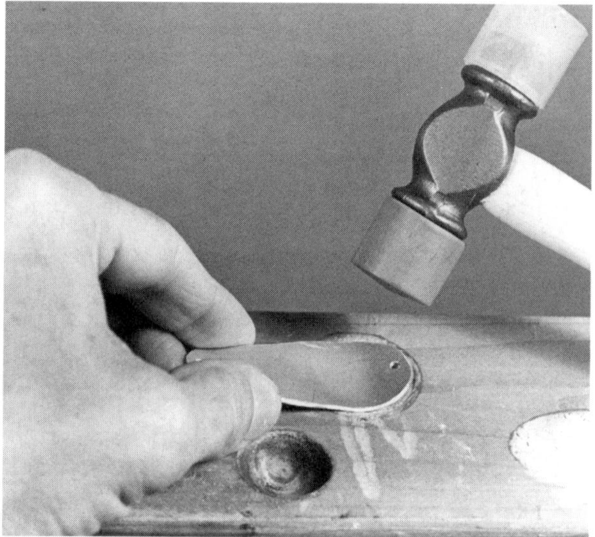

Shallow depressions cut into a block of wood make it easy to deepen the curvature in a spoon blank. Here the rubber face of the hammer is used to avoid marks on the spoon blank.

Using a nylon-head hammer to begin hammering a spoon to shape. Hammering on a flat block of wood like this will produce a concave surface in the spoon blank.

Using a ball-peen hammer to make marks on the spoon blank after it is shaped. To prevent the blank from being hammered flat again, you must hold the spoon blank on a convex surface—here half of a darning egg glued to a wood block.

To add hammered finish marks to the convex side of the bent spoon requires a special anvil or support. You can't hammer in finish marks unless the blade is supported directly under the hammer area or you will just flatten the blade. Even with a special anvil or support, it is difficult to hold the blade on the support while also holding the chisel or marking tool and a hammer.

Hammering the finish first tends to put a curve into the blade, thus putting the finish on the concave side. If you want the finish on the convex side, the finished blade must be hammered flat again and then rebent to the desired shape.

There are several ways to hammer the spoon blade into shape. One way, suggested by my

Using a nail set to make scale marks on a spoon blank before it is bent into shape with convex and concave curves.

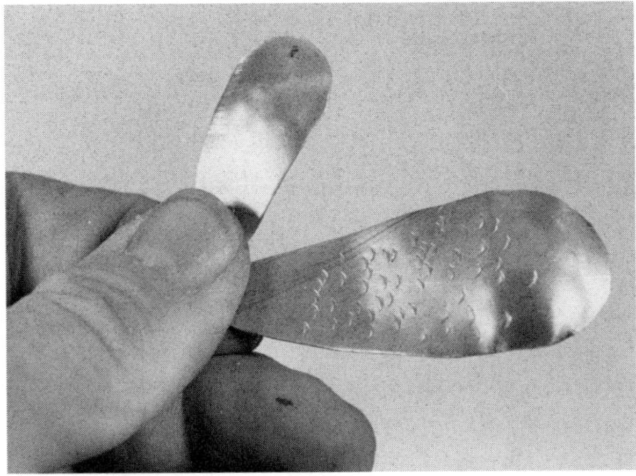

Hammered thin-metal spoon blanks, one with scale marks hammered into it with a large nail set. The half-circles are cut into the blade by hammering the nail set at an angle. Though crude, these spoons have good action in the water and do catch fish.

friend and fishing buddy Norm Bartlett, is to place the blade on a block of wood, put a large steel ball (like a ball bearing) on the blade where you want curvature, and then hit the ball with a heavy hammer. (In this as in all shop operations, be sure to wear goggles and follow other safety guidelines.) To accentuate this curve further, first carve (or hammer) a depression into the supporting block of wood so that the spoon blade has a pocket into which it is pressed when the steel ball is hit. Different size balls can be used for different curves and shapes. You can also place a large concave curve on one end of the spoon blade and then turn it over and, with the same or a smaller ball, make a reverse curve on the other end.

You can use a homemade wooden anvil with a curved, carved pocket in it and a ball-peen hammer to shape the blade into the proper curvature. Small anvils are available from hobby, craft, and hardware stores. Make sure the anvil has a "horn," or curved end, on which to hammer shapes.

You can make your own anvil by using hardwood carved to shape and pinned to a larger wood block for support. One easy way to do this is to use a hardwood darning egg used for repairing socks. Cut the egg in half and pin and glue this half to a larger block of wood.

If you want a smooth finish, or if some other type of finish will be added later, use a rubber- or plastic-head hammer, working the spoon on a hard flat or shaped wood block, like those described above. Hammer evenly all over the part of the spoon to be curved. The hammering will gradually produce a concavity on the hammered side, so the anvil or block must be concave. With practice you will be able to hammer spoons into almost any degree or type of curvature, including reverse or S-shaped curves.

Hammered and Cut Finishes

Although chapter 15 covers painting and finishing, some types of finishes for spoons are best covered here because they involve hammering and marking methods using a hammer and anvil.

One easy way to decorate a spoon is to give it a hammered finish, either while forming the curve in the spoon or after the spoon is shaped. If the hammered finish is to be on the concave side of the spoon, it is easy to place the spoon on the wood block and hammer until the desired effect is achieved.

If you wish the hammered finish to be on the convex side of the spoon blade, there is a problem. Hammering on the convex side of the spoon will destroy the curve without some type of support *directly under* the hammered area. You can use an anvil, a homemade wood block, or a similar support. Place the spoon blade concave side down on the anvil or support, and hammer the finish with a ball-peen or cross-peen hammer. The former will leave small polished marks, although they will vary with the material on which the spoon blade is hammered and the makeup of the side of the ball-peen head. The cross-peen hammer will leave straight-line marks, much like a chisel. These also will vary with the material used as a base for the hammering operation.

As previously described, you can hammer the finish on a flat support before the blade is shaped. In this case, a rubber- or plastic-head hammer must be used for shaping in order to prevent scarring the finish and the blade after decorating.

You can make different kinds of finishes, either before or after shaping, using punches, nail sets, prick-punches, and chisels to get different effects. A finish of small circles—much like fish scales—is easy to make by hammering in a pattern with a large nail set held at an angle. Made-to-punch (or "set") finishing nails just beneath the surface of wood, a nail set has a small cuplike depression on its face. A similar effect is achieved with a flat-end round punch or drift. A punch, drift, or nail set can be used straight on (at right angles to the spoon blade) to make various sizes of circles if desired.

Various straight lines and designs on a spoon blade can be made with a cold chisel. Hammer the chisel into the spoon to make parallel lines, herringbone patterns, or random marks as desired.

You can make your own special stamps and punch patterns from hardened nails following the directions in chapter 2.

Spoons and spinner blades can be painted. At one time most fishermen preferred metallic-finish spoons and blades, but that is changing. Today brightly painted spoons and spinners, along with those decorated with glitter or prism tape, are preferred in some areas or for certain types of fishing. Painting spoons, as well as applying other finishes of tape, glitter, and flocked materials, is discussed in chapter 15.

MAKING FIXED-HOOK SPOONS

Many spoons are made with the single, double, or treble hooks added to the spoon blade with a split ring and thus swinging free. It is also possible to make spoons in which the single hook is fixed to the concave surface of the blade instead of swinging free. This method is used commercially for large trolling spoons, weedless spoons for bass fishing, and some surf-fishing spoons. There are no commercial blanks for this, although there are many for swinging-hook spoons, but blanks can be made in the same way that all spoons blades are cut out from sheet metal.

Once the spoon is cut out, the hole for the hook is drilled to a larger than normal (or larger than needed for a swinging hook) size, through which the hook point is inserted. The metal at the edge of the hole is bent toward the inside, or concave side, of the spoon so that the hook shank will fit through the hole and be straight or parallel to the spoon blade. This bend must be toward the concave surface of the blade.

Once the hole is drilled and its edge is bent, insert the hook point through it and position the hook eye on the center of the spoon blade or at a position to allow good exposure of the hook point. Mark through the center of the hook eye where it falls on the blade with an indelible-ink or felt-tip marker. Remove the hook, clamp the blade to a wood block or into a vise, and drill the marked spot. Use a drill bit that will allow you to fasten the hook eye to the blade with a small rivet (like a ⅛-inch-diameter pop-style rivet), split rivet, or small bolt and nut. Before drilling make *sure* you have a method of fastening that will fit through the hook eye; match the hole in the spoon to this fastener. Shape the blade and add any finish desired, if this has not been done previously. Insert the hook, and then place the hook eye over the hole in the spoon and fasten, using a hammer for a regular rivet, a pop-rivet tool, or a screwdriver and wrench for the bolt and nut. If possible use a stainless steel or brass bolt and nut to eliminate or reduce future corrosion problems.

One advantage of using a bolt and nut is that the hook can be changed as desired. If a hook becomes hopelessly dulled, the feathers or skirt are chewed off a hook by a bluefish, or a hook rusts in the off-season, it is easy to replace. If you won't ever replace the hook, use the rivets or hammer the end of the small bolt to peen it and make it impossible to remove the nut.

You can also use standard commercial blades by enlarging the rear hole. Drill the hole out larger, preferably on a drill press. To insert the hook point, bend the metal to allow clearance for the hook shank and drill the central hole for the hook-eye attachment. Then proceed as above to finish the assembly.

An even simpler method of fastening a hook to a spoon blade is to drill a hook-attachment hole at the tail end of the spoon and larger than you would need for a swing hook attachment and then fasten the eye of the hook to this hole. You can use a pop-rivet tool, a standard rivet, or a tiny bolt and nut. Some of these spoons are sold with a skirted tail (the skirting material fastened or wrapped onto the hook shank). You can also use fly-tying methods to tie any natural or synthetic skirt material to the hook shank before fastening the hook to the spoon blade.

This method can also be used to drill out the tail hole on any commercially available spoon blade to fasten a hook by the hook eye as outlined above.

One additional fastening method is to solder the hook to the spoon blade. This method makes for a weaker connection, however, so use it only as a last resort and check it frequently. If you solder to stainless steel, you will have to use silver solder, which is more difficult to use in most cases and definitely more costly.

Regular stainless steel teaspoons can be used for making simple fixed-hook and swinging-hook spoons. Here a spoon is held in a vise by the handle, which has been cut off with a hacksaw.

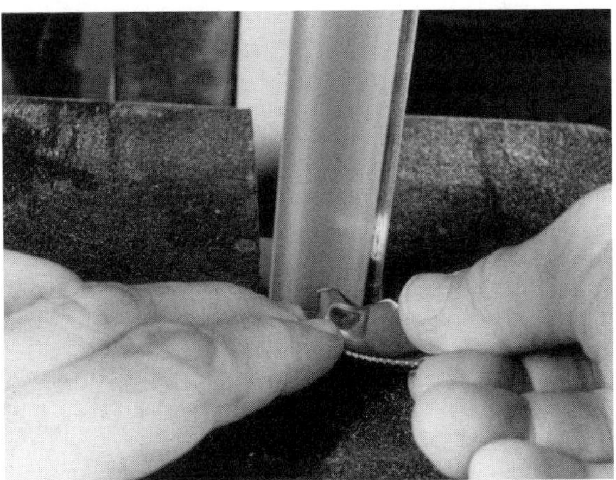

Using a sanding belt to polish the cut edge of the spoon.

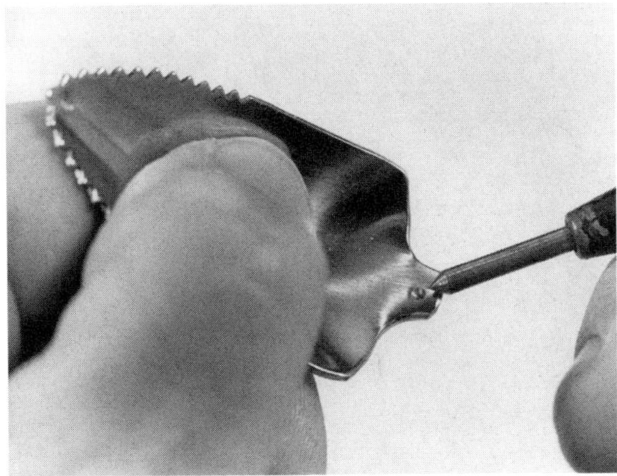

A punch must be used to make a small depression in the spoon blade for drilling; otherwise the bit will drift.

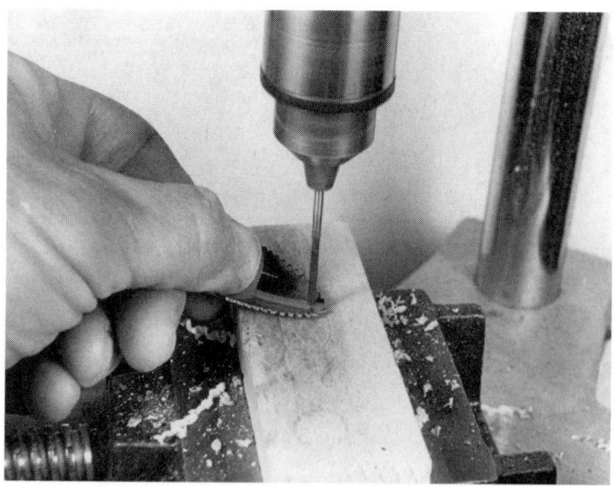

Drilling a spoon for the line-tie attachment split ring using a small hobby drill press.

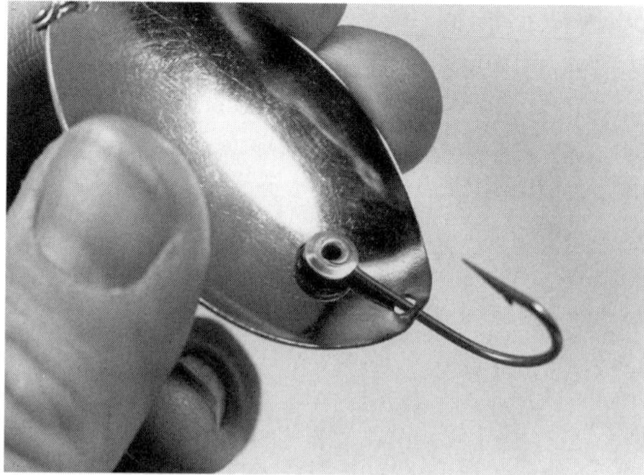

Here a spoon is finished using a pop rivet through a hole in the spoon blank to hold the hook eye in place. Tiny bolts and nuts can also be used.

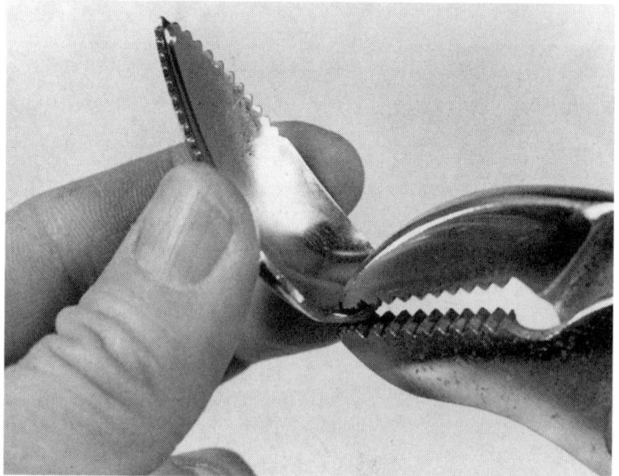

After drilling both ends, use pliers to bend up one end before adding the hook.

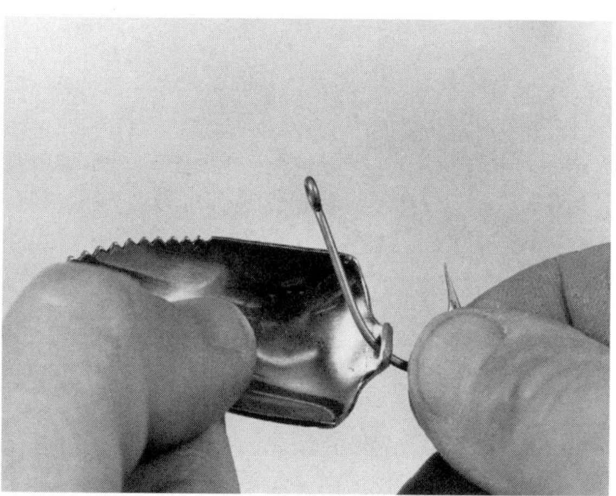

Threading the hook through the folded-up eye for the fixed hook attachment. Once this is done, the position for drilling the hook-eye attachment is marked with a felt-tip marker and then with a punch.

VARIATIONS IN MAKING SPOONS

Many variations in making spoons are possible. For swinging-hook spoons, add a special worm hook in place of a standard hook. This way a worm or long grub can be fastened to the spoon Texas-style as an added attracter and also to make the hook weedless. Using a toothpick through the worm and hook eye, you can fasten the head of the worm to the hook eye, or you can attach a HitchHiker to the spoon attachment or hook eye. This holds the worm head with the small wire corkscrew of the HitchHiker, the hook point buried in the body of the worm, to make for a weedless Texas rig. Some commercial spoons have red glass or plastic eyes (beads) on each side of the forward part of the spoon. These can be added to a spoon by drilling and making some simple additions. First decide what size of red plastic or glass eye bead you wish to add. Choose a drill bit slightly larger than the eye to drill holes through two premarked spots on the blade. To do this safely and properly, first mark the spot with a felt-tip marker, and then use a prick-punch to mark the spots and prevent the drill from walking. Then, with a *small* drill bit, drill the holes on each side, using successively larger bits to expand the hole until the finished size is reached. If desired or necessary, polish the hole edges with a larger drill bit or countersink.

Once the final holes are made, mark, punch, and drill tiny holes (⅓ or 1⁄16 inch will do) immediately to each side (ahead and in back or side by side) of each large hole. Cut light stainless steel wire about ½ inch longer than the distance between the small holes that bracket each large hole. Slip the wire through the red eye (bead) and bend it in a U or staple shape with the bends precisely at the distance between the holes. Place the ends of this "staple," with the red eye attached, through these small holes (the eye/bead will lodge in the large hole) and use pliers to secure the ends of the wire to hold the eye in place.

An alternative method of adding eyes is to use glue made for doll eyes, available from craft shops. This involves no drilling—just gluing with a good epoxy glue. Other doll eyes, such as the snap-on type, can be used for spoons. These eyes have a short stem that is smaller in diameter than the eye, and the eye is held in place with a backing plate that is pushed in place on the stem. To use these for spoons, drill a hole or holes slightly larger than the diameter of the stem. Do not drill any side holes, as for bead eyes. Insert the eye stem through the hole and add the backing plate, pushing it on securely to hold the eye, and then cut off the excess stem. You must leave a little bit of the stem in order for the backing plate to hold. For added security add some epoxy glue to the stem, or use a soldering iron to melt and flatten the plastic against the backing plate. These bright and colorful eyes can also be glued in place, in which case you can cut the stem off

Drilling holes in the center of the spoon for adding a red plastic bead that will show from both sides of the spoon.

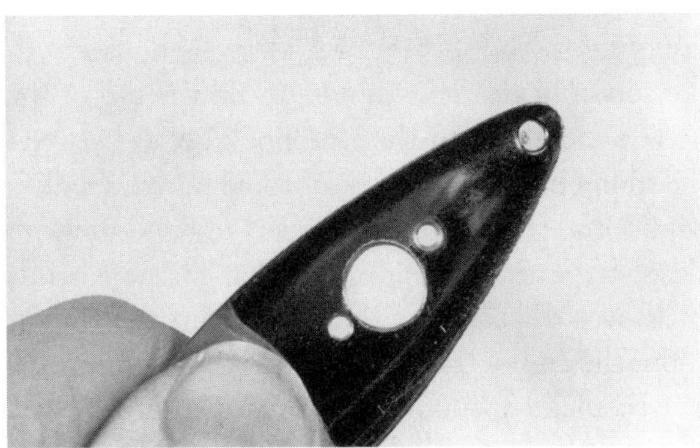

The larger center hole holds the bead; the two smaller holes secure the wire holding the bead.

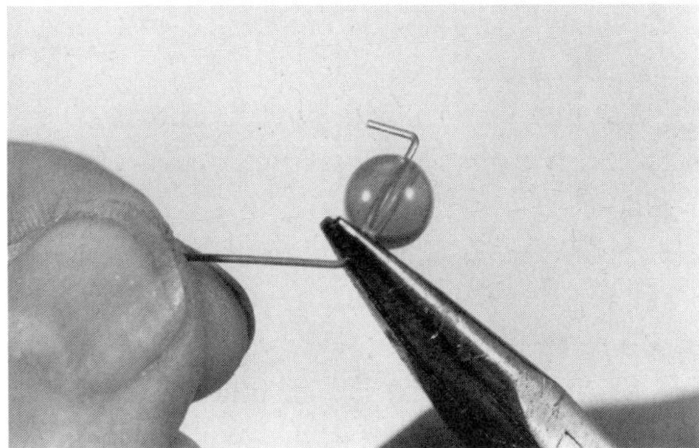

Use pliers to bend the wire once the bead is in place. These bends must correspond with the distance between the two holes.

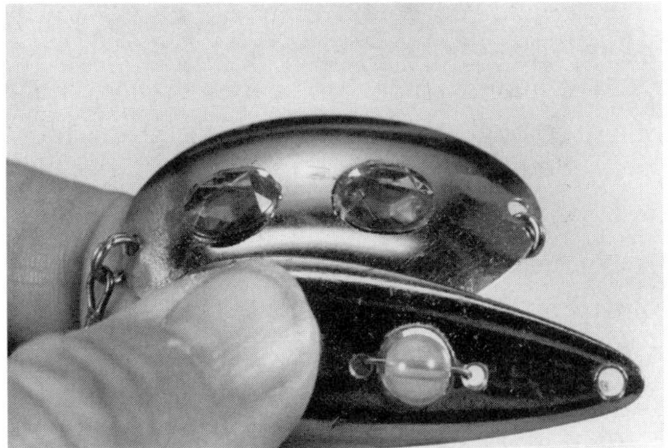

The finished lure with the bead in place and wired to the spoon blank. A simpler way to get a similar effect is shown in the top spoon—using plastic craft "jewels" glued to the blade.

completely. Or just buy flat-back eyes that are easily glued in place.

Another way to add more flash to a spoon is to attach a smaller size spinner blade—usually a willowleaf—to the forward (line-tie) split ring. Tie the line to the split ring; the willowleaf blade will hang down and twist, turn, and flash as the spoon is retrieved.

To add small willowleaf or other blades to the tail of the lure, add one to the split ring holding the hook as in the above method. Another option for some lures is to drill two small holes at the rear of the spoon on either side of the hole made for the swinging or fixed hook. Add small willowleaf blades to these holes using small split rings. (Other types of spinner blades can be used in these variations, although the willowleaf blade is the most commonly used because of its slim shape.)

Two or more short, stubby spoon blades can be connected with a split ring to make a long jointed spoon, with the end blade holding the fixed or swinging hook. A variation of this is to make a jointed spoon: Cut out a long spoon blank or use a standard commercial spoon blade. Cut the spoon blade in half horizontally (or into thirds, if you like), and then round and smooth the cut edges. Drill center holes in these parts and join them with a split ring. Jointed spoons like this can be made using different colors, finishes, metals, shapes, and in swinging- or fixed-hook styles. Swinging-hook styles are most common.

Spoons, with either a fixed or a swinging hook, can be combined with spinner attachments.

Two small spinner blades have been added to the sides of the back of this spoon for added noise and flash. The split ring for the hook is being added here.

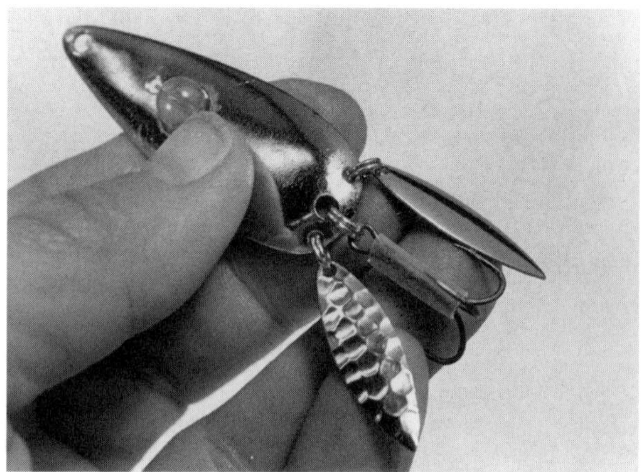

Completed lure with plastic tubing on the treble hook.

Add a spinner wire to the eye of the hook or to the forward split ring and build up the wire with beads (at least one used for a bearing) and a clevis-fitted blade or two. This makes for a spoon with a rotating spinner part on the front end.

Any spoon can be made weedless. Swinging-hook spoons are easily assembled using weedless hooks. These are widely available and have a small wire weed guard over each point of the hook. They are available in single-, double-, and treble-point styles. For making weedless fixed-hook spoons, use light weed guard wire. Light-wire weed guard wire is available from most component-supply houses. It averages about 0.016 inch in diameter, but lighter or heavier wire can be used—some as light as 0.012 inch or as heavy as 0.020 inch. Heavier wire could be used for heavy muskie-style spoons or saltwater spoons. Form the wire into a small circle at one end. Fasten this circle onto the spoon blade when fastening (by bolt, rivet, or solder) the hook eye to the spoon blade. This should go on the top of the hook attachment so that the hook eye is between the spoon blade and the eye formed in the weedless wire. Once this is done, use pliers to bend the wire close to the attachment eye so that the wire bends back over the point of the hook. Clip the wire at about the end of the hook bend.

To make a double weed guard, use the same wire and bend a length into a V. Fasten the bend of this V at the eye of the hook as above, and bend both wire stems back over each of the two hook points. Clip where desired. To avoid wasting wire, figure the length that will be required and cut it to length in advance.

Any hook on any spoon can be dressed with fur, feathers, or similar artificial materials. Use standard fly-tying or bucktail-making methods (see chapter 4) to tie in the materials, wrap off the thread, and secure the wrap with fly-head cement or sealer. If you dress fixed-hook spoons, be sure you make the dressing sparse for easy fastening of the hook to the spoon blade. Add this skirting to the hook before adding the hook to the spoon blade.

Whether you are making fixed-hook or swinging-hook spoons, the hook should be dressed separately and before it is added to the spoon.

Stinger hooks can be added to spoon hooks just as they can to spinnerbaits and buzzbaits; standard or stinger hooks can be dressed with fur, nylon dressing, artificial fur, or feathers for more attraction.

MISCELLANEOUS SPOONS AND METAL LURES

In addition to the standard types of free-swinging and fixed-hook spoons, other easily made metal lures fall loosely into the spoon category. For example, small-diameter copper tubing and similar small conduit can be cut into 2- to 6-inch lengths, hammered flat, drilled at each end, and fitted with hardware. This is easy to do with a hacksaw blade to cut the tubing, a hammer to flatten it, a drill to make the holes, and a file to round and polish the ends.

A variation of this type of tube lure can be made by hammering the tube only partially flat, leaving the other end with a round or elliptical cross section. You can leave it this way for maximum action or fill it with molten lead (see chapters 4 and 5 for details on molding) for more weight to get the lure deeper or to achieve more casting distance.

Instead of filling the hollow end with lead, you can glue in some open-cell foam, being careful not to seal off the end so that while you are fishing the foam can be filled with various fish scents that will leach out into the water for more attraction.

Another possibility is to hammer both ends flat, leaving the center hollow and round, before the second end is flattened, and then fill the tube with rattles for weight and sound. Different rattles will make different sounds: Lead shot makes a dull sound; steel ball bearings make a heavy, sharp sound; and glass or plastic beads (the lightest of these materials) make a light, sharp sound.

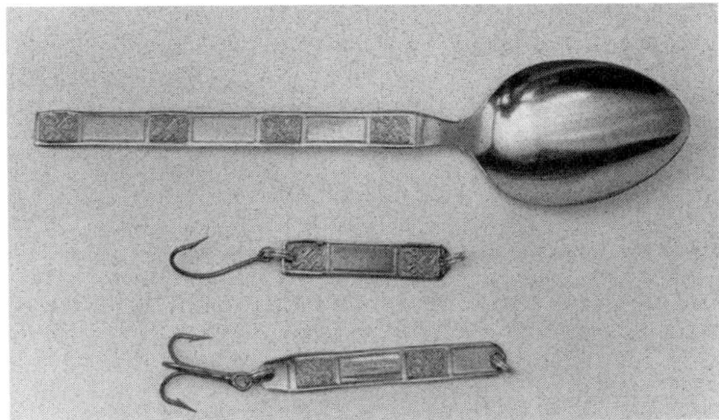

Two lengths and sizes of structure-type spoons made from the handle of a teaspoon. The spoon handle has been cut into two lengths and drilled for swinging-hook and line-tie split rings. By choosing spoons with the right handle, it is possible to get several lures from each spoon. The bowl part of this utensil can be used for making a swinging or fixed-hook trolling or casting spoon.

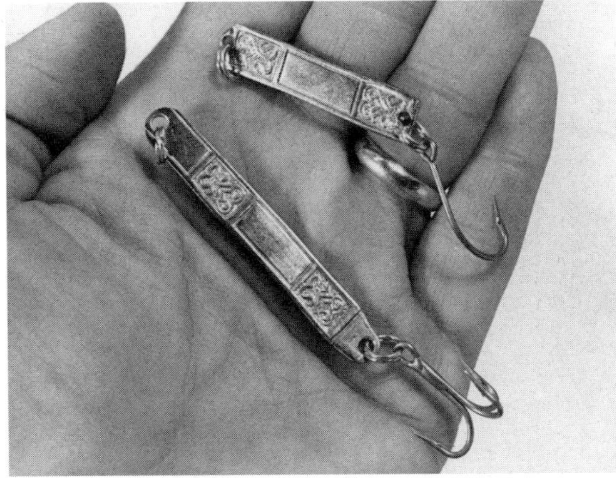

Two structure spoons made from a spoon handle. Single, double, or treble hooks can be used, undressed as shown or dressed with feathers, fur, or surgical tubing.

The same type of tubing in a larger size can be cut on a sharp diagonal to create a wobbling type of swinging-hook lure. Square, rectangular, or round bar stock can be cut on the diagonal to make a heavy slab-sided lure. It will, however, take time to cut through the bar stock with a fine-tooth (metal) hacksaw blade. Old discarded knife and other utensil handles can be used for jigging spoons after a hole is drilled in each end for the line-tie and hook. Best are those bulky handles that will result in a lure resembling some of the vertical jigging and structure spoons.

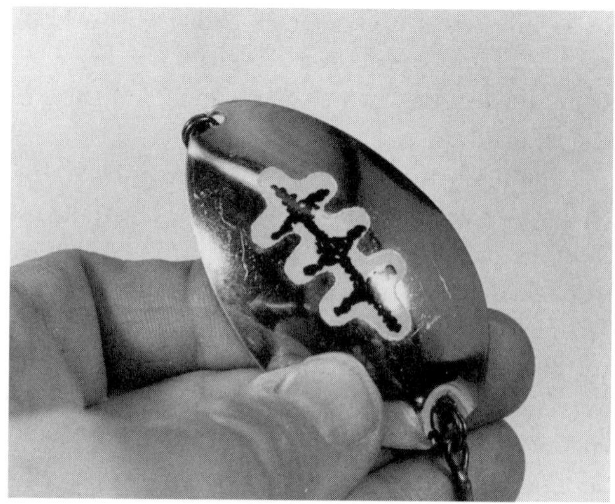

A simple way to finish a simple spoon is with self-adhesive decal stickers, available in many shapes and colors from several manufacturers.

SPOON KITS

Unlike those for some other lures, kits for spoons are not that prevalent. Some supply companies do sell kits that include painted or finished spoon blades, split rings, and hooks to make up a number of swinging-hook spoons. Most companies have wide assortments of spoon blades available in many styles, sizes, finishes, and painted colors. Lakeland, for example, has trolling and casting spoon blade patterns that include plain, hammered, fine diamond, diamond, special diamond, rib, hex, scale, prism, ripple, half-diamond/plain, and half-rib/plain. With most of these individual spoons, the companies note the size of the split ring and hook to be used to make ordering these parts easy. Individual spoons are available variously in packs of five through one hundred. These are very easy to finish into completed lures with only split-ring pliers.

9
Wood Plugs

Introduction • Tools • Plug Hardware • Wood Plug Bodies • Wood Stock for Making Plug Bodies • Carving Wood Bodies • Using Power Tools to Make Wood Bodies • Through-Wire and Plate Construction • Sealing and Painting • Adding Plug Hardware • Variations in Making Wood Plugs • Plug-Making Kits • Costs

Basic Safety Requirements

Safety goggles

Carpenter's apron

Work gloves

Basic Tools for Assembly

Small screwdriver

Pliers

Split-ring pliers

Basic Tools for Carving

Pocketknife

Sandpaper

Countersink

Helpful Tools for Carving

Electric drill

Wood rasp

Long-shank electrician's or aircraft drill bits

Electric-drill routers (such as Dremel Moto-Tool)

Lathe

Lathe chisels

Band saw

Carpenter's saw

Knife

File set

Sandpaper, assorted grades

Glue

Contour gauge

Calipers

Rule

Awl

Saw

INTRODUCTION

When I was a boy, plugs were almost all wood and sold for about 75 to 85 cents each. That was pretty steep for a lad with a paper route as his only source of income. Today plugs cost much more, and some of them are very expensive indeed. If they catch fish and you can afford the cost, that's okay; but there are lots of ways you can make your own wood plugs as a wintertime hobby and a cost saver. The savings, custom finishes, special shapes and sizes, and similar advantages are offset only by the time it takes to make the plugs.

At one time all plugs (today called crankbaits, particularly in bass-fishing circles) were made of wood. Then, from the introduction of plastic plugs in the 1940s until recently, most were made of plastic. There were always some wood-plug holdouts, such as Smithwick, A. C. Shiner, the popular Rapalas and their balsa imitations, and Bagley. Today, however, there is a resurgence of wood plugs, with outdoor-magazine articles noting not only the nostalgic interest in wood plugs of the past but also the effectiveness of wood plugs of the present.

Wood plugs for both fresh and salt water are available from Heddon, Poe's, Gibbs, Acme, Dennis Gilmore, Ozark Mountain, Capt. Andy, Gags Grabbers, Arbogast, Fudally Tackle, Great American Fishing Supply Co., Luhr Jensen, Martin Tackle, Mouldy's Tackle, Nica, Smithwick Bait, Stidham Enterprises, Strike King, Suick Lures, and Trader Bay. Wood is back—maybe bigger than ever.

There are several ways to get into making your own wood lures. Some preshaped wood-plug bodies are available. These are easy to paint and assemble into finished plugs. You can also buy wood blanks—wood blocks cut into the widths and lengths most practical for making wood-plug bodies. Most of these are available in 4-, 6-, and 8-inch lengths. You can also buy wood boards and cut them to size. Regular pine and oak are available at home repair stores such as Lowe's and Home Depot. Basswood is available in some woodworking shops and hobby shops, and various size blocks of balsa are available from hobby shops.

Once you have your materials, you have the choice of either carving out the finished plug with a pocket or carving knife or turning it on a lathe. Once they're shaped, painting and final assembly are the same for all plugs.

TOOLS

The tools required vary, depending on the method chosen for making the plugs. If you work only with preshaped wood-plug bodies, then you may need only a small screwdriver to insert the screws used to attach the hook hangers and plate holders onto some lures. For plugs that require only screw eyes for the line-tie and hook attachment, you won't even need a screwdriver. If you use long screw eyes for work with hardwood, you may want a drill and small drill bits to predrill pilot holes in the plug for the screw eyes.

A start-from-scratch plug-builder could equip himself with a lathe to turn out lures quickly or, at the other extreme, with nothing more than a pocketknife. If you have a lathe, this is an easy way to turn out plug bodies with a round shape. The best lathes for this would be relatively large, with a universal or self-centering chuck (all three jaws close at once with one operation) for working with round stock such as large dowels or closet rods, or a four-jaw chuck (each jaw is operated independently) for holding square stock such as the wood boards and blocks previously described.

It helps if the lathe has a through-center head, which allows stock to be held and passed through the head and jaws of the lathe. This way, you can

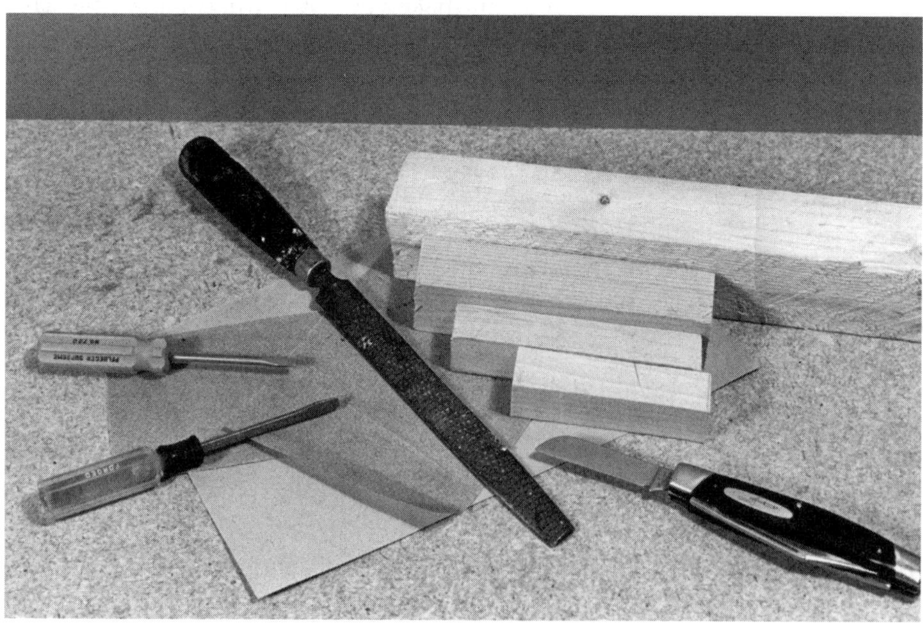

Tools and materials needed for hand-carving wood plugs. The blocks of wood are stock for making plugs. Tools include various carving and pocketknives, pliers, a rasp, and several grades of sandpaper.

seat round stock in the jaws, turn one plug body of the shape desired, cut it off with a cutting tool, open the jaws to move the stock up, and repeat the process. However, a tail stock must be used at all times to hold the free end.

Small hobby-style lathes may also be used, if the swing (clearance between the center of the lathe and the bed) and the length of stock they allow are large enough for any fresh- or saltwater plug. Small lathes like this are sometimes available inexpensively, and used lathes are sometimes available through classified ads.

If they are not supplied with the lathe, you will need to buy special chisels to cut the wood. Many styles are available, but you can probably get by with four or five, including a gouge, round-nose, skew, spear-point, and parting tool. The gouge is used for roughing wood to general shape and for carefully rounding off square stock. The round-nose, skew, and spear-point chisels are all used for the final shaping of the stock; the parting tool is used to cut off the stock when it is completely finished.

Sandpaper is useful for finishing wood-plug bodies. Special lathe sandpaper in narrow widths (1 to 1½ inch) and long coils makes it possible to tear off a strip and work while the lathe runs—in effect turning the stock against the sandpaper.

Kits are available that have a drill handle held up in a clamp, which in turn mounts on a board or bench top for lathe work. Some of these are just simple clamps; the better ones include a simple tail stock and tool rest. Although they will not do precision work, these small drill clamps are okay for limited use in making wood-plug bodies.

A drill with a long bit (called an electrician's or aircraft bit) is handy for making plugs that require through-wire construction, in which a strong cable or wire runs through the plug to prevent loss to toothy or destructive fish. The bits are available in 6- and 12-inch lengths; the 6-inch lengths are suitable for all but the longest plugs.

A band saw is also useful for making wood plugs. You can use a template to trace an outline on two sides of the wood-plug blank (of square stock) and then use the band saw to saw out the blank to the desired shape. The result is a squared-off plug in the general shape desired. To finish, it is easy to remove the corners of the rough cut with a carving knife, whittling knife, pocketknife, rasp, sandpaper, sanding wheel, or a combination of these.

For finishing rough cuts or carving a wood plug from scratch, carving, pocket, and whittling knives are fine, even if time-consuming to use. The best are those with straight blades for straight cuts. Many styles of small wood-handled carving knives are available at hobby shops, and some whittling knives have similar straight blades. Folding knives should have a locking blade for safety.

Electric stationary (bench-mounted) belt sanders are handy for finishing and forming plugs. To form the bodies, such as removing the corners from sawed stock, use coarse sandpaper; finish with finer sandpaper.

Other tools to consider include a countersink for recessing a slight depression in the wood to hold the screw eye or a cup washer for a line-tie or hook hanger. A carpenter's contour gauge is also handy. A contour gauge, through a series of thin pins held in a special bracket, will allow exact duplication of a shape that can then be traced onto a block of wood or used to make a reusable template. If you have rough-carved a plug that seems to have great action, you can trace it to make more plugs exactly like it. It is best not to trace commercial lures, as some have design copyrights or are otherwise protected. You'd probably be okay for your own use, but as soon as you give some to friends or sell to a local shop you could be in violation of the law, not to mention being liable for the excise tax on lures. (For more details on this problem, see appendix B.)

Calipers are a good second choice for checking plug dimensions. A wood saw is a possibility if you are cutting wood to make your own blocks; it's a necessity if you cut a slot in a plug for through-wire construction or add a metal plate for this same purpose.

PLUG HARDWARE

All plugs require hardware. For wood plugs this can include everything from simple screw eyes or hook hangers to hold the hook to some sort of bill or lip to make surface lures wobble or diving lures dive deep. Screw eyes come in nickel-plated brass or stainless steel, with the nickel-plated brass more common. Use the stainless steel fittings for saltwater plugs. Both closed- and open-eye styles are available: The closed-eye type is used for the line-tie, the open-eye type for attaching the hooks. (Although it's seldom done, you can use closed-eye screw eyes and open-eye hooks—trebles, doubles, or singles—on the completed plug.)

Both styles of screw eyes come in a variety of lengths and wire thicknesses, and the length and wire thickness are related. For example, in one catalog the smallest screw eye (open or closed) with a ¼-inch-long shank is made of 0.040-inch-diameter wire; the larger sizes, ranging from ¾ inch to 1½ inches, are made of 0.062-inch-diameter wire.

Generally speaking, the longer screw eyes will hold better, although the wood used for the plug also has a definite bearing on screw-eye strength. Do not confuse these small screw eyes with the larger hardware-style eyes that are available at hardware and variety stores. The screw eyes for plugs are much smaller, are made specifically for plug and lure construction, and have thin wire and small eyes for hook attachment.

The proper screw-eye length for the size and type of plug varies with the size of fish the plug is meant to attract and the type of wood used in its construction. Generally the harder the wood, the shorter the screw eye required; the softer the wood, the longer the shank necessary to hold the screw in the wood. In general a ¼-inch shank should be used only in the smallest plugs, used for relatively small fish. Screws with a ½-inch or ¾-inch shank are better for standard bass, big bass, walleye, pike, and catfish plugs. For larger fish go with the 1¼-inch shanks; beyond that, or for saltwater use, employ through-wire or plate construction to hold hooks.

If you work with hardwood and a long shank, you will need to drill a pilot hole. The best pilot holes for the smallest screw eyes of 0.040 or 0.050 wire are 1⁄32 inch (0.031250). For the larger and thicker screw eyes of 0.057, 0.063, or 0.072 wire, drill a pilot hole of 3⁄64 or 1⁄16 inch (0.046875 or 0.062500, respectively).

The cost of screw eyes is minimal, and because they are used in all plugs, they should be ordered by the hundred. I order only the open-eye hooks because it is easy to close them for line-ties with pliers at the same time I add hooks. This will reduce your inventory of screw eyes, particularly if you need different lengths for different-size plugs. Fortunately they are inexpensive, although the stainless steel screw eyes are slightly more costly than the nickel-plated styles.

Screw eyes are often used with cup washers, although this is not absolutely necessary. Cup washers look like tiny regular washers bent into a bowl-like shape. Disc washers are similar but look like small derby hats with a hole in the top. A countersink depression is necessary for the cup washers, and a straight-sided, shallow drilled hole is necessary for proper seating of the disc washers.

The washers supposedly give the plug a more "finished" look, but they also have an important role: They can help limit the swing or movement of the hooks, thus preventing or reducing the instances of the hook points scratching the paint finish. The disc washers are more effective in this regard than are the cup washers. Usually the disc washers are used in the belly of the plug, where free-swinging hooks can cause the most damage, and cup washers are used for the line-tie and the tail hook.

Cup and disc washers are usually made of nickel-plated brass and range in size from 5⁄32 to ¼ inch in diameter. The depths usually range from 1⁄16 inch for the cups to 3⁄16 inch for the discs, and the hole diameter is about 0.072 or 0.082 inch, enough to accommodate the largest screw eye.

Hook hangers are small devices in the shape of a bent gardening trowel. They are designed to hold a hook and limit its forward swing and are held in place with two small screws. Their main advantage is that they sharply limit the forward movement of the hook to help prevent it from tangling with other hooks on the plug or from swinging forward and catching the line. Hangers are usually available in two or three sizes and are made of nickel-plated brass. They are inexpensive, although slightly more costly than screw eyes and cup washers.

The screws used for hook hangers and for lips and bibs (described below) are nickel-plated steel, usually in a ¼- or ⅜-inch shank length and about half the price of the hook hangers.

Plates, bibs, lips, and bills are plastic or metal devices used to increase the action of any lure. Those that create more surface splash on top-water lures are often called plates, scoops, or bibs. They are usually screwed into the plug at an angle so that any jerk or movement of the lure will create surface splashing, gurgling, or popping. Devices used to control the depth and movement of underwater crankbaits are usually called lips or bills. Some are metal, attached with small screws (the same kind used for the hook hangers listed above). The line-tie is sometimes attached to the lip; other times it's a screw eye in the nose of the plug. Metal lips are usually nickel-plated steel or brass.

Plastic lips are usually made of Lexan or a similar tough, clear plastic. A new type of lip is made of circuit board, the same material used as a base for connections in electronic devices. This new material, made of fiber and resins, supposedly lends more flexibility and vibration to the lure, increasing its attractiveness to fish. Tests have shown that the lure gets as much or more action from these smaller lips than they do with the Lexan lips; however, the circuit board lips are much more expensive. These lips are set into slots cut into the plug body to control the depth to which a lure will run. The size of the bill and the degree of the angle it makes with the long axis of the plug determines the general depth to which the plug will run. Short bills and those at a pronounced angle to the lure axis run shallow; long or larger bills set almost parallel to the axis run deep.

Connectors are often used for greater movement in plugs. Connectors are figure-eight metal attachments with one part of the eye attached to the lure or lure bill and the other part used as the line-tie. A tight knot to the line eye or figure-eight link will not impede the action of the crankbait, since this figure-eight attachment provides a loose connection for maximum action.

Connectors should *always* be used in the case of lips with punched-out holes for line attachment. The edges of the holes are sharp and may cut any line tied through the holes. Connectors can include a wide variety of attachments such as split rings, welded jump rings, figure-eight attachments, connector links, and Berkley or Duo-Lock snaps. The most common attachments are the split rings, figure-eight connectors, and connector links. All are commonly used on commercial deep-diving lures. Connector links are generally not used on top-water plugs unless there is a punched hole in the bib or scoop, in which case a split ring is the best connector.

Hooks for plugs, top-water lures, and crankbaits must be chosen with care. Treble hooks are most often used, but double hooks and single hooks are sometimes found on commercial plugs and used on homemade ones for specific purposes.

Treble hooks are made by all the hook manufacturers, including Mustad, Eagle Claw, Gamakatsu, and Tiemco. Sizes range from the tiny #14 and smaller up through the huge 6/0, and even larger. Obviously there is a full range of hooks for use with any size or type of lure. The most popular sizes for freshwater lures will be from #10 through 1/0, and big-water freshwater (salmon, muskie) sizes might go to 3/0. Some saltwater plugs might carry hooks to 5/0. Finishes include solid stainless steel (ideal for saltwater plugs) and bronze- and nickel-plated styles. Both straight and curved (beak) points are available, and the hooks also come in short or regular shank lengths. The short shank lengths are best where a separate split ring is used between the screw eye or hook hanger and the hook eye, because the split ring will add some length to the total hook arrangement.

Split rings for treble-hook attachment are usually not necessary unless you are replacing hooks on a commercial plug featuring molded-in hook hangers or adding a hook to through-wire or plate-style construction for a saltwater or big-water plug. Even in these cases, it is possible to use open-eye treble hooks. Mustad makes an open-eye hook that can be added to any hook hanger and the eye then closed with pliers. Mustad also manufactures a split-shank treble hook that can be slid in place just as are continuous-wire double hooks. Treble hooks range widely in price, depending on their size, finish, and style.

Double hooks are less often used for wood plugs. They are sometimes used for top-water lures, with the two hook points up to the rear so that when the plug is moved, the hooks will tend to ride up close to the plug body and not hang up on weeds. Some bass pros, when encountering a weedy section that they want to fish with a top-water plug, will use compound-action cutter/pliers to cut off the forward point of a treble to provide the same weedless action of a double hook. Double hooks have a split shank, so the hook can be slid in place onto any hook hanger, screw eye, or split ring. They are *not* like the solid-shank salmon double hooks used for fly tying. Both nickel- and bronze-plated styles are available, in sizes ranging from about #16 through 3/0. Prices depend on style and size.

Single hooks are rarely used in plugs, although there are some notable exceptions. Some bass anglers use single hooks with wire weed guards to fish crankbaits or top-water lures in weedy areas. Some saltwater anglers prefer single hooks for the improved hooking power (usually a single hook one size larger than the appropriate treble hook is used) and because they are easier to unhook from fish, a particular advantage when toothy critters such as barracuda, mackerel, or bluefish are being sought.

Eyes on lures have become increasingly popular, particularly since some biological reports indicate that gamefish seem to react to the eyes of prey and that prey species often have large eyes, obviously for spotting danger and predators. Eyes for wood plugs can take all manner of forms. Small round-head tacks are useful for eyes and were the type of eyes first used on wood plugs at the turn of the twentieth century, before glass eyes became available and popular. Map tacks—small, round-headed plastic pins used for marking maps and business reports—are also good. They stick out with a pop-eyed effect, although if this is not desired it is easy to use a small drill or countersink to cut a recess for one-half of the plastic bulb. Because they are plastic and come in many colors, tacks do not have to be painted and can be added after the plug is completely finished.

Glass eyes are available from some mail-order outfits. They come on a wire shaft with one eye on each end. To use, cut the shaft so that about ¼ inch of wire with the attached eye is inserted into the plug at the appropriate spot.

Decal and self-adhesive eyes are available from companies that make vinyl and prism tapes for decorating lures. These eyes are added after the plug is complete and painted.

Craft stores and some tackle-supply houses sell "wiggle eyes," which are flat-back, clear-front "bubbles" containing a small pupil that rattles around in the bubble. Black pupils are most common and popular, but pupils of red, yellow, blue, and green are also available, if you think the fish care. Sizes range from a tiny 2 millimeters up to 1½ inches. The larger sizes are best as inserts in clear plastic for offshore lures; the smaller sizes are best for smaller freshwater lures.

Stemmed eyes used for craft dolls are solid plastic with a stem and a metal backing plate that holds them on the doll or stuffed animal. They are good for wood plugs when small enough sizes can be found, since a hole drilled in the wood allows the stem to be easily glued in place.

Eyes can be carved into a plug. One easy way is to hammer a dull round punch into the wood and then paint this depression to make it an eye.

WOOD PLUG BODIES

Some wood plugs are available to the tackle builder. Mail-order houses sometimes stock them, and local tackle shops may have some that are locally made. Usually these plug bodies are round in cross section and are mass produced on assembly-line lathes in the same way round table legs are produced.

Most wood plug bodies are made of white cedar or basswood, although other woods can be used. Typical lures from recent catalogs include chuggers, shallow divers, jerk or stick baits, and jointed divers. Usually these are nicely sanded and finished, ready for assembly. In some cases it does help to touch up the ends (end grain), where they were held in the lathe and might be a little rough.

WOOD STOCK FOR MAKING PLUG BODIES

A large variety of wood types is used to make commercial wood plugs, including cedar, California cedar, sugar pine, basswood, teak, birch, oak, balsa, African odom, abachi, jelutong, and ponderosa pine. Basswood, cedar, and sugar pine seem to be the most common, especially for freshwater plugs. All three are easy to work, finish well, hold screws and attachments securely, are easy to seal and paint, and float well for top-water and floater-diver plugs. Balsa is very popular for some commercial lures, but it requires care in finishing. Although it is soft and easy to work and carve, it is also difficult to finish. In addition, it requires special consideration in attaching screw eyes, with through-wire construction recommended because of the wood's softness. Balsa also requires special care in sealing and painting, because the soft wood requires more than the usual number of coats to protect the lure and prevent nicks and cuts that would swell the wood and ruin the lure.

Harder woods, such as birch, oak, and teak, are sometimes used, most commonly with saltwater plugs that are subject to more abuse than are freshwater models. These harder woods are more difficult to carve and finish, sometimes are more resistant to sealing, and do require pilot holes for screws and screw eyes to prevent the screw eye from twisting off or splitting the wood. Through-wire construction is often used anyway for saltwater plugs, even with these tough woods, so this may not be a consideration. Any of these woods—and others—can be used for making plugs at home.

Homemade plugs can be cut from small blocks of wood obtained from lumberyards, hardware stores, hobby shops, tackle stores, and fishing-tackle mail-order outfits. One such mail-order/retail operation carries small basswood blocks that range in size from ¾ × ¾ × 3 inches to 1 × 1 × 6 inches and 1⅛ × 1⅛ × 8 inches, all of which may be used for a variety of plug styles and sizes.

Cedar is the traditional plug wood and was used at the turn of the twentieth century for those venerable old plugs by Heddon, Shakespeare, South Bend, and others. Although now more scarce than it once was, white cedar is still available in the small sizes required by lure carvers. Some companies offer small blocks about 1 × 1 × 4 to 1 × 1 × 6 inches long. You can also get it in boards 4 to 8 inches wide and 1-, 2-, and 3-inch thicknesses, which can be ripped (sawed) to size.

Other woods are available in similar widths and thicknesses from hardware, lumber, and specialty wood shops. To try exotic woods, find a specialty wood shop that caters to a woodcarving and furniture-making clientele. They often will have small scraps (though they still charge for them) of exotic woods with which you can experiment. Some such shops advertise in the specialty wood-carving/furniture-making magazines. Also check the Yellow Pages

Wood dowels are another possibility for plugs but work best only if you have a lathe or band saw or both. Wood dowels are available in 3-foot lengths, ranging from very thin up to the ¾-, ⅞-, 1-, 1¼-, and 1½-inch sizes most useful for making plugs. Although they come in a round cross section, dowels are very hard and are thus difficult to carve by hand.

They are okay to use if you have access to a lathe, because they can be held with a spur center or three-jaw chuck and turned down to the required size and shape. If you don't have a lathe, you can use rotary rasps mounted in an electric drill or hobby motor tool such as a Dremel to shape dowels.

CARVING WOOD BODIES

Anyone can carve plugs or crankbaits from wood blocks using nothing more than a pocketknife or wood-carving knife. Essential to the use of any of these tools is knowing how to work safely with sharp tools, knowing how to whittle or carve, and having a sharp blade on the tool of choice. Carving and cutting with the blade worked away from you and your other hand out of the way is mandatory. To maintain a sharp blade, you will need a good sharpening stone, hone, or diamond sharpening steel.

Sharpening instructions come with most good knives and with the better sharpening sets. In picking a sharpening set, be sure to choose one that has a fine grit so that it will sharpen the blade properly. Most blades need only a touch-up now and then to bring them back to razor sharpness, so coarse stones and hones are seldom needed. Some sophisticated sharpening sets have special brackets to hold the knife at a set angle to sharpen it properly. Before you buy one, check first to be sure that your knife will fit it for proper sharpening. Many of these sets are designed primarily for larger blade fishing and hunting knives.

Before beginning, first decide on the type, style, and design of the plug to be carved from each stock piece of wood. Random carving on a block in hopes of producing a lure usually results in a pile of wood chips. Before touching knife to wood, make templates or determine the exact design you wish to make.

Often the best way is to begin by copying an existing plug. One easy way to do this is to use a carpenter's contour gauge pressed into the side of a lure to exactly duplicate the shape of the plug. A contour gauge consists of a series of short rods or pins mounted in a clamped bracket. Pushing the contour gauge against anything pushes in the pins to exactly match the shape of the object being copied. In using a contour gauge for plugs, make sure you push it into the centerline or center axis of the plug to copy the full shape and width of the lure.

Carpenter's contour gauges can be used for copying existing plugs to make similar or identical wood plugs. Note, however, the cautions concerning trademark registration and patents in appendix B, "Sales of Tackle."

If the plug is not uniformly round, you will have to trace its shape. Sides are almost always symmetrical; the back and belly are often different shapes in diving lures. Trace these patterns on cardboard, making a different pattern for the top (showing the two sides) and the sides (showing the back and belly). In the case of lures such as stickbaits or top-water chuggers, all sides may be identical in size, requiring only one template.

These templates can be either "positive" (the cardboard piece is in the shape of the lure) or "negative" (the shape of the plug is cut out of the surrounding cardboard). The former is easiest to line up on a block of wood but is harder to handle.

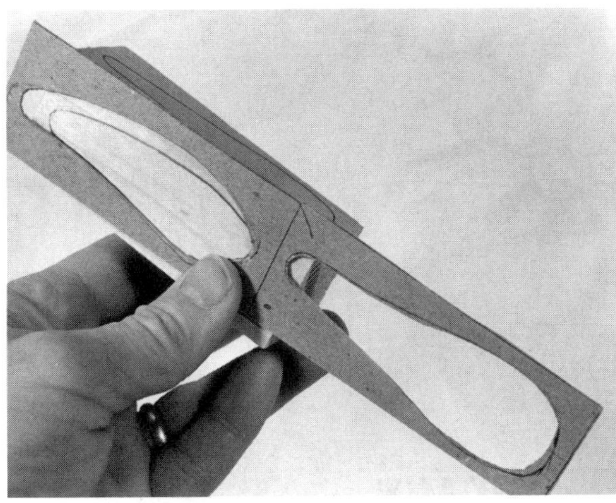

Templates are different for the top/bottom and sides of a plug in all but cigar-shaped surface plugs. Both templates can be made on one sheet of cardboard, as shown, for easy filing of basic designs.

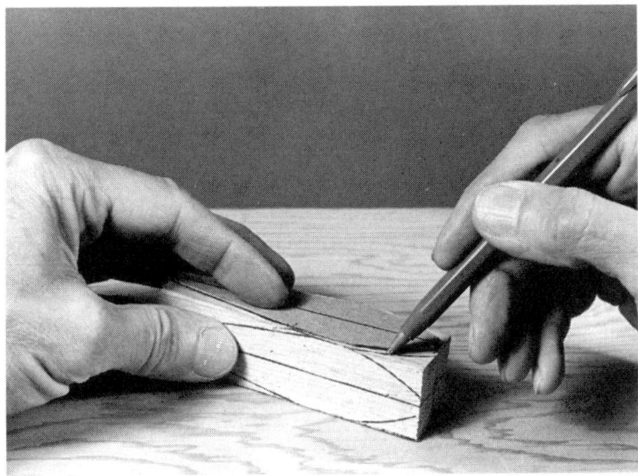

Using a template to trace the design for a wood plug onto the wood stock. The design must be traced on both planes of the wood, as shown.

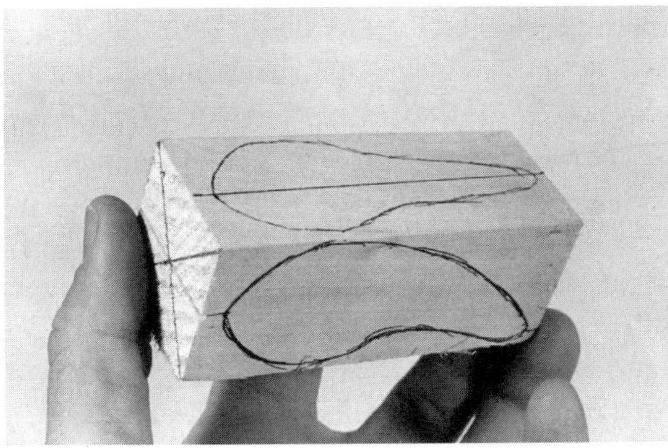

Plug with design roughly drawn on the wood stock rather than using a template. Such freehand plug designs are fun to experiment with.

One tip for making templates is to try a plug first to determine if it will have the action you desire. If it does, you may wish to make templates out of sheet metal for long-term use. To do this, trace the plug's outline from cardboard to the sheet metal—tin or aluminum are both readily available. Then cut the outline out of the metal with tin snips. You may have to begin outside the template area if you're making a negative template, but this will not affect the final result. Flexible sheet plastic also works for this and can usually be cut with scissors. When making templates—whether from cardboard, sheet metal, or plastic—accurately mark the centerline of the long axis of the plug.

Plugs can be designed freehand, but it helps to use graph paper to make sure both sides of the plug design are symmetrical. First draw a centerline on the graph paper, mark the length of the plug, and let your imagination go wild. When drawing outlines use simple shapes and lines as much as possible. Wildly varying shapes and curves are difficult to carve and usually are no more effective in catching fish than are simple shapes.

One other way of making or testing an outline is to draw one side from the centerline, fold the paper in half on the centerline, and then trace the other half of the pattern on the other side of the paper. It also helps to use a rule or precise calipers to check the dimensions.

Once the outline is traced to cardboard and the cardboard is cut for either a negative or positive template, prepare the wood block. First find the centerline of the plug by drawing diagonal lines from corner to corner on each end of the block. Use a square to draw a straight line through the center mark, which falls at the point where the diagonal lines intersect. Continue this straight line along all four sides of the wood block. Place the template on this continuous line, lining up the centerlines of the template with the centerline of the wood block. Trace the plug outline on all four sides of the block for ready reference while you are carving.

Once the pattern is traced on the wood, begin carving. Use safe carving technique and carve a little at a time, being careful to cut away from you. First cut away those parts of the plug pattern that are noticeably thinner than the wood block. For example, in a stickbait both ends will be thinner than the center, while in a chugger only the tail end will be thinner. Carve these portions before you round off the plug. In other words, in the first phase of carving the wood should still be blocky and square but formed in the general shape or silhouette of the plug. Once this is accomplished, begin to round off the plug, working a little at a time so as not to take away too much wood.

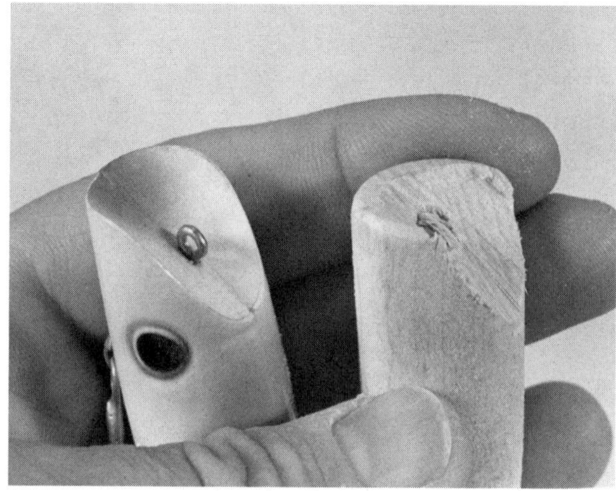

Wood plug body (right) with shaped lip similar to that of a commercial plug (left).

Carving the block of wood with a carving pocketknife, following the template lines.

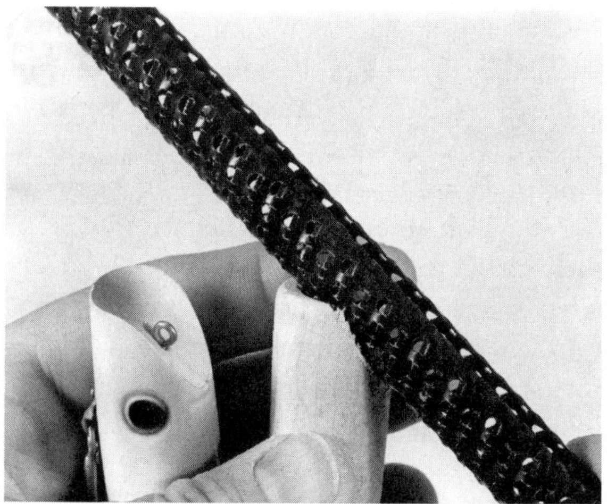

Round rasps or woodworking tools can be used to shape lips such as this sloping lip in a plug, similar to the commercial plug shown to the left.

When the plug is completely roughed out, start the final rounding with a wood rasp. Remember that the final finishing with sandpaper will also remove some wood, so don't try to rasp the block down to the final, finished dimensions. I prefer to leave the plug about $\frac{1}{16}$ inch larger than the final dimensions after it is rasped to shape; I then remove the remaining $\frac{1}{16}$ inch with sandpaper. (If $\frac{1}{16}$ inch sounds like too much wood to leave on, remember that it translates to only $\frac{1}{32}$ inch per side.) This is a good time to check all dimensions with an outside caliper or vernier caliper for accuracy against the plug model or drawn template.

Now start sanding with grade 1 sandpaper, progressing to finer grades until you are using grades 6/0 or 8/0. You do not have to use every grade along the way; you can jump several stages, since there are six additional grades between 1 and 6/0. You can buy sandpaper in coarse, medium, and fine grades or by the grit, which indicates the number of grains that would equal 1 inch if they were laid on top of one another.

A rough comparative chart of sandpapers follows:

Grit	"O" Size	Description	Basic Use
220	6/0	Very Fine	Final sanding
180	5/0	Fine	Final sanding
150	4/0	Fine	Final sanding
120	3/0	Medium	General sanding, light wood removal
100	2/0	Medium	General sanding, light wood removal
80	1/0	Medium	General sanding, light wood removal
60	½	Coarse	Rough wood removal, shaping, rounding the plug shape
50	1	Coarse	Rough wood removal, shaping, rounding the plug shape

There are grits and grades of sandpaper other than those above, both coarser and finer. Also, various abrasives are used in all of these grades, including flint, garnet, and aluminum oxide. Abrasives such as silicon carbide are usually used for wet work, while emery cloth and crocus cloth are used on metal.

For a final smooth finish, take a tip from cabinetmakers. Save some fine sawdust, sprinkle it on the sandpaper backing and on the plug, and then use the back of the sandpaper to polish the wood. At this stage the shaping of the plug is complete.

At this point the plug may still not be complete and ready to seal for painting. If you wish to carve out special sockets for eyes, make gill plates behind the head, carve a dorsal fin, or make other additions, do it now. This can be done by hand or by using small power tools such as the Dremel Moto-Tool. The small cutters and grinders on such tools make quick work of modifications and additions.

Balsa requires special treatment because it is a very soft wood; screw eyes, even long screw eyes, might pull out of it over time. Some commercial plug manufacturers use through-wire construction (which I recommend, although mono can be used just as well on most freshwater plugs) or insert a dowel or plug of hardwood into the center of the long axis of the lure to hold the screw eyes. This works great but is a lot of added trouble for amateur plug builders. If you use balsa, be sure to use some method to ensure the integrity of the hooks and line-tie.

If you make a plug with through-wire or plate construction, you will need to use a power tool to drill holes or a hand or power tool to make the slot for a plate. The methods and techniques for doing this will be discussed later in this chapter.

Once the carving of the plug is complete, you can still make additions by adding metal or plastic parts. For example, dorsal fins of metal or plastic can be fitted to a slot cut into the back of the wood lure and glued in place using a good 24-hour epoxy. Any sheet metal will work, as will durable plastic fins cut from coffee-can lids, plastic bottles and containers, or scraps of acrylic plastic such as that used for some storm windows and hobby parts. If you use the flexible plastic from coffee cans, cut the fin with extensions, or "wings," at the base so that the glue will completely cover them when the fin is glued in place. Glues do not stick well to these plastics; if you omit this step, the fins may come out easily.

USING POWER TOOLS TO MAKE WOOD BODIES

Before you use *any* power tool for making plugs or other tackle operations, make sure you completely understand the tool, read the complete operator's manual, and follow established shop-safety procedures. This is mandatory.

Generally safety means using goggles for eye protection, rolling up your sleeves to prevent them from catching in power tools (remove your tie for the same reason), and taking off all jewelry (chains, bracelets, watches, rings).

A number of power tools can be used in the construction of wood plugs.

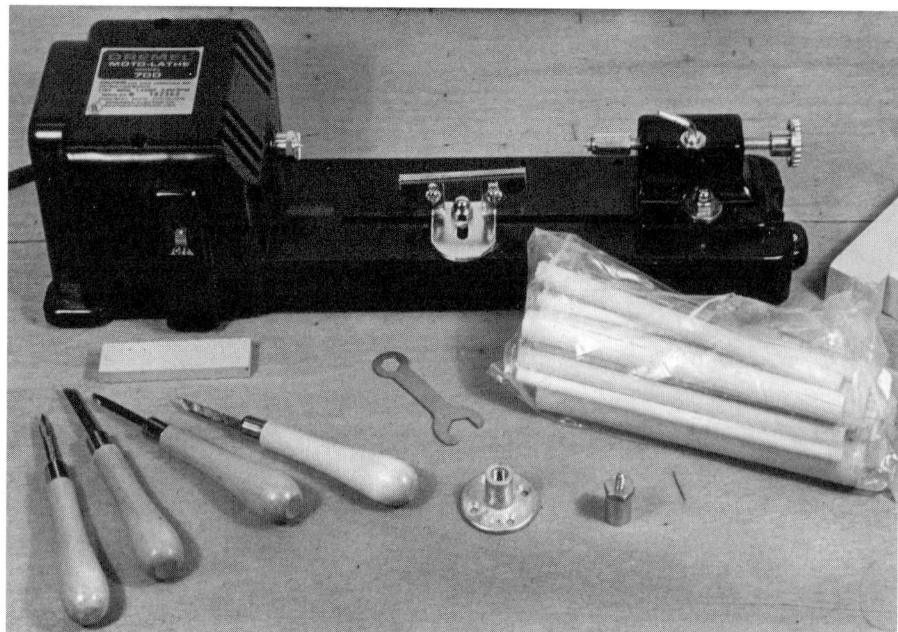

A Dremel Moto-Lathe and small lathe chisels are ideal for turning plug bodies. This particular lathe has been discontinued by Dremel, but some may still be available through used-tool outlets.

Lathe

Any wood lathe can quickly turn out a number of plug bodies. The possibilities include working with a standard lathe with a spur center on the head stock and dead center on the tail stock, using a through-head lathe (the stock will go through the head of the lathe and chuck) and chuck to hold the stock in conjunction with a dead center on the tail stock for quick turning. If you work with round stock, such as a dowel, you can use a three-jaw chuck. If you work with square stock, you can only use a four-jaw chuck, on which each jaw must be adjusted independently. In all cases you must use a live (moving) or dead (stationary) center or taper on the tail stock to hold and support the wood while working it.

Practice good lathe operation, and begin with a gouge to rough the wood to shape and to remove all corners or unevenness from square stock. Shape with the appropriate round-nose, skew, or spear-point tool. Sand with strips of sandpaper, either cut for the purpose from sheets or from the coils of special lathe sandpaper. Use the finer grades until the plug is completely polished. Use calipers or a template (cardboard, sheet metal, or sheet plastic) to check the work for shape and dimension, but do this *only* when the lathe is turned off and has *completely* stopped. Do not attempt to check your work while it is turning.

Lathes are ideal for turning out rough cross-section plugs used for top-water lures (propeller baits, stickbaits, chuggers, poppers) or underwater diving lures to which a lip or bill is attached. They can even be used to make thin-sided lures: Turn the plug to shape, and then use sandpaper or a belt or disc sander to remove material from both sides to make it slimmer from side to side than from top to bottom. Because of the way in which stock is held in a wood-turning lathe, it is often necessary to sand and polish both ends once the finished piece is removed from the lathe with a parting tool.

Band Saw

A band saw can be used to rough out wood plugs for final shaping with a knife, sander, rasp, or router. First outline the shape of the plug on a square wood block, marking the outline on all four sides. Install the narrowest possible blade in the band saw. One-quarter-inch blades are often the smallest a saw can handle, although some better band saws can use blades as narrow as 1/16 inch, enabling them to cut in the smallest radius possible. Set the saw-blade guide for the height of the

Checking a wood surface plug shaped on a lathe.

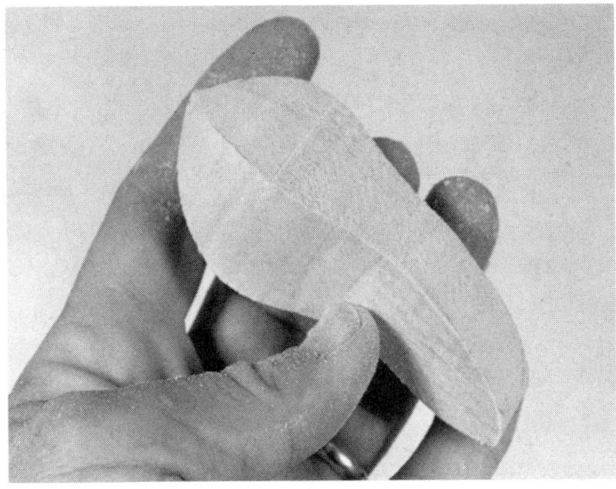
Rough plug body after being sawed out on both planes.

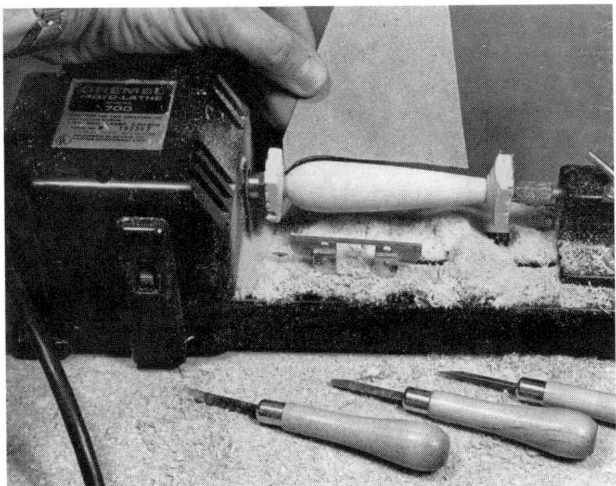
Wood plug shapes can be checked with a cardboard template. The lathe must be stopped for this check or any other adjustment.

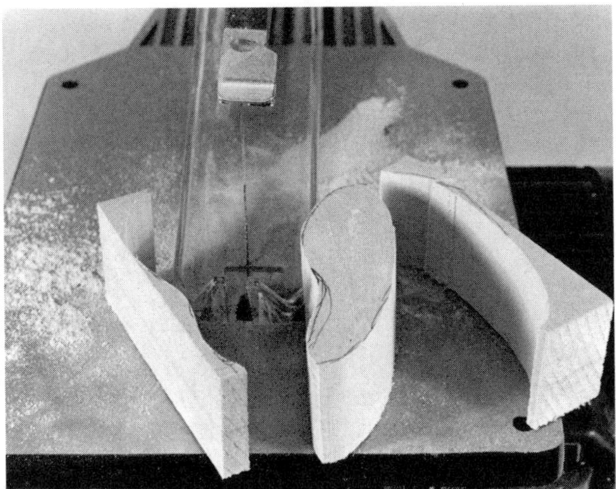
The sawed-out plug with the resultant scrap wood. Tape can still be seen on the wood parts.

wood block to minimize any bowing or twisting of the blade.

With the blade guide set and the saw on, run the block carefully through the saw, following the entire pattern outline on one side. If it proves difficult to go all the way around the outline, first saw one half of the outline and then the second half, working always with the same side up. Save both of these scrap pieces. Then turn the wood block 90 degrees to the side, keeping all the wood pieces (plug, block, and scrap) together. This way you will have a square block of wood to saw the second time, even though the plug blank has already been shaped by the saw. In essence you are using the scrap piece of wood as a base, or cradle, to hold the plug body as you make the second set of cuts. Often it helps to tape these sections together before making the second set of cuts.

If you saw out the two sides with the first cut, the 90-degree turn allows you to cut the back and belly of the plug. The result will be a silhouette of the plug from the top, bottom, or sides. By rounding off the corners and angles with a knife or rasp, you will begin to come close to the final shape of the plug. The rest of the shaping and finishing is just like that for carving a plug: Use the rasp or knife to shape and the successively finer grades of sandpaper to bring out the finished form.

Scroll Saw

Although roughing out can be done with a scroll saw, this is not recommended. Scroll saws have a reciprocating action with their short blades (as opposed to the continuous action and blade of a band saw) and thus are designed for cutting thinner material, primarily sheets of wood and plastic. They are not designed for, nor do they work well with, wood in the ¾- to 1½-inch thicknesses used to make plugs. If you must use a scroll saw, be sure to use it slowly and carefully, and use blades with the least number of teeth per inch for the fastest cutting. The resultant plug bodies will require final shaping and polishing as previously described.

Dremel Moto-Tool

Dremel makes a number of different models of their Moto-Tool, a high-speed specialty drilling and grinding tool. These are versatile tools; the special collets will hold not only small drill bits but also cutoff wheels, routers, grinders, cutters, diamond wheel points, wire brushes, sanding discs, sanding drums, and polishing wheels. All these accessories come in a variety of shapes and sizes. Close to 150 of these bits and accessories are listed in the current Dremel catalog.

The Moto-Tool itself is available in single-speed, two-speed, and variable-speed models, the variable-speed models with settings from 5,000 to 30,000 rpm. There are cordless models, although this feature would probably not be important to the tackle crafter. A flexible-shaft attachment allows you to hang up the Moto-Tool and use its 36-inch-long cable for precise working control. Other attachments allow you to convert the Moto-Tool to a router, shaper/router, and mini drill press; a holder and base allow you to secure the Moto-Tool so that you can work the wood plug against the stationary tool.

The best bits for making plugs seem to be the ½-inch-diameter sanding drum, which makes it easy to sand and shape plugs; the cylindrical tungsten carbide cutters, for fast removal of excess material; the high-speed steel cutters; and the cutoff wheels. Although you cannot easily work a plug from start to finish with these tools (though it *is* possible—decoy carvers use these and similar flexible-shaft tools in their work), they are ideal for shaping and finishing after the plug is roughly blocked out or sized to a general shape.

Electric Drill

An electric drill is a versatile tool for drilling and similar operations, but clamped down or with the addition of a flexible shaft like the one mentioned for the Dremel Moto-Tool, it is also handy for shaping and carving. Special router, grinder, and polishing bits, along with sanding drums larger than ½ inch (1- and 2-inch sizes are readily available), allow easy shaping and polishing of plug bodies. Even the smallest drills are too awkward to hold by hand for this work. A flexible shaft or a permanent holder for the drill allows you to use both hands to hold and work the plug with a foot-control switch or locked "on" setting for the drill. It is easier to work the wood block against a stationary tool than it is to work the tool against a stationary wood block.

Belt or Disc Sander

Sanders are ideal for the final polishing of plugs. I find the small belt sanders most useful; the disc sanders will only sand on a flat plane and thus have limited use for the curved surfaces of plugs. Bench-type belt sanders usually have a backing plate. Most also have an area with no backing where the curves of the plug are more easily shaped because the sandpaper there will flex and give to match the plug curvatures. Fine sandpaper is best. Usually some final hand sanding is also required because these tools will not always allow a final, complete sanding

Any of these tools would be handy to have for the purposes just outlined, but there's no need to buy them solely for tackle building. These tools can be used for other tackle-crafting purposes as well: drills and Dremel Moto-Tools with router bits can clean flash from bucktails; a drill mounted as a lathe can turn rod handles and wood reel-seat inserts; a grinder can carve sprue holes in aluminum block molds for soft-plastic or lead lures. Such tools also have many other general workshop purposes, which would help amortize their cost.

THROUGH-WIRE AND PLATE CONSTRUCTION

Through-wire or plate construction is possible on any wood lure for fresh or salt water. It can be done with homemade and preshaped, purchased wood bodies. Through-wire and plate construction are the means by which a plug's line-tie and hooks are connected, by a wire or metal plate, to preclude the possibility of losing a fish to a pulled screw eye or a ripped-out line-tie, or a plug to the forceful strike of a particularly vicious fish. This reinforcement is done on most saltwater plugs; it is better to have a shattered plug but land the fish than to lose both the plug and the fish. (You might lose the fish some other way, but it should not happen because of the plug or hardware.)

There are several methods for through-wire or plate reinforcement, most of which involve drilling a long hole through the plug or cutting a slot into its back or belly. Neither is done on plastic plugs, since forming the slot or hole for the wire or metal plate and sealing the plug up again isn't worth the extra effort.

This section might seem a little out of order here because it includes information on the assembly of plugs, but you first have to know how you are going to make and assemble the parts before knowing what, where, and how to cut or drill.

There are several ways to rig through-wire or plate construction. The first, and simplest—and one that can be done with any plug, commercial or homemade, wood or plastic—involves using twisted-wire cable appropriate in size to the plug and the fish sought. This is done after the plug is finished and the hooks added and can also be done with any commercially available plug or lure. Use leader sleeves to connect the line-tie to the cable with a simple crimped-loop connection. Then bring the wire through the eye of the belly hook or hooks and repeat the sleeve and crimped-loop connection to the eye of the tail hook. The result will obviously show, but it will also guarantee that you won't lose a fish to a shattered plug.

You can drill a hole through the center of the long axis of a shaped and finished plug (before painting and finishing) and thread wire through the plug. Use a long-shank drill bit, often called an electrician's or aircraft bit. These are usually 6 to 12 inches long, with the ⅛-inch-diameter size best in most cases. In this method you must also drill a short, larger diameter hole through the belly of the plug for each belly hook used (usually only one treble). For construction use heavy (about 1⁄16-inch diameter) wire, twisted into a loop eye at one end and threaded through the hole drilled into the plug. Use a short connector link or barrel swivel in the center of the belly hole (one for each hole drilled and hook used) so that the wire passes through the eye of the connector link or barrel swivel and the barrel swivel is attached to the hook with a small split ring. (Brass swivels are the best and strongest.) Use a barrel swivel of a size that will allow the eye on the opposite end to remain clear of the belly surface of the plug and hold the hook securely.

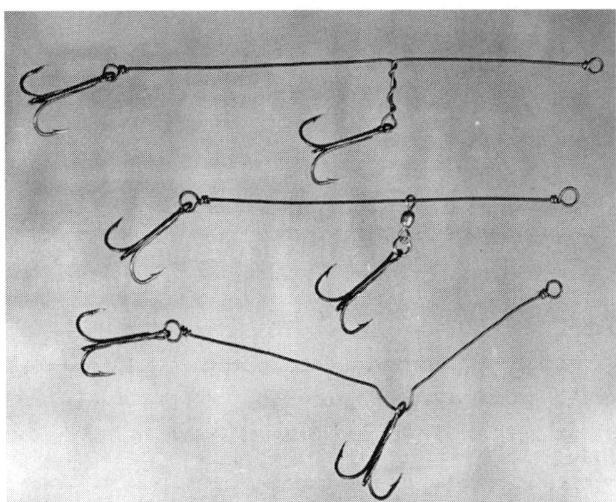

Through-wire construction involves using wire or plates through the body of a plug to prevent loosing the fish should the plug shatter on the strike or break during the fight. These are some examples of wire rigs.

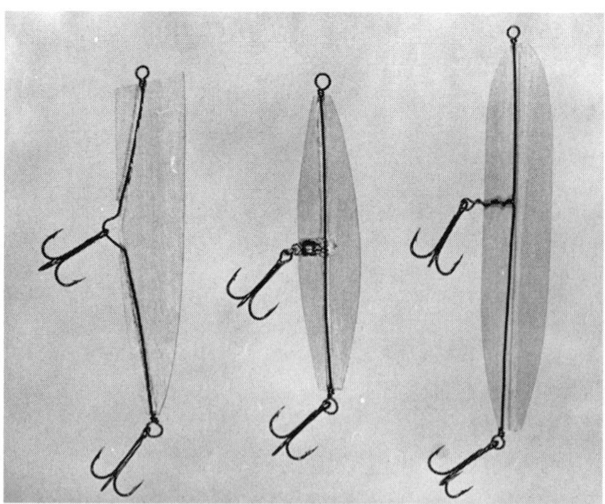

Wire rigs shown in cross sections of wood lures, showing the drilling directions and types of hook-hanger rigs used.

Continue threading the wire through to the end, cinch it up tight, make a loop, and add the rear treble or hook (just like adding a hook to a spinner wire). Wrap the wire shaft to secure it. Finish by adding the belly hook to the swivel with a split ring or by using an open-eye or split-shank hook. Single hooks, doubles, and trebles can all be added this way.

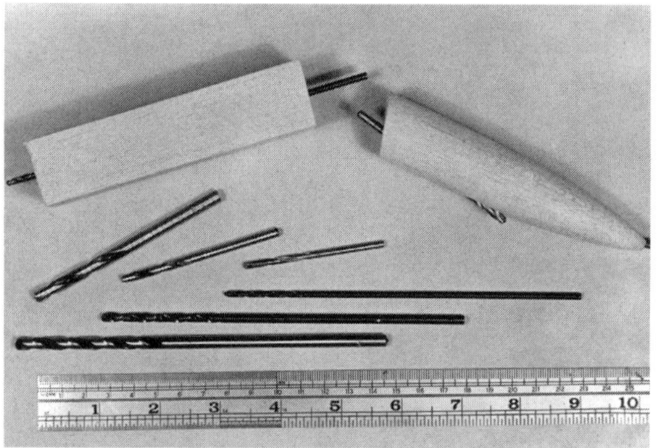

Long bits, sometimes called aircraft or electrician's bits, are best for drilling straight through wood plugs. Standard and long bits are shown here.

This method of making wired plugs is most suited to small (or at least short) plugs. Most 1/16- or 1/8-inch drills are not long enough to drill all the way through long plugs. And the longer a plug, the easier it is to drill off-center and end up with an eccentric hole in the plug, ruining it for all practical purposes. Even with short plugs this is a problem, because most 1/16- or 1/8-inch-diameter drill bits are no more than 1 to 2 inches long—hardly long enough for any but ultralight spinning plugs, where this construction is seldom necessary.

To drill longer holes, use the aircraft, electrician's, or extra-long bits. These are available in both 6- and 12-inch lengths, with the 6-inch bits the most practical for making plugs. They are more readily available now than when the first edition of *Tackle Craft* came out in 1974 and should be available at many good hardware stores and through specialty mail-order hardware houses. The best sizes for plug drilling are those that are 1/16, 3/32, and 1/8 inch in diameter.

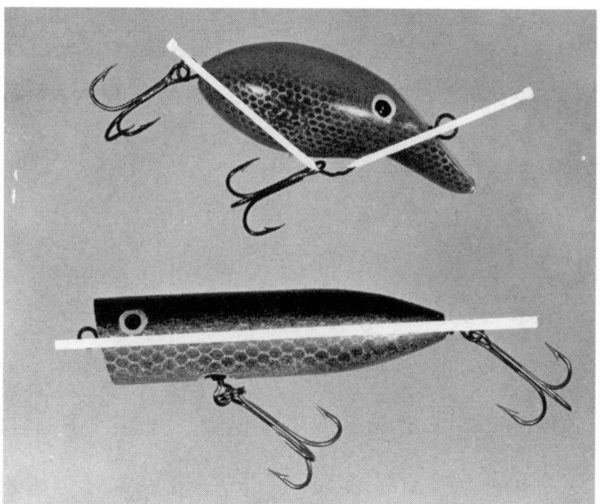

Drilling directions for two types of rigging operations. The top involves two separate drilling operations and can sometimes be done with standard drill bits. The bottom plug requires a longer bit and accurate, straight-through drilling.

Drill the plug from either end, preferably with a drill press for accuracy. If you don't have a drill press, you can get a small inexpensive drill press holder for most electric drills. Use a bench vise or some other support to hold the plug absolutely in line with the drill bit. If you don't have a special vise, you can make a three-board corner that can be clamped to the drill press table, with the plug body clamped or held in place in this corner. When you make such a corner from scrap shelving, make sure all the pieces are square and straight and that the jig made forms an accurate right angle.

You also may wish to do this before the plug is completely finished; a plug roughed out on a band saw will have the scrap that can serve as a "cradle" to hold the plug, with the flat side of the scrap resting against a vertical support. If you work with completely finished plugs, you may wish to make such a support so that the two ends are in a perfectly vertical plane.

Another way to make longer holes is to cut blocks of wood in the correct sizes, drill the center holes, and then carve or saw the plug around these holes. In this case you would use the holes as the axis of the plug, the centerline if you will, on which the rest of the plug shape and design will be based. The advantage of this is that even if the holes are drilled slightly off-center, the plug can be carved accordingly and will end with an accurate, on-center hole at each end.

The same methods can be used to make plugs with twisted cable in place of single-strand wire. The advantage to the cable is that it will be thinner and slightly easier to handle in making loops with leader sleeves in place of wrapped eyes, but it will have a tendency to slip out of the plug or to have more "slop" when the plug is worked. It is simpler too in that a loop with leader sleeves can be formed in one end and the other end of the wire slipped through the long axis hole, run out the belly hole, through a leader sleeve, through the eye of the center hook and back through the same leader sleeve, up into the belly hole, and down to the tail. The wire is pulled snug, the leader sleeve is crimped to hold the belly hook in place, and the tail hook is added with a leader sleeve in the same way. To keep this light-wire arrangement from sliding around, it helps to use some epoxy glue or gel in the hole to hold the wire in place.

You can use heavy mono in the same way, tying secure knots or using mono-safe leader sleeves. In most cases single-strand wire or cable is better, because most fish that can shatter a plug can also bite through mono.

You can use short or long (6-inch) drill bits in another procedure, drilling a hole in each end but not going through to the other end of the plug. The hope here is that both holes will be close to if not exactly on-center all the way through, and by drilling a belly hole for the swivel, you can connect all the parts with the straight wire or cable. The advantage is that you definitely get on-center holes on the axis at both ends. If the wire goes in a slight angle or dogleg through the center, it will not affect performance.

Although these methods work well for all plugs and especially for slim plug bodies, there is another method that can be used with fat-bodied lures such as the so-called pregnant minnow or Big O styles. This method involves first drilling a hole straight through the plug body from nose to tail and then making a second hole from the opening through the nose, angled down to exit at the belly. Bend the wire with round-nose pliers into the shape of a V, and insert the cut ends so that one end of the wire goes through the straight nose-to-tail hole and the other angles down to exit at the belly. Slide the wire into place, leaving enough exposed for the line-tie (thus the need for the round-nose pliers in forming the V). Use pliers to make loops at the belly and tail, add the hooks, and finish the eye by wrapping around the standing part of the wire.

This method can also be used with heavy twisted cable and leader sleeves to close the wire loops holding the hooks. Add a split ring to the nose wire for a line-tie.

A method that avoids the belly drilling for the swivel and belly hook is to drill a hole from each end that angles in such a way that the drill exits through the center belly of the plug. Drill from each end, making sure the belly exit holes are as close together as possible. This assures that the end holes are exactly on-center. The one disadvantage here is that it is often difficult to place the belly holes precisely. Once drilled, assemble the lure by making a wrapped eye with single-strand wire, running it through the plug, and then through the hook eye as it comes out one hole. Bend the wire slightly to guide it into the other belly hole and help push it through the tail hole, where a tail hook can be added and the wire twisted securely. The same technique can be used with flexible cable or heavy mono. It will be easier with the cable or mono to make the change of direction at the center of the plug.

A similar result is possible by cutting a slot into the plug and adding a completed wire assembly or a precut metal plate. If you use single-strand wire, you will not need the swivel because the two (or more) hooks can be added to the tail and center of the plug at the right positions by using a wrapped eye for the tail hook and a slightly twisted wire (like a haywire twist) for the belly hook or hooks. With this arrangement you can preassemble the wire assemblies so that they are ready to go into the slot.

Slots can also be cut into the belly of a plug for through-wire or plate hook hangers. This slot would hold a plate but would have to be widened for a wire rig.

Once the plug shape is complete and sanded, you can only cut the slot with a handsaw. Using a power saw is definitely too dangerous! Cut the slot by holding the plug body in a vise, using soft wood on the jaws to protect the plug. Cut down to and slightly past the center axis line so that there is room for the wire assembly. Make sure you use a saw that will cut a wide-enough slot, or "kerf," into the wood for the wire, including any wire wraps. Once you have a proper fit, place the complete assembly in place and use epoxy glue or gel to fill up the hole.

If the plug is not painted when you install the assembly, you will have to mask the wire eyes and hooks during the painting process. You can also wrap only the line-tie eye and twist the center hook eye, but do not add the center hook or tail hook. Place the assembly into the slot, add the glue or gel, and then paint. Once the plug is completely painted and finished, use an open-eye hook to add to the belly, and finish twisting the wire eye for the tail hook, also to be added at this time. Another alternative is to make all the eyes—line-tie, belly hook, and tail hook—and add the hooks later, using the open-eye hook style or split rings.

The same techniques can be used for flexible cable; use leader sleeves to make the loops for the line-tie and hooks. To use mono, tie the mono or use mono-safe leader sleeves.

The slotting method is ideal for working with plates. A plate accomplishes the same thing as wire does, but a single sheet-metal plate is used. Any tough metal plate of aluminum, sheet steel, copper, or brass will work. It must be thick enough so that the hooks or line-tie split ring will not pull out of it under severe stress.

Cut the slot as before, and make a cardboard template of the plate you wish to make. Usually this plate need be nothing more than a long slim triangle with drilled or punched holes at each corner. Each of these corners will protrude from the

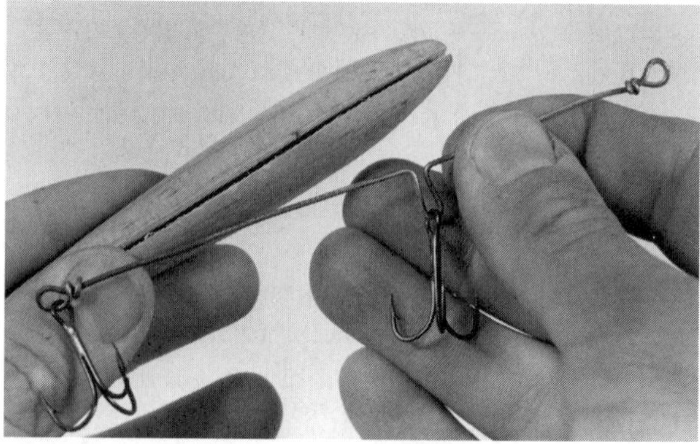

Wire hook hanger made for insertion into a slot in a wood plug body.

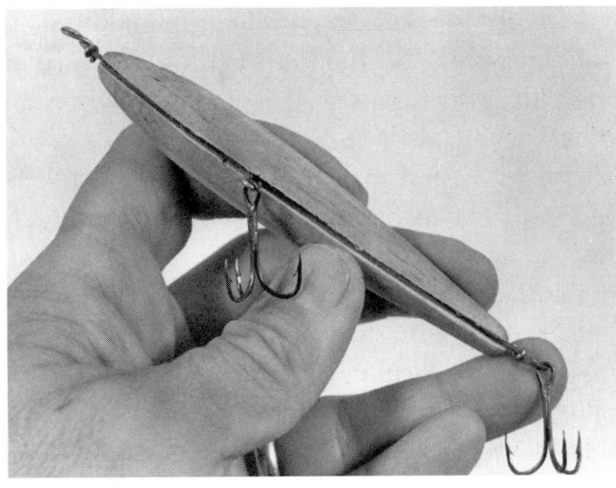
Wire rig inserted into the plug body. The wire rig must be glued to the body.

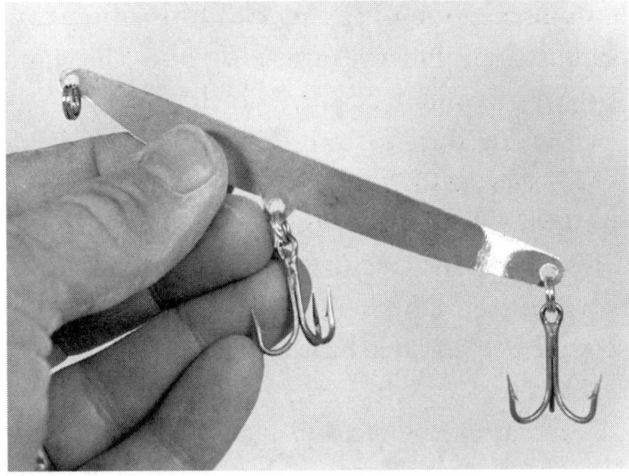
A typical plate cut from sheet metal and shaped and drilled to hold hooks and line-ties using split rings. The plate is glued into a slot in the plug.

body of the plug when it is complete, with the rest of the plate hidden and glued in place. Similar plates can be made in the shape of a very low, wide T, but any shape used for this purpose will require that the drilled, eyed ends for line-tie and hooks protrude from the plug body.

Fill the slot with glue, add the plate, and fill up the slot with additional glue or epoxy gel. Remove any excess glue. Finish painting the plug, and then complete the assembly by adding a split ring for the line-tie and split rings or open-eye hooks for the belly and tail hooks. In this construction, *always* use a split ring or strong snap on the end, because line tied to any drilled or punched hole will wear through in time.

One additional way to prevent the plate from coming out of the slot is to drill several large holes in the plate's center. Glue will fill these holes and help cement the plate to the slot in the wood body.

A variation involves cutting the slot before the plug is carved or shaped. You can use a power table saw for this, provided you cut an entire length of wood and only afterward cut it into the short lengths that will be used for each plug. Trying to cut the short lengths used for plug construction is too dangerous with a power table saw.

Using a billet measuring 1¼ × 1¼ × 4 feet long, first set the power table saw blade for just slightly more than half the depth of the wood, a little more than ⅝ inch. Then set a table guide

Plate being checked against the plug body for length and position of hooks.

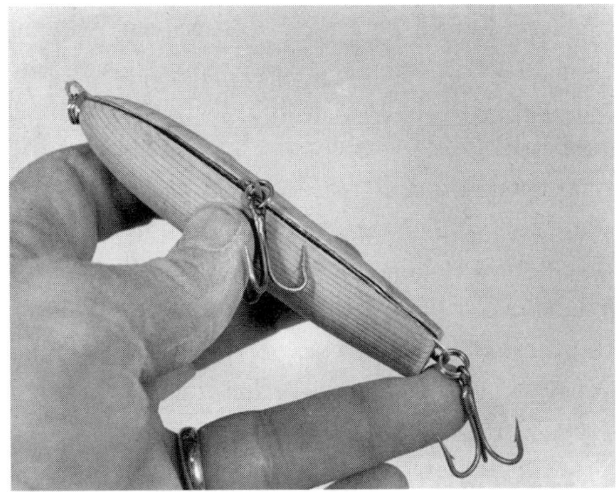
Plate hook hanger in position in plug showing hooks and line-tie in place. The plate must be glued in the slot.

(a rip fence to guide the wood through the saw blade at a specific measurement) to cut the wood strip in the center, exactly ⅝ inch.

Make a test cut, and then cut all the wood for this series of plugs. Remove the rip fence from the saw, replace with a miter gauge to cut cross-grain, and cut the wood into the lengths required for each plug. Carve or shape the plug around the slot and finish, paint, and assemble as described.

The sizes of wire and plate to use in these assemblies are not precise, but as a general rule single-strand brass or copper wire of 0.060 diameter is good, and brass wire of this size is used on many commercial through-wire plugs. South Florida anglers who make their own plugs are using stainless steel #15 leader wire with equally good results.

Any relatively thick scrap sheet metal can be used; stainless steel, copper, brass, and aluminum are better than sheet steel, which will rust. Stainless steel is the hardest to work, although it's tougher than brass, copper, or aluminum. In most cases sheet metal of about 0.030 thickness is fine, but other sizes will work provided they are thick enough to hold the fish but not too thick to fit into the sawn slot.

SEALING AND PAINTING

Once the shaping of the plug blank is complete, it should be sealed with a clear lacquer, base paint, or special wood sealer before any further work is done. Before doing this, make sure you have completed all possible carving or shaping operations. For example, make sure you have drilled any necessary pilot holes for screw eyes, drilled holes or slots for through-wire/plate construction of saltwater plugs, countersunk the screw-eye holes for the cup washers, and made any carving for eyes or gills. Only when all such operations are done should the plug body be sealed.

Usually sealers are slightly thinner than paints because they are designed to penetrate the wood. Permeation will vary with the wood; soft woods are penetrated more thoroughly than are hardwoods. Sealing also helps to waterproof the plug, which is why it is done only after all other carving, drilling, and cutting operations are complete. Several coats of sealer are best. Add one coat, allow it to dry, and then lightly sand with fine sandpaper or steel wool to bring down any grain that might have been raised. This action will also vary with the wood and is more common in soft woods. Sealing prevents the final coats of paint from being absorbed, sometimes unevenly, into the wood and provides a good finishing coat.

After this point the plug is painted or finished in some other way. A variety of finishes are available, including paints and lacquers, scale finishes, glitter, masked patterns, prism tapes, fluorescent paints, phosphorescent paints, and metallic dust finishes. (Since finishing methods for plugs, spoons, jigs, and other lures are similar, chapter 15 has been devoted to this subject.)

After the plug is painted or otherwise finished, it is completed by the addition of the necessary hardware: through-wire hook hangers, hooks, hook hangers, screw eyes, lips, cup washers, and so on.

ADDING PLUG HARDWARE

There is no particular order in which the hardware must be added to plugs, top-water lures, or crankbaits. I prefer to start at the front end and add the closed screw eye to which the line or leader is tied. Use a closed screw eye, preferably one as long as possible for added "bite" in the wood to keep it from pulling out. Some of those supplied in kits and even some found in commercial plugs are a bit too short for my taste. I particularly like a long screw for the nose and tail, because these are usually screwed in parallel to the grain of wood rather than across the grain as in a belly hook, which holds better for a given length of screw thread.

I may be slightly overcautious on this. As a test I once screwed a ¼-inch-long screw eye into the end grain of a 1-inch-thick block of basswood used for making plugs and pulled it against an industrial-grade tension tester accurate to plus or minus 0.5 percent. It did not pull out, and it finally deformed at 24 pounds pull. This is far more tension than would ever by exerted on a small plug with such a screw eye in landing a fish.

On the other hand, I have heard too many tales of screw eyes coming out of homemade plugs to be complacent about them. Plugs are not just thrown into the water to occasionally retrieve a fish. They get hooked on snags and stumps and knocked about in tackle boxes and boats. Lines are snapped off sharply to the side to change lures, and plugs are cast into rocks and rubble, brush and boat docks. All this can weaken and loosen the hold of screw eyes in plugs—especially over a period of time.

Using long screw eyes does create some other problems however. I have occasionally had the eye part of the screw eye twist off while I was still turning the thread into the wood. This will happen with hardwoods or with long screw eyes; thus the suggestions made previously to drill pilot holes for all long screw eyes used in hardwoods. Some suggestions for pilot-hole sizes were made, but it is always best to experiment and determine what is best for you, since there are too many variables in screw-eye size and wood density. Another tip is to use a bit of soap on the threads to lubricate them for easier turning.

Cup washers through which the screw eyes are fastened into the plug are not absolutely necessary, but they do help limit any swinging of the treble-hook points and thus help prevent damage to the plug finish. They also add a professional touch. Deeper cup washers, called disc or derby washers, serve the same purpose as cup washers but even further limit hook movement and reduce or eliminate the possibility of hooks tangling on short or small plugs. Often the deeper disc washers are used at the belly of the plug and cup washers at the nose and tail.

Countersink the area for the cup washers, and drill a small depression for the disc washer. Do this before painting.

If wiggle plates are to be added on surface plugs, they must be lined up properly and attached with the small ¼- to ⅜-inch screws used for the purpose. Metal lips are added the same way, using small screws to hold them in place. Some of these have a built-in hook hanger for holding the belly or center hook, which must be added before the lip is secured.

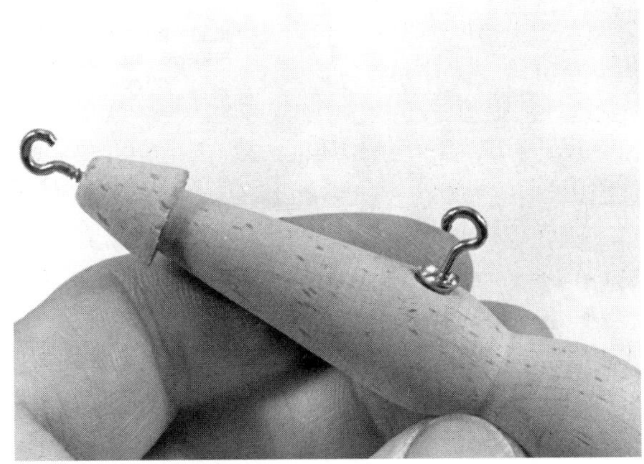

Open screw eyes in the plug body to check for position before painting and assembling. The belly screw eye uses a cup washer, fitted into a hole countersunk into the wood body.

Plastic lips are usually inserted into the plug, and for this a slot must be cut into the wood either before or after painting. If the slot is cut before painting, you may have to cut or resize it again, because some paint will have soaked into it. To fasten the lip, use a good grade, long-setting 24-hour type of epoxy, not the 5-minute kind. For best results drill a pilot hole before gluing so that you can insert a small screw for additional strength and security. This screw must go into the plug body and then into or through the glued-in base of the lip. When gluing, make sure the lip is perfectly lined up with the body and then mop up any excess glue. One way to prevent glue smearing onto the plug finish is to use masking tape around the edge of the lip, insert the lip, and then remove the masking tape with the excess glue on it. Then do any final cleanup.

When using metal and plastic lips, be sure the line-tie is rounded—a round wire in the case of some plastic lips. If it is not, then be sure to add a split ring, Duo-Lock snap, or connector link for the line attachment.

Add the tail screw and cup washer to complete the lure. Use open screw eyes to add all treble hooks and screw eyes. Insert the screw eye into the wood until about three turns from the end, then add the hook, close the screw eye with pliers, and finish turning the screw eye into the plug. Line up the plane of the screw eye with the axis of the plug. Both the belly and tail hooks can be fastened with hook hangers and the small screws used to hold them. With these the "trowel" blade part of the hanger is always faced forward so as to limit the forward swing of the hook.

Some surface plugs have propellers for added flash, noise, and splash. On some plugs they are on the tail; on others they are on both ends. Add these to the shaft of the nose and tail screw eye before inserting into the wood. Since part of these screw eyes will protrude from the lure, you will need screw eyes about ¼ inch longer than you would otherwise use. Use small cup washers both fore and aft of the prop for bearing surfaces. Take care not to draw the screw up tight, because this will prevent the prop from turning.

Another tip if you make plugs with props both fore and aft: Get counter-rotating blades, or twist the blades of one prop to spin in the opposite direction of the second to eliminate any torque that might otherwise tend to spin or rotate the lure and cause line twist. This is particularly a problem with small, lightweight lures, but it can happen with large saltwater lures as well.

Using a hobby tool with a cutting disc to cut a slot in the top of a wood plug body for addition of a plastic or metal dorsal fin.

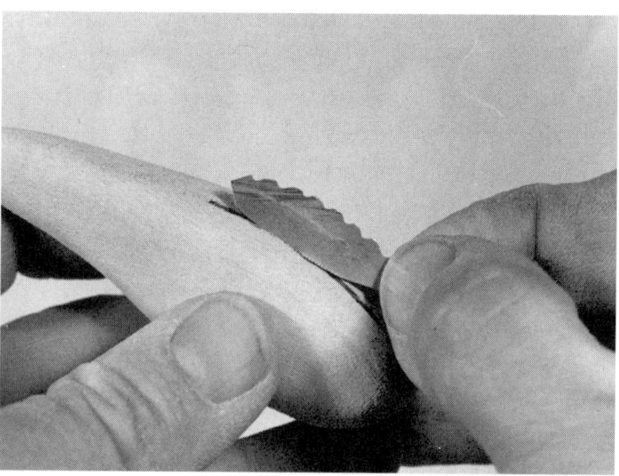

Dorsal fin, cut from scrap metal, being checked against the slot.

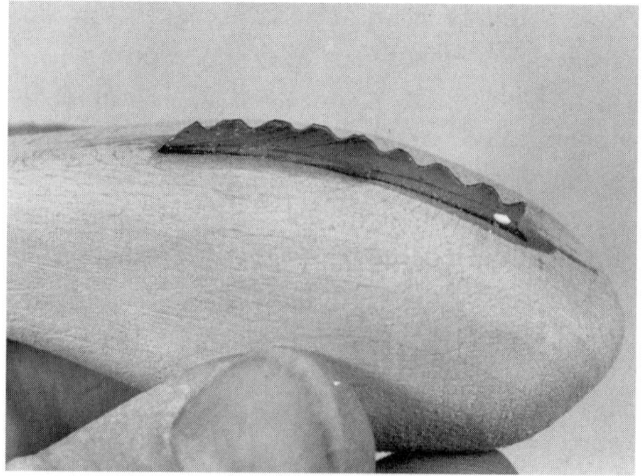

Metal dorsal fin glued in place on top of plug body.

VARIATIONS IN MAKING WOOD PLUGS

Variations in shape, style, running depth, and design of wood plugs are unlimited. Anything that is similar to commercial designs, or anything that you imagine, can be carved on wood and rigged for fishing. Some simple variations on the basic construction of a basic plug include:

Jointed plug. These are easy to make because they are really nothing more than a plug cut into two or more parts, with the parts joined by connectors. In most cases jointed plugs consist of only two parts. In some, three or even more parts are used, although these usually make for excessively long plugs that have limited use and are little, if at all, better than single or two-part plugs.

A simple way to make jointed plugs is to plan for this in the design, carve or shape the plug, and then cut it in half at the desired spot to make the two parts. Whether carved by hand, shaped with a band saw, or turned on a lathe, this is far easier than making each part separately.

Once the parts are cut, use a rasp, knife, or sander to slightly round or angle the sides of the connecting surfaces. This will allow the side-to-side movement of the two parts, giving them clearance.

There are several ways to connect the parts. The easiest way is to use long screw eyes centered in the two parts, with one eye arranged vertically, the other horizontally. Another method is to use a short connector link or to make a similar thin connector plate with holes at each end. Cut a horizontal slot into the center of the connecting surfaces, insert the connector link or plate, and secure it with a thin, long screw fastened vertically through the plug and the holes in the link or plate. A large split ring could be used as a connector in the same way.

Both parts must be painted before the assembly, and the proper connections are part of the final assembly process, along with the addition of line-ties, hooks, and any finishing parts.

Rotating tail section. This is similar to the two-part lure, but instead of a wiggling jointed lure, the second part rotates on a shaft for a different action or more flash. This is not often seen on commercial lures, and when used it is primarily for muskie and saltwater lures.

For this variation, make the lure as previously described, and cut it in half. Drill a center hole through both parts, but make the hole in the forward section just barely large enough for brass wire, and make a larger diameter hole through the rotating rear section.

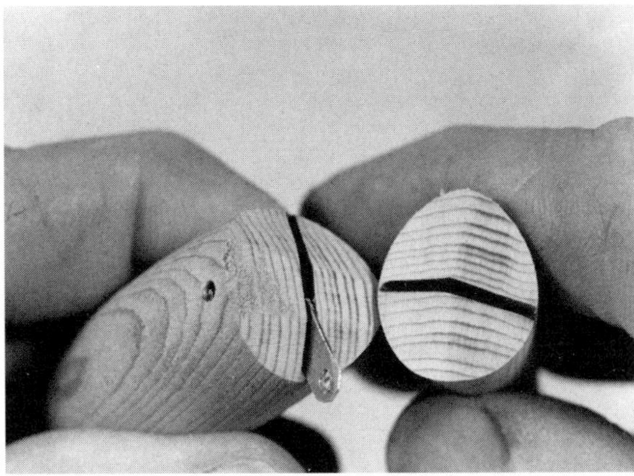

Another way of making a jointed body is to place a small plate, cut from sheet metal and drilled at both ends, into a slot cut into the plug body and then pin it to each part of the plug body.

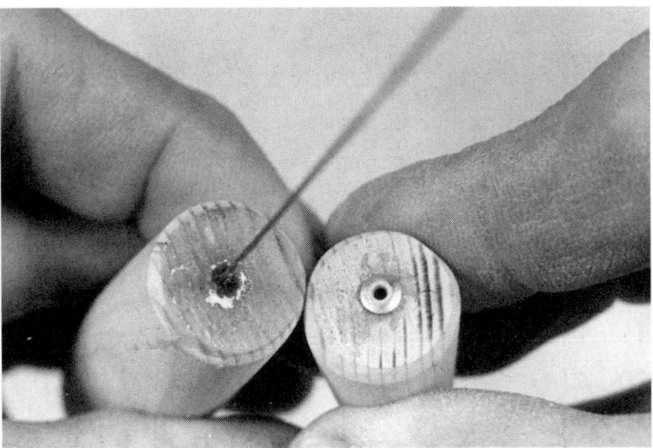

Rotating tail sections on two-part plug bodies are possible by through-wiring and then making fins for the tail section to rotate. Here the wire is glued into the front body and a collar (pop rivet head) is placed on the tail as a bearing.

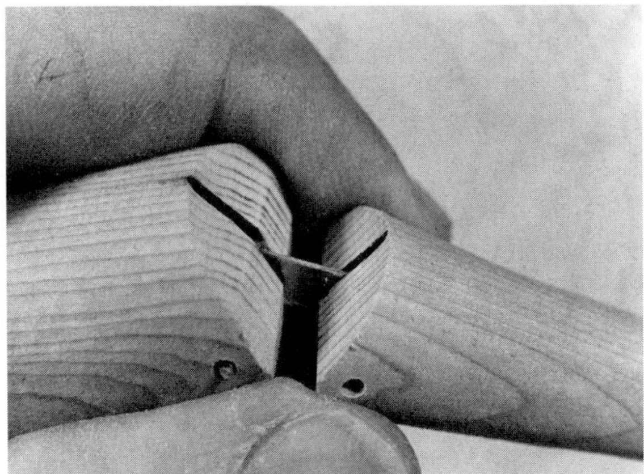

Jointed plug body showing the taper on the facing ends of the jointed parts and the plate pinned in place. Pins are easily glued in place.

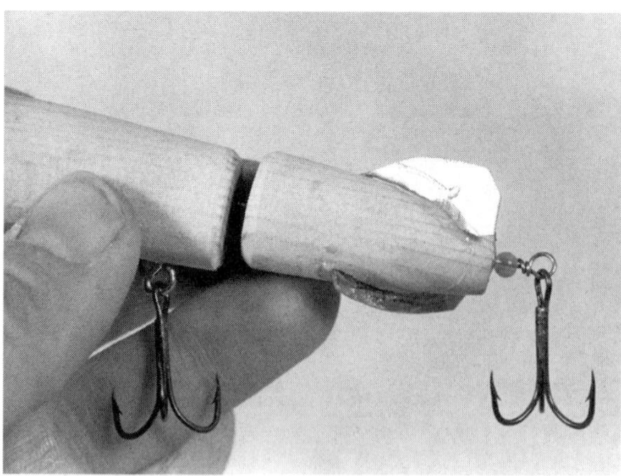

Fins glued into place on the tail section to cause this tail section to rotate. Note the bearing bead between the tail section and wrapped wire eye for easy rotation.

Rig as with through-wire construction, but make sure the hole in the rear section is large enough for it to rotate easily on the wire. Glue the wire in place in the forward section to prevent it from sliding back and binding against the rear rotating part. Use a small plastic bead as a rear bearing on the wire for the rear section, and finish with looped eyes to hold the hooks.

To make the rear section rotate you will have to add metal or plastic fins or cut planes into the section that will make it like a propeller. Another way to get good rotation to the lure is to drill slightly larger holes in each end of the rear section and insert glass or plastic beads or derby washers that will serve as bearings on the wire for the lure tail, preventing the lure from binding on the wire.

One easy construction method for some lures involves making two at one time by carving the lures or turning them on a lathe and then cutting them apart. This way you can get the same taper on each end and save time and effort. This is best when making chuggers, since the two lures on the lathe will be fat in the middle (where the two faces are) and tapered at the ends. These lures can be cut apart square or cut at an angle to make an angled face.

Adding weight. Many lures are completed without adding weight. In some cases weight helps get the lure deep or gives it a certain action. Even surface lures can benefit by the addition of weight, because many surface lures, stickbaits, chuggers, and the like will work differently when they float flat on the surface than when they float vertically, tail under and head above the water. Weight in the tail section allows for this difference.

Deep-diving lures, even floater-divers, often need weight to work properly or to make them a "neutral buoyancy" lure, which will neither rise nor sink but will remain suspended at rest at a given depth. One point about these lures—whether homemade or commercial: Neutral buoyancy is a goal that can be approximated but seldom exactly achieved. Water temperature and salinity, among other properties, affect lure suspension. Thus a lure that will suspend perfectly at one water temperature and salinity (or lack of it) will rise or fall under slightly different conditions.

Usually lead is used as weight, and it is almost always added to the belly of the lure, although for surface lures the tail is favored. Be sure to experiment with other locations when adding lead, but realize that the lower part of a plug body is best in order to prevent the lure from turning over and losing stability.

To add weight, drill a hole in the belly of the lure and add the chosen amount of lead. A good way to add lead is to use split shot glued into place

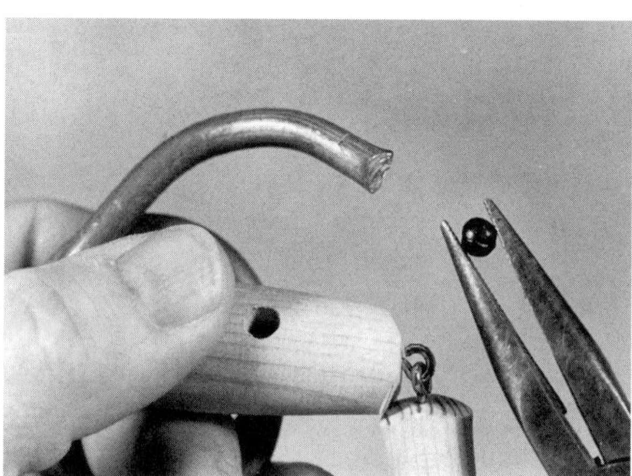

Plugs can be weighted for balance by adding pencil lead (left) or split shot to holes drilled into the belly. Molten lead can also be poured into drilled holes.

in the hole or to use short, cut lengths of the pencil type of lead used in T-type rubber tubing holders for West Coast drift fishing. This lead is readily available in the Northwest, but it can be bought through catalogs as well. The lead comes in ⅛-, 3⁄16-, ¼-, and ⅜-inch diameters, in coils, and can be easily cut to size and glued into drilled holes in plugs. For added security the pencil lead with a hole through the center can be used; a screw should be run through the hole and into the body of the plug to secure it. It should also be glued, if for no other reason than to smooth the surface of the lure prior to painting. If you do this, be sure to measure and/or weigh the lead used in a given lure so that you will later be able to duplicate it exactly.

In all cases be sure to use epoxy glue to hold the lead; smooth the glue surface once it's cured and before painting.

Another way to add lead to a lure is to drill the hole for the lead weight and then use a smaller drill to poke holes in the side of this larger hole and rough up the inside surface. With a batch of these lures, use lead-molding techniques to melt lead and pour a little into the belly hole of each lure. Roughening the inside of the hole is necessary to keep the lead from slipping out later.

Adding rattles. Rattles will always contribute weight to a lure, but because the rattles must be in a loose chamber, the added air pocket helps offset the added weight. Rattles can be lead shot, copper BBs, or tiny 2-millimeter glass or plastic beads such as those from Woodies Rattles. Rattles are often found in hollow plastic lures and less so in wood lures because of the added manufacturing cost. Basically you must drill a relatively large hole into the plug, into which rattles can be added and the hole then plugged or sealed. The best way to do this is to drill the hole, clean it, and add enough rattles to make a noise (check this by placing your thumb over the hole and shaking the plug).

Wood will tend to deaden the sound of the rattles somewhat, but there are ways to increase the noise. One way is to make a "liner" from a sleeve cut from a discarded ballpoint pen and placed in a drilled hole. This will help the rattles make a sharper clicking noise.

Another way to add rattles is to obtain some of the rattling worm and lure weights (plastic, metal, or glass), drill an appropriate size hole, and glue one of these weights into the lure. Coat the hole with glue, and smooth it off after the glue has cured and before painting.

Adding spinner tails. Spinner-blade tails will add some flash to a lure and are easy to add by using a Duo-Lock snap to attach the spinner blade to the rear hook hanger or screw eye in the plug.

Changing hooks. Hooks are easily changed by using split rings or the open-eye style of hook, available in single, double, and treble styles. If you don't have these, the split ring can be opened and the old hook taken off and the new added at the same time. Single hooks are often used for some types of fishing; a single hook one or two sizes larger than the treble is often the best choice.

This means a larger gap for better hooking, more strength in the wire for big fish, and easier unhooking of toothy fish such as bluefish, mackerel, and barracuda. The use of double hooks instead of trebles is often best for fishing in weeds. Arrange the hooks with the points up to minimize snagging.

Adding soft-plastic tails. Soft-plastic tails, including grubs, spinnerbait tails, and short worms, add attraction to plugs. The one problem with this is that the soft plastic will often react adversely with the paint used for wood lures (or with the plastic used in plastic lures), so the paint surface and plastic tail should be kept separate in storage if at all possible.

There are several ways to add soft-plastic tails to plugs. One is to add a soft lure corkscrew to the rear screw eye of the lure and twist the worm or grub onto this screw eye. To make your own use a small ⅛- to 3⁄16-inch-diameter compression spring (the type with each coil separated by a space), bend one end to fit onto the screw eye, and twist the worm into the open wire of the other end. If the free end is not open, use wire cutters to remove some of the spring, or use pliers to bend out a free point of wire. You don't need a long spring for this—about six full coils will do fine. HitchHikers are the same thing and are designed for lures and adding soft plastics; they are commercially available from tackle shops and mail-order catalogs.

Another way to do this is to replace the standard treble hook on the tail with a bent-shank worm hook, designed specifically for Texas-rigging worms. Use your choice of worm hook for the tail hook in the lure. Then add the worm or grub tail to the worm, slide it up to the head of the hook, and Texas-rig it to make it weedless. To help prevent the worm from sliding down on the hook shank, use the bass fisherman's trick: Peg the worm to the eye of the hook with a toothpick, and then break off the excess toothpick. A variety of hooks are available for this from all the major hook companies. Check their catalogs or your tackle shop for the best choice.

PLUG-MAKING KITS

Plug-making kits are available from a number of catalog companies, including Cabela's and Jann's Netcraft, although kits for plastic lures are more common. Most come with the unfinished but shaped wood lures and include the lips, bibs, hooks, screw eyes, or hook hangers necessary to complete the lure. Some include paints; others are already painted.

COSTS

Costs for wood plugs can range from only a few cents each to several dollars for commercially shaped wood bodies in large sizes. If you carve or shape them yourself from raw wood stock, the cost is only pennies each—mainly the cost of hardware, hooks, and paint. Kits and preshaped and prepainted wood plugs add to the cost.

10
Plastic Plugs

Introduction • Tools and Materials • Plug Hardware • Plastic Plug Bodies • Assembly of Plug Parts, Gluing, and Sealing • Plug Bodies from Solid Plastic • Adding Plug Hardware • Painting and Finishing • Variations in Making Plastic Plugs • Plug-Making Kits

Basic Safety Requirements

- Safety goggles
- Carpenter's apron
- Gloves

Basic Tools

- Pocketknife
- Sandpaper

Basic Tools for Assembly

- Small screwdriver
- Pliers
- Split-ring pliers

Helpful Tools

- Electric drill
- Long-shank electrician's or aircraft drill bits
- Lathe
- Lathe chisels
- Dremel Moto-Tool
- Band saw
- Carpenter's saw
- Knife
- File set
- Sandpaper, assorted grades
- Glue
- Contour gauge
- Calipers
- Rule
- Awl
- Saw
- Polyethylene lure models

INTRODUCTION

There are pros and cons to making plastic plugs versus wood plugs. First there is no way a hobbyist can make injection-molded plugs such as the floater-divers or top-water models that are made by modern lure manufacturers. They can't be "poured" as plastic worms can, and the equipment for making them runs into tens of thousands of dollars, perhaps ten to twenty thousand for the mold alone. A method of casting plugs and poppers using a type of polyurethane foam developed by Roy Hilts of Hilts Molds was taken off of the market some years ago. This was different from injection molding in that the material used expanded to twenty times its liquid volume, in the process becoming very light to make surface lures or floater-divers.

You can turn plastic plugs on a lathe using clear acrylic plastic rods, but these end up as solid plugs that sink and are thus limited in their usefulness when compared to modern commercial floating/diving plugs.

You may be able to find plastic plug bodies in two parts, which must be glued together. Often this is how commercial plugs and crankbaits are made, with the two sides molded and then welded together with liquid glue or through electronic ultrasonic vibrations to make the finished lure.

They are also available in finished but unpainted lures, and in finished painted lures that require only the addition of hooks for completion. They are generally a lot easier to make and also have somewhat of a "guaranteed" action in the water. These plastic lure bodies sometimes come from the same molds in which commercial lures are made.

Plastic lures do not have the versatility of wood lures. You can't easily change their length, shape, or action. Unless you make the lures from plastic rods, what you buy is what you get, finish, and fish with. With wood you can make up any shape or design you wish, including the standard proven designs available in commercial wood lures or some offbeat experimental model that may work great—or not at all.

TOOLS AND MATERIALS

The tools and materials for making plastic lures are usually far simpler than those needed or frequently used for making wood lures. For example, if you purchase finished, painted, plastic plugs, you don't need much of anything at all—just pliers or split-ring pliers to insert the hook-hanging screw eyes into the lure and/or attach split rings to the screw eyes and hooks.

The list of tools at the beginning of this chapter does, however, indicate the extent to which you can go in making plastic plugs if you work from raw plastic such as a plastic rod. You can use a lathe to turn a cast plastic rod to shape the plug, use an electric drill to drill pilot holes for the screw eyes, and use a Dremel Moto-Tool for final carving and making eye sockets for solid-plastic plugs. The basic operations of these tools on plastic plugs are no different from those mentioned in chapter 9 on wood plugs, and you should review the appropriate sections in that chapter before you work on plastic.

One basic suggestion in working plastic is to use the proper speeds. Lure and tackle makers who have worked with cast acrylic rod suggest speeds of about 1,400 to 1,800 rpm, using scrapers rather than cutters for tools. The use of higher speeds can result in the plastic melting or charring, damaging the resulting lure. Check your tool's owner's manual for suggested speeds for drilling, turning, or working acrylic plastic.

Acrylic plastic rod is available in several diameters, with the most useful being about 1 inch to 1½ inches. Popular sizes include ¼-, ½-, ¾-, and 1-inch diameters. The cost varies with the diameter, and the material is priced by the foot. Six-foot lengths are standard. Clear is probably the best choice, but colors are sometimes available. Look for this material under "Plastics" in your phone book Yellow Pages.

In all your acrylic purchases, make sure you have *cast* acrylic rod, not *extruded* acrylic rod. Cast acrylic rod is ideal for working in a lathe, using a universal three-jaw chuck and a through-hole head: The rod can be run through the head, shaped, cut off, and the next section run out of the lathe chuck for shaping. Extruded acrylic rod is subject to shattering, cracking, and breaking. All this will result in a damaged lure and could even be dangerous, depending on how and how badly it breaks.

Other necessary tools and materials include only a few hand tools. For example, you might want a knife to gently scrape away any flash or excess glue that forms along the seam lines of preassembled plugs. If you glue the parts together, you will need the same tool for the same purpose. If you work with solid plastic (acrylic rods shaped into plugs), you will find final-shaping uses for a wood rasp, sandpaper, and countersink, the latter to make recesses for screw eyes.

If you make plugs from solid plastic rod, you may also want to drill it for through-wire construction, requiring 6-inch-long aircraft/electrician's bits for the drill.

Glues for assembling the two halves of a plastic body must be chosen carefully. Special glues that will glue to butyrate or PVC plastics used in most plug bodies are a must. Check the labels to determine the best choice. Regular hobby-style Duco Cement is fine, along with the vinyl glues

Some ultralight plugs are available in two parts and must be glued together before adding line-ties and hooks. Since they are available with red heads and white bodies, no finishing is required.

designed to "hold everything" and the so-called superglues made of cyanoacrylate. You can also often use some special solvents of these plastics that will in essence "weld" the two halves together. Often various ketones work for this; acetone is the most common and is sometimes available from pharmacies or hardware stores. Acetone is also the major component of some finger-nail-polish removers. You can try some, but experiment first with this or any other solvents not specifically designed for plug "welding."

Pliers are handy for inserting screw eyes into the plug and also for closing the open eyes to hold hooks or to make the closed-eye line-ties for the front of the plug.

Again, review the more-extensive discussion of tools in chapter 9, or refer to the section on tools in chapters 1 and 2.

PLUG HARDWARE

Plug hardware for plastic plugs is no different from that used for wood plugs. Lips are separate in wood lures but are generally molded into shallow or deep-diving plastic lures. So while lips are seldom used for plastic plugs, you will need the same screw eyes, hook hangers, propellers for surface lures, hooks, and the like used in wood plugs. The one difference is that for most wood lures long screw eyes are best, and lengths can vary depending on the type of wood (its hardness) used and the presence or absence of a pilot hole. Injection-molded plastic plugs usually require a specific length of screw eye, since most have molded-in sockets or recesses for this specific length. Shorter screw eyes will only make for a weaker hook attachment; longer screw eyes will go through the bottom of this molded-in recess and penetrate the hollow interior of the lure, perhaps weakening it or allowing water to enter. I've even seen cases where long screw eyes have split these plug bodies.

As with wood plugs, you may want split rings, connector links, or Duo-Lock snaps to serve as a line-tie for the plug and to give the plug additional action. This is particularly important when using heavy line, since a tight knot to an immobile line-tie will impede lure movement.

For making plugs of acrylic rod, you can use any length of screw eye but must drill pilot holes appropriate to the diameter of the screw eye. The hard acrylic plastic will not yield as wood will, and thus the pilot hole is mandatory to ensure proper holding without the hole stripping or twisting off the screw eye from too tight a fit.

You can also through-wire acrylic rod plugs by straight-drilling a hole through the plug body, through which a wire can be run to connect hooks and line-ties. (The techniques are the same as for wood plugs but will be briefly discussed later in this chapter.) Either stiff wire or twisted cable can be used. Heavy wire should be chosen, and braided wire is best, in thirty- through fifty-pound test sizes for most plugs. Either bright or black wire can be used. Leader sleeves for making the necessary loops for line-tie and hook attachment are also necessary. If using stiff wire, you only need to form eyes and wrap them as is done when making spinners or wood plugs.

You can cut a slot along the long axis of a solid plastic plug to insert a metal plate for the line-tie and hook attachment, but this is only done infrequently.

Eyes for plastic plugs are similar to those for wood plugs, except that wire-mounted glass eyes can only be used on acrylic-rod plugs or plugs that are solid in that area, because holes must be drilled to hold the glued-in wire. Eyes can also be painted, decals, wiggle craft-type eyes (doll eyes), or self-adhesive reflective tape.

PLASTIC PLUG BODIES

Most molded plug bodies available from tackle shops or mail-order catalogs today are composed of butyrate or ABS. Both are hard, tough plastics; butyrate is clear and ABS is opaque. The choice of plastic by commercial lure manufacturers is often based on whether the final lure will be completely opaque, clear, or with a translucent finish.

As previously stated, plastic plug bodies come several ways. Some are available complete—molded, sealed together, with molded-in hook hangers, and painted with a professional finish. Others are available just as complete but unpainted. Others are available painted or unpainted and without hook hangers or line-ties; these are added by installing screw eyes of the correct length and size. Some plugs are available in two parts, right and left, which are then glued together or sealed with a supplied or separately purchased sealer.

The shapes available include most of the basics, such as top-water stickbaits, top-water propeller lures, chuggers, poppers, shallow-running minnow imitations, shad, deep-diving plugs, banana-shaped plugs, surface poppers, and salmon-trolling plugs.

Some plugs have separate bodies and bills or lips. The lips are usually clear butyrate or Lexan,

Examples of commercially available plug bodies that come finished, requiring only the addition of hooks using split rings.

the bodies made of an opaque plastic, probably ABS. These are easily glued in place. Plugs that come in two parts have molded-in registration pins along the sides so that the two parts will be in perfect alignment when glued together. Some two-part plugs also include a small weight of molded lead to be glued inside the plug in a special cavity for proper weight and balance in the water. Plugs of the several types listed are currently available from such major component mail-order catalogs as Jann's Netcraft, Mud Hole, and Hagen's.

These are all available in standard crankbait and top-water lures in both painted and unpainted models. In addition, companies such as Jann's Netcraft also sell the hardware for plates and lips, for both wood and plastic bodies, along with hooks, screw eyes, hook hangers, mounting screws, and figure-eight line-tie links for completing any of these lures.

Two-part lures in which the two sides or ends are glued together are also sometimes available. Most companies that sell the two-part plastic plug bodies also sell the solvent or glue for affixing these two parts to each other. Incidentally, solvent and glue are different. Glue binds to each of the two parts and holds them together. Solvents soften the two parts, or seam lines in this case, so that when properly softened and then joined, the two parts are in effect welded together. The solvent eventually evaporates to leave the two parts joined permanently.

Commercial plugs are usually made in one of two ways. One is to use a solvent as described above, allowing the joining edges to sit for a specified time on a pad soaked with solvent and then joining and clamping the parts together for the few minutes necessary to achieve a good bond. The other method can't be done by the home tackle maker because it involves expensive ultrasonic equipment to produce vibrations (15,000 to 20,000 cycles per second) that create friction, which in turn creates heat, which in turn welds the two parts. Lures to be sealed this way are made slightly differently, with a small triangular ridge molded on the edge of both halves. This ridge serves as an "energy director" to "aim" the ultrasonic energy. The ridges are small—about 12/1,000 of an inch wide and 8/1,000 of an inch high—but will melt under the ultrasound vibration cycles to form a solid welded unit.

If you can't find solvent to weld lure bodies, special plastic cements are available (often from hobby shops) that will work best with these plastic parts.

ASSEMBLY OF PLUG PARTS, GLUING, AND SEALING

Plugs that come in parts must be assembled. Most of these are lures in two halves. Some require only the addition of a clear lip to an opaque body. For this, you must use glue or a solvent, the solvent often one of the ketones, such as acetone. Be sure to follow the plug manufacturer's or seller's instructions and use only the glue or solvent recommended. Plastics differ, and the glue or solvent required for one type of plastic may not work on another type or may even react adversely and ruin the plug. Failure to use the right glue might cause the lure to pull apart later.

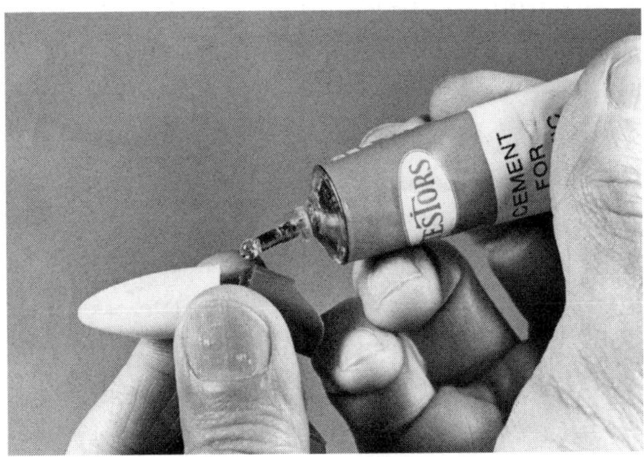

Gluing the two parts of an ultralight plug.

In most cases the solvents used are very liquid; glues are usually a little more viscous. In both cases use a small brush to coat the adjoining lure surfaces with the glue or solvent. If using a solvent you must do this rapidly and press the parts together immediately because solvents evaporate fast. Failure to work quickly can cause future failure of this joint. You do have a little more time with glues, since they will not set up as quickly as solvents evaporate. Many glues come with a small brush in the container lid for quick and easy application. Don't get solvent on your hands during this operation; solvents are harmful to skin, and any transferred from your hand to the plug body will leave a distinct, disfiguring mark.

If you make a lot of plastic plugs at once, you can use the technique of the lure manufacturers and prepare a small metal pan with a thin sheet of foam or sponge, pour solvent in the pan, and set the two plug parts on the foam or sponge pad to soften or soak up the solvent for the welding. Do not use a plastic pan for this—the solvent might react with it. Some plastic foams and sponges also will react. If you're unsure of your material, use a felt pad to soak up the solvent.

Use solvent safely, with adequate ventilation and under controlled conditions. This should not be done just anywhere, anytime. Lure manufacturers using this technique keep pans under large vacuum-ventilation hoods to vent fumes from the shop and protect their workers. You won't have access to equipment like this, so work with solvents outside only—on a patio, in a carport, or in similar shaded but open area. It does help to place a small cover over the pan to prevent excess evaporation of the solvent. Consider cutting down one side of a large cardboard box and inverting it over the pan. The open side will allow you room to work.

Whether using the pad or brush technique, try to avoid getting too much solvent or glue anywhere on the plug except the fine seam lines where the plug snaps together. Although glue can be wiped off and solvent will evaporate, both will leave a mark. The fish won't notice of course, but it's best to try to do the best job you can during every stage of tackle crafting.

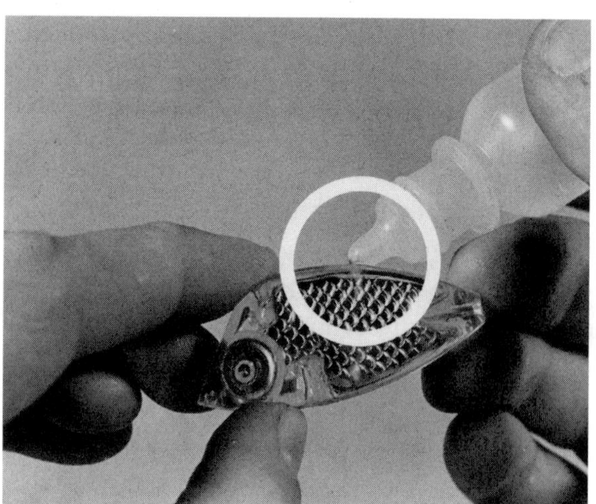

Gluing together two halves of a plastic plug after foil insert sheets have been added. The foil sheets show through the clear sides, eliminating the need for painting or other finishing.

PLUG BODIES FROM SOLID PLASTIC

Plug bodies can be made from solid plastic such as acrylic rod or acrylic block. Rod is easier to work with because you do not have to round off the corners before shaping. Just remember that it must be *cast* rod, not *extruded* rod. Block or square stock can be used; use care in rounding off the corners to get the block to a round shape. The best way to do this is with a lathe, using safe and standard lathe practices to place the rod in the lathe and shape it. Use a three- or four-jawed chuck with a live or dead center tail stock. (A live center will turn; a dead center does not turn.) Both types come to a point to hold the plastic rod at a small hole punched or drilled into the center of the stock. A live (turning) center is much preferred, because most plastics of this type will expand when heated and can cause binding with a dead center, which will heat up and create more friction.

Original turning speeds for plastic will vary, and you should consult a good lathe operation book for advice here. This book covers making lures in a variety of ways, including lathe operations with plastics, but it is not intended as a complete guide to working all types of materials with all types of machine tools. However, a good starting point with most acrylic and acrylic-type plastics is to run the lathe at a speed that will turn the material at about 200 feet per minute. Thus with a 1-inch stock, one turn will equal approximately 3 inches. Three inches into 200 feet would be a rotation of about 800 rpm. Too slow a speed may not cut properly, but too fast a speed will melt or burn the plastic. Also, if you use a dead center, be sure to check the material periodically (with the lathe off) to see if binding between centers is occurring from plastic expansion due to heat or if any melting or burning of the plastic is occurring.

Once you are set up for the lathe operation, cut the plug to shape using standard cutting tools, but cut with a thin bite to prevent the tool from digging in—a potential problem with plastic.

If you make cupped faces for chuggers, consider mounting the plastic rod into a three-jawed chuck with no tail center and working on the face to cup it. Then the stock can be placed between centers to finish the shape of the rest of the plug.

Once the plug body is finished, use a drill (again at a slow or medium speed to prevent burning or melting) to make the holes for the screw eyes for the line-tie and all hooks. If you desire through-wire construction, use a drill press and vertical support (see chapters 1 and 9 for details) to drill through the long axis, using 6-inch-long aircraft or electrician's bits. Note that it is important *before* drilling to decide the size of the screw eye you will be using and to drill an appropriate size (diameter) pilot hole. If you are unsure of the proper size pilot hole, drill a few different size holes in scrap plastic and test them with the screw eyes you intend to use. The screw eye should go in firmly, without any looseness and without twisting or weakening the screw eye itself. Plug hangers using the small screws can also be used, again held in place with screws after drilling tiny pilot holes. All holes to be drilled should be marked first with a fine-tip felt-tip marker or can be marked with an awl or punch. The latter will also provide a guide for the drill bit, preventing slipping.

ADDING PLUG HARDWARE

In general plug hardware is added after painting and finishing, but there is no particular order in which various pieces of hardware must be added to the lure. With plastic lures it is important to pick the right hardware. Most injection-molded plastic plugs have specific diameter and depth recesses to hold screws or screw eyes. Shorter or thinner screw eyes or fasteners will not hold securely; longer or thicker (or both) screw eyes may split the plug, cause it to crack, cause it to leak, or cause the screw eye to twist off or weaken as it is added.

Cup washers, although generally used with wood lures, are not used much with plastic lures. There is nothing wrong with adding them, but they do not help seal the lure, protect the countersunk area, or otherwise add to lure appearance or function. Cup washers are used in plastic plugs with propellers, for instance top-water lures that require props. Here the cup washers are used as bearings to help the propellers turn, just as they are in wood plugs. A cup washer both in front of and behind the propeller is required, the convex sides facing the propeller. If you use two props, consider turning the pitch of one counter to the other to reduce the possibility of the lure spinning.

With finished assembled plug bodies, the hook hangers are usually molded in place. They need only split rings and hooks (usually treble hooks) to finish the lure. Use split-ring pliers to open the split ring and start it on the wire hook hanger. As soon as it is started on this wire form, add the treble hook eye and continue to turn the ring with the pliers until the hook is loose on the ring and plug. It also helps to add a split ring to the line-tie wire to add action to the lure.

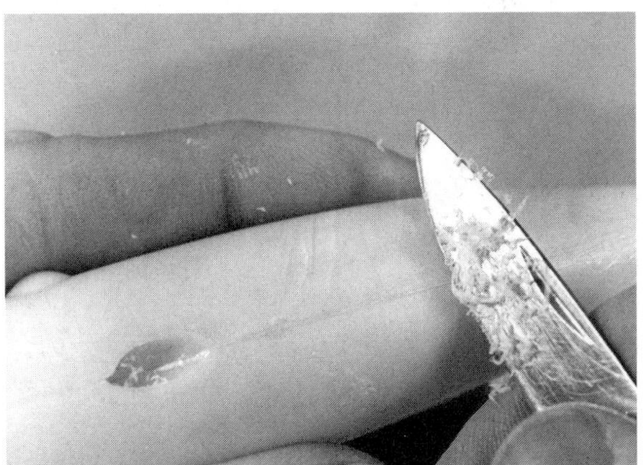

Some plastic plug bodies might need some work before painting and finishing. There may be some flash along the seam lines, easily removed by scraping with a knife.

Solid-acrylic plastic plug bodies are generally sinking lures and made with sloping faces to help them dive and run deep. Metal or plastic lips are available but are often too difficult to attach to be worth it. Some saltwater top-water plugs can be made of acrylic plastic, even though this plastic sinks. This seeming incongruity is a result of the different way in which saltwater surface chuggers are worked. They are worked fast, and a heavy lure actually helps hold the plug in the water, making it splash through the surface. A hollow lightweight plug will often bounce around, sometimes hanging the line on the hooks and causing missed fish. The sinking top-water plug has enough weight to hold position, while the sloping chugger face keeps the plug on the surface with rapid jerky retrieves.

If you make through-wire construction acrylic plastic plugs, the best method to follow is that for wood plugs, in which a straight, thin hole is drilled through the body, front to rear, and a larger hole is drilled in from the belly. The size of this second hole should be just large enough to contain the barrel swivel used to hold the belly hook using a split ring. Cable or single-strand wire is formed into a line-tie (often a split ring is added to the loop with cable), and the wire is run through the body to engage one eye of the swivel and then out the back, where a second loop or twisted eye is formed to hold the tail hook. The hook can be attached to the belly swivel using a split ring or an open-eye hook that can be closed with pliers once on the swivel eye.

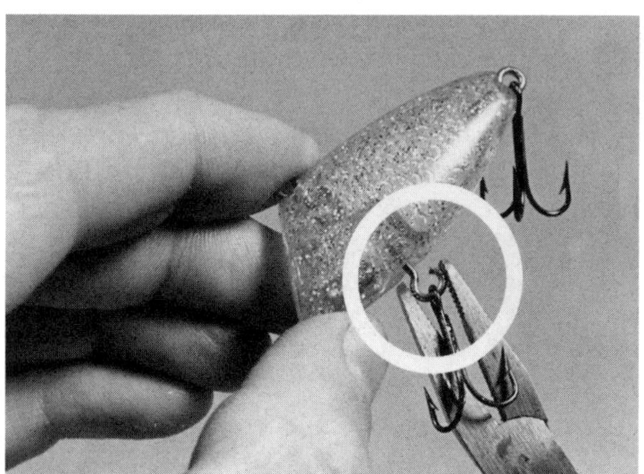

Assembly of plastic plugs is really no different from that of wood plugs. Here an open screw eye and hook (circled) are being added to a plastic sonic-style plug body. The pliers will close the screw eye before it is completely screwed into the lure.

PAINTING AND FINISHING

Painting and finishing with tape, eyes, and so on is covered in chapter 15. Generally speaking, painting and finishing are done before adding the plug hardware and hooks to the lure in order to prevent painting and masking difficulties.

VARIATIONS IN MAKING PLASTIC PLUGS

Many of the variations outlined for wood plugs can also be accomplished with plastic plugs. Refer to those sections in chapter 9 for details. Some of these variations include adding spinner blades to the tail, adding soft plastics (though the soft plastic may react with the lure plastic just as it may react with the paint on wood lures), changing hooks, and so on.

PLUG-MAKING KITS

As with spinners and spoons, kits for plastic plugs are available and contain complete plug bodies and hardware for a number of lures. Most kits include all parts needed to make a number of lures. Major lure-component parts companies, such as Jann's Netcraft and Hagen's, have charts in their catalogs that suggest the right hook, hook size, and split ring size for each of their available painted or unpainted plastic plug bodies.

11
Offshore Lures

Introduction • Tools • Materials • Step-by-Step Assembly of Bead Lures • Bead-Lure Variations • Molded-Plastic Lures • Plastic Lure Molding Steps • Molding Offshore Lures Using Epoxy Casting Compound • Step-by-Step Construction of Wood Lures • Soft-Bodies Lures • Adding Skirts • Rigging Hooks • Variations

Basic Safety Requirements

Goggles

Respirator mask suitable for protection from casting resins

Apron

A clean, clear place with a heavy countertop on which to work

Basic Tools

Waxed cups for mixing plastic

Stirring sticks (Popsicle sticks or craft sticks)

Electric drill and long-shank drill bits

Machinist's vise or Vise-Grip pliers for hook-rigging

File

Leader-crimping pliers

Wire cutters

Pliers

Carving knives for making wood lures (see tools in chapter 9)

Helpful Tools

Drill press

Lathe (for making wood lures)

Scissors (for cutting, preparing skirts)

INTRODUCTION

Offshore lures were not included in the first edition of *Tackle Craft,* but they were included in *Modern Tackle Craft* and *The Complete Book of Tackle Making*. Offshore lures can be made with ease by any tackle tinkerer. In fact, with the existing diversity of offshore lures, there are several ways they can be made and made radically different in construction methods, even if the end result is for skipping or trolling lures for inshore and offshore species.

Offshore lures by definition are those lures that are used primarily (but not always) offshore for ocean pelagic species such as dolphin, wahoo, billfish, shark, tuna, and mackerel. Although they are often referred to generically as "offshore lures," in smaller sizes they are equally useful when trolling inshore for species such as bluefish, barracuda, false albacore, snapper, mackerel, bonito, and roosterfish.

While smaller sizes can be cast, most of these lures are large and bulky and really designed to be trolled. Some are skipped on the surface in the wake of a fishing boat, either chugging along on the surface or alternately diving and skipping. The action is determined by the basic design, the shape of the head, and the cut of the face. Others, in a size and construction to take heavy saltwater fish, are fished deep and are more like large wood or plastic bass lures.

Skirts, hooks, various beads, chain, monofilament and wire, and egg sinkers for making offshore bead-style trolling lures.

One of the simplest ways to make offshore lures is to thread a series of large plastic beads on a leader/hook rig and add an egg sinker, which in turn is covered and hidden by a vinyl or similar skirt. Wood lures like the offshore billfish heads and skirts can be made by carving, turning on a lathe, or cutting the lure out of a large-diameter dowel or closet rod; painting and finishing; and finally wrapping with a skirt. The same applies to the offshore cedar plugs favored for early-season tuna fishing. Molded hard-plastic heads of clear casting resin molded with eye inserts, prism reflectors, glitter, and other materials for flash and color are also easily made in one- or two-step molding processes.

While the creation of any lure requires care (as continually emphasized in this book), there is an additional concern with using casting resin: It is highly volatile and gives off noxious and potentially dangerous fumes. When I bought some at a hobby shop recently, the owner related tales of the liver damage and near death of a hobby magazine editor who was using a similar compound under confined conditions. Only a casual comment made in the hospital about the hobby led his doctors to the true nature of his condition and thus the cure. As with any material, but especially with these casting resins, use extreme care and follow all manufacturer's directions and safety instructions *exactly*.

TOOLS

Tools for making offshore lures vary with the type of lure and its construction. In most cases only a few tools are needed, although some helpful tools will allow you to make the lures quicker or easier.

The tools used in making the lures in this chapter include:

Crimping pliers. These are used to make crimps in the leader sleeves used in wire and mono riggings. They are useful for virtually every style of offshore lure, unless of course you are buying prerigged hooks and adding them to your homemade lures. Although knots and snells can be used for rigging smaller lures for smaller species, leader sleeves are typically used for most connections when attaching hooks and making leader end loops. This is particularly true for the heavy mono often used in making lures for big-game fishing.

In virtually all cases, the mono used for such lures will vary with the size of the lure, the size of the fish sought, and the experience of the angler. This applies whether the mono or leader is an integral part of the lure or the lure is added to the leader when fishing with the hook, an afterthought when threading the leader through or into the lure.

Leader-crimping pliers come in several styles and sizes. It is important, as noted by outdoor writer Mark Sosin in an October 1989 column in *Salt Water Sportsman*, to choose the right kind of crimping pliers for the sleeve to be used. Sleeves are made in two styles: one a round cross section, the second shaped like an elongated 0, an open 8, or an hourglass. The pliers designed for the open-8 or hourglass style are a cup-opposing-cup style and are usually compound action for greater leverage and swaging force, with the rounded sides of the sleeve fitting into the matching cups of the pliers' jaws. Pliers for the round sleeves are the point-opposing-cup style, in which the sharp ridge of one jaw pushes the sleeve into the cup or trough on the other jaw. Be sure to match pliers and sleeve-type properly. Popular crimping pliers are the Nicopress and Hi Seas brand (these two are often rated the best by many serious captains, mates, and anglers). Smaller but also excellent pliers for most applications are made by Mason, Sevenstrand, Berkley, and other companies. For more information see chapter 13.

Wire cutters. Often compound-action fishing pliers or crimping pliers will have wire cutters built into the side or end. If not, you will need a good pair of compound wire cutters for finishing offshore-lure riggings. Be sure to get wire cutters that will cut the tough braided or twisted wire used in leader riggings and not just soft copper electric wire. A good cable cutter is the Felco model C-7, but many others are also available.

Snap-ring pliers. These are required for slipping short sections of surgical tubing over the leader and down onto the hook and tagline (the cable running from the eye of the forward hook to the eye of the trailing, or gaffer, hook). Long straight-jaw pliers are best for this.

File. A file or two are handy for a variety of tasks, including coarse cuts for roughing and finishing. They are good for smoothing the edges of molded-plastic lures and roughing out wood plugs and trolling heads. An 8- to 12-inch file is a good length for most tackle tasks.

Vise. A good vise is necessary for many tasks, including tightening mono knots and wire connections, sharpening large offshore hooks, and holding molds for pouring plastic.

Drill. A good electric drill with a ⅜-inch or larger chuck, variable speed and reversible, is ideal for drilling the long holes necessary for rigging offshore lures or constructing the molds and jigs necessary to make them. Both standard bits and longer 6-inch-shank aircraft bits are best.

Drill press. A small drill press is ideal for many drilling operations, though it is not mandatory. The best are those that are fitted with a sturdy drill press vise to hold materials for accurate drilling.

Lathe. A small lathe for turning cedar or hardwood dowels into offshore trolling heads or cedar tuna plugs is handy but certainly not necessary. A lathe makes it easy to turn out identical plugs and heads quickly.

Scissors. These are necessary for cutting skirt material to finish tolling lures. Good long-blade scissors are available from most hardware and general stores.

Knife. A whittling knife is a must (unless you have a lathe) for carving out wood heads and plugs. The techniques involved are similar to those used in making freshwater plugs, as outlined in chapter 9.

Stirring sticks. Popsicle sticks, also called craft sticks when sold in bundles in craft and hobby shops, are disposable and ideal for stirring glue and the two-part molding plastic used for making offshore trolling heads.

MATERIALS

Materials for making offshore lures vary widely depending on the type of lure to be made. Although some materials are basic to all lures (skirts, wire or mono rigging and leader material, hooks), others vary according to the type of lure.

Beads. Beads vary widely and are available from tackle shops, mail-order component houses, and craft/hobby shops. Although any type of bead can be used for these and other offshore lures, the most popular are the nesting tri-beads. These are small triangular beads that, when threaded on mono or wire, match the angles of one bead to the flat edges of the adjoining bead in order to nest. Two sizes and many colors are available. Round, oval, square, and many other types of beads can be used, although for offshore use they should be of a large diameter—10 to 12 millimeters or even larger is not too large for these lures. They are strung on the wire or mono under the skirt. In addition to the color they give a lure, they also serve as spacers to properly position the hook and lure head of the skirt in relation to the hook.

Monofilament and wire leader material. Leaders for offshore lures can include single-strand wire, braided or twisted cable, and nylon-coated cable. Each has its enthusiasts and critics, often reflections of the type of fishing done, species sought, or lure used. Mono or single-strand wire is often used with cedar plugs for early-season tuna. Mono is often used for marlin, tuna, sailfish, and dolphin, along with smaller inshore species, but is not good for toothy critters such as king mackerel or sharks. Nylon-coated cable is favored in some ports but becomes unusable if the nylon coating becomes frayed. Cable is fine for big game but is often a disadvantage for leader-shy fish such as marlin. Single-strand wire is thin and almost invisible, but if kinked it will break readily and then becomes completely unusable.

The leader material must match up with the size of the lure and the fish sought. Thus there is no need for 200-pound or heavier mono for inshore trolling. Generally leaders will range from about 50 to 400 pounds, although there are no minimum or maximum limits. Often commercial prerigged mono leaders are 125-, 200-, or 250-pound test. Most mono specifically for leaders is tough and stiff, with high abrasion resistance. The stiffness is especially required for big-game offshore trolling by anglers who use a two-hook rig, with the trailer hook at 90 or 180 degrees to the main hook. The stiff mono prevents the hook from changing position when properly snelled in place. Clear, mist-colored, and black mono is available for leaders.

Single-strand wire such as Monel or stainless steel ranges from as light as size 2 (29-pound test) to as heavy as size 19 (400-pound test). It usually comes in large coils that are restraightened, which means that when uncoiled the leader will be straight. Stainless steel comes in bright silver, black, or coffee (bronze) color, in lengths ranging from 25 feet, to quantities sold in ¼-pound or 1-pound bulk spools.

Cable is available in stainless steel in silver or coffee (bronze) color in various pound tests and configurations. Although it's often called "braided," cable is really a twisted wire, and saltwater leaders range from 1 × 7 (one cable formed by twisting seven separate strands together), to 3 × 7 (three of the 1 × 7 cables twisted together to make a single cable of twenty-one strands of wire), and 7 × 7 or 49-strand wire (seven strands of the 1 × 7 cable twisted to make one heavy cable of forty-nine strands).

The 1 × 7 wire can test as high as 250-pound, while the 7 × 7 will range from as light as 175- to as high as 920-pound test, all depending on the size of the wire used.

Nylon-coated cable is identical to wire and cable, except that it has a thin nylon coating. It comes in bright or camouflaged (bronze or coffee) wire with a clear or black nylon coating. Coils of cable are available in lengths of 30, 100, 150, 200, 300 feet, and up. Not all manufacturers will make all types of cable or offer it in coils of every size.

Leader sleeves. Leader sleeves are used to make eyes in leader material to which hooks are attached and to make the eyes for double-line or snap attachments. Leader sleeves are used with all cable, nylon-coated cable, and mono, although knots and snells can be used in mono provided it is not too heavy. Single-strand wire requires only a haywire twist to make a strong and effective eye or loop, something far simpler and often quicker than working with sleeves. But it only works on single-strand wire.

Different companies label sleeves differently, although it is mandatory to have a sleeve that matches the size of the mono or cable. Thus a size A3 Sevenstrand sleeve would fit ninety-pound test Sevenstrand cable, forty-pound test Sevalon (nylon-coated cable), and fifteen- and twenty-pound test monofilament. A size A7 would fit 90-pound test Sevalon, 275-pound test Duratest (forty-nine-strand cable), and 100- to 125-pound test monofilament. Similar ranges will be found with other manufacturers. Note that in all cases, these sizes are based on two strands (to form an eye or loop) fitting through the sleeve. If you use a sleeve as a spacer only on a single strand of leader, a smaller size will often work. In addition, some companies make special sleeves for monofilament leader, with sizes for 100- to 500-pound test mono. Sleeves for wire and mono range from small freshwater sizes to heavy saltwater varieties. Sevenstrand products range from A1 sleeves for cable to 27-pound test, to A12 for 800-pound test Duratest (forty-nine-strand), to A14 for 250-pound test mono. Check out all these specifications carefully when buying wire, cable, or mono for these offshore lures, and be sure to use the right size and style of crimping pliers.

Sinkers. Egg sinkers are best for use as weights in beaded, vinyl-skirted trolling lures because they have a center hole, fit easily under the molded vinyl skirt, and can weight the lure properly. Egg sinkers in sizes too small to use in trolling up to several ounces in weight are readily available at most tackle shops or can be molded easily (see chapter 5).

Hooks. Hooks for salt water must be strong and corrosion resistant, with sturdy, often-welded eyes. All the hook companies make hooks in styles, materials, designs, and sizes specifically for heavy-duty saltwater fishing. Favored hooks include models 254SS and L9021 from Eagle Claw, the Perma Steel 9729 and 9730 from VMC, and the 7732 and 7754 from Mustad.

Molded vinyl skirts. These skirts are molded to slip on the lure. In essence they look like long, tough, brightly colored glove fingers, with the tail section sliced into individual skirt strands. Weber, Sevenstrand, and other companies make these skirts, and they are often sold as replacement skirts for commercial lures. They can, however, be used for homemade lures.

Sizes generally range from about 4 to 16 inches long, with proportioned diameters. Colors are usually bright, with red, pink, orange, blue, bright green, yellow, and purple prevalent, although black and white are also available. Solid colors, multiple colors, two-skirt multiple colors, and skirts with molded-in glitter are all readily available. In use the skirt head is cut or punched with a small hole to take a leader, as for a bead lure, or a larger hole to be fitted and tied onto a separate lure head. The shape of the head end of these skirts will vary with the manufacturer: Some are pointed, others rounded, and still others rounded but with a narrow waist or bell shape.

Wrap skirts. Some companies also make wrap skirts—skirt material that looks like a frayed strip of sheeting. The unfrayed, or head, end is tied or wrapped to the rear of the trolling head. Often several of these skirts are used for a multiple-color look, for more bulk in the skirt, and to completely fill in large heads that might not be covered with just one wrap. Excellent skirts are available from Mold Craft.

Molding plastic. This is a liquid plastic that when combined with the right amount of catalyst produces a hard, clear casting. The polyester resin is available in 16-ounce, 32-ounce, 1-gallon, and 50-gallon-drum containers—the latter for commercial users. It does require a small amount of catalyst, available in ½-ounce, 1-ounce, and 1-gallon sizes. The 16-ounce container of resin and ½ ounce of catalyst will make several lures, depending on their size. Although there are no standards as to sizes for offshore or inshore trolling lure head, small lures will require about 2 to 3 ounces, medium lures about 5 to 6 ounces, and larges lures for big game about 8 to 10 ounces of resin. Since the catalyst is measured in drops per ounce to the resin, it is easy to measure the volume of resin required and mix it to the catalyst for precise results with no waste.

The resin must be stored properly, according to its manufacturer, Environmental Technology, Inc. (ETI). High heat will cause the resin to solidify even without the addition of the catalyst. "If you take the 16-ounce can and place it in a window where it will get the sun every day, in a couple of weeks it can set up," said Ed LaFley, national sales manager for ETI. Normally the casting resin will have a useful shelf life of about nine months. A dating code on the bottom of each can indicates both the manufacturing date and control number. The code consists of numbers to indicate the date the batch was made. For example, a code of 10365 (a kit I currently have) indicates that it was made in 2010 (the first two numbers of the code) on the 365th day of the year (yes, they work on New Year's Eve). Thus, the first two numbers are the last two numbers of the year when made and the following numbers the day of the year when that batch was produced. By understanding the code you will know if you are getting fresh casting resin and how long the container can sit on your shelf.

ETI now makes an epoxy casting compound. This has both advantages and disadvantages to their casting resin mix.

Mold Builder. This product, also manufactured by ETI, consists of a pure latex compound that can be used to make molds for casting resin lures. Thin coats of the compound are brushed on a model lure or prototype in many layers to build up a mold. The latex mold is then pulled off the model and filled with casting resin to produce a copy exactly like the

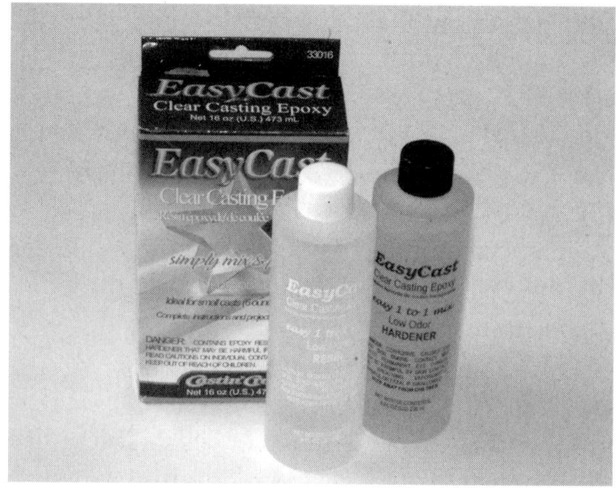

This 50/50 epoxy mix for making offshore lures uses the same steps but is easier to use than casting resin. Inserts can be added to any clear or colored lure.

original. (For more details on making molds this way, see chapter 16.)

Other additions for lures. Molded lures can include prism or mirrored inserts, glitter, eyes, scalelike tape patterns, and other features. Eyes for big-games lures can be found in component-parts catalogs, some tackle shops, and most craft shops, where they are sold for dolls and other art/craft items. Eyes can be molded into clear-plastic heads or glued onto wood bodies. Self-adhesive or glue-on tape eyes can be added to vinyl skirts or soft-head lures. The molded-in eyes commonly used are the craft-style "wiggle eyes," with the black (or

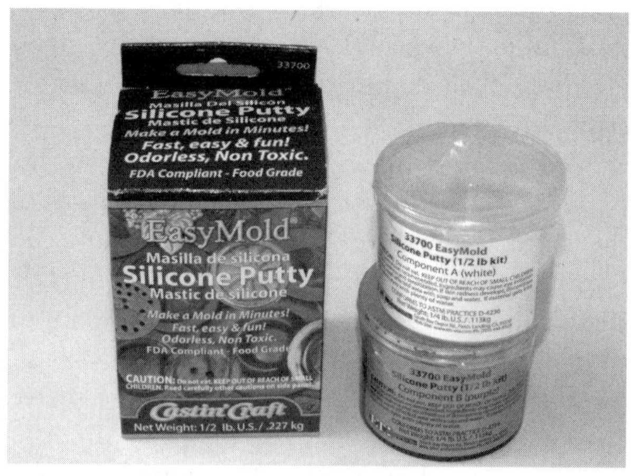

Following the three-step instructions, mixing two-part epoxy mold maker, such as this Silicone Putty from ETI, makes it easy to form molds for making lures.

colored) pupil loose inside a clear, bubblelike case. These eyes are available in many sizes, from 2 or 3 millimeters up to 1-inch-diameter ones ideal for big-game lures. Plastic "crystal eyes," sold in similar sizes, are solid and feature a post (for attachment to stuffed animals through a backing plate) that can be glued onto the outside of a molded-plastic lure for a pop-eyed look or molded into the clear head. Round acrylic stones on a metal base are also available in a variety of sizes and are usually sold in multicolor packs. With a contrasting head color, they can be used as "eyes" when molded into a lure. Most of these items are available at craft stores or from craft catalogs.

Tape eyes, available in many sizes from craft and tackle stores and catalogs, are thin self-adhesive strips that can be stuck onto the outside of a lure or molded into its center. Since water pressure will tend to strip off anything on the outside of a lure, these are best used in the center of a clear-plastic lure.

Prism tape is available in dozens of different colors and patterns. This tape, available through tackle shops and made by companies like Phantom Tape Products, is easily cut to size and placed on a center insert for molding into a plastic head.

Craft shops sell packets of small mirrors in various shapes, including round, square, rectangular, and diamond. These can be glued to an insert placed into the mold for additional flash. Small metalized plastic sequins, often labeled "palettes," are available in many colors and can be molded into a lure. Sequins are another possibility, either loose and mixed with the resin or on a string (they are sold this way) and glued into place to resemble cheek or head scales. They must be glued to the insert brass rod (through which the leader will run) or to an insert plug or plate placed in the mold for this purpose. Buttons have also been used as eyes or decorative inserts, as has aluminum foil crinkled and glued to insert plates: The crinkling adds to the flash produced by the lure in the water.

Glitter, available in many colors and occasionally different particle sizes, can be added to casting resin when it is mixed with the catalyst for random flash in an otherwise clear lure. Resin may also be colored with transparent dyes available from craft stores or the shop where the casting resin and catalyst are purchased. If these dyes are used properly, prism, mirrored, eyed, or other molded-in inserts will still show through, even though the head has a definite color.

Tubing. A hole is necessary for running the leader through the lure. Brass tubing is most often used, with the tube placed in the mold used to make the lure. Brass tubing of about ⅛ to ¼ inch in diameter is good; 3⁄16-inch tubing is a good compromise. Make sure the tubing is large enough to accommodate the diameter of the leader you plan to use. A little play to get the leader through the tubing is fine, but avoid too much play. Although other tubing could be used, brass tubing is best. Copper or aluminum would be close second choices because these metals will deburr easily to prevent leader abrasion and cutting and are easy to cut and shape in the home workshop. Brass tubing is available at hobby shops, copper tubing at hobby and automotive shops.

Wood. Cedar is the most commonly used wood for making offshore wood plugs, which is why they are usually called cedar plugs. Other wood can be used, including basswood, fine-grain pine, oak, and poplar. These woods differ in quality, and some require more care in drilling and shaping. Some, such as oak, are tough but prone to split if not worked carefully. In all cases wood choices and construction methods are identical to those covered in chapter 9.

STEP-BY-STEP ASSEMBLY OF BEAD LURES

Trolling skirts of bead lures, often called "hoochies," "hoochy trolls," or just plain "vinyl-skirt" lures are effective and have lots of action. They come in a wide variety of sizes and colors and will take anything from inshore bluefish to offshore tuna, wahoo, and marlin.

To make these lures you need only the skirts, egg sinkers for weight, single saltwater hooks, beads (usually tri-beads), and wire, mono, or chain for the rigging. Crimping pliers are necessary if you work with wire and leader sleeves.

Necessary hooks range from sizes 4/0 to 10/0, although smaller or larger hooks are possible. Make sure they are saltwater style; stainless, tinned, or cadmium-plated; and with a welded eye in the larger sizes.

Mono and cable can vary from as light as 40-pound test to as heavy as 200- or even 400-pound test, depending on the size of the fish sought and the size of the lure.

Beads come in a number of styles, colors, and sizes. The tri-bead style is usually chosen for these lures; they stack up easily and give the appearance of a segmented, scaled body. The similar "snowflake" beads also stack up and create a lifelike, flashy, and scaled appearance, though they are more fragile than tri-beads. Bags of beads, both mixed- and same-color beads, are available in various sizes. All are available at craft and hobby shops and through some tackle shops.

The advantage of tri-beads or snowflake beads on these lures is that they will stack up almost like bricks or building blocks, giving the lure body some bulk and "life." Regular round, tapered "spaghetti," or other beads will not do this and will create only a thin line of color in the lure. T-style beads will work but are not generally used. Because of how they lock together, the stacking beads give a segmented or scaled appearance. As the sun strikes the surface of the stacked beads, it creates flash and specular highlights, similar to the flash that would occur with a live baitfish. The snowflake beads in particular will catch the water as they skip on the surface and will leave a trail of bubbles—"smoke" in the parlance of the big-game angler. This trail of bubbles is particularly good for attracting gamefish.

The beads serve several purposes. First, they make an easy-to-construct spacer on the leader to separate the hook from the egg sinker weight. This sinker gives the lure some trolling weight and also fills out the head of the skirt. Second, the beads provide lifelike flash and color that resemble ocean baitfish. You can build this up with colors that are attractive to a particular species or effective in a particular geographic area. Third, they give the leader between the egg sinker and the hook some stiffness, or body.

Vinyl skirts come in lengths ranging from about 3 to 16 inches and in single or double style. The single styles are of a single color; double skirts are essentially two skirts "welded" together. Often these contain a single color underskirt with a slightly shorter overskirt in flake or glitter colors.

The egg sinkers that fill up the head of the vinyl skirts and give the lure trolling weight and bulk range from ¾-ounce sinkers for small, thin skirts to 3- and 4-ounce sinkers for large skirts.

We'll work with mono to make a basic lure (variations will be covered later). Begin by choosing the right size mono for your quarry. This might be 50- to 80-pound test for inshore species to 100- or 200-pound test for offshore species.

Tie or snell one end of the mono to an offshore hook, again picking a size consistent with the size of the fish sought and the finished lure. Use a secure knot such as a clinch, Palomar, or improved clinch, or use crimped leader sleeves to fasten the loop.

Another excellent alternative is to use a hook snell (see the section on rigging hooks in this chapter, as well as the drawings in appendix E); this will provide a straighter connection between the hook and the leader.

At this point decide whether you want the lure with or without a leader. Many offshore lures come built on the leader so that you have a coil of mono or wire ranging from 10 to 20 feet long. This is probably the best way to make lures, since by means of a loop tied in the end, the leader can be snapped directly and quickly onto a heavy snap at the end of the double line of any offshore outfit. An alternative is to make the lure with a short leader of only a foot or two, this to be tied to a heavy shock leader. The advantage here is in lure storage, either in tackle drawers on the boat, in a large saltwater tackle box, or in a soft roll-up lure pouch.

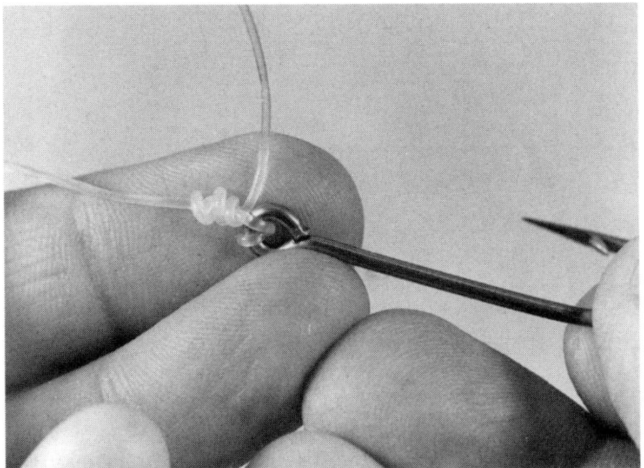

The first step in making any bead-style trolling lure is to use a good knot or snell to attach the hook.

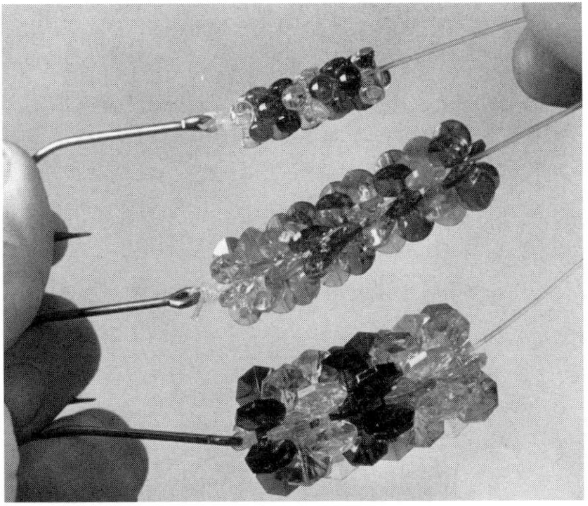

Various sizes and colors of beads can be used, but most are the tri-beads or snowflake beads that nest together when stacked. Different colors are shown here, although beads can be single- or multicolor.

Once you decide on leader length, cut off the appropriate length of mono and begin threading the beads one at a time onto the mono leader. The beads can be mixed in color, a single color, or in segments of several beads of a particular color separated by segments of other colors and repeated as desired.

There is no rule for the number of beads that go onto the leader, but because beads serve as spacers, check length frequently. For most lures you will want the end of the skirt to hit at just about the end of the bend of the hook, although each angler has a preference for this. Add beads until you get to the point where the addition of the egg sinker will allow the skirt to fall at this point.

Add the egg sinker, checking to make sure that there are no burrs that might interfere with the straight axis of the lure. Then add the skirt. Because most vinyl skirts are made by dipping forms into liquid vinyl, you will have to punch a hole through the end of the point in the head of the skirt or use scissors or cutters to cut off the tip end to make a hole.

Check again to make sure the skirt length is appropriate for the lure, and make adjustments as necessary. Adjustments can include adding or removing beads or slightly trimming the skirt. Cut the end of the mono or wire (if this was not done before) to the length required. Make this

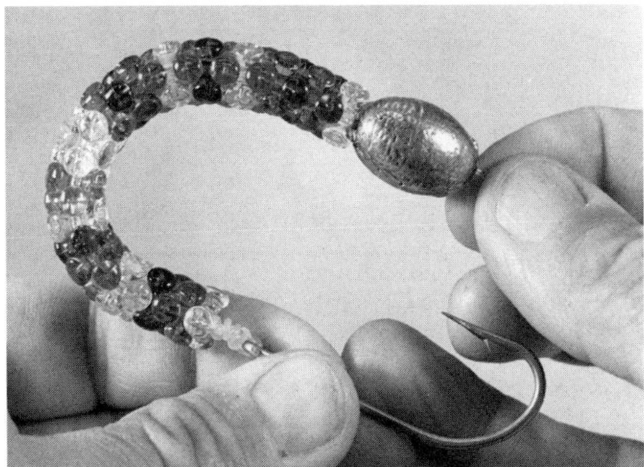

Completed bead body with nesting tri-beads and egg sinker for weight and to hold the skirt.

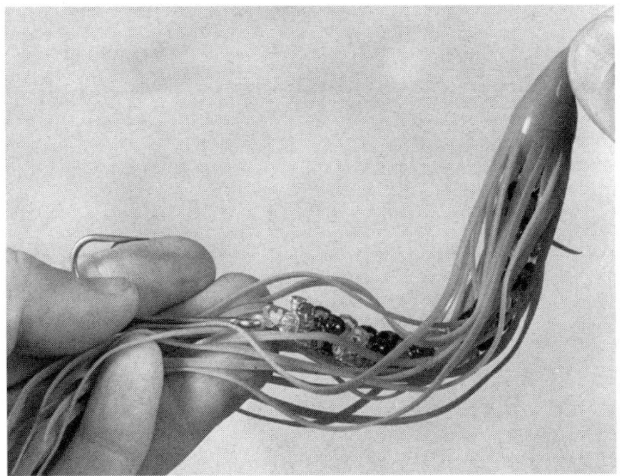

Completed lure with vinyl skirt added to the lure. The egg sinker is hidden under the skirt head.

long for a leader attachment, short—1 foot at most—to use as a lure separate from the leader.

To finish, make a loop in the end using a perfection knot, surgeon's knot, or figure-eight loop knot. Another alternative is to use a double overhand knot pulled into a tight loop and secured with two leader sleeves. This reinforces the loop to make it more abrasion resistant.

BEAD-LURE VARIATIONS

There are variations to the above. One is to use two or more skirts in line with bead spacers between them to create a longer lure or one with more bead and skirt colors. To do this proceed as before. In place of one large egg sinker, add a small one that together with all the egg sinkers under the skirts will total the desired weight and balance of the lure. Once the first skirt is added, add more beads; then add a second sinker and second skirt. Continue with more beads, an egg sinker, and another skirt if you wish to add a third skirt for a longer lure. For this fewer beads are usually used ahead of the main skirt, as well as a shorter skirt.

If you do not wish to add additional weight to the lure, you can use a large bead or poly-foam ball (available from craft shops) as a "stop" to make up some bulk on which the head of the skirt can rest. In this case be sure to use a large egg sinker at the head of the forward skirt. Although the poly-foam balls are worth a try, often it is best to use sinkers to give the middle and tail of the lure some bulk and weight to prevent it from flopping and possibly tangling when trolled.

Another variation is to use a few beads and a tubing spacer to separate the beads from the egg sinker and keep the skirt in the right position. Any type of flexible plastic tubing can be used for this, provided it is stiff enough to prevent the lure from collapsing under the pressures of all-day trolling. Plastic tubing from craft stores and tackle shops, the handles of shopping bags (these are vinyl tubes of varying colors), and even thin clear-plastic tubing from hardware, hobby, and pet shops will all work well. Thick tubing of ¼ inch or larger diameter is often available from hardware stores; clear thin tubing is available from pet stores (as aquarium air hose) or hobby shops (as model airplane fuel line).

To use tubing, begin as before to tie or snell the hook, and add several beads. Then cut a length of tubing that will serve as a spacer between the beads and the egg sinker. Add the tubing and then the egg sinker and skirt, as before. Check for proper length, and adjust as necessary by cutting the tubing, adding or removing beads, or trimming the skirt. A variation of this is to use clear-plastic polyethylene tubing, threaded with an inner core of braided Mylar, as is used for saltwater fly tying. Remove the cord core of the braided Mylar and then thread the Mylar through the plastic tubing. Thread the mono leader through the center of the Mylar. You may wish to add some waterproof glue to the plastic tubing to prevent the Mylar core from sliding out.

You can also use mono with a section of chain as a spacer. This will lack beads but is an advantage if trolling for toothy fish such as bluefish, king mackerel, or wahoo.

If you build a lure this way, first choose chain that will hold up in salt water. Interlocking copper or brass safety chain works well. Also be sure to check the pound test of the chain to make sure it is the strongest part of the lure. Add the hook to the chain by using a large split ring, preferably in brass for long life in salt water. If possible weld it shut to prevent its opening during the hard fight of a big fish.

Measure the chain for the right length as a spacer between the hook and the egg sinker. Cut the chain, add a welded or heavy-duty split ring, and tie in mono; or use leader sleeves on heavy mono or braided wire. If you use safety chain or some other type of interlocking chain links, a split ring is a must because the sharp chain surfaces can cut mono and even abrade wire. Tie the mono or sleeve the mono or wire (using a double overhand loop knot and two crimping sleeves) to the split ring, add the egg sinker, and finish with the skirt.

An alternative is to use heavy single-strand wire as a connector link on which the egg sinker, beads, and skirt are placed. The wire is secured to the hook with a wrapped eye, and a second eye at the forward end is used as a line-tie or a leader tie.

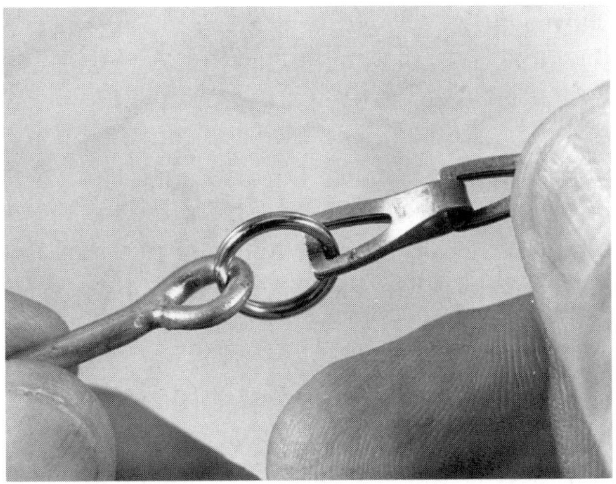

For toothy fish or more durability and strength, chain can be used in place of mono. Use welded jump rings or heavy-duty split rings (shown) to attach the chain to the hook eye.

Using any of these methods, you can make a complete assortment of offshore lures in one evening. This simplicity even makes it possible to thread or assemble the lures while watching television, and their effectiveness makes them well worth the little bit of time it takes to put some together.

Best of all, these lures can easily be changed or repaired. If some snowflake beads get broken in a hard strike, a skirt becomes damaged or torn, or a hook becomes rusted or bent, it is easy to cut either end of the wire or mono, remove the damaged parts, and replace with new beads, skirts, or hooks. Thus there is no such thing as a lure that is "bad" and has to be thrown out. Any lure can be repaired by having parts added or, if in really bad shape, stripped and used for parts for other new lures or lures needing repairs.

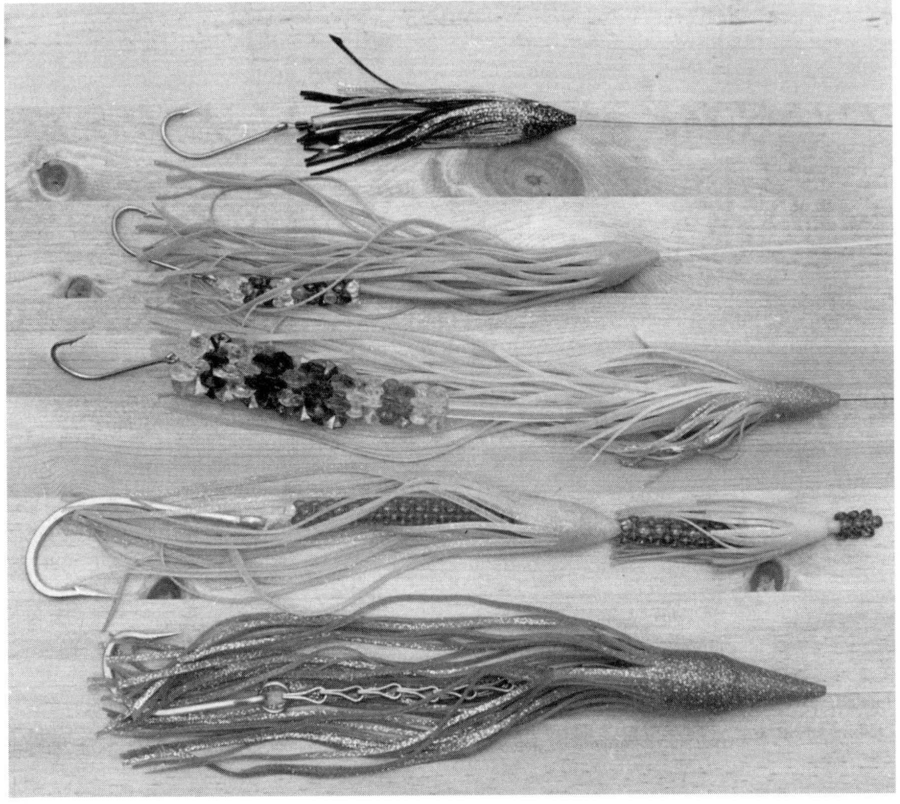

Various sizes and styles of single- and double-skirt bead and chain-spacer trolling lures. All are easy and quick to make.

MOLDED-PLASTIC LURES

Although casting resin can be used for making almost any type of solid lure, it is usually reserved for offshore trolling lures. Casting resin is heavier than water and thus will sink. Most bass, walleye, and other freshwater and saltwater lures are floating/diving styles—they will float at rest and dive as a result of a bill or lip built into the front of the lure. Casting resin could be used to make clear, glitter-filled, or colored (opaque or translucent) jig heads, sinking plugs or crankbaits, saltwater surface lures (these are worked rapidly, usually have a sloping face, and thus will not sink when fished), spinner bodies, spinnerbait and buzzbait heads, some "spoons," and various miscellaneous lures. In most cases there are easier, quicker, better, and cheaper ways to make these lures or parts. There are no alternatives for offshore lures, however, other than in the wood bodies that are occasionally used (and discussed later in this chapter).

Molded offshore lures are typically short, stubby cylinders of molded casting resin with molded-in tubes for leaders and rigging and cast-in color, prism tape, glitter, eyes, or other attractors. As heads they are finished into lures with the addition of a slip-on or wrap-on skirt, usually of vinyl.

ETI, the major manufacturer of casting resin for hobby and fishing use, suggests that any number of materials can be used as molds for such lures (in addition to their Mold Builder latex material). They do suggest that it is best to stay with polypropylene materials for molds. They recommend avoiding plastic foams (such as foam coffee cups or similar containers) and also avoiding any plastic that night be harmed by the high heat generated by the curing resin-and-catalyst mix. The problem here is not so much with the mold, which is usually disposable and which can be replaced, but with the finish on the completed lure, which can be made rough or pitted as the resin attacks the mold.

PLASTIC LURE MOLDING STEPS

A good workplace for molding is a must. You will need a bench or bench-type work space in an area with adequate ventilation. Casting resin is highly volatile and emits a potentially harmful vapor. Without proper ventilation, severe headaches and possibly other medical problems could result from prolonged and continued inhalation. Since the product is combustible, do not use it near an open flame. A kitchen countertop completely covered with heavy cardboard or scrap

Materials needed for molding cast plastic offshore lures. The mold builder to the right allows making a mold from an existing lure, discussed in chapter 16, "Making Molds for Lead and Soft-Plastic Lures."

plywood will work well. **Make sure the stove is not gas and does not have a flame pilot light.** Do not use casting resin around any gas stoves or ovens or even near a gas clothes dryer. If you work in the kitchen, be sure to use the stove's exhaust fan and avoid using the kitchen for food preparation until all resin fumes are completely removed. Make sure there is no food open or improperly stored near the work area. As with lead-molding in the kitchen (see chapters 4 and 5) make sure no one else will be using the kitchen at the same time. To avoid possible accidents and spills, make sure children and pets are kept from the work area at all times.

If your kitchen is not suitable as a work space, consider other well-ventilated areas, such as a garage (with open doors), carport, deck, patio, or porch. If you work in a basement or any other room in the house, make sure several windows are open and that there is plenty of cross ventilation. Ed LaFley of ETI says there should be no problem for hobbyists using casting resin for 30 minutes or so at a time, but those working with the resin repeatedly or for long periods should consider getting a good mask. This does *not* mean a simple filter-type painter's mask but rather a good laboratory/industrial-style respiratory mask.

Before beginning the casting, have a definite plan for the lure you will make, the number to be cast, and the steps involved. In addition, you must have sufficient molds for the number of lures you plan to make in one session. Molds can be disposable—destroyed when removing the lure—or reusable, in which case the lure must slip or pop out of the mold. Mold possibilities include the plastic bottles and jars that originally contain spices, herbs, decorative cake granules, bouillon, film, and so on. The best are about 1 to 2 inches in diameter and about 2½ to 4 inches long. In some cases—particularly with the spice containers—the bottles will have varying constrictions, such as necks and decorative indentations, that require them to be destroyed in order to remove the lure, but they do make good workable molds. For example, a plastic bottle currently used by McCormick for spices is a little over 4 inches long and 1¾ inches in diameter, with a long constricted neck. That neck is ideal for attaching a wrapped skirt. Since these bottles are completely clear, it is also possible to fill them with the casting resin (colored or with additives as desired) and leave them on as a "skin" over the body of the lure. You will have to completely remove the paper label if keeping the lure in the spice container. With colored or frosted containers you may want to remove the mold. Several other spice companies have similar small clear-plastic bottles that have constricted necks for easy skirt attachment.

You will need to plan how to make the lure. In an article in the February 1986 issue of *Salt Water Sportsman*, Jim Rizzuto outlined a method of first molding inserts to hold eyes and prism tape from Tic Tac breath-mint boxes and a plastic 35-mm film canisters to mold a tail piece (to hold the skirt) and then inserting the cast results into a larger bouillon container to make the finished lure. These lures can be further enhanced with a large prism and eye insert and smaller round tail stock for the skirt. In essence this molding process becomes a two-step operation: first molding the rectangular Tic Tac and round 35-mm can inserts, and then completing the lure in the bouillon container. Jim suggests drilling the completed lure in order to glue in a brass- or copper-tubing leader hole.

Other tackle makers suggest carefully drilling the mold to hold the 3⁄16-inch (the typical size used) brass or copper tubing for the leader. Before adding the tubing, add insert eyes and prism tape to the tubing, and then mold the lure in one shot.

Other possibilities for inserts include natural materials such as the fishy-like shell materials and veneers offered by Aqua Blue Maui. These are principally sold for use as decoration in building custom rods (along with arts and crafts, flooring, musical instruments, etc.) and are available in many colors through custom tackle catalogs. In addition to the raw, ThinLam and Flex Pearl abalone shell, the company now also has a translucent material called Tranz-Pearl. Scotty Ventura of Aqua Blue Maui described this as being like a stained-glass window and highly usable as an insert in clear resin offshore lures. The result can be a lure suitable for daytime but also useful for night-time swordfishing when building a lure with sockets that will take chemical light sticks. Natural materials such as abalone shell (500 colors possible) and translucent natural materials both can be used as inserts in homemade offshore lures using the techniques described here. The opaque abalone can be used just like you use Mylar, prism sheets, or other additions to the center of the lure by gluing the abalone onto a balsa strip or center sheet for molding into the casting resin or epoxy. The translucent Tranz-Pearl should be used alone without a center sheet so that the light will show through it as it is trolled on the surface.

Note that the use of these materials by rod or lure makers does *not* require sanding or grinding. You need only cut the shell material to size and shape. Grinding or sanding this material can be highly dangerous, creating fine abalone or shell dust that, according to Ventura, is more dangerous than asbestos. The calcium carbonate that results from grinding shells is a strong lung irritant and can also trigger allergic and asthmatic attacks. If you must grind or sand abalone or any other shell, protect yourself by wearing a National Institute for Occupational Safety and Health (NIOSH)–approved N95 respiratory mask.

There are endless variations of the two basic methods of making lures. Let's take each of them and cover all the procedures step by step.

One-Step Lure Molding

1. You will need the following: a short length of brass or copper tubing about 3⁄16 inch in diameter, a mold of the proper shape and size for the lure you wish to make (spice jar, Silastic rubber mold, latex mold), casting resin, casting catalyst, mixing cup (usually a paper cup, not a poly-foam cup), stirring stick (such as a craft or Popsicle stick), and any insert materials you wish to use (plastic eyes, prism tape, mirrors, glitter, dyes or opaque pigments for the casting resin, sequins, etc.). You will also need a vinyl skirt or skirt wrap material, hooks, leader material (cable, single-strand wire or mono), leader sleeves, crimping pliers, and bead spacers, if necessary, for positioning the hook.
2. Gauge the amount of plastic needed by filling the mold with water and measuring the water. This will give you the volume of plastic needed—less any inserts. If the inserts are large, you may wish to add them to the mold before adding the water (they do not have to be glued onto the brass tubing at this time) to more accurately determine the volume required. Dry the mold thoroughly and any insert materials completely before casting.
3. Most plastic bottles or jars of the type we will use have a small mold mark in the bottom center. Some jar tops (used to help center the inserted metal tubing) have a similar mark. Drill through both the bottom and the top with the exact drill size required to insert the brass or copper tubing. Carefully measure the tubing diameter first.
4. Add the insert materials to the brass tubing. You can do this using double-sided tape (carpet tape), craft adhesives or glues, airplane glues, or epoxy. If you use tape, be sure the insert materials will stay in place in the mold and will not loosen while the plastic is curing. Heavy items such as large plastic eyes and mirrors are best glued in place using a 5-minute epoxy.
5. Glue the inserts onto the brass rod, making sure inserts on both sides of the tube are in the same position and parallel. Carefully insert the brass tube into the mold through the hole in the bottom. If there is play in the hole, use masking tape to stop leaks. Use masking tape to secure the tubing in the proper position

in the mold so that the inserts are accurately placed. Do this with all the molds you will fill at one time.

6. Using the measurements you previously determined with water, pour casting resin into the waxed-paper-style cup, which you have marked at the precise level where the correct volume is reached. Add the catalyst, following the manufacturer's instructions for the proper amount. For ETI resin products, this will be about two to five drops of catalyst per ounce of resin, based on a resin and room temperature of 70 degrees Fahrenheit. Do not add excessive catalyst, because this can cause the completed lure to fracture. In this case less is better than more: Too little catalyst will simply prolong the curing process, not ruin the lure.

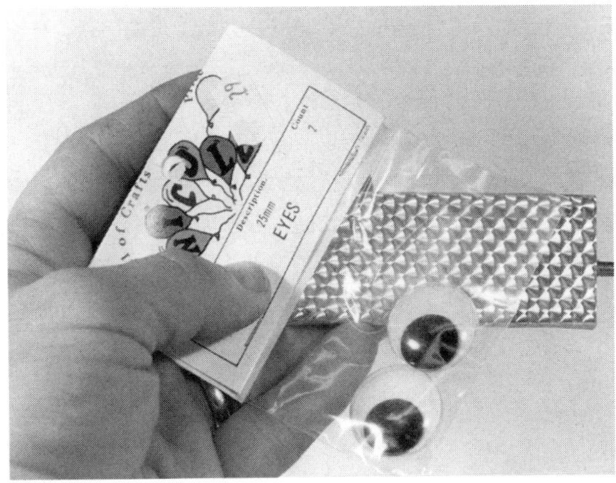

Eyes from craft stores, such as these large 1-inch craft eyes, are often used on foil and other inserts that go into offshore cast plastic lures.

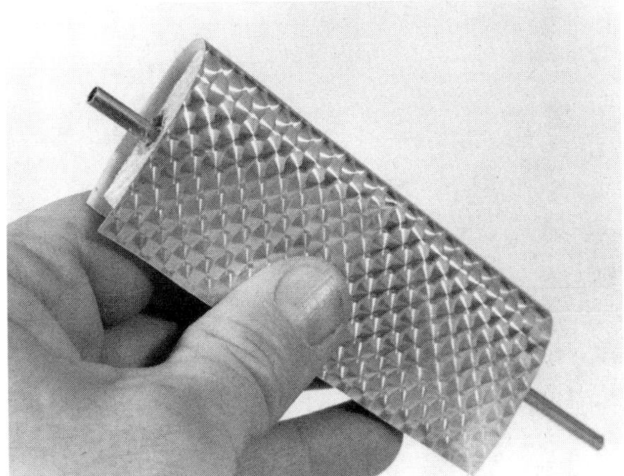
Checking a strip of self-adhesive foil to see if it will go around a wood insert body made for insertion into a cast plastic body.

Insert sheet made from several layers of wood, built up and glued together around the central tubing sleeve.

Use a stirring stick to carefully and thoroughly fold the catalyst into the casting resin. Be sure to scrape along the sides and bottom for a thorough mix, stirring for about 1 minute. Do not beat the resin to a lather, since this will add bubbles that are unattractive and difficult to remove. At this time, and according to the manufacturer's directions, add any dyes or pigments to the liquid plastic. Dyes are usually used because they will make for a translucent lure in which the inserts and eyes will show. Pigments make for an opaque lure, eliminating the need for and use of inserts.

If you use a release agent to ease removal of the lure from the mold, add it now. Once the resin is properly mixed, pour it slowly and carefully into the mold. You may wish to tilt the tubing holding the inserts to one side for easier pouring and to lessen the possibility of spills. Once the mold is filled, slowly return the tubing to a straight upright position. Place the drilled cap over the tubing, and rest it on the bottle to hold the tubing in a straight vertical position. If there is no cap on the bottle, use masking tape to support the tubing.

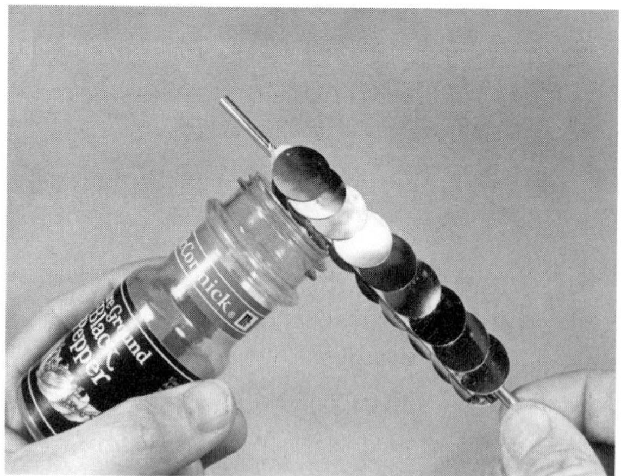

Insert in which shiny sequins are glued to a small strip of wood, through-drilled to receive the tubing shown.

Insert sheet and tubing in the spice bottle ready for molding.

Adding solid eyes from craft supplies often requires cutting off the stem to glue the eye onto the flat insert sheet.

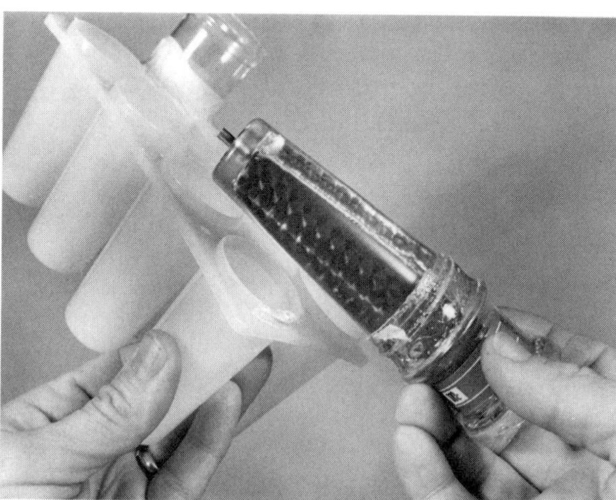

Other plastic containers can also be used for molding. Here a Popsicle tray makes tapered lures. The collar around the back, not yet removed, is from a spice bottle.

Eyes glued to a flat insert sheet, covered first with self-adhesive foil and designed to fit into a discarded spice bottle for molding the lure.

To mold, first pour out a measured amount of casting resin sufficient for the mold or molds to be filled.

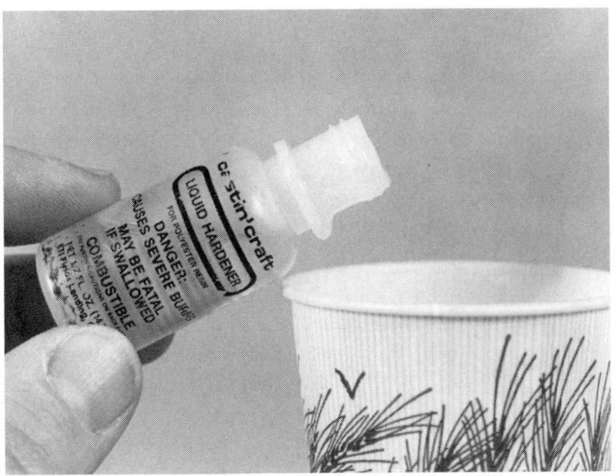

Add hardener or catalyst, using only a few drops per ounce. Too much catalyst will cause the lure to cure too rapidly and crack. Experimentation is a must here to develop the right proportions for your particular molds and conditions.

Completed head with foil insert and eyes, still in the spice bottle and with the tubing not yet trimmed.

In all of the above, work at your arm's length to keep from inhaling fumes from the casting resin. Curing time will be at least a few hours and will depend upon the amount of catalyst used, the volume and size of the casting, room temperature, the resin temperature when it was poured, the color additives used, and humidity.

7. Once the lure has cured, remove it from the mold. In some cases, for instance as when using spice bottles, the mold will have to be broken off the lure. Do this with care, using pliers to peel the mold off of the lure, or use a knife or razor blade to partially score the mold lengthwise (carefully!) on both sides before you peel it off. Do not cut all the way through the mold, because this will score the lure—the fish won't mind, but it will make for a less-attractive lure.

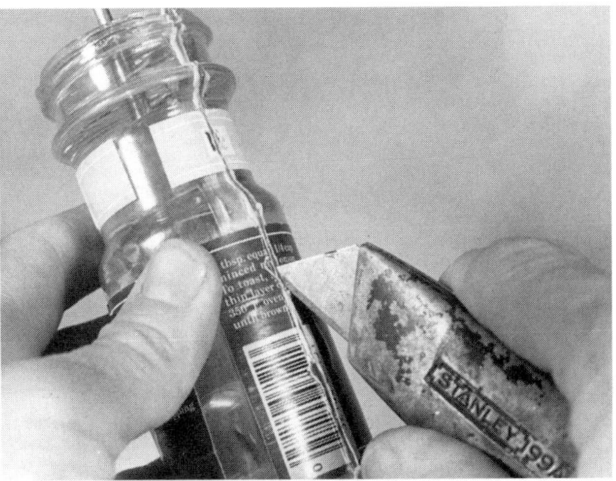

To remove the lure from the spice bottle, use a sharp utility knife to cut carefully along the sides to pry out the lure. Do not cut deeply, as this will scar the lure.

If the mold does not have constrictions that require you to break it, it can usually be separated from the lure and the lure worked free. Often you can roll the mold between your hands to separate it from the lure, gradually working the lure out. Once the mold and lure are loose, you can also pull on the leader tubing to force the lure out of the mold.

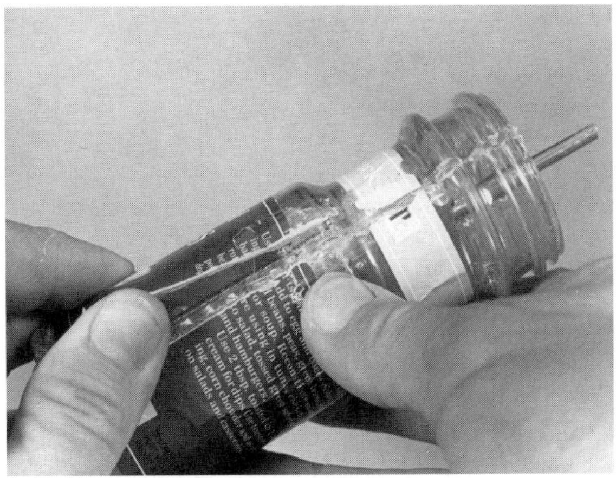

Begin removing the cut spice bottle by prying it off the lure. Often rolling the mold between your hands first will ease separating the mold from the lure.

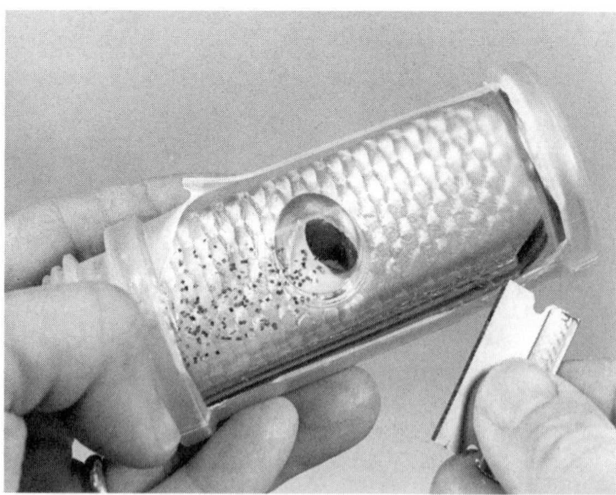

Mold partially removed, using care and a razor blade to cut away a little of the mold at a time.

Cracks in a lure, often a result of too much catalyst. This may or may not harm the effectiveness of the lure, depending upon the extent and location of the cracks.

One way to smooth the area where the skirt will be attached is to turn the lure on a lathe.

8. Once the lure is out of the mold, examine it and make sure that it is completely dry and hard. If not, set it aside to cure completely. Do not handle it. If it is completely dry, shiny, and hard, wrap it in rags, clamp it lightly in a vise, and cut off both ends of the leader tubing flush with the ends of the lure. If necessary, polish the ends of the tubing with a file and then use a countersink to polish the hole in the tubing and remove any burrs.

There are variations of this basic method. For example, you can mold the lure without tubing and drill a hole through it later. This does have some disadvantages. First, it is not always possible to drill straight through the lure unless you have a drill press, something not every angler has. And even this requires construction of a rig to hold the lure absolutely vertical while drilling. Second, most lures use inserted flash materials and eyes, which still have to be placed in the lure in some way. These can be built or assembled on wood or plastic sheets and inserted into the mold before pouring, but they must be kept in the center for best results. And there still must be enough space in the middle to drill the leader-tubing hole. Third, once the lure is molded and drilled, the tubing must be added and glued into place.

Multiple-Step Lure Molding

The second method of making offshore cast-resin lures involves several steps, such as those mentioned in Jim Rizzuto's article. In this method the basics are the same; there are two or more extra steps to complete the lure.

1. Use a small Tic Tac breath-mint container and 35-mm film canisters as molds to fill with resin. If desired, these can be filled with colored resin, which will create a contrasting inner color to the clear-resin outer lure coat.

2. Once these lure components are cured, remove the mold from them.

3. Glue the Tic Tac mold component to the film-can component end to end.

4. Glue any eyes, prism tape, or similar additions to the sides of the flat Tic Tac component.

5. Place these glued inserts into a larger mold (usually a round bouillon jar), with the tail stock (film-can component) up. Add clear casting resin to fill this mold, and allow it to cure.

6. Once it has cured, pop the lure out of the mold, drill straight through it (preferably with a drill press), and glue a brass or copper leader tube into place.

7. Cut the ends of the leader tubing, file to smooth them, and polish with a countersink; the lure is ready to have the skirt added.

Drilling a cast plastic insert piece for the brass or copper tubing that will serve as a leader guide and sleeve. This cast piece was molded from a Tic Tac box.

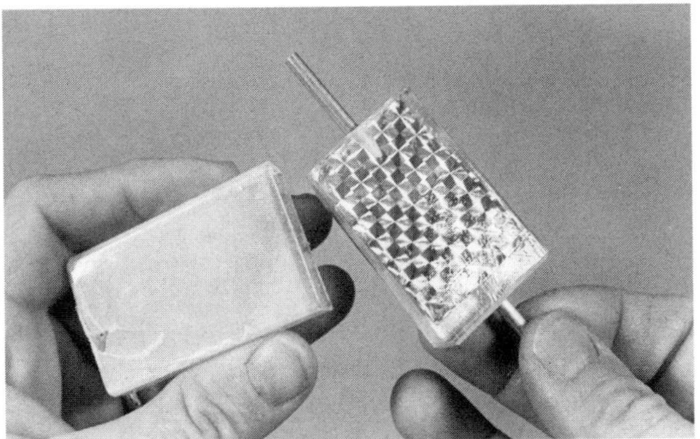

Molding insert piece, with tubing inserted, removed from a Tic Tac box. The box is cracked as a result of hammering on the mold to remove the insert.

Variations of this method are to use shaped wood slats, available in various widths at any good lumberyard, cut to the appropriate length with one end cut down to fit into a film canister or similar mold used for the tail stock. This eliminates the need to cast the first component, reducing the amount of casting resin needed for any one lure. The insert eyes and any prism or tape can be glued to the side of the wood insert and the cured insert placed tail stock up into the round bouillon jar (or similar) mold.

Another alternative is to drill the wood and tail stock, insert leader tubing, and then complete the casting in the larger mold. Other possibilities are bound to occur to you. To avoid the use of constructed molds that must be destroyed and the several steps involved in the second method, some anglers mold a single cylinder with inserts and tubing and then use a coarse sander or grinder to shape a thinner neck or flange, to which the skirt is attached. Finally, polish the lure with boat or car polish to shine the plastic.

The main thing is to consider all the steps and requirements first, plan completely, and try one lure before committing to many lures in one pouring.

MOLDING OFFSHORE LURES USING EPOXY CASTING COMPOUND

You can use the same steps listed above for working with epoxy casting compound, also available from Environmental Technology, Inc. But there are subtle differences in the two materials.

First, the casting resin (polyester) requires only a few drops of catalyst to harden into a finished lure. The epoxy is a 1:1 mix, with one 8-ounce bottle each of resin and catalyst or hardener in one 16-ounce kit. In addition, it is suggested that the maximum casting size for the epoxy compound be no more than 6 ounces total. To make lures larger than this, casting resin is better. An alternative is to make the larger epoxy lure in two parts: pouring one part, letting it cure overnight, and then adding a second part that can be molded so that it will adhere to the first part.

If you use the two-part system with casting resin, it will not adhere to itself; the epoxy resin and compound will adhere to itself in a second pour. The casting resin will stay clearer for a long time, whereas the epoxy will stay clear and transparent but will turn slightly yellow or amber with age.

The polyester casting resin will release air bubbles a little more readily than epoxy, but there are solutions for dealing with this in mixing and using the epoxy. This is particularly true of epoxy resin for finishing rod wraps. The epoxy will also remain more flexible and thus be less likely to split or break as the lure is banged around on a boat.

Otherwise, follow the steps above for mixing and working with epoxy for making offshore and other lures. More information on the use and mixing of epoxy is provided in chapter 25.

STEP-BY-STEP CONSTRUCTION OF WOOD LURES

Several types of offshore lures can be made from wood. Though they will lack the visual appeal of the clear-resin cast offshore lures, wood heads can be carved or turned on a lathe and painted. The lathe is the best way to go, using the techniques outlined in chapter 9. With a wood lathe and using closet rods, hardwood dowels, or blocks of poplar and oak sold specifically for lathe work, such lures are easy. Although the shapes are different, they aren't much longer or more difficult to make than a big freshwater plug. Most offshore lures will vary from as small as about ¾ inch in diameter to as large as 2 inches and range from about 2½ inches to about 6 inches long. Some teasers—hookless lures used to attract fish to the baits—are larger.

Using standard lathe practices, you can make blunt-nose, round-head, or cup-faced lures, all with necks or flanges for adding skirts. Cutting the completed lure face at an angle once it is out of the lathe will make slant-headed lures that alternately skip, bounce, and dive.

In addition, you can drill a number of holes straight through the heads or at an angle, using a hand drill, although a drill press is better, to make lures that "smoke" (the multiple holes cause bubbles). If you're not accurate with a hand drill and don't have a drill press, you can take a square cross section block, run a centerline down each face, and carefully cut wide slots (about ¼ inch wide, ¼ inch deep) with a handsaw. Make four ¼-inch slots, one on each face. Then place the block in a lathe and turn it to size and shape. Cut it to a size that will just fit into a piece of PVC, CPVC, or ABS pipe of about 1 inch to 1½ inches in diameter. Make sure the slots in the side of the block remain so that you will have straight-through holes in between the wood block and the wall of the pipe. The result will be smoke holes that will create bubbles. The outside of the lure will be the plastic pipe, painted; the inside will be the wood core. The wood is glued into the plastic pipe and then the whole lure painted with several base coats of white followed by a finish color.

In addition to offshore trolling lures, cedar plugs are also easy to make. These are popular for early-season trolling for tuna on the Northeast coast and are just what they sound like: cedar wood plugs, usually in a chunky cigar shape, with multiple hooks or a single hook.

These can be made by using the same methods outlined in chapter 9. Typically they have a metal or lead head and a cedar body with a line-tie in the head for the line and one single hook in the tail. The cedar body can be turned on a lathe, the head molded in a plaster or Silastic rubber mold (using the type required for high-heat lead molding), and the two parts glued and fitted together. For saltwater fishing, the completed lure should be through-drilled with a wire leader run through the lure for a solid line-to-hook connection.

Making a bubbler for a lure by cutting four grooves around the perimeter of a dowel for passage of air and water through the lure.

Using a file to smooth the cut grooves for the bubbler.

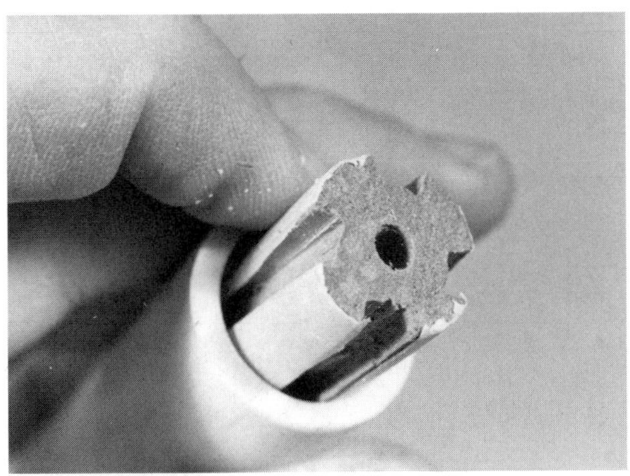

Completed bubbler insert, here ready to be glued into a piece of PVC pipe to make a bubbler that is part of a lure or can be threaded onto the leader ahead of the lure for added froth—"smoke" in the parlance of the offshore angler.

SOFT-BODIED LURES

You can make soft-bodied lures using plastic bottles and jars, aluminum, wood, or Silastic rubber RTV molds. The methods of molding are almost the same as outlined in chapter 7. The differences are as follows:

Because you will be making saltwater lures, you must add a considerable amount of hardener to the plastic to make a tougher lure. You will have to experiment with this, but remember that commercial soft-vinyl lures are very tough for the severe trolling conditions under which they are used.

You will be making far larger lures than the soft-plastic worms used for freshwater fishing, so use a sufficiently large pot and melt enough plastic to fill the mold.

Molds for these lures are basically cylinders that are similar in size to molds for trolling lures. You can use bouillon jars, other small jars, 35-mm film canisters, or spice bottles, as previously outlined. You can also make your own molds using wood, Silastic rubber, or small aluminum juice cans. If you use Silastic rubber, you will have to make the mold using a model of the lure you wish to duplicate.

You will not be able to mold the skirts that are a part of commercial lures. All you can effectively make is the cylindrical head—the skirt must still be added or wrapped on later.

You can use inserts such as plastic or wood slats, to which eyes, mirrors, prism tape, sequins, or other additions are attached. These will not show nearly as well as they will through the clear, hard-plastic casting resin.

ADDING SKIRTS

Once the molded parts of the lures are complete and polished, skirts are added. There are two basic ways to do this: One involves using a ready-molded skirt, such as those used on bead-chain lures and resembling a large, thick, shredded glove finger. The second involves using strips of skirting material wrapped and sometimes glued in place.

For the first method, buy ready-made vinyl skirts such as Psychotail replacement skirts or similar brands. Cut the head off so that you get a tight fit onto the tail or lure or tail stock, whichever method you use. For one method use a good vinyl glue on the flange or neck, and slide the skirt onto this area. If the glue is not holding securely, or if there is no neck or step-down to the skirt area to prevent water pressure from ripping the skirt off, you may wish to secure the skirt with wire, cord, dental floss, or braided-nylon fishing line. Use many wraps, but do not wrap too tightly, which will tend to cut the skirt.

Another method is to cut the head off the skirt, reverse it, and glue the reversed side (the outside) to the neck or head flange. The head end will be pointed toward the tail, and the skirt end will be up over the forward part of the plastic head. Secure with a wrapping of cord, nylon fishing line, or wire. Many commercial lure manufacturers use fifty-pound test Dacron line.

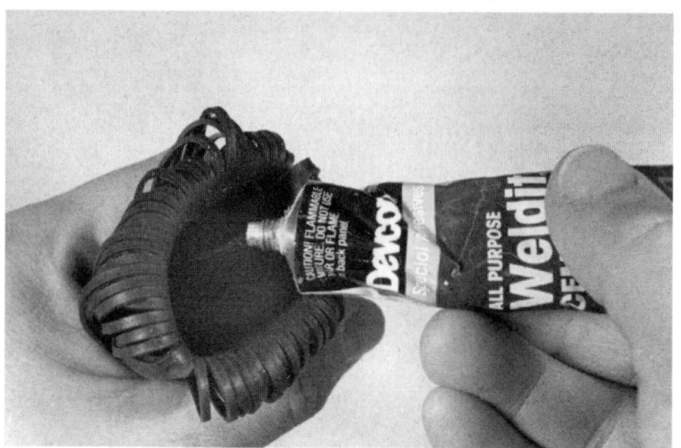

Usually several skirts are combined, using flexible glues to cement one skirt inside of another.

Here a silver skirt is being glued inside a black skirt.

A dowel placed inside the head allows cutting the skirt at the right position for stretching and gluing onto the head.

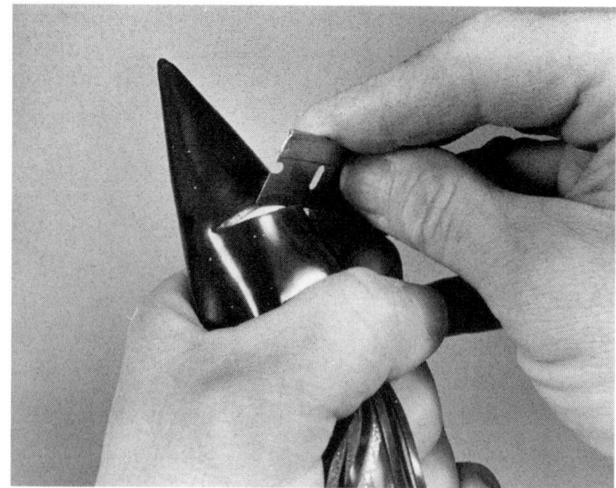

Using a razor blade to cut around the perimeter of the skirt's head for attaching to the cast plastic head.

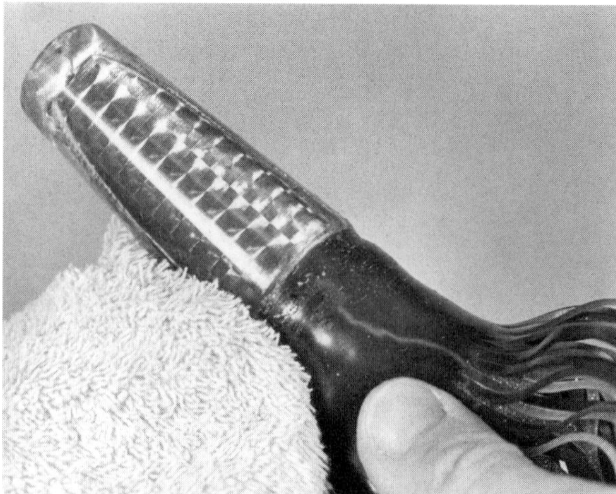

Using automobile polish to clean and polish the head after the skirt is glued in place.

If you use wire, twist the ends to secure them and lay them flat against the body. Slowly and carefully roll the skirt (almost as if you were rolling off a pair of rubber kitchen gloves) to pull the outside down over the neck and hide the wrapping holding the skirt in place.

You can use both methods with two or more skirts, making the inner skirts of different colors than the outer skirt. Although three skirts are sometimes used, two skirts are more common. You can also find single skirts in which the underside is a completely different color (usually white or light) than the upper side, giving the appearance of two colors in one skirt.

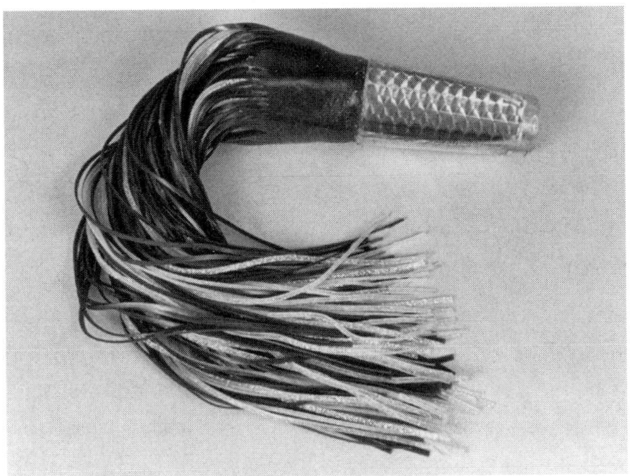

Completed lure, unrigged but otherwise ready to fish.

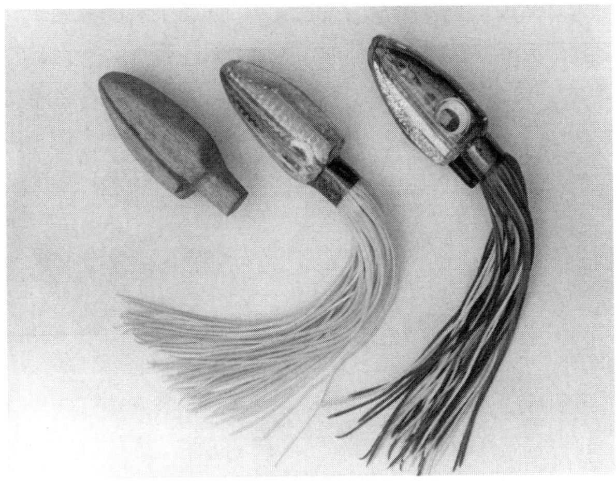

Example of steps in making a lure from a wood prototype. The wood prototype serves as a model for using Mold Builder (see chapter 16, "Making Molds for Lead and Soft Plastic Lures"), with examples of completed lures to the right.

Another method involves using strips of skirts and wrapping them around the neck or flange of the lure head. These strips are available from Mold Craft in an 11½ × 3½-inch size and in twenty colors. The strips are tied in place after being glued to the neck. Most commercial lure manufacturers use Zap glue. Similar to the various "crazy" glues, Zap glue (originally the highly expensive Eastman 910) is not completely waterproof, but it is highly water-resistant and has proven the best so far in gluing the soft vinyl skirts to the hard casting-resin heads.

One skirt about 3½ inches wide will wrap one lure with a neck of about 1 inch in diameter. If you work with larger lures, the skirts can be cut with a razor blade, glued, and wrapped in place. In both methods, some anglers use a foil tape wrapped around the head of the skirt to cover the cord wrappings. The tape can be glued in place with the Zap glue or with a PVC glue that serves as a good "weld" to the soft-vinyl skirts.

RIGGING HOOKS

Rigging is done with single-strand wire, mono, or twisted-wire cable. Twisted-wire cable and heavy mono are most commonly used. You will need an offshore hook appropriate to the size of the lure and the fish sought. Leader sleeves are a must with wire and usually with mono as well. Be sure to use the right leader sleeves with the right tool (point-opposing-cup with the round sleeves, cup-opposing-cup with the oval or figure-eight sleeves). Be sure also to use the right size sleeve to hold the wire or mono securely. Heavy mono can be snelled to the hook to make single or tandem rigs.

To make single-hook rigs, first decide on the test and type of leader to be used. Then snell, tie, or secure the hook to the leader with leader sleeves. If you work with mono, you have all three choices; if you work with cable, you can only use leader sleeves.

To use leader sleeves to attach the hook, make a double overhand knot around the hook eye. The easy way to do this is to first place two leader sleeves on the leader. Run the leader through the hook eye twice, and then wrap the end of the wire twice around the resulting loop. Pull the cable into a small loop, and adjust the length of the end to fit the two leader sleeves a few inches apart. Run the end of the leader through the first sleeve and slide the sleeve close to the loop. Crimp tight with crimping pliers. Twist the end of the leader about 180 degrees around the standing wire, and slip the second leader sleeve in place. Make sure the end of the wire is not exposed through the leader sleeve. Crimp to secure.

The method just described results in a free-swinging hook, but there is a method to make the hook straight and stiff with the wire cable. This rig or a variation is often called a "pro rig," in reference to the number of serious anglers who use it. For this rig first place two sleeves on the leader and then run the leader through the eye of the hook toward the gap or hook point. Wrap the cable up, over, and around the hook shank in back of the hook eye and back out the eye down toward the point. Make these wraps as tight as possible. Secure with the leader sleeves as before. The result is a hook that remains stiff and in line with the leader cable.

If you use mono, you can sometimes tie knots, such as the clinch, improved clinch, and Palomar knots, although these become more difficult with large size mono. Tie these knots carefully and tightly, and use pliers to pull up the ends. You can also use leader sleeves (some special leader sleeves are made just for mono) using the same connections (double overhand loop knot and figure-eight wrap) previously mentioned for cable.

Snelling is often the preferred way to rig hooks on heavy mono. Instead of the mono being run through the eye of the hook, the eye is used as a "stop" to prevent the snell from sliding off. To make a snell, hold the mono on and parallel to the hook shank, and allow it to extend past the bend of the hook. Loop the mono in a circle so that the end lies next to the first part of the loop of mono on the hook shank. Holding the mono securely, use the resulting loop to wrap around the two overlapping strands of mono and hook shank. The wrap is from the bend toward the eye, with the first wrap crossing over the mono and subsequent wraps evenly made around the two pieces of mono and the hook shank. Make at least five turns, and then finish by holding the shank and mono loops securely while pulling the end strand of mono. This will gradually decrease the size of the loop until there is no loop and the mono ends are completely under the wrap. Position this so that the snell is up against the eye of the hook and the leader runs from under the eye. Finish by grasping the tag end with pliers, holding the leader end securely and pulling both simultaneously to tighten the knot.

Tandem hooks are common in offshore lures; the second hook is on the same leader or is attached by a second short section of cable. With cable you will need a short length of cable and the appropriate sleeves, along with some straight-jawed snap-ring pliers and some short lengths of surgical tubing of a size that will hold the leader on the hook securely. An alternative to the surgical hose method is to use shrink tubing, which will tighten with heat, or to tie the rig in place with braided fishing line or cord.

Note: Although this description comes after the description for making a single-hook cable rig, in actuality you would make the second rig first and then attach it to the forward hook. This reduces cable waste and also makes it far easier to slip the one or two pieces of surgical hose onto the forward hook. Otherwise you would have to run the surgical tubing down over the complete cable leader.

Begin by securing the hook with the tight figure-eight pro-rig wrap. Then run the cable forward and through the eye of the forward hook. Slip a sleeve or two onto the cable. Position the cable through the eye at the exact position desired for the two hooks. How you hold the cable and hooks now is critical to the resulting rig. Most anglers like a rig in which the two hooks are at 90 or 180 degrees to each other. To achieve this you must position the hooks this way before making any bends—any changes will be impossible later.

Remember that if you fish by the International Game Fish Association (IGFA) rules for tournaments or records, you cannot have the eyes of the hooks less than a hook's length apart and no more than 12 inches apart (eye to eye) in lures (18 inches in baits).

At the chosen position for the hooks, bend the cable into a loop; slip the end through the leader sleeve, and crimp. Repeat with the second sleeve (if one is used), and crimp. Place a small piece of the surgical tubing onto the snap-ring pliers and slip the tubing over the forward hook eye, leader, and crimped sleeve (moisten with saliva or suds for easy application). Slide the tubing down on the hook close to the bend, where it will hold the hook shank and cable in alignment. Add a second piece of surgical tubing the same way, placing it directly over the hook shank and crimped leader.

Other alternatives for securing the cable to the first hook are to use shrink tubing, which can be slid in place and then shrunk by applying heat or attached by wrapping with self-adhesive tape or tying with dental floss or cord. Once this is done, the leader can be added to the forward hook as per the original description.

You can also make a free-swinging hook rig, using the previously described method of using a double overhand knot and two leader sleeves for a free leader/hook eye connection. Usually the short length of cable is still firmly attached by surgical or shrink tubing to the hook shank of the forward hook.

To add a second hook using snelled mono, the second hook is attached after the first, opposite the method for making the two-hook cable rig. You use the same method described for snelling a hook, beginning with the eye of the second hook held in position at the bend of the forward hook. Since the excess line is pulled through the wraps to the rear, the position will change only slightly as any slack is taken out of the snell upon tightening.

Single-strand wire can also be used for big-game offshore lure riggings, with a simple haywire twist typical of connections to the hook. Because of the tendency of single-strand wire to kink and the frantic antics of a hooked fish, cable is typically used for two-hook rigs even when the rest of the leader is single-strand wire.

Note that in making any of the two-hook rigs, there is plenty of room for experimentation. As this is written, serious offshore anglers are experimenting with two-hook rigs by varying the angles of the planes of the hooks, using a larger hook for the tail hook, a smaller hook for the tail hook, and different hook styles. The goal of these experiments is to achieve better and more secure hooking, though the ultimate, perfect rig is still elusive.

VARIATIONS

Given the nature of offshore lures and offshore fishing, there are almost endless variations in lures, not to mention the constant arguments regarding speed, action, and the best color head and skirt for a given game species. Consider these possible variations:

1. Casting a basic clear or dyed resin cylinder-lure head, with eyes and molded-insert prism material; turning it on a lathe to the desired shape and size; and finally polishing it with a polishing or rubbing compound. This results in an absolutely accurate round lure, with the center hole dead on-center as a result of the live centers used on the lathe. You can duplicate a commercial or homemade lure using a template or contour gauge or experiment with different shapes for different action, bubbling, or flash when trolled. You can also cut a lure flange or neck to the exact size needed for a given vinyl skirt. For the groups of plastics that include cast resins, cutting speeds of about 200 to 300 feet per minute are rated best, with cuts and feed no more than 0.010. No lubrication is required, but it is important to check the tightness between centers; these plastics often expand with heat and may have to be adjusted.

2. Clear- or colored-plastic CAST acrylic rods (such as Plexiglas) can be similarly turned on a lathe to make lures. As with the cast lures, the result is a perfect cylinder in relation to the lure center, and any shape can be cut. Finish with a polishing or rubbing compound. These lures have to be drilled, which is best done on a drill press, following the marks made by the lathe centers while turning. Since these lures begin as solid-plastic rods, any eyes or other attractions must be added to the outside of the lure, using Zap glue or a similar glue designed to work with acrylic plastics.

3. Soft-style offshore trolling lures can be made from large diameters (1¼ to 1½ inches are usually the largest sizes available) of foam rod-handle material, commonly called EVA or Hypalon. Often these are available with a small hole of about ¼ inch through the center, but they are more commonly available with larger holes up to about ¾ inch. This material is available in up to 18-inch lengths, often in various colors. To make a lure with EVA, use a core tube of copper, brass, or polyethylene plastic, and glue it into the hole in the foam rubber. If the hole is larger than ¼ inch in diameter (the right size for 3⁄16- or ¼-inch tubing), you must build up the difference. One way to do this is with inner-tube rubber or rubber gasket material, cut to the right length for the lure and wrapped tightly around the tubing, using rubber cement while wrapping to secure the material. To do this properly, first measure the amount of flat rubber material required, coat both sides with the rubber cement, allow the cement to become tacky, and then tightly roll the rubber material around the tubing. Add rubber cement on the inside of the rubber foam and around the rubber core, and insert the core into the foam body. Wait until the cement has cured, and then use a lathe or work a rasp manually to shape a neck or flange on which to add the skirt. The skirt can be made with flat strip material such as Mold Craft Tuff Tails or by using a vinyl skirt such as the Sevenstrand Psychotail replacement skirts. Glue the skirts with a PVC glue or rubber cement and/or wrap with floss or cord.

The wide range of and uses for offshore lures still leave plenty of room for experimentation and testing. This chapter outlined only a few of the methods that can be used to construct what are today considered standard lures. Tomorrow new techniques and methods will no doubt be discovered and tested.

12
Miscellaneous Lures

Introduction • Plastic-Pipe Lures • Metal-Tubing Lures • Swaged-Pipe Lures • Metal-Bar Lures • Pipe-Slab Lures • Surgical-Hose Lures • Split-Shot Jigs • Egg-Sinker Jigs • Rope Jigs, Flies, and Lures • Ice "Flies" • Trolling Rigs • Other Lures

INTRODUCTION

For this chapter we will abandon the listing of tools and materials, although step-by-step instructions will be included with each lure example. That's because these lures are unusual and defy categorization.

In most cases the lures here are simple to make or involve methods that have been discussed in previous chapters. In some cases they require experimentation to perfect the best action. They are not "miracle lures"—there is no such thing—but they are fun to make and fish and often take as many fish as other lures. Sometimes they will take fish when nothing else works. In any case, most are easy to make, very inexpensive, and well worth a try.

PLASTIC-PIPE LURES

Plastic pipe can be used for an unusual type of tube lure. Many types of plastic pipe are available, including pipe of PVC, CPVC, ABS, and similar plastics. Some are available only in large sizes. The pipe you will want for this lure ranges from ½ inch through about 1½ inches in diameter and is usually PVC or CPVC. The lure is simplicity itself to make.

Simple lures can be made by wiring cord or nylon strands onto the wire leader ahead of a hook as shown.

To make a plastic-pipe lure, choose the diameter of pipe best suited for your fishing. Generally this will be a diameter about the same as that of a plug or crankbait you would use. Use a saw to cut the pipe into lengths, again choosing a length about the same as for a crankbait you would fish.

Here are some suggested diameters and lengths: ½-inch-diameter pipe in a 3-inch length for bass and pike; ¾-inch pipe in a 4-inch length for light-tackle saltwater trolling; 1-inch pipe in 4- or 6-inch lengths for saltwater trolling and light surf casting; and 1½-inch pipe in 6- to 8-inch lengths for offshore trolling, heavy surf casting, and heavy saltwater fishing.

You can cut the pipe square at both ends, cut one end at an angle, or cut both ends at an angle. The degree of cut will affect the action in the water, although at any angle the lure will have an erratic action in the water or when trolled on the surface. The angle does help in attaching the hooks, through-wire leader, and line-tie though. After cutting the pipe, smooth it. You can do this by using a large reamer, sanding lightly, or scraping with a knife blade on both the inside and outside of the cut edge.

Once the edges are smooth, drill a ⅛- to 3/16-inch hole through each projecting end of the tubing. Smooth these holes with a countersink. Next prepare a through-wire leader of cable, single-strand wire, or heavy utility wire (the kind available in small coils at any

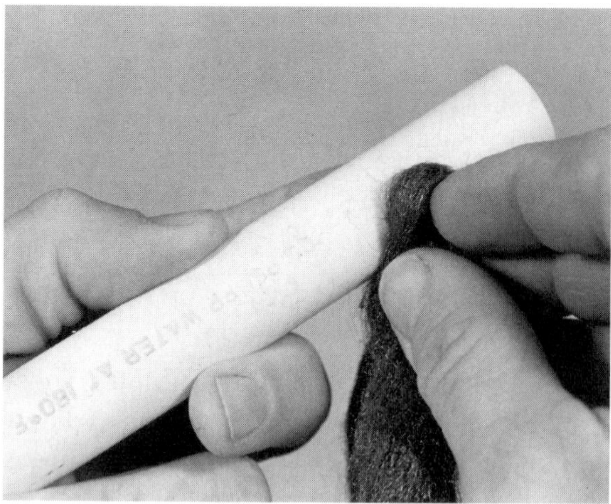

Making a plastic PVC-pipe lure first requires removing the printed markings on the side of the pipe. Steel wool is ideal for this.

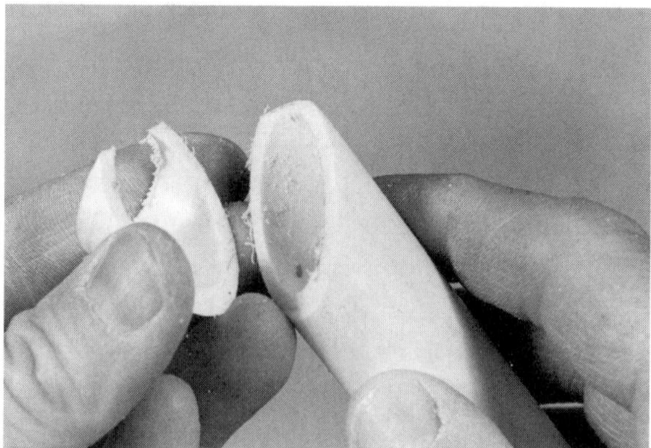

To make a sloping-face lure, use a saw to cut one end at a sloping angle.

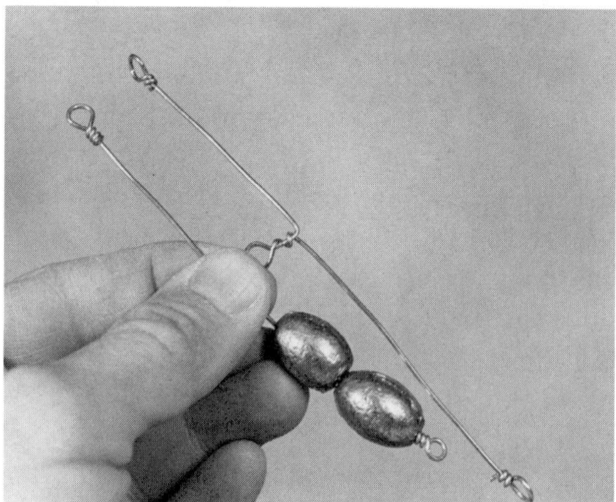

Rigged wire forms that serve as a connection between the line-tie and rear and belly hooks. This is necessary for strong fish.

hardware store). The leader, with formed or sleeve-crimped eyes, must measure the same as the distance between the two drilled holes. If you wish to weight the lure for casting, deep-jigging (requiring lots of weight), or a special action while trolling, add it to the leader at this point. The easiest way to do this is to use a series of egg sinkers or one large egg sinker on the leader. The sinkers must be small enough to fit into the plastic pipe. Use a leader sleeve to hold the sinkers in place on the leader. The position of the weight on the leader—essentially at the head or tail of this tube lure—will change the action and retrieve or trolling depth somewhat.

In place of the egg sinker, you can mold small "ingots" of lead in a homemade mold of wood or plaster of Paris (quality won't matter here). Use a small pan-head sheet-metal screw to hold this lead weight inside the tube, inserting the screw through the outside of the plastic pipe and into the lead ingot or molded weight.

Once the through-wire leader is prepared, the last step is to slip the leader into the tubing and secure it in place by using large split rings at each end—the split rings go through the leader eye and the tube hole. Use the same step to add the hook—treble, double, or single—at the tail end. If desired, you can also add a belly hook by making the wire form with a loop in the center and drilling a hole through the plastic pipe so that the loop in the wire fits through the hole for hook attachment. This can be done using a split shank hook or adding a treble, double, or single hook with a split ring. Another way to do this is to drill a hole through the PVC tubing and use a hook on a barrel swivel (connected with a split ring), with the swivel placed inside the lure where the leader wire runs through it. These methods secure all the hooks—tail and belly—to the wire leader.

Running the split ring through the hook eye, tube eye, and leader eye all at the same time saves time and also prevents excessive spreading of the split ring. The addition of the egg sinker(s) gives the lure some weight for casting, and the leader prevents the loss of a fish should the eye

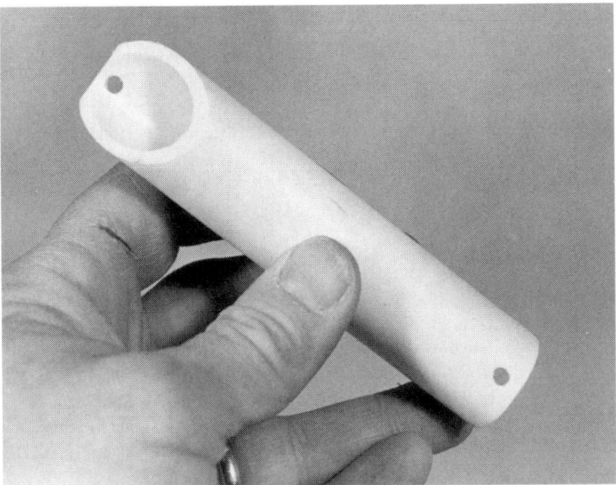

Pipe lure with sloping face and holes drilled for line-tie and hook attachment.

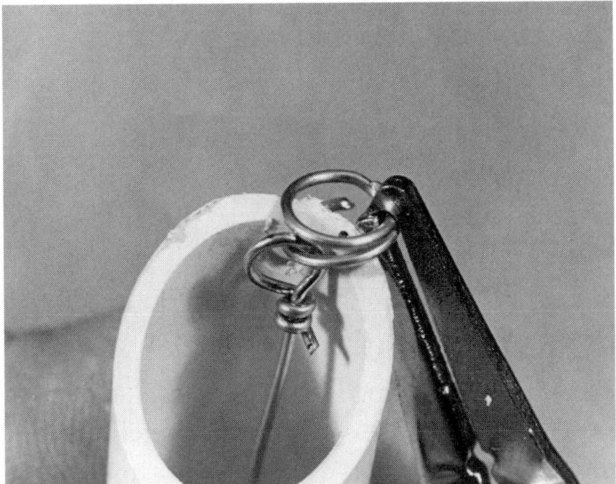

Adding the internal wire rigging to the pipe form with split-ring pliers. On the tail and belly attachment, the hooks would be added at the same time.

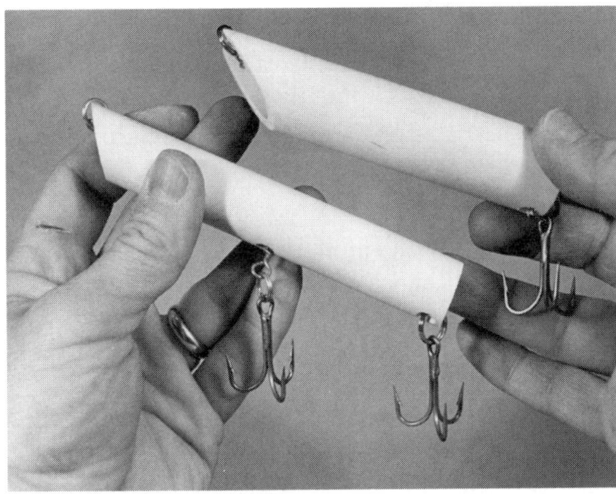

Examples of finished lures.

in the plastic tubing pull out in a fight. Ideally it is best to rig the lure so that the stress of fighting the fish is on the leader—not on the drilled holes in the plastic pipe.

One added touch to increase action is to make a saw cut or slot partway through the lure at a right angle to the tube's length. This can be at different angles in different lures to hold a glued-in "lip" of plastic or metal. Sturdy scraps of metal or plastic, cut into shape and glued in place with epoxy or plastic pipe glue, work well and give the lure added action. Experiment with different lip materials, lengths, and angles to find the best action for your lures. The best and toughest material for lure lips is clear Lexan, often available at plastic-supply houses (check the Yellow Pages) as scrap and sold by the square foot in ⅛- and ¼-inch thicknesses.

Final finishing (discussed for all lures in chapter 15) can include painting, coloring with felt-tip markers, adding prismatic tape, and so on.

METAL-TUBING LURES

The same techniques described above can be used with metal tubing such as copper, brass, and aluminum pipe. Any pipe can be used. For a very bright lure, try using sections of chrome-plated bathroom pipe such as used for drain

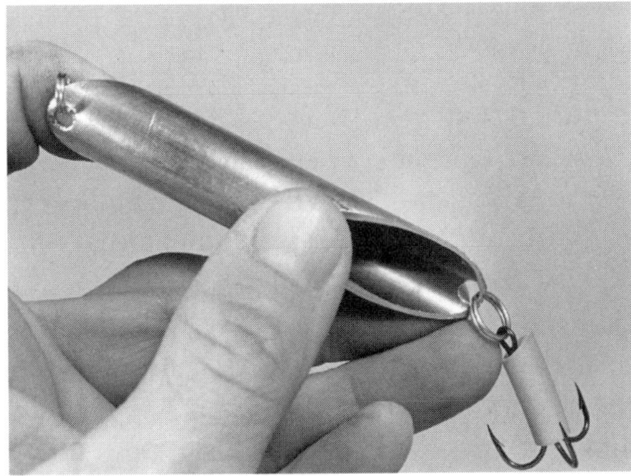

Finished metal-tubing lure, this one made from copper water pipe. The metal is strong, so no internal wire rigging is required.

An anvil and heavy hammer are necessary for swaging flat lures from pipe. Either one or both ends can be swaged, or the entire lure can be flattened.

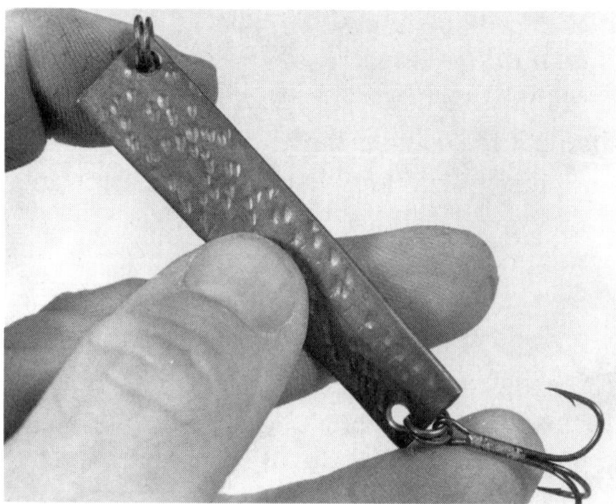

Flattened pipe lure, with hammer marks made with ball-peen hammer.

pipes (though this is large—about 1¼ inches in diameter) and inlet water pipes (about ½-inch diameter). Cut the pipe at an angle for the split-ring attachment, smooth the cut with sandpaper or a file, and drill a hole in each projecting end. Since this pipe is metal and should not crack as can plastic pipe, you do not need the leader wire for protection against loss. Also, because it is metal you can add weight by plugging one end and pouring melted lead into the lure and allowing it to cool. (Be careful when doing this, and be sure to read all safety precautions in chapters 4 and 5.)

Use a section of dowel, a cork stopper, or similar plug to stop up one end of the tubing. Since the lead may eventually slide out if it's not secured, drill a hole through the sidewall of the tubing where the lead is located and insert a short stainless steel or brass sheet-metal screw to hold the lead in place. Add a split ring to one end for a line-tie, and add a split ring and hook to the tail end. You can add a belly hook (as described with the PVC lures) by drilling a hole in the body and adding a hook on a swivel or wire form, using a leader wire to run through the swivel eye as it runs from the tail hook to the line-tie. Another method of attachment is to drill a hole to take the swivel, run a large split ring through the eye of the swivel, and slip the swivel through the hole in the pipe from the inside. The large split ring will prevent the swivel from pulling through. Then use a split ring to attach the hook to the external swivel eye.

Finish by polishing the lure and coating it with a clear lacquer, paint, a clear prism tape cover, plastic tape, or whatever suits your design.

SWAGED-PIPE LURES

Metal pipe also is used for these lures, which consist of a short length of pipe completely swaged into a flat lure or left round by swaging at each end for the hook and line-tie attachment. If you make a lure that will be completely flattened, remember this when choosing the diameter of the pipe: Any round tubing will flatten out to about one and one half times the round diameter. Thus a 1-inch-diameter pipe will make a flattened swaged lure that is about 1½ inches wide.

You can flatten copper, brass, or aluminum pipe or tubing in one of two ways: One is to squeeze the pipe in a large vise, preferably one that has jaws as wide as the tubing lure is long. Otherwise, squeeze gently in several steps. The second way is to place the tube on an anvil or suitable substitute and hammer the tubing flat. Do this also a little at a time, turning the tubing over often for an even result.

Once the tubing is flattened to your satisfaction, make sure the ends are completely flat, and then round the end slightly with a file or grindstone. Drill a hole straight through each end, smooth with a countersink, and add a split ring at one end for a line-tie and a split ring and hook to the other end.

To make a round lure with swaged ends, use the same techniques above, except use the vise or anvil and hammer to flatten the very ends only—not the middle. Hammer alternately from both sides to make them even. Drill a hole through the ends, and finish as above.

This method also allows the easy addition of lead to make a heavier lure or a specialized jig or to change the running depth or action of a trolling or casting lure. To do this, crimp one end shut and make sure that it is *completely sealed* to prevent any leakage of molten lead. Secure the lure with the open end up (you can make a special rack for this or just stick it in a bucket of sand), and add the desired quantity of lead. Once the lead is cool, crimp the open end and continue as above. A simpler alternative is to crimp one end; add sufficient scrap-lead pieces, birdshot, old lead sinkers, or split shot; pour in some glue to hold the scrap securely; allow the glue to cure; and hammer the open end shut. Finish by drilling and adding the hooks and line-tie split rings. The same method can be used to add BBs, shot, and other rattles, which can be particularly effective in these lures when they are used for vertical jigging. Particularly good for this are the commercially available rattles in glass, plastic, and metal.

METAL-BAR LURES

Metal bars and rods of any type can be used for casting, trolling, and jigging lures. Scrap bars, metal rods, and bars available from hardware stores, the handles of old discarded kitchen utensils, even threaded rod can all be used for making metal-bar lures. In the case of flat metal bars, such as the do-it-yourself materials available at hardware stores that average about ⅛ or ¼ inch thick, this involves nothing more than cutting the bar to length, grinding or filing the ends to smooth, drilling a hole in each end, and adding a line-tie and hook with split rings.

If you use round stock such as threaded or smooth rods (both available at hardware stores) you will have to grind or file the end flat—to a thinner diameter—to make it possible to add the split ring and hook easily. The handles of old kitchen knives, spoons, and forks are ideal because they are usually stainless, heavy enough for casting with a slight bend for some action, and flat enough to drill easily for hook and line-tie attachment.

Any of these lures can be bent slightly to give them more action in the water. Such lures, in large sizes to cast easily (several ounces), are ideal for surf fishing and often resemble the best tin squids or metal surf spoons you can buy.

PIPE-SLAB LURES

Pipe-slab lures can be made of lead-filled metal or resin-filled plastic pipe. The metal lures are filled with lead but are not used or made in the same way as the ones above. They end up like an angled slab of metal—not round but oblong, the degree of oblong depending on the angle at which the pipe is cut. To make them, first plug one end of a pipe that has the diameter you want in the finished lures. Then fill to the top with molten lead or tin. (Tin will be lighter in weight but also shinier.) Allow the lure to cool, and cut the pipe at an angle and into very thin sections. The angle of the cut will determine the length of the lure; the thickness of the cut will determine the action and weight of the lure. Once the slabs are cut out (using a hacksaw or working carefully with a metal-cutting power or band saw), smooth the cut sides with a file, grinder, or belt sander. Once the sides are smooth, you might find that the lead or tin center is loose in the outer ring of metal. You can pull this material out and glue it in place with epoxy glue, or you can just drill holes on each end through the lead and the metal rim to secure the center in place with the split ring. Add split rings at each end for the line-tie and the hook.

A variation is to use the metal pipe but fill the center with casting resin, the same material used to make offshore trolling lures (see chapter 11). You must plug the end of the metal pipe, just as when filling with molten lead. Follow the directions in chapter 11 for care, handling, and safety in working with the plastic and also for suggestions on the proper amount of catalyst to use for a large mass of casting resin. For colorful lures, add dye (for translucent lures) or pigment (for opaque lures) to the casting resin before pouring.

Once the plastic is poured in the metal tube, allow it to cure and then carefully cut at sharp angles to make the slablike lures. These will differ from those containing lead in that they will be lighter and also transparent or translucent, giving a completely different effect. In addition, while the metal pipe adds weight and a shiny surface to these lures, you can also make resin-filled lures using PVC, CPVC, ABS, or similar plastic pipe. Leave the pipe bare or paint it after pouring but before cutting into the oblong slabs. Since you are working with clear casting resin, you can create color variations by adding opaque or translucent coloring to the plastic or by adding glitter, small aluminum or Mylar craft mirrors, or colored or shiny sequins to the mix. When adding particles like this, you must rotate the tubing periodically to keep the material from settling.

SURGICAL-HOSE LURES

Surgical-hose lures go by a lot of names—hose lures, surgical hose, and surgical eels—and are readily available commercially. Although the basic concept behind these surgical-hose lures is an old one, they continue to be popular and work well. They are good for striped bass, bluefish, and other saltwater species when trolled and for barracuda when rigged straight and cast on tropical flats. Basically nothing more than a length of rubber or plastic tubing over a hook and short leader attached to a barrel swivel, such "surge" lures are extremely simple to make.

The tubing comes in a variety of sizes and colors, including the natural amber color as well as red, yellow, black, blue, green, pink, and other colors. Fluorescent colors are sometimes available. Similar hose is also available in clear plastic, which can be used with insert materials such as colored or shiny tinsel or Mylar tubing. Some anglers even use the very thin catheter tubing for special fishing applications. Diameters range

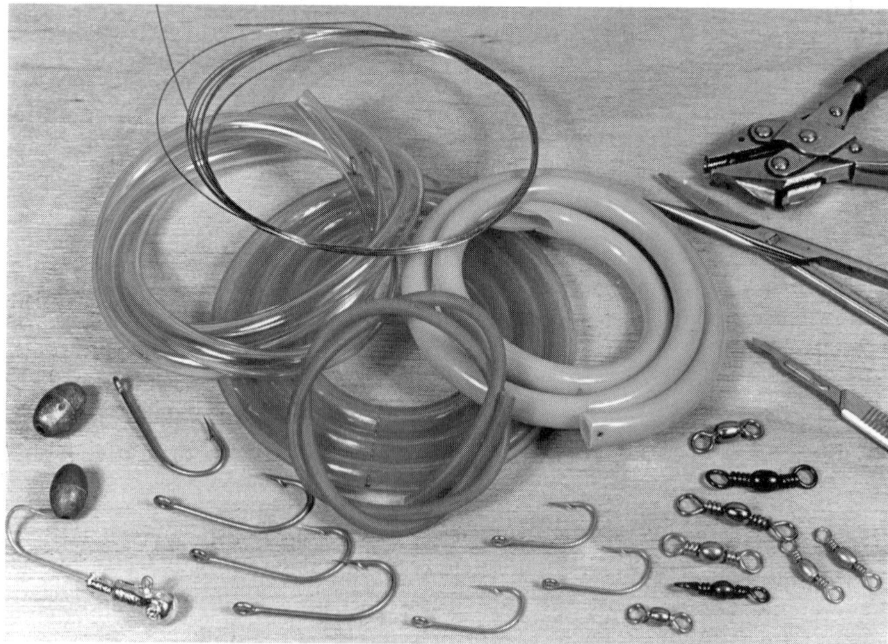

Materials needed for making surgical-hose lures.

from as thin as ⅛ inch to larger than you would want to use. You can get the tubing from most mail-order houses and many saltwater-area tackle shops. In making these lures use strong saltwater single hooks. Use either wire or heavy mono for the leader, with wire usually getting the nod in case of hits from toothy critters such as bluefish.

Determine the length you desire for a given lure. Most of these lures will vary between about 6 to 24 inches, with 14 to 18 inches being a good average for saltwater striper and bluefish use. For the hook connection, use forty- to fifty-pound mono and similar sizes of braided or single-strand wire. Use a haywire twist (single-strand) or leader sleeve (mono or braided wire) to fasten the hook to the leader. The size of the barrel swivel is determined by the inside diameter of the tubing. The tubing should fit snugly around the center barrel of the swivel. Cut one end of the tubing on a sharp angle, using sharp scissors, so that this short "tail" will extend beyond the hook bend. Lay the tubing alongside the partially prepared hook and leader, placing the forward part of the slanted cut at the bend of the hook. Cut the

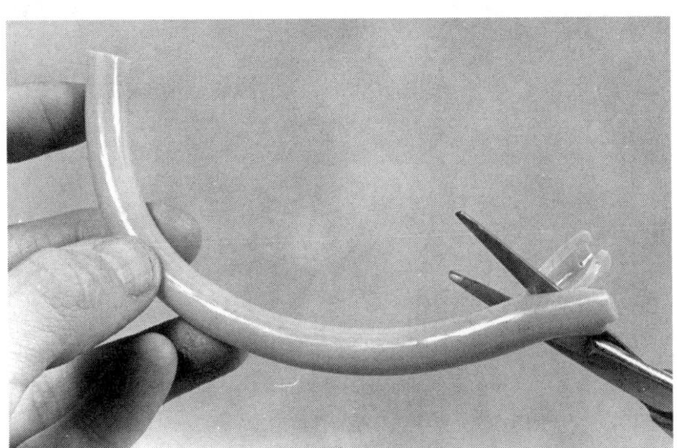

Cutting the end of the surgical hose on a slant to make a tapered tail for the lure.

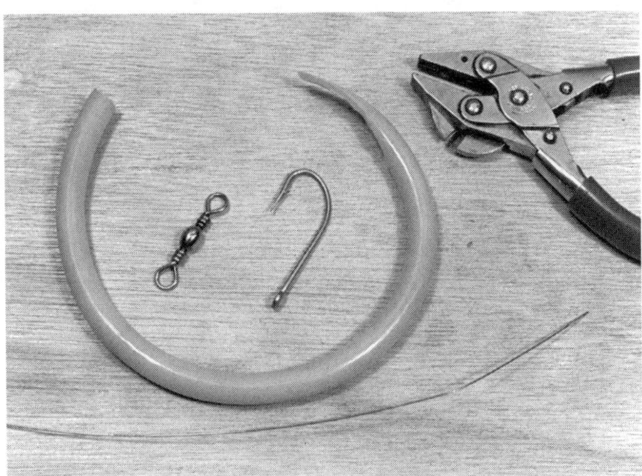

Wire, swivel, hook, hose, and pliers are all that you need for making simple "surge" lures.

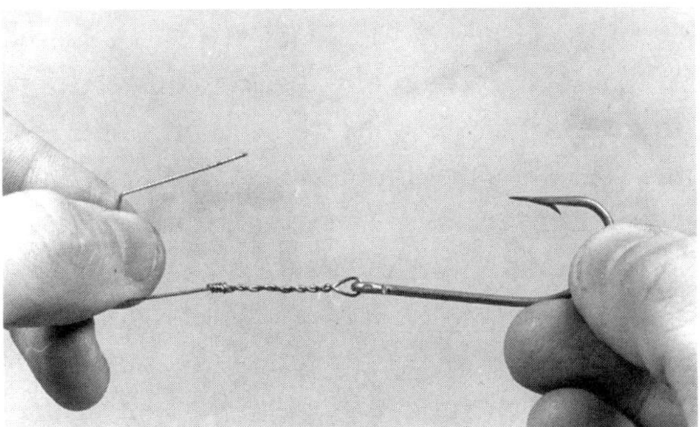

The hook is attached to wire with a haywire twist. Here the excess wire has been broken off to allow for a tight wrap.

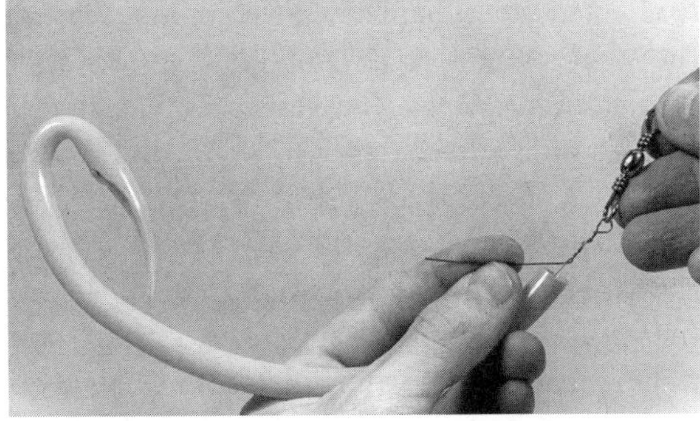

Hose being threaded onto the completed wire/hook rig. The excess wire at the head end can be used to wire the hose to the swivel, or it can be clipped off and then a separate wire used to secure the hose to the swivel.

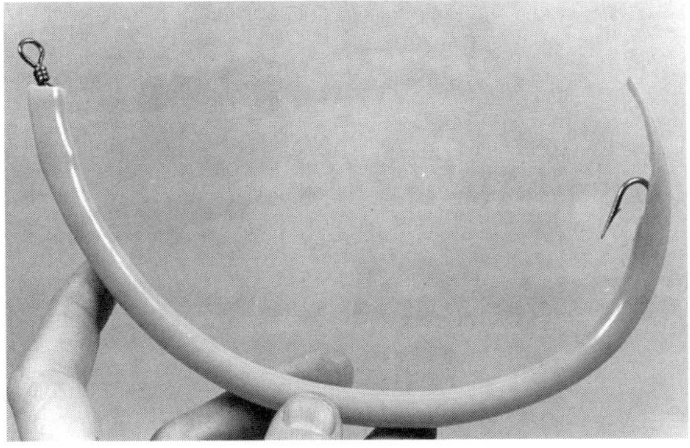

Completed hose lure.

leader, leaving enough wire or mono to finish the eye for the barrel swivel.

Run the leader through the tubing, allowing enough wire or mono to form the eye at the end. Grasp the leader with pliers, and roll the tubing back onto the leader wire and up onto the bend of the hook. This is to allow room for making the eye in the leader and to attach the barrel swivel. While holding the tubing back in this position, run a leader sleeve onto the wire or mono, run the wire or mono through one eye of the barrel swivel, form the loop or eye, and run the leader back through the leader sleeve. Position and crimp the leader sleeve. Slide the tubing back up onto the wire, placing the end of the tubing over the center part of the barrel swivel.

It is also possible to premeasure the tubing against the complete wire-leader rig (complete with hook and swivel). Slip the swivel eye of the completed leader rig over a strong doubled wire (straightened coat hanger will do fine), and thread the surgical eel over the double wire, pulling it down (carefully—watch the hook!) onto the leader and the hook. Once the eye of the swivel is clear of the end of the tubing, remove the doubled wire.

Since the tubing fits tightly around the barrel swivel, be especially careful not to slip and run the hook into your hand. A little warm soap solution, Teflon spray, or similar lubricant rubbed on the barrel swivel, or soaking the tubing briefly in a soapy solution, helps greatly. The lubricant or soap is easily washed off.

To secure the swivel to the tubing, some anglers use several wraps of single-strand wire around the tubing and the swivel, or through the tubing and the lower eye of the swivel, to hold it in place.

By using hooks with extra-long shanks, you can rig surgical hose without a wire leader. To do this get hooks as long as possible and make the surgical-hose lure the length of two or three hook shanks, depending on how many hooks you wish to use and the length of the surgical hose desired. Hooks with turned-down eyes are best. You must be able to run the point and shank of one hook through the eye of the second hook. You

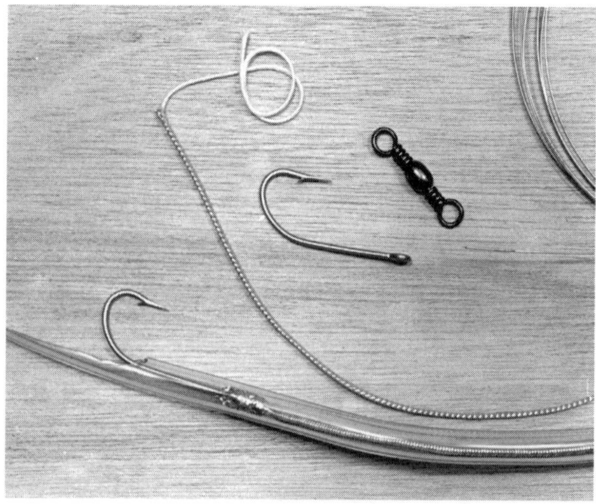

Using clear, or translucent, plastic tubing allows Mylar or other braided tubing to be used over the wire and in the plastic tubing for added flash.

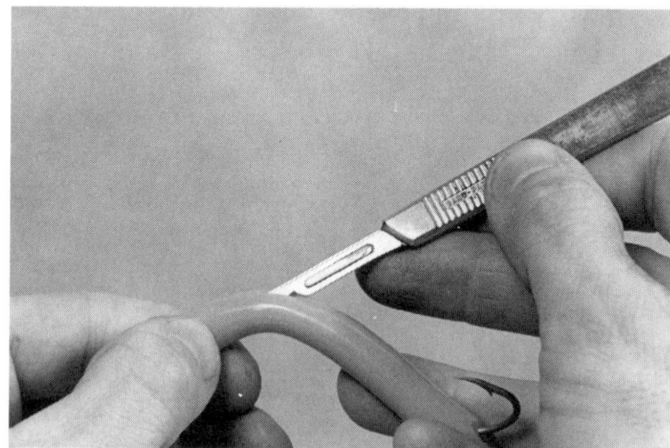

To add additional hooks without using wire, use long-shank hooks and thread the rear hook in the tubing first, making a cut at the point where the hook eye is located.

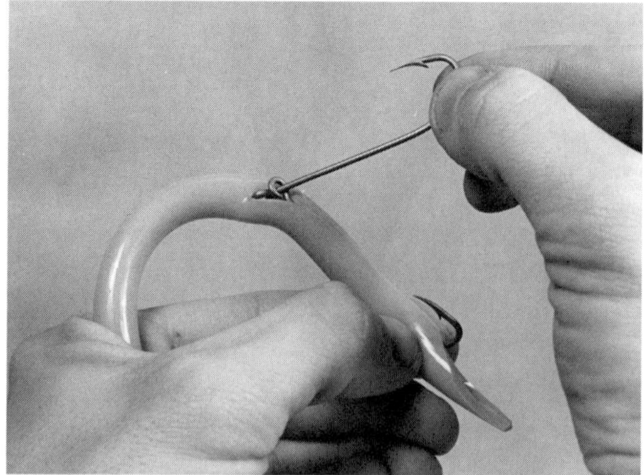

At this point, force the hook eye out of the hose, thread a second hook through this hook eye, and then force the second (forward) hook up through the tubing. This essentially connects the first and second hooks.

can slightly open the eye or bend down or file the barb of the hook point to make this possible.

To rig, hold the tail hook alongside the surgical hose and make a small cut in the hose at the point where the hook eye lies. Next run the hook up the hose and the eye of the hook out through the small cut. Run the second hook through the eye of the tail hook; slide it all the way on so that you can force the eye of the front hook through the hole in the hose and slide the hook forward. This will place only the point and bend of the forward hook through the hose and will hide the rest of the hook in the hose. Once all the hooks are attached this way (three is about the maximum you will want), attach the forward hook eye to a hookless jig head, Japanese feather-style jig head, or similar setup. To finish the hose lure without adding weight (as in the originals), use a split ring to attach the forward hook eye to a barrel swivel; wire the hose to the swivel to prevent slippage.

You can also rig a surgical hose to a heavy tin squid, jig head, or fixed-hook swimming spoon. To do this with a hook at the end, use a wire or mono leader to fasten the tail hook to the head. The leader eye can be used to fasten to the forward hook in the lure. Sometimes some imagination and ingenuity are required here, depending on the type of lure desired and the fastening necessary to complete the lure. Japanese feather-style hole-through-the-center jig heads also can be used—the surgical hose wire-wrapped around the collar on the head to hold it in place and the leader wire through the hose and the lead head.

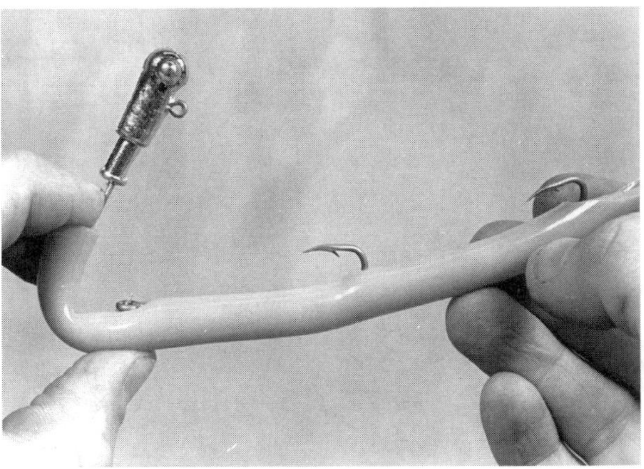

Repeat the above as required, finally forcing the hook eye onto a jig hook or attaching it to a swivel with a spilt ring.

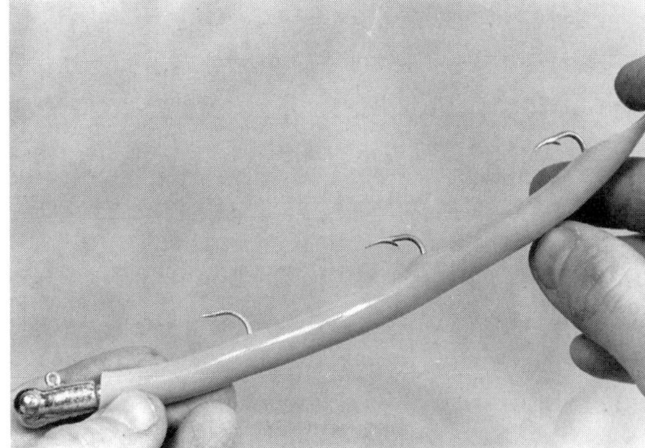

Completed lure with three hooks—one the jig hook and two connected to each other through the hook eyes.

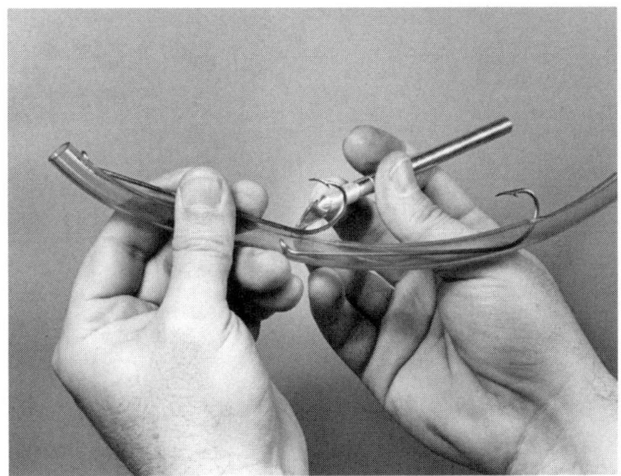

Details of the above in transparent plastic tubing, showing the cut in the tubing.

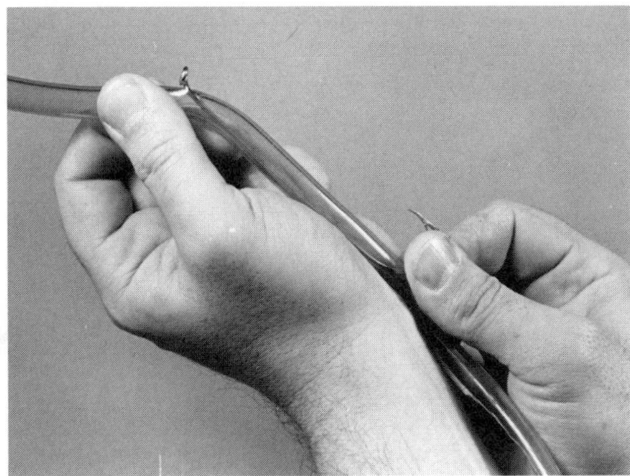

Forcing the eye of the hook through the cut in the tubing.

Another possibility with surgical hose is to use bead chain in place of the mono or wire. This will definitely allow twisting of the hose portion of the lure without affecting the jig head or twisting the line. Use a bead-chain rig of the right length for the lure you are making, adding a hook to one end with a split ring. Cut the tubing about 1 to 1½ inches short of the length of the bead chain, depending on the lure you are making. Run the bead chain hook rig through the hose, beginning at the sloping-cut tail end. At the upper or forward end, use a short section (about 1 to 1½ inches long), run the bead chain through this short length of hose, and then hook the eye of the bead chain to the lure. For a jig this can be to the forward eye of the jig. Use the short length of surgical tubing to hold the bead chain in place on the lure. If you're making a hose with a jig head, you can run this over the molded-in jig hook. With a spoon, this can replace the standard tail hook or be in addition to that hook.

Small "banana"-type hose lures are made using a short length of hose cut at the rear at an angle and threaded onto a long-shank saltwater hook. The secret here is to use a tube and hook combination in which the hole in the hose is just slightly smaller than the diameter of the hook eye. That way you can slip the tube onto the hook and it will not slide and slip off.

If you use mono in place of wire for any of the previously mentioned tasks, you can use knots to attach the leader to the hook and barrel swivel or to snell the hook with the mono (see chapter 13 and appendix E).

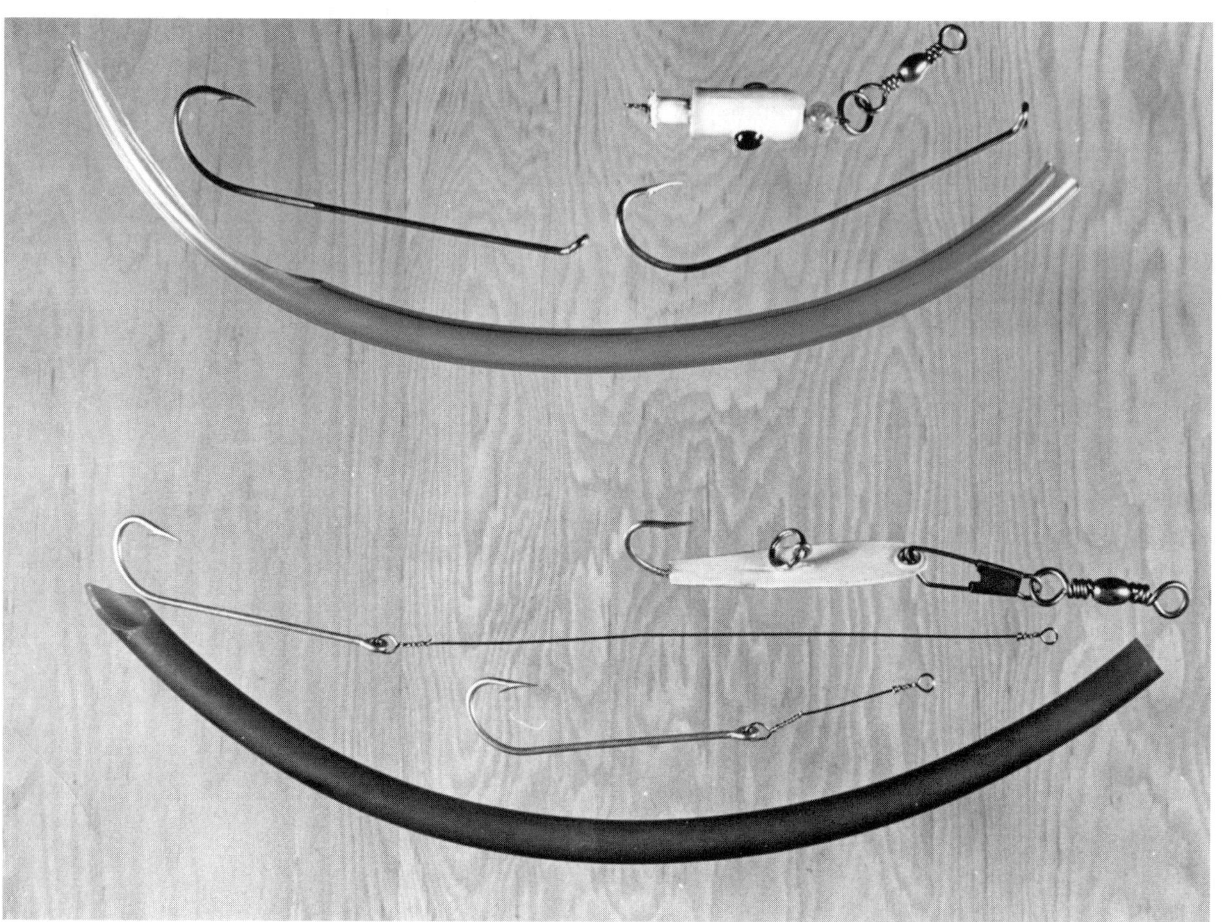

Parts required for making various types of multiple-hook surgical-hose rigs. Top, a two-hook through-rigged surgical hose with a lead head; bottom, a three-hook rig, each of the hooks attached to the main jig head with separate leader wires of the appropriate length.

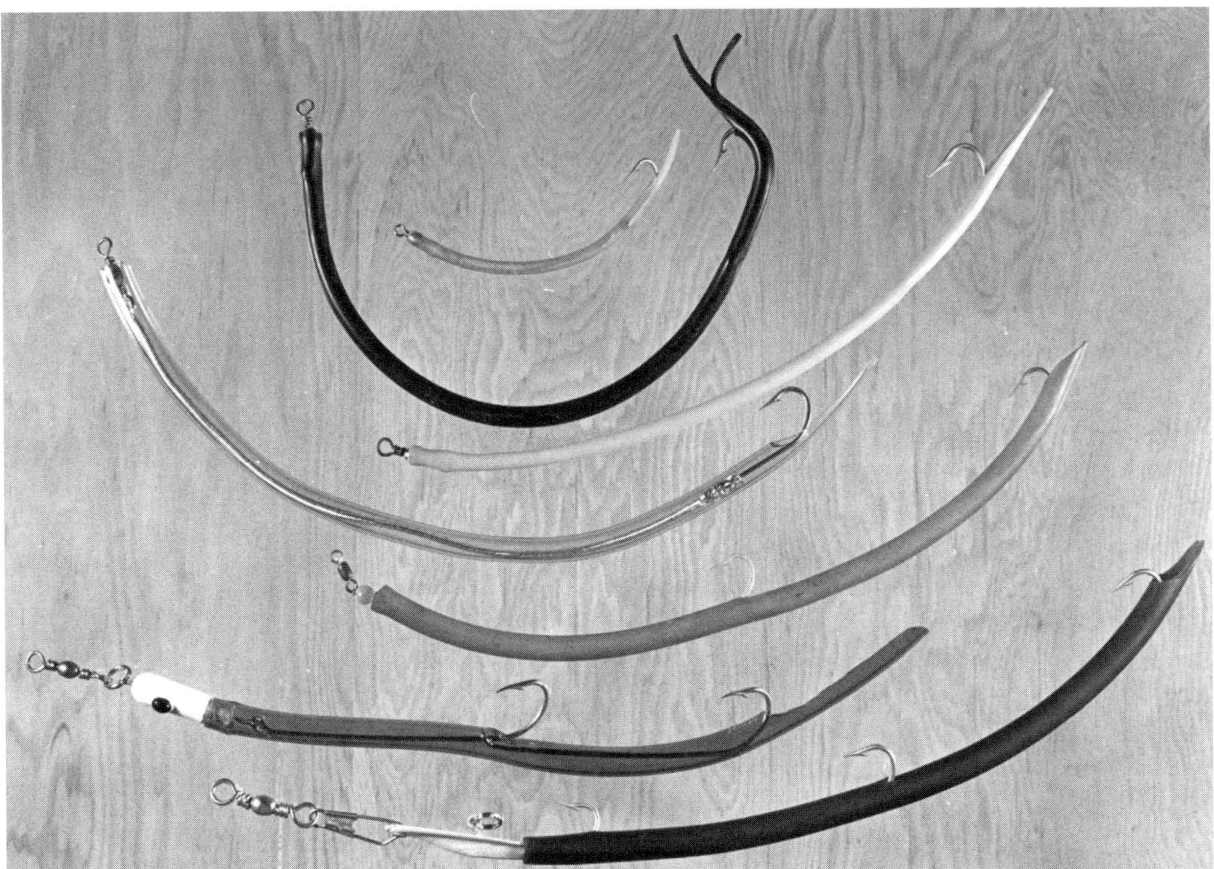

Examples of various surgical-hose lures.

SPLIT-SHOT JIGS

A standard saltwater hook, fixed with one or two large split-shot sinkers, securely crimped on and with a tail of tied-down feathers, fur, or nylon, will make a passable jig. The jig head can be painted, but this is not required. And you do not have to have a tied-on tail but can instead use a slip-on piece of surgical hose, soft-plastic grub, or similar tail. These jigs are simple, effective, and, best of all, can be made in the field in only a few seconds with a pair of strong pliers for crimping the sinker in place. The sinker might become loose in time, but for something this effective and easy, it is a quick fix.

EGG-SINKER JIGS

These are nothing more than a variation of the split-shot rig in which an egg sinker or two are threaded onto a wire and eyes are formed in the ends of the wire, with one eye used as a line-tie and the other attached to a straight-eye hook. The hook can have a tied-on tail, slip-on soft-plastic tail, or short length of surgical hose for a tail. As with the split-shot jigs, the egg-sinker body can be painted or left unpainted.

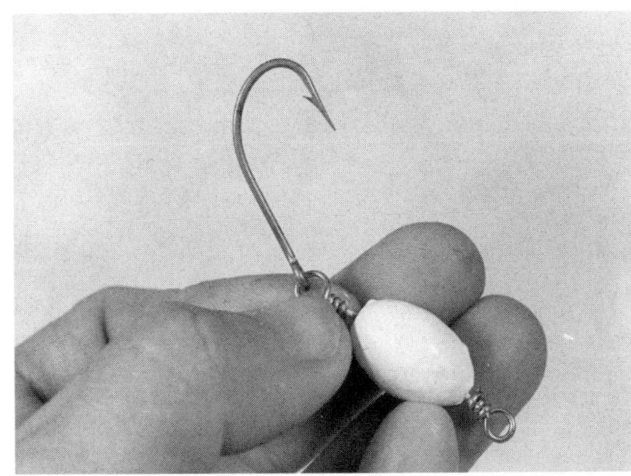

A simple swinging hook jig made from a lead egg sinker (here painted white) and stiff utility wire.

ROPE JIGS, FLIES, AND LURES

One type of rope lure consists of nothing more than multiple strands of soft cotton or nylon rope with the strands tied in the middle to the lure or rig with a wire wrapping and the strands frayed out. Usually these are made so that they are about 12 inches long and are used primarily for billfish or gar. No hook is used, since when the fish hits, the rope strands get tangled in the rough bill or teeth, holding the fish as securely—probably even more securely—than would a heavy hook. While these lures might work for other fish where teeth or bills could get tangled, this is the only use I have heard of for them. There are disadvantages in that this lure may be illegal in some states or areas because it is an entangling device. It is prohibited under IGFA rules, and fish caught by these lures cannot be entered in IGFA events. Also, since the "mop lure," as it is sometimes called, will become entangled with a billfish bill, it must be cut free to release the fish. This can injure the fish by keeping it stationary and with the head out of the water for the time required to free it. With billfish becoming increasingly rare, these lures should not be used for offshore fishing. Also, since you must cut out the lure to free the fish, you tend to destroy the lure.

My fishing buddy Norm Bartlett was the first angler I know of to use rope for lures and flies (with a hook), though I am sure many have tried it. Norm uses several methods of making these, depending on whether he is making flies or lures. He uses a heat glue gun for attaching the rope to the hook but more recently has gone to jig hooks—the type with a bend in the shank—and uses a cigarette lighter to seal the rope on the hook. To do this, cut a length of rope appropriate to the jig hook being used. Both braided nylon and polypropylene rope work well, although with poly rope you may wish to remove several straight core strands for easy threading on the hook. Run the hook through the rope, and position the rope's end near the bend in the hook shank. Use the lighter to melt and seal the rope around the bend to prevent it from slipping. Then use the lighter lightly on the body of the shank to slightly melt the rope and give it some body. For the part of the rope that extends beyond the hook bend, use a pick or comb to fray the strands to make a "tail." Tip: Use the side of the flame against the rope to heat and melt it and to prevent the rope from getting soiled by smoke or residue from the flame.

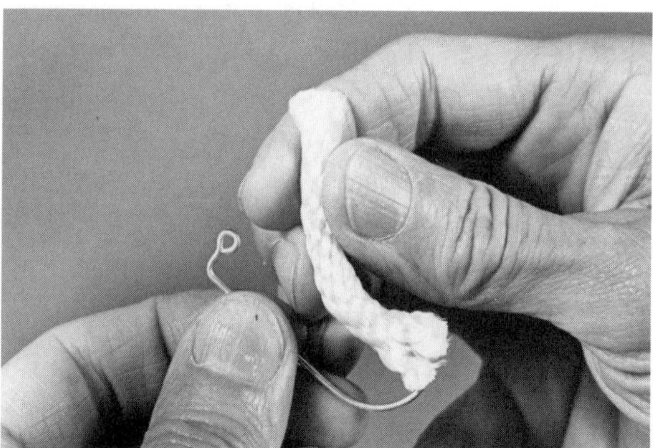

Rope jigs, here made by threading braided rope onto a jig hook.

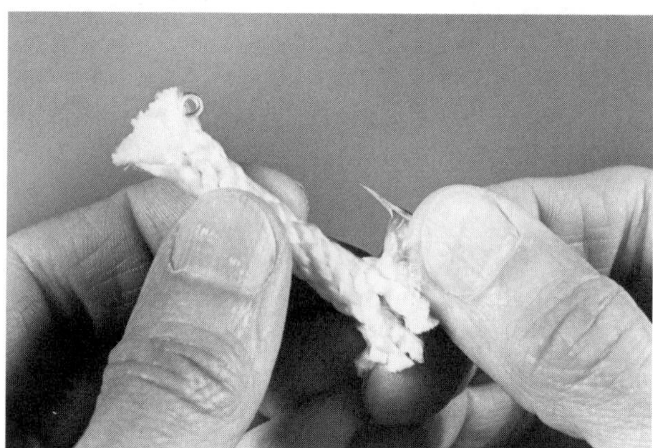

Rope in place on the jig hook.

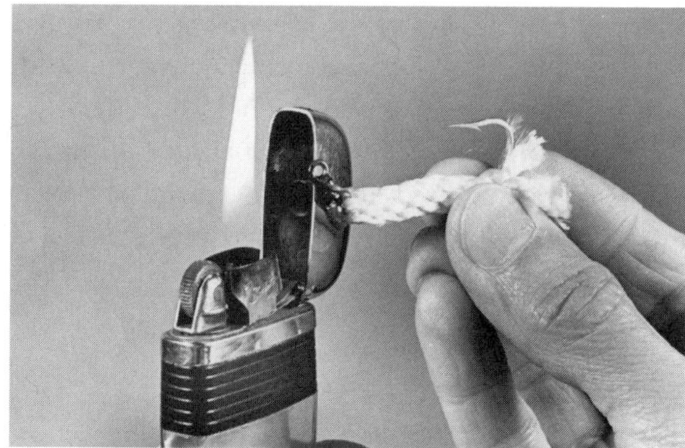

Using a lighter to melt and fuse the nylon rope to the bend in the jig hook. The jig hook and this bend help prevent the rope from sliding back.

You can use these same techniques with a long strand of rope for a needlefish imitation or barracuda lure. Although white rope is often used, you can buy colored rope (poly rope often comes in white, yellow, red, blue, and other colors) or dye the rope (braided nylon rope) with household dyes such as Rit or Tintex.

ICE "FLIES"

Ice flies are really small lures for jigging with ice-fishing tackle and are sometimes used for panfish and crappie the rest of the year with ultralight spinning tackle. Most are made on hooks no larger than #10, although #12, #14, and #16 hooks also are used.

Ice flies are tiny weighted jigs or spoon-jig combinations that you can easily make yourself. There are lots of ways to make them. One is to use small spinner blades and solder a small hook to the blade, adding enough solder to fill the spinner concavity and add some weight. You will have to flux the spinner blade first for a good bond or use a solder with a built-in (core type) flux. The resultant ice-fishing fly can be left bright or painted; you can even affix some tail material (marabou, fur, feathers, or artificial fur) to the bend of the hook for added attraction.

You can also make tiny versions of split-shot jigs, again painting and tying in tails if desired. You can mold your own of lead, using an open-face mold (see chapter 16) of plaster of Paris, wood, or RTV Silastic rubber. Environmental Technology makes several types of materials (in latex and other compounds) for creating molds that can accommodate hard plastics such as their casting resins and epoxy casting materials.

Another method is to cut out small circles or strips of aluminum from cans with scissors, or punch them out with a paper or leather punch, then fold the circles over and glue them onto a small hook. Folding and crimping, with a little bit of epoxy glue applied to the hook first, will hold these small bits of metal in place on the hook. These jigs can be left bare, painted, or have a tail tied on.

TROLLING RIGS

Trolling rigs are long wire (or sometimes mono) leaders rigged with a series of trolling blades ending with a snap by which lures or a baited hook can be added or ending with a spoon or spinner lure. They are primarily used for slow, deep trolling to take trout and salmon in the Upper Midwest, but they can be fished anywhere. I've used them to take trout on large ponds and lakes in several states.

The blades used are similar to those used for making spinners but are usually larger, sometimes fluted and often painted. The distinction between special blades for trolling rigs and those for spinners is blurring though, and any blades that work can be used. This includes all the standard spinner blades, such as Colorado, Indiana, willowleaf, and other styles. Often several sizes are used in a trolling rig, starting with a larger blade and gradually working to smaller ones toward the rear of the rig.

In addition to the spinner blades, the only other parts needed are appropriate size clevises, twisted-wire leader material, leader sleeves, snaps, and swivels. Begin by deciding on the length of the rig desired, and then cut a length of thirty- to fifty-pound test twisted-wire leader to that length (most finished rigs are about 3 to 5 feet long). Slide a leader sleeve onto one end, add a swivel, and then reverse the leader wire through the sleeve to make a tight loop holding the swivel. Crimp the leader sleeve. From the other end, slide on a clevis and spinner blade with the concave side of the blade against the wire when facing the rear, and position the clevis just behind the swivel. Add a bearing bead or two, and then add a leader sleeve to hold the blade in place on the leader. Crimp the leader sleeve where you want the blade, usually a few inches from the swivel. Continue this process, adding successive spinner blades on clevises and bearing beads and leader sleeves in the same way, using several of one size smaller than the first, then a few more one size smaller still. All should be arranged a few inches or more apart so that a six-blade rig will be about 2 to 3 feet long.

You can use as many blades and beads as you wish and then end the rig with another sleeve; run the leader through the sleeve, then through a snap (to attach a lure or bait), and then back through the sleeve to crimp it.

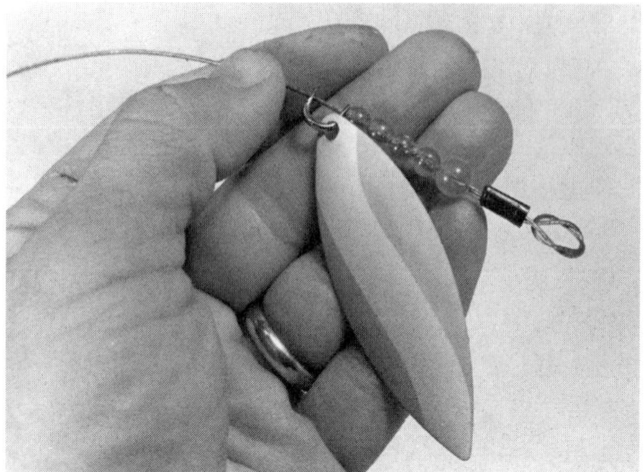

Typical arrangement for making a trout or salmon trolling rig in which spinner blades are attached separately and in series along a several-foot-long leader wire. Leader sleeves are used here to form the rear loop. Leader sleeves are also used on the single leader wire to position the beads and spinner blades on clevises.

Variations of this include using different sizes, colors, styles, and numbers of blades. In addition, you can rig a keel-type sinker to the front of the lure either in the rigging or by crimping the leader wire onto the eye of the sinker and then adding a split ring and swivel to the front of the keel sinker. This will help get the rig down deep and also prevent line twist from the many blades.

OTHER LURES

Although the foregoing covers some of the more typical variations of lures that can be made by tackle tinkerers, lures can be made from virtually anything, as proved by the occasional bass angler who fashions a hook to a clothespin and catches a bass just to prove it can be done. Here are some other possibilities we hear about or occasionally see in magazine articles:

CO2 jigs. Old CO2 cartridges can be made into shiny, smooth, oblong, albeit somewhat large, "jigs" by taking the old cartridge (make sure it is empty), drilling it at both ends, running an eyed spinner wire through it (such as the 0.030 wire used for making spinners and small spinnerbaits), and fixing a hook to the end. To drill these hard-metal containers, you generally have to use a drill press and vise with a punch to slightly indent the end of the cartridge to prevent the drill bit from sliding across it. Drill straight through both ends with a 1⁄16-inch bit, and enlarge one end with a larger bit so that you can pour molten lead or tin into the cartridge to weight it. Run the wire through the lure, tape one end to prevent leakage, and then add the molten metal. Single, double, or treble hooks can be attached to an eye formed in the wire at the end of the lure. The completed lure can be left as is, covered with shiny lure tape, painted, or coated with glitter.

Shell-casing lures. Casings from small-caliber bullets can be made into simple jiglike lures. Any size can be used, but those in calibers of .22, .25, or .32 are best for most freshwater fishing; larger sizes can be used for saltwater fishing. Remember, we are talking about casings—spent after shooting—*not* live ammunition!

To make these lures, clean the casings and drill a hole at one end large enough to pass a hook eye through. Using fly-tying methods, tie a tail or feathers, fur, or artificial fur to the hook, making sure the wrap is a little back from the hook eye to give it clearance through the casing hole. Place the hook into the casing, and position it so that the casing completely covers the thread wrap over the tail. Tape the hole and eye to prevent leakage, turn the casing up on end, and fill it with thick waterproof glue or epoxy or casting resin. (Thick glue will not run out of the hole at the end.) Make sure the glue completely covers the tail wrapping to seal it in place. Allow the glue to cure, remove the tape from the front end, and the lure is ready to fish.

Lures in different lengths and weights can be made by using different shell casings. Shell casings of .22 caliber, for example, come in short, long, and long-rifle lengths.

Ballpoint pen lures. The two-part click-on-and-off pens can sometimes be fitted with replaceable ink cartridges but often are thrown away. The front ends of these pens can be used to make small squidlike lures for trolling or casting. Since these already have a small hole in one end and are made of colored plastic (pick your pens by the color you like to fish), an easy way to rig them is to attach a small trolling skirt to a mono or wire leader and use the pen half slipped over the wire as a head. An easy way to weight the lure for casting or deeper trolling is to pinch split shot onto the wire leader just above the trolling skirt. The split shot will be covered by the pen half. Just make sure the split shot is smaller than the inside diameter of the pen so that it can be completely covered.

Another method is to use a large hook with a very long shank and at the rear of the hook shank use fly-tying methods to tie on a tail or fur or feathers. Coat the wrap with waterproof glue, fly-tying head cement, or fingernail polish to seal it, and then slide the pen half over the hook. If the hook is large and long enough, use an ice pick to enlarge the hole in the end of the pen through which to fit the hook eye. An alternative is to use a wire or mono leader on the hook and run the pen half over the leader to butt up against the hook eye. Make a loop in the end of the leader.

Natural shell lures. Natural shells are available throughout the country. In saltwater areas the shells of clams, oysters, mussels, and similar shellfish are readily available for making lures. In freshwater areas freshwater clams and mussels can be found in most river systems. The thinner shelled freshwater clams and the thin-shelled saltwater mussels are better than the larger clams and thick-shelled oysters. And the natural curve in the shells of these shellfish makes for a natural curve in the lure, which will cause it to wobble, as with any commercial spoon. To make this task easier, and to prevent needlessly killing live shellfish, you can often find empty shells that are completely cleaned naturally and are ready for the workshop. Such shells are ideal for spoons and spinner blades. In fact, back in the 1930s and through the 1950s commercially made shell spoons and spinners were in high demand. Today they are probably too labor intensive for commercial concern.

To make these spoons and spinners, use a template of the size and shape you want and trace it onto a shell with a felt-tip marker; soft, heavy pencil; or grease pencil. Using proper safety procedures, drill the hole or holes for the hook and line-eye (or clevis in the case of a spinner blade) attachment. The reason for doing this now is that shell tends to splinter and split, and drilling before shaping the shell provides a thick-edged wall to reduce such problems. Use a sharp bit, slow speed, and very light pressure to drill through the shell. Then use a bench grinder or bench sander to remove the excess shell and shape it into the spoon or spinner blade. Hand-sand to round and smooth the edges.

Since shell blades are subject to breakage, rig the spoons by running a wire through the holes at each end for line-tie and hook attachment. That way, should the spoon shatter on a strike or during a fight, you won't lose the fish. The best way to do this is to make a wire form with eyes at both ends of the proper length to absorb the strain of the fight when split rings are run through the eyes in the wire and the holes in the shell. You can also run the wire through the holes at each end and make a slight bend or kink in the wire. Although this works fine in most cases, the strain of the fight could straighten the wire and break the hole in the shell spoon. This is not a problem with spinner blades, because the blade is attached only at one end to a clevis (usually), and there is no stress on the blade.

13

Wire Leaders And Rigging

Introduction • Tools • Safety Equipment and Procedures • Materials • Using Leader Sleeves • Working with Single-Strand Wire • Bait and Lure Riggings • Sinker Riggings • Knots, Splices, and Snells

Basic Safety Requirements

- Safety goggles
- Work gloves
- Work apron

Basic Tools

- Pliers
- Round-nose pliers
- Wire cutters

Helpful Tools

- Wire former (various ones are available from Worth, Netcraft, and others)
- Bench-style professional-type wire former (e.g., Cabela's)
- Leader-sleeve crimping pliers
- Homemade wire-eye former and bender

INTRODUCTION

Even though rods and many lures have been considered the proper domain of the tackle craftsman for years, wire rigging and such are equally easy to accomplish and just as important. Fortunately some booklets in recent years have been devoted to wire-rigging procedures, as well as several excellent books by Vlad Evanoff on dozens of bait and lure-rigging arrangements for fresh- and saltwater fishing.

Wire leaders and terminal tackle rigs of all types are among the easiest of all tackle items to make, requiring only the simplest tools and no expensive materials. There are special wire-forming tools on the market that cost several dollars or more, but they are not required except by the angler whose hobby might turn into a part-time business, by a fishing club for community use, or by anyone fishing extensively (perhaps a guide or charter-boat captain) who must constantly replace a lot of terminal tackle and riggings.

Trying to define this chapter is somewhat difficult, like trying to wrestle a bag full of basketballs. Wire leaders, rigs, terminal-tackle items, and rigged lures can encompass a wide range of tackle ideas often diverse in both use and construction. Simple wire leaders, bottom-fishing spreaders, surf-fishing bottom rigs, spinner shafts for making spinners, hook lears for bottom rigs, drop-sinker trolling rigs, sinker releases, spinnerbait rigs, wire weed guards for weedless hooks, and a host of other small items all fall into this broad category. To further confound things, there are often several ways in which each of these items can be made.

TOOLS

The tools required will vary widely with the tackle to be made. Let's look at some possibilities and their uses.

Needle-nose pliers. Needle-nose pliers are handy for general bending operations, making eyes in wire, making hook lears, and so on. They do have a disadvantage in that the contact surfaces of the jaws are flat, not round, and thus make it difficult to make a neat rounded eye. Many have side cutters that work well for cutting wire and heavy mono.

Round-nose pliers. These are often long or with tapered or step-type jaws that are completely round. Those round on one side (jaw) and flat on the other also work well. They are best for making precisely round eyes.

Worth wire former. This small hand tool allows the tackle crafter to make several types of eyes for spinners, spinnerbait rigs, wire rigs, spreaders, and other items. It comes with instructions and is easy to use.

Netcraft wire former. This wire former, or wire winder, as Netcraft prefers to call their Model 20 Tack-L-Tool, works on a slightly different principle than the one above and can be handheld or mounted on a workbench. The supplied instructions described how to make a number of eye types along with springs, coil fasteners, and various other wire bends.

Professional-style wire formers. These are available from several outfits. A typical one from Cabela's is not unlike one Herter's used to carry years ago. It clamps to a workbench (up to 1¾ inches thick) and has two separate handles with which all types of wire forms can be made. It is primarily designed for making various spinner, spinnerbait, bait, and similar rigs, not for working with long fishing wire or leaders. Made of cast iron, this tool is far heavier and also more expensive than the smaller handheld wire formers listed previously. It will handle a variety of wire sizes, but different heads are required for the various ranges of wire sizes. Heads are available for wire sizes 0.018 through 0.025, 0.026 through 0.029, and 0.030 through 0.035.

Single-strand wire benders. These are small devices for easily making haywire twists or barrel twists in single-strand wire. Three sizes are available, each for a different wire size range. There is a small size for wire sized from 0.012 through 0.020, a medium size for 0.022 through 0.031, and a large size for 0.033 through 0.045.

Compound-action fishing pliers. These fishing pliers are made by a number of companies—Berkley, Manley, and others—in several sizes. They are ideal as on-the-water fishing pliers stored in a belt holster. Since the jaws remain parallel when opened and closed (unlike regular pliers, in which the angle of the jaws changes), they are also ideal for tackle work. They all have side-action cutters for mono and light wire and hooks, and most have a small hole drilled into the jaw with which wire can be bent and formed.

Crimping pliers. These vary widely by type, size, and the force they bring to crimp a leader sleeve, even by the type of leader sleeve used. They are made by Berkley, Sevenstrand, Mason, C and H, PFC, Felco, and other companies. Some of these are small hand tools that are ideal for crimping leader sleeves for light-tackle fishing. Big-game anglers generally do not like this type, however, and opt for the Felco model or similar large, long-handled pliers with a stop that predetermines the exact amount of pressure needed for a given leader sleeve.

One of the most important aspects of choosing crimping pliers is not only the size and usage of the pliers but also the type of leader sleeve on which it will be used. Often problems result from mismatched sleeves and pliers. There are two types of jaws on crimping pliers. One, with two cups or sockets opposing each other, or the cup-opposing-cup style, is designed specifically for single and double oval sleeves. The other type, in which a point is opposite a socket, or the point-opposing-cup style, is designed only for round sleeves. Mixing sleeve and pliers styles can result in inadequate force in crimping the sleeve and thus early failure of the crimp. In addition, it is vital that you match the size of the crimping pliers' jaw to the crimping sleeve used. Most pliers have several positions at which sleeves can be set. More expensive ones have an adjustable stop that can be changed to adjust the degree of pressure on the sleeve.

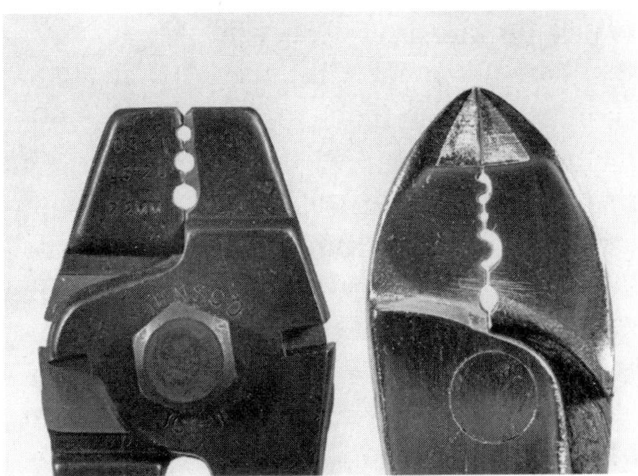

Examples of cup-opposing-cup pliers (left) and point-opposing-cup pliers (right) for crimping leader sleeves.

Leader sleeves (oval, left; round, right) held in place in their respective crimping pliers.

SAFETY EQUIPMENT AND PROCEDURES

As with any tackle-building task, some safety equipment is required. These requirements are minimal and include the following items:

Goggles. These are the main requirement, since cutting wire often causes end pieces to fly off. Safety goggles protect the eyes and should be worn during all wire-working operations, especially when cutting wire with wire cutters or side cutters on pliers.

Work gloves. These are suggested but not absolutely required. The advantage is that they protect your hands from scrapes and possible puncture wounds. The disadvantage is that they make it more difficult to work with the wire, since you lose a sure sense of feel and the ability to pick up strands of wire easily.

Work apron. This helps keep your clothes clean. Some wire has a slight oil residue from the manufacturing processes or to keep it from rusting or corroding; cutters and crimping pliers can also leak oil that can get on your clothes. Wearing a work apron for *all* tackle-making tasks is just a good idea.

MATERIALS

Materials for making wire rigs can encompass a wide range, including surgical hose used to stabilize hooks in some double-hook offshore rigs and electrician's tape used for the same purpose.

Some typical materials for most leader and wire rigs include:

Twisted wire. Braided wire or cable is really twisted and has a lot of advantages for anglers. First, it is very strong. Second, it is very flexible, far more so than single-strand wire. Third, although it will kink, this is not as much of a problem as with single-strand wire, where a kink means the wire is markedly weakened and must be cut and thrown away and new wire spooled onto a reel or rig. Twisted wire comes in a number of configurations, depending on the manufacturer and strength. Sevenstrand, Mason, American Fishing Wire, and PFC are among the large manufacturers of this wire for the tackle industry.

This wire is often listed as to its fabrication, using symbols such as 1 × 3, 1 × 7, 3 × 7, and 7 × 7. The figures indicate how the wire was made. For example, a 1 × 3 is three separate strands of wire wound or twisted into one wire; 1 × 7 indicates seven strands to make one wire. In 3 × 7 wire seven strands of wire are twisted into one strand, then three of the resulting strands are twisted into the final wire. In 7 × 7 several strands are twisted into one strand, then seven of these are twisted together. Often the lighter fabrications are considered wire; the heavier 7 × 7 is considered cable. The type of fabrication varies with the test of the wire. Type 1 × 3 is often light eight- to twelve-pound test, and 1 × 7 ranges from 18- to 250-pound test. Type 7 × 7 can range from 175- to 920-pound test and is primarily used for big-game leaders. The single-strand wire size of each also varies with the pound test.

Wire is available plain in bright, bronze, coffee, or dull black finishes; nylon coated; or black-nylon coated. It is sold in both spools and coils: The heavier pound-test sizes used for leaders are often sold in coils, the lighter tests in spools. Coils of 30 feet are standard for most wire, with large spools ranging from 100- to 5,000-foot spools.

Note that while most mono line is measured by the yard, wire is generally measured by the spool. Although it is widely used for fishing line and big-game leaders, twisted wire can also be used effectively for various riggings. Each manufacturer of wire may have slightly different designations for its wire products. This even includes leader sleeves and diameters and types of wire. Thus, if using a particular brand of wire, stick to its brand of sleeves and crimping pliers for best results.

Single-strand wire. This is used for some trolling but can also be used for riggings. Sizes vary from 2 through 19, with size 2 of about 29-pound test and size 19 of about 400-pound test. Most is made of stainless steel in coffee, black, or bright silver and sold in 25- or 30-foot coils and larger bulk spools.

Monofilament line. The mono used for riggings is no different from the mono used for line. Depending on the rigging, you might pick a line specifically known for abrasion resistance, thin diameter, or other qualities, but these qualities are also available in standard fishing line through many manufacturers.

Single-strand spinner and spinnerbait wire. This type of wire is used to make spinners as described in chapter 3. It can be tinned or stainless steel (both are about the same price, so it makes sense to buy the stainless steel type) and comes in various short lengths and also pre-straightened coils. (It is sold in coils but when uncoiled becomes a straight-shaft wire.)

Sizes range from about 0.024 to about 0.040, with the 0.024 and 0.030 sizes used most for making spinners, as in chapter 3.

Single-strand weed guard wire. This is a lightweight wire of about 0.009 to 0.012 in size for most lures. It is no different from # 2 single-strand leader wire (measuring usually about 0.011).

Utility wire. Utility wire in brass, copper, steel, aluminum, and other metals is available from hobby and hardware shops and is often ideal for tackle riggings, hook lears, bottom rigs, spreaders, keel sinkers, sinker releases, and other tackle riggings. It is available in various diameters ranging up to about ⅛ inch thick, the largest suitable for most tackle rigs. Regular 14-gauge electrical wire can be used (it measures about 0.065—the same as for some bottom spreaders I have checked with a micrometer). Some companies (Jann's Netcraft, for example) sell straightened 14-gauge spring-brass wire, which would be better for most spreaders and hook lears.

Some wire is very flexible and thus ideally suited for the twisting and turning required in making hook lears and keel sinker rigs. Other wire is springier and thus better suited for making spreaders and long, extended hook lears. Although not designed specifically for fishing, this wire is handy to have around and ideally suited for many rigging operations and much experimentation.

Leader sleeves. Leader sleeves are available in many sizes, materials, and styles and are usually made by the same manufacturers that make and sell wire. They are available in round, oval, and double-oval styles, and each style must be matched to the proper crimping pliers.

Different manufacturers rate sleeves in different ways. Sevenstrand uses a letter and number system: from size A1 through A14 for wire, cable, nylon-coated wire, and cable and mono. Its AM9 through AM14 sizes are made for mono. Mason uses a number system of from 1 through 14 in the round sizes and 11 through 71 in the double-oval or double-connector sleeves. PFC labels its sleeves in inch diameters—1⁄32 inch through 5⁄32 inch, with extra long (one and a half times the standard length and designed for mono sleeves) in the same sizes. Berkley uses a letter and number system that ranges from B2 to B6 for general sleeves and MS1 to MS4 for monofilament sleeves.

Sleeves are often available unplated in zinc finish or black oxide in small packs of fifteen to forty (depending on size) or in bulk one-hundred-count packs. Copper and brass are the two most commonly used materials for making leader sleeves, with copper getting the nod for saltwater fishing because it is more resistant to corrosion.

Terminal fasteners. Terminal fasteners or tackle include the variety of snaps, swivels, and other devices used in making up rigs. Two excellent references on terminal fasteners are

Hook, Line and Sinker and *Soucie's Fishing Databook*, both by Gary Soucie. Some of the more important terminal tackle parts include:

- *Safety snap.* These can be of steel or stainless steel and are sold everywhere. The big disadvantage with safety snaps is that they can be pulled open under heavy stress, unlike the interlock snap. A range of small to large sizes is available.

- *Interlock snap.* Also called the lock snap, this is similar to the safety snap with the addition of a small bend at the end of the snap wire that fits into a hole in the lock mechanism. This makes it far stronger and harder to pull open under stress. Small to large sizes are available.

- *Duo-Lock snap.* This is a simple wire snap that does not have a metal plate as do the safety and interlock styles. It is strong and can be opened from either end, which has many advantages in the construction of many types of fishing tackle. It is usually stainless and so is good in fresh or salt water. Sizes are more limited than for safety and interlock snaps.

- *Cross-Lok snap.* Developed by Berkley, this snap is similar in some ways to the Duo-Lock snap in that it consists only of wire and can be opened from either end. It differs in that the locking tangs are both on the same side rather than opposite sides of the snap and that the locking pieces overlap each other to make this snap very strong for its size.

- *Coastlock snap.* This is a long snap with a wire-wrapped eye and locking tang that fastens over the wire of the snap. It is popular for saltwater fishing and comes in large sizes.

- *Pompanette snap.* This is almost identical to the Coastlock but with a tighter bend in the end. It is popular for saltwater fishing. Under high stress, this and the previous four snaps will deform slightly before opening.

- *Lockfast snap.* This is a snap similar to the Coastlock snap but with a bend that is in line with the snap eye rather than slightly off to the side, as with the others. It is most useful for saltwater fishing.

- *McMahon snap.* This is made of wire and resembles a pair of closed ice tongs. Because the overlapping ends are tight, it requires snapping onto whatever is being fastened to it.

- *Pigtail or corkscrew snap.* This is not really a snap but a type of end-fastener with a spiral or corkscrew design that allows a loop of line, swivel, split ring, or other device to be threaded onto it quickly. It is not as readily available as the other snaps but can be made using spring wire and a small homemade tool (the tool construction is described in chapter 2).

- *Barrel swivel.* This is a simple swivel with a twisted eye on each end. The shaft of the eye is inside the central barrel. Available in black, brass, and nickel plate, it comes in a range of sizes.

- *Box swivel.* This works like the barrel swivel but has an open box into which the shafts of the two eyes fit. Once popular, it is seldom seen today.

- *Three-way swivel.* This is nothing more than three eyes, all swaged and held in place in a small flat ring. It is used for many bait and bottom-rigging situations.

- *Cross-line swivel.* This has three eyes, but unlike the three-way swivel, in which the eyes are all at an identical angle to one another (120 degrees), this swivel has two eyes in line with each other (at 180 degrees) and one eye at a right angle (90 degrees) to these. If the swivel is to be stressed in a straight line, this swivel is far better than the standard three-way style but is much harder to find. It is made in barrel, box, and bead-chain styles.

- *Ball-bearing swivel.* Made by several companies (Sampo, Berkley, Rome, and others), this swivel incorporates small ball bearings in the barrel for easy turning, even when under stress. Many sizes are available, most with split rings for line and lure attachment. In larger sizes for offshore trolling, larger welded rings are used.

- *Snap swivel.* This incorporates a snap and a swivel. In almost all cases it can be found in a variety of styles, including those with standard or ball-bearing swivels; with safety, interlock, Duo-Lock, Cross-Lok, Coastlock, Pompanette, and pigtail fasteners or snaps; and in bright, brass, and black finishes.

- *Bead-chain fastener.* The Bead Chain Company makes many snaps and snap swivels in many styles and lengths. All incorporate the unique series of multiple beads, as is used in some electric-light and ceiling-fan pull-cords.

- *S-connector.* This S-shaped connector is designed for fastening but not for anything that might come under great stress. It is not commonly seen in most tackle shops.

- *Solid connector.* This is used mostly as a permanent addition to a lure or plug line-tie and resembles various lengths of open figure-eight wire shapes. It is strong when closed with pliers.

- *Slide-link connector.* This is used on some lures and saltwater bottom rigs and consists of a single length of wire, bent, with an eye at each end and with the two ends turned to the middle, where they are secured with a sliding link, hence the name. It is secure and strong but somewhat unwieldy.

USING LEADER SLEEVES

To construct a basic leader using leader sleeves, you must have the right size sleeve for the wire, nylon-covered wire, or mono used. (A listing of these sizes may be found in appendix D.) You must also have the right type of crimping pliers for the type of sleeve being used (cup-opposing-cup for the oval or double-connector sleeves; point-opposing-cup for the round sleeves).

Run the leader through the sleeve and any additional part that is being permanently attached to the leader and then back down through the sleeve. Position the end of the wire so that it is slightly hidden in the body of the sleeve, place the crimping jaws of the pliers over the center (not the ends) of the sleeve, and crimp hard *once.* Do not try to make several crimps because this will weaken the sleeve.

Crimped leader sleeve making a double loop in the end of a wire leader.

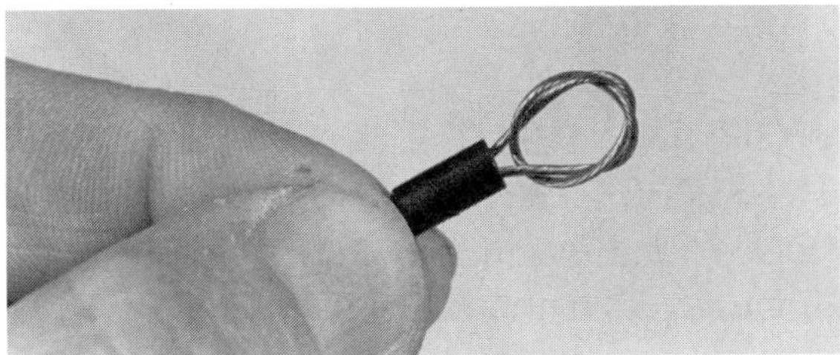

Completed end of the wire leader loop formed in the above photo.

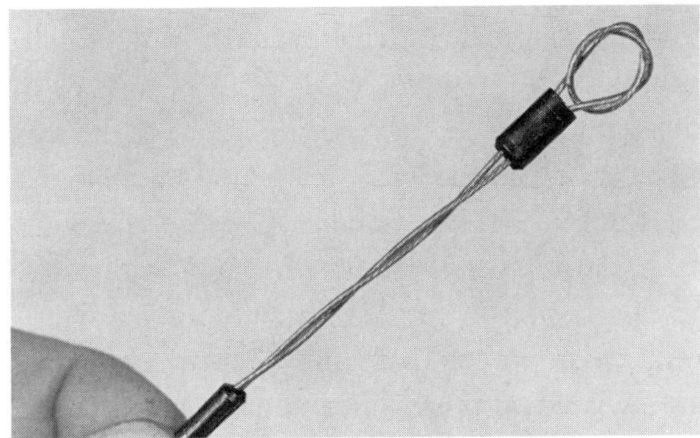

For added insurance, many leader connections use a second leader sleeve placed several inches above the first.

For an even stronger crimp, use two leader sleeves (take the leader through the two sleeves first, make the loop, then run it back through the sleeves). Crimp the first sleeve (the one adjacent to the leader loop) and then twist the wire end several turns around the standing wire, place the second sleeve so that the end of the wire does not protrude from it, and crimp. These sleeves should be about 1 to 2 inches apart.

For a variation of making a loop, run the leader through a sleeve, make a double overhand knot by passing the mono twice through the loop (this is almost like a surgeon's knot), pull it up into a small loop, and then run the end of the wire back through the sleeve or sleeves and crimp. This additional step is best with heavy wire or cable, such as the 7 × 7 fabrications or with very heavy mono.

When using leader sleeves this way, it is a simple matter to make loops, connect two lengths of leader wire together, attach hooks to leaders, make short leaders with snap-and-swivel ends (as for pike or bluefish), construct one- and two-hook bottom rigs for surf fishing, and accomplish similar tackle functions.

WORKING WITH SINGLE-STRAND WIRE

Single-strand wire is also easy to work with, although different methods are used depending on the size of the wire and the intended fishing purpose. Light wire such as that used for trolling, big-game leaders, and such does not require (in fact can't use) leader sleeves. The proper connection here between two lengths of wire or to make a loop is the haywire twist. To make this twist, first fold the wire over to make a loop and lay the two lengths parallel. Overlap the wires and gently twist them together repeatedly. The key is to make a gentle twist, not a hard wrapping twist, and to make sure that the two wires are twisted *together*—not one twisted around the other. If that happens, cut off and start again, since the connection will not work. After about four turns of twist, bend the tag end of the wire at a right angle to the standing wire and make several wrapping turns that are *tight* against one another and around the standing part of the wire. After several turns bend the end of the wire into a right angle to make a "handle" by which to break off the end of the wire. Use this handle to bend this tag end back and forth against the shoulder of the last wrap. After several back-and-forth bends, metal fatigue will snap the wire close to the wrap. *Never* use pliers or cutters to cut the wire, since this will leave a protruding burr that could injure you when you are handling the wire or landing or unhooking a fish.

Although this connection works well for lighter wire and terminal-tackle rigs using this wire, probably the most important single-strand wire techniques involve heavier spring wire in sizes from 0.024 to 0.040, and averaging 0.030, for making spinner shafts and forming different eyes for spinners and similar lures.

To form eyes with this heavier wire, you can use round-nose pliers, needle-nose pliers (though they will not make a neat rounded eye), or various wire formers that are available from tackle shops or through mail-order catalogs. One advantage of working with the wire formers is that you will waste far less wire than you will by working with pliers, since the wire former can work and bend wire right up to the tag end. Thus, while you will need extra wire for the wraps and eye, you will not need it for the leverage of finishing the wrap.

The basics can be done with round-nose pliers. Wire formers all include directions for making specific eye types. First select a piece of wire, leaving about 1½ to 2 inches extra length on the end or ends on which you wish to form an eye. (If you are making eyes on both ends, you will need a wire about 3 to 4 inches longer than the rig or lure.) The eye will not take up this much wire, but you will need it for leverage in working the wire with pliers and to make a neat, tight eye.

To make a wrapped eye, grasp the wire 1½ to 2 inches from the end with the pliers and bend the main end (the longer or lure end) at a slight angle. An angle about 30 to 45 degrees off the straight wire is about right. After a wrap or two, experience will dictate the right bend. Continue to hold the wire in the same spot with the round-nose pliers, and bend the short end tightly around one jaw of the pliers. You will only be able to go about two-thirds of the way around, because the other jaw will block continued movement. Shift the jaws of the pliers on this eye until you can make a complete 360-degree turn around the one jaw with the wire to form a complete circle. Now the reason for the first bend becomes obvious—making that bend places the wire shaft in line with the center of the eye. At this point you will have a complete wire circle and the tag end of the wire will be at a right angle to the main wire shaft. Remove the pliers jaw from the eye and hold the eye between the two jaws, allowing clearance of the tag end. Using your fingers or another pair of pliers, tightly wrap the tag end of the wire twice around the main shaft. Use the cutters on your pliers or wire cutters to cut the tag end of the wire close to the wrap. (This wire is usually too heavy to snap through the metal fatigue of back-and-forth bending.)

To make a self-lock snap eye, begin with the steps just outlined and make the sharp bend and then the bend around the one jaw to form about two-thirds of a circle. Shift the jaws of the pliers so that you can make a second sharp bend, like the first, in the tag end of the wire. You should have about 1 to 1¼ inches of tag-end wire remaining. About ⅜ inch from the end, make a sharp right-angle bend toward the main wire shaft. Hold this section of the shaft and, using the fine ends of tapered round-nose pliers, make a small (as small as possible) U-shaped bend in the very end of the wire, positioned to catch on the main shaft. If there is excess wire, clip it. At this point the bend and eye are complete and in an open position for addition of a hook or lure. To close, spring the end of the wire close to the main shaft and catch the small U on the main shaft.

Making a coil-lock snap is identical to this except that there is no final bend to hook the main wire shaft. Begin by sliding a proper size coil spring onto the wire shafts. The coil spring, usually about ½ inch long, must have an inside diameter that is slightly larger than the diameter of the two wires. Several different sizes are available in both tinned and stainless steel. After the coil spring is slid into place, make the sharp bend with the pliers, bend the wire about two-thirds of the way around one of the jaws, and make a second bend. The result will look like the Greek letter omega (Ω) or the outline of a keyhole. A coil spring is used to close this eye: Hold the main shaft and the end parallel, and slide the coil spring over the open end.

BAIT AND LURE RIGGINGS

Wire can be used for a wide variety of bait and lure riggings, including spreaders, hook lears for single- and two-hook bottom rigs, and umbrella trolling rigs. Some of these, and some options in making them, include:

Spreaders. Bottom spreaders consist of a long, flexible (but springy) wire fitted with snelled hooks on each end; the line is fastened in the middle of the wire and a sinker added to this middle area to hold the rig on the bottom. Heavy brass wire, copper wire, and light but bendable stainless wire are all used to make spreaders. To build these simple rigs you can use either round-nose pliers or a homemade wire former consisting of a nail or two hammered into a block of wood, with the heads

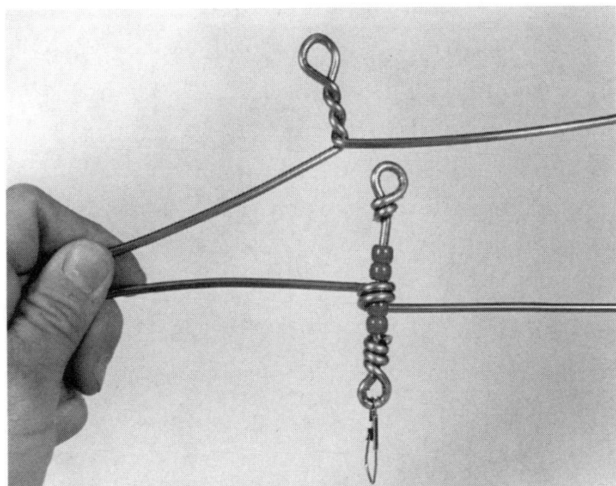

Bottom spreader rig bends. These are made with long side arms for holding snelled hooks, the line attached to the eye. The bottom one includes a snap for holding a bank or pyramid sinker.

cut off the nails and the block of wood held in a vise. The wire is wrapped around the nails to form the eyes and loops needed and then is slipped off.

One easy way to make a drift spreader that does not include a sinker is to take a long section of wire, make a simple twist for a line-tie in the center, and then make several circular wraps on each end to attach the snelled hooks. These end wraps are similar to a spring or the coils found on most key rings. The loop of the snelled hook can be threaded onto and around

Using a homemade wire former to make a hook lear. The first bend is made by twisting heavy utility wire around the two adjacent posts. This homemade wire former, previously described, is made by hammering nails into end-grain wood blocks and then sawing off the heads.

Another wire former, this one used to form the brass wire eyes used in tin squids and some saltwater sinkers.

this spiral. Any length of wire can be used to make this type of spreader, and most spreaders are about 18 to 24 inches wide. Allowing for the extra wire needed for the central line-tie and the end twists, you will need to start with wire about 4 to 6 inches longer than the desired result.

To make a spreader with a sinker snap, first use a short length of wire to form a large open eye and a loop to hold the sinker. Then make a second smaller eye, the function of which is to hold the beads in place that will allow the rotation of the spreader on the central shaft. Once this part is made, use round-nose pliers or the nail wire former to make a double wrap in the center of a long length of wire. This bend should be at a right angle to the plane of natural bend in the wire. Finish the two ends with spiral loops or snaps, or snap swivels to attach the snelled hooks. Once this is complete, add a bead to the partially completed central shaft. Usually the small hole–diameter beads used for making spinners will not work on this heavy wire, but pony beads, available from craft and hobby shops, have a larger diameter hole and work fine. Slip the round eye over the central shaft, add a second bead, and finish the central shaft with a wrapped eye for the line-tie. If the spreader doesn't need to rotate on the central shaft, you don't need the beads.

Hook lears. Hook lears are the devices that hold a snelled hook out and away from the main line or tackle rig to prevent tangles. They are used on single-, two-, and multiple-hook bottom rigs. In essence a hook lear is a short length of wire that works as an arm to hold the snelled hook. It can be incorporated into the bottom rig or added to a leader or line to extend the snelled hook.

One easy way to make a hook lear is to take a length of wire 8 to 12 inches long, fold it in the middle, and wrap it like a loose haywire twist. At the ends make two tight wraps at a right angle to the plane of the eye at the middle of the wire. These eyes will then ride and rotate on a leader wire used for the main bottom rig. Thus the rig can rotate without twisting line.

Another way to make a hook lear is to use a slightly longer length of wire, fold it in the middle, and twist as above, but about 2 inches from the end make a right-angle bend so that the two ends are angled 180 degrees to each other. Form an eye in the end of each wire and attach the bottom leader to these eyes with knots or leader sleeves, or run the leader through the two eyes using a leader sleeve and bead on the leader to hold the hook lear up in place.

Another method is to take a length of wire and make an eye at each end and one on the shaft, with the shaft bent at a right angle at the central eye. The eye on the shaft should be offset

Making a hook lear: After the first bend is made, make a second and then a third bend.

Completed example of hook lear made from heavy utility wire on a homemade wire former. Each wire former must be set up for making a specific type of bend.

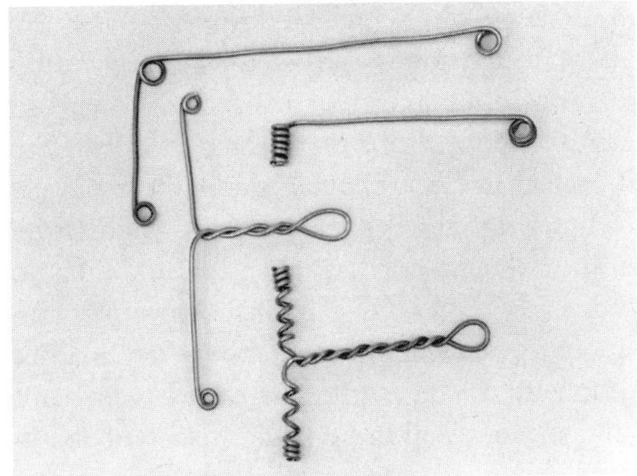

Examples of wire hook lears formed with homemade wire formers. Any type of bend or wire rig can be made this way.

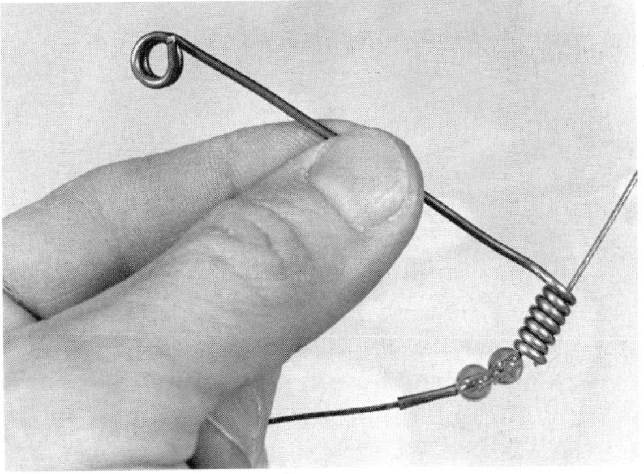

A hook lear in use. The beads serve as 360-degree rotation bearings above a leader sleeve crimped onto the wire bottom rig.

to one end so that there is a long arm to extend the snelled hook and a shorter arm for tying into the leader. Usually these ends will be about 2 inches and 4 inches, respectively, although other lengths can be used.

Umbrella rig. These rigs are used for trolling and consist of several arms—similar to the ribs of an umbrella—extending out from a central eye or line-tie, with various lightweight trolling lures on long snells attached to the end of each arm. These arms are similar to spreaders but with two or three spreaders attached at a central point to make a rig with four or six arms.

One easy way to make an umbrella rig is to use a small stainless steel screw-eyebolt (available at hardware stores) and two larger washers (usually called fender washers) to fit it. Make up long arms like spreader arms but with a central eye large enough for the eyebolt (usually ⅛- to ¼-inch diameter). The bolt should be about 1½ inches long. Slip a nut onto the threaded part of the bolt, add one fender washer, and then, in order, add the two or three spreader arms. Finish with the second fender washer and finally a wing nut. To prevent loss of the spreader arms (and the attached lures) while trolling, bend or

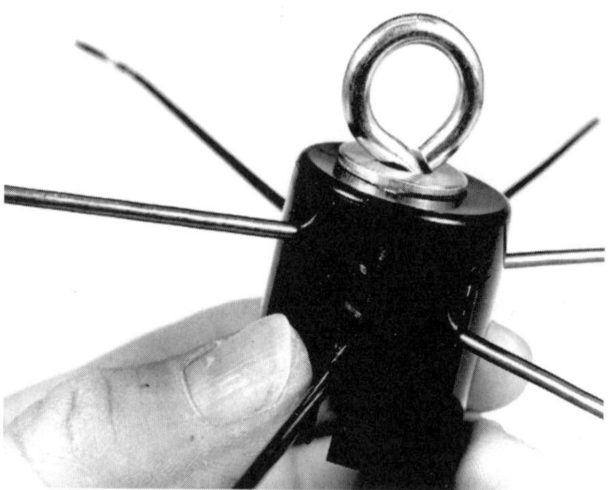

"Umbrella" rig made from spring utility wire, an eyebolt, and a plastic film canister. Bends in each of the three arms fit onto the eyebolt, and slots in the film canister hold the arms in a spread position for trailing lures while trolling.

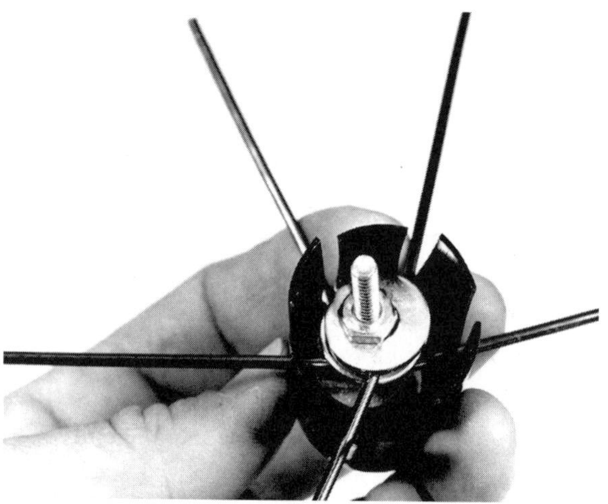

Underside of the above rig, showing the washers that fit between each of the wires. While a hex nut is used here, you can also use a wing nut so that the arms can be loosened to fold together for storage.

deform the last threads on the bolt to prevent the wing nut from coming off. The wing nut then allows you to adjust the umbrella from a spread (fishing) to folded (stored) position. Since the lures used for this fishing will often twist, be sure to use snap swivels on the end of the spreader arms for the snell or mono attachment.

To prevent the arms from tangling together while fishing, you can make a small separator out of a 35-mm film canister. While becoming rarer with the popularity of digital cameras, film canisters are still available from many photo shops. Drill a hole large enough for the bolt through the bottom of the can. Then, using scissors, carefully cut six slots evenly around the perimeter of the can's top. The result should look like the battlements on a castle's walls. Slide the arms onto the bolt, followed by the separator. Position the slots on the separator under the arms to hold them in position.

Weed guards. Weed guards to protect the point of a hook from snagging are easy to make. Size 0.009 or 0.012 spring wire should be used for most fishing and most fishing conditions. Cut a piece of wire about 1 inch longer than twice the distance from the eye of the hook to the barb. Double the wire in the center; hold this bend with pliers, and bend slightly about ⅛ inch from the doubled end. This will form the "loop" that fits at the hook point. Hold the wire bend at the hook point, with the end positioned between the point and the barb, and measure to the eye of the hook. Bend the wire again at this point so that the two ends of the wire can be slipped through the hook eye and fastened to the shank of the hook.

Obviously the length of wire needed for each size and style of hook will differ slightly, so if you're going to make any number of weedless wires for specific hooks, keep a record of the length of wire needed for each hook size.

There are several ways to fasten the weed guard in place. The two ends of the wire can be wrapped onto the hook shank using mono or size A, D, or E thread. The technique used here is the same used in fly tying, wrapping a guide on a rod, or snelling a hook. (See chapter 22 for this method.) However, instead of tying off the wrap

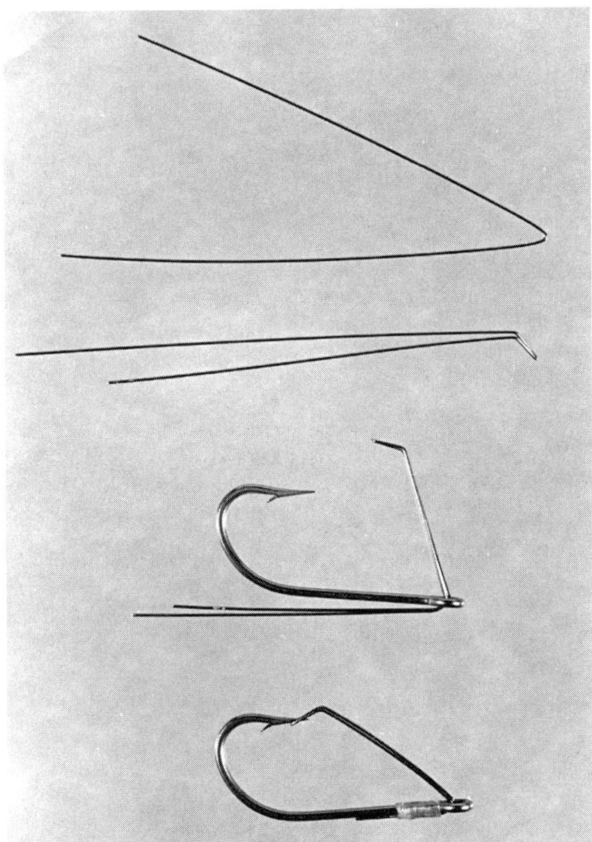

Making a wire weed guard from light wire. Steps, from top to bottom, show bending the wire in half, forming the kink that fits over the hook point, fitting and bending the wire into the hook eye, and wrapping the weed guard in place on the hook shank.

by pulling the end of the thread under the last wraps, finish with a series of half-hitches, commonly used in finishing a fly in fly tying. Add several coats of epoxy rod finish or fly-tying head cement to the wraps to seal them.

Other techniques to fasten the weed guard to the hook are to solder the wire in place, wrap the ends with wire, wrap with wire and solder it to the hook, or use thin-diameter shrink tape or tubing (the kind that shrinks with the application of heat—usually from a cigarette lighter). Incidentally, clear shrink tape and tubing are now available—you don't have to use black exclusively anymore.

There are other methods of construction. One is to cut the wire and make the first center bend exactly as above but then position the two ends of the wire over the point of the hook. Bend the remaining wire to fit through the hook eye, and fasten in place. Once the wire is wrapped or soldered in place, spread the two wires and, if desired, slightly bend the ends to make a spread-V weed guard.

You can also use just one length of wire, wrapping one end around the shank of the hook with the wire going through the hook eye and extending over the hook point. The result will be the wire bent on an acute angle—one leg wrapped to the hook shank, one extending down and in front of the hook point.

SINKER RIGGINGS

Sinker riggings from heavy brass or copper wire are easy to make; follow the techniques for making eyes with the homemade wire former.

Keel sinkers. These are easy to make from simple egg sinkers: Form wire into a large D shape with an eye at each end, and thread egg sinkers onto the bend in the D. Use a length of wire, form an eye at one end, and then add a second eye about a third of the way up the shaft. Add egg sinkers to the shaft, bend this wire into an arc, and wrap the end of the wire close to the first wrapped eye. The result is a large D with an eye at each end for placing in-line on a line/leader trolling rig.

You can also make a keel trolling sinker that is adjustable for weight by making the D-shaped wire like a large safety pin so that egg sinkers can be added or subtracted at will. The end of the wire is held in place with a bent wire catch.

Trolling sinkers can be made by forming an eye on each end of wire that holds one or more egg sinkers, but these sinkers do not have a keel and will tend to rotate if there is any lure or bait twist.

You can make a triangular-shaped wire with eyes at each corner, an eye for the line-tie, leader-tie (to lure or bait), and drop-sinker tie for hanging a weight (for a trolling sinker). You don't have to make these in a triangle shape though; a similar effect can be achieved with three eyes on the ends and bends of L- or T-shaped wire.

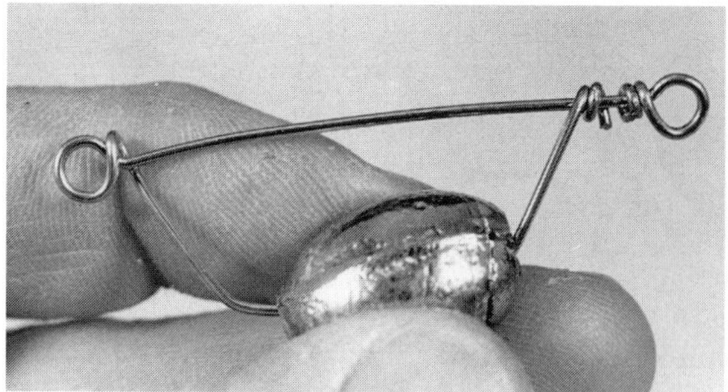

Brass or copper utility wire can be used to make sinker rigs, such as this keel-style rig made with an egg sinker. Line is tied to one eye of this rig, the leader to the other; the sinker prevents line twist.

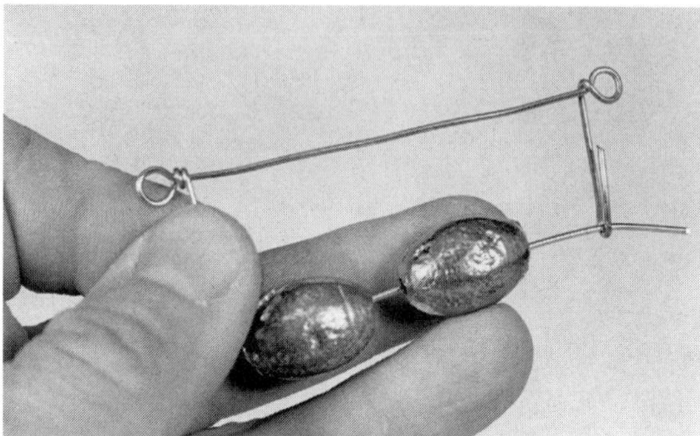

Another example of a keel sinker rig, this with a clip fastener for removing and adjusting the number and weight of sinkers used.

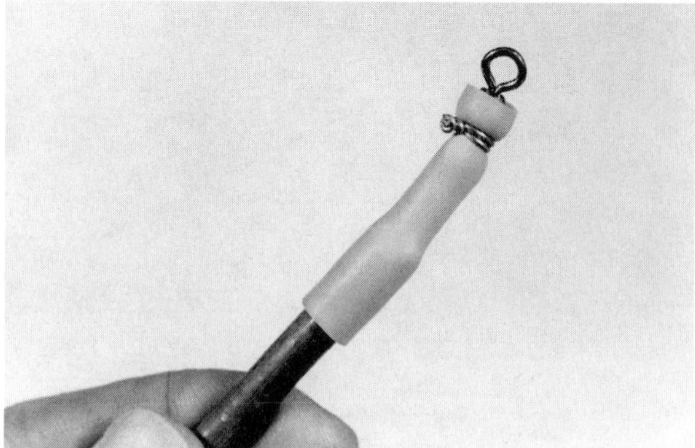

Making a sinker rig using a swivel, a short length of wire, and a short length of surgical hose. The surgical hose is slipped and wired onto the swivel and then holds any size and length of pencil lead for river fishing and drifting.

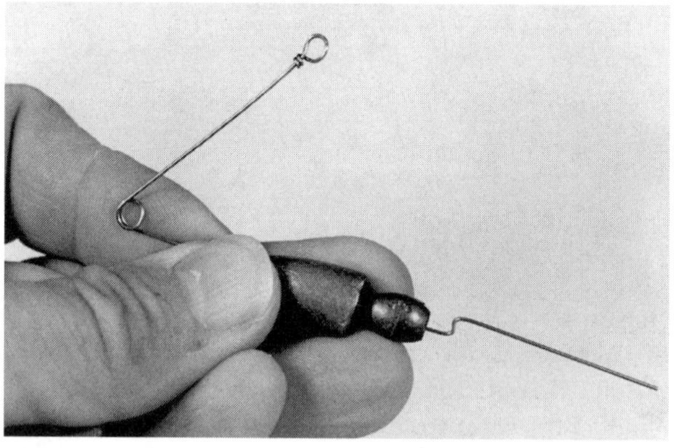

"Bait walking" type of sinker rig. The sinkers added to the lower wire (these can be changed and adjusted) allow the lure (tied to a leader at the top eye) to swim close to the bottom. The line is tied to the eye in the center of the rig.

Eyes for molding sinkers and tin squids are easily made from heavy or copper wire using the nail wire former to make eye forms in the shape of a keyhole or figure eight.

Rigs using pencil lead, like those used for West Coast steelhead fishing, are possible with a cross-line swivel (three eyes in the shape of a T) and a short length of surgical hose. Using surgical hose slightly smaller than the diameter of the swivel eye, run the hose onto the 90-degree-angle swivel eye, and secure it in place with a wrapping of thread, cord, or wire through the eye and the end of the hose. It is then easy to tie the line and leader to the other two eyes. The pencil lead is easily cut to the length (weight) required and slipped into the surgical hose.

Another way to make a river-type drift sinker is to use utility wire, preferably with a slight curve in it, and form an eye at one end. Then thread on egg sinkers to obtain the weight you need. After these are added, make a very *slight* bend in the end of the wire to just barely keep the sinkers in place. If they get hung up, a strong continued pull on the line will pull the sinkers off the wire and free the rig. This sinker has to be adjusted each time you change the weight being fished.

KNOTS, SPLICES, AND SNELLS

Proper knots, splices, and snells are vital for any good rig. Knots are listed in appendix E along with drawings and text. It is important to use a knot for its stated purpose, since not all connections will work with all materials at all tests.

14
Tackle Accessories

Introduction • Tackle Boxes • Bait Box • Chum Pots • Birds • Planers • Floats • Nets • Net Frames • Cradles for Big Fish, Long Fish • Sand Spikes, Rod Holders, Rod Racks, and Rod Cases • Surf Belts • Surf Gaffs • Gaffs • Tailers • Priests • Wading Staffs • Dehookers • Snubbers • Fishing Markers • Lure Retrievers

INTRODUCTION

There is no listing of tools, basic materials, or safety equipment in this chapter. That doesn't mean tools and materials and safety equipment are not used, only that this chapter is a "catchall" that includes easy-to-make items that do not fit well into other chapters.

Tools and methods are suggested where practical, and safety must be paramount, as in any tackle-making operation. Use a safe workplace, goggles, and any special safety equipment or protective clothing or gloves. Be sure you know how to use the tools needed before attempting any task.

TACKLE BOXES

It is possible to make tackle boxes—I've done it—though to be perfectly honest, it usually isn't practical. Today there are plenty of options in tackle containers from the major tackle-box companies such as Plano, Flambeau, and Woodstream, as well as special boxes designed to be built into boats and often seen advertised in boat and saltwater sports magazines. Some box styles are just plain impractical to build. Single- or double-side satchel boxes would be difficult at best and too heavy for practical use.

A homemade tackle box using thin shelving and dovetailed compartment dividers.

You can build drawer-type boxes—I built these long before the tackle-box companies came out with their models—but they are still heavy and best when designed for semipermanent use in a boat or as a basic box to be kept in a beach buggy or fishing vehicle.

In building this type of box, I did not use a hinged front-lid cover but instead opted for magnetic strips in the back of each drawer to hold them in place in a closed position. They worked well, although I did use a pin-type catch mechanism to hold the drawers for extra security.

Basic for any boxes is to use the lightest wood possible and to design drawers for the size of the lures you plan to carry or the type of tackle to be stored in the box. For fasteners, use a good grade of carpenter's glue and brass or stainless steel screws.

BAIT BOX

Bait containers or boxes are preferred by some boat and bank fishermen for minnows and other aquatic bait. They are available commercially but can also be made. A floating bait box can be constructed in any size and will keep minnows in the water where they are to be fished—reducing loss through changes in pH, temperature, or salinity. There is no need to use battery-operated air pumps or to change the water at regular intervals. Basically a floating wood bait box is like a small boat except that the bottom is made of hardware cloth (wire-mesh screening) to facilitate the free flow of water. While commercially available bait boxes and containers are good for most fishing applications, these wood bait boxes are ideal for anglers with waterfront property to keep a supply of bait secured to a private dock.

General dimensions of an average bait box are about 10 inches wide, 18 inches long, and 6 inches deep. Scrap wood can be used for the sides, end, and top, with standard shelving or plywood most popular. If you do use plywood, it should be the marine type to resist delaminating. Any wood box should be coated with a good water sealer and painted. The bottom of hardware cloth is simply stapled or nailed into place; the lid is cut from the top, hinged, and closed with a simple toggle latch. Stainless steel toggles and hinges are best, although brass and sometimes plastic are available. Fasten the box together with brass screws to prevent rusting. Fasten a large screw eye or through-eyebolt to one end of the bait box for line to tie the box to the boat, stake it to the bank, or secure it to a private dock. Varnish or paint it and it is ready for use—just be sure to allow several days of curing time to prevent the paint from harming minnows.

Parts necessary for making a floating bait box. This bait box is easily made from scrap lumber and hardware cloth (metal screening).

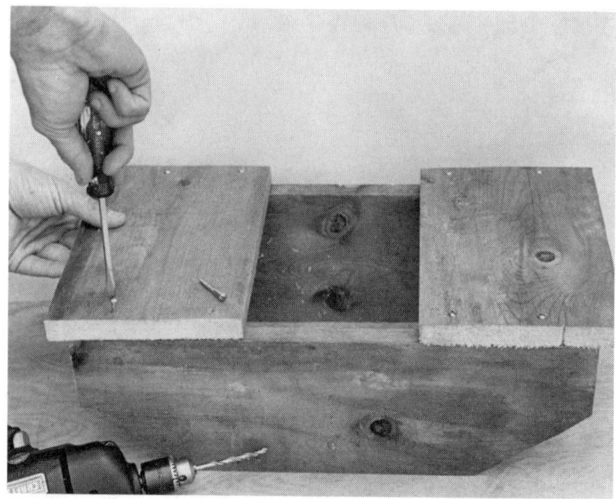

Simple tools are all that are necessary to complete the box. The bottom will be completed with hardware cloth.

Using a stapler to staple the hardware cloth to the frame of the box.

Completing the box top with hinges and a lock on lid.

Floating box. This bait box is ideal for use at docks or attached to a boat for still or drift fishing.

CHUM POTS

There are several ways to make chum pots. These useful pieces of tackle have their place in freshwater fishing for carp and catfish as well as in much saltwater fishing. Flounder, bluefish, striped bass, white perch, and other species are readily attracted to a chum line. Sometimes chum is broadcast behind an anchored boat, but a chum pot is preferable for most fishing because it concentrates the chum in a specific area and thus concentrates the fish that are attracted to the chum.

One easy way to make a chum pot is to use a large, wide-mouthed plastic jar. Gallon sizes for mayonnaise or mustard used by restaurants are ideal for this. (Check with a restaurant, school, church, or other large user for these.)

Wash the jar thoroughly, and drill or punch a hole in the center of the cap. Punch more holes, all in the size preferred for the chum used, in the sides and lid. Use a drill, awl, reamer, red-hot nail, or hot soldering iron (though heated tools will make the plastic smell!). Make two more holes, one on each side at the jar's top and just below the lid. Weight the pot with several ounces of lead bars or sinkers screwed to the bottom. Knot a rope handle to run from the top center hole in the lid down through one hole in the top and around the outside to the other topside hole. This will serve as a handle and a tie point for the pot and prevents the loss of the lid.

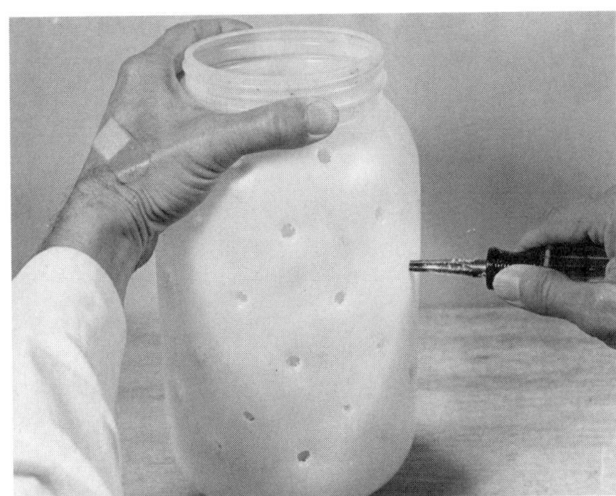
One way to make a chum pot is with a gallon-size plastic container. Use a drill or reamer to punch holes throughout the side of the container.

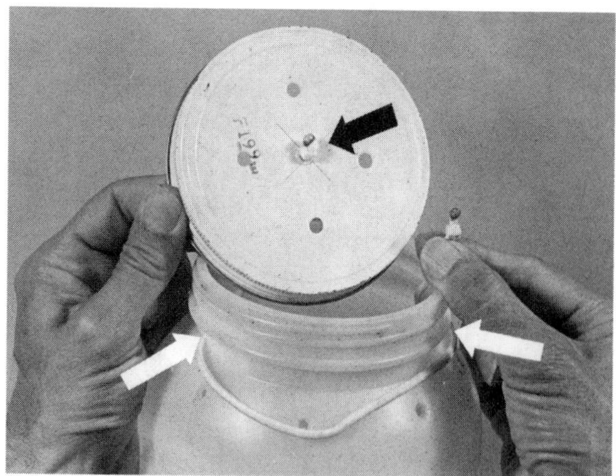

The top should also be drilled; a rope threaded through the side and knotted to the top prevents loss of the top. Arrows point to the attachments in the lid and through the sides of the container.

Various sizes of hardware cloth (metal screening) can be used for chum baskets, based on the size of the chum particles.

Use pliers to crimp the edges of the hardware cloth into a circular container to make a chum pot.

Another way to make a good chum pot is to use hardware cloth (wire mesh), available from hardware and building-supply stores. Hardware cloth comes in different mesh sizes, from about ¼ to 1 inch—choose the mesh size best suited to the chum you plan to use. With pliers, join the mesh edges to make a container of any shape desired. Square (like a crab trap), rectangular, and cylindrical are typically good shapes. Making such a container is easy, since you can cut the mesh with wire cutters so that you have wire "fingers" along each edge to be wrapped around the edge to be joined. In all cases, make the container with the top open. Use more hardware cloth for the top, making hinges of heavy wire (copper or brass is good and easily worked) so that you can open the top to add chum. Use a simple large snap or large safety pin to secure the lid. Attach a rope to the chum pot, and add several large sinkers to it to weight it.

An alternative is to mold the weight into the pot. One easy way to do this is to use a disposable mold, such as an old metal pie tin, for the bottom of a cylindrical chum pot. Make a cylindrical wire-mesh pot that will just fit into the pie tin. Melt lead (see the proper procedures and safety rules listed in chapter 4). Pour the molten lead into the pie tin, and immediately immerse the wire mesh cylinder in it. The lead will cool around the bottom of the wire to create a solid lead-weighted bottom. Make a top of mesh for the pot.

A simple way to weight the chum pot is to set the tubular screening into a metal pie plate and fill it with lead so that the screening is embedded in the bottom.

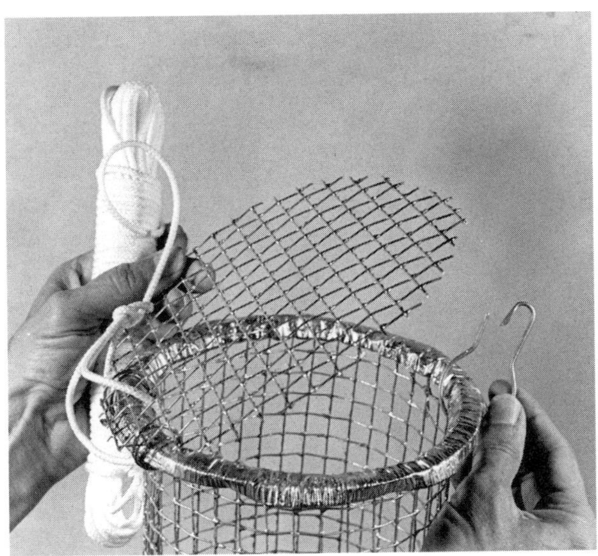

The simple top with a rim of lead and screen top secured with a shower-curtain clip.

Two types of chum pots, with lead for weighting and rope.

A third possibility is to use PVC tubing or 4-inch-diameter pipe. Make it as long as you wish, but about 12 to 18 inches is best. Use one solid end or cap and a threaded clean-out flange and clean-out plug. Use the proper glue (special glues for these plastics are available at hardware stores) to attach the solid cap to one end and the threaded clean-out flange to the other. The clean-out plugs usually have square ends, so they may be opened with a wrench, but you will not have to secure the end tight enough to require this. To prevent loss of the plug, drill a hole in the top center of the square end, run a knotted rope through this (with the knot on the outside), and secure the rope (again knotted on the outside) through a hole drilled into the opposite side of the pipe. Make sure you have enough clearance in the rope to remove and replace the plug. Drill holes throughout the rest of the pipe, using a drill size and reamer that suits the type and size of chum you will be using. Holes of about ¼ to ¾ inch are best.

In use, add some large sinkers to weight the chum pot. Fill the pot with your chum of choice, and lower it over the side of the boat by a short rope. The weights in the pot will sink it, and the holes will allow the chum to dissipate slowly. Periodically jiggling the chum-pot rope helps to spread the chum.

Another technique is to rope the chum pot on the boat just at water level, where the waves and rocking of the boat will regularly wash over the pot to maintain a continual chum stream.

BIRDS

Birds are not lures, but they do deserve a place here because they are used *with* lures to attract fish when lures are trolled. They are primarily used offshore but can be used inshore and even for some forms of big-water freshwater trolling.

Birds have been popular for about fifty years now. Their precursors were the cola bottles and similar devices that were used in offshore trolling for the bubbles and smoke they created, followed by the large trolling birds used in the Asian and Pacific fishing methods.

Birds are basically nothing more than a long strip of wood with some angled crosspieces that create bubbles and surface disturbance and may cause the bird to rock or wobble when trolled. They are all made and rigged to troll on the surface; a lure is trailed behind them to hook the fish. Birds can be any length, and some as small as several inches long have been used. Others are as long as 3 or 4 feet. Most average about 10 to 18 inches.

Birds can be made of any type of scrap wood of almost any reasonable thickness. Standard shelving is ideal. They can be drilled with holes to make them lighter, have rattles added (either commercial or homemade with ball bearings and 35-mm film canisters), have lead poured into cavities for greater weight and more water disturbance, and have more than one wing added for additional surface splashing. From the top, a typical one would look like nothing more than X or a cross.

Good stock to use is 1-inch shelving (actual size about ¾ inch) or similar wood about ¾ to 1 inch thick. You can use thicker wood, and a two-by-four works well for the body. The wing can be 1-inch shelving on the large birds made on two-by-fours or lathing or furring strips for the smaller sizes.

There are only a few critical factors to consider in making a bird. The wing is placed into the top by cutting a slot in the body. While there are no absolutes, the angle of the wing should be about 30 degrees from vertical, or about 60 degrees from horizontal. Make the wing about one-third to one-half the length of the body. Generally the front and tail of the body are tapered to allow the bird to skip easily and not plow into the water. The farther the wing is placed to the rear of the bird, the better it will track; too close to the front and the bird may dip and dive. A wing placed deep or low in the body will cause the bird to roll and wobble more than will one placed higher up.

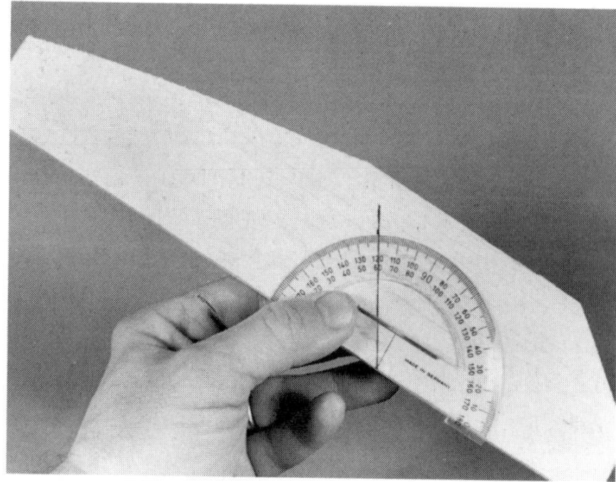

Most birds—attractors for offshore fishing—are made with the short wings at about a 60-degree angle, as shown and drawn on this bird body.

Completed bird with wing glued in place, before painting and rigging.

Cuts to hold the wing do not have to be very accurate—the fish won't care; a good epoxy will hold the wing in place. You can cut out the parts in minutes with a handsaw or on a band, scroll, saber, or other power saw. When using any power tool or saw, be sure to practice proper safety procedures. Small items like this should be cut out with a table or radial saw.

Once the parts are cut out, round off the edges, soak the slot for the wing with glue, and set the wing in place. You can paint it bright colors to add to its attractiveness.

There are several ways to rig birds. One is to cut a slot longitudinally through the body during construction, epoxy a heavy wire into place, and form wrapped eyes on both ends once the lure is complete and painted.

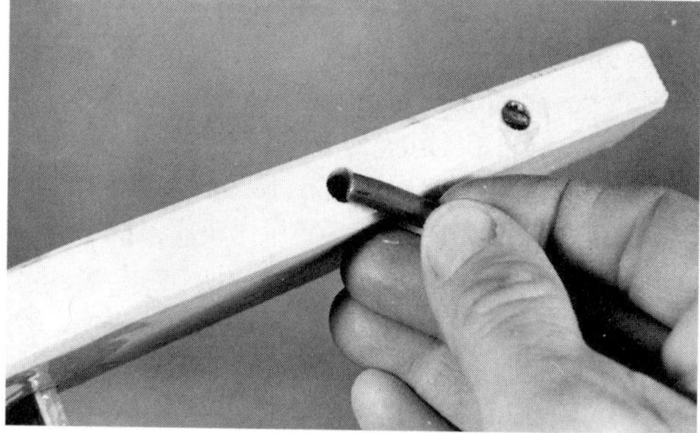

Weight can be added to a bird using pencil weights glued into holes drilled into the bottom of the bird.

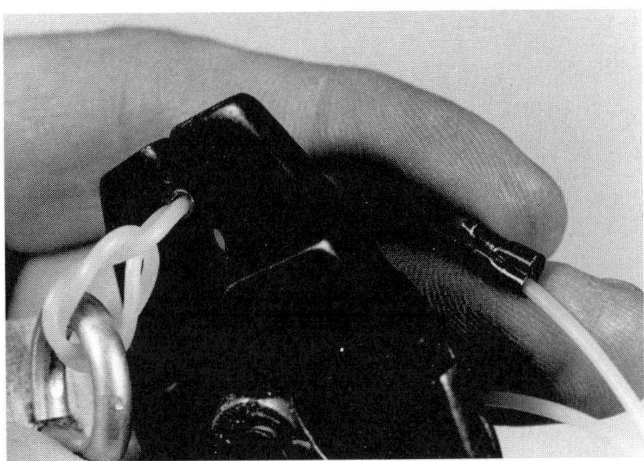

Using Mason leader pliers to crimp the leader sleeves to hold the heavy mono on the bird.

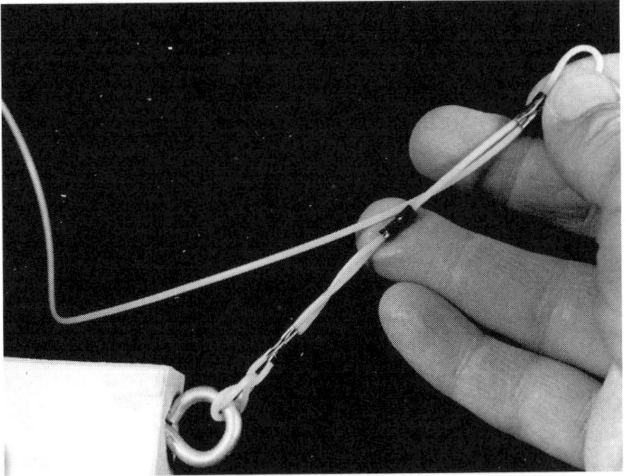

Close-up showing the rigging for one end of the bird. The line is tied to the loop held by the thumb and index finger.

Another method is to use a separate short length of leader from which the bird will hang at both ends. This places the strain from the lure on the leader and allows the bird more movement and action. Use heavy wire or mono, about 200-pound test and about one and a half times the length of the bird when loops are added at each end using leader sleeves. When making these loops, add a good swivel to the front end of the leader and a snap or snap swivel to the rear. It is this leader that will take the strain of trolling, with the line fastened to the front swivel, the leader and lure fastened to the rear snap. To attach the bird to this separate short leader, use short lengths of mono or Dacron for flexibility. You will need two of these lengths of line, and when it's complete the bird should hang down from the taut leader no more than several inches. Tie each length of material to the swivel eye, and then fasten it to the other end of the bird. (Alternatively, use a longer length for the suspension leader, make a loop at each end using a leader sleeve, and use the ends of the mono as the attachment from the leader to the front or back of the bird.)

Attachment can be made four ways: through a screw eye fastened at each end; a heavy wire with an eye formed at one end, run through a hole drilled through the wood; the line directly through a hole in the wood and knotted in place; or a small eyebolt run through the bird with the nut secured with Loctite or glue.

Variations may be made in size or general shape (consistent with the basics of bird construction), with holes in the side to reduce weight, lead poured into the body for added weight, holes in the wing for added surface disturbance, and the addition of rattles and bright finishes, including glitter, mirrors, and prism tape. Rattles are best added by drilling holes through the main body of the bird and inserting canisters holding ball bearings or BBs. Film canisters are good for this, as are any small metal cans. Ideally these should be shorter than the width of the bird so that you can use an epoxy gel to cover the rattle and make the outside finish smooth.

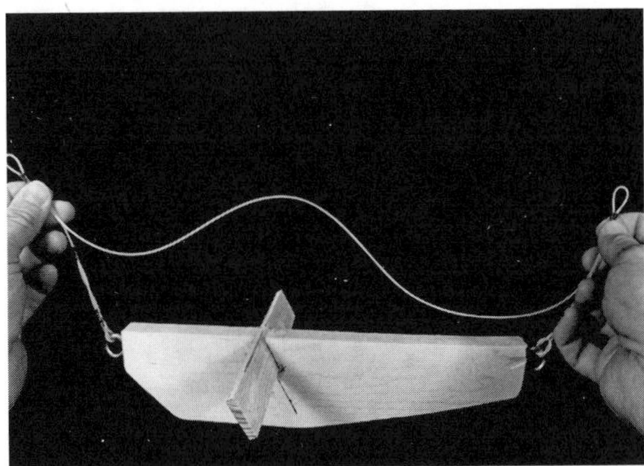

Complete rigged bird with heavy, offshore mono leader attached to both ends, rigged as a "trolley" from this leader section. When rigged with an additional teaser behind it, the stress of trolling this bird will be on the leader.

PLANERS

Planers provide a way of trolling more fishing lines, increasing the chances of catching fish. For charter boat captains, they provide a greater chance for more hookups. They can also be used by bank and shore fishermen to fish lines in the middle of the river or farther out than it is possible to cast.

They are in essence a floating, water-surface equivalent of offshore outriggers in which several lines are run from outrigger clips to skip lures and teasers in the boat wake.

Planers are almost like small catamarans. They are run to the side of a boat by means of a very heavy line. Outrigger clips, or simpler clip-like devices, are used to run lines from rods and reels to the lures that are trailed through the water to the side of the boat. One planer and planer line can be run on each side of the boat. In my area of the Chesapeake Bay, charter captains use them to run up to four lines on each side of the boat, in addition to the four to six lines fished from the boat cockpit. Some boats can troll up to fourteen lines this way.

Planers are not used—or are only rarely used—for offshore fishing for wahoo, billfish, sailfish, dolphin, etc. The attendant problems of necessary dropbacks for a hookup, tangles with hooked fish, fish running all over the ocean, and such make this technique pretty much useful only for big freshwater, coastal, or brackish water for stripers and bluefish and similar situations.

These planners are commonly used in freshwater lakes when fishing for walleye and lake trout.

You can buy them from a number of different companies, but you can also make them from shelving boards or "2X" construction boards.

In essence they consist of two boards, each on its side and about a foot apart, fastened together with a bolted, threaded rod that has an eyebolt on one side. The boards should "swim" as close as possible to a 90-degree angle to the boat. It also helps to have a vertical fiberglass rod with a bright flag attached to the planer to alert other boats in the area that you are fishing planers.

While dimensions can vary, a basic materials list for these would be two 8- to 10-inch shelving boards, each about 24 to 28 inches long; 3 feet of threaded ¼ × 20-inch rod; a bunch of nuts and fender washers to fit; a ¼-inch eyebolt; 150 feet of 0.080 weed-cutting line; a fiberglass pole; and brightly colored pennants to signal other boats.

Assembly is simple. First cut the two boards at an angle like the bow (the front) of a boat. Then chamfer or cut the edge at an angle to help the planer pull out from the boat or shore. Cut the threaded rod into three 12-inch lengths. Drill a ¼-inch hole through the boards in order to attach them together like a catamaran. For this drill two holes through the rear of each board and one in front for the rod attachment. The three lengths of rod will hold the two parts together. For this planer to work correctly, the board outermost from the boat must be staggered in front of the inner board. The two holes for the rear of the outer board will be about 2 inches from the rear edge, while the equivalent holes on the inner board should be about 6 to 8 inches forward of the rear edge. This staggering will make the planer work better and pull harder to the side. The easiest way to do this is to place the outer board on top of the inner board, positioned about 4 to 6 inches forward, and then drill all three holes through both boards at once.

Drill a hole for the eyebolt about 4 inches forward of the midpoint but only on the inside board. Attach all the parts using nuts and fender washers (wide flange washers to prevent pull-through of the bolts).

To finish the planer board, paint with a good waterproofing sealer, then with white, and finally with a bright Day-Glo orange or fluorescent paint.

To make the line holding the planer, use heavy mono or weed-cutting line (available at any hardware store), cut to the length desired, and knot. If using leader sleeves, attach a dog-leash snap to each end.

To use, attach one line snap to the eyebolt on the inner side, pay out the planer on the line, and attach the second snap on the end of the line to an eye in top of a vertical pole placed in a rod holder in the center of the boat. Do the same on the other side of the boat with the second planer and a second pole.

This keeps the planer line up and off of the water and makes it easier to fill with the rings or fishing line releases. If the boat has a cabin or canopy, you also can add a ring or eyebolt to the top center of the boat at the cabin or canopy and attach the planer line there.

To hold the fishing lines, you can use outrigger release clips or simple releases made from rubber bands and shower-curtain rings. The best of these rings are round plastic. For this rigging, run out the line behind the boat from the reel to the length that you want the line to run behind the planer line. Then double a rubber band around the line, place the loop formed into the shower-curtain ring, and clip the ring closed around the planer line. Position the rubber band on the round part of the ring and the flat closure part of the shower-curtain ring to run against the planer board line. With this rig you can probably fish about three to four fishing lines to each side of the boat. For shore or bank fishing, one or two lines are about the comfortable maximum.

Two 1 inch x 10 inch x 3 foot-long boards with the saw used to cut and make them into a side planer for trolling more lures.

Here the boards for the side planer have been cut at an angle and sloped to make the assembled planer troll properly when used.

To complete the side planer you will also need threaded rods, fender washer, and nuts as shown, along with an eyebolt to tie to the planer to secure it to the boat.

Here the four threaded rods (here 18 inches long) have been added to the one side of the planer, with fender washers on each side of the nuts to prevent pull-through and wear when fishing.

Fender washers, larger in diameter than regular washers, are used here on each side of each board and hole to secure the threaded rods.

Side view of the planer with the eyebolt.

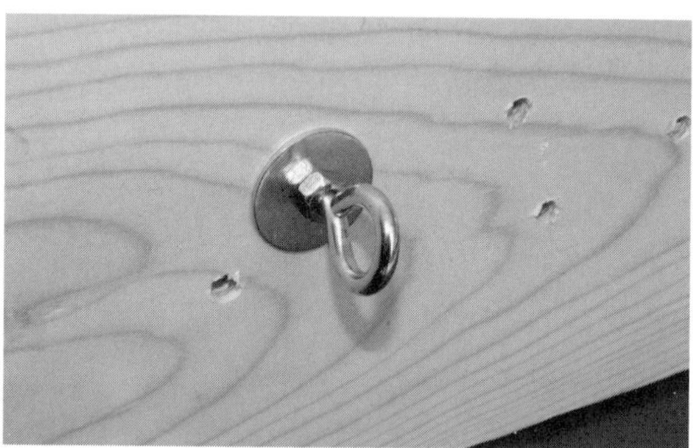

Here the eyebolt is shown to secure the planer to the boat. Note that several holes have been drilled into the board to provide for adjustment with the planer when deciding the best place to position the eyebolt.

View of side planer. Note that this one is made for trolling off the starboard side of a boat.

The above is fine for fresh water, but for choppy water, offshore, and light saltwater bay fishing, modifications of this basic design work better. Captains Buddy Harrison and Buddy Jr. found that a trimaran design of three heavier and slightly longer boards works better than the above. The Captains Harrison fish for stripers and blues out of Chesapeake House on Tilghman Island, Maryland, in Chesapeake Bay.

They build their own planers using 2 × 10-inch boards, with each planer board 36 inches long, and with three boards each separated by 12-inch threaded rods to make a planer 2 feet wide. They use the same construction as above to cut the angled prow of the planer and the chamfered edge to help the planer cut into the water and pull against the boat. The major exception, apart from the heavier boards, is that they use three boards, each one staggered 6 inches in front of the board to the inside of it. These are staggered 6 inches each so that the outside of the three boards runs 12 inches forward of the inside board—a 6-inch staggering for each board addition. For the eyebolt they have found that a position about 4 inches forward of the midpoint of the inside board works best—or about 22 inches from the rear on a 36-inch-long board. For planer line they use 150-foot spools of 0.080 weed-cutting line, using the entire line for each planer to run these 150 feet out from the boat on each side. As with the planer mentioned above, a vertical pole with a bright pennant is necessary to alert other trolling boats of the added width of the trolling area. Using these, the Harrisons often fish up to six lines on each side of the boat in addition to the lines run from the cockpit of the boat.

FLOATS

Fishing floats can be made in a number of different ways. The simplest version is to get a cork ball, drill it (if it does not come with a through-drilled hole), glue a length of dowel of the right diameter into the hole, and wrap several turns of wire around one or both ends of the dowel for line attachment. Most such floats are painted, and if this is desired, do so before adding the wire. In addition to cork, balsa is also a good high-floating wood, and craft stores sometimes have small plastic-foam balls that can be used as floats. If you use plastic foam, use only epoxy glue for any attachments, since other glues may break down some foams.

Refinements can include using floats of various shapes: round, oblong, tapered, football shaped, cone shaped, and so on. You can weight the finished product with lead so that it just barely floats. This way the float is more sensitive to light nibbles and thus better for fishing. In some cases you might want to make floats of different sensitivities for different fish species and fishing situations. If you add lead, do so symmetrically around the bottom, adding it little by little until the desired sensitivity is reached. Epoxy the lead in place, and paint the resulting float. A good way to add lead is with small split shot, lead bird shot, lead wire, or BBs.

Porcupine quills are often used for delicate floats: They can be bought from some tackle dealers and most fly-tying outlets. Wrap a loop of mono or wire to the lower end of the quill, and use a small twist of spring wire or a small rubber band (such as those used for orthodontic braces, or you can make your own by cutting thin sections of rubber surgical tubing left over from making hose lures) placed around the center to complete the quill float. To use, run the line through the loop and then clip it in place in the center of the float with the spring wire. If you use a rubber-band fastener, the line must be run under the rubber band and through the loop at the bottom.

NETS

As inexpensive as both original landing nets and replacement bags are, it might seem foolish to even consider making one. However, there are several advantages to doing just that. First, the net can be made in any size or dimension desired. It can be made of any thickness of cord, with any size mesh, of either cotton or nylon. And once you learn the basic net knot, you can make any style of net you wish. A medium-size net bag can usually be completed in one evening.

Several tools are required, but all are inexpensive. You will need shuttles to hold the netting cord and mesh gauges to keep the net mesh (openings) even and uniform. Both individual and sets of these items are readily available from Netcraft.

Either nylon or cotton cord can be used for nets. Nylon is more expensive but also longer lasting and stronger for any given size. One consideration in this age of conservation awareness and catch-and-release is that cotton nets are less damaging to fish than are those made of nylon. Polypropylene nets are even more damaging, although polypropylene cord is not used for hobby-net construction.

Bonded nylon, such as is available from Netcraft, is the easiest material to use because it has a slight "tackiness" that helps "lock" the knots securely and prevent them from slipping. It is not sticky or difficult to work with. Regular nylon can be used, but it is more difficult to work with and more likely to slip, both in construction and while landing fish.

Cord for making nets comes in different sizes, and these sizes differ with each type of cord. Bonded nylon ranges from size 3, testing 20-pound strength with 2,200 feet per ¼-pound spool, to size 48, testing 430 pounds with 380 feet per pound. The smaller sizes are sold in ¼- and 1-pound sizes, the larger sizes in 1-pound spools. Sizes include 3, 6, 9, 12, 18, 24, 30, and 48, with the largest size best for making hammocks.

Tools required for making and repairing nets. The shuttles and mesh gauges at the top are from Netcraft; those on the bottom are homemade from stiff cardboard.

Details on these cords (available from Jann's Netcraft) are as follows:

Size	Pound Test	Diameter	Feet/Pound
3	20	0.020	8,800
6	50	0.030	3,840
9	86	0.040	2,160
12	101	0.045	1,876
18	165	0.060	1,131
24	260	0.075	697
30	309	0.080	585
48	430	0.095	380

This nylon is available in both white and green.

Netcraft offers the following suggestions on the size of cord to use for various projects:

Net Type	Nylon Twine Size	Approx. Quantity
Cast Nets	3	⅛ lb.
Landing Nets	9 or 12	¼ lb.
Turtle Traps	18	½ lb.
Hammocks	48	2 lbs.

In addition to the cord, you will need some tools, including a shuttle or two. Plastic shuttles vary by length and thickness, the thickness determined by the mesh size to be made. A small size for minnow nets is 6 inches by ⅜ inch; the largest measures 10¼ inches by 1³⁄₁₆ inches. They are inexpensive—a set of eight shuttles of all sizes costs only a few dollars.

Mesh gauges are required to measure and check the size of the mesh while working. These are also made of plastic, and a set of eight costs only a few dollars. Mesh sizes include ¾, 1, 1¼, 1½, 1¾, 2, 2½, and 3 inches. These are for *square measure,* one of the two methods of measuring net mesh size.

Parts available for net-making include wire frames for making landing nets, net weights for minnow seines, live-bag rings (for making live bags to hold catches and to keep the net expanded), floats for seines, "swivels," and thimbles for cast nets.

Before beginning, the cord must be transferred from the spool or skein to the proper size shuttle, which is determined by the size of the

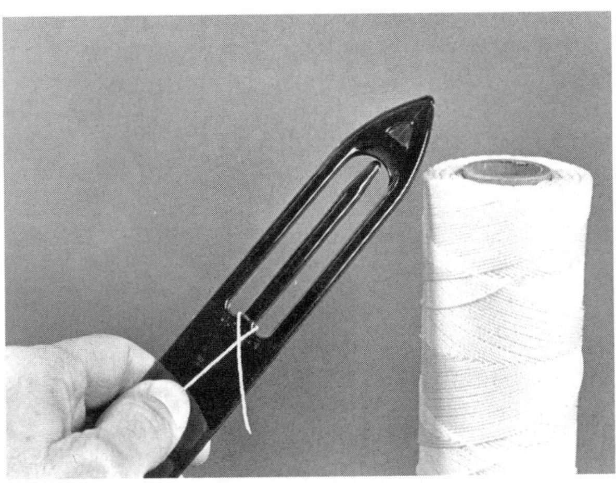

The netting cord is locked in place on the shuttle to fill the shuttle.

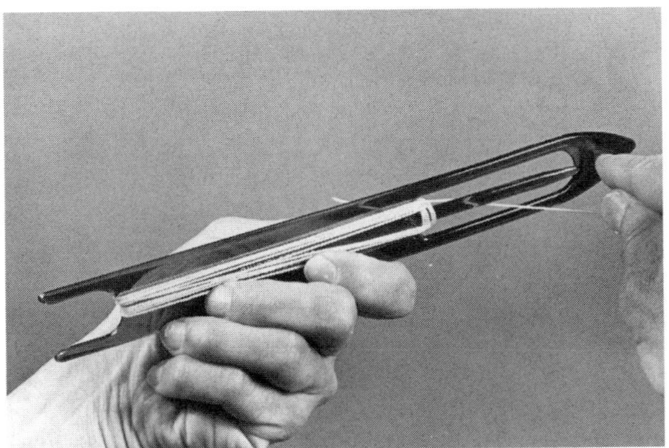

The shuttle is filled with net cord by wrapping alternately from side to side, wrapping the cord around the tongue of the shuttle each time.

net. Most nets have a large mesh at the upper end and gradually progress to a smaller mesh at the bottom. The plastic shuttles are flexible, and the cord should be placed with as little tension as possible to avoid building tension and twisting the shuttle. Begin by locking the cord over the center "tongue" on one side of the shuttle, then alternate the cord back and forth around the end (foot) and up over the tongue each time. Quite a lot of cord can be placed on a shuttle this way. In practice I find it easiest to hold the shuttle by one edge in my left hand, pushing the tongue out from the main body of the shuttle to slip the cord over it. You can push the tongue back and forth this way with your finger and thumb to rapidly fill the shuttle.

Once the shuttle is loaded, you can begin in one of several ways. One is to make a short, square net (a little like a short commercial gill or minnow net). Once the square net is finished, join the edges with net knots to make a completed round landing net. Jann's Netcraft also sells various parts and tools for making nets, including rings, weights, and floats. In addition they sell a small book on making nets with tips and techniques for all net types.

Netcraft used to make a net wheel that held cord in place at the frame position, allowing the net to be constructed from the frame position to the bottom. Some of these tools are still in use and allow the making of round nets as well.

Net meshes are measured in two different ways—stretched and square. Square measurement is the size of each square of mesh from one side of the square opening to the other (from one knot to the next knot). A net measuring 1 inch from one knot to the next would have 1-inch-square mesh. The same mesh would be 2-inch *stretched* mesh, since this type of measurement is taken with the mesh stretched and the length of the slit of mesh thus formed measured.

The mesh gauge you use determines the square-mesh measurement. Thus a 1-inch-thick mesh gauge would form a 1-inch-square mesh netting, or 2-inch stretched netting.

To begin any net, the cord must be held, secured, or clipped in place, with enough loops for the net desired. If you make a flat net, you will need a metal or wood rod on which to lay the first row of loops. Metal rods are probably best, and plain metal rods in diameters of about ¼, ⅜, and ½ inch, usually about 3 feet long, are available at most hardware stores. At the same time, buy two screw eyes or screw hooks with eyes larger than the rod. These are screwed into the edge of the workbench to hold the rod. The screw hooks are better because they make it easier to attach and remove the rod and working net.

Although you can make a series of open meshes that can then be transferred to the rod for making the net, you can also use a small

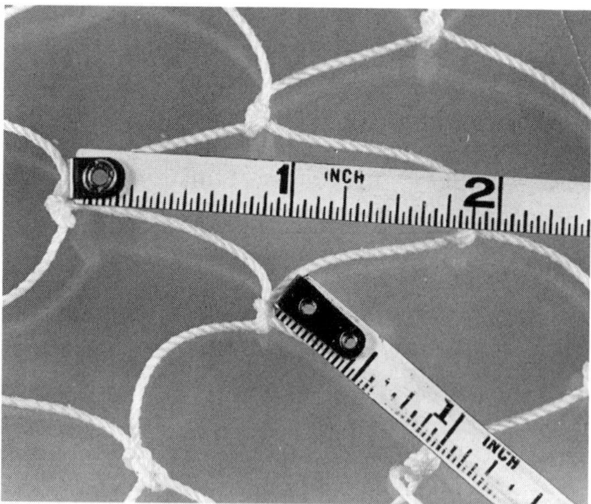

Measuring net mesh size. Top, measuring the meshes stretched into a slit; bottom, measuring the sides of the square mesh opening from one knot to the next.

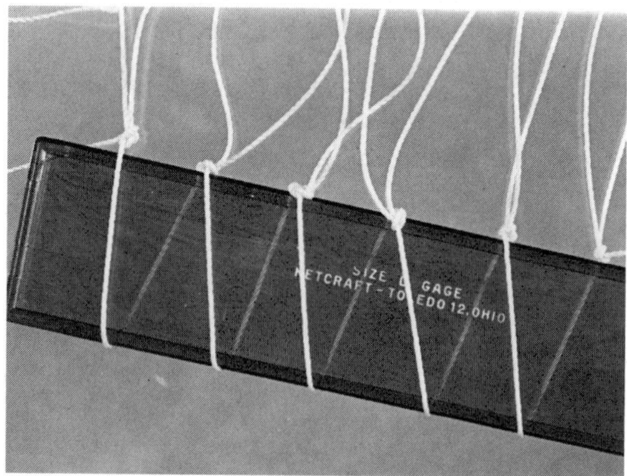

A mesh gauge is used to assure even mesh size while working.

Simple homemade tool for beginning net making consists of a strip of wood with a series of fasteners 1 inch apart. The fasteners for fastening the first row of the net cord consist of a spring-loaded washer held in place with a screw.

helpful homemade tool. The tool is the mesh-net starter, and it consists of a series of screws or nails secured about 1 inch apart in a straight line onto a block of wood. Each nail or screw holds a compression spring and washer. With this tool, each loop of cord can be held in place between the wood and the spring-loaded washer: The tension keeps it from slipping as you adjust the mesh size. This also allows the use of double cord, or double selvage, to combat the added wear of the meshes on the frame or top row.

You can get by with as little as three of these spring-loaded holders, but the more you have, the easier the job will be. I like at least ten. Using this tool, you have one cord attached and spaced to these holders. Begin the meshes with a second cord wrapped on the shuttle. Make sure you have enough cord for the top row to complete the length you want. If you run short it won't be a disaster, but it will require a knot.

Begin by wrapping the cord around each nail or screw under the washer to hold it in place. Use the chosen mesh gauge to check for the proper size loop. (*Note*: If you place this net on a larger size frame, you may wish to begin with a larger mesh size that will slip easily onto the aluminum or metal frame of a handled landing net. If so, adjust for that size and then switch to a smaller mesh gauge for the remainder of the net.)

Once you have the holders filled, use the shuttle to add meshes to begin making the net. But remember that you only have loops prepared for as many holders as you have. For this first row you will be making a mesh row attached to the top loops for the length of the holders, then you will be removing the loops from the holders and rerigging the holders with the remaining cord, making more meshes, and repeating these steps until the first two rows (the row of loops on the holders and the first row of "real" meshes) are complete. At this point transfer the top loops to the rod held with the screw eyes for working the rest of the net. If the net is long, you may have to do this in stages or get a longer rod to hold the meshes.

To make the meshes, knot the shuttle cord to the bottom of the end loop, taking care that

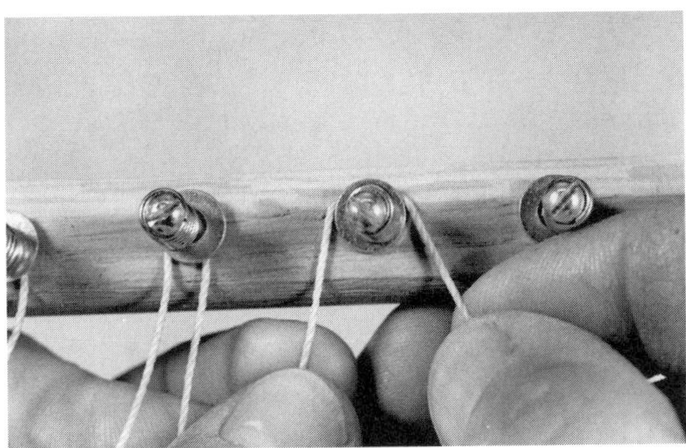

Detail of slipping the net cord onto the spring fastener of a homemade net starter. Loops have to be adjusted for length with a rod or mesh gauge.

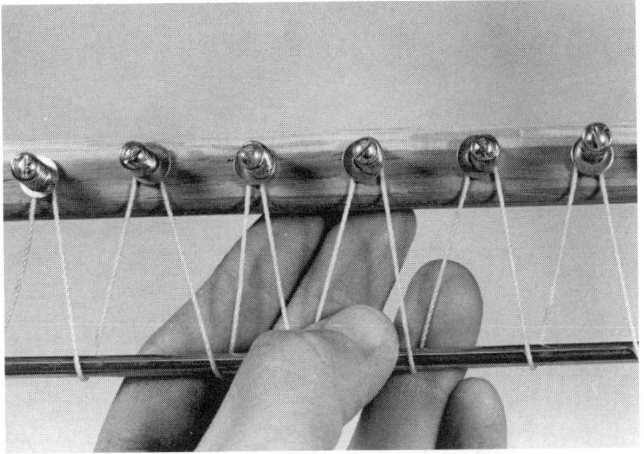

Adjusting and checking the loop length of the initial row of loops using a rod.

this knot does not slip. Then hold the mesh gauge so that its top edge hits this knot, take the cord around the mesh gauge from front to back, and bring the shuttle up through the second loop, back to front. Pinch the cord at this point while holding the mesh gauge with the cord tight around it. Take the shuttle around in back of the upper loop (now pulled into a V) and around in front of the loop just formed. Pull the knot tight to make a knot on the V of the upper loop.

Let's consider the steps. I find it easiest to work from left to right, bringing the shuttle up under the mesh gauge with my right hand, taking it through the upper loop with my right hand and crossing the hand over my left, pulling tight, and holding the taut cord with my left thumb. I then flip the loose cord above the mesh row, taking the shuttle right to left behind the two cords forming the upper loop and through the loose cord loop just thrown up by my shuttle hand. Pull the shuttle down and to the right and tight to make a knot on the upper loop. If the knot is going to slip, it will be at this point; the just-formed knot may slip below and off of the loop. Correct this when it happens, because the slipped knot will make for uneven meshes.

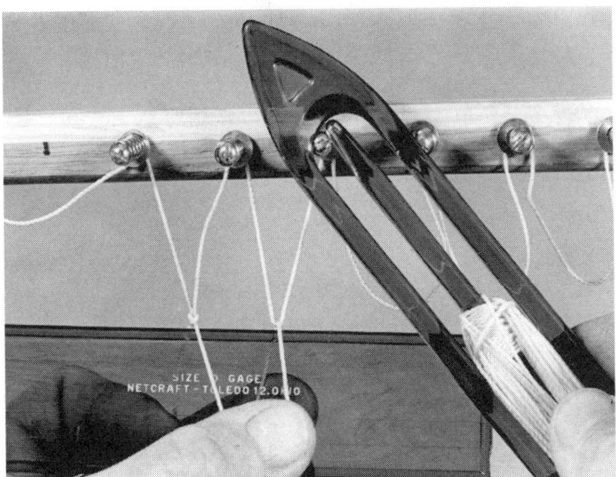

Beginning the second row of mesh loops using the mesh gauge and shuttle.

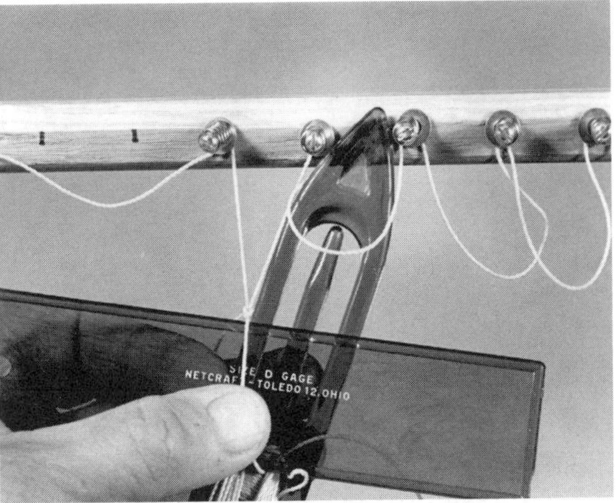

The shuttle is passed through the upper loop from behind and pulled tight to form the loop.

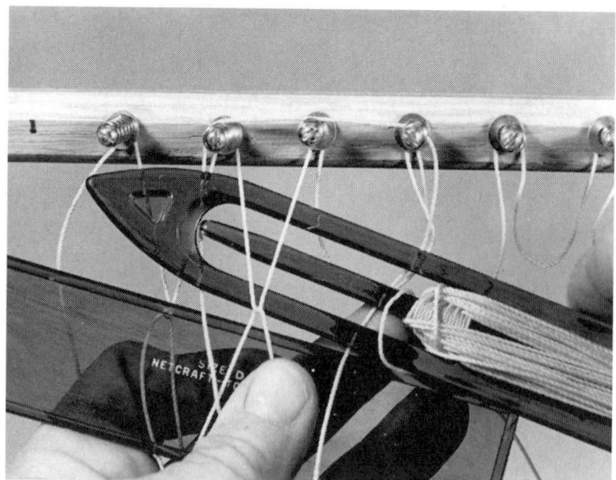

Once the loop is formed, the excess cord is held up and the shuttle passed in back of the upper loop, as shown, but in front of the loose cord.

The loop net knot ready to be pulled tight.

Another view of a net knot being pulled tight correctly.

Repeat this procedure with the adjoining loops all the way to the end of the net. Once at the end of the row, reverse the rod position so that you can continue working from left to right. If you are left-handed, you may wish to completely reverse these instructions.

If you make a minnow seine or square drop net, these steps are all that is required, although you may wish to add a perimeter row of double selvage or heavier cord to guard against wear. If you make a minnow net, you will need a heavier cord at the top and bottom for the floats and weights. For this, string the proper number of floats or weights onto a cord of the proper length. Use the standard netting knot to attach the cord to the top or bottom of the net, and use half-hitches on either side of the float or weight, around the cord on which they are strung, to hold them in place on the net. Plan equal distribution of the floats and weights along the net perimeter.

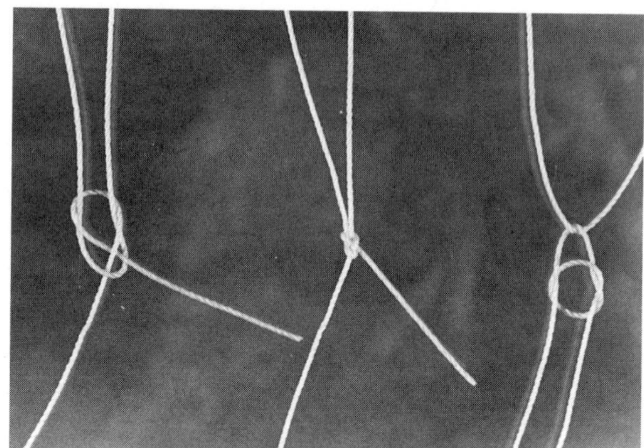

Good and bad net knots. Left, open view of proper knot; center, proper knot pulled tight; right, knot that has slipped and must be corrected.

If you make a landing net, you may wish to decrease the size of the mesh as you proceed toward the bottom. This is simple to do by beginning a new row with a smaller mesh gauge. Continue for several rows, decreasing mesh size as desired.

If you make a square or rectangular net and convert it to a circular landing net or live net, bring the two edges together and run a row of netting knots to join the two edges. To close the bottom,

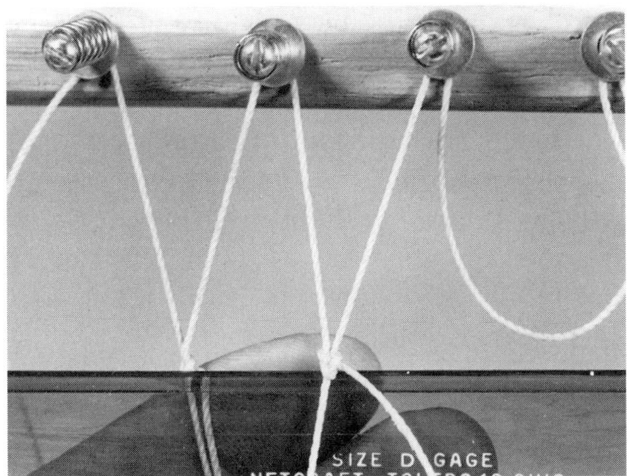

Tight net knot ready for the next loop and knot.

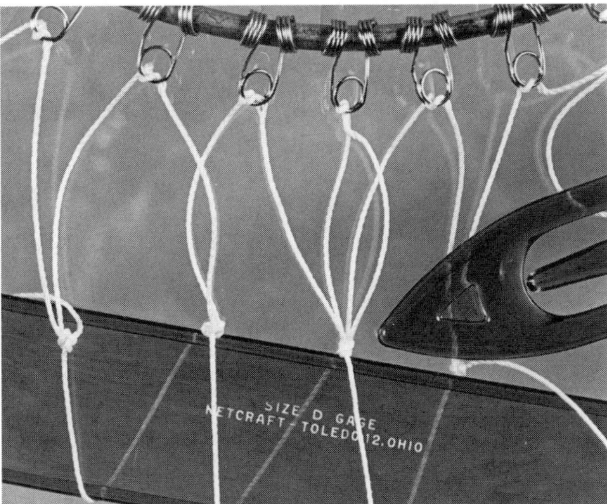

Net size can be decreased by knotting the two upper loops as shown. This is usually done several times in a single row, evenly spaced around the net.

use a brass or heavy-plastic ring and with a length of cord form a series of half-hitches around each loop and the ring to secure it in place. Half-hitch all the way around the ring, including all the loops, and then tie off with a square knot.

To attach the completed net to the frame, you must remove the hoop portion of the frame from the handle, thread the top row of loops or meshes onto the frame, and then reassemble the net. An alternative method is to use a heavy cord to loop through each top mesh and around the frame, going completely around the frame and tying off at the yoke (where the hoop meets the handle). Wood net frames, whether for long-handled boat nets or short trout nets, require a different technique. Most have small holes through which the top loop (mesh) is threaded. The loop is prevented from coming out by means of a cord that runs the outside perimeter of the net hoop frame in a slot cut into the wood. To make a bag for these frames, you *must* make the replacement bag with the exact number of loops as the number of holes in the frame, because each loop must be threaded through one of these holes.

To make a landing net, beginning on a circular frame is easier. For this you will want a frame to make the first row of meshes and to hold the net bag while you work on it.

If you work on a circular frame to make a circular or landing net, you will want to decrease the number of loops to form a tapered shape as you work toward the bottom. This is easy to do. Begin by running the shuttle through two loops of the upper row and then form the net knot. Do this systematically around the net, perhaps at three, four, or five equidistant points around the perimeter, depending on the total number of meshes in the existing row. If you start with a series of forty meshes, you could decrease to thirty-six by picking up two loops at four equidistant points around the bag (every ninth loop), decrease to thirty-five meshes by picking up two loops at five points (every seventh loop), and so on.

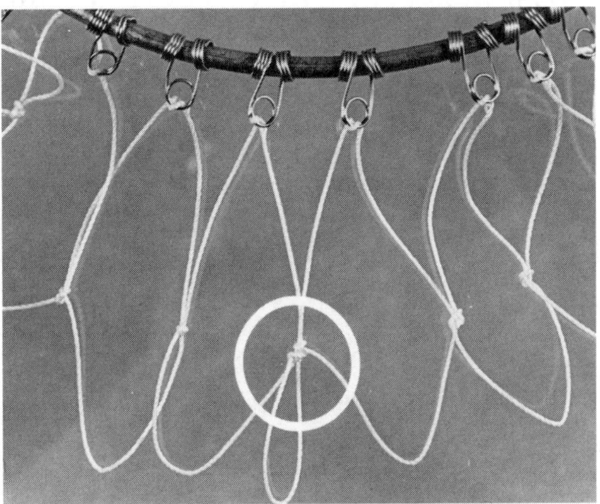

Nets can be expanded (as when making a live-bag net) by adding a second loop to the same upper loop as shown. Additional loops like this are spaced evenly around the net perimeter.

You can also widen a net by adding extra loops. To do this, tie in an extra loop between the regular loops. Make these equidistant around the net also. Thus you could go from forty to forty-four or forty-five or forty-eight, if desired. Although it is not mandatory to have these additions or deletions of loops exactly equidistant, doing so will make the bag more uniform and professional looking.

The final type of net discussed here is the bridge net. This is simply a net in a circular frame, which is suspended by three lines running to a main line. The net is dropped when fishing from high places such as bridges (thus the name), piers, bulkheads, and jetties. The best frame here is not aluminum but heavy steel rod, since you want the net to sink rapidly so that the fish can be led to it for landing. Often it helps to place pinch-on sinkers around the bottom of the bag to sink it and prevent it from ballooning in the water.

NET FRAMES

Woven nets can be used in several different ways. First, they can be used for replacing rotted nets in standard landing-net frames. Alternatively, they can be placed in discarded tennis-, squash-, and badminton-racket frames. Almost every house has an old racket or two somewhere that may be easily converted into a landing net.

Frame sizes of the three types of rackets will vary, and some odd sizes, such as in oversize tennis rackets, are also available. Of the three, the badminton racket is perhaps the most useful, since a tennis-racket frame is a bit heavy and the squash-racket frame is a bit on the small side.

First remove the webbing from the frame, and then cut the handle to the length desired. This will be necessary on any of the frames if you are making a short-handled landing net; it will not be necessary if you are making longer handled nets.

A cork fishing-rod grip (preformed, or built up as described in chapter 20), a plastic or rubber-foam fishing rod grip, or a plastic bicycle grip can be used as a new handle over the racket shaft.

Once it is finished, attach the new landing net to the frame by threading the net loops through the holes in the net frame (just as described for wood-frame landing nets) or by looping the net to the frame with lacing cord spiraled around the net frame.

You also can make your own wire rims or hoop frames. Use heavy steel or aluminum rod or wire. Steel rod comes in 3/16-, 1/4-, 5/16-, 3/8-, 7/16-, 1/2-, 5/8-, and 3/4-inch diameters, often in 36-inch lengths (limiting you to a net diameter less than 12 inches) but with longer lengths available. A hoop of this wire attached to a wood handle makes a fine frame. Or the entire net may be made with aluminum tubing.

The net frame must be bent into a circle, a job best accomplished with tube benders or a wood jig that can be made to bend tubing or steel wire to different radii. Tube benders for bending conduit for electrical work are available for 1/2-inch and 3/4-inch tubing, but these are really designed for the tightest possible radii for making sharp turns and bends. Although it can be accomplished, it would be difficult to make an even circle or a larger diameter with these tools.

Steel or aluminum frames should be sized to the strength you feel is needed for the size of the net and the weight of fish to be landed. The larger and heavier the fish, the stronger the hoop frame must be. The length can be determined by multiplying the chosen rim diameter by 3½ to 3¾. (The circumference of a circle is 3.1416 times the diameter—the additional length is used for the lugs that will bind the net-hoop frame to the wood or aluminum handle.)

The wood jig for bending net frames is not really worth making unless you will be constructing a large number of net frames or if you're making it for a fishing-club project to be loaned to members for their tackle-making needs. The jig consists of wood cut into a curve; the radius of the curve is determined by the size of the net you wish to make. You can use thick plywood (or several sheets of plywood); several layers, sandwiched, of wide shelving; a two-by-six or two-by-eight (or larger) piece of lumber; or similar scraps. Use a saber or band saw to cut the wood into an even curve. To bend the aluminum or steel wire or rod, clamp the jig into a vise and clamp one end of the hoop material to one end of the jig. A good way to do this is with a C-clamp. Bend the rod gently. Once it is bent sufficiently, remove the C-clamp, shift the rod, and bend a new section. Repeat these steps until the frame is bent into a circle.

Once the frame is bent into a full circle, bend the two ends at right angles to and away from the frame rim, making each straight piece 3 to 4 inches long. At each end of these pieces, bend short lugs inward to fasten into the wood frame or into a wood plug if the net is used with an aluminum handle. This will keep the net from canting sideways when you are landing a big fish. To make these final bends, you may have to clamp the wire ends in a vise, hammering over the short lug. It is possible to use a longer length of wire, bending it over the lugs and then cutting to length; although this is an easier method, it is more wasteful.

The same jig can be used to make hoop frames from aluminum or other tubing. For some years the Reynolds Metal Company, and more recently other companies, has marketed do-it-yourself aluminum materials, including tubing, strap, rods, bars, channel, and sheets. The tubing comes in 6- and 8-foot lengths in ¾-, 1-, and 1¼-inch diameters. Before choosing it for your hoop frame, make sure that the tubing will not create too much resistance when you swing the net under a fish for landing. Some specialty shops carry ½-inch-diameter aluminum tubing.

As with wire, choose the framing length by multiplying the diameter of the net by 3½ or 3¾ to determine the length of the rim material required. Take care not to bend the tubing into too sharp a bend. Tubing bent at too sharp an angle will deform or crack—examples of which can be readily found in old and abused aluminum-frame lawn furniture.

The smallest bending radii recommended for the three diameters of aluminum tubing are as follows: ¾-inch tubing, 6-inch radius; 1-inch tubing, 11½-inch radius; 1¼-inch tubing, 13-inch radius. If required, these radii can be cut in half by tamping damp sand into the tubing before it is bent. The damp sand prevents the tubing from collapsing.

Once the tubing is bent in a full circle, remove it from the jig, tamp damp sand into both ends, and place the tubing on a jig with a smaller 3-inch-radius circle (or bend around a large pipe or similar object of this size). **Note:** The sand should be damp—not so dry that it falls apart when cupped in the hand, but not so wet that water can be squeezed from it.

Plug the end and then bend the end of the tube in the jig, making the bend opposite the curve of the frame. Repeat with the other end. The two ends of the hoop frame will now be parallel so that they can be slipped into an aluminum handle. Knock out, and then wash out, the sand.

Flatten the inside edges of the frame's ends until they slip inside the 1-inch or 1¼-inch aluminum handle. Take care that you do not completely flatten and thus weaken the sharp bend you've just made. Once the ends of the frame hoop are securely in the handle, drill two ⅛-inch holes; each hole goes through the handle and one of the frame ends. Add self-tapping sheet-metal screws to the handle through these holes, and the frame is finished. (Unless you spiral cord around the net frame to hold the bag on the frame, add the bag before completing this step of fastening the hoop to the handle.) The screws make it possible to remove the hoop frame and add the net or replacement bags.

Cut the handle to the desired length. Nine-inch handles are standard for stream nets; 24-inch to 48-inch handles are standard for boats and canoes, the exact length to be determined by the fish sought, water, and conditions. The handle can be finished with an aluminum spring snap cap (designed for this with do-it-yourself aluminum), but I prefer a crutch tip, chair tip, or, best, a bicycle handlebar grip of the proper size. In addition to smooth aluminum tubing, there are also oval-, hexagonal-, and rib-embossed patterns. These patterns make a more attractive net handle, one that will less readily show scratches, and, more importantly, one that will provide a better grip than the smooth tubing.

Frames of wire or rod can be finished the same way, but you might have a problem in securing smaller diameter rod into a relatively large-diameter tubing. One solution to this is to use a short section of dowel as a spacer between the rod lugs and the internal diameter of the handle.

For this, first select a short length of dowel that will fit snugly into the aluminum-handle tubing, or cut a dowel down to size. The dowel should be about 6 inches long for most nets. To fit the hoop frame to this plug, cut, saw, or rasp grooves along two sides of this insert dowel the diameter and length of the net wire or rod. Cut an additional hole or depression (it can be drilled straight through the plug) at one end of the dowel to hold the short inward-bending lugs that will keep the frame from twisting. This hole must be the diameter of the net rod or wire.

Place the net frame into the plug (add the net bag first unless you intend to tie it on with cord), and slip the plug with the lugs in place into the end of the aluminum handle. This should be a snug fit, and you may have to hammer the plug a little to get it into place. Once the end of the plug is flush with the end of the handle, drill two ⅛-inch holes on each side of the handle over the plug area. Use four pan head sheet-metal screws to hold the plug in place. By removing these screws you can remove the hoop frame for bag replacement.

The same technique for making the wood plug can also be used to attach the hoop frame to a wood handle. In this case, however, you will have to use a sleeve of aluminum to hold the lugs in place in the wood-handle grooves, or you will have to wrap the handle/lug area to secure it. If the wood handle is the right size, you can use a sleeve of aluminum tubing left over from other projects or perhaps salvaged from old discarded lawn furniture. If you wrap, use light wire of brass, aluminum, or stainless steel and the same method as for wrapping a rod (see chapter 22) or whipping a rope.

Because the wire is stiff and harder to work than thread, it may be necessary to wrap the wire by securing the end in a vise and rotating the handle under tension to maintain pressure on the wrap. To begin the wrap, you may wish to use a small nail, wrapping the wire one or two turns around the nail before beginning to wrap around the wood handle and the frame lugs. Also, you usually cannot finish by pulling the wire under the previous wraps, as with rod wrapping, but must use a long staple or another nail or wood screw to hold the end securely.

CRADLES FOR BIG FISH, LONG FISH

A cradle is another type of net that is becoming increasing popular with anglers seeking big fish and long fish and those anglers interested in catch-and-release. You can use any kind of square or rectangular minnow netting material or, as described above, even make your own netting. If you are making this for catch-and-release, it would be best to buy rubber-coated netting to prevent damage and stress to the fish.

You can think of a cradle for fish almost like a stretcher for the injured. It consists of two long poles, one on each side, with netting attached to each side and center handles added on each side to aid in lifting the fish. These are particularly good for big and long fish such as pike and muskie, striped bass, wahoo, and the larger mackerel species.

To use a cradle net, submerge the net below the water alongside the boat, and lead the fish into one end of the cradle. Then lift the cradle evenly out of the water. These nets can be made in any size but typically are as large as 4 feet long by 3 feet wide or as small as 3 feet long and 2½ feet wide.

Attach the netting to the long handles by making a doublewide net, sewing or lacing it together, and then running both handles through the net, stretching it out to support the fish.

Another way to do this is to run the handles through the mesh in one side of the netting to hold it and then add a center handle. A good center handle can be made of a section of old hose, with a length of wide nylon strapping, or with a length of clear hosing. Use a hose clamp or series of small cable ties to secure the handle to the lengths of wood.

The handles can be made from long 1-inch diameter wood dowels or any straight length of rod.

SAND SPIKES, ROD HOLDERS, ROD RACKS, AND ROD CASES

ABS, RS, PVC, and CPVC plastic pipe, along with plastic conduit used in electrical work, can be used for a number of fishing-tackle items. You are not limited to the four plastics listed, but they will illustrate uses and applications in tackle making.

CPVC is chlorinated polyvinyl chloride pipe, PVC is a similar polyvinyl chloride pipe, RS is rubber styrene plastic, and ABS is acrylonitrile butadiene styrene. These materials are all rigid and will not rust, rot, or corrode. They are lightweight, easy to cut and work with hand tools, and are readily available at hardware and plumbing-supply houses.

Plastic pipe comes in different wall thicknesses. PVC, for example, comes in different "schedules" of 80 (very thick and strong), 40 (medium strength and thickness—ideal for rod cases), and 120 (thinner and ideal for lightweight rod cases and rod racks in boats). (There are also "SDR" sizes of PVC pipe, which are not generally found on the homeowner market but which include SDR 13.5, SDR 21, and SDR 26.) I like the schedule 120 PVC pipe for lightweight projects (rod cases, rod racks, tubes to hold lures in surf bags) and the heavier schedule 40 only for sand spikes and large-diameter rod cases for airline travel.

Diameters of plastic pipe range to 10 inches or larger, but the most useful sizes for tackle building are ½ inch to 6 inches, usually available at hardware, plumbing-supply, and lumber-supply houses. Both PVC and CPVC pipe come in these size ranges, including ½-, ¾-, 1, 1¼-, 1½, 2, 2½, 3-, 4-, 5-, and 6-inch pipe in both schedule 40 and 80. The lighter wall schedule 120 comes in all these but the 5-inch size. ABS, a black plastic pipe, is useful in sizes of 1½-, 2-, and 3-inch diameters.

Most of the pipe comes in different wall thicknesses made for specific purposes, such as meeting health standards for carrying drinking water, burial underground, or high temperature. For example, a 6-inch pipe that you might want for a large travel rod case will come in eight different types of pipe, each with a different wall thickness and each requiring different end fittings and caps.

The size of pipe needed will vary with the project. In all cases you need the pipe large enough to hold the rod. For example, with most sand spikes or rod racks, you will want 1½- or 2-inch-diameter pipe, but for some rods with large butt caps or large grip diameters, you may need 2½-inch diameter. For the sand spikes, the larger, heavier, schedule 40 pipe is best; for rod racks that just support rods, the lighter schedule 120 is fine.

Pipe is generally available in 10- or 20-foot lengths, but often hardware stores will sell you exactly the length you need. In addition, you might check the trash bins of plastic-pipe distributors or construction contractors. (Ask at the front desk first and explain your interest—many companies are understandably opposed to people just randomly rooting through their trash bins.)

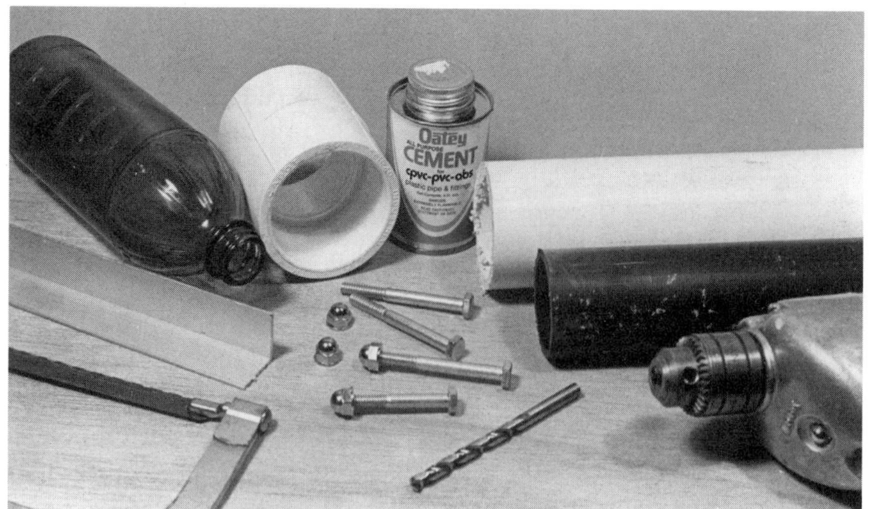

Tools and materials for making sand spikes, rod holders, rod cases, and similar items from plastic pipe include the pipe, some hardware, and simple saws and drills. A bottle is necessary for flaring the pipe for some uses, and PVC cement allows you to weld parts together.

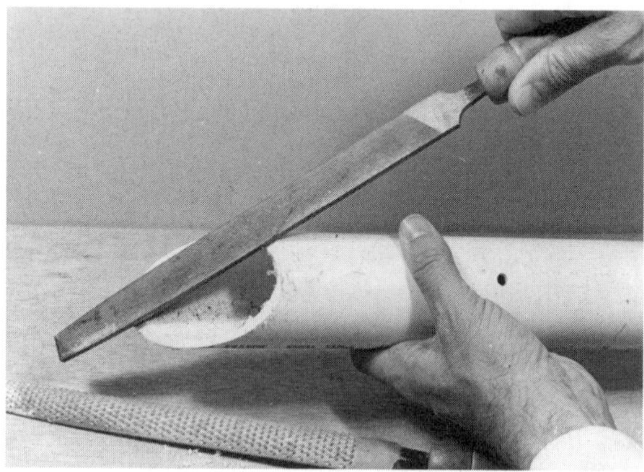

Rasps and files can be used for smoothing cut ends of pipe after sawing with a wood or hacksaw. Here a tapered cut has been made for the end of a sand spike.

Heat applied to the end of the plastic pipe allows flaring the pipe with a bottle. Use sufficient heat to flare the pipe—pressure is not necessary and should not be used. The towel is used for safety should the bottle break.

Working with Plastic Pipe

The basics for working with this material are simple. The pipe is easily cut with any type of saw, including wood or handsaws. While these will leave some rough edges (the coarser the saw, the rougher the edges), these can be smoothed with a wood rasp or half-round coarse file. Often it is best to flare the pipe for easier insertion of the rod butt into the sand spike or rod rack. To do this, you must first heat the pipe. Heat it over a stove or propane-torch flame, taking care to keep the pipe away from the flame, which could scorch it. You want the pipe hot and flexible with the heat, not burned. One way to do this is to hold the pipe to the *side* of the flame, not over the top of it. This will provide sufficient heat to soften the pipe without the flame that could char it. Rotate the pipe slowly to heat evenly. Be sure to heat only the end of the pipe you wish to flare. Heating the pipe over too large

Examples of collapsible sand spikes made in two parts for easy storage in a surf bag. The parts are reversed and clamped in place to use. One uses angled aluminum held in place with a hose clamp; the other (right) consists of telescoping tubing, held in place for use or travel with a through-bolt and wing nut.

an area will cause it to bulge and deform when you try to flare it.

When the pipe is hot enough to flex very easily, quickly press the end firmly onto the neck of a glass soda bottle you've chosen for its taper. Take care when doing this to hold the pipe well up and away from the bottle and to wrap your hand with a towel for protection in case the bottle should break. While I have never had this happen, it is always possible. Be prepared and protected for this possibility, even if it is a remote one. Also, make *sure* that the pipe is hot enough to flare evenly and with little pressure. Once the pipe end is flared properly, hold it in place on the bottle until it cools sufficiently to hold the flare. Plastic pipe has a memory and will return to its original shape and diameter if it's removed from the bottle neck while still hot. If necessary, repeat this process with more heat until the pipe is properly flared for your purposes.

Sand Spikes

Sand spikes are nothing more than tubular rod holders most often used for surf fishing but also suitable for other shore and bank fishing. Use 1½-, 2-, or rarely 2½-inch plastic pipe to make them. Generally 2 feet is a serviceable length for sand spikes, although commercial ones range from 20 inches to 36 inches. Five 24-inch-long sand spikes or four 30-inch sand spikes can be made from one 10-foot length of pipe. If you cut the pipe end (the bottom end) at a 30-degree angle, you will end up with sand spikes slightly longer than the above dimensions. For this, do not cut the pipe into four or five equal lengths, but instead alternate the angled (30-degree) and squared (90-degree) cuts so that there is no waste, except perhaps for one small section at the end. To get the sand spikes of identical lengths, measure and mark the pipe, but when making the angled cuts (30-degree), use these marks for the *center* of the cut and cut an angle across it.

Now flare the upper end of the pipe using the bottle technique. To complete the sand spike, drill a ¼-inch hole straight through the pipe about 12 to 15 inches down from the upper end. (You can make this hole higher or lower if desired—check your rods before drilling.) Insert a ¼-inch stainless steel or brass bolt through the hole. If possible make the bolt exactly the right length to just slightly protrude through the far side of the pipe, and use a cap nut (blind nut) with some glue or Loctite. The bolt keeps the rod from falling completely into the sand spike.

You can also make a longer sand spike of longer plastic pipe to place the rod higher, an advantage when fishing heavy surf where raising the

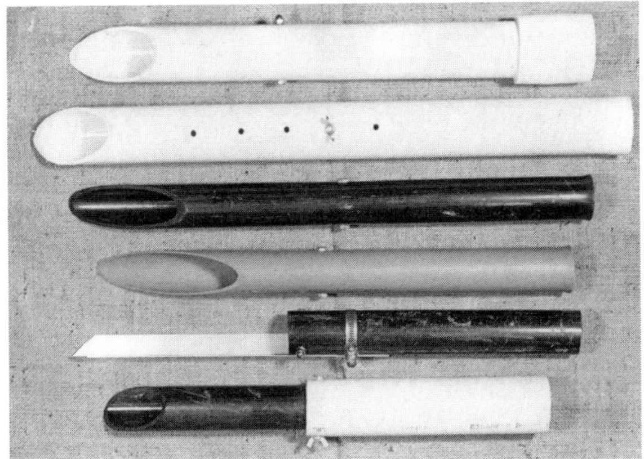

Different types of sand spikes using different kinds and diameters of plastic pipe with flared, straight, and collared ends. The second from the top uses a series of holes and a bolt and wing nut as an adjustable rod stop for different length rod handles. The bottom two holders collapse for travel or storage.

Rod holders on the front of a beach buggy. Such rod holders are typically made of plastic pipe, clamped to a board that is then fastened to the vehicle's front bumper.

line will help prevent the waves from dragging the line and thus the bait.

While it gets off the subject of plastic pipe a little, there are other ways of making sand spikes. Aluminum tubing of the right diameter (perhaps an old but damaged aluminum rod case?) can be cut at an angle, drilled for bolt placement, and used as a sand spike. Similarly, a 2-foot length of plastic tubing can be fastened to a 3- or 4-foot length of 1- or 1¼-inch aluminum angle using two hose clamps. (An alternative is to use a hose clamp on the upper part of the pipe and run the bolt through the pipe and the aluminum angle to secure the lower end.) Cut the aluminum angle at a sharp angle at the end to make a spike or point that can be sunk deeply into the sand. Such a sand spike will provide a high "reach" for the rod, as will long plastic-pipe tubing.

Rod Holders for Boats

Use the same techniques to make vertical rod holders for boats. Cut a 12-inch-long section of pipe and insert a bolt, long rivet, or similar pin to prevent the end of the rod from dropping below the holder. Because of the variety of boat materials and boat construction methods, no exact mounting method can be described. In some cases you may be able to run the bottom bolt through an aluminum or a fiberglass gunnel overhang. Other usual methods for the top of the rod holder, or for both ends, are to use pipe strap (available in metal or plastic—plastic is better to eliminate corrosion) or short lengths of aluminum strap or U bolts around the sides of the rod holder at two points. Drilling two holes through the sides of the rod holder (straight through both sides), enlarging the hole on one side to take a screwdriver, and screwing the holder to the boat (be sure you have a solid base for this) also works. Another good method for mounting such rod holders on vertical aluminum tubing in boats (grab rails, Bimini tops, etc.) is to use two hose clamps, each large enough to fit around both the rod holder and the aluminum tubing of the boat.

If you are going to use spinning tackle, cut and file a notch in the upper part of the holder for the foot of the reel to prevent it from swinging around. This is important both for boats and also for the front-mount racks on beach buggies. This will not interfere with carrying conventional or trolling rods.

Rod Holders for Beach Buggies

Surf anglers always like to have rods at the ready, but the 8- to 14-foot length of some surf sticks makes it hard to carry them in a beach buggy while roaming the beach in search of fish or birds working over bait.

Rod holders fixed to the front bumper of a beach buggy hold rods vertically and ready for instant use. ABS, PVC, or CPVC plastic pipe is ideal for this; choose a diameter (1½ to 2½ inches) suitable for the grips and butt caps on your rods. Lengths can be cut, flared, and drilled as above and attached to the front bumper or a removable board to make an excellent surf-rod holder. Up to ten rod holders can be rigged together. Leave several inches between each holder so that the rods and reels do not rub together while you are traveling the beaches.

There are several tips for making these. First, you can make them long enough to hit the reel at the upper end of the pipe to prevent the reel from swinging and hitting other tackle. You can cut a notch, as described above for boat rod holders for spinning outfits, or you can just cut a wide, deep V into the upper flared pipe to stabilize any rod and reel combination. Second, although you might be carrying rods on long pipes, run a ¼-inch bolt through the bottom end anyway. There might be a time when you wish to carry a reel-less spare rod in the rack that would otherwise drop straight through. Third, make sure the pipes and the basic rack are no lower than the lowest part of the bumper on the beach buggy. A lower board or pipes invite trouble by reducing clearance under the vehicle.

Slot cut into the upper end of a beach-buggy rod holder to receive the shaft of a spinning reel. This will prevent it from rotating and knocking into other reels.

A fourth tip, one that I picked up years ago from Ken Lauer, then a guide on the Outer Banks of North Carolina at Cape Hatteras, will prevent tangles of the bottom rigs and sinkers often used in the surf. Mount a small length (6 inches) of pipe, capped with a plastic pipe cap or drilled to take a through-bolt, to the base of the rod holder in between each pipe holder. Use this to hold the heavy sinkers used in surf fishing and prevent them from swinging around and possibly damaging rods, the car finish, and the windshield.

One easy way to mount the pipe and rod holders to the vehicle is to use a large 2 × 10- or 2 × 12-inch board and through-bolt the pipes to the board. A through-bolt through the bottom of the pipe and a U-bolt around it at the top work well. Use similar J-bolts or strapping to bolt the board to the vehicle bumper.

Horizontal Rod Racks for Boats

Rod racks for boats may be constructed using plastic pipe. The design is for horizontal racks on the sides of small boats, usually just below the gunwale or under an overhanging walk-around gunwale. For this, use light schedule 120 plastic pipe as a sheath for the tip section of the rod, much as you would use a sheath for a sword. Cut a length suitable for the rod you plan to carry in the rack, and flare both its ends. (**Note:** Flare both ends so that if you're racking a rod longer than the tube, you will have a flare to prevent catching the guides or tip-top as you pull the rod from the rack.)

For the handle end, use a wood or metal platform on which the handle can rest at the reel position. To keep the rods from bouncing around in rough water, use bungee cord (braided-cover elastic cord) in a loop to stretch over the platform and secure the handle. Another possibility that I have used is hook-and-loop fastener. The loop side is glued to the underside of the handle platform, and a long strip of the hook side is secured to the back of the platform, where it can be secured over all the rod handles.

Use a platform wide enough for the pipe sheaths you plan to use. Most boats will hold quite a few of these to carry rods ready-rigged. Even on my small johnboat I have six racks to a side (racks for twelve rods in all), arranged in two layers of three racks each.

Rod Cases

Plastic pipe can be used for rod cases, either individual-rod or large multiple-rod travel cases. The 1½- to 2-inch pipe is best for most individual rod cases (check handle diameter and guide size on spinning rods). For travel cases for multiple rods, you will want 3-, 4-, 5-, or 6-inch-diameter pipe. Schedule 40 is probably best, but if you won't be shipping rods by commercial airline, the schedule 120 will be fine and is much lighter in weight. For any size rod case, glue-on end caps are available for the closed end. There are several options for the removable end. You can get a threaded adapter, glue it onto the end of the pipe, and then use threaded end caps (sometimes called plugs) to close the rod case. You can also get a slip-on (really glue-on) cap and rout out part of the inside to take a riveted, hinged hasp and then rivet the staple onto the pipe. That way you can slip the cap on and off and lock it in place when required. This is most feasible with the larger diameter multiple-rod cases.

Whenever a permanent cap is required, be sure to use the appropriate glue for the plastic pipe you are using. Most often PVC or CPVC pipe is used, and a special glue (really a solvent) is available that works on both these plastics. Follow directions, use with plenty of ventilation, swab the pipe with the glue (a swab is provided in the cap of the glue can), and immediately add the cap. Hold for the few seconds the glue takes to cure.

An alternative is to obtain some of the square plastic pipe that comes in 4- and 6-inch sizes. These have a little bit more usable room than the round cases, but the square pipe is harder to get. I used this in the 4-inch size to make travel cases for four-piece 9-foot travel fly rods. I cut wood shelving the exact size necessary to fit into the base of the case and held this wooden bottom in place with eight pan head screws, two to each side. I made a similar size lid and hinged it with nylon strapping, held in place with Velcro hook-and-loop fasteners. (**Note:** If you want to use a lock, make sure it's one of the TSA-approved ones.) Of course you can make longer cases for three- or two-piece rods or for a few spinning rods. The 6-inch size of square tubing is also ideal for larger guide spinning rods.

Rod cases can be made from do-it-yourself aluminum tubing, available in a 1¼-inch-diameter and 6- or 8-foot lengths. By choosing the right length for maximum usage, you can get two or three rod cases from each piece of aluminum. Special aluminum end caps are available, or you can use the plastic slip-on caps available for plastic tubing (check for the proper size). One easy way to make a permanent bottom-end cap is to cut a small plug of wood sized to fit snugly in the aluminum tubing, secure it in place, and fasten it tight with three small pan head screws through the aluminum and into the wood. Paint the wood to seal and protect it from moisture.

Tools and materials needed for making one type of travel rod case.

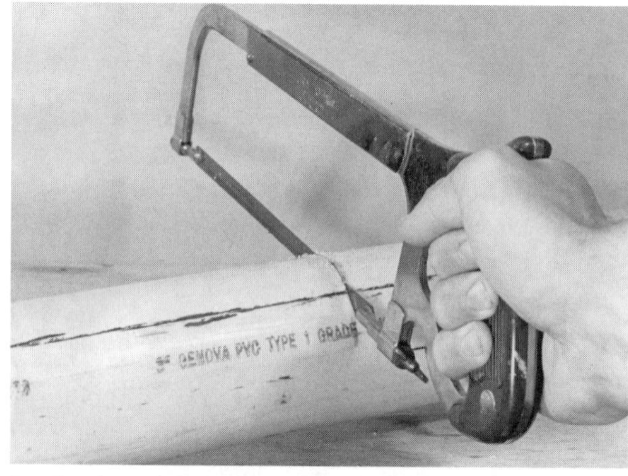

Sawing large-diameter PVC pipe for a rod case. Cut the pipe several inches longer than the longest rod or rod section you wish to carry.

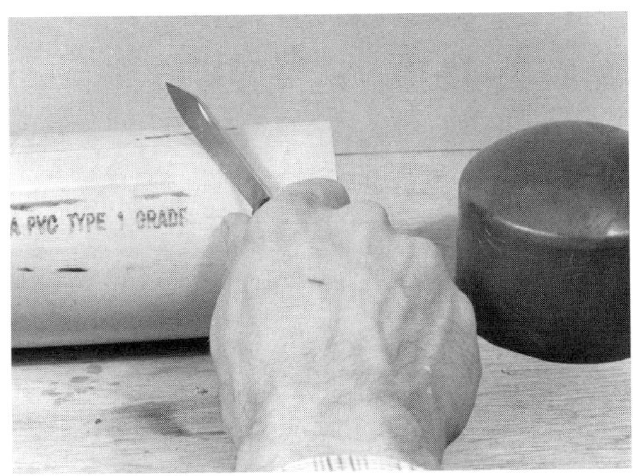

A slip-on pipe cap provides a removable cap—scrape the side of the pipe for added clearance.

Completed cap end, with lock hasp parts in place.

Use a rasp to cut space in the cap for the lock hasp. The hasp can be bolted or riveted into place.

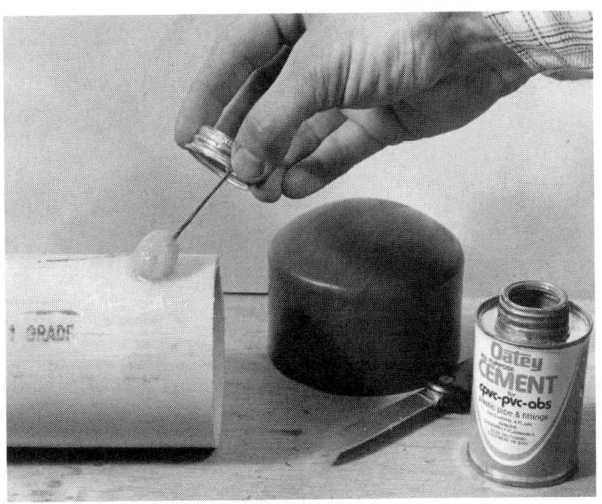

A second slip-on cap can be cemented to the other end using special PVC or other pipe cement.

Hasp in place, with foam used as a cushion on the end of the cap.

The main disadvantage of the aluminum tubing case is that the largest-diameter tubing generally available—1¼-inch—is only large enough for fly rods or ultralight one-piece spinning rods.

SURF BELTS

A surf belt is a belt for carrying all the items needed for surf fishing; these belts are usually worn over waders in high (deep) surf. There is no standard surf belt or even standard items to carry on it, although accessories might include a short surf gaff, small bags of plugs and tin squids, a fillet or bait knife, pliers in a holster, and a dehooker.

Surf belts can be made of almost anything. Often they are assembled from surplus or surplus-style armed-services belts that have quick-lock snaps to fasten in front. Often small surplus bags can be converted to surf bags for plugs and squids. Since these belts are wide, it is frequently necessary to jury-rig a method of holding pliers holsters on the belt.

Another and frequently seen possibility is the use of 1½- to 2-inch-wide nylon straps or belting, secured with the quick-lock snaps available in camping, mountaineering, and outdoor-equipment stores. Small belt bags and cases are available at the same stores, and the pliers holsters will usually fit on these narrower belts.

One way to convert a small bag into a plug bag is to use schedule 120 or lighter PVC or CPVC tubing as vertical compartments for the lures. Alternatives to the PVC tubing are 1¼-inch aluminum tubing and the rigid plastic sleeves used over electric candle lights, available from lighting stores.

SURF GAFFS

Surf gaffs are short gaffs used in the surf and are usually carried on a surf belt during wading. The gaff can be made in the same way as other gaffs but has a short handle—usually less than 12 inches long. Too long and it becomes unwieldy. It is best to have a coiled cord to attach the gaff to the surf belt. An old phone cord will work fine for this, but it should have a light breakaway attachment at one of the ends—either the belt or the gaff handle. That way, should the gaffed fish pull the gaff free of your hand, the attachment will break and you won't be pulled into the water.

Make a holster for the gaff by using a base plate of aluminum or plastic with a bolted-on screw eye to hang the gaff. A better alternative is to use hook-and-loop fasteners to secure the gaff hook to the base plate. Instead of hook-and-loop

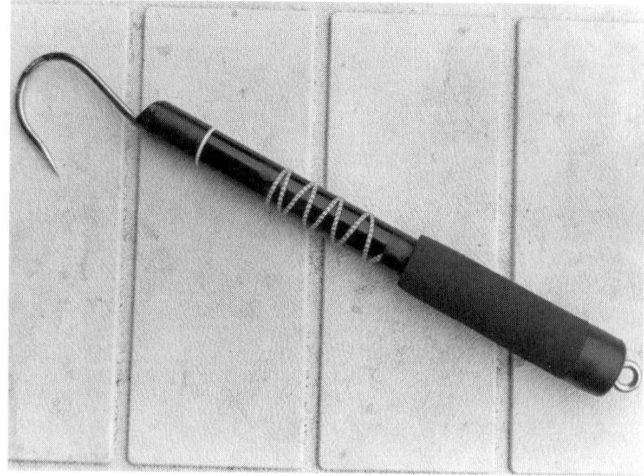

Gaff made by outdoor writer Charlie Most using a length of discarded rod blank, foam grip, and a gaff hook cemented into the end of the rod. The decorative wraps match his rods.

Making a long-handled gaff using a regular gaff hook placed in a dowel. Here the wood dowel has been marked for routing to hold the tang of the gaff hook; the dowel plug is then inserted in an aluminum handle.

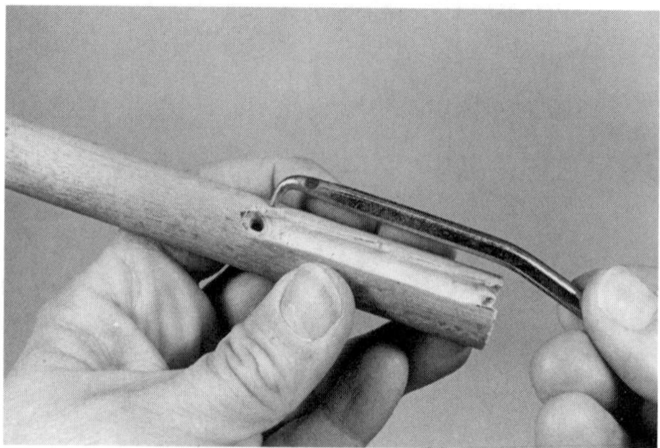

Routed and drilled wood dowel ready to receive the gaff-hook tang.

fasteners, you can use snap fasteners, available from sewing and fabric stores. In all cases the point should be sheathed to avoid accidents.

GAFFS

You can buy steel or stainless steel rods and wood handles and make a gaff from scratch, but I can't recommend it. Proper construction of such a gaff would require equipment for bending and tempering ¼- or ⅜-inch rod—processes generally not done by the home craftsman.

The best way to make a gaff is to buy a ready-made gaff hook and secure it to a wood or aluminum handle. Gaff hooks are made from both ¼- and 5⁄16-inch stock, are properly tempered, and have a built-in tang for attaching to the handle. Gaff sizes from 1½ to 2½ inches are commonly available from tackle stores and mail-order outlets.

Wood handles can be made from 1-inch or larger stock dowels, replacement shovel or hoe handles (hickory and very sturdy), or similar wood stock. Wood handles made and sold specifically for gaffs are also available. To make a wood-handle gaff, groove the gaff end of the handle, sizing and drilling the groove to fit the tang of the gaff. Notch or drill the end of the groove to fit the right-angle bend at the end of the tang. Then place the gaff hook into the groove to check for fit, add 24-hour epoxy glue to the groove and hole, and cement the gaff hook in place. Once it has cured, use a file to remove any excess glue from the surface of the handle. Wrap the tang area with stainless steel or brass wire, using a small screw or nail on which to wrap the wire as a starting point. Wrap tightly, and use a similar nail or staple to hold the wire once the wrap is complete. Often shovel handles used for gaffs and gaff handles are tapered at the end. If this is the case, begin at the gaff end or lower end, and wrap up the handle.

If you wish to begin the wrap by wrapping over the wire (as is done with thread in wrapping a guide in place), use a small nail or staple to hold the wire down as you begin the wrap under pressure. One way to maintain high tension on

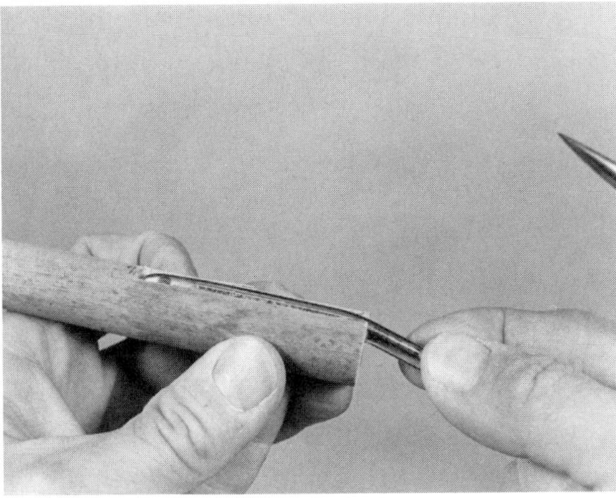

Gaff-hook tang in place in the dowel. The tang should be almost flush with the surface of the dowel as shown.

An alternative in building gaffs is to use a wood handle and wrap the end of the handle and gaff-hook tank with wire as shown.

After completely wrapping the tang, the wire can be held in place using a small screw as shown.

the wrap is to hold the end of the wire in a vise and wrap with your hands, leaning back against the gripped wire to create tension. To finish the wrap, work with tight tension up to about ten wraps from the end, use Vise-Grips or a C-clamp to hold the wraps in place (so that they do not loosen with the next step), and make ten loose wraps, sliding the end of the wire under these wraps. Then go back to the first of the ten wraps and wrap tightly, using pliers if required to get maximum tension. Work along all the wraps until you get to the end, and then use pliers or a vise to pull the wire end tight. Another, easier way is to use a long staple or nail to secure the end of the wire.

Another possibility to secure the tang, provided the end of the gaff handle is not tapered, is to use a short length (about 6 to 8 inches) of aluminum tubing as a sleeve over the end of the handle to hold the tang in place. For this, glue the tang into the groove, and use a block of wood and hammer to gently force the aluminum sleeve into place. Use one or two pan head sheet-metal screws or round-head wood screws to secure the sleeve in place on the wood handle. This is sort of a reverse of the method in which a wood plug is used in an aluminum handle.

Gaffs can be made with aluminum handles, using 1- or 1¼-inch smooth or embossed aluminum tubing. You will still need a gaff hook with a tang. You will also need a short length (about 6 inches) of dowel or hardwood that will fit snugly into the tubing. Groove and notch the wood to fit the tang, making sure the tang will fit into the groove so that it is flush with the outer circumference of the wood plug. Fit the tang into the wood plug, and start working the wood plug into the end of the aluminum tubing. It should fit snugly but not be so tight that it will risk splitting or deforming the metal wall of the tube. Now hold the aluminum handle vertically on the floor (with a block of wood under it to prevent scarring the floor) and gently hammer the dowel and gaff hook into the tubing until the dowel is flush with the end of the aluminum handle. Use a block of wood between the hammer and dowel

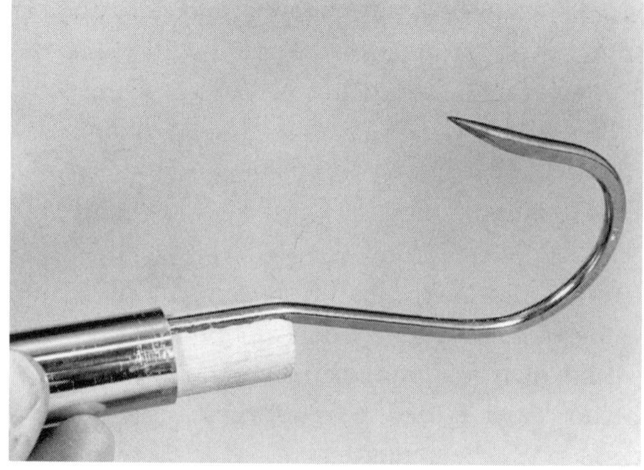

Gaff hook with the tang in a dowel being inserted into an aluminum handle.

One way to hold the dowel in the aluminum handle is to use several pan head screws as shown.

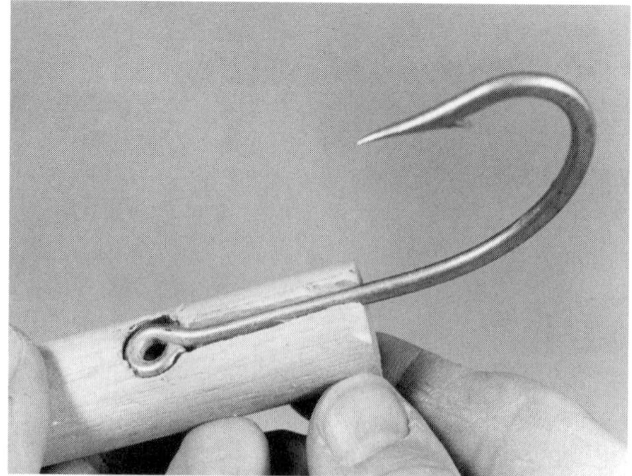

Dowel drilled and routed to hold a big-game hook as a gaff hook. An aluminum sleeve or wrap of stainless or brass wire holds the tang in place. Later the barb will be removed from the hook point.

to prevent deforming this plug. Once the plug is hammered home, drill the tubing and the wood dowel through at two points, with both holes at a right angle to the plane of the gaff hook. Secure the gaff hook with long solid-aluminum or brass rivets, sheet-metal screws (four are used—one at each hole on each side and each no more than half the thickness of the dowel), or wood screws used in the same way as the sheet-metal screws. If possible use noncorrosive materials as fasteners—stainless steel, brass, or aluminum.

Another way to make a gaff is to get a large hook and use this for the gaff hook. There are two possibilities for this. One is to get a needle-eye hook (commonly used in saltwater fishing), file the barb off, and use a wood plug as above. But in this case drill a hole the diameter of the hook shank through the center of the wood plug and hammer the hook shank into place. Before beginning, measure the length of the hook shank so that you know where to drill to secure the hook. If possible seat the hook so that the drilled hole that secures the hook will go across the grain to prevent the possibility of splitting the wood. Then gently hammer the wood plug and hook into the aluminum handle. Measure and drill a small hole to go through aluminum, wood plug, and hook eye. Insert a thin bolt or pin through the hole and hook eye to prevent the hook from pulling out, and the gaff is finished. (The same technique can be used to place this hook into a wood handle with an aluminum sleeve.)

The second possibility is to use a large size standard hook with a standard ringed eye. File off the barb. For an aluminum handle, groove a wood plug to fit the hook shank. Use a larger drill to drill a hole at the end of the groove large enough to receive the hook eye. Unlike the previous procedure, make sure the groove and the hole for the eye are deep enough to receive the hook and a pan head screw that will secure the hook into the wood plug. Place the hook in the groove and secure it with the right size screw. Then gently hammer the plug into the aluminum handle and secure the handle with four wood screws or pan head screws through four pilot holes drilled through the aluminum into the

Another way to make a gaff using a hook is to drill a hole in the end of a dowel, insert the gaff hook, and drill a hole through the dowel to hold a pin through the eye of the hook.

wood plug. This can also be done in a wood handle, but you will have to slip the aluminum sleeve over the hook shank first (before sliding it onto the wood handle) and then work the hook shank into the previously made groove. As a result, this type of sleeve is often shorter than normal.

The best handles for most gaffs are bike handlebar grips, available from bike shops and variety stores. These are best glued onto the handle using vinyl glue. For long gaffs—those usually 4 feet long and longer—two grips are often used, one at the end and the other a foot or two down the handle. For this second handle you can also use a bicycle grip. Use a razor blade to cleanly cut the closed butt end of the grip off, and use vinyl glue to secure the handle where you wish. Then add the end grip.

You can also use the foam grips (EVA or Hypalon) used for rod grips. These provide a good grasp, especially if they are glued in place, but they are more difficult to slide in place on the blunt tubing end. Instructions can be found in chapter 20 but basically consist of using an appropriate size dowel, tapered and lubricated, as a guide to open the tubing and slide the grip into place. Another alternative is to use a longer aluminum handle than is needed, taper it with a long angled cut, slide the grip in place, and then cut the aluminum flush (cutting off the tapered portion) and cap it.

Another handle alternative is to wrap heavy braided nylon cord securely around the handle to form a grip where and of the length you wish. To do this, wrap just as you would wrap a rod guide, beginning under high pressure to overwrap the end of the cord and then wrapping securely and tightly along the handle. Finish by wrapping over a separate loop of cord six or eight times, cut the end of the wrapping cord, tuck the end through the loop, and pull through. Since this will by necessity be a tight wrap, you may need to use pliers on the cord loop or fasten it in a vise to pull it and the cord under the previous wraps.

There are many variations to these methods, as well as to gaff styles and sizes. For example, some anglers use heavy-wall rod blanks for handles, choosing blanks that have a butt diameter similar to that of a gaff handle—about 1 inch. The gaff hook is placed in a wood plug, grooved for the tang, and the plug is glued into the small end of the rod blank. A lot of glue is necessary, because rod blanks are tapered and the plug can only be as large as the hole in the tip end. The plug should be pinned with a rivet, fastened with small flathead screws (so as not to impede the subsequent thread wraps), and then the tip end of the rod should be double- or triple-wrapped with heavy rod-wrapping thread (size E or EE) for hoop strength.

Gaff lengths are usually in even feet, but you can make them any length you wish. Short hand gaffs, sometimes called release gaffs for their purpose in some fishing, have virtually no handle at all and consist of only a hook in a short handle, most of which is covered by a bike handlebar grip. Longer surf gaffs are about 12 to 18 inches long, while boat gaffs will vary with the type of boat, the height of the gunwale, and the size and type of fish being landed. Typical lengths are 2, 3, 4, 6, and, rarely, 8 feet.

It is also possible to make a hand gaff or release gaff that does not have a handle. It is nothing more than a large hook fastened to a braided rope looped through the hook eye. To make one, file or grind off the hook barb and sharpen the point. Run the rope loop through the eye of the hook. Knot the ends or secure the rope by wrapping it down along the hook shank with lighter cord. The important dimension in this hand gaff is the size of the rope loop. It is *not* used to put your hand through—if you use it to unhook a tarpon, this could result in your being pulled into the water, an unpleasant experience at best and highly dangerous at worst. It is used to loop around your thumb: The rest of the loop goes around the back of your hand, with the loop and hook shank held in your hand. That way, should a fish threaten to pull you

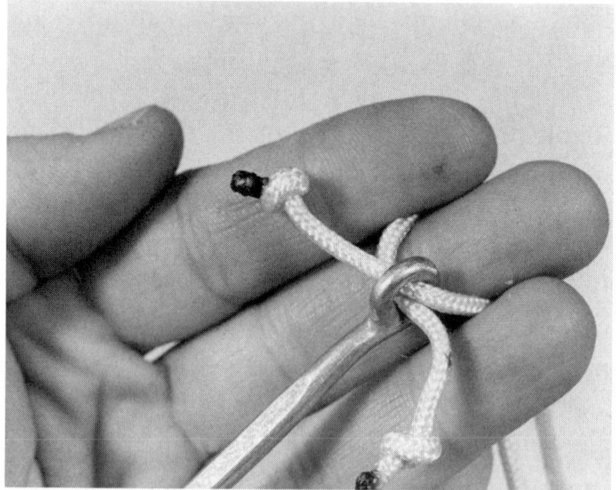

A simple hand gaff made with a loop of cord knotted through the eye of a big-game hook. The loop must be the right length, as described in the text.

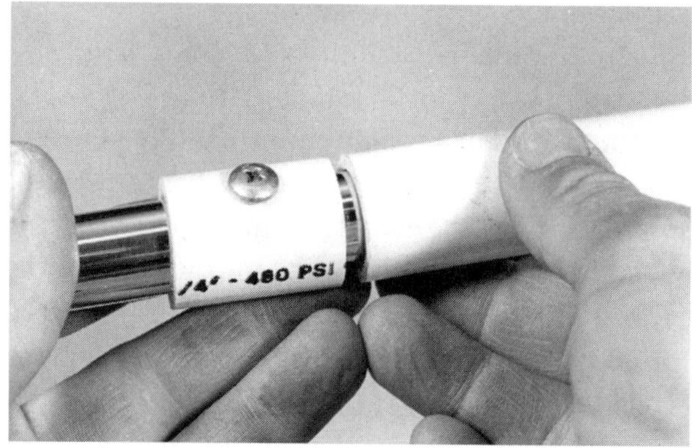

For shark gaffs, rotating handles prevent a spinning shark from twisting the gaff from your hands. One way to make these is to use a loose-fitting plastic pipe for the handles, with short lengths fastened to the aluminum handle as stops at each end.

out of the boat, simply opening your hand allows the fish to pull the gaff off your thumb. Naturally such a gaff, or any short gaff, should *never* be used to land or unhook any toothy critter such as a shark, bluefish, pike, muskie, or barracuda.

Sharks often roll when gaffed in the body (if you plan to release your shark, cut the leader). Some commercial gaffs are made with additional grips that rotate. Holding these grips allows the fish to twist, and the gaff will rotate without danger of ripping out of your hands. To make a gaff that will accomplish this purpose, use a long-handled gaff, preferably of large-diameter (1¼-inch) aluminum tubing. If you can get heavy-wall aluminum tubing for these big-fish applications, so much the better. Add the regular grips, but immediately adjacent to them add two additional grips. These are made by using PVC or CPVC pipe just large enough to fit over and rotate on the aluminum tubing. (Remember, these plastic pipes will vary in type and thus wall thickness and inside tube diameter.) An ideal inside diameter for the plastic pipe used on 1¼-inch aluminum tubing would be about 1⅜ inches. For better gripping it is best to make these grips a little longer than the average 6-inch-long bike grip—a length of 8 to 10 inches is best. In addition, cut two small sleeves from the plastic pipe, each about 2 inches long for each grip. Cut lengthwise through the wall of these short sleeves to remove just enough material so that the sleeve will fit tightly on the aluminum tubing when screwed in place. (Another alternative is to cut sleeves from the next size smaller plastic tubing, cut the wall lengthwise, and expand the pipe to fit onto the aluminum tubing. Any slight gap that results will not affect performance.)

Make sure the end cuts on these sleeves and on the rotating grip sections are completely smooth and clean. Assemble by adding one sleeve and screwing it in place with two or three small pan head sheet-metal screws. Add the rotating grip and then add and fasten the second sleeve. Be sure to leave about ⅛- to 3/16-inch clearance for easy rotation. Add the regular bike grip (with the closed end cut off) above this, and then at the end of the handle add one more rotating grip and one more stationary bike grip. The result is a long gaff (usually about 6 feet) that you can hold with the firm bike grips when sinking the hook into the fish, immediately grabbing the adjacent rotating grips should the fish start to spin. Often it helps to add nonskid materials (available in strips for bathtubs and for boat steps and ladders) to the smooth plastic grip for better grasping.

A completely different form of gaff, but one with the same purpose and function, is the "bridge gaff." While often called bridge gaffs, these tools are ideal for fishing from any high place where it is impossible to pull a fish up with the rod or to get a regular gaff to the water. Bridges, piers, some jetties, and bulkheads are all ideal spots for such a gaff.

A bridge gaff is nothing more than a series of gaff hooks connected to a snap that can be attached to the fishing line: The gaff hooks are connected to a rope to pull up the catch. There are endless varieties of these. Some consist of two or more hooks placed to face in opposite directions and attached to a snap link (available at hardware stores in different sizes); the snap link is also attached to a large fishing snap, shower-curtain clip, or spiral loop of wire that allows quick attachment to the fishing line. The gaff is lowered to the hooked and spent fish on a rope. The snap on the fishing line keeps the gaff hooks close to the fish. Once at the water level, manipulate the rope to get the hooks under the fish, use a quick jerk to hook the fish, and then pull it up to you. Some anglers leave the barbs on these hooks for a more secure hold; most file or grind them off (see also bridge nets).

TAILERS

Tailers are also used to land fish, but by catching the tail of the fish in a noose rather than gaffing it with a hook. Although this might initially seem less damaging to the fish than even lip-gaffing (if you plan to release it), a tailer can damage the tail of the fish, as well as the fish's muscles and ligaments, if it is lifted out of the water. Used in combination with a lip gaff to help stabilize a fish in the water to remove a hook, a tailer is usually safe for the fish.

A tailer is nothing more than a noose on the end of a handle (such as a lightweight gaff handle); the noose is held open so that it can be quickly slipped over the tail of a fish. The noose is held open by means of a short length of light flexible cable or braided rope with a ring at the end and a longer length of stiffer spring-like cable or spring steel that will bend into a U shape. This requires smooth attachment of the short length of flexible cable or rope to the end of the larger, stiffer cable or spring steel, something usually difficult for the home craftsman to accomplish. (The problem is with the *smooth* attachment of the two parts.)

An good alternative way to make a tailer is to bind the two cables together, allowing the lighter, more flexible one to extend well beyond the stiffer cable. Thus for an average salmon tailer, you would want about 3½ feet of lightweight cable and about 2½ feet of stiff cable or spring steel. Using the plug method described for gaffs, cut a piece of wood 6 inches long with a diameter equal to the internal diameter of the handle. For this landing device you can use lighter aluminum tubing; ¾-inch is fine. Most tailer handles are about 3 to 4 feet long, but you can customize to any length. Groove the plug for the two cables, running the groove along opposite sides of the plug. Butt the two cables and run them along the groove, around the end of the plug, and down the groove on the other side. This wraparound will hold the cables in the handle securely. Drive the plug into the end of the handle and secure with four pan head sheet-metal screws. You can also cement these parts into the end of a short length of strong rod blank scrap. Use heavy cord to wrap a "bump" of cord at the very end of any handle used. This bump will hold the ring in place when the tailer is in an open, ready-to-use position.

For the other end attach a bike grip, cord wrapping, or EVA or Hypalon foam rod grip

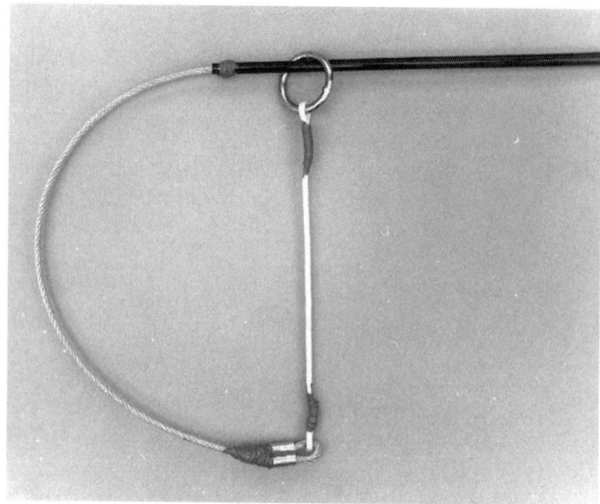

Tailers to land fish by the tail can be made in several ways. This one is made using an old hollow rod blank through which is run some cable, which is then secured to rope or lighter cable. Braided rope is used here; light cable would be used for sharks and large fish. The ring along the rope or cable slides tight and tightens around the fish's tail. The small built-up ball of thread on the end of the tailer rod serves as a stop to prevent the ring from prematurely sliding off the rod.

material. (See chapter 20 for details on getting the foam in place on the handle.) At the point where the cables exit the handle, wrap to the end of the two cables with cord or plastic (electrician's) tape, or secure with a clear plastic polyethylene tubing sleeve. Choose tubing that will fit over the two cables smoothly. (To slide the sleeve in place if the tubing is a close fit, you may have to tie a cord to the end of the long, lighter cable, run it through the tubing first, fasten it in a vise, and then pull the tubing against tension to slide it up to the end of the handle. Lubricating the sleeve or the tube with an antimoisturizer such as WD-40 will also help.)

Once the two cables are secured, you will have about 12 inches of light, thinner cable extending from the end. Attach a welded ring to the light cable by looping the cable around it and wrapping with wire, or use a sleeve (like an oversize leader sleeve for wire fishing-leader construction) hammered into place to hold it.

To use the tailer, slip the light cable through the ring to form a loop, and then slide the ring up over the doubled cables and the end of the handle and over the wrapped thread bump. This will cause the cables to form a rough D-shaped opening that may be slipped over the tail and body of the fish. To trigger the tailer, pull it quickly against the side of the fish once you have the fish's tail in the loop. This causes the ring to slip off the handle and slide down, closing the open loop as you pull on the tailer to catch the tail of the fish. If the loop slips too easily, you may wish to add a round-head screw to the end of the handle as a stop or detent to hold the ring in place until the tension against the fish pulls it free.

Alternate methods of making a tailer include using spring steel in place of the heavier cable to trigger the tailer and telescoping the spring steel (or heavy cable) into the body of the handle for travel and storage. The basics of this telescoping method are to use two wood plugs. One wood plug is made small enough in diameter to slide along the internal diameter of the handle, with the spring steel and/or cables securely fastened to (not just looped over) the plug. The second, shorter plug has a hole through its center loose enough for the cables to run through and is fastened with screws to the handle. It serves as a "stop" for the sliding plug to keep the cables from coming out and to hold the tailer in an open position.

PRIESTS

A priest is nothing more than a club used to kill a fish. While perhaps sounding brutal, this tool is actually humane. If you plan to release a fish, it should not be harmed and should be released immediately—preferably by unhooking it without taking it out of the water. If you plan to keep a fish, it is far kinder to kill it immediately and get it on ice (or, if permitted, gut or fillet it and place on ice) than to allow it to suffocate in the water on a stringer or out of the water in a cooler or fish box or on the deck. (Some regulations prohibit filleting fish on the water, so check local laws before doing this.)

To make a club, there are a number of possibilities, all easy to accomplish. Hardwood turned on a lathe to your personal design is one possibility. Other, simpler, ones include using a broken tool handle (shovel, rake, or hoe) cut to length, smoothed, and sanded. For added weight drill a cavity in the end of the priest; run a pin, nail, or screw or two into this open cavity from the outside; and then fill it with molten lead. A few ounces are generally plenty, and the screws or pins will hold the lead in place. Do *not*—repeat, *not*—hold the priest while filling it with molten lead. Instead place it in a hole in the backyard, in a sand pile, or in something equally sturdy. Then pour. (Be sure to first read and then follow all the safety tips and instructions for melting lead in chapter 4.)

A similar alternative is to use a short length of pipe or aluminum tubing, plug all but a few inches at one end (with sand or a cork or wood plug), add a screw or two to keep the lead from sliding, and fill the space with lead. Add a bike handlebar grip to the other end for a handle.

WADING STAFFS

A handy item for any river angler, a wading staff is easy to make using the same do-it-yourself aluminum tubing previously mentioned. One-inch tubing is best; the length is dependent on your individual preference and height. I am 6-foot, 1-inch tall and find 55 inches a good length. Parts needed for a wading staff include 1-inch aluminum tubing, a heavy-duty crutch tip, a bicycle handlebar grip, 30 inches of plastic or nylon strap, short wood plugs or dowels to fit the aluminum tubing, screw eyes, 4 feet of light braided rope (about ⅛-inch diameter), and a dog leash or French-style snap.

Use a hacksaw to cut the aluminum tubing to length. If you have any doubt about the proper length, cut it long—it can always be shortened later. Add the crutch tip to one end. (The best type of crutch tip, with a metal plate molded in place to prevent the aluminum tubing from cutting through, is available from some medical-supply houses and larger drugstore chains.) Cut a 4-inch length of wood

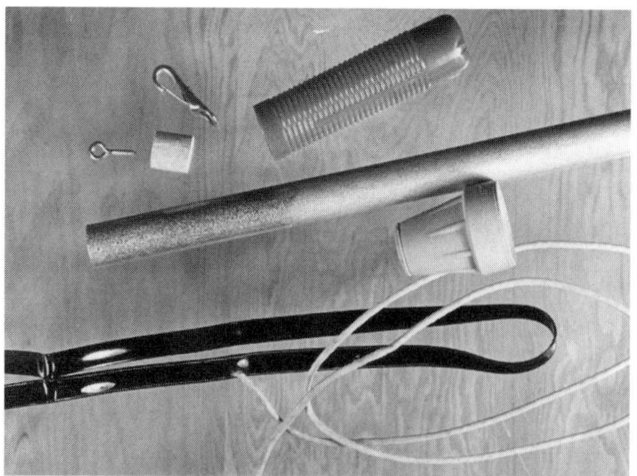

Materials required for making one type of wading staff.

To add a strap handle to the wading staff, use a cork or small wood dowel that has been cut along one side for the strap, pushed into the end of the aluminum shaft.

dowel to fit snugly into the other end of the tubing, and plane one side to wedge the strap into place. Take 2½ feet of strap, fold it in half, and place it along the flat side of the dowel as the dowel is tapped into place in the tubing. Inserting 3 inches of the strap ends into the tubing will leave enough strap for a serviceable loop extending out from the handle.

Tap the wood dowel home, and fit the 1-inch-diameter handlebar grip. Since the grip will have to fit over both the aluminum tubing and the plastic strap, soak it first in hot, soapy water to soften and lubricate it for an easier fit. Glycerin and special aerosol-spray lubricants will also help the grip slide onto the tubing.

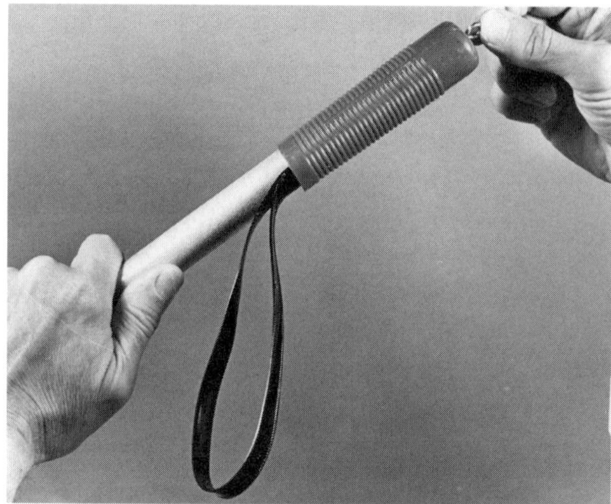

Add a bicycle-type grip as a handle on the wading staff. A screw eye added to the top will allow you to attach a tether to prevent loss. A crutch tip goes on the other end.

Add a screw eye to the top of the staff through the hole in the plastic bike grip and into the wood plug.

Attach one end of the 4-foot cord (⅛-inch parachute cord, available from surplus stores, works well—polypropylene rope will float and is good for this reason) to the screw eye or to the plastic-strap handle, if you desire. Tie the other end of the cord to the snap. A dog-leash snap is okay, but a French snap, which opens at the center, is far easier to use when fishing. The cord will prevent the wading staff from floating away while you're fishing, and the snap will make it easy to secure the staff to clothing such as a fishing vest.

An alternative is a modified ski pole with the ring and webbing removed from the bottom. For certain river bottoms, the sharp pointed end holds better, and some anglers like the molded handles with which most ski poles are equipped. Ski poles come in different lengths and often can be found in secondhand thrift stores like those of the Salvation Army and Goodwill. As with any wading staff, use a cord and snap to attach it to your clothing.

A good alternative to the cord attachment to your belt or wading vest is to use one of the heavy-duty snaps made by HammerHead Industries.

These are like Zingers on steroids—heavy-duty examples of those spring pull-cord tools by which fishermen (mostly fly fishermen) attach small items to a fishing vest.

With a heavy-duty HammerHead snap, you can secure a wading staff, lock the cord in place where you want, or allow the cord to run back and keep the wading staff next to you when not in use.

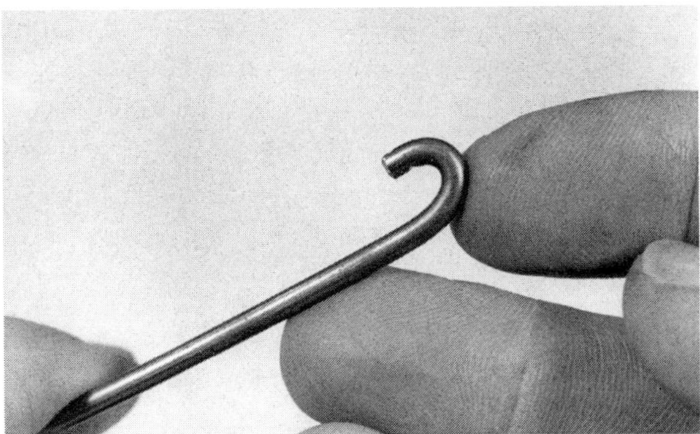

Make a dehooker by using steel or brass rod and bending one end into a tight J shape.

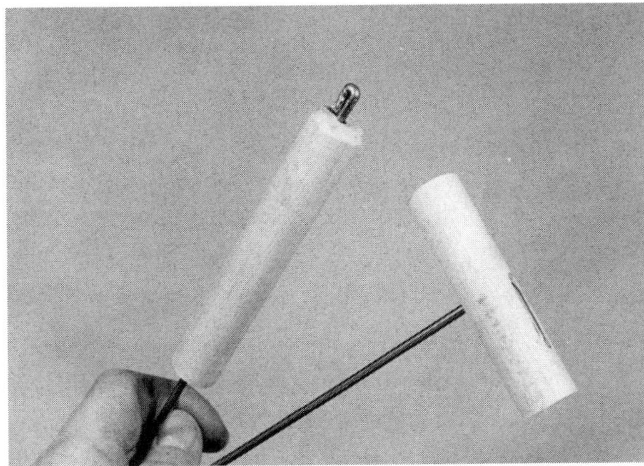

Two types of handles on dehookers. The T shape gives a better grip for use with big fish.

DEHOOKERS

Several types of dehookers are possible. They can be nothing more than a stick, forked at the end, used to catch the bend of the hook and lever it backward out of the fish's mouth for removal. Such dehookers (often called disgorgers) can be made by notching the end of an old toothbrush handle (for small fish), a ¼- or ⅜-inch dowel for larger fish, or the end of a thin but sturdy strip of any metal.

A better disgorger for quick hook removal, provided the hook is not too deep, is to use a length of round-stock steel or brass rod, bent into a sharp J shape. Welding rod is ideal for this, since it is strong but also bendable. Obtain a foot or two of steel or brass rod ⅛ to 3⁄16 inch in diameter or a length of welding rod. (Base the diameter on the rod material and size of fish to be caught.) Use a vise and pliers to bend a sharp, small J shape in one end of the rod. This should be very small, with a gap no larger than about ⅜ to ½ inch at most, or large enough to allow passage of the hook eye.

Secure the other end of the disgorger into a handle. There are several ways to do this. One method is to drill straight through the end of a 1- to 1¼-inch dowel, 6 to 8 inches long, using a long aircraft or electrician's bit. Run the straight length of rod through the dowel, and make a bend in the rod at the end.

Another method is to use a similar dowel 4 to 5 inches long and drill straight through the center of one side. Drill a second blind hole alongside the first hole. Insert the rod through the first hole, and make two right-angle bends to fit the end of the rod into the blind hole. Add glue, and seat the rod in place.

You can also bend the rod into an elongated D-shaped handle by bending the rod back on itself with three right-angle bends. Wrap the end once around the main shaft of the dehooker, or weld or solder the end to the main shaft.

John Page Williams of the Chesapeake Bay Foundation has come up with an improvement on this D-shaped wire model. He makes the same basic shape of dehooker with the rod and then adds a section of flat insulation foam to the center part of the handle. This makes the dehooker floatable so that you can't lose it while using it. To keep from losing the insulation, wrap it and the wire rod part of the handle with tape. Williams uses duct tape, but electrician's or masking tape would also work fine. This all takes no more than a few minutes to make.

Dehookers with wood handles are easier to hold and use, particularly with heavy fish. However, the flat all-metal rod model takes up less space in a tackle box or gear bag.

To use the dehooker, lift the hooked fish into the air, slide the J-shaped hook down the line to the bend of the hook (or grab the bend of the hook with the dehooker), and hold the hook while you pull the line and hook down. Often the weight of the fish will pull the hook free. If it doesn't, a sharp jerk will snap the fish free of the barb and you can drop the fish into a fish box or back into the water.

SNUBBERS

Used when trolling for trout and salmon with long lake trolls, snubbers are nothing more than surgical latex tubing secured with braided line running through the center and a swivel or snap swivel on each end. The line is connected to the swivels at the ends. In use, snubbers are placed between the long lake-trolling rig and the short leader/lure to take up some of the shock of the strike of a strong fish.

To make a snubber, first gather the parts: two swivels or snap swivels, a 6-inch length of light surgical tubing, 15 to 20 inches of heavy (fifty- to one hundred-pound test) braided fishing line, and some light copper or brass wire. Any size surgical tubing can be used; thicker tubing will require a stronger pull (strike) to reach full stretch.

First tie the braided line to the eye of one swivel or snap swivel using a clinch, improved clinch, or similar knot. Use a long upholstery needle or fine doubled wire to run the end of the braided line through the 6-inch length of tubing. Pull the tubing up close to the eye of the swivel, slip it over the swivel, and wrap and twist light copper or brass wire around the tubing and the covered swivel eye to hold it in place. Now pull the tubing out to a full stretch, allowing the braided line to run freely in the center of the tubing while doing so. Pinch the end of the tubing to hold the line and release the tubing.

Tie the loose end of the braided line to the eye of the second swivel. If some slack occurs while you pull the knot tight, adjust for this before tying the knot by pulling some of the braided line out of the tubing. Trim any excess. Pull the rubber tubing out to full stretch again, and slip it over the second swivel eye. Secure the tubing around

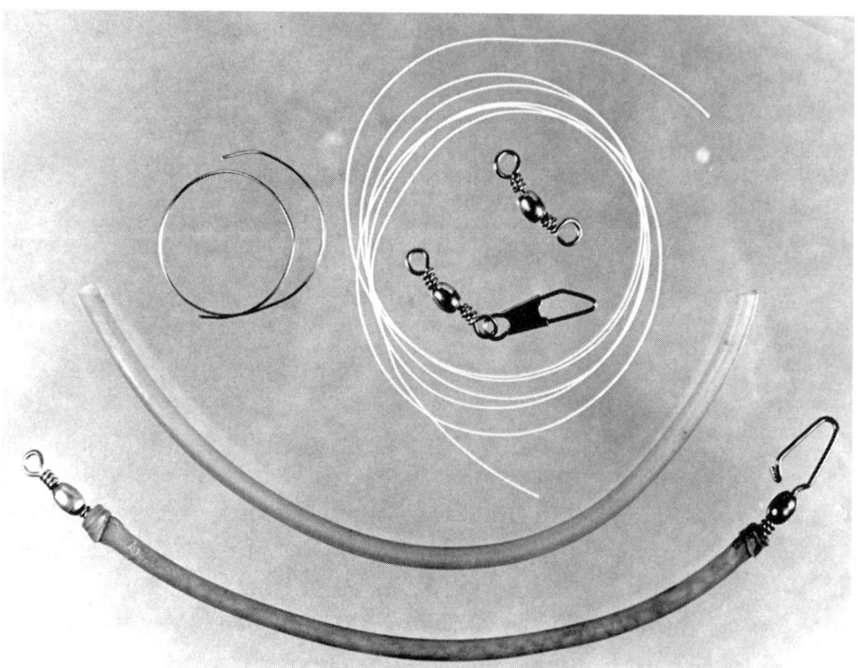

Materials for making snubbers include surgical hose, Dacron line, snaps, swivels, and wire. The line is threaded into the surgical hose and tied to the snaps and swivels, which are fastened to the hose with wire.

the eye with copper wire. Fold the ends (about ¼ inch) of the tubing back over the wire wrappings to protect them, and the snubber is ready for use.

To use, connect the snubber by means of the swivels to the line and the leader holding the trolls. The purpose of this is to lessen the shock of a strike when a fish hits the troll. The line in the middle of the snubber serves as insurance to land the fish should the surgical hose pull free from one swivel or break.

FISHING MARKERS

Fishing markers have a number of uses in both fresh- and saltwater fishing. Essentially a marker is a float with a line and sinker or weight attached. Admittedly, some types can be bought cheaply enough, but you can make your own if you so desire. Markers serve to mark channels, fishing reefs, stream bottoms in man-made lakes, drop-offs, points, breaklines, FADs (fish attractor devices), and other fishing spots—most located first with a depth-finder.

Carried on a boat, markers make it easy to mark a fishing spot temporarily because they can be thrown out immediately once you spot fish or see them on a depth finder. This marks the chosen spot, and the attached line unwinds to hold the marker in place. In fresh water it can hit the bottom to hold the marker in one spot, while in saltwater fishing it might drift but will still mark the area where fish were spotted. Once you are through fishing, they are picked up, rewound, and saved for the next trip.

Freshwater markers are smaller and lighter than those used in salt water because the area covered is usually smaller and the chop on the water usually less. The buoy or marker for saltwater fishing must be larger, both for buoyancy and easy visibility.

There are many ways to make markers. For a freshwater marker, cut a 1 × 4 × 5-inch board or similar size plank into an H pattern. The center of the H is used to wind the cord, and the "wings" prevent the marker from unwinding further once the sinker hits the bottom.

The dimensions of the H depend on individual preference. However, if you make the H too big or cut the center core too narrow, you will need a heavier sinker to unwind the board.

Once the board is cut out, paint it white, fluorescent orange (over a white base coat), or a similar bright color that will contrast with the water. Tie on and wrap light nylon cord on the center bar of the H, wrapping on enough cord to allow the sinker to hit the bottom of the deepest hole of any fishing water. For freshwater fishing, this is usually 25 feet for ponds and shallow rivers; 50 feet in deeper ponds, rivers, and shallow lakes; and 100 feet in the deepest lakes. Tie a sinker of several ounces to the end of the cord to complete the outfit. Since these are simple to make, it is best to cut out several at once, in case you have to mark several fishing spots in one area, or to mark the border of a breakline, channel, or streambed.

For saltwater markers, a larger, more visible buoy is desirable. One-half to 1-gallon bleach or similar household-product bottles serve well as buoys. Clean off the labels, rinse out the bottle, and glue the cap in place. If the bottle has a handle, tie the nylon cord to it and then wrap the cord around the middle of the bottle. (Otherwise, fasten the cord securely around the middle of the bottle and glue it in place.) Depending on the depth of water fished, this line may be from 50 to 200 feet in length.

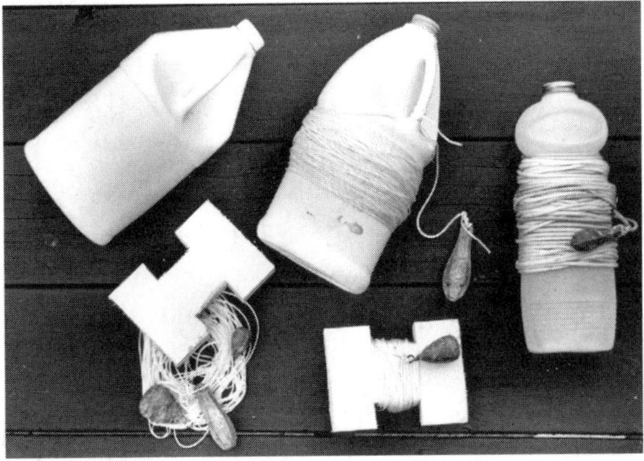

Examples of various types of fishing markers made from bottles and scraps of wood cut into H shapes.

The one disadvantage of this method is that, because some bottles are not flat, the entire cord unwinds once the bottle is thrown out of the boat. For this reason, do not make the cord any longer than necessary. However, even with the entire cord unwound, the cord angle that is caused by tides and wind will not be enough to misrepresent the marked location significantly. Because of the larger size and more rugged intended use of saltwater markers, a heavier sinker might be necessary to hold bottom.

One solution to the problem of the cord completely unwinding is to use a flat bottle that will be less likely to turn over once the sinker hits bottom. These flat bottles are usually smaller than round ones—about 1 quart is a common size—but white ones will still be readily visible and will float high enough to be seen.

An alternative is to take one of the ½- to 1-gallon round bottles and partially fill it with wet plaster, concrete, or gravel mixed with glue. Run a couple of large screws through the side of the bottle, fill it about one-fifth to one-quarter full with the material you've chosen, and turn it on its side with the screws down so that the material covers the inserted screws. Allow the mixture to cure. The screws will prevent the weight—which serves as a keel—from rolling. Coat the screws on the outside with silicone sealant to prevent leaking.

You can also make markers from the dense closed-cell foam used for packing delicate instruments. The brittle type of foam will break with time, but the flexible rubbery type (such as Dow Ethafoam) will last forever. It can be found as supports and packing shims for TV sets, DVD players, and other electronics and is easily cut to shape with a sharp knife.

Still another method is to buy two 3-inch-diameter polystyrene balls (though other sizes can be used) and drill a blind hole in each to accommodate a short length (4 to 6 inches) of dowel or broom handle. Use epoxy glue (other glues might "melt" the plastic) and glue one ball onto each end of the wood dowel. To give the marker an off-center weight to keep it from unrolling cord completely, drill two additional holes in the foam balls (both holes at the same relative position on the balls) and glue in ½- to 1-ounce lead weights. Drill a small hole through the center of the wood dowel, and insert nylon cord, wrapping it around the wood dowel. Add a sinker or lead weight at the end of the cord that is sufficient to cause the marker to roll when it is thrown into the water. If desired you can paint the marker, but use caution because some paints will dissolve some foam plastics. If possible use an epoxy paint.

An important tip on weights for any markers: Although you can use lead sinkers, old sparkplugs, or other such weights for markers, it's best is to use a weight than can be attached or wrapped onto the marker to prevent the cord from becoming loose while the marker is stored. You can use pure lead and pour out a thin layer of it or fill a small discarded cookie sheet to a depth of ⅛ inch. Allow the lead to cool, and cut the lead into strip about 1 inch wide by 4 to 6 inches long. These will be similar to the strips used in some commercial markers and will wrap around the center core. A second method is to obtain (or mold) hollow pencil lead, such as that used for West Coast steelhead and salmon fishing. Run a screw eye into the hollow core, and cut off the length you need for the marker weight desired. Since this material comes in several diameters, you can adjust weight by varying its size. (Before molding lead strips or pencil-lead weights, be sure to check the instructions, general tips, and safety rules in chapters 4 and 5.)

LURE RETRIEVERS

Lure retrievers, used to retrieve lures caught on the bottom, can be made in a variety of ways. All involve a weight to get down to the bottom, some way to temporarily attach the retriever to the fishing line to act as a "trolley," and a heavy line to pull up the lure.

One of the best retrievers is one that I designed years ago. It consists of the attributes just listed, with some chains on the weight to help catch and

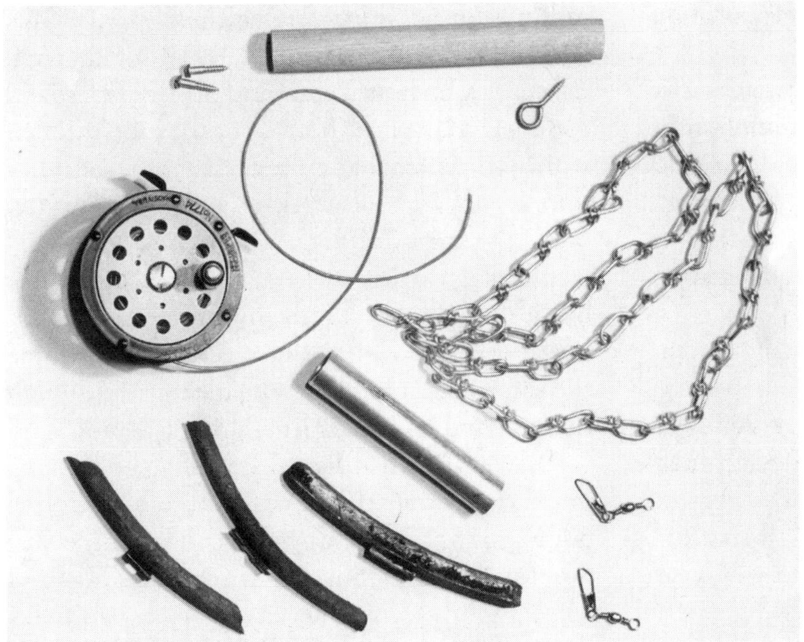

Tools and materials needed to make plug retrievers.

Drilling the aluminum tubing to accommodate the chain.

Wrapping the hole openings with tape.

Slipping the chains into place in the drilled holes.

Pouring the plug retriever full of lead. Note that the plug retriever is placed in a can of sand and that the top link of chain is held in place with a nail.

pull the lure free. The heavy line is spooled on an old fly reel for storage.

To make this retriever you will need 4 feet of light chain, a short length of aluminum tubing, a little lead, some heavy nylon cord, part of a broom handle, and a cheap or discarded reel. Construction is simple. Take a 4-inch length of ¾- or 1-inch aluminum tubing and drill two holes completely through the sides. Make each hole large enough to thread the chain through. (I like # 3 Inco Coil chain, a double-loop weldless wire chain, but similar-size jack chain or other types will also do. For this chain, a ⅜-inch hole is just about right.) Make the holes at right angles to each other and separated so that the chains threaded through the tubing will clear each other.

Drill two smaller holes in line through one wall of the tubing. Cut the chain into three equal 12- to 14-inch lengths. Run one length of chain through the center of the tubing, leaving one link exposed at the upper end. Then run the other lengths through the larger holes so that you have a total of five chains hanging down from the lure retriever (one from the center tube and one from each hole). Make sure you have equal lengths of chain hanging from each hole. Getting the last length of chain into position might be a little difficult, but if you twist the chain, it can be worked through.

To make a hanger that can be attached to the fishing line, use stiff wire, preferably stainless steel, about 15 inches long. Bend a curve or fold in the middle. Then, holding it in a vise or with pliers at this bend, make several complete spiral turns with each end. Position the ends of the wire into the smaller holes in the tubing, and use needle-nose pliers to bend these at right angles once they are inside the tubing. This special twist of wire allows you to place the lure retriever onto the fishing line with ease at any point on the line.

At this point wrap the lure retriever with masking or electrician's tape to hold the chain and the wire in place and to prevent lead leakage around the holes. Paper tape, such as masking tape, works better than plastic tape, which tends to burn when lead is poured. Wrap as securely as possible around all the holes, and completely cover the bottom of the tube through which the chain hangs. Place the lure retriever into a container of sand, leaving only the top opening exposed. The sand prevents additional lead leakage, absorbs the lead's heat, and safely holds the tube upright during the lead pouring. If the top link of the chain slides down inside the tube, hold it in place with a nail run through the link and laid across the top of the tube.

If you have a ladle for pouring the lead, so much the better. If you don't, an old discarded pot or coffee can (held with a pair of pliers) will do. Junk lead is fine for this, including lead wheel weights from service stations, printer's lead, and other lead alloys. **Before you go further, be sure to read all the pouring instructions and follow the safety directions found in chapters 4 and 5.**

Melt and pour the lead outside the house—lead fumes are dangerous. When pouring the lead, make sure it is hot and completely molten—not just slushy.

Pour the lead rapidly into the tube until it is filled. Make sure the top link of the chain is centered in the lead. It can be positioned in the liquid lead with a pair of pliers if necessary. Allow the lead time to cool, and then remove the retriever from the sand and unwrap the tape. If all has gone well, the tube will be completely filled with lead and no lead will have leaked through the wrapped openings. Remove any such excess lead with wire cutters, pliers, or a file.

While the above describes the original lure retriever as noted in *Tackle Craft* (with the variation of the bent wire in place of snaps for adding the fishing line), there is an easier way to make the same tool. For this use aluminum or PVC tubing for the retriever, run the chain through the tubing, and add additional chains at the end using large split rings or chain repair links. Make sure the chain goes all the way through the tubing so that the upper link is the tie for the heavy cord. Add the bent wire used for placing the lure retriever onto the fishing line.

Tightly wrap masking tape around the bottom of the tubing to seal off the area where the chain links exit. A better alternative is to use some flexible kids' clay (the kind that does not harden) and pack it around the end of the tube and chain. Use a nail across the tubing to hold the upper link out of the tube and then alternately add a little resin, then some lead, some resin, some lead, and so on until the tube is completely filled. For this you can use regular or 5-minute epoxy glue or casting resin (the same kind used for offshore lures). For the lead you can use old sinkers, scraps from the molding operation, old solder, or other heavy materials. Allow the resin or glue to cure before removing the tape or clay.

Another simple version is to buy or mold a very large (several ounces) egg sinker, form an eye in heavy wire, and run the wire through the egg sinker. Then form another eye, but instead of cutting the wire after wrapping this eye, extend the wire at a right angle to the main wire, make a second 90-degree bend, and bend this wire into loose coils. These loose coils make it easy to add the fishing line to track the lure retriever down to the hung lure.

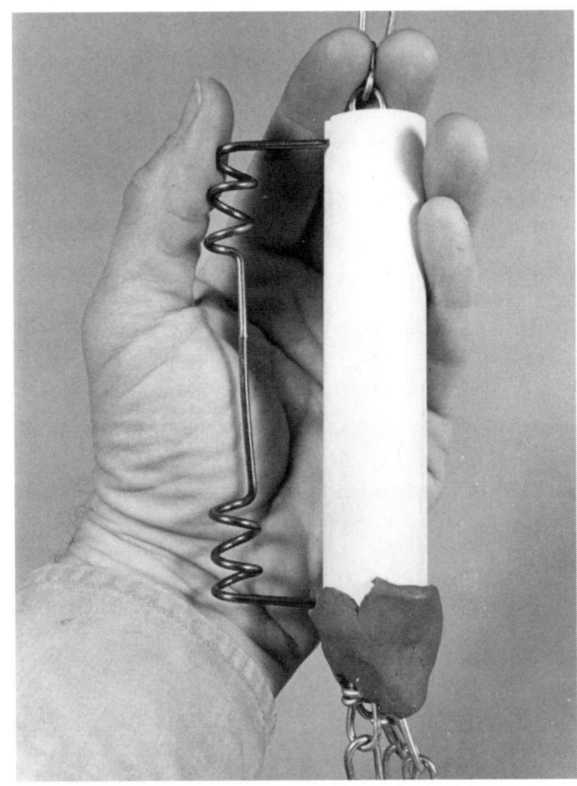

Plug retriever ready to pour. The clay at the bottom prevents leakage of the resin or glue where the chains are attached. One chain goes all the way through the pipe.

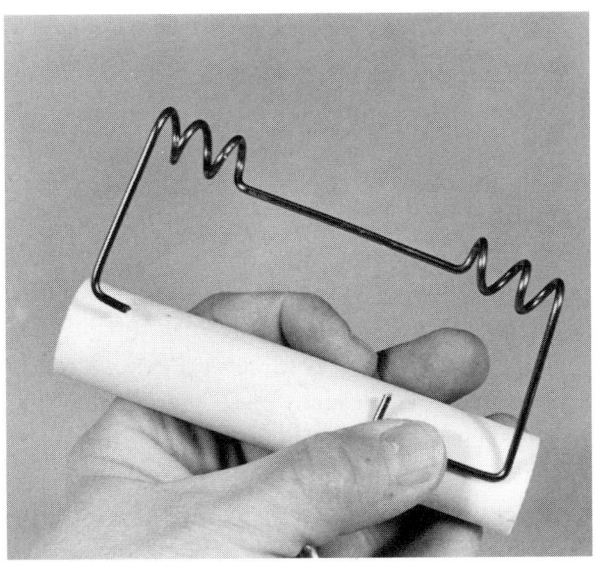

Another way to make a plug retriever with an improved line attachment is to use PVC pipe, filling the pipe with lead bits or sinkers glued in place with casting resin or glue. The twisted rod/wire to be inserted into the pipe makes it easy to add or remove fishing line.

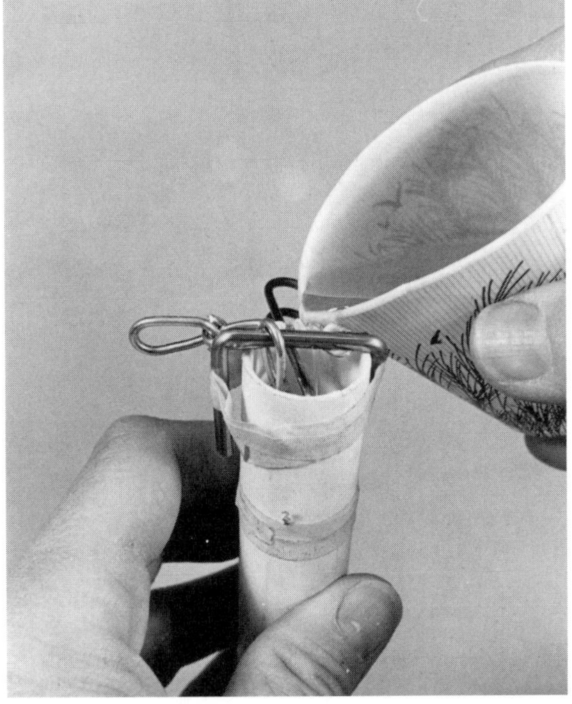

Pouring the casting resin.

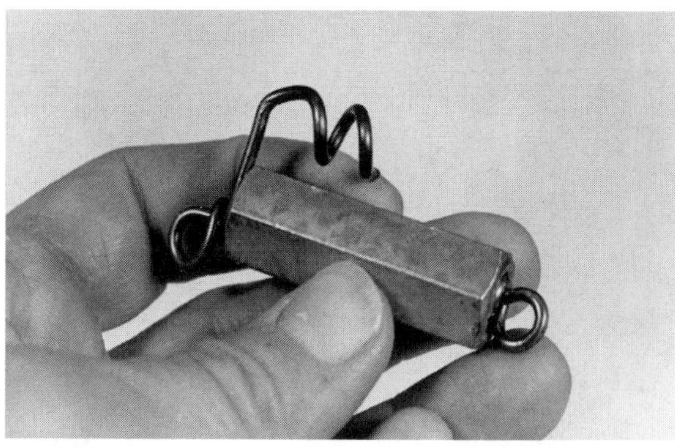

Another type of plug retriever can be made with an egg sinker or large bolt link as shown. The wire goes through the bolt link or egg sinker, with the twisted rod used as a guide on the fishing line. Heavy cord can be attached to either end.

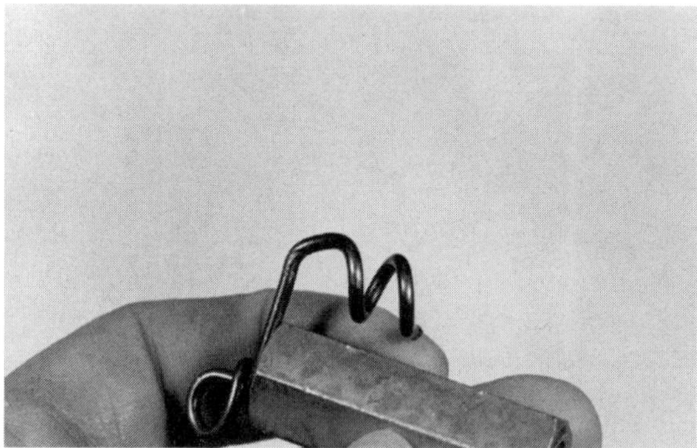

An 18-inch length of flexible plastic tubing at the terminal end of the cord prevents the cord's fraying on rocks while retrieving lures.

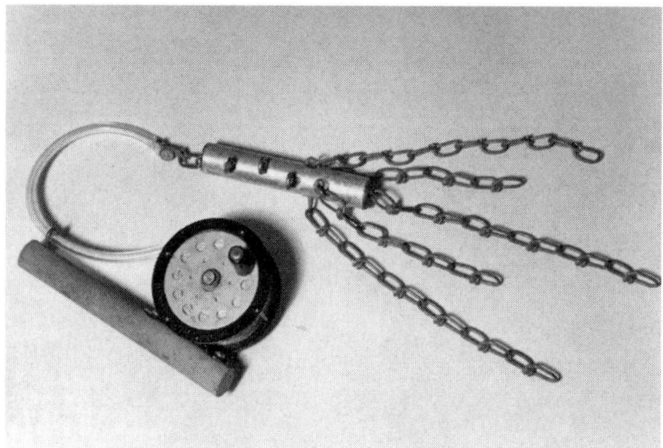

Completed plug retriever.

Tie heavy cord to the eye or attachment of the lure retriever. If desired, chains can be added to the other eye to catch the hooks of a lure.

To make it easy to use the lure retriever, mount a cheap fly reel onto a 6-inch length of broom handle (1-inch dowel will do fine also) for a handle, using a screw to attach each end of the reel foot to the wood handle. At the end of the dowel, attach a screw eye through which to run the heavy cord. Fill the reel with heavy nylon cord, or at least enough cord to reach the bottom of your fishing waters.

To protect the end of the cord from rocky ledges, stumps, and rocks, cover it with plastic tubing. Use an 18-inch length of thin vinyl tubing over the end of the cord. To get the tubing over the cord, run a thin doubled length of wire through the tubing, catch the end of the cord with the doubled wire, and pull the cord through. Knot the heavy cord securely to the top link in the lure retriever, and slide the clear tubing down over the end of the cord. To prevent the tubing from slipping up and exposing the cord to damage, rivet or wire the tubing to the top chain link.

Using the lure retriever is simplicity itself. Once you are hung up on the bottom, wrap the fishing line through the spiraled wire holder on the lure retriever and drop the retriever to the bottom, spooling line off the reel. Often, just the heavy lure retriever knocking against the lure will be sufficient to jog it free. If the lure remains snagged, jig or bounce the retriever up and down a few times to knock it free. If this does not work, continue jigging the lure retriever until the chains catch on a hook or some other part of the lure. Wrapping the heavy cord several times around the wood-dowel reel handle to prevent line cuts to your hands, pull the lure up. Usually you can pull the lure to the surface easily, although you may bend or break one of the hooks on a treble-hook crankbait. Once while using this retriever, I pulled up my plug but left one of the treble hooks in a log. This was a minor loss when compared with the cost of a new lure.

15

Painting and Finishing

Introduction • Tools • Types of Paint • Other Finishing Materials • Painting Methods: Dipping • Painting Methods: Spraying • Painting Methods: Brushing • Painting Wood Lures • Painting Plastic Lures • Preparation of Metal Lures for Painting • Painting Metal Spoons and Spinner Blades • Painting Lead Bucktails and Lures • Painting with Powder Paints • Painting Patterns and Using Stencils • Painting Scale Finishes • Craquele Paint • Adding and Painting Eyes • Baking Paints • Adding Glitter to Lures • Flocking Lures • Adding Tapes • Coloring Plastic Worms and Lures with Felt-Tip Markers • Field Painting and Dyeing • Final Lure Finishing • Kits

Basic Safety Requirements

- Goggles
- Painting facemask
- Rubber or plastic gloves
- Apron or protective smock

Basic Tools

- Paintbrushes
- Scale netting
- Finishing nails and pins

Helpful Tools

- Airbrush
- Masking tape
- Embroidery hoops
- Felt-tip markers
- Various stencils
- Disposable brushes
- Sponge makeup applicators
- Butane torch (for use with powder paints)

INTRODUCTION

It is not enough to turn out fine wood plugs; assemble a series of plastic lures; cut, bend, and finish spoons; or mold bucktails by the hundred. Before any of these can be fished, they must be painted or finished in some way. Admittedly, lures can be fished unfinished and will still catch fish. But these cases are more the exception than the rule. Day in and day out, well-finished lures will catch more fish than those left unfinished.

There are numerous ways to finish lures, depending on the lure material, the method used, your choice of colors and patterns, scale finishes, and the use of tape, glitter, and reflective materials.

TOOLS

Very few tools are needed for finishing lures. The best methods involve dipping or spraying the paint to prevent paint buildup or brush marks on the finished lure. If brushes are used, they should be the best obtainable. Having said that, there are small packs of inexpensive brushes available from craft and hobby shops, some tackle-component supply houses, and other outlets that are ideal for small items or for use with thicker paints, in which the brush marks will disappear before the paint cures. They are also ideal for touching up paints on lures, painting some eyes and patterns, and similar tasks. The one big advantage of such brushes is that they can be thrown out after one use without pangs of economic conscience. Packets of sponge-tip makeup applicators are also fine for quick touch-ups and for painting a few lures. They are disposable and work well with most paints used for lures.

If brushes are to be reused, and if the highest quality job is desired, the best brushes are flat brushes of ¼- to ½-inch width, available from artist supply stores.

You can use aerosol sprays, but there are increasing environmental concerns about such products. Airbrush guns can be used, but simpler, cheaper air-gun sprays that are operated with a can of air or propellant are available. The cost of air-gun kits has come down markedly in recent years. Kits that include a spray gun, hose, and can of air are available for about one-half to one-quarter the price of a complete system that also includes a compressor. The disadvantage of these systems is that you must constantly buy the cans of propellant. Currently a large can is good for about 1 to 2 hours. The cost of ten cans, or about 20 hours' use, comes close to the current cost of a low-priced compressor system. Another disadvantage is that using the propellant chills the can, so usually you can work for only about 30 minutes before you have to stop to allow the can to warm up.

The compressor systems work with an AC motor and air compressor to provide a constant source of air pressure for the gun. The lower priced compressors require rests, since too much continuous work will accelerate motor wear. The most expensive are those that have an automatic cutoff—when you release pressure on the gun trigger, the compressor stops. Others are stopped by a separate on-off switch or by removing the plug from the wall outlet. Also, the less-expensive models have a control that, when opened, releases air and paint at the same time (called "single action"). In short, open the control and you are painting.

The more expensive models have a control that when pushed down releases the air from the nozzle, and a separate pullback switch (like a small trigger, but operated by the thumb) releases the paint (called "double action"). Thus, these models have finer control.

There are a half dozen manufacturers of such air-compressor equipment, including Paache, Thayer/Chandler, Badger, Iwata, and Devilbiss.

The big advantage of this relatively expensive type of spray system is in the versatility of the spraying operation. Unlike a can of spray paint, the guns allow adjustment of the spray area. Some are capable of spraying a line no wider than that made with a standard pencil. Others have minimum spray areas of ⅟₁₆ or ⅛ inch. Most also have maximum widths, ranging with the gun model from about 1 to 2 inches. The choice of a nozzle or gun, based on the type of spraying you plan to do, is important. If you will be spraying entire lure bodies, spoon blades, spinner blades, and larger jig heads, choose a spray gun that will cover an area the size of the lure. If you plan to paint fine designs on the lure body, spray patterns, or "draw" gill plates, fins, and so on, then choose a gun with a head that will make fine lines.

One other thought: These airbrushes are designed for use with water-based paints, primarily for artwork and retouching. This does not allow for the use of enamels or lacquers but does allow acrylics, which wash up with water (actually a water-vinegar or water–window cleaner mix is used) but are waterproof when dry. Many use these paints for decorative work on motorcycles, autos, and trucks. One machine, which holds the paint externally in a small pan, would probably allow use of solvent-based enamels and lacquers.

In any case such equipment—cans or compressors—is a must for serious finishing of large numbers of lures. Initial setup costs are high, however, so consider the depth of your involvement in making lures and painting before investing.

Standard aerosol-paint cans are also good for painting lures, and some of them have a nozzle that can be adjusted to a thin or broad spray pattern. If you are planning on more than a solid coat of color on your lures, you will need masking tape. You can also use other patterns, scale finish nets, templates such as broad-tooth combs, and other such devices to make patterns on lures. It is possible to cut patterns in masking tape, tape the pattern on the lure, spray, and remove the tape. Tape is also necessary when you spray-paint the head of a lure a different color than the body of the lure, as in the popular red-head, white-body topwater lures and crankbaits. Masking tape is readily available in the standard widths of ¾ inch and 1, 2, and 3 inches. Thinner masking tape is available from art supply or rod making stores in ¼-, ⅜-, and ½-inch widths.

To add a scale finish to a crankbait, top-water plug, spoon, or spinner blade, you'll need a special netting pattern. This netting is available from most component suppliers and from some tackle shops. The pattern from the hexagonal mesh simulates the scales of a fish. The cost is low, the material is usually sold by the yard, and different sizes are available for different lure patterns. Other types of netting can be obtained from craft stores. Just check the mesh closely to determine the size and type of pattern that will result.

There are several ways to use the finishing netting, the handiest of which involves stretching it over an embroidery hoop so that the lure can be held against the netting and sprayed with the scale color. Embroidery hoops consist of two rings, one fitted inside the other; material is stretched tightly between them. They come in both oval and round styles, either spring-loaded or with a small screw to tighten the outer rim against the inner hoop. Sizes suitable for spraying lures range from about 4 to 12 inches in diameter. Embroidery hoops are very inexpensive and available from sewing, notion, and department stores.

Eyes can be painted on lures using simply made tools. These tools are nothing more than several sizes of finishing nails or straight pins pushed into the ends of short wood dowels, which serve as handles. The different size heads on the pins and nails, when dipped into paint and then touched lightly to the lure, make different size eyes and/or pupils.

Since painting can be a messy job, cover the workbench or work area with oilcloth, newspapers, or other coverings to make cleanup easier. Spraying is especially messy, since the fine paint mist tends to float in the air. If you use spray paints, use some sort of "trap" to keep the paint in a confined area. One way to make a simple no-cost trap is to place a cardboard box on its side behind the lures to be painted. A length of bead chain, pipe strap, or small-link chain hung horizontally along the front top edge of the box will serve to hang the lures during spraying. Even a box like this, in which only the front is open, will allow some of the paint spray to bounce back out of the box. One way to lessen this is to line the back and sides of the box with an old Turkish towel. Better still, hang a second towel, cut into fine strips, in front of the backing towel. The backing and strips will serve to trap much of the excess spray paint and prevent it from filling the room.

When using spray paints, wear goggles to protect your eyes and cover your nose with a small facemask. Both are available at hardware and paint-supply stores and are very inexpensive. If possible, an exhaust fan should be employed during extensive spray painting, or the painting should be done outside on a *calm* day. Another possibility is to use an open garage or protected carport or patio. If you spray lures extensively, consult the book *Ventilation: A Practical Guide for Artists, Craftspeople, and Others in the Arts* for ideas on reducing or eliminating any dangers or problems.

TYPES OF PAINT

Standard paint is supplied in two basic ways: as a liquid in a container and in aerosol sprays. Powder paints are completely different in packaging and use. The spray paints are generally more expensive for several reasons. First, packaging the paint with an aerosol propellant adds to the initial cost. A quick look at the net weights and costs of aerosol paints versus liquid paints will show this to be true. Also, because of the spraying technique, much spray paint does not cover the lure but instead is dispersed into the air. This is particularly true when spraying small items such as lures. For this reason it is best to use some sort of rack to hang the lures close together (but not touching) and spray many lures at once to reduce waste as much as possible.

To its advantage, spray painting gives a very good, smooth finish on a lure if it's done correctly and in several light coats. Too heavy a coat will cause running and dripping and can also cause crackling of the resulting finish. Spray painting is also the only way that scale finishes, "feathering" (blending two coats), and painting through stencils and masks can be effectively accomplished.

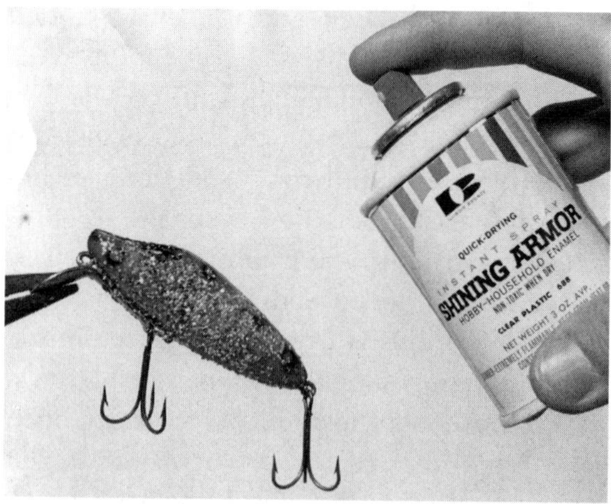

Spray cans of clear finish make it easy to paint and refinish lures. This lure with added glitter is being protected with a clear plastic coating.

Paint sold in a container (usually a can but sometimes in bottles or jars) can be used with a brush or for dipping lures. If you are dipping, thin the paint to prevent streaking or the formation of a solidified paint drop at the lower end of the lure. Lure companies using dipping techniques (most do, at least for base coats and clear finish coats) avoid this by employing a mechanized conveyer chain that dips the lure and slowly removes it from the paint rough to prevent solidified drops. Usually the rate of withdrawal of the lure from the paint is the critical factor—it must match or be slightly slower than the rate at which excess paint runs off the lure. However, since such a device is generally beyond the scope of the home tackle craftsman, thinner paint is a must.

Since paints of different types and manufacture can vary greatly as to their viscosity, no definite thinning directions can be given. For dipping baits the best method is to thin the paint slightly and experiment with small quantities of paint (on scrap pieces of wood—not on a completed lure!) and the proper thinner until good results are achieved. For those using airbrush equipment, the basics are to thin paint with thinner in a 50:50 ratio. In all cases, keep records so that you can duplicate your results with other colors and larger quantities.

Another factor to consider when dipping lures is that larger quantities of paint will be needed than for brushing or spraying. Even 1-pint cans are seldom deep enough for larger lures. The paint must be transferred to a taller, thinner container to allow the lure to be completely submerged. This is not necessary when using brushes; even the small ¼-ounce bottles of Testor's PLA enamel, available in hobby shops, can be used with a brush to paint large saltwater lures.

Both types of paint, container and aerosol, vary greatly in their properties. Some are best for wood lures, some for plastic, and some for metal. Mail-order companies specializing in do-it-yourself fishing supplies often offer different paints for different purposes. It is particularly important to choose the appropriate paints for foam lures—lures made from hard polystyrene foam and found in some bass bug bodies and some bass and saltwater lures. In some cases standard paints may react with the body and cause it to partially dissolve. (This is also a problem with glues, since standard household waterproof glues will do the same thing. Epoxy glue usually works well, but test it on one or two lure bodies before gluing or painting a gross or two.)

The term "lacquer" can apply to clear finishes and also to a colored nitrocellulose base paint of thin consistency. Sometimes these color lacquers are called lacquer enamels. They are usually excellent for painting metal (such as spinner blades, spoon blades, and lead bucktails) and are very fast drying. Often they are not acceptable for plastics, since the solvent in some lacquers may react chemically with the plastic or the plastic solvent (plasticizer). But they vary widely. Check the fine print on the label or the catalog copy. Some companies carry standard, fluorescent, pearlescent, and similar lacquers that can be used on all lure materials. Lacquers can usually be bought in ounce-size bottles and several sizes of larger containers.

Automobile touch-up lacquers are excellent for dipping or spraying, and they come in aerosol and liquid. Hardware and auto-supply stores carry them in the same colors to be found on the late-model cars of most manufacturers. For metal lures and lead jigs, they offer a durable, tough finish.

Enamels are usually heavier, thicker paints, often advertised as "covering in one coat." They can generally be used on any type of lure material but are not available in the same variety of colors as lacquers and auto touch-up paints. They are also slower drying than lacquers. Prices are about the same as for lacquers, and enamels are available in many container sizes in bottles, cans, and aerosols.

Alkyd and acrylic enamels are modern enamels. They are available in small cans from lure suppliers as well as from home repair and paint stores. They can be used on metal, wood, and some but not all plastics.

Epoxy paints, like epoxy glue, are sold separated into two parts that must be mixed together before use. These paints are very tough, but many have the disadvantage of a flat finish rather than the gloss preferred for most lures. This can be overcome by using either a finishing gloss coat of clear lacquer over the epoxy or a finish coat of clear epoxy.

Vinyl paints are also good for lead lures because they are slightly rubbery and flexible and thus will not chip as readily as many other paints when the lure is knocked against a hard rock or is otherwise dented. Unlike epoxies, vinyl paints do not require mixing but are used straight out of the container. Vinyl paints in a variety of colors are readily available from mail-order suppliers. Most of these paints are available in basic colors such as yellow, red, orange, blue, green, white, black, and brown, although Do-It sells more than thirty different colors of vinyl paint, including a clear gloss. These paints are available in 1-, 4-, and 16-ounce containers. As with painting any lures, two base coats of white are suggested to make sure that subsequent colors retain their brightness for a professional-looking lure.

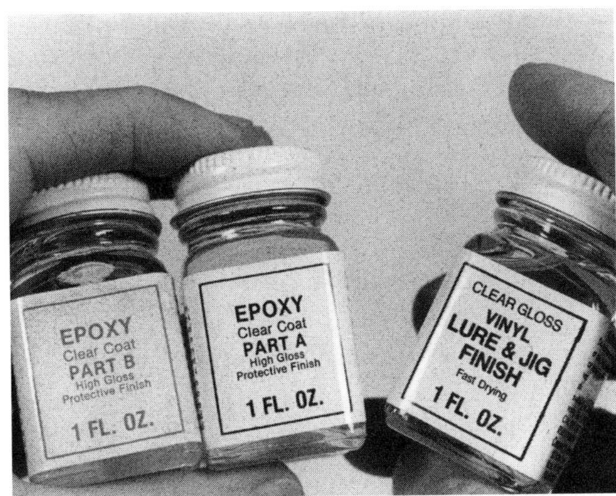

Paints for finishing lures include epoxy and vinyl clear-coat finishes over the paint to protect the finish.

In addition to the standard range of colors in the paints, there are also special colors and paints that make even more elaborate lures possible. Fluorescent paints in red, orange, pink, yellow, green, blue, and purple are available. These paints are sometimes referred to as "neon" colors.

Do-It has glitter in ten colors that can be added to a clear finish to add more sparkle and life to a lure; both fine and coarse glitters are available in craft, art, and hobby shops.

Many times multiple colors of paint and glitter can be found either in cans or aerosols in drug, hobby, department, and stationery stores. For obvious reasons, avoid buying fluorescent paints that are water-based and designed only for poster work.

For best results fluorescent colors must be used over a base coat of white. Painting them over any other color or even over bare metal or wood will not produce the expected bright color.

Phosphorescent paints, which glow in the dark, are also available for lure finishing. In some states or areas they might be illegal on lures or when fished in certain waters, so be sure to check local laws and regulations before using them.

Phosphorescents also come in standard colors. The most common are yellow and white, but blue, green, red, and orange are also available. Any lure painted phosphorescent will not glow indefinitely but must be "recharged" with light periodically. Therefore this paint works best on lures that are frequently cast or exposed to the sun rather than on lures used for continual deepwater trolling, such as downrigger fishing. (It is not necessary to fish phosphorescent lures only on sunny days or to avoid dawn, dusk, or night fishing. Any light can be used to recharge such lures—flashlights, camp lanterns, cigarette lighters, matches. One great way to recharge lures is to "hit" the lure with a small photographers' electronic flash by using the "open flash" button. If your camera lacks this function, short out the hot shoe with a key or wire to get a flash. To avoid hurting the flash, be sure the flash recharges completely before firing again. A couple of flashes on the lure are as good as 10 minutes in bright sun.)

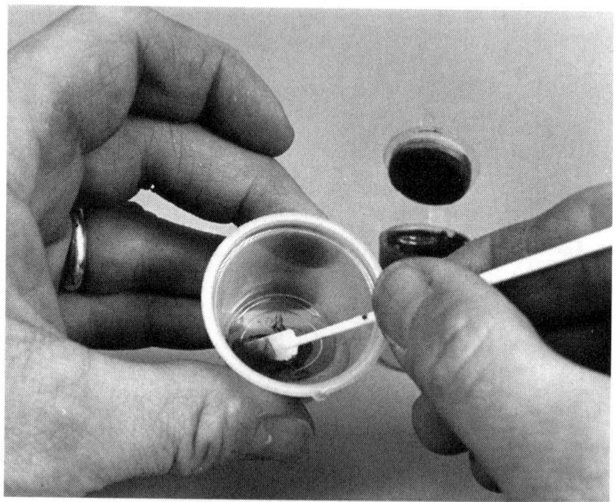

Mix the pigment in with a clear finish coat using a small mixing or disposable condiment cup.

Various dyes for coloring lures are also available. They can be used on hard baits but work best on plastic worms and skirts, where the dye can penetrate slightly.

There are also phosphorescent pigments that can be added to regular paints to give an underwater phosphorescence in addition to a daylight color. These are usually sold by the ounce. Any of the phosphorescent paints should be used over a base coat of white for best results.

Pearl pigments and similar paint additives give lures a shiny mother-of-pearl look. They can be combined with paints and used to paint plugs, spoons, spinner blades, and bucktails. They are most often seen on spoons and bucktails.

Don't neglect other paint possibilities. At Christmas and Halloween I have found special paints, additives, and paint coverings that are designed for holiday decoration but also do well on a lures. Some of these include colored spray paints that contain fine bits of bright metallics to imbue the base color with a silvery, glittering overcoat. Paints are also available that, when dry, make a crystal pattern on a lure. These are sold at Christmas to simulate the crystal patterns formed by ice on windowpanes. Prices are reasonable, but remember that any of these items will be drastically reduced in price immediately after the holiday season. Also make sure these paints are waterproof.

Another possibility that is particularly good for lead heads, although limited in variety and color patterns, is plastic dips. These are primarily designed for building up a rubberized coating for pliers and other tool handles but will also work well as a tough, thick, durable coating on lead heads (since these are particularly prone to chipping, flaking, and other damage as the lure bounces off rocks). The only disadvantage is that colors are limited, although white, black, red, yellow, and clear are commonly available. Since these dips are thick, only one coat is necessary.

While powder paints have been around for about thirty years now, for the do-it-yourselfer they are still the newest thing in the paint and finishing area. Originally there were only a few basic colors available, but that has fortunately changed. Most tackle shops and do-it-yourself catalogs now carry these paints. Barlow's Tackle carries forty different colors of standard powder paint, ten topcoats of powder glitter paint, six phosphorescent powder paint colors, and seven transparent metallic colors of powder paint. Powder paints are just what they sound like—paints in powder form. Usually they are about the consistency of talcum powder, perhaps a little coarser.

Powder paints are used completely differently than are other paints and can only be used on metal lures, including lead and metal jigs, lures of tin, chromed finish, sheet metal, etc. They are available in both standard and fluorescent colors. Depending on your source, about twenty different colors are available.

No liquid is involved in painting with these. Instead the lure is headed up to 350 degrees Fahrenheit and then dipped rapidly into the paint container, where the powder paint sticks, melts, and seals onto the lure. You can heat lures in a toaster oven, using a quick shot with a butane torch, over a gas stove burner, etc. An additional way to get maximum durability from these paints is to hang the painted lure in a toaster oven or regular kitchen oven for another 15 minutes to allow the paint to bake on the lure. The result is often so durable that the paint will not chip even after a lead lure has been dented by being thrown into a rock pile. Commonly these paints are used on lead head jigs, tin squids, metal spoon blades, metal spinner blades, and blades for buzzbaits.

OTHER FINISHING MATERIALS

Other materials for finishing lures can be used in place of paint or in combination with it. Reflective and colored tape can be added to fishing lures, including plastic and wood plugs, spoons, and spinner blades. Some tapes, such as the many types of prism reflective and scale-finish tapes, have shiny mirrorlike finishes in metallic colors (silver, gold, copper, and brass), along with many bright-colored finishes. Most have a self-adhesive backing and are easy to add to any lure. Some come in solid sheets, others in small packs of several sheets, and some are precut into patterns specifically designed for lures.

The red reflective tape designed for use as car-bumper reflectors can be used on lures with the same results. Some supply houses carry other tapes, such as glitter-flake tape that is available in several colors. Similar glitter tape is available from hardware and hobby shops in rolls, usually about 6 feet long and available in several widths of ½ inch and wider.

Reflective tape made with microscopic glass beads is available in a variety of colors in both sheets and rolls. Fluorescent tapes are also available in bright colors (many colors are available), along with some phosphorescent tapes.

Pigments and glitter materials also make it possible to add flash to any drab or scarred lure or to design new lures with extra fish-attracting flash. Most popular are the glitter materials in gold, silver, red, green, blue, and other colors. These are tiny metallic bits or, more frequently today, Mylar that looks metallic. These can be glued in place, sprinkled on a fresh coat of paint or clear finish, or added with a special glitter adhesive. They come in small bottles and tubes and are low in cost. This material is also available in tubes of clear glue that can be squeezed onto or spread over a lure. Once cured, this material won't come off—and it's waterproof.

Fluorescent, phosphorescent, and standard-color pigments can also be added to lures by dipping the lure into a clear lacquer or thin adhesive and rolling or sprinkling the pigments onto the lure where desired (detailed methods follow).

Electroplating spinner and spoon blades is also possible, and there are kits available for this.

Caution: Once you begin to paint any lure, follow through the entire process with paints of the same type, or at least paints that will not react adversely when mixed. This includes base coats, finish coats, scale finishes, masked sprays, eyes, and clear protective coats. Switching from one type of paint to another, even though the underlying coats are dry, may cause a chemical reaction. The result could be that the new coat may never dry, or it might wrinkle, crinkle, crack, peel, blister, or bleed. Unless it is clearly stated that a particular paint (of any type) can be used over other types of paint, it's best not to do so. If you must mix paint types, test the combination on one or two lures, or on scrap pieces of wood, to determine results.

PAINTING METHODS: DIPPING

For most lures, dipping is perhaps the best method to get a base or single-color coat of paint. Wood and plastic lures, spoon and spinner blades (where it is desirable to cover both sides of the blade with paint), and bucktails can all be dipped.

The paint must be thinned with the proper thinner. It is hard to give exact directions on thinning because of the infinite variety of paints and thinners available, but a one-to-one mix is a good place to start. If in doubt, experiment with small quantities first, adding minimal amounts of thinner. It is usually easier to add more thinner than it is to double or triple the amount of paint to get the right paint-to-thinner mix.

Since the entire lure must be dipped into the paint, often the paint must be transferred from the original bottle or can into a deep container. This is especially true with long plugs and spoons. Cheap juice glasses, olive jars, and similar tall containers are excellent for this. You can also make your own by using short sections of PVC, CPVC, or ABS plastic pipe fitted with a flat glued-on end cap. You need

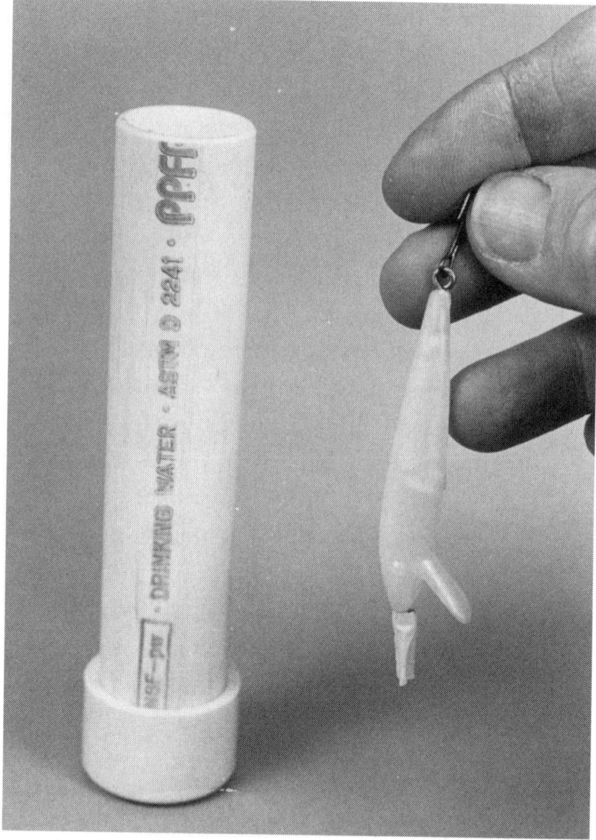

One simple aid for painting slim lures is to make a pipe container with a short length of plastic pipe and a cemented-on end cap. This requires less paint for coverage when dipping. Note that the lure line-tie is masked for this.

the flat end cap, not the rounded style, so that the container will stand upright. Even so, it is best to support the pipe container in some way to prevent spills. Insert it into a bucket of sand, wedge it upright into the corner of a cardboard box, or tape it to an L-shaped bracket clamped to the workbench or held in a vise.

Be sure to cover the work area with old newspapers, and have a rack handy on which to hang the lures to dry. A simple length of wood shelving with two end supports (to make a wide U shape) works fine. Use metal L brackets to support the end pieces. At the top, string a length of bead chain, pipe strap, fine-link jack chain, or similar chain from one leg of the U to the other, from which to hang the lures. Bead chain (available in several sizes from any hardware store, where it is sold by the foot for electric light pulls) is ideal because it is inexpensive, separates the lures, does not allow them to slide together and touch, and will not catch the lure when it is removed as might chain link. Do *not* use wire or cord for a hanger, since the weight of any lure will cause all lures to slide to the center; the lures will stick together, ruining the painted finishes. Make sure the rack side supports are higher than the length of any lure, including the hook, paper clip, or hanging wires.

Bucktails and spoons can be hung by their hooks. Since plugs must be painted before any hardware is added, you'll need to use open-end screw eyes partially turned into the tail or head of the lure, or a straight pin or thin nail pushed into the plug with the shaft of the pin or nail turned in a J shape, for hanging on the rack.

Dip each lure carefully and slowly into the paint. Dipping slowly is necessary to prevent the formation of air bubbles on the lure. Cover the lure completely with paint and then withdraw it slowly to minimize running streaks or dripping. Once the lure is completely out of the paint, hold it over the container briefly to allow any excess paint to run back into the container.

It helps to touch the lower part of the lure to the top of the paint surface here to remove the last drop. If the paint is thin enough, or if the lure has been removed slowly enough from the paint, this may be sufficient to prevent a dried droplet of paint on the finished lure. If the paint is not thin enough, it may be necessary to check the drying lures later, carefully touching the lower part of the lure with a rag or absorbent towel to remove any drops of paint. The proper time to do this will depend on the paint's drying time: With lacquers it may be necessary in a matter of minutes; with slower-drying enamels you might have to wait an hour or longer.

Dipping can be used for sealer coats, base coats, and a series of finish coats. Sealer coats are coats of sealer, designed to penetrate wood lures and to allow for a good, even coat of finish paint. Base coats are designed to take a finish coat of paint. Base coats are primarily white, and

Drying rack for holding painted lures. The bead-chain racks prevent lures from sliding together, while the spring on each end maintains tension on the bead chain.

they *must* be white when the finish coat is to be a light color or when any of the fluorescent or phosphorescent colors are used. Once a base coat or two is added, you can then add finish coats by dipping, brushing, or spraying.

PAINTING METHODS: SPRAYING

Spraying, provided it is done correctly, has the advantage of covering a lure evenly, without streaks or droplets. Do it incorrectly (too heavy a coat, too light a coat, spraying too soon after a first coat) and you can end up with runs, drops, crackling, crinkles, or gaps in the finish. Spraying should be done lightly and evenly, with several light coats sprayed over a sealer or base coat.

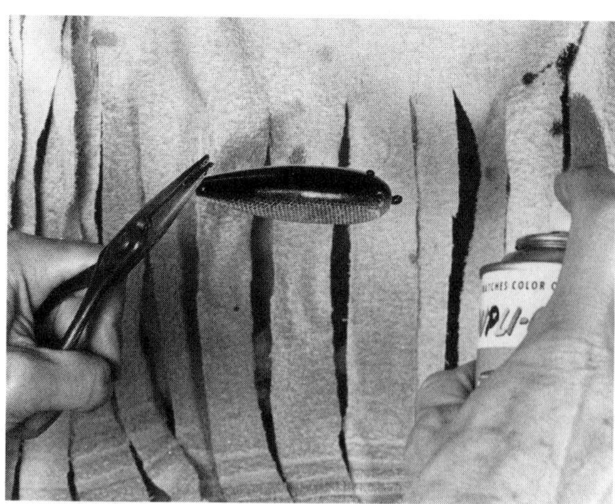

Once the sides are sprayed on a plug, the back is sprayed a dark color. The strips of cloth in the background are part of the spraying box described in the text to contain excess spray.

Use a spraying box, and line up the lures to be sprayed as closely as reasonable to prevent waste of the aerosol paint. Since one spray coat will cover only one side of a lure, the lures must be turned. There are several methods to accomplish this. One is to use a small spraying box and a separate hanging rack. Spray each lure evenly and thoroughly by holding the lure's support pin with pliers and turning the lure to cover all sides with the aerosol spray. Then hang the lure up on the separate rack. If you rack all the lures to be painted in the spraying box, consider using an overhead frame that will hold beach-chair or pipe-strap hanging strips so that you can reverse the lures 180 degrees after the first spraying. Another possibility is to use a spraying box that has a fold-down front and back. Keep the hanging racks stationary, but spray from both sides; reverse the positions (up or down) of the front and back flaps when spraying from the opposite side.

Once sufficient finishing coats are on the lure, add secondary coats by spraying. Each plug or lure will have to be done separately. This is usually the case whether spraying freehand or using a mask or scale-net finish for more lifelike results. This does give good results, since the second coat of color can be "feathered" to blend with the first coat, giving a professional appearance.

If you are spraying with an airbrush gun, you can often add details with the gun adjusted to a fine spray, avoiding the need for masks or stencils. For expediency and consistency, most lure manufacturers use special, precisely cut masks and stencils for spraying details in different colors.

Since lures must be held individually, by hand or with cheap long-nose pliers, wear rubber or plastic painting gloves to keep the spray off your hands. Medical-type rubber gloves purchased in bulk (hundred- or gross-count boxes) are ideal because they can be worn on either hand. Heavier rubber gloves are available in housewares departments of department or discount stores; plastic painting gloves are available from hardware and paint-supply stores.

Spraying does have some disadvantages. When spraying a base coat on the lead head of a bucktail (before the tail is tied down), you may get paint on the hook point. Unless the paint is removed, hooking a fish becomes more difficult. One way to avoid this is to use a bit of petroleum jelly on the hook point (though be careful to avoid getting it on the lead head, because it will not allow paint adhesion) or to use a small bit of masking tape on the hook point. A better way is to use a flat shield behind which the hook point is held, exposing only the lead head to be painted.

Before you put a finishing coat on a bucktail, tie the tail in place. This is done for the specific purposes of later covering the thread winding with a protective layer of paint and giving the lure a uniform color. However, paint must be kept off the tail. Cover it with masking tape or use a flat cardboard shield.

Spraying does not have to be limited to just one color or coat. In fact, it is at its best when several colors are used to blend, or feather, one color into the next. For example, one way of making an attractive underwater plug or crankbait is to first coat the lure with a base coat of paint, and then paint a belly color of white, yellow, ivory, pink, light blue, or some other light color. Then follow with the side color of a darker shade, perhaps dark yellow, orange, light red, medium blue, medium green, or tan. To do this make a quick swipe or two with the spray can or air gun to hit each side of the lure (turn the lure to do this) without coating the belly. Complete with a quick swipe along the top or back of the lure with black, dark blue, dark green, or a similar dark-color paint. Do this lightly so as to not affect the side colors and shading. The result of this is a very professional-looking, lifelike lure with a dark back, medium-color side, and light belly—just like the natural coloring and shading of a live baitfish. This can be combined with eyes, scale finishes, vertical bar marks, or other embellishments. Once you know the basics of spraying, the possibilities are limitless.

PAINTING METHODS: BRUSHING

Brushing is not generally advisable for painting lures. It can leave brush marks, and there is a chance that a bristle will come off the brush and stick to the painted lure surface. In reality this is more an aesthetic than a practical concern, since the fish are not going to examine the degree of expertise of your paint job. They do not care if you are good or bad at brushing paint onto a lure. The lure either will look lifelike to them, in which case they will hit it, or it won't, in which case they will avoid it.

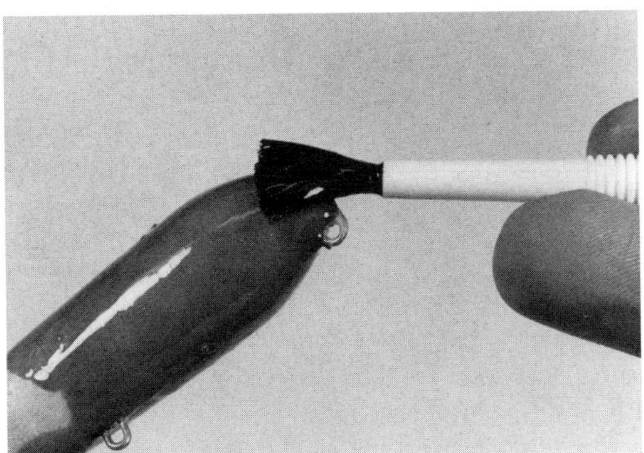

Brushing mixed epoxy finish onto a lure.

Brushing has two advantages over dipping and spraying: It requires no special quantities of paint or special containers, as does dipping, nor does it require room for a spraying box or that you waste paint, as ultimately happens with spraying. That being said, brush painting has no other advantages over dipping or spraying. It does not allow professional-looking fine details, even when a fine brush is used. Delicate bars, stripes, spots, and similar markings can be made—but generally not as well or as accurately as when they are sprayed through masks or stencils.

PAINTING WOOD LURES

Once they are carved or turned, wood plugs should be finished with a fine 7/0- or 8/0-grade sandpaper in order to get good results from painting. Once sanded smooth, the plug should be dipped, sprayed, or brushed with a wood sealer to seal the pores of the wood and prevent subsequent coats of paint from soaking into the wood. If a wood sealer is not used, the paint will soak into the wood in an uneven pattern (soaking more into end and summer grain than into the denser winter grain), making several more coats of paint necessary. Usually one coat of wood sealer is sufficient; if it isn't, use a second coat and allow it to dry completely before proceeding with the next step.

Once the wood sealer is dry, rough the surface with fine sandpaper or steel wool to give the sealer some "tooth" so that the next coat of paint will adhere to it. Each subsequent coat of paint, except for the final coat, should be buffed lightly with fine steel wool to give it tooth for the next coat. Both spraying and dipping work particularly well on wood lures; spraying is best for final touches and patterns applied through stencils.

PAINTING PLASTIC LURES

Plastic lures are painted in the same way as wood lures, except that additional care must be taken in the choice of paint. Some plastics react chemically with certain paints, so the paint you use should be clearly marked as suitable for plastic. If it is not so marked, test it first on an old plug or a small corner of one you are painting to be sure that the paint cures properly without softening the lure or otherwise causing a chemical reaction. While softening or dissolving is the most common effect when solvents react, other effects could be a softening of the surface of the lure or a crinkling of the lure surface to make a smooth final finish difficult or impossible. Ideally, what you want is a paint that will *just slightly* soften or dissolve the surface enough to allow a penetration of the paint into the plastic and a "binding" of the paint with the plastic surface.

Spraying, brushing, or dipping techniques can be used for painting plastics, with spraying the best method.

PREPARATION OF METAL LURES FOR PAINTING

Preparation for painting bucktails, spoons, spinner blades, and similar metal lures is extremely important. Some paints will be affected by light oils, which can prevent good paint adherence. As a result, all rust, grease, oils, perspiration, and dirt must be removed from metal lures before painting. Use an acid or metal cleaner, dipping the spoon, spinner blade, or bucktail body into the solution according to directions. Several types of acid cleaners are available from mail-order supply houses. Some are used undiluted; others are diluted with water. Most of these cleaners are of an "inhibited" acid type that will prevent any damage to the surface of the metal.

Because of the acid content of these cleaners, they can be used only in plastic (polyethylene), glass, or crockery containers; they will attack metal containers. The solutions are often irritating to the skin and toxic if breathed extensively, and they are volatile, with low flashpoints. Handle them with care, and *use them only with proper ventilation or outdoors.* Don't smoke when using these cleaners, and don't use them around any pilot lights (from hot-water heaters, stoves, gas clothes dryers, or the like) or where a motor is in use (air conditioner or heater) that may spark.

A weak acid, such as white vinegar or acetone, can be used as an alternative to clean and prepare metal lures. These materials are less dangerous to use than the commercial preparations but should still be used with caution. These acids are best used only on lead surfaces or those with zinc (some lead alloys); they will have far less effect on the nickel-plated surfaces of most spoons and spinner blades. They also work on copper and copper-plated metals.

One danger, and a concern of painting professionals such as Jeff Janos of Rustoleum, is the possibility of "wiping" the surface with a solvent- or acid-soaked rag and in the process leaving more oils or dirt than are being taken up by the wipe. In addition, enough wipes with the same rag will eventually soil the rag and dirty the surface you think you are cleaning.

Another cleaning alternative, and perhaps the simplest and best one, is a good wash with soapy water, which will remove oils and grease, and then thorough drying. When washing, strong dishwasher detergent is better than plain soap. Soaps serve as a solvent for grease and oil, but detergents actually "encapsulate" oils to remove them completely without leaving a residue.

Shortly after the metal surface is cleaned, it should be painted. Waiting only allows additional accumulation of dirt, oil, grease, and fingerprints, all which prevent good adhesion of the paint. Lead lures begin to oxidize on the surface shortly after being molded, and this oxidation also interferes with good paint adhesion. To protect lures of lead or other metals, clean and then paint them immediately, using a white paint as a base coat. White paint as a base is good under any additional paints and is required for maximum brightness with fluorescent or phosphorescent paints. In addition, after you paint a base coat of white on a lead lure, that lure will no longer oxidize. The lure can be set aside as long as you like before finishing with other colors and finishing touches.

PAINTING METAL SPOONS AND SPINNER BLADES

Painting any metal surface, such as the plated surfaces of spoons and spinner blades, is best only after cleaning. Often spinners and spoons are painted only with a few stripes, dots, or bars or with a solid color on one side of the blade only. As a result, dipping is seldom used, except in those rare cases when you want both sides of the spoon or spinner painted the same color.

Spraying is the best method to cover spoons and spinner blades with a single coat or to apply a pattern of stripes or bars. Brushing can be used if aerosols are not available. To spray a solid color on one side of the spoons or spinner blades, lay the blade on old newspapers in front of the spraying box, and spray evenly with several light coats. This same technique will work if you use masking tape or stencils to paint stripes, bars, or similar patterns on the blade.

The best paints are those that provide a hard, durable finish. The best way to do this is with an epoxy primer—preferably one made specifically for metals—and end with an enamel or lacquer finish coat. Baking the paint also helps give it a hard finish.

As described before, you can heat the metal lure to 350 degrees Fahrenheit in an oven or toaster oven and then dip it rapidly into powder paint, swishing the lure back and forth for a few seconds to assure adhesion of the paint. Since these lures are hot, the best way to hold them is to use a pair of needle-nose pliers and hold the spoon or spinner blades by the hole for the line-tie, hook, or clevis.

PAINTING LEAD BUCKTAILS AND LURES

Before you apply a base coat to any lead lure, the head should be dipped into a mild acid (acetone or vinegar solution), rinsed with water, and dried thoroughly. Bucktails can be painted either before or after the tail is tied down. The advantage of painting before tying is that the entire paint job can be finished and the tail then tied on with an identical- or contrasting-color thread. The thread is then protected with epoxy finish or fly-head cement or by painting it after it has been tied off.

If you paint lead-head lures or bucktails after tying on the tail material, you have to take some special considerations. For example, you can paint on the tail materials and then tie off the thread with several half-hitches or a whip-finish. To paint the lure you can spray, dip, or brush. If you brush you can paint without any lure protection by brushing the lure head and then the thread wrap. Be careful not to get paint onto the tail materials.

If you dip, dip down to the edge of the thread wrap so that you completely cover the wrap without the paint bleeding up into the tail materials. If you spray, use masking tape or a template to protect and shield it while spraying the lead lure. The advantage of any of these methods is that the paint serves as a sealer and protective coat for the thread wrap.

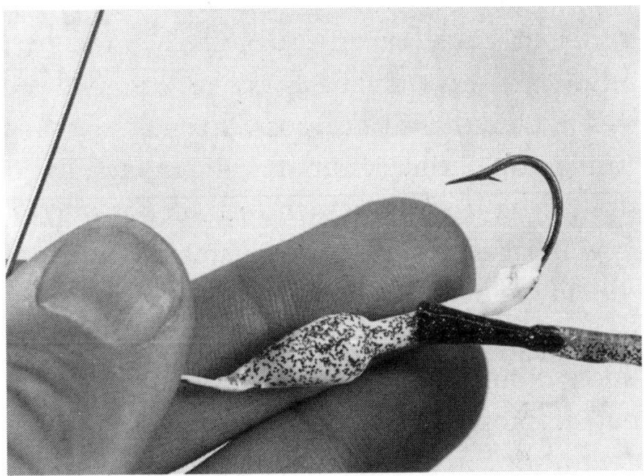

Glitter is available in a clear base for painting on lures. Here glitter in a clear finish is added to a dry base coat of white on a spinnerbait body.

Templates are available from a number of sources to create painted patterns on lures. Here are two examples and the templates used.

It is most important to paint lead heads as soon as possible after molding. This is impossible if you buy your lead heads but not if you mold your own. Try to paint the heads the same day they are molded. The less time that elapses between molding and painting, the less chance there is of oxidation buildup. Paint a base coat even if you won't finish the lead heads immediately, because once this base coat is on, the lure is protected and can be painted and finished at any time in the future.

Generally the adherence of paint to lead lures is not good, even on most commercial lures. The problem is that pure lead is soft and malleable and thus deforms when the lure hits any structure. Automobile touch-up paints work well, but paint experts suggest that the best solution is a plasticized epoxy primer followed by a polyurethane finish coat. The polyurethane paints stay flexible and thus will tend to give as the lure hits rocks and such and will not chip off as will harder, brittle paints. Painted lead heads should *not* be baked, since this makes the paint more brittle, even though it does make it more durable. Spraying or brushing will work well, but dipping is ideal because most lead heads are finished in one solid color, perhaps with the later addition of eyes.

The same flexibility can be found in the powder paints, which are highly durable and which do not chip or flake off even when a lead lure is seriously dented. Here extra baking of the paint onto the lure is recommended.

PAINTING WITH POWDER PAINTS

Painting with powder paints is not like painting with any other type of paint. You heat the lure to about 350 degrees Fahrenheit, dip the lure into the powder, stir it around, and then take it out for an instant, smooth, durable finish. You can go an extra step by baking the painted lure for an additional 15 minutes in the oven at about 350 degrees. This makes the finish even more durable.

There are several ways to heat the lead jigs and bucktails prior to dipping in the powder paints. You can hang them from racks and heat in a regular oven, set to about 350 degrees. You can also place them in a toaster oven. Heating on an outside propane grill is also an option, although it is more difficult to control the heat so that you do not end up melting the lead. A fourth method is to heat each lure individually as you paint it, using a torch such as a handyman butane torch, available from any hardware store.

In all of these methods, be careful of overheating. Lead has a melting point of 621 degrees Fahrenheit, while tempered hooks (according to the industry experts at Mustad) would have to be heated to about 900 degrees to damage the point temper.

If making jigs with a brush-type weed guard, mold them with the small pins designed to make a socket for the brush guard, but only add the brush guard after painting with powder paint.

These pins or core rods are usually supplied with the molds used to make brush guard jigs. If the jig's nylon brush guard is in place, placing a jig head in a heated oven will result in the brush guard curling up like the head of Little Orphan Annie. Since the powder paint might fill up or clog the socket for this weed guard application, it helps to have a drill bit the same diameter as this socket hole to ream out the paint after the jig head is painted but before trying to glue the brush guard into place in the lead head.

For the same reason, you cannot finish or tie tails on a lead bucktail before painting with powder paints. First, the heat would burn the tail materials, and it might burn the thread holding the tail materials in place. Second, the addition of a tail might impede dipping the lure head into the small jar of powder paint.

In heating the lures prior to painting, the lures obviously become too hot to handle with your fingers. The easy way to handle lead jigs is to hold the hook by the bend with a pair of long-nose pliers. Once the lure is heated, dip the lead part of the lure into the powder paint. Another way of heating lead lures is to hold them by the bend of the hook and then place them rapidly into the flame of a butane torch. I often use this method, although I am careful to keep the hook bend and point away from the flame, heating only the lead body of the bucktail.

The big advantage of the oven method of heating is that all the lures in the oven will be at the same temperature. Testing one to see if you get good powder paint coverage after pulling the lure from oven assures that you'll get the same results with the others. When using a butane torch, you have to be careful as to the placement of the jig head into the flame and also the time it takes to get a good even coat.

To paint two colors onto a lure, first paint the entire lure a solid color. Then reheat the lure and dip the head only partway into the second color to make a two-color lure. Powder paints and the heating painting method prevent the use of additional stencils, guides, or fancy patterns, as you can with other paints and finishing methods.

PAINTING PATTERNS AND USING STENCILS

Lures are seldom painted one solid color. Underwater plugs, some bucktails, and some spoons may be a solid color, but most lures are given a scale finish, bars, mottled-pattern markings, fishlike vertical lines, or similar finishes. Stencils and various masks can be used over any base coating on any plug, crankbait, spoon, spinner blade, or even bucktail head.

Stencils and masks are essentially sheets of flat material cut out in various designs. Often the sheets are of plastic, cardboard, masking tape, or paper that has been cut or punched with the design you want on your lure. Stencils aren't restricted only to flat sheets of cardboard and plastic though. One of the best ways to make vertical perchlike bars on a lure is to spray paint through the coarse teeth of a large comb—a method used by at least one major lure manufacturer!

Some typical stencil patterns include bars added to the sides of plugs and spoons in wavy lines (such as in the popular red-and-white casting and trolling spoon), dots, mottled patterns, and stripes. Gill slits can also be masked and painted red.

Some plug and spoon kits come with stencils for painting included, but most do not. You can make your own stencils by a number of simple methods. One is to use a paper punch and punch out holes in paper, cardboard, or lightweight plastic sheets (available at art supply stores). You can even punch some of these holes off center to make them irregular for a mottled froglike pattern. Irregular patterns can be found almost anywhere. I've found them in fly swatters and various grocery wrappers—you just have to keep your eyes open. In addition, craft shops often sell plastic stencils that will make dots and diamonds. These are sold for tole and other stencil work on wood and fabric.

Stripes and strips can be created easily by using a razor blade to cut the shapes to be painted into paper or plastic. For example, to make a mask for a wavy line on a red-and-white spoon, cut out two triangles (one side wavy) large enough to cover any spoon to be painted. The trim area will mask all but the central wavy strip on the spoon. Thus you will have two triangle cutouts with the strip in between. This is best for painting any stripe when spraying a dark color over a light base coat. For the reverse—a dark spoon with a light or white centerline—just cut out the center wavy stripe in a separate mask. Paint the spoon white, allow it to cure, lay and secure the wavy-stripe mask over the center, and then spray again with the darker color paint. Any similar stripes—wavy lines, multiple patterns, etc.—can be cut the same way.

The best way to use a stencil is to tape one side of the stencil or mask to a base of cardboard so that the tape acts as a hinge. Lift the free side of the stencil, slip the lure under it, and hold or tape down the other side. Spray the lure, and then lift the stencil and remove the lure. Once the paint is cured, do the lure's other side. Both

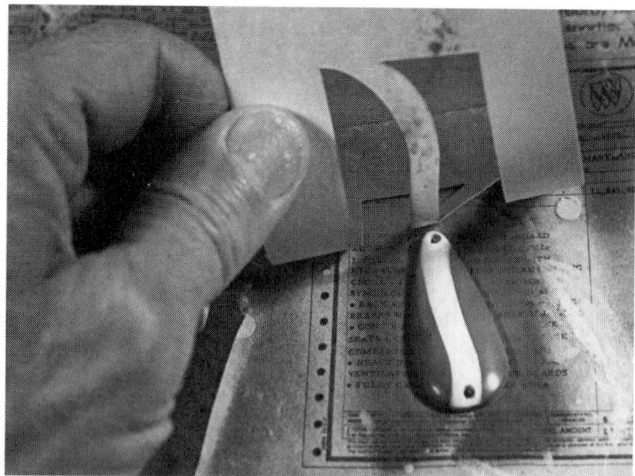

The best way to use templates is to tape them down so that the lure body can be placed under them in turn for painting as shown here. This commercial template produces this particular stripe on a spoon blade.

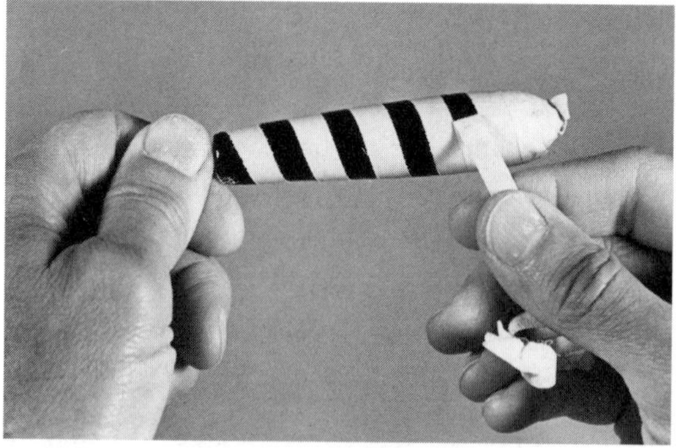

Spiral patterns can be made using thin strips of masking tape. Here a lure has been painted and then masked in a spiral pattern and repainted.

sides are stenciled on plugs, top-water lures, and bucktails, but usually only one side is stenciled on spoons and spinner blades.

This method works best with flat lures, since a fat crankbait will not allow close contact with the spraying mask. The method will still work, but the finish will be slightly blurred or fuzzy at those areas where the mask is separated from the lure. You can adjust the sharpness of the line or border of the painted area by making a "nest" to hold the lure precisely, with the masking stencil in a frame an inch or two above it. Spraying this way creates softer lines. Experiment for the effect you want—the distance of the mask to the lure and of the spray gun to the mask will affect results.

This is not as time-consuming as it sounds, but it does point out the necessity of making lures in a mini-mass-production assembly line. If you are painting both sides of a lure, you often need two templates (mirror images) and must allow time for one side of the lure to dry before reversing the design and spray-painting the other side. (In the case of spoons, only one side is painted, usually the convex side.)

Masking tape can also be cut into a stencil and taped onto a lure before spraying. It takes a little more time, and the results are not as long-lasting as a flat stencil (the tape will deform or tear after a few uses), but it does work well on small lures or on large round lures where you want sharp lines.

PAINTING SCALE FINISHES

Scale finishes are added over the base coat or over a selected base color on a lure. Where a scale finish is to be added, it is best to use a light color for the base, covering it with a darker or contrasting color for visibility.

The scale netting used for these finishes is available from most mail-order tackle companies and some tackle shops. You also can get this or very similar netting from fabric stores. The netting can be used in two different ways. One is to dip the net into paint thinner and wrap it tightly around the lure. The paint thinner in close contact with the net will tend to cut into the base paint of the lure and make a more pronounced scale effect. Once the net is wrapped around the lure, spray the lure with the chosen finish or partially *with the net in place*. With most spray enamels or lacquers, this will take only a few minutes. Remove the netting and dip it in the thinner again for the next lure. Failure to wash the netting each time will result in smeared lures, since the paint from the spraying operation will get on the next lure. This is a slow and messy operation, but it produces good results. Be sure to use protective gloves (rubber or plastic) to avoid contact with the paint thinner.

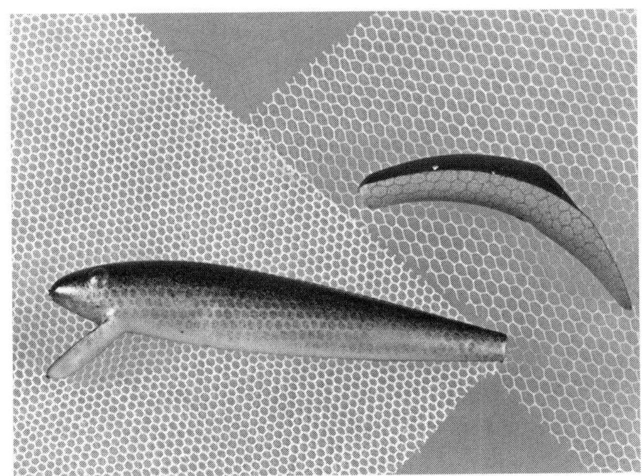

Two different styles of scale netting with the resultant finish on lure bodies.

Spring- or clamp-style embroidery hoops hold scale netting securely for spray-painting lures. Different sizes and shapes are available.

A quicker, better method with very similar results is to fasten the scale netting in a frame and hold the lure in place behind and in contact with the netting for spraying. You can build a frame out of wood strips, but an embroidery hoop works just as well. (Embroidery hoops work several different ways, but all have an outer ring clamped around an inner ring. They are available in a variety of sizes in both round and oval shapes. The best for tackle crafting are about 4 to 12 inches in diameter.) Clamp the netting in the hoop, and hold the hoop in a vise or base support to hold it vertically. In any of these frames or hoops, the netting must be slightly loose, because you want it to fit tightly against the curved side of the plug or lure. The plug can be held by hand (wear gloves) or by a screw eye (even better) screwed into one end of the plug; hold the eye, and thus the plug, with a pair of inexpensive pliers. Keep in mind that you will be spraying paint, so buy inexpensive tools or mask them with tape or cardboard shields. Hold the side of the plug or lure tightly against the netting, and spray through the netting with one or two passes of the spray gun or aerosol can.

The usual procedure for painting a plug with a scale finish is to spray or brush the entire plug with a chosen light-color base coat. Then spray the sides through the netting with a slightly darker shade. Finally spray the top of the plug (*not* through the netting) with a dark color for contrast. The result is very similar to a baitfish—dark on top, medium on the sides, with a light-colored belly.

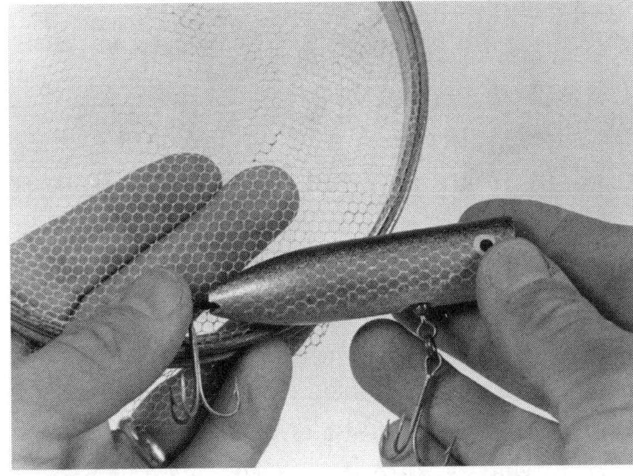

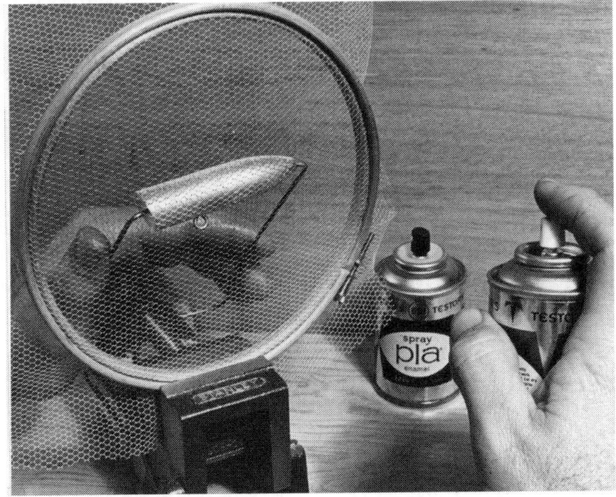

An embroidery hoop with scale netting held in a vise makes it possible to create scale finishes on lures. Hold lures tight against the netting for best results.

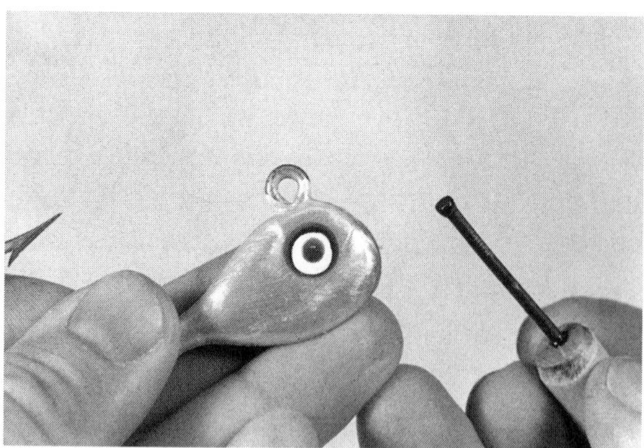

Painting the pupil of an eye using a nail head. A larger nail head was used for the base eye color.

Scale finishes can be used on any lure, including spinner blades, spoons, bucktail heads, and spinnerbait and buzzbait heads and blades.

CRAQUELE PAINT

Craquele paint has a cracked look and is often used to create a crazed or antique furniture look. Recently it has also been used on fishing rods (see chapter 25). This paint comes in special kits, usually readily available from art supply and craft stores. Some thirty years ago lure manufacturers used this method to create lures—mostly crankbaits. It was popular for several years before falling out of favor.

The method uses two different paints—a base coat and then an overcoat that will crack and craze to show the base coat. To create this effect, first brush, dip, or spray a base coat on the entire lure, and then finish the lure with the craquele paint or kit. Use durable paint for the base coat. Many lure makers use spray automotive paint.

Once this base coat is cured (overnight), use the craquele kit to add the special varnish, followed by the craquele paint a few hours later. Usually about 90 minutes of curing time is best, but be sure to follow the instructions in the kit you are using. In time (usually a few hours) the surface craquele paint will crack or craze to create this unusual effect. To protect this finish add a coat of light epoxy rod varnish or other protective clear finishing coat. While this is a pretty straightforward technique, it's a good idea to try all these steps on an old lure to make sure there are no unwanted chemical reactions that will affect the final result. Since this is a two-paint process, often the best results are obtained by using a base coat and a finishing craquele paint in contrasting colors so that the cracked finish will show. You can use this effect over the entire lure or just over the sides, with a dark plain-color back and light plain-color belly. For this look you can just paint the base coat followed by the craquele coat on the sides of the lure after painting the back and belly, or you can paint the entire lure with the craquele finish and then lightly spray the back and belly as desired.

In addition to kits available from craft and art stores, you can also use a nail polish available from Sally Hansen. The result is the same, with a crackled topcoat and a contrasting-color base coat showing through. First use a standard nail polish to create a base coat or undercoat. Once this base is cured and dry, paint the crackle polish on top. As this cures and dries, it will crack to show the undercoat polish. You can use clear nail polish or a clear rod-building epoxy finish on top for protection. If using anything other than a crackle finish made by the nail polish manufacturer, try it first on scrap material to make sure the dissimilar finishes to not react with each other.

ADDING AND PAINTING EYES

Eyes in baitfish have been proven by biologists to be a triggering factor in strikes or attacks by gamefish and other predators. Thus large, prominent eyes are a must for any lure. They won't ever hurt, and they might possibly affect how crowded your live well is at the end of the day. Generally, if there is a question between eyes or no eyes, add eyes. If it is a question between little eyes or big eyes, make them big.

Eyes can be painted on any lure, and there are several techniques for doing this. If you are really expert, you can use the finest spray nozzle of an airbrush and spray a small eye, following later with a contrasting color for a smaller pupil. You can also use two different templates or masks, spraying first through the larger of the two for a background eye color and following later (after the first coat has dried) with the smaller template for a dark contrasting-color pupil. The only difficulty with this method is in positioning the second template to center the pupil on the eye already painted. You can use clear plastic and small punched holes for this so that you can see through the plastic to position the mask. You can also position the pupil at an edge of the background eye to make a forward-, backward-, up-, or down-looking eye. Some lure companies do this as a special design or identifying characteristic on their lures.

You can make simple "tools" for this process, these tools being nothing more than different size pins and nails. The best nails and pins for this are those with flat heads, such as regular straight pins and small flathead brads, common nails, and box nails. Seat them in a small dowel or cork, which acts as a handle.

Dip the head of a larger pin or nail into the background color paint. Make sure you do not submerge the nail or pin head but only touch the top of the head to the surface of the paint. Then lightly touch the paint-covered head to the lure. Do this on both sides with top-water plugs, crankbaits, and bucktails.

Once the paint is cured, follow with a smaller pin or nail head in a darker contrasting paint to make the pupil. Since you can see the background eye, you will be able to position the pupil exactly where you wish. Even a third color can be added with a still-smaller head.

Eyes are added after all other coats of paint have been applied because they are a finishing touch. The only addition after eyes would be a coat of clear or epoxy finish over the entire lure. For the eyes to show up properly on a lure, it is important to use contrasting colors. Thus you would want a color contrasting with the plug for the background eye color and then a color contrasting with that for the pupil. Good background colors include white, yellow, orange, and red; for the pupil use black or white. Of course you can reverse this, using black for the background color and then adding a yellow pupil.

There are a number of other ways eyes can be added to lures. Doll eyes are ideal for this. These come in several styles, including the glue-on styles with moving pupils, also called "rattle" eyes. These doll eyes come in sizes from 3 millimeters up to about 25 millimeters—the latter for big-game lures. Most come with a white background eye and a black pupil, although eyes with pink, blue, green, or red pupils are starting to become available. Most have a flat back that is easily glued onto any lure, although some stemmed doll eyes are also useful. With wood plugs you have an added advantage in that you can slightly recess the body with a hole the diameter of the eye and glue the eye into the recessed area. These eyes can be glued onto any lure though—bucktails, spinnerbait heads, buzzbait blades, plugs, top-water lures, and spoons.

Eyes have proven to be very important on lures. Here doll eyes have been glued onto several lures. The eyes come in several sizes, shapes, and colors.

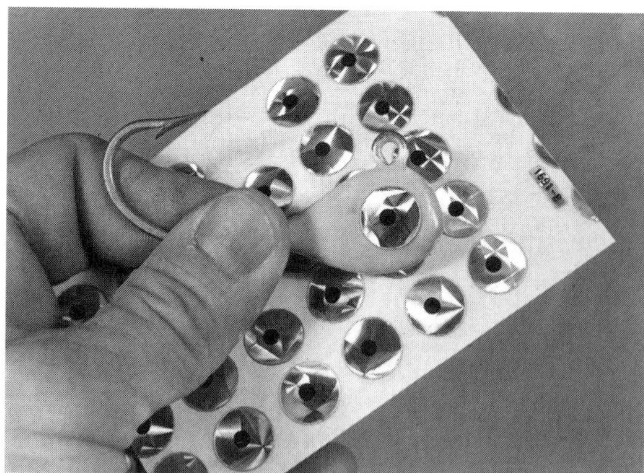

Example of decal eyes available for lures. Many sizes and colors are available. For best results protect the eyes with a clear finish.

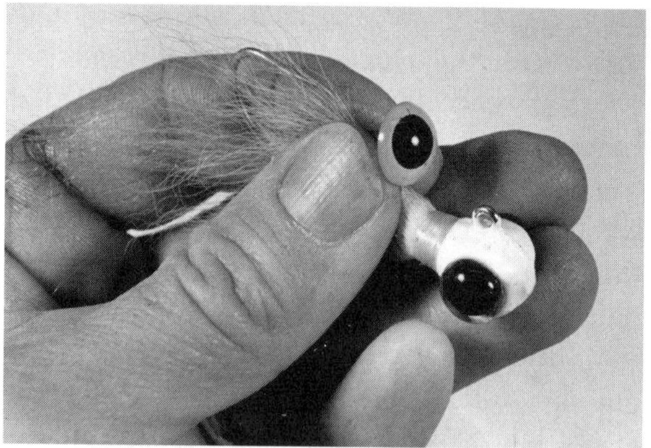

Sew-on doll eyes are also good for lures, but cut off the stems before gluing the eyes to the lure. An alternative with wood plugs is to drill a hole to receive the stem. These bulging eyes are used on a bucktail.

Solid doll eyes on a plastic stem (with a hole in the stem for sewing onto the doll or with a friction-fit back for fitting through a hole in the doll fabric) or movable plastic eyes on a stem are also good. The solid eyes come in sizes from about 5 millimeters to 25 millimeters, often with a yellow background color and black eye. If you can find them, eyes with a clear background and black pupil are best, since this allows you to paint the back of the eye in any color desired. Since these eyes have a stem, they must be mounted by drilling a hole into the lure (on lead bucktails or wood plugs only) and gluing the stem in place or by cutting the stem off to glue the flat back to the lure (on spoons, spinner blades, and plastic plugs).

Another interesting eye material is the half-round beads with no holes that are sold in craft stores and catalogs. These can be painted any color desired and are often best when used in small sizes as pupils against contrasting-color background eyes painted on lures.

Map tacks are another possibility. These are sold in stationery and office supply stores and consist of a round head on a pin. They come in many colors but only in small sizes. They are fine to create a bug-eyed appearance on small lures and especially fly-rod popping bugs. Because map tacks are completely round, it often helps to countersink a hole in the lure slightly to recess the tack.

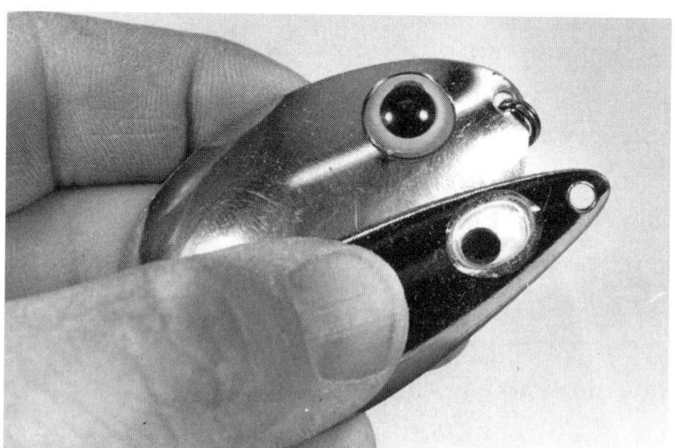

Examples of solid plastic eyes (top) and "rattle" doll eyes (bottom) used on spoon blades.

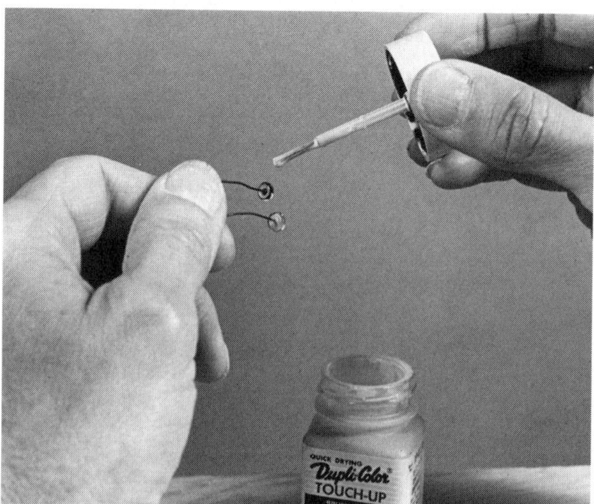

Glass eyes are available for lures (and taxidermy work); the backs of the eyes can be painted to make different color eyes with black pupils.

Glass eyes are available from some craft stores and catalogs, mail-order-component tackle-supply houses, and taxidermy shops. They are usually fastened to a wire stem, which can be glued into some lures (wood plugs and bucktails) after you've drilled a small pilot hole, or the stem can be removed and the glass eye glued on the lure surface. They are more expensive than any other type of eye, and styles are somewhat limited in small sizes. Some are colored, but others can be painted on the back to provide a background eye color. To use, cut the stem of the eye to about ½ inch long and glue it in place in a small pilot hole drilled for this purpose.

Another possibility is the decal eyes that come in sheets. Cut out the pair of eyes to be used, moisten them, and slide them onto the lure. For permanence they have to be covered with a coat of clear finish.

BAKING PAINTS

One method of increasing the durability of lure finishes is to bake the painted lures in a kitchen oven. This can only be done with metal lures, such as spinner blades and spoons. You risk burning wood lures and will definitely melt and destroy plastic lures if you bake them.

Baking paint does have disadvantages as well as advantages. You will note that in the list of metal lures above, bucktails were left out. This is because baking increases the brittleness of paint as well as its durability. Since bucktails are made of a malleable metal (lead) that is often deformed when it hits rocks during fishing, baking would only cause the paint to chip off more readily. Baking is an ideal method for increasing paint durability on hard-metal lures such as spoons and spinner blades.

Baking must be done as the paint is drying. Also, since paints vary widely, baking procedures will vary accordingly. Automotive touch-up paints are especially suitable for baking. Experiment with small quantities of lures, or even with a scrap piece of metal, to determine the results with any given paint and color under specific time and temperature conditions. As a starting point try baking paints in a preheated oven at 175 to 200 degrees Fahrenheit for about 15 to 20 minutes. Some paint experts suggest that baking times can be lengthened and temperatures increased, but do this with caution, experimenting first with painted scraps to check results.

Baking is highly recommended with power paint finishes and on all types of metal lures. Bake in an oven at about 350 degrees Fahrenheit for about 15 minutes.

ADDING GLITTER TO LURES

Metallic or plastic Mylar glitter flakes can be added to any lure to increase its attractiveness. This glitter, available from tackle, craft, and variety shops, is available in small tubes and shaker bottles. It is also available combined in a tube with glue that can be squeezed onto lures. Available colors include red, blue, green, silver, gold, copper, and multicolor mixes. In addition, both standard sizes and micro-glitters are available to adjust the appearance of your glitter-coated lures.

There are several ways to add glitter to lures, depending on the desired effect. For an overall glitter effect, coat the entire lure with special glitter cement (available separately), or use a clear adhesive coating or a clear finish coat. Then shake the glitter out of the bottle onto the lure, turning the lure if necessary to cover it completely. If the glitter you buy does not come in a shaker bottle, you can transfer it to an empty spice or herb shaker bottle. If necessary, ream out the holes in the bottle to make them large enough. The holes in salt or pepper shakers are usually too small to allow passage of the glitter.

Use a base of newspaper or a large tray under the lure during glitter application. Some of the glitter will not stick to the lure, and any excess that falls to the paper or tray can be funneled back into the shaker bottle.

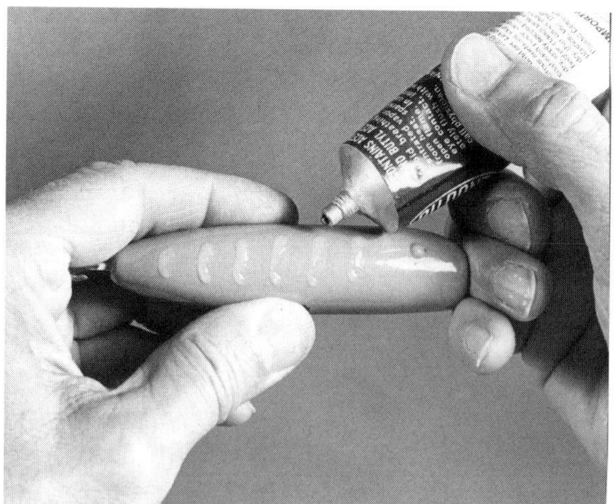

Adding glitter in patterns is easy to do by coating the lure with patterns of glue and then rolling the lure in glitter. Here the glue is applied to the lure.

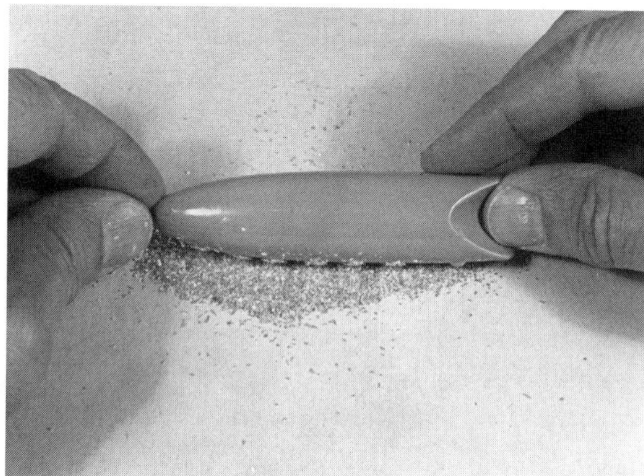

Rolling the lure in glitter.

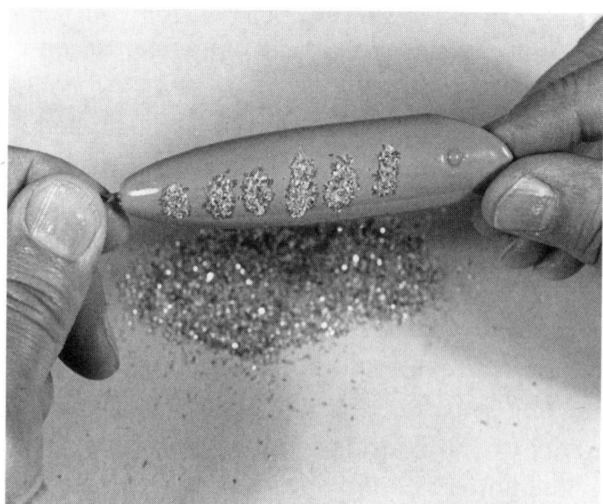

The finished glitter pattern. This method will make for a denser, more compact glitter finish than sprinkling will.

Another method of adding glitter is to paint the lure with clear cement or adhesive on selected parts and then shake glitter over these parts. The glitter will stick only to the adhesive, resulting in a predetermined pattern.

For a denser coat of glitter, paint the lure with adhesive either totally or selectively and then roll the lure in a bed of glitter, previously deposited onto a clean surface. Waxed paper is good for this because it will not discolor the lure (as might newsprint) and will allow easy funneling of the glitter back into the bottle. If you cover the entire lure with adhesive, you will need some sort of lure-holder—pins or screw eyes in both ends or split rings in spoon blades.

Add a final coat or two of clear finish to the lure to protect the glitter finish and keep it from flaking off.

FLOCKING LURES

While flocking is principally done on fishing rod handles in the fishing tackle industry (see chapter 20), it is also possible to flock lures. Flocking is a method of adding a soft fuzzy material to a surface by blowing short strands of nylon or rayon onto a surface prepared with a cement or glue.

Information on working with this material is available from DonJer Products Co., 13142 Murphy Rd., Winnebago, IL 61088; (800) 336-6537 or (815) 247-8775.

Rayon strands (0.030) and nylon strands (0.040) are available, but you only want to use nylon for fishing lures and rods. Because of its wood fiber base, rayon will break down with weather, water, and use; petroleum-based nylon is more durable. Nylon is available in fifteen different colors, with matching color Super-Tex Undercoat Adhesive. The flocking is sold in 3- ounce and 1-pound bags, and different colors can be mixed if desired to get a special color. This does require experimentation, however, so be careful; use small mixed amounts until you get the result you want. DonJer also suggests that you can get darker or lighter color flocking by experimenting with the adhesive and the flocking fiber colors. For example, you can get a darker green than the supplied flocking by using a black adhesive.

There are several ways to add the flocking material to a product once the product (lures in this case) is prepared with a brushed coat of adhesive. One is a commercial method using an electrostatic charge to deposit the flocking. For large-scale use at home, you can use an air-assisted spray gun attached to an air compressor with a 1-quart drum holding the flocking material. When released through the trigger pull, air mixes the flocking and shoots it out through a special nozzle. To use, half fill the 1-quart drum with the flocking material, hook up the spray gun to the air compressor, and spray the lure. Another method uses a device called the Mini-Flocker Applicator. The applicator has two telescoping tubes, which are pumped to spray the flocking through five holes in one end of the tubes to coat the lure.

DonJer sells a low-density polyethylene squeeze bottle with a nozzle end. This bottle can be half filled with flocking and squeezed to shoot the flocking onto a lure. Other types of squeezable bottles can also be used.

To use any of these methods, you must have a rack or other means of holding the lure as it's sprayed. One of the easier ways is to hold the lure by the lip or bill, brush on the adhesive, and then use the squeeze bottle to puff the flocking onto the lure, turning the lure in the your hand for complete coverage.

You can't use this method with the Mini-Flocker Applicator, since you will need both hands to work the pump to spray the flocking. In this case secure one end of the lure in a vertical lazy Susan and turn it slowly while pumping the spray device.

Another method would be to put a screw eye into the tail of the lure, hang it vertically, and spin it slowly while puffing the flocking onto the lure. In both of these methods, be sure to have a box or bag to catch for reuse any flocking that does not stick to the lure.

A simple method for a few individual lures would be to put flocking into a paper bag, coat the lure (do one lure at a time) with waterproof adhesive, and drop the lure into the bag. Fold the bag to seal it, and then shake the bag. Remove the lure and hang to cure overnight. With any of these methods, you have about 10 to 15 minutes of working time to coat the lure with flocking.

A final method used for flocking lures is to coat the lure with adhesive, spread flocking out on a sheet of wax paper, and then roll the lure through the flocking. This allows you to put flocking precisely on the parts of the lure you want and makes it easy to recover any unused flocking left on the wax paper. This method also allows you to use two different colors of flocking. For example, you can roll the back of the lure through dark blue flocking and the belly of a lure through separate ivory or white flocking. If doing two colors this way, it is best to coat half the lure (back or belly), allow the lure to cure overnight, and then add adhesive to the bare half of the lure and roll it through the second flocking color. This method isn't as effective as puffing or shooting the flocking onto the lure with an air-powered delivery method. Rolling the lure in the flocking will tend to make the fibers lie down or flatten to the lure instead of standing up like an imitation fur.

This furlike material is ideal for any surface lures, where it can be used in dark natural colors to make imitations resembling mice, shrews, moles, voles, lemmings, etc.

ADDING TAPES

A number of tape products can be used to dress up lures. Some of these, such as prism and colored tapes, are available from Luhr Jensen, Al's Goldfish, Les Davis, Wapsi Fly and Gator Grip (from J & L Tool & Machine Company), and Flasher Lures (from Five Star Products) and are made specifically for lure application. They come in large and small sheets in a variety of different prism patterns and colors. Most have adhesive backs; some, such as the specific shapes available from Gator Grip, peel off easily for application. Many tapes are also available from craft and art stores.

To use tapes that are not precut, cut the tape into the desired shape and size, remove the backing, and position the design over the lure. Since most of these adhesives are permanent upon contact, take care that the tape is properly positioned before contact is made. In the case of large pieces of tape used on large spoons or plugs (or any lures with severe or complex curves), it may be necessary to cut slits into the tape to help it conform to the shape of the lure. Another alternative is to use several smaller, thinner strips of tape on the lure instead of one large piece of tape. The smaller strips are easier to handle and lessen the problems of placing flat tape on curved lures.

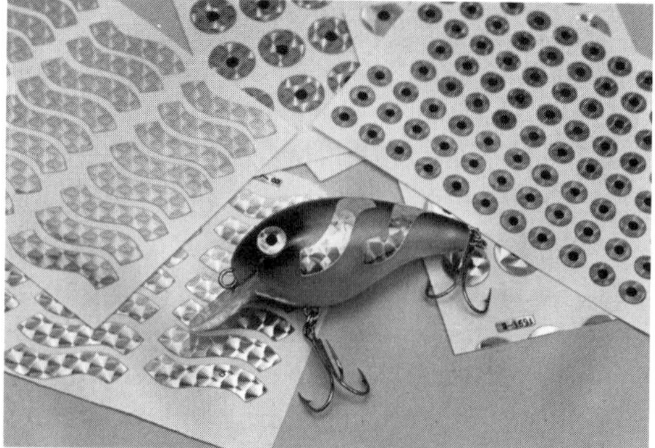

Many tapes are available for adding to any lure—homemade or commercially available.

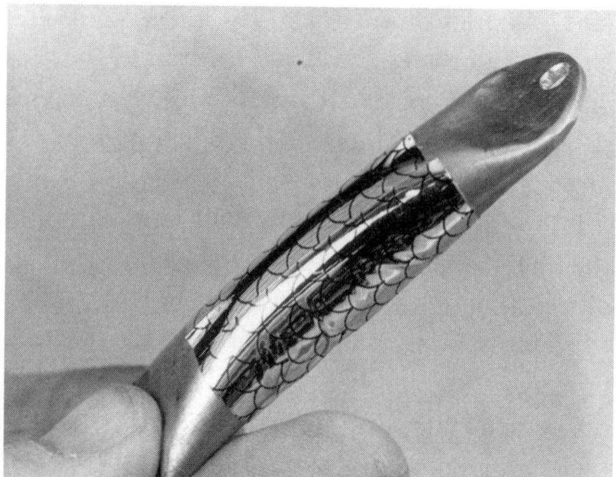

Prism-scale finish tape, here added to a structure lure made from copper pipe.

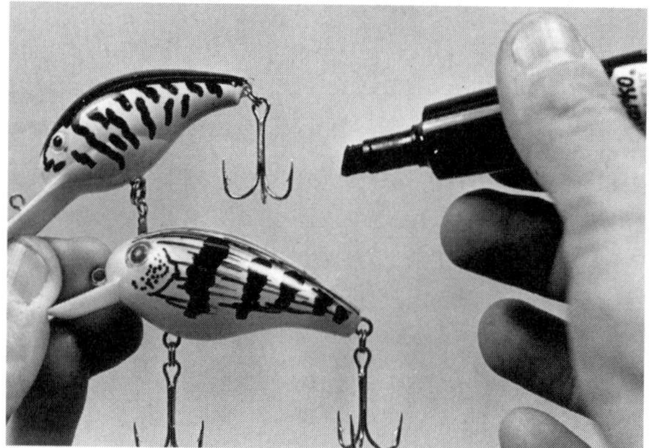

Simple lure finishes on base-painted plugs are easy to do using different colors and sizes of waterproof felt-tip markers.

Finishing up this book, I just discovered Sally Hansen Salon Effects Real Nail Polish Strips. These are another way to add color and patterns to spinner blades and spoons, perhaps even crankbaits if the application surface is not too curved. These brightly colored and patterned self-stick strips—sixteen to a box—come in twenty-four styles, including solid and patterned designs. They are about the size and shape of a #5 or #6 French spinner blade (and smaller), although several sizes are included in each box of patterns. On nails they are said to last up to ten days, so do not consider these permanent. They might be made permanent if coated with a spray or brush-on clear finish. The manufacturer suggests that the strips be applied to nails over a coat of clear nail polish, so perhaps the same would be best with spinner and spoons blades, finishing with a clear coat of fingernail polish or epoxy finish.

Sally Hansen and other nail polish manufacturers make other decorative nail decals, coatings, and such, along with self-application pens and brushes. Check all this out for possible use—and experiments—with lure finishes.

COLORING PLASTIC WORMS AND LURES WITH FELT-TIP MARKERS

Permanent felt-tip markers are good for painting lures. They contain the only type of color (other than dyes) that will effectively color plastic worms or any soft-plastic lure. Plastic worms have color molded into them, but if you wish to make an on-the-water change of that color to a darker color, you can usually do it with felt-tip markers. The final color may be slightly affected by the base color of the worm or by how dark that base color is, so don't expect perfect colors or perfect results. If you plan on changing colors in the field a great deal, the solution is to buy or mold clear worms or worms that are very light in color—smoke, yellow, any light-colored shade. That way you can change color as desired and get as close as possible to the color of the felt-tip-marker.

Felt-tip markers will also work on other lures. They are least effective on bare metal, such as on spinner blades and spoons, but will work over painted, finished plugs, top-water plugs, crankbaits, and bucktails. They work best if a dark color felt-tip marker is used over a light color. However, on soft-plastic and other lures, be forewarned that these colors are difficult to remove later on. Alcohol or lighter fluid works in some cases, but experiment first before going wholesale with felt-tip color changes. Also check the felt-tip-marker label, since some of these products contain solvents that will remove color from soft plastic.

FIELD PAINTING AND DYEING

Just as felt-tip markers are ideal for field-coloring lures, so are some dyes and paints made just for this purpose. Companies that market these colors change, but Spike-It and perhaps some other companies carry quick-dry paints specifically designed for field use on both hard and soft lures.

Most of these paints come in small bottles (1 or 2 ounces) with a lid-attached brush for immediate, no-problem application. Kits of these colors are also available.

For field applications make sure the lure is dry. If you have recently used the lure, dry it completely (be careful of the hooks) or allow it to lie in the sun for a few minutes to dry after shaking off the excess water. If it's bright, hot, and sunny, use your body to shade the lure as you apply the paint—otherwise it will dry too rapidly. Use rapid brushstrokes to cover the whole lure, working first on one side and then on the other. If you are making bars, stripes, or dots, use the brush as evenly as possible. Often it helps to hold the lure on something stationary like a boat deck and support your brushing hand on the same surface to produce even strokes. Although these paints will dry in a few minutes, you can fish almost immediately if you do not touch the painted finish. Just drop the lure in the water and start trolling, casting, or fishing again. After a few minutes in the water, the lure finish will be dry to the touch.

Dyes are available that allow you to dye your lures. These products are best on permeable lures such as rubber skirts and on feather and fur tails. They will lightly color hard lures though. These dyes are designed for field use and applied the same way as the paints just described.

FINAL LURE FINISHING

All lures, whether plugs, spoons, spinners, or bucktails, will look better and last longer if several final finishing coats of clear lacquer or epoxy finish are added to protect the paints. These finishes will also protect lures to which eyes (painted or applied), tape, and other final touches have been added. These clear finish coats should be added only after all the base coats, scale finishes, eyes, tapes, glitter, and other finishing procedures have been completed.

Make sure the clear finish coats are chemically compatible with the previous coats used on the lures to prevent a reaction that might damage all your work. Dipping or spraying is the best method of application for these final coats. The toughest are those finishing coats of two-part clear epoxy.

KITS

Painting and finishing kits provide an easy way to get the proper colors and finishing materials for lures at minimal cost. Cabela's, Bass Pro Shops, Jann's Netcraft, Hagen's, Mud Hole, Merrick, Do-It, and others listed in appendix F offer these kits. Kits are a great way to start finishing lures; you can later add replacement paints or different colors for your specific needs.

16

Making Molds for Lead and Soft-Plastic Lures

Introduction • Aluminum Bucktail Molds • Silastic Rubber Bucktail Molds • Plaster Bucktail Molds • Miscellaneous Sinker Molds • Tin-Squid Molds • One- and Two-Piece Soft-Plastic Lure Molds • Molds for Offshore Lures

INTRODUCTION

The basic tools for making a wide variety of molds are no different from the basics we have already described. You can make many of these molds with no tools at all; others will require only the basics.

To make most molds you will need odds and ends of scrap aluminum, wood, nails, and other bits and pieces found in most shops. Most of these molds require little time, talent, or materials and can add greatly to the ease with which you can construct tackle and to the variety of lures you can make. Although the basics are discussed here, your imagination will no doubt suggest variations.

As with all lure-making and rod-building tasks, safety procedures must be followed. Be sure you know how to use any of the tools described in this chapter before you use it. Use a work apron, roll up your sleeves, and remove jewelry when using machinery. Use protective clothing and gloves when working with potentially irritating mold-making compounds. Wear an appropriate face mask if fumes are likely to result from some of these processes. Wear safety glasses at all times.

ALUMINUM BUCKTAIL MOLDS

If you have a design for a bucktail and want to make a commercial-type aluminum mold for it, there are ways this can be done. The easiest way is to get a "blank" mold—one with hinges and handles but no cavities. These are available from Do-It, Hilts Molds, and Li'l Mac. Do-It makes a standard-size blank mold (4⅝ × 2⅛ × 9⁄16 inch on each side) that is hinged and handled. Li'l Mac blank molds are 1 inch thick on each side. You must be able to fit the finished lure into the length, width, and depth of the mold, and you must be able to machine the cavities for the lure yourself or contract with a small machine or tool-and-die shop for this work. If you do not machine the mold yourself, it may be relatively expensive (maybe four or five times the cost of a standard bucktail mold) to have it done. It is wise to check out this cost before ordering a blank mold.

The Perfect Replica Mold from Hilts Molds is a large aluminum mold, hinged and handled, with several gates and a large rectangular cavity (2 × 5 × 1 inch). It comes with two pieces of silicone that are worked like modeling clay to make the mold and then vulcanized in the oven at 375 degrees Fahrenheit for 45 minutes, after which the gates are cut with a knife. Extra silicone inserts are available for making molds with several different cavities for use in the accompanying frame.

You can make your own molds from aluminum blocks or by using a Do-It or Li'l Mac blank mold. You will need block aluminum, special drills, rotary files, and routers. Do-it-yourself aluminum in the ¼-inch thickness is okay for small lures; larger blocks of aluminum are available from scrap-metal dealers and some hobby shops. A portable drill on a light drill stand, a drill press, or a rotary grinder is necessary for machining the cavities in the two aluminum mold halves. A Dremel Moto-Tool also works well, since a number of small routers, sanders, drill bits, and grinding bits are available for these versatile tools.

The basic technique is as follows: First cut out the two blocks of aluminum to the size needed for the bucktail or bucktails. Allow for at least a 1-inch margin on all sides of the jig. Allow a wall

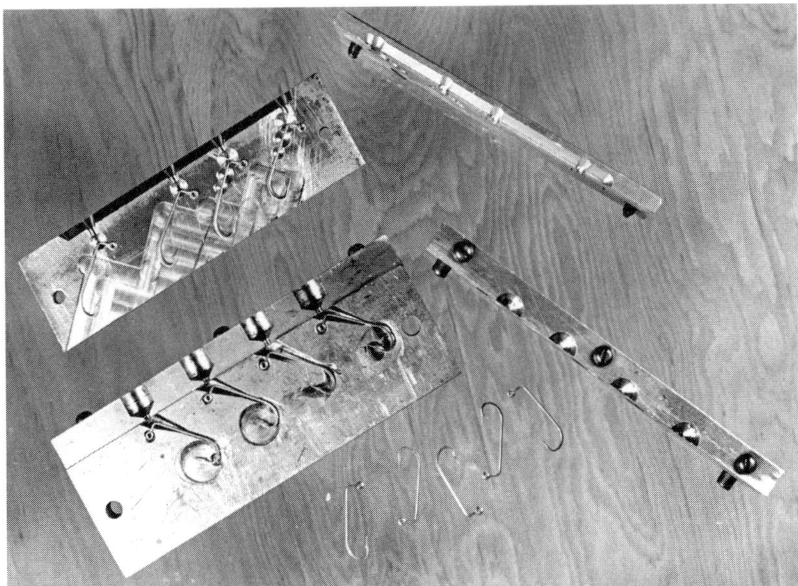

Aluminum molds for making lead lures can be made from block aluminum but require innovative construction methods. To make this mold for shad darts (bottom mold), the builder first drilled angled, tapered holes and then added a separate plate separately drilled for the sprue hole. The separate place is permanently screwed in place on the base block. Note the registration pins also placed in each mold.

thickness of at least ⅛ inch at the widest (thickest) part of the lure. Clamp the two blocks together, and drill a ⅛-inch hole through opposite sides of the two blocks (the sprue holes will be on one of the other sides), drilling the blocks together. Insert a #10 finishing nail (or other stiff ⅛-inch wire) through each of the two holes in one block, tapping it firmly in place. Cut the pins flush on the outside of the mold and leave about ¼ inch exposed inside to fit into the holes on the other block. These form registration pins. You may wish to sand the protruding pins a little for a good fit without binding; you may also wish to tap or swage the pins in place a little to secure them in the one block. This procedure will ensure proper registration of the two mold halves for the rest of the work and for pouring the lead heads once the mold is completed.

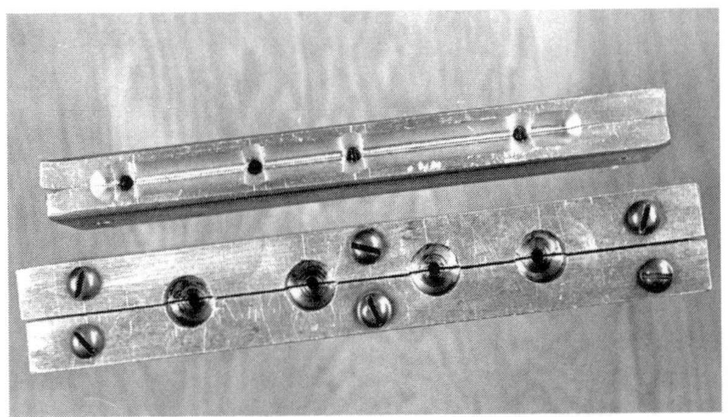

Top view of above two molds, showing the sprue holes.

You can use the mold as is, or you can finish it with hinges and handles. To do this, drill and tap holes for the machine screws to hold the hinges in place. You can also cut the heads off the screws and glue wood handles in place. Or you can avoid this step by using the Do-It or Li'l Mac molds, which already have handles and hinges.

Place a sheet of paper between the two mold halves and clamp them together so that the two pins (or nails) cut holes into the paper. (If you use the Do-It or Li'l Mac mold, trace the mold outline on both sides, because there are no registration pins.) Outline the block on the paper and remove the block. Draw an outline of the chosen bucktail shape in the center of the paper square. Cut the bucktail outline out of the paper and retrace it on both sides of the mold halves, taking care that the paper is *exactly* positioned on the pins or on the outline of the mold.

Using rotary files in a rotary grinder (such as the Dremel Moto-Tool), cut out the shape of the bucktail from each half of the mold. Periodically check the shape of the mold by pressing a small piece of beeswax or children's modeling clay between the two mold halves. Continue cutting and shaping until the two cavities are symmetrical, with the edges in perfect alignment.

Similarly, rout out a sprue hole or gate (the tapered or funnel-like opening through which lead is poured into the mold cavities). Mark the proper position for the jig hook, cut slots for the hook shank and holes for the eye, and make any other additions as required. These additions could include space for molded-in weed guards. Once the mold is completed, it can be used in the same ways as any commercial mold. Follow the techniques outlined in chapter 4.

SILASTIC RUBBER BUCKTAIL MOLDS

Silastic RTV mold-making rubber from Dow Corning is an ideal medium for making molds of unusual bucktails and other lead lures. (RTV stands for "room temperature vulcanizing," a method of curing the silicone rubber mold with a catalyst.)

In the past you could buy this material directly from Dow Corning. Today it is only available from distributors (check the Yellow Pages), which in turn might refer you to local stores or outlets to get the small quantities needed by lure makers.

There are a number of different Silastic rubber compounds, each of which consists of a liquid that sets up into a solid with the addition of a catalyst. All the Silastic compounds would work for making bucktail molds, but some are better suited than others because of their viscosities. Some, such as types C and D, are very thick or viscous and would not pour well. The types most often made available for bucktails molds are the Silastic RTV A and B. These have good temperature stability of up to 500 degrees Fahrenheit (600 degrees with the type B), which is suitable for the intermittent heat of molding lead bucktails. (Lead melts at 621 degrees Fahrenheit.)

You will also need a catalyst, and the catalyst must match the rubber compound used. Usually catalyst type #1 is best for compound types A or B, the, since it promotes a standard cure rate and good working time. A #4 catalyst promotes a fast cure rate and should be avoided because it will give you far less time to work.

EasyMold Silicone Putty from Environmental Technology, Inc., is good up to 400 degrees but would be questionable for use with lead, even with intermittent heat. Lead melts at 621 degrees Fahrenheit and for even a small sinker or bucktail might burn or melt the molding material.

Note that safety must be paramount when working with these or any mold-making materials. Check the safety precautions supplied by the manufacturer.

To make a mold, begin with a bucktail head that is as perfect as possible. If you are working from a finished lure, you must carefully cut off and remove all the tail materials and wrappings. You can make a model of almost anything—good possibilities for models include wood, modeling clay, and carved plastic. Naturally the hook for the finished lure must be included, so a cavity for the hook are left in the finished Silastic mold.

Make sure the model—regardless of what it's made from—is free of grease, oil, fingerprints, or anything you don't want reproduced on the molded lures. Select a container to hold the mold material and the bucktail model. If possible allow for about ½ inch all around the sides but no more, since more will just waste the Silastic rubber. Good containers include film canisters, small juice cans, any plastic kitchen container with the top cut off, and plastic disposable bottles or jars with the tops removed. Cut the container to a height that will allow you to hang the bucktail by the hook on a pencil or toothpick laid across the top of the container. Since the bucktail model will land head down, this makes it easy to later cut a gate or sprue hole into the tail of the lure, where it will be hidden by the skirt or tail and make a clean, perfect bucktail head.

Mix the Silastic rubber according to directions, using a 10:1 (Silastic rubber to catalyst) mix for best results. More catalyst will decrease

Materials and supplies needed for making molds from Silastic rubber compound. Even though these molds are made of rubber, they still allow you to mold lead lures.

working time; less will increase working time. Dow Corning lists the following working and cure times for various mixes:

Silastic RTV Type A

Ratio	Working Time	Cure Time
20:1	4 hours	48 hours
10:1	2½ hours	24 hours
5:1	1 hour	18 hours

Silastic RTV Type B

Ratio	Working Time	Cure Time
20:1	4 hours	36 hours
10:1	2½ hours	24 hours
5:1	1½ hours	12 hours

These cure times are for when Dow Corning catalyst #1 or #16 (used with type A or B rubber only) is used. Dow Corning catalyst #4 is faster acting, with working times as short at 4 minutes and cure times as short as 15 minutes. (Cure times for other types of RTV rubber are available from Dow Corning.)

The two parts of the Silastic rubber compound are added and mixed. Different colors make complete mixing easy to determine.

Mix thoroughly, using a gentle folding or stirring motion. Beating, whipping, or frothing the mix will increase the possibility of air bubbles—and defects—on the surface of the mold. Mixing to a uniform consistency is easy because the rubber and catalyst are two different colors; a smooth uniform color indicates a complete mix.

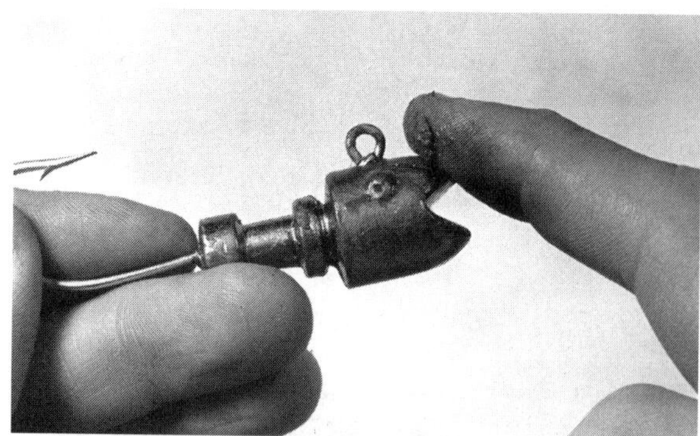
The first step in making Silastic rubber molds is to coat the master lure with a parting compound.

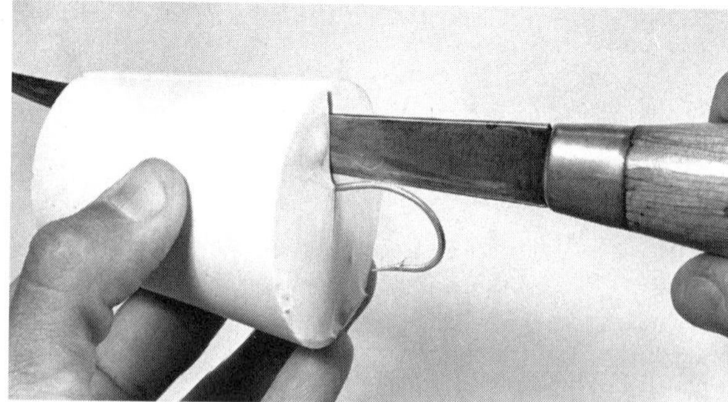
The best way to separate the mold is with a fillet knife, cutting along normal seam lines and in plane with the hook.

One way to prevent air bubbles when pouring the Silastic rubber is to first slowly dip the master lure into the mold compound for complete coverage. Once dipped it can be hung from a pin in a mold container, in this case a paper cup. Then the rest of the Silastic compound is added to complete the mold.

Once the molding compound is added and allowed to cure, the bucktail mold can be removed as shown here.

To make sure the model will separate from the mold, coat the mold with a releasing compound such as Johnson's Paste Wax or with a mix of petroleum jelly and rubbing (isopropyl) alcohol in a 1:20 ratio. (Because of its flammability, take care when using alcohol.) To lessen the possibility of air bubbles even further, coat the model lure with Silastic rubber before placing it into the container. Do this by slowly dipping it into the mixed rubber or, better still, by gently and thoroughly brushing the liquid rubber on the model. This latter method is particularly good if the lure has a lot of intricate detail. Then hang the lure into the container by its hook from a rod or pencil, and slowly pour the Silastic rubber around it into the mold.

Allow this to cure at least overnight, preferably for two nights. At this point you must get the lure model out of the mold by cutting the mold apart. You must do this exactly (or as close as possible) on the same lines or plane of the model so as to free not only the lure but also the hook shank and eye.

One easy way to do this is to cut down along the plane of the hook with a fillet knife until it hits the rear of the model, then cut along this plane until you are close to the bottom of the mold. For best results do not cut the mold completely in half; instead leave the bottom intact. The model (and later the molded heads) can be popped out of the mold by peeling it back from the top. This also eliminates the need of registration pins to line up the mold halves. (If you wish to cut the mold completely in half and use registration pins, first position the bucktail in the container and then push finishing nails through the pouring container in at least two points, preferably four, to properly line up the two mold halves later. These essentially create registration pins to properly line up the mold halves. Pull the finishing nails completely out before you cut the mold in half, and then reinsert them in one side, with about ½ inch protruding. When using registration pins or nails, it is best to use a disposable plastic or cardboard drink container for the mold. That way the nails can be pushed directly and easily through the container to function as registration pins.)

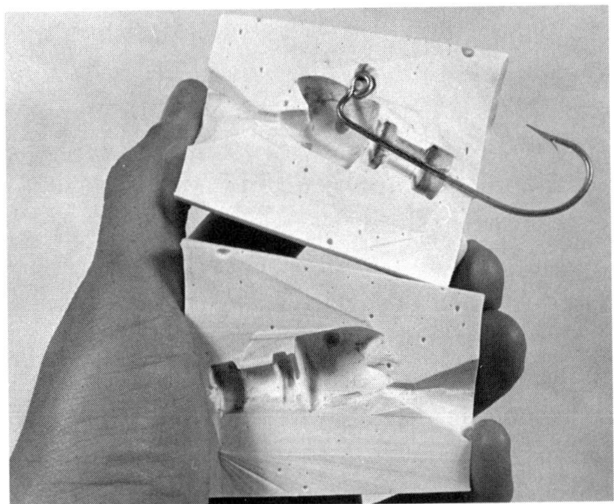

Completed mold in two parts. The sprue hole has been carved into one end for pouring, and a hook has been added.

Pouring lead into the Silastic rubber mold. Note the rubber bands used to hold the two mold halves. An alternative method to using rubber bands is to mold registration pins into the mold.

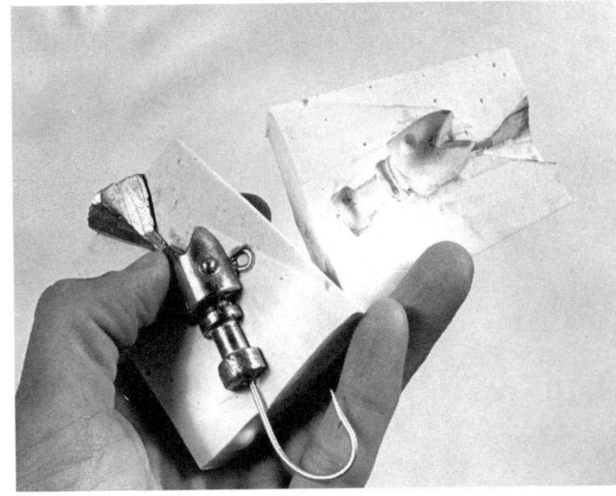

Completed mold with cast lead head.

After the model is out of the mold, use a sharp knife to cut a funnel-like gate or sprue hole into the tail or head of the lure (the top of the mold). Make this funnel about ⅛ inch at the bottom (where it connects with the lure body) and about ½ to ¾ inch at the top.

Once the mold is finished, it can be used just like any other bucktail mold. Place a hook in the mold before pouring, and line up the registration pins or use a rubber band around the top of the mold if it is only split partway through. Follow the instructions in chapters 4 and 5 when melting and pouring the lead. Pay particular attention to the safety instructions, since these *must* be followed, regardless of the type of mold used.

PLASTER BUCKTAIL MOLDS

Bucktail molds made from plaster require no special tools or skills. Plaster of Paris, small boxes or containers for pouring the plaster, a couple of nails for registration pins, petroleum jelly or liquid soap, and a model of a bucktail head are all you need. If it is an original design of a bucktail head, make a sample body of wood, plastic wood, modeling clay, liquid steel, liquid aluminum, epoxy, or a similar easy-to-work material. If you are using a standard commercial bucktail, strip off all the thread and tail material before proceeding. Although we are

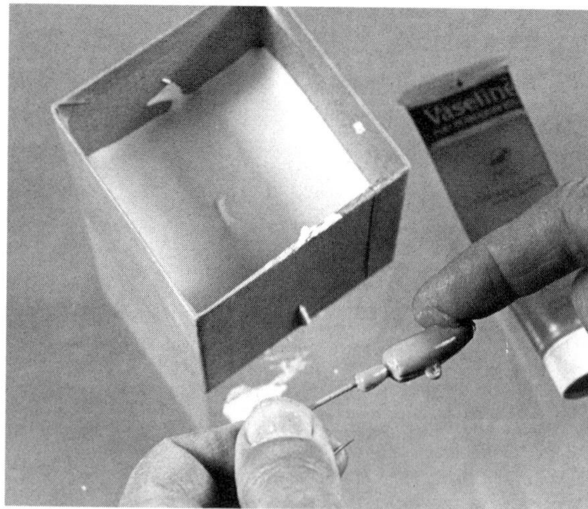

Making a mold from plaster. First half fill a box with plaster, then coat a master lure with petroleum jelly and lay it on its side in the mold.

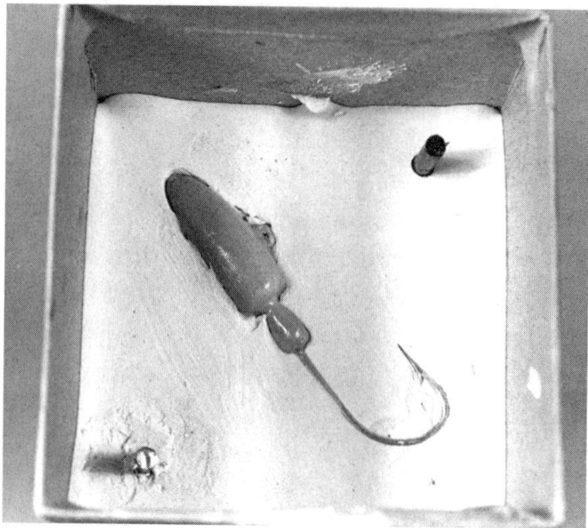
Master lure in mold half, with registration pins (nails with the heads cut off) added.

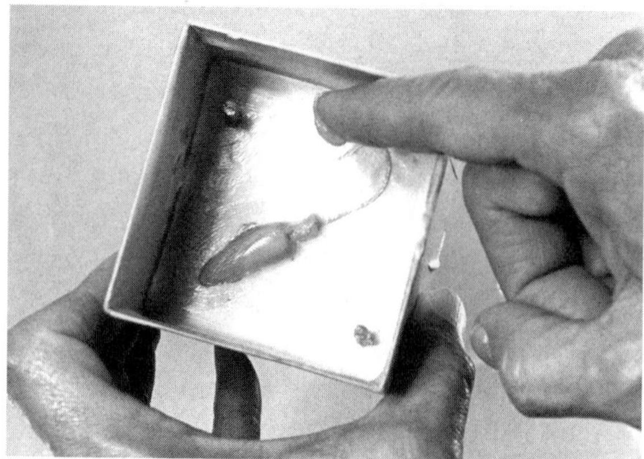
Once the plaster is cured, the rest of the mold is coated with plaster to allow for easy separation.

describing making a mold for a bucktail here, the same technique can be applied to molds for lead sinkers or tin squids.

Find a suitable small box into which the plaster can be poured. Small plastic boxes, cardboard boxes, even cut-down disposable plastic bottles and jars are ideal. A good size for a single-cavity mold for a ½-ounce bucktail would be about 4 × 3 × 1½ or 2 inches deep. Mix the plaster with water to a consistency resembling thick, smooth pancake batter. (Plastic mixing bowls are ideal for this, since any hardened plaster is easily cracked out by bending or twisting the bowl.) However, the plaster should flow, not drop or "plop" into the mold box. Mix only enough to fill half the box, since the mold must be made in two separate parts. It is important to make the plaster as smooth as possible, without air bubbles that can cause defects in the mold cavity. (To remove air bubbles, rap the mixing bowl sharply with a spoon or tap it on a table.)

At this time you can either lengthen or shorten the curing time of the plaster if it seems to be too thick (setting up too rapidly) or too thin (curing too slowly). Add a little salt to speed up the curing process; add a little vinegar to slow it.

Pour plaster evenly over the bottom of the box, filling half the box. While the plaster is starting to set, cover the entire bucktail body, hook, and eye with a thin coating of petroleum jelly to prevent them from sticking to the plaster. Place the bucktail on its side in the plaster. It is critical that the lure be set only halfway into the plaster. If the lure is too shallow, the top part of the mold will contain too much of the lure body and might not mold properly. If the lure sample is too deep, it might wink, which could also make the mold less usable or perhaps not usable at all. An easy way to control this first step of molding half of the lure is to stick a molded "rod" of Fun Tac to one side of the bucktail sample. Fun Tac is a moldable material (like play putty) that sticks to anything yet is easily removed. By using this plug of Fun Tac on one side, it is easy to place the lure and also to hold it in the proper position and depth as the plastic cures. Once the plaster

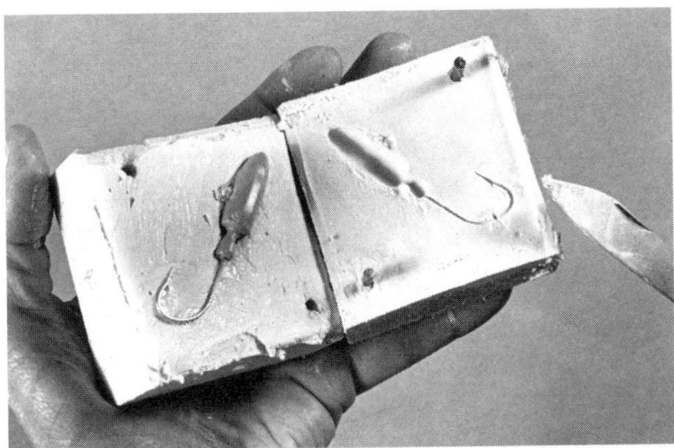

Completed mold after opening by scoring with a knife along the seam lines.

As with Silastic molds, a sprue hole must be carved into the end.

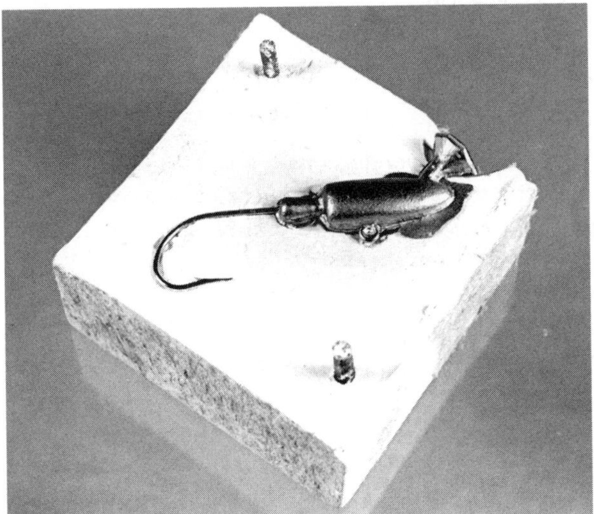

Completed mold with cast lure. Flash is not uncommon with these molds, and ultimately the molds must be discarded as they wear and chip with use.

cures, the Fun Tac also makes it easy to remove the lure and then replace the sample lure for the second part of the molding method.

There is a critical time for doing this: If it is done too early, the bucktail may sink into the still-liquid plaster. If it's done too late, you may not be able to push it halfway into the plaster. Before the plaster sets, take two thick 1- to 1½-inch nails and sink them vertically—head end first—into the plaster at opposite corners of the mold. Leave about ¼ inch of the point end extending out of the plaster. These nails will ensure proper registration during casting. Allow the plaster to set for 30 minutes to 1 hour, and then coat the entire cured exposed surface of the mold with petroleum jelly. This helps the two parts of the mold separate when the plaster is cured.

Now mix another batch of plaster and pour it evenly over the bucktail and the first half of the mold. When the second pouring of plaster has set—in about 1 hour—break or cut apart the box used for the mold, and remove the solid block of plaster. Carefully separate the two mold halves by running a knife blade along the joint. Remove the bucktail from the mold carefully, and allow the mold to cure and dry thoroughly. Plaster holds a great deal of water for a long time, and the curing cannot be hurried. For average-size molds, allow about two weeks to cure.

Caution: Don't ever pour molten lead into a plaster mold that has not been properly or completely cured. The water in the plaster will cause the molten lead to splatter dangerously and the mold to crack and become ruined.

During the two-week curing time, finish the mold by carving a sprue hole. Sprue holes, or gates, allow the molten lead to reach the bucktail cavity. Usually they are placed at either the head or tail end of the bucktail and between the two halves. (Placing a sprue hole at the tail end is best, since any imperfections caused by cutting off the lead sprue after molding will be covered by the bucktail skirt.) Taper the hole, leaving an opening of no more than ¼-inch diameter at the entrance to the cavity. You can, if desired, carve slots in the mold for weedless hooking arrangements, spinnerbait wires, or similar additions.

Once the mold is complete and cured, place a hook in it. Clamp the mold together with woodworkers' spring clamps or C-clamps. If you use C-clamps, fasten them very lightly; because excessive pressure will crack the mold. Plaster molds will not last indefinitely, as iron or aluminum molds will, but with care they are usually good for at least several dozen lures. In time the mold cavity will start to chip around the edges, causing excessive flash in the castings. If you are making sinkers, this is less of a concern, because sinkers do not have to be finely finished or smooth. You can get more from this method by making a multiple-cavity plaster mold that will make several or more bucktails or sinkers at one pouring.

MISCELLANEOUS SINKER MOLDS

While many sinkers are designed and shaped for a specific type of fishing, it is possible to mold a common sinker by drilling a hole in a wood block and using this hole as a mold for pouring in lead. The result is rough in appearance, but for holding a lake or shore bottom, it works as well as a sinker bought in a tackle store or made from a commercial mold.

To make a two-piece wood mold, clamp together two pieces of 1- to 2-inch-thick wood. With a large-diameter drill bit, drill on the centerline between the two blocks so that each block will have a half-hole. Depending on the size of the wood block, you can drill several holes for sinkers. No sprue hole is needed. Fill the drilled hole with molten lead. Hold a brass eye in the center of the sinker with pliers (it will get hot!) until the lead cools. Once the sinker has cooled, separate the two parts of the mold, and pry the sinker out with an awl or pliers. The hole in the wood will burn slightly, but you can make many sinkers before the wood is rendered unusable. These cylindrical sinkers in various sizes can be used for many types of fishing.

A crude type of egg sinker can be made the same way. Drill a ⅛-inch-diameter hole to hold a core rod (usually made from a coat hanger or nail—make this hole deeper than the sinker hole), and then drill the larger diameter hole (big enough to make a crude sinker—perhaps ½-inch to 1-inch diameter, depending upon the sinker size desired) for the sinker. Place the core rod into the mold cavity, and pour the lead around it. Remove the core rod as soon as the sinker cools enough to open the mold.

Carving also allows you to make different sinkers. For example, it is easy to lay out and carve a flat-sided pyramid sinker in two-part wood blocks. With skill and practice you can also carve out examples of bank sinkers or shallow-sided dollar-style sinkers or carve in sprue holes for more precise molding. If you're not handy with a whittling knife, small routers such as the Dremel Moto-Tool make these tasks easy and quick.

A split block of wood like this, drilled with a larger diameter drill bit and also drilled to take a core rod, works to make simple egg or net-type sinkers. The split wood allows removal of the sinkers.

TIN-SQUID MOLDS

Using the techniques for making plaster molds, you can make one-piece (one-sided) tin-squid molds. Tin squids are usually flat on one side and thus lend themselves to one-piece molds, even though commercial molds for them are generally available only in two parts.

Using a tin squid as a model, mix and pour plaster as outlined, placing the tin squid into the mold so that the top flat side is level with the surface of the plaster. If the squid is of the fixed-hook variety, make sure the hook point is up. If the lure uses a swinging hook, remove the hook and any split or jump rings prior to making the mold.

Since these lures are very simple, another technique is to mold a block of plaster, allow it to cure, and then lay out a design and carve or rout the shape into the hardened plaster. You can also use a tin squid or follow a drawing or design pattern to trace an outline on a block of wood or aluminum, carving it to the shape desired. A small whittling knife can be used for carving wood, while electric tools (such as the Dremel Moto-Tool) are ideal for shaping the cavity in an aluminum block. Take care when using this type of mold, since the mold must be filled completely with tin or lead but without any overflowing. A small ladle for pouring helps in this.

ONE- AND TWO-PIECE SOFT-PLASTIC LURE MOLDS

Following the directions given for making two-piece plaster bucktail and one-piece tin-squid molds, you can make plaster molds for molding soft-plastic lures.

There are two possible methods of making a one-piece plastic-lure mold from plaster, but both require a good commercial or homemade lure "master," or model. In most cases these molds are used for making soft-plastic worms, and the model worm, or any lure model, must have one flat side. One method is to lay the model on a flat sheet of glass. This is best when using a lure model that can be glued or stuck to the glass. (Try a small bit of petroleum jelly for this.) With this method it is possible to get a completely flat mold that is very easy to work with.

Stick the worm or worms or other lures to be used to the glass sheet. An 8 × 10-inch glass sheet is fine for all but extra-large lures. Cover the glass sheet with a thin layer of petroleum jelly. Place a plastic or cardboard box, open at the top and bottom, over the lures and onto the glass to contain the plaster. Weight the box to prevent plaster leakage, or tape the box in place.

Fill the box with mixed plaster, following the previous directions. Allow it to set overnight, and

Open-face plaster molds for making jigging spoons and tin squids. Here master lures have been used to make the mold cavities.

Making plaster molds for molding soft-plastic lures. The salt and vinegar can be used to adjust curing times.

After mixing the plaster, pour it into a simple container. This mold is made from aluminum foil.

then carefully remove the box sides, lift the plaster block from the glass, and carefully remove the model lure or lures. If you have difficulty removing a worm or lure, stick a pin or nail into one end at an angle, and carefully pry the lure out of the mold. Any small pieces of plaster that may crack off the edges should be shaken or brushed away before using the mold.

For the second method, a box (with bottom intact) is filled with plaster. Place the master lure carefully onto the plaster with the flat side up. Take care to push the worm down into the plaster until the flat surface is flush with the surface of the plaster. Allow the plaster to cure overnight, and then remove the model lure and clean as before.

Once the mold is cured and dry, it can be used just as commercial soft-plastic molds are used, as described in chapter 7.

However, if the plaster mold is used without further treatment, the resulting worms or lures will have a dull, or matte, finish. A shiny lure finish is possible by first painting the mold cavity with heat-resistant gloss or semigloss paint. These paints resist heat up to 400 degrees Fahrenheit (they are often sold for painting auto engine parts) and are readily available in both spray-on and brush-on containers. One important point: These plaster molds can't be slipped into a pan of water to cool, as can plastic molds. Molding will be slower in a plaster mold because it will take more time for the lure to cool enough to remove.

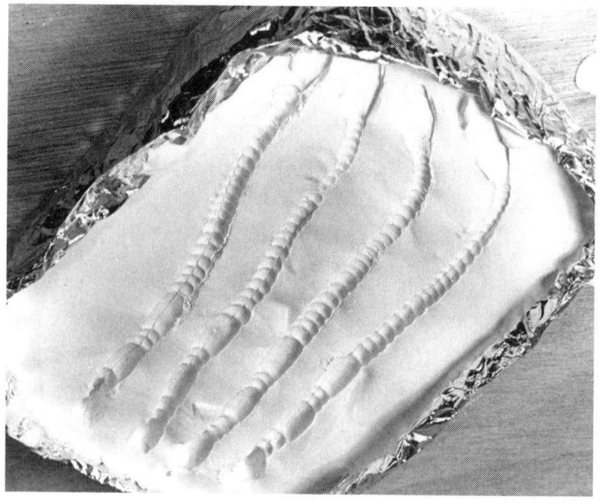

Completed plaster mold for molding worms.

Various worms and soft lures can be combined as shown here to make up new designs of soft-plastic lures. Here a worm and twin spinnerbait tail have been combined in an open-face plaster mold.

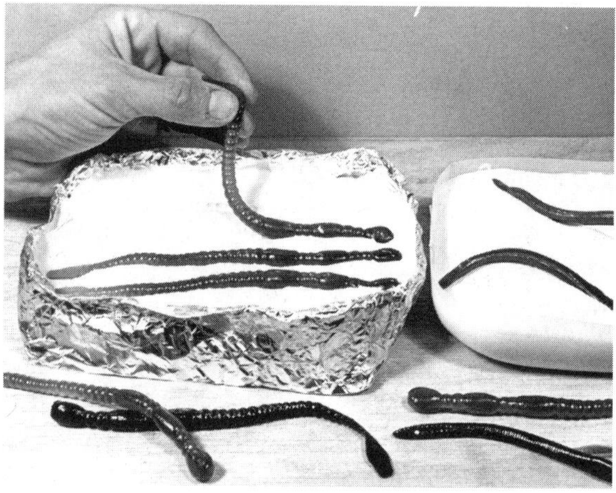

After the plaster is poured, the worms are laid in the liquid plaster. After curing, the worms are removed.

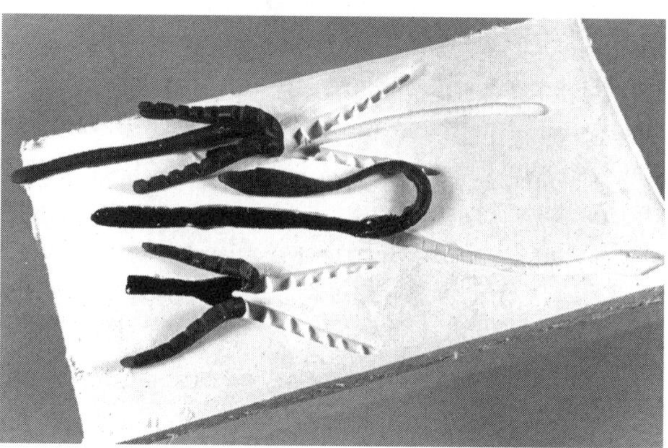

Result of the above molds, with the new triple-tail worm at the top.

Using these methods you can make molds for worms, spring lizards, spinnerbait tails, and other lures by *combining* parts of several different soft-plastic lures. For example, you could take a standard twin-tail spinnerbait tail and add a worm tail to the fork where the two tails meet to make a three-tail spinnerbait tail. The parts do not have to be welded together. Just placing the parts in proximity in the mold will produce a good connection, although you can use heat or a Wormizer to weld the parts together.

Two-piece plaster molds for soft-plastic lures may be made by following the directions for making two-piece bucktail or sinker molds. The plastic must be poured in two parts, and you should pick a box shape that will match the lure shape. Since worms are made frequently, this often means a long, thin box for a one-cavity mold. Be sure to pick master or model lures that are completely round; otherwise a simpler one-piece open-face mold will work just as well with less trouble.

When placing a round worm in the bottom part of the two-piece mold, make sure you position it so that the seam line on the worm is level with the surface of the plaster. Otherwise your molded worms will have two seams—one from the original master worm and the second from the plaster mold. If you mold a curved-tail worm, the curved tail will have to lie out flat on the surface of the mold so that it can be removed easily. Also, as with the bucktail molds, use short nails—at least two of them—to serve as registration pins for the two parts of the mold. These must be placed before the first pouring of the plaster.

Once the first bottom part of the mold is partially cured (30 minutes to 1 hour), cover the mold surface and the model lure with petroleum jelly, and pour the second portion of plaster. Allow this to cure for about 1 hour and then open or cut apart the box and run a knife around the mold joint to open it up. Carefully open the mold, remove the model, and allow the mold halves to cure overnight.

At one end of the mold, carve a sprue hole through which to pour the molten plastic. If this is a worm mold, place the sprue hole at the head

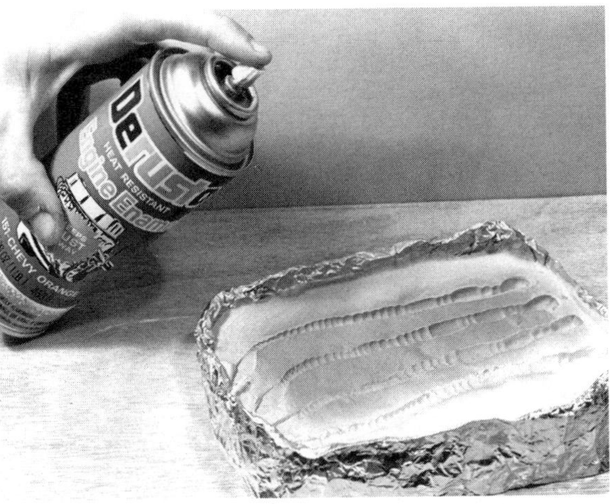

To prevent dull matte finishes in soft plastics, the mold cavities must be sprayed with a semigloss or gloss paint. Any color will work, but heat-resistant engine enamel is best.

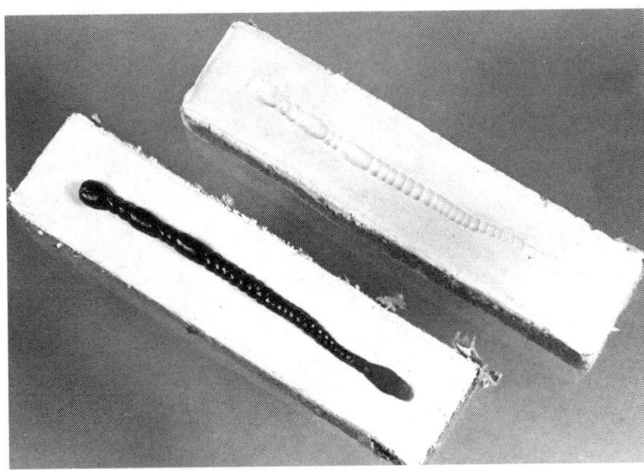
Completed mold showing the worm in place and the mold opened. A sprue hole has not yet been cut in the mold.

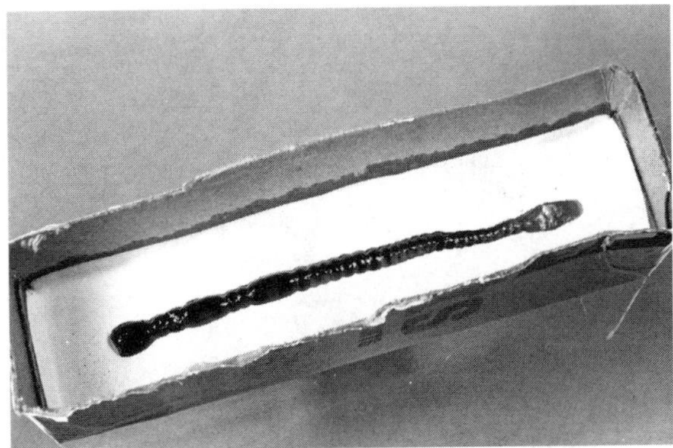
Making two-piece plaster mold for soft plastics. Here the worm has been laid on the first part of the two-piece mold.

The completed two-part mold is secured with rubber bands and filled with liquid plastic.

Making a mold from an offshore lure using Mold Builder is easy but time-consuming. The Mold Builder is brushed onto the master lure—here a plastic spice bottle.

end. For other lures place the sprue hole at widest part of the mold cavity. Since molten plastic is more viscous than the lead used for molding bucktails, the opening from the sprue to the mold cavity must be relatively large. If the mold does not fill completely, carving the sprue hole larger will usually correct the problem.

Pour the molten plastic in slowly, holding the mold at an angle so that the plastic will flow all the way to the bottom and fill the mold from the bottom up. As with open-face molds, the cavity and sprue hole can be painted with glossy heat-resistant paint to give the molded lures a shiny finish.

Completed round worms from the two-part mold. The sprue has been cut from one of the worms.

MOLDS FOR OFFSHORE LURES

Molds for offshore trolling lures are easily found: Use plastic spice bottles, film canisters, bouillon jars, and the like, as outlined in chapter 11. In addition, you can make a mold for your favorite offshore lure by using Mold Builder, a liquid latex-rubber compound manufactured by ETI. You can also carve or use modeling clay or plaster to make a master prototype of a lure, using the Mold Builder to make the mold. The compound, available in 16-ounce jars, can be used as is over metal, plastic, or glass. Copper or brass should be shellacked first; plaster, clay, or similar porous materials should be sealed with a sealer or paste wax.

To use Mold Builder you must have an exact model of the lure you wish to copy. If you use a commercial lure, first remove all the skirting and rigging. Mount the model tail down with glue on a level work surface, preferably glass or plastic. Use a brush to coat the lure or model with the Mold Builder. Make sure there are no air bubbles; if any air bubbles form, pop them to prevent flaws from occurring. Also coat the base surface in an area of about 2 inches all around the lure. This will form a flange by which the mold is supported when polyester resins are poured to make the lures.

Mold Builder, which is white in color when wet, will dry to a translucent tan in time. Allow the material to cure to this tan color before adding second coatings. To prevent damaging the brush, wash it with soapy water between coats. After the first two or three coats, additional coats can be applied more thickly, or strips of gauze can be added to the mold for reinforcement and strength. Usually about six to eight coats are sufficient for a small lure of up to about 3 inches long; more may be required for larger lures.

After the last coat, allow the mold to cure for 24 hours. Remove the cured mold, first coating the outside with talcum powder to prevent it from sticking to itself. To strengthen the mold, vulcanize it by boiling it in water for 20 minutes.

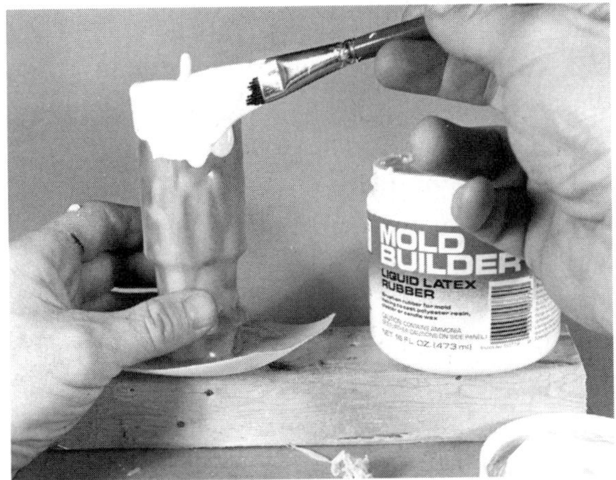

Repeated coatings of Mold Builder are necessary to give the mold strength

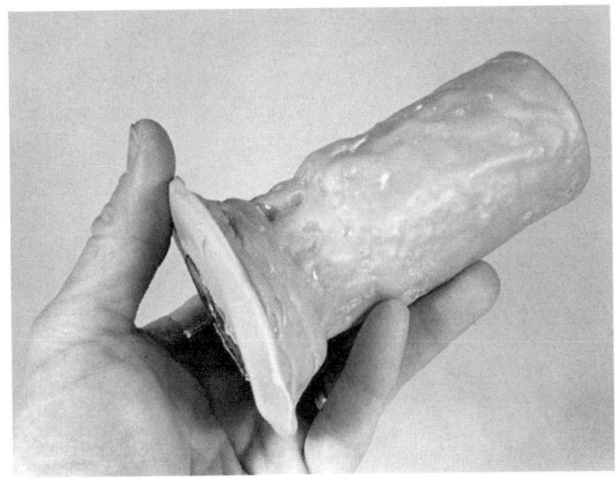
When lures are poured, this completed mold will be supported on an inverted cardboard box through a hole cut into the box.

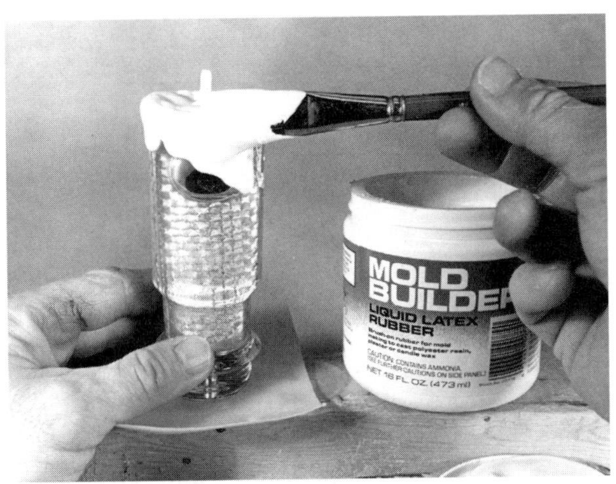

Brushing Mold Builder in place on the lure. The liquid latex is white but cures to a tan color.

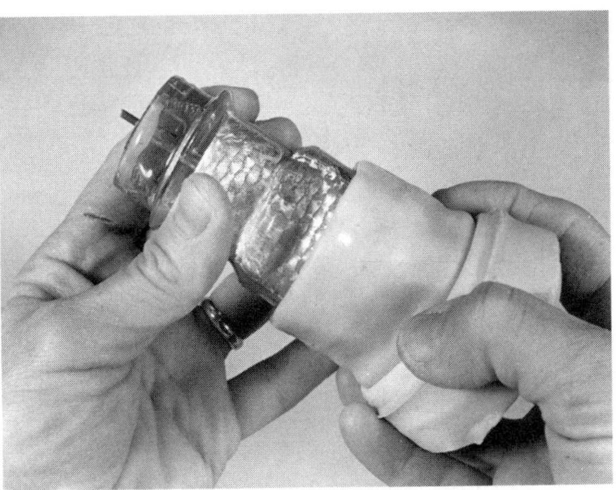
The mold being peeled off of the master lure.

To make the castings, prepare a cardboard box with a hole in the center top, through which the mold can be suspended. Make sure the box is high enough to accommodate the mold. With the box upright, place the mold in through the hole and tape the flange of the mold in place with masking tape. Follow the directions outlined in chapter 11 for mixing and preparing the plastic resin and adding any previously prepared inserts to the mold. (If you wish to mold in a center hole, you can make the mold with a socket for this. Use an unrigged lure and place a snug fitting, short 1-inch-length rod into the forward part of the rigging hole. Coat this rod at the same time you are coating the lure. When molding, place thin tubing, which becomes part of the lure when it is cut off at both ends, into this socket and tape it to the center of the supported mold when pouring the plastic.)

Any inserts molded into the lure will have to be drilled for this core tubing (about 3⁄16 inch in diameter) and placed there at the same time.

Molds can also be made from the latex-rubber material used to make nonslip grips on pliers handles or by using previously described techniques of making molds using the Dow Corning Silastic RTV rubber compounds. The latter, however, will usually produce lures with a duller finish than those produced with the latex-rubber compounds.

17
Rod Blanks and Rod Parts

Introduction • Blanks • Guides and Tip-Tops • Reel Seats • Grips • Handles • Butt Caps and Gimbals • Ferrules, Collets, Hosels, and Winding Checks • Thread • Finishes, Color Preservers, Sealers, and Glues • Miscellaneous

INTRODUCTION

Building rods really means assembling them. Unless you are into splitting your own cane and milling the six strips that go into a split-bamboo rod, you are really combining or assembling parts when you are "building" a rod. This is not to demean the skill required in this hobby, but only to put it into proper perspective. Assuming you follow directions and use proper care, building any type of basic fishing rod is no more difficult than assembling and gluing a plastic model plane and is probably less complicated than constructing most home decorations as taught in arts and crafts classes.

All the rod parts are built around the blank, and while the parts might seem to vary widely, all rods require the basics of a blank, butt cap, reel seat, grip or handle, guides, and tip-top. What these parts are and how they vary is the subject of this chapter; how these parts are assembled on the blank is the subject of the remaining chapters in this book.

BLANKS

Bamboo Blanks

To understand blanks properly, it helps to know a little about how they are made. Six-strip split-bamboo rods were developed by Samuel Phillippe in 1859, according to the earliest printed evidence. There are differing views on this: In his book *Classic Rods and Rodmakers,* Martin J. Keane notes that rods with three- and four-strip bamboo tip sections were developed by the British as early as 1801.

Even though entire books are devoted to these rods and their building, repair, and restoration, the basics are easy to understand—if harder to implement. Culms of Tonkin cane bamboo, one of the 2,000 species of this unique member of the grass family, are cured, seasoned, split into rough strips, and then split again into finer strips. These are placed on special V-blocks that have tapered Vs cut into the bed at a 60-degree angle. The strips are measured and cut to fit together with five other identical strips. The strips are then glued, crisscross wrapped with heavy cord, and slow-baked to cure. The cord is removed, the resulting blank is cleaned and trimmed, and the appointments are added to the blank to make a fine rod. Other rods of split bamboo are made in four, five, eight, and other strip methods with obviously different angles than the strips made on other milling blocks.

Finished bamboo blanks are available for rod builders through some companies and custom builders.

Synthetic Blank Construction

Rods from synthetics are made in one of three basic ways: pultrusion, Howald process, and cut-and-roll. Pultrusion is used for making solid-glass blanks and results in an inexpensive, heavy, but very strong rod. These blanks are often used for heavy boat rods and shark rods. The process begins with raw glass, which is melted and blown to produce fine glass fibers. The strands of this fiberglass are then pulled (thus the name) through a bath of resin adhesive and then through a small die that compresses the fibers into a round rod form. During the assembly-line process, the straight, continuous glass rod goes through an oven to cure, the resin and glass fusing into a single, continuous, and uniform-diameter fiberglass rod. The rod continues through the manufacturing facility, where it is cut into predetermined lengths. These uniform-diameter rods then go to a centerless lathe that uses abrasive wheels to taper the blank to predetermined butt and tip diameters.

A mandrel design helps to determine the type of rod blank that is made and is required for both the Howald process and cut-and-roll manufacture. Large-diameter steel mandrels, or tapered rods, are used for large blanks such as would be used for heavy fishing or saltwater use. The large diameter helps the blank resist breaking as a result of the hoop strength (just as a large-diameter pipe or tube resists bending and breaking more than does an otherwise identical small-diameter tube or pipe).

Thinner mandrels are used for freshwater blanks and fly rods. Mandrels can also vary with their taper. A straight-taper mandrel results in a rod (everything else being equal) with an even progressive bend from butt to tip. A mandrel with a nonlinear taper that becomes sharply thinner in the tip end will result in a rod with more tip action. Where this taper begins will determine the degree of tip action—moderate, fast, or extra-fast.

A single mandrel can be used to construct several different styles of rods, making them more cost-effective. Mandrels are often longer than the rod that is made on them, so the position of the rod material on the mandrel will determine the degree of taper, the action of the blank, the length of the blank, and in part the power or strength of the blank. For example, an 8-foot-long mandrel with a sharp taper in the middle could be used to make an 8-foot rod with moderately fast action. By placing the rod material on the lower 6 feet, or butt end, of the mandrel (leaving the upper portion of the mandrel bare), a 6-foot rod with a fast or extra-fast tip would result. Making a 6-foot rod on the tip end (leaving the 2 feet at the butt bare) would result in a smooth-taper parabolic rod but one with a very strong butt section. Naturally all these rods would be for different purposes and have different power, since the diameters throughout would vary.

Rod blanks in a factory ready for shipment. Blanks are separated by type and length.

Howald-Process Blank Construction

The Howald process, used by the Shakespeare Company and named for its developer, Dr. Arthur M. Howald, uses a mandrel machined to precise tolerances. The taper and dimensions of the mandrel determine the inside diameter of the resulting rod.

In the first step of the Howald process, the mandrel is coated with a releasing agent—silicone or Teflon—to allow the blank to be removed when finished. Then a machine wraps rod material around the mandrel in a tight spiral. This material can be graphite, glass, other material or combinations thereof, but in the case of Shakespeare it is graphite. A second machine, which looks like a lathe, feeds individual longitudinal strands of rod material onto this spiral inner wrap. These strands, which again may be graphite, glass, or other materials, go through a resin bath just before being placed on the wrapped mandrel.

The longitudinal strands are wrapped with clear tape to keep them in place. One important point is that as the rod is fed through the Howald process machinery, some of the longitudinal strands are cut in a precise sequence. This results in less rod material at the tip end than at the butt end, resulting in the typical arc or bend in a rod. The action (how a rod blank bends) and power (how it resists bending) are a result of the type of materials used, the amount of material added in each step, the taper and diameter of the mandrel, and the number of strands cut during the Howald process and the position at which they are cut. Cutting most of the strands high up on the rod results in a rod that is stiff but with a very fast tip action. Cutting the strands regularly throughout the blank results in a parabolic-action rod.

Blank Materials

The cut-and-roll method is used by most rod-blank manufacturers. It uses similar steel mandrels, but instead of individual fibers, sheets of materials are cut to specific geometric shapes and then wrapped in place. The materials can be glass, graphite, or combinations, but they are always in a sheet form, much like cloth fabric. The fabric used is just like other cloth, with a fiber warp and woof going in two directions. (This is usually the case. Some materials used today have all longitudinal fibers and use no cross- or right-angle fibers.) Materials differ in this construction. Typically fiberglass is a 400 denier cloth, but glass that is finer and coarser is available. The standard glass in the industry, and one used for years, is E glass. A higher quality glass with a higher modulus (for stiffer action) is called S glass (T glass by Japanese manufacturers).

Graphite varies as to modulus, a term used to describe stiffness, or resistance to and recovery from bending. Modulus is really a term for the stiffness of the material—its resistance to breaking or to tearing apart longitudinally (the tensile strength). It is this tensile strength modulus that is used by most of the industry in determining low, medium, and high modulus rods and blanks. According to one supplier of graphite fibers to the rod companies, low modulus is in the range of 32 to 35 million pounds per square inch (msi), medium or intermediate modulus is in the range of 40 to 46 msi, and high modulus is more than 50 msi. Msi is the measurement of modulus. The higher the number, the stiffer and quicker the recovery from bending for any given rod. Some rods have been made in the past as high as 70 msi.

Regardless of the modulus, graphite is manufactured in several ways. It can be laminated or manufactured with the warp and woof of graphite or with a warp of graphite and woof of glass (this is seldom done). Or glass may be laminated to graphite cloth, the glass providing right-angle fibers to the length of the rod and as a result providing hoop strength to the rod to prevent or reduce breaking. Some of these combinations result in the hybrid or so-called graphite/glass blanks in which both materials are used. As of this writing, several attempts by the American Sportfishing Association to define several grades of graphite and/or glass composition in finished rods and blanks have failed. Thus a "graphite" blank or rod can be wholly graphite or only 10 percent graphite. Generally you get what you pay for in rods and blanks.

Graphite cloth is made by proprietary processes in which some graphite fibers run perpendicular to the cloth's main fibers. Another proprietary method involves "collimated" fibers, in which all the fibers are parallel, with no scrim or right-angle fibers. This produces a blank in which all the fibers run longitudinally for maximum strength yet without any loss of hoop strength. The finished rod is lighter and has increased sensitivity and power for its weight.

Most of these materials go through a "pre-preg" operation in which resins are added to the cloth so that the wrapped cloth on the blank will stick to itself when baked.

Polyester or phenolic resins once were typically used with fiberglass; they are still used today, although epoxy resins are more prevalent. Epoxy resins are used with graphite materials because they stick better to graphite. The results are better bonding and less bubbling than with the phenolic resins. Usually these pre-preg materials are kept chilled to prevent the resins from setting up and curing. If this happens, the cloth becomes stiff and brittle and impossible to wrap on a mandrel.

Other materials are sometimes used in rods and rod blanks. Boron, once widely popular, is rarely used today because it is extremely expensive and difficult to work with. Generally longitudinal fibers of boron are placed with graphite or glass (generally graphite). Silicon carbide is also sometimes used in rod blanks. This is made of short fibers and "whiskers" and resembles a dust in the rod material. Kevlar has been used as an outer coating or scrim on some blanks for hoop strength and blank protection.

Cut-and-Roll Construction

Construction of the blank begins on the cutting board with the glass, graphite, or composite-fiber cloth. A steel template or pattern outline is placed over the cloth and used to cut the cloth to a precise geometric (often trapezoidal or triangular) shape. These templates are basically triangular in shape. One long edge is placed on the edge of the cloth, and this edge is tacked to the steel mandrel. The butt end of the material is wider than the tip end, and the taper can be straight, producing an evenly bending rod blank, or have a complex bend. For example, a template and material cut with one side in an S shape—the wide end at the bottom, the thin end at the tip—will result in a heavy-butt fast-tip rod. Just where the S curve is placed on the material will determine the action of the rod—moderate, fast, or extra-fast. Moderate rods will have the S curve near the butt end; for a fast-tip rod the S curve will be at the tip end, usually about one-fifth to one-quarter of the way down from the tip. The degree of curvature in the S will also determine the rod action: A gradual curve results in a gradual change of action; a sharp curve causes a rapid and pronounced change of action.

In some cases extra strength is required in the butt end. While this can be done by widening the rod material (making a broader triangle), doing so may result in wrinkles in the resulting blank. It also takes more time, resulting in higher labor costs and often in more material waste. A preferred way, and one that allows more economical use of the material, is to add a small piece of material, variously called a "pennant" or "flag." The pennant may be of a different material, such as a glass reinforcing flag for a graphite blank.

The same technique is used to add small pieces of reinforcing material to high-stress ferrule areas. Often this material is visible on the blank as a spiral line running around the rod for a few inches close to the ferrule, regardless of whether it is a spigot or slip-over (Fenwick-style) ferrule. The spiral is indicative of a small triangular piece of material used to reinforce this area and give it more hoop strength.

Once the material is cut to shape and prepared, a hot iron is used to tack the material to the mandrel. The impregnated resins serve as a glue for this. The mandrel and material then go to a rolling table—much like a broad, padded ironing board with a free-swinging, swiveling flat top. The mandrel is positioned, and then the top is lowered to push and roll the mandrel so that the material wraps tightly around it. The swiveling and rotating top helps the material roll around the mandrel regardless of the taper or amount of material involved.

The next step is the cellophaning process, by which a polyester tape is wrapped in a spiral around the blank to secure the material and prevent it from unsticking. Holders on the end of the mandrels then allow the material-wrapped mandrels to be hung vertically in huge high ovens for baking. The blanks are baked for 1 hour to several hours at temperatures of from 250 to 350 degrees Fahrenheit. Polyester resins used for glass are baked in the higher range; epoxy resins for graphite are baked in the lower temperature range.

The blanks are removed from the oven, and special machines pull the mandrel from the blank. The mandrels go back to produce more rod blanks. The rough tip and butt end of the blank are cut off, and the polyester tape is removed from the blank. Some blanks—primarily of glass—are left this way, with the spiral wraps of the tape showing on the blank. Lamiglas manufactured some of their glass blanks this way. Most rods are sanded, allowing the manufacturer to inspect the blanks for any defects. Sanding smoothes the blank, which in the minds of most people makes it more attractive; when properly done, it will not affect the strength of the rod blank.

Several methods are used to finish the rod blank. Some rods are given a clear epoxy or polyurethane finish; others are painted prior to finishing. Most rods have a glossy finish, although some are marketed with a matte finish, based on the theory that a dull rod will not cause glare on sunny days and thus won't scare fish.

Today a number of companies make rod blanks for the rod-builder. These include Lamiglas, Sage, Talon (LCI), American Tackle, Calstar, St. Croix, Temple Fork, Phenix, Seeker, PacBay, Winston, Orvis, North Fork Composites, Batson, Mud Hole, and Colt (Cape Fear). Many of these companies also carry other components, such as reel seats, grips and handles, guides, ferrules, and glues and finishes.

Available blanks include everything from solid-glass pultrusion blanks (discontinued, but a few are still around) for heavy fishing through E and S glass blanks, various composite blanks of mixed graphite and glass, and various forms of graphite. Often these various graphites are of different moduluses, or stiffnesses. At this writing, for example, G. Loomis manufactures glass blanks acceptable for IGFA trolling rods; hybrid blanks that are a blend of regular graphite, woven graphite, and glass; 96 percent graphite; IM6 graphite, which has a higher modulus; and IMX graphite, the company's highest-modulus blank. Lamiglas offers IM700 high-modulus graphite blanks, G1000 graphite blanks of slightly lesser modulus, and LHS Esprit graphite blanks.

Rods with Self-Ferruling Systems

Ferrules vary with rods. Some are of the slip-over type first developed by Jim Green of Fenwick and used exclusively on their rods for years. Today the patents have run out and other companies are using the same system. Basically it consists of a rod tip that at its lower end is sized precisely in taper and diameter to fit over the upper end of the butt section.

A sort of "reverse" Fenwick-style ferrule is also found in rods but generally not in rod blanks. In this the lower section of the tip end is a straight tube (parallel to the outside diameter) that slides into a fitted opening in the upper end of the butt section.

Spigot ferrules are different. These consist of a short section, usually a solid plug of graphite or glass, that is glued and fitted into the upper end of the butt section and precisely sized to fit the inside diameter of the lower end of the tip section. These rod blanks are usually made in one piece and then cut in half (or almost in half—room must be allowed for the ferrule extension on the lower section to have the two, or more, sections equal overall in length). The butt section then has the plug ferrule glued in place. In multipiece rods such as three-piece rods and four- or more-piece travel and pack rods, a plug ferrule is added to the upper end of each section (except the tip) to match the adjoining section. With rare exceptions almost all blanks available to the rod builder today have the built-in or "self"-ferrule of the spigot or Fenwick style or a combination of both.

Most rod blanks today are supplied with these self-ferrules of glass-to-glass or graphite-to-graphite. Most are also ferruled for equal section lengths, regardless of the number of sections in the blank. A few two-piece rod blanks are off-center ferruled. In these the tip section is always longer, the theory being that placing the ferrule closer to the butt preserves more of the sensitivity of the rod in the tip section or upper end. One disadvantage of blanks with off-center ferrules is that the sections are of different lengths, which requires a longer rod case than equal-section (center-ferruled) rods. From a practical point of view, I find little difference in fishing the two styles of blanks.

Sometimes off-center-ferruled rods are termed "butt-ferruled." This term should not be confused with the special ferrules or collets that go onto the butt end of older style casting rods and are designed to take an appropriately ferruled casting-rod handle. These are at the very end of the rod blank and fit the handle to the blank.

Metal ferrules are rarely used except on some traditional quality fly rods—usually bamboo. These can be added to any rod because they are tubes that are slipped over the cut blank ends. In addition, ferrules to make a spigot type of ferrule for rods can be constructed from scrap blanks, a procedure described in chapter 26.

Some anglers insist on one-piece rods without any ferrules, claiming that a ferrule anywhere weakens and desensitizes the rod. This is true with some one-piece fly-rod blanks (primarily short rods for chalk-stream fishing or some of the new 8-footers for heavy big-game fishing and specifically made for IGFA 20-pound class tippets) and some heavy one-piece East Coast surf rods.

In all honesty I find little if any real, demonstrable difference between good one-piece rods and good two- or multi-piece rods. My argument has always been that if you close your eyes and cast any rod without knowing what it is, you cannot tell if it is a one-, two-, or multi-piece model, provided everything else is equal. In fact, fly-rod guru Lefty Kreh points out that sometimes a two- or multi-piece rod is better than a one-piecer because the ferrules add stiffness to the rod at critical points, improving the action and power.

Making long one-piece rods is difficult for the manufacturer. It requires longer mandrels and exponentially increases the possibility of wrinkles and defects. It also makes complex blanks and the addition of flags and pennants and complex S-curve cuts more difficult. In addition, the reject rate (and thus the cost to the consumer) of long one-piece rods goes up rapidly. Long, lightweight one-piece models tend to have curves, kinks, and twists that are unacceptable to the consumer. Understand that we are not talking about short one-piece bass rods of perhaps 5 feet, 6 inches or so, but 8-foot one-piece fly rods and 9-foot noodle rods.

Blank Design

Although most rod blanks are of two or three pieces, travel and pack-rod blanks of four or more sections are also available. Most companies carry them in four pieces, such as those by Sage, Lamiglas, Powell, G. Loomis, and others. Also, some rod blanks are designed for specific purposes. For example, some IGFA-style rod blanks are made so that the lower 10 or 12 inches have a uniform diameter, designed specifically to fit one of the several Unibutt handle systems without shimming. Most IGFA offshore rod blanks are 68 inches long, allowing for cutting and modification

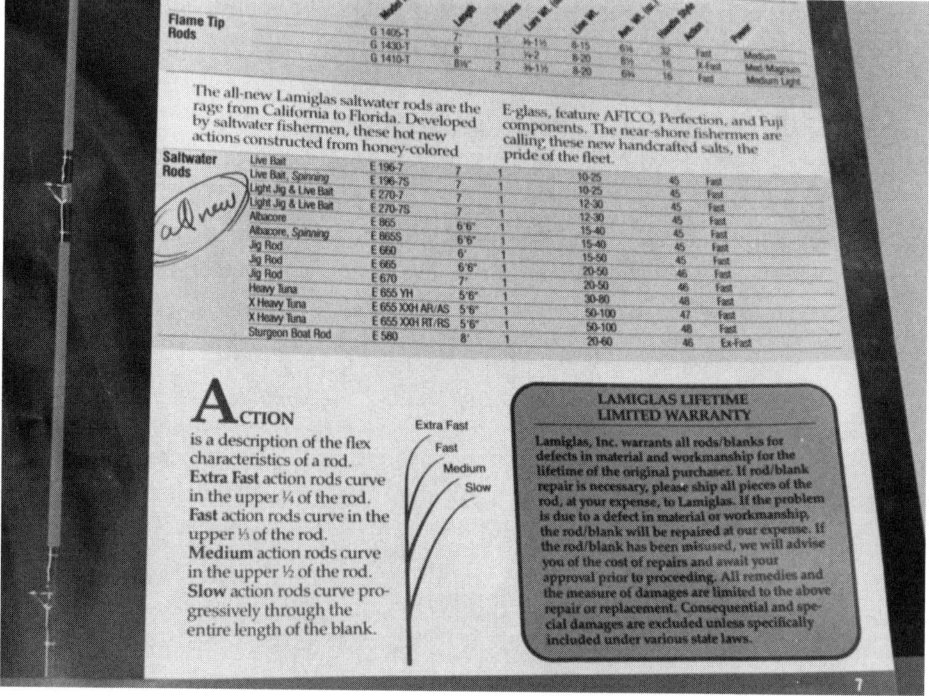

Flame Tip Rods

G 1405-T	7'	1	[illegible]	6-15	6¼	32	Fast	Medium
G 1430-T	8'	1	½-2	8-20	8½	16	X-Fast	Med Magnum
G 1410-T	8½'	2	[illegible]	8-20	6¾	16	Fast	Medium Light

The all-new Lamiglas saltwater rods are the rage from California to Florida. Developed by saltwater fishermen, these hot new actions constructed from honey-colored E-glass, feature AFTCO, Perfection, and Fuji components. The near-shore fishermen are calling these new handcrafted salts, the pride of the fleet.

Saltwater Rods

Live Bait	E 196-7	7'	1	10-25	45	Fast
Live Bait, Spinning	E 196-7S	7'	1	10-25	45	Fast
Light Jig & Live Bait	E 270-7	7'	1	12-30	45	Fast
Light Jig & Live Bait	E 270-7S	7'	1	12-30	45	Fast
Albacore	E 865	6'6"	1	15-40	45	Fast
Albacore, Spinning	E 865S	6'6"	1	15-40	45	Fast
Jig Rod	E 660	6'	1	15-50	45	Fast
Jig Rod	E 665	6'6"	1	20-50	46	Fast
Jig Rod	E 670	7'	1	20-50	46	Fast
Heavy Tuna	E 655 YH	5'6"	1	30-80	48	Fast
X Heavy Tuna	E 655 XXH AR/AS	5'6"	1	50-100	47	Fast
X Heavy Tuna	E 655 XXH RT/RS	5'6"	1	50-100	48	Fast
Sturgeon Boat Rod	E 580	8'	1	20-60	46	Ex-Fast

all new

ACTION is a description of the flex characteristics of a rod. **Extra Fast** action rods curve in the upper ¼ of the rod. **Fast** action rods curve in the upper ⅓ of the rod. **Medium** action rods curve in the upper ½ of the rod. **Slow** action rods curve progressively through the entire length of the blank.

LAMIGLAS LIFETIME LIMITED WARRANTY

Lamiglas, Inc. warrants all rods/blanks for defects in material and workmanship for the lifetime of the original purchaser. If rod/blank repair is necessary, please ship all pieces of the rod, at your expense, to Lamiglas. If the problem is due to a defect in material or workmanship, the rod/blank will be repaired at our expense. If the rod/blank has been misused, we will advise you of the cost of repairs and await your approval prior to proceeding. All remedies and the measure of damages are limited to the above repair or replacement. Consequential and special damages are excluded unless specifically included under various state laws.

7

Many blanks come in several different actions, as indicated by this Lamiglas catalog.

from 58 inches to 68 inches without affecting the action or power specified for the blank or the fit into the collet for the handle assembly.

Action and Power

"Action" and "power" are terms used to describe how and to what degree a rod bends. In my opinion these terms are used incorrectly in many cases. Some rod companies refer to their blanks and rods as having a "light action," "medium action," or "heavy action," referring to the range of lure weights possible or degree of stiffness of the rod. Actually action refers to the way in which the rod bends—parabolic, moderate, fast, extra-fast, and so on. These are degrees of stiffness of the *sections* of the rod, parabolic being a gradual bend all along the length of the rod, and extra-fast being a stiff rod with a light tip (sometimes called a "worm" action for the action built into worm spinning and casting rods).

Power refers to the rod's resistance to bending. Thus a stiff rod has more power than a light rod, but both could have a specific action or type of bend when under stress. By the same token, a rod of a certain power or stiffness could be built with completely different actions. Fenwick used to differentiate between these by describing the action and then using a number for the power—the higher the number (usually from about 1 through 7) the stiffer the rod. Today many companies differentiate between these separate blank characteristics with specific listings for action and power in their catalogs. Even so, each company usually describes its rods' actions slightly differently.

Lamiglas describes its rods as follows:

Extra-fast: bending in the upper quarter of the blank

Fast: bending in the upper third of the blank

Medium: bending in the upper half of the blank

Slow: bending or curving progressively throughout the entire length of the blank

G. Loomis describes its rods' actions as:

Extra-fast: bending in extreme tip of blank

Fast: flexing in upper third of blank

Moderate: bending in upper two-thirds of blank

Slow: flexing or bending in upper three-quarters of blank

Note that in all cases, this does *not* mean that the lower part of the rod is as straight as a poker when under stress, only that the most pronounced bending occurs as described. Note also that the terms "light," "medium," and "heavy" have no place in describing action, only in describing the power or relative stiffness of a rod. In choosing a rod, it is also important to select a rod or blank by the weight it is designed to cast or, in the case of offshore and boat rods, the line weight recommended for trolling. Otherwise the terms light, medium, and heavy are meaningless. A very heavy freshwater spinning rod that might cast a 1½-ounce weight, for example, would still be more flexible and lighter than a light surf rod used off Hatteras designed to cast a 2-ounce sinker or a light offshore rod of 20-pound class designed to troll large and heavy lures for white marlin, sailfish, and wahoo or dolphin.

GUIDES AND TIP-TOPS

Sometimes called eyes by novice fishermen, guides force the line to run the length of the rod from the reel, allowing for easy casting. They also distribute the strain on the rod blank when a big fish is played. They can be broken down into a number of basic styles according to the rod on which they are to be used or the materials from which they are made.

Materials

At one time guides were made with wire rings and frames. Some of the better guides were and are today made of stainless steel to resist corrosion. Others are made of carbon steel. Some, such as the Fuji titanium-frame guides, use a titanium–stainless steel alloy. These are rated as being 35 to 40 percent stronger, more corrosion-resistant, and more flexible and resistant to metal-fatigue failure (particularly important in one-foot guides) than stainless steel. They are teamed with ceramic rings of various materials and come in a dozen different styles of frame and foot configurations.

Snake guides are still made of carbon or stainless steel. Forecast and PacBay, two companies making these guides, use only stainless steel in their construction, although different finishes are available. Small ringed guides for fly rods are also available and made by PacBay, Forecast, and Fuji. Most of these are additionally chromed for added smoothness and protection.

Snake guides and guide frames are often made with chrome plating over the stainless steel or carbon steel. The chrome is harder and thus more resistant to grooving and is also smoother and thus reduces friction on the line. Some guides have special coatings, often more for appearance and to match the finish of the rod than for any functional purpose. For example, snake guides can come in black or bright finishes, sometimes even gold finishes. Some even have a Teflon coating for reduced friction. Similarly, frames and outer wire rings of ceramic guides can be chemically finished in gold, black, bright, gunsmoke, and other colors.

AFTCO and Batson even make roller guides in different colors to match specific rod and trim colors. AFTCO guides, for example, come in a standard chrome-plate finish, black chrome-oxide finish (both with stainless steel–finish rollers, screws, and pins), and a black-and-gold finish with a frame of black chrome oxide and rollers, screws, and pins coated with gold titanium nitride, along with similarly made roller guides of silver/gold and gold finish. All are of stainless steel plated with the specific finish. Mildrum rollers also come in several styles with choices of chrome, black, or gold frames and side plates (which hold the roller and bearings) of chrome, gold, or black, for up to nine color combinations. PacBay stocks roller guides in blue/silver, gold/silver, gold/black, black/silver, black/gold, silver/gold, and silver/black, in listing the frames and side plates, respectively.

Carbide guides use carbide only in the ring of the guides; the frames are stainless steel, chromed stainless steel, or nickel silver. Carbide, Carboloy, or Mildarbide (the latter two are trade names) are very hard materials and extremely wear- and corrosion-resistant. Like wire rings, these guides are welded or brazed to the frame, eliminating the need for a shock ring.

The popular ceramic guides come in a number of slightly different materials. Unfortunately "ceramic" can have several meanings. At one point ceramic meant the less-expensive, poorer quality white inner-guide ring used on low-quality rods. It can still mean that, but ceramic is a general term for the wide range of a half dozen or more earth materials used in guide-ring construction. These materials include the original quality guide-ring material, aluminum oxide, along with more recently developed materials such as silicon carbide, silicon nitride, Hardloy (a trade name of Fuji for an aluminum oxide with an additional harder ceramic material added), sterite (also called E-rings), neo-aluminum (also called O-rings), and a U-ring that is not currently sold in this country. The white ceramic is often called a "cera ring."

With the exception of the white rings, all of these are dark colored, although white aluminum oxide rings under the Mildrum Milumina brand used to be available. Each of these rings has its specific uses. Important factors in guides are hardness (to resist grooving), smoothness (to reduce or eliminate friction and heat), heat dissipation (to prevent line damage during long fights), and weight (heavy guides adversely affect rod action, particularly on light rods).

Hardness is one important consideration, since it is a function of how resistant a guide ring will be to grooving by a line. The Vickers scale, used to measure very hard materials (as opposed to the Rockwell C scale, used primarily to measure metals and with a more limited upper range), shows the following range of approximate guide hardness, according to spokesmen from Fuji:

Silicon carbide rings: 2,200 to 2,400 Vickers hardness

Blue Zirconium rings: 1,750 Vickers hardness

Ti Gold Zirconium rings: 1,750 Vickers hardness

TiCH Zirconium rings: 1,750 Vickers hardness

Zirconium rings: 1,600 Vickers hardness

Carboloy rings: 1,500 Vickers hardness

Silicon nitride rings: 1,300 to 1,500 Vickers hardness

Aluminum oxide rings: 1,200 to 1,400 Vickers hardness

Hardloy rings: 1,200 to 1,400 Vickers hardness

Neo-aluminum rings: 1,100 to 1,300 Vickers hardness

Sterite or E-rings: 750 to 850 Vickers hardness

White or cera rings: 550 to 650 Vickers hardness

By comparison, knives are considered very hard if they are tempered to a Rockwell C scale of 52 to 54, which is about 600 to 650 on the Vickers hardness scale.

In heat dissipation, silicon carbide also comes out best, followed by Hardloy, aluminum oxide, and silicon nitride (all are similar) and then cera and sterite. Heat dissipation in a guide is important to prevent line damage. Heat buildup in a guide through the friction of line running over it can damage the line, particularly if the fish stops and the unmoving line continues to touch a hot guide ring.

It is also important to have light guides. Silicon carbide again wins according to Fuji, since six identical rings of its silicon carbide guides weigh the same as one aluminum oxide ring of the same size.

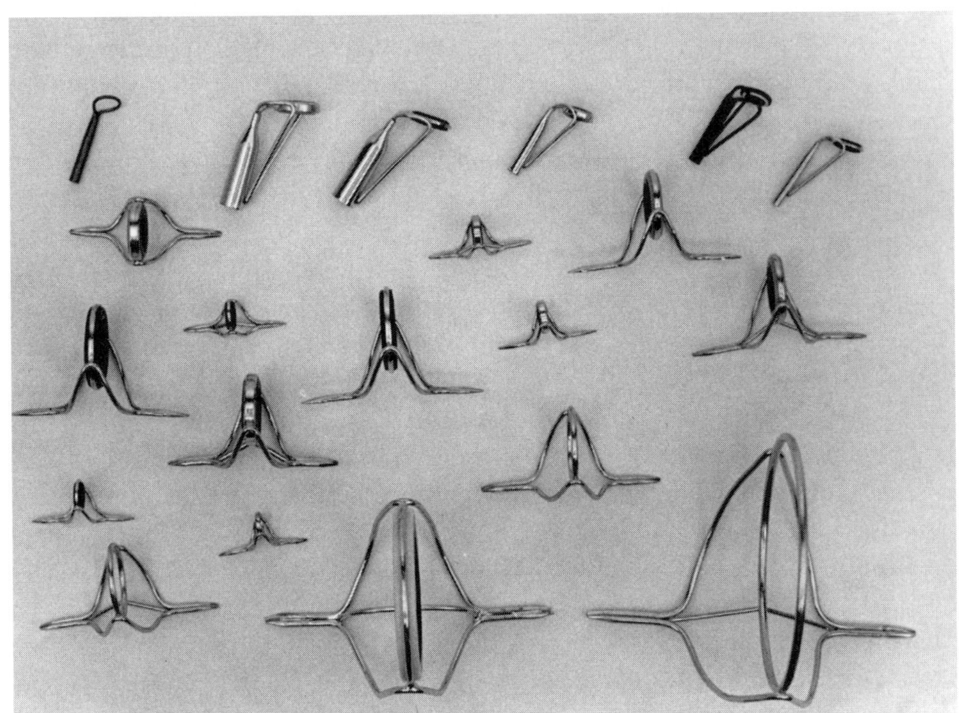

Many types of guides and tip-tops are available. These are just some available from Perfection Tip.

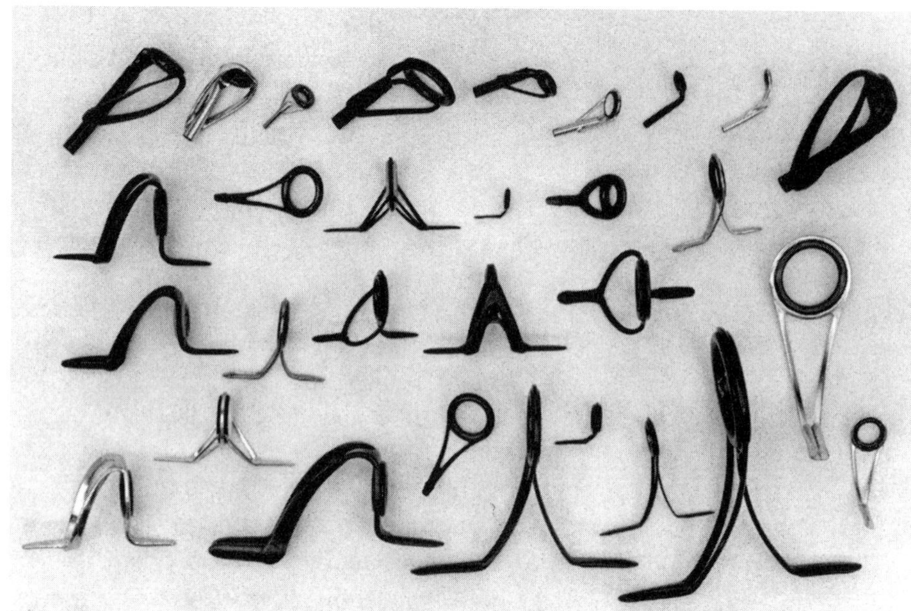

Some of the many types and sizes of Fuji guides available. They include traditional styles along with heavy-frame boat and trolling guides, high-frame spinning guides, and tip-tops to match.

Another important characteristic is the inner diameter of the guide. Initially this was a problem, because the original aluminum oxide guides had (and most still have) a shock ring between the wire ring frame and ceramic guide ring. Silicon nitride guides sometimes use shock rings. Silicon carbide and Hardloy guides may or may not have shock rings, in part because they are less brittle than the aluminum oxide and silicon nitride, which need a shock ring for protection, even though this results in a slightly bulkier ring.

Shock rings also vary, although most are made of a firm but pliable plastic or nylon. They must be firm to hold the ring, which is snapped into the shock ring. Usually the shock ring is held by a groove that secures it into the thin wire-frame ring.

Shock rings used to be available in only two colors. Guides from Fuji were available in a light luminous green, which appeared a light cream in daylight and glowed in the dark with a light yellow-green color. It was used primarily with aluminum oxide and silicon nitride guides. Black shock rings were used with aluminum oxide and hard-ring economy guides.

Other guides now have black or natural shock rings. The natural color is a translucent light gray. Natural-color rings can sometimes be colored by dyeing with regular household dyes such as Rit or Tintex to match a rod or trim color on a rod. As a result of the rings' naturally cloudy appearance, any dyed colors will not be pure and bright, but they will be recognizable. The best colors are basic blue, green, and red.

Many guides today do not use shock rings but instead are fitted and glued directly into the aluminum frame. In some cases these frame rings have a lip that prevents the guide ring from slipping out on one side, with custom glues to hold the ceramic ring securely in place. Roller guides typically use stainless steel rollers with a system of bushings underneath for easy turning and special stainless steel (usually) screws and bushings. Some also have nonconductive and self-lubricating side plates to prevent problems with electrolysis and corrosion.

Tip-tops are just like guides in the materials used for them, including the frame materials, ceramic rings, and shock rings. The only difference is that the tip-top frame and ring is fitted onto a tube; the tube comes in different sizes to fit accurately onto the end of a rod. Usually these tubes have a slight taper to them similar to that on the rod and are constructed of the same materials—chromed or blackened stainless steel in most cases—as are the guide frames.

Most guides, including fly, casting, spinning, surf, offshore, and offshore roller are all stainless steel for maximum durability. Usually this is an SS304 or SS316 stainless. The SS304 frame is generally used for guides and tops that are used in fresh water. For salt water Batson recommends guides with the SS316 frame, since they hold up better in saltwater use. The standard test for this is an industry ASTM-B117 test, wherein tested materials are placed in a chamber and subjected to a continual saltwater spray or fog. According to Batson, even their SS304 guide frames show no corrosion after twenty days or 480 hours of constant spray, the equivalent of 68-hour saltwater fishing trips without washing the tackle. The SS316 guide frames are tested in a similar test for fifty days, equaling 150 8-hour trips without washing tackle. Fly rod guides (no separate ring or frame) are mostly made with the SS316. Some companies such as Batson also made very heavy-duty boat rod guides using a frame of marine-grade brass.

Ring Sizes

The lack of a shock ring in a guide allows for a larger inner diameter. Originally all guides were wire rings, and the guide size was the inner diameter of that ring. That was fine at the time, but the same system of measurement was used on the wire-ring frame even with the addition of a nylon shock ring and ceramic inner-guide ring. The result was that a nominally 12-millimeter guide ring seated with a shock ring would have a true internal diameter of about 8 millimeters.

In part this is more complicated now as a result of the different sizes of the inner ceramic rings used by some manufacturers and the fact that while some guides have a shock ring, many do not. Thus there are light or standard rings, heavy rings, and flanged rings, the latter with a slight ridge or flange to help prevent the inner ring from popping out. These are used on tip-tops where the line can make a sharp bend the ring. The flange provides line protection throughout the radius of this bend. At one time having inner rings pop out was a problem, particularly for the silicon carbide guides (also called SIC guides), because no shock ring was used. Today the pressure used to force inner rings into the metal frame ring has been doubled by many manufacturers, which also use special glues to seat these rings.

Ring size in guides and tip-tops is very important. It is necessary to consider the true internal diameter of the ring, not just the nominal size of the guide, which is far larger, particularly with ceramic-ring guides, and even more so with those using shock rings. Ring size is important primarily for knot and line clearance. Too small a guide on a rod will impede the line flow, particularly on spinning rods, where the line tends to flow off in loops. (An exception to this is when a high-frame, small-ring guide is used for the first of the butt guides, removing all the loops at this point and allowing the rest of the line to flow in a relatively straight line.)

There are no real rules on guide size, since line sizes and limpness vary and require different minimum ring diameters. For fly rods it is also important, since fly lines are very thick and require good clearance to flow freely through the guides for casting and shooting line.

Knot clearance is equally important to consider for some rods. If you are making a spinning, casting, or spin-cast rod in which the line will always be tied only to the end of a lure, then this is of no concern. However, for an equally light rod in which you need doubled line through a Bimini twist, a leader tied with an Albright, a wire leader, or a shock leader used to cushion the line during the force of casting a surf rod, larger guides and tip-tops are a must. The guides must be large enough not only to clear the knot but also must be extra large because knots tend to jump around as the line goes through the guides and tip-top.

Such considerations are particularly important in the design of surf rods, light-tackle tropical rods for shark and barracuda, muskie rods, or any rod that might be used

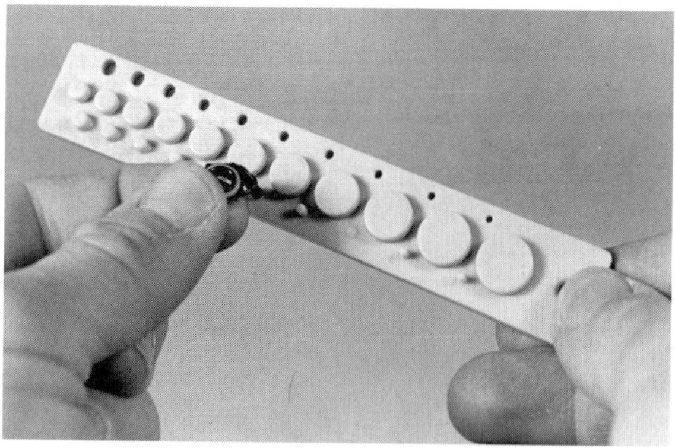

Tip-top gauges, such as this one, make it easy to check tip-top sizes. The sockets in this gauge are designed to fit rod tips for measuring tip-top size; the "plugs" are used for measuring the tubing of the tip-tops.

with a leader at any time. It is equally important for fly rods, because there are knots at the line-leader and line-backing connections. Use a long leader and you might have to bring the leader knot through the top and guides to land the fish. Hook a big fish and it will take the 100-foot fly line plus the backing, zigzagging the line-to-backing knot and the line-to-leader knot through the guides several or more times before landing the fish.

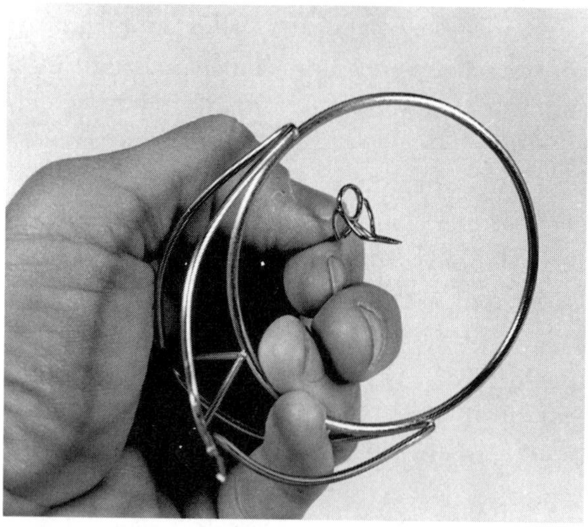

In the past guide manufacturers and fishermen dealt with fishing and casting problems through the ring size of guides. Here two old wire guides are shown—an 8-millimeter guide for casting and spinning tips and a 75-millimeter larger ring guide used at one time as the butt guide for surf-fishing rods.

Although guides of any ring size can be used on any rod blank (within realistic limits of guide type, size, and rod weight and power), tip-tops are another problem. Most tip-tops are of a specific ring size on a specific tube size. You must use the correct tube size to fit the rod top. Fortunately many companies have recognized the need for larger ring sizes on some tubes and for fly-rod fishing. Today you can find tip-tops for light spinning and casting rods that will fit rod tips of varying rods such as fly and spinning. These tip-tops are available now in a choice of ring diameter sizes, such as choices of a size 6-, 7-, or 8-millimeter ring. Many companies make these choices available.

For those interested in specific sizes, the following chart shows sizes for Fuji guides both with and without shock rings. One point of explanation: The outside diameter in the guides refers to the outside diameter of the ceramic ring or shock ring—or the same as the internal diameter of the wire-frame ring. In most cases it is very close but not identical to the nominal size of the guide.

Fuji guides without shock ring

Size	O/D	I/D light	I/D heavy	I/D flanged
2.5	2.0	1.0		
3	2.4	1.3		
3.5	2.9	1.7		
4	3.4	2.2		
4.5	3.9	2.5	1.7	
5	4.6	3.0	2.8	2.6
5.5	5.3	3.5	3.3	2.9
6	6.1	4.1	3.7	3.3
7	7.0	4.8	4.2	3.8
8	8.0	5.6	4.8	4.4
10	9.8	7.0	6.2	5.8
12	11.5	8.3	7.5	6.7
16	14.5	10.6	9.8	8.8
20	18.3	13.7	12.8	12.0
25	23.5	18.1	17.5	
30	29.4	23.2	22.8	
40	33.5	28.5	28.3	

Fuji guides with shock ring

Size	O/D	I/D light	I/D heavy	I/D flanged
5	4.6	2.6		
5.5	5.3	3.2		
6	6.1	3.7	2.8	
7	7.0	4.3	3.3	
8	8.0	5.0	4.1	
10	9.8	6.4	5.2	
12	11.5	7.5	6.2	
16	14.5	9.4	8.8	
20	18.3	12.3	11.4	
25	23.5	16.3	15.1	
30	29.4	21.5	20.1	
40	35.5	26.5	24.6	
50	38.4	35.4		

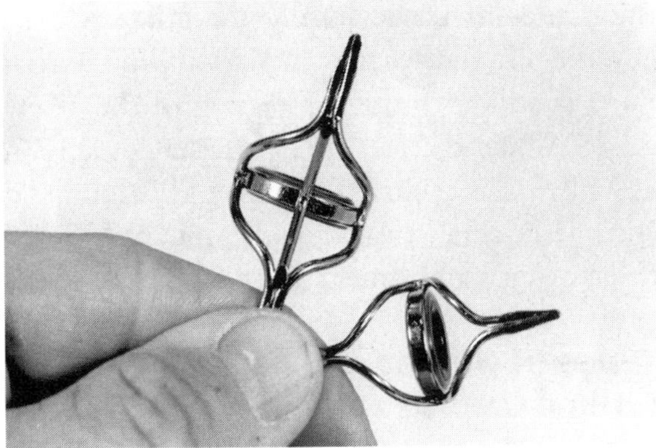

Often the same type of guide can come in several different frame configurations. This heavy-rigged boat and casting style guide is available in standard (right) and reinforced (left) models. The reinforced model has an additional bar under the frame to protect the ring from hard use. This guide also comes with a lighter metal ring holding a lighter shock ring for spinning rods.

Frame Styles

Guides vary widely in frame style. Simple snake guides are nothing more than wire twisted into the guide shape and with flattened ends for easy placement and thread wrapping. Simple guides for casting, spin-cast, and spinning rods and strippers on fly rods vary widely. They can be double-foot or single-foot, high frame or low frame, reinforced or supported with an additional frame support running from the bottom of the guide ring to the frame end of the guide foot, made with three frame supports (two running to one foot and one to the other foot), of light materials or heavy materials (for strength or lightness), in straddle styles in which two feet on one end of the guide bracket the rod blank, or of stamped or round-wire frames. Wire frames running from the foot to the wire ring can be in a U or V shape. Some guides are even completely wire, formed like a snake guide with an additional turn (like the earlier Foulproof sold by Gudebrod). Tip-tops for these guides are similar, with a double wrap of wire for the ring and the two ends of the wire flattened and designed to straddle the rod for wrapping in place.

One important consideration in guides is the width of the guide feet. For example, rod builders using split-bamboo blanks usually want guides with wide feet so that the guides will set evenly on the flattened sides of the blank. In contrast, those using graphite blanks—particularly thin or very lightweight graphite blanks—like narrow guide feet that will not "hang over" the side of the blank when wrapped in place. One style of guide is not made in two widths of feet, but any wide-foot guide can be filed to a narrower width for use on a thin graphite-blank section.

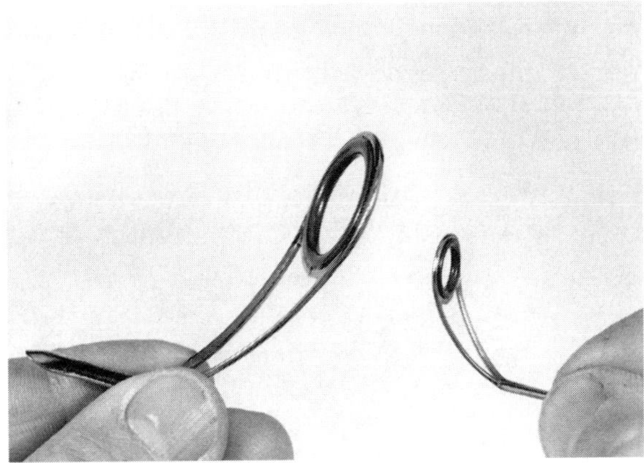

Example of high-frame, one-foot spinning guides from DNY.

One recent change in guides is the trend of manufacturers to file the guide feet, making for a smoother transition of thread from the blank to the guide foot while you're wrapping the guides in place. Ideally the guide will be chrome plated after the guide foot filing so that there is still corrosion protection of the entire guide. When the rod builder files a guide foot, any plating is removed with the file and could corrode in time, even though protected by the thread wraps and thread finish.

Types of Guides

Fly-Rod Guides

Snake guides are small guides used on fly rods and presumably are so named because of their twisted appearance when viewed from the top or side. Sizes vary with the manufacturers that continue to make these guides. There used to be two different sizing methods—one used by Mildrum (called "Mildrum size"), the other used by other companies. Mildrum sizes include a small of 4 through a large of 9. The alternate method—and the one used universally today—ranges from a small 4/0 through a large of 6. A comparison of these sizes is as follows:

Size	Mildrum	Other
Small		4/0
		3/0
	4	2/0
	4½	1/0
	5	1
	5½	2
	6	3
	7	4
	8	5
Large	9	6

Fly-rod snake guides are made by most guide manufacturers, including PacBay, Batson, and REC.

These snake guides are just like a snake in shape—a wire twisted into an arc and with the two ends flattened to make feet to wrap the guide onto the rod. Thus there is a wire "arch" for the line flow, with the guide very lightweight for the fly rod use. Two wrappings are required, one for each of the two feet. Today these are available in sizes 4/0 (small) through 6 (large), with sets of fly-rod guides in graduated sizes also available.

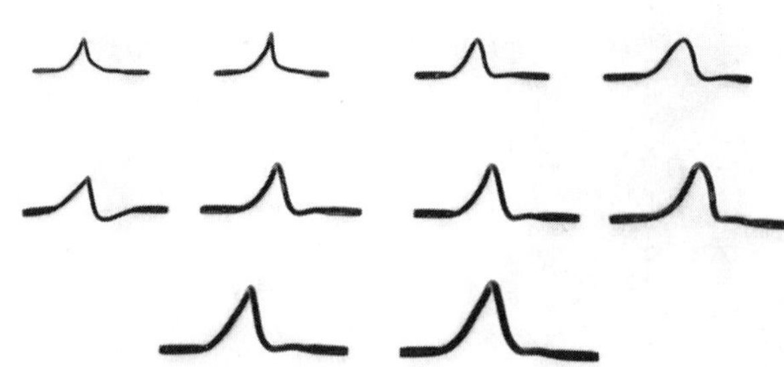

Snake guides come in a variety of sizes, such as this range of guides in sizes 4/0 through 6. Several finishes are available.

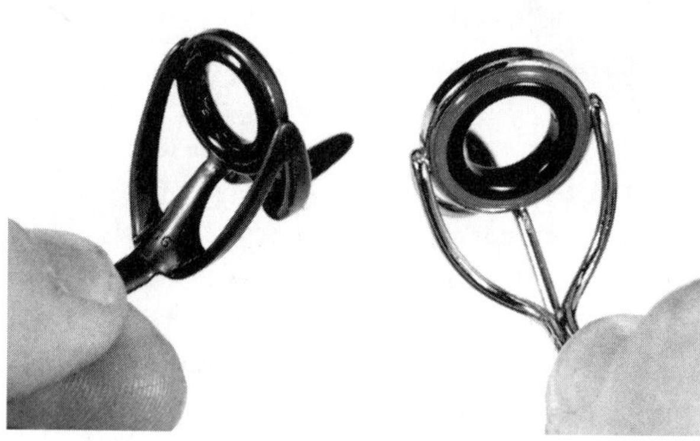

Two styles of guides. The Fuji guide on the left is stamped from one piece of metal with the ring secured in place. The Perfection Tip guide on the right is welded from wire rods.

A newer type of wire guide is one in which the wire is formed into a complete wire circle with the two ends folded parallel and next to each other to make a single foot. These guides have a ring through which the line flows. They require only one wrap, slightly reducing the weight and any dampening effect of the second wrap. These ring wire guides are available in size designation of 2/0 to 6.

The stripper guides for these two types of wire guides are usually made with a matching-finish stainless steel frame and ring. These are available in sizes 7 through 12 millimeters.

Many guide manufacturers also make fly rod, small, low-frame, one-foot, ceramic-ring guides using one of the many ceramic materials available. In most catalogs these are available in 4- through 12-millimeter ring sizes. Matching stripper guides from about 8- through 12-millimeter ring sizes are available for these ceramic-ring guides. These usually have two feet for strength. In addition, for those rod builders restoring old classic rods such as old bamboo fly rods, classic agate stripper guides in sizes 8 through 16 millimeters are available.

To match wire fly-rod snake guides, fly-rod tip-tops have a simple wire ring—no frame support—attached to a tube sized to fit the rod tip. Tube sizes for these range from 3.5 to 7.5 millimeters. Some are made with larger than standard rings for large lines, principally in saltwater fly rods. The rings are round or a very slight pear shape.

For matching with ceramic fly-rod guides, tip-tops have a ceramic ring of 6 or 8 millimeters in size and are available in tube sizes from 4 to 7.5 millimeters. These usually have a slight elevated split frame to hold the ring and keep the line elevated off the rod blank.

Casting Guides

Guides for casting rods include any standard style of frame and guide ring of any material. Most are low-frame because the line comes off the reel in a straight line, not in loops, as with spinning line off a spinning reel. Although any size guide can be used for this, most range from about 6- through 16-millimeter ring sizes. Most will be light styles, although heavy-frame or reinforced guides are used for saltwater casting or popping, muskie, and similar heavy-duty rods. Standard sizes for tip-tops for casting models range from 31/2/64 up to large sizes used for surf and boat rods, with most casting rod tip-tops in the 5⁄64 to 8⁄64 range.

Casting guides are available in all types of ring material, usually with a stainless steel frame. Tip-tops to match the guides are available from every fishing gear manufacturer.

Spin-Cast Guides

Spin-cast rods are very similar to casting rods, with the differences sometimes found in the guides and lower profile reel seats. Since the line comes off the reel in a straight line, the same low-frame, small-ring guides used for casting rods are used for spin-cast rods. Some spin-cast reels do have a very large hole in the nose cone, resulting in some slight looping of the line during the cast. For this reason spin-cast rods sometimes have a slightly larger butt guide—say a size 16 instead of a size 12 or a size 20 in place of a size 16. Other than these somewhat subjective choices, the guides used are exactly the same as those for casting rods. Most frames are stainless, and rings of stainless or all types of ceramics are available. Matching tip-tops for a given guide series are available.

Microguides

Microguides are new to the market in just the past few years. They most resemble casting rod guides and can be found in one- and two-foot models. Their ring sizes range from about 2 to 3.5 millimeters, or about half or less of the 6-millimeter guide, which in the past was the smallest ring guide available. They also all have very low frames and rings so that the line runs very close to the rod blank.

Since these guides are smaller, they are also lighter. They are also shorter in length and thus create less of an effect on the rod during casting and fighting fish. They do not impede casting in any way, since the line in any casting situations only touches a small portion of the ring of any guide and then only infrequently as the line is cast and flows out from the rod guides.

Against this argument is the fact that by being smaller, it would be impossible in most cases to use a knot in the line to attach a leader, or at least a knot above the point where the line hangs down from the tip-top preparatory to casting. Thus for much freshwater fishing and some saltwater fishing wherein the line is tied directly to the lure, these small microguides would not be a problem. In some saltwater fishing or any fishing where you would have a knot or connection a foot or more above the lure tie or bait rig, casting would be impossible. The guide rings are small enough to impede a knot in most of these casting situations.

Currently these guides are primarily used for casting tackle, but at this writing designs with a higher frame are being tested for use with spinning tackle. For spinning, the line loops coming off the reel would be choked down on almost immediately with the first guide, after which the line would run straight and the microguides would be no problem.

Spinning Guides

Spinning guides are essentially like lightweight casting-rod guides, with light frames and light rings. But they do differ in two important ways: They generally have much larger rings to accommodate the loops of line that come off the reel, and high frames are a must to reduce or eliminate line slap against the rod blank as the line loops flow off the reel. Sizes used range from a small of 6 millimeters up through a size 75-millimeter wire ring for the butt guide on a surf-spinning rod. Some companies still make large reinforced-frame wire ring guides up to 70 millimeters in diameter. Remember that this 70-millimeter ring size is an outside diameter, not an inside diameter. Today most guides are made with a stainless steel (SS304 freshwater or SS316 saltwater) frame and a ceramic ring of one of the many materials available. Many are also available with or without (most often without) a shock ring. Most of these are in a 50-millimeter (OD) ring size or smaller. Most for freshwater fishing will range from 6 millimeters through 30 or 40 millimeters. The frame can be U or V shaped, stamped or wire, using the same ring materials already covered. Guide weight and thus frame style, ring style, and guide size are very important considerations, particularly with light and ultralight rods. Such rods are light, and the addition of any unnecessary weight makes them slow, logy, and "heavy."

There is a trend to higher frames and relatively smaller rings for spinning rods. Guides such as the PacBay Minima Model M series are very high for their size and also have smaller than normal rings than would be expected for their given frame height. These are also one-foot guides with split-frame sides for lightness coupled with strength.

One additional thought on spinning guides, which I expressed in the first edition of *Tackle Craft* (1974), concerns the large rings used on spinning rods. They may not be necessary—a point I first discovered decades ago while fishing in Florida. Then some expert anglers were using special long-distance spinning rods that incorporated a butt guide with a small Carboloy ring on a very high frame. Since nothing was available commercially at that time, all these special guides were custom-made. The rest of the guides were standard, though small, spinning models. The theory then and now is that the small guide clears the line immediately and that the line then runs straight through the rest of the guides. Using a series of standard spinning guides with a large butt guide and successively smaller rings, the line usually continues to flow in loops, retaining the possibility of increased guide friction and line slap all the way up the rod.

Shortly after this, Heddon, then still in the rod business, sold spinning rods with small-ring, high-frame guides. Its tests showed that the smaller rings made no difference in casting distance and in fact might have improved on it over the use of regular guides. Unfortunately the company could not convince the angling public of this and eventually discontinued the rods. Today Fuji, Batson, PacBay, and others are manufacturing and selling guides with the high-frame and small-ring style, and they are being accepted. This also confirms in part the idea of the spinning-style microguides currently being talked about and tested.

Surf rods can be built as spinning or casting (revolving-spool) models. The guides for spinning surf rods are the same as for the standard spinning guides already covered, with the exception that they are larger, unless built according to the small-ring, high-frame theory. Often revolving-spool surf rods are used for the heaviest of surf fishing, so these guides are often reinforced and have a heavy or flanged ring. The principal consideration with any surf rod is to use large-internal-diameter guides and tip-tops at the tip end of the rod that are sufficient to allow the smooth flow of knots and shock line through the guides on a cast. Often this means 16- or 20-millimeter rings to take care of and allow flow of Biminis and Albrights often used in surf-fishing shock and bite leaders.

Boat Guides

Typically boat-rod guides are similar or identical to the heavy revolving-spool guides used for surf fishing. Though spinning rods are used for boat fishing and trolling, traditionally this term refers to revolving-spool tackle. The guides are low with an extra-heavy frame and heavy rings and are reinforced for the heavy-duty work required. Since knots, double lines, and leaders are often used with boat fishing, large-ring guides are a must for clearance.

Although stainless and ceramic rings on boat guides are popular, some anglers still like (they are available) guides with Carboloy or Carbide rings for strength and hardness. Matching tip-tops are available for any of the boat-guide options.

Noodle-Rod Guides

Noodle rods are long and very soft, almost like fly rods in blank design but built as spinning rods and used with very light lines (typically two-pound test) and spinning tackle. Guides for these rods must be very light and small and typically use silicon carbide or Hardloy in the small-ring, high-frame styles such as are used for match fishing and ultralight fishing. Slightly extended tip-tops with wire frames to hold the ring extended are available for these high-frame, small-ring guides.

Roller Guides

Roller guides are just what they seem: guides in a frame with a roller on which the line runs, thus eliminating the friction of the line against an immovable-ring guide. They are used on high-quality offshore trolling rods. All are similar in function, although the brands available are different in frame design, roller design, bearings and frame materials used, and so on.

The Stuart roller guides have four frame finishes: stainless steel, silver anodized aluminum, gold anodized aluminum, and black anodized aluminum. Mildrum rollers come in chrome, gold, or black on silicon bronze-cast frames, with silver, gold, or black side plates for many finish combinations. There are also several models: the Lite for lightweight fishing (six- to fifty-pound-class tackle); the Hi-Rollers, rated for rods of fifty-pound class and heavier; and the Roller Flex, which is a one-foot design for less of a "footprint" and greater flexibility on rod blanks used for stand-up fishing to fifty-pound class. Roller Flex is specifically designed for flexible tip, high-leverage rods such as stand-up rods and West Coast tuna-style rods.

AFTCO roller guides come in several sizes and finishes. The Super Heavy Duty roller guides and top are available with ball bearings; gold nitride rollers; and pin and screw frames of chrome, black chrome oxide, or black and gold. There are also regular Super Heavy Duty roller guides and tops with sleeve-type AftCote bearings. These are ideal for eighty-pound class through unlimited tackle. The Heavy Duty rollers and tops are designed for twenty- through eighty-pound-class rods, and all are available with AftCote bearings, in chrome-and-black chrome oxide frames with standard stainless rollers, pins, and screws, or in black-and-gold with black frames and gold rollers and fittings. The regular roller guides and tops designed for six-through fifty-pound-class tackle come with AftCote bearings in the same choice of finishes. In addition, rollers are available with special hardened rollers and frames for use with wire line that might in time groove regular rollers. These rollers are also suitable for regular monofilament and Dacron line as well. AFTCO also has a one-foot roller guide that is very small and designed for freshwater and very light saltwater rods.

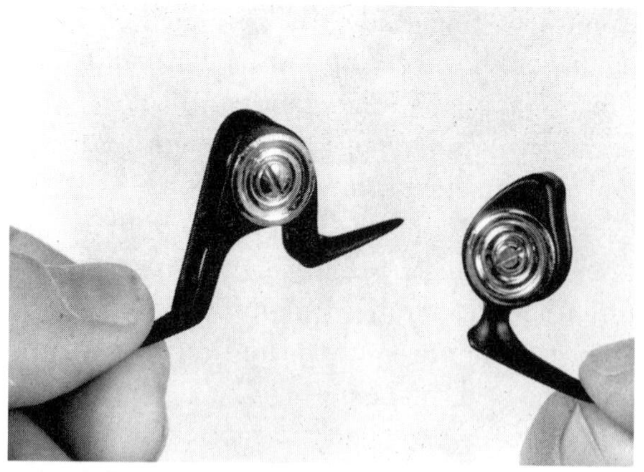

Roller guides from Mildrum are available in both one- and two-foot styles. Both are for light-tackle fishing.

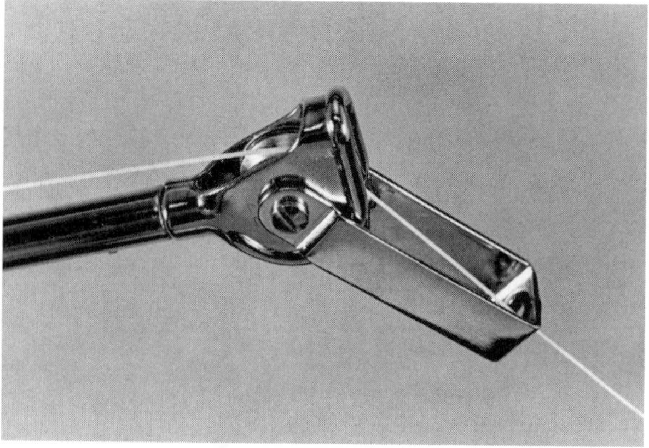

Some guides are designed to prevent the line from rubbing the side of the frame—such as this one by AFTCO used mostly for wire-line fishing. The top swivels to keep the line in the center of the roller.

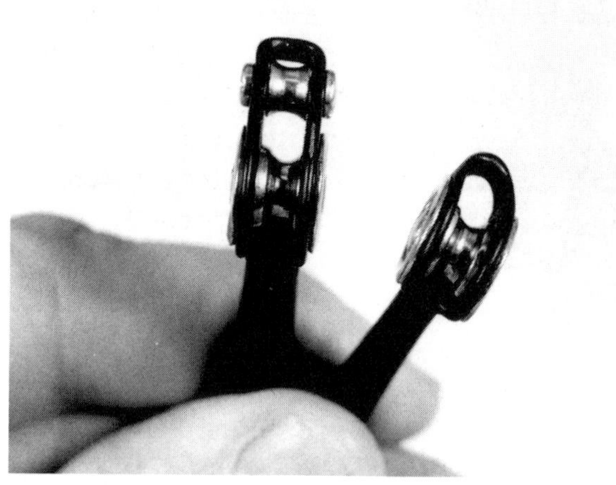

Frames of representative Mildrum tip-tops. The heavy-duty model to the left includes a roller for the line and a spacer bar above.

The tip-tops for these guides match in materials, finish, and rollers. To allow for line and knot clearance, in some cases guides are available both with standard and larger heads (in the same size roller) for greater space and knot clearance around the roller. Tube sizes range from $\frac{5}{64}$ through $\frac{32}{64}$, with different frame and roller sizes based on the top size.

In addition, there are special tip-tops for wire-line fishing in which the tip-top swivels on the tube so that the roller can track the direction of the line. The roller would not do this, however, without the addition of an extended bail ending in a small carbide ring through which the line

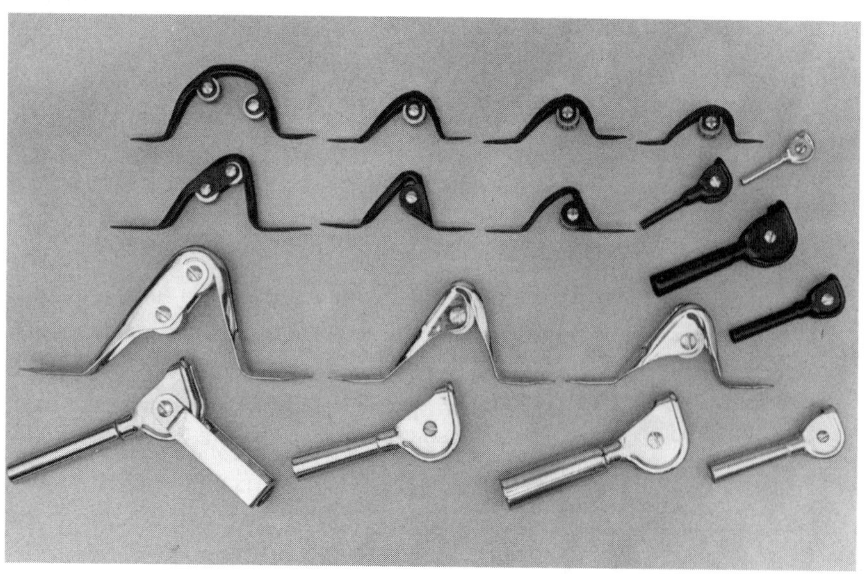

Guides from AFTCO include three different size ranges, each in several finishes. Tip-tops to match are also available.

travels. This bail travels with the line to cause the roller to turn as the line moves. The sizes for this swivel top, from AFTCO, range from $^{20}/_{64}$ to $^{32}/_{64}$. The advantage of this for wire-line fishing is that it prevents the wire from wearing against the side of the frame or in turn wearing grooves in the frame.

Final Thoughts on Guides

Guides continue to change and advance. Some final thoughts on the current state of guides follow:

Once there were only a few basic styles of guides for fly fishing, casting rods, spinning tackle, and boat gear, but they continue to evolve. Today guides are available in a dozen different ring materials, all superior to the ceramic rings originally developed in the 1970s. These include different reinforcing methods, grinding the guide feet before chrome plating for added protection and corrosion resistance, and methods of stamping out frames to lower the cost of manufacturing. All this gives the customer a better product at the least-expensive price.

Colors were once nonexistent on guides unless you wanted a chromed or stainless steel finish. Today you can get guides with varying ring colors, although often these ring colors are a function of the ceramic ring material used. With these varying ring and frame colors, custom rod builders have more choices than ever to make a unique rod. Typically ring and guide colors can be used to match thread colors used in the thread wraps holding the guides in place. These colors can also tie in with the many varied anodized colors of reel seats, fixed and movable hoods, butt caps, ferrules for saltwater rods, etc.

Manufacturers' information is more readily available today for those custom rod builders who want precise information about the products they order. Sometimes you can find this information in dealers' catalogs, such as those by Barlow's, Jann's Netcraft, Merrick, and Mud Hole. For example, with PacBay you can often find the following information for standard guides: overall height, overall length, height to the bottom of the guide ring, and length of each foot. Tops are also listed by the length and height. This of course is in addition to the nominal and/or true ring size of a guide. Batson offers similar information on its guides. In many cases there is a listing of both the outside diameter and the inside diameter (OD and ID) of the rings used.

More and more experimentation is occurring with guides, as per the current trend to microguides. Guide manufacturers are starting to make guides in which the ring slopes toward the tip end of the rod to reduce or eliminate line tangles on the guide frame or ring. At the same time, manufacturers are also making rings that are not round as guide rings were in the past. They are now making guide rings that are rectangular in shape with rounded corners. In a vertical mode, when placed into a sloping frame guide as above, this rectangle allows for more clearance for the line as it goes through the ring. Whether this makes any difference is not known, but it can't hurt. In addition, guide manufacturers are constantly looking for harder, better ring materials and new ways for making and stamping out frames.

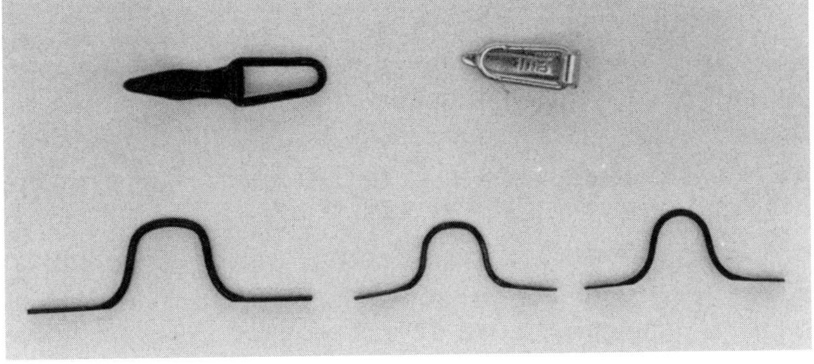

Various types of hook-keepers. Traditional styles in three sizes are shown below; a more modern fold-up/fold-down style from Fuji in two finishes is above (enlarged view).

Examples of Fuji reel seats that range from large, heavy-duty models (left) to medium-size models and a skeletal design (right). The skeletal model requires an insert of wood, cork, or foam.

Heavy-duty aluminum reel seats. These are skeletal style and require an insert and come with a specially cut cork ring (left) for hiding the fixed hood.

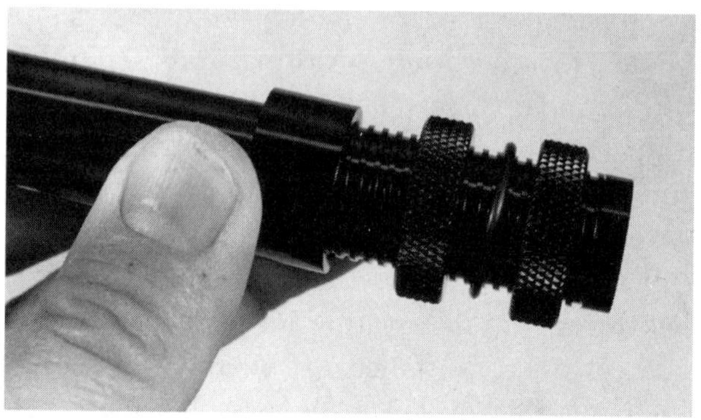

Reel seats for saltwater fly rods usually have double lock nuts. This one from Struble has an additional O-ring between the locking nuts to help secure the nuts in place.

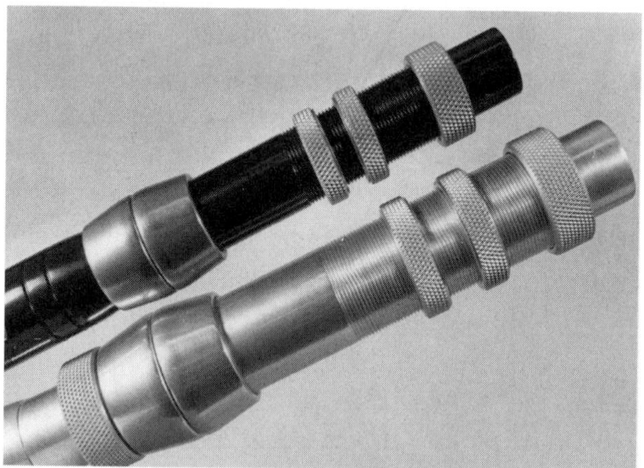

Different sizes and styles of reel seat/handle combinations are available for boat and trolling rods. These are from AFTCO.

REEL SEATS

A reel seat holds the reel in place on a rod. It is part of the rod and has the simple function of securing the two reel feet. Within this basic function, however, there are many varieties and styles. These also vary widely with the type of rod and function of that rod.

Spinning-Reel Seats

Spinning-reel seats are mostly simple tubes designed to fit onto the rod with shims that adjust for the diameter differential of the outside of the blank and the inside of the reel seat. A simple reel seat consists of a tube with a fixed hood at one end to hold one of the reel feet and a sliding hood at the other end to fit over the other reel foot. Single- or double-screw collars or locking nuts are fastened finger-tight against the sliding hood to hold the reel in place. There is no trigger, as is found on casting-style reel seats, and the hoods and locking nuts are usually made as low-profile and unobtrusive as possible, since in spinning the hand holds the rod at the reel seat with the fingers on either side of the reel shaft and around the reel feet and reel seat.

Basic reel seats like this are made of aluminum and also molded in nylon or plastic with graphite fibers (often called “graphite,” “graphite fill,” “composite,” or, if they lack graphite, “graphite-style”). They come in a wide range of sizes, from a small of about a 16-millimeter internal diameter to a large of about 32-millimeter internal diameter (although sometimes these vary; sizes are sometimes off by a millimeter or two).

Today many reel seats are made far fancier than in the past. These two have inserts and some metalworking, making them among the special reel seats for deluxe rods.

End view of seven reel seats showing the ribbing that many manufacturers are adding to their products today. These internal ribs are designed to grip the glue when the reel seat is glued to a rod blank so that the reel seat will never twist or turn, as was a problem in the past.

Sizes will vary with the function, with size 18 being about the smallest comfortable for most male adults. A size 16 may be best for some women and children. For freshwater fishing, sizes 18 through 22 are about the best, with the largest sizes of 28, 30, and 32 best for big, boat, and surf-spinning rods.

There is a wide variety in the quality of such reel seats, with some having graphite (molded) hoods, others with molded hoods covered with stainless steel or gold-plated stainless, and some with a keyway that keeps the sliding hood in line with the reel foot at all times.

The trend in spinning-reel seats today is for more variety in barrels, colors (painted or anodized aluminum), vented spinning-reel seats with or without wood inserts, spinning-reel seats with resin impregnated wood inserts, ventilated spinning seats with braided or infinity barrel designs, and other features.

These are often skeletal-type spinning-reel seats that consist of the fixed hood and a separate threaded portion, lock nut, and sliding hood. Most often these are anodized aluminum, black or bright. Missing is the smooth, plain barrel in the center. For skeletal reel seats, this missing center is replaced with same-diameter

Rod makers can see lots of examples of available parts for making rods at the High Point, North Carolina, International Custom Rod Building Exposition. This is a display from one manufacturer of the many types of reel seats they have available.

foam, cork rings, wood, or similar material. Often the same material used for the grips is used here to keep the design of the whole rod complementary.

In addition, reel seats for spinning rods include various types of skeletal styles, such as simple sliding rings that will slide on a cork or foam grip but will hold securely when slid up onto the sloping reel foot. In some each ring is really two rings that, when rotated, will lock down the reel foot through a cam mechanism.

Casting-Reel Seats

Reel seats for casting (revolving-spool reel) rods have all the same features as spinning models. They have a fixed hood, barrel, sliding hood, and threaded lock nut or nuts. They also have a trigger that is usually fixed to or molded with the fixed hood. These are made of aluminum or molded of plastic (with or without graphite). Several sizes are available but not usually in the full range of sizes of the spinning (no-trigger) reel seats. This does not mean that plain or spinning-style reel seats can't be used with casting rods, only that those with the trigger for an index-finger grip are more typical. Skeletal styles are also available in which the fixed-hood ring includes a trigger with a separate threaded barrel, hood, and nut.

As with the modern spinning-reel seats, these casting-reel seats are also available in a wide variety of colors, materials, sizes, and styles. Many of these are molded of graphite-resin material and thus are basic casting reel seats. These basic styles come in low-profile styles in which the blank is exposed through an opening in the bottom just in front of the trigger. In all of these, various finishes of the metal sleeve over the sliding hood are available, adding to the variety of possible choices.

Big-Game, Boat-Rod, and Trolling-Rod Reel Seats

The basic design of a big-game reel seat is no different from that of a spinning rod. What *is* different is the strength and reinforcement of the reel seat and the hoods. What is required will of course vary with the size and type of rod. The graphite-fill reel seat that might work great for a light trolling rod will be completely inadequate for a heavy 80- to 130-pound-class offshore trolling rod.

Graphite-fill reel seats come in boat- and trolling-rod models, with thicker walls and heavier, sturdier hoods. For offshore trolling rods, slipover aluminum reel seats, such as those from AFTCO, are best because they have the highest strength-to-weight ratio of any reel seat. These are machined, rather than stamped or rolled, using marine-grade aluminum (usually 6061 or 7071 aluminum). The hoods, both fixed and sliding, are heavy, thick walled, and milled for the reel foot in order to hold under the heavy pressures of this type of fishing. Double lock nuts hold the sliding hood in place. Aluminum reel seats are anodized. AFTCO reel seats are available in silver-anodized or hard-coat black. Sizes range from 13/16 to 13/16.

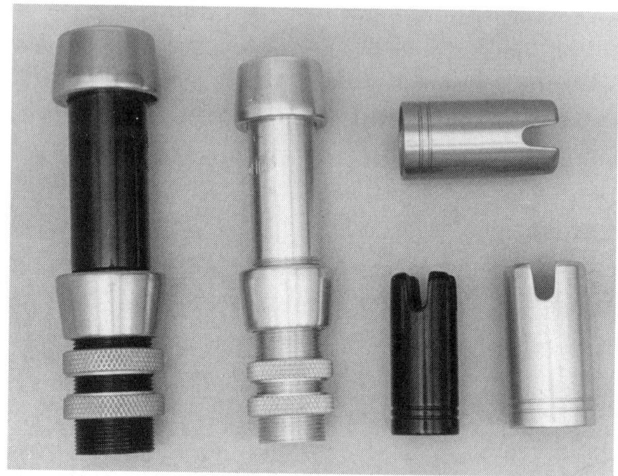

Examples of AFTCO reel seats and gimbals for big-game rods.

One important point: The slipover reel seats described are designed only for one-piece rods in which the rod blank goes completely through the reel seat and the grip is built up on the blank as well. They are not designed for the detachable-butt rods, which require reel seats that include a ferrule that slips into the upper end of the reel seat and into which the butt of the rod blank is fastened via a locking nut. Usually these reel seats are threaded at the upper end to take a special collet nut that fits over the ferrule and that secures the rod-tip section to the detachable butt. One model is available from Fuji in a molded graphite-fill seat; others, made of chrome-plated brass, are sometimes available. In all of these the reel seat is glued to the rod butt and remains part of the rod butt when the tip is detached. They are also available from Lakeland.

These reel seats are chrome-plated over brass, heavily reinforced, and milled and swaged hood styles.

Similar big-game reel seats with ferrules and collet nuts are made as an integral part of aluminum butts. They are discussed as handles later in this chapter.

Fly-Rod Reel Seats

Fly-rod reel seats run the full range of sizes, styles, designs, and materials. Their difference from other reel seats is that they are all designed to fit at the end of the rod—below the grip—and thus have a closed end or a plug at one end. The exceptions would be those designed to take an extension butt or those with a built-in nondetachable short extension.

The simplest and least-expensive reel seats are those made of aluminum or graphite-fill plastic. For example, the size 16 FPS-style reel seats from Fuji can be used as fly-rod reel seats with the addition of a special rubber plug that fits into the bottom. Other than the plug or a closed fitting at one end, these reel seats resemble—or are identical to—small-diameter slipover reel seats used for spinning rods. Most of those that have a separate or removable plug can be used as up-locking or down-locking types; those that have a permanent fixed plug or closed end cannot. These can be either down-locking or up-locking. Those that are down-locking have the nuts and the sliding hood at the upper end so that they lock the reel seat in place as the nuts are tightened on the movable hood. I prefer the up-locking style, since it provides a little more room between the end of the rod and the base of the reel, in essence providing a very slight extension on the butt end of the rod as an advantage in fighting a fish.

Reel seats that allow removal of the plug or fixed-hood end can usually be used either way—up-locking or down-locking—and there are advantages to each. Down-locking reel seats are more traditional and are commonly seen on most finished rods. Up-locking reel seats, in which the threaded part of the barrel and the sliding hood are at the base of the rod and the fixed hood is at the upper end, have two advantages. One is cosmetic: The upper fixed hood can be hidden under the last of the cork rings (special cork rings with a milled cutout for the hood are available). The other advantage is more practical: Locking the reel in place leaves a short extended portion of the reel seat to help prevent the reel from catching in clothing when the rod is braced against the angler's body.

In addition to the basic plain-vanilla fly-rod reel seats, there are reel seats that are highly individualized, almost custom-crafted, and extremely beautiful. Some are moderately priced; others are relatively expensive. Examples include reel seats with cork or wood barrels, such as those available from PacBay, Batson, and others. Some of these have anodized-aluminum threads, locking nuts, and fixed hoods in silver, black, brown, and nickel silver, the latter obviously more expensive. Usually these are made with a recess in the threaded portion of the barrel so that the reel foot rests on a plain metal barrel, not on threads.

Spacers, or the wood inserts, include a wide variety of exotic woods such as bubinga, cocobolo, walnut, English walnut, zebrawood, bird's-eye maple, imbuya, rosewood, teak, mesquite, ebony, vermillion, Bastogne walnut burl, California burled walnut, spalted maple, padauk, snakewood, ash, black ash, butternut crotch, grenadil, thuja, olive, and brier. Distributers and suppliers are now selling blocks of some of these woods so that tackle builders who have a lathe can make their own inserts or modify them for separately available skeletal reel seats. Cork is also an option, as are laminated woods and scrimshaw done on bone or plastic.

Some skeletal fly-rod reel seats are nothing more than a cork or wood body that is swelled at the ends to prevent loss of the rings, with sliding rings of nickel silver or aluminum to secure the reel. These reel seats are very attractive and very lightweight, especially when used with a cork spacer or barrel, but they run the risk of loosening in time during fishing. They also have the disadvantage of the rings slightly cocking at an angle when they are slid onto the reel foot, thus marring the barrel material over time. This is more pronounced on cork than on wood spacers, but it will affect the finish of wood spacers.

In addition to the solid graphite or aluminum fly-rod reel seats, some manufacturers are now making reel seats that require a wood insert but are not true skeletal styles. These reel seats have complete metal barrels, but the barrel is drilled with large holes or milled out to take the foot of the fly reel. This provides maximum venting of the reel with the added plus of different color barrels or wood inserts for more variation.

The possibilities in all this are endless. Between the dozen or more styles of reel seat, the dozen or more wood inserts, and the finishes of the aluminum reel seat parts, there are perhaps hundreds of variations of any reel seat for any fly rod.

Saltwater fly-rod reel seats are similar but for durability and strength are made mostly of continuous barrel aluminum with up-locking double lock nuts and sometimes with slightly heavier swaged hoods. For the larger reels used in salt water, they are usually longer and slightly larger in diameter than freshwater models. Some have built-in extension butts, which are usually short and sometimes permanent. Others have open ends or removable butts so that a plug-in or screw-in extension butt can be placed in the reel seat when a fish is fought. The easiest and most secure of these have double O-rings to hold the extension butt in place and still allow instant attachment and removal. While it used to be difficult to find a short manufactured extension butt for a saltwater fly-rod reel seat, one manufacturer alone now has close to eighty different fly-rod reel seats, not counting the variations of wood inserts for some models.

Some of the larger, tougher reel seats for saltwater fly fishing have an O-ring between the double lock nuts to help secure them and hold them in place to prevent the reel from becoming loose.

Steelhead and salmon fly-rod reel seats are similar and are designed to accept extension butts. Some of these extension butts are very short—only about 1½ to 2 inches long—while others range up to 6 inches long. Any extension butt of any length can be used, but 6 inches is about the maximum available and is the maximum allowed for IGFA-record catches. Just remember that the longer the extension, the more likely it is that the fly line will flip around and catch on it at the end of that perfect cast when a tarpon eats the fly as soon as it lands. Most serious fly anglers, if they like or use an extension butt at all, use a short extension butt of about 1½ inch to 2 inches.

Typically the extensions are of the same material used for the barrel insert—cork or one of the exotic woods.

Other Reel Seats and Reel-Holding Methods

Skeletal reel seats and rings are really a modification of standard reel seats and have already been discussed. In addition, there are plate-type reel seats that are usually thread wrapped onto a larger rod (like a surf rod) or held in place with electrical tape for temporary use. These fit onto a rod blank in any position, are wrapped or taped in place (special recesses on the plate are designed for this), and hold the reel by means of a fixed hood and a sliding hood that is locked in place with a cam-functioning lever.

Reel-Seat Bushings

Since reel seats almost always have a considerably larger inside diameter than the outside diameter of the rod blank, some sort of bushing or shim must be used to fill up this space and keep the reel seat centered on the blank. Bushings of cork, graphite, fiber, and sometimes fiberglass are available. To fit properly they must be of the correct internal and outside diameter in order to fit the reel seat and the rod blank. They are often available in several outside diameters to fit internal diameters of specific and standard reel seats and in many internal-diameter sizes for rod blanks.

Although not usually purchased as bushings or bushing material, other materials may be wrapped around a blank to fill up space, including masking, paper, and fiberglass tape; cord; and string. In addition, cork rings and wood or fiber discs can be shaped and sized for bushings. (The details are covered in chapters 18 and 20.)

GRIPS

We've made a differentiation here between grips and handles: Grips fit onto the rod blank and are designed for gripping the rod; handles incorporate the grips, reel seat, and butt cap. Grips are typically of wood, cork, various types of foam, and graphite tubing. Today modern rod builders are also making grips (and handles) of wood turned on a lathe, and more and more rod builders are going into lathe work for part of their tackle making. Shaped foam is also used, with a graphite sleeve over the foam for durability. Aluminum is used in offshore rods and is available as a complete handle.

Wood grips are more typically found in complete handles incorporating the reel seat and butt cap but are also available individually. Most are of hickory and are designed as long rear grips for inexpensive boat rods. Aluminum grips or butts are available with a built-in gimbal knock and a section sized to hold a standard reel seat. Bored aluminum butts are available, again with a gimbal knock and reel-seat bushing, but are bored for through-handle construction of one-piece trolling rods and the so-called stand-up rods as popularized in Southern California long-range fishing boats and trips. Both are available from AFTCO and other manufacturers.

Cork is used both in ring form and in preshaped grips. Rings are widely used to make grips for all types of rods—fly, spinning, casting, boat, downrigger, noodle, surf, popping—and as foregrips on offshore rods. Cork is more common in some rods than in others. It is almost a must in fly rods and is popular in spinning, casting, popping, downrigger, noodle, and some surf rods. Foam or leather-covered foam is more prevalent and works better as a foregrip on big-game offshore rods.

Cork is a natural material, very light (about one-fifth the weight of foam, although this will vary with foam type and hardness), relatively hard, and easy to hold when wet or dry. It comes from Portugal, where it grows as the bark of the cork tree and may be peeled every few years. Cork trees are not a quick crop; they must be ten years old before the cork bark may be harvested. After harvesting, the cork is cut into rings, divided as to quality, and sold as is or used to make preshaped cork grips.

The best cork rings are "specie" cork, in which the natural cork pits run parallel to the handle—the same direction as the center drilled hole in the cork. (Mustard cork rings, rarely seen today, are made of lower quality cork with the natural pits running at right angles to the drilled hole or handle direction.) Better quality rods grips and the cork available for custom rod building are almost always specie cork. There are different grades of specie cork, based on the number and size of the natural pits. The fewer and smaller the pits, the higher the quality of cork and the more expensive it is. Unfortunately there is no standard cork-industry rating of grades, so you must depend on the reputation of the store or mail-order company from which you buy and the grading system they use. Most will use the grading of the importers from which they buy the cork. Some importers use a rating system with "Flor" as the best, followed by Super, A, B, and C grades. Other companies use a system of letters, beginning with AAAA and continuing through AAA, AA, A, and B. Ratings of Super Fine, Extra Fine, and similar descriptions are used by still other companies.

Cork rings are almost always ½ inch thick but come in different ring diameters for sizing to any rod with minimum waste. (Some suppliers may have rings of ¼ inch thick, which some rod builders like because it makes for a different laminated-type look in the finished grip. When available, these rings are most often used in fly rods.)

Most rings are available with drilled holes, which also differ in size, although some rings are available solid and not drilled. Diameters include 1⅛, 1¼, 1½, and 2 inches. The 1⅛-inch size is typically used for most freshwater fly rods; 1¼-inch rings are used for light spinning and casting grips and noodle rods; 1½-inch rings are used for light boat, saltwater, and heavy muskie rods; 2-inch-diameter rings, which often have a large 1-inch hole, are used for thick-diameter surf blanks and some foregrips on big-game rods.

The internal diameters on the rings vary from about 0.25 to 0.75 inch; larger rings usually have a larger range of hole sizes. If you buy cork rings for a number of rods, the best way to buy them is in quantities of one hundred or a gross, with a large enough outside diameter to make up the grip you want for any rod and a small enough internal diameter to fit the thinnest rod planned. Often it is best to buy rings with a 0.25-inch internal-diameter hole, since this can be easily enlarged to fit any blank. Building up a blank to fit a larger hole in the cork can be done, but it is far more difficult and subject to mistakes.

In addition to the individual cork rings used to build up a handle of the diameter and length desired, preshaped cork grips are also available. Often these are available through tackle shops or catalog houses, which purchase them from cork importers and wholesalers. Very high quality preformed grips are available (again through local or mail-order dealers) from Lamiglas, Struble, Mud Hole, Jann's Netcraft, Barlows, Merrick Tackle, and similar supply houses. Many of these are in standard fly-rod grip shapes such as cigar, half wells, full wells, and Western.

Many rod/blank manufacturers and mail-order suppliers also carry cork grip kits that include everything that you need for the reel seat, butt cap, etc., for a variety of rods styles, including fly, spinning, steelhead and salmon, casting, muskie, flipping, and popping. Cork grips usually come with a small-diameter hole and are finely finished. Both

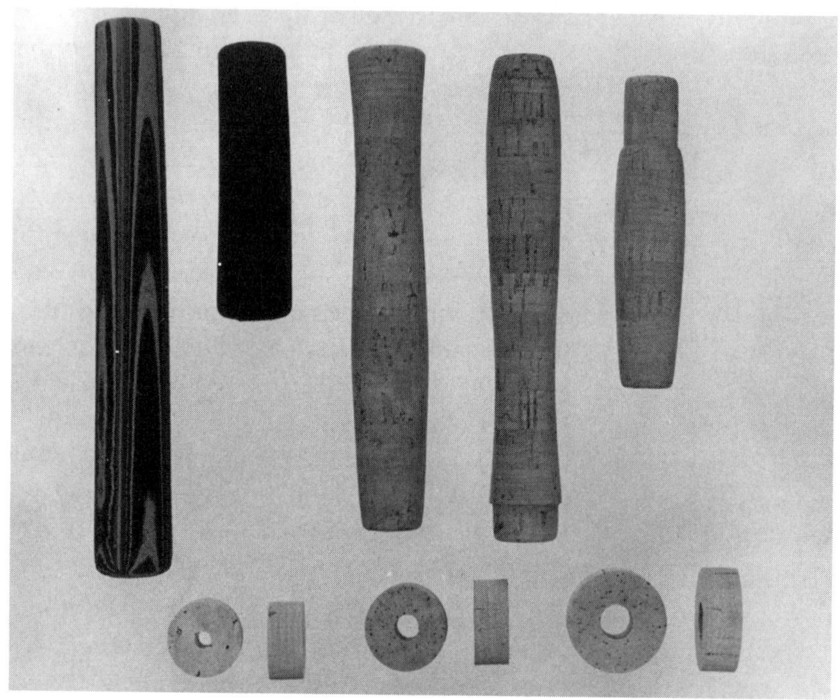

Examples of foam and cork grips and cork rings available for rod building. The cork rings come in several sizes, as shown.

fore- and rear-grip styles are available. Adding them to the blank requires tapering the hole to size to fit the blank and gluing the grips in place.

Foam grips include different materials, as well as foam, under different trade and brand names. All are dense open-cell foams. EVA is a urethane foam that comes in a variety of degrees of softness or hardness (measured using a device called a durometer) adjusted by the manufacturing process. Cork measures about 60 or 70 on this scale; EVA foam varies from about 20 to 80. Hypalon, a similar-looking material developed originally for pipe insulation, is made with a skin on the outer surface. This skin must be removed and the material shaped on a lathe or similar machine to form it into a recognizable rod grip. The shaping is done by the manufacturer or subcontractor so that the final result is a shaped grip that looks and feels similar to the open-foam EVA grips. Hypalon is often harder and thus preferred over EVA for offshore, boat, and stand-up saltwater rods.

Foam is available in a wide variety of colors. Black, brown, and gray used to be the most popular and sometimes the only colors available. Today you can get all types of foam and EVA in many colors. Hypalon comes in popular red, black, green, brown, and blue. EVA foam is available in about fifteen colors, including black, brown, gray, red, yellow, light blue, blue, dark blue, and dark green, and in grain (striated) colors of red, brown, green, blue, dark gray, light gray, and tan grain. EVA foam is also available in reddish or greenish camouflage colors that will match the camo reel seats being placed on some custom rods.

Foam grips are available in a wide variety of internal diameters, because the proper diameter is necessary for fitting the grip onto a rod by one of several methods. Considering the extremes, internal diameters range between ¼ inch and 1⅛ inches. Usually only straight sections or grips are available in the largest internal diameters; shaped grips are not available in as wide a range. The internal diameters for foam grips can range from as small as ¼ inch to as large as ¾ inch, but not all lengths, colors, and shaped grips come in a full range of internal diameters.

The outside diameters also vary, usually between about 1 inch and 1½ inches. Because these are foam grips, the internal- and outside-diameter measurements are not as precise as measurements on cork, wood, or any other more-solid material. There is a certain amount of give in the foam as it is worked. Fortunately this does not matter a great deal, since the foam's internal diameter must expand to properly fit the grip onto the blank, and the outside diameter can in part be shaped and controlled by the degree of compression or stretch of the foam grip. Straight-grip lengths are sometimes available up to about 30 inches long. Shaped grips have shapes similar to those found on cork grips and are often built with a recess at one end for a reel seat or, with rear grips, a recess at both ends for a reel seat and butt cap.

Graphite grips are only rarely used, usually in the straight-style Tennessee handle in which the reel is usually taped onto the rod handle. The idea is that the straight grip and taping the reel in place leads to greater sensitivity and greater comfort (there is no metal or graphite reel seat to hold) and is better in cold weather because it lacks a metal or molded reel seat that can conduct cold. This type of grip can be made of straight-length cork, but graphite is more common. These are nothing more than straight sleeves of graphite with graphite bushings to center and position the grip. Graphite bushings are mandatory to get optimal transmission of impulses through the rod blank to the grip. Some anglers are now also shimming the blank into a straight graphite Tennessee handle with the blank off-centered so that the blank itself touches the inside of the graphite handle and is glued in place to provide maximum sensitivity from the blank, through the handle, and to the hand.

HANDLES

Handles, at least in our definition, differ from grips in that a handle consists of the entire butt cap/rear grip/reel seat/foregrip assembly. Some may not include the foregrip, but the general concept is of a complete unit.

Handles vary as to type as follows.

Casting

When the first edition of *Tackle Craft* and the greatly expanded *Modern Tackle Craft* and *The Complete Book of Tackle Making* were published, most casting rod anglers were building rods with detachable handles made by Featherweight, Fuji, and similar companies. These separate handles consisted of a rear grip, a trigger-style reel seat to hold the reel, and a small hard foregrip that consisted of the socket to hold the butt ferrule of the rod that was attached to the butt end of the rod blank. With Featherweight these included a movable-screw three-jaw chuck to hold a then-standard ⅜-inch plug to fit the blank for assembling the rod for fishing. The Fuji style included a similar chuck but with a larger plastic butt plug permanently fastened to the end of the rod blank. These were both designed for use with casting or spin-cast rods with several variations.

One type of rod required a slip-in or lockdown type of ferrule or adapter. Most required a chuck to lock the adapter in place. The rod blank was glued into the adapter, which then allowed the rod to be removed from the handle through this chucking system. These handles came in graphite or fiberglass, sometimes in different colors (with black the most popular), with a pistol or straight grip, and were one- or two-handed. The thinner adapters had a series of smaller internal diameters for easier fitting to thin graphite blanks, and the larger outside-diameter adapters had larger internal diameters for larger diameter blanks. In the Fuji system the thin-diameter "GA" adapters came in internal diameters of 9 through 10.5 millimeters; the larger diameter "NA" adapters were available in internal diameters of 11 through 14.5 millimeters. Similar adapters from other manufacturers had internal diameters as small as 7 millimeters. (Handles are specific to a given type of adapter.)

Other handles used adapters but were designed so that the rod blank glued into the adapter; the adapter was then glued into the handle. While this might seem to be an extra, unnecessary step, it makes sense from a cost standpoint. Molds are expensive, and it is far cheaper to the consumer to make one handle type with several different simple molds (only the core rod is changed to make the different internal diameters) than it is to make and inventory several different handles. Adapters for Fuji glue-ins ranged in size from 6 to 11.5 millimeters for the "LA" style and 9.5 to 15 millimeters for the "EA" style.

Handles also were available through-bored for a glue-fitting onto a rod: The result was a one-piece rod in which the handle could not be removed. For through-handle construction, skeletal-type casting rod handle kits were available that consisted of the preshaped rear cork grip, the trigger/hood section, the cork insert, the threaded barrel, the hood and locking ring, and a short foregrip.

Today almost all casting rods are made with through-handle construction and handles that are an integral, permanent part of the rod after construction is complete. A depiction of twenty-one current handle kits from one rod/blank company alone (St. Croix) features eight kits for casting rods. Most of these are the same or similar, except for the length of the rear grip (4¾ inches to 14 inches) and the foregrip (2 to 5 inches) cork handle/grip parts. They all have the same butt cap, same graphite composite trigger reel seat, and choices of three winding checks.

Boat-Rod Handles

Boat-rod handles of wood with a glued-on reel seat and mushroom butt cap are sometimes available; usually hickory wood is used. When available these come with a sized ferrule and collet nut to fasten the rod blank to the detachable handle. They are sometimes available in through-bored models in which the rod blank can be shimmed or the handle sized with a reamer or file so that the two fit together properly. In these cases the handle cannot be detached from the rod blank.

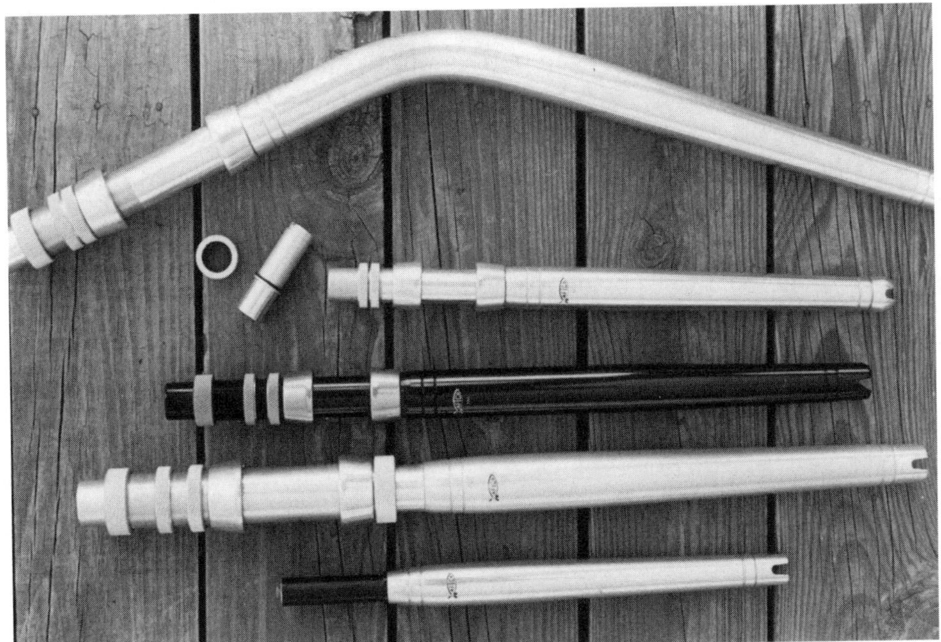

Examples of various sizes and types of offshore trolling handles from AFTCO. Each is made of aluminum and designed with a collet (second rod from top) to fit the rod.

Offshore Trolling-Rod Handles

Offshore rods are available from several companies, including AFTCO, Stuart, and Wright. The AFTCO handles come in several styles and models. Most popular are the Unibutts, which incorporate handle and reel seat into one unit. The handle is similar to a standard swaged handle, with a built-in gimbal reel seat and ferrule/collet. A pinning system assures that all parts are straight and in line. The hoods are milled from heavy-wall aluminum for strength, and two shouldered nuts hold the sliding hood in place. The ferrules are interchangeable so that one handle or butt system can be used with several different rod tips. Another advantage is that the ferrule and collet incorporate a rubber O-ring on the ferrule that acts as a watertight seal to keep salt water and corrosion away from the internal parts.

The advantage of the Unibutt system is that the reel seat is an integral part of the handle, thus there are no dissimilar metals that can facilitate electrolysis and corrosion.

The Unibutt system, along with other AFTCO handles and butts, is made of high-strength 6061-T6 aluminum. Sizes available include models designed for six-pound-class through unlimited-class tackle. Both straight-handle and curved-handle models are available; the curved-handle models are designed for heavier tackle such as thirty-pound through unlimited-class. Curved-butt handles are designed to lower the rod tip and allow up to 30 percent more pressure during a fight for the same power and pull on the part of the angler. The result is a quicker fight, a quicker landing of the fish, and less strain on the angler. Finishes available include silver anodized, hard-coat black anodized, and hard-coat black body with gold-anodized hoods and rings. The ferrules allow these butts to take rods with butt diameters of from 0.750 to 1.188 inches. In addition, the rods are available with ball gimbals to reduce deck damage that might occur with the straight gimbal and the option of slipover reel-seat sleeves that fit between the reel seat and foregrip to reinforce that area when forward reel braces are used.

While these standard rod butts serve well for most fishing, there are some additional specialized items on the market. One is the Extend-A-Butt by AFTCO, which allows stand-up rods to be used in fighting chairs. Stand-up rods, by definition, must have a short butt for handling the rod in a rod belt. The Extend-A-Butt slides over this short butt to extend it and make it suitable for a fighting chair.

One additional problem-solver by AFTCO is the Storabutt. This is essentially a handle-and-seat arrangement that not only has a ferrule and collet nut on the upper end for the rod blank but also a ferrule extension of the butt that fits into the reel seat and is secured with a collet nut. In essence the reel seat is ferruled at both ends. The result is that butts can be removed from rods without disturbing the reel or line/terminal tackle as it runs through the rod guides. The Storabutt is made with curved or straight butts and in 80- and 130-pound-class sizes. It is most useful with the curved butts, since these are more difficult to store or rack in overhead or vertical rod racks.

Handle Kits

Handle kits are available for a number of light-tackle fishing-rod styles. For example, Lamiglas lists more than forty different handle kits, including those for fly, saltwater fly, steelhead, salmon, casting, two-hand casting, boat, downrigger, Tennessee-handle spinning, spinning, and offshore rods.

BUTT CAPS AND GIMBALS

Butt caps and gimbals are designed to finish the butt end of the rod. Butt caps are used on most rods; gimbals or gimbal knocks (two terms for the same item) are used on offshore and big-game rods that are used with fighting chairs and crossbar-style rod belts. Gimbals are longer, sturdier for heavier fishing, and have two crossed slots—like an X—in the bottom to fit the crossbar in fighting chairs or belt rod sockets. Their purpose is to keep the rod from twisting or torquing under the strain of fighting big fish.

Butt-cap styles range widely. The simplest are a simple rubber or flexible plastic socket—like a crutch tip or chair leg. The rubber crutch-tip type is usually available in short and long styles, in black or white, and in diameters of ¾, ⅞, 1, and 1⅛ inches. While these are okay, similar but more streamlined butt caps specifically designed for rods are available in dark colors and several styles and diameters to match most rods. One butt cap has a spread end designed to give extra leverage with forearm support. Even caps lacking this specialized shape have some swelling at the butt end. Longer slim, tapered butt caps, primarily designed for larger rods such as surf and boat rods, are available in black or brown. They are about 3 inches long, with an inside diameter ranging from about ¾ to a little over 1 inch. Rubber mushroom caps are used on the ends of wood boat rods and also at the ends of some heavy rods, such as some fly-rod extension butts.

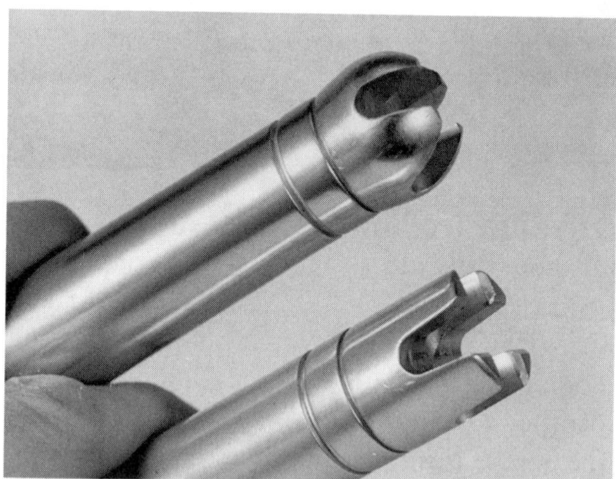

Regular (bottom) and ball gimbals are available on some offshore handles. These are from AFTCO.

Though they are more brittle and thus not as sturdy, small tapered butt caps of a harder plastic are also available. Some butt caps incorporate both metal and rubber or wood. These look more European—they are the type found on some long-handled European-style rods and are readily available for custom rod building. Wood caps are more attractive, but rubber is durable and doesn't slip and is more practical for most applications.

Some butt caps are simple swaged aluminum sockets, though these are harder to find and are used less frequently. Aluminum butt plates are popular, mostly as the butt ends on fly rods with short, built-in extensions of 2 inches or less in length; on the ends of fly-rod extension butts; and as the butt ends of ultralight spinning rods incorporating all-cork sliding-ring reel-seat assemblies. Sometimes two sizes can be found: a smaller diameter for fly rods and a larger diameter for spinning. Most have a short stem by which they are securely glued into a cork handle. Several anodized colors are available, and some caps come in nickel silver.

The most popular gimbals for boat and big-game rods are made of machined aluminum, such as the gimbals by AFTCO that come in silver or hard-coat anodized black in ⅞, 1, and 1⅛ inches inside diameter. Brass gimbals are also sometimes available, as are gimbals of hard molded plastic (nylon), tough polyethylene, or graphite (usually graphite fill). For true big-game fishing, the machined-aluminum or brass models should be the only choice. For lighter fishing, where the stresses, length of the fight, and size of the fish are all less, any of the other materials will do fine.

Molded plastic and graphite gimbals are lighter, a sometimes important consideration in lighter rods. Some gimbals have, or have as an option, a soft-plastic or rubber butt cap that slips over the gimbal to protect decks, boats, and other tackle from damage.

FERRULES, COLLETS, HOSELS, AND WINDING CHECKS

Most ferrules used on rods and blanks today are built into the blank or rod: You buy the blank and the ferrule comes with it. You do need to wrap the female portion of the ferrule for hoop strength, but you get the ferrule as an integral part of the rod blank. Ferrules are available separately but usually only in two extremes of quality. Nickel-silver ferrules are available for high-quality fly rods and are usually used only on bamboo blanks, since the others have built-in ferrules. They are expensive and available in a smaller range of sizes for bamboo blanks.

Chrome-plated brass ferrules are also available. Another type of ferrule is used for big-game reel seats. These are designed to fit specific reel seats, such as the ferrules and locking collet nuts on AFTCO Unibutts. Most of these ferrules have a notch to fit a pin in the reel seat, which assures proper alignment of the reel-seat hoods on the handle and the rod guides. Collet nuts fit over the ferrule to lock the rod tip onto the handle and prevent loosening or loss.

Rod hosels serve the same purpose as winding checks in providing a finishing touch between the upper end of the foregrip and the rod blank. Rod hosels are extended or cone-like winding checks that are primarily used on big rods, mostly inshore boat rods. Sometimes they are used on offshore tackle, heavy freshwater tackle, downrigger rods, and heavy salmon rods. They are available in larger internal diameters, usually in sizes of $^{20}/_{64}$ through $^{40}/_{64}$.

Winding checks are thin rings of metal, rubber, polyethylene, or nickel silver that serve as trims between foregrips and rod blanks. They are used on virtually all rods, from fly rods to big-game rods. Depending on the style they are sized in 64ths (often from $^{13}/_{64}$ to $^{60}/_{64}$) and in millimeters (typically from 6.5 to 16 millimeters in nickel-silver rings).

Functionally they are not necessary, but they work aesthetically to eliminate an unfinished appearance at the grip-to-blank junction. Aluminum winding checks are available in anodized colors; nickel silver are polished; rubber are almost always black; and the polyethylene are usually available in brown, black, and similar dark colors.

THREAD

Thread is required to wrap the guides in place, make underwraps, and wrap ferrules, as well as to fashion decorative wraps such as trim wraps at the handle and tip-top and to make any decorative diamonds, chevrons, weaving, or other fancy wraps.

The principal material used for wrapping guides is a special rod-wrapping thread. The main company making such thread today is Gudebrod, although threads sometimes are available from Kreinik, PacBay (RodSmith), and American Tackle (Pro Wrap). Some of these are strictly fly-tying threads and, because they are very thin, would be suitable only for the lightest rods. (Most of these companies offer rod-wrapping thread in sizes A and D; some have a wider range of thread.)

Rod-wrapping thread comes in a variety of sizes, ranging from 00 through FF, although not all sizes are available from a single manufacturer.

Nylon thread is standard for rod wrapping and is available from several companies. For a long time Gudebrod thread was considered the standard. It has recently gone through some changes, going out of business in fishing line but reorganized as Wel-Tec, LLC (508 North Lewis Rd., Royersford, PA 19468; 610-792-7310), buying all the braiding machinery and tools necessary for making its thread and rod-building products. Kreinik is another manufacturer of threads and stranded materials for rod building and fly tying. Newcomers to the thread market include American Tackle with its Pro Wrap threads, PacBay with its RodSmith threads, and FishHawk with its line of silk, nylon, metallic, and variegated threads for rod building.

Silk thread is available but is not as widely used or available in as many sizes and colors. The advantages of nylon are that it will not rot and break down and that the slight amount of stretch inherent in the material can be used to place any wrap under tension. Tension helps you get a good secure wrap, so this *is* an advantage.

Nylon thread comes in several sizes and many colors and spools, but not all sizes are available in all colors or spools. Regular nylon does not come in C, however, and the NCP thread (requiring no color preserver) comes only in sizes A, C, and D. NCP thread is made with special colorfast processes and dyes that resist the color changes caused by the strong epoxies, varnishes, and polyurethanes used on today's wraps. Both regular and NCP threads come in dozens of colors. In addition, metallic thread in sizes A and D is made with an aluminized film wound over a nylon core for strength. Metallic thread comes in regular colors but has far greater sheen, sparkle, and brilliance. Trimar thread, available in size C only, uses a base of NCP thread twisted with Mylar to make a distinctive sparkle-color thread.

Thread colors currently available from Gudebrod in regular nylon and NCP include black, white, light blue, cobalt blue, peach, rose pink, spring green, sunburst, garnet, goldenrod, orange, royal blue, dark blue, rust, blue dun, tan, scarlet, candy apple, maroon, gold, dark brown, hot pink, charcoal, purple, medium brown, medium gray, gunmetal, chestnut, dark green, lemon yellow, and medium green. Metallic thread colors include gold, black, silver, pearl, old gold, ice blue, lime, fuchsia, aquamarine, royal blue, aqua, red, dusty rose, green, copper, purple, and bronze. Trimar thread colors include black/silver, white/silver, blue/silver, green/silver, brown/silver, red/silver, black/gold, white/gold, blue/gold, green/gold, brown/gold, and red/gold.

The threads are available in spools of 100 yards (50 yards for size FF), 1 ounce, and 4 ounces. Not all colors are available in all thread sizes, nor are all sizes and colors available in all spool sizes. The best spool size for most hobbyists is the 100-yard spool or, for serious rod-builders, the 1-ounce spool. The 4-ounce spool is primarily for rod manufacturers or commercial jig wrappers because it holds a lot of thread. A 4-ounce spool of size A thread contains 4,800 yards (about 2.8 miles); 2,300 yards (about 1.3 miles) in size D; and 1,200 yards (about 0.66 mile) in size E.

Gudebrod recommends the following uses for their various thread sizes (reprinted with permission from the Gudebrod catalog):

> *Size 00.* Wrapping delicate fly rods and ultralight spinning and spin-cast rods; wrapping and tying jigs from 1/32 ounce through 1/8 ounce.
>
> *Size A.* Recommended for fly rods and freshwater spinning and casting rods; wrapping and tying jigs from 1/2 ounce through 1½ ounces.
>
> *Size C (NCP) and D nylon.* Wrapping saltwater rods and medium-weight spinning, casting, boat, and trolling rods; wrapping and tying jigs from 5/8 ounce through 2 ounces.

Size D (NCP) and E nylon. Wrapping 80- and 130-pound trolling rods, as well as heavy-duty boat and surf rods; wrapping and tying jigs from 2¼ to 3½ ounces.

Size E. Wrapping heavy-duty trolling, boat, and surf rods.

Size EE. Wrapping extra-heavy-duty trolling rods and extra-long (14 to 16 feet) surf rods.

Size FF. Special wrapping effects on gaffs, outriggers, and antennas; wrapping heavy-duty rod butts for friction grip. Size FF is the recommended size for wrapping pool-cue handles.

Gudebrod also makes a special, heavy rod-butt cord that is used for wrapping rod butts on heavy casting, boat, trolling, and surf rods and for gaff handles. It provides a colorful and non-slip grip. Available colors include black, blue, brown, white, red, and yellow. Although it's not designed for rod building, a similar heavy cord is available from craft stores, where it is sold as macramé cord in 1½- and 2-millimeter diameters and many colors.

Most of the thread companies make a wide variety of thread colors for rod wrapping and custom effects. Of the thousands of thread colors available, most companies have a good selection for rod builders. For example, Pro Wrap has eighty colors available in both A and D sizes and in both nylon and colorfast (no color preserver required) types. These are available in 100-yard spools, 1-ounce spools, and 4-ounce cones. Pro Wrap has thirty-nine metallic colors available. RodSmith (PacBay) thread is available in nylon and no-color-preserver-required thread (Stay True) in thirty-two colors and in sizes A and C. The company's metallic thread is available in sizes A and D in twelve colors.

FishHawk threads come in a variety of different styles the company calls "collections." Its nylon threads for rod wrapping and jig tying come in forty different colors in 100-yard, 1-ounce, and 4-ounce spools. Its nylon ColorLok threads require no color preserver. The thirty-six available colors come in sizes A and C in 100-yard, 1-ounce, and 4-ounce spools.

For those who like silk threads or who need them for bamboo rod restoration, FishHawk's collection of silk threads from Japan are pure filament silk. The threads come in sixty-seven colors, including six colors in a silk sparkle collection. The silk sparkle is available in size 3/0 in 100-yard spools; the rest of the silk threads are available in size 3/0 in 200-meter spools along with A in 100-meter spools and D in 50-meter spools.

The FishHawk "Metallic" collection is made on a nylon core under rice paper and with a silver alloy finish. These come in twenty-two colors in size A thread in 100-yard and 1-ounce spools.

The "Metallic (P)" threads are similar to the Metallics but manufactured over a polyester core with a metalized foil wrap. Twenty-four colors are available in sizes A and D in 100-yard, 1-ounce, and 4-ounce spools.

A final "Variegated" collection is available with variegated color threads in twenty-five colors in size A 100-meter spools.

To add to this complexity, not all colors and styles of thread from all manufacturers are available in all sizes.

Note: For more details on yards-per-spool and the break strength of threads of different manufacturers, check the thread color and spec charts of each manufacturer.

FINISHES, COLOR PRESERVERS, SEALERS, AND GLUES

Glues are necessary to fasten some rod parts together; color preservers, varnishes, and rod finishes are necessary to protect rod wraps. Glues are used for fastening cork rings together to form a handle on a blank, gluing preformed cork grips into a blank, gluing foam grips to a blank, securing ferrules (where used) onto rods, fastening tip-tops to the end of a rod, gluing reel seats onto rod blanks and handles, gluing butt caps, and assembling reel-seat parts such as the fixed hood, barrel insert, and threaded barrel. Color preservers are necessary when using regular (not NCP-type) nylon thread, and a final coating of varnish or, more typically, epoxy rod finish is also applied.

Everyone has his or her own theories and ideas on the best glues for all the above tasks. Any such glue should be easy to work with, not too thick or thin for the task at hand, waterproof, easy to clean up, not toxic or dangerous to work with, and capable of a secure hold.

My preferences are as follows, but new adhesives and glues are coming out all the time, so be sure to check for the latest available products that will suit your tasks, keeping the above criteria in mind.

Glued Materials

Butt cap to the rod blank/handle. A good waterproof glue, such as U-40 Cork Bond, Duco, Devcon, Ambroid, or the various 24-hour epoxies, is ideal for this when the butt cap is aluminum, metal, or plastic. For gluing rubber butt caps onto a rod, extension butt, or wood handle, use glue that will bond with rubber as well as with the other materials. Most glues state on the package the best usage and gluing purposes for that particular product.

Gimbal to rod butt. These are going to be under much greater stress than plain butt caps, so use 24-hour epoxy. Lacking that, use a very strong glue such as a Gorilla Glue or a similar product.

Foam grip to rod blank. Foam grips, whether EVA or Hypalon, always use a smaller diameter hole than the size of the blank on which they are placed, but gluing is still required. However, because the grip must be forced over the blank, and because glue is often used both as an adhesive and a lubricant, a product that cleans up with water is best. The seeming contradiction of a water-based glue on a fishing rod is not as great as it seems, since the glue is under the foam, and water penetration through the foam would be rare if not impossible. For this reason I like water-based glues such as Elmer's Glue-All and similar craft glues. They glue well and hold well and clean up completely if washed immediately after the parts are set in place. Solvent glues also work well but require more cleanup, usually with an acetone product or denatured alcohol.

Gluing cork rings together to make a rod grip. In my opinion, epoxy glue is not the best for this task. Epoxy glue is so strong and cures so hard that the necessary filing and shaping of the rings to the handle becomes difficult. Unless you are careful, you could end up taking off more cork than glue between the rings, resulting in a slightly scalloped look and an uncomfortable gripping surface. For this use I prefer a cork glue or cement, such as U-40 Cork Bond, Elmer's Glue-All, Duco cement, Pliobond, or similar "softer" and gentler glues. I *have* used epoxies for this, but if you do so, make sure the glue is completely wiped off the cork surface so that you do not have to cut through glue when you try to shape the cork rings.

Gluing preformed cork grips onto the rod blank. Epoxy is best for this: Smear the epoxy onto the rod blank at the proper position, and then slide and rotate the cork grip into place. Of course you first have to check the hole diameter and taper on the cork grip to make sure it fits properly. Here the taper and fit must be very close if not exact to the preformed grip (or ring) and the blank, since the cork will not expand and stretch as will foam, EVA, and Hypalon grips.

Reel seat to rod blank. Reel seats require shimming (in most cases) to fill the space between the rod blank and internal diameter of the seat. Glues should be 24-hour epoxy or other very strong glues.

Tip-top to the tip of the rod blank. There are two possibilities here. Heat-set glues such as glue-gun materials or stick ferrule cement from Fuji and other companies are all ideal for light rods. For heavy rods I like 5-minute epoxy. The epoxy will set up rapidly yet still provide time to work, and it will hold far more securely on big rods under extreme stresses when fighting fish. If necessary you can still remove the tip-top from the rod with heat, as will be described.

Although these suggestions are good for most rods built by hobbyists, rod manufacturers generally use either 5-minute or 24-hour epoxy glue for all their gluing operations (with the possible exception of gluing cork rings together for a grip). They even use it for the often-messy job of gluing foam grips onto rod blanks. Commercial rod builders have the distinct advantage of being able to use acetone or other ketones as solvents for quick cleanups. Home rod builders should avoid extensive use of these solvents without adequate ventilation and protection. Check with your local Occupational Safety and Health Administration office or similar agency for proper usage and safety requirements.

Sealers

Sealers are sometimes used with cork grips to seal the cork pores on the outside of the grip, to help give the grip more of a nonslip surface, and to protect it against undue soiling. Several cork sealers are available: U-40 Urethane Cork Seal is one.

Color Preservers

Color preserver is necessary on regular nylon thread (not threads treated with color preservers, which make this step unnecessary). Varnish or an epoxy finish used over thread without a color preserver will result in the thread changing color. Light-colored threads will turn lighter, with white often becoming completely transparent. Dark colors will turn darker, and all colors will become translucent, allowing the guide foot to show through in some cases.

Color preserver must penetrate the threads completely to be effective. Often one coat is sufficient, but occasionally two coats are required. Many companies make color preserver, with perhaps the current best-known products available from Flex Coat and U-40. They are usually available in 1-ounce, 4-ounce, and 1-pint bottles.

Finishes

Once the color preserver is completely dry or a "no color preserver" thread is used, a protective finish must be applied to the thread wraps. Varnish, epoxy, and polymer are all used. Once the standard, varnish today is used primarily for bamboo rods when an old, traditional look is wanted or for a quick finish without a two-part epoxy or polymer. Varnish is not as durable as epoxy or polymer and requires more coats to build up the thick, glossy finish that is available with one coat of epoxy. Many brands also have a tendency to yellow or turn brown in time.

Epoxies and polymers include Flex Coat Finish, Flex Coat Lite (designed for a thinner finish of epoxy on fly rods and ultralight rods), Bullard rod finish, U-40 Perma Gloss, and U-40 Dura Gloss Polymer Rod Finish.

Most of these types of finishes have the disadvantage of requiring the mixing of two parts (an exception is the U-40 Perma Gloss), although in some cases the color-coded syringes and bottles (such as those of Flex Coat and U-40) make this easier. The advantage is a one-coat application that affords high build and excellent protection, is highly durable, and does not markedly yellow or turn off-color. One additional disadvantage is that most of these finishes are thick and heavy and thus require slow rotation of the rod to prevent sagging and dripping.

Depending on the brand, these finishes come in 1-, 2-, 4-, 8-, 32-, and 64-ounce containers.

MISCELLANEOUS

Some small items such as protective gloves, razor blades, and ferrule treatments are also handy for rod building.

Protective gloves, such as disposable surgical gloves (often available from better drugstores and some mail-order companies), are ideal for working with glues, color preservers, and epoxy finishes. They are very thin and easy to work in, allow easy cleanup, and are inexpensive. Most manufacturers discourage skin contact with glues and finishes. In addition, some people are allergic or have reactions to prolonged contact with these materials. If such is a problem for you, gloves are especially recommended. Note that if you are allergic to latex, gloves are also now available in latex-free material.

Razor blades are handy for trimming and cutting operations in rod building. A razor blade makes it easy to trim excess glue, cut thread when wrapping rods, or scrape a rod to size it into a ferrule or collet. Scalpels and X-Acto knives are also handy, but razor blades are cheaper, disposable, and readily available in "industrial" packs of one hundred units.

Some companies (U-40, for example) make a ferrule treatment that is designed to help smooth and hold the self-ferrules (glass-to-glass or graphite-to-graphite) of modern rod blanks. These treatments are fine, but a good substitute is candle wax rubbed over the male portion of the ferrule to aid in fitting and holding.

18
Basic Rod Building

Introduction • Calculations for Rod Parts and Assembly • Assembling Parts, Materials, and Tools • Determining the Spine • Mounting the Rear Grip • Mounting the Butt Cap • Mounting the Reel Seat • Mounting the Foregrip • Mounting the Winding Check • Mounting the Tip-Top • Preparing and Wrapping Guides • Protecting the Wraps: Finishing Coats

Note: You should read chapter 17 before reading this chapter and before you purchase items to build the rod described here. This chapter will provide detailed information about the parts and materials available and the assembly of those parts into a finished rod.

INTRODUCTION

Building any rod is really an assembly process that is not unlike tying a fly—in which the various materials are added and tied down in sequence—or building a model plane or car. There is some fitting, some sizing, lots of checking, some measuring, a little gluing, a fair amount of cleaning up, and, initially at least, a lot of following directions. Taking it slow and easy, particularly for a first rod, is also very important.

Building a rod is not hard. In this chapter we will construct a 6½-foot two-piece spinning rod with a simple foam grip, graphite blank, aluminum oxide two-foot guides, graphite-style reel seat, and rubber or plastic butt cap. The basics for all the steps in building a rod are essentially the same, regardless of the type of rod. There are some special tips for handling certain types of guides or the different materials used in grips, and so on, but these are easily learned.

Variations of these basics, along with some professional tips and greatly expanded directions and details, are covered in subsequent chapters.

CALCULATIONS FOR ROD PARTS AND ASSEMBLY

When you buy a rod of a known pedigree from a major manufacturer, you get that manufacturer's assurance that the rod is what the company states it is. You get the length, power, action, and suggested range of line test and lure weights. If it is a fly rod, you get the suggested fly-line weight and maybe the ounce weight of the rod blank or rod. Fly-line weights matched to rods are determined by industry standards, based on the first 30 feet of the fly line. This is based on the grain weight of the line, with each rod size (from 1 through 15, or higher) taking the appropriate line in the same size.

Some expert fly anglers use either heavier or lighter weight lines on a given rod for specific reasons. For example, a fly angler casting very short line lengths for fishing on small streams might go with a heavier than suggested line weight, since he or she will never be casting the first 30 feet of line. Often the chosen line for this is one line size heavier but can be two line sizes for some anglers in some cases.

As an example, a 4-weight line will weigh 120 grains, with a plus or minus manufacturer's tolerance of about 6 grains. If you are casting only 15 feet of line instead of the 30 feet on which the line weight is measured, you are not casting 120 grains but only 60 grains. Similarly, if you are casting half the 30 feet a 5- or 6-weight line, you are casting 70 or 80 grains, respectively. The nominal grain weight of a 5- and 6-weight line is 140 grains and 160 grains, respectively. Admittedly you are still not casting the 120 grains of line called for in the first 30 feet of a 4-weight line, but you are closer to that weight with the 70 or 80 grains than with the 60 grains that would be the first 15 feet of a 4-weight line. This all of course assumes a level line (which very few fly anglers use), but the principle still stands.

A lot of other factors can affect a fly rod and line and how they are cast. For example, even ambient temperature might play a role in casting. While there are tropical and cold-weather lines to cope with hot weather and winter conditions, any line will be stiffer in the cold and more flexible or even limp in heat. That can affect how the line flows through the guides and casts in the air.

Within reason and with compensation in your a fly-casting style, you can use almost any rod to cast almost any line. The casting may not be easy, and a lot of compensation will be called for, but it is possible. By compensating with slower strokes and careful line control and line length in the air, you can cast a 10-weight line with a 4-weight rod. Get enough line in the air, and a cast with a 4-weight line using a 12-weight rod is possible.

This is accomplished by shortening the line out while slowing and lengthening the stroke with a light rod and heavy line or by speeding up the stroke while lengthening the line with a stout rod and light line.

A number of other factors can affect rods, lines, and how they cast. On a windy day you might want a slightly heavier line to punch into the wind and get through it to put a fly on the water. Going with a lighter line is best to gently and softly present a dry fly on calm water on a calm day.

The mass/air resistance of the fly or bug with fly tackle can also affect lines, leaders, and how you punch out a cast. A lighter line and leader combination can be used to cast a Quill Gordon that has little mass and a slim profile and air resistance. Switch to a Humpy or unweighted Muddler, and you might find that a heavier line or even heavier line/rod outfit will work better. This is why charts and formulas that match a fly size to a leader type to a line size/type to a rod weight are all generalities. There are exceptions to everything, and you can't make absolute rules for all the vagaries of fly fishing.

Similarly, fly casting requires a constant change in line length to reach different spots on a stream or lake. Change a casting length (line in the air) from 30 feet to 31 feet to 35 feet to 40 feet, and the casting force, angle of arc and thrust, line speed, line loop, and other factors will be different on each line length. Of course the difference between casting 30 feet and 31 feet (or even 35 feet) might be technically different but of no practical experience or importance, but it is there. Adjustment of these many factors is also required when switching from floating line to a sinking line, since the mass/air resistance is changed between the two line types.

To a lesser degree the same factors would also apply to a casting or spinning rod or even a surf outfit or noodle rod. With these and a line used with a lure of a given weight on the end of a constant style, type, and pound test of line, and with a specific rod and spinning or casting reel, factors can still change. The angle through which you move the rod, the force of the cast, the wind, the timing of the release (which in turn is again different for both spinning and casting tackle), the weight and type of lure, and the length of line all make a difference. Even if you are casting to the same target point each time, these factors will change, albeit very slightly and obviously involuntarily.

The reason for all this information is to point out that, as good casters, we usually adjust our casting style to meet the conditions of the outfit, day, wind, length of cast, and lure or fly. You can find various formulas and charts to help you adjust your rod building in terms of guides, numbers of guides, locations of guides, lures, and line weights, but in my view these do not work. Casting and fishing require a lot of adjustments all day long as conditions, waters, wind, casting targets, and lines and lures are changed and adjusted.

Trying to put all of this into one formula for all fishing for a given rod is not going to accomplish the task desired. Try these charts and formulas if you like, but the basics of simple, standard rod building for a rod blank designed for a specific fly line or casting/spinning line test and lure range will work fine all the time.

ASSEMBLING PARTS, MATERIALS, AND TOOLS

Before beginning you will need all the parts, materials, and tools necessary for all steps through the final finish. In this case we will be making a 6½-foot graphite freshwater spinning rod; the directions will be generic but applicable to any materials or brands you might choose.

Rod Parts

Two-piece 6½-foot graphite spinning rod. Freshwater style, designed for ¼- through ⅝-ounce lures.

Set of aluminum oxide, silicon carbide, or Hardloy spinning guides. Bought either as a set or individually to match the rod. We will use aluminum oxide for our rod. Six or seven guides are recommended, along with a tip-top. The tip-top tube will have to fit the end of the rod tip, and the guide sizes should be 40, 20, 16, 12, 10, and 8 millimeters. With seven guides add one more 8-millimeter or one 7-millimeter guide. There can be variations in these sizes, particularly if you use the high-frame small-ring guides currently in vogue, since these will allow for good funneling of the line through the guide ring; the high frame helps prevent line slap and the resulting friction and loss of distance. With these guides the largest size is often about a 20-millimeter ring on a high frame. Here a suggested guide set would include 20-, 12-, 10-, 8-, 7-, and 7-millimeter rings, plus the tip-top. For seven guides, one more 7-millimeter guide is added. Another configuration of guides for such a rod could be ring sizes of 20, 10, 7, 7, 7, and 7 millimeters and the tip-top. These latter two guide configurations are lighter weight than the first listing but will still funnel line easily—the first guide will choke the line down; the rest just allow the line to flow along the rod and out the tip-top.

Rubber or plastic butt cap. These are a simple slip-on, glue-on style that is quite standard on this type of rod. Most are about ¾ to ⅞ inch in diameter for freshwater model rods.

Foam rear grip. These are Hypalon or EVA or a similar open-cell foam material drilled to fit tightly on the blank and available in many colors. For this rod we will pick one that is 6 inches long. This must be of the right inside diameter for the blank. Since these are a tight fit (not like cork grips, which must match the taper and diameter of the blank), you must choose a foam grip with the right hole size. The best guide to this is to choose a grip with a hole of about two-thirds to three-quarters the diameter of the blank. This provides for ample gripping of the blank without extreme stresses or mounting problems.

Foam foregrip. This will be of the same material and color as the rear grip, 4 inches long, and sized with an internal diameter to properly fit the rod blank, usually about two-thirds to three-quarters of the blank diameter. Note that with steep-taper rods, this internal diameter of the foregrip might be slightly different than the internal diameter of the rear grip, since they will be separated by the length of the reel seat.

Reel seat. For a light rod like this, a graphite-fill reel seat of about 18 to 20 millimeters is best.

Winding check. Although it's not absolutely necessary, this nicety makes for a decorative trim between the grip and blank.

Materials

Thread. For this example we will use regular nylon in size A. One small spool will be enough.

Color preserver. This will be necessary to protect the color of the thread you choose and keep it from changing. The color preserver must be compatible with the finish used. A 1-ounce bottle will be sufficient.

Rod finish. For this we will choose a two-part epoxy finish. The smallest available container will be sufficient.

Twenty-four-hour epoxy glue. Necessary for gluing the tip-top, reel seat, and butt cap.

Water-solvent glue. A glue such as Elmer's Glue-All will serve as an adhesive and lubricant to slide the foam grips onto the blank and secure them in place.

Masking tape. Necessary in a ¼-inch width to hold the guides in place while the threads are wrapped. A larger size (1-inch width) is best if the tape is used as a shin or spacer for the reel seat. Better possibilities for these shims are cord, paper tape, cork rings, cork bushings, and fiber bushings.

Tools

Rod-wrapping tool and support of some type. As previously described in chapters 1 and 2. The rod-wrapping device can range from the simplest to the most complex, but it is necessary to do a good job. Must-have features include the ability to wrap any guide in any position, to support the length of the rod or rod section even when you are wrapping a tip-top or close to one end, and a maintainable and adjustable thread tension.

Razor blade or scalpel. To cut the rod-wrapping thread at the completion of each wrap.

Basic rod-building wrapper for hand-wrapping rods, with two V-supports to hold the rod blank and a sewing machine–type thread tension device. Courtesy of Flex Coat Company.

Handle seater. This item, or a piece of wood with a hole in it, helps push the foam grip down into place on the rod blank. Not absolutely necessary, but it does make this task easier.

File. This is a must to file the ends of the guide feet to slope them and prepare them for the rod wrap. Today some manufacturers supply rod guides with filed and tapered feet, making this step unnecessary.

Brush. You will need two—one to apply the color preserve to the wraps, the second to apply the epoxy finish.

Rod-curing motor. Whether jury-rigged from a barbecue motor or bought as a curing motor, this is a must to turn the rod constantly during the process of curing of the epoxy to prevent sags and drips.

Once the parts, materials, and tools are assembled, you are ready to begin. As with any tackle-building task, make sure you have a completely clean workplace and that you are familiar with all the following steps of building before beginning.

DETERMINING THE SPINE

Rod blanks made with the cut-and-roll method have glass or graphite material wrapped around a removable steel mandrel to make the equivalent of a thin-walled, hollow jelly roll. The material spiraled around the mandrel during construction results in a slight unevenness in the blank and thus a slight unevenness in the blank's strength or resistance to bending in different planes. The spine then—sometimes erroneously called the spline—is that plane of maximum stiffness, or resistance to bending, on the blank. Generally the guides are lined up on this spine or plane of stiffness or on the opposite, or "softer," side.

Because of this construction, all rods of this type will vary in stiffness in different planes. Factors controlling this are the diameter of the mandrel and also the number of wraps of material around the mandrel making up the wall. If you have a blank made with two and a half wraps of material around the mandrel, some parts of the mandrel will have three wraps and the rest will have only two wraps. Thus one part of the blank will have 50 percent more material than the rest of the blank. On this area the spine and stiffness differential can be pronounced. Conversely, a big-game rod might have twenty and a half wraps of material around the mandrel, resulting in most of the rod having twenty wraps and one section having twenty-one wraps. The result is only a 5 percent differential between the various planes and thus a much less pronounced spine.

It would seem that rods made by the pultrusion process (solid-rod blanks) and the Howald process would have equal distribution of material in the blank and thus not have a spine. As a general rule these processes do come perhaps as close as possible to this ideal, but absolutely even distribution is impossible in any blank. Also, a blank that is not absolutely straight—and very few are *absolutely* straight—will be under tension when it is straightened. Thus a blank with perfect distribution of material but with a slight curve would have a spine, or plane of stiffness, in line with the concave side of its curvature.

In some cases the spine will be very pronounced; in other rod blanks it will be very minimal or almost nonexistent. Some rods will have two spines—one more pronounced than the other—as a result of some of the factors mentioned above. In addition, in all blanks the spine will vary in different sections of the blank. If you were to cut a blank into four equal parts, the spine could be on a different part of the blank in each part. The spine that we measure is really an average of the total spine distribution and stiffness forces in the rod blank.

It is extremely important to determine the spine in a blank before beginning to build the rod. It is on this plane that the guides must be placed with light-tackle spinning, casting, spinning, and fly tackle. The softest side of the rod, or the side opposite the plane of stiffness (usually, but not always), must be used for guides on big-game rods, trolling rods, and similar heavy tackle.

The reasoning for this is as follows: As just outlined, the torque of the rod will always tend to turn the rod to bend on the softest plane. This is countered with rods that have the guides on the underside during casting—spinning and fly rods—since the rod is light enough and the guides pronounced enough to prevent this from having any great effect. However, some rod manufacturers like to mount their guides for spinning and fly rods on the softest side (the convex side of the rod's natural bend) or the side of natural bending, mounting guides for casting and spin-cast rods on the side opposite this (on the concave side of the rod's natural bend). Trolling-rod guides are mounted on the soft side (the convex side of the rod's natural roll when it is bent), because these heavy rods, under heavy stresses, will tend to jump and torque if the guides are not lined up to allow the rod to bend naturally on the softest side.

In all cases, even with light rods, it is important to mount the guides in line with this plane of stiffness, since mounting them off to one side by design or accident may result in a rod that casts inaccurately to one side. This is particularly true with spinning rods, since during a normal cast the rod loads as it starts to come forward; at this point the guides can twist off to the side, causing the lure to cast at a slight angle as the guides torque around on the completion of the cast.

Before determining the spine of the rod, first check to make sure the butt end is completely smooth, free of any burrs or imperfections, and cut at a right angle to the blank's axis. Wrap a layer of masking tape around the rod blank so that it can be marked with the spine plane. The easy way to check the spine is to place the butt end of the blank on a smooth, laminated countertop, leaning the tip section against your right hand and pressing down on the blank with your left hand to flex the rod. Using your left hand, rotate the rod blank so that it rolls along the counter. As you roll the rod, you will feel a marked difference in its resistance to bending at one point. Mark this side of the rod, and make a small note that this is the stiff side. Now allow the blank to roll naturally so that you find the side of least resistance, or the softest side. Mark this side also, with an appropriate designation as to resistance. Often, but not always, these marks will be completely opposite each other. The critical factor with big-game rods is to mount these guides opposite the soft side (or on the convex side of the rod as it naturally rolls with the least pressure) so that the rod flexes naturally as the guides bend when trolling or fighting a fish. Other rods can usually be mounted either way, following this general rule: Mount spinning and fly-rod guides (or any fishing when the reel hangs underneath during fishing) on the soft side; mount casting and spin-cast guides (with the reel on top) on the stiff side, or opposite the soft side.

In our case of building a 6½-foot graphite spinning rod, check each section separately, and mark the sections so that they are assembled in line with the stiffness. This process of checking each section of multipiece rods is important in any rod, because the spine must be determined for each section for proper guide line-up and so that the rod works most efficiently. In some cases rod-blank manufacturers or custom component shops may mark the spine on rods and rod sections.

One final note on spines: You may wish to check the spine in different areas of the rod, depending on the rod type and the most important flexion portion of the rod. For a tippy-action worm rod, you may wish to flex only the upper end of the rod, supporting the very tip end with your right hand and pressing down with your left to check the spine. For a heavy flipping rod or similar rod where the lifting power of the butt end is important, support the rod at the middle and press down at the butt end to check the spine in the lower section of the rod. Naturally this is more difficult with heavier and stiff rods, because any spine is more difficult to determine on a very stiff rod.

MOUNTING THE REAR GRIP

The rear grip is added to the lower section of the rod first. This provides a base on which the butt cap is easily glued. Since we are using a foam grip, there are several mounting possibilities. One is to use air pressure. Manufacturers do this with a special tip on an air hose; they slide the foam grip partially onto the upper end of the blank and insert the hose tip between the foam grip and the blank. Hand-controlled air pressure allows the foam grip to be slid down the blank (the air pressure pushes the foam out to allow it to be positioned on the blank) until the grip is in place.

Another way to mount the grip is to use a water-based glue that will serve both as a lubricant and an adhesive and also allow easy water cleanup. You can use any water-based glue (I like Elmer's Glue-All), diluting it slightly with water. I like a dilution of about one-third water to two-thirds glue. Use a dowel or rod to spread the glue evenly on the inside of the foam grip and over the rod blank. As much as possible, try to keep the outside of the foam grip clean. To help with this you can cover the grip with paper towels, taped in place. Wrapping masking tape around the entire rear foam grip is another way to keep it clean.

Place the grip over the rod blank and, using a continuous motion, push the foam grip down on the blank. Do not try to pull the foam grip down, because it will grab the blank and work like a Chinese finger puzzle. Push from the top only. You may wish to use a handle seater, as described in chapter 2, or you can simply use a scrap piece of wood with a blank-diameter hole drilled into it as a grip-pusher. Either will work fine.

Depending on the differentials between the outside diameter of the blank and the inside diameter of the foam grip and the firmness of the grip, you may find that the grip retains its shape during this step. Most likely the foam grip will tend to compress and bunch a little, sometimes even ending up like a little foam football at the bottom of the blank. Don't worry about this—it is easy to "milk" out the foam grip to the desired shape, length, and diameter. Make sure the foam grip covers the entire butt end of the blank, because you will need the end of the grip on which to mount the butt cap.

As soon as you have the grip in place, use warm water to remove all the excess glue from the blank, especially any that might have gotten on the foam grip. If the glue dries, it will be far more difficult to remove from the porous foam grip than from the smooth blank finish. Warm water and a rag work best for removing excess glue.

The same procedure can be followed using epoxy glue as the lubricant and adhesive. This is what rod manufacturers use. Epoxy performs much better but is also messier because epoxy requires a solvent cleanup—usually acetone or a similar ketone. Some glue manufacturers sell epoxy cleaners (designed to clean brushes used with epoxy), and these may also work well.

You can also seat the grip using various lubricants to help slide the foam grip into place. Gasoline has been mentioned in some magazine articles, and although it will work well, do *not* use it. It is just too dangerous and can only be used outside under strictly controlled conditions. Safer lubricants that work almost as well include soapy water, shaving gel or foam, alcohol, various lubricant sprays, and some demoisturizers. These liquids must be cleaned up, and any left under the grip will evaporate and disappear in time. It helps to use a handle seater or push-board to help slide the foam grip in place quickly, particularly with rapidly evaporating solvents.

MOUNTING THE BUTT CAP

We will use a simple socket-type, slip-on plastic butt cap. These are designed to fit onto the rear grip and make for a finished end to the rod. For an attractive rod the outside diameter of the butt cap must be no larger than the outside diameter of the rear grip. Often they are slightly smaller. To properly fit the butt cap onto the rod grip, you must cut a recess out of the end of the rear grip for the butt cap. Because the foam is slightly spongy, this does not have to be a precise fit, but it must be close. (A precise fit would be required for a cork grip.)

First measure the depth of the butt cap and mark the rear grip with this measurement. The best way to do this is to tape the grip with several layers of masking tape to both mark the grip and protect the exposed portion of the grip while you remove material to make the recess. Measure the inside diameter of the butt cap, and then measure the outside diameter of the rear of the grip to determine how much material to remove.

There are several ways to remove the material after the grip is taped for protection. The best way is to place the rod on a through-center lathe, wrapping the grip material to keep from marring it and using supports to the side of the lathe to hold the rod blank and prevent it from whipping around and becoming damaged. Support the end of the hollow blank with a live or dead center. Then use a simple tool rest (like that used with a wood lathe) to support a wood rasp for removing the material at the exposed area. Go slowly and carefully with this, being careful not to damage the taped portion of the grip. Use calipers often to check the diameter, but be sure to take any measurement *only* after turning the lathe off and waiting for it to come to a complete rest. Make a final check with the butt cap.

If you lack a lathe (as most of us do), there are alternatives. One is to use a grinder to remove the required foam, holding the grip sideways against the grinder with only the recessed area in contact with the wheel, and turning the grip while applying light pressure against the grinder. Check frequently, and make sure you make complete 360-degree turns to remove material evenly.

Another method is to use a wood rasp and remove the material by hand. Because it is difficult to hold or clamp the grip and use the rasp against it, a better way is to clamp the rasp, flat side up, in a bench vise. Use two boards—one on each side of the rasp—to protect the rasp teeth. Work the recessed area of the grip against this fixed rasp, rotating the grip slightly while doing so. Work completely around the grip, checking measurements frequently.

One danger of both the grinding wheel and rasp methods is the possibility of taking more foam off one side than another. One way to prevent this is to work in sequence, counting strokes, and then rounding off the result. To do this count several strokes taken on one side of the foam to remove a flat portion. Do not take off too much. Repeat the same number of rasp strokes on the opposite side. Repeat at 90 degrees and then at 180 degrees to the two worked sides to end up with a squared-off area. **Note:** Do *not* take the foam down to a square shape—only slightly square off the sides consistent with the material that you must remove for a good fit. Once you're at this point, square off the corners slightly and check measurements. This gives you an octagon and a shape with which you can work. Repeat this process if you need to remove more material. Once you're close to the final size, round off the corners and check for a final fit.

Don't worry if this recess is not precise and smooth, because you only need it sized to fit the butt cap properly. The upper edge must be smooth to properly mate with the butt cap, but the rest does not have to be smooth. It does not even have to be completely round—it only has to fit the butt cap properly. It must be on-center with the rod blank to make the butt cap fit properly.

If you cut away too much and the recessed area is too small in diameter, you will have to make adjustments. The simplest and best solution is to soak the area with glue and then wrap heavy cord around the butt-cap recess with an even wrap or two to fill in any gap area. Soak the cord with glue, and then twist the butt cap in place.

Another problem that sometimes develops is cutting the recess too high up so that the butt cap bottoms out before the upper edge mates with the handle. To solve this, use a fine-blade hacksaw (32 teeth to the inch) and evenly cut off enough material at the end of the blank and grip to eliminate the gap.

One problem with the above methods is that you may end up with a slight unevenness at the edge of the recess—where the edge of the butt cap meets the rod handle. To smooth off this area after checking for size and fit, remove the masking tape and use medium-grain sandpaper or an emery board to finely polish and dress the area.

Another method of adding a butt cap does not require cutting out a recess in the foam grip. Instead it relies on leaving a short length of rod blank exposed at the end of the grip and then fitting a bushing onto the end of the blank that is sized to fit the butt cap. One or two cork rings are ideal for this: First ream out the hole in the cork to fit the end of the rod butt, and then file down the outside of the cork to fit the inside diameter of the butt cap. In neither case must this filing be precise, because the cork will be completely hidden under the butt cap. Use enough cork rings (each ½ inch thick) to make up the height of the butt cap. Butt caps vary in size from about 1 to 3 inches, so two to six rings will be required. Once the rings are sized, spread epoxy glue on the blank end and then glue each cork ring in place. Add glue to the cork faces, and twist adjoining rings to assure complete bonding with one another and the rod blank. Once the rings have cured and, assuming they are sized to the butt cap, glue the butt cap in place.

Other materials can be used for the butt-cap bushings. Wood spacers, wrapped cord, paper tape, and fiberglass tape are just a few. Cork is readily available for rod building, however, and is easy to work with.

This step can be done before or after the rear grip is added. If it's done before the rear grip is added, completely assemble and glue the bushings on. Then add the butt cap and allow it to cure overnight. Add the rear grip as above, sliding it into place against the top of the butt cap for a tight, even fit. If this step is done after the rear grip is added, mark the blank for the position of the bushing corks, then slide the rear grip into place at this mark. Clean up as before; then add the cork bushings or spacers and glue the butt cap into place as above.

When you are gluing the butt cap onto the bushing, one additional step will make this a professional job and also make it easier and prevent glue from smearing on the butt cap or grip, where it is especially difficult to remove. This step is to add three wraps of regular 1-inch masking or painter's tape to the edge of the rear grip and also to the butt cap. Do this right to the edge of these parts—not over them and not leaving any areas showing. For additional good adhesion, use a rasp, Dremel tool, or rasp bit on a drill to roughen and scar the inside of the butt cap. Make sure the cork bushings or recessed foam is similarly roughened.

Then, with the masking tape in place, add Gudebrod Liquid Rod Cement or 24-hour epoxy glue, thoroughly mixed, to the sides and bottom of the butt cap and to the sides and bottom of the recess. Do not add too much glue. Then gently twist the butt cap onto the recessed area prepared for it. To prevent air pressure from blocking proper seating of the butt cap, use a slight pinching motion with the butt cap to allow air to escape from one side. Another way to eliminate air is to puncture the bottom center of the butt cap with a needle to allow air to escape.

Once the butt cap is in position, glue will ooze from the joint with the grip. This will happen no matter how careful you are with the glue, how evenly it is spread, or how little you use. However, by placing the tape on the edges of the butt cap and grip, you eliminate cleanup problems. Any glue will ooze out onto the protective tape. To get a clean edge, first use an old rag to remove any excess glue, *then* gently remove the tape. Finally, use a clean rag to touch up and clean any remaining glue.

MOUNTING THE REEL SEAT

Once the foam rear grip and butt cap are in place, the next step is to mount the reel seat. In our case we are using a graphite-fill reel seat. Because the reel seat must sit comfortably under the hand, we have chosen a 20-millimeter-diameter seat. This will hold any freshwater reel securely and not cramp the hand. However, the internal diameter of the reel seat is considerably larger than the outside diameter of the rod blank, thus a bushing or shim to build up this space is necessary. There are several possibilities for this, including cork-ring and special cork bushings; formed-fiber bushings; wraps of paper, masking, and fiberglass tape; and wraps of string.

For cork-ring bushings use one cork ring for each ½ inch of reel-seat length, less ½ inch. Thus for a 5-inch reel seat (standard for a graphite-fill seat), you will want nine cork rings to make a 4½-inch bushing. The shorter bushing will allow the foregrip to firmly seat up against the mounted reel seat. A 5-inch-long bushing might be a fraction of an inch longer than the reel seat and would thus create a gap between the reel seat and the foregrip or rear grip.

Use the poorest grade of cork rings because they will be hidden and are only used to shim the reel seat. You might also check suppliers for cork bushings made to serve as a bushing under a reel seat. You do not need flawless top-quality rings for any bushing you make. Use a reamer or rat-tail file to ream out the cork rings to fit snugly onto the rod blank. Keep the cork rings in order or number them with a pen, because the degree of reaming will vary from one end to the other with the taper of the rod blank.

Once the cork rings are reamed to size, wrap the top of the rear grip with three layers of masking tape to protect against excess glue. Mix some 24-hour epoxy glue and spread a small amount evenly on the rod blank in the area of the reel seat. (More glue can be added while you work, but too much at this point will only drip and cause problems.) Slide the first cork ring into place and, if needed, add a small amount of glue to the face that will butt against the top of the foam grip. Check first before doing this, because in most cases sliding the cork ring in place will also push the glue down the rod blank. (This is why tape is wrapped around the top edge of the foam—to protect it from excess glue.)

Once the first cork ring is in place, add subsequent rings in order, making sure there is enough (but not too much) glue on the blank and also on the faces of adjoining rings. Twist each ring against the adjoining ring to assure good adhesion and a tight fit. Once all the rings are in place, use a paper towel to clean up any excess glue. Remove the tape from the end of the rear grip, and complete any final cleanup. Allow the cork to cure overnight.

Once the rings have cured, wrap the end of the rear grip again with masking tape, but make five or six turns to protect the grip. (If you leave the previously wrapped tape on overnight, it may become stiff and difficult to remove.) At this point you must remove the excess cork in order to size the bushing to fit the reel seat. To do this, use internal calipers to check the internal diameter of the reel seat against the outside diameter of the cork to get an idea of the amount of cork to remove. There are several ways to remove the cork—by grinding on a wheel, using a wood rasp, or turning on a lathe. Turning on a lathe assures that the cork bushing will be on-center but is not necessarily any better or faster than the other methods. If you use a lathe, mount the rod blank with the rear grip carefully chucked (use layers of tape to protect the grip and butt cap), and secure the free end to prevent it from whipping around as the lathe turns. Use a slow lathe speed. Carefully remove the cork with a rasp or file; check frequently for size with calipers but only when the lathe is turned off and the work has stopped turning.

To remove cork without a lathe, use the "four-square" system, by which you count strokes to remove equal amounts on all four sides, slightly squaring off the cork rings. Check frequently for size so that you do not remove too much cork. Once the rings are squared off, take off the corners; round off the resulting octagon, making any adjustments for size. Counting strokes and removing the same amount of cork on each side is important with this system to keep the bushing on-center with the rod blank.

You can use a file or sandpaper in place of a wood rasp, but the rasp is quickest and easiest. The same system can be used with a grinding wheel or sander: Remove the cork, and check it for size in the process. In this case use the same number of back-and-forth strokes against the turning wheel or sanding belt to assure equal cork removal.

Once the cork is sized, check it with the reel seat. It should fit snugly and be easy to slip on, but not be tight or loose. At this point remove the tape from around the end of the rear grip (it was used to protect the grip while you were working on the bushing) and replace with three layers of fresh masking tape wrapped around the end of the grip. This will protect the grip from excess glue when you're gluing the reel seat in place. Decide if you want the reel seat to be up-locking or down-locking. Most reel seats on spinning rods are up-locking, with the threads at the butt end of the rod. At the same time make sure you will still have the mark indicating the spine of the rod and proper position of the guides, since the reel-seat hoods must line up with this.

Before mounting the reel seat, use a rat-tail file or rasp to roughen the inside of the seat for more "tooth" and better adhesion of the glue. Some reel seats, like those from Fuji or similar graphite-fill seats, have longitudinal ridges inside the hole for better adhesion, but roughening the inside of any reel seat won't hurt and can only help.

Make sure you have three tight wraps of masking tape around the upper part of the rear grip. Make another three wraps of masking tape around the lower end of the reel seat. Use well-mixed epoxy glue, and coat the bushing evenly and thinly. Slide the reel seat down the rod (check that the sliding hood is at the end you prefer) and onto the glue-coated bushing. Work the reel seat down onto the cork bushing, twisting and working it up and down as you do so to assure complete distribution of glue. Gradually slide the reel seat to butt against the rear grip. At this point some glue will ooze out from the two parts and onto the two wraps of masking tape—one around the grip and the other around the reel seat. Clean this up with a rag or paper towel, then line up the reel-seat hoods with the spine or guide mark.

There are several ways to line up the hoods with the guide mark. One way is to use a bright overhead light and hold the rod in your lap so that the light makes a reflected streak on the shiny finish of the rod. Without moving your head, rotate the rod so that the guide mark lines up with the light streak. Then, moving your eyes but not your head to check the hoods, line up the reel-seat hood by rotating the reel seat. Check again. Then remove the tape from around the end of the reel seat and the end of the rear grip. Use a clean rag for a final cleanup of the junction of these two parts. Allow the work to cure overnight.

MOUNTING THE FOREGRIP

The foam foregrip is mounted in the same way as the rear grip. Various gels, foams, or glue (water-solvent Elmer's or epoxies) can be used to help seat the foam grip in place. As with the rear grip, the internal diameter of the hole in the grip must be slightly smaller than the outside diameter of the rod blank, because the grip will expand to fit tightly in place.

To prevent glue from flowing over onto the reel seat, wrap the top edge of the reel seat with three layers of masking tape to protect it. At the same time wrap three layers around the butt end of the foregrip. Smear a thin coating of glue onto the rod blank where the foregrip will seat, and slide the grip in place on the rod blank. As with the rear grip, use a push-board or make a board with a hole of about the outside diameter of the blank to help push the foam grip down in place.

Use one smooth motion to push the grip down until it is within about 1 inch of the upper end of the reel seat. Stop at this point and use a clean rag or paper towel to mop up any excess glue. There *will* be excess glue, because the tight grip fit pushes the glue in front of the grip. The short bushing leaves about ¼ to ½ inch of space at the upper end of the reel seat for glue to flow to, but it is still best to mop up any excess. After cleaning this area, work the foam grip down into position, touching the top of the reel seat. "Milk" the grip out, if necessary, to a cylindrical shape. At this point there may still be some glue that oozed from the reel seat and grip joint junction. Clean this with a clean paper towel. Once the grip is set in place and the joint is cleaned, carefully remove the masking tape from the reel seat and the foregrip. Any excess glue that spilled will have flowed onto the masking tape, demonstrating the value of this protection in keeping the reel seat and foam grip clean.

MOUNTING THE WINDING CHECK

The winding check is not absolutely necessary to the function of the rod, but it's a nice finishing touch. Winding checks are available in aluminum, nickel silver, rubber, and plastic. Any of these will work, but rubber currently seems to be the most popular. Slide the winding check onto the rod blank, and add a tiny bit of glue with a toothpick around the upper end of the foam grip to rod blank joint. Then slide the winding check in place. If it's rubber it will expand to fit. Tip-tops of other materials can be added the same way, although some tip-tops of metal, wood, or hard plastic have to be precisely sized to fit the rod at the point where the winding check will be positioned.

MOUNTING THE TIP-TOP

The tip-top must be mounted onto the rod in line with the reel-seat hoods and the spine of the rod. There are several choices of glues for gluing the tip-top tube in place. Ferrule cements (basically heat-set cements) have long been popular, but more and more rod builders are going to epoxy glue. (Even if you use epoxy glue, a careful application of heat to the tube—and tube only—allows removal of a damaged tip-top without harming the rod blank.)

Make sure the tip section of the rod is completely clean. Sometimes you may find an excess of epoxy at this point as a result of the blank construction process. This is easily removed by sanding with an emery board.

Make sure the tip-top fits and is neither too loose nor too tight. Use a toothpick to spread epoxy glue inside the tube and also lightly on the end of the rod blank. Slide the tip-top onto the end of the rod blank. Some glue may ooze out of the end of the tube and require cleanup with a rag. Also, you may get some glue that oozes through the upper end of the tube. This is because some of these tubes are tapered and swaged and may have a small gap or hole in the end. If this occurs there are two ways to clean up the excess glue. One is to use a heavy cord or string and run it through the end of the tip-top frame to mop up the excess glue. The other is to wait until the glue cures and then use a razor blade to cut away the excess. In any case the excess glue should be removed to prevent it from touching the tip-top ring and possibly damaging the line.

Before the glue sets, line the tip-top up with the spine or reel-seat hoods. The best way to do this is to use the same technique used for lining up reel-seat hoods. Use an overhead light that will create a streak of reflected light on the shiny rod blank, and line up this streak (moving your eyes but not your head) first with the hoods or spine mark and then with the tip-top. Once this is set, make sure you place the rod or tip section horizontally, with the tip-top facing down. Otherwise the weight of the tip-top will cause it to rotate on the rod blank and become misaligned during curing.

PREPARING AND WRAPPING GUIDES

Before the guides are wrapped in place, the guide feet must be filed to a sharp end. At one time manufactured guides did not end in a sharp edge but in a rather blunt end. That has changed with many manufacturers today, since many file the guide feet and advertise this as a selling point for their guides. But check the feet in any case.

Without filing the feet, thread will not smoothly cover the end of the foot, resulting in a gap as the thread jumps from the smooth rod blank to the raised guide foot. In these cases the end of the guide foot often will show through. This blunt end also makes it harder to wrap guides, because it is difficult to get the thread up onto the exact end of the foot, even though previous wraps are already on the rod blank.

To prevent these problems each guide foot must be filed down at the end (not the sides—we are not trying to make a knife edge). Note, however, that you also may wish to file the sides of the guide feet when mounting guides on very thin tip sections of skinny graphite rods. This will reduce the bulk and width of some guides and make for a more aesthetically pleasing guide and guide wrap without sacrificing strength. File each guide foot with a clean, smooth file until it tapers to a sharp edge. Thus the size of the file will vary with the size of the guide. A jeweler's file may be all that is needed for a fly-rod snake guide, while a coarser workshop file will be necessary to dress a big-game roller guide.

Although there are definite wrapping advantages to doing this, there are also some disadvantages. For example, with black-frame or other colored guides, the finish will be removed, leaving the filed end bright and shiny. Normally this is not a problem, because the thread will cover and hide the guide foot. This may be an aesthetic problem if you use very light colors (white, light yellow) of thin-diameter (size 2/0 or A) threads of if you use regular (not NCP) thread without color preserver (this will turn light colors lighter and translucent).

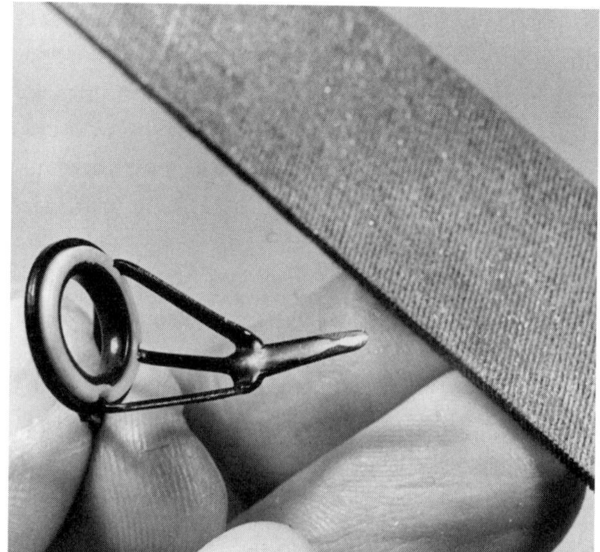

Use a regular file to file all guide feet for smooth thread wraps.

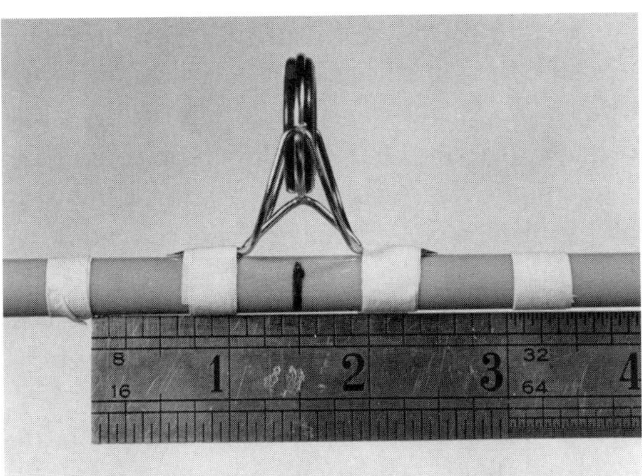

Beginning the thread wrapping by using masking tape to hold the guides in place—with the feet ends exposed for easy wrapping—and tape holding the guide foot for the beginning of each wrap. Use a rule or calipers to check measurements on both sides of two-foot guides.

There is also a slight problem with plated guides, even when the plating is the same color as the base metal. By cutting through the plating, you potentially expose the guide foot to corrosion and oxidation. The likelihood of this is slim, however, and more theoretical than actual, because the guide foot is completely covered with thread, which in turn is protected by a thick coating of epoxy rod finish.

When you file the guides, check them over carefully. Check the bottoms of the guide feet for burrs and imperfections that might scar or damage the rod (these could even cause breakage in severe cases), and use the file to remove and smooth any such spurs.

The guide frames should be straight, the guide rings properly seated in the wire frame or shock ring, and the two feet in a straight line. If the guide feet are bent slightly up or down, gently bend them in line and check with a straight edge or against the rod blank.

Once the guides are all checked and the feet filed smooth, they are temporarily fastened to the rod for wrapping. Prior to this of course, proper guide spacing must be determined (see chapter 21). We will use six guides and place them 5, 11, 18, 26, 35, and 48 inches from the tip. This means the butt guide will be 30 inches up from the butt end of the 6½-foot rod (30 inches plus 48 inches equals 78 inches, or 6 feet, 6 inches).

These spots are marked on the rod with a grease pencil or piece of masking tape. Since we are using two-foot guides, these spots will mark the positions of the guide rings. The best way to secure the guides for wrapping is to use thin strips of masking tape. Masking tape in a ¼-inch width is best. You can get this from rod-building supply shops or from a local art supply store. As an alternative you can cut short strips from a standard roll of ¾- or 1-inch masking tape. Hold the guide in position in line with the spine (tip-top and reel-seat hoods), and wrap the tape around the foot at the frame end of the guide so that the end of the foot is exposed. This is necessary so that the thread wrapping can begin on the end of the guide foot without removing the tape, which would loosen the support for temporarily holding the guide.

Tape both guide feet on each guide, checking each time to be sure the guides are lined up properly. If the guides are slightly off, they are easily adjusted by slightly sliding the foot sideways or removing and readjusting the tape.

At this point it helps to discuss ways to properly line up guides, because the methods used will be required when taping the guides down and at each step of wrapping each guide foot. The secret to good guide alignment is to check constantly and to make adjustments as necessary.

It helps to assemble the rod at this point and exactly line up the spine marks so that the tip-top and the reel-seat hoods, previously aligned on the separate sections, are in alignment when the rod is put together. Then use a strong overhead light as before when making these alignments for the spine. There are several methods, and all should be used at one time as a check against one another.

1. Hold the rod by the butt and sight along it so that the overhead light makes a reflected streak down the length of the rod. Then turn the rod so that the reel-seat hoods and tip-top

are straight up or on top of the rod. The guide or guides taped or wrapped on the rod should be in this alignment also.

2. A variation of this, when you have several or all guides taped or wrapped in place, is to sight along the rod and look through the guide ring. If the guides are properly aligned, each smaller guide ring (looking from the butt to the tip end) will appear to be inside and concentric to the larger rings. The guides may be slightly off, but this is because the frame heights vary and also because of the natural curvature from the weight of the rod as it is held horizontally. Any guide that is out of alignment may be easily adjusted by sighting this way.
3. Often the best way to sight is along the rod with the rod held horizontally as before but with the guides hanging straight down and the hoods and tip-top beneath the rod blank. This allows you to easily check the amount of the ring that appears on each side of the blank. In other words, the blank will hide part of the guide ring but will allow you to see the two sides of each ring. Each ring has an open area on each side of the blank, and rotating the rod adjusts the butt guide until these two areas, or the amount of the ring showing on each side of the blank, are equal. With the butt guide in alignment, and without moving your head or the rod, run your eyes up the rod to successive guides to check each in turn. Make adjustments as necessary, and recheck using this method and the other methods.

Note again that this checking is done with the guides taped in place and again after each guide foot (not both feet or the entire guide) is wrapped in place.

Once the guides are lined up and taped down, make additional markings to indicate where to start the rod wrapping. The wrapping is always begun on the rod blank and progresses up onto the guide foot toward the center of the guide. It helps to use thin strips of masking tape to make these marks. Also, you will want to use calipers or a rule to mark these spots evenly so that they are the same on both sides of each guide. For a tastefully wrapped rod, the length of the wrap on the blank alone (before reaching the end of the guide foot) will vary with each guide size because the guide feet will vary in length. Usually the best way to think of this is as a proportion of the guide-foot length.

A good general rule is to use a wrap on the blank of about one-half the length of the guide foot, or a total guide wrap of one and a half times the length of the guide foot. You can use more or less as desired, but a length of about one and a half, one and a third, or one and a quarter the length of the guide foot is best and makes for a neat wrap. This also makes each wrap proportional to the guide. A big guide with a 2-inch-long foot would have a wrap of 3 inches under the one-and-a-half ratio, while on the same rod a smaller tip section guide with a foot length of ½ inch would have a total wrap of ¾ inch long.

Using a rod wrapper or wrapping system as previously described (see chapters 1 and 2), pick the color you desire in size A thread.

Place the rod in the rod wrapper on the support arms or V-block, and place the edge of the guide directly over the thread-tension device. Adjust the tension so that you wrap under pressure, but not so much pressure that you risk breaking the rod or forcing the guide foot into the blank or so little pressure that you can't hold the guide foot securely. (The risk of using tension so tight that you push the guide foot into a thin-walled blank is a real one. I've seen it happen among rod builders with the philosophy that if a little pressure is good, more is better, and a whole lot is great. The thread should be under reasonable tension but pull from the thread-tension device as you would pull line off a reel with a smooth drag.)

Although you must always wrap from the blank toward the guide, you can wrap either from left to right or right to left. Either way works fine. Most right-handers like to wrap from left to right, left-handers from right to left. Doing this does require constantly flipping the rod, so some rod builders never flip the rod but wrap the left side of the guide feet from left to right and the right side of the guide feet from right to left.

One other requirement: The rod must be rotated away from you so that the thread laid down on the blank is visible to you at all times. If you wrap the rod rotating toward you, the thread will be laid down in back of the rod—out of sight—and can lead to gaps and overlapping. Before beginning, cut a 10-inch length of thread from the end, fold it over, and knot the two ends. This serves as the loop to be used later when you tie down and finish off the wrap.

Begin the wrap by taking one turn of thread around the blank, with the end of the thread ending on the side of the guide. Wrap over this turn of thread, and continue with several more wraps to secure this end of thread. After three or more turns, stop rotating the rod; use a razor blade to cut the end close to the wraps. Continue wrapping evenly and smoothly, covering the rod blank with the thread wrap. One tip to getting a tight wrap with no gaps is to keep the thread at a slight angle so that the thread being laid down is tight against the previous wraps.

Continue the wrap up onto the guide foot. At this point work slowly, since even a smoothed and filed guide foot will at first tend to cause the thread to cross over previous wraps. Once the end of the guide is secured with several wraps, remove the masking tape. Wrap along the guide foot toward the center of the guide until a point about six to eight wraps or turns away from the end, or at the point where the frame or support bars are attached to the foot.

Now pick up the previously made loop of thread and lay it down along the blank, with the loop end at the center of the guide. It often helps to tape the knotted end of the loop to the rod blank with masking tape to prevent tangles. Carefully rotate the rod and wrap over the loop, making sure the wraps are tight and even. Continue to the frame or support bars. Holding the end of the wrap with a spare finger, cut the thread several inches from the rod. Tuck the end of the cut thread

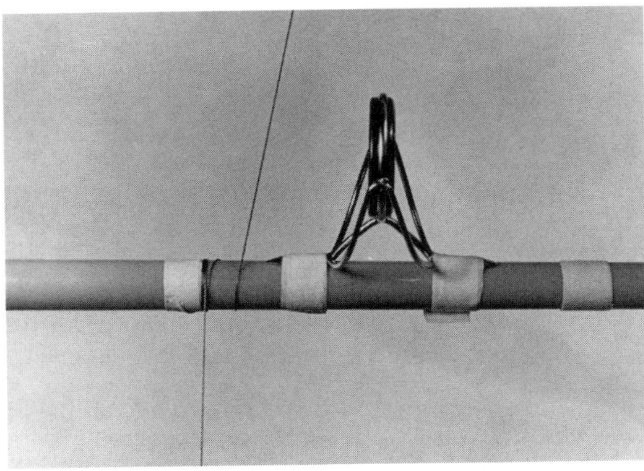

Start the thread by wrapping around the rod with constant tension, crossing over the thread with several turns to "lock" it in place.

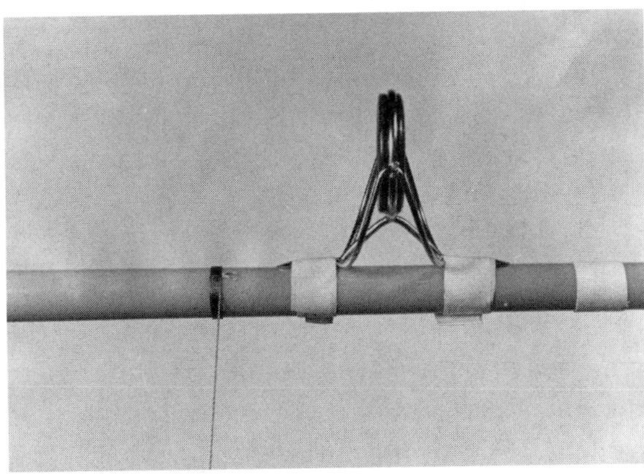

Begin thread wrapping with several turns of thread, the excess clipped off and the tape marking the beginning of the wrap removed.

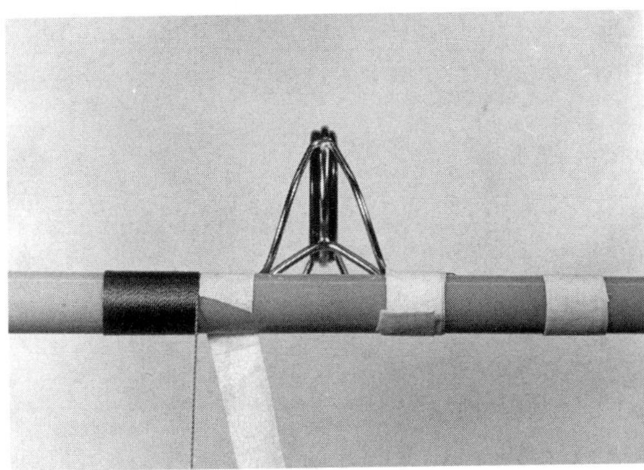

Continue the wrap until the thread begins to cover the exposed guide foot, at which point the masking tape is removed to allow further wrapping.

through the loop and slowly pull the loop tight, gradually pulling the loose thread end along with the loop beneath the thread wraps. This fastens the wrap end in place.

After pulling the loop and all the excess thread through, you must cut the thread to hide it. The method I like best for this is to alternately work the loose end of thread right and left to open up a gap in the wraps where the thread exits. Then hold a razor blade parallel to the thread wraps (at a right angle to the rod blank) and cut straight down on the thread end. Do *not* use pressure, which might harm the rod blank. An easy way to do this is to rock the blade back and forth slightly to be sure of cutting the thread completely with no frays and fuzz. Use a burnisher or the side of a smooth ballpoint pen case to close the gap in the wraps and smooth them. Burnishers for this purpose are also available and work well.

Once the one guide foot is wrapped down, check the guide for alignment. Make any necessary adjustments, then replace the rod in the rod wrapper and wrap the other foot using the same techniques. When doing this, make sure the guide—the two feet of the guide—is in a straight line with the rod blank.

Note: There are other ways of wrapping, adding underwraps, and making variations of wraps. There are also variations of tucking the end of the thread under the wrap and finishing the wrap. These are outlined in detail in chapter 22. Check this chapter for more details and information.

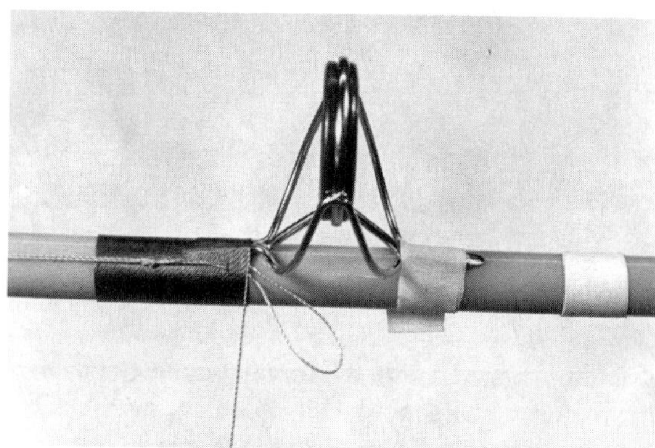

Close to the end of the wrap, a loop of thread is laid down and then wrapped over. It is used to pull the end of thread under the wraps.

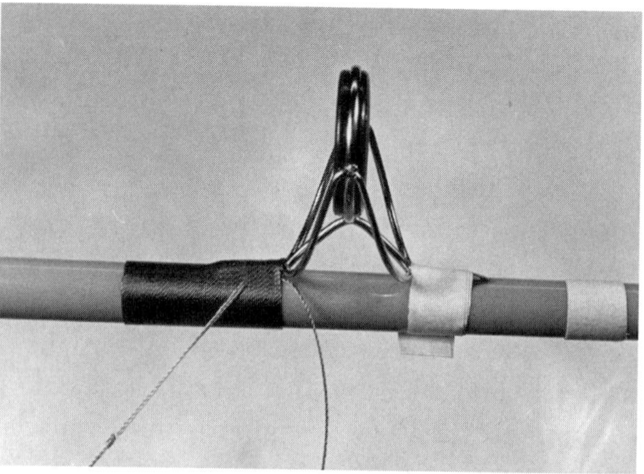

Pull the loop of thread under the wraps after the end of the thread is tucked into the loop.

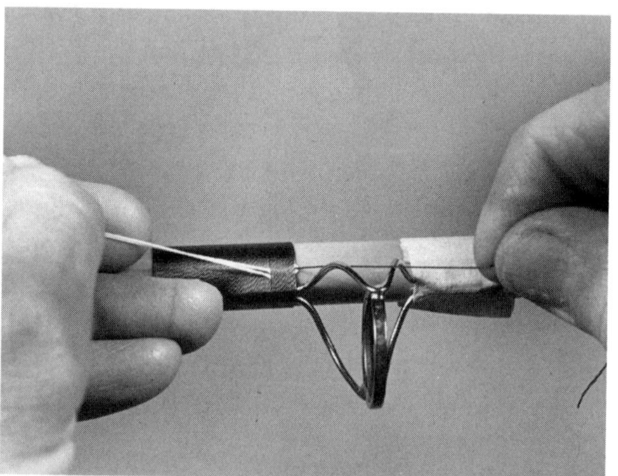

A heavier and different color thread, as shown here, helps avoid tangles when tucking the thread into the loop and pulling the loop through.

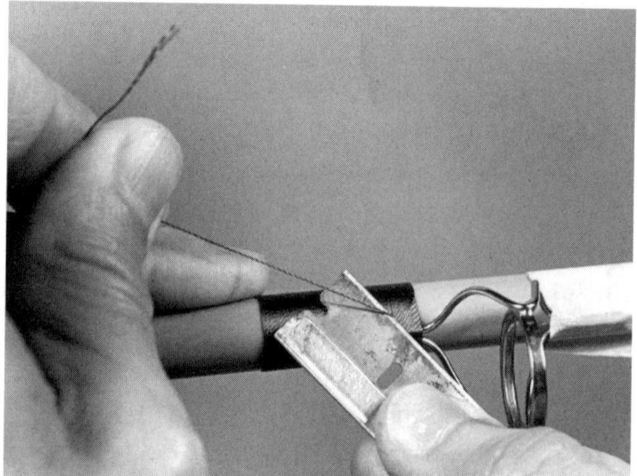

Once the end of the thread is pulled through the wraps, use a razor blade or scalpel to trim the excess. It can be cut flush like this, but there are better methods, as outlined in chapter 22.

Other Wraps

In addition to the wraps made to hold down each guide, other wraps are necessary. A similar wrap, made by the same procedure above, is done at the tip-top. For standard tube tops this is strictly decorative because it is done on the blank. It meets but does not go over the tip tube and does not help to hold the tip-top in place. There are exceptions to this: Some tube tops have slight extensions on the sides that are wrapped down with thread, and the one-piece wire flexible-frame guides have two wire legs on the tip-top that fit on either side of the blank and are wrapped in place, this wrapping serving to hold the tip-top to the blank. There is no tube with this style of tip-top. The length of these wraps must be sized as are guide wraps (about one and a half to one and a quarter the length of the legs on the flex-guide tip-top or, for tube tops, about the length of the wrap on the uppermost guide).

A trim wrap is also typically placed immediately above the winding check and handle. This can be fancy (see chapters 23 and 24), or it can be just a simple wrap of the same color used in the guide wraps. That's what we will do for this first basic rod: Make the wrap at the winding check the same way as for the guides, finishing with a loop of thread, and make the wrap aesthetically pleasing—usually about 1 to 3 inches long.

For this two-piece rod, one additional wrap is most important and is functional as well as decorative. This is a wrap at the female portion of the ferrule to give the rod additional hoop strength at this important junction. Most manufacturers recommend this, but it should be done regardless. To do this use normal tension and wrap no more than about 1 to 1½ inches along the blank. Current trends are to make an even shorter wrap of perhaps ¼ to ½ inch at the very end of the female ferrule section, since this is where splits would occur if the blank end is not protected. If you are using a blank with a spigot ferrule, make a similar, short wrap on the male side. In both cases begin on the body of the blank and work the wrap up to the edge of the blank. Attempting to begin the wrap at the edge of the blank and work in the other direction is too difficult and will not result in the wrap being close to the blank edge. Begin and end the same as for a guide wrap. Although this is a decorative wrap in addition to being functional, some rod builders like to "hide" it by making it the same color as the blank. To do this choose a thread color that is close to the blank color, but when finishing the rod do *not* add color preserver. When the epoxy finish is added, the epoxy will cause the wrap to become translucent, causing it to further disappear into the blank.

PROTECTING THE WRAPS: FINISHING COATS

Once all the wraps are completed, they must be protected with some type of finish. Today the best choices are the various epoxy and polymer resins that provide high-build clear coatings that are very durable. Most are two-part with a 50/50 mix; some are single solutions. Before adding any protective finish, however, you must consider whether you want to use color preserver.

Color Preservers

Color preservers are often specific to a particular brand of finish (companies that make finishes also produce color preservers) and may or may not work with other brands of finish. For starters, stay with one brand of finishes.

Color preservers have some advantages and some disadvantages. Color preservers, as the name indicates, will preserve and protect the bright color of the thread used. Thus the color you see on the spool is the one you will get on the rod when color preserver is used. Without a color preserver, the thread will become translucent and change color slightly when coated with epoxy or polymers. Dark colors will become darker; light colors will become lighter or in some cases almost transparent.

Second, color preservers will seal the thread against the absorption of the epoxy and thus make it easier to do rod repairs. Preventing the epoxy from soaking into the thread and "gluing" the thread to the blank aids you in removing the wrap with a razor blade.

Some rod builders think the wrap is better protected by the epoxy finish soaking through the wrap, which also provides a protective coating. This is probably true technically, although the practical difference in the durability of epoxy- or polymer-protected wraps with or without color preserver seems to be nonexistent. A more serious disadvantage is that sometimes the use of color preserver can eventually cause cracking or crazing around the guide feet or at the connection of the foot with the frame. If this is a serious consideration, the only solution is to finish without a color preserver.

Some rod builders prefer the translucency and color changes in the thread caused by using finish without color preserver. This seems to be particularly true with fly-rod builders, who often like traditional and muted tones rather than the bright colors found on other rods. The translucent wraps resulting from using no color preserver are more like the darkened silk wraps of early bamboo rods.

One compromise solution on rods on which an underwrap is needed is to use the color preserver on the underwrap to make for easy repairs when required but use no color preserver on the guide wrap. If good color combinations are chosen, the result can be very attractive, with a light-colored underwrap and a darker yet translucent guide wrap.

There are several ways to apply color preserver. One is to use a small piece of sponge and pat the preserver in place. This is not the best method for the lacquer-based color preservers made by some companies but works fine for others. A brush can also be used for any type of color preserver. You can spread the color preserver with your finger, but this is best for water-based preservers. A paper towel or rag works well but tends to be wasteful.

When coating with color preserver, first follow the manufacturer's directions. Use plenty of color preserver, completely covering the entire wrap, and add enough color preserver to soak well into the threads. This soaking will require more color preserver for heavy-thread wraps, such as for size E or EE, than it will for the thin size A thread. Apply evenly, and blot up any excess with a paper towel. Even when using NCP thread, one coat of color preserver as additional protection against blotching or uneven finishes is suggested. However, you do not want puddles of color preserver to rest on the wrap and form a thick coating, or skin. Add several coats this way, at least two and possibly three on heavy wraps when using regular (not NCP) thread. Blot the final coat thoroughly and allow to cure for 24 hours, or until you no longer smell any of the solvent or color preserver odor.

If you work with underwraps or double wraps, add color preserver after each layer of wrap: on the underwrap, after the guide wrap is added, and again after a second guide wrap (double wrap, if used) is added.

Finish Coats

Finish coats today consist of varnish, two-part epoxies, and similar coatings. Be sure to use only those products designed for rod finishing. Epoxy glue is not the same as epoxy rod finish. Some finishes, such as the U-40 Urethane Rod Finish, are one solution and require no mixing. Others, such as Flex Coat and Gudebrod finishes, High Build Polymer Rod Wrapping Finish, and U-40 Dura Gloss Finish, are two-part, requiring mixing to produce a thick, clear, one-coat (in most cases) rod finish.

With all of these, follow the manufacturer's instructions, but here are a few tips. All of these work best at room temperature, and some mix better at a slightly higher temperature, such as 80 to 90 degrees. Heat thins the liquids and makes for more accurate measuring and easier, faster mixing and also reduces the possibility of bubbles in the mix.

For easier mixing use craft sticks, small disposable cups (of the type used for dispensing liquid medicine), and syringes. One point about syringes and plastic mixing cups: Most syringes available for medical use, and thus available in drugstores, have a light silicone coating for better lubrication. However, silicone in any form reacts adversely with epoxy and polymer finishes and may cause the finish to separate from the rod blank and wrap. Flex Coat sells syringes without silicone. Another advantage is that these syringes are color-coded to correspond with the cap colors on bottles of two-part epoxy finishes. Use only these syringes or others that are silicone free. Avoid paper or wax-coated cups, which will tend to introduce bubbles into the mix. Use nonporous plastic disposable cups, but check to be sure that the epoxy will not eat through the plastic. I've had this happen with epoxy finishes and paints when using plastic cups. Disposable or artist's brushes for brushing on color preserver and epoxy are useful. (You must use different brushes for each material or clean them thoroughly between uses. Special epoxy cleaners are made for this. The disposable brushes are best because they are inexpensive and allow for one-time use with no possibility of cross-contamination.)

You might also want to prepare a smooth surface on which to spread the epoxy mix. Aluminum foil is often suggested, but I like plastic sheets cut from the sides and bottoms of disposable plastic food and drink bottles. Aluminum foil can wrinkle and tear, while the flat plastic cutout sheets make it easy to mix, stir, and use two-party epoxies.

To mix the two parts of the epoxy, make sure the liquids are at room temperature or slightly warmer. Use the graduated mixing cup or syringes to measure equal amounts of the two parts. (If you use syringes, do not attempt to clean them afterward. Just be sure you reserve one syringe for each liquid part used.) Also make sure you mix *exactly* according to directions, usually in a 50/50 ratio. If the mix proportions are off, you can end up with too brittle a mix or a mix that is soft and even sticky. In some cases the terms used for the parts are misleading. With most companies "part A" in the finish is the resin, and "part B" is the hardener (catalyst). However, if you get too much hardener in the mix, the result will be a soft or sticky finish. Often rod builders try to correct this by adding a second coat with even more hardener, on the theory that the more hardener is added, the harder the resulting finish will be. If you do by chance get a finish that is slightly soft or sticky, mix a new batch with exact 50/50 measurements, using at least 5 cubic centimeters of each liquid, and apply this over the first finish. This usually solves the problem.

ETI president David Fonsen notes that in their two-part epoxy kits and in their use of epoxy, the two parts have slightly more of the hardener. Any additional hardener in the two-part mix is often too much and will lead to a sticky finish. You can be off by about 5 percent in either of the two parts, but more than that starts to spell trouble. As does Roger Seiders of Flex Coat, Fonsen notes that mixing too small a total quantity makes it difficult to get a good 50/50 mix.

Mix the two parts thoroughly, using a round or flat mixing stick. Seiders likes a round stick; I prefer a flat craft stick that I think mixes the two parts more rapidly and completely. Either is okay, provided that the mix is thorough. Mix evenly and thoroughly but not rapidly or with a whipping motion, because this will form bubbles in the mix that are difficult to remove and will make for an unattractive finish.

When you are sure the solution is thoroughly mixed (after several minutes), pour the solution out on aluminum foil or the plastic sheets cut from bottles and jars. Pouring out this mix will extend its working life. Another way of extending the life is to place the sheet on a tray or dish of ice cubes. Keeping the mix on a flat surface will also allow any small bubbles to pop to the surface easily. Other tips that work for most of epoxies include:

1. If you have some bubbles in the mix at this point, hold the sheet close to your mouth and blow on the solution slowly and evenly. The purpose is not to make a breeze but to allow your breath to drift over the puddle of epoxy. Opinions differ as to the reason, but this will usually cause any small bubbles

to pop to the surface and dissipate rapidly. (David Fonsen says this works due to both the heat of your breath and the CO2 exhaled. Both help bring air bubbles to the surface and help them dissipate.)

2. A hair dryer or heat lamp briefly held over the epoxy will accomplish the same thing. Personally I do not like using a hair dryer, since it pulls air in from the surrounding atmosphere and can possibly draw in dust that will be blown onto the wet epoxy. That's not good.

3. Use at least 5 cubic centimeters of each solution to get exact measurements and a good mixture. Use less than that, and the chances increase that the mix will be off more than the 5 percent leeway suggested as the maximum by ETI's Fonsen.

4. You can sometimes extend the working life of the mixture to about one week by placing the puddle of epoxy into the refrigerator or freezer. In some cases a freezer will ruin the mix, so the refrigerator is the safer choice.

5. Sometimes one part of the epoxy resins will crystallize. Often this occurs when the parts are stored in a cold area. Sometimes the solution can be restored by heating the bottle or jar in hot but not boiling water.

6. If you wish to check the flexibility of your chosen rod finish, mix up a small batch, pour it onto a flat surface, and allow it to cure overnight. You can then peel it off and check for stiffness, flexibility, clarity, and durability (the latter by pushing on the finish with a thumbnail and subsequently trying harder objects, such as a nail or knife blade).

7. You can sometimes thin epoxy or other finishes with the appropriate solvent or other methods to make a thin coat on light rods. Flex Coat recommends using a stiff brush to spread the epoxy thinly, using heat to thin the epoxy mix, and using solvents. For their products Flex Coat recommends using acetone or epoxy thinner in a ratio of one to four drops of solvent per 6 cubic centimeters of epoxy mix. Other products may also be thinned but will require experimentation or following the manufacturer's recommendations.

Once the epoxy or finish is mixed—or when using a single-solution mix—use a small brush to add the finish to each wrap, with the rod held in a horizontal rack. Often the rod-wrapping rack is fine for this. Strong light is necessary. I like to begin with the wraps at the tip end of the rod, because the thinner mix will work better on the thin-diameter wraps. That way, if the mix does thicken up slightly by the time you get to the other end, you will be doing the largest or longest wraps and the large butt decorative wrap, where a thin mix is less important.

Begin by rotating the rod and adding a thin coating of finish to each end of the wrap, in essence making a circular band of clear finish that just barely overlaps the edge of the wrap at each end. After this is done, fill in the rest of the wrap area with the brush, first working around the wrap and then working at right angles to this, parallel to the blank. The result should be complete coverage of the wrap.

To check the coverage, rotate the rod slowly and watch the streak of reflected light that forms on the shiny liquid finish. If there are any gaps, these will immediately show up. Continue working on each wrap this way, from the tip end toward the butt end.

Once you have completed all the wraps, check again with the light to be sure there are no gaps. Also check the underside of each wrap to see if there is any sagging from the application of too much finish. If there is, remove any excess with the brush, and distribute the remainder of the finish evenly from one end of the wrap to the other.

At this point you will need a curing motor to slowly turn the rod so that the finish will not sag and drip during curing over the next several hours. Special motors are available for this, or you can jury-rig a slow-rpm motor from a barbecue grill or an old clock motor. Speeds can range from about 1 rpm to about 20 rpm, with 10 rpm a good average.

Chuck the rod butt into the jaws or rod holder of the device (see chapters 1 and 2 for details on this), add a support to the rod two-thirds of the way up from the butt (and between guides), and allow the finish to cure in a dust-free environment. The best way to ensure this is to use a vacant room or cure at night, when there is little human traffic through the house and the rod can rotate undisturbed. If you allow the rod to rotate without supervision, make *sure* the rod is chucked so that it will not come out and that the upper rod support will not move (clamp it down). The finish can be ruined or the rod broken if it slips off the motor or support while the motor continues to turn.

Once the finish has cured overnight, the rod is ready to be fished. For best results use a small coating of paraffin, candle wax, or U-40 Ferrule Lube on the male section of the ferrule before assembling it for fishing. This coating will aid in keeping the joint tight and will protect the mated areas. Although wax has been widely used, U-40 emphasizes that their Ferrule Lube can be used on any ferrules (including metal ferrules) and does not collect dirt (as does paraffin), which can harm ferrules. It is a thinner material than paraffin or wax, yet it fills the pores of the blank to aid in creating a tight joint when the parts are joined. This ferrule treatment also allows the ferrule to be easily loosened for takedown of the rod.

Additional finishing touches can be added to the rod as outlined in chapters 23, 24, and 25.

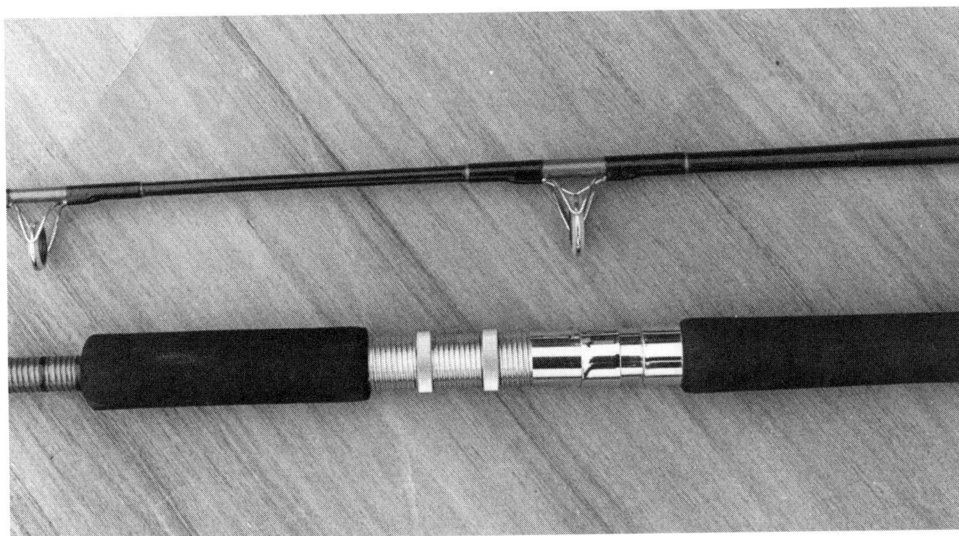

Completed basic spinning rod with simple wraps and foam handle but with a chromed reel seat in place of the graphite fill model mentioned in the text.

19

Building Specific Rod Styles

Introduction • One-Piece Rods • Multipiece Rods • Ultralight Spinning Rods • Light Spinning Rods • Tennessee Handle Rods • Surf Spinning Rods • Conventional Surf Rods • Boat Spinning Rods • Noodle Rods • Casting Rods: Detachable-Handle Style • Casting Rods with Permanent Handle • Casting Rods with a Spiral Guide Wrap • Popping Rods • Spin-Cast Rods • Light Fly Rods • Heavy Fly Rods • Fly Rods with Extension Butts • Boat Rods • Offshore Trolling Rods: One-Piece • Offshore Trolling Rods: Detachable-Handle Style • Stand-up Rods • Notes on Microguide Rods

Note: You may wish to refer to specific sections of this chapter for general ideas for building specific rods after reading chapter 27. For details on specific aspects of rod construction, check chapters 20, 21, 22, 25, and 26.

INTRODUCTION

All rods have the same basic parts as outlined in the previous chapter: blank, butt cap, grips, winding check, guides, tip-top, essential and decorative wrappings, and protective finishes. These parts all vary quite widely in the wide range of sportfishing tackle and sportfishing rods that can be built. All types of rods are built just as easily as the rod in the previous chapter, although some require slightly different handle treatments, guide wraps, and order of assembly. This chapter discusses differences in turn, with an outline of suggested order of assembly. In some cases this suggested order can be changed slightly. For example, in the 6½-foot spinning rod of the previous chapter, the butt cap could be put on the rod first and followed by the grip. Things like that can be considered somewhat subjective. Putting the handle on the rod before wrapping guides on the same blank section is not, however, because obviously the handle cannot be slid down the blank once the guides are in place.

More and more modern rods are being made with two-part rear grips, with the exposed rod blank between the two sections. This is not a major problem at all and is explained in this chapter.

ONE-PIECE RODS

The differences in building a one-piece rod of any style over a two-piece rod are few. First you will need a longer bed and working area for the rod wrapping, because you cannot do the rod in sections as you can with two-piece rods. You will also need more rod supports for long rods to support the ends and maintain balance as you wrap the rod. Naturally this length and the number of rod supports required vary with the type of rod. You won't need much space with a one-piece 6½-foot spinning rod. You need less space with a two-piece 6½-foot rod, since the sections will be about 3 feet, 3 inches, plus a few inches for the ferrule. More space is needed for a two-piece 9-foot noodle rod or a 14-foot two-piece surf rod.

For a one-piece rod there is no reinforcing wraps at the ferrule, since there is no ferrule. Each style of rod has specific requirements and components. These specifics of components and assembly order are followed with one-piece rods just as they are for two-piece models.

In some cases one-piece rods are lighter than equivalent two-piece rods, since they are often designed for casting lighter lures. In these cases you may need to position the rod supports of your rod-wrapping machine closer together and also lighten up on the tension of your thread device to prevent getting a bow in the rod that would interfere with easily wrapping the rod.

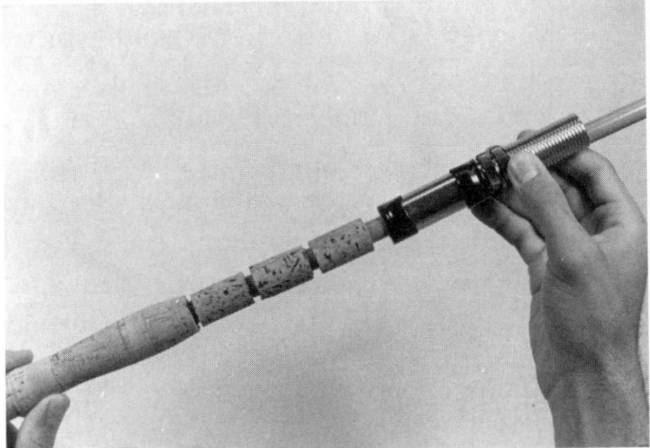

Gluing a reel seat onto a spinning rod, using cork bushings to hold the reel seat in place.

MULTIPIECE RODS

Multipiece rods are rods that are collapsible into short sections. Most are pack or travel rods in three-, four-, and five-piece models. The difference in building these is that you will need a rod-wrap machine in which the supports can be placed close together to accommodate these short sections. Lacking this you can ferrule two or more sections (any adjoining sections) to make for a rod length that is easy to work with on the rod-wrap machine. In addition, you will need to make a reinforcing wrap at each ferrule, at least on the female ferrule, as specified earlier. You should also do this on the male section of a spigot ferrule unless this step is specifically indicated as not necessary by the blank manufacturer.

Careful consideration must be made as to guide placement on multipiece rods. If possible and if ferrule wraps are suggested as necessary, it is always good to incorporate a guide wrap with a ferrule wrap. This way you can minimize the number of wraps necessary on the rod. This also reduces stiffening of the rod, because all such pairings of guide and ferrule reduce the number of wraps.

Any style of rod can be built in multipiece fashion, although some require that you cut the blank and build your own ferrules to make a two-piece rod into a four-piece pack rod. (To make ferrules, see chapter 26.)

The order of assembly in any multipiece rod is the same as for any rod of that style. There is one exception: With some multipiece rods there is no guide on the butt section, so the butt assembly can be done before or after you wrap all the guides on the other sections. It does not make any difference, but I like to make the butt assembly of any rod first—including the handle, grips, reel seat, and butt cap—and then wrap the guides. Most multipiece rods are of the light variety, such as light spinning, fly (very popular today), light to medium light spinning, and some light casting rods. Rarely will you find a multipiece heavy boat rod or offshore rod, although they are occasionally available and can be made by buying, cutting, and ferruling blanks as outlined in chapter 26.

ULTRALIGHT SPINNING RODS

Ultralight spinning rods differ from standard spinning rods in that they are generally short; designed for very light reels, line, and lures; and thus built with very lightweight components.

The length of such rods varies but usually ranges from about 4 feet to 6½ feet. Most are in the 4- to 5½-foot range. The blanks are light and usually designed for lures of about $\frac{1}{64}$ to $\frac{3}{16}$ ounce. Line weights used with such rods are typically from one- to four-pound test.

As a result, components are light. Butt caps typically are of the lightest plastic or the aluminum butt-plate style. Often the grips are skeletal cork with sliding rings for less weight than the standard reel seats used with larger rods. If sliding rings over cork are not used, then the reel seats are usually graphite or graphite fill, often with skeletal parts with a separate fixed hood position and movable hood position with a cork insert between them to keep the weight down. Usually the grips are short; 9 to 10 inches is often standard. Foam grips are heavier than cork grips and are usually avoided with these light rods. Guides are also light, with the single-foot silicon carbide style or very lightweight ring flex-guide style often preferred.

Because of their short length, blanks are usually made in one piece, reducing both the cost (adding ferrules costs the manufacturer more) and the weight of the blank, as well as the possibility of any dead spots, which would be particularly critical on a light rod like this.

Assembly of an Ultralight Spinning Rod

Determine the spine of the rod, and mark it for guide placement. Although other grip materials (foam, wood) may be used, cork ring grips with sliding rings are standard. Mount the preformed cork grip by first reaming the hole in the grip to fit the blank using a rat-tail file, reamer, or dowel wrapped with sandpaper. Once the grip is sized to fit snugly, add epoxy glue to the blank and slide the grip in place. Often these grips come in two halves (since both ends are swelled to prevent loss of the sliding rings) or with a swelled cork for the end. Add one half or the main part of the grip, and mop up any glue. Add the sliding rings, add more glue to the section covered by the remainder of the grip, slide the grip part or cork ring in place, and add a small amount of glue to the cork faces. Twist the cork pieces together, mop up any excess glue, and allow the glue to cure.

If you make the cork grip from individual cork rings, follow the instructions in chapter 20 to make and shape the grip, adding the sliding rings at the same time.

Add a winding check with a little glue. Glue the tip-top in place in line with the spine. Place the rod on the wrapping machine and wrap the guides in place, using the spacing chart provided in chapter 21 or a spacing that you copy from a similar commercial rod or otherwise devise. Once the wraps are complete, add color preserver and finish; turn on a rod-curing motor overnight, and the rod will be ready to fish the next day.

LIGHT SPINNING RODS

Building light spinning rods is very similar to building ultralight spinning rods, with a few variations. By general definition, light spinning rods are slightly heavier than the ultralight models and are often longer—5½ to 6½ feet is more typical. They will cast lures ranging from about ⅛ to ¼ ounce, and a fair number of two-piece models are available. The guides are the same; the grip is typically cork but often with a fixed, glued-on tubular reel seat instead of sliding rings. Foam grips can be used, but they are heavier than cork for the same length and diameter. Wrapping and assembly instructions are otherwise the same as for the ultralight spinning rod or standard spinning rod discussed in chapter 18.

Spinning-rod handles don't have to be made of foam or cork. This handle is of wrapped heavy cord with a glued-on reel seat.

Reel seats are eliminated on some rods—the "Tennessee" handles on commercial spinning rods are an example. This similar wood handle uses a taped-on reel.

TENNESSEE HANDLE RODS

Most rods with "Tennessee" handles are made with cork grips, although other materials can be used. These are light, often long rods used in the Southeast, primarily for light fishing for crappie and perch and also for bass, white bass, Kentucky bass, and smallmouth.

In essence they are spinning rods with a longer than normal grip or handle and with no reel seat. The reel is taped in place using masking tape, blue painter's tape, electrician's or similar tape, or even wrapped in place using heavy (size D or E) rod-wrapping thread. If using rod-wrapping thread, the mount is meant to be permanent or semipermanent. The thread wrap can of course be cut off, but it is usually left in place with the reel mounted to the rod. For permanent protection of a thread wrap over the reel seat and grip, coat it with color preserver and epoxy finish for protection.

If using tape, electrician's or similar nonsticky tapes are best, and they are available in many colors from most hardware stores. Masking tape tends to get hard and brittle and is also difficult to remove if left on too long or exposed to the elements. The blue painter's tape is better because it does not stick as readily when left in place for a long time.

The construction of these rods in terms of grips (remember—no reel seat), guides, and other concerns is no different from that of standard rods. The standard method of making these rods is to add the grip first, using cork, wood (built to shape and drilled to fit), wrapped cord (like the handle construction of some surf rods), graphite/graphite-fill tubes, or even thin-wall PVC or CPVC plastic pipe. In most cases when using tubes, the tubes are sized to be comfortable, such as 1-inch diameter. Use cork bushings for these tubes as a spacer on the rod blank and to hold the tube centered on the blank.

An alternative method was described in a *RodMaker* magazine article in which the spacer was used to hold the blank not on-center but hard against one side of the tube. The purported advantage of this is that with the tube off-center of the rod blank, and with the rod blank and tubing grip in contact with each other, there is more sensitivity through the rod and grip to the angler. For this construction, glue bushings to the blank and then, with a rat-tail file, file one long groove in the outer edge of the bushing and on the opposite side of the guide position to allow the rod blank to maintain this rod-to-grip contact. Then by taping or thread wrapping the reel foot onto the tubing grip and right over the contact spot with the rod blank, you achieve maximum sensitivity.

SURF SPINNING RODS

Surf spinning rods are essentially giant-size versions of standard spinning rods. Typically called surf rods, they are also used for coastal fishing from bridges, piers, jetties, and bulkheads. Although length will vary depending on the application (shorter for pier and jetty, longer for high surf from the beach), most will be between 8 and 12 feet long. Some shorties of about 7 feet are sometimes available—more for pier and jetty fishing—along with some long beach models of up to 15 feet.

Often these rods are two-piece, although those in the 12- to 15-foot range are sometimes three-piece. Some are one-piece, especially those in the 8- to 10-foot range, because some anglers feel this makes a difference in strength or action. In my opinion it doesn't make a difference, but one-piece blanks (and rods) are found in some beach shops.

As a result of this range, models can be found to throw everything from 1-ounce lures to 10 ounces or more. This heavy-duty purpose requires heavy components. Most of the guides are high-frame, two-foot models of aluminum oxide or silicon carbide. Cork is a good grip material but tends to get chewed up under the harsh conditions of surf fishing and sand-spike use, so foam is often preferred. Other grips can be of wrapped, varnished cord (popular mostly on thick-diameter blanks), leather or synthetic wrapping materials (such as typically used on bike grips), and cork tape (also spiral-wrapped around the blank). These thin wrap-on materials are especially good for surf rods because the thick-diameter blanks do not require a large buildup for comfortable holding, merely the addition of a comfortable nonslip material for gripping. These materials often add only about ⅛ inch to the diameter of the rod.

Reel seats are also a problem, because large-diameter models of the slip-on style are required to fit the large blanks. The graphite-fill style is popular, as is the wrap-on plate style. Because the reel seat is placed so far up the blank for leverage, often the rear grip is divided into two parts, with the bare blank showing between the two. This is more common with foam grips than with cork tape, cord, or spiral wraps. A foregrip, usually of foam, is standard.

Assembly of a Surf Spinning Rod

First determine the spine of the rod or rod sections and mark for guide and reel-seat placement. Although the cork tape, cord, and spiral bike wraps can be added to the blank after the guides are wrapped in place, it is usually best to follow the same order of assembly as for any basic rod. This helps establish the proper position and alignment of the reel-seat hoods, which in turn aid in lining up the guides.

If you mount cork rings, a preformed cork grip, or a foam grip, follow the instructions previously outlined. Slide the grips down on the blank and glue them in place, leaving enough room to add the butt cap. Note that the shorter length of the two-part rear grip (one section at the butt cap and one immediately beneath the real seat) will make it far easier to slide in place than if you were using a full-length rear grip, which often measures up to 22 inches long on rods like this. Thus add the lower rear grip, mark the rod for the reel-seat position, and add the second rear grip. (Often a good way to decide on the spacing for these grips is to hold the rod at arm's length to the side, with the butt end in your armpit and your hand comfortably on the blank. This marks the position for the reel seat; the upper rear grip goes immediately below this. It often also helps to check the positioning of the reel seat on a comfortable commercial rod.)

Glue the reel seat in place and then add the foregrip. Add the butt cap (which, because of the large diameter of the rod blank, often does not require shimming).

If you are making a cord-style rear grip, first determine the position of the reel seat, glue it in place, glue the butt cap on, and then wrap the cord on up to the reel seat (which was previously glued in place), using the detailed instructions in chapter 20. Actually this is just like making a guide wrap: Wrap over the tag end of the cord at one end, and wrap to the other end (butt cap to reel seat), securing the end just as for wrapping a guide or whipping the end of a rope. Some companies make special butt cord in various colors for this type of wrap, although you can use a macramé cord or a "craft cord," available in craft shops in 1½- and 2-millimeter diameters and also available in many colors.

Most rods with a cord rear grip still have a foam or cork foregrip for comfort. Follow the instructions just outlined to wrap on the spiral bike tape or special self-adhesive cork tape. These do have to be secured at both ends with a short (½-inch) wrap of heavy thread. A variation of this is to first wrap the entire grip area (from the end of the rod up through the foregrip area) with the cork tape, cord, or spiral tape, and then glue the butt cap over this, using the grip materials as a shim. Similarly, the tubular or wrap-on plate-style reel seat is mounted over the grip material. The grip material is secured at the upper end with a short wrap of heavy thread.

Guide wrapping is best with an underwrap (see chapter 22). Finish with two coats of color preserver followed by one or two coats of epoxy thread finish; allow them to cure properly before you use the rod.

CONVENTIONAL SURF RODS

Conventional surf rods are similar to spinning surf rods, except that they are often built on heavier blanks. You usually won't see the excessive lengths used in surf spinning with many conventional surf rods in the 9-foot to 12-foot range. The choice of a conventional surf stick over a spinning rod is often made on this consideration of power and length, with the shorter, more-powerful conventional rods used for heavier fishing such as drum fishing or when surf conditions and fishing conditions dictate a heavy sinker and chunk of bait that would be difficult to cast with a spinning outfit.

The basics of building the handle and wrapping the guides are the same, except that the guides are smaller ring two-foot styles, and one or two more are often added to the blank to reduce line rubbing (because the guides ride on top of the blank when the angler is fighting a fish). The handle is the same, and there is no difference in the reel seat, because these rods do not use trigger-style reel seats, as do shorter casting rods.

BOAT SPINNING RODS

Boat spinning rods can range from fairly simple, inexpensive models used for inshore and Great Lakes trolling to more carefully finished, finely crafted models used for offshore trolling for big game. Most are about 7 feet long, one- or two-piece, and built on strong heavy-wall blanks for heavy-duty fishing. The methods of building them are no different from those outlined in chapter 18, except that all the parts are larger, stronger, and heavy duty. They are standard spinning rods in parts, construction, and appearance, albeit heavy "industrial strength" models. Foam grips are typical, along with heavy-duty graphite-fill, anodized aluminum or chrome-plated-brass reel seats. Guides are typically two-foot heavy-duty models. Often an underwrap, sometimes even a double overwrap (see chapter 22), is used on these rods.

Assembly of a Boat Spinning Rod

Determine and mark the spine. Use standard rod-building methods to slide the foam grip in place (chapters 18 and 20), and then glue the butt cap on the end of the blank. (Although cork grips can be used, they are chewed up rapidly in trolling-rod holders and thus are seldom used on these rods. Even the foam grips take a fair share of abuse from this type of fishing and the constant pressure on the grip where the edge of the rod holder hits the foam.)

Add and glue the reel seat in place, then the foregrip as previously outlined. Glue the tip-top on, add the guides, and wrap them in place. Because this is a boat rod for heavy-duty fishing, consider using an underwrap (see chapter 22). Complete the job with color preserver and a wrap finish, and allow the finish to completely cure before using the rod.

One consideration is in the style and size of the guides. Large high-frame guides are a must, including a large tip-top. This is necessary because these rods are used for inshore and offshore trolling, where it is often necessary to reel doubled line through the guides when fighting a fish. Considering the large-size line in use (thirty-pound, sometimes even fifty-pound along with a Bimini or similar knot), the knots are large and knot clearance is a must. Often a size 16 is the smallest guide that should be used, and the largest tip available should be standard.

NOODLE RODS

Noodle rods can be either casting or spinning style but comprise a general type of design that is similar in both styles. Basically noodle rods are long, limber rods designed for light-line fishing. Most noodle rods range from about 9 through 12 feet, although this will vary with the manufacturer. Most are very light—some are designed for lines as light as two-pound test and usually for line no heavier than six- or eight-pound test. They are long and limber so that the shock absorbency of the blank can prevent break-offs of big fish on the light tackle and line.

As a result, noodle rods are basically not unlike heavy fly rods but are used for spinning and casting tackle and built like spinning or casting rods. With their light, limber design, they must be built with light components. Building a noodle rod is really like building a light or ultralight spinning rod in component selection, although with the length, more guides must be added to the rod to distribute the stresses and balance the line strain.

The secret is to pick light components, particularly in the guides at the upper end of the rod. Because even on spinning rods the line funnels down rapidly, the guides on the upper end of the rod can be very light, small-ring-diameter one-foot guides, such as those made of silicon carbide. The handle is usually cork but often includes a threaded-barrel fixed reel seat rather than the sliding-ring style.

Assembly of a Noodle Spinning Rod

First mark the spine of the rod sections and mark for guide spacing and handle placement. Assemble the handle just as you would for a standard spinning outfit. Use cork rings or a preformed cork rear grip, and glue and slide them in place. Add the butt cap, then shim the blank above the rear grip for the reel seat and add the fixed reel seat. Add and glue the foregrip. The grips should be cork for lightness. The best reel seats are those that are lightweight graphite-fill or light aluminum. Choose one-foot guides that are light in weight, and get the smallest rings suitable for the tackle. Since the guides are under the rod, you will not need them very close together, but you will need enough to distribute strain. (Check suggested guide spacing in chapter 21). Use light thread for the wraps, with 2/0 a good possibility. To save weight, do not use an underwrap. Protect with one or two layers of color preserver and one coat of light epoxy rod finish.

Making a casting-style (revolving-spool) noodle rod is identical, with a few differences. First the reel seat will have to be a trigger style, although the handle length (long rear grip and standard foregrip) can remain the same. The small one-foot guides using light guide wraps are also identical, although you will usually need more guides at the upper end of the rod to reduce line rubbing against the blank, since these guides are on top of the rod as you fight a fish. The smallest, lightest one-foot guides with the lightest wrap are thus imperative to keep from ruining the action of these light rods.

CASTING RODS: DETACHABLE-HANDLE STYLE

At one time almost all casting rods had detachable handles. Detachable handles were sometimes specific to certain manufacturers of finished rods. In other cases generic-style handles, such as those from the now-defunct Featherweight company, were available, in which a special butt ferrule (available in sizes to fit all rods) was available for gluing onto the butt of a blank, the standard (usually ⅜-inch) ferrule fitting into a special handle collet. Fuji followed with a similar style with a plastic ferrule, and some modern versions of these are still available. Fenwick had a similar style and function handle.

Today virtually all these designs are gone from the market, although if you find one of the older type of detachable handles and the appropriate ferrule, you can still build one. Most casting and spin-cast rods today are one-piece with a through-built blank running through the handle or in two-piece styles with a center ferrule as with most spinning rods. Occasionally you can find a so-called spinning/fly model rod in which the detachable handle reverses end to end to make a handle that will take a fly reel for fly casting or, when reversed, a spinning reel for spinning.

In the original design, what you had was a casting rod that might vary from 5 to 6½ feet, with a long one-piece blank and a separate handle. The handle included the grip, reel seat, and the female ferrule or collet to receive the blank ferrule. Most grips were vinyl, with a plastic or graphite-fill trigger reel seat and collet. Grips were available in pistol grip or straight trigger style, and in one- and two-handed casting lengths. I've seen some handles with cork grips, but these and all such handles are rare at this writing. Note that even during their popularity two decades ago, the handles and ferrules of Fuji, Featherweight, and Fenwick were not interchangeable.

The advantage of these rods was that rod building involved only wrapping the guides and gluing the ferrule or butt adapter in place. The handle fit onto the adapter and was bought, not built. There was a slight fishing advantage for the traveling angler: Since the handle could be detached, the one-piece rod blank could be stored easily in a slim travel-rod case or PVC-tubing case. Because the handle was removed (and because the handle makes up most of the bulk in a rod like this), you could get more rods in the case without risk of damage. The handles were easily stored and carried in a duffle bag or suitcase. Construction and assembly of a detachable casting rod was thus simple.

Rods were built simply and quickly by marking the spine, gluing (using a 24-hour epoxy glue) the appropriate adapter or ferrule onto the butt end. Then the guide were positioned and wrapped in place. After which (or before, if preferred) the tip-top was glued to the end of the rod. The guides could be one-foot or two-foot style. Often this choice was made based on the power of the rod. Light rods were and are best with one-foot guides; medium to heavy rods better stand the strain with two-foot guides. Make sure you have enough guides, based on guide-spacing charts. Cover the wraps with two coats of color preserver and then one coat of epoxy rod finish. Allow the finish to cure 24 hours before using the rod.

CASTING RODS WITH PERMANENT HANDLE

With both commercial and custom-build rods, this is how casting and spin-cast rods are made today. The butt cap, rear grip, reel seat, and foregrip are all mounted on the rod blank and then the guides wrapped on and finished.

Casting rods of this style might be one-piece or two-piece center-ferruled rods, but the handle is a part of the rod, not separate. There are different choices of handle style. In the simplest styles, the handle kits are available from component suppliers, or it is possible to choose and custom build with grips, reel seats, and butt caps of your choice. These parts are all simply glued onto the rod. However, because every rod has a different diameter butt end, sometimes different inside diameter grips of EVA, Hypalon, or cork are necessary to fit the blank chosen for the rod being built.

The big advantage of rods such as this, together with the reel seats available today, is increased sensitivity. Many of the available reel seats are the so-called skeletal type in which the reel seat is designed to fit the rod blank so that the angler gripping the rod maintains direct finger and hand contact with the part of the rod that is exposed through the reel seat.

Another way to make permanent-handle casting rods is to use the separate handle components available from manufacturers such as PacBay and Batson and then glue them onto the blank. The blank runs through the handle (just as for the handle on the basic spinning rod in chapter 18).

Handle components vary widely. Most grips are cork in the straight style, since the pistol-grip style of the past is not much used today. The rear cork grips available vary widely, from the short one-hand-casting style to the long steelhead-and-salmon style.

Trigger reel seats with or without cork inserts are also available, as are cork foregrips.

Building a rod this way is much like building the spinning rod previously described.

Begin by marking the spine of the rod for the guide alignment. Then in turn add the handle and reel seat parts, just as you would in making a spinning rod as described in chapter 18. First glue on the preformed cork rear grip (or use foam or cork rings to make your own), then add the butt cap, glue on (with shimming if required) the reel seat, and finally glue on the short foregrip and winding check.

Wrap the guides in place, include a trim wrap at the adapter and the tip-top, and finish with two coats of color preserver and a coat of epoxy rod finish.

CASTING RODS WITH A SPIRAL GUIDE WRAP

Regardless of type, length, or style, casting (conventional casting reel) rods can be made with a spiral wrap. This design has been around a long time and periodically gets "reinvented" by someone unfamiliar with tackle history.

Basically there is nothing different about these casting rods or casting rod construction other than the fact that the guides are not wrapped onto the rod in a straight line, as they are with most other rods.

The spiral wrap begins with the first or butt guide slightly to the side of the normal guide plane of the rod, usually by about 30 degrees. The second guide is usually about 120 degrees from this normal guide plane, or about 90 degrees from the first guide. The remaining guides are placed about 180 degrees from the normal guide plane or on the bottom of the rod as the rod is held with the reel centered on top.

As the rod is cast with the normal position of the reel handles up (or down, depending on your right- or left-handedness and style of casting), the line comes off the casting reel and flows through the guide partly around the rod blank. It still casts just as well this way as with the guides lined up on top of the blank. The main advantage and purpose for this guide and rod design occurs when fighting a fish, when light tackle trolling, or when reeling in a lure. For these actions there is no possibility of line contacting the rod blank, since the guides are positioned to prevent this and the guides along the tip end of the rod are basically underneath the rod as they are with spinning tackle. While this design is mentioned again in chapters 21 and 22, there is no real difference in wrapping on these guides or building these rods other than the careful positioning of the guides spiraling around the rod to prevent line contact.

POPPING RODS

Popping rods are nothing more than very tough saltwater casting rods. They are usually about 6 to 7 feet long with a stiff power and designed for heavy saltwater lures for inshore fishing for big fish such as snook, tarpon, shark, stripers, and redfish. Most are in one piece, though some two-piece models are available. They are built just as are the rods using handle components. Any differences between these and standard casting rods of the same construction are in the components, which are tougher and heavier for the rougher fishing. Heavier two-foot guides are a must for the heavier fishing and line stress. Large guides are also helpful, even with these casting rods, because this type of fishing often requires a heavy line and a doubled leader and line and shock leader, resulting in knots that must clear the tip-top and upper guides. Thus a size 12 or 16 ring is often the smallest used on these rods. They also have thick handles with a rear grip slightly longer than found on one-handed casting grip rods. These rods also usually include larger trigger-style reel seats.

SPIN-CAST RODS

Spin-cast rods are very similar to casting rods but often have a slightly larger (by one size) butt or stripper guide. Another difference sometimes found is the use of a recessed or lowered reel seat to better allow for gripping and palming the spin-cast reels used. With the permanent handles on rods today, this requires a reel with the lowest possible profile to fit the reel and for the casting style required. Other than that, spin-cast rods are built about the same way as casting rods. They can be in one piece or two pieces.

LIGHT FLY RODS

Although there is no real separation between "light" and "heavy" in fly rods, those that are designed to throw up to 7-weight lines can be considered light. Thus the components must be lightweight and designed for the angler, the rod, and the fishing. Fly-rod reel seats for these rods can be as simple as a graphite-fill or aluminum-barrel seat or as fancy as those with nickel silver hoods and exotic-wood barrel inserts.

Grips should always be cork—foam and other materials do not transfer energy as well, lack sensitivity from the blank, and lack good loop control on the forward cast. Cork rings or preformed grips can be used in standard shapes as preferred.

Guides can be snake or the small one-foot ceramic-ring guides—traditionalists will opt for the snake guides, though these will wear in time and require replacement. Best of these snake guides are those with a hard chromed finish that will provide the maximum long wear. Guide sizes must be chosen with care. Too large a snake guide is not necessary and on the lightest rods may even slow the action. Too small a guide, however, will restrict the flow of the thick fly line through the guides and thus limit casting distance, the ability to shoot the line on the cast, and double-hauling. The current trend is to make and fish with very light fly rods that will take the lightest possible lines, such as 3- and even 2-weight. For these you need the lightest possible snake guides, thin cork grips, and even skeletal reel seats that consist of a cork base and sliding rings to hold the reel. Another way to cut the weight on fly rods is to use looped-ring single-foot guides that reduce the amount of thread on the guide, since only one foot per guide has to be wrapped instead of two.

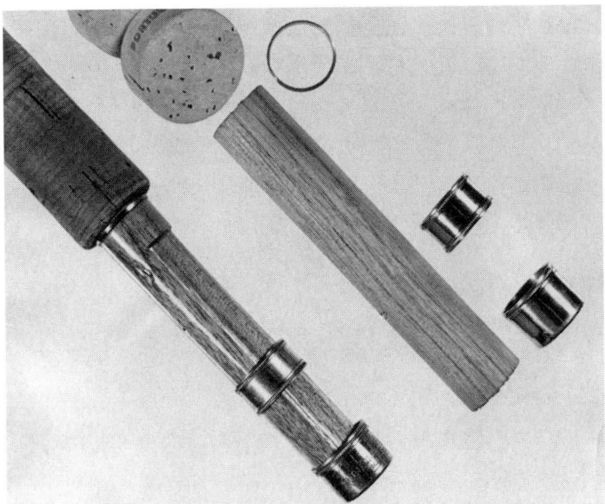

Typical light reel seat used on a very light fly rod. This reel seat uses metal sliding bands to hold the reel instead of locking nuts.

Examples of fly-rod reel seats include down-locking (far right) and up-locking models with aluminum and wood inserts. Some, such as the third from left, have a built-in extension butt.

Examples of other fly-rod reel seats. The one on the far right has sliding hoods rather than the locking-nut hoods as shown on the other three reel seats.

Assembly of a Light Fly Rod

First determine the spine, and mark the rod sections accordingly. Then, since a fly rod has the reel seat below the grip, glue the reel seat in place. You will usually have to shim this for most fly rods, although if you use a reel seat with a wood-insert barrel, this is usually minimal and may not be necessary. If you work with a wood-insert reel seat in which the parts are separate (that is, the fixed hood, wood barrel, and threaded portion with sliding hood and lock nut), glue the reel seat together first and then glue the completed assembly onto the rod. In all cases make sure the butt of the rod blank seats all the way to the bottom of the reel seat. Use a good 24-hour epoxy or similar strong glue.

Next, if you are using a preformed cork grip, make sure the grip is reamed out to comfortably fit the blank. Glue the cork grip onto the blank using a strong glue, and tape the reel seat and the cork grip ends to prevent glue from contacting finished surfaces of the grip or reel seat. If you are not using a preformed cork grip, ream and glue in place the cork rings necessary to make the grip. Immediately wipe up any excess glue from the cork grip. Once the glue is cured, place the rod in a lathe and use successively finer grades of sandpaper to shape the grip. Pick from among the various shapes such as a full wells, half wells, half wells placed on reverse, cigar, Western, and straight.

Glue on a winding check. Mark the rod for the guide spacing, and wrap the guides in place with light thread. Size A thread would be standard for most rods; if it is available, use 2/0 thread for the very lightest models. Glue the tip-top in place and add trim wraps at the ferrules and just above the winding check. Add and wrap a hook-keeper if desired (this is traditional on most rods). Finish with two coats of color preserver and one coat of rod finish.

HEAVY FLY RODS

Building heavy fly rods (those of size 8 and over, for this discussion) is no different than building light fly rods except in the choices of the components used. For example, heavier reel seats are used, along with stouter (usually thicker and slightly longer) cork grips, larger guides, and more and larger stripper guides. The same reel seats are used, along with similar types of preformed grips. The choice of snake guides or one-foot ceramic-ring guides also remains. Often you will want to go to a slightly larger tip-top ring for better clearance of the line and shooting ability on the cast. Such larger ring tip-tops are available from several companies such as PacBay and Batson. Other than this, the steps in building are exactly the same.

There is one exception: the very heavy saltwater or tarpon rod. These rods are designed for sight-fishing, in which a cast is not made until the fish is sighted (usually); thus these rods are built for strength and power, not all-day-long casting ease. They are built on powerful blanks with good lifting power. The reel seats are heavy duty, often like the larger sizes of Fuji, PacBay, and Batson reel seats designed for such fishing. It is also possible to find a suitable butt cap to use with a larger style spinning-type reel seat built of anodized aluminum throughout, with double-locking nuts and extra length to accommodate the longer reel foot of saltwater fly reels. Handles are also thicker and longer to prevent hand cramps during the long fights that occur with any hookup of a big fish. In some cases heavy fly rods even have a small additional grip above the handle as an added grip for lifting big fish out of deep water and into release or gaffing range. Often there are three stripper guides, sometimes beginning with a 16 or 20 ring size for better clearance of the line when the fish is hooked and first takes off and before the surplus line is in the water or on the reel. Snake guides are traditional running size 6 guides attached along the full length of the rod and culminating with the largest tip-top available (largest ring) for line clearance. Some anglers even use the braced-frame tip-tops traditionally used for spinning rods because of their greater strength and larger ring size.

Construction is exactly the same as for light fly rods, including the use of strong 24-hour curing glues for the tremendous pressures and strains exerted on the equipment. If a lifting grip is added, it will be glued in place on the rod immediately after building on the handle and before any guides are wrapped on the butt section.

FLY RODS WITH EXTENSION BUTTS

Heavy fly rods are sometimes built with permanent or removable extension butts. In some cases this is easy; in others a little more care is required. The easy part is when the reel seat purchased includes a permanent extension butt.

In this case the reel seat is glued onto the rod exactly as for any other reel seat. If the extension butt is a removable one that is part of or an option to a reel seat, then you must use care in building the rod.

First the male portion of the extension butt that fits into the reel seat (it may screw in or slip in with O-ring fit, depending on style) must have clearance to fit. Thus the rod blank *cannot* extend all the way to the base of the reel seat, because this will not allow insertion of the extension butt.

First measure the length of insertion of this portion of the extension butt, add about ¼ inch, and then cut back the rod blank by this amount on the butt end. This is assuming you are working with identical-length sections of two- or multipiece fly rods. Failure to make this cut back will result in the end of the reel seat extending perhaps 1 to 2½ inches beyond the length of the other sections. Glue the reel seat onto the rod blank, but be sure to leave clearance for the extension butt as outlined above.

Most reel seats made for this option have an all aluminum barrel; the wood-insert types with the threaded barrels, even in an up-locking mode, would not be strong enough to hold the extension butt were it really needed.

Example of a homemade extension butt made by adding a handle to a wooden dowel and then sizing the dowel to fit into the butt of the reel seat. An open-end reel seat or one with a removable rubber butt cap is required.

You can also make your own slip-in extension butt by building up cork rings (for the grip part) on a suitably sized dowel that is in turn cut on a lathe to friction-fit into the open-end barrel of an aluminum reel seat (more on this in chapter 20). In this case you still have to leave clearance in the barrel of the reel seat for the full insert section of the extension butt.

BOAT RODS

The term "boat rod" is a catchall term, since it can be argued that any rod used from a boat is a boat rod. In the parlance of most angling, however, a boat rod is a heavy rod, usually for salt water, often simply built, and designed for a variety of heavy and utility boat-fishing tasks from trolling to bottom-bouncing to chumming to drift fishing.

Often boat rods have simple wood handles, and it is this style of rod we are discussing. There are two ways to build these rods. One is to use a separate handle, in which the reel seat is attached to the wood handle with a mushroom butt cap on the bottom, and a ferrule—with or without a locking collet nut—included to fit the blank to the handle assembly. Construction is just like that for a detachable-handle casting rod.

Glue the ferrule onto the butt end of the rod blank, and add a foregrip of foam or cork. Foam is the most common and readily usable material for these rods. Finish by wrapping the guides in place. Because ferrules usually come in only one size to fit the upper part or sleeve of the reel seat, you may have to shim the blank to fit the ferrule (details are covered in chapter 20). In some cases the wood butt and the reel seat are separate and the reel seat must be glued onto the wood handle. In this case use a 24-hour epoxy glue to glue these parts, and make sure the grain in the wood handle is lined up on a plane with the reel-seat hood for maximum strength. Once the reel seat is glued onto the handle, glue the blank onto the ferrule and wrap the guides in place.

Another possible construction method involves the use of wood handles that have been drilled so that the handle is glued directly onto the blank. Naturally you must choose the right blank for each of these applications. In making a 7-foot rod, for example, you would choose a blank of about 5½ feet to fit onto a ferrule to make up a 7-foot rod with an 18-inch handle, whereas you would need a 7-foot rod for the straight through-the-handle construction. Since handles are not drilled for each specific size and taper of rod blank, you must often shim the blank slightly to achieve this fit.

Guides used on boat rods are typically two-foot, heavy-frame boat-rod guides, although sometimes rollers are found. Also, it is not uncommon to have a boat rod with a double-roller stripper and roller tip-top but with ring guides on the rest of the rod or a rod with ring guides exclusively but a roller tip-top. When you wrap these guides, it is best to use an underwrap, though the functional necessity of this will vary with rod power and function. Heavy rods should have an underwrap; lighter boat rods can have it but generally do not require it. The guides must be protected with color preserver and rod finish.

Making offshore and boat rods requires additional attention to strength in assembled parts. This gimbal butt cap from AFTCO has special grooves on the inside for additional glued strength.

OFFSHORE TROLLING RODS: ONE-PIECE

The construction of offshore trolling rods is really identical to that of boat rods, with a few exceptions. First, in most cases the one-piece rods are about 7 feet long, which is standard for most offshore trolling and boat rods.

To build a rod this way, first check the rod blank for the spine and mark it for guide placement. Assuming that you have a wood or aluminum handle, glue the butt cap or gimbal knock onto the end of the handle. Use 24-hour epoxy glue for this, following instruction earlier for gluing butt caps. Then use 24-hour epoxy glue and earlier instructions to glue the reel seat onto the handle. Do this by smearing glue on both the inside of the reel seat and the outside of the reel-seat recess on the handle. Coat the shimmed rod blank with 24-hour epoxy, and insert and glue it into the handle assembly. (For this, shim the rod blank to fit the drilled hole in the handle. Smear the bottom 18 inches of the blank with glue, and slide the blank into place in the handle.) With the rod blank in place, finish the handle assembly by adding a cork (preformed or cork rings built up and sanded smooth) or foam (EVA or Hypalon) grip onto the rod above the reel seat as a foregrip. After this, position the guides. Generally roller guides are used for offshore trolling rods, with a double roller used for the first or stripper guide and single rollers for the rest. Often these are sold in sets of five and are specifically designed for most trolling rods of this length. Wrapping roller guides requires an underwrap first, followed by a guide wrap and sometimes even a double wrap for very heavy rods. See chapter 22 for more details.

Once the guides are wrapped in place, protect them with color preserver and two coats of rod finish.

OFFSHORE TROLLING RODS: DETACHABLE-HANDLE STYLE

These rods are more typical today, since most offshore anglers are using rods with detachable blanks from the handles. Offshore trolling rods with detachable butts are far more common than one-piece models. Many use an AFTCO or similar aluminum butt, either straight or curved (curved only in the heavy-duty models). Since the detachable handle takes up about 18 inches, rod blanks for this style of rod are about 5½ to 6 feet long.

Construction is the same as for a detachable-handle casting rod or detachable-handle boat rod. The butt is usually all aluminum, with an inclusive reel seat. Some butts do not include the reel seat, and for them a reel seat must be glued on. In all cases the handle or reel seat takes a slip-on or usually collet locked-down ferrule; the ferrule and collet nut are a permanent part of the butt end of the rod blank. To build this type of rod, first glue the reel seat onto the aluminum butt, if the reel seat is not included. Then glue the ferrule (with collet nut and any O-rings or washers) onto the butt end of the rod blank, shimming at this point with fiberglass tape if required. Use a very strong or epoxy glue for this step, because this joint will be under tremendous pressure and strain during trolling and especially during a fight. Often the ferrules used for these heavy rods have a slot that is keyed to a pin in the handle to prevent turning and torquing. If this is the case, make sure the ferrule is lined up properly so that the spine of the rod is properly aligned for guide placement and the slot in the ferrule is aligned with the pin in the handle for proper alignment.

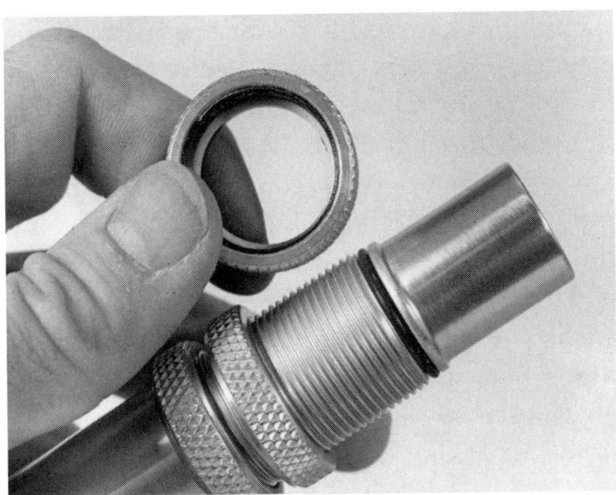

To guard against corrosion from salt water, this AFTCO collet on a reel seat/handle assembly has O-rings and special seals to prevent water intrusion into the collet/reel seat joint.

Add a foregrip to the blank. Foam is typically used, although on some very heavy rods a leather wrapping over cork is preferred because it is firmer and provides a better grip. Flocking a cork handle is another possibility.

At one time guides for most offshore rods (both one-piece and detachable grip/reel seat) were roller guides from companies such as AFTCO and Fin Nor. Today more and more anglers are switching back to hard ring guides for their offshore rods. As one angler told me, "The worse thing in the world for big-game fishing is to have a roller guide that won't roll. And I don't need something else in my fishing tackle that I have to maintain." He makes a good point, since even with bearings and bushings, rollers do have to roll to be effective and not damage line. Many anglers today, at least for rods up to fifty-pound class, are using ring guides. Some are using ring tip-tops, although roller tip-tops are still popular.

For these guides, those that are two foot, with heavy reinforced frames, are best for the heavy-duty work of offshore angling for big gamefish.

As with roller guides, using five or six is usually standard, although this can be varied at will when the rod is being built. Stand-up rods (covered later) often have a few more guides for the tip action of the heavy rods used and typically use ring guides rather than roller guides.

Once the grip is in place, position the guides on the rod, add an underwrap to the rod at these spots, and then wrap the roller guides in place using a single or double wrap. Coat with color preserver, allow the preserver to dry, and then protect the rod with a rod finish.

STAND-UP RODS

Stand-up rods are a new design of trolling rod in which the angler stands up to fight the fish, holding the rod in a specially designed harness and on a special belt that holds the gimbal at the butt end of the rod.

These can be built as one- or two-piece rods using the same methods used for trolling rods. There are a few differences, however. First the rods usually have a different action, with more flex at the tip end. The design is to allow for flexion to place the fish under constant pressure, with power occurring in the butt of the rod for lifting the fish and levering it in when pumping. The result is that the rod requires more guides, particularly at the upper end. Often seven guides will be used in place of the five typically used with a standard trolling rod. The roller guides (or ring guides), wrap, and underwrap requirements are the same.

The second difference is that the butt sections are slightly shorter for the stand-up fishing than are the butt sections on rods used for fighting fish from a fighting chair. Most are about 2 inches shorter, but this will vary. Rod-handle manufacturers such as AFTCO have responded to this with handle models that are shorter and designed for stand-up fishing. These rods usually have detachable handles, and construction of the rod with these parts is exactly the same as for trolling rods.

NOTES ON MICROGUIDE RODS

The most recent development in guides are the so called "microguides" now being produced by manufacturers such as Fuji, Batson, and PacBay. These are basically very small, single-foot guides for use on casting and—with a proper butt guide—spinning rods.

The sizes of these microguides range from as small as a nominal 3.5 (Fuji) or 4 (PacBay or Batson). The true internal diameter ring sizes are smaller than these nominal guide sizes, with a size 3.5 ring having a true internal diameter of 2.14 millimeters in some guides.

Being small, these guides are very lightweight compared to other standard guides. Most standard guides have a minimal size of about a 6-millimeter ring size, with about a 4-millimeter internal diameter.

Because of their small size and the low frame holding the tiny ring, more of these microguides are required on a rod than are the more standard guides. Even with more guides, this still reduces the weight of the total guides on the rod and thus the total rod weight. It also increases the sensitivity of the rod.

Note that the guide formulas and charts in chapter 21 are for standard guides. A good general starting point for microguides is that you should use about 50 percent more guides than recommended for standard guides on a rod. Thus for a casting rod where six standard guides might be recommended, perhaps nine would be better for the microguides. These guides have to be closer together, which allows the rod to still flex completely but with less contact of the line with the blank than if the microguides were used with standard guide spacing. Obviously, preventing line contact with the rod is a good thing.

Microguides are also starting to be used with spinning tackle now, but with one major difference. This difference is the necessity of a larger funneling or choking guide at the butt end (the first guide through which the line travels) to choke down the line from coils coming off the spinning reel spool to a straight or almost straight line going through the guides. Once the line is choked down and funneled to a straight line, the smaller guides are fine. At this writing, developments and experiments of a suitable high-frame, small-ring butt guide for matching these microguides on spinning tackle are taking place. The best possible design may be available as this book comes off the press or should be available shortly.

20

Handle and Grip Assembly

Introduction • Tools and Materials • Professional Tips • Glue Mixing and Application • Cork Grips • Foam Grips • Decorative Foam Grip Work • Foam Core/Graphite Sleeve Grips• Graphite Grips • Wood Grips • Aluminum Grips • Plastic and Acrylic Grips • Cord and Wrapped Grips • Cork-Tape Grips • Miscellaneous Grips, Reel Seats, and Variations • Butt-Cap Assembly • Reel-Seat Mounting • Ferrules and Adapters

INTRODUCTION

It seems as if everyone looks at the guide wraps on a rod, yet little attention is paid to the handle or grip and reel seat assembly. Although perhaps not as decorative and colorful as the fancy wraps, these parts are still vital to any good custom rod. A mistake made here can be costly in terms of rod performance. It can also be difficult or impossible to repair. For example, a loose reel seat on a rod is almost impossible to repair without tearing apart the whole handle assembly or drilling one or more holes into the reel seat to inject glue. The drilled holes mar the finish and look of the completed rod. Doing nothing results in an outfit where the reel will rotate out of line with the guides as the reel seat slides around the rod while the angler is fishing or fighting a trophy. A well-mounted and firmly glued reel seat is a must for solid rod function.

Although there are many handle types used for many different types of rods, there are some basics in construction. Using the right glues, having the right tools (though few are needed), using the right shim materials for reel seats, and taking time for all the steps necessary to build the handle correctly are vital to a good job.

TOOLS AND MATERIALS

A complete discussion of tools for tackle crafting can be found in chapters 1 and 2. Here is brief rundown of tools you may wish to consider for making handles:

Rod-handle seater. These are available commercially, or you can build one as outlined in chapter 2. It allows seating of foam grips made of EVA, Hypalon, and similar materials. It can be as simple as a piece of shelving board with a hole in the center slightly larger than the diameter of the blank at the point where the grip finally seats. A second possibility is a board with a series of different size holes. A third possibility is an 18-inch-long board in which a long V is cut from one end; this tapered slot is slipped over the rod blank and used to push the foam grip in place.

Note: If you use this tool be sure to leave some clearance around the V—do not shove it up until it fits the blank tightly. The blank is

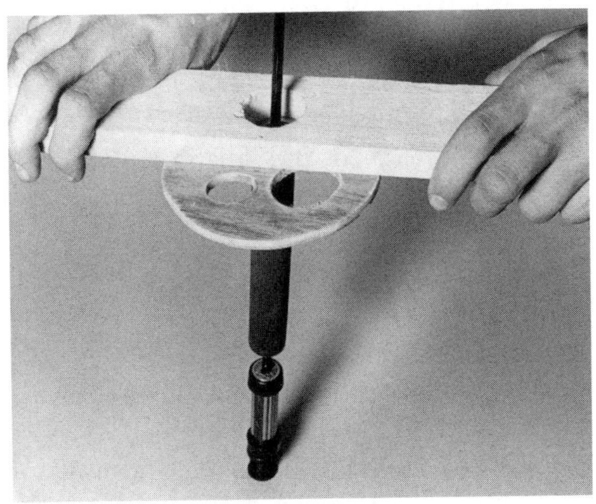

A board with holes in it to fit the blank is ideal for pressing foam grips into place. Here a board with a disc holding a series of different size holes is used to push a foam grip onto a rod.

tapered, and pushing down with the V tight at the top can jam the board on the blank or even crack it. Also, do not cut the V close to the end of the board, because this will leave little wood as a frame, and the tool might split. A solution is to use thick plywood, because the cross-grain of the several layers will prevent splitting.

Cork-handle gluing clamp. This item also is available commercially, or you can make one by following the directions in chapter 2. It consists of two boards with holes in the center that are connected by long threaded rods or a combination of chain (adjustable with hitch clip pins) and screw eyebolts. Wing nuts allow adjustment and tightening. This tool allows firm clamping of any cork handle after the rings are glued together. It helps make for a professional job, eliminates any possibility of gaps between the cork rings, and also allows easier cleanup because the handle is glued in place on the rod.

Wood rasp. This is the first tool you will need to shape the cork rings after the gluing clamp is removed. A rasp can be used with a lathe or for removing cork by hand.

File. A number of files can be used for rod-handle work and are used mostly on cork handles where cork removal is necessary after roughening has been done with a wood rasp. Files should be 8 to 12 inches long, flat or half-round, and with a coarse or medium cut. If you don't already have one, buy a file card—a small wire brushlike tool for cleaning the file teeth. Because the teeth of files fill up rapidly with cork dust, this tool is a must.

Sandpaper. Sandpaper is necessary to finish cork grips and can be used for some shaping of cut lengths of foam grips. For cork grips you will need medium-fine and extra-fine grades. For foam grips, coarse or medium sandpaper is best for shaping the tapered and rounded ends.

Masking tape. Masking tape is a must for keeping grips clean while they are glued. Standard ¾- or 1-inch masking tape is fine for wrapping the ends of reel seats and grips to prevent oozing glue from touching the grip. After the oozing glue is cleaned off, the tape is removed and final cleaning is completed.

Reamer. Reamers are a must only when a cork grip or preformed cork grip must be enlarged to fit onto a blank. Although long commercial reamers are available, they are very expensive. The best reamers for rod building are those in which a thin strip (¼ to ½ inch wide) of coarse or medium sandpaper is wrapped around and glued onto an old scrap rod blank or tapered wood dowel.

Rotary rasper and bit extender. Rotary raspers on a ¼-inch shaft are available from any hardware store. With this you will need a 12-inch-long bit extender. The rasper fits into the bit extender and is secured with an Allen set screw. The extender has a ¼-inch shaft to fit any drill chuck.

This combination allows for hole enlargement of any foam grip. With a variable-speed hand drill (recommended) you can run this extended rasp bit into the foam hole to enlarge it. Do this carefully, since you can feel the bit working under your hand holding the foam grip. Done carefully, there is no problem of the bit drilling eccentrically and off-center.

Flex Coat pilot drill bits. These are spade drill bits to which an aluminum sleeve is added to serve as a pilot to keep the cutting part of the bit centered on the hole in the foam grip. These come in sizes ranging from 5⁄16 to ⅝ inch, and special-order sizes are available. They are ideal for drilling out foam grips to the size needed for your rod.

Contour gauge. This is the same contour gauge described for tracing the shapes of plugs and crankbaits for duplicating. It consists of a series of metal rods in a frame: The rods are pushed against the item to be traced to duplicate the item's shape. This tool can also be used for tracing or copying the shape of a cork grip.

Glues. Glues are a must for attaching a grip or reel seat to any blank. A number of different glues are available for rod building and sold for that specific purpose. A number of glues for general household or workshop purposes are also readily available from hardware and variety stores.

The best glues for cementing butt caps, reel seats, or grip materials to blanks (directly or through bushings and shims) are the strongest glues available. Usually this means standard epoxy glues, not the quick-set "5-minute" types that although quicker and easier to use, have less strength.

Good glues include any of the standard epoxies on the market, such as those by Duro, Devcon, and Flex Coat. These are all two-part; some are available in double-joined syringes for easy, accurate measuring and mixing, and all to my knowledge are a 50/50 mix.

Five-minute epoxies are similar but often not as strong. Different companies rate them differently. Of two manufacturers consulted for this book, one rated its 5-minute epoxy as 95 percent as strong as regular 24-hour epoxy; the other company rated its epoxy as 80 to 85 percent as strong.

Ribbon, paste, and clay-type epoxies are also available. They have been well received in the past by some rod builders but are generally not as strong as the standard 24-hour epoxy. The reason is that although the paste and claylike epoxies won't run and thus are handy for filling large voids and gluing reel seats in place, they also won't "wet" as well—one of the important characteristics any glue needs to form a good bond.

Paste, clay, or other high-viscosity epoxies, such as PC-7, Duro Master Mend Ribbon, and Devcon 5 Minute Epoxy Gel, can be used for roughly forming bushings that are sized to fit a blank and reel seat. Allow the epoxy to cure, and then glue the bushings to the rod blank and reel seat using standard 24-hour liquid epoxy glue.

Another problem with the high-viscosity glues is in the mixing. Even though the two parts of the mixture are two different colors to aid in determining a complete mix, they are by their nature difficult to mix completely. In the words of one manufacturing spokesman, if they are not mixed completely, "You have big problems. They don't cure well and are very messy."

Acrylic glues are also very strong—just as strong or stronger than epoxies, according to one manufacturer—but they are more difficult to work with. In short, they allow less working time. They come in two separate parts. One part, the resin, is applied to one surface; the other part, the activator, is applied to the second surface. When the two surfaces make contact, the resin and activator mix and the glue bond is complete. You do have a few seconds to adjust the parts and move them, but this is not normally time enough to adjust reel-seat-hood alignment. These glues would be impossible to use when sliding a foam or preformed cork grip in place on a blank and are best suited for gluing reel seats to bushings or butt caps to blanks or bushings. Thus, instead of mixing different glues for different parts of the assembly process, it is generally better to use epoxies throughout.

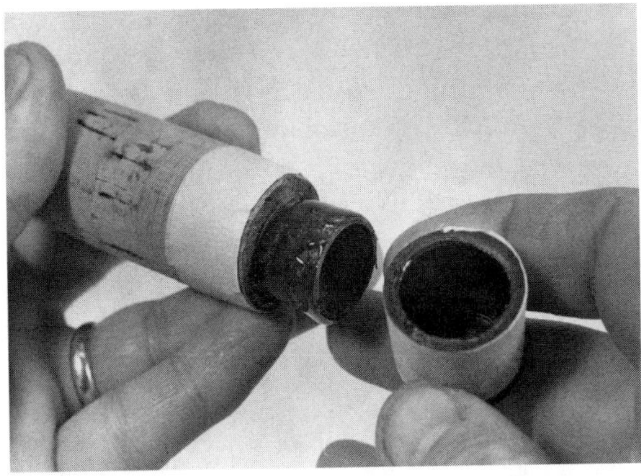

Using tape around both parts when gluing is a professional tip for gluing parts together. It is ideal for gluing on butt caps (shown), grips, reel seats, and foregrips.

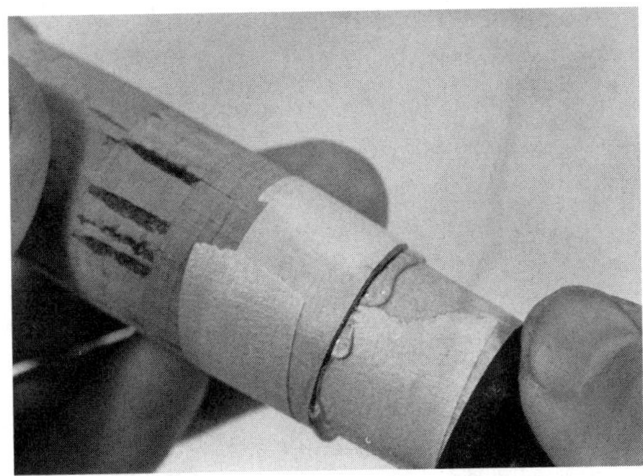

Once pressed together, any excess glue oozes out onto the previously wrapped parts. A quick cleanup with a rag, then removal of the tape, makes for clean joints.

PROFESSIONAL TIPS

There are several tips for assembling rod grips and reel seats. One of the best is to wrap two to three layers of standard ¾- to 1-inch masking tape around the end of parts that are to be joined, such as a grip and a reel seat, or a grip and a butt cap. The technique for this is to wrap the tape tightly and make sure that one edge of the tape touches the edge of the grip or reel seat. In the case of reel seats, it also helps to try to force the tape into various indentations in the reel seat, such as keyways for sliding hoods and the ends of threaded barrels. When you are wrapping around the fixed end of the reel seat, the bulk of the hood may force you to stretch the tape (masking tape is slightly flexible), or you may have to wrap as tightly as possible around the bulk of the hood but then push the masking tape into place at the edge of the reel seat. In some cases, using thinner tape, such as ¾- or ½-inch tape (available in art supply stores), in place of 1- or 2-inch tape will make this step unnecessary.

It also helps to fold over about 1 inch of tape at the end so that you have a tag end to pick up for removing the tape once the two parts are joined together.

This step must be done on both parts to be joined. The purpose is to prevent glue from marring the parts and to make cleanup quick and easy. Let's assume that you have a rear cork grip on a blank and are adding a reel seat. Tape several times around the end of both the reel seat and the cork grip. To glue the reel seat in place, you usually must shim the blank with a wrapping of thread or cord. Do this to build the blank area up to the internal diameter of the reel seat and then soak it with a good 24-hour epoxy glue. Slide the reel seat onto the blank and over the shimmed area. As you slide the reel seat in place, rotate it to spread any glue, working slowly to minimize air gaps and bubbles.

Slowly join the two parts, at which time glue will ooze out and usually build up on both the end of the reel seat and the end of the cork grip. This is the reason for the tape—the glue will be on the tape, not the grip or reel seat. Use a soft rag or paper towel to carefully remove any excess glue. Take care that glue does not get on the reel seat or cork grip while you are doing this. Once the excess glue is removed, line up the hoods of the reel seat with the glue alignment marks (the spine of the rod). Then carefully remove the tape first from one part, then from the second. This will remove all the glue that otherwise would have smeared on these parts or required a cleanup with acetone or fingernail-polish remover. (Make sure you use a fingernail-polish remover that has an acetone or ketone base—not the more environmentally friendly polish removers that are also available today.) The result is a clean, perfect joining of the two parts that requires no lengthy or special cleanup procedures.

Another tip is to sand or otherwise roughen all parts that are to be glued. First remove the gloss finish from the rod blank where any grips, butt cap, reel seat, or reel seat shims are to be placed. Because almost all rods have a glossy finish, removing this finish with steel wool or light sandpaper will give the rod more "tooth" for a better adhesion of the glue to the blank. Al Jackson, rod designer for much of the industry over his years in the business, strongly recommends fine (maroon color) 3M Scotch-Brite, because it will remove the finish without destroying the graphite or glass fibers.

Measure exactly the location of the grip, grips, or reel seat on the blank, and mark the spot with a pen or masking tape. To prevent slips and damage to the exposed portion of the blank, cover a few inches of the blank above the grip/reel seat area with masking tape. Then use fine sandpaper or steel wool to remove the gloss. Sand longitudinally, across, and at angles to assure a good roughening of this area of the blank. Do this only until the blank looks dull. The purpose is not to sand down to the fibers but only to remove the shiny finish.

Also sand or file the inside of the reel seat. Depending on the size of the reel seat, there are several ways to do this. For large reel seats such as might be used on saltwater rods, the simplest way is to wrap sandpaper around your index finger and work your finger around on the inside of the reel seat with a rotating motion to thoroughly abrade and scour the finish. Some reel seats, such as the Fuji, Batson, American Tackle, and PacBay brands, have longitudinal grooves inside to aid in gluing, but additional abrasion also helps. For small reel seats you can use a rat-tail file to abrade the inside surface or use sandpaper wrapped around a file or wood dowel. A rat-tail file can also be used to abrade the smooth surfaces sometimes encountered on the insides of some foam grips and to roughen the insides of preformed cork grips. The best way to do this is to fasten the file or dowel sander in a vise and move the reel seat against the tool rather than try to hold the reel seat (you can't clamp it—it will scratch) and work the tool at the same time.

If you are making a grip from cork rings, usually the hole in the cork will be rough enough from reaming to fit the blank. If it isn't, use a file or reamer. It also helps to slightly abrade the faces of the cork rings, laying the sandpaper and the cork-ring face flat on a work surface and sanding with a rotating motion. Make sure this is a light sanding only, however—sandpaper that's too rough might roughen the adjoining faces so much that they allow noticeable glue gaps between the rings.

Butt caps can also be roughened for better adhesion. Aluminum butt caps are easily abraded with medium sandpaper. Rubber or plastic butt caps are best abraded with coarse or rough sandpaper moved in a circular motion to scour the inside.

Another tip is to *never* touch the blank, inside the reel seat, inside the butt cap—or inside any other surface that will be glued—after you've removed the gloss finish or roughened the surface. Touching these parts at this point can introduce body oils and otherwise contaminate the blank surface so that there is poor glue adhesion. Hold the rod blank above or below the sanded point, and do not touch it or the reel seat internal diameter or any other parts to be glued.

Remove any sanding dust with a clean cloth. One good way to thoroughly clean these parts (after sanding and abrading) is to use regular drugstore isopropyl alcohol. Isopropyl alcohol is a cleaning solution for liquid epoxy glue and will not harm the blank or any of its parts or affect the glue or bond. Be sure to allow all the alcohol to evaporate before using glue.

GLUE MIXING AND APPLICATION

Two-part glues must be mixed thoroughly before use. This includes epoxies, acrylics, and any similar glues. In almost all cases the mix is 50/50, but always follow the manufacturer's instructions as to percentages or proportions by volume or weight. Most glues include mixing and application instructions in the package.

Often it helps to slightly warm the two parts of epoxy glues. Roger Seiders of Flex Coat suggests using a lightbulb or heat lamp to heat the resin and hardener to about 80 to 90 degrees Fahrenheit. This heat makes for a quicker mix and also helps reduce the micro bubbles in the mix. Too much heat, however, will make for a weaker bond.

For any glue, hold the tube or syringe upright (tip up) to allow for any air bubbles at the tip to rise. Puncture the tip or cut off the end (in the case of the syringe types).

There are several options for mixing surfaces. One is to use aluminum foil, paper, or cardboard. Some rod builders like to use the larger size Post-It notes from 3M, because these are large enough for mixing and will peel off easily for a new surface with each new mix. Cardboard is also good and, because it is stiffer than paper, will not wrinkle or fold on you as paper might. I like to use small sheets of scrap plastic cut from the sides and bottoms of milk, juice, and other disposable food and drink containers. They are smooth, easy to mix on, do not allow absorption of the glue into the mixing surface, and cost nothing.

Begin by spreading out two equal ribbons of each part of the glue on the mixing surface. If you are using the syringes, the glue is measured for you. If you are using glue supplied in separate tube containers, it's easy to roughly measure the same amounts of resin and catalyst. If you are mixing a lot of glue, spread the glue in several double ribbons instead of one long ribbon, because this will concentrate the glue and make it easier to mix.

Once the glue is spread out, your working time will be about 5 minutes for the 5-minute epoxies, and about 30 minutes to 1 hour for the 24-hour epoxies. The best spreaders are tongue depressors (though they are a little wide for this), Popsicle sticks (also called craft sticks and sold for this purpose in craft and hobby shops), craft picks (small and thin, almost like a toothpick, but about 3 to 4 inches long), and cooking skewers (available in food markets for kabob and skewer cooking and ranging from 4 to 12 inches long). I like the craft or Popsicle sticks best because they are flat and allow for easy folding, blending, and mixing. Use the mixing stick to fold back and forth, mix in circles, and even scrape along the mixing surface to thoroughly mix both parts of the glue.

Note that glue and finish expert Roger Seiders prefers to use a round plastic stirrer, such as the end of a discarded finishing brush. He claims the wood stirrers tend to add air bubbles to the mix.

With glues as well as with wrap finish, mix until all cloudiness is gone and the mixture is completely clear with no streaks or swirls. Once the glue is mixed, apply it to both surfaces to be glued. Apply it evenly, but use a thin coat; otherwise the glue might drip and run even before you get the two parts together. This method is best for gluing butt caps to rod blanks and bushings and gluing reel seats to bushings. It is not good for gluing cork rings or foam grips to the rod blank or when the internal diameter of the reel seat is close to the outside diameter of the blank. In these cases, adding glue to the lumen of the part to be slipped over the end of a rod blank will only end up smearing glue on the rod blank, which has to be cleaned up before the glue sets up and hardens. The best procedure in these cases is to add a little excess glue to the blank or bushing and then use a rotating and reciprocating (back and forth) motion on the slipover preformed grip, reel-seat cork ring, or other part to assure good wetting of that part and a good glue bond.

In gluing parts be sure to use the taping method to keep excess glue from the blank, reel seat, or grip materials.

Once the parts are glued, it is important to *immediately* line up critical parts such as the reel-seat hoods, tip-top, and perhaps the grain of wood handles. Line these up with the spine of the blank and future position of the guides. Once this is done, *do not* touch or move these parts, because the glue bond will begin to gain its strength almost immediately; in the case of 24-hour epoxies, the glue will gain 60 to 70 percent strength within the first few hours. Often it is best to prop the rod blank straight up, using masking tape to attach it to a workbench temporarily while the glue cures overnight.

Heat has often been suggested for increasing strength and decreasing curing time with glues. Heat will decrease curing time because it will increase the catalytic reaction. It may also *slightly* increase the strength, although glue technicians have different opinions on this. Some suggest there is no real strength advantage; others claim there is a slight increase in strength with the molecular changes caused by the heat. The decrease in curing time is generally not important, because overnight curing is not really an inconvenience. All glue technicians agree that *too much* heat will *decrease* the strength of a bond. Most who recommend heat suggest using temperatures of from 100 degrees Fahrenheit to 120 degrees maximum. Higher than that will weaken the bond and cause it to become brittle and shrink somewhat—causing the two parts to separate. Some ways to heat include using heat lamps, any lightbulb at close range, a 250-watt photoflood lamp kept several feet away, or even a hair dryer propped to blow hot air onto the glued area.

Epoxy cleanup can be easily accomplished when it is still liquid using acetone or isopropyl (regular rubbing) alcohol. Acetone is more expensive, more difficult to get, and more dangerous to use (because of the fumes and the chance of skin contact), and when used in excess it can dissolve or react with the resins used in the gel coat of a rod blank, possibly ruining the blank. Alcohol will not create such a reaction and will clean up any spilled glue equally well. Using a rag dampened with alcohol (or acetone), wipe rapidly and firmly to remove the liquid glue *before* it sets up.

CORK GRIPS

Cork grips are made from cork rings ½ inch thick (some ¼-inch rings are available) and are available in diameters of 1⅛, 1¼, and 1½ inches. Occasionally 2-inch-diameter rings are available for extra-heavy rods and surf rods. Buy the best-quality cork rings possible. There are no standard cork-industry terms for the best-quality rings, but catalogs will usually indicate quality, as will the price of the rings. Cork can be used for shimming reel seats, in which case lower quality, less-expensive rings can be used.

Buy cork rings that are larger than the diameter of the cork grip you intend to make. Regardless of the care you exercise, the cork rings will not line up exactly and will have to be rasped and sanded into final form and shape. Use 1⅛-inch-diameter cork rings for fly rods; 1¼-inch rings for spinning, casting, spin-cast, and most freshwater rods, some heavy fly rods, and light-tackle saltwater rods; 1½-inch rings for heavy boat rods, medium to heavy saltwater rods, and medium surf rods; and 2-inch rings for the heaviest of offshore rods (80- and 130-pound class) and very heavy surf and specialty rods. It is best to choose rings with the smallest available hole size, because it is far easier to ream out a ring to fit a blank than to build up or shim the blank to fit a large-hole ring. The exception to this might be with heavy rods or heavy surf rods; the diameters on these are large, and a larger ring hole will mean less reaming and rasping.

Unless just making one rod or making a rod very occasionally, I like to buy cork rings in bags of one hundred at a time, since this will be the lowest bulk price. If making a lot of rods, try to buy cork rings in larger quantities to get a lower bulk price. I also buy rings in the largest outside diameter for the rods that I will be making and the smallest hole diameter for possible use on a light graphite fly rod. If I am only going to make spinning, casting, and fly rods, the largest rings I buy are 1¼ inch. To make large-grip surf rods, offshore rods with cork foregrips, etc., I would buy rings in 1½- or 2-inch outside diameter. For making a lot of different rods of varying handle sizes, consider getting a bag or pack of bulk rings in several sizes each of the outside diameter required and with a small inside diameter to fit any rod blank.

Steps in adding cork rings to make a grip are simple, yet some tips will make it easier. Begin by selecting top-quality rings, two for each inch of grip length. Slide the ring over the blank to the handle area to check for size. Remove the ring and ream it to fit, checking frequently on the blank to get a snug but not too-tight fit. Use a pencil or pen to number this ring (number it 1) on its face. Repeat with each ring in turn, and continue numbering to keep the rings in order. The rings should be kept in order because the taper of the rod blank will dictate a slightly different internal diameter for each ring.

Using a reamer to ream out each cork ring to fit the rod blank.

Once all the rings are reamed to fit, they are ready to slide in place, usually butting up against a butt cap (as with a rear grip) or reel seat (as with a foregrip). Wrap several layers of masking tape around these parts so that the glue used does not touch the reel seat or butt cap and the joint can be cleaned as previously outlined.

Use a good bonding glue, such as 24-hour epoxy glues, Flex Coat Rod Builders Epoxy Glue, U-40 Rod Bond, or U-40 Cork Bond. I like the epoxies best for the general bonding of all handle, reel-seat, and grip parts. After mixing the glue (if necessary) according to directions, smear a light coating onto the blank in the grip area. Do *not* place any on the cork rings or into the cork-ring hole, which will only smear glue onto the blank as you slide the ring in place.

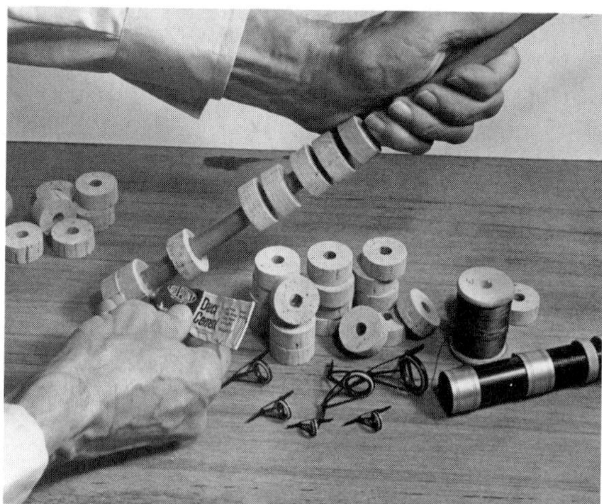

Gluing cork rings onto a rod blank.

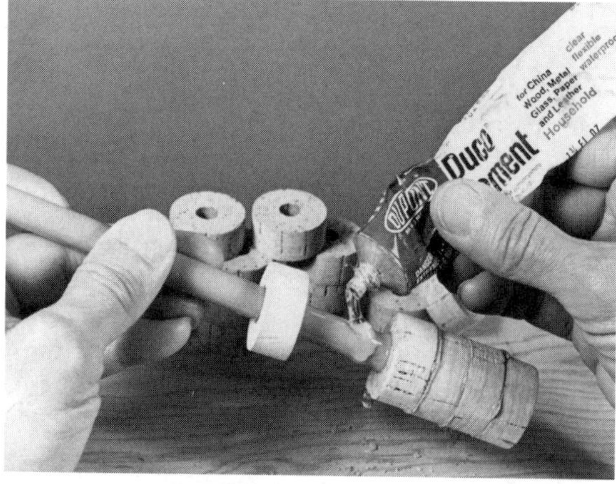

For proper gluing, each cork ring must be glued to the rod blank and to adjacent cork rings. Once all the corks are added, excess glue must be wiped off and the grip allowed to cure.

With the glue *on the blank,* slide the first ring onto the blank, twisting and rotating it to assure good glue adhesion to the blank. Once the first ring is in place against the reel seat or butt cap, use a cloth or paper towel to wipe any excess glue off the masking tape. This will prevent the glue from flowing onto the covered part and making cleanup more difficult. Slide the second ring in place, but before seating it against the first ring, smear a small amount of glue onto the adjoining faces of the two rings. Bring the rings into contact with each other and twist them together to assure good bonding. It also helps to use a push-board such as that used for pushing foam grips into place. This tool can be made with the hole in the center of the board, with different-sized U-shaped slots in a side, or with a long V-slot cut into the long side. Any of these variations will work well.

Continue with each ring in its turn until the grip is complete. At this point wipe up any excess glue from the cork rings, again wipe the glue from the masking tape, and then remove the masking tape.

While it's not absolutely necessary, it helps to use a gluing clamp on the grip during the curing process. The clamp can be used just on the grip itself or can be extended from the upper end of the cork-ring grip to the end of the rod. Tighten the grip and wipe it free of any glue that oozes out from between the cork rings. Do *not* overtighten—this will squeeze glue out from between the cork faces and could lessen the strength of the glue bond.

If desired, an additional step can be taken for more strength in the grip. Cut each cork ring with a slight bevel or taper on each face for an additional gluing surface in this area. To do this, size and ream each cork ring and then, using a countersink or small half-round file, cut a bevel into each ring face on each side. This slight bevel allows for a buildup of glue at the cork and blank junction for greater bonding strength. Be sure to add a little (not too much) glue to this area and to twist each new ring against the adjoining one to spread the glue for maximum bonding.

Another good tip is to use a triangular file to cut several (three or four) grooves on the inside of the hole in each cork ring so that there is a buildup of glue in this area to keep the bond from breaking free and the ring—and grip—from rotating on the rod blank. Both of these steps can be used for additional bonding. Just be sure that you do not make too much of a bevel or too deep a groove, which will prevent contact of the cork internal diameter with the blank.

Once the cork grip is cured, remove the clamp. There are several ways to finish the cork grip. One is to place the rod into a lathe, making sure you have plenty of rollers to support the rod blank and prevent it from whipping around (and breaking) as you turn the grip down. Also, even though you have rollers on a lathe, wrap the blank with several layers of masking tape at the blank/roller contact point to protect the blank finish. That way the taped blank, not a bare blank, runs on the rollers. It helps if you have a lathe with rollers that surround the blank to prevent it from coming loose. The usual arrangement is to have two rollers for the blank to ride on, with an additional one or two above the blank to hold it down and prevent it from jumping out and whipping around. Turn the lathe on at the lowest possible speed to see if the rod blank will run without whipping. Then gradually increase the speed. Once the lathe is running at the right speed, begin shaping the cork.

Note: Although any lathe speed can be used, manufacturers use about 3,500 rpm for shaping cork. Keep in mind that cork is an extremely abrasive material that will dull cutting tools quickly. If you are using a cutting tool, be sure to check it frequently and to keep it sharp.

One of the best ways to shape cork is with a rasp or file. To do this, with the blank secured in the lathe, first use a rasp or coarse file along the length of the cork grip to bring the rings to a uniform diameter. Then use the same tools to lightly shape the cork grip into the desired shape. For spinning and casting rods, this will likely be a smooth uniform cylinder or fat cigar shape. For fly rods there are a number of choices of grip shape, including full wells, half wells, cigar, reverse half wells, Western, and Payne. Do *not* take the cork down to the final diameter desired. Since the rasp or file is rough, you will need to use successively finer grades of sandpaper to smooth the grip. Stop the initial shaping when the grip is about 1/8 to 3/6 inch larger in diameter than the final size desired. Be sure to stop the lathe before checking the diameter with a template, calipers, or rule.

Methods of assuring that cork rings are securely glued to the rod blank include cutting three or four grooves into the hole in the ring (left) or cutting a bevel (right, using a countersink as shown) into the two edges of the ring. Both methods assure a bead of glue at these points to lock the cork ring in place.

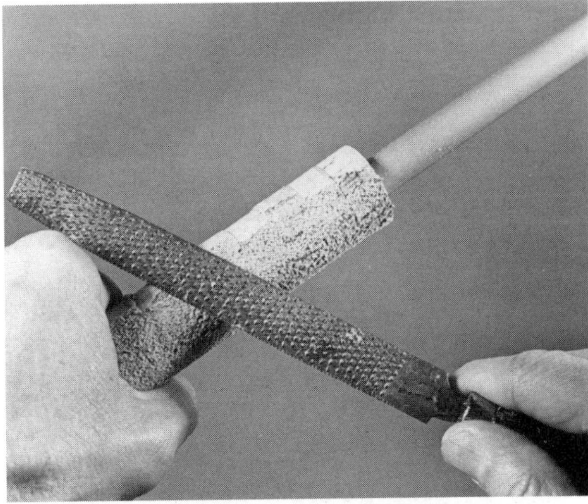

Using a rasp is one easy way to remove excess cork when shaping the grip. Follow directions in the text to remove cork evenly around the perimeter of the grip.

A small simple lathe can also be used for making cork grips. The tools and materials needed are shown.

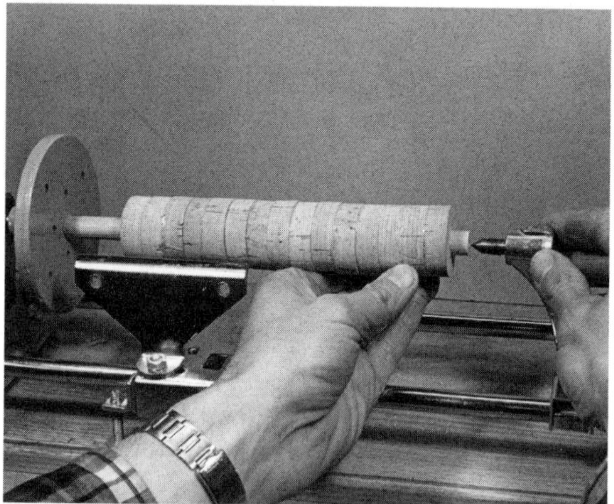

Cork rings glued to a wood dowel are mounted in the lathe.

Using a rasp for initial shaping of the cork grip.

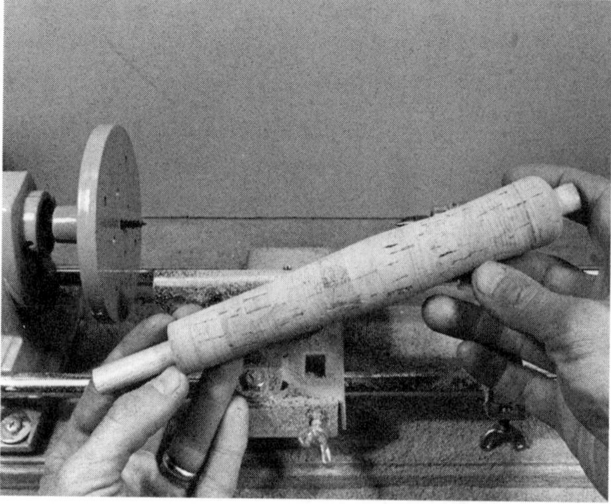

Finished shaped cork grip on wood dowel. The dowel is then removed to glue the grip onto a rod blank.

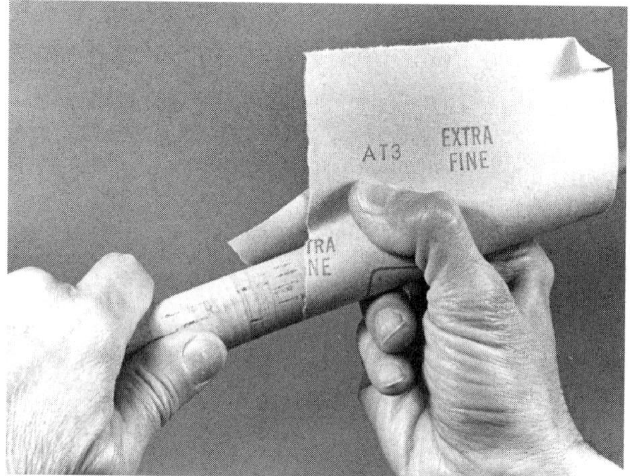

Successively finer grades of sandpaper are best to polish the cork grip.

Once you have the general shape, start the lathe again and use medium sandpaper on the grip, then switch to finer grades until you are using the finest possible grade for the smoothest finish. A tip from lathe woodworkers is to finish by using the lathe dust and the backing of the sandpaper to get the smoothest finish.

One tip, which I hope will not be necessary, involves the possibility of uncovering a pit in the cork while initially turning the cork to shape. If this occurs, stop and fill the pit with a mixture of cork dust and glue, but do not use the very hard glues, such as epoxies. Mix the dust and glue, and fill the pit to slightly overflowing to allow for some shrinkage. Allow this to cure overnight and then continue the shaping, using the lathe tools and sandpaper. Use care, because some glues are so hard that the cork around the filling will cut away, leaving a "bump" of filler in the grip. If the repair is done right, the patched area will be as smooth and level as the rest of the grip.

Another way to do this is to wait until the cork grip is complete and smooth and then fill the pit with the cork-dust-and-glue mixture and allow it to cure overnight. Sand to shape using an emery board. The stiff emery board allows sanding in the immediate area so that you do not affect the previously shaped grip, as well as rapid shaping and finishing. Begin with the coarse side of the emery board; finish with the fine side.

If you do not have access to a lathe, you can shape a cork grip with hand tools. First use a rasp to remove cork, using even strokes from one end of the grip to the other. Do this along one part of the cork grip so that you slightly flatten that side. Then turn the grip over 180 degrees and do the same on the opposite side. Now turn the cork grip 90 degrees and remove cork again to slightly flatten the area, and then turn this 180 degrees for more removal of cork. The result at this stage is a cork grip with four slightly flattened sides. Do *not* take this down until you have a square cross section, since this will remove too much cork to make a comfortable handle! Now remove cork from the "corners" to make a grip that is slightly octagonal. Then use the rasp to knock off the corners to make the cork grip truly round. Working this way assures that the cork grip will not end up either angled or off-center.

Once the grip is roughed out this way, use the same technique to shape and taper the ends or middle, depending on the type of grip you want. Finish by hand sanding with successively finer grades of sandpaper, beginning with a medium grade and working to the finest grade available.

Preformed cork grips are available in a variety of styles and lengths for spinning, casting, spincast, fly, noodle, and saltwater rods. These do not require any finishing but do require slightly different mounting methods.

First buy the grip with a hole diameter similar to—but smaller than—the diameter of the blank where the grip will be mounted. Slide the grip onto the blank to check for size.

If the grip does not fit, remove it and use a long reamer or sanding reamer to taper the hole in the grip to size and shape. Sanding reamers for this purpose are sold commercially, or you can make your own with strips of sandpaper cut thin and glued in open spirals onto a tapered scrap rod blank.

Remember that you must remove more material from the butt end of the grip than from the forward end due to the taper of the rod. Take care in doing this, because it's a natural tendency to end up removing more from each end than from the middle. Try to work evenly and smoothly to remove cork from all parts of the hole uniformly. Since you will be sliding the entire grip into place, it is generally best to have a slightly looser fit than you would with individual cork rings. Otherwise the tendency of the cork grip will be to act as a squeegee and push the glue ahead of it down the blank.

Another solution is to wait until the epoxy glue is fairly close to setting up so that the glue will be stiffer and less likely to be pushed along the blank. This method is also a little more hazardous, because you do not want to get to the point where the glue is so stiff that it will not adhere to the cork or so close to setting up that you cannot push the cork grip completely into place.

Once the grip is sized to fit, cover the adjoining butt cap or reel seat with masking tape to protect it. Smear glue onto the blank, and then slide the grip onto the blank. Slide it over the glued area, working it back and forth and rotating it to get complete glue distribution and good adhesion.

Another possibility, although it's seldom done, is to make your own preformed grips by building up cork rings on a dowel, old scrap blank, or threaded rod, and then remove the grip for gluing onto the blank. Do *not* add glue to the mounting surface, because this will not allow removal of the grip from the dowel, blank, or rod. The main advantage of this method is that you can make grips in advance. You can also turn the grips on a lathe for easy, quick shaping without fear of damaging the rod blank. It is an additional advantage if you wish to make a preformed grip that is completely different from one commercially available—one with insert rings of plastic or wood or of an unusual shape, for example. To make this easy, you can buy checkered or plain wood rings in ⅛- and ¼-inch thickness from places such as J. P. Timberlake. These can be drilled and then glued in place with cork rings on a mandrel or dowel to make your own lathe-shaped preformed cork grip.

FOAM GRIPS

Foam grips of EVA, Hypalon, and similar dense-foam materials are readily available. They are used for rod-blank grips, bike handlebar grips, and some tool-grip applications. They are heavier than cork grips (sometimes up to five times heavier) and thus are not recommended for ultralight and light rod blanks, nor are they recommended for fly rods where a firm grip is required to punch forward on the final cast.

In some cases you may find that you have to ream out a foam grip to fit a blank. As stated earlier, foam grips should be bought with a hole diameter about two-thirds to three-quarters of the blank diameter where the grip is to fit. This allows for expansion of the foam grip onto the blank for a solid fit. If the hole in the foam is too small, however, it will not fit, will not allow the grip to go on completely, and could even split or crack the blank, particularly light-wall blanks. To prevent this, ream out any foam grips that may be too small. One easy way to do this is to get a drill-bit extender and some rotary-rasp drill rasps. The bit extender is usually about 12 inches long and will fit into any ¼-inch chuck electric drill. The other end will hold (by means of a set screw adjusted with an Allen wrench) any ¼-inch-shank of a rotary bit or file. Start the drill and slowly run the rotary rasp in and out of the hole in the foam. The foam will expand around the bit (you can feel it under your hand as you do this), but the bit will in time ream out the entire length of the grip. If the grip is longer than 12 inches, work alternately from both ends.

Another possibility is to get some pilot drill bits, available from Flex Coat. These are spade bits in sizes available from 5⁄16 to ⅝ inch, with a special aluminum pilot sleeve mounted to the front of the bit. The pilot sleeve follows the ¼-inch hole of most foam grips, and the spade bit teeth on the side cut out the hole to the size desired. These are self-guiding so that you do not drill off-center. Flex Coat also sells a kit you can use to make your own pilot drill bits using spade bits that you have on hand or can easily purchase.

The best way to add a foam grip to a blank is to use a lubricant—preferably of glue, which will also hold the grip in place—and to push the grip down the blank using a push-board. Another solution is to use a lubricant of isopropyl alcohol on the foam grip (with glue on the blank) and immediately slide the foam grip in place. Because the alcohol is a solvent for the glue, the effect on the glue will be minimal. The alcohol will, however, aid in lubricating the blank-to-foam-grip surface, particularly if the foam grip starts to "grab" the blank above the glue. Once the alcohol reaches the glue, the glue will serve as additional lubricant.

Naturally this will push glue ahead of the foam grip, because the grip will act as a squeegee on the blank. Tape both the end of the foam grip and the adjoining part (usually a butt cap or reel seat) so that the glue ends up on the masking tape for easy cleanup, not on the rod component.

DECORATIVE FOAM GRIP WORK

While EVA and Hypalon grips are attractive and useful for most rods, you can add decorative designs to EVA grips. It is not as useful for Hypalon grips, since these are manufactured differently than EVA and only come in dark colors such as black, brown, and gray.

Billy Vivona of North East Rods Builders (XLrods@yahoo.com) has several designs and has learned several different ways in which EVA foam can be customized. These are his instructions to get the best possible results for the various methods of working with foam grips. These include the addition to trim rings into the foam, making inlays into the grip, cutting the foam to create oblique/oblong designs, and making checkerboard patterns in a foam grip.

All of these procedures require a band saw for cutting the foam to get a clean gluing surface. A good saw has a blade with about 12 teeth per inch. Small, hobby-style woodworking lathes are ideal for shaping and cutting the foam for these decorative additions. To sand the foam, grits working down from 80 (80, 120, 150, 220) are ideal.

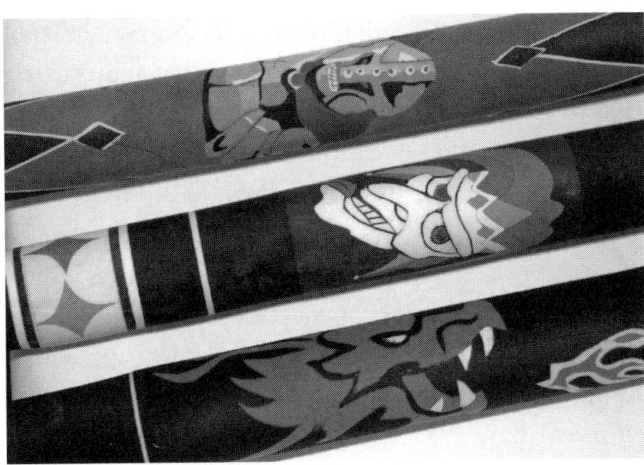

Examples of EVA and Hypalon grips by Billy Vivona making cutouts and then using contrasting color 3-millimeter foam to create a picture in a foam fishing rod grip.

Trim rings are relatively easy and involve cutting, gluing, and then sanding foam grips. One or more trim rings of contrasting colors are added to the foam grip, making for a unique design. These can be added to preformed foam rings or to foam blocks that are about 2 × 2 × 18 inches long and then sanded to shape and size when finished.

To start you need EVA sheeting (readily available from tackle supply stores and catalogs as well as from craft stores such as JoAnn Fabrics and Michaels). These come in many colors in 2-, 3- (⅛-inch), and 6-millimeter (¼-inch) thicknesses. You will also need WeldWood Contact Cement regular—not the thicker gel formula. Begin by using a band saw or lathe to cut the foam grip or block in half, using a straight cut at right angles to the blank/grip axis. To do this with a lathe, put the foam on a mandrel or scrap rod blank, mount in the woodworking lathe (hobby lathes are ideal for this), and use size D thread as a cutting tool to cut the turning foam.

Cut the foam sheeting into small squares (2 × 2 inches is often fine) that you will glue into the foam grip. To glue, brush a thin coat of the contact cement on the clean cut end of the foam grip or block and on one side only of the cut square of trim foam. Allow the glue to cure and dry briefly, and then add a second coat. Allow this second coat to cure (5 to 10 minutes), and then touch the foam sheet to the cut-foam grip. Note that no adjusting or positioning is possible—touch it to the right spot the first time, since it cannot be moved.

Push hard on the glued surfaces. One way to do this is to first punch a small hole in the center of the foam sheet square, add a mandrel to the foam grip or foam block, and then push the trim piece onto the handle. Then you can use a push-board to push hard down on the surface to make for a firm glue bond. A push-board for this is just like that used to push a foam grip onto a blank, but with a smaller hole for pushing on the thin mandrel. If using a ¼-inch mandrel for this step, consider a ⅜-inch hole in the push-board.

Add another two coats to each surface of the foam sheet and the other end of the foam grip, and repeat to glue the handle together with the contrasting color foam sheet in the center of the grip.

Use a razor to cut off excess foam sheeting, place the grip (still on a mandrel) on a lathe, and shape with sandpaper. Using this method and taking time with each layer of foam trim, you can add trim layers individually or in groups, in the middle or at the ends of the foam grip.

A second way to make a fancy grip is to add inlays of a design or picture to the foam surface.

This is very attractive but can be very time consuming, according to Vivona, depending on the complexity of the inserted inlay. To do this, first find a suitably sized drawing, print it out from a computer, photocopy machine, or magazine, and then cut it to size. As an example, let's make a simple outline of a fish. Cut out the fish shape, tape it to a sheet of 3-millimeter (⅛-inch) foam of the color desired. (Six-millimeter foam will not work, since in the contact gluing process, the foam will likely stick to the side of the insert space and cannot be positioned properly into the prepared recess in the foam grip.) Cut out the fish-shaped foam on the grip with an X-Acto knife, or grind it out with a router or Dremel tool. For this example, let's use a white fish shape on a blue foam grip. Place the fish shape on the preformed grip and draw the fish outline on the grip. Use a razor blade, X-Acto knife, or (carefully!) a Dremel tool with a grinding bit, to cut out the outline shape to a depth of 3 millimeters. Test this cut depth repeatedly with the cut-foam fish sheet. When ready to glue in place, add the contact sheet as above, using two coats of glue in turn to both the recess and the back of the fish-shaped foam. Use masking tape to tape the fish down, and then roll it on a flat hard surface, almost like rolling out dough with a rolling pin. When cured, put the rod or mandreled foam grip on a lathe and sand lightly to remove any rough edges. Make sure you do not sand too much to remove all the 3-millimeter depth of the white fish.

A third method for making designs is to cut and add an angled insert to a foam grip to make an oblique or oblong design in the form grip. Done properly, this will form a long elliptical shape of a foam trim color in a foam grip. To do this, work with a block of foam, mark it, and cut it on a band saw on a long diagonal, from one corner to the opposite corner at the other end of the block. In this case let's assume a red foam block and an insert of white. In this design you will need a long rectangular shape of sheet foam of 2-, 3-, or 6-millimeter thickness. As before with the rings, add two coats of contact cement to the angled cut block and also to one surface of the sheet insert.

Place the contact glue surfaces together, and press hard enough to cement the pieces firmly. Make a second band saw cut parallel to the first to remove a strip equal to the thickness of the foam sheet. If you used a sheet 2 millimeters thick, remove 2 millimeters. This step assures that the crossing of the strip of sheet foam to make the "X" will line up to make an accurate "X" along the cut. Add another two coats of contact cement to the surface of the sheet foam and also the cut foam block. Then seat these together and push on them to cure them into a firm bond.

To make a crossing elliptical, cut the block in the opposite direction with the band saw, cutting corner to corner as before. Use a second sheet of foam, and glue it to one side of the cut foam using two coats of the contact cement. Then make a second angled band saw cut in the block, parallel to the first and as thick as the sheet foam being used. This will assure that the "X" being formed to make the elliptical in the finished grip will line up properly.

Glue these pieces together as above to make the finished grip with two X's to form ellipticals when sanded to shape with the lathe. To make two more elliptical bands on the other side, rotate the block 90 degrees and repeat as above to place two crossing strips of foam angled through the foam grip.

Finish by placing a mandrel through the foam block, place the block in the lathe, and, using successively 80- to 220-grit strip-type sandpaper, sand to shape and size. The final result is a grip with long ellipticals running at angles and the length of the grip.

A fourth Vivona method of grip decoration is to make a grip in a checkerboard pattern. To do this you will need the Vivona-designed checkerboard jig by which round foam sections up to 4 inches long can be cut into sections of checkerboard design. These designs can be positioned to make a final checkerboard pattern in a foam grip once glued together.

To do this put a 4-inch length of round foam grip material onto the bolt of the jig, with the slotted spacers (cutting guides) at each end. Put the supplied saw into the slots at each end, line them up properly, and securely tighten the bolt (¼ or ½ inch) holding the jig. Then cut the foam into eight sections, using the slots on the jig, and cutting almost all the way through.

Remove the foam from the jig, and with the supplied saw continue cutting through the foam to make eight long, pie-shaped strips. Do the same thing with a separate 4-inch length of foam in a contrasting color. With the strips cut apart, use contact cement to cement the strips together, with colors alternating in each glued strip. Once the strips are glued together and cured, use a band saw to cut into sections ¼ to ½ inch wide. Assemble and glue these with contact cement, positioning the sections opposite a contrasting color to make a checkerboard design in the final grip. Place the rod or grip mandrel on a lathe for a final shaping and polishing.

FOAM CORE/GRAPHITE SLEEVE GRIPS

A different type of foam is used to make foam core composite grips that can be shaped on a lathe, sealed with epoxy, covered with a composite sleeving—carbon, fiberglass, or carbon-fiberglass hybrid—and finished with epoxy to make a shaped custom grip for any type of rod.

This is a system first tried by Tom Kirkman, editor of *RodMaker* magazine, and written about in *RodMaker* volume 10, issue 6 (articles by Andy Dear and second article by Tom Kirkman). The process has since been further developed by Mike and Vikki Pedersen of North Carolina and utilizes their blend of a six-pound expanding polyurethane pour foam—parts A and B. They have also developed tools and materials for the rod builder to make his/her own grips.

Operating under the name of Riley Rods, the Pedersens have developed a method that utilizes a rubber silicone mold and expanding pour foam to create a "foam core." This foam core is shaped, sealed, covered with a composite sleeving, and finished with epoxy.

The pour foam is not unlike the foam used for flotation by boat builders. It comes in a two-part pour, mix, and mold procedure. For a majority of rod grips, six-pound foam is best, although lighter (four-pound) or heavier (eight-pound) pour foam can be used. The foam designation is based on the weight of a cubic foot of the finished foam. Six-pound foam is recommended for most rods, with the four-pound foam satisfactory for very light spinning and fly rods and eight-pound foam best for very heavy saltwater rods.

The basic Riley Rods kit for pouring foam cores includes the two-part expanding six-pound foam, a 15 × 1¼-inch rubber silicone mold with two PVC halves and end reinforcing caps, a ¼-inch steel mandrel, a drill-held mixer to mix the foam solution, black pigment for tinting the foam cores gray (versus their natural

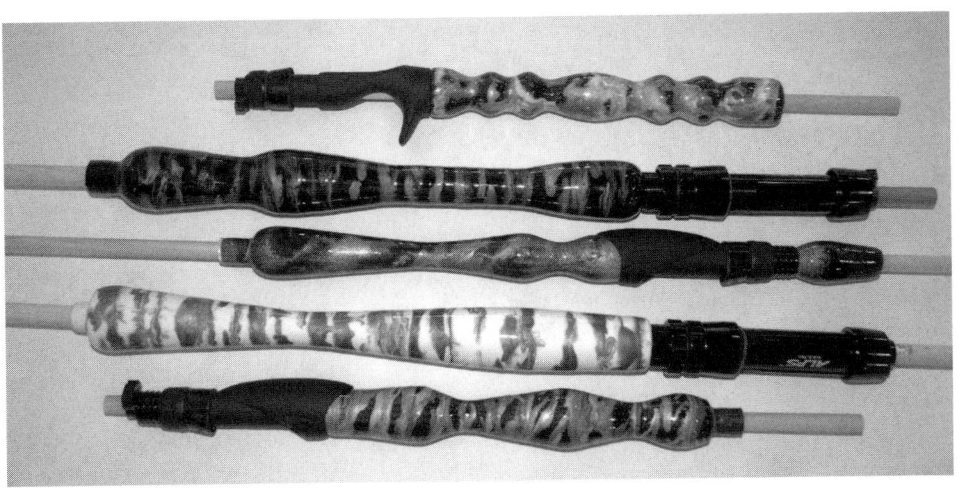

Examples of foam grips with mottled epoxied skins. Note that these grips by Mike and Vikki Pedersen can be made in any shape, length, or diameter and with any plain or mottled color. Directions in text.

cream color), and RR-321 two-part epoxy. The epoxy is used for sealing the foam core, applying the composite sleeving, and finishing the completed grip. The composite sleeving to cover the shaped core is purchased separately.

The mold is silicone rubber so that it will not stick to the foam core, allowing for easy removal of the core from the mold. The mold's end caps have a center hole to hold the center mandrel. The silicone rubber mold has a slit in one side for easy pouring of the foam and removal of the cured foam core. Be sure to season the mandrel with a release agent before inserting it into the mold.

To make a foam core, mount the drill mixer on a drill and mix the two parts of the pour foam (50/50 mix) for 20 seconds at high speed—1,500 to 2,500 rpm.

Once mixed, and with the bottom PVC half and silicone rubber mold horizontal on a table or support (and with the center mandrel in place), open the slit at the side/top of the mold and rapidly pour the liquid into it. Place the other PVC half on top of the mold, and put on the securing end caps. Wait for the foam to expand and fill the mold. The foam core is cured after 40 minutes and can be removed from the mold. (As a substitute for the rubber silicone mold, you can use light-wall 1½-inch-diameter PVC pipe [schedule 120] sprayed with a silicone lubricant, release agent, or PAM and capped with PVC caps as above.)

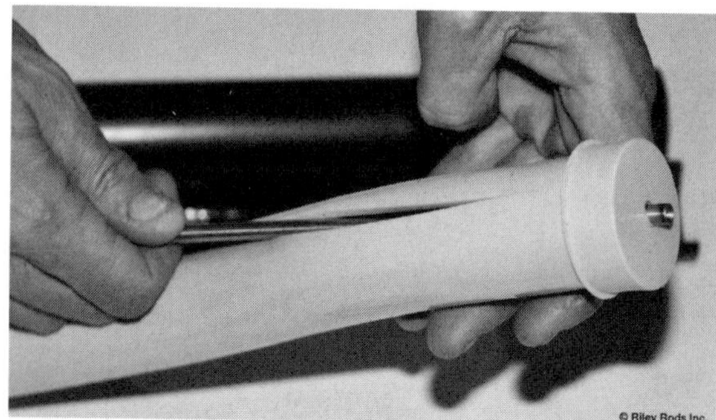

Credit: Riley Rods / Vikki Pedersen

Placing a mandrel into the Riley Rods mold for making foam grips. Note that the end cap is shown on one end of this flexible mold.

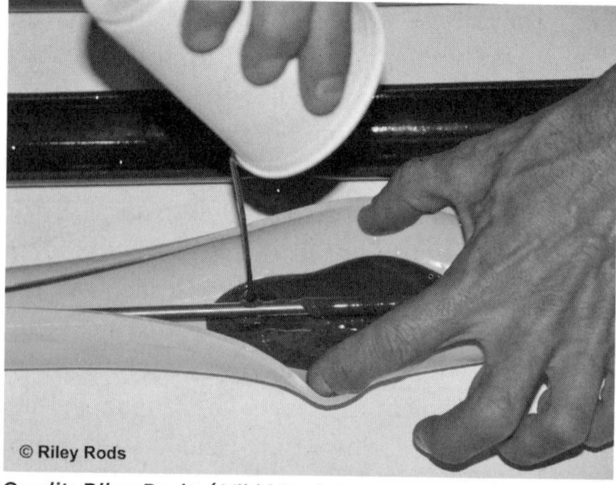

Credit: Riley Rods / Vikki Pedersen

Pouring the mixed foam into the mold with the mandrel in place. The mold is flexible to allow spreading it open with the fingers as shown to pour in the foam mix.

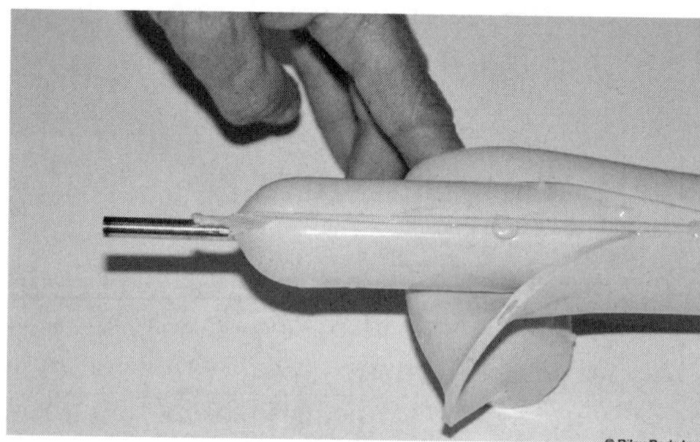

Credit: Riley Rods / Vikki Pedersen

Pulling the cured foam grip out of the flexible mold by peeling the mold back.

Credit: Riley Rods / Vikki Pedersen

Foam core with the mold peeled back and almost removed.

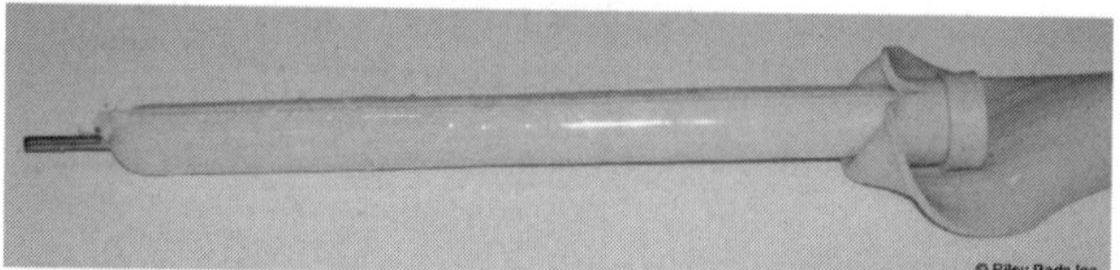

Credit: Riley Rods / Vikki Pedersen

Completed molded foam grip—before shaping—with the mandrel still in place.

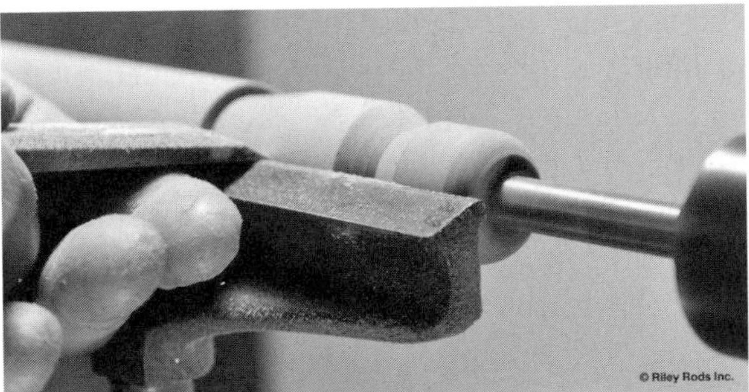

Credit: Riley Rods / Vikki Pedersen

Shaping the completed foam grip on a lathe to create the handle shape desired.

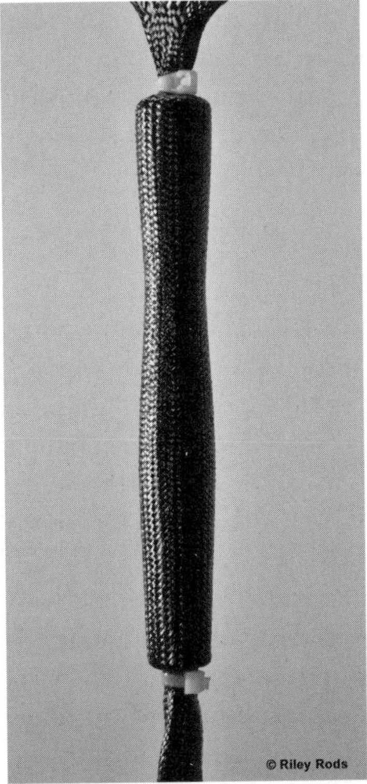

Credit: Riley Rods / Vikki Pedersen

The carbon skin in a wet lay-up placed over the shaped mold grip and secured in place at each end for curing.

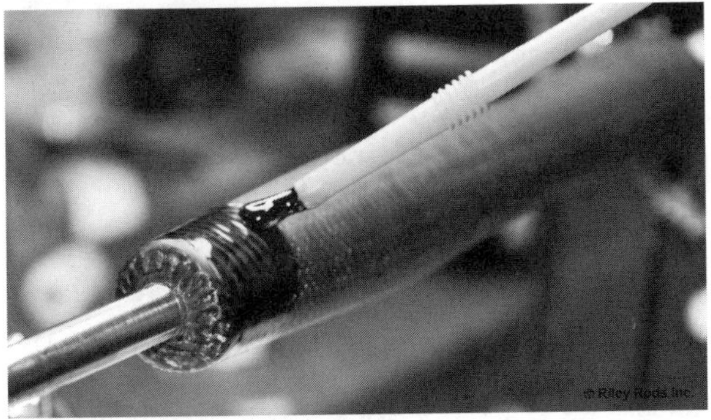

Credit: Riley Rods / Vikki Pedersen

Final coat of epoxy on the outside of the carbon skin of the completed foam grip to complete the grip or handle.

Credit: Riley Rods / Vikki Pedersen

Completed grip (two parts in this case) on the rod and with the finishing accessories and touches to complete the handle.

The foam core will be cylindrical—15 inches long and 1¼ inches wide. Remove the ¼-inch mandrel, and drill out the core hole with a spade pilot bit (such as is available from Flex Coat); insert a mandrel that is just slightly smaller in diameter than the rod blank on which the finished grip will be added. With the appropriate mandrel in place, secure it to a wood lathe and use lathe tools to make the foam core concentric and worked to size and shape. Finish using 400-grit sandpaper, Very Fine Scotch-Brite (maroon), and Ultra Fine Scotch-Brite (gray). Note that the subsequent layers of epoxy and composite sleeving will add about 0.5 millimeter to the finished grip's outside diameter. Thus, if you want a very specific diameter to the finished grip, sand and shape the grip to about 0.5 millimeter outside diameter less than the outside diameter desired.

Use the Riley Rods RR-321 epoxy with a 2:1 mix (resin to hardener), and skim coat the foam core to seal it. (Be sure to wear nitrile rubber gloves. Latex gloves often have a powder in them, which would contaminate the epoxy.) Place the foam core on a curing motor to prevent sagging, and let it cure for three hours. While this is curing, choose the composite sleeving to be used.

The composite sleeving comes in a variety of sizes and is chosen by the desired grip diameter. The sleeving is woven, biaxial, and works like a Chinese finger puzzle. Use a 1-inch-diameter sleeving for grips with an outside diameter of 1 inch or less. Use 1½-inch sleeving for those grips greater than 1 inch. Cut the composite sleeving 3 inches longer than the desired grip length. Open the cut composite sleeving and place it over a cylindrical object that's a bit larger than your grip size. Straighten weave and set aside.

Mix RR-321 epoxy for 5 minutes. Place the mandrel with foam core on a horizontal rod stand. Put on nitrile gloves, and while constantly rotating the foam core, use a small brush to fully wet it with epoxy until it reaches a consistent, glasslike finish.

Then move the mandrel with foam core to a vise and secure it vertically. Lower the cut composite sleeving over the wet foam core. Loosely conform the sleeving to the foam core, and gently pull ends (like a Chinese finger puzzle). Start at the top, and secure the sleeving to the mandrel using a cable tie. Work your way down the grip, smoothing the sleeving onto the foam core and "milk" it out to fit evenly and securely. Add a cable tie at the bottom of the grip. Place the skinned foam core on a curing motor and gently heat with a heating gun (constantly moving) until sleeving is fully saturated (about 1 to 2 minutes). It will cure to a non-tacky state in about 3 hours, to a fully usable state in about 7 hours.

Place the mandrel with foam core on a lathe, trim cable ties, cut off the excess sleeving, and clean up with a paring tool. Use Scotch-Brite or lightly sand with 600+-grit sandpaper. Clean with denatured alcohol to remove all residue.

Put the grip on a curing motor, and apply one to two finishing coats of RR-321 epoxy to reach the desired finish. If you want to use pigments (to add color/marbling), add to the epoxy while it is mixing (and before you apply the finishing coats). The carbon sleeving is black, but other colors are possible using either natural fiberglass sleeving, which otherwise dries clear, with pigments or the carbon-fiberglass hybrid sleeving.

Once the grip is cured, remove the mandrel and prepare the handle for gluing onto a rod blank. Using epoxy glue, cement the finished handle onto the rod blank as described elsewhere in this book.

GRAPHITE GRIPS

Graphite grips are available from some component-parts houses. These are essentially cylindrical tubes of graphite material—almost like graphite tubes—that are used for the popular tape-on Tennessee-style handle used in the South to tape spinning reels to rod handles. (Standard clamping-type reel seats are not used.)

Although the same thing can be done with cork grips, one of the advantages of graphite is that it will provide greater sensitivity through the handle, provided graphite or hard bushings are used. Some kits are available that include the graphite tube, two end caps (one is either drilled for the blank or must be drilled for the blank), and graphite bushings that must be drilled to fit the blank but are sized for the grip. Some, designed for removal of the reel, include two slip-on bands to hold the reel foot.

Building these is a simple two-step operation: First glue the bushings in place on the rod blank, and then glue the graphite tube or sleeve to the bushings. Measure the position of the grip, and mark it on the blank. Then mark the positions of the bushings, because these usually are not as long as the handle. Use regular 24-hour epoxy glue to glue the bushings onto the blank. Allow the glue to cure overnight, and then glue the graphite grip to these bushings. In both cases use plenty of glue for a secure bond.

Sometimes bushings are not available and must be made. In this case use the tips suggested later in this chapter. Be sure to use firm bushing materials, such as graphite material (this is best) or cork rings, wood bushings, or molded epoxy bushings (made from paste-type high-viscosity epoxy glues).

WOOD GRIPS

Although wood grips can be used on any rod, they are generally used for the rear grip on boat and inshore trolling saltwater rods. This is because these rods are primarily used in rod holders and are not held except during the fighting of a fish, and then they are held mostly by the foregrip, which is usually a more comfortable cork or foam. Thus the weight of wood is not a problem. Wood is durable and a good grip material from that standpoint, but it is too hard to be comfortable for rods that are held and repeatedly cast.

Some rod builders like to make grips of wood, which requires turning them on a wood lathe as shown here. After the grip is shaped, it must be center-through drilled and reamed to a taper in order to be glued onto a rod blank.

Wood grips are available drilled straight through for through-handle construction or undrilled for use with a reel seat and ferrule arrangement as previously described. In the latter case they are primarily used with reel seats that have a built-in slip-on or screw-down ferrule; the end of the rod blank stops at the ferrule, and the rod breaks down at this point for storage or travel.

Most of these wood grips are about 18 inches long and include some sort of recess at the bottom for a gimbal knock or mushroom-style butt cap and a recess at the upper end to hold the reel seat. Often they are made specifically for certain reel seats, which will glue on without shimming or requiring the recess in the wood handle to be cut to a smaller diameter.

To glue the drilled wood grips onto a blank, first check the fit of the blank and grip. If the blank is too large to go completely through the hole in the grip, use a long reamer, rat-tail file, or 12-inch drill bit (known as electrician's, aircraft, or extended bits) to drill out the wood grip close to the size of the blank. It is also possible to use a rotary rasp (as used with foam grips) on a bit extender and electric drill to enlarge the hole as needed.

Blanks are tapered, and this sometimes requires some additional consideration. Often this means drilling the top end with one size bit and using a larger bit to drill the butt end. Use calipers first to check the diameters of the hole in the grip and the outside diameter of the blank before drilling.

Once the grip is drilled and sized properly (with no play or slack), measure the wood handle's length on the blank, remove it from the blank, and spread mixed epoxy glue thoroughly over this measured portion of the blank. Slide the grip down into place, using a rotating motion to assure a good wetting of the inside of the grip and a good bonding of the two parts. Do this over old newspapers, because excess glue will be squeezed out during this procedure. Once the grip is in place, mop up any excess glue and rotate the grip so that the wood grain is in line with the spine of the rod blank. Allow the glue to cure overnight.

Wood grips that are not drilled are intended to be used with blanks that end in the ferrule–reel-seat combination. These require no installation and are covered later in this chapter.

ALUMINUM GRIPS

Aluminum grips are available straight or curved, bored (for blank through-construction) or unbored, with reel seats (such as the AFTCO Unibutt) or without, in sizes to fit any saltwater fishing need, and in anodized finishes of black, silver (natural), and black-and-gold.

Most of these grips have been described in chapter 17. Assembly of the unbored grips involves gluing the rod butt into the ferrule that comes supplied with the reel seat. Because these assemblies are used on heavy saltwater rods and because of the excessive strain to which these rods are subject, matching the rod butt to the ferrule is critical.

For example, many rod manufacturers include special bushings as an integral part of the butt end of trolling-rod blanks; these bushings fit specifically into special ferrules from those companies making these ferrule fitting reel seats. In turn, manufacturers of the reel seats and grips usually have specific ferrule internal diameters so that rod manufacturers and custom rod builders can match them or so that rod builders can slightly cut down the rod-blank butt end, if necessary, to precisely fit the reel seat. Typical ferrule internal diameters on such reel seat/ferrule sets measure 0.750, 0.875, 1.000, and 1.188 internal diameter (AFTCO). For Batson these measure 0.750, 0.787, 0.873, 1.0, and 1.188.

Occasionally you have to fit a rod blank with a small butt end into a ferrule with an internal diameter that is too large for the blank. In these cases the best solution is to get a boat repair kit of fiberglass resin and tape and build up a bushing around the butt end of the blank, allow it to cure overnight, and then rasp, file, or lathe it down to size and a smooth cylindrical shape. After this, it is a simple matter to use 24-hour epoxy glue to glue the butt into the ferrule. Other bushing materials, such as epoxy putty, epoxy glues, and synthetic tapes built up with epoxy glue around the butt of the rod, can also be used. In all cases these *must* be firm and solid. Never use string, masking tape, or similar materials for these bushings, even with epoxy glue.

The best way to glue a blank into a bored aluminum butt is to drop the rod blank into the bored butt, making sure the blank goes all the way through to the bottom of the butt section. Use a pen or masking tape to mark the point where the blank exits the butt section. If the blank is loose at this point (it usually is), remove the blank and use the previous methods (fiberglass boat tape and resin, epoxy and synthetic cloth, epoxy putty) to build up the blank at this point to precisely fit the hole in the butt section. If necessary build this oversized, allow it to cure overnight, then work the section down to size and shape with a rasp, file, sandpaper, or lathe.

Next add enough liquid epoxy to the rod butt through the hole in the top to fill up the bottom to a level of several inches. (If there is a hole in the bottom, tape this over temporarily.) Usually an ounce or two is enough. Then smear glue on the bushing that has previously been sized to snugly fit the upper end of the bored butt. Slide the rod blank down into the butt and mop up any excess glue.

PLASTIC AND ACRYLIC GRIPS

In volume 13, issue 6 of his rod-building magazine *RodMaker,* Tom Kirkman describes a method of making clear acrylic grips. In his article he points out some things that are not initially obvious. First, acrylic plastic is not a light material, and acrylic grips are at least as heavy as grips made of hardwood. Second, while most acrylic stock available is extruded, this will shatter, crack, or break if used and turned on a lathe for rod grips. Thus you must use acrylic rod or stock that is cast, not extruded.

Once you have a suitable piece and size of cast acrylic stock, keep it at room temperature or above. Anything below about 60 degrees

Fahrenheit can lead to brittleness and possible problems. You can turn acrylic on either a wood or metal lathe, using tools such as a round-nose scraper and a parting tool for cutting off. Scraping the surface is better and safer than cutting. According to Kirkman, a wood lathe is best for turning if you have any curves in the grip. Resharpening tools frequently (maybe once per minute) is necessary for optimal results.

Since you will have to bore a hole to fit the grip onto a rod blank, this can be done before or after turning the grip. Best speeds are about 1,400 to 1,800 rpm. For boring you can use standard twist drill bits, preferably aircraft or electrician's bits for their added length, necessary for the grip length. Make sure you can completely drill through the acrylic from one end to prevent a two-end approach, which can lead to checkering and difficulty. To keep the removed cut stock from building up, remove the bit about every ½ to 1 inch.

To turn the stock, use about 1,300 to 1,800 rpm. Once the stock is sized, start sanding by working with successively finer grades of sandpaper until reaching about 2000 grit. Kirkman suggests using, in turn, sandpaper grades of 320, 400, 600, 800, 1200, 1500, and 2000. Finish by buffing to a clear finish using Duco plastic polish (blue) for maximum clarity.

To make the grip completely clear, sand and buff the interior hole drilled. Attach sandpaper to a slotted dowel placed in a hand drill to run the sandpaper dowel back and forth through the hole, using successively finer grades of sandpaper and using HUT plastic polish (white) in and out of the bore. Each time you move to a finer-grit sandpaper, be sure to blow out the hole to remove any grit residue.

Since you will want the interior gluing to the blank to show, Kirkman recommends Flex Coat Rod Builder's Epoxy for gluing the blank to the grip. Regardless of the glue used, make sure there are no bubbles in the mix, since these will show magnified through the clear grip.

CORD AND WRAPPED GRIPS

On thick rod blanks, such as those for surf and other heavy rods, wrapped grips are possible. In all cases you must start with a blank that has a diameter that will be comfortable to hold, because the wrapping will not add much to the diameter—only to the gripping quality. In most cases this will vary between about a 1- and 1¼-inch blank diameter. Adding a foam, cork, or wood grip will make the diameter too large to be held comfortably.

One simple solution is to use hard cord, wrapping it around the blank using the same technique as for wrapping guides in place. Several types of cord are available for this. Some companies (such as Gudebrod) make a butt cord for this purpose or a decorative cord that's usually used above the foregrip but is also useful for this handle wrap. Most of these are available in basic colors and in spools long enough to wrap a handle.

Craft stores, hobby shops, and sewing shops often carry hard cords that are used for craftwork, macramé, or similar hobbies. Some that I have seen are 1.5 or 2 millimeters in diameter and ideal for wrapping grips. Larger diameter cord is sometimes available.

Regardless of your choice of cord, it must be hard and stiff so that it will not stretch and will allow a firm grip. If color is important, the cord must be colorfast, because most anglers do not coat cord with color preserver or rod finish. Doing so would make for a slick surface, something that would not allow a firm, comfortable grip. Other anglers like to soak the grip with varnish (several coats until it soaks in and builds up on the grip) or thin epoxy glue.

If you use any other cord for this, test it first by soaking samples in water or exposing them to the elements for a few weeks before wrapping on the rod.

To wrap cord on the rod, first choose the area to be covered. In the case of surf rods, often this is from the butt cap all the way up to the top of the grip area. In some cases it is easiest to wrap the entire grip area and then use the grip as a shim on which to mount the reel seat or a plate-type reel. Most companies make these, and component parts catalog houses carry them. Fuji has ten different models of plate-type reel seats in black, silver, and chrome finishes and with the ability to take any casting (squidding or surf) or spinning reel foot.

In other cases it is best to mount the reel seat directly on the rod blank and then add wraps both above and below this for a rear and foregrip.

The technique of wrapping is the same as that used for a guide. Begin by crossing over the main cord, continue for several turns, and then cut the excess thread. To prevent a lump where the cord is wrapped over, fray out as much of the cord here as possible, making sure the frayed portion is wrapped over and not a part of the final wrap. Continue the wrap until you are about four to six wraps from the end, then lay down a separate loop of the same cord or of heavy monofilament. Continue wrapping, cut the cord, and place the end through the loop. Pull the loop hard to pull the tag end under the wraps where it can be cut off. Open up a gap where the thread exits between two wraps, cut the thread off by cutting straight down with a razor blade, and then close the gap formed.

Another way to complete this wrap is to use the Leonard style of wrap finishing, as described in chapter 22 on guide wrappings.

Fraying out the end of a cord wrap for a rod handle makes for less of a lump at this point. Heavy cord is used for this handle wrap.

CORK-TAPE GRIPS

Cork tape serves the same purpose as cord: as a thin grip material on surf blanks that are of large diameter. As with cord, the cork tape can be run the length of the area of the rear grip and foregrip, and then the reel seat can be placed over this with the cork tape used as a shim. In most cases the reel seat is mounted and then the cork tape is added. Most cork tape comes with a self-adhesive backing.

Before starting, be sure the blank is clean. To get complete coverage without gaps, achieving the proper angle of attachment is a must. To get this for each individual rod, leave the backing paper in place and wrap the tape several times around the blank. This will adjust to the correct angle with only a short length of the tape. Make several turns, making sure the cork-tape edges abut. Now hold the wrap, and unwrap several turns at the blank end. Peel off the backing paper from the unwrapped tape. Rewrap the peeled cork tape around the rod. Then unwrap the tape that still has backing paper and peel the backing off a few inches at a time, wrapping the cork tape on the blank as you do so. The result is that you get the exact taper and angle the cork tape must take when it's wrapped around any particular rod.

Once you finish this wrap, cut both ends of the tape so that they are square with the butt end of the rod. To keep the ends from unwrapping, add some masking tape temporarily to hold each end down. For the butt-cap end, remove the masking tape, add some epoxy glue to the cork tape and the butt cap, and slide the butt cap in place over the cork tape. To finish off the wrap below a reel seat or at the end of a foregrip, hold the end of the cork tape in place with masking tape. Use a razor blade or a coarse emery board to taper the end of the cork tape all the way around the blank. This will serve as a base for the wrap that will hold the end of the cork tape down. Use heavy cord or thread (E or EE) and begin a wrap around the blank, just as you would a guide wrap. Continue wrapping up onto the tapered cork tape, but use a very light pressure to avoid cutting into the cork tape with the thread. Continue wrapping for a dozen turns or so, and then finish with a loop of thread as you would any other wrap. These wraps must be coated with color preserver and epoxy finish, as must any other rod-guide or ferrule wrap.

Method of making a cork tape grip on a rod. The spiral is formed on the rod with the backing in place and then the backing removed while holding some of the tape in place to maintain the correct spiral without gaps or overlapping. Here the lower part of the cork tape has been fastened to the rod; the backing is being removed from the rest of the tape.

Completed cork tape grip with butt cap.

MISCELLANEOUS GRIPS, REEL SEATS, AND VARIATIONS

The grips already mentioned are standard, but nonstandard grips are possible. They can be made of almost anything that can be fitted to a rod blank and that will provide a good gripping surface. Possibilities include drilled acrylic rod (clear or in colors), fancy woods (for casting-rod pistol and straight grips), bicycle handlebar tape over a cork base, wood dowels, and so on. Construction for most of these is the same as for typical rod grips in terms of measuring, sizing, and gluing. Some, such as the bicycle or leather tape over cork grips, are sometimes used for the foregrips on big-game rods and can be used on other rods. The best method is to glue the cigar-shaped tapered cork grip to the blank, taper it sharply at each end, and then wrap the tape around the cork grip, holding it in position with a band of rod-wrapping thread.

Variations of grips most often include inserts of other materials in the grip. The techniques are pretty basic and the possibilities endless, including the following:

Inserts of plastic or wood into a cork grip. These are most often small discs of contrasting-color material such as plastic and exotic wood. You can include these inserts into a grip you are making from cork rings or into a preformed cork grip. However, if you are using a preformed cork grip, you will need to make the grip slightly longer (the length of the insert material), or you will have to remove that much cork from the insert position to keep the same length.

If you use a preformed cork grip, carefully and accurately cut the cork grip through at the point where you want the insert material. Use a fine saw and, if the shape of the grip allows it, a small miter box. Once you make the cut, use sandpaper to smooth the surface and correct for any inaccuracies.

Next pick out the insert material. This can be slices of wood; clear, translucent, or opaque plastic; or similar materials. Drill the material to fit the blank at the position where it will be placed. Another good method is to use a hole saw, which will not only drill the hole but also cut the plastic or wood to the diameter you want for the rod grip. Shape the diameter of the material close to, but not exactly the size of, the grip (if you have not already done this with the hole saw). You will have to wait until the grip is glued on the blank to do the final shaping.

Another possibility is the checkerboard-style light and dark wood insert rings (⅛ inch thick and ¼ inch thick) from J. P. Timberlake of Sticks & Bones Custom Rods.

To position these in a rod, drill slowly and carefully through the center of each ring for placement into the preformed grip. Slow drilling is important to avoid splitting the insert or splitting apart the light and dark portions of the rings.

Glue the cork rings in place one at a time, as for making a standard cork ring grip, or glue on the lower half of the preformed cork grip. Add the insert material, making sure you get a good glue bond to the blank and also to the adjoining cork surfaces. Glue the rest of the rings or the remainder of the grip in place. Once this is done, allow the glue to cure overnight.

Next you must shape the insert material to the diameter and form of the grip. For best results, roughly file and shape the cork grip (if it's made from cork rings) until it is close to the final diameter. Then use a hard file, sandpaper backed by a board, or a stiff emery board to shape and size the insert ring. You can't just sand the cork and the insert ring at the same time, because the softer cork will be sanded away faster than the hardwood or acrylic insert. The result would be a scalloped or dished appearance to the cork on each side of the insert. Once the insert is shaped, sand the cork grip to meet this diameter. When working with a preformed cork grip, use a layer or two of masking tape to protect the cork on each side of the insert, then use the hard files and sanders to sand the insert to shape and size. Remove the masking tape and do any final sanding with fine sandpaper.

An alternative is to use a hole saw and saw out insert materials to the exact diameter needed, then polish the edges, enlarge the hole to fit onto the blank, and glue the insert in place when gluing the foam or cork rings onto the rod blank. Assuming the cork rings are larger than the insert, the cork can then be shaped and sized to the diameter of the insert ring, using methods previously described.

Inserts can be of one, two, or more materials. One common method is to use a cork grip with one or more insert materials, with each insert area composed of alternating material bands. Often white material is used for light bands. One variation is to use insert materials in colors that will match or blend with the color of the thread to be used in the guide wraps.

Another popular and easy insert can be composed of burnt cork—a dark brown cork that is available from most tackle-component suppliers. It can be inserted as a single ring or thinner slice of contrasting cork in a reel-seat insert or grip on spinning, casting, or fly rods.

Inserts of rubber foam in foam grips. Rubber foam comes in several colors, and inserts of contrasting colors can be cut in short sections and then inserted into foam grips. Cut the foam grip where you want the insert, then trim the insert accurately with a razor blade. For an accurate lineup of the two foams, which must be glued together, you must use the same material and the same inside and outside diameters. The best procedure is to glue the parts together with rubber cement and then glue the completed grip onto the blank with epoxy glue. Use care, however, because the glued grip will be more fragile than will a solid, uncut grip.

In addition to using different colors of foam, you can cut foam from the center of old thong-type sandals. Many of these are colorful, with several layers of bright color, and can be added to grips for a decorative touch. For best results use a hole saw run at a very slow speed to cut out the rings of material from the sole.

Any inserts of wood, plastic, foam, or other material can be placed into the grip at an angle by cutting the grip on an angle and allowing for the change in dimensions in the insert material. The insert material will require an oblong hole—or a hole cut at an angle to the axis of the material—and must be oblong in shape to fit the angled cut.

Skeletal reel seats. Skeletal reel seats can be bought and can also be made. Start with a plain reel seat of aluminum or graphite fill. Then use a fine-blade hacksaw (32 teeth per inch) to cut out the barrel section between the fixed hood and the threaded barrel holding the adjustable hood. After cutting these, use a fine file to smooth the cut edges and remove any burrs. If you are working with an aluminum anodized reel seat, use a permanent felt-tip marker of the same color as the reel-seat anodizing to touch up the edges. You can then make an insert of wood or cork.

For a wood insert the best procedure is to turn the wood on a lathe until it is of the right diameter and length and has a slight recess to go under the fixed hood, with a longer recess to go under the threaded barrel. The outside diameter of the wood insert should be the same as for the aluminum or graphite. The recesses at both ends must fit snugly into the remaining reel-seat parts. If you are making an insert of cork, glue several rings together on a threaded rod and shape them as an insert to fit the reel seat. It is possible to place insert discs in these for added decoration. In making these inserts for skeletal reel seats, be sure you make them the correct length; once the barrel is cut out, you will have no reference as to the proper length that will accommodate the feet of reels you plan to use with the rod.

You can also buy skeletal reel seats without the barrel insert and use these parts (barrel, fixed hood, sliding hood, one or two locking nuts) to make a special barrel insert and make your own special reel seats.

It is also possible to place graphite or graphite-fill reel seats in a jig and drill holes through the sides using a drill press with a pilot drill bit and then larger bits until reaching the size hole you wish. Just do this with care and careful planning as to the size of the holes you wish either for appearance or weight reduction.

Wood handles on casting and spinning rods. Exotic woods can be used for handles, although for most tastes these are too hard and firm for comfort. If you wish to try them, do it on one rod and fish with it before changing all your rods or building a whole new stock of tackle with wood handles.

Any exotic wood can be used. Some exotic woods are available from well-stocked lumberyards, as well as special woodcarving and wood-hobby shops. Popular woods include those used for fly-rod reel-seat inserts, such as walnut, cocobolo, mesquite, and ebony. To make a spinning or straight handle—such as that for a trigger-stick-style casting rod—use a lathe to shape the wood.

You will have to drill a hole for the blank, and there are two ways this can be done. One is to drill the hole first, using a drill press and a long-shank drill bit. These bits come in 6- and 12-inch lengths so that you can make any but the longest grips. Make a jig for your drill press that will hold the wood stock (usually square in cross section) perfectly vertical and in line with the drill bit.

Essentially this jig is nothing more than a precise corner made of wood scraps. By clamping the base of this corner onto the drill-press table, the two sides will be made vertical. Placing the wood stock into this corner assures vertical drilling. To drill long grips you will probably have to position the wood stock in this jig on the drill press, place the drill bit into the chuck, and then position the drill bit in line with the center of the wood stock. Then drill as deeply as possible, periodically raising the drill bit to clear the wood chips and dust. Because most drill presses will not feed a bit a full 12 inches, you will probably have to stop the drill press with the bit still in the wood, raise the drill-press table in line with the bit, and then continue drilling. Once the wood stock is drilled, place it in a lathe and shape it to size.

An alternative method is to drill with the wood in the lathe. Usually this is easily accomplished by using a drill in a chuck in the tail stock, with the wood stock held in a four-jaw or three-jaw universal chuck.

Once the wood is shaped and drilled, a reamer or other drill bits can be used to further drill the hole to the proper taper to fit the rod blank.

To make pistol-grip casting-rod handles, first decide on the type of wood you want and on the length required. A general size would be about 5 to 6 inches long, about 3 inches wide, and about 1½ inches thick.

First drill a hole lengthwise through the wood, gradually enlarging it to fit the blank. Once this is done, trace the general shape of the grip on the wood. Often a good way to start is by using a pistol grip you like as a template. If you wish, you can make the grip unique by adding finger-grip indentations. Once you are satisfied with the shape, cut the wood on a band saw. Once the grip is cut out, use a rasp, sanding belt, or files to roughly shape the body of the grip, finishing with various grades of sandpaper. For those with the inclination and tools, checkering, such as is done for gunstocks, will add security to the gripping surface and also make it more decorative.

Extension and fighting butts on fly rods. Extension butts on fly rods can be made of varying lengths, permanent or detachable. They are available commercially with some fly-rod reel seats—or as a separate option—such as those by PacBay and Batson. They can also be made using standard fly-rod reel seats. The purpose is to provide for extending the fly reel from the body when fighting big fish. Usually the rod butt is held against the body for leverage in fighting such fish, and the extension butt allows this while keeping the turning reel spool away from clothing.

To make a permanent extension butt, you must use an open-end reel seat (open at both ends, like that for spinning rods) so that the blank can fit straight through. Begin building such a permanent extension butt by first deciding on materials. Classic design dictates a small aluminum butt cap or butt plate, above which are mounted several cork rings to make up the extension butt. (If you will be mounting a socket type of butt cap, first mount the cork rings, sand them to size and shape to form a recess for the butt cap, and then glue the butt cap in place. If you are mounting a plate-type butt cap, add the cork rings and then glue the plate in place.) You can make any length of extension butt you want, using one cork ring for each ½ inch of butt length. Generally the shorter the extension butt the better, and for tournament or record purposes, the IGFA does not allow an extension butt longer than 6 inches. In most cases 6 inches is longer than you would want anyway for comfort and practicality.

Longer extensions will catch the fly line more, get caught in sleeves of shirts and jackets, and get in the way of casting. Fly-rod guru Lefty Kreh states that each inch over 2 inches of extension butt adds another problem to casting and fishing. A short permanent extension butt of about 2 inches is far better, because it will still extend the reel away from the body yet not be so long as to interfere with casting.

After gluing on the cork rings to make the extension butt, add the reel seat or reel-seat bushing to hold the reel seat. In this you have a choice between up-locking or down-locking seats. Up-locking (locking up toward the tip of the rod) seats are better, because they will add another inch or so of space between your clothing and the reel. Down-locking seats push the reel down toward the extension butt.

Add the reel seat, first gluing together any component parts (wood or cork insert, fixed hood, and threaded barrel with adjustable hood), and then ream out the reel seat to fit snugly on the blank. Make sure you use the masking-tape method of taping outer edges to protect the parts from glue. Allow the parts to cure, and then glue the completed, assembled reel seat onto the rod blank and seat against the corks making up the extension butt. Align the hoods with the spine of the rod. Then add the adjoining cork to finish the rest of the handle. Cover the reel seat with several layers of masking tape to protect it and then, using hand or lathe methods, shape and size the cork grip and the short cork extension at the same time.

You can make an extension of other materials, such as foam or wood. I do *not* recommend using foam for the fly-rod grip because foam, regardless of type, is too flexible and gives too much on the forward part of the cast for you to maintain good loop size and line control. Foam or wood can be used for the extension fighting butt because this is nonfunctional on the cast. For this proceed as above, adding the foam or wood in place of the cork. The foam should have an outside diameter approximately equal to that of the rear of the reel seat and an inside diameter slightly smaller than the outside diameter of the rod blank for smooth fitting. Fit the foam on with epoxy, using the same methods as for adding a foam grip on other rods.

Extensions of exotic woods to match the fly-rod reel-seat-insert wood can also be made. The best technique is to drill a short length (the best extension butts are only about 2 inches long, so this does not require long drill bits) and then place it on a lathe. Shape the exposed portion of the extension butt, and then make any appropriate recesses to fit into a butt cap or halfway into the open-end fixed-hood reel seat. If you are using a skeletal-type reel seat like this, you will also have to cut off a portion of the recess of the wood-barrel insert to allow for the partial recess of the extension butt.

Note that if you build the rod this way, you will move the grip and reel seat slightly forward (the length of the extension butt), but both sections of the blank (or several sections) will remain the same length. If you do not wish to shift the position of the reel seat and grip, you can add a permanent extension to the end by using a scrap of blank epoxy glued into the butt end of the rod, on which you can build the extension. If you do this, make sure the tapers are identical or similar and that at least 4 inches of the scrap blank fits into the rod blank. Substitutes for a tapered rod blank include tapered wood dowels. This method is not really recommended for permanent extensions because it does add to the overall length of the butt section of the rod.

I like removable extension butts best. You can leave them off when you don't want or need them but can still carry them in a hip pocket or fly-fishing vest to plug into the rod when desired. If you make your own, you can make and carry several different lengths, say, 2 and 6 inches.

There are several ways to make a removable extension or fighting butt. They all must use an open-end reel seat so that there is an opening into which the extension butt can slide. In essence, all are made using some sort of ferrule system, even though it may be very crude when compared to a rod ferrule. For example, one simple way to make an extension butt is to build the rod normally, with the butt of the rod blank extending all the way to the end of the reel seat.

An exception to this would be if you are using a special button or butt cap—such as the button for the Fuji FPS 16 fly-rod reel seat—that requires fitting to the reel seat, not to the blank. In this case leave space for the button, with a little extra for clearance. You *must* clear all the glue from this open end so that the butt cap or button will fit. This means not only the glue on the inside walls of the reel seat but also any bulge of glue at the end of the rod blank that might interfere with proper full seating of the button. If you use this method, cut off as much of the rod blank as you plan to recess the blank for clearance for the button. Check and measure against the tip section first—some rod sections are not exactly identical, and you may not have to cut off any rod blank at all.

Once the reel seat and grip are glued in place, you can add a removal extension butt using a scrap of blank or a tapered wood dowel. Either the scrap blank or tapered wood dowel must have the proper size and matched taper to fit securely into the blank for about 3 or 4 inches. If you have a piece of scrap blank that is not exactly the right taper, a little sanding will quickly match it to the rod-blank taper. Wood dowels must be tapered with sanding or scraping methods to get the insert portion of the dowel shaped and sized to fit. This is easy to do but requires a little work and trial-and-error fittings. One way to check your work is to insert the extension into the rod blank end and twist it several times with moderate pressure. When it's removed you can usually spot the glassy rub marks, indicating high points that require more sanding.

Once you have a good fit, build the cork, wood, or foam body on the extension butt; add a butt cap; and shape the cork or foam if necessary. Once the extension is glued and completed, add a little paraffin or candle wax to the plug-in part (this helps it to grip and hold) and you are ready to fish.

An alternative, for use with a regular aluminum open-end fly rod or light-spinning-reel seat (with no wood or other inserts), is to measure the reel seat and cut off half this amount from the end of the rod blank. In many cases these reel seats are about 5 inches long, so cut off about 2½ inches of the butt end of the rod blank. Check the length of the butt section against the length of the tip section to make sure the two remain equal.

Then glue the rod blank into the reel seat (see later description for suggestions), making sure the rod blank leaves about 2½ inches of clearance at the end. Completely clean the end of any excess glue.

You then have a straight shaft of opening, 2½ inches long, into which you can insert a straight-sided plug holding an extension butt. You can use a straight dowel, cut for a snug fit on a lathe if necessary, to fit into the end of the reel seat and serve as a base for the removable extension. Build as before with cork, foam, or wood.

Because the size of the dowel is critical for this friction fit, a variation is to make for a slightly looser fit and then cut two or three grooves around the dowel, using a pointed parting tool and a lathe. This will place two or three even grooves, into which you can stretch small O-rings that will serve to make a tight friction fit. Naturally this requires some trial and error in getting the right depth to the grooves for the size of the O-ring used. Small O-rings for this purpose are available at all good hardware stores. In essence this is a homemade copy of the same O-ring fitting of the removable extension butts available from some commercial reel-seat manufacturers.

Though I do not like it as well, you can also make a threaded fitting. There are several ways to do this. One of the easiest is to get a ¼-20 or 5⁄16-20 threaded rod fastener. These are like a nut but long—usually about 1 to 1½ inches. Use epoxy glue to glue this inside the blank at the end of the reel seat (if it will fit), or in the reel seat if the blank is cut and recessed. Then glue a same-size bolt with the head cut off or a short section of threaded rod into the center of the blank used for the extension or into a straight hole drilled for the purpose into a wood dowel.

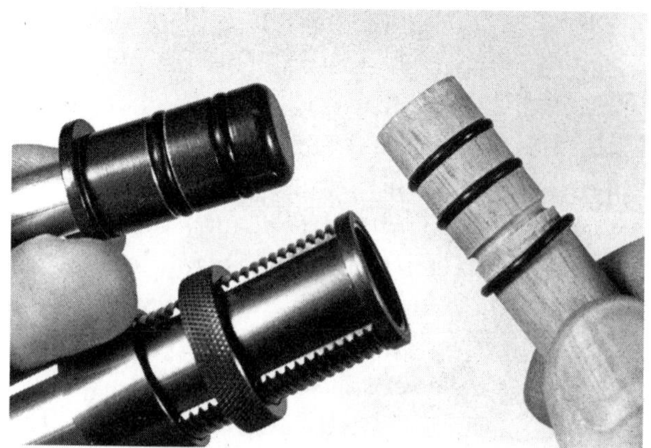

This method of making an extension butt for a fly rod involves cutting grooves around a dowel (a lathe is best for this) as shown; O-rings, available at hardware stores, are placed in the grooves for friction and centering. In essence the insert becomes similar to a commercially available insert (left top). One of the O-rings on the wood dowel has been moved to show the groove. Fit is by trial and error, and the wood dowel is then built up with cork rings.

Another, though heavier, alternative is to use a short bolt of the right length, building the extension onto the bolt with the threaded end exposed to fit into the reel seat. In all cases extend the threaded rod (bolt) about ½ to 1 inch, enough so that it will thread into the rod fastener. Then build up the extension butt so that the forward end of the butt meets the beginning of the threaded rod. For best results use a sander or grinder to carefully point the end of the threaded rod so that it will be easier to begin to thread the extension butt into the end of the rod.

If you add this type of screw-in extension butt to the rod before fishing, it is easy but has no real advantage over previously described systems.

Trying to do this after hooking a big fish—say a tarpon jumping all over the county—is almost impossible. Some commercial reel-seat/extension-butt combinations use this system, but in my opinion there are better, simpler ways.

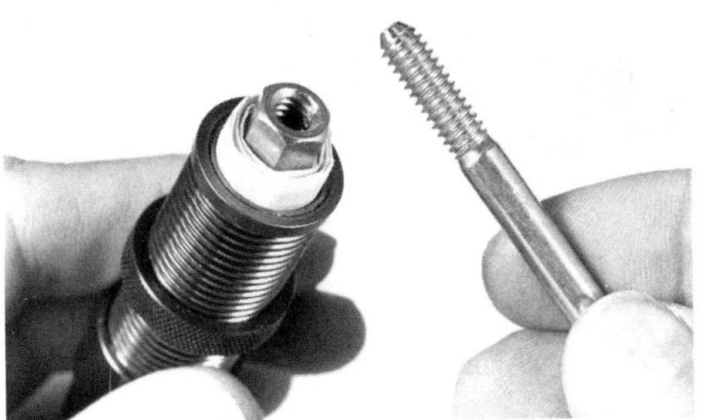

Method of making an extension butt for a fly rod. A nut extension is glued into the reel seat end (not yet glued at this point) and the cork rings built up on a shoulder bolt. The best size for this is ¼ inch by 20 (¼-20) threads, although any size can be used. Cork rings are built up on the shoulder bolt and the extension threaded into the end of the rod when needed.

Fly-rod fighting grips. These are commonly used on the largest fly rods, such as those used for billfish, tarpon, big sharks, and other large gamefish. These are nothing more than slim cigar-shaped grips mounted forward of the standard grip. They are usually about 5 to 6 inches long and slimmer than a normal grip, because they are only used for a second hand-support to help raise the rod to lift a big fish from the depths or in a sideways motion to turn the head of a big fish.

They are built in the same way as standard grips on a fly rod. Cork rings are built up on the blank and then shaped on a lathe (preferably). Usually they are mounted about 2 to 4 inches above the standard grip, with a decorative trim wrap and hook-keeper in between the two grips. Some big-game anglers do not add a hook-keeper, avoiding anything that might interfere with the line or smooth landing of a big fish.

BUTT-CAP ASSEMBLY

Butt caps are easy to add to any rod handle, but there are some tricks and considerations with them. Some butt caps are designed to fit over the end of the handle, so the process is one of simply gluing the butt cap onto the end of the handle with a strong epoxy glue. Be sure to use a file, sandpaper, or rasp to roughen the outside of the end of the handle to be covered by the butt cap and the inside of the butt cap. Use a layer or two of masking tape around the open edge of the butt cap and also around the handle *at the point where the butt cap will stop.*

Some butt caps require—or look better with—a recess in the handle so that the edge of the butt cap is flush with the edge of the handle rather than slightly overlapping it. These types of grips can be done with any rod, any style butt cap, and any style handle. Cork handles can be sanded, cut, or turned to allow for such a recess. Some preformed cork handles and some foam handles are made with specific recesses for butt caps and reel seats. The gluing procedure is exactly the same for this type of handle. Roughen the glued surfaces, and add a layer of masking tape to the butting edges of the handle and butt cap.

Some butt caps are really butt plates, in that they are aluminum or plastic buttons with a plug in the center; the plug is designed to be glued into the hole in the rod blank that extends to the rear of the rod handle. Most often these are used on cork handles for ultralight or light spinning rods, although they can be used on any type of rod and any type of materials. Use sandpaper to roughen the inner flat surface and also the extending plug. Roughen the flat end of the rod handle. Then add a good quantity of 24-hour epoxy glue to the hole in the rod blank and smear some glue on the end of the rod handle and on the inside surfaces of the butt plate. Push the butt plate into place, wipe up any excess glue around the edges, and stand the rod absolutely vertical.

One good way to do this is to stand the rod vertically alongside a bench and hold it in place, using masking tape to tape it to the bench edge. Often it helps to add some weight to the rod to keep pressure on the bond as the glue cures. One way to do this is to add a reel to the rod (if the reel seat has been mounted) or to slide some weights down the rod blank so that they jam at the handle. If the guides are in place, you can hang weights over the rod where they will jam at the guide frame.

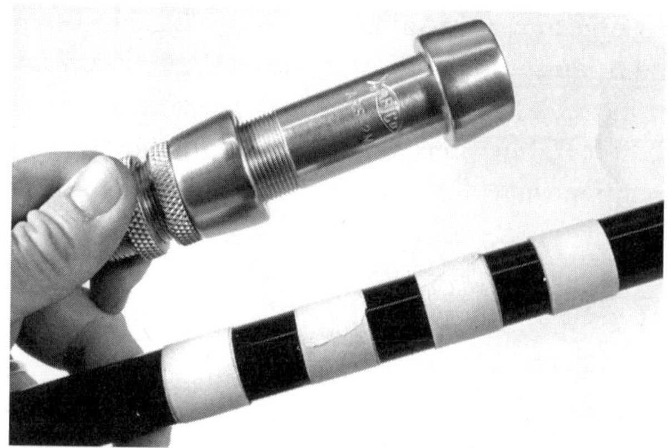

In some cases only a very slight shimming of a reel seat is required, such as this fitting of a heavy-duty reel seat onto a rod blank. Masking tape is ideal for this, but space should be allowed for a direct glue bond of the blank to the reel seat—not just gluing the reel seat to a solid layer of masking tape.

REEL-SEAT MOUNTING

Reel seats require specific methods of mounting on a rod blank, because the outside diameter of the rod blank on which they are mounted is almost always thinner than the reel-seat barrel. (Exceptions today in commercial rods are the skeletal reel seats that are specifically designed for a given blank diameter and thus are glued directly to the blank. These are becoming increasingly popular.)

In essence what you have to do is add a bushing of some sort to the rod blank, with the internal diameter of this bushing sized to the outside diameter of the blank and the outside diameter of the bushing sized to the internal diameter of the reel seat. In some cases bushings or shims can be drilled, tapered, and sized to fit; in other cases tape and cord can be used

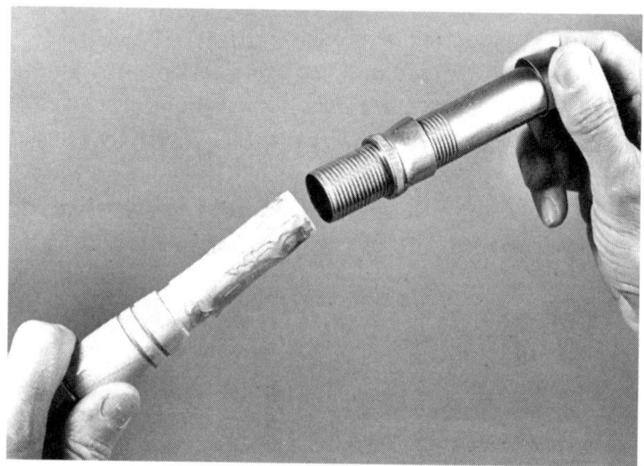

Adding a reel seat to a wooden boat-rod handle. For best results these parts should be taped, as previously outlined, to prevent smearing of glue.

Graphite bushings are available for shimming reel seats when there is a lot of space to fill. These are ideal since they transmit any impulses from the rod blank to the grip and reel seat. Several sizes are available, and all can be reamed or drilled to fit any rod blank.

Some bushings or fittings for reel seats require shimming. On this wood handle this is done by adding crossed cords to take up space between the wood and the reel seat. The ends of the handle and reel seat are taped, glue is added, and the reel seat is slid on.

to build up the area on the rod blank to fit the reel seat. Some possibilities for bushings of all types include materials that are slid and glued in place and those that are wrapped around the blank to build it up to the reel-seat diameter. Those that can be wrapped around the blank include thread; cord; and masking, paper, fiberglass, and self-adhesive cork tape. Those that are slipped onto the blank include cork rings; cardboard, graphite, and wood bushings; and old thread spools sized to fit.

Although you can wrap thread or cord around the blank using the standard rod-guide-wrapping method to start and finish, it is not necessary. One easy way is to smear epoxy glue onto the blank, lay a short length of cord parallel to it, then start with light pressure to wrap around the blank and cord. The glue holds the cord in place. After each wrapped layer, add more glue to make a solid cement bond of the cord or thread bushing. Once the layers produce the thickness prescribed by the reel-seat internal diameter, finish with a half-hitch or two, cinching them down to hold them in place and to prevent ridges in the finished bushing. Finish with a final layer of glue.

Another method I like is to spiral-wrap up and down the section of rod blank so that large lattice-like gaps are left in the wrap, to be filled with glue as the wrap progresses. This goes rapidly, reduces

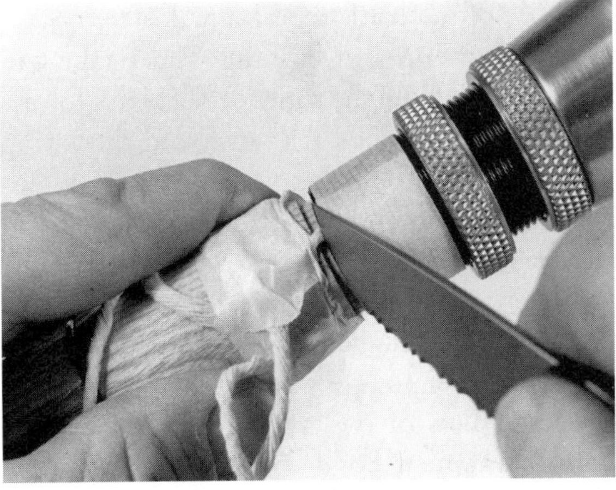

Once close to a final mounting of the reel seat, any excess cord is cut away and the reel seat pushed home on the handle.

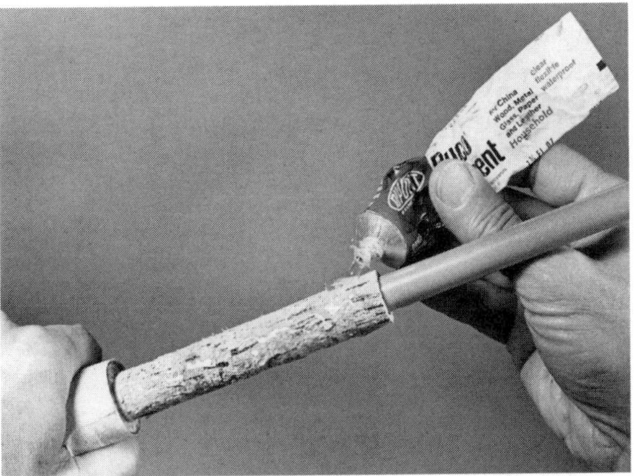

Additional cork rings or cork bushing (or other types of bushing) are added to the rod blank above the rear grip to glue the reel seat in place.

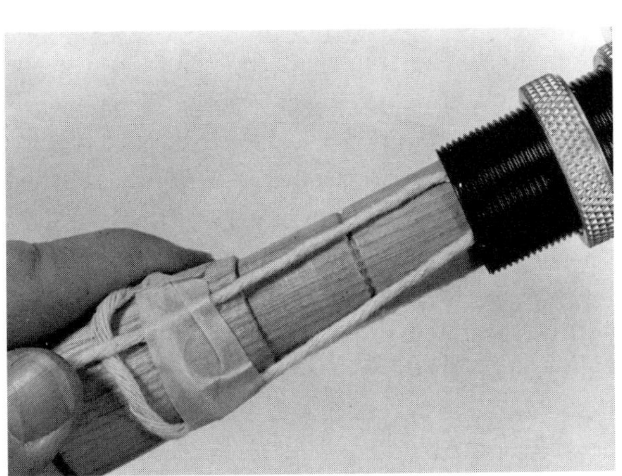

Checking a bushing for fitting after the longitudinal cords are added as a shim.

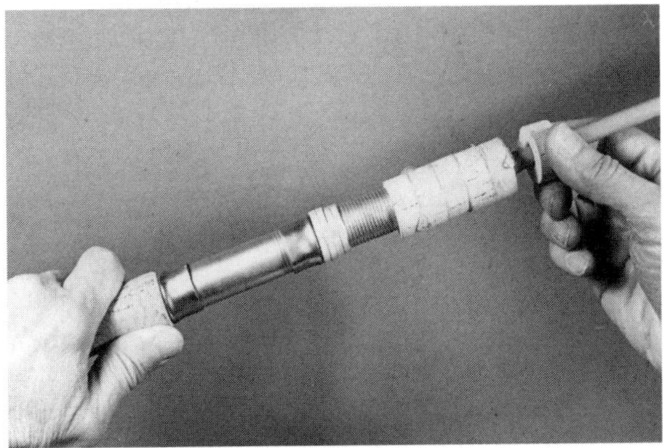

The reel seat glued in place, with corks added to make the foregrip on this spinning rod.

the bulk of the cord, and also makes for a solid epoxy-like bond and bushing. Paper tape can also be used: Glue the paper to the blank (or use self-adhesive or glue-back tape), and then wrap tightly around the blank until the paper wrapping is the diameter of the internal diameter of the reel seat. Fiberglass tape can be used in the same way: Wrap it around the blank, but in this case use epoxy glue or fiberglass resin to glue it in place.

Regardless of the type of bushing used, a good permanent bond of the reel seat to the blank through the bushing requires a solid bushing properly glued to the blank and reel seat or made from cord, thread, paper tape, or other tape but with a solid bond of epoxy glue from the blank all the way out to the reel seat. Thus, for "soft" materials such as cord, paper tape, and especially masking tape, the bushing material can only serve to keep the reel seat centered on the rod blank, while the epoxy, resin, or other glue forms the solid base for a permanent reel-seat mount.

An additional suggestion, particularly if you use tape products, is to use thin bands of tape around the blank so that you have a series of three or four or more bands, each about ½ to 1 inch thick and an equal distance apart. That way a lot of glue can be added to these spaces between the bands while the reel seat is being slowly slid onto the blank. The glue then bonds the reel seat to the blank.

If you are building up a solid bushing of any type, allow it to cure overnight. Then add glue to the bushing and slide the reel seat gently and slowly onto it. Make sure you first wrap the end of the grip and the lower end of the reel seat with several layers of masking tape to make a smooth, clean joint when the tape is later peeled off, along with any oozing glue. Slide and rotate the reel seat back and forth several times when adding it to the bushing to get a good distribution of glue. If you use a bushing made up of several bushing bands, add glue to them, slide the reel seat onto the bushing until the first bushing ring is hidden, then add as much epoxy glue as possible and slide the reel seat on farther. Continue until the reel seat is in place, and then allow the glue to cure overnight with the rod held vertically. This allows the liquid glue to flow and form a block of epoxy between the rod blank and reel seat.

FERRULES AND ADAPTERS

Methods used to add ferrules and adapters are similar to but far simpler than the methods used to add reel seats. First, the ferrules we are talking about here are not the self-contained ferrules found on most center-ferruled rod blanks but are the metal ferrules that used to be found in all rods and are today most common in older or older style rods and in bamboo fly rods.

Other examples would be the adapters that are permanently glued to rods and are designed to allow the rod to fit into a specific handle—usually a casting rod handle. In addition, there are the ferrules that are glued to offshore rods and designed to fit into the Unibutt handles by AFTCO and similar handles by other companies. In most cases these ferrules or adapters are available in 1⁄64th size increments, so no special sizing of the blank or parts is needed.

If additional sizing is needed, here are some tips to make this easy. First, do not count on building up the space between a ferrule and rod blank with excess epoxy glue. It might work, but a bond with only a thin amount of glue is better and stronger. (You can go too thin with the glue. Because the blank and ferrule are made of impervious materials, you must count on a surface coating of glue for proper bonding. It is important to lightly sand the blank to give it some roughness and tooth to hold the glue. If the ferrule or adapter is large enough to do so, it also helps to roughen the inside of the hole with a rat-tail file, rasp, or sandpaper strip glued to a dowel chosen for the purpose.) There are several steps to take in checking and correcting any looseness of these parts:

1. First recheck the size of the blank or ferrule and make sure that a smaller size ferrule or

adapter will not fit. A proper fit is one that will slide on snugly without any appreciable looseness but also without requiring forcing or pushing to get the ferrule completely on the rod.

2. If the ferrule or adapter is not the best size for the rod (and the next size smaller is too small), then you can correct the situation in one of several ways. The first is to wrap a single tight layer of thread around the rod—just like a guide wrapping—to build up the thickness of the blank in this area. Soak the area with glue, and slide the ferrule or part in place.

3. A second method is to make a thread wrap. Spiral the thread for most of the wrap, keeping it tight only at both ends, where you start and finish. That way the thread wrap serves as a shim to keep the ferrule or adapter centered on the blank; the gaps in the spiral wrap allow glue to bond the rod blank to the ferrule. In other words, you are not running the risk of just gluing the ferrule to the surface of the thread wrap.

4. Another method, which I like very much, is to lay thread or cord longitudinally along the blank, taping it in place several inches above the end, running it over the end and up the opposite side, and taping it again. Repeat this several times so that you end up with four (the minimum), six, or eight taped-down strings, threads, or cord. Soak the cord and blank with glue, and slide the ferrule in place. The advantage of this method, particularly if the fit is tight, is that there is no way to push the thread wrap out of place, as might occur with circular wraps. If the fit is too tight, the ferrule won't go on but the cord can't dislodge, as can a wrapped-thread shim.

5. Another method to use, if the fit of a ferrule is slightly loose on a blank butt section, is to cut the blank back slightly. This produces a slightly decreased blank diameter as you slide the ferrule on. However, it pays to take some careful caliper or micrometer measurements before you do this; otherwise

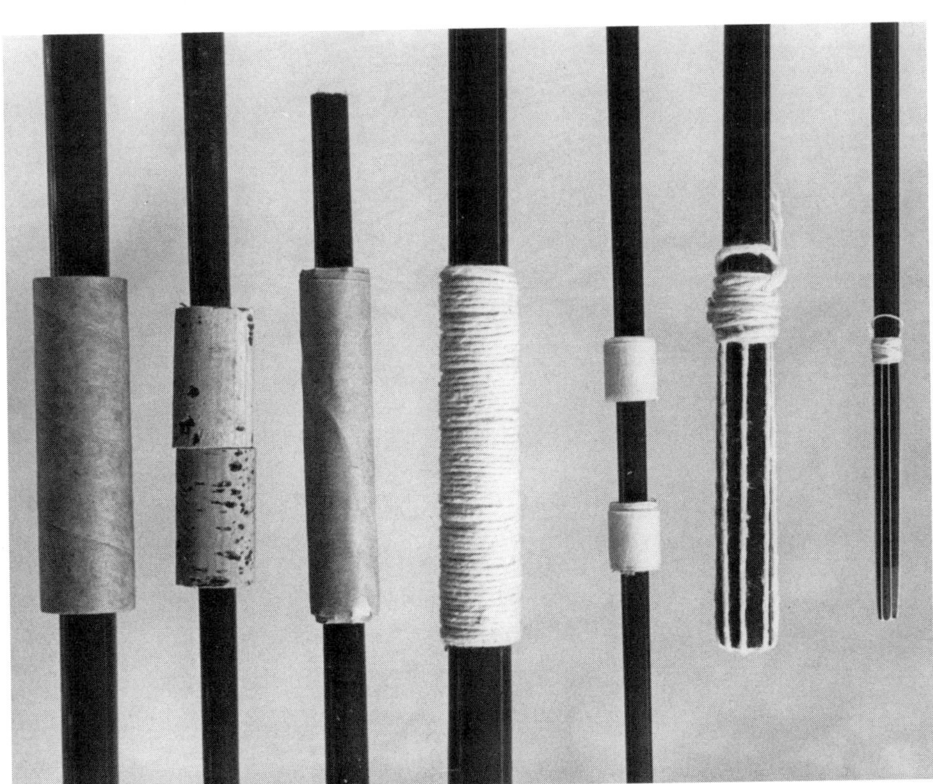

Types of bushings for reel seats and metal ferrules. Left to right: fiber bushing, cork bushings, wrapped paper tape, wrapping of cord, built-up rings of masking tape, spines of cord over the end of the rod, and spines of thread over the end of the rod.

you risk cutting the blank back too far and thus shortening the blank and possibly even changing the action of the rod at this critical ferruled point. The rationale of course is that with the increasingly smaller diameter of the blank, you will get to a point where the ferrule will fit perfectly.

6. If you are using two-part ferrules as you would with a two-piece rod or bamboo fly rod, try to get the best possible fit of the ferrules. Usually these ferrules today are only made in the fine, 18 percent nickel silver material, available in differences of 1⁄64 inch and thus able to get an exact or almost exact match for each ferruled section. If you are using bamboo, you can often file down the edges of the six-strip section so that a too-tight ferrule will fit or run some thread longitudinally (as above) over the ferruled part so as to shim a slightly loose section and make for a good glue bond.

Once the ferrule or adapter is glued onto the rod blank, clean any excess glue with a solvent-soaked rag and, if necessary (as with the longitudinal-cord method), trim off any exposed cord or thread shim material. Then the ferrule or adapter can be wrapped with thread (see chapter 22) as desired.

Note that some metal ferrules have a slight shoulder or recess acting as a stop point for a thread wrap that begins on the blank and partially wraps up over the ferrule. In some cases the ferrules are wrapped completely as part of the decoration of the rod or to hide the shiny metal portion. If this is the case, the male portion that slides into the female ferrule must be kept clean and free of any thread work.

21
Guide and Part Spacing

Introduction • Tools and Materials • Using Other Rods for Spacing • General Considerations • Other Sources for Guide Spacing • Formulas • Guide-Spacing Charts • Checking Guide Spacing

INTRODUCTION

An important note: All guide spacing should be checked before the guides are wrapped down and coated with epoxy. After this it is a little late to make easy adjustments. Even if you are sure of the guide spacing, check anyway, using one or more of the methods noted at the end of this chapter. When you're finally satisfied, proceed to the wrapping bench.

Guide spacing is critical in making a custom rod. If the guides are spaced wrong, casting distance, accuracy, and pleasure can be hindered severely. Poor guide spacing can turn a good blank into a terrible rod. Having too many guides on a light rod, or the wrong guides, can make the rod sluggish and unusable. If there aren't enough guides on a rod, the line can rub against the rod excessively or, because the stresses haven't been distributed evenly, the rod can break.

There are no absolutes in terms of the exact number, size, or position of guides; there are, however, some general rules and guide-spacing charts. That's what this chapter is all about: understanding the concept of guide spacing and getting the best spacing available for the rod blank and type of rod you have chosen to build.

TOOLS AND MATERIALS

Tools for guide spacing are few. You will want some masking tape to mark the location of the center of each guide. Also, you will want an accurate ruler to measure the distances on the rod blank you've taken from rod charts or other formulas to determine guide spacing. For this a straight metal or wood rule is best. Roll-up measuring tapes can be a little awkward to work with, particularly if you are determining the space from tip-top to a butt guide for proper spacing of the intermediate guides.

If you plan to make a number of rods of the same design with the same guide spacing, you may want to make an additional tool—a board or strip that serves as a template for the exact measurement of all the guides on that rod. For example, a length of wood with the blank number marked at the top and marks measured from the top for the position of each guide (along with the reel-seat position) will make a good template. You do not need a strip of wood as long as the rod—only a strip that is as long as the distance between the first and last guides. You can include information as to guide size and type, if desired. Thus the strip of wood would contain a list of numbers beginning with the distance from the tip-top to the first guide followed by guide information, reel-seat position and, for safety, the measurement in inches. An example might look like this: "#1-SHG 10-6¼." That would indicate the first guide, the type of guide used, the size of the guide in ring size, and the distance from the tip-top or the previous guide. Another easy way to do this is to use a discarded venetian blind strip and mark the measurements with a permanent felt-tip pen. The curve of the blind strip will cradle the rod blank while you are transferring the measurements from the blank to the blind strip to create a measurement template and then from the blind strip to the next rod of this design that you are building.

USING OTHER RODS FOR SPACING

Once you have the handle glued on, or the exact measurements for the length of the handle, one of the easiest ways to determine guide spacing is to copy it from a *good* existing rod. I emphasize the word *good,* because a poor rod—or one made with compromises, with too few guides or the wrong type of guides, or a poorly positioned reel seat—will result in an equally poor copy.

A good rod with good guide spacing and good guides that was made with attention to quality and performance should result in a rod equally good or better when you copy the same dimensions. Naturally the rod must be of the same power (the strength, or resistance to bending), the same action (the way in which the rod bends—parabolic or fast-tip), and the same length, and it must have the same type of handle assembly.

Assuming these things, copying guide spacing is a perfectly acceptable way to start. I say start, because even with the same type of rod, it pays to tape guides in place and then bend and lightly and carefully cast the rod to assure that it works the way you want. If it doesn't, some adjustment of the guides may be required.

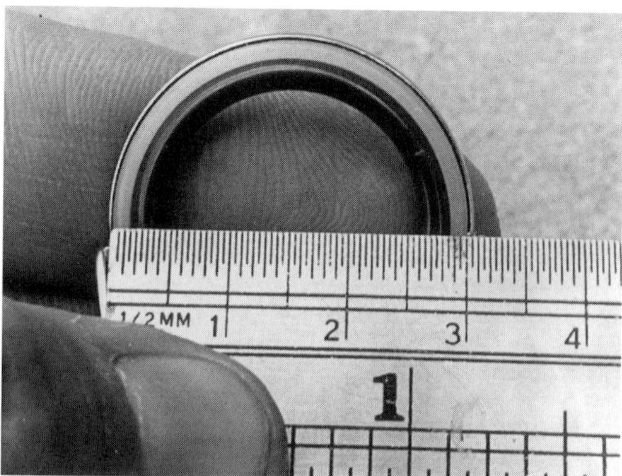

In choosing guides it is important to note that with the new ceramic guides, the true size of the opening in the ceramic ring is often far smaller than the nominal stated size. This 30-millimeter guide, for example, actually has an interior diameter of about 23 millimeters. Ring diameter is important for line flow and knot clearance, particularly in small guides.

GENERAL CONSIDERATIONS

If you do not have a rod to copy from, you can start from scratch, assuming some general considerations. The first step in any such calculation is to determine the position, or approximate position, of the butt or first guide up from the reel seat. The best way to figure this is from the center of the reel seat, or center of the reel, to the guide. This is the only unchanging measurement and the only one that counts. The presence of long or short rear grips or the length of the foregrip does not matter. What does matter is the distance from the reel, where the line leaves and travels along the rod, to the first guide, where it is gathered (thus the term "gathering guide") to continue through the rest of the guides.

This location can be critical. Some years ago I did some testing for a major rod and rod-blank manufacturer in which I was asked to start from scratch and determine the best possible guide spacing and size for its line of fly rods. In the process I tried some ridiculous butt- or stripper-guide positions, including some as close as about 20 to 24 inches above the center of the reel seat. In these cases the first guide was only about 11 to 15 inches above the top of the handle. Up to about 27 inches from the center of the reel seat, the guide position usually would cause line waves and rod shock to the point that the rod could not be cast effectively. The rod blanks were first-rate designs, but this extreme of guide positioning made them impossible to cast. I also tried placing the first guide much higher than normal—ranging from about 35 inches or more from the reel-seat center. In these cases the line slap was so great that it also reduced casting distance and accuracy. It did not create the same line shock, line waves, and rod shock as did the shortened distances, but it did adversely affect an otherwise fine rod. These tests were done with the guides taped on, the way you should do them also, until I was absolutely sure of the best possible guide spacing.

Other types of rods are also affected by extremes of butt-guide placement. Thus the position of this guide is really the most important of

Tip-tops must also be chosen for line clearance. The two on the left are the same tube size to fit the same diameter blank, but the center guide has a larger ring than the one on the left. When possible, choose tip-tops with the largest ring size.

all. It can control how well your rod casts and also determine in part the amount of spacing between the rest of the guides used and thus the distribution of stress.

There are some approximate figures for positioning the butt guide. The following are all measured from the center of the reel seat to the butt guide:

Fly rods: 28 to 32 inches. Use the shorter distance for light, short fly rods; the longer distance for larger, longer, and heavier fly rods.

Ultralight spinning rods: 16 to 24 inches. Shorten the distance with very light 4½-foot rods; lengthen with longer ultralight rods.

Freshwater spinning rods: 19 to 27 inches.

Saltwater spinning rods: 20 to 27 inches.

Bait-casting rods: 17 to 25 inches.

Popping rods: 18 to 26 inches.

Boat rods: 22 to 26 inches.

Trolling rods, East Coast style: 20 to 25 inches.

Trolling rods, West Coast style: 22 to 26 inches.

Surf rods: 27 to 33 inches.

Once the basic butt-guide location is determined, you can determine the positioning of the rest of the guides. There are also some general considerations as to the location of the guides and the number of guides used on each type and length of rod. Note, however, that these are *general* considerations. There are exceptions to all the following based on a specific rod, rod action, rod power, handle length, type of rod, and so on. These basic considerations are:

1. In all rods the number of guides is important but not critical. If you have one too many or too few guides (according to someone else or a formula), it is not the end of the world. However, it is best to have the "right" number. Too many guides and the rod can become sluggish. Too few and the rod may not distribute stresses properly.
2. Fast-tip rods will need more guides than even-bending parabolic rods, and these guides will have to be closer together, with more at the tip end. This will help distribute the stresses of the light-rod action better. In the case of revolving-spool tackle in which the guides are on top of the rod, it helps to minimize line contact with the rod blank between the guides.
3. For fly rods use one guide for each foot of length or fraction of a foot of length, exclusive of the rod's tip-top. Thus an 8-foot rod would have eight guides, an 8½- or 9-foot rod would have nine guides, and a 9-foot-3-inch rod or 10-foot fly rod would have ten guides.
4. For spinning rods use one guide for each foot of length, not including fractions of a foot but exclusive of the tip-top. Thus a 4½-foot ultralight would have four guides, a 6- or 6½-foot medium spinning rod would have six guides, and a 7-foot rod would have seven guides.
5. Casting and spin-cast rods should have one guide for each foot of rod length or fraction

of a foot of rod length. Thus a 5-foot casting rod would have five guides; a 5½- or 6-foot casting rod would have six guides.

6. Surf rods should have one guide for each two feet or fraction of that of rod length, exclusive of the rod tip-top. An 8-foot surf or jetty rod would have four guides, a 9- or 10-foot rod would have five guides, and a 12-foot rod would have six guides.
7. Offshore and heavy boat trolling rods of standard lengths of about 6½ to 7½ feet would have five guides plus the tip-top.
8. West Coast–style and action trolling rods in which there is a pronounced tip action (stand-up rods) but the same lengths as standard or East Coast–style trolling rods (6½ to 7½ feet) would require six or seven guides plus the tip-top. The greater number of guides is required to help distribute the stresses of the tip-action rod, and the extra guides are located in this tip area.
9. Stand-up rods would have one or two more guides than trolling rods as a result of their fast tip actions and usage.
10. Long, thin, light so-called noodle rods would have more guides than similar-length casting or spinning rods to help distribute stress and reduce line rubbing. Generally most noodle rods would have one guide for each foot of length or fraction of a foot in length, plus two or three additional guides, plus the tip-top. Thus a noodle rod about 9 feet long would have eleven or twelve guides. These guides would be very small and lightweight, in keeping with the rod's power and action.
11. Opinions differ with the new microguides that are coming into the marketplace and being used on commercial rods and by custom rod builders. These are mostly being used on casting and some spinning rods, with a micro-wave or similar butt guide to funnel the line straight to microguides that might be as small as 3 millimeters. I like the idea of about 50 percent more guides than the guide numbers suggested for so-called standard guides. Thus for a 6-foot casting rod that would take about six standard guides, I would put on nine guides. However, I have tremendous respect for the knowledge and opinions of longtime rod designer Al Jackson (and developer of microguides), who would use no more microguides on a rod than he would standard guides.

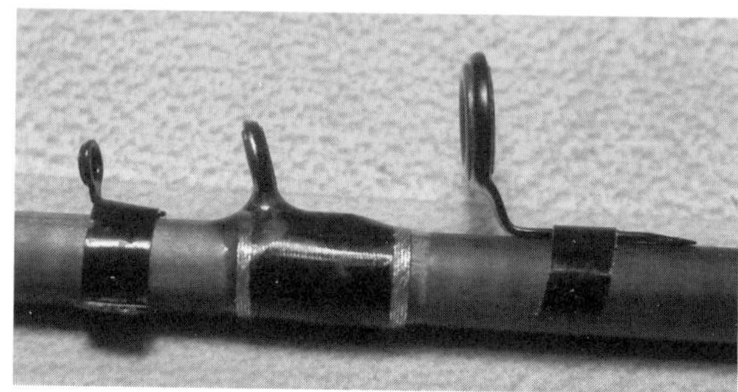

Left to right, a 1-millimeter and a 3- millimeter microguide, which are now being used in the commercial and custom rod markets. The third guide to the right is a 6-millimeter guide, which used to be the smallest guide available for any rod, custom or commercial. Microguides reduce weight and stiffness of a rod without affecting line friction or casting ease. ***Photo by Mike Harris.***

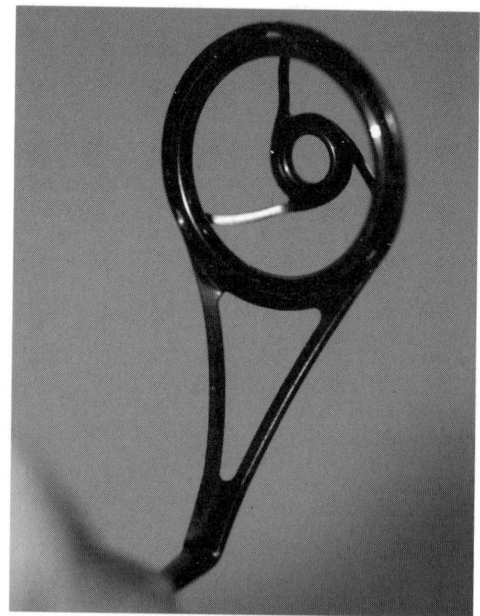

Tiny microguides are now being used for both casting and spinning rods. To choke down the line with the first guide on a spinning rod, innovative guides are being designed and used, as per this example.

OTHER SOURCES FOR GUIDE SPACING

If you are experienced in fishing and rod building, then perhaps the easiest way to determine guide spacing is to simply lay the rod blank on a flat surface, determine the number of guides needed, and begin to position the guides along the blank, adjusting as you go. The best way to do this is to first position the butt guide where you think it belongs, going perhaps by the measurements above for suggested butt guide spacing above the reel seat. Then position the rest of the guides, with less spacing between guides at the tip end and more at the butt end to adjust for the rod taper and type of bend. I do this but still check with a rule and make any adjustments as required; then I tape the guides in place and check them.

Other information for guide spacing is available. If you don't have a rod from which to copy spacing, specific guide information is often available from the source of the rod blank. Mail-order companies will often provide suggested guide spacing for the specific rod you buy. Other sources will sometimes determine guide spacing for you, based on the rod blank, the guides chosen, the type and length of handle to be used, and the position of the reel seat for your planned rod. Tackle shops will often have the same information or provide the same service.

Fishing clubs that are heavily into rod building as a club project or as a service to members also sometimes keep information on guide spacing for specific rods.

Some mail-order and rod-blank-manufacturer catalogs include guide-spacing information obtained from the rod manufacturers. Similar information, where it was possible to get it, is available in the remainder of this chapter.

There are two important factors to consider in using any such information. The first is that although the information is accurate, it is based on the rod being built to certain specification. For example, if you begin with a 6-foot casting-rod blank and use charts for a blank through-handle construction with a short handle but modify it for a long flipping- or steelhead-type handle with a 12-inch-long rear grip, the reel seat position will change and thus the guide spacing will change. In effect the longer handle moves the entire grip and reel-seat assembly forward about 4 or 5 inches on the rod blank, shortening the distance between the reel and the first or butt stripper guide by this much. The result may be more line friction on the cast and when line is retrieved, particularly when a wide-spool reel is used. Conversely, a rod designed for a through-the-handle construction with a long steelhead-type rear grip that is built with a 5-inch rear grip will have increased distance between the reel and first guide, thus increasing the possibility of line-slap and rod friction.

The second factor is that you do not have to match the exact brand and power of rod if you use a chart from a ready-built commercial or custom rod. For example, a rod built on a blank by manufacturer A will generally work fine with the guide spacing taken from the same length, action, and power of a rod built by manufacturer B. Similarly, most rod-blank manufacturers will have rods of the same length and action but in several different power, or strength, ranges—for instance, light, medium, and heavy. In general the same guide spacing will apply to all three rod blanks, even though you might want to go with a light one-foot guide on the light-power rod; a two-foot guide on the medium-power rod; and a reinforced, braced two-foot guide on the heavy-power rod.

The same rule may not apply to rods with different actions. For example, a manufacturer may have a rod blank of the same length, basic purpose (say, casting), and power (designed for the same general range of lure weights) but with an even parabolic action—different from the second rod, which has a stiff butt and fast-tip action. This often requires different guide spacing for the two rods. The parabolic rod may require even guide spacing from tip to butt (though the distance between guides will increase from tip to butt). The fast-action rod may require closer guide spacing at the tip end to better distribute stress at this light, whippy area, requiring greater distance between guides at the butt end, or perhaps even one more guide than the parabolic rod of the same length.

One method used years ago to determine guide spacing, and still accurate as a starting point, is to use a deflection chart. This involves checking rods against a large wall-mounted chart. The chart must be as long as any rod you will test and generally several feet high, since it will be used to measure rods and rod deflection and strength when the rod is positioned horizontally. The chart must be exactly horizontal on the wall; check with a level.

The chart must have horizontal stripes or lines to determine guide position. You can make such a deflection chart from a wide strip of paper. The 54-inch-wide background paper used by photographers (and available from good photo-supply stores) is ideal for this. Pick white or a light color, and draw in the lines you need. A more colorful and easier alternative is to pick wallpaper with even vertical stripes and attach it to the wall so that the stripes run horizontally. Narrow stripes about 1 inch wide are ideal, but any even striping will give you an easy way to check the points where the bent rod blank intersects the chosen line measurement.

The deflection chart must have a bracket or pegs on which to hold a rod horizontally with the handle *exactly* straight and horizontal. This can be done with a series of adjustable pegs or by using a tube or rod holder (such as those that fit onto the side of a boat for fishing or trolling) to hold the handle. Rod-building companies and component houses have such sets of equipment to hold and position rod handles horizontally for these checks with a rod deflection chart.

With the rod in the horizontal position, hang a weight from its end. This can be done by first gluing the tip-top in place and then tying a weight to it or by taping cord or line to the tip end of the rod and then adding a weight to that. The weight will vary with the rod but should place a pronounced curve in the blank similar to what it would get during casting or playing a fish. Often this will result in the tip end pointing straight down or almost straight down, with the rest of the rod curving until gradually becoming horizontal at the handle. You want a weight that will arc the rod but not be so heavy that it will only bend the butt end while pulling the top end straight down for several feet.

Guide positioning can be done in a couple of ways. One way is to determine a deflection measurement—say, 5 inches—that you wish to use between the tip-top and the first guide. Measure 5 inches straight up from the position of the tip end or tip-top to a horizontal line that will intersect the bent rod blank. This intersection (bent rod and the horizontal line 5 inches up from the tip end) is the point for the first guide. Measure 5 inches to the next line. Continue doing this—measuring 5 inches (or whatever measurement you determine best) to where the horizontal lines intersect the rod blank. Do this until you are at or close to the position for the first (butt) guide. Naturally this measurement will vary with the rod and will be determined by the rod type. A surf rod might have an initial distance of 8 to 12 inches, a freshwater spinning rod about 6 inches, a fly rod about 5 inches, and a very light noodle rod about 4 inches.

An alternative method is to place the rod on the chart, hang a weight from the tip, and then measure along the rod from the center of the reel seat to determine an approximate placement of the first guide (see the lists in manufacturing rod charts for suggestions here). With the weight hanging from the rod tip, mark this point on the deflection chart, and then measure straight down the chart to a point where the bent tip end intersects a horizontal line. Measure this distance and divide it by the number of guides you plan to use. For example, if a particular rod had 30 vertical inches between the tip end and the position of the first butt guide and you were planning to use five guides, then the *vertical* distance between guides (not the distance on the rod blank) would be 6 inches. This method eliminates the possibility of getting a butt guide positioned too high or low on the rod blank and having to redo the measurements and calculations.

A simpler way is to mount the rod horizontally with a bracket or clamp and then stretch a string horizontally (check it with a level) so that the handle and reel seat are centered on the string. Then hang a weight from the rod to bow it and, using a straight rule, measure down from the string to the tip end. Move up a set amount (based on the rod type) and then measure down, moving the rule until the second measurement intersects the bowed rod blank. Repeat this until you are at the first position for the location of the butt guide. Alternatively, you can use the second method, measuring along the rod blank to position the butt guide. Measure straight down to this point, take a second measurement to the end of the rod, and then divide the distance between the two by the number of guides to determine the first spacing.

Perhaps the most important point is that *all* formulas for guide spacing should be considered as starting points. All guide spacing should be checked, as will be outlined later in this chapter.

FORMULAS

There are formulas for determining guide spacing, or at least to serve as starting points for guide spacing. Some of these are simple; others are quite complex. Some take into account the positioning of ferrules and make allowances for them; others do not and thus sometimes require adjustment of guide positions.

One simple formula calculates the distance between guides after the position of the butt guide is determined. It also allows for the gradually increasing distance between the guides as they progress from the tip to the butt. The simplest way to understand this is to consider a standard spinning rod 6 feet long with six guides and a tip-top. Assuming the butt guide to be 2 feet up from the end of the rod, this would place the bottom guide 4 feet, or 48 inches, below the tip-top. This then creates six spaces between the adjacent guides, starting with the space between the tip-top and the first guide. If we assume this first distance to be a constant factor—"X"—then we can figure the remaining guides by adding to this X factor. Using the addition of 1 more inch per guide is a good starting point. Thus the position between the tip-top and first guide would be X, the distance between the first and second guides would be X plus 1, the distance between the second and third would be X plus 2 (1 plus 1), the distance between the third and fourth would be X plus 3 (2 plus 1), the distance between the fourth and fifth would be X plus 4 (3 plus 1), and the distance between the fifth and sixth or last guide would be X plus 5 (4 plus 1). This formula would look like this:

$X + (X + 1) + (X + 2) + (X + 3) + (X + 4) + (X + 5) = 48$ inches (the space between the tip-top and butt guide)

If we subtract the inches from the formula, it becomes:

$$6X + 15 = 48$$
$$6X = 48 - 15 = 33$$
$$6X = 33$$
$$X = 5.5$$

Going back to the formula, we then see that the distances between the guides are as follows: Between the tip-top and the first guide, 5.5 inches (X); between the first and second guide, 6.5 inches (X + 1); between the second and third guide, 7.5 inches (X + 2); between the third and fourth guide, 8.5 inches (X + 3); between the fourth and fifth guide, 9.5 inches (X + 4); and between the fifth and sixth or last guide, 10.5 inches (X + 5).

You can use any additional spacing factor you desire. While the formula is simple by adding 1 more inch with each guide spacing, you could just as easily use 1¼ inches, 1½ inches, or 2 inches (though you would not use such large spaces on this standard medium freshwater spinning rod). If you used 1½ inches, for example, using six guides, the spacing would be X, X + 1½, X + 3, X + 4½, X + 6, and X + 7½.

The three factors that would change the guide spacing and positions would be the length of the rod (or the length between the tip-top and butt guide), the number of guides, and the constant number that would be added to the spacing of each previous guide. This can be done using millimeters or centimeters as well as inches. Just be sure you keep all numbers in the same measuring system.

Note that the above does not take into account the number or positioning of ferrules. In some cases with multiple-piece rods, you may have to adjust the position of a guide slightly to avoid it sitting right over a ferrule. It is permissible to place a guide just above or below a ferrule so that the guide wrap also becomes the ferrule wrap, reinforcing the blank for hoop strength. This change in position usually requires some slight adjustment of guides above and below the guide in the ferrule area.

GUIDE-SPACING CHARTS

The following companies have been most helpful in providing guide spacing charts for all their rod blanks. Unfortunately space limitations allow only a small sampling of these listings. These companies make more rods for a variety of line sizes and casting weights than those listed. When choosing between different rods of the same length but of different power (line size in fly rods and lure weight in others), I usually chose the lighter. In most cases the guide spacing would be identical or very similar to that of heavier rods, although the guide sizes might change. Realize that you *must* use the same style handle and position of reel seats as used by the manufacturer in its finished model; otherwise the guide spacings will be invalid. Complete information on any rod blank is available directly from the manufacturer or from vendors selling the rod blank. (See appendix F for complete addresses.)

St. Croix Rods

Suggested Guide Size and Spacing Chart

STYLE	INCHES FROM TIP-TOP	SIZE
CASTING (BASS & WALLEYE)		
5'6"	4.5-9.5-15.5-22.5-30-39	12-10-8-6-6-6
6'0"	4.5-9.5-15.5-22.5-31.5-42.5	12-10-8-6-6-6
6'2"	4.5-9.5-15.5-22.5-31.5-42.5	12-10-8-6-6-6
6'6"	4-8.5-13.5-19.5-26.5-34.6-44.5	12-10-8-6-6-6-6
7'0"	5-10.5-16.5-23-31-40-50	12-10-8-6-6-6-6
7'6" tel.	4-9-15-22-30-39-49	12-10-8-6-6-6-6
CASTING (MUSKIE)		
6'0"	5-10.5-16.5-24-34.5	20-16-12-10-8
6'6"	5-10.5-16.5-24-32.5-42	20-16-12-10-8-8
7'0"	4.5-9.5-15-21-28.5-37.5-48	20-16-12-10-8-8-8
7'6"	4.5-9-14-19.5-25.5-32.5-41-51	20-16-12-10-8-8-8-8
CASTING (LIGHT SALTWATER)		
7'0"	5-11-17-24-31.5-40-49.5	12-10-10-10-8-8-8
7'6"	5-10-15.5-21.5-28-35.5-44-55	12-10-10-10-8-8-8-8
8'0"	4.5-9.5-15-21-28-36-45.5-57	16-12-10-8-8-8-8-8

St. Croix Rods

Suggested Guide Size and Spacing Chart

STYLE	INCHES FROM TIP-TOP	SIZE
CASTING (SALMON/STEELHEAD)		
8'0"	4.5-9.5-15-21-28-36-45.5-57	16-12-10-10-8-8-8-8
8'6"	4.5-9.5-15.5-22.5-30.5-39.5-50-63	16-12-10-10-8-8-8-8
10'6"	4.5-10-16.5-24-32-41-50.5-61-71.5-83	16-12-10-8-8-8-8-8-8-8
SPINNING (BASS & WALLEYE/TROUT & PANFISH)		
4'6" UL	5-11.5-20.5-31	20-10-8-6
5'0" UL	5-10.5-17-25-34.25	20-16-10-8-6
5'6" L-M	5.5-11.5-18.5-26.5-37	25-16-10-8-6
6'0" L-M	4-9-15-22-30-40	25-20-16-10-8-7
6'6" L-M	4-9-15-22.5-31.5-42.5	30-20-16-10-8-7
7'0" L-M	4-8.5-13.5-19.5-27-36-49	30-20-16-10-8-7-6
7'6" L-M	4.5-9.5-15.5-22.5-30.5-41-54	30-20-16-10-8-7-6
SPINNING (SALMON/STEELHEAD)		
7'6"	4.5-9.5-15.5-22.5-30.5-41-54	30-20-16-10-8-7-6
8'6"	5.5-12-19.75-28.5-38-50.75-65	30-20-16-10-8-7-6
9'0"	5-10.5-16.5-23.5-32-42-53-68.5	30-20-16-10-8-7-7-6
FLY (LIGHT TO MEDIUM FRESHWATER)		
6'0"	4-8.5-13.5-19-25-32-40-50	10-4-4-3-3-2-2-2
6'6"	4-8.5-13.5-19-25-33-41.5-52	12-4-4-3-3-2-2-2
7'0"	4-9-15-21.5-28.5-36.6-45.5-56	12-4-4-3-3-2-2-2
7'6"	4.5-9.5-15.5-22.5-30.5-39.5-49.5-61.5	12-4-4-4-3-3-3-3
8'0"	4.25-9.5-15-21.5-29-37.25-46.25-55.5-65.5	12-4-4-4-4-3-3-3-3
8'6"	4.875-10.375-17.375-25.125-33.125-41.625-50.875-60.875-71.875	12-4-4-4-4-3-3-3-3
9'0"	4-9-15-22-29.5-37.5-46.625-56.75-67.25-78	12-10-4-4-4-4-3-3-3-3
9'6"	4-9-15-22-29.5-37-45-53.25-62.125-71.375-81.25	12-10-4-4-4-4-3-3-3-3-3
10'0"	4-9-15-22-30-39-48-57.5-68.375-79.375-90	12-10-4-4-4-4-3-3-3-3-3
FLY (HEAVY FRESH- & SALTWATER)		
8'6"	4.875-10.375-17.375-25.125-33.125-41.625-50.875-60.875-71.875	16-12-5-5-5-4-4-4-4
9'0"	4.5-9.5-15.5-22-29-36.5-44.5-54-64-76.5	16-12-5-5-5-5-4-4-4-4
9'0" salt.	4.5-9.5-15.5-21.625-28.875-36.5-44.75-53.25-64-76	20-16-12-6-6-6-5-5-5-5
9'6"	4-9-15-22-29.5-37-45-53.25-61.125-71.375-81.25	16-12-5-5-5-5-4-4-4-4-4
10'0"	4-9-15-22-30-39-48-57.5-68.375-79.375-90	16-12-5-5-5-5-4-4-4-4-4

Lamiglas Guide Spacing Chart

Revised 4/22/10

ROD MODEL	ALL MEASUREMENTS ARE IN INCHES FROM TIP														BLANK MODEL
XMG 50 TRAVEL															
XMG 904	4	9	15 1/8	21 1/2	28	35 3/4	43 3/4	53 3/8	63	75 1/8					ET 1084-4
Guide Sizes	1	1	1	2	2	2	3	4	10	12					
XMG 905	4	9	15 1/8	21 1/2	28	35 3/4	43 3/4	53 3/8	63	75 1/8					ET 108 5
Guide Sizes	1	1	1	2	2	2	3	4	10	12					
XMG 906	4	9	15 1/8	21 1/2	28	35 3/4	43 3/4	53 3/8	63	75 1/8					ET 1086-4
Guide Sizes	1	1	1	2	2	2	3	4	10	12					
XMG 907	4	9	15 1/8	21 1/2	28	35 3/4	43 3/4	53 3/8	63	75 1/8					ET 1087-4
Guide Sizes	1	1	1	2	2	2	3	4	12	16					
XMG 908	4	9	15 1/8	21 1/2	28	35 3/4	43 3/4	53 3/8	63	75 1/8					ET 1088-4
Guide Sizes	4	4	4	4	5	5	5	6	12	16					
XMG 909	4	9	15 1/8	21 1/2	28	35 3/4	43 3/4	53 3/8	63	75 1/8					ET 1089-4
Guide Sizes	4	4	4	4	5	5	5	6	12	16					
XMG 910	4	9	15 1/8	21 1/2	28	35 3/4	43 3/4	53 3/8	63	75 1/8					ET 108-10
Guide Sizes	4	4	4	4	5	5	5	6	12	16					
XMG 912	4	9	15 1/8	21 1/2	28	35 3/4	43 3/4	53 3/8	63	78 1/8					IMT 108-12
Guide Sizes	4	4	4	4	5	5	5	6	16	20					
XMG 967	4 1/2	9 1/2	15 3/4	22 1/4	29	36 7/8	45 3/8	56 1/4	67 1/2	81 1/2					ET 1147-4
Guide Sizes	1	1	1	2	2	2	3	4	12	16					
SPRING CREEK															
AT 663	4	9	15	22	30	39 1/2	50								ET 783
Guide Sizes	1	1	1	2	2	3	10								
AT 703	4 3/8	9 3/8	15 1/2	21 3/8	28 1/2	36 1/2	45	56							ET 843 3
Guide Sizes	1	1	1	2	2	3	4	10							
AT 764	5 1/2	12	19 1/4	27 1/4	35 1/2	43 1/2	52 1/2	62 3/4							ET 904
Guide Sizes	1	1	1	2	2	3	4	12							
AT 803	4 1/2	9 1/2	15 1/2	22 3/4	30 1/2	38 3/4	46 7/8	56 3/4	67 3/4						ET 963
Guide Sizes	1	1	1	2	2	3	4	10	12						
AT 805	4 1/2	9 1/2	15 1/2	22 3/4	30 1/2	38 3/4	47	57	68						ET 965
Guide Sizes	1	1	1	2	2	3	4	10	12						
AT 865	5 1/2	10 7/8	17 3/4	25	32 3/8	41 1/8	50 1/8	59 3/4	70 1/4						ET 1025
Guide Sizes	1	1	1	2	2	3	4	10	12						
G1000 GRAPHITE FLY															
G 1298-4	4	9	15 1/8	21 1/2	28 3/8	35 3/4	43 3/4	53 3/8	63	75 1/8					GF 108-4
Guide Sizes	1	1	1	2	2	2	3	4	10	12					
G 1298-5	4	9	15 1/8	21 1/2	28 3/8	35 3/4	43 3/4	53 3/8	63	75 1/8					GF 108-5
Guide Sizes	1	1	1	2	2	2	3	4	10	12					
G 1298-6	4	9	15 1/8	21 1/2	28 3/8	35 3/4	43 3/4	53 3/8	63	75 1/8					GF 108-6
Guide Sizes	1	1	1	2	2	2	3	4	10	12					
G 1298-7	4	9	15 1/8	21 1/2	28 3/8	35 3/4	43 3/4	53 3/8	63	75 1/8					GF 108-7
Guide Sizes	2	2	2	2	3	3	3	4	10	12					
G 1298-8	4	9	15 1/8	21 1/2	28 3/8	35 3/4	43 3/4	53 3/8	63	75 1/8					GF 108-8
Guide Sizes	3	3	3	4	4	4	5	6	12	16					
G 1298-9	4	9	15 1/8	21 1/2	28 3/8	35 3/4	43 3/4	53 3/8	63	75 1/8					GF 108-9
Guide Sizes	4	4	4	4	5	5	5	6	16	20					
G 1298-10	4	9	15 1/8	21 1/2	28 3/8	35 3/4	43 3/4	53 3/8	63	75 1/8					GF 108-10
Guide Sizes	4	4	4	4	5	5	5	6	16	20					
Ti2000 TITANIUAM/IM700															
TBC 86 MT	3	6	9	12	15	18	21 1/4	25 1/2	29 3/4	35 3/4	42 3/4	50 3/4	62 1/2		TIMSH 102 2MT
Guide Sizes	6	6	6	6	6	6	6	7	7	8	8	10	12		
TBC 86 H	3	6	9	12	15	18	21 1/4	25 1/2	29 3/4	35 3/4	42 3/4	50 3/4	62 1/2		TIMSH 102 2H
Guide Sizes	7	7	7	7	7	7	8	8	8	8	10	12	16		
TBC 96 MT	3	6 1/8	9 1/4	12 1/2	16	20	24 1/2	29 1/4	34 1/2	40 3/4	48	56 1/2	64 3/4	74 1/2	TIMSH 114 2MT
Guide Sizes	6	6	6	6	6	7	7	7	8	8	8	8	10	12	
XMG 50															
EXC 89 MT	3	6	9	12	15	18	21	24 1/4	28	32 1/2	38 1/8	44 7/8	52 1/2	63 3/4	XMG 105 2MT
Guide Sizes	6	6	6	6	6	6	6	6	7	7	8	8	10	12	
EXC 92 M	3	6 1/8	9 1/4	12 1/2	16	20	24 1/2	29 1/4	34 1/4	40 1/4	46 1/4	53 1/2	61 1/2	70	XMG 110 2M
Guide Sizes	6	6	6	6	6	7	7	7	8	8	8	8	10	12	
EXC 92 M-C	3	6 1/8	9 1/4	12 1/2	16	20	24 1/2	29 1/4	34 1/4	40 1/4	46 1/4	53 1/2	61 1/2	70	XMG 110 2M
Guide Sizes	6	6	6	6	6	7	7	7	8	8	8	8	10	12	
EXC 96 M	3	6 1/8	9 1/4	12 1/2	16	20	24 1/2	29 1/4	34 1/2	40 3/4	48	56 1/2	64 3/4	74 1/2	XMG 114 2M
Guide Sizes	6	6	6	6	6	7	7	7	7	8	8	8	10	12	
EXC 10 M	3	6 1/8	9 1/4	12 1/2	16	20	24 1/2	29 1/4	34 1/2	40 3/4	48	56 1/2	64 3/4	74 1/2	XMG 120 2M
Guide Sizes	6	6	6	6	6	7	7	7	7	8	8	8	10	12	

Lamiglas Guide Spacing Chart

Revised 4/22/10

EXS 92 M	4 1/4	8 1/2	13	18 5/8	24 5/8	32 3/8	41 3/8	54 3/8	70 1/2							XMG 110 2M
Guide Sizes	6	6	7	8	8	10	12	16	20							
EXS 92 M-C	4 1/4	8 1/2	13	18 5/8	24 5/8	32 3/8	41 3/8	54 3/8	70 1/2							XMG 110 2M
Guide Sizes	6	6	7	8	8	10	12	16	20							
EXS 96 LL	4 1/4	8 1/2	13	18 5/8	24 5/8	32 3/8	42 3/8	56 3/8	73 1/2							XMG 114 2LL
Guide Sizes	6	6	7	8	8	10	12	16	20							
EXS 96 L	4 1/4	8 1/2	13	18 5/8	24 5/8	32 3/8	42 3/8	56 3/8	73 1/2							XMG 114 2L
Guide Sizes	6	6	7	8	8	10	12	16	20							
EXS 106 ML	4 1/8	8 3/8	13	18 5/8	24 5/8	33 1/2	44 1/2	56 1/2	69 3/8	83 3/8						XMG 126 2ML
Guide Sizes	7	7	7	8	8	8	10	12	20	25						
							CERTIFIED PRO									
X 80 MBC	3 1/4	6 1/2	9 3/4	13	17	21 1/4	25 3/4	30 1/2	36	41 1/2	47 1/2	56				XLB 96 1MT
Guide Sizes	7	7	7	7	7	7	7	7	8	8	10	12				
X 80 MBC GH	3 1/4	6 1/2	9 3/4	13	17	21 1/4	25 3/4	30 1/2	36	41 1/2	47 1/2	56				XLB 96 1MT
Guide Sizes	7	7	7	7	7	7	7	7	8	8	10	12				
X 86 MC	3	6	9	12	15	18	21 1/4	25 1/2	29 3/4	35 3/4	42 3/4	50 3/4	62 1/2			XSH 102 2M
Guide Sizes	6	6	6	6	6	6	6	7	7	8	8	10	12			
X 86 MTC	3	6	9	12	15	18	21 1/4	25 1/2	29 3/4	35 3/4	42 3/4	50 3/4	62 1/2			XSH 102 2MT
Guide Sizes	6	6	6	6	6	6	6	7	7	8	8	10	12			
X 89 MTC	3	6	9	12	15	18	21	24 1/4	28	32 1/2	38 1/8	44 7/8	52 1/2	63 3/4		XSH 105 2MT
Guide Sizes	6	6	6	6	6	6	6	6	7	7	8	8	10	12		
X 89 MTC GH	3	6	9	12	15	18	21	24 1/4	28	32 1/2	38 1/8	44 7/8	52 1/2	63 3/4		XSH 105 2MT
Guide Sizes	6	6	6	6	6	6	6	6	7	7	8	8	10	12		
X 90 MC	3 1/4	6 1/2	9 3/4	13	17	21 1/4	25 3/4	30 1/2	35 1/2	41	47	53 1/2	60 1/2	68 1/2		XSH 108 2MMT
Guide Sizes	6	6	6	6	6	7	7	7	7	7	8	8	10	12		
X 90 HC	3 1/4	6 1/2	9 3/4	13	17	21 1/4	25 3/4	30 1/2	35 1/2	41	47	53 1/2	60 1/2	68 1/2		XSA 108 2H
Guide Sizes	7	7	7	7	7	8	8	8	8	8	8	10	12	16		
X 96 JC	3	6 1/8	9 1/4	12 1/2	16	20	24 1/2	29 1/4	34 1/2	40 3/4	48	56 1/2	64 3/4	74 1/2		XSH 114 2MJ
Guide Sizes	6	6	6	6	6	7	7	7	7	8	8	8	10	12		
X 96 MC	3	6 1/8	9 1/4	12 1/2	16	20	24 1/2	29 1/4	34 1/2	40 3/4	48	56 1/2	64 3/4	74 1/2		XSH 114 2M
Guide Sizes	6	6	6	6	6	7	7	7	7	8	8	8	10	12		
X 10 MC	3	6 1/8	9 1/4	12 1/2	16	20	24 1/2	29 1/4	34 1/2	40 3/4	48	56 1/2	64 3/4	74 1/2		XSH 120 2M
Guide Sizes	6	6	6	6	6	7	7	7	7	8	8	8	10	12		
X 10 MHC	3	6 1/8	9 1/4	12 1/2	16	20	24 1/2	29 1/4	34 1/2	40 3/4	48	56 1/2	64 3/4	74 1/2		XSH 120 2MH
Guide Sizes	6	6	6	6	6	7	7	7	8	8	8	8	10	12		
X 10 MTC	3	6 1/8	9 1/4	12 1/2	16	20	24 1/2	29	33 3/4	39 1/8	45 1/4	52 1/8	59 5/8	68 7/8	80 1/2	XSH 120 2MT
Guide Sizes	6	6	6	6	6	7	7	7	7	8	8	8	8	10	12	
X 106 MC	3	6 1/8	9 1/4	12 1/2	16	20	24 1/4	29	34	39 1/4	47	55 1/2	63	72	84	XSH 126 2M
Guide Sizes	6	6	6	6	6	7	7	7	7	8	8	8	8	10	12	
X 106 MLC	3	6 1/8	9 1/4	12 1/2	16	20	24 1/4	29	34	39 1/4	46	53	62	72	84	XSH 126 2ML
Guide Sizes	6	6	6	6	6	7	7	7	7	8	8	8	8	10	12	
X 106 MHC	3	6 1/8	9 1/4	12 1/2	16	20	24 1/4	29	34	40	47	54 1/2	63	72	84	XSH 126 2MH
Guide Sizes	7	7	7	7	7	7	8	8	8	8	8	8	10	12	16	
X 110 MHC	5	10 1/2	16 1/2	23	30	37 1/2	46	55 1/2	66 1/2	79	92					XSH 132 2MH
Guide Sizes	8	8	8	8	10	10	10	12	12	16	20					
X 113 MCP	3	6 1/2	10 1/2	15	20 1/4	27	34 1/2	43	52 3/4	64 1/4	75 1/2	89				XSH 135 2M
Guide Sizes	8	8	8	8	8	8	8	10	10	12	12	16				
X 86 MTS	3 3/4	8	12 3/4	18 1/4	24 1/4	32	40 1/2	50 1/2	64							XSH 102 2MT
Guide Sizes	7	7	8	8	8	10	12	20	25							
X 86 MS	3 3/4	8	12 3/4	18 1/4	24 1/4	32	40 1/2	50 1/2	64							XSH 102 2M
Guide Sizes	7	7	8	8	8	10	12	20	25							
X 89 MTS	3 3/4	8	12 3/4	18 1/4	24 1/4	32	40 1/2	51 1/2	66							XSH 105 2MT
Guide Sizes	7	7	8	8	8	10	12	20	25							
X 90 HS	3 3/4	8	12 3/4	18 1/4	24 1/4	32	40 1/2	52 1/2	68							XSA 108 2H
Guide Sizes	7	7	8	8	8	10	12	20	25							
X 96 LLS	4 1/4	8 1/2	13	18 5/8	24 5/8	32 3/8	42 3/8	56 3/8	73 1/2							XSH 114 2LL
Guide Sizes	6	6	7	8	8	10	12	16	20							
X 96 LS	4 1/4	8 1/2	13	18 5/8	24 5/8	32 3/8	42 3/8	56 3/8	73 1/2							XSH 114 2L
Guide Sizes	7	7	8	8	8	10	12	20	25							
X 96 JS	4 1/4	8 1/2	13	18 5/8	24 5/8	32 3/8	42 3/8	56 3/8	73 1/2							XSH 114 2MJ
Guide Sizes	7	7	8	8	8	10	12	20	25							
X 96 MTS	4 1/4	8 1/2	13	18 5/8	24 5/8	32 3/8	42 3/8	56 3/8	73 1/2							XSH 114 2MT
Guide Sizes	7	7	8	8	8	10	12	20	25							
X 10 MTS	4 1/4	8 1/2	13	18 5/8	24 5/8	32 3/8	42 3/8	58 3/8	76 1/2							XSH 120 2MT
Guide Sizes	7	7	8	8	8	10	12	20	25							

Lamiglas Guide Spacing Chart

Revised 4/22/10

X 10 MS	4 1/4	8 1/2	13	18 5/8	24 5/8	32 3/8	42 3/8	58 3/8	76 1/2							XSH 120 2M
Guide Sizes	7	7	8	8	8	10	12	20	25							
X 106 MLS	4 1/8	8 3/8	13	18 5/8	24 5/8	33 1/2	44 1/2	56 1/2	69 3/8	83 3/8						XSH 126 2ML
Guide Sizes	7	7	7	8	8	8	10	12	20	25						
X 12 MS	4 1/4	8 3/8	13	18 5/8	23 3/4	31 1/2	41	51	63	75 1/2	89 1/2	104				XSH 144 3M
Guide Sizes	7	7	7	7	8	8	8	8	10	12	20	25				
CERTIFIED PRO FIBERGLASS																
XCF 801	3	6	9	12	15 1/4	18 3/4	22 3/4	26 3/4	31	35 3/4	41	48 1/2	56			BSP 961
Guide Sizes	6	6	6	6	6	7	7	7	7	8	8	10	12			
XCF 803	3 1/4	6 1/2	9 3/4	13	17	21 1/4	25 7/8	30 1/2	36	41 5/8	47 1/2	56				BMB 96 1E
Guide Sizes	7	7	7	7	7	7	7	7	8	10	12	16				
XCF 862	3	6	9	12	15	18	21 1/4	25 1/2	29 3/4	35 3/4	42 3/4	50 3/4	62 1/2			BXCF 102 2M
Guide Sizes	8	8	8	8	8	8	8	8	10	10	12	12	16			
XCF 864	3	6	9	12	51	18	21 1/4	25 1/2	29 3/4	36 2/3	42 3/4	50 3/4	62 1/2			BXCF 102 2H
Guide Sizes	8	8	8	8	8	8	8	8	10	10	12	12	16			
XCF 903	3 1/4	6 1/2	9 3/4	13	17	21 1/4	25 3/4	30 1/2	35 1/2	41	47	53 1/2	60 1/2	68 1/8		BXCF 108 2MH
Guide Sizes	8	8	8	8	8	8	8	10	10	10	12	12	12	16		
XCF 904	3 1/4	6 1/2	9 3/4	13	17	21 1/4	25 3/4	30 1/2	35 1/2	41	47	53 1/2	60 1/2	68 1/2		BXCF 108 2H
Guide Sizes	8	8	8	8	8	8	8	10	10	10	12	12	12	16		
XCC 934	3 1/4	6 1/2	9 3/4	13	17	21 1/4	25 3/4	30 1/2	35 1/2	41	47	53 1/2	60 1/2	70 3/8		XSH 111 2H
Guide Sizes	7	7	7	7	7	7	7	8	8	8	8	10	12	16		
XCF 1064	3	6 1/2	10 1/2	15 1/8	20	25 3/4	32	38 1/4	45 1/2	54	63 1/2	74 1/4	86			BSH 126 4F
Guide Sizes	8	8	8	8	8	10	10	10	10	12	12	12	16			
XCC 1064	3	6 1/8	9 1/4	12 1/2	16	20	24 1/4	29	34	40	47	54 1/2	63	72	84	XSH 126 2HC
Guide Sizes	7	7	7	7	7	7	8	8	8	8	8	8	10	12	16	
XCF 1065	3	6 1/2	10 1/2	15 1/8	20	25 3/4	32	38 1/4	45 1/2	54	63 1/2	74 1/4	86			BSH 126 5F
Guide Sizes	8	8	8	8	8	10	10	10	10	12	12	12	16			
XCF 106 4F	4 1/2	10 1/2	17	25	34	44	55	67	80							BSH 126 4F
Guide Sizes	8	8	8	8	10	10	10	12	16							
XCF 1065F	4 1/2	10 1/2	17	25	34	44	55	67	80							BSH 126 5F
Guide Sizes	8	8	8	8	10	10	10	12	16							
G1000 SERIES																
G 1300-T	4	9	15	22	30	39	51									GSH 90 2MT
Guide Sizes	6	6	8	10	10	12	16									
G 1302-T	4 1/2	9 1/2	15	21	27 1/2	34 3/4	42 3/4	52 1/2								GLB 90 2M
Guide Sizes	8	8	8	8	10	10	12	16								
G 1303-T	5 1/2	11 1/4	18 1/2	26	34	43	53 1/4									GLB 90 1M
Guide Sizes	8	8	8	10	10	12	16									
G 1336-T	4	8 1/2	14	20	27	35	44	54								GFP 90 MH
Guide Sizes	6	6	6	8	8	10	12	16								
G 1382-T	4	9	14	19 3/4	26	33 5/8	41 5/8	50 5/8								GLB 96 1MH
Guide Sizes	6	6	6	8	8	8	10	12								
G 1330-T	4	9	15	22	30	39	49	60								
Guide Sizes	6	6	6	6	8	8	10	12								
G 1306-T	4 3/4	9 3/4	15 3/4	22 3/4	30 3/4	40 3/4	51	63 3/4								GSH 102 2M
Guide Sizes	6	6	6	8	8	10	12	16								
G 1308-T	4 1/2	10	16	23 1/4	32	41	51 1/4	64								GSA 102 2H
Guide Sizes	6	6	6	8	8	10	12	16								
G 1310-T	4 1/2	9 1/2	15 1/2	22 1/2	30 1/2	39 1/2	50 3/8	63								GSH 102 2MH
Guide Sizes	6	6	8	8	10	10	12	16								
G 1313-T	4	8 1/2	13 1/2	19 1/2	26	33 3/4	42	51 3/8	63 3/4							GSH 102 2MT
Guide Sizes	6	6	6	6	8	8	10	12	16							
G 1314-T	4 1/2	10	16	24	32	41	51 1/4	64								GSA 102 2
Guide Sizes	8	8	8	10	10	12	12	16								
G 1342-T	4 1/2	9 3/4	15 1/2	22	29	37	45 1/2	54 1/2	64 1/2							GSH 102 2HX
Guide Sizes	8	8	8	8	10	10	10	12	16							
G 1318-T	4 1/2	9 3/4	15 1/2	22	29	37	45 1/2	54 1/2	64 1/2							GSH 102 2X
Guide Sizes	8	8	8	8	10	10	10	12	16							
G 1324-T	4	8 1/2	13 1/2	19	25	32	40	49	59	70						GSH 108 2M
Guide Sizes	6	6	6	6	8	8	10	10	12	16						
G 1326-T	4 1/2	9 1/2	15	21 1/2	28 1/2	37 1/4	47	57 1/2	69							GSH 108 2H
Guide Sizes	8	8	8	8	8	8	10	12	16							
G 1344-T	4 1/2	9 1/2	15	21 1/4	28 1/2	37 3/4	47 1/2	58 3/4	70							GLB 108 2ML
Guide Sizes	8	8	8	8	10	10	10	12	16							

Lamiglas Guide Spacing Chart

Revised 4/22/10

G 1316-T	4 1/2	9 1/2	15	21 1/4	28 1/2	37 3/4	47 1/2	58 3/4	70				GLB 108 2MH
Guide Sizes	8	8	8	8	10	10	10	12	16				

G 1348-T	4 1/2	9 1/2	14 3/4	20 5/8	27 1/8	34 1/2	43 3/8	54	66				GSH 108 2HX
Guide Sizes	8	8	8	8	10	10	10	12	16				
G 1218	4 7/8	11 7/8	19 3/4	28	37 9/16	52							GFW 90 2M
Guide Sizes	8	10	12	16	20	25							
G 1359	4 7/8	11 7/8	19 3/4	28	37 9/16	52							GLB 90 2ML
Guide Sizes	8	10	12	16	20	25							
G 1307	5 1/2	11 3/4	19 1/2	28	38 3/8	50 1/2	64						GSH 102 2M
Guide Sizes	8	8	10	12	16	20	30						
G 1311	5	11	18 1/4	26 1/8	36 1/8	48 1/8	62						GSH 102 2MH
Guide Sizes	8	8	10	12	16	20	30						
G 1313-S	5	11	18 1/4	26 1/8	36 1/8	48 1/8	62						GSH 02 2MT
Guide Sizes	8	8	10	12	16	20	30						
G 1315	5	11	18	26	36	48	62						GSA 102 2H
Guide Sizes	8	8	10	12	16	20	30						
G 1342-S	5	11	18	26	36	48	62						GSH 102 2HX
Guide Sizes	8	8	10	12	16	20	30						
G 1319	5	11	18	26	36	48	62						GSH 102 2X
Guide Sizes	8	8	10	12	16	20	30						
G 1321	5	11	17 1/8	24 1/8	32 1/8	41 1/16	51 15/16	67 1/4					GSH 108 2LL
Guide Sizes	6	6	8	10	12	16	20	25					
G 1355	4 3/4	9 3/4	15 3/4	22 7/8	30 7/8	39 7/8	49 3/4	61 3/16	72 1/2				GSH 108 2L
Guide Sizes	6	6	6	8	10	12	16	20	30				
G 1325	5	11	17 1/8	24 1/8	32 1/8	41 1/16	51 15/16	67 1/4					GSH 108 2L
Guide Sizes	6	6	8	10	12	16	20	25					
G 1365	4 11/16	8 15/16	15 7/8	22 3/4	29 7/8	37 1/4	45 3/16	53 1/4	62 11/16	73 3/8			GHS 114 2L
Guide Sizes	6	6	6	8	8	10	12	16	20	25			
G 1367	5	11	17 1/8	24 3/4	33 1/4	43	56 3/4	73 3/4					GSH 114 2L
Guide Sizes	6	6	8	10	12	16	20	25					

XMG 50 SERIES

EXC 703	3	6	9	12	15 1/4	19	23	27 1/4	32	37 1/2	44	53	LMB 843
Guide Sizes	6	6	6	6	6	7	7	7	8	8	10	12	
EXC 704	3	6	9	12	15 1/4	19	23	27 1/4	32	37 1/2	44	53	LP 844
Guide Sizes	6	6	6	6	6	7	7	7	8	8	10	12	
EXC 705	3	6	9	12	15 1/4	19	23	27 1/4	32	37 1/2	44	53	LMB 845
Guide Sizes	6	6	6	6	6	7	7	7	8	8	10	12	
EXC 722	3	6 1/4	9 3/4	13 3/4	18	23	28 1/4	34 1/4	42 1/2	52 3/4			LC 862
Guide Sizes	6	6	6	7	7	7	8	8	10	12			
EXC 724	3	6 1/4	9 3/4	13 3/4	18	23	28 1/4	34 1/4	42 1/2	52 3/4			LMB 864
Guide Sizes	6	6	6	7	7	7	8	8	10	12			
EXS 661	3 1/2	7 1/4	11 3/4	17	23 1/2	32	42 1/2						LSJ 781
Guide Sizes	6	6	7	8	10	12	20						
EXS 663	3 1/2	7 1/4	11 3/4	17	23 1/2	32	42 1/2						LSJ 783
Guide Sizes	6	6	7	8	10	12	20						
EXS 702	3 1/2	7 1/2	12 1/2	19	27	36 1/2	48 1/2						LSJ 842
Guide Sizes	6	6	7	8	10	12	20						
EXS 703	3 1/2	7 1/2	12 1/2	19	27	36 1/2	48 1/2						LMB 843
Guide Sizes	6	6	7	8	10	12	20						
EXS 722	3 1/2	7 1/2	12 1/2	19	27	37 1/2	50 1/2						LSJ 862
Guide Sizes	6	6	7	8	10	12	20						

CERTIFIED PRO GRAPHITE SPIN & CAST

XC 661	3	6 1/8	9 1/4	12 1/2	15 3/4	19 1/8	23 1/8	28 5/8	35 5/8	45			IMC 781
Guide Sizes	6	6	6	6	6	7	7	8	10	12			
XC 664	3	6 1/8	9 1/4	12 1/2	15 3/4	19 1/8	23 1/8	28 5/8	35 5/8	45			IMC 784
Guide Sizes	6	6	6	6	6	7	7	8	10	12			
XC 703	3	6	9	12	15 1/4	19	23	27 1/4	32	37 1/2	44	53	DTIMC 84 M
Guide Sizes	6	6	6	6	6	7	7	7	8	8	10	12	
XC 704	3	6	9	12	15 1/4	19	23	27 1/4	32	37 1/2	44	53	IMP 844
Guide Sizes	6	6	6	6	6	7	7	7	8	8	10	12	
XC 704 J	3	6	9	12	15 1/4	19	23	27 1/4	32	37 1/2	44	53	IMS 843
Guide Sizes	6	6	6	6	6	7	7	7	8	8	10	12	
XC 705	3	6 1/4	9 3/4	13 3/4	18	23	28 1/4	34 1/4	41 1/2	50 3/4			IMC 845
Guide Sizes	6	6	6	7	7	7	8	8	10	12			
XC 724	3	6 1/4	9 3/4	13 3/4	18	23	28 1/4	34 1/4	42 1/2	52 3/4			IMC 864

Lamiglas Guide Spacing Chart

Revised 4/22/10

Guide Sizes	6	6	6	7	7	7	8	8	10	12						
XC 725	3	6 1/4	9 3/4	13 3/4	18	23	28 1/4	34 1/4	42 1/2	52 3/4						IMC 865
Guide Sizes	6	6	6	7	7	7	8	8	10	12						

XCC 724	3	6 1/4	9 3/4	13 3/4	18	23	28 1/4	34 1/4	42 1/2	52 3/4						CCB 86 4M
Guide Sizes	6	6	6	7	7	7	8	8	10	12						
XCC 725	3	6 1/4	9 3/4	13 3/4	18	23	28 1/4	34 1/4	425 1/2	52 3/4						CCB 86 5MF
Guide Sizes	6	6	6	7	7	7	8	8	10	12						
XC 734	3	6 1/4	9 3/4	13 3/4	18	23	28 1/4	34 1/4	42 1/2	52 3/4						IMP 904
Guide Sizes	6	6	6	7	7	7	8	8	10	12						
XC 767	3 1/4	6 1/2	9 3/4	13	17	21 1/4	25 3/4	30 1/2	36	41 1/2	48 1/2					XLB 96 1MH
Guide Sizes	7	7	7	7	7	7	7	7	8	10	12					
XC 807	3 1/4	6 1/2	9 3/4	13	17	21 1/4	25 3/4	30 1/2	36	41 1/2	47 1/2	56				XLB 96 1MH
Guide Sizes	7	7	7	7	7	7	7	7	8	8	10	12				
XPC 703	3	6	9	12	15 1/4	19	23	27 1/4	32	37 1/2	44	53				IMP 843
Guide Sizes	6	6	6	6	6	7	7	7	8	8	10	12				
XPC 704	3	6	9	12	15 1/4	19	23	27 1/4	32	37 1/2	44	53				IMP 844
Guide Sizes	6	6	6	6	6	7	7	7	8	8	10	12				
XFT 764	3 1/4	6 1/2	9 3/4	13	17	21 1/4	25 3/4	30 1/2	36	41 1/2	48 1/2					IMC 905-T
Guide Sizes	7	7	7	7	7	7	7	7	8	10	12					
XFT 766	3 1/4	6 1/2	9 3/4	13	17	21 1/4	25 3/4	30 1/2	36	41 1/2	48 1/2					IMC 906-T
Guide Sizes	8	8	8	8	8	8	8	8	10	10	12					
XFT 797	3 1/4	6 1/2	9 3/4	13	17	21 1/4	25 3/4	30 1/2	35 1/2	40 3/4	46	51 3/4				IMC 937-T
Guide Sizes	8	8	8	8	8	8	8	8	10	10	10	12				
XFT 806	3 1/4	6 1/2	9 3/4	13	17	21 1/4	25 3/4	30 1/2	36	41 1/2	47 1/2	54 1/2				XC 96 HT
Guide Sizes	8	8	8	8	8	8	8	8	10	10	10	12				
XS 661	3 1/2	7 1/4	11 3/4	17	23 1/4	32	42 1/2									IMS 781
Guide Sizes	6	6	7	8	10	12	20									
XS 663	3 1/2	7 1/4	11 3/4	17	23 1/2	32	42 1/2									IMS 783
Guide Sizes	6	6	7	8	10	12	20									
XS 703	3 1/2	7 1/2	12 1/2	19	27	36 1/2	48 1/2									IMS 843
Guide Sizes	6	6	7	8	10	12	20									
XPS 662	3 1/2	7 1/4	11 3/4	17	23 1/2	32	42 1/2									XP 783
Guide Sizes	6	6	7	8	10	12	20									
XPS 702	3 1/2	7 1/2	12 1/2	19	27	36 1/2	48 1/2									IMP 843
Guide Sizes	6	6	7	8	10	12	20									
XPS 702 X	3 1/2	7 1/2	12 1/2	19	27	36 1/2	48 1/2									LP 842
Guide Sizes	6	6	7	8	10	12	20									
XPS 703	3 1/2	7 1/2	12 1/2	19	27	36 1/2	48 1/2									IMP 843
Guide Sizes	6	6	7	8	10	12	20									
XPS 704	3 1/2	7 1/2	12 1/2	19	27	36 1/2	48 1/2									IMP 844
Guide Sizes	6	6	7	8	10	12	20									
XPS 763	3 1/2	7 1/2	12 1/2	18 1/2	25 1/2	33 3/8	43 1/8	54 1/4								IMP 903
Guide Sizes	6	6	7	8	10	12	16	20								
	CERTIFIED PRO FIBERGLASS															
XCF 665	3 1/8	6 3/8	9 3/4	13 1/4	17 1/4	22 1/4	28 1/2	36	45							BXC 785F
Guide Sizes	6	6	6	7	7	8	8	10	12							
XCF 705	3	6 1/4	9 3/4	13 3/4	18	23	28 1/4	34 1/4	41 1/2	50 3/4						BXC 845F
Guide Sizes	6	6	6	7	7	7	8	8	10	12						
XCF 705R	3	6 1/4	9 3/4	13 3/4	18	23	28 1/4	34 1/4	41 1/2	50 3/4						MBM 84 1E
Guide Sizes	6	6	6	7	7	7	8	8	10	12						
SR 705R	3	6 1/4	9 3/4	13 3/4	18	23	28 1/4	34 1/4	41 1/2	50 3/4						MB 84 1E
Guide Sizes	6	6	6	7	7	7	8	8	10	12						
SR 765R	3	6	9	12 1/2	16 1/2	21	26	32	38 1/2	46	55 3/4					MB 90 1F
Guide Sizes	6	6	6	6	7	7	7	8	8	10	12					
	EXCEL SERIES															
XL 703C	3	6 1/2	10 1/2	15	20	25 1/2	31 1/2	39 1/2	50							XL 843
Guide Sizes	6	6	6	7	7	8	8	10	12							
XL 704C	3	6 1/2	10 1/2	15	20	25 1/2	31 1/2	39 1/2	50							XL 844
Guide Sizes	6	6	6	7	7	8	8	10	12							
XL 705C	3	6 1/2	10 1/2	15	20	25 1/2	31 1/2	39 1/2	50							XL 845
Guide Sizes	6	6	6	7	7	8	8	10	12							
XL 705GLASS	3	6 1/2	10 1/2	15	20	25 1/2	31 1/2	39 1/2	50							XL 84 1E
Guide Sizes	6	6	6	7	7	8	8	10	12							
XL 734C	3	6 1/2	10 1/2	15	20	25 3/4	32	40 1/4	51 1/2							XL 874
Guide Sizes	6	6	6	7	7	8	8	10	12							

Lamiglas Guide Spacing Chart

Revised 4/22/10

XL 735C	3	6 1/2	10 1/2	15	20	25 3/4	32	40 1/4	51 1/2			XL 875
Guide Sizes	6	6	6	7	7	8	8	10	12			
XL 7116C	4 1/2	9 1/4	13 3/4	19	24 1/4	31	38 1/4	48	58 1/2			XL 966
Guide Sizes	6	6	6	7	7	8	8	10	12			

XL 702S	3 5/8	7 5/8	12 1/2	19	27 1/8	36 5/8	48 1/2					XL 842
Guide Sizes	6	6	7	8	10	16	25					
XL 703S	3 5/8	7 5/8	12 1/2	19	27 1/8	36 5/8	48 1/2					XL 843
Guide Sizes	6	6	7	8	10	16	25					
XL 704S	3 5/8	7 5/8	12 1/2	19	27 1/8	36 5/8	48 1/2					XL 844
Guide Sizes	6	6	7	8	10	16	25					

MUSKIE

LGM 70 MH	4	9	15	21 1/2	28	35	44					LGM 84 1MH
Guide Sizes	10	10	10	10	12	12	16					
LGM 70 H	4	9	15	21 1/2	28	35	44					LGM 84 1H
Guide Sizes	10	10	10	10	12	12	16					
LGM 70 XH	4	9	15	21 1/2	28	35	44					LGM 84 1XH
Guide Sizes	10	10	10	10	12	12	16					
LGM 76 H	5 1/2	11 1/4	18 1/2	26	34	43	53 1/4					LGM 90 1H
Guide Sizes	8	8	8	10	10	12	16					
LGM 80 H	4 1/2	9 1/2	15	21	28	36	46	56 1/2				LGM 96 1H
Guide Sizes	8	8	8	10	10	12	16	20				
LGM 80 XH	4 1/2	9 1/2	15	21	28	36	46	56 1/2				LGM 96 1XH
Guide Sizes	8	8	8	10	10	12	16	20				
LGM 86 XH	4 1/2	9 1/4	13 3/4	19	24 1/4	31	38 1/4	48	58 1/2			LGM 102 1XH
Guide Sizes	8	8	8	10	10	12	12	16	20			
LGM 90 H	4 1/2	9 1/2	15 3/4	22 1/2	30 1/4	40	50 1/2	63				LGM 102 1XH
Guide Sizes	8	8	10	10	12	12	16	20				

G1000 GRAPHITE SPIN & CAST

G 1208	5 5/8	14 1/2	24 5/8	38 1/2								GUL 662
Guide Sizes	8	12	16	20								
G 1210	4 7/8	11 1/2	20	29 1/2	40							GFW 72 2L
Guide Sizes	8	10	12	16	25							
G 1212	5 1/2	13	21 1/2	32	45							GFW 78 2ML
Guide Sizes	8	10	12	16	25							
G 1213	5 1/2	13	21 1/2	32	45							GFW 78 2M
Guide Sizes	8	10	12	20	30							
G 1214	4 7/8	11 1/2	20	29 1/2	40	52						GFW 84 2ML
Guide Sizes	8	10	12	16	20	30						
G 1215	4 7/8	11 1/2	20	29 1/2	40	52						GFW 84 2M
Guide Sizes	8	10	12	16	20	30						
G 1218	4 7/8	11 7/8	19 3/4	28	37 9/16	52						GFW 90 2M
Guide Sizes	8	10	12	16	20	25						

ULTRA LIGHT CASTING/TROLLING/SPINNING

FC 76 UL	3 1/2	7	10 1/2	14	18 3/8	22 7/8	28 1/2	35	42	49 1/2	58 1/2	FL 904-1
Guide Sizes	6	6	6	6	6	6	8	8	8	8	10	
GC 792 UL	3 1/2	7 10	10 1/2	14 1/2	18 3/8	22 7/8	28 1/2	35	42 1/2	51 1/2	61 3/8	GFW 93 2UL
Guide Sizes	6	6	6	6	6	6	8	8	8	8	10	

SUPER SURF SERIES

SS 101 MHC	4	8 1/2	13 3/8	19 3/8	27 1/2	36 1/2	46 7/8	59 1/2				SSU 120 1MH
Guide Sizes	10	10	10	10	12	12	16	20				
SS 12 MHC	7 1/2	16 1/4	26 1/4	37	49	64	81 1/2					SSU 144 2MH
Guide Sizes	16	16	16	16	16	20	25					
SS 91 MLS	5	11 1/2	19	27	38	51 1/2						SSU 108 1L
Guide Sizes	12	16	20	25	30	40						
SS 9 MS	5	11 1/2	19	27	38	53						SSU 108 2ML
Guide Sizes	12	16	20	25	30	40						
SS 91 MHS	5	11 1/2	19	27	38	51 1/2						SSU 108 1M
Guide Sizes	12	16	20	25	340	40						
SS 101 LS	5	11	18	26 1/2	36	46 1/2	60 3/4					SSU 120 1L
Guide Sizes	12	12	16	20	25	30	40					
SS 10 MHS	5	11	18	26 1/2	36	46 1/2	60					SSU 120 2MH
Guide Sizes	12	12	16	20	25	30	40					
SS 101 MS	5	11	18	26 1/2	36	46 1/2	60 3/4					SSU 120 1M
Guide Sizes	12	12	16	20	25	30	40					
SS 101 MHS	5	11	18	26 1/2	36	46 1/2	60 3/4					

Lamiglas Guide Spacing Chart

Revised 4/22/10

Guide Sizes	12	12	16	20	25	30	40		
SS 106 MHS	5	11	18 3/4	27 1/2	37 1/4	49 1/8	62 1/2		SSU 126 2MH
Guide Sizes	12	12	16	20	25	30	40		
SS 11 MHS	5	10 1/2	16 1/2	23	30 1/2	39 1/2	50 1/2	66	SSU 132 2MH
Guide Sizes	12	12	12	16	20	25	30	40	

SS 10 MHS DH	5 1/2	14 1/4	24 3/8	35 3/8	47 5/8	60 3/4		SSU 121 2MH
Guide Sizes	12	16	20	25	30	40		
SS 105 MHS DH	5 1/2	14 1/4	24 3/8	35 3/8	47 5/8	60 3/4		SSU 125 2MH
Guide Sizes	12	16	20	25	30	40		
SS 108 MHS ACDH	5 1/2	14 1/4	24 3/8	35 3/8	47 5/8	60 3/4		SSU 126 2MH
Guide Sizes	12	16	20	25	30	40		
SS 11 MHS DH	5 1/2	14 1/2	24 3/4	34 3/4	47 5/8	60	72 3/4	SSU 132 2MH
Guide Sizes	12	16	20	25	30	40	50	
SS 115 MHS DH	5 1/2	14 1/2	24 3/4	35 3/4	47 5/8	60	72 3/4	SSU 137 2MH
Guide Sizes	12	16	20	25	30	40	50	
SS 118 MHS ACDH	5 1/2	14 1/2	24 3/4	35 3/4	47 5/8	60	72 3/4	SSU 140 2MH
Guide Sizes	12	16	20	25	30	40	50	

RON ARRA SURF SERIES

XCRA 1205	6 1/2	14	23 1/2	34 1/2	48	63 1/2	XRA 1205
Guide Sizes	12	12	16	16	20	25	
XCRA 1322	5 3/4	13 1/8	23	35 5/8	51 1/2	71 1/2	XRA 1322
Guide Sizes	12	12	16	16	20	25	
XSRA 961	7	17	31	50			XRA 96 1M
Guide Sizes	10	12	20	40			
XSRA 1022-2	7 1/4	17 1/2	31	49 3/4			XRA 102 2M
Guide Sizes	10	12	20	40			
XSRA 1083	8	19	33	53			XRA 1083
Guide Sizes	10	12	20	40			
XSRA 1083-2	8	19	33	53			XRA 1083-2
Guide Sizes	10	12	20	40			
XSRA 1084	8	19	33	53			XRA 1084
Guide Sizes	10	12	20	40			
XSRA 108 4-2	8	19	33	53			XRA 1084-2
Guide Sizes	10	12	20	40			
XSRA 1203-2	7 5/8	15 7/8	26 3/8	40 3/4	58		XRA 1203-2
Guide Sizes	12	16	25	40	50		
XSRA 1204	7 5/8	15 7/8	26 3/8	40 3/4	58		XRA 1204
Guide Sizes	12	16	25	40	50		
XSRA 1205	7 5/8	15 7/8	26 3/8	40 3/4	58		XRA 1205
Guide Sizes	12	16	25	40	50		
XSRA 1205-2	7 5/8	15 7/8	26 3/8	40 3/4	58		XRA 1205-2
Guide Sizes	12	16	25	40	50		
XSRA 1321-2	7	19	32 1/2	46 1/2	65 1/2		XRA 1321-2
Guide Sizes	12	16	25	40	50		
XSRA 1322	7	19	32 1/2	46 1/2	65		XRA 1322
Guide Sizes	12	16	25	40	50		
XSRA 1322-2	7	19	32 1/2	46 1/2	65 1/2		XRA 1322-2
Guide Sizes	12	16	25	40	50		

GRAPHITE SURF & JETTY

XS 101 MHC	4	8 1/2	13 3/8	19 3/8	27 1/2	36 1/2	46 7/8	59 1/2	GSB 120 1M
Guide Sizes	10	10	10	10	12	12	16	20	
XS 10 MHC	4	8 1/2	13 3/8	19 3/8	27 1/2	36 1/2	46 7/8	59 1/2	GSB 120 2M
Guide Sizes	10	10	10	10	12	12	16	20	
XS 111 MHC	5	11 1/4	18 1/2	26 3/4	36	46 1/2	58	72	GSB 132 1M
Guide Sizes	10	10	10	10	12	12	16	20	
XS 11 MHC	5	11 1/4	18 1/2	26 3/4	36	46 1/2	58	72	GSB 132 2M
Guide Sizes	10	10	10	10	12	12	16	20	
XS 12 MHC	7 1/2	16 1/4	26 1/4	37	49	64	81 1/2		GSB 144 2MH
Guide Sizes	16	16	16	16	16	20	25		
XS 15 MHC	6	12 1/2	20 1/2	30 5/8	44 1/2	59 7/8	78 7/8	100 3/8	GSB 180 2MH
Guide Sizes	16	16	16	16	20	20	25	30	
XS 81 MS	7	17	31	50					GLB 96 1M
Guide Sizes	12	20	30	40					
XS 91 MHS	8	19	33	53					GLB 108 1MH
Guide Sizes	16	25	40	50					

Lamiglas
FISH WITH CONFIDENCE

Lamiglas Guide Spacing Chart

Revised 4/22/10

XS 9 MHS	7 3/8	16 1/2	27	39	52 1/4							GLB 108 2MH
Guide Sizes	12	16	25	40	50							
XS 96 MHS	6	15	25	39	56							GLB 114 2MH
Guide Sizes	12	16	25	40	50							
XS 10 MS	7 5/8	15 7/8	26 3/8	40 3/4	58							GSB 120 2L
Guide Sizes	12	16	25	40	50							

XS 10 MHS	7 5/8	15 7/8	26 3/8	40 3/4	58							GSB 120 2M
Guide Sizes	12	16	25	40	50							
XS 101 MS	7 5/8	16 7/8	28 3/8	44 3/4	64							GSB 120 1L
Guide Sizes	12	16	25	40	50							
XS 101 MSAC	8	23	41	62								GSB 120 1L
Guide Sizes	16	25	40	50								
XS 1061 PP	5	13	24	36	49 1/2	63 1/2						CSB 126 1M
Guide Sizes	12	16	20	25	40	50						
XS 11 MS	7 1/2	18 1/4	30	45	64							GSB 132 2L
Guide Sizes	12	16	25	40	50							

TRI FLEX GRAPHITE SURF

TS 86 MS	7 1/4	14 1/2	22 3/4	33 3/4	49 3/4							CSB 102 2L
Guide Sizes	12	16	25	30	40							
TS 9 MHS	7 3/8	16 1/2	27	39	52 1/4							CSB 108 2M
Guide Sizes	12	16	25	40	50							
TS 96 MHS	6	15	25	39	56							CSB 114 2M
Guide Sizes	12	16	25	40	50							
TS 10 MHS	7 5/8	15 7/8	26 3/8	40 3/4	58							CSB 120 2M
Guide Sizes	12	16	25	40	50							

SURF LITES

LSU 762	4	9	185	22	31	41 1/2	52					XSH 84 2L
Guide Sizes	7	8	10	12	16	20	30					
LSU 802	5 1/2	12 1/2	20 1/2	38 1/2	47 3/4	60 1/2						XSH 96 2MMT
Guide Sizes	8	10	12	12	16	2						
LSU 862	5 1/2	11 3/4	19 1/2	28	38 3/8	50 1/2	64					XSH 102 2MMT
Guide Sizes	7	8	10	12	16	20	30					

BIG BANG HEAVER

NW 1310	5	11	17	23	29	37	46	56	67	83	100 1/4	SB 166 5F
Guide Sizes	12	12	12	12	12	16	16	16	20	20	25	
NW 1310-2	5	11	17	23	29	37	46	56	67	83	100 1/4	SB 166 5F-2
Guide Sizes	12	12	12	12	12	16	16	16	20	20	25	

TROPIC PRO JIGGING AND POPPING

TP 5630 CJ	3 7/8	8 3/8	13	18 1/4	24 3/8	31 1/2						CHJ 6630C
Guide Sizes	10	10	12	12	16	20						
TP 5650 CJ	3 7/8	8 3/8	13	18 1/4	24 3/8	31 1/2						CHJ 6650
Guide Sizes	10	10	12	12	16	20						
TP 5630 SJ	4	8 1/4	13 1/2	19 1/2	26 5/8							CHJ 6630
Guide Sizes	12	16	20	30	40							
TP 5650 SJ	4	8 1/4	13 1/2	19 1/2	26 5/8							CHJ 6630
Guide Sizes	12	16	20	30	40							
TP 7030 SP	3 1/2	7 1/2	12 1/2	19	27	36 1/2	48 1/2					NZ 84 2M
Guide Sizes	8	8	10	10	12	16	25					
TP 8040 SP	5 1/2	12	21	31	41 1/4	53 1/4						NC 96 2H
Guide Sizes	10	12	16	20	30	40						
TP 8650 SP	5 1/2	12 1/2	21	31	42	55 1/2						NZ 102 2XH
Guide Sizes	12	16	20	25	30	40						
TP 8080 P-SG	5 1/2	12 1/2	21	31	42	57						NZ 102 2XXH
Guide Sizes	16	16	20	25	30	40						

TRI FLEX GRAPHITE SALTWATER

BL 5630 CPO	4 7/8	9 3/4	14 3/4	20	25 7/8	32 1/4						CHJ 6650
Guide Sizes	6F	6F	8F	8F	10F	10FH						
BL 5630 C	4	8 1/8	13	18 3/4	25 1/2	33						CHJ 6650
Guide Sizes	10	10	12	12	16	20						
BL 5650 CPO	4 7/8	9 3/4	14 3/4	20	25 7/8	32 1/4						CHJ 6680
Guide Sizes	8	8	8	10	10	10FH						
BL 6080 CPO	4 1/4	9	14 1/2	21 1/2	30 3/8	40 1/2						GFC 72 XXH
Guide Sizes	8	8	8	10	10	10						
BL 6620 C	4	8 3/4	13 1/2	19	25	32	40					CGBT 78 1L
Guide Sizes	8	8	8	10	10	12	16					

Lamiglas Guide Spacing Chart

Revised 4/22/10

BL 6625 C	4	8 3/4	13 1/2	19	25	32	40		CGBT 78 1ML
Guide Sizes	8	8	8	10	10	12	16		
BL 6630 C	4 1/2	8 3/4	13 1/2	19	25	32	40		CGBT 78 1M
Guide Sizes	10	10	10	12	12	16	20		
BL 6640 C	4 1/2	8 3/4	13 1/2	19	25	32	40		CGBT 78 1MH
Guide Sizes	10	10	10	12	12	16	20		
BL 7020 C	4	8 3/4	14	20	27	34 1/4	45 1/4		CGBT 84 1L
Guide Sizes	8	8	8	10	10	12	16		
BL 7020 CG	4	8 1/2	13 1/2	19 1/2	26 1/4	33 3/4	43 3/4		CGBT 84 1L
Guide Sizes	8	8	8	1	10	12	16		
BL 7025 C	4	8 3/4	14	20	27	34 1/4	45 1/4		CGBT 84 1ML
Guide Sizes	8	8	8	10	10	12	16		
BL 7025 CPO	3 3/4	8	12 3/4	19	26 3/4	35 1/2	47 1/8		CGBT 84 1ML
Guide Sizes	5.5	5.5	6	6	6	8	10		
BL 7025 CGH	4	8 1/2	13 1/2	19 1/2	26 1/4	33 3/4	43 3/4		CGBT 84 1ML
Guide Sizes	8	8	8	10	10	12	16		
BL 7030 C	4	8 1/2	13 1/2	19 1/2	26 1/4	33 3/4	43 3/4		CGBT 84 1M
Guide Sizes	10	10	10	12	12	16	20		
BL 7030 CGH	4	8 1/2	13 1/2	19 1/2	26 1/4	33 3/4	43 3/4		CGBT 84 1M
Guide Sizes	8	8	8	10	10	12	16		
BL 7030CGH-SP	4	8 1/2	13 1/2	19 1/2	26 1/4	33 3/4	43 3/4		CGBT 84 1M
Guide Sizes	10	10	10	12	12	16	20		
BL 7040 C	4	8 1/2	13 1/2	19 1/2	26 1/4	33 3/4	43 3/4		CGBT 84 1MH
Guide Sizes	10	10	10	12	12	16	20		
BL 7040 LB	4	8 1/2	13 1/2	19 1/2	26 1/4	33 3/4	43 3/4		CCB 84 7M
Guide Sizes	10	10	10	12	12	16	20		
BL 7040 W	5	11	18	26	34	43 3/4			CGBT 84 1MH
Guide Sizes	12	12	12	16	16	20			
BL 7050 LB	4	8 1/2	13 1/2	19 1/2	26 1/4	33 3/4	43 3/4		GFC 84 H
Guide Sizes	10	10	10	12	12	16	20		
BL 8050 C	6	13	21	31	41 1/2	53			CGBT 96 H
Guide Sizes	12	12	12	12	12	16			
BL 6620 S	5 7/8	11 3/4	19 7/8	29 1/4	39 1/2				CGBT 78 1L
Guide Sizes	10	12	16	25	40				
BL 6640 S	5 7/8	11 3/4	19 7/8	29 1/4	39 1/2				CGBT 78 1MH
Guide Sizes	10	12	16	25	40				
BL 7020 S	5 3/4	11 3/4	18	26 1/4	35 1/4	45 3/4			CGBT 84 1L
Guide Sizes	10	10	12	16	25	40			
BL 7025 S	5 3/4	11 3/4	18	26 1/4	35 1/4	45 3/4			CGBT 841 ML
Guide Sizes	10	10	12	16	25	40			

INDIAN RIVER

IRFA 703C	3	6	9	12	15 1/4	19	23	27 1/4	32	37 1/2	44	53	TLP 84 3
Guide Sizes	6	6	6	6	6	7	7	7	8	8	10	12	
IRFA 764 C	3	6	9	12	15 1/4	18 3/4	22 3/4	27 1/4	32 1/4	38 1/4	45 3/4	55 3/4	TLP 90 4
Guide Sizes	6	6	6	6	6	7	7	7	8	8	10	12	
IRFA 702S	3 1/2	7 1/2	12 1/2	19	27	36 1/2	48 1/2						TLP 84 2
Guide Sizes	6	6	7	8	10	12	20						
IRFA 703S	3 1/2	7 1/2	12 1/2	19	27	36 1/2	48 1/2						TLP 84 3
Guide Sizes	6	6	7	8	10	12	20						
IRFA 704S	3 1/2	7 1/2	12 1/2	19	27	36 1/2	48 1/2						TLP 84 4
Guide Sizes	7	7	7	8	10	12	20						
IRFA 763S	3 1/2	7 1/2	12 1/2	18 1/2	25 1/2	33 3/8	43 1/8	54 1/4					TLP 90 3
Guide Sizes	6	6	7	8	10	12	16	20					
IRFA 764S	3 1/2	7 1/2	12 1/2	18 1/2	25 1/2	33 3/8	43 1/8	54 1/4					TLP 90 4
Guide Sizes	7	7	7	8	10	12	16	20					

TRI FLEX GRAPHITE INSHORE

TFX 7020 C	2 5/8	5 7/8	9 3/4	14 3/8	19 7/8	26 1/2	34 1/2	44 1/8		TXC 84 1ML
Guide Sizes	7	7	7	8	8	10	12	16		
TFX 7020 CT	4	8	12	16	20	25	30	36 1/2	44 1/2	TF 8430
Guide Sizes	7	7	7	7	8	8	10	12	16	
TFX 7030 C	2 5/8	5 7/8	9 3/4	14 3/8	19 7/8	26 1/2	34 1/2	44 1/8		TXC 84 1M
Guide Sizes	7	7	7	8	8	10	12	16		
TFX 7030 CT	4	8	12	16	20	25	30	36 1/2	44 1/2	TF 8440
Guide Sizes	7	7	7	7	8	8	10	12	16	
TFX 7040 CT	4	8	12	16	20	25	30	36 1/2	44 1/2	GTF 84 1M
Guide Sizes	7	7	7	7	8	8	10	12	16	

Lamiglas
FISH WITH CONFIDENCE

Lamiglas Guide Spacing Chart

Revised 4/22/10

TFX 7650 CT	3	6 1/8	9 1/2	13 1/2	18	23 1/4	29 1/2	37 1/2	48				GTF 90 1MH
Guide Sizes	7	7	7	7	7	8	10	12	16				
TFX 7820 C	2 3/8	5 1/4	8 3/4	12 7/8	17 7/8	23 7/8	31	39 5/8	50				TXC 92 1ML
Guide Sizes	7	7	7	7	8	8	10	12	16				
TFX 7830 C	2 3/8	5 1/4	8 3/4	12 7/8	17 7/8	23 7/8	31	39 5/8	50				TXC 92 1H
Guide Sizes	7	7	7	7	8	8	10	12	16				
TFX 8020 C	2 1/8	4 1/2	7 1/2	11 1/8	15 1/2	20 1/2	26 7/8	34 3/8	43 1/4	54			TXC 96 1ML
Guide Sizes	7	7	7	7	8	8	8	10	12	16			

TFX 8030 C	2 1/8	4 1/2	7 1/2	11 1/8	15 1/2	20 1/2	26 7/8	34 3/8	43 1/4	54			TXC 96 1M
Guide Sizes	7	7	7	7	8	8	8	10	12	16			
TFX 7020 S	3 1/4	7 1/4	12	17 3/4	24 1/2	32 1/2	42 1/2						TXC 84 1ML
Guide Sizes	8	8	10	12	16	20	25						
TFX 7030 S	3 1/4	7 1/4	12	17 3/4	24 1/2	32 1/2	42 1/2						TXC 84 1M
Guide Sizes	8	8	10	12	16	20	30						

GRAPHITE INSHORE CLASSIC SERIES

IC 66 MH	4	8 1/2	13 1/2	19	25	32	40						IC 78 MH
Guide Sizes	8	8	8	10	10	12	16						
IC 66 H	4	8 1/2	13 1/2	19	25	32	40						IC 78 H
Guide Sizes	8	8	8	10	10	12	16						
IC 70 M	4	8 3/4	14	20	27	34 1/2	45 1/4						IC 84 M
Guide Sizes	10	10	10	12	12	16	20						
IC 70 MH	4	8 3/4	14	20	27	34 1/4	45 1/4						IC 84 MH
Guide Sizes	10	10	10	12	12	16	20						
IC 70 H	4	8 1/2	13 1/2	19 1/2	26 1/4	33 3/4	43 3/4						IC 84 H
Guide Sizes	10	10	10	12	12	16	20						
IC 70 MLS	4 1/2	11	18 1/2	26	35	47							IC 84 ML
Guide Sizes	8	10	12	16	25	30							
IC 70 MHS	5 3/4	11 3/4	18	26 1/4	35 1/4	45 3/4							IC 84 MH
Guide Sizes	10	10	12	16	25	40							
IC 70 HS	5 3/4	11 3/4	18	26 1/4	35 1/4	45 3/4							IC 84 H
Guide Sizes	10	10	12	16	25	40							

CERTIFIED PRO POPPIN'

XPC 703	3	6	9	12	15 1/4	19	23	27 1/4	32	37 1/2	44	53	IMP 843
Guide Sizes	6	6	6	6	6	7	7	7	8	8	10	12	
XPC 704	3	6	9	12	15 1/4	19	23	27 1/4	32	37 1/2	44	53	IMP 844
Guide Sizes	6	6	6	6	6	7	7	7	8	8	10	12	
XPS 662	3 1/2	7 1/4	11 3/4	17	23 1/2	32	42 1/2						XP 783
Guide Sizes	6	6	7	8	10	12	20						
XPS 702	3 1/2	7 1/2	12 1/2	19	27	36 1/2	48 1/2						IMP 843
Guide Sizes	6	6	7	8	10	12	20						
XPS 702 X	3 1/2	7 1/2	12 1/2	19	27	36 1/2	48 1/2						LP 842
Guide Sizes	6	6	7	8	10	12	20						
XPS 703	3 1/2	7 1/2	12 1/2	19	27	36 1/2	48 1/2						IMP 843
Guide Sizes	6	6	7	8	10	12	20						
XPS 704	3 1/2	7 1/2	12 1/2	19	27	36 1/2	48 1/2						IMP 844
Guide Sizes	6	6	7	8	10	12	20						
XPS 763	3 1/2	7 1/2	12 1/2	18 1/2	25 1/2	33 3/8	43 1/8	54 1/4					IMP 903
Guide Sizes	6	6	7	8	10	12	16	20					
XPS 764	3 1/2	7 1/2	12 1/2	18 1/2	25 1/2	33 3/8	43 1/8	54 1/4					IMP 904
Guide Sizes	6	6	7	8	10	12	16	20					

TRI FLEX GRAPHITE SALTWATER

LK 7620 C	3 1/2	7	10 1/2	14 1/2	19 1/2	25 1/2	32 1/2	40 1/2	50				TF 90 20
Guide Sizes	8	8	8	8	10	10	10	12	16				
LK 7625 C	3 1/2	7	10 1/2	14 1/2	19 1/2	25 1/2	32 1/2	40 1/2	50				TF 90 25
Guide Sizes	8	8	8	8	10	10	10	12	16				
LK 7230 S	3 1/2	7 1/2	12 1/2	19 1/2	27 3/4	37 1/2	50 1/2						TF 8630
Guide Sizes	8	8	10	10	12	16	25						
LK 7615 S	4 1/4	9 3/4	16 3/4	26 1/4	37	49 3/4							TF 90 15
Guide Sizes	8	10	12	16	20	25							
LK 7620 S	4 1/4	9 3/4	16 3/4	26 1/4	37	49 3/4							TF 90 20
Guide Sizes	8	10	12	16	20	25							
LK 7625 S	4 1/4	9 3/4	16 3/4	26 1/4	37	49 3/4							TF 90 25
Guide Sizes	8	10	12	16	20	25							

TRAVEL SERIES

XTC 704	3	6	9	12	15 1/4	19	23	27 1/4	32	37 1/2	44	53	IMP 844-3

Lamiglas Guide Spacing Chart

Revised 4/22/10

Guide Sizes	6	6	6	6	6	7	7	7	8	8	10	12				
XTC 7025	3	6	9	12	15 1/4	19	23	27 1/4	32	37 1/2	44	53				XT 8425
Guide Sizes	6	6	6	6	6	7	7	7	8	8	10	12				
XTC 865	3	6	9	12	15	18	21 1/4	25 1/2	29 3/4	34 1/4	39 1/2	46	53 1/2	62 1/2		XT 102 3H
Guide Sizes	6	6	6	6	6	6	6	6	7	7	8	8	10	12		
XTS 703	3 1/2	7 1/2	12 1/2	19	27	36 1/2	48 1/2									IMP 843-3
Guide Sizes	6	6	7	8	10	12	20									
XTS 704	3 1/2	7 1/2	12 1/2	19	27	36 1/2	48 1/2									IMP 844-3
Guide Sizes	6	6	7	8	10	12	20									

XTS 7025	3 1/2	7 1/2	12 1/2	19	27	36 1/2	48 1/2									XT 8425
Guide Sizes	6	6	7	8	10	12	20									
XTS 865	3 3/4	8	12 3/4	18 1/4	24 1/4	32	40 1/2	50 1/2	64							XT 102 3H
Guide Sizes	7	7	8	8	8	10	12	20	25							
XTS 105	6	12	19	27 3/4	39	52	67 1/2									GSB 120 4M
Guide Sizes	10	10	12	16	20	30	40									

CHECKING GUIDE SPACING

In all checking of guide spacing, you should work with the guides taped in place. By using narrow masking tape to hold the guides on the rod, you can change guides or guide positions easily until the guides are positioned properly and the rod is exactly right.

There are several ways to check guide spacing. In fact, some of these methods can be used to *determine* guide spacing. One of the easiest ways is to first determine the guide spacing by any method you prefer. Then tape the guides in place at these locations and glue the tip-top in place. Mount this tip-top in line with the spine that was previously determined. Mount a reel on the rod (the handle and reel-seat assembly will be complete at this point), thread the line through the guides, and tie on a practice plug.

Pick a sunny day, and make a soft careful practice cast at right angles to the direction of the sun. Make this a gentle cast, because the guides are only taped in place. Do not watch the plug (a natural tendency) but instead hold the rod out and look in the direction of the sun (do not look *at* the sun) as the line comes off the reel and flows through the guides. This shows up best against a dark background, but in any situation the glint of the sun on the line shows exactly what the line is doing during the cast. It is best to have an experienced angler cast while you watch the line flowing through the guides. That way you can adjust your position to best see the line at different angles. Do this several times so that on each cast you can examine closely the line flow through and around each guide. For example, you might find that there is excessive line slap on the rod between the reel and the first guide on a spinning rod, indicating either too low a frame on the first guide or too much space between the reel and the guide. By changing the guide position, or the guide itself, you will see the results of your adjustments.

If you want to check the degree of friction coming through a set of guides in comparison with a similar rod of the same length, you must have (or beg or borrow) two identical spinning reels, spool them with identical (in brand, type, and line-test) line, and have two identical practice plugs or sinkers. You will also need to find a spot with a straight drop where you can drop the sinkers or practice plugs. Ideally this drop should be 20 feet or more. This is sometimes called a "drop test" and is used by some manufacturers to test their spinning rods against the competition. (You can also test spool-lip friction on a spinning reel in two different reels by using identical rods.)

At a place with a straight vertical drop, fasten the rods horizontally by clamping the rod handles or otherwise supporting them. I find an easy way to do this is out of a second- or third-story

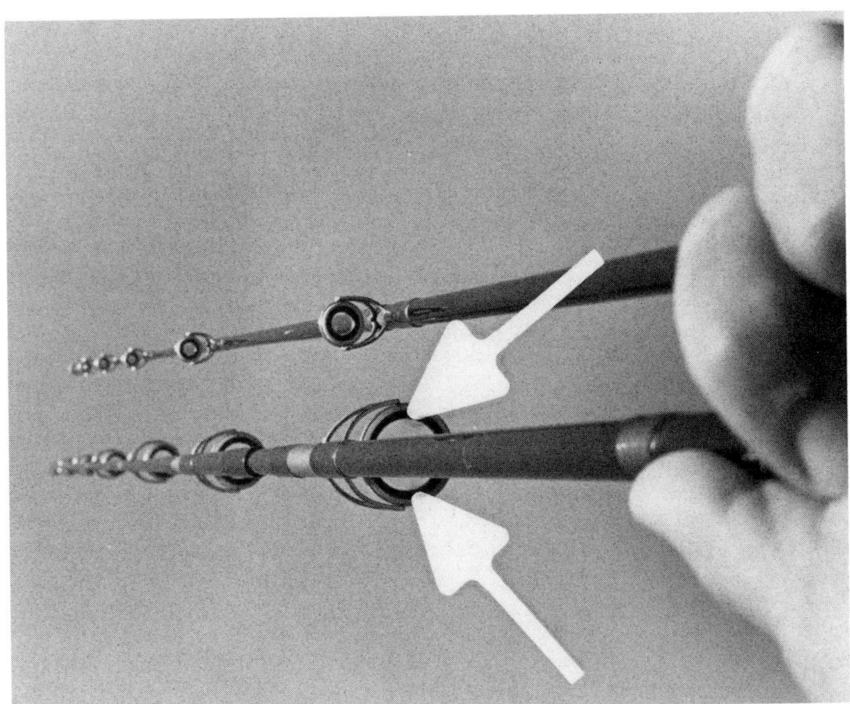

Sighting along rods to check guide alignment. Two methods are shown: left, with the rod guides under the rod; right, with the guides on top of the rod. Note that on the left rod, slightly more of the guide ring and space can be seen to the right (note arrows) than to the left. This would have to be adjusted and then this guide used as a check against all the other guides without moving the rod.

window in a home. Run line through both rods, and tie the identical practice plugs to the line. With the plugs hanging down 6 inches from the tip end, lift both lines above the horizontal rods between the reel and the first guide. Then, holding the line, open the bails. With the bails open, release both lines at once (hold both lines together between your index finger and thumb). The practice plug that hits the ground first from the high drop will have experienced the least guide friction. Check this several times to be sure. The principle is that because the reels, line, and practice plugs are all identical, any differences in the drop will be the result of friction as the lines run through the guides.

A third method of checking rod guides is to use a deflection test. For this you would use a chart as previously described for positioning the guides. Mount a reel on the rod, run the line through the guides, and tie a weight to the end of the line. This should be slightly heavier than the weight of a lure or sinker balanced for the rod. This will bend or deflect the rod, and you can check visually for evenness in the distribution of stresses and of bending.

Once you are completely satisfied with the positioning, size, and type of the guides on the rod, tape them down securely and proceed to wrap them in place.

22
Guide Wrappings and Variations

Introduction • Tools • Materials • Mounting the Tip-Top Guide • Preparation for Guide Wrapping • Measurements • Wrapping Methods • Underwraps • Double and Triple Wraps • Variations and Special Effects and Wrappings • Wraps on Rod Parts Other Than Guides

INTRODUCTION

Careful guide wrappings are a must for any custom rod. Guides are wrapped on with thread on virtually every type of rod, from ultralight spinning and 2-weight fly rods up to heavy surf and 130-pound IGFA-class offshore rods.

The technique of wrapping guides is the same on all rods, although variations and additions to this technique abound. The important thing to remember is that once the basic guide-wrapping technique is learned—and it can be learned in only a few minutes—it is basic to any wrap for any guide, using any size thread, and may be applied to any of the many variations that can be used.

TOOLS

Tools for rod wrapping can be costly and complex, inexpensive and simple, or you can make uncomplicated tools from wood scraps—or even a cardboard box—in only a few minutes that will suffice for one or two rods. The main tool of course is the rod wrapper or rod winder.

The simplest tool isn't actually a tool but rather a methodology of wrapping. One method involves dropping a spool of thread into an empty cup or bowl then running the thread between several sheets of clean typing paper placed in the center of a phone book. The phone book—or books piled on top of it—creates the necessary tension, while the bowl or cup keeps the thread spool secure. By placing the spool of thread on a table and resting the phone book on the near edge of the table, the thread can be brought straight up and over the front of the rod blank for wrapping. (Bringing the thread up behind the rod does not allow you to see the position of the thread to prevent gaps or overlapping.)

A better way is to make a rack or supports to hold the rod blank while you are wrapping it. There are several ways to make racks. One is to use a heavy wire (all-wire) coat hanger. Pull the wire out straight, and then bend it so that it will clamp onto a worktable; the hook will support the rod. You'll need at least two of these, and for long rods you might need a third or possibly even a fourth hanger to support the long end of some blanks.

A rod blank support can also be made from a cardboard carton. Use a large, sturdy carton and cut off the top to the level on which you want the rod to rest. Then cut out the front, but leave a margin around the two sides and bottom so that the box will retain its box shape. Cut V-shaped notches into the two sides to serve as supports to hold the rod. If the box is large, you may wish to place the phone book and the cup with the spool in the box. If the box is not large enough for that, cut a hole in the back of the box, place the phone book and bowl outside the box, and run the thread through the hole. Hold the box in place by C-clamping it to the table or holding it down with a few heavy books. To keep the thread in front, where you can see it when the cup is inside or in back of the box, tape a guide to the C-clamp or the front edge of the cardboard box and run the thread through it. This brings the thread straight up in front of the rod blank for easy wrapping, regardless of the position of the thread spool.

A third variation is to use scraps of wood to make a support rack that can then be clamped to the table. Although any size wood can be used, a good start is old shelving, 4 inches or more wide. Make a base about 18 inches long and two end supports about 8 to 12 inches high. Nail or screw the upright supports to the base. For added permanence and strength, use metal corner brackets. Cut a V-shaped notch into the top end of each upright support. To protect the rod, line this notch with self-adhesive felt or with a strip of plastic cut from a plastic bottle, or wrap the rod with masking tape where it will touch the wood wrapping support. The first two methods are better because they are one-time solutions. With the third method, because the wrapping position changes with each new guide, the protective masking tape must be constantly changed. You can still use the cup and phone book, but mount a spare guide to the center base of the wood support through which to run the thread while you are wrapping.

Simple rod-wrapping tools are sold commercially and are widely available. Most of these consist of a clamp-on support with two arms to hold the rod; in the center of the support is a small combination thread holder and tension device. These are fine for one or two rods, provided they are lightweight freshwater rods. The small distance between the two supports makes them impractical for building large or heavy rods or long sections of rods. They can be used for long and heavy rods with an additional rod support, such as one made from coat-hanger wire or by making a V-cut upright on a short base similar to that described above for supporting a rod blank on a wrapping tool.

Other simple and inexpensive rod-wrapping tools consist of finished commercial models very similar to the scrap-wood tool just described. Usually there is a base with two upright supports. Often one or both of these upright supports are adjustable, as is the center thread holder and tension device. In addition, it is easy to cut a cardboard box to size to hold one end of a long or heavy rod to be placed in these tools, since they are used on top of the worktable, not clamped to it.

Larger and more complex rod winders are available. Often these have longer bases on which to make larger, longer rods; have rollers to help turn the rod without potential damage to the rod blank; and have adjustable blank supports and thread-tension devices. These are available from most tackle shops, custom rod shops, and suppliers and are made by Flex Coat, PacBay, Batson, and other companies. These include simple wrappers in addition to the motorized rod wrappers described in the following paragraphs.

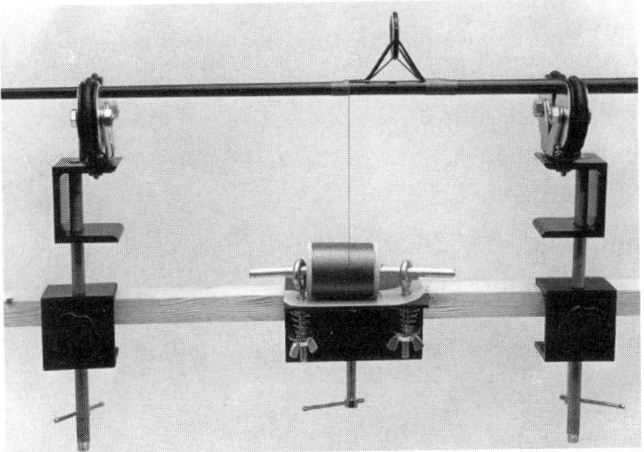

Homemade, adjustable rod wrapper with rollers to support the rod. The thread-tension device is adjustable for any size thread spool.

Rubber rollers such as those on this rod wrapper prevent scratching or damage to the rod blank. If using plastic wheels, cover them with several layers of masking tape to protect the blank.

The next stage of rod winders incorporates motors to control the thread-wrapping speed. The motor is usually controlled by a foot-operated rheostat. Most of these have rollers both above and below the rod blank, so as to both support and hold down the blank to keep it from whipping around at higher speeds. They are available with extensions for extra-long rods (such as one-piece surf rods), and some have an option of standard or self-centering three-jaw chucks to hold the rod butt in place while wrapping on the guides. All have thread tension devices, and most have carriages that will hold several spools or cones of thread for multiple thread wrapping.

These motorized wrappers are built with a rail or extruded aluminum base or sometimes with a long wood base. The motor at one end is usually fitted with a three-jaw chuck to easily hold the rod blank. To protect the rod butt cap in these situations, be sure to wrap it with several layers of masking tape before placing the rod into the chuck.

Some of these wrappers have dual motors or dual controls for either wrapping with the foot control or for slow and continuous turning of the rod when curing finish on the rod wraps.

These are expensive—or more expensive than simple hand wrappers—and thus are best suited as a purchase for a fishing or rod-building club, the serious angler, or a small-scale custom rod-builder.

Other tools will help to make the wrapping task easier. Separate motorized curing motors with a simple lightweight chuck for holding the butt end of the rod are also available. These include an additional rod support for holding the rod at some point (the rod turning at slow speeds or up to 200 rpm as the commercial rod companies do it) to keep the finish from sagging or dripping as the finish cures on the rod wraps.

In addition, a file is a handy tool for filing the ends of the guides into a sharp, flat point for easy transition of the thread from the blank up onto the guide foot. A fine or medium file works best for this. A file is also good for removing any burrs on the base of the guide foot to prevent damage to the rod blank. Many of the guide manufacturers now advertize their guides as being prefiled, or polished to a fine edge or point to make this step unnecessary.

Masking tape is required both to hold the guide in place and to mark the ends of the wrap, at which point the thread wrap is begun. The best sizes are ⅛ or ¼ inch. Masking tape is available from art supply stores and some tackle and mail-order companies specializing in rod-building supplies.

Scissors are necessary for general thread work: cutting thread for wrapping and making up the loops of thread used to pull the end of the working wrapping thread through and under the wraps. Almost any type of scissors will work, although special rod-wrapping scissors are sold by many custom catalog houses and stores. Fly-tying scissors are also fine for this purpose.

A thread puller, described in chapter 2, consists of hook-and-loop strips (Velcro) joined at one end by a rivet or grommet, to which is attached a loop of monofilament of about eight- to fifteen-pound test. Use finer sizes of mono for finer thread, such as size A, and larger mono for larger thread, such as sizes D, E, and EE. The thread-puller hook-and-loop strips are separated and attached around the rod with the loop of mono pointing to the center of the guide. This loop is placed on the rod wraps when the wrap is about four to six turns from the end, or finishing. The thread wrap is continued, wrapping over the loop pointing toward the center of the guide. Once you reach the end of the wrap, cut the wrapping thread and place the tag end into the wrapped-over loop. Then hold the tag end straight and pull the loop through and under the overlapping threads to pull the tag end through and out before cutting the excess thread. Unlike thread loops, this tool is reusable, although in time the mono loops do have to be replaced.

A scalpel or razor blade is needed to cut the end of the thread after it has been pulled under the end wraps. Either will work, although disposable razor blades are less expensive and more readily available.

Add a burnisher for rubbing over the wrappings to remove any small gaps or unevenness that might have occurred during wrapping. Burnishing tools are sold by most custom parts stores or catalogs. The same tool is also available from art supply and stationery stores. Any smooth round tool can be used for this purpose. Plastic pen barrels are ideal—avoid aluminum or other metal that might discolor or flatten the thread.

A simple rule helps to measure rods for guide positions, wrap lengths, equalizing wraps on both sides of a two-foot guide, and similar tasks. One of the best of these, manufactured by C-Thru Ruler Company, is sold in stationery stores as a center rule. One side of the rule is a standard metric rule measuring 0 to 15 centimeters from left to right. The other side has a grid pattern in tenths of an inch, with the edge of the scale measures from 0 to 6 inches. The important part of the rule for rod builders is the center of the transparent plastic, which has an "O" in the center of the rule with measurements in tenths of an inch in both directions from this central point. This makes it easy to determine equal wrapping positions for a two-foot guide by taping the guide in position, holding the rule against the rod blank and guide with the center O of the rule on the center of the guide ring, and then measuring out on each side to mark the beginning of the wrap on each guide foot.

MATERIALS

The principal material for wrapping guides is special rod-wrapping thread. The companies making such threads today include Gudebrod, Kreinik, RodSmith (PacBay), Pro Wrap (American Tackle), and FishHawk. Some of these are strictly fly-tying threads, and because they are very thin would be suitable only for the lightest rods. (Most of these companies have rod wrapping thread in sizes A and D; some have a wider range of thread.)

Rod-wrapping thread comes in a variety of sizes, ranging from 00 through FF, although not all sizes are available from a single manufacturer. Thread sizes and their suggested uses follow:

Size 00. Wrapping delicate fly rods and ultralight spinning and spin-cast rods; wrapping and tying jigs from 1⁄32 ounce through 1⁄8 ounce.

Size A. Recommended for fly rods and freshwater spinning and casting rods; wrapping and tying jigs from ½ ounce through 1½ ounces.

Size C (NCP) and D nylon. Wrapping saltwater rods and medium-weight spinning, casting, boat, and trolling rods; wrapping and tying jigs from ⅝ ounce through 2 ounces.

Size D (NCP) and E nylon. Wrapping 80- and 130-pound trolling rods, as well as heavy-duty boat and surf rods; wrapping and tying jigs from 2¼ ounces to 3½ ounces.

Size E. Wrapping heavy-duty trolling, boat, and surf rods.

Size EE. Wrapping extra-heavy-duty trolling rods and extra-long (14 to 16 feet) surf rods.

Size FF. Special wrapping effects on gaffs, outriggers, and antennas; wrapping heavy-duty rod butts for friction grip. Size FF is the recommended size for wrapping pool-cue handles.

Most of the thread companies make a wide variety of thread colors for rod wrapping and custom effects. Gudebrod is the main supplier of wrapping thread, so we'll deal primarily with their products. Of the thousands of thread colors available, most companies have a good selection for rod builders. For example, Pro Wrap has eighty colors available in both A and D sizes and in both nylon and colorfast (no color preserver required) types. These are available in 100-yard spools, 1-ounce spools, and 4-ounce cones. Pro Wrap offers thirty-nine metallic colors. RodSmith (PacBay) thread is available in nylon and no color preserver required thread (Stay True) in thirty-two colors and in sizes A and C. Their metallic thread is available in sizes A and D in twelve colors.

FishHawk threads come in a variety of different styles they call "collections." Their nylon threads for rod wrapping and jig tying come in forty different colors in 100-yard, 1-ounce, and 4-ounce spools. Their nylon ColorLok threads require no color preserver. The thirty-six available colors come in sizes A and C in 100-yard, 1-ounce, and 4-ounce spools.

For those who like silk threads or who need them for bamboo rod restoration, the collection comes from Japan in pure filament silk, and in sixty-seven colors including six colors in a silk sparkle collection. The silk sparkle is available in size 3/0 in 100-yard spools; the rest of the silk threads are available in size 3/0 in 200-meter spools, size A in 100-meter spools, and size D in 50-meter spools.

The FishHawk "Metallic" collection is made on a nylon core under rice paper and has a silver alloy finish. These come in twenty-two colors in size A thread in 100-yard and 1-ounce spools.

The "Metallic (P)" threads are similar to the Metallics but manufactured over a polyester core with a metalized foil wrap. Twenty-four colors are available in sizes A and D in 100-yard, 1-ounce, and 4-ounce spools.

The company's "Variegated" collection comprises twenty-five variegated-color threads in size A, available in 100-meter spools.

To add to this complexity, not all colors and styles of thread of all manufacturers are available in all sizes.

Note: For more details on yards per spool and the break strength of threads of different manufacturers, check the thread color and spec charts of each manufacturer.

MOUNTING THE TIP-TOP GUIDE

The tip-top, or tip guide or top guide, as it is variously called (I like, and most manufacturers use, the term "tip-top"), should be mounted before the guides are wrapped in place. Although this is really a gluing operation, it is considered here with the guides because sometimes the glues used are different from those used for handle and reel-seat assembly. Also, it is a guide and does get a wrapping, even though this wrapping is strictly decorative. (Though there is one exception where it is functional, which we will discuss.)

Tip-tops must match the guides. All manufacturers make tip-tops that match their guides in color, style, and construction. Some manufacturers, such as Fuji, PacBay, and Batson, have different tip-tops to match different guide styles. Some even have fly-rod tip-tops in regular ring sizes and then larger ring sizes to accommodate the larger size weight-forward fly lines such as 10 and up to 15-weight. Almost all tip-tops consist of a ring and frame that is mounted on a tube. The tubes are available in different sizes to fit the tip end of different size rods. The tube should fit the rod tip firmly, not tightly or loosely. It should slide on easily, without any slack or play. Naturally you must first check the tip end of the rod to be sure it is even and not splintered, flattened, or damaged in any way. If it is, you may have to cut the tip section back slightly, anywhere from a fraction of an inch to an inch. Cut back more and you are into the custom cutting and chopping of the blank. (For details on cutting see chapter 26.) Briefly, the technique requires using a fine triangular file to groove and then cut through the blank where you wish it cut. Or you can use a fine-tooth hacksaw blade (preferably with 32 teeth per inch) or a jeweler's saw with a very fine-toothed blade, applying light pressure to drag the blade toward you to prevent the teeth from catching on the thin-diameter graphite blank. Rotate the blank until the blade or file cuts through.

Adding tip-tops. One easy way is to melt the ferrule and tip-top cement, smear the cement on the rod tip, and immediately add the tip-top.

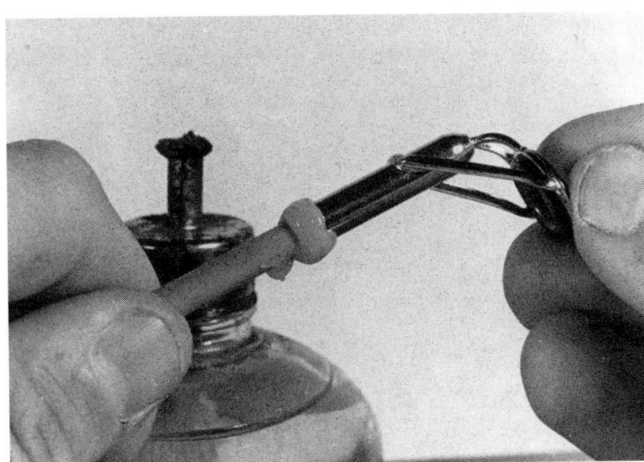

If liquid enough, the hot rod-tip cement will flow as the tip-top is added and ball up at the base of the tip-top tube.

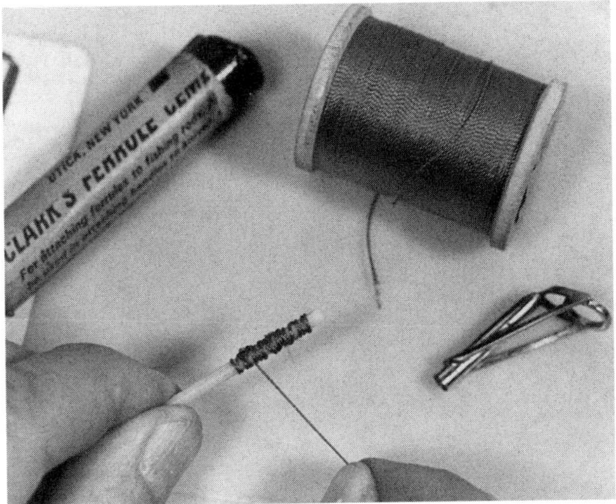

If some shimming is required, it is possible to wrap the rod blank at the tip or lay threads over the end and along the sides of the blank.

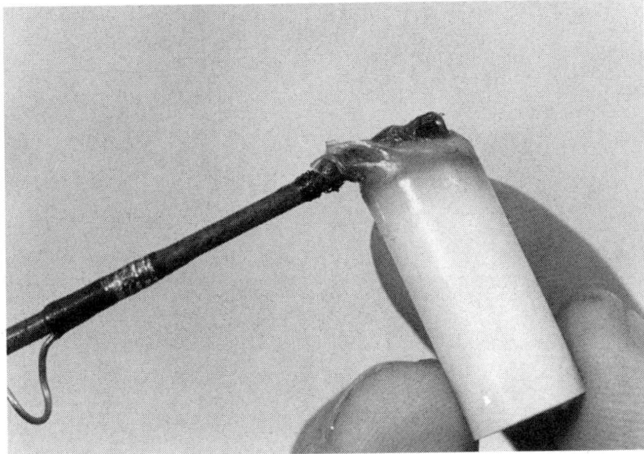

Adding melted tip-top cement to the wrapped rod blank.

For a good bond of the tip-top to the end of the blank, use steel wool or fine sandpaper to lightly roughen the end of the blank. To prevent scratching the blank, wrap the end with masking tape so that you sand only that portion that will be glued into the tip-top tube.

You can use 24-hour epoxy or other glues for gluing the tip-top. One caution in gluing on the tip-top is that tip-tops are subject to breakage and damage and sometimes have to be replaced. To be replaced, the tip-top must be removed from the end of the rod without damaging the rod blank. For this reason I like glues that are not quite as strong as the 24-hour epoxies. For light freshwater rods and light fly rods, I like to use a stick-ferrule or tip-top cement. For heavier freshwater rods, heaver fly rods, and light saltwater rods, I use a 5-minute epoxy glue that will be stronger than the heat-set cements but only about 80 to 90 percent as strong as the 24-hour epoxy glues. One advantage is that these 5-minute epoxies, according to the glue manufacturers, will break down under heat more rapidly than the stronger epoxies and thus will be easier to remove from the rod tip. For heavy surf rods, heavy trolling rods, and other heavy tackle, I use the regular 24-hour epoxy glues.

While I use the above glues in most situations, rod designer Al Jackson likes the CA glues—super, or cyanoacrylate, glues. He finds them easy to use and also easy to remove the tip-top with a little heat (just on the metal part of the tube though) when needed.

When you use the ferrule cements or other heat-set cements (the glue sticks from craft stores also work well), you will need a heat source. A butane lighter, match, or similar *small* heat source will work fine. In all cases use the *side* of the flame to melt the glue or heat the tube. If you hold the rod end or tip-top over the flame, the heat covers a broad area and is more likely to damage the rod or ring in the tip-top. There is also the increased possibility of soot or unburned particles smoking or darkening the blank parts.

There are several ways to add a tip-top using heat-set cements. First use the flame to melt the end of the ferrule cement or cement stick. When the cement is molten, coat the end of the rod tip with it. Don't worry if you get too much on the end of the rod. Do *not* use the flame around the rod tip. Once the molten cement coats the rod end, immediately slide the tip-top tube onto the rod blank, making sure that the rod tip goes completely to the end of the tube and that the tip-top is immediately lined up with the spine and guide placement on the rod blank.

If you are not quick enough, the cement might solidify on the end of the rod. If this happens, there are two possibilities to consider. One is to use the side of the flame previously used to heat the cement by bringing the rod tip close enough to the flame to melt the cement. Rotate the rod while doing this to assure complete melting. Then slide the tip-top on the rod blank or rotate the tip-top to line up with the spine.

The second possibility is to hold the tip-top gently with pliers and heat the tube with the flame. When the tube is hot, slide it onto the rod tip. The hot metal tube will melt the cement on contact and glue the tip-top to the rod.

A completely different method involves using a knife blade to shave off fine slivers of the ferrule cement and slip these into the metal tube of the tip-top. Once you have the tube filled, heat it with the flame and immediately slide it onto the end of the rod. Heating the tube causes the cement to melt and allows gluing the tip-top to the rod.

In using any heat-set cement, do not try to wipe up the glue while it is still molten. It can burn you and usually only strings out and makes a mess. Instead wait until the cement is completely cured and cool. At this point the cement will be hard and can be easily peeled or knocked off the rod end.

Although I haven't seen any yet, the possibility exists that someone will produce a tip-top with a composite tube instead of a metal tube (guides with composite graphite/glass/resin materials are produced at this time). If this happens, then naturally you cannot use heat on the tube when gluing with heat-set cement but must rely on the other methods just described. (AFTCO currently has a composite tip-top for use on rods with their composite frame lightweight roller guides for two- to thirty-pound test line. They state that you can carefully use a small propane or gas torch to heat the tube but also state that overheating can melt the tube. Be careful and only smear the molten heat-set cement onto the rod tip and then immediately add the tube, or use the CA glue as suggested by Al Jackson.)

Using 5-minute epoxy is simple. Mix the epoxy as described in chapter 20, and then smear the glue on the roughened tip section of the rod. At the same time, use a toothpick or straightened paper clip to smear a little glue inside the tip-top. Then slide the tip-top on the rod tip, use a rag to remove any excess glue, and align the tip-top with the guide alignment. One problem with this is that the liquid glue often allows the tip-top to rotate on the rod blank if the blank is not placed exactly vertically (held vertically against a workbench with masking tape) or laid at an angle (butt down, tip up, and with the guide position facing directly down) so that gravity will hold the tip-top in line with the guide/reel-seat position. As an alternative you can just hold and check the tip-top until the glue sets up, usually in about 5 minutes.

The technique for using 24-hour epoxy glue is exactly the same, only additional care must be taken to keep the tip-top in line with the position of the guides during curing, which is much longer.

A few tip-tops do not come with a tube but instead are made of a double-wrapped wire—the ends of the wire extending parallel and at an angle to the loop to form "legs" that are wrapped in place. These are filed to a smooth edge, taped in place with thin masking tape, and wrapped down using the same thread size, color, and proportion as is used for the guides on the rod.

Tip-tops are sometimes damaged and must be removed. If the tip-top is one of the rare types that is wrapped in place, the technique for removal is the same as that for a guide. Use a razor blade to plane down the threads and finish until reaching the blank. Then peel the wrap off just as if you are peeling the shell from a steamed shrimp. Wrap the new tip-top using standard guide-wrapping methods.

Tube tip-tops, by far more common, require a different technique. Heat must be used—use the least heat necessary for the ferrule-cement/heat-set cements and the most possible for the 24-hour epoxies.

You must use care in all steps of removing tip-tops, because failure to follow exact directions can result in damage to the rod blank. First you must shield the wrapping and the exposed portion of the rod blank from the heat. This can be done in several ways. One is to make a shield that you can hold against the rod so that only the tip-top is exposed. A shield can be a groove cut into a scrap piece of wood, a small wood angle made for this purpose, or a similar device. A simpler method is to use several layers of masking tape wrapped around the blank, beginning the tape right at the edge of the metal-tube tip-top. Build this up to serve as insulation against the heat.

Using a small flame, heat the metal tube on the tip-top, rotating the rod as you do so. Use only the side of the flame (a flame under the tip-top will produce too broad a heat source), and try to keep the flame toward the end of the tip-top. You might melt or damage any glues or shock rings holding the ring in place, but this won't matter because the tip-top is damaged anyway.

Keep pliers handy, and check frequently for looseness on the tip-top. Using pliers (the metal tip-top will be hot enough to burn you), remove the tip-top as soon as possible to avoid applying any more heat to the rod blank than is necessary. In the case of all glues (heat-set, epoxy, CA), the heat will break down the resins and allow you to remove the tip-top.

Once the damaged tip-top is removed, clean the blank and add a new tip-top using previously described gluing methods or the wrapping method. Once the old tip-top is off, remove the shield or the masking tape as soon as possible. Use alcohol to clean up any remaining masking-tape adhesive. If the tip-top is the tube type and the wrap is properly protected, you will not need to rewrap the thread. Just use a new tip-top of the right size and glue it in place, butting the new tip-top against the thread wrap. Clean up the glue; the rod is ready to use as soon as the glue cures.

PREPARATION FOR GUIDE WRAPPING

Before you begin to wrap the guides in place, there is a little preparation required. First you must check the position of the blank's spine. At this point you will have the handle assembly in place, with the reel-seat hoods lined up with the spine and the tip-top in place. Both help determine the alignment of the guides. An exception to this would be rods in which the handle is separate from the section with the guides, such as offshore two-part trolling rods where the handle separates from the blank, pack rods in which the butt handle section is so short that it does not include any guides, casting rods in which the handle separates from the blank, and spinning rods with a sliding-ring reel-holding system that is not lined up with the guides. For these types of rods, you need to retain the masking tape or mark that indicates the spine and guide alignment or to determine the spine location again.

Once you have the spine and alignment of the guides located, you may wish to clean the rod with alcohol. This will remove any greases, dirt, hand lotions, or body oils that would later harm the wrapping or cause blotching or mottling of the thread wrap. To be honest, in building many rods without taking this step, I have never seen a problem, but theoretically it is probably best to follow it. One of the big problems with almost all rod finishes is the presence of silicones on your hands or a part of the blank or when mixing epoxies to cover the thread wraps. The next few steps should be done while you are wearing light cotton gloves, such as are available for camera and darkroom work, or rubber gloves like those used by lab and medical workers. These are generally available through camera shops, medical-supply stores, and from better drugstores. Both latex and nitrile rubber gloves are available.

A final preparation involves checking the guides for wrapping. Basically this means filing the ends of the guide feet (if needed and if the manufacturer has not done this), checking and filing the bases of the guide feet, and, if necessary, adjusting the guide feet for straightness.

Filing the guide feet is necessary to provide a smooth, gradual "slope" for the thread to follow as it is wrapped from the bare blank up onto the guide foot. For this the feet must be ground down. A fine flat file is perhaps the safest tool to use for this because it is handheld and can thus be controlled at all times. However, instead of working the file against the guide, I find it best to work the guide against the file. I also find it easier to slightly twist or rotate the file to follow the convex curvature of the top of the guide foot while filing it to a knife edge. To do this, place the file in a vise, protect it with scrap wood or rags, and work the guide foot against the flat file face.

Other methods of filing guide feet include using a small rotary grinding tool such as a Dremel Moto-Tool. These tools come in several different styles and models and will chuck small diamond-wheel points, aluminum-oxide grinding stones, aluminum-oxide abrasive wheels, silicon-carbide grinding stones, and various drum sanders.

Standard bench-type grinders can also be used, although in most cases the stones supplied with them are too coarse and the motors too fast for good control. Although any motor-operated grinder will work faster than hand filing, the danger is in loss of control and excessive cutting, which might ruin the guide foot. I like the drum sanders used with the Dremel Moto-Tool; they are small enough for me to hold easily while I'm working on the guide and allow good control and guide-foot shaping. Small bench-type belt sanders, fitted with a fine sanding belt, will also work fine. They are perhaps the best of the motorized tools because they allow you to hold the guide securely with both hands and work the guide foot against the moving belt.

In addition to sanding the top of the guide foot, you should at the same time check the guide foot for straightness. Hold the guide on a tabletop, strip of wood, or rod blank to check the guide feet. If the two feet are not straight, slightly bend them up or down until they are straight and parallel to each other so that they will be parallel and straight with the rod blank.

Once the guide feet are straight, rub the bottom of the two feet lightly over a piece of sandpaper to remove any slight burrs that might have occurred in manufacture. Most guides have a crosswise concave curvature on the bottom of the foot, so be sure to check this also for any slight burrs or imperfections. If you feel any burrs, remove them with a slim round file run along the length of the guide foot. Note that some or all of the above may not be necessary today, since more and more of the guide manufacturers are prefiling the feet of their guides to make them smooth for an easy transfer of the thread from the rod blank up onto the guide foot.

MEASUREMENTS

Guide spacing was covered in chapter 21. However, for a careful, neat job, you still must establish the measurement of the wrap for each guide, considering such factors as underwraps, trim wraps, and so on. Let's consider a standard two-foot guide. You will want the guide wrap to look right, you'll want sufficient wrap to begin on and hold the blank before being taken up on the guide foot, and you'll want the guide to be proportional to the wrap, the size of the guide, and the size and type of the blank.

Measurement must be made for underwraps that will match the guide wraps to be placed on top of them. Calipers or a rule helps to check these dimensions.

In all cases you must wrap over the entire guide foot. Also, you must begin the wrap on the blank. There are two methods of considering such measurements. In the one that I prefer, I make the entire wrap proportional to the length of the guide foot. This also becomes proportional to the diameter of the blank, because smaller guides with shorter feet are used on the thinner tip end than on the butt end of the rod. I measure the distance between the ends of the two guides and multiply this by a constant factor, usually about 1¼. Thus for a large butt guide measuring 2 inches between the end of the feet, the total length of the guide wrap would be 2½ inches. The total length of the wrap on the blank only would be ½ inch or ¼ inch on each end. For a smaller guide that would measure about 1 inch between the guide feet, the total length of the guide wrap would be 1¼ inches long, a total length of ¼ inch—or ⅛ inch on each end. Thus all of this stays proportional to the rod and to the guide. What you do not want is a 2-inch-long guide wrap on a big butt guide and a 2-inch-long guide wrap on a very small size 8 guide at the tip end. In this case, because of the shorter length of the guide foot, the wrap on the blank before reaching the guide foot would be excessively long and unnatural looking. Naturally you can adjust this proportional guide wrapping to any constant factor you desire, depending on your preference for the total length of the wrap and the length of the wrap on the blank before it reaches the end of the guide foot. Some rod builders prefer to use a constant of 1½, thus doubling the amount of wrap on the blank in the above examples.

If you use an underwrap, you must figure this first in addition to the length of the guide wrap, which should also be in proportion. For the above examples to be wrapped with an underwrap, I would use a constant of 1½ for the underwrap and a constant of 1¼ for the guide wrappings. This allows a small portion of the underwrap to show at the end of the wrap in addition to showing under the center of the guide ring and also providing a smooth base on which to wrap the guide. Again, such constants can be anything you wish, but the constant for the underwrap must always be a larger figure than that for the guide wrapping. Also note that these constants are figured on the basis of a simple one-color wrap, or a simple wrap with a simple trim wrap, and include the total length of the wrap. If you use these figures for the base wrap alone and then add a trim wrap, the underwrap constant factor will have to be larger to allow for the additional trim on the end of the wrap.

Where you will be making fancy or multiple-thread trim wraps at the end of a guide wrap, you may want to make the constant far larger to accommodate these additional wraps. Because this is often difficult to plan initially, one solution is to first measure the length of the guide feet on the largest guide to be wrapped (the butt guide) and to wrap that guide in place, using whatever fancy trim wraps, multiple-thread wraps, or additional wraps you wish to make.

Note that if you get very fancy, you may have to count and note thread colors and turns in order to maintain symmetry on both sides of the guide. Do one side of the guide and then measure the total length of this wrap with an accurate scale or rule. Make the same measurements on the other side of the guide, measuring from the junction of the foot and the frame. Mark the end of this measurement with masking tape. Then measure the total length of this distance—from the masking tape on the one side to the end of the wrap on the other side. The proportion of this figure within the length of the guide feet is the constant you will use.

As an old-timer, I prefer a slide rule (remember them?) to figure this constant, but other proportional rules and methods are available. If you can't find your school slide rule or other proportional scales, you can always revert to basic math, as follows:

In this example, we will use a total guide-foot length of $1\frac{5}{16}$ inches and a total guide wrap of $1\frac{29}{32}$ inches. The formula then becomes:

1 is to $1\frac{5}{16}$ inches as X is to $1\frac{29}{32}$ inches

1 is to $^{21}/_{16}$ as X is to $^{61}/_{32}$

1 is to $^{42}/_{32}$ as X is to $^{61}/_{32}$

$^{42}/_{32}X = {}^{61}/_{32}$

$42X = 61$

$X = 1.4523$, or $1\frac{29}{64}$ inches

This also points out why it is far better to develop a basic, simple constant first, because using a constant of 1⅜, 1½, or the decimal equivalents of 1.375, 1.5, or ½ 5, is far easier than using an awkward constant multiplier such as 1.4523 or $1\frac{29}{64}$.

Although I like this method best and think it makes for attractive wraps that are proportional to the size of the guide and the diameter of the blank, it does have some problems if you want fancy trim wraps or single-thread trims at the end. Since the length of the wrap on the bare blank changes with the guide (the foot length, really), it also might change the proportions of the number of rotations of the thread around the blank in fancy or detailed trim wraps. Thus if you had a trim wrap of four turns on a large guide, this might have to be reduced to three turns or two turns on the smaller guides and shorter wraps to remain in proportion to the rest of the guide wrap. The same would apply to inlaid wraps.

An alternative method of determining measurements is to use a constant measurement of the length of the wrap extending beyond the guide feet. In this method you would use a constant in inches or millimeters that would be added to the total length of the guide feet for any wrap. For example, using a constant measurement of ¼ inch of wrap on the blank alone at the end of each guide, you would have a total of ½ inch. For a larger guide in which the total length of the feet might measure 2 inches, the total guide wrap would be that 2 inches plus ½ inch, for a total of 2½ inches. For a smaller guide used farther up the blank in which the total length of the guide feet might be only 1 inch, the total length of the guide wrap would still be that ½ inch plus the 1-inch guide-feet length, for a total of 1½ inches. Personally I feel that the proportional method is best, though this second method does have some advantages. The main advantage is that the proportions or number of thread rotations of trim wraps and inlaid wraps do not have to be changed with the guide, because the space for this remains constant regardless of which guide is being wrapped in place.

WRAPPING METHODS

Any guide wrapping or wrapping associated with a guide is simple, although there are some variations to finishing and adding trim wraps and single-strand wraps inlaid in a guide wrap. For the basics let's first describe a simple guide wrap—no underwrap, no trim wraps, no fancy inlays. These additions can be added to rods and wraps later as you gain experience.

Once guide spacing is determined, you must tape the guides on the rod blank. For this use thin masking tape. I like ⅛-inch-wide tape, although ¼-inch-wide tape will work for large guides and for guides on large rods. If tape in these widths is not available, measure out several inches of standard masking tape (usually 1 inch wide) on a plastic base (a standard kitchen cutting board works well), and use a razor blade to cut thin longitudinal strips.

Once you have the strips cut, place each guide on the rod blank at the predetermined position, line it up with the spine of the rod, and tape it in place. Tape the guide down close to the frame using the thin strips. In other words, leave the end of the guide exposed. By doing so, it will be easy to leave the tape in place until after the guide wrap begins on the guide foot to hold it securely and in line with the spine. If you tape over the end of the foot, you will have to remove the tape before the thread gets to that point, in effect negating the purpose of the tape.

Although it is a small point, you should wrap the tape in the same direction in which you will rotate the rod when wrapping. Many rod builders turn the rod for each guide foot on two-foot guides (so that they always wrap from left to right, for example). If you do this, then the wrap for each side of the rod must be opposite the previous wrap.

A final tip is to fold over the end of the tape so that you have a small tag end to grab when you wish to remove it. This makes tape removal easier if you are also controlling the tension and position of the guide-wrap thread.

Tape both guide feet, making sure they are lined up with the rod blank and with the spine of the rod. With the flexibility of masking tape, you usually can make slight adjustments as required at this point. Tape all the guides in place, but remember that you can make final alignment adjustments immediately before wrapping each guide and as you start the guide wrapping.

Another possibility used by many rod builders today is to use thin-diameter surgical hose tubing, now available from many custom rod shops and supply houses. Usually this has about a ⅛-inch lumen. To use, cut it very thin with a razor blade and then slide it over the rod blank to hold the foot of a guide. Position the ring of tubing close to the frame so that the thread wraps can begin over the end of the guide foot after several or more wraps on the rod blank. Once the guide foot is being wrapped and the guide held securely, use fine-point scissors to cut off the surgical hose ring. Another possibility for holding the guide is to use a small rubber band, loop it over the center ring of the guide, wrap it around the guide and blank several times, and then loop it again on and over the center ring of the guide. This works well on most two-foot guides but not so well on single-foot guides, where the guide foot might rise up above the blank surface.

Use the measurements for each guide (determined by previously mentioned formulas) to mark the center position of the guide with a rule, and use strips of masking tape to mark the beginning point for each wrap. Alternatively, some rod builders suggest using a small scratch mark in the rod finish or a felt-tip marker or grease pencil. I don't like any of these methods. I don't like scratching the blank at any time, and the various marking pens either leave a permanent mark or are too broad and wide to be accurate for fine custom rod work. The taping or the surgical hose ring method allows for precise measurements, leaves no mark once removed, and can be adjusted infinitely until placement is exactly right.

Once the guide is positioned and held in place, position the rod in your rod wrapper with the guide centered over the thread-tension device. Make sure the rod will rest without your having to hold it. If necessary, use extra end supports to hold the longer end of the rod securely. After all, you want to concentrate on wrapping the guide, not on holding one end of the rod up or down.

Most rod builders like to wrap from left to right, meaning they always wrap the left-positioned guide foot. Some like to wrap from right to left; others wrap in either direction, wrapping from left to right for the left-positioned guide foot and then, without moving the rod, wrapping from right to left for the right-positioned guide foot. Any of these methods is satisfactory. Choose the one that is most comfortable for you.

I'll assume we'll be wrapping from left to right on the left-positioned guide foot in these directions. First bring the thread up from the thread-tension device and over the rod blank. At this point you may want to check the tension, adjusting it for the thread and the type of blank. Naturally you will want more tension for a larger guide on a heavy-wall surf blank when using size D thread than you will for wrapping a snake guide on a fly-rod tip section using size A thread. Although you will want enough tension to hold the blank, do not use too much. With the strong threads available today and the thin-wall graphite blanks, too much tension will compress the wrap and in effect push the guide foot into and through the wall of the rod blank, ruining the blank. Be particularly careful of this with thin-walled graphite and thin-walled S glass blanks.

Once the thread tension is correct, bring the thread up over the blank next to the tape marking the beginning of the wrap. Bring several inches of the thread around the blank until this first wrap makes at least a 360-degree circle. Keeping tension on the end of the thread, push the thread with your thumbnail so that it crosses over the thread underneath. Continue with tension on the end of the thread, and rotate the rod so that the thread wraps around the rod and over the thread end. Continue maintaining tension until about four to six wraps around the rod blank are completed. Cut the tag end of the thread close to the wrap and continue the wrapping. One tip here for all wraps is to maintain the wrapping thread at a slight angle so that it is constantly pulled in toward the existing wrap and thus is wrapped tightly, with no gaps between it and the previous wrap of thread.

Continue wrapping by rotating the blank. When you reach the end of the guide foot, slow down, because even with the smooth taper to the end of the foot, care is required in this area. Make sure the thread is tightly wrapped, does not have any gaps, and traverses smoothly up the slope of the guide foot.

After a few wraps around the blank and the end of the guide foot, grab the tag end of the masking tape and pull the tape off while rotating the rod. (This is why you want the tape wrapped in the same direction as the rod rotation. It will come off as you rotate the rod.) Once the masking tape is removed, continue wrapping as before until about six to eight wraps from the end of the guide foot and the beginning of the frame. If you are using a surgical hose ring to hold the guide in place, cut it off to the point where the thread wraps hold the guide foot down.

To finish the wrap lay down a loop of thread or monofilament to wrap over with the final wraps and finish the guide wrap. To do this, prepare a loop of mono or thread, knotting the two ends to make a loop. If you use thread, it should be the same size used for wrapping. If you use mono, use approximately the same size as the thread. Although monos vary widely today based on purpose, the following comparison chart, based on Gudebrod thread, shows clear similarities:

Thread Size	Thread Diameter	Mono Size
00	0.0045	two-pound test
A or NCP A	0.0070	four-pound test
D or NCP C	0.0104	eight-pound test
E or NCP D	0.0132	twelve-pound test
EE	0.0154	fifteen-pound test
FF	0.0175	twenty-pound test

I rarely use anything lower than six-pound test and usually stick to about six-, twelve-, and twenty-pound test for most mono loops. You can lay these loops down on the rod and just wrap over them, you can tape them down with a small square of masking tape, or, in the case of the mono loop, you can buy or make a hook-and-loop fastener (see chapter 2) that will hold the mono loop to the rod blank while you continue to wrap. Make sure the end of the loop faces the center of the guide.

Wrap over this loop with the working thread until you reach the end of the guide foot where it touches the frame. Use your thumb or finger on the thread wrap to maintain tension and cut the end of the thread a few inches from this last wrap. Tuck this end into the loop and pull the loop up slowly. Make sure the thread is straight as you pull the loop snug against the thread wraps. At this point release the tension on the thread, hold the blank with one hand, and slowly pull the loop under the previous wraps. This also pulls the tag end of the thread free, securing the end of the wrap.

There are several ways to cut the end of the thread. One is to pull the end of the thread snug and use a razor blade to cut the end of the thread close to the thread wrap and parallel to the axis of the blank. Although this will hold the thread wrap securely, it is the poorest way to finish a wrap because it leaves the stub of the tag end showing between the two thread wraps.

A better way is to pull the end of the thread snug and then work it back and forth to open up a slight gap where the thread exits between the wraps. Then use a razor blade or scalpel blade to cut straight down on the blank, using a slight rocking motion with the sharp blade to cut cleanly through the exiting thread. Take care that you use only enough pressure on the blade to cut the thread. Do *not* use hard pressure that might score or cut the blank. This is extremely important in order to avoid cutting through the resin coat and into the blank's longitudinal fibers, which could affect the rod's action and power. Also, if you make a guide wrap over an underwrap, then you *must* be very careful when cutting down with the razor blade to avoid cutting into the underlying threads of the underwrap. If there is an underwrap, you will find it more difficult to open up a gap to trim the thread. The thread beneath the guide wrap will prevent side movement of the guide-wrap threads. Also, in any cutting with a razor blade or scalpel blade, you must cut at right angles to the rod blank axis so that you do not inadvertently cut or nick the threads you have just wrapped in place.

Another method involves a slightly different technique. For this it is best to make about eight to ten wraps over the thread loop instead of the six to eight previously suggested. Cut the end of the thread, tuck it through the loop, and pull the loop snug. At this point use fine-point scissors to cut the end of the thread so that the length extending from the snug loop to the end of the thread is slightly *less* than the distance between the end of the wrap and the exit point of the loop. Once this is done, slowly pull the loop through. The loop pulls the end of the thread under the wraps, but the short thread end never exits through the wrap with the loop. There is no end to cut or stubs of thread to worry about. There is a slight gap in the thread wrap from the loop, but this may be burnished closed easily using a burnisher or the plastic barrel of a pen.

A fourth method of finishing involves any of the first two methods of cutting but does not involve the use of a loop to pull the thread

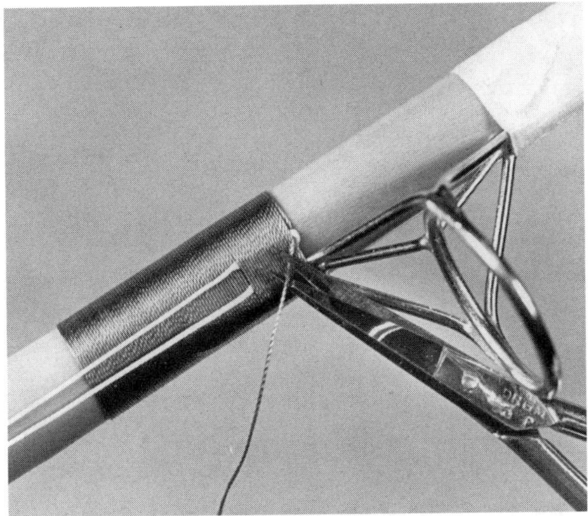

Another method of finishing a wrap with a loop is to pull the loop snug as shown and then clip the end of the thread so that it will be completely hidden under the thread wrap. This eliminates any cutting or trimming after the loop has been pulled through, since the end is too short to pull all the way through the wrap.

through. I first learned this method years ago at the Leonard rod factory, which has used this method for years for wrapping snake guides onto split-bamboo fly rods. In all honesty, I don't think this method offers any great advantage over the loop method. The steps are the same for wrapping the blank and guide foot in place up to the point at which the thread is pulled through. Do not use a loop of thread at this point. Instead place your finger on the wrap to maintain tension at this point, and remove the thread spool from the tension device.

Spool off some thread and then lay a length of this thread over the blank toward the far side of the guide. Then bring the spool of thread around the blank in the same direction as the previous thread wraps, but wrap inside this length of thread and back toward the guide. Make a number of turns equal to the number of turns you want around the blank to secure the thread. Once you reach this point, bring the spool of thread back over the original length of thread to the side of the guide being wrapped, but now reverse the thread direction. If you were wrapping over the rod blank and

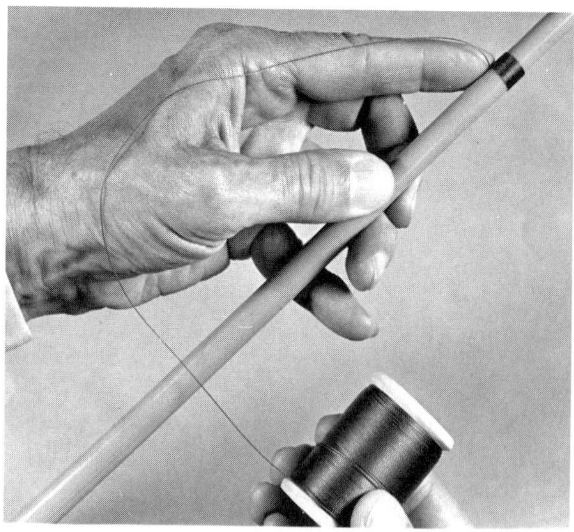

Making the Leonard style of finish on a thread wrap, here shown without guides for clarity. When you're within several turns of completing the wrap, make a larger loop of thread well ahead of the main wrap.

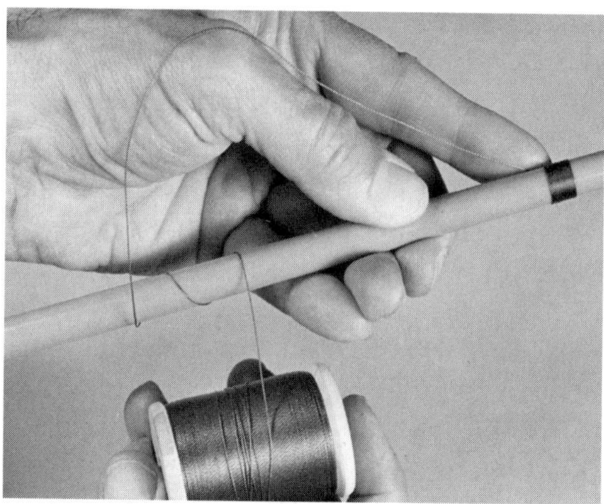

Continue by wrapping back around the rod blank toward the guide or wrap, wrapping in the same direction as the thread wrap.

away from you on the far side of the guide, you would now wrap over and toward you. Make turns equal to the number of turns on the other side of the guide.

Set the thread spool down on the workbench, and with your free hand grab the loose thread at the point immediately above where you are holding the wrap to maintain tension. Holding this end, rotate the rod to wrap over the portion of thread you just crossed to the opposite side of the guide.

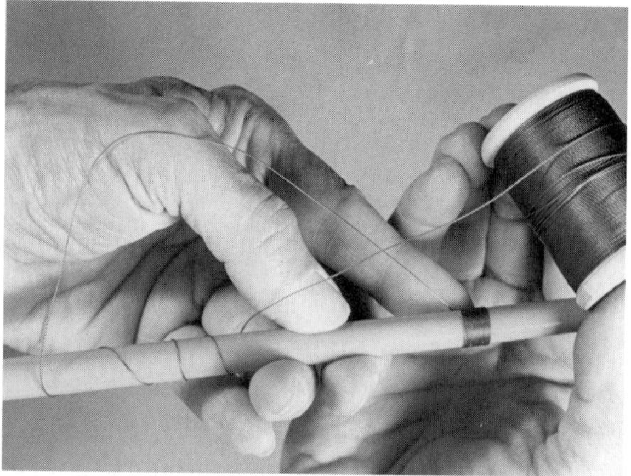

After several turns, bring the excess thread back across the thread wrap and make several turns around the rod blank in the opposite direction of the thread wrap. This just helps to keep the thread and spool out of the way when completing this wrap.

Continue doing this and you will notice that you are decreasing the excess loops on both sides of the guide wrap. Ultimately you reach the point where all the loops are removed (by rotating the rod), and you have only to maintain tension and pull the loose end of the thread through the wraps.

The end result is exactly the same as with other finishing methods, except that it does not involve a loop. The excess thread must be cut off by one of the several methods already suggested. The one

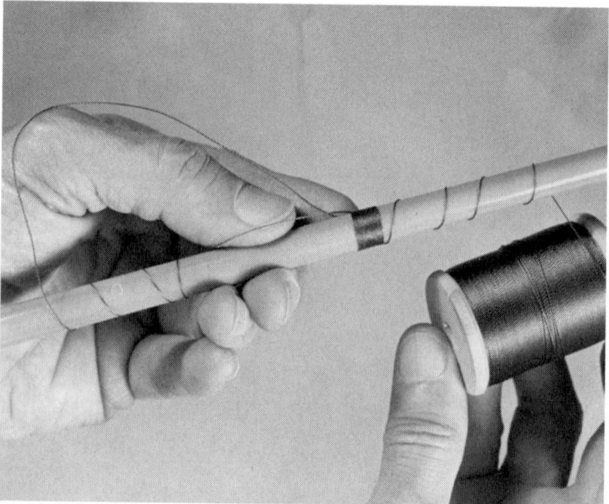

Turns around the rod blank in the opposite direction of the thread wrap help keep the end of the thread out of the way when finishing this wrap.

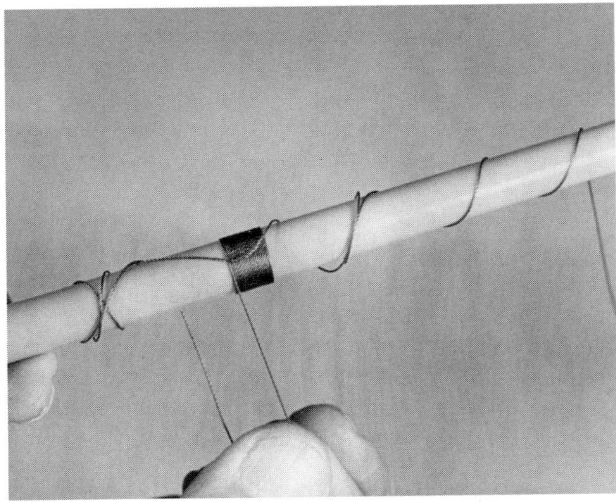

At this point continue the thread wrap, using the loose wraps made above the guide wrap as shown.

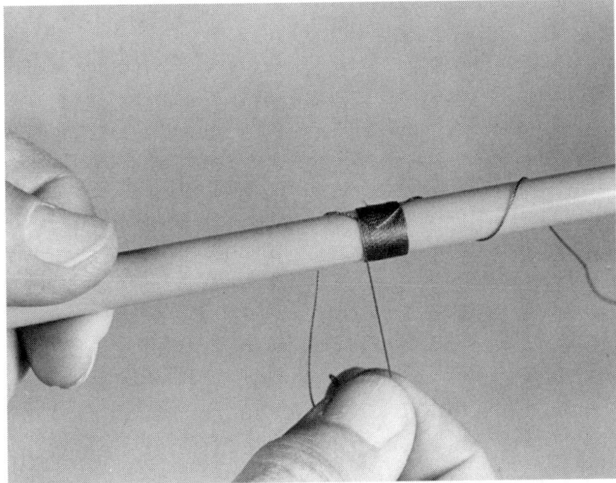

Continue until all turns are removed and the thread is completely wrapped around the blank.

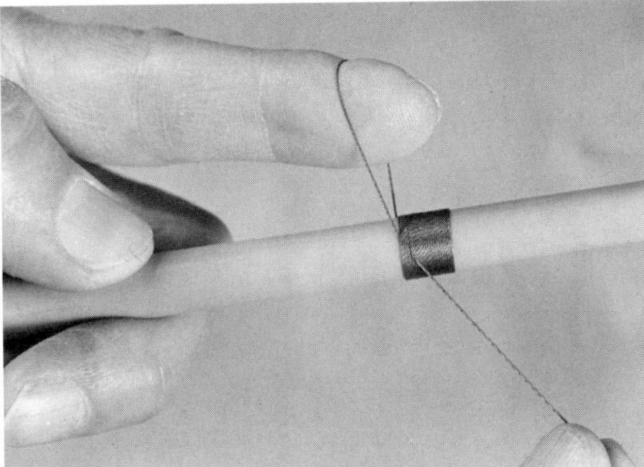

Hold the loop of thread, and pull the excess thread through the wrap.

main disadvantage to this method if you are wrapping anything other than fly rods where small snake guides are used is that the larger guides of other rods are sometimes awkward to make the thread wraps over while turning the rod. The larger the guides, the more thread you need for this step.

In all the above methods, use a burnisher to polish the wrap and close up any slight gaps that might have occurred during the wrapping process. An ideal tool for this is the various burnishing tools offered by custom rod supply houses or the similar plastic-letter-transfer tool made by C-Thru Ruler Company and sold in art, stationery, and now tackle-component shops. Plastic ballpoint pens and similar smooth-plastic tools are ideal for this. You can use anodized-aluminum crochet and knitting needles, but make sure you do not use anything that might leave a stain or mark on the thread wrap.

These methods are basic for any rod, any wrap, any size thread, and any type of guide. However, you may wish to consider the following tips:

1. If you use heavy thread on heavy rods, such as sizes E, EE, or FF, you may wish to cut the end at the beginning of the wrap and then fray out the cut end so that there is a smooth transition of the thread wrap over the cut end. In most cases this will not be noticeable, however.

2. When using standard nylon rod-wrapping thread, you should have no problems with "frizzes"—tiny fibers of the thread. However, in some cases these fibers will interfere with a perfect wrap and epoxy finish. To remove them use a flame from a cigarette lighter, fireplace lighter, or alcohol lamp, holding the side of the flame against the finished wrap while rotating the blank. The flame will burn off these fine fibers to leave a smooth surface. Make sure you rotate the rod, and use only the side of the flame to avoid damaging the wrap or soiling it with soot.

3. Do not finish the thread so that the wrapped-over portion ends up in the gap alongside the guide foot. By necessity, this is a small space, and the thread end cannot be held tight there. You must snug it up under a tight wrap on the top of the guide foot or on the blank.

4. When it is examined carefully, the beginning and end of any wrap can be seen—both where the end tucks through and also at the beginning of the thread wrap. You can't eliminate this, but you can position it where it will not normally be seen during fishing. For example, on a fly rod or spinning rod, you can position the beginning and end of every wrap in line with or on top of the guide foot. Because the guides hang under the rod during fishing, this will place the ends of the wrap out of view. For casting rods, traditional trolling rods, and revolving-spool tackle, place these spots directly opposite the guide foot and thus away from view during fishing. The same thing can be done with any part of any wrap—underwraps, trim wraps, inlaid wraps, and single- and multiple-thread wraps.

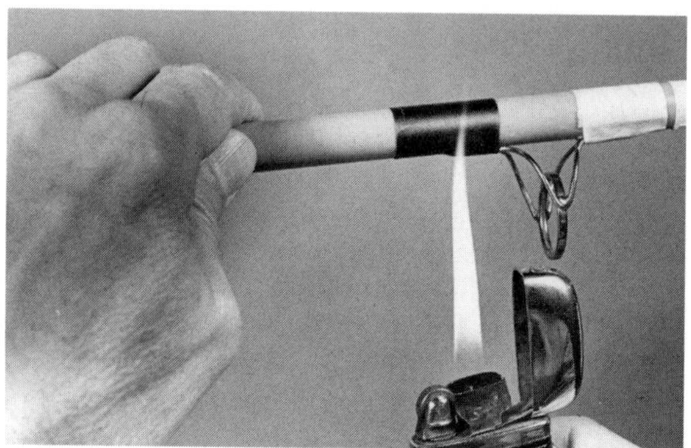

Using the side of a flame to singe any thread fibers remaining after wrapping. Usually this is not necessary. Use only the side of the flame; otherwise the thread might burn or become soiled from smoke.

UNDERWRAPS

Underwraps are wraps placed on a rod prior to the guide wraps. They are directly underneath each guide wrap and have several purposes. They are decorative because they are almost always a different color than the guide wraps and thus provide contrast and additional color. They are also functional in that they provide a cushion between the blank finish and the metal foot of the guide.

Underwraps are made using exactly the same techniques as guide wraps, except that no guide is wrapped down. An underwrap is usually a plain, continuous wrap, although decorative wraps to make the center ring of the guide or to dress up the end are also possible, just as they are on any guide wrap. An underwrap must be slightly longer than the guide wrap, thus the need for care in measurements for underwraps previously mentioned. An underwrap must be exactly centered for guide positioning. Mark the center position of the guide, and then use this mark and a center rule to mark both ends of the underwrap (use masking tape). Begin as for a guide wrap, wrap the whole length of the underwrap, and finish as described. You can begin and end underwraps so that you will not see these areas while fishing.

Color choice in underwraps is important. Generally it is always better to use light colors for underwraps and darker colors for guide wraps. Using a dark color for the underwrap and a lighter color for the guide wrap can result in a show-through of the darker color underwrap. It would be the same as using one layer of light paint over a dark paint—the darker color could affect the lighter color. Any effect of the underwrap color—light or dark—will be accentuated unless color preserver is used on the underwrap

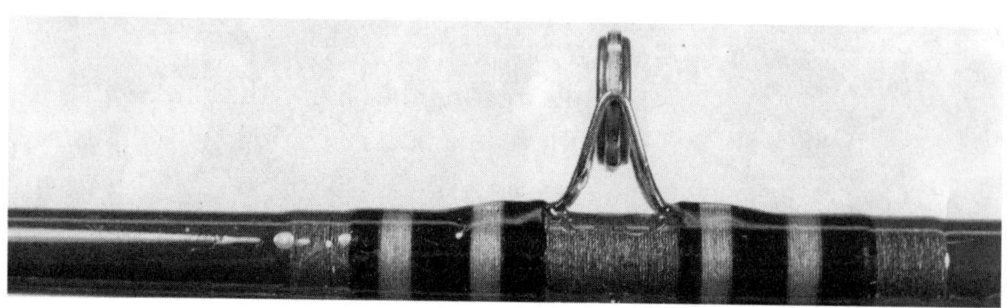

Completed thread wrap with finish added.

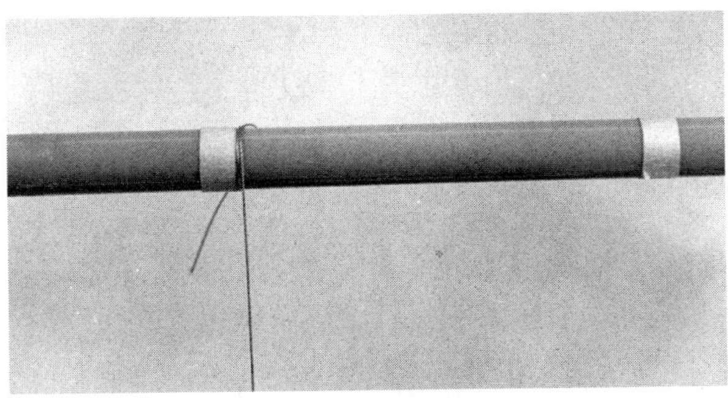

Beginning an underwrap by wrapping around the blank and over the previous thread wraps several times.

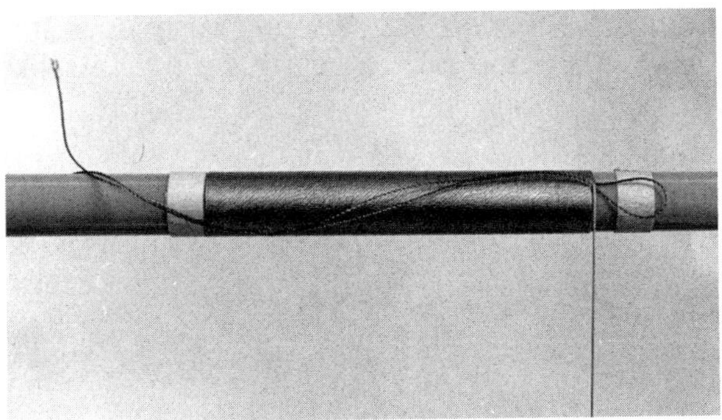

The wrap is completed close to the end, where a loop of thread is laid down to finish the wrap.

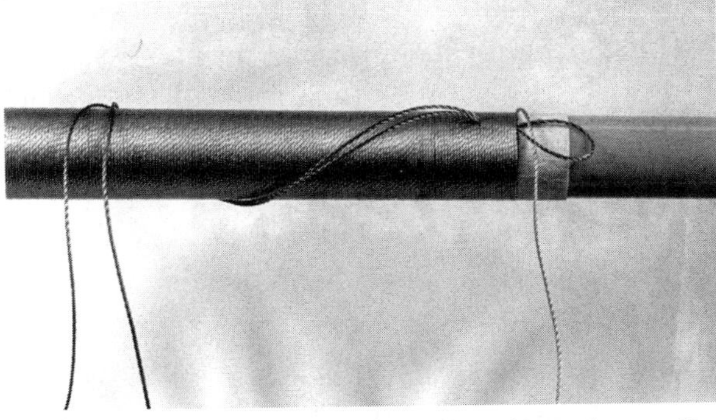

Here the thread has been wrapped to the end, over the loop, and the thread cut and tucked into the loop.

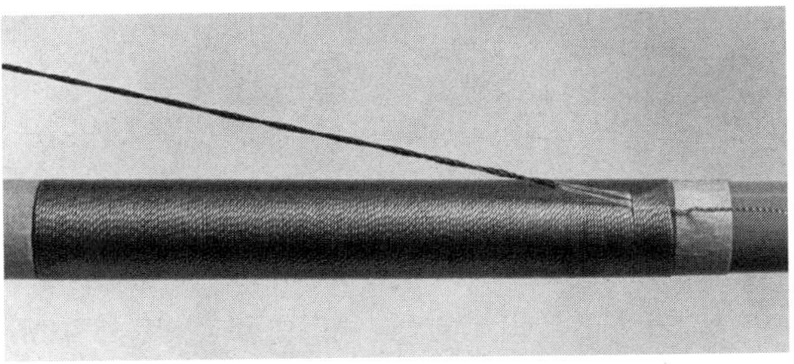

Pulling the loop through eventually pulls the end of the thread under the wrap to secure the thread. Note that the masking tape is still in place and must be removed at this point.

before the guide is wrapped in place. Often one coat is best over NCP thread (though you are probably reasonably safe without it), and two or three coats of color preserver are best over regular nylon thread. Be sure to use a color preserver that will match the final finish used. In most cases this means using the same brand of both color preserver and finish.

Some rod builders go even further, adding one coat of epoxy rod finish to the underwrap before wrapping the guide wrap. There are several advantages and some disadvantages to this. The advantages are that the underwrap is completely protected from any show-through or blotching of color; the smooth finish provides a smooth working base on which to wrap the guide; and if you make this smooth base of finish, you can then use the same size thread used for the underwrap. Otherwise you should use different thread sizes for the underwrap and the guide wrap—say, size A for the underwrap and size D for the guide wrap, or size 2/0 for the underwrap and size A for the guide wrap on a large rod. Doing this when you do not use the epoxy rod finish prevents the guide-wrap thread from wedging in between the underwrap threads, as would happen with threads of the same size used without a finish. A larger thread size for the guide wrap spaces each individual wrap differently, preventing this problem. A disadvantage is that the coating of an epoxy over the underwrap and before the guide wrap might make the surface slippery and thus allow for some gaps in the overwrap over the guide feet.

Although finishing wraps and rods is covered in chapter 25, we must consider finishing here before adding guide wraps over underwraps. One of the problems with underwraps is a splotching or mottling if the underwrap shows through the overwrap, particularly if the guide wrap is a medium rather than a dark shade.

One way to prevent this is to use NCP thread on the underwrap or to use one or two coats of color preserver on the underwrap before adding the guide wrap. This seals the underwrap colors and prevents show-through.

One other possible cause of blotching and mottling is contaminants on the wraps. Before beginning any wrap, make sure your hands are clean, that you use no hand lotion or other lotions, and that you do not come in contact with any chemicals that could cause problems. Silicone is a particularly bad substance; it can create bad reactions with any epoxy and can mar the finish. Also, if you have very sweaty hands, consider wearing cotton gloves during wrapping operations.

DOUBLE AND TRIPLE WRAPS

Guide wraps can be made single (as previously described), or they can be made double or triple. Usually multiple wraps are done for added strength when using light thread on heavy-duty rods or just as added insurance, even with heavy thread, on heavy-duty rods. It can also be decorative if separate thread is used of a different color than the basic guide wrap.

There are several ways to do double and triple wraps (several layers of wraps over the initial wrap) on a guide. The simplest way is to continue using the same thread as for the main guide wrap. For this technique begin and proceed as for the single guide wrap, but do not lay down a loop of thread near the end. Instead proceed to the end of the guide foot and, at this point, cross back over the thread to begin making a wrap of thread on top of the wrap just completed. You are only reversing the direction of the thread on the guide foot—the rotation direction continues the same. Often you can begin within about one or two wraps of the end. You may find that you will have to use a slightly reduced thread tension during this step to prevent the thread from pulling through the previous wraps and into the gaps between. The problem here is similar to that of making a guide wrap on top of an underwrap. Continue wrapping as far as you like. Some rod builders like to stop about halfway along the guide foot; others continue along the guide foot almost to the original beginning of the wrap. If you continue this far, remember that you will be going down the slope of the end of the guide foot. Use care here to prevent gaps, although this won't cause as much of a problem as it would on a bare guide foot. The previous thread wraps provide a base that will grip the next layer of threads.

Once you reach the guide frame and the end of the first wrap, you can rapidly spiral back over the completed wrap to the beginning or near the beginning of the original wrap and then start again with a wrap up the blank and onto and over the guide foot. Usually you can make such a spiral wrap in about one-half turn of the rod so that the spiral will be hidden on one part of the rod, opposite where you will visually see the rod. This spiral will also be covered by the continuing wrap over the first wrap as you wrap up again from the blank and onto the guide foot.

A triple wrap is done in the same way, by first making the single wrap from the blank up to the frame end of the guide foot, reversing the wrap, and then reversing it a second time to begin a third wrap, this time going back toward the center of the guide. You can also use the spiral method mentioned above, making the first wrap from the blank to the guide frame, then a rapid spiral back to the beginning for the second wrap and finally another spiral wrap back to the beginning to start a third wrap. All these additional wraps should be made with less pressure than that used for the first wrap to prevent the possibility of the thread cutting down between the threads of a previous wrap. Finish as for any wrap, using a loop of thread or mono.

Regardless of where you plan to stop, lay down a loop of thread or mono about six to eight wraps from where you want to end, with the loop pointed away toward where you will continue to wrap and finish the wrap. Wrap over the loop for six to eight turns, cut the thread end while maintaining the tension, tuck the end through the loop, and pull the loop through. Cut the end using one of the methods described for the single guide wrap.

Although I still like the method best, there is an additional problem and danger if you use a razor blade to cut straight down between the wraps. First, the thread base here will make it harder to spread the wraps apart. Second, you must cut carefully so as not to cut the threads beneath, which make up the first layer (or second layer with three wraps) of the guide wrap. The problems are easily handled once you understand them and are no different from cutting through a single wrap made over an underwrap.

In addition, double and triple wraps can be made as separate wraps: The first, second, and third layers of the wraps are made with separate thread colors for a decorative as well as strengthening effect. The advantage is that all the guides can be wrapped in place and color preserver added as is done for underwraps to prevent blotching. Then the second-color wrap is added, with more color preserver; finally a third-color wrap is added if desired. The color preserver helps seal the wraps and makes for a more solid and level base on which to make the subsequent wrap. In most cases a small edge of the previous wrap is left exposed at each end, or at least at the outer end of the guide wrap, for decorative purposes. If preferred you can use the no-loop method described earlier as Leonard and other bamboo companies used to use for finishing their snake guide wraps.

VARIATIONS AND SPECIAL EFFECTS FOR WRAPPINGS

The foregoing describes some good but basic ways to make single wraps, double wraps, triple wraps, and underwraps. There are a number of variations that will not hold the guides any more securely but will make the guide wraps more decorative and have more of a custom look.

Some of these variations follow:

Wrapping a single-foot guide. The technique for wrapping a single-foot guide is really the same as for wrapping two-foot guides, whether using a basic bare-bones method as previously described, using a double or triple wrap, or using some of the fancy techniques to be covered here. The one concern is that since there is only one foot, it is not stabilized as easily when taped in place, so that there is a greater likelihood of its being wrapped at a slight angle to the rod axis. There is no real way to prevent this other than to check the guide and guide-foot alignment frequently while wrapping. The wrap beginning, wrapping method, wrap ending, and finishing methods are all the same as for two-foot guides.

Pfeiffer bump wrap for single-foot guides. One variation of this that I have sometimes used is to add a small "bumper" of thread in front of the guide foot, both for decoration and to prevent the guide foot from sliding out from beneath the wraps. If the guide is wrapped tightly, this is not really a problem, but I still like to add the bumper. One way to do this is to wrap up to the end of the guide foot and then jump the thread over the front of the guide and finish on the bare blank in front of the guide foot. You have to work at a slight angle to get the thread around the guide, because all the frames lean slightly forward. Sometimes I will end this way; other times I go about four wraps and then reverse the thread, laying down a loop at the same time, to double-wrap this bumper area.

An alternative is to make a short wrap (four to six turns of thread) first, butt the guide foot against it, tape the guide in place, then finish with the same thread or a different color or size thread. To do this you must lay down the loop first and make the whole wrap over the loop; otherwise the wrap is too short to finish. If you double-wrap this bumper, do not lay down the loop until the first layer is complete.

Forhan single-foot locking guide wrap. This is a locking loop and bump developed by Rich Forhan. It is another variation of wrap for single-foot guides only. To do this, tape down and begin the wrap on a single-foot guide as you would normally. Start the wrap on the blank and then, with the guide foot filed and tapered (if necessary), continue the wrap up onto the foot. About eight thread wraps from the end, lay down a loop with the loop end pointing toward the end of the guide wrap. After several more wraps, and with the guide on top of the horizontal rod, take the thread wrap by hand

and wrap it around the junction of the frame with the guide foot. Then continue around the blank and make this same step again, with the thread wrapped around the guide frame/foot junction. Do this a third or even fourth time, and then make a final wrap or two around the blank, the guide foot, and the loop before cutting off the tag end of the thread and then tucking it into the loop and pulling the loop through before cutting off the excess thread as previously described. A variation of this is to make two wraps each time around the frame/guide foot junction before again going around the rod.

Trim wraps. Trim wraps at the end of the guide wrap or at the end of the underwrap are generally several thread wraps in width, although they can be more or less. They can be done in several ways. The basic wrap (the guide wrap or underwrap) can be completed and the trim wrap then added to the end. Or you can make the trim wrap first and then begin the basic guide wrap or underwrap at the end of the trim wrap. In both cases it helps to mark the end of the wraps with masking tape to help maintain proper alignment and accurate spacing.

One problem with trim wraps is that they are generally very short and thus are perceived as difficult to begin and finish because there is a very narrow wrap under which to pull a loop of thread for finishing. If the wrap is fairly wide—say, six or eight turns of thread—you can begin as with a regular wrap, continue for a turn or two, then trim off the thread end and lay down a loop of thread or mono, continuing to the end of the wrap (another four to six turns). Then cut the end and tuck it through the loop, pulling the loop through. Make sure you burnish this well but lightly. Too heavy a pressure on these wraps can sometimes pull threads loose. For best results with any burnishing, burnish *toward* the center of the wrap, not away from it, which might create gaps in the last turn of thread.

It is also possible to make several trim bands at the end of the wrap with different colors of thread. Treat each of these the same way to begin and end, using separate loops for the endings but keeping the loops close together so that the endings are all in line.

It is also possible to make two or more bands using one finishing loop. To do this, wrap down two different additional colors of thread when making the beginning of the main guide wrap. For most wraps use threads about 12 to 18 inches long. Finish the main wrap and then begin the trim wraps. Take the thread to be used for the end trim band and tape it down to the blank at the end of the thread wrap. Tape down a loop of thread or mono at the same time, with the loop pointing away from the guide center. Then wrap the first thread around the loop and taped-down thread for several turns. Cut the end and run it through the loop. Pull it back toward the guide, and tape this end down. Then tape down the end of the loop to help maintain tension on this wrap. Begin the second wrap with the previously taped-down thread, wrapping over the loop. Continue for several turns and then cut the end, tucking it through the loop. Take up the tape over the loop and pull the loop slowly through. In doing this, the loop will first pull through the end thread and then pick up and pull through the first thread. Both threads will exit through the same gap in the main-wrap threads. Cut and finish.

A variation is to use thread for the trim wrap that is one size smaller than the wrap thread. When used at the ends of the wrap, this makes for a more tapered effect with the wrap and also allows for the thinnest possible wraps, including the single-thread wrap as described next.

Single-thread trim wraps. For a delicate look you can make a trim wrap of only one or two threads at the end of the main wrap. These are too narrow to finish with a loop of thread in the traditional way, so an alternative method must be found. There are two.

One is to first lay down a loop of thread pointing away from the guide center. Do this so that the loop is at the location of the beginning of the wrap. Then lay down a length of thread that will be the one- or two-turn trim wrap. Begin the main guide wrap or underwrap with a different color thread, wrapping over the loop and the thread to be used for the single-thread trim. After about five turns, cut the end of the main-wrap thread, cut the end of the trim-wrap thread, and flip the knotted end of the loop up and over so that subsequent wraps will not be over the loop. Continue the main wrap to the end, and finish with a separate loop of thread.

To complete the trim wrap, make one, two, or as many turns as you want around the blank. Then cut the end of the thread, tuck it through the original loop, and pull the loop through. Because the loop has several turns under the main wrap in addition to the trim wrap, the end of the thread will be completely secured. Cut the end and finish.

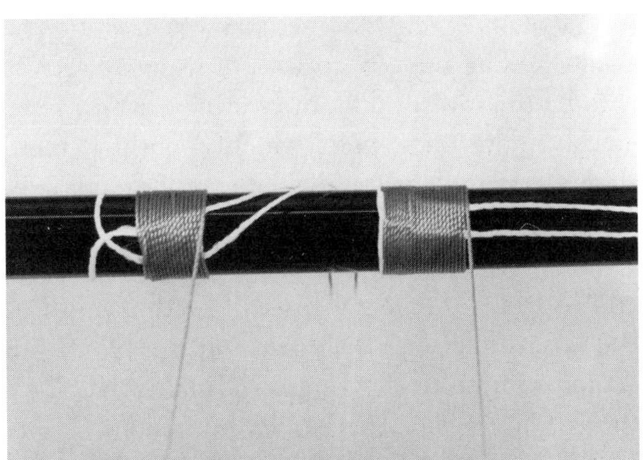

Making a single wrap of thread at the end of a guide wrap. Left, the single contrasting-color thread is held in place (using masking tape) to the blank and the main wrap begun over it. Note that the thread is crossed over itself. After the wrap is complete, or after several turns are made, the single wrap can be pulled tight against the main wrap. Right, the single thread pulled tight but before the ends of the thread are cut.

A second method does not involve loops and is actually much easier to accomplish. Before making the main wrap, use tape to secure one end of the trim-wrap thread. Use another piece of tape to hold the thread about 2 inches away from the beginning of the wrap, and make one or more turns around the blank. (The number of turns you make here will determine the number of turns the trim wrap will make around the blank upon completion.) Then lay the thread down parallel to its end and tape it in place. These wraps must be loose at this point; you will be rewrapping them when the main wrap is completed.

Begin the main wrap between the tapes holding the thread and at a predetermined point—preferably marked at this time with tape after measuring. Continue the wrap for six to eight turns, cut the end of the main-wrap thread, remove the tape from the trim-wrap thread, and pull these two threads out so that they are free of subsequent wraps. Continue the wrap to the end, and finish and cut the thread. Make sure the two parallel threads cross over each other at the point where they were wrapped around the rod. Keep them in this position, and then wrap the topmost thread around the wrap so that it is tight against the main wrap just completed. Continue wrapping; the loose wrap will unravel until you are at the point where the thread goes under the main wrap. Gently pull this thread while maintaining light tension on the loose thread loop. Pull tight, tighten both threads, and then cut them with a razor blade.

Note that this wrap can be done on the end of a guide wrap or underwrap and can be one, two, three, or more threads in width when complete. It is very important to have the parallel wrapped-over threads crossing each other at the end, particularly for a one-turn wrap. This will prevent the two ends from being pulled apart when they are pulled tight, thus eliminating part of the complete "circle" of this single-strand wrap.

This same method of making one- or two-turn wraps in the center of a wrap can be applied anywhere along a guide wrap or underwrap for decorative effect. Often such wraps are placed near the end of a wrap to give a decorative or trimmed look to the wrap.

Guide-center single-thread wraps. Guide-center wraps are sometimes added to an underwrap to indicate in a decorative way the center of the guide or position of the guide ring. These are often single- or double-turn wraps and thus require care.

Begin the underwrap in the normal manner, and proceed until within about six to eight turns of the center. Check the exact position of the center with a rule or caliper, and mark the spot with a pencil. Once you are several turns from the center, cut a 12-inch length of thread to be used for the center wrap. Lay down one end of this thread. Continue wrapping over this thread with the main underwrap thread until it is right at the center. Check again for the center position at this point. Now make one or more turns of the center thread around the rod blank, wrapping over the main-wrap thread at the same time. Once you have made the desired number of complete turns, use the main-wrap thread to wrap over the loose end of the center thread. Continue for several wraps; make sure the center wrap is tight, or adjust it by slightly pulling the wrapped-over thread. Cut this thread and then continue to the end of the wrap. The effect is to secure both ends of the center wrap, with one end on each side of the center mark and wrapped over by the main wrap.

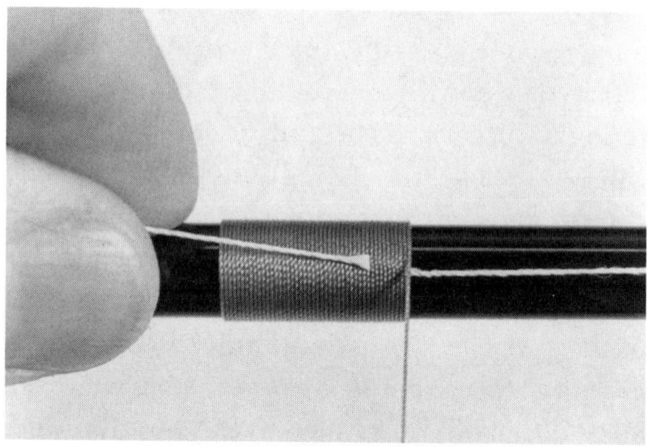

Beginning a center thread in the middle of an underwrap. Here the contrasting thread is wrapped down.

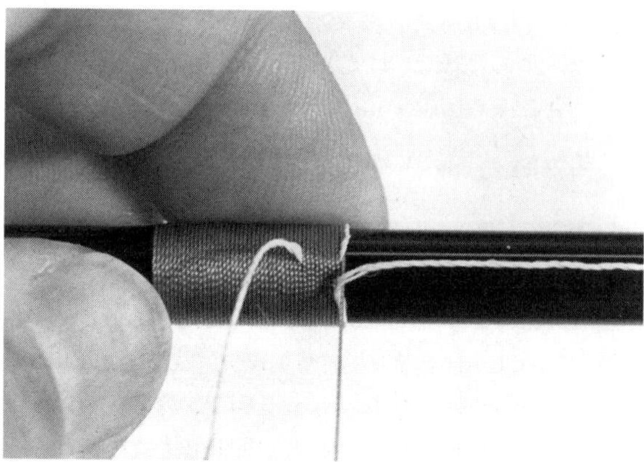

The contrasting thread is wrapped around the rod and over the other thread, then the main thread is wrapped over this.

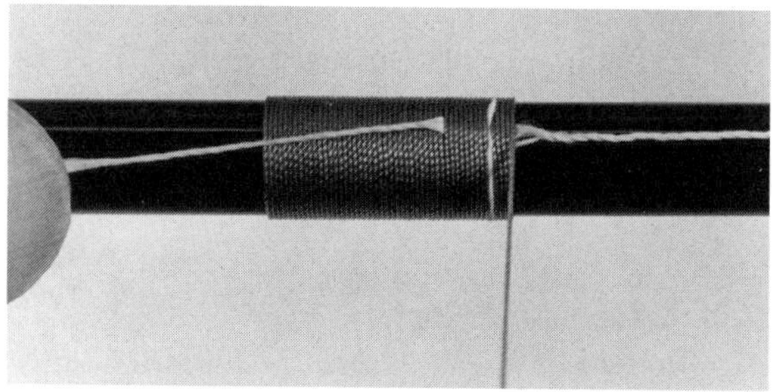

Completed center wrap in place. Both ends of this contrasting thread must be cut at this point.

False underwraps. Sometimes you might want the look of an underwrap within the extra layer of thread. This is easily done by creating what has been called a false underwrap, which is nothing more than a wrap underneath the center of the guide covering what would be an open, exposed area.

First measure the distance between the inside ends of the guide feet. This will be the length of the false underwrap. Measure on the blank the center position of the guide, and mark the blank there. Place a tape marker on both sides of this mark, each marker to be at one-half the inside guide-foot spacing. Make this wrap, which can be plain or a center-guide wrap. Once this wrap is complete, position the guide on the top center of the wrap, tape it in place, and mark the beginning point of each guide. Complete each guide wrap, making sure you wrap up to the frame edge to meet the previous false underwrap. The completed effect is just like an underwrap, particularly if you add a simple, short trim wrap to the outside end of the guide wraps. This is ideal for light rods where you do not want or need the added weight and stiffness of the underwrap.

Double-, triple-, or quadruple-thread wraps. You can use more than the four threads indicated, but most rod builders do not. In effect, what you are doing here is wrapping with two, three, or four threads, all of different colors, and all at the same time. The effect is an almost shimmering look. Once started, this wrap is no problem other than in the handling of several threads at one time and in keeping them from crossing. One way to simplify this is to use a standard hair comb, mounted in the rod-wrapping thread carriage, to keep the several threads in the proper relationship to one another.

There are several ways to start this thread wrap. Let's assume a wrap of three threads, although the same principle would apply with fewer or more threads. One way to begin is to treat all three threads as one: Wrap them around the blank, and then cross them over to lock them down. Make several turns while holding the ends of the threads to maintain tension, then cut the excess and continue wrapping.

This type of wrap can be finished off using a loop of mono or thread. To do this, wrap until you are several turns from the end (this can be just one or two turns, because one turn will be three threads for a trim wrap and two turns will be six threads). Lay down the loop, wrap two turns over it, and then cut all three threads while continuing to maintain tension. Keep the threads in order (do not mix or cross them), and tuck all three into the loop. Arrange the threads in order,

Wraps using two or more solid-color threads at one time: top, a wrap with two threads; center, a wrap with three thread colors at once; bottom, a wrap with four color threads at one time. Such wrapping is tedious, since all threads must remain parallel and remain under equal tension.

and pull the loop to pull the threads through. Cut as before, and burnish to close the resulting gap. Obviously two threads will be easier to pull through than three, three will be easier than four, and so on.

Another method is to begin with one thread and make two wraps, then add the second thread (by wrapping over it with the first wrap) and make two more wraps, then add the third thread (by wrapping over it with the first two wraps), and continue. After several more wraps, cut the excess thread and continue to the end, where you reverse the process with three loops, all close together. Use one loop to tuck under the closest thread, make two more wraps or turns with the remaining two threads, and use the second loop for tucking in the second thread. Then, with two more wraps, finally finish the last thread by tucking it into the remaining loop and pulling it through. Cut the exiting threads as outlined.

Variations of simple guide wraps. Variations of simple guide wraps (with one thread color) are easy to do using several techniques. These include spiral wraps, spiral wraps over tape or Mylar, and band wraps. A spiral wrap is a single thread spiraling over a bare blank, underwrap, Mylar tape, or even abalone. Begin it as for a standard wrap, but after about six turns of thread begin to spiral the wrap toward the guide. Stop spiraling before the end of the guide foot is reached, and return to the standard wrap. Finish normally.

This same wrap can be made over a band of Mylar or tape. The Mylar or tape provides underlying color to the spiral part of the wrap. First measure the position for the wrap, and then add tape to the point that will be exposed by the spiral wrap. Make sure the end of the wrap is located on the side opposite where it will be viewed during fishing. Begin as above, starting and ending the spiral wrap over the top of the Mylar or tape. Finish normally. Other tapes and coverings other than Mylar wrap can be used for this method.

A band wrap is like a spiral wrap, but instead of a continuous spiral, one spiral turn is made, then the thread is wrapped tightly to make a short band, a second spiral is made, another band is wrapped, and so on. The number of separate bands is limited only by the total length of the wrap.

One final method of making a wrap is to begin at one end, but instead of finishing at the frame/foot junction, the thread is "jumped" around the base of the guide and continued on the other side. The difficulty here is that it is hard to maintain tight wraps on the downslope of the second guide foot. It can be done, but it requires less tension in order to avoid pulling the threads down the slope. Finishing with a loop is accomplished as for any wrap.

Spirals, bands, and similar wraps are not usually found on custom rods. They are more common on less-expensive factory rods but are included here for those who would like to try them.

WRAPS ON ROD PARTS OTHER THAN GUIDES

The basic wrappings just described are used in other ways than wrapping guides. In all cases the wraps are made in exactly the same way as for guides. The same techniques, the same variations, the same several methods of finishing—all are applicable.

As previously described, the tip-top is always wrapped. This is for decoration only in the case of the tube-type tip-tops, because the tubes are glued in place. The wrapping does not hold anything but only covers the last inch or so of the rod blank below the edge of the tube.

Ferrules also have to be wrapped, even when they are built into the rod. This is necessary to give the rod blank hoop strength in order to prevent the tubular blank from splitting under the pressure of bending. In most cases an inch or two here is enough of a wrap, but in all cases follow the specific directions of the individual rod-blank manufacturer. There are several types of self-ferrules, but all should be wrapped.

The spigot type is made by cutting through a one-piece blank and then inserting a short plug or ferrule into the larger butt section. This plug is usually solid and must be of the same taper as the lower end of the tip section or upper section (in the case of multiple-piece rods) in order to fit and mate properly. Wrap on both sides of the ferrule to reinforce both the lower male end with the plug and the upper female end. This spigot-type ferrule is no longer found on factory blanks anymore, but it can be made and used by any custom builder and is included here for that purpose.

The "Fenwick" (so-called because Fenwick developed this ferruling system back in the early 1960s), or slipover, style involves a blank made on two mandrels—the upper end has an internal diameter that will match the outside diameter of the lower section for an easy slipover and mating. Naturally the tapers must be the same. Most of these require wrapping only for the female section to give it hoop strength, because the female section provides hoop strength for the male end.

Making these wraps is just like making an underwrap or making a guide wrap without the guide. In any of them, begin on the body of the blank and work up to the edge. This will allow you to make the wrap much closer to the edge of the blank than would be possible if it were started at the edge. Some manufacturers suggest that a wrap is not necessary on their rod blanks, but unless otherwise suggested to not include a wrap, a slight, short wrap is recommended. Rod builders and manufacturers vary on this, with some suggesting a wrap of about ¼ to ½ inch, others suggesting a rod wrap of about two to three times the diameter of the rod blank at the point of the ferrule, and still others suggesting 1 inch or more for a complete wrapping of the female section of the ferrule.

If you will be using metal ferrules (as when rebuilding an old rod or when making a bamboo rod, which requires a metal ferrule), these too must be wrapped. This is more for decoration than strength, but it does help impart some strength to this joint. Begin as for a guide wrap on the blank, and wrap up to the ferrule. Ferrules vary in manufacture. Most have a slight shoulder about ⅜ to ½ inch above the end, which is a marking for the end of the thread wrap. Wrap up to and finish off at this point. The wrap will completely cover the end of the ferrule and provide a decorative touch. If you wish to hide a metal ferrule or prevent glare from a bright ferrule, you can wrap the entire ferrule. Most female ferrules have a rolled edge, and the thread can be wrapped up to that point. The male ferrule should be wrapped to the point where the male section enters the female ferrule.

Many rod builders also use hook-keepers on their rods. These are small loop-, hooklike-, or folded-metal holders that are wrapped to the blank just about the foregrip and are used to hold the hook of a fly or lure to prevent it from catching anglers or objects when not in use. Some of these are small, two-foot wire devices with a separate ring that are wrapped on just like two-foot guides. Others have only one foot and are wrapped on as a one-foot guide would be. Some fold out of the way when not in use. They are easy to wrap. Alignment is a matter of choice, but most rod builders place the hook-keeper in line with the guides. Some in the past have placed the hook-keeper to the side or directly opposite the side with the guides. Although it rarely happens, I have seen situations where a hook-keeper opposite the guides can cause casting problems. With both fly and spinning rods, sometimes the line can loop around or fly up to catch the hook-keeper and slow or stop the cast. With the hook-keeper in line with the guides, this can't happen. Hook-keepers are wrapped exactly as are guides, following all the same steps. The hook-keeper feet must be filed and polished, in proper alignment, and the foot must be taped down to the rod blank with the end of the foot showing to receive the first thread wraps.

Examples of spiral wraps (top) and band wraps (bottom) with basic solid-color thread.

Rods also have a wrap immediately above the foregrip. This is again strictly decorative and tends to finish the look of the rod and to cover any roughness or unevenness that might have occurred when the grip or the winding check was mounted. In all cases where a hook-keeper is used, these wraps are usually combined. In these cases the upper (tip) end of the foregrip wrap is usually combined with the lower (butt) end of the hook-keeper wrap.

Begin the wrap at the winding check, using a burnisher to push the beginning wrap well back against the winding check or grip to eliminate any gaps. Then continue for an inch or so until you've wound up onto the foot of the hook-keeper. Then tie off and begin a wrap again (if necessary) for the other end of the hook-keeper. An alternative is to start an inch or so above the winding check and wrap down to the winding check to make sure the threads are tight against it with no gaps.

These simple thread wraps are completely different from the decorative wraps used on the butt section of some rods, as will be described in the next two chapters.

23
Simple Butt Wraps and Decorative Wraps

Introduction • Tools and Materials • Simple Butt Wraps • Basic Theory • Rod Preparation • Underwraps • Layout of Decorative Wraps • Basic Wrapping Techniques • Diamond Wraps • Chevron Wraps • Cross Wraps • Flag Wraps • Checkerboard or Snakeskin Wraps • Other Variations of Simple Wraps

Basic Safety Requirements

Safety goggles

Basic Tools

Flat, sturdy workbench

Rod-wrapping supports; thread-tension device or rod-wrapping tool

Ruler

Razor blades

Burnisher

Masking tape

Helpful Tools

Circle template and angle aluminum or plastic angle

Proportional-scale ruler

Bobbins for holding thread, particularly when making simple and complex wraps with multiple thread colors

INTRODUCTION

Decorative wraps on rods are just that—strictly decorative. Decorative wraps can be placed at the butt of a rod just above a foregrip, between the hand grip and lifting grip of a saltwater fly rod, above the winding check or foregrip of a bait-casting rod, filling the space between the foregrip and first guide on an offshore rod, or even woven in between the frame and foot of guides to make a "mini diamond" (or similar wrap) on each and every guide. All such wraps are decorative and contribute nothing to the strength or function of the rod. They are, however, beautiful; done tastefully and well, they contribute to the appearance of the rod and mark it as truly a work of individual craftsmanship.

Such decorative wraps are not hard to do but require careful planning, particularly when laying out and designing unique custom wraps that involve intricate placement and order of the threads. They also require layout and careful thread work throughout the wrap. Other than that, all they require is thread, careful measurement, a lot of time, and some simple tools that are easily obtained or made.

The time required must be emphasized. To make a simple diamond wrap might require only an hour. More-complex wraps with more thread, more colors, and more intricate designs can require much more time—hours and hours. As with any aspect of tackle craft and rod building, decorative wraps can be as simple or as complex as you like.

If you have not made a decorative wrap before, start simple before going on to design your own patterns or getting into complex multiple wraps or weaving. One suggestion is to add a simple diamond or chevron to an existing rod, whether that rod is custom built or factory made. Existing simple butt wraps—usually just a band of thread above the foregrip—are easily removed using a razor blade as a carpenter's plane to shave off the thread and peel off the finish to expose the bare blank. Making a simple basic diamond wrapped here can help you determine your level of interest in making other wraps. Some rod builders love—almost live for—the custom wraps and touches they can create on their rods. Others are interested only in plain, serviceable, highly functional rods that have little in the way of decoration—and nothing in the way of decorative wraps.

TOOLS AND MATERIALS

Tools and materials for underwrapping are few and simple. Most often they are found in craft and stationery stores and then adapted for decorative wraps. Some possibilities include:

Circle template. This is a clear-plastic template sold in stationery stores and used for drawing circles. It consists of a series of different size circles, in inches or millimeters. One I use has holes in millimeters, from 2 through 10 millimeters in half-millimeter increments and then from 11 through 30 in full millimeters. Another measures from 1 millimeter (about 1/25 inch) through 45 millimeters (about 1 3/4 inches). These tools help create proper alignment of the decorative wrap, but you must buy the right kind. Such templates *must* have quadrant marks that mark each 90 degrees of every circle. This is mandatory to properly line up a wrap.

Clear right-angle plastic strip. This is nothing more than a strip of the clear-plastic corner protection sold in hardware stores and designed to protect outside corners of walls in heavy-traffic areas. They are popular with young couples to protect household walls from tricycles and other abuse by young children. They can be cut into strips of any length. They are used with the circle template for laying out the wrap and later checking it for straightness. Several strips of about 6, 9, and 12 inches are ideal for most work and can be cut with a hacksaw from a standard 4-foot strip of this material.

Proportional rule. This is a clear-plastic rule that, in addition to having an inch rule on one side and a millimeter rule on the other (the rule is very wide), has grooves cut into the middle for easy measurement of odd increments. The ones I use from C-Thru Ruler Company are unfortunately no longer made, although you might occasionally find a leftover in a stationery store. One is for architectural work (model AR46 or AR56), the other for engineering (EN46 or EN56). The central grooves have no other markings than the incremental marks. Standard marks include not only 1/4, 1/2, and 1 inch but also 3/16 and 5/8 inch (in the architectural model). Because these are the only marks on the grooves, the layout of the design is easy. Otherwise you would almost have to calculate as you go along. With 3/16 inch, for example, such calculations would be 3/16, 3/8, 9/16, 3/4, 15/16, 1 1/8, 1 5/16, 1 1/2, and 1 11/16 inches.

You can make your own proportional rule if you do a lot of this type of work. My suggestion is to obtain a cheap, readily available clear-plastic rule and use a permanent felt-tip marker to mark those incremental measurements you want for a given decorative wrap. You could use a different rule for every different set of incremental measurements or a different color felt-tip pen for different measurements. Using a standard rule in which the measurements are marked makes for far more accurate spacing than marking cardboard, although this is another, less-expensive possibility.

Standard rule. A standard ruler will work for making measurements along a rod for proper layout of the design—just be sure to measure very carefully.

Rod-wrapping support. You will not need the tension device used for standard guide wrapping, but you will want a support to hold the rod while you rotate it when spiral-wrapping the thread up and down to make a decorative wrap. You will need the thread-tension device when you make the band wrap at the end of each decorative wrap. These band wraps are made with the same method used for guide wraps and are used to hold spiral wraps securely in place. You will also want a rod-wrapping tool or lathe for wrapping thread around the blank when weaving, although this is really covered—along with the Renzetti Wonder Weaver designed by Jim Upton—in chapter 24.

Other rod-wrapping tools. You will also want the other tools associated with guide wrapping, such as a razor or scalpel to cut the thread, a loop of thread or mono to pull the tag end of the binding thread through the wraps, and a burnisher to smooth threads.

Materials are not complex, and about the only requirements are masking tape to hold the thread at the end of each wrap and double-stick tape, which will serve as a substitute for the masking tape and will also hold threads in place.

SIMPLE BUTT WRAPS

Simple butt wraps, by our definition, do not involve crossing threads or weaving. They are variations of the basic guide wrap in which the thread is wrapped around the blank—begun and finished in the same way as a guide wrap. These butt wraps can involve all the variations of guide wraps: one-color wraps; trim wraps at the end; two-, three-, four-, and more-color wraps; spiral wraps; spiral wraps over Mylar; spiral wraps over an underwrap; spiral wraps over ribbon material; band wraps; band wraps over Mylar; band wraps over an underwrap; and so on.

There are other variations. For example, most butt wraps (and for that matter, other decorative wraps) are combined with the wrap for a hook-keeper, if one is placed on the rod. In addition, butt wraps are sometimes separated so that there is a wide band just above the foregrip; then information about the blank, rod, or blank manufacturer; and then another short band wrap. This latter band wrap, when applied, serves to "frame" the written information on the blank. (See chapter 25 for details about adding inscriptions to the blank.)

These wraps can be made over the bare blank or over a contrasting-color underwrap or Mylar tape, allowing the tape to show through band or spiral wraps.

Other possibilities include short bands, usually only about three to five threads wide, that serve as measuring points for fish caught with that rod. This is most common on trout or salmon fly rods (sometimes long spinning rods) with the marking on the blank serving as a measurement for a minimum size when measured up from the upper end of the grip; for a personal size limit; for a trophy-trout size limit; or for a slot-limit size where applicable on certain waters. Other anglers will mark other rods—casting or spinning—with small bands of thread, using different colors for the size limits of different species. This is particularly popular with wade fishermen, who are less likely than boaters or shore anglers to carry a rule or tape for quick reference.

Other than that, these simple butt wraps are no different from basic guide wraps. They are simply circular bands of thread of varying lengths (widths of thread wrap) around the blank to serve decorative purposes, to frame inscriptions or information, or to serve as measuring points for legal sizes of fish species. The same methods of starting and finishing are used, as are the procedures listed in chapter 22.

BASIC THEORY

The basic execution of decorative wraps (other than the simple wraps above that are like guide wraps) is to cross threads back and forth to make up a decorative pattern on the blank. Thread is spiraled up the blank then back down the blank. As the thread is spiraled down the blank, it crosses over the threads made on the up-spiral. This causes intersections of thread that are the basis of all decorative wraps, except in weaving. These crossing threads are used to form and develop diamonds, double diamonds, chevrons, double chevrons, flags, Maltese crosses, spiders, plaids, snakeskin patterns, and so on. How the threads are run up and down, their position in relation to previous wraps, and what colors are used at which time in the wrap determine the ultimate pattern and design.

Naturally these crossing wraps must be straight—the intersection in line with the rod blank—and the measurements between each intersection of thread must be accurate and identical in order for the completed wrap to look right.

This points out one of the basics of any decorative wrap: The intersections of the first thread wrap *must* be properly aligned with the rod and *must* be accurately measured. If the first intersection is properly aligned and accurately measured, all the rest of the thread wraps follow in proper alignment and accurate measurement. If the measurement or alignment of the first thread (intersections) is off, all the rest of the threads will be off.

The basic design involves alternately crisscrossing one thread after another alongside the basic initial spiral wrap or adjacent threads. The added threads may be positioned at the tip end of the previous thread crossing, at the butt end, or to one side or the other. In almost all cases one thread is used at a time, although two, three, four, or more (if you can handle them) threads can be wrapped at once. Doing so imparts a different look to the wrap and also makes for wider bands of color where this is done and when it is desired. Using several threads at one time speeds up the wrapping process as well. Even if wide bands are made with single threads, the two methods make for completely different looks in the final wrap.

ROD PREPARATION

There is little rod preparation for making butt or decorative wraps other than in the basics of any wrap. The rod should be clean, smooth, free of dirt and any previous wraps or finish (should it be a previously wrapped rod), and without any marks or lettering. Lettering, however, can be a problem. Many rod blanks have silk-screened or stamped lettering to indicate manufacturer, model number, and specifications such as blank weight and length, action, lure, and line range. Depending on the length of the handle, this lettering may end up just above the foregrip, where you will want to frame it with simple butt wraps or a complex decorative wrap and forward band wrap. Or you may wish to remove or cover the lettering completely.

The removal and covering of lettering have their problems, although they are possible. Removal may be easy or difficult. Some rod manufacturers have a clear stick-on label for the specification information. If this is the case, it is usually easy to pull off the label and then clean the blank with alcohol, acetone, or lighter fluid.

If the label is silk-screened onto the blank, you may be able to remove it with lighter fluid or acetone. If you use acetone, be very careful: Use it outside or with good ventilation, keep it away from flames, and use it rapidly to avoid any possibility (although slim) of damaging the resins in the blank. This will *not* work if the lettering is covered with a clear epoxy rod finish. Removing a clear epoxy finish over lettering requires either repeated scrubbing with acetone or using another solvent, which could damage the resins in the rod blank. It is best to avoid this.

A better procedure is to lightly sand or scrape the finish off, removing the lettering at the same time. You can use regular very fine sandpaper, a fine file, or similar abrasives, but take care to work only in the area of the lettering to be removed. One way to prevent damage to the rest of the blank is to mask the area with several layers of masking tape. When this step is necessary, I use a small emery board that is stiff enough to work one small area and that has both coarse- and fine-grit sides. Another removal method is to use a sharp knife blade, but instead of cutting with the blade, scrape the blank by holding the blade in such a way as to scrape off the finish coat and ultimately the lettering.

Once the lettering is removed, a general sanding with very fine sandpaper removes any lumps or imperfections and makes it easy to wrap and finish the blank.

You may choose not to remove the lettering but to wrap over it, particularly if it is in an area that will be wrapped anyway. However, this is best only if the wrapping thread is dark enough to cover any possible show-through of the lettering. If you will be working on a white rod blank with black lettering, a wrap of light yellow or light blue would probably not work because the black lettering would likely show through. Using a dark blue, dark green, dark brown, or black wrap would likely prevent this show-through. Light-color lettering (white lettering on a dark blank) is easily covered by any wrapping, although for a dark rod a dark wrap would be a must (to prevent the blank from showing through and marring the color of the wrap). If a medium-color wrap is to be used on a dark blank, a light or white underwrap should be placed on the rod blank first.

To minimize show-through, you can paint over the lettering with a latex or acrylic paint. The paint should be the color of the blank or white, which will help prevent the blank color from bleeding through light-color wraps. Be sure to use paints that will not react with the epoxy rod finish.

UNDERWRAPS

Some rod builders like underwraps; others do not. Underwraps have advantages and disadvantages. The advantages are:

1. An underwrap helps keep the blank color from affecting the thread-wrap colors in the decorative wrap. By using an underwrap—which will usually be light in color—the blank color is visually separated from the decorative wrap color and allows more of the true color of the wrap to show. It is like giving a dark-color object a light or white base coat before painting it, or painting lead-head jigs white before adding bright or fluorescent colors.

2. An underwrap will give more tooth to the blank and thus will hold or grip crisscrossing threads more easily. On a bare blank these threads will tend to slide, making it more difficult to keep them accurately aligned and measured.

3. The lack of an underwrap can also be an advantage in making these decorative wraps. The fact that the thread can slide around a little more allows more adjustment of the threads as you make the decorative wrap. If you are unsure of your alignment or think that alignment will be difficult, then working on a bare blank can help by allow thread movement as you build up the decorative wrap.

4. An underwrap will show through the spaces left in any decorative wraps (unless the entire blank area is filled with the decorative wrap, as with snakeskin wraps). This allows an additional color in the decorative wrap. Also, when the underwrap is in a strongly contrasting color to the decorative wrap (as they usually are), this allows the decorative wrap to stand out far more than it would on the blank alone.

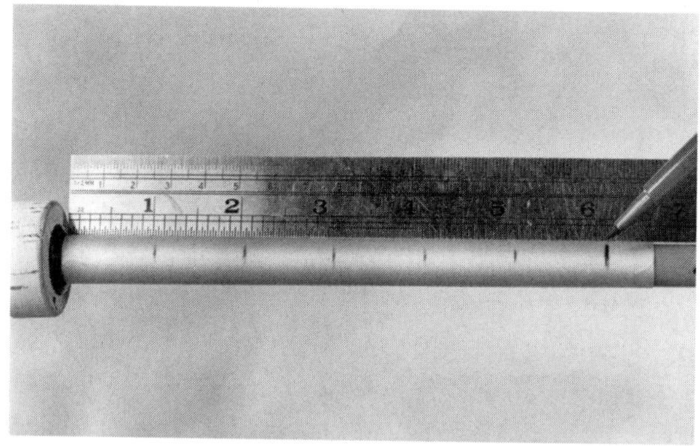

Laying out a basic decorative wrap. If making a diamond wrap, the marks made will be hidden. If making a chevron, the marks must be as small as possible to prevent them from being seen at one edge of the wrap. Marks are laid out at even intervals on one side of the blank and at equally even intervals on the opposite side but spaced halfway between the original marks.

The disadvantages of using an underwrap are:

1. The advantage of the underwrap providing tooth for overlying crisscrossing threads can also be a disadvantage. If the wrapped threads are tight, this makes it difficult to move or change the position of the crossing threads to adjust alignment. A wrap over the bare blank—which is somewhat slippery—makes this easier.

2. If you will be making a wrap in which all the spaces will be filled in, there is no decorative

advantage to using an underwrap, because it will be completely hidden. This won't apply if the light underwrap helps preserve and maintain the bright colors of the decorative butt wrap.

Underwraps for decorative wraps are done exactly as are underwraps for guides, only they are longer for the butt decorative wraps. They must be slightly longer than the decorative wrap, so you must first measure and decide on the length of the decorative wrap (including any tie-down wraps at the butt end and possibly the tip end) and then calculate the length of the underwrap. This does not have to be a complicated calculation—just one that will allow you to make the wrap of the length you desire. Often this is more a feel or estimate than an actual measurement—at least that is how I do it most of the time.

You can begin the underwrap either at the winding check to work up the rod or at the upper limit of the wrap to work down to the winding check. Either way will work fine. Note that if you are going to do an underwrap and also add a hook-keeper, do the underwrap first and then add the hook-keeper, incorporating it as a part of the butt-thread wind-off to hold the decorative wrap in place.

Begin by using rod supports and thread tension, just as for guide wraps. Use a light color (preferably) with darker colors for the overwrap, because this will reduce the possibility of blotching, mottling, or show-through. Wrap the thread around the blank, cross over this first wrap, maintain tension, and then continue for several turns. Clip off any excess thread. Then continue to wrap the full length you decided upon with this underwrap. Although this can be done with any method of rod wrapping, it is one procedure for which a motorized wrapping tool is very handy. Otherwise wrapping around the blank for 6 or 8 inches gets monotonous in a hurry.

Once you are at the end, lay down a loop of thread, wrap over it for about five or six turns, hold the last wrap in place, clip the thread, tuck it through the loop, and pull the loop through, along with the thread end. Open up a gap, and use a razor blade to cut straight down through the gap (parallel to the thread wraps—at right angles to the rod blank) to cut the thread beneath the surface of the underwrap.

As mentioned earlier, underwrap colors should be lighter than the overwrap to prevent show-through. Good colors include white, light blue, tan, yellow, light green, orange, and any very light shade of any color. It also helps to give the completed underwrap a coat or two of color preserver before continuing with the decorative wrap. Some rod builders go even further, applying an additional coating of epoxy rod finish to completely protect and finish the wrap before proceeding with the decorative wrap. To do this, follow the suggestions in chapter 25. The advantage of applying color preserver on the underwrap before adding the decorative wrap is that it helps seal the wrap to the blank and also reduces or eliminates the possibility of show-through. The epoxy finish gives even more protection, but it also adds a layer of finish to the wrap and makes the area slightly slippery—reducing in part the advantage of the extra tooth that holds decorative wraps in place while the thread is wrapped in the up-and-down spirals.

LAYOUT OF DECORATIVE WRAPS

Whether working on the bare blank or with an underwrap, you must lay out the alignment and crossing points of the decorative wrap. This applies to everything from the simplest wrap to the most complex. The first step of laying out the wrap is to determine a straight line on the blank or underwrap that is also in line with the guides and reel-seat hoods. There are several ways to do this, as follows:

1. *Sighting along the rod.* One of the easiest ways to determine a line on the rod, and one that requires no tools, is to sight along the rod. Place one band of masking tape at the butt just above the winding check, with a

second band above the underwrap or where you plan to end the decorative wrap. Support the rod horizontally directly under a strong overhead light. Long fluorescent lights that are hung in line with the rod are ideal for this. Looking directly over the rod, close one eye. Then, watching with your open dominant eye, rotate the rod until the guides are straight up. If your eye is directly over the rod, the glare from the light should form a streak on the blank precisely in line with the guides and reel-seat hoods. Mark the position of the light streak on the tape at both ends. The glare won't be visible on the tape, but it will extend along the rod blank to the tape.

(**Note:** If you are using an underwrap, it won't reflect the light, and the streak might be difficult to see. To adjust for this, place a long strip of cellophane tape on the blank. This shiny surface will reflect the glare, and the resulting streak can then be transferred from the clear shiny tape to the masking tape bands.)

Once you have marks on these two bands, it is easy to line them up with thread or a rule so that you can mark the rest of the decorative wrap area. Once you do this, however, you must turn the rod over and position the guides directly down (you can position butt guides so that equal parts of the guide rings are visible on either side of the rod blank), then repeat the marking procedure.

If you plan to make double diamonds (see chapter 24 for details) you must make additional alignment marks on the sides of the blank so that you have four alignment marks—all 90 degrees apart. For single diamonds and chevrons, such as are discussed in this chapter, two marks 180 degrees apart are all that you need.

2. *Working from the first streak.* An alternative to sighting these separate streaks is to determine the first streak or line and then work from this. Place another band of masking tape around the rod, making sure that the tape overlaps a little, the overlapping is a little out of line, and this overlapping occurs where the alignment has already been determined. (Do not remove or use the original masking tape for this, or you will have to start all over.) Mark the second tape band with the same alignment mark (based on the first mark), making a permanent mark on both parts of the overlapping tape. Remove the second band of tape, lay it out on a rule, and determine the distance between the two marks that indicate a "0" point on the rod. Mark this tape halfway between these marks for single wraps, in quarters for double wraps. Then carefully replace the tape on the rod at its original position, making sure the original overlapping marks are in line with the originally determined line.

Do this at the other end of the wrap, also 6 or 8 inches up from the handle, since the taper of the rod will preclude using the same tape or measurements at both positions. Once this is done, it is easy to use a rule or thread to line up the 90-degree or 180-degree marks for single or double decorative wraps.

3. *Using a circular template.* Another method of laying out decorative wraps involves the use of circle templates and a short length (about 6 inches is good) of right-angle aluminum or plastic. The circle template *must* have quadrant marks on each circle in order for this method to work. First make a tight wrap of masking tape at both ends of the decorative wrap. Then slide the appropriate size circle on the template onto the rod blank. (**Note:** This is possible on many two- or multipiece rods that do not have guides on the butt section. If the rod does call for a guide on the butt section, this method can only be done prior to wrapping the guide or guides in place, because it requires that you slip the circle template onto the rod.)

Make sure the circle used is closest or identical to the diameter of the rod at the winding check. If you can't get an exact fit, wrap several layers of masking tape around the rod blank until the fit is snug. Once the circle template is in place, sight down the rod section from tip end to butt end, and line up the quadrant mark on the circle with the hoods of the reel seat. Sometimes it helps to place a reel in the seat to get an exact alignment. Once this is done, mark the position of the required two- or four-quadrant marks on the masking tape. (Two should be 180 degrees apart if you are making a single decorative wrap; four should be 90 degrees apart if you are making a double wrap.)

Once these marks are made, place a short length of right-angle aluminum or plastic on the blank. Line up the sharp bend of the angle with the main quadrant mark on the circle template. Place a mark on the upper masking tape wrap (which should be positioned at the end of this strip or angle) in alignment with the angle of the metal or plastic strip. Remove the angle, remove the circle template, and replace the template on the rod blank using another, slightly smaller, circle that will fit onto the blank or masking-tape wrap. Line one of the quadrant marks on this circle with the mark on the masking tape, and then make the other mark or marks on the tape for single or double decorative wraps. You can also double-check this second mark by aligning the circle quadrant mark with the reel on the reel seat.

With these marks in place, you can make straight lines with a rule or thread. White thread is good because you can use a black felt-tip marker to mark it at the crossover points and then tape the thread onto the rod in line with the previously made marks. After the first several spiral wraps up and down have been made (and thoroughly checked and measured in the process), the thread can be pulled out and the wrap completed.

Another method is to make small marks with a lead pencil at the crossover points. If you do this, make these as small as possible, particularly when making a chevron. All marks should be small for accuracy; this is especially important for chevrons, in which the first wrap—where the mark is located—is at the edge of the decorative pattern, not at the center, which will be covered, as with the diamond pattern.

Because the threads spiral and create a pattern on both sides of the blank, those on the reverse side are exactly half the distance of those on the top side. For example, if the marks on the guide side of the rod were at 1, 2, 3, 4, 5, and 6 inches, then those on the opposite side would be positioned at ½, 1½, 2½, 3½, 4½, and 5½ inches. If you will be making a double wrap, the wraps will be the same when on opposite sides of the rod (say at 0 and 180 degrees) and halfway between at the halfway positions (90 and 270 degrees).

The positioning of these marks is relative to the diameter of the rod but can be adjusted so that the patterns are either tight together and bunched up or spaced far apart and stretched out. The closer together the marks are, the smaller the pattern will be; the more stretched out they are, the larger the pattern will be.

Although there are no rules as to spacing, a general guide is to use spacing that will be about double the diameter of the rod blank. Thus for a rod blank about ½ inch thick at the handle, the marks to indicate the first crossed thread should be about 1 inch apart.

Once the wrap is laid out, we are ready to begin.

BASIC WRAPPING TECHNIQUES

Before considering types of rod wraps, some basics must be discussed that are applicable to all decorative wrappings. The basic technique is to spiral or wrap thread up and down the blank to form crossing threads that will develop into a colored pattern. You begin on the handle or just above it and spiral thread up and down. When the spiraling is complete, a simple band wrap around the blank finishes off the decorative wrap, and the excess thread used to begin each thread wrap is cut away in the process. The upper end of the decorative wrap can be finished off the same way, or you can make a turn of the threads there to bring them back down the blank so that no finishing wrap at the upper end is necessary.

Let's look at beginning the wraps. You have a choice of wrapping thread crudely around the blank or grip and then cutting it away or of using masking tape or double-sided tape to fasten the thread down at this point. Both methods work well, but if I begin on the handle, I like to use tape, while I usually wrap the thread down if I start just above the handle on the blank. The reasoning here is that if I wrap around the handle, in time there will be enough thread and enough pressure to cut or scar the rod handle. This is particularly true of cork handles but can apply to any handle. If you are at all concerned about this, begin on the blank or lay down a layer of tape before wrapping the thread in place on the handle (the tape should protect the grip). The reason for beginning on the handle in the first place is that it allows for a shorter "back wrap" of thread to secure and finish the spiral wraps. If you start on the blank, this is more difficult to do.

If you are making the turn at the upper end of the wrap to avoid finishing there, it is best if you work with an underwrap. The underwrap gives some tooth to the surface so that you can make the turn easily. Trying this over a bare blank will often result in thread slippage and problems later on in the wrap. One solution is to use a little color preserver on the first wrap of thread or two, because this will tend to "tack" these threads down. Once the first thread is down, all the rest will follow in order. Naturally this requires that the first threads to be tacked down are in perfect alignment and measurement, because it will be very difficult to move them later.

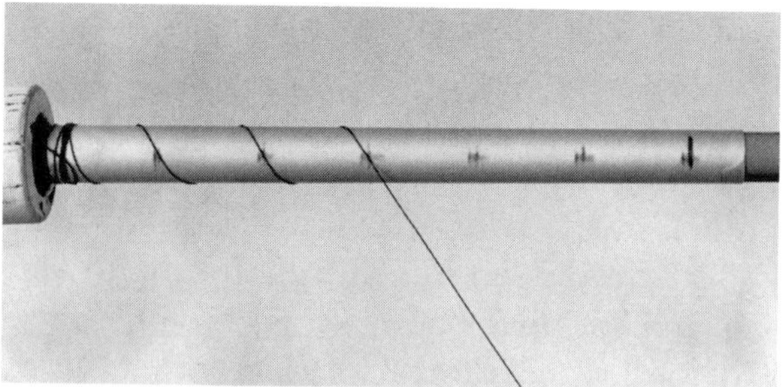

Beginning the wrap by tying down the center thread (for a diamond) and then spiral-wrapping up the blank, crossing all the marked points.

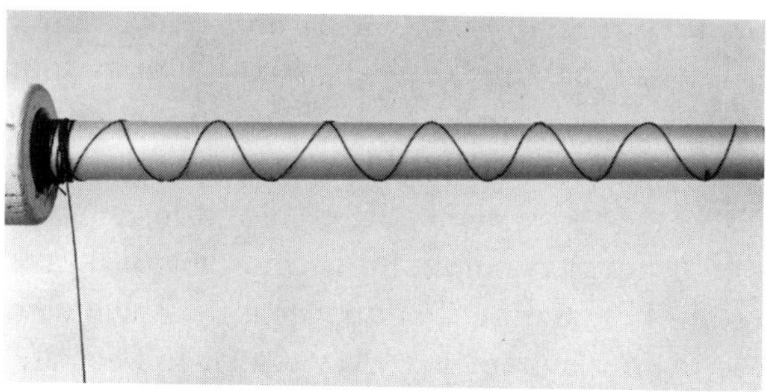

At the top the thread can be turned to come down the blank (as shown here) or wrapped up onto the blank, where it can later be wrapped down. This is a side view, showing the first thread up and down and tied off at the handle.

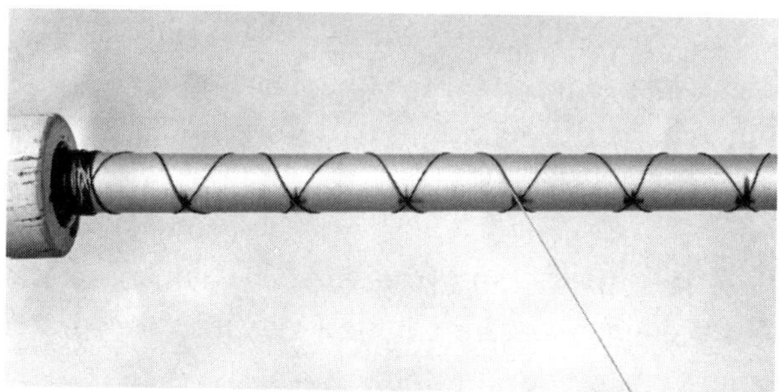

Beginning the second wrap of thread up the blank. Two courses up and down the blank are needed for each successive wrap of thread—one on each side of (or above and below) the original central thread.

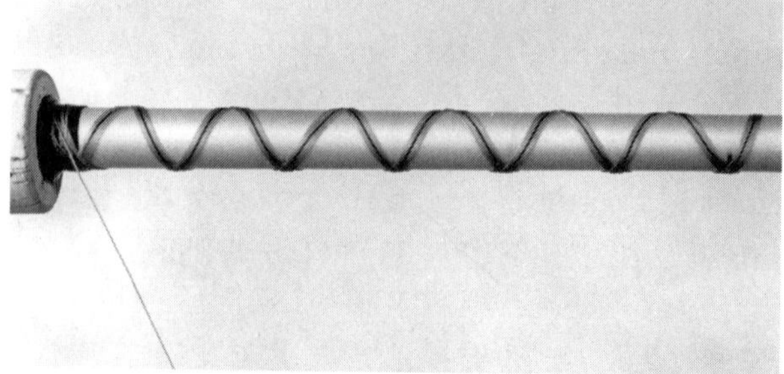

Continue the wrap of thread in one color up and down the blank. Care must be taken to prevent gaps.

DIAMOND WRAPS

Once the wrap alignment and thread crossings are laid out, it is easy to begin a simple diamond wrap. In fact, one of the simplest uses a kind of wide-band thread. Various wide Butt Wind (Gudebrod) threads or even ribbons from sewing and craft stores can be used for these simple decorative wraps. One craft or sewing ribbon that I have found good for these wraps is soutache braid. This decorative ribbon is wide (about ⅛ inch), and when wound up and down the rod (taking care for proper alignment and measurement), the effect is like a several-threads-wide diamond or chevron wrap of one color. Additional colors will build up a very wide diamond wrap quickly, although it will have a different look from those done with just one thread at a time. When using this or similar materials, follow the same directions as for the basic diamond. Note that repeated runs are not required, since just a few runs up and down with the wide-band ribbon are enough to create a decorative pattern. Test these materials on a scrap blank for any reactions to color preserver or epoxy finish before doing a just-finished rod with these—or any untried—materials. They often are combinations of cotton and rayon and thus must be tested for color reactions to finish coats.

Creating regular decorative diamond wraps with thread is simple, though time-consuming. For illustrative purposes we will use a white underwrap and make a diamond with a red center over it, bordering it with bands of white, blue, and a final outline thread of black. We'll begin by using masking tape to secure the end of the red thread to the blank just above the grip. If possible, use a fly-tying bobbin for this wrap. These are available to fit small, 100-yard spools of thread from any fly-tying shop; some larger bobbins are available for larger 1-ounce spools in addition to the standard 100-yard spools. Using bobbins eliminates the necessity of handling the thread, and bobbins are particularly useful for working with several colors simultaneously, as with complex wraps.

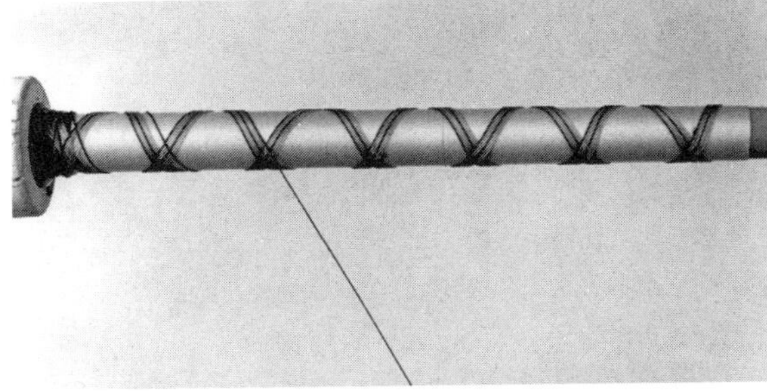

Continuing with another color thread. One course of thread has been made up and down the blank; this is the second wrap which, when completed, will bracket the other thread colors.

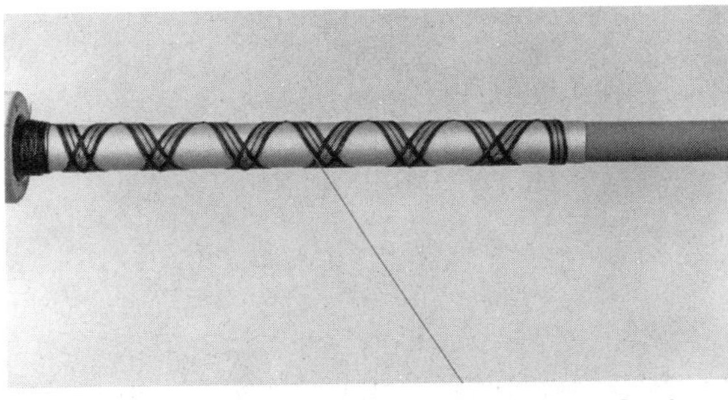

Continuing the wrap to broaden the bands of colors.

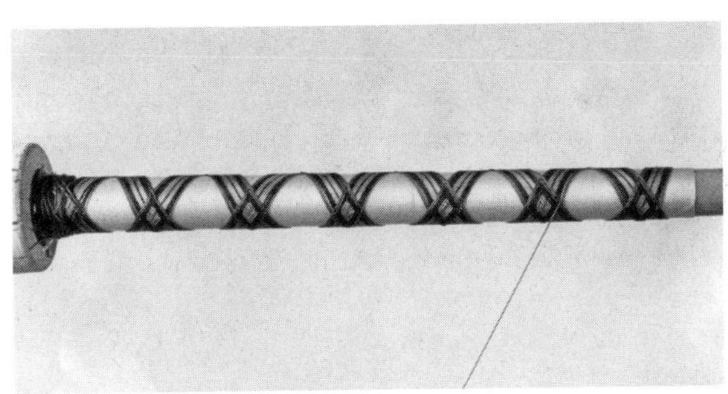

Another color thread added. Diamonds formed this way can be as small or large as desired and as simple or complex as the number of color threads used.

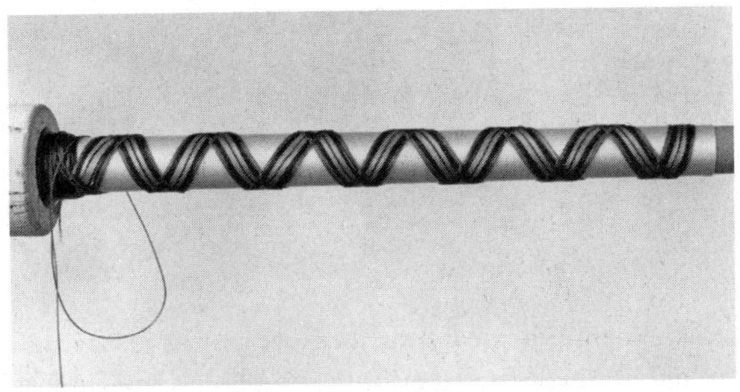

Once the thread wraps are complete, all the thread is tied off at the end. Each thread color must be tied off in turn as the wrapping proceeds.

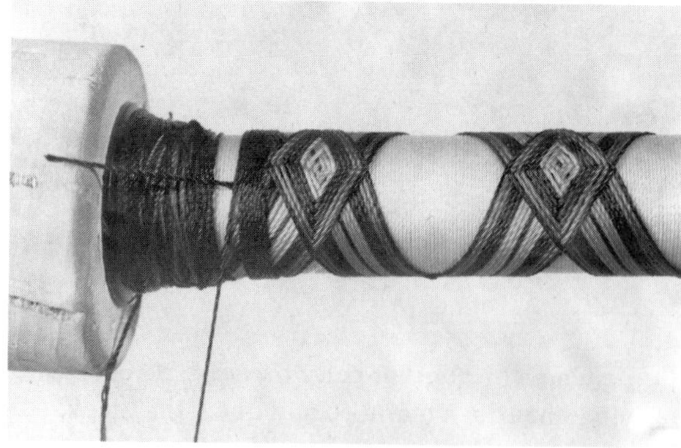

Beginning the band wrap that will hold the decorative wrap in place. This is identical to a guide wrap or underwrap, begun on the decorative wraps and worked down to the rod handle.

Examples of simple wraps made on a wood dowel to check patterns and wrapping techniques. This is a method used by master rod builder Cantwell Clark in teaching clients how to wrap. Wrap by Cantwell Clark.

Once the wrap is complete and the loop pulled through (it is finished the same as a guide wrap), the excess thread is cut. The wrap is now complete, and adjustments in the thread or thread gaps can be made.

Different spacing in these wraps will result in a different look. This is the same wrap as above but with a closer spacing. Wrap by Cantwell Clark.

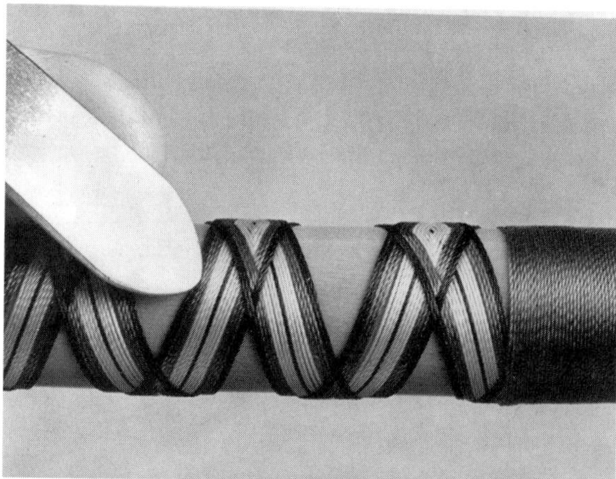

A scalpel handle or burnisher can be used for adjusting threads and closing any gaps that might have occurred while wrapping.

To begin a basic wrap, spiral the red thread up the blank, making sure the thread crosses exactly in the center of each previously made mark on both sides of the rod. We'll wrap off at the upper end, so above the underwrap we'll make a couple of turns and then reverse the direction of the thread and spiral back down the blank, crossing over the previous wraps exactly where the measured markings are located. Once at the butt (just above the grip), make several turns around the blank and then spiral up the blank again, making sure the thread is laid down next to the previous wrap with no gaps. Bring the thread down the same way, wrap around the butt end a few times, and then spiral up again. This time, however, keep the thread on the *other* side of the first wrap. Thus the first wrap is below—on the butt side—of the initial thread crossing, and the second wrap is up and above—on the tip side—of the initial threads. Wraps continue this way—up and down—always using the first thread as the central thread on any diamond.

At the end of these wraps, tie (with half-hitches) or tape the thread to the rod. Then start with a white thread, again in a bobbin if possible, and wrap up and down the blank, first on one side and then with a second up-and-down wrap on the other side to bracket the red band. Continue this two more times to make a frame of three threads of white around the central red band. Tie this thread off, tie down a blue thread, and wrap up and down with the blue thread to bracket the white band. Continue this to make three thread wraps around the white thread, and then tie off. Finally, tie down a black thread and spiral up and down twice with it to finish and frame the completed red, white, and blue diamond wrap.

At this point the diamond is completed, but it must be finished with a regular wrap (rotating around the rod, like a guide wrap or underwrap). This is a critical step, because a slight mistake here can cause some of the diamond threads to loosen and ruin the wrap. One way to reduce this possibility is to coat the diamond with one coat of color preserver and blot it dry. The color preserver will tack the diamond wrap to the rod and help prevent loosening.

Once this is done, place the rod on a regular rod wrapper and wrap thread around the wrap at the butt, but above where the threads are no longer lined up properly. Begin this wrap and make about five to six turns before cutting off any excess thread. Maintaining constant tension on this wrap, begin to carefully cut away the tie-down threads and tape of the diamond. (One way to maintain tension on the rotary wrap is to secure it in place tightly with masking tape. Another way is to use a heavy rod anchor—a tapered hook that fits over the rod with a heavy weight, such as a heavy sinker, on the end to hold the rod and keep it from moving. For best results, the tapered hook should be rubber coated to prevent the rod blank from sliding.)

Use scissors, a razor blade, or a scalpel to cut away all threads to a point above the winding check. Then remove the masking tape or rod anchor from the rotation wrap and continue wrapping, working all the way to the winding check. About six turns before the winding check, lay down a loop of thread. Make sure the loop is pointed toward the butt end of the rod. Wrap over the remaining threads and the loop to the end. Maintain tension, cut the end, and tuck it through the loop. Pull the loop through and, with it, the end of the thread. Then open up a gap and use a razor blade to cut down into this gap to cut the thread end. The technique is just like finishing a guide wrap.

An alternative to this is to wrap down to the winding check and then double back, finishing by making a double wrap of thread. Another possibility is to wrap down a hook-keeper at the same time, finishing off on each side of the hook-keeper or spiraling the thread around the hook-keeper to finish in one wrap.

Make a similar wrap on the upper end of the rod, beginning on the decorative wrap and working up (away from the wrap) to secure the thread. Tape the thread down, and then carefully cut away the excess thread of the diamond wrap. Finish as described. The final result will be a fine simple, single diamond (diamonds on the top and bottom of the rod—but not on all four sides) finished by a band of thread between the winding check and the diamond and a band of thread wrap at the upper end.

The various combinations of thread colors and types and spacing of the diamonds make for endless possibilities.

CHEVRON WRAPS

Chevron wraps are started and completed in the same way as diamond wraps. The main difference is in the method and order of working with the threads to form the chevron pattern. Making this wrap is just like making half a diamond. To begin, first decide whether you will work with an underwrap; then lay out the wrap as previously described. The layout of this wrap is exactly the same as for a diamond. For our example we will pick the same colors as for the diamond and make a red, white, and blue chevron.

Begin by tying or taping the black framing thread to the rod, and run up and down the blank with that thread, making sure it is exactly aligned and measured. Tie the black thread off and then tie down the first red thread. Wrap up and back down again with the red thread, just as with the diamond wrap. Make sure this first red wrap of thread is to the *tip side* of the first black thread. Continue with four more wraps to make a total of five wraps, all placed to the tip side of the previous wraps. Tie the red thread off, tie in a white thread, and repeat the wrap to the *tip side* of the previous wrap. Tie the white thread off and then tie in the blue thread. Continue with five wraps of this thread, again to the tip side of the previous wraps.

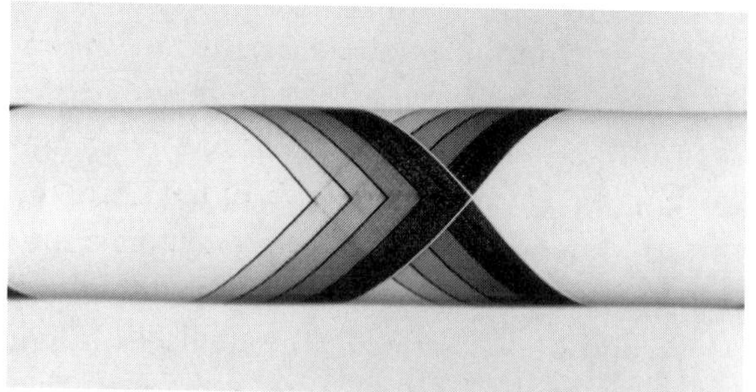

A simple but attractive chevron wrap. This is done just like half a diamond—all thread wraps are placed sequentially on one side of the first thread. This wrap progressed from the first dark thread on the left, through the successively darker wraps, and finished with the white thread on the right. Wrap by Cantwell Clark.

Example of a single chevron with an additional single thread wrap (the black thread crossing the center of the white space) to make it look more complex. The black crossing thread is added last. Wrap by Cantwell Clark.

To frame or block off the finished wrap, use a black thread to go up and down—again to the tip side—of the previous wraps. This, together with the first black thread, will bracket or frame the wrap. Tie off, and then make the finishing band wraps on the butt end just above the winding check to hold down the chevron-wrap threads. The result will be a chevron of red, white, and blue, just like the colors in the diamond. The difference will be that the diamond is diamond- or square-shaped, while the chevron is an inverted V shape as you look from the butt of the rod toward the tip.

There are several variations to this basic wrap. The first is to make all the wraps described but make them on the *butt side* of each previous thread rather than on the *tip side*. This will result in a V-shaped chevron, in essence running in the opposite direction (toward the butt) of the original design described here.

Another possibility, but one that's seldom seen, is to make a chevron that points sideways. For this continue as described, but always make each wrap to one side of the previous wrap so that the V is worked to the side. If you make wraps to the right as you look from the butt to the tip end of the rod, the V will point to the right. If you make the wraps to the left, the V will point to the left. The one disadvantage of right- or left-pointing chevrons is that they might not seem lined up properly on the top of the rod. To correct for this, you might wish to make four quadrant marks on the rod, as if you were making a double wrap, and begin the right- or left-pointing chevron at the appropriate 90-degree quadrant mark. Then work around the rod to end up with the final thread making the point of the V at the top center of the rod, or at the position of the mark aligned with the guides and reel-seat hoods.

Just as with diamond wraps, there are endless thread combinations for chevrons. And chevrons can be made pointing in any of four directions. Also, as with simple diamonds, simple chevrons can be made with soutache braid or similar materials.

CROSS WRAPS

A cross is essentially a diamond done backwards—starting from the outside threads and working to the inner or central thread. The layout can be the same, but the wrap is a little more difficult because you must lay down the outside and then work to the center. The two outside threads must be parallel throughout the wrap so that there are no gaps when the wrap is complete. To use the three colors of red, white, and blue, begin with two wraps up and down with the red thread to bracket the wrap area. These wraps must be parallel, and you must try to figure out the total width of the wrap with five threads each of red and white on each side and then five threads of blue in the center: five plus five red, five plus five white, and five blue, for a total width of twenty-five threads. (If you don't get this spacing exactly, don't worry; any of the thread bands can be made with more or less thread as desired. If you have too little space, you can use a thread pick or pointed burnisher to open up the wrap for an additional thread wrap or two. If you have too much space and some gaps, you can use the burnisher to close up the total wrap.)

Once these threads are in place (using one thread on the markers on the underwrap or blank) and parallel, continue with the rest of the four red threads up and down twice, always laying down the thread on the *inside* of the bracket wrap. Tie off and then tie down the white thread, and continue with two bands each of five threads. Finally, tie off and finish with a five-thread wrap of blue for the center. If you calculated the spacing correctly, there will be room for all the thread wraps and no gaps in the process. However, this is one wrap you might want to do a little loosely so that you can use a burnisher to tighten up the wraps if necessary. You also could allow for some adjustment in the number of thread wraps as you work, adjusting as you go along so that you end up with a tight no-gap wrap with no overlapping. One possibility if you have too much space at the end but not enough for an additional double up-and-down wrap is to wrap with two threads at the same time to fill in gap areas. Combinations of thread (including the wide-braid materials), number of wraps, thread types, and thread colors lead to unlimited possibilities in these various cross patterns.

FLAG WRAPS

Flag wraps that look like an American flag are popular and attractive. They are done using standard solid red and white thread along with blue or metallic blue thread to create the sparkle of the star-filled upper left corner of the flag. These wraps require the same precise layout methods as other wraps, because the area around the flag is usually filled in with a background-color thread. The marked point in this case will be the lowermost right corner of the blue, star-filled portion of the flag.

Begin by laying out the wrap. You can work with several threads at once if you want to make this wrap quickly—it will not affect the appearance. You can also work one thread at a time if you wish, or one color in three or four threads, depending on the width of each band of red and white.

Let's assume you will be working one band of color at a time, with three threads. Tie or tape down a band of three strands of solid red, and spiral them up the blank, going from left to right around the blank as you look toward the tip end. Make sure the lower part of this band just touches the measurement mark. Once at the top of the wrap area, do not come back down; instead tie or tape off and cut the thread. Continue this way, working alternately with three strands of white, three strands of red, and so on, until you have a solid field of four red bands and three white bands.

At this point begin the blue star field, working with blue metallic thread. Again, you can work with one thread or several at once. We'll work with three threads at a time again, because this will help us determine the correct proportions of the parts of the flag. Begin by spiraling three strands of the blue or blue/silver thread up the rod, working from right to left as you look toward the tip. Make sure the upper edge of this thread just touches the measurement mark. Each of these marks will be a corner made by the lower part of the lowest red band of color and the upper part of the blue. Continue with the blue thread until you have twenty-seven strands laid down. Since the red and white bands make up twenty-one bands (three each of four red and three white), this will make the proportions for the flag correct. All these wraps are tied down or taped off at the top of the wrap area—not continued down the rod.

Return to the three strands each of white and red. Begin with white, spiraling up the rod from left to right so that the white thread covers the lower part of the blue (to now be completely covered) and just touches the red band previously made. Alternately lay down three strands of white and red to finish the flag colors (for a total of thirteen horizontal stripes—seven red and six white). The flag is blocked off by using another color of thread to border first the bottom and left side of the flag and then the top and finally the right side of the flag. The right side of the flag is done last, because the position of the border wrap here will determine the proportions of the flag.

Roughly the flag is in a proportion of 3 × 5. Exact dimensions can't be given, because much depends on the size of thread used, how tight the wraps are, how many threads are used for each band of red and white, and so on. The border can be broadened a little to outline the flag, with the rest of the wrap exposed, or the rest of the wrap can be completely covered with a border.

This American flag wrap appears far more complex than it really is. First three bands of red and white are spiraled up the rod to make the top of the red and white stripes of the flag directly opposite the blue field. There are four red and three white to this band. Next a spiral wrap of blue or metallic blue is laid down to form the blue field with "stars." More bands of red and white follow, these parallel to the first bands and consisting of three bands each of white and red. Finally a gold "flag pole" band is added to the left. The wrap is completed by boxing in the rest of the wrap with a wrap of contrasting color. Wrap by Cantwell Clark.

Another "flag" pattern done with spiral wrappings of thread.

Usually this latter method is used to make the flag stand out.

An alternative method is to lay down a gold band of two or three threads on the left of the blue field to resemble a flagpole. Then block in the rest of the flag with a background color. You can also make a wrap in which a series of small flags like this runs all along the wrap or surrounds the butt end of the rod. These can be done only on the top, on the top and bottom, or on all four quadrants of the rod as desired.

CHECKERBOARD OR SNAKESKIN WRAPS

Checkerboard or snakeskin wraps are simple. They are not really a checkerboard but a solid color broken up into small squares by single threads in a contrasting color. To make this wrap, lay out the design as previously described. The wrap simply involves wrapping several bands of a chosen color up and down the rod, as with a standard diamond or chevron. There are several techniques that can be used to obtain the final result. One is to make a solid block of color and then come back with a single thread of a contrasting color and go up and down the rod to lay out small squares with every few threads. These must be equal in size for the wrap to look right. Once this is done, the whole block can be bracketed with a border of the same color as the individual threads or with a third color. The result is that the individual threads of contrasting color sit on top of the base-color wraps.

Another method is to first make the base-color wraps under lessened tension. The secret here is to make them slightly slack but not so much that they are noticeably loose. When the individual contrasting color thread is laid down, it can be forced in between the existing threads. Because these individual threads are laid down under more tension, it is important to begin at the center of the wrap and then to work out; forcing the individual threads into place will slightly push the base-color wraps to both sides. The wrap is bracketed as previously described.

A third method is to make the base-color wraps with bands of two, three, four, or five threads, separating each band one thread width from the next. After this is complete, it is easy to lay down one thread to block out the checkerboard pattern.

OTHER VARIATIONS OF SIMPLE WRAPS

Variations of these simple wraps are endless. Here are some possibilities:

1. Make individual thread cross-wraps between any of the above wraps—diamonds, chevrons, Maltese crosses, flags, or checkerboards. You can measure for these, but if you do them after the main wrap is complete, it is easy to estimate measurements. These can be a simple, single-thread wrap or two or three threads of the same or contrasting colors. If you do these before the main wrap (which will cover some of this thread work), you will want to measure for them.
2. Build up this cross-wrap into a mini-diamond, mini-chevron, or other wrap. This is completely different from the technique of double wraps as described in the next chapter. It will add another row of wraps on the rod but in the same line and on only two sides, as with any single wrap—not at 90-degree angles, as with the true double wrap.
3. Make the mini-wrap of a diamond or chevron on the wrap but at 90 degrees to the main wrap so that it will closely simulate a double wrap. It won't be exactly like it, because the variation is done with the two wraps completed separately, as opposed to double wraps, which are done simultaneously.
4. Mix decorative wraps, such as making a chevron and then adding cross-wrap threads between the original threads and building up these cross-wraps to make a mini diamond. Any combination of wraps is possible.

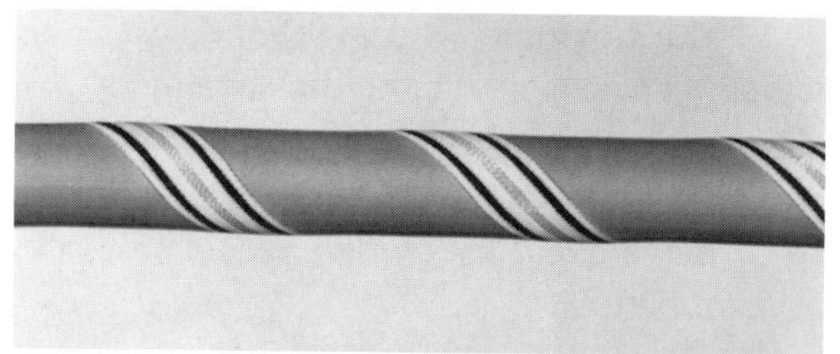

Decorative wraps can be made using simple spiral bands, tied in using a basic guide-style wrap at both ends. Such wraps avoid complex spacing and the necessity of lining up crossing threads. Wrap by Cantwell Clark.

5. Use one thread at a time. The end result, look, and effect of a wrap are completely changed when you use one thread at a time. Working with one thread gives more of a detailed, intricate look to most wraps, although with some, such as the checkerboard, it will not make a noticeable difference. For the checkerboard wrap, working with bands of threads may even make the wrap easier and result in a better final appearance.

As with any decorative wrap, there is no limit to the number of wrap combinations, widths of bands, thread colors, or number of colors that may be used. And there is no distinct separation between simple decorative wraps and complex decorative wraps, as will be discussed in the next chapter. They are all accomplished by a buildup of knowledge and experience, just as each wrap is accomplished by a buildup of thread.

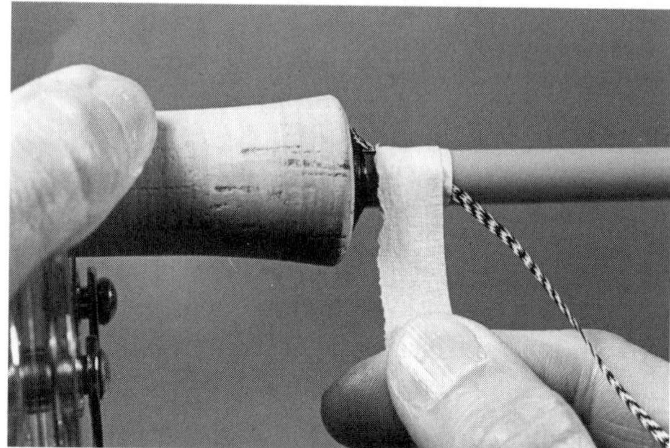

A simple wrap of wide, flat sewing materials called soutache will make for a simple butt wrap. Begin by taping this material in place, spiraling up and down the rod as shown here, and tying off as previously described.

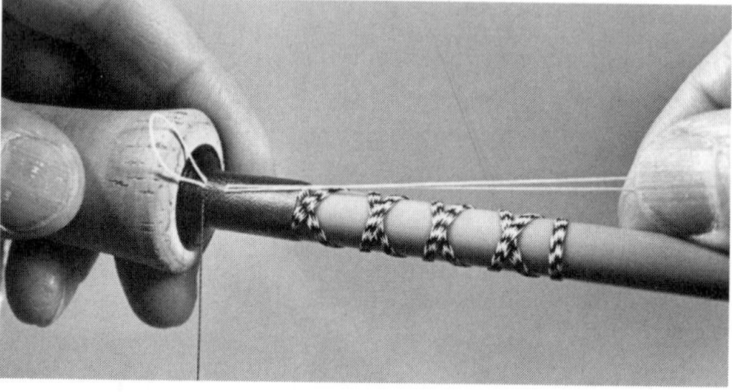

Once complete, the braid is wrapped in place using a basic guide wrap as shown.

24

Complex Butt Wraps, Decorative Wraps, and Weaving

Introduction • Tools and Materials • Layout and Design • Multiple Wraps • Plaids • Split Diamonds • Split Chevrons • Weaving Letters and Numbers • Weaving Scenes and Designs • Beading Wraps and Scenes • Decorative Wraps on Guides • Further References on Complex Wraps and Weaving

The safety equipment, basic tools, and helpful tools for making complex wraps are exactly the same as for the simple wraps described in chapter 23. Consult that chapter for details. To understand complex wraps, read chapter 23 before this chapter.

INTRODUCTION

Complex decorative and butt wraps are essentially just an extension of simpler wraps. In fact there is no clear separation between the two, even though I've created a separation with two chapters here. Complex wraps are just that—more complex in design and execution than the simpler wraps, but where you draw the line between the two is a subjective decision. Complex wraps are for the most part built on the same concept as simple wraps: intersecting threads that in turn are built up into designs and patterns.

As with simple wraps, complex wraps are not difficult, but they do require care and planning. Particular attention must be paid to the first crossing wraps, which will determine the accuracy and spacing of all subsequent wraps.

In addition, the more complex a wrap becomes, the more planning must go into it and the more care in design and step-by-step production must be taken to make sure the result is the color scheme and design desired.

The method of weaving is another aspect of complex wraps, and woven wraps take on a totally new design methodology. For weaving letters and numbers, the design and layout of each letter and number must be planned in advance in order to know how many wraps to make over and under each horizontal thread (horizontal as the rod is held in or on a rod wrapping machine—longitudinal with the rod blank).

Weaving scenes is almost a matter of trial and error, because you have to have a basic concept of what you want to do, of the scene you wish to make, and of the thread colors and arrangements possible for the scene. In all such cases it helps to keep notes so that designs can be repeated if desired. It also helps to start with very simple scenes, fish, designs, etc., so that you can become confident with the basics before getting into more complex designs. In the case of numbers and letters, simple charts are available that will allow you to repeat figures of the same size and shape.

TOOLS AND MATERIALS

Tools and materials used for these complex wraps are exactly the same as those for simple wraps. The only addition might be some chart tape, available in stationery stores and art supply shops. This tape is ideal for testing designs before beginning the actual wrapping process. An alternative is to use various colors of construction paper cut into strips. You could also use different colors of a heavy cord—like a macramé cord—to lay out and cross or weave sections of different colors of cord to get a concept of the final result.

The fly-tying bobbins mentioned in the previous chapter become even more useful here, because many of the more complex wraps involve different thread colors. Using a bobbin for each color makes wrapping easier.

If you're seriously into weaving designs, consider the Renzetti Wonder Weaver designed by Jim Upton. This tool holds the rod blank in place and, with a series of wheels with slits (180 of them) along the outer edge of each wheel, makes it easier to clip threads back and forth to weave the crossing wrapping threads so that they are above or covered up with the longitudinal threads along the axis of the blank. This is what makes the weaving process on rods possible. These wheels, which cover 360 degrees, also make it possible to easily weave completely around the blank . Weaving around the blank is possible without this machine, but it's far more difficult.

LAYOUT AND DESIGN

The layout and design of complex wraps are exactly the same as for simple wraps. You still have a choice of wrapping on a bare blank or over an underwrap, still must measure the center stripe of the rod for proper alignment with the guides and reel-seat hoods, and still must accurately measure the position for the crossing threads that are the basis for any subsequent wraps.

To use the chart tape as a guide for wraps, first make an "X" on a sheet of paper or white cardboard (cardboard is better, because you can keep the resultant design for reference). Then use this X as the basis for the first crossing threads. From this it is possible to lay down subsequent wraps of any color of chart tape in any order to make any possible design or to test any design. It is really better for the latter—testing designs where you are unsure of the final result. It helps to make accompanying notes that list in order the wraps made, the numbers of threads to be used, and the color used for each final wrap.

A good and more readily available substitute for chart tape is construction paper. I buy assorted-color packs, use a paper cutter to cut the paper into ¼-inch-wide strips, and use the various strips to lay out and plan wraps. Unlike chart tape, which has a sticky side, this paper allows you to lay down strips and remove them to start over if you don't like the result. If you do like the result, it is easy to use clear tape to secure the edges of the strip to make it stationary.

One simple way to keep a permanent record of your designs is to use 8½ × 11-inch paper for the base, plan the wrap as above, tape on the paper base, trim off any strips that extend beyond these borders, and place the taped-down result into a clear plastic sheet protector. These are designed for three-ring notebooks, so you can make up your own book of personal designs. If you are a custom rod builder making designs and rods for customers, this also serves as a good reference book to show clients possible designs that might be used on their custom rods.

In most cases the strips of paper can provide a general idea of the design appearance, if not the exact number of threads you might use. On the same paper you can write notes as to the number of threads used for each band in an actual wrap, the suggested number of threads in a planned wrap, and even the exact thread colors by stock numbers. Most thread companies use a number or letter/number system for the color of each of their threads, so you can match these notes to your favorite thread manufacturer.

It is important to understand the basic differences between making a single diamond or chevron wrap, as described in chapter 23, and making double or multiple wraps. With a single wrap, one spiral of thread up and down the blank serves as the basis for all other thread wraps and the formation of the pattern being developed. The ultimate effect is that of a series of patterns forming on the two sides of the rod, 180 degrees apart. With double or multiple wraps, the thread must be spiraled up and down several times to form the basic thread wrap. Note that this effect is completely different from the effect described in the last chapter, in which a single wrap is made and additional cross-wraps or mini-wraps are added

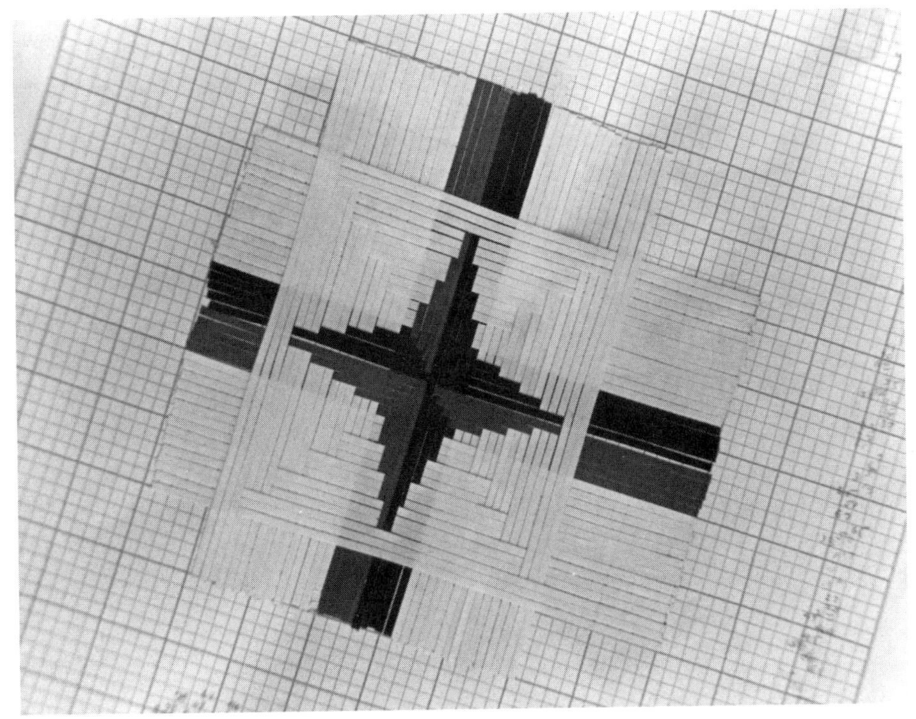

Complex designs are often best laid out first using chart paper strips or strips of different color construction paper. This is a design to show the sequence of wraps for a cross pattern done by Cantwell Clark.

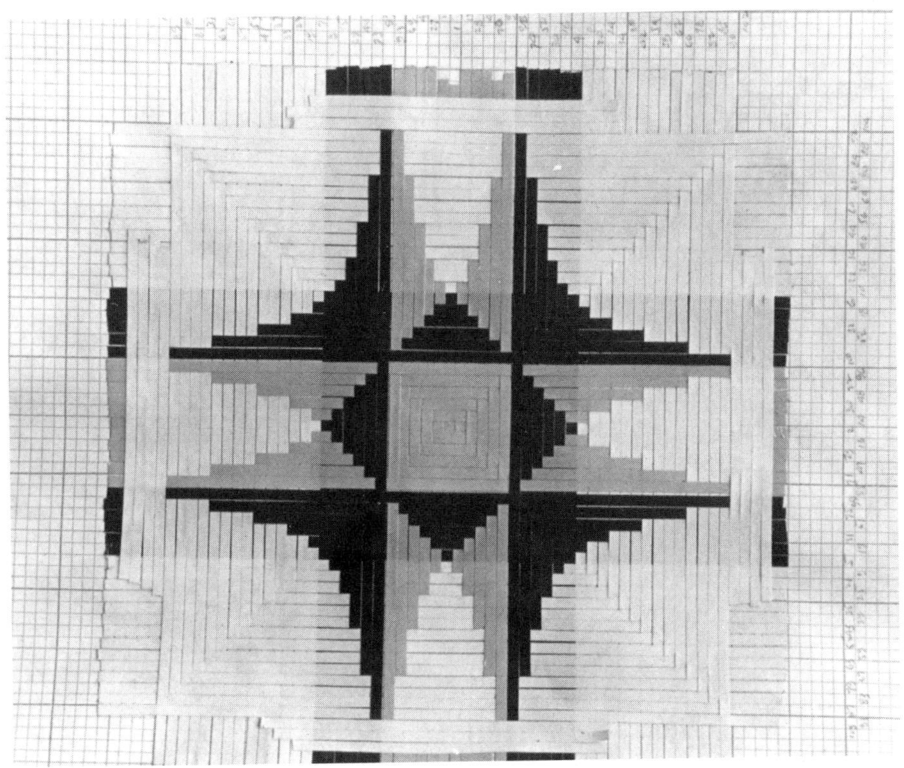

Another complex design by Cantwell Clark. Making such designs on paper helps to develop the sequence of wraps and helps define widths of bands and colors used.

Another design by Cantwell Clark, this of a stylized fish.

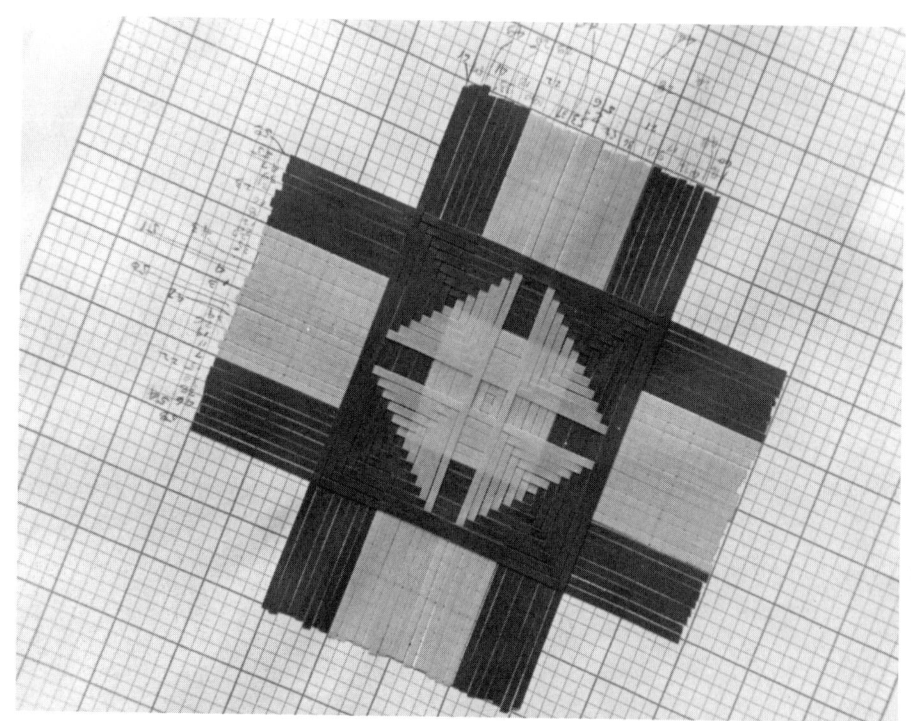

Notes along the margins of wraps, as shown in this photo, serve as helpful reminders of wrapping steps and procedures, thread colors, and numbers of thread wraps. Wrap by Cantwell Clark.

later as additional decoration. The effect there is of two separate wraps, one made over the other. The effect of the double wrap or multiple wrap is that of a totally integrated set of patterns.

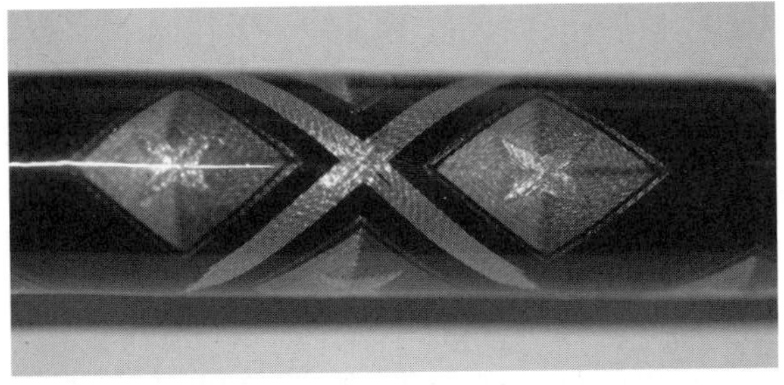

Fancy thread wrap placed above the foregrip of a rod. Today greater emphasis is on fancy wraps and weaving to dress up rods.

MULTIPLE WRAPS

Double and multiple wraps involve the same turns of thread up and down the blank, as was outlined for single wraps, to get identical band widths, but several turns up and down the blank are made with each thread. Thus while one spiral turn up and down is required for a single wrap in which patterns end up on both sides of the rod, two turns up and down are required for a double wrap, three turns up and down are required for a triple wrap, and so on.

The difference in these wraps is both in the number of turns made and in the position of the patterns. Thus with a single wrap, although the patterns on the two sides of the rod are 180 degrees from each other, they are not directly opposite. If the positions of the top patterns, measuring from the foregrip, are 1, 2, 3, 4, and 5 inches, the position of the patterns on the opposite side of the rod will measure ½, 1½, 2½, 3½, 4½, and 5½ inches.

In making a double wrap, the thread is wrapped up and down twice. This results in a layout with the wraps at 0 degrees and 180 degrees directly opposite each other (at the 1-, 2-, 3-, 4-, and 5-inch positions). Those on the sides will be at 90 degrees and 270 degrees and

Finished woven dragon by Jim Upton.

Fancy wrap of a diamond incorporated into an overall chevron wrap.

Simple weaving design of two fish woven into a butt wrap on a fishing rod.

are at halfway spots such as ½, 1½, 2½, 3½, 4½, and 5½ inches.

For this double wrap you have to lay out the straight lines not only on the top and bottom of the rod (0 degrees and 180 degrees) but also on the sides (90 degrees and 270 degrees). This is easily done using the circle quadrant marks on circle templates or the marked masking tape method, both outlined in chapter 23. After this layout is done, lay out and measure the position of the crossing thread. In making the marks for these patterns, we can think of the four lines as 1, 2, 3, and 4 turning clockwise around the cross section of the blank at 0, 90, 180, and 270 degrees. Making the wrap requires two spiral wraps up and down the rod—the first wrap crossing at 0, 2, and 4 inches on top and at 1, 3, and 5 inches on the bottom or underside. The second wrap up and down will fill in these areas, crossing on top at 1, 3, and 5 inches and on the bottom at 0, 2, and 4 inches, all measured from the foregrip.

Making quadruple wraps is similar, because you end up with eight instead of four patterns around the rod. The lines, based on the cross section of the blank, will be at 0, 45, 90, 135, 180, 225, 270, and 315 degrees.

If we think of these lines as traveling clockwise and numbers 1 though 8, the number 1, 3, 5, and 7 lines will pattern at the same position, as measured lengthwise from the rod grip; those at the 2, 4, 6, and 8 positions will pattern at the same position as well, although this second batch of patterns (lines 2, 4, 6, and 8) will intersect halfway between lines 1, 3, 5, and 7. Thus if we are to make all the patterns 1 inch apart, the markings on lines 1, 3, 5, and 7 would be 1, 2, 3, 4, 5, 6, 7, and 8 inches. Those for lines 2, 4, 6, and 8 would be at ½, 1½, 2½, 3½, 4½, 5½, 6½, 7½, and 8½ inches. The markings for each line remain 1 inch apart; they just vary in comparison to the adjacent lines. (In all these examples the measurements are only hypothetical—you will often need more or less space between wraps, based on the appearance of the wrap and the diameter and type of rod used.)

Methods of laying out simple and complex wraps. Here the first thread wrap of these patterns is shown. Top to bottom: a single wrap (patterns on opposite sides of the rod), double wrap (two courses of thread up and down to result in patterns on four sides of the rod), triple wrap (three courses of thread up and down the rod to result in patterns on six sides of the rod or every 60 degrees), and quadruple wrap (four courses of thread up and down the rod to result in eight patterns around the circumference of the rod). Note that these wraps are not precisely measured but simply spaced by eye—often a good way to check the complexity and "business" of any wrap to be developed. Spacing, or distance along the axis of the rod, can be adjusted for any of these wraps.

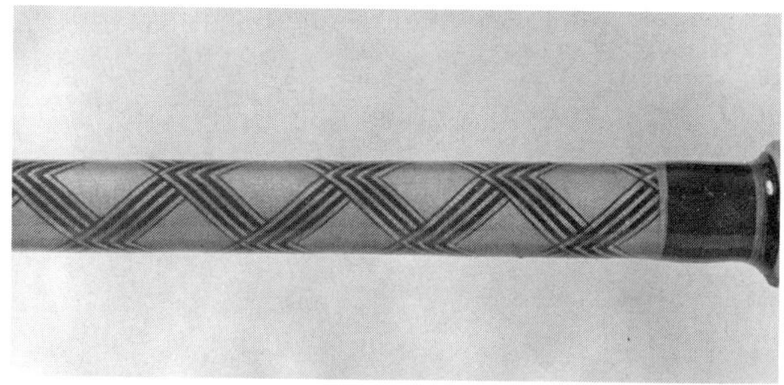

Multiple wraps (this is a chevron) require two wraps up and down the rod for each band of color. The result is a wrap that crosses at the side so that a double chevron will have chevrons at each 90 degrees rather than at only 180 degrees, as with a simple wrap. Six- and eight-sided wraps can be made similarly.

For a quadruple wrap, four spirals in the first wrap are required, beginning at 0, 4, and 8 inches (measuring from the top of the rod). A second wrap at 3 and 7 inches is followed by a third at 2 and 6 inches and a fourth at 1 and 5 inches. Only then are the crossing threads for all eight wraps complete. Subsequent thread wraps must follow the same pattern up and down the rod four times for each wrap.

Making this many wraps creates unique problems First, because the distance between the marks for each course of the thread is somewhat far apart (4 inches in the example we have been using), the resulting patterns tend to get a stretched-out look. You can move all the markings closer, but this causes the patterns to fill up the allotted area and cover the underwrap or bare blank. Often this can be used to advantage in filling up the rod area completely to make a snakeskin effect of repeated patterns, usually diamonds (similar to that found on some snakes), chevrons (similar to scales on other reptiles), or a latticelike diamond or checkerboard. The easiest way to think of this quadruple wrap, however, is as an extension of the double wrap previously described. In essence it is an extension of a double wrap as previously described, with additional wraps of thread used to fill in the blanks that occur on a standard double wrap.

If you will be making triple wraps, a different layout has to be planned. You must plan for crossing thread wraps to allow for three turns up and down the rod to make three different crossing points on three different locations on the rod blank.

For this there are six lines of patterns around the rod. These will be positioned at 0 degrees and each successive 60 degrees (thus at 0, 60, 120, 180, 240, and 320 degrees). There are also different measurements for the start of each pattern. Let's assume a final position where the wraps are ½ inch apart. Marks made on the three straight lines will have to be ½ inch apart; however, not all will have the same positioning, even though all the measurements will be the same length apart. If we envision a cross section of the rod blank, we can number the straight lines used for the crossing threads at the 0-, 60-, 120-, 180-, 240-, and 320-degree positions around the blank. If we number these in a clockwise direction, we would have patterns on lines 1, 2, 3, 4, 5, and 6. The markings for the 1, 3, and 5 line positions will be at ½, 1, 1½, 2, 2½, 3, and 3½ inches. Those for the lines in the 2, 4, and 6 positions will similarly be 1½ to 2 inches apart *but will begin with a ¼-inch measurement then follow with the successive ½-inch measurements.* Thus the measurements for this second set of wraps will be ¼, ¾, 1¼ inches, and so on. An easier way to think of and measure these is to make the first ¼-inch measurement and then reset the rule so that all subsequent measurements are ½ inch apart.

The first thread wrap up and down the rod will not be at each crossing point but at every *third* crossing point. To continue with our final measurements ½ inch apart, the first course of the single thread wrap up and down will be at 0, 1½, 3, 4½, and 6 inches, and so on. Once the first course is made, the second course up and down will be at 1, 2½, 4, and 5½ inches, and so on. The third course will be at ½, 2, 3½, and 5 inches, and so on. Any sequence of order can be made, provided the constant distance of 1½ inches is maintained between all wraps.

At this final point all the threads will have crossed all the measurements made on the wrap to complete the first, single-thread, stage of the wrap. Subsequent wraps of thread will be made up and down the rod in the same sequence, using three courses up and down the rod for each thread color (unless several threads are used at once).

Any multiple wrap is finished the same as a single wrap. Thus you first have a choice of turning a corner at the upper end of the wrap, in which no locking-thread wrap is used at the upper end, or of continuing up onto the rod blank and finishing off both ends of the wrap with a simple band wrap to lock the threads in place. As with any wrap of this type, it often helps to add a coating of color preserver before laying in the band locking-thread wrap. Doing this does not allow you to just rip away the excess thread, but it does allow you some insurance that threads will not loosen as you make the band wrap at the rod handle and, if required, at the upper end.

PLAIDS

Plaids are made by using a combination of NCP (no color preserver required) and standard thread. You must have a white base, which you can create by using a white blank, by using a white underwrap, or by painting the blank white. Working with a white rod is the easiest. If you paint the blank, paint it only in the area of the plaid wrap and use only a latex or acrylic paint that will not react with the epoxy rod finish. If you use a white underwrap, use NCP white thread and add one coat of color preserver, or use regular white thread and two or three coats of color preserver. The color preserver or NCP thread and color preserver is necessary to prevent the white thread from showing through when you add epoxy finish to the main wrap.

Once the white base is prepared, lay out your cross marks for a double diamond and begin to build the pattern. Usually these plaid wraps look best if they closely simulate Scottish tartans, so you might wish to check a fabric pattern or a book of tartans from the library. Tartans can be of any color combination but are often blue and green, green and red, red and black, yellow and red, and yellow and blue. Build up the double diamond, trying to use as little tension as is necessary because you might have to adjust some thread positions later.

Once the diamonds are complete, use regular white thread in between to build up and cover all of this blank area. Here is where you might have to adjust some thread positions and push some threads around, because the taper of any blank seldom allows for an easy fill-in of this area between decorative wraps. Assuming everything else to be equal, the taper of the blank allows for less room between the perimeters of the diamonds at the upper end of the wrap than at the lower end. Use continuous up-and-down spirals of white to fill this in completely, using the point of a burnisher or similar tool to push threads out of the way and to allow for threads with no crossover or overlapping.

Once the regular white thread is completely covering all the space between the diamonds, coat the area with a thin epoxy finish such as Flex Coat Lite or some other thinned rod finish. This allows for complete penetration into the wrap and a bleed-through of the darker colors in the plaid. Once this coat is complete and cured, finish with trim wraps of individual NCP threads, generally using a white over the dark diamond as an accent point and dark over the white wrap in between the diamonds. Once these are completed to your satisfaction, protect the entire wrap with a final coat or coats of epoxy rod finish.

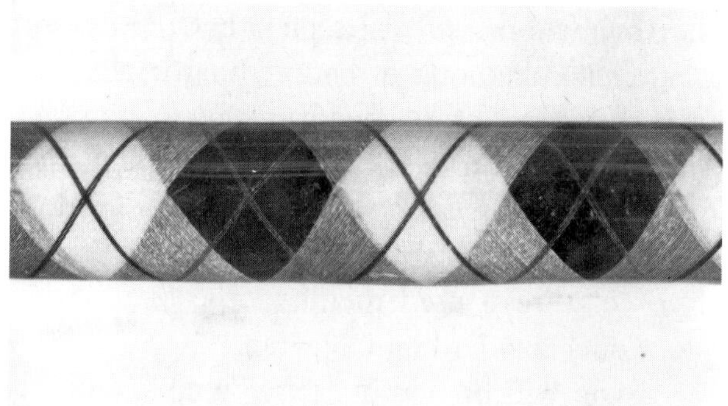

Plaid wrap, by Cantwell Clark, using different colors and regular and NCP thread. Note the plaid effect by the use of both NCP thread (no color preserver) and standard threads finished with epoxy and no color preserver.

SPLIT DIAMONDS

Diamonds can be split so that they develop a completely different look—that of two different colors. This can be done around an existing diamond (usually made small) or as a completely separate pattern in which the splits become the central block, which in turn are blocked in with other color wraps. They can also be done so that the split occurs along the axis of the rod or at right angles to the axis of the rod.

Let's first consider a split of diamonds across the axis of the rod. First lay out a central crossing thread, using one of the two colors you want for the diamond. Let's assume red for this example. Then you lay out to one side (above, toward the tip, or below, toward the butt) of this diamond crossing wrap a second up-and-down wrap of the other color—let's say green. Standard diamond wraps are made with one central thread and separate bracketing threads on each side so that you always have an odd number of threads. I prefer to think of these first two threads as a set and add equal numbers of same-color thread on each side of this set. I think of this as starting with one color and ending with the second color. Thus if your first color is red, the last color—regardless of the size of the pattern—will be green (in this example). This keeps the diamond equal in size on both sides and also does away with any separate-color central threads, as are used with standard diamonds. (The central thread may not always be a separate color—in fact it is often the same color for several wraps to build up a central block of one color to be surrounded by separate-color diamonds.)

A Cantwell Clark split wrap in which different colors are used on each side of the original thread wrap. Side-to-side split wraps can be made by using a different color thread going up the rod than the thread coming down the rod.

Once this basic set of thread colors is laid out—one color up and down as an initial thread followed by one contrasting color up and down on one side—you have the basis for the rest of the wrap. Continue laying down one red thread up and down, always on the red side, and one green thread up and down, always on the green side. The result ultimately is a diamond consisting of the shapes of two abutting triangles of different colors.

To finish this diamond you can bracket it with a third color—let's say black. This bracket can be one or two threads, or as thick or thin as you wish it to be. You can also make additional diamonds of uniform colors (as with a standard diamond wrap) so that the split diamond becomes blocked in with successive bands of contrasting colors.

You can develop a split diamond with the split along the axis of the rod. To do this first lay out the initial crossing thread (we'll use red for the first color, green for the second, as before). Then wrap the second color (green), making the course up the rod *below* the initial red thread and the course down the rod *above* the red thread. Continue this way, with the next red thread kept above the red thread going up and kept below the red thread going down. The colors continue this way, with the green always next to the green, the red always next to the red. In essence you are working to the side of the rod from the center axis, keeping green on one side and red on the other. Once you have the split diamond sized as you desire, bracket it with a third color to frame the pattern, or build up other bands of color as previously described.

Although the above description is for simple split diamonds using one color on each side of the split, you can also make multicolored patterned diamonds by building up a split diamond and then, after a given number of thread wraps, changing colors. This is how a standard diamond is usually done: starting with a block of color and then one or more times shifting to different colors and band widths of colors to make the diamond more decorative. For this you can use totally new colors for each of the new bands or simply reverse the colors so that a split diamond that starts with red above (toward the tip) and green below would reverse to a second band of green above and red below. When using reversed bands or different colors, you can continue as many times as you wish, using as many colors as you wish, with identical or different size band widths.

An alternative is to make each band up and down of a different color, but keep the colors consistent for each side of the diamond. The result will be a four-sided diamond with each of the developing sides a different color. Thus you can have a diamond in which each little triangle that makes up the diamond is different—say red, green, blue, and yellow. Of course any combination of colors is possible.

SPLIT CHEVRONS

Just as diamonds can be split, so can chevrons. Chevrons are really easier, because they are only half a diamond. To make a split chevron, work with two colors (let's use red and green again), but in this case one color (let's say red) spirals up the rod and the second color (green) spirals down the rod. For the initial wrap the two crossing threads will not be the same color but will be red and green. After these threads are properly checked and positioned on the premarked underwrap, the rest of the wrap is easy and involves nothing more than running the same colors up and down the blank: red up and green down.

But unlike a diamond, in which the central threads or sets of threads are bracketed on both sides, for a chevron all the subsequent threads are to one side (above or below—toward the tip or the butt) of the initial wrap. If all the wraps are below the initial wrap, then the point of the chevron will be aimed toward the butt of the rod. If all the wraps are above the initial thread, then the point will be aimed toward the tip. As described in chapter 23, you can also make a chevron to the right or left simply by tracking all the threads after the first thread to the right or left. If you make all the wraps to the right, the point will aim right; if you make all the wraps to the left, the chevron will point left.

Regardless of the direction to which the chevron points, you can also make additional bands of color, just as you would on a standard chevron. One way I like to do this is to reverse the colors so that if there is a split chevron with red left and green right in an initial band, I can switch to green left and red right in a second band, back to red left and green right in a third band, and so on. These bands can be of the same width each time or of varying widths each time, although each side is identical in the number of threads used.

A variation is to make the bands of different widths and colors on each side or to vary their positioning so that there is a more fragmented zigzag pattern to the chevron. One easy way to do this is to start with the red and green to make two bands up and down with each color, then continue with two more bands of green on the one side, white on the other. Continue the white for two more on one side, with two of blue on the other, then two more of blue on one side, red on the other. The final look is of a chevron but with the two stripes on each side not lining up exactly.

Another way to get a similar effect, even if the bands are lined up, is to work with bands of several threads rather than individual threads. The individual threads will make a neater wrap, but bands will make for a different zigzag look.

If you wish to frame these chevrons, the best way to do it is to first lay down a framing thread (let's say black) and then lay down the chevron threads, finally framing with black threads again. If you place the entire frame after completing the wrap, it will have a diamond frame and lose some of the chevron look, although this is a matter of personal taste.

Simple chevron by Cantwell Clark, boxed in with white thread that separates the wrap from the crossing threads required to make it.

Sometimes simple wraps appear more complex than they really are. This three-dimensional looking "box" pattern is really a multiple chevron in which different colors are used in each direction (a light color in one direction, dark color in the opposite direction) to make it appear shaded and to give it a three-dimensional look. Wrap by Cantwell Clark.

Long simple chevron with crossing threads in the open white space.

Complex wrap developed by Cantwell Clark.

WEAVING LETTERS AND NUMBERS

Weaving letters and numbers can be tedious but is relatively easy once the principles are understood. The purpose for weaving numbers and letters is to provide a way in which various information can be added to the rod. In most cases the owner's name is added to the blank. Other information, such as the rod maker, rod length, rod weight, line and lure size, and date, is written onto the blank using one of the several means outlined in chapter 25. However, if you have the time and wish to do it, all this information can be woven into a base wrap on the rod using standard simple weaving techniques.

To weave numbers, letters, and scenes, you will want not only the rod supports used for making various diamonds, chevrons, and other decorative wraps but also the thread-tension

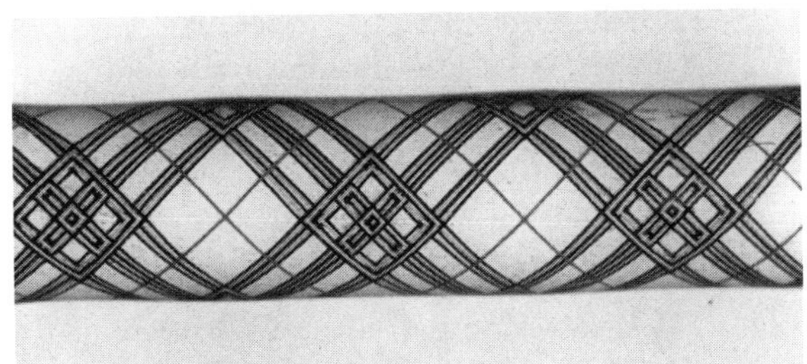

Another complex wrap by Cantwell Clark.

Example of letter weaving on a rod blank. In this weaving the light-color (white in this case) longitudinal threads are evenly laid out on the rod and taped in place, with these individual threads lifted up and laid down under and over the dark (black) circular wrapping threads to make the woven design of letters shown here. Wrap by Cantwell Clark.

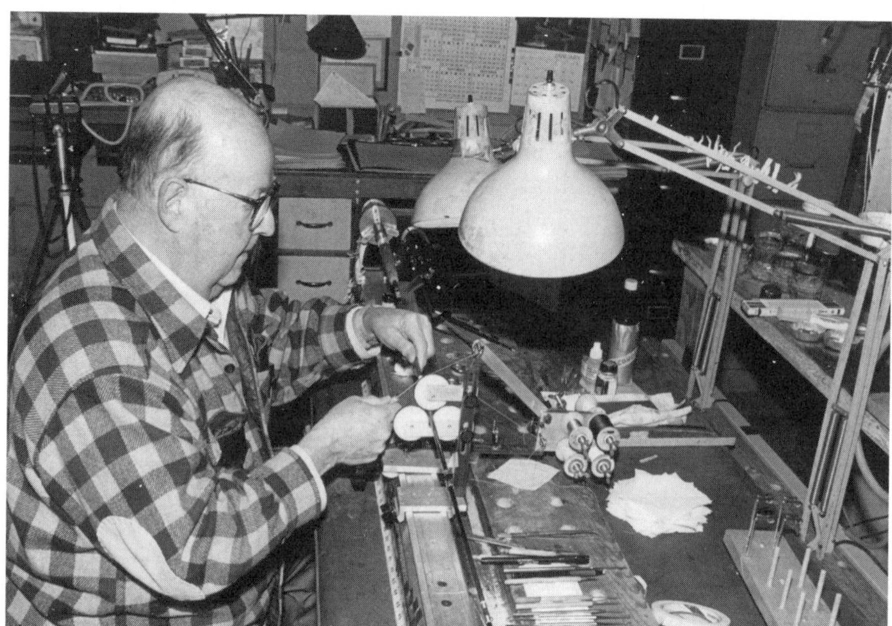

Cantwell Clark at his rod-building table.

device you use for making regular guide wraps. This is a must for making a rotary wrap of base thread as you work the horizontal threads (as the rod sits in a rod lathe or holder) back and forth along the rod to form the letter, number, or scene.

The technique of weaving letters and numbers involves a basic wrap like an underwrap and longitudinal threads (parallel to the rod blank) that are wrapped over the base wrap to form the letters and numbers.

Weaving is not like making diamonds, chevrons, or other decorative wraps in which threads are spiraled up and down the blank. It is a true woven process, different from spiraling threads or bundles of threads at an angle up and down a blank. For weaving, serious rod builders consider the Renzetti Wonder Weaver, developed by Jim Upton, for their weaving tacks. This not only allows weaving completely round the rod blank on all sides but also makes it easy to lift and hold

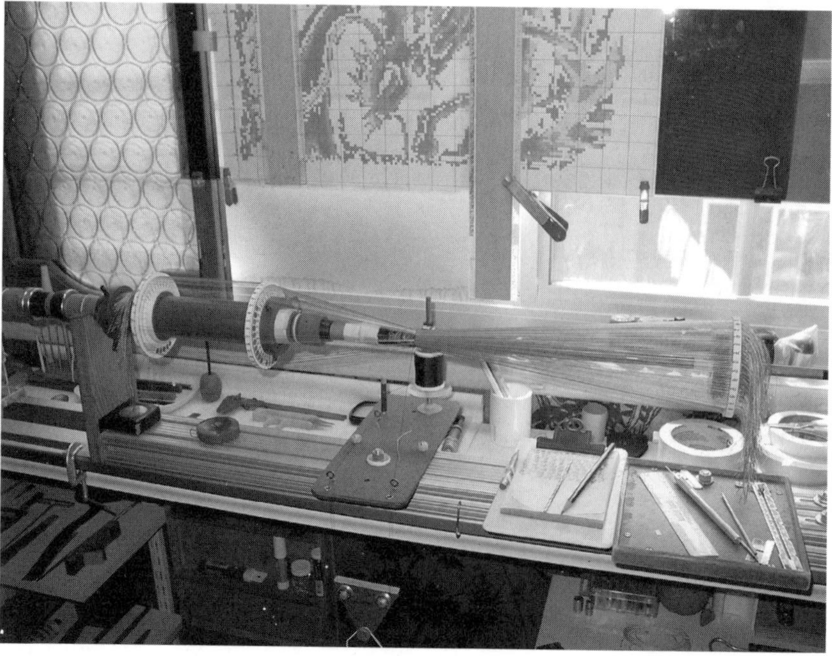

Jim Upton designed and Renzetti made the weaving machine used by Upton to weave a dragon—his specialty—onto a rod blank.
Photo by Jim Upton

Woven dragon on rod mostly complete. Dragon by Jim Upton. ***Photo by Jim Upton***

or secure the threads or put them back in place as you continue the weaving process.

In weaving, all the letters are made of threads that are laid down parallel to the blank, over the base wrap, which is formed by a tight wrap around the blank. Using this weaving method, different sizes of letters and numbers as well as different fonts or styles can be used. It just takes time and careful design before starting.

The number of parallel threads used determines the height of each letter, and the number of wraps around the blank behind the parallel threads determines the width of each letter. Although you can make any letters you want by stretching or compressing them in width, a general rule would be to make the letter width about 80 percent of the height.

The letters can be made any height but are usually made in proportion to the type of rod and to the rod-blank diameter at the butt. Thus for a freshwater spinning rod, you might want a letter height of only ⅛ inch, while for a big-game rod you might want larger letters of about ¼ inch. Usually the height is determined first, because the width is proportional to the height, not the other way around.

Just how high the letters will be depends on the size of thread used. Different rod builders have different views on this. Ted Bingham, writing in an excellent series on the subject in *The Fisherman* magazine, for Atlantic Coast anglers, notes that he likes a height of fifteen threads and a width of twelve threads. Dale Clemens, in his book *Advanced Custom Rod Building,* suggests seven threads high and eight wide, although the eight-thread width is used primarily for wider letters, such as M, N, Q, T, V, W, X, Y, and Z.

The point is that you can vary the height and width of letters and numbers, but you must have a plan for what you want to do and how you will do it. If you will do a lot of weaving, make up your own outline of letters and numbers, using graph paper. I use 10 × 10 graph paper (ten squares in each direction per inch) on which to draw out the letters. I use one horizontal line for each horizontal thread and one vertical line for each wrapping thread, keeping the scale of the width to about 80 percent of the height. I draw only the horizontal threads that will make up the letters. Another possibility is to buy or borrow from the library a book of letter and number fonts from which you can copy or design the letters required for your rod building.

One way to determine a reasonable arrangement for threads is to figure letter size based on the width of the thread. This won't hold up completely because thread will become slightly compressed when wrapped, but it will provide a starting point. Some manufacturers of threads provide the width of their threads in both decimal inches and millimeters. From this we can figure out the width of a band of a certain number of threads or the number of threads that will make up certain band widths. For inches the chart from older Gudebrod thread would look like this:

NCP Thread	Reg. Thread	Dia.	10 threads	20 threads
A	A	0.0070	0.070	0.140
C	D	0.0104	0.104	0.208
D	E	0.0132	0.132	0.264

In millimeters the same chart would be:

NCP Thread	Reg. Thread	Dia.	10 threads	20 threads
A	A	0.175	1.75	3.50
C	D	0.260	2.60	5.20
D	E	0.330	3.30	6.60

If such a chart is available for the thread that you use, you also can multiply the number of threads that will be required for a certain height in inches or millimeters. A chart showing also the approximate width of the letter based on the 80 percent formula (height/width) would be as follows:

Letter Height	Thread Size		
	A	C (NCP)/D	D (NCP)/E
0.125–⅛ inch	18/14	12/10	9/7
0.250–¼ inch	36/29	24/19	19/15
5 millimeters	29/24	19/15	15/12
10 millimeters	57/48	38/30	30/24

In some of the above there will be just too many threads to handle. This would apply to most thread wraps where more than twenty horizontal threads would have to be handled. You could work with larger thread sizes—EE for example—but often this makes for a coarser-looking wrap and should be avoided if possible.

In principle weaving letters and numbers is easy. In practice there are a couple of tips that will help. Begin by deciding where you will make your lettering wrap. Often this is just above the foregrip and done in conjunction with or in place of a diamond or some other crossing wrap. Use masking tape to tape to the rod blank the number of horizontal threads (the vertical threads along the axis of the rod blank) to be used. Do this close to the foregrip or on the left side of the wrap, because we write and read from left to right. Then, about 2 inches to the right (or leaving enough space for the writing you have planned), tape down the threads again. In doing this make sure they are all parallel. Because you will constantly lift and tape down these threads, using double-sided tape is better than using masking tape. Double-sided clear tape and masking-type drafting tape are available for this operation. To hold the threads to the left as you lift them up for making the thread letters, place another strip of double-sided tape to the left of the original tape and at the beginning of the wrap.

One trick I use to make this easier is to tape the left side in two steps. First I just gather a short length of the correct number of threads and tape them down in a bunch. Then, immediately to the right of this, I straighten out the threads so that they are parallel and tape them a second time, making sure they are all touching in a straight, flat bundle. If you are worried about getting close enough to the foregrip, you can tape the bundle down on the foregrip, straighten out the threads, and make the second taping (with the threads parallel) on the blank just above the foregrip.

Once these threads are in place, run them between the teeth of a comb to keep them parallel for taping down straight and parallel on the right side.

Following the above, begin wrapping with a base wrap around the rod, just as you would for an underwrap. Begin on the left, over the parallel threads, leaving the taped ends exposed. Make several turns, or wrap until you wish to begin the letters. At this point let's assume you will make an L—certainly an easy letter to make using 15 horizontal threads. Where you wish the letter to begin, remove all the parallel threads from the right side (which is why the double-sided tape is better here) and place all 15 threads completely to the left. Continue the base wrap for three complete turns. Bring parallel threads 1 through 12 (counting from the top) back to the right, and wrap over them with the base wrap. Make nine complete turns (which now gives you 12 complete turns of thread from the beginning of the letter L) and then bring the last three threads (13 through 15) back to the right. Wrap over these threads to complete the L. Now all the parallel threads are wrapped over, and after making several more turns of the base wrap (usually about one-half of the letter's width, or six turns in this case), you begin the next letter.

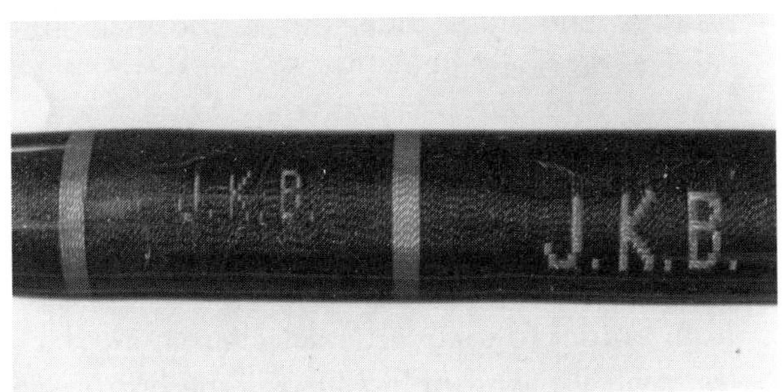

Sample letters by Cantwell Clark, woven into a rod. Note the two sizes used in this sample.

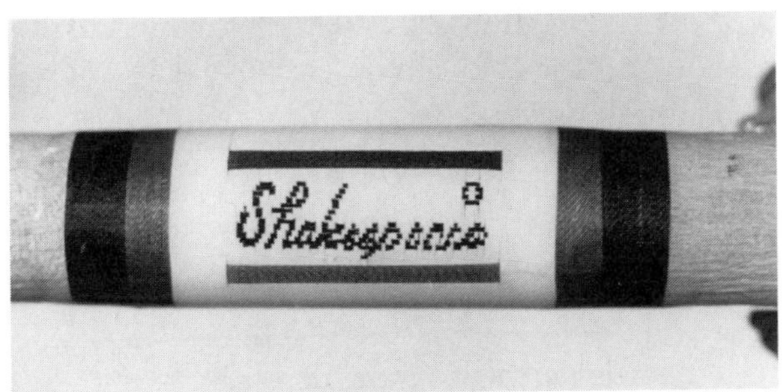

Example of extreme skill by Cantwell Clark in this script lettering for a rod-blank manufacturing company. Wrap is a sample, built on a wood dowel.

Other letters would be made similarly. A letter C would be just like an L except that the top three threads in addition to the bottom three would be held to the left and brought over at the same time as the bottom threads. Doing so would make a very squared off C. An O is the same as a C except that the right stroke of three threads is made to complete the letter. A U is the same as an O except that the top is left open. H, A, E, F, and P are similar. Other letters are pretty obvious and follow suit, once you understand the principle: Any thread flipped to the left will ultimately be exposed; any to the right will be hidden.

Note that in the L, with a 15/12 size configuration, we have arbitrarily chosen three threads as the width of the lettering strokes. That lettering can be made narrower, with only one or two thread widths, or wider, with four or five threads for the width. (In our example the lettering can't be wider than four or five threads. In an H, for example, a width of five would only allow for a space of two threads between the two vertical strokes—each vertical stroke would be five, for a total of twelve threads in width.)

Although not usually done, it is also possible to get into unusual letters, such as letters with very thin vertical strokes (one thread) and very thick horizontal strokes (up to four threads) or very thick vertical strokes (up to five threads) and very thin horizontal strokes (one thread).

It is always best to first outline on graph paper a complete alphabet of those letters you plan to use. This will quickly point out any problems you have in spacing or planning before you start to wrap—and possibly get into trouble. For some letters you will have to plan on making a series of small connected blocks of thread for diagonal lines, as in A, K, M, N, Q, R, V, W, X, Y, and Z. Often these will have to be considered "extra width" letters, requiring a little more space to complete them properly and proportionally.

In some cases you can partially round off letters, as when leaving out a corner for the right side of a D, B, P, or R, or you can round off all the corners of an O or Q, the top of an A, or the corners of a G. This is done by flipping over (to the right) the top and bottom threads in these spots so that they are wrapped down and are thus hidden.

Numbers are made the same way and are best blocked out first on graph paper to determine the best shape and appearance before the wrap is begun.

Here are some tips for making letters and numbers:

1. Proper alignment of the completed name or message is extremely important. One way to aid this process is to make alignment marks on the blank. Hold the rod blank in a horizontal position, and place a piece of masking tape at each end of the letter area. Using a strong overhead light, and without moving your head, use the streaks of light cast by the overhead light to mark the pieces of tape. Then rotate the rod to the bottom of the lettering area and mark the tape again. When you wish to check the alignment, use a rule to line up the top and bottom marks to serve as a guide.

2. Leave the end of the parallel threads out until you are finished. That way you can pull on all the threads together to tighten the lettering, or you can pull individual threads to help straighten and smooth the resulting letters. Do not make the base wrap too tight, or it will be difficult to move any of the parallel threads. If you can move the parallel threads, you can sometimes shift them back and forth enough to remove any crossed threads that might have resulted while making a letter. Such crossing should be avoided, but if it does occur, pulling the thread back and forth may help remove it.

3. Use contrasting-color threads for the base and lettering wrap. It is best if you do not use a very light thread color for either wrap. If you were to use white or a very light color for the base wrap and a very dark color for the parallel threads, you could end up with a wrap in which the dark strands of thread would show through the base wrap. Try to use similar shades of contrasting colors—red and blue, yellow and medium brown, gray and pink, orange and light blue, green and red, and green and blue.

4. If you wish to get fancy, you can use different colors for the parallel threads. Thus you could have green letters with a red central thread or threads, red letters with a black top and bottom border to each letter, letters that are dark blue on top and light blue on the bottom, a similar-color Mylar or metallic shimmering thread in the middle of each letter, and so on. Remember, however, that you will have to consider the colors in order to avoid any show-through once the wrap is finished.

Stylized fish wrap by Cantwell Clark.

WEAVING SCENES AND DESIGNS

Scenes and figures can be woven just as letters and numbers are woven—although making scenes is more of an advanced method. Master lettering first to understand completely what is involved in weaving.

Some possible figures involve stylized fish, a fisherman with an arched rod and a fish on the end of the line, dock scenes, and boats (particularly offshore rods on offshore boats). Some custom-rod builders are so adept at this that they can make very lifelike fish of different species on a blank using the same basic threads.

Any number of threads can be used. In most cases the colors used, the number of threads of each color, and the arrangement of each color will depend on the scene desired. Most fish, for example, have dark-color backs blending into light bellies. Thus the top of a wrap depicting a fish would use dark colors, and these colors would gradually change into lighter colors near the bottom of the weave. The thread colors chosen will depend on the fish species and personal preference. To make a bonefish you might start at the top with a light gray, shift to a blue-silver metallic thread, and end up with a white or silver thread. The appearance will be of a bonefish with a gray back, blue-silver sides, and a white-silver belly. A blue marlin might have a medium or dark blue top with a light blue belly. A channel bass or redfish might have a medium brown back and gold or tan belly. A shark might be a uniform medium or gunmetal gray.

Other scenes, such as a river and sky with a boat and fisherman, would more typically use light blue threads at the top to simulate the sky and other colors in the middle and bottom to simulate other subjects in the scene.

Unlike the various formulas and charts sometimes seen for weaving letters and numbers, there are few if any charts for scenes or figures. As with developing patterns for letters and numbers, the best method for working out a pattern for a scene is to draw it out on graph paper, using one vertical graph line for each vertical base thread and one horizontal graph line for each horizontal thread used in the scene. Often it is best to first sketch out the scene with a pencil and then to come back with crayons, colored pencils, or colored felt-tip markers to draw in threads of each color.

While you can make weaves of anything just by wrapping thread around the rod and throwing selected threads to the right to be covered by the thread wrap or off to the left to make up part of the design when covered later, the Wonder Weaver designed by Jim Upton is a much better way to go. This machine, available through Renzetti, allows precise holding of thread in place, either out of the way or to be wrapped over. This excellent design allows for weaving 360 degrees around the rod blank if you like. Without this specialized loom design, it is usually only possible to wrap one face or side of a rod blank, or about 30 to 40 degrees.

The Wonder Weaver works with three wheels of plastic, each with an outer rim of hard rubber slotted 360 times to hold threads. Ninety of the slots are numbered for convenience when moving threads around. Each wheel fits onto the rod blank, and the rod blank can be held separately from a rod lathe by propping it onto a simple rod holder such as a few V-block rod holders. Thus you can make woven designs at leisure without interfering with rod wrapping or other rod work on a separate rod lathe. The Wonder Weaver does require a thread tension device to hold and control thread that is wrapped around the rod blank either over or under the longitudinal threads (with the longitudinal threads flipped out of the way). The numbering system on each wheel allows you to make up a design for the weave using a number of longitudinal threads and notes as to when they are wrapped over or pulled to the left to make the design.

The Wonder Weaver allows weaving with any number of threads up to the extreme of 360 with the 360 slots available for threads and weaving.

The less-expensive Wonder Weaver II has only two wheels instead of three. This makes it less costly to start weaving and also includes one wheel with a large bore that can be used on large handle grips, such as those for bait-casting rods, as well as skinny rod blanks like those for fly rods. A large bore hub is also available separately that will take large handles such as those for bait casters, but it does not include the foam wheel and plastic discs of the basic Wonder Weaver.

Jim Upton and Andy Renzetti are currently working on a simpler version of the Wonder Weaver that will work on one side of a rod only and may take 20 to 30 longitudinal threads for simpler weaves.

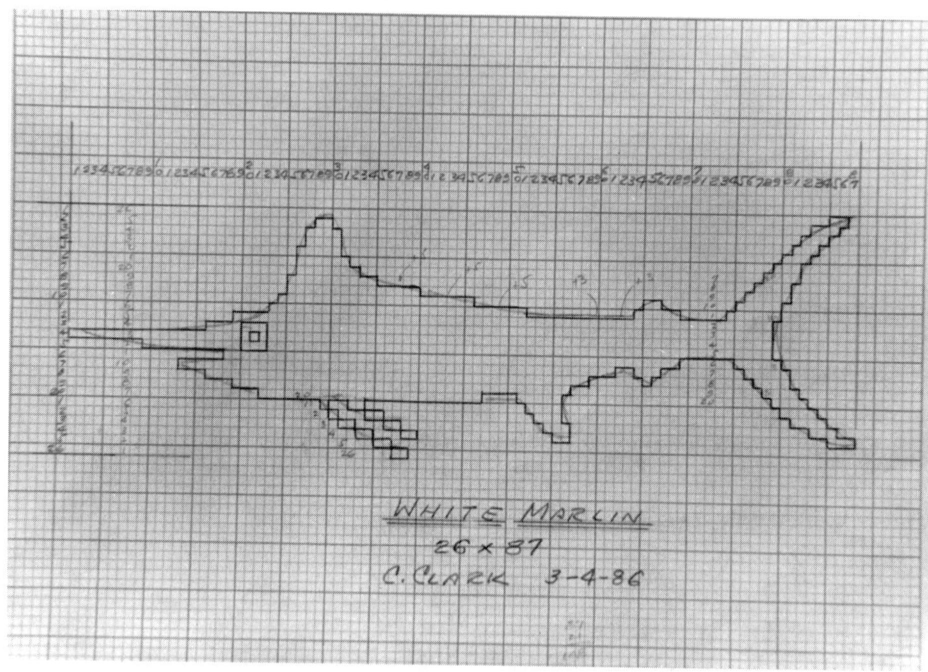

Cantwell Clark design layout for weaving a white marlin into a butt wrap. Each thread and step is laid out on graph paper.

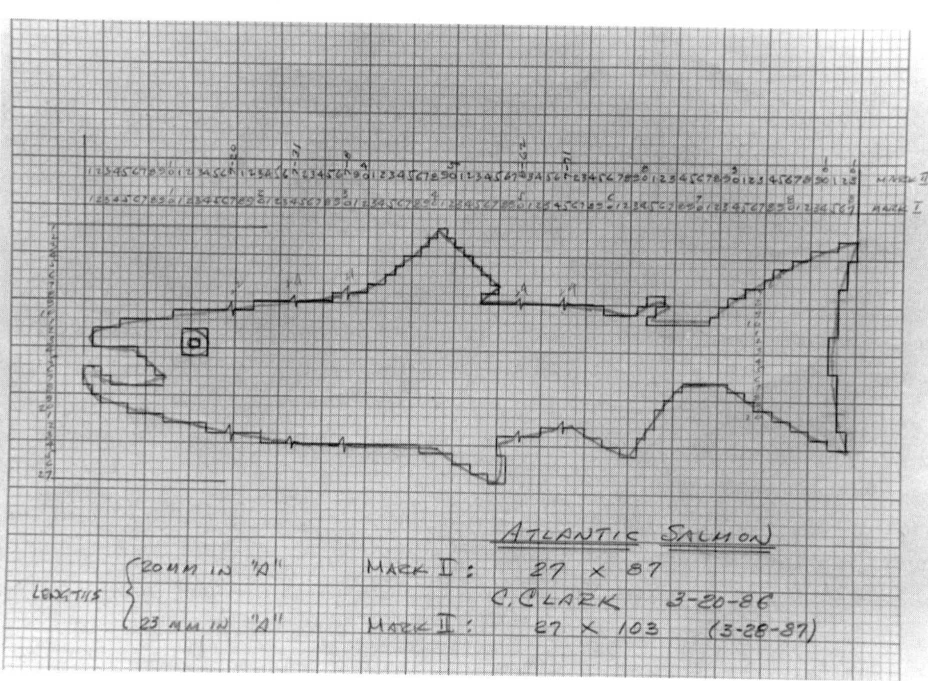

Another Cantwell Clark design, this for an Atlantic salmon.

SPERM WHALE, MARK II, 28 × 87

C. CLARK 3-27-84

1	15-22	⊗ ✓	23	14-28	⊗ ✓	45	(15-27) DO	⊗ ✓	67	(18-22) DO	⊗ ✓
2	14-23	⊗ ✓	4		⊗ ✓	6	DO	⊗ ✓	8	DO	⊗ ✓
3	14-23&27	⊗ ✓	5		⊗ ✓	7	DO	⊗ ✓	9	18-21	⊗ ✓
4	DO	⊗ ✓	6		⊗ ✓	8	15-26	⊗ ✓	70	17-21	⊗ ✓
5	13-23&27	⊗ ✓	7		⊗ ✓	9	DO	⊗ ✓	1	DO	⊗ ✓
6	DO	⊗ ✓	8		⊗ ✓	50	DO	⊗ ✓	2	16-21	⊗ ✓
7	3&13-23&26-27	⊗ ✓	9	DITTO	⊗ ✓	1	15-25	⊗ ✓	3	16-20	⊗ ✓
8	2&13-23&26-27	⊗ ✓	30		⊗ ✓	2	16-25	⊗ ✓	4	15-20	⊗ ✓
9	1&13-23&26-27	⊗ ✓	1		⊗ ✓	3	DO	⊗ ✓	5	12-20	⊗ ✓
10	DO	⊗ ✓	2		⊗ ✓	4	16-24	⊗ ✓	6	10-21	⊗ ✓
1	2&13-24&26-27	⊗ ✓	3		⊗ ✓	5	DO	⊗ ✓	7	8-21	⊗ ✓
2	3&13-24&26-27	⊗ ✓	4		⊗ ✓	6	DO	⊗ ✓	8	6-22	⊗ ✓
3	[illegible]24&26-27	⊗ ✓	5		⊗ ✓	7	DO	⊗ ✓	9	6-25	⊗ ✓
4	3&13-24&26-27	⊗ ✓	6	14-28	⊗ ✓	8	DO	⊗ ✓	80	5-10&15-23	⊗ ✓
5	2&13-24&26-27	⊗ ✓	7	14-27	⊗ ✓	9	17-24	⊗ ✓	1	5-6&18-24	⊗ ✓
6	1&13-27	⊗ ✓	8	DO	⊗ ✓	60	17-23	⊗ ✓	2	20-25	⊗ ✓
7	DO	⊗ ✓	9	DO	⊗ ✓	1	DO	⊗ ✓	3	21-26	⊗ ✓
8	2&13-27	⊗ ✓	40	DO	⊗ ✓	2	DO	⊗ ✓	4	22-26	⊗ ✓
9	3&13-20&24-28	⊗ ✓	1	DO	⊗ ✓	3	DO	⊗ ✓	5	23-26	⊗ ✓
20	13-20&22&24-28	⊗ ✓	2	15-27	⊗ ✓	4	DO	⊗ ✓	6	24-25	⊗ ✓
1	DO	⊗ ✓	3	DO	⊗ ✓	5	17-22	⊗ ✓	87	25	⊗ ✓
2	13-20&24-28	⊗ ✓	4	DO	⊗ ✓	6	18-22	⊗ ✓			

Weaving notes, this for a Cantwell Clark design for a sperm whale. Notes are a must for designs to be repeated.

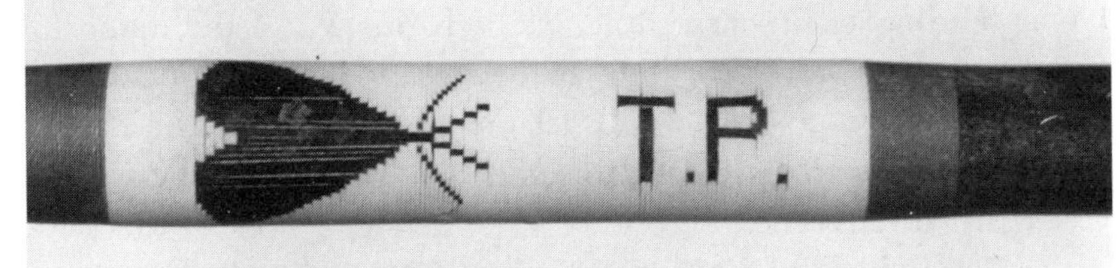

Example of stonefly and letters by Cantwell Clark.

Woven fishing scene of two fishermen in a boat. Design by Cantwell Clark.

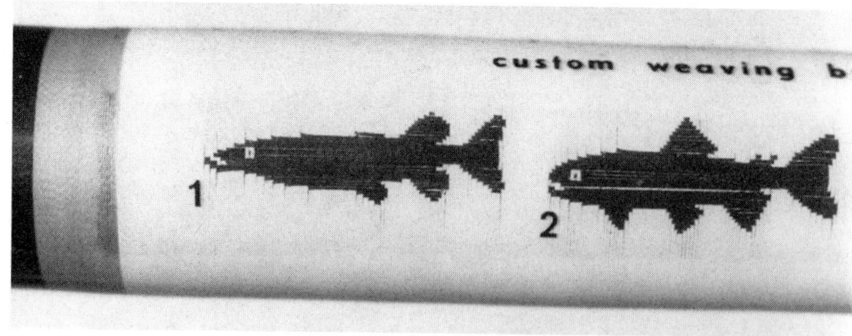

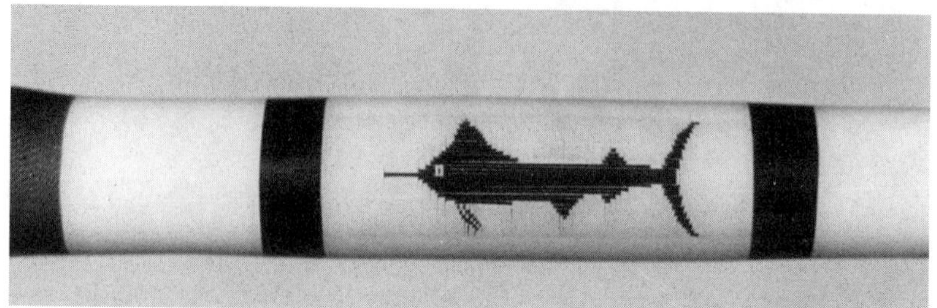

Sample fish designs by Cantwell Clark.

BEADING WRAPS AND SCENES

Rod builders Lana and Ken Preston have expanded the possibilities of decorative designs and weaves on rods. Ken introduced his wife, Lana, to rod building. She in turn introduced bead work as it's done for decorative dresses, party dresses, wedding gowns, and similar clothing and accessories.

Lana creates a "3-D" effect by adding depth to the wrap or woven scene through the addition of small beads. She uses basically two different beading techniques, although both use fine needles and very small 15/0 Japanese beads threaded on one- to two-pound-test monofilament fishing line to outline the thread design or create the woven scene.

For outlining and emphasizing a decorative pattern wrap, Lana first creates the wrap design using standard thread techniques. This can be a diamond, double diamond, chevron, double chevron, Maltese cross, or any other type of simple or complex pattern wrap.

Once this is finished, the next step is to outline or cover this pattern using beads strung on one-pound-test monofilament using a fine needle. The process uses just enough beads each time to outline the part of the thread wrap on which you are working. First begin by completing the thread pattern wrap just as you would if this were the final step of a decorative wrap. Then run the needle through a part of the thread wrap adjacent to the point where you begin adding beads.

With the monofilament anchored down, add clear or colored beads. Use just enough beads to outline one side of the pattern wrap. If using clear beads, this will allow the colors of the thread wrap to show through. If using colored beads, these augment the color of the thread wrap over which the beads are being added. Add just enough beads to the mono for this one wrap leg length. This might be three to seven (or fewer or more) beads, based on the size of one leg of the pattern wrap. Run the needle through a thread or two on the end of this leg of beads to finish this one small part. Then continue, adding more beads for the next leg of the wrap, etc., until you've filled in the outline of that wrap or completed the amount of beadwork for that part of the pattern wrap. Continue as above for other sections of the pattern wrap until the entire wrap is completed as desired with a pattern outline or covering of beads.

Once the beadwork is complete, add one to two coats of color preserver and, once cured, finish with a coat of epoxy rod finish. If necessary, add a second coat.

For making bead scenes similar to that of a woven scene, a slightly different technique is

Design for the butt of an offshore fishing rod. This design was originated and created with beads by Lana Preston to create a three-dimensional effect.

Beaded flag design by Lana Preston for the butt of a rod.

Close-up of a billfish design by Lana Preston, showing the beadwork and the beads that are tied into the thread wrap to make the design.

used. For this Lana first wraps the blank section with a continuous double wrap, almost like a long simple guide wrap. The purpose is to lay down an even, continuous thread base (underwrap and overwrap) for both a background of the weave and also as a base on which to secure the mono using the beading needle.

This double wrap allows for a better color base and also for a thicker thread base by which to sew through to hold the mono and beads in place against the background. The length of the continuous wrap must be based on the length and complexity of the beadwork that is

Detail of Lana Preston working with beads on a rod butt design.

to follow. Fish are popular, and one of Lana's best-known works is a large and complex blue marlin. Begin by scanning onto a computer a photo, clip art from an Internet page, or from a magazine. Scale the image to the size desired. Print it onto a 10 × 10-square graph paper. Use this as a template or design for the beading work. If you're artistic, you can draw directly onto the thread background, using lightly penciled lines or reference points for specific parts of the design.

Once the picture is outlined, begin by running the needle through the base thread to lock the mono in place, and then add beads of the color desired. Note that colored beads are a must here. Once you run a length of beads and lock them down with the needle, run the needle back through the last and first beads to secure the beads and the line or color bead pattern in place. Continue as above, following along the lines and pattern point reference marks to create the scene.

As with a beaded pattern wrap, finish with color preserver and a coat or two of epoxy thread finish.

For beads Lana recommends craft and art shops such as Michaels, JoAnne Fabrics, and Hobby Lobby; also check the Internet or eBay. At this writing, two articles on this technique have appeared in *RodMaker* magazine, in volume 14, issue 1, and volume 14, issue 2. For additional information on this innovative technique, call Ken or Lana directly at (410) 360-1730 or e-mail them at kpres375@aol.com.

DECORATIVE WRAPS ON GUIDES

Some anglers like the look of custom decorative wraps on guides. These are basic wraps to hold down the guides and are used as underwraps for subsequent wrapping techniques. A standard diamond, chevron, or double diamond would be placed over this underwrap. This is a very tedious wrap to create, however, because it is relatively short (the length of the guide wrap), and each one must be finished off with a band wrap at each end of the guide. This is not normally done with separate wraps on each guide foot but rather with a long underwrap that is completed by running the decorative wrap from one end of the guide wrap to the other. Because these are tedious and time-consuming, they are usually done on large rods, such as fancy offshore big-game rods and IGFA-style trolling rods.

They are tedious also because the threads used for making the diamond or chevron must be laced through the frame and around the guide feet. This requires careful planning, because the guide size and type used must allow for the size, style, and positioning of the pattern. Too large a pattern, for example, might run into the frame or not allow proper positioning at the sides of the rod or under the center of the guide. Although I have seen such wraps where the diamonds or chevrons matched those on the butt of the rod above the foregrip, most of these have been on offshore and similar large rods.

FURTHER REFERENCES ON COMPLEX WRAPS AND WEAVING

While a complete bibliography is listed at the end of this book, the subject of weaving and complex wraps has grown so much over the past twenty years that some special reference is deserving for those interested in more detailed information. These books include *Custom Rod Thread Art* by Dale Clemons and *A Guide to Thread Weaving for the Custom Rod Builder* by Jim Upton.

DVDs are also available that address lots of aspects of rod building and custom wraps and weaving. For more on custom wraps, you can reference *Decorative Wraps and Pattern Animations, Collection #1*, by Dave Boyle and Billy Vivona, available by e-mailing davidboyle@visualwrap.com.

25

Finishing Touches and Finishing Rods

Introduction • Tools and Materials • Finishing Touches • Abalone, Decal, and Feather Additions • Hydrographic Printing • H • Craquele Painting of Rod Blanks • Color Preserver: Pros and Cons • Applying Color Preserver • Mixing Rod Finishes • Applying Rod Finishes • Unusual Finishing Touches for Blanks and Rods • Finishing Problems and Solutions

Basic Safety Equipment

Safety goggles

Cotton or rubber gloves

Respirator mask

Basic Tools

Mixing cups

Stirrers, round plastic sticks, Popsicle sticks, craft sticks, or wood skewers

Brushes

Smooth, flat surface onto which to pour epoxy

Good light (for viewing rod finish on rod)

Helpful Tools

Rod supports

Rod-curing motor

Hair dryer or clean torch

Fine nibs and pen holders

INTRODUCTION

The guide wraps and decorative wraps of the most elaborate and well-built rod in the world won't last long if the rod is not protected with a long-lasting finish. That finish usually involves a color preserver (to preserve and protect the thread colors) and an epoxy (to protect the wraps with a clear, hard coating).

Sometimes additional finishing touches are made to dress up a rod and impart a custom look. Executing these final steps well by working carefully and following all manufacturers' directions can make the difference between a fair-looking rod and a beautiful one.

TOOLS AND MATERIALS

Tools and materials for rod finishing are specialized yet simple. Tools can include mixing cups to combine the two-part epoxy finishes. Throwaway or good-quality brushes are used for applying the color preserver and the epoxy finish. Flat craft sticks or wood kitchen skewers can be thrown away after mixing the epoxy. A curing motor is not completely necessary but will help you get a good, smooth, drip-free finish on any rod. A drying box is a simple or fancy long box in which a rod can be placed to cure completely. These boxes have curing motors built in or a hole at one end to allow the butt end of the rod to extend into the box. They allow complete curing in a relatively dust-free environment. A hair dryer or torch may be used to heat the epoxy in order to remove bubbles after the finish is applied to the rod.

The materials used for finishing involve several different brands of color preserver and epoxy finish. Popular brands include Flex Coat, U-40, American Tackle Clear Coat Rod Epoxy, AftCote, Mud Hole ProKote, and similar epoxy and hard finishing compounds. Often these vary as to type. Some companies, such as Flex Coat, offer both high-build epoxy rod finishes for larger and heavier rods and a lighter, thinner finish for light rods, such as light and ultralight spinning and all fly rods. American Tackle has both high-build and light-build rod epoxies. All of these have matching color preservers available. In most cases you will need both a color preserver and a finish coat. Other finishes, such as varnish, are available, although varnish is most often used for finishing traditional bamboo rods.

If you are adding an inscription of any type to your rod, you need the right kind of ink to write on the blank. A good ink is one that will contrast with the color or finish of the blank. White ink is a good contrast to a dark brown or black glass or graphite blank; black ink contrasts well with white, honey, yellow, or other light-color blanks. Good possibilities include India ink for the dark ink and diluted typewriter correction fluid or water-based latex paint in light colors for the light-color "ink."

In addition to tools and materials, you will need a good, flat, clean work area, particularly one that is dust free. In most homes the best time to apply a finish is in the evening, when human activity in the home has lessened, and in a room or part of a basement that is clean and out of the way of human traffic.

A good strong light is also a must, because a light helps you to detect any gaps in the finish and aids you in adding an inscription to the finished rod.

FINISHING TOUCHES

In addition to decorative wraps and weaving, other finishing touches can be added to a rod before applying the protective wrap finish.

One of these finishing touches is the addition of information on the rod. Typically this includes the length and weight of the rod, line range, lure-weight range, the date the rod was completed, name of the owner, etc. In some cases some of this information is on the blank already and can be left in place if it has not been covered by a decorative wrap. In other cases you might want to add to the information, including your name and address or, if you're making the rod for a friend, a notation as to the maker and recipient. An example of a typical inscription would be "Custom-built for John Doe by Tom Smith, March 3, 2011."

This information can be inscribed on one line but more typically is inscribed on several lines around the circumference of the rod, with each line printed on the rod's longitudinal plane. Thus a typical arrangement would be:

Custom-built for
John Doe
by Tom Smith,
March 3, 2011

Usually these lines would be sized to be placed about 90 degrees apart around the rod, with the recipient's name on the top of the rod where he or she will see it. If the blank is of a thin diameter, then these four lines might be too much to include. If this is the case another possibility would be:

Custom-built for John Doe
by Tom Smith, March 3, 2011

These lines provide the same information and vary only in the arrangement for the given rod. You could also simply inscribe *Custom-built for John Doe* on one line.

There is a variety of ways to add such information to a rod. Perhaps the best and easiest is to write on the rod. Such information must be printed on the bare blank and must be covered with a clear rod finish to protect it.

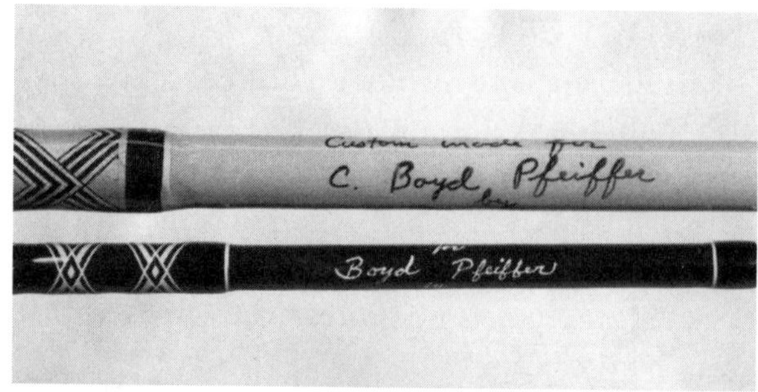

Examples of writing on a rod blank. Both white and black inks can be used, depending on the color of the blank.

Example of using dry transfer letters for labeling a rod blank. Sample by Cantwell Clark.

One problem that can occur is that the clear finish added to the rod can smear the writing. Often this occurs when a water-based ink is combined with a water-based finish or a solvent-based ink is combined with a solvent-based finish. The similarity of solvents—whether water or chemical based—seems to cause the problem, with the solvent in the finish loosening and smearing the writing. One simple solution is to use a water-based ink for writing and a solvent-based finish, and vice versa. Most finishes are chemical solvent based. This includes Gudebrod Hard 'N Fast II, Flex Coat, Flex Coat Lite, Classic Rod Coat, U-40 Perma Gloss, and U-40 Dura Gloss. Others, such as Gudebrod Speed Coat, are water-based finishes.

Writing can be done with any type of pen, but because the writing must be delicate, usually a small fine-point pen is best. You may find, however, that certain pens or pen points work better with certain inks or fluids, so it pays to experiment.

Although any ink can be used, a water-based black or dark ink is best for light-colored blanks. For dark blanks light-colored writing is a must. I like slightly diluted (about one part water to two or three parts of fluid) water-based typewriter correction fluids. These are available in a water base or a solvent base (the trend is to water-based correction fluids—be sure to get the water-based kind if you will be using a chemical-solvent-based finish coat) and are available in a wide variety of colors. Current manufacturers include Wite Out, Liquid Paper, Pentel, Universal, and Benchmark. In addition to white, available colors include blue, canary, yellow, goldenrod, regular green, ledger green, ivory, gray, pink, and buff. Another advantage to using the water-based fluids is that mistakes can be easily wiped up with a wet paper towel and inscriptions can be redone until they are perfect.

The key is to experiment. You must experiment with the best dilution formula for writing. Add a small amount of water at first, because it is easier to add more water and increase the dilution than it is to add more fluid to a too-watery solution. It also helps to experiment with pens. I like the inexpensive pens with detachable nibs best—those with a slightly rounded end seem to write best on blanks—but perform your own experiments to find the best writing combination. Pens are available individually (this is the best way to get them) or in sets that include a variety of nib styles and are designed primarily for calligraphy.

You also need to experiment to make sure the finish will not smear the writing. Practice on a scrap piece of blank, although any similar surface will do. Write on the scrap piece, allow the solution to dry completely, and then carefully add a coating of rod finish.

Once the solutions are tested, here are some tips to make any inscriptions easier:

1. Place masking tape around the area of the blank to be inscribed, and lightly roughen this blank area with very fine steel wool. Do this only enough to take the sheen and gloss off the blank—not enough to cut into the blank or damage the underlying fibers. This will make it easier for you to write on the blank, because the pen will be less likely to slip. Use a tack cloth or similar means to completely wipe the blank free of all steel-wool dust. It helps to wipe the blank in this area with acetone or alcohol to completely clean it. Note that any clear finish added on top of the writing will remove any dullness to this area.

2. It is always easier to write on the same level on which the hand rests. Use a small support—a stack of cardboard, a block of wood, an old book—that is approximately the same thickness as the blank. If the blank is ½ inch thick, use a support for the heel of your hand that is ½ inch thick. This will help prevent many mistakes and slips that might otherwise occur.

3. If you are making a lot of rods and doing a lot of writing on these completed rods, you may want to make a writing support board. This is nothing more than a 1-foot-square board with a squared groove cut along one edge, about 1 inch away from the edge. This allows you to place the rod in the groove and then place the rod surface on the same level as your hand, making it easier to write legibly. If you are making many rods of similar diameters, you can cut one groove to the depth needed—the diameter of the rod blank where you will be writing. If you are making rods of different diameters, you can cut different grooves along each edge, such as grooves with depths of ¼, ⅜, and ½ inch. With four edges to a 1-foot-square board, you have four possibilities. If you do not have a router to do this, or a friend with a wood shop, consider going to your local high school and giving the shop teacher a few bucks to make this tool for you. (Be sure to check school policy before doing this.)

4. Plan each line of the inscription, as well as the size of the writing. This is especially important for thin blanks, such as those for light fly rods and ultralight spinning rods.

5. If you have trouble lining up your writing or writing in a straight line, use a strip of masking tape along the axis and write just above its edge. Keep the writing about 1/32 inch above the masking tape—do not let the ink touch the masking tape, or it will bleed. An easy alternative if the blank is relatively thin is to split or cut in a straight line a 2-inch length of plastic straw, then slip the straw around the blank and line up one of the straight edges to serve as a bottom guide for writing. As with the masking tape, the writing does not touch the straw; the straw serves only as a guide to maintain relatively straight lines. You can use two straws—one as a guide for the bottom, the other as a guide for the top edge of the writing.

6. Another alternative for getting straight lines while writing is to use the glare from an overhead light to form a streak on the rod and thus a line (this only works if you do not move your head) or to inscribe a faint line with a pointed awl. The scratch formed will be filled in with the finish coat.

7. Another option is to use a commercially available lettering guide. Both the C-Thru and Alvin companies make guides of clear plastic, and both have slots that provide guides for various sizes of lettering. Both metric and fractional sizes are available, and the fractional Alvin model TD-1119 includes slots for ⅛, 5/32, 3/16, and ¼ inch.

8. Once you've written on the blank using a previously tested formula of ink or correction fluid, allow the inscription to dry completely.

9. Often inscription areas are bracketed with thin thread wraps or are placed at the upper end of a decorative wrap (the other side is bracketed with a simple wrap). Such wraps can be added before or after the inscription. Often they are best added before, after the proper planning of the size and space needed for the given inscription.

10. Once the inscription is completely dry, coat this area of the blank with rod finish when you are coating the rest of the rod wraps. To prevent any possibility of smearing the inscription, do this early to make sure the finish is completely liquid and not beginning to stiffen. Use a clean brush and the lightest possible touch of the finish to the blank to prevent too much contact with the inscription.

A good way to do this is to pick up a large blob of finish on the brush and add it immediately over the inscription, then lightly use the brush on top of the finish (not enough to drag the bristles of the brush over the inscription) to spread the finish over the area and any bracketing thread wraps.

11. As with rod finish on thread wraps, use a strong overhead light to create a glare on the shiny finish and help detect any missed spots. Use care and a light touch in filling in any spots you find.

The same basic techniques are applied when using calligraphy or India-type inks, such as those from Higgins (Faber-Castell) or Stradtler. Red and black are generally available, and these inks all seem to be chemical solvent based. Use a small-nib pen for the writing.

In addition to writing inscriptions, there are other ways you can add information. One is to use gold or silver foil that is usually sold with a small round-point burnisher (not a pen) with which the foil can be laid on a surface, taped or held in place, and, using the burnisher, transferred by pressure to the writing surface, in this case a rod blank. The result is any information you wish on the rod, but in a gold or silver finish.

Dry-transfer letters and numbers are available from stationery stores in sizes from about ⅛ inch and larger. These come on sheets that include capital and lowercase letters, numbers, and some punctuation marks. They are transferred to the rod blank by holding the sheet containing the letters on the blank and using a burnisher (such as the plastic burnishers available from most custom-rod catalog houses) to transfer the letters to a clean and dry rod blank. Use care—the rod is round, and the letter must be transferred completely to the blank. Once the letters are burnished completely, add a finishing coat of epoxy to hold them in place and protect them.

One way to add transfer letters easily is to first lay down a strip of masking tape in a straight line to serve as a guide for the bottom of the letters.

Another possibility is to use the gold or silver foil that is transferred by means of a heated pen used for bookbinding or woodworking.

It helps to use some of the previously mentioned tips for writing with ink, including sanding the rod blank and working from a surface at the same level as the surface of the rod blank.

Other ways in which information can be added include stick-on or self-adhesive labels. The information is written on the label (printed labels for your custom rod business are also available), which is then applied to the rod blank and then coated with a rod finish.

The one advantage to a label is that all the information can be written on a flat surface, making it easier to get straight lines of script. You also could use small ink stamps with a name or name and address and use them to stamp a label for a printed effect. Make sure the ink pad is new and the stamp is thoroughly covered with ink for a good, dark impression. If you have a stamp with your name and address and wish to use only your name, it is easy to mask the address lines with a sheet of paper or an index card.

Another possibility, particularly if you have trouble writing on the curved surface of a rod blank, is to write on a piece of clear tape (cellophane or similar tape) with the tape stretched out onto a smooth surface, such as a laminated countertop. Make sure you do not touch the adhesive side of the tape. Once the information is written on the tape and the writing has dried, lift the tape, trim any ends, and apply it to the blank. Finish with a regular rod-finish coat.

One potential problem with these systems is not only that the ink from the stamp pad or pen might smear but also that the label, once applied, must not lift up or curl around the edges. Experiment with a scrap blank to check the results before using these methods.

ABALONE, DECAL, AND FEATHER ADDITIONS

Not all decorations for rods are regimented thread designs or decorative fishing scenes. Some can involve natural materials from various flora and fauna sources. An abalone veneer can create patterns that are natural, beautiful, and not unlike the marbleizing technique accomplished with epoxy and paint pigments.

After seeing a photo on the Internet of a rod sporting some abalone, rod builder Kevin Knox of Queen Anne, Maryland (www.anglersenvy .com), started to play with this material. He subsequently wrote an article on the use of abalone veneer in rod building for *RodMaker* magazine (volume 11, issue 5). As Knox explained in his article, abalone is a type of marine snail with more than one hundred species throughout the world. Resembling a big, rounded, bowl-like oyster, internally it has a beautiful nacre or mother-of-pearl appearance. For use in decorations or crafts, abalone is cut into thin veneers of about 0.15 millimeter thick and usually coated with an adhesive backing to be used in such decorative applications as flooring, fishing lures, musical instruments, and wall murals.

Aqua Blue Maui, of Kula, Hawaii, has been supplying this material for about ten years. The company can color or dye the abalone veneer in more than 500 shades. Several dozen colors are currently available with the abalone mother-of-pearl appearance.

While the material is very thin, it is still somewhat brittle and must be carefully cut to size to wrap around a rod and secure it in place. Use very sharp scissors, a guillotine-style paper cutter, or a laser cutter such as used in a trophy or awards shop. The cost of this latter cutting option might be a bit steep. Scissors can be used, but the blades will dull rapidly.

Once cut to size to fit evenly around a rod, the veneer has to be treated to make it slightly flexible. In his original *RodMaker* article on the topic, Knox suggests soaking the veneer in a bath of distilled white vinegar for several hours and then removing the veneer and discarding the vinegar (do not use again). To remove any build up of calcium on the veneer, lay the prepared sheet on a paper towel and rub the surface with denatured alcohol. Once the veneer is clean, carefully place it on the rod, making sure the adhesive backing is in proper alignment. Once you begin to place the veneer in position, you will not be able to move or adjust it. To secure the abalone on the rod, wrap it temporarily but completely with a heavy (D or E) thread wrap to "clamp" the abalone in place and allow it to cement to the rod securely.

While Knox provided the above instructions for applying raw abalone veneer, he suggested that the Aqua Blue Maui ThinLam veneer be soaked in distilled white vinegar for three days and then dipped in boiling water to make the laminate as flexible as possible.

In a subsequent *RodMaker* article (volume 12, issue 6), Knox suggested a simpler way of processing the abalone for rod building: Boil the ThinLam abalone veneer for 10 minutes in distilled white vinegar. Remove the pan and veneer from the stove and allow to cool enough to handle. Remove the backing, wrap the abalone around the rod, and then clamp as above with a wrap of thread.

Once the veneer is at this point—regardless of the raw or ThinLam abalone used—remove the clamping thread. Using sanding boards or a scraper, remove and sand any excess adhesive that might have oozed out. Add a final wrap of thread at each end of the abalone, then coat with a rod wrap finish, and place on a curing motor for 24 hours. Remove the rod, flex it (this will produce some hairline cracks that will not be noticeable), and then finish with final coating of rod finish.

Scotty Ventura of Aqua Blue Maui says an even better and simpler version of his company's abalone veneer is now available and is easier to work with than the original material.

The Flex Pearl abalone is far more flexible and, when prepared properly, can be wrapped easily around a rod blank no thicker than ¼ inch. The Flex Pearl comes in many colors and is available in the standard 9½ × 5½-inch sheets. To make the material a little more flexible, place the desired sheet or cut size in a water bath and place it in a microwave for 3 to 5 minutes. This will warm the sheet and make it easy to apply to any rod. The material has a 3M adhesive on the back, protected with a peel-off backing sheet. Soak and microwave it with the backing sheet in place, and then remove the backing as you place the Flex Pearl onto the rod.

Knox uses this process and product only and has an article on the product's use and preparation in *RodMaker*, volume 14, issue 4.

Most anglers rim such decoration with a decorative wrap at each end of the abalone addition. This can be a simple wrap started on the blank and wrapped up over the abalone, or it can be a longer—but still short—chevron or diamond wrap. Knox adds a simple thin diamond that goes over the entire abalone decoration. Almost all the abalone shows, since the wrap is thin, with only a few crossing threads to form a minimal diamond.

Note that the use of abalone or other shell materials by rod or lure makers does *not* require sanding or grinding. You need only cut the shell material to size and shape. Grinding or sanding this material can be highly dangerous, creating fine abalone or shell dust that, according to Ventura, is more dangerous than asbestos. The calcium carbonate that results from grinding shells is a strong lung irritant and can also trigger allergic and asthmatic attacks. If you must grind or sand abalone or any other shell, protect yourself by wearing a NIOSH-approved N95 respiratory mask.

For more details on this material and how to use it, contact Kevin Knox or purchase the relevant issues of *RodMaker* magazine: volume 11, issue 5; volume 12, issue 6; and volume 14, issue 4.

A simple and bare-bones way to add decoration to the butt section of any rod (usually just above the foregrip) is to use readymade decals. These are available from most of the catalog companies, including Mud Hole, Jann's NetCraft, Merrick, and Angler's Workshop. Available decals include dozens of species of fish and fish shapes in laser-cut abalone. Mud Hole carries more than fifty fish shapes alone. Some companies, including Mud Hole, carry stickers for mermaids, U.S. and other national flags, state flags, military insignias, and even college logos.

These decals are added to rods using standard decaling methods and then coated with a clear rod finish.

Some rod builders think the idea of adding feathers, coated with a clear finish, is new. I have seen rods from the 1940s and earlier that incorporated the same idea. Most of these earlier rods were fly rods and often incorporated only jungle cock feathers, usually one, two, or three of them. These feathers were and remain popular; they are a standard finishing feather for trout streamer flies and are particularly appropriate for fly rods. Today some rod builders are placing jungle cock feathers over guinea fowl or other feathers or making up combinations and designs of feathers for decoration just above the grip of a rod. The easy way to do this is to coat the rod area with a clear finish, add the feathers and adjust their position, and then place the rod onto a drying motor overnight. Finish with a final clear coat, allowing it to cure on a drying motor. With care you may be able to do this in one coat of finish—adding the finish, then placing the feathers, and then brushing over the area carefully with an epoxy-coated brush.

A tradition among rod builders—particularly fly-rod builders—is to include a jungle cock or other feather as part of the decoration, just above the grip. This rod has a design of four feathers, but many variations of design and feather type are possible.

HYDROGRAPHIC PRINTING

Hydrographic printing, or hydropainting, is another way to dress up a rod. It's a process by which any design printed on a special film can be transferred to any object, regardless of the shape or size of the object. Guns, for example, are often printed in a camouflage design. This process alone can cost up to $200 or more for a rifle or shotgun.

The process is obviously less expensive for fishing rods, but it is still expensive. It involves purchasing the chosen printing film and also the activator spray solution that allows the printed design to be transferred to the rod blank.

An article in *RodMaker* (volume 14, issue 1) by editor Tom Kirkman outlines the process. The process was first described by J. P. Timberlake, who, along with Tom Kirkman, has done seminars on the process at various rod-building shows.

Basically this is a process in which print on a thin film is floated on water, the film dissipated with a solvent, and an object dipped into the water to which the printing adheres. The film for making patterns on rods comes in hundreds of different patterns, available in a minimum of 1 square yard. An activator is needed to dissolve the printed film when it floats on a bath of water. When dissolved, only the print remains, which then adheres to the object being coated or printed.

Kits are available with different print films and include the spray-on activator. You will need a face mask, latex or nitrile gloves, a dipping tank, the activator or a spraying process, a base or primer coat, the hydro film, and a spray-on top protective coat.

Although specialized tanks are available, a good substitute is one or more wallpaper wetting tanks. These can be bought at paint and wallpaper stores and are lightweight, disposable, and inexpensive. Cut off one end each from two of the tanks and tape (duct tape) or glue (silicone sealant) them together to make a tank long enough for a rod. Cut both ends off the center tank if you are using three tanks for a very long rod.

Prepare the rod blank using a citrus-based paint remover to remove the paint. Wash the blank with water, and scrub the finish with a fine gray Scotch-Brite pad to ensure a "water break free" surface.

Paint the rod blank with a base coat of enamel or the paint provided in a hydrographic kit. Most hydrographic films have a clear base, so you will want a base coat color that contrasts with the pattern of the hydro print film.

Once the paint is dry and cured, you are ready to create the hydrographic pattern on your rod. Half fill the dipping tank with warm water of about 75 to 85 degrees Fahrenheit. Since you only need enough film to cover a rod, strips of about 4 inches wide are ideal. After cutting, cover the edges with masking tape to create a "frame." Holding the frame by the ends, touch the belly of the film to the water and slowly lower the film onto the water.

Kirkman notes that the film must be added to the water with the right side up. To test this, he recommends wetting your thumb and forefinger and touching a corner of the film for 30 seconds. Release the film and one side of it will stick to your skin. The side of the film that sticks to your finger goes *down* onto the water's surface.

Spray activator over the film to remove it and leave the print floating on the surface. This activator often comes with a hydrographic printing kit, or an activator (check with the film manufacturer on this) can be added to a Preval aerosol sprayer, available at hobby shops. Be sure to wear your face mask and goggles while doing this.

Once you start to spray, timing is critical as to when you dip the rod blank into the water. Allow about 1 minute for the film to disperse, and then dip the rod blank. If you wait too long, the film pattern will begin to disperse, making for an indistinct pattern. Once the activator removes the film, dip the rod. The best way to do this, says Kirkman, is to hold the rod at both ends and, keeping the rod parallel to the water surface, touch the rod to the water and roll the rod along the floating film. Keep the rod blank underwater, and swish it around to help "set" the film onto the rod blank.

Continue swishing the blank around for 30 seconds and then remove it from the water bath. Once the blank is completely dry, add an aerosol finish (which may be supplied in the hydrographic printing kit). If you plan to use a finish other than that provided or suggested by a hydrographics company, prepare a small scrap blank and try the finish first to be sure you do not get an adverse reaction. Do not use an epoxy thread wrap finish; it is not designed for this and is too heavy for coating on an entire blank.

You can also hydropaint other components such as reel seats, metal or plastic butt caps, aluminum rod handles, and carbon skin foam handles. You could probably hydropaint other rod parts as well, but adhesion of the print and the firmness of the material would probably govern the longevity of the hydrographic pattern. If you plan on dipping a reel seat or other item, you must have a hanger to hold it as you dip and the film encircles the product. These can jerry-rigged, with coat-hanger wire being a top contender for a temporary holder when dipping.

Hydrographics kits suggested by Kirkman include those available from www.mydipkit.com, with films available from www.alsacorp.com and www.liquidconcepts.com.

CRAQUELE PAINTING OF ROD BLANKS

Craquele is a method of creating a cracked or crazed finish on a rod blank. It can be done on only the butt end of the rod at the finishing stage of rod making or on the entire rod blank before the additions to the rod (handle, reel seat, guides, guide raps, tip-top, etc.) are added. To avoid problems, this technique is usually best used only on the butt of the rod and after the rod is finished, with the handle, reel seat, butt cap, and guides/guide wraps already added.

Basically it involves using a "craquele" type of painting technique using products found in craft and art stores. The result is a cracked or crazed finish to the rod that is both different and attractive. It is not unlike the cracked or crazed finish used on lures several decades ago.

This is a painting technique in which the rod or rod section (usually the base or butt of the rod blank) is first painted with a base coat of paint of any type. For the best and most striking results, this base paint color should be a marked contrast with the external coat to be added, which will crack or craze to expose the underlying base coat color. Thus a light blue–dark blue or orange-red combination will not show up as well as a black-white, red-white, or blue-white combination.

Begin the process by wrapping with tape, or tape and plastic, any part of the rod and all the handle assembly that you do not want affected. Clean the base application area with alcohol and then sand lightly with fine-grit sandpaper or Scotch-Brite. Dust the area, and then apply a base coat of paint. Spray paints, such as durable automotive colors, work best. Allow the spray paint to cure overnight, and then apply by soft brush the craquele varnish from the craquele kit. Follow the kit directions to allow the varnish to cure or dry (usually about 90 minutes) before adding a thin coat of the finish paint. This paint is designed to react with the base coat and separate out and craze. Airbrush application is best here. Note that you can adjust the type of appearance you want. A thick, heavy coat results in fewer but wider cracks. A thin coat creates more and finer cracks. Finally, after the paint has cured (about 3 hours), apply a coat of a light epoxy rod finish to protect the finish.

In addition to kits available from craft and art stores, you can also use a nail polish available from Sally Hansen. The result is the same, with a crackled topcoat and a contrasting-color base coat showing through. This "Crackle" nail polish, available at any drug or variety store, is easy to use on small portions of rod blanks.

To use this product, first create a base coat or undercoat with a standard nail polish. Once this base coat is cured and dry, paint the Crackle polish over the top. As this cures and dries, it will crack to show the undercoat polish, with the same results as the paints in craft kits. You can use a clear rod-building epoxy finish or a clear nail polish on top of this for protection. If using anything other than a finish by the nail-polish manufacturer, check first on scrap material to make sure the dissimilar finishes do not react with each other.

More information on this technique can be found in the article "Craquele!" by Marco Antonio da Silva (*RodMaker* magazine, volume 14, issue 1).

COLOR PRESERVER: PROS AND CONS

Color preserver has both fans and critics. On the plus side, color preserver is designed to do exactly what it says—preserve and maintain the color of the thread wrap. One or two coats of color preserver on a rod wrap will do this, even though the wrap will turn darker when it's wet. When the color preserver dries, the wrap will return to its original color.

Another plus is that the use of color preserver will help in removal of the thread wrap, should this be necessary. The color preserver prevents penetration of the epoxy into and through the wrap to bind the thread to the rod, making removal easier. Color preserver does help in cementing the thread wrap to the blank, although not as securely as does epoxy finish. In this respect color preserver helps in fancy thread work—it will bind the wrap to the rod and thus prevent threads getting moved or jostled out of position before the epoxy finish coat is added.

Color preserver also soaks into the thread and dispels air bubbles from the wrap, making it easier to get a perfect finish without a haze of bubbles in the epoxy finish. By soaking into and coating the thread, color preserver provides a smooth base on which to add rod finish, unlike the spongelike base of untreated thread wraps.

Detractors of color preserver correctly say that color preserver will prevent the penetration of the rod finish (usually epoxy) into the thread and that this penetration of the epoxy rod finish into the thread to bind the wrap to the rod blank and protect and coat the surface is what is important. In essence, without color preserver the rod finish glues the wrap to the blank as well as coating and protecting it. Critics of color preserver feel—probably rightly from a technical standpoint—that the lack of color preserver makes for a stronger, more durable wrap and finish. Countering this is the fact that even the finest threads are plenty strong (2.8 pounds break strength in size A Gudebrod) when formed into a tight wrap.

There is a reason for using color preserver: Lack of it will result in permanent thread-color changes when varnish or epoxy finish is applied. In most cases dark-color threads (blue, red, green, purple, brown) will become darker than the original color, while lighter color threads (white, yellow, goldenrod, pink, orange, light blue) will become lighter in color. And all thread will become translucent, allowing a partial show-through of the guide foot. In some cases this is not bad, and some rod builders deliberately omit color preserver to get this effect. For example, among traditionalist fly-rod builders some years ago, and even with some companies and custom builders today, color preserver is omitted and the bright feet of the snake guides and matching stripper guides are allowed to show through the wraps. It does look funny, though, on black frame guides in which the end of the guide foot has been polished or filed to a knife edge for a smooth transition of the thread from the blank onto the guide foot. One solution is to use only bright finish guides or to color the filed end of the guide foot with a permanent felt-tip marker. Allow this coating to dry completely before wrapping the guide in place.

APPLYING COLOR PRESERVER

Color preserver comes in two styles: water based and chemical solvent based. At one time most color preservers were solvent based, but the water-based styles are becoming more popular. If there is one key to using color preservers, which must be covered with a rod finish, it is to stick with the same brand for both products or to be *sure* the two products are compatible. For example, Flex Coat cautions against using a lacquer color preserver under its Flex Coat Rod Finish; U-40 ColorLok can be used under its urethane one-part Perma Gloss rod finish and Dura Gloss epoxy resin finish; Gudebrod Color Preserver can be used under its Hard 'N Fast II or Speed Coat Rod Finish; and Gudebrod's Speed Coat Color Preserver and Sealer can be used under its Speed Coat Rod Finish or Rod Varnish. The lesson here is to follow the manufacturer's directions for application and compatibility of products. No manufacturer is going to recommend using another brand with its products, but such combinations often work. If you wish to try, conduct compatibility experiments first with a simple wrap on a scrap piece of rod blank.

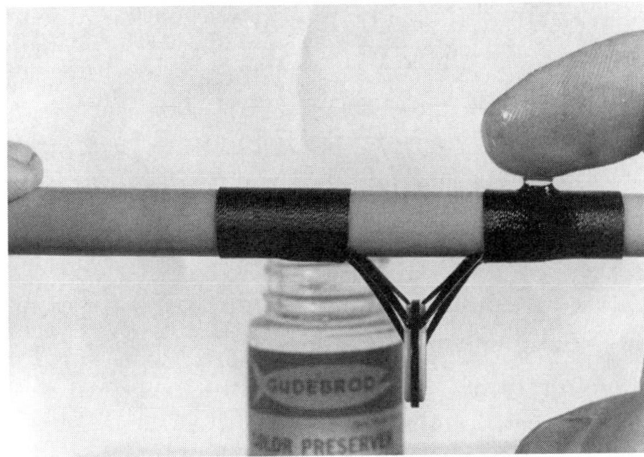

Using color preserver. Solvent color preserver can be added with a fingertip as shown here. Avoid too much contact with the solvent.

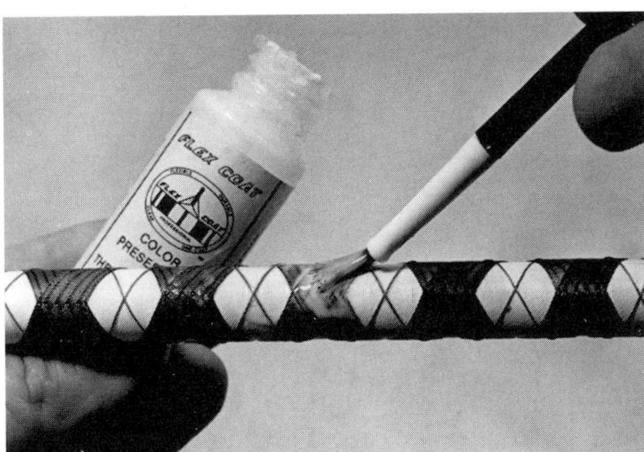

Using a brush to apply water-based color preserver. This white color preserver will dry clear, but it must be blotted after allowing it to soak into the wrap.

There are different ways to apply color preserver. Often the best, neatest, and cleanest method is to use a brush, mix the color preserver well if required (it sometimes is with the water-based preservers), and then liberally coat the rod wrap with the color preserver. To keep the color preserver from building up and causing blushing or mottling of the wrap when the finishing coat is applied, blot off any excess with a paper towel. Blot—don't rub. Rubbing may move some of the threads (particularly with decorative wraps), and some of the towel might rub off onto the wrap and into the color preserver.

Follow manufacturer's directions for how much preserver to apply. Some suggest one coat, others two coats; some even suggest three coats for heavy threads. Some manufacturers suggest using one coat as a protective measure, even when using NCP thread, and two coats for regular thread.

Other debates concern the use of color preserver: how much and when, and when to apply on underwraps and double and triple wraps. One method is to complete the entire wrapping process and then add several coats of color preserver, allowing each coat to be absorbed before adding the next. Often it is best to wait at least an hour for the water-based color preservers and overnight for the solvent-based types. One key, especially for the solvent types, is to smell the color preserver. When there is no smell, it means the color preserver has cured or all the solvent has evaporated.

When creating several layers of wrapping, make the underwrap and then apply one or two coats of color preserver, allowing it to cure completely before adding the guide and wrapping it in place. Then the guide wrap (single, double, or triple wrap) can be protected with color preserver and later coated with rod finish. This same technique can be used with decorative wraps: First coat the underwrap and allow it to cure, then add the decorative wrap, coat it with color preserver again, and finally add the finish coat.

An alternative is to leave the color preserver off the guide wrap (after adding it to the underwrap) and coat only with rod finish. This allows for color protection of the underwrap and easy removal of the wrap, should it be necessary, while also providing for the durability and extra strength of the bond on the overwrap and slight translucency in the colors.

Once the final coat of color preserver has been added, wait 24 hours to be sure of complete curing before adding the final rod finish. If you use water-based color preservers, the time to clean up the brushes is immediately after finishing wrap coatings. Wash them thoroughly to remove all color preserver, and then rinse the brush and allow it to dry. I even do this with so-called disposable brushes with no problems.

MIXING ROD FINISHES

Some rod finishes do not require mixing. Rod varnish and some one-part finishes are ready to use from the bottle. Examples are U-40 Perma Gloss, Gudebrod Rod Varnish, and Gudebrod Speed Coat Rod Finish. Usually these are not epoxy; the U-40 Perma Gloss is described as being a nonyellowing, flexible, noncracking, thin-coat aliphatic urethane polymer.

Other finishes (usually epoxy) are in two parts that must be mixed. These include Gudebrod Hard 'N Fast II, Flex Coat Polymer Rod Finish, Flex Coat Lite Rod Finish, and U-40 Dura Gloss. Fortunately most of these two-part mixes use a cap-coding systems to prevent placing the wrong cap on the wrong bottle, a situation that could cause contamination and hardening/curing of the bottle contents.

All the two-part mixes I know of for custom-rod builders are a 1:1 mix, which makes for easy mixing. There are two ways of mixing these finishes. One is to use small mixing cups; the other is to use syringes. The syringes are best for very small amounts of finish; mixing cups that hold an ounce or more are best for larger quantities of finish.

It should be noted here that some rod builders have advised against using plastic in any mixing process for epoxies. This would include mixing cups, syringes, working surfaces, and nylon- or plastic-bristle brushes. Although it is a good practice not to use odd or offbeat plastic products in the mixing process, I have never had a problem using plastic, provided that I apply common sense. I use medical mixing cups, medical syringes (sold by Flex Coat with no silicone lubricants), nylon-bristle brushes, disposable brushes, sometimes plastic brush handles for mixing sticks, and plastic coffee lids and plastic mixing surfaces cut from drink and milk containers. In fact, many finish manufacturers use plastic and sell plastic products for use with their epoxy or other rod-finish resins. Gudebrod offers nylon-bristle brushes; Flex Coat has plastic brushes, mixing cups, and non-silicone syringes; and U-40 has plastic mixing syringes.

One key to using any solution is to keep it warm. An easy way to do this is to place the bottles into a pan of hot water for about 15 minutes, checking the temperature from time to time. Other possibilities include using a hair dryer or an incandescent lightbulb or placing the solutions in the sun on a warm summer day. Just a hand check for temperature will do—you don't need a thermometer. Warmer temperatures make the solutions more fluid and thus aid in pouring and mixing. Other advantages are that the hotter fluids will help dissipate any bubbles that form, and heated finish will soak better into wraps to protect them. Flex Coat recommends at least 75 degrees Fahrenheit for its rod finishes, with an ideal of about 80 to 90 degrees.

The best way to add epoxy to a mixing cup is to hold the cup level with your eye against a light background that allows you to clearly see the measurement markings. Then add one of the two solutions to the mixing cup until it reaches the mark indicating one-half the total amount needed. Roger Seiders of Flex Coat recommends first adding Part B to the cup and then adding Part A. Part A is heavier, so it will tend to sink and thus mix better with the Part B already in the cup.

Two-part epoxy finishes require a mixing cup, as shown, for accurate measuring and mixing.

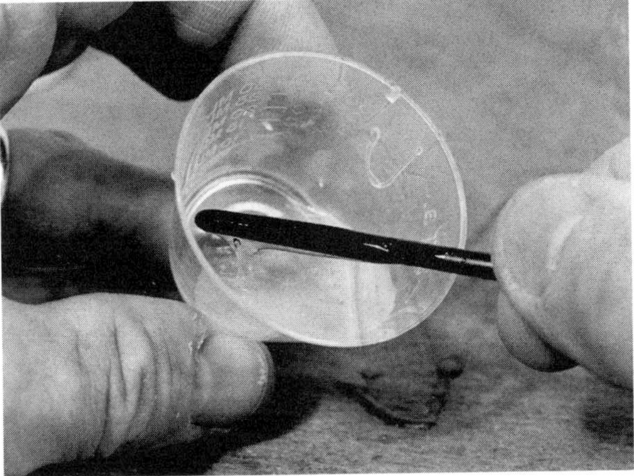
Thorough mixing of all epoxy is necessary to assure a good finish. Avoid whipping the finish, which will add bubbles that must be removed later.

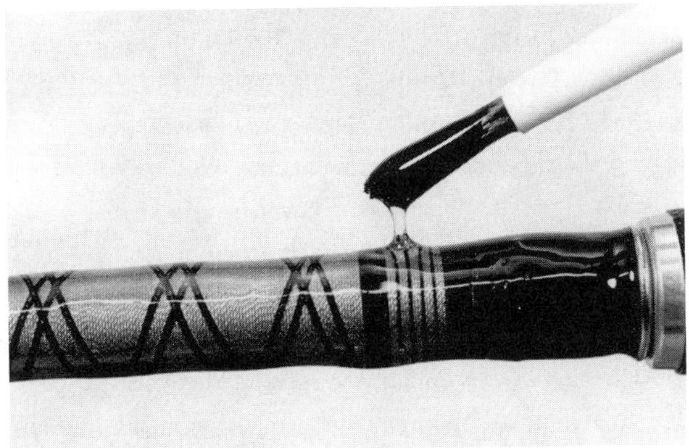
Adding two-part epoxy to a decorative wrap. When wet the finish will be very shiny, and a bright light will help to show any gaps, bubbles, or missed spots.

Make sure you add the liquid to the center of the mixing cup and that none splashes on the sides of the cup above the marks, since this will make the mix inaccurate. Also make sure you pour slowly, because thick viscous liquids often require a little time to self-level for accurate measurement. Once the first solution is added, close the bottle, open the second bottle, and add that liquid until the full measure is reached. Close this bottle before mixing the solution.

There are varying theories as to mixing. Seiders likes a rounded stick for mixing, arguing that the round stick is less likely to create bubbles, which must be removed at some time in the future. I like flat sticks, such as some craft sticks, that allow folding of the mix onto itself and a thorough scraping of the sides and bottom of the mixing cup to assure that all of the solution is completely mixed. Small, flat craft sticks and kitchen skewers are ideal. Some of the stiff little plastic coffee stirrers are also ideal because they are flattened but with rounded edges. They are available everywhere and are disposable.

Obviously a disposable mixing stick is best, as are disposable mixing cups. However, avoid using paper cups, waxed cups (the wax can come off and contaminate the mix), and aluminum foil (some recommend it, and it is disposable, but I find it difficult to mix in without tearing or puncturing). Also, epoxies can dissolve some food service disposable cups.

Mixing with syringes is easy, because two identical syringes are used to pull up identical amounts of the respective resin and hardener or catalyst. But be careful. According to Seiders, silicone and epoxy will not mix, and medical syringes available at drugstores often have a silicone coating. These cannot be used with epoxy—at least not with Flex Coat. Flex Coat syringes do not contain silicone lubricant.

Once the syringes are filled with the right amounts of solution, slowly discharge the contents into a mixing cup. An alternative is to spread the liquid on a flat mixing surface, but this often makes mixing more difficult.

Note: Don't try to clean the empty syringes. Keep them separate and marked (if they are not already color-coded) for use the next time. Do not allow the tips to touch, because the two solutions will mix slightly and "glue" the syringes together or contaminate them.

To mix the solution, use the mixing sticks of your choice to fold and stir. Do not beat the solutions into a lather, which will create bubbles in the mix that may be difficult to remove later.

At first the solution formed with most brands will become cloudy, and often you can see the combining of the two parts as they begin to mix. Sometimes streaks form at this stage. Ultimately the solution will become completely mixed and turn clear. In all parts of the mixing, make sure that you fold the mix over and over, side to side and top to bottom, and that you scrape the sides completely as you fold. This assures a good mix.

You will need a flat surface on which to pour the rod finish once it is mixed. Ideal surfaces include scraps of paper, glossy cardboard stock (like poster cardboard—not skirt cardboard that might fray and contaminate the mix), aluminum foil (though I don't like it because it has a tendency to tear), or plastic sheets. I like plastic surfaces best because they can be bent in order to pop off the dried mix and used repeatedly. Good sources are well-cleaned plastic surfaces from juice, milk, drink, and food containers. I use milk containers, cutting out the sides and bottoms and stacking several for use when needed. The thin sides are ideal for rod finish, the thicker and tougher bottoms for rod glues.

PacBay sells an automatic epoxy mixer that consists of a slow (24 rpm) A/C motor and angled stand that will hold a standard 2½-ounce mixing cup. It also includes a stainless steel mixing rod/ball that rolls around the base edge of the cup while the motor turns the cup to mix the epoxy. This mixes any two-part epoxy in a few minutes.

As soon as the finish is completely mixed, pour and scrape the complete solution onto the flat surface. This accomplishes several things. First it prevents the mix from curing too rapidly. As you end the mixing process and hold the cup, you may feel some buildup of heat. This is a result of the solution being in a confined space and indicates the catalyst is reacting with the resin and beginning to cure the mix. Pouring the solution out on a flat surface will slow this reaction and allow you a reasonable working time. Also, pouring the solution out onto a flat surface makes for a much shorter distance that any bubbles will have to travel upward to get out of the mix—and you must remove the bubbles to keep them from getting into the finish of the rod.

Another way to further slow the curing process (and extend the solution's working life) is to place the flat surface on a tray of ice cubes to cool it. This extends the solution's working life longer than the typical 30 minutes of most standard mixes.

An added advantage to pouring the mix on a flat surface is that it will then be easy to accomplish one of the methods of removing bubbles: exhaling onto the mix. As you do this you can see bubbles rapidly popping to the surface. Theories on this are that the dispelled bubbles are caused either by the carbon dioxide, the moisture, or the warmth of your breath.

Another way to remove air bubbles is to use a hair dryer. Even though it's often recommended, I don't like this method because a hair dryer blows air, and air contains dust. I don't want to blow dust into my finish before it goes on a rod (or after it is on the rod but not yet cured, for that matter). Another method is to use a flame, because the heat of an alcohol lamp or propane or butane torch will cause bubbles to escape. This works great, but I don't like the idea of an open flame around epoxies. Use extreme care if you use this method, and move the flame constantly to avoid potentially dangerous heat buildup. Breathing on the mix and stabbing the occasional large stubborn bubble with a bodkin seems to work fine for me.

APPLYING ROD FINISHES

Once the solution is completely mixed and free of bubbles, it is ready for applying to the rod wraps. For this you will need a good-quality brush or a disposable one. Whatever kind you use, make sure it doesn't shed bristles when being used. If it does, you'll have to pick the bristles out of the mix; even worse, they might dry in the mix if not detected in time. A number of companies, such as Gudebrod and Flex Coat, have good brushes (ox hair and disposable brushes from Gudebrod, disposable from Flex Coat). Suitable brushes are available from craft stores, art supply stores, and hobby shops.

Before beginning, make sure the rod is on a rack that is ready to be attached or plugged into a slow-rpm curing motor. Some companies make motors just for this purpose, or you can use any low-rpm motor provided you can jerry-rig it to hold the rod. Good ways to do this include using different sizes of butt caps or crutch tips to hold the rod butt or using a 2-inch-diameter PVC cap with thumbscrews tapped (a ¼-20 tap and thumbscrew works well) into the edges and set equally around the perimeter to grip the rod butt. Both connectors must be attached to the motor shaft, and the best system uses a small coupling or a threaded rod coupler as required. Often some imagination is

Commercial rod turner for turning a rod slowly while the thread finish is curing. This model uses three neoprene O-rings to create tension in the middle hole to hold the rod gently for slow turning. This design can also be made at home using a plumbing PVC end cap with screws to hold the O-rings and with the cap mounted on a slow-rpm motor.

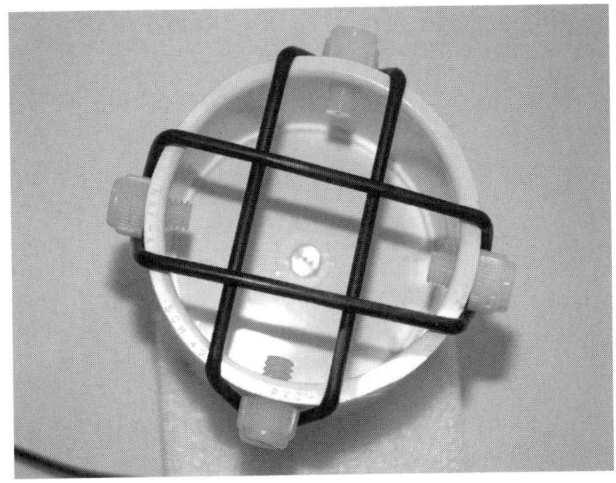

Same as bottom left, using two O-rings to create a square hole to hold a rod butt or blank while slowly turning it to allow the rod finish to cure without sagging. This is commercial, but a similar one can be made using a PVC end cap, O-rings, and screws.

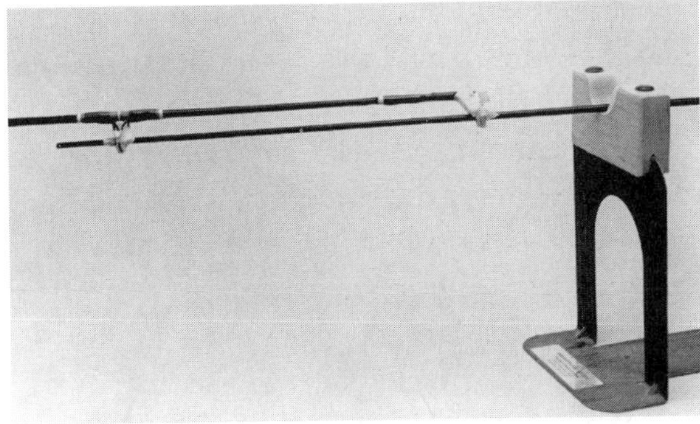

When an entire rod is finished or refinished, sometimes the tip section cannot ride on a support. For this an additional dowel or blank, stuck through and taped to the guides, will allow turning the rod without making contact with the rod.

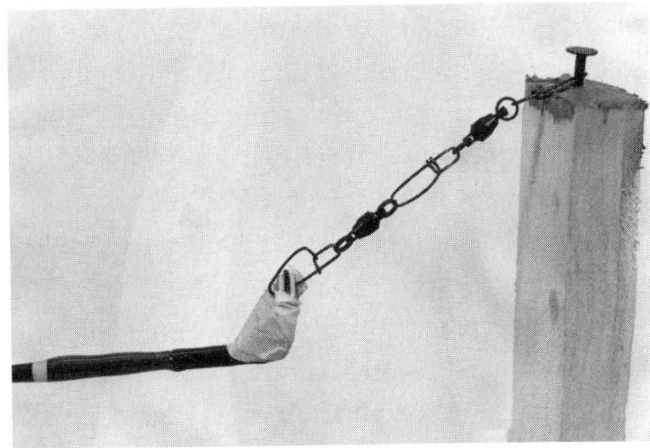

An alternative to the above is to use several swivels (preferably ball-bearing) and a snap to attach the rod tip-top to a vertical stand for complete turning without rod contact.

required for this. Good motors are A/C although, if you don't mind the expense of batteries, D/C hobby motors are also available. Make sure the motor is sufficiently powerful to turn the largest rod you wish to make. A good speed for such motors is about 10 rpm, although anything from 1 to about 60 rpm will work. Commercial manufacturers use motors that turn multiple rods at about 200 rpm.

Begin by dipping the brush into the epoxy, taking care to avoid creating more bubbles with the bristles. Load the brush well. Then add the epoxy to the rod wraps while rotating the rod. Begin with a band of epoxy around the outside edge of each wrap. This band of epoxy should cover the wrap and just barely overlap the edge so as to touch the blank and thus seal the wrap from the elements. Ideally the finish will completely coat the wrap so that there can be no intrusion of water or moisture. Pay particular attention to the area around the open gaps formed by the thread going over the guide feet. Try to fill these gaps with epoxy, and make sure this area has a complete seal of finish for complete protection. One way to do this is to push the brush bristles into the small tunnel formed by the thread wrap bridging from the guide foot to the rod blank.

Once this is done, continue adding finish to the wraps as needed until you fill in the entire area between the two "bands" of finish first applied. This allows you to completely fill in each wrap as you rotate the rod after you've made sure the bands around the end seal the rod wrap. Be certain to add equal amounts of finish to each wrap, based on the surface area of the wrap. You want an even thickness of finish so that more finish will be added to a wrap on the butt guide, which has more surface area, than to the wrap at the tip end of the rod.

Make sure the finish is evenly spread around the blank and from one end of the wrap to the other. Failure to do this can produce a wrap finish that looks slightly pregnant. To avoid this, after brushing around the blank, brush along the axis of the rod to even out finish buildup in any one area.

Because the finish will begin getting slightly stiffer as you add it to the blank (though in most cases this will be almost unnoticeable), I find it best to begin adding finish to the tip end of the rod and then work down to the butt guides and finally to the decorative wraps just above the handle. That way, if the finish does begin to stiffen, it will be on the heavier butt end, where it is easier to spread rapidly with broad strokes. Be sure to cover all wraps—not just guide wraps but also the wraps at the tip-top, ferrules, or hook-keeper, as well as decorative wraps and wraps bracketing inscriptions.

For best results rotate the rod as you work (this will be necessary anyway to get the finish on all parts of each wrap) to keep the finish from sagging and beginning to drip. Once you are through, you can place the rod on the curing motor if the rpm's are slow enough, or stop the curing motor and closely examine each wrap under the glare of a strong light. The strong light makes it possible for you to detect any gaps in the finish. When you spot these areas, add finish and brush it out to blend with the existing finish. Check each wrap several times with the light to ensure that there are no gaps.

Then place the rod on the curing motor and allow it to cure for several hours. In most cases the rod will cure enough to allow you to stop the motor in about three or four hours, but be sure to check the manufacturer's directions for details. If you don't have a completely dust-free environment in which to cure the rod, use a drying box. This can be nothing more than a long cardboard box, or a couple of boxes with the ends mostly cut out, that completely covers the curing part of the rod. You do not have to cover the curing motor or the rod-handle section.

Other suggestions are to finish rods late at night when house traffic is lowest and when pets and children are not around. Make sure you have enough humidity (you can spray the area with a water mister before curing any rods).

If you do not have a curing motor, sometimes you can jerry-rig something from A/C rotisserie motors that come with barbecue grills. Most of these motors turn at about 10 rpm and are ideal for curing rods. If you don't have a motor, you can hand-turn the rod, but continuous hand-turning gets old in a hurry. One solution is to hand-turn the rod about 90 degrees every 5 minutes for the first 20 minutes and then about every 15 minutes for the next 2 hours. A good way to do this is to watch a miniseries on TV and turn the rod each time there is a commercial break. Often you can judge the amount of turning needed by the tendency of the finish to sag between turns. Exact figures can't be given because of the many variables, including brand of finish, epoxy, or urethane; ambient temperature; humidity; and the amount of finish on each wrap.

In some cases one coat of epoxy rod finish is enough. With other finishes and other rods, you may want to add two or three coats. If this is the case, repeat the mixing and adding of finish after allowing the previous coat to cure for 24 hours. Often the lighter finishes used on fly or light spinning rods require only one coat, but any coating applied should lightly but completely cover each thread wrap.

Not all finishes are two-part formulas. Gudebrod Speed Coat Rod Finish and U-40 Perma Gloss are one-part finishes; other than the mixing process, they are applied just as the previously outlined steps indicate. Because these finishes are often thinner, you may need more than the one coat that is often enough with epoxy finishes. For example, U-40 recommends using two coats of a Perma Gloss over two coats of its ColorLok size A thread and two or three coats of ColorLok followed by four coats of Perma Gloss on size E thread wraps. Most of these finishes also cure and dry quicker; Perma Gloss is tack-free in 30 minutes, and Gudebrod Speed Coat Rod Finish sets up in 1 hour. Both finishes require additional time to cure completely.

UNUSUAL FINISHING TOUCHES FOR BLANKS AND RODS

Marbling

This is a method by which swirls of color can be added to any rod blank or even to hard solid handles. Marbling cannot be added to soft foam grips but can be added to hard foam-core grips, cork, wood, and tubular Tennessee handles. It could be added to an entire rod blank, but the added weight of the necessary epoxy base and the pigments added would make for a sluggish, heavy rod when the trend today is toward lightweight rods and maximum sensitivity. It can be added as a small decorative touch just above the grip or foregrip and perhaps bracketed by bands of thread. Any marbling can be done over the bare material (rod blank or grip), or the material can be painted first to provide a base coat for the surface marbling coat.

You can marble over any base coat of a blank or painted grip or reel-seat insert. Just add pigment to the epoxy to be used, stir thoroughly, and then add to the desired surface. Once this is cured you can marble on top using a clear epoxy to which has been added a mix of pigment. Powdered automotive pigments are best and are available from Riley Rods or locally from an automotive parts distributor.

Mix up a small puddle of epoxy, and add the pigment. Several puddles of different colors (pigment) can be added this way, all at the same time. Spread these onto different parts of the base epoxy finish and swirl around as desired with a toothpick or spatula. Put the rod on a curing motor and allow to cure overnight.

Painting

Normally you would not paint a blank, although you might want to paint an area just above the grip to provide a base area of white or color for a particular finishing touch. This could be for a decorative wrap in which the blank shows through or as a base for giving information about the rod and owner, etc. One additional reason for painting an entire blank is for camouflage. While you can use hydropainting to get a paint screen in camouflage, you can also very simply paint the blank.

I did this for a completed trout rod, and it worked very well. From a hobby shop, I bought the flat finish paints used to paint small hobby military vehicles. Best were the foliage tones for a spring trout fishing rods, including matte-finish black, gray, brown, tan, light green, dark green, yellow, and dark yellow. Using a disposable brush at home, paint these randomly onto the blank to completely cover the blank, including the rod wraps. The result was not unlike the camouflage of hunter's clothing. Since the purpose was camouflage, I did not bother changing or cleaning the brush.

Decals

Decals can be put on rods and rod parts just as decals are added to car windows, bicycles, or anything else. To use the decal, cut it out (or away from other decals) and follow application directions. Usually this means soaking the decal in warm water and then sliding it off of the base and onto the rod or sticking the decal face down and then slowly removing the base sheet and carefully washing off any residue. Decals can be added quickly and easily anywhere on rod blanks. Decals of fish, college logos, military insignia, zodiac signs, mermaids, and national and state flags are all available through catalog houses such as Mud Hole and Merrick Tackle. To finish, once the decal is in place and dry, coat the decal with a clear epoxy rod finish of your choice.

Abalone

These 0.15-millimeter-thick strips of abalone in various colors and finishes are one of the latest things in rod building. Prepared properly, the abalone can be cut to shape and applied to rods, rod butt areas, handles, and reel-seat inserts. Abalone is sold in strips and sheets and can be cut and prepared by any rod builder.

Feather and Skin Inlays

Every few years the idea of a feather decoration or inlay on a rod just above the grip or in the reel seat or handle gets "reinvented." But it is an old idea. I have seen rods from the 1940s on which feathers were used—usually a jungle cock feather (popular in fly tying) glued and varnished (no epoxy back then) to the rod, usually a fly rod. This is still done today with fly-tying feathers of all types, either overlapping or in a design pattern. To do this, coat the rod area to receive the feather with epoxy rod finish, carefully lay the prepared feather in the spot, position and adjust the feather, add a thin coat of epoxy over the feather, and allow to cure.

The same technique can be used to add small sections of snakeskin to the rod for a patterned look. This is done the same way as adding the feather, or the snakeskin can be laid down and wrapped in place at each end with a thread band. Protect the snakeskin with a thin coat of clear rod-finish epoxy. If you do not have your own snakeskin, cobra, rattlesnake, and diamondback rattlesnake are all available from custom rod shops such as Mud Hole, Jann's Netcraft, and Merrick Tackle.

FINISHING PROBLEMS AND SOLUTIONS

Sometimes problems occur during the rod-finishing process. Some of these problems follow, along with possible causes and suggested solutions:

1. In some cases the finish will still be tacky even after it should be completely dry. Often this is caused by an inaccurate mix of two-part finishes so that the finish never really cures. If the tackiness is just borderline, a wait of a day or two can help, as can adding heat to help the finish cure. In other cases nothing can be done to dry the finish. One solution is to mix new finish and coat the rod a second time. Often this will solve the problem—but only if you make an accurate mix. One tendency (I did it once) is to figure that if the finish is not cured, it needs more hardener. So the second mix contains more hardener, which is exactly the wrong thing to do. Although many brands call one part of the mix "hardener," it is really a catalyst, and more of it will make the finish even stickier the next time. Mix the two parts exactly, and if you have to err, do so on the side of using slightly less hardener.

2. If the cured finish is smooth and hard in some areas and tacky in others, this indicates incomplete mixing. In other words, some parts of the epoxy were thoroughly mixed (and thus are hard and smooth) and other parts had too little resin or catalyst (and thus are still tacky). The solution here is to make up and measure accurately a new batch of finish, mix it thoroughly this time, and recoat the blank.

3. In some cases blotching or mottling of the rod wraps will occur. This can be caused by several things. One possibility is contamination of the wraps by oils from your skin, hand lotions, or various other substances that are passed from your hands to the wraps while you wrap the rod. To avoid this, clean your hands thoroughly before wrapping, or wear cotton gloves (available from photo stores, for handling negatives, or art stores) or rubber gloves (available from surgical-supply houses and some drugstores).

   Another possible cause is the use of too much color preserver and allowing it to puddle on the rod wrap. To avoid this, add a coat of color preserver and allow it to soak in completely then blot to remove the excess. Do this with each coat of color preserver added.

   A third possible cause of blotching is incompletely applying color preserver to the wraps so that some areas of the wrap receive more preserver than others, causing the underlying threads to react differently when coated with rod finish.

4. Sometimes finishes appear lumpy. Usually this is a result of the rod not being turned evenly enough after the finish was applied, resulting in some sagging, which then cures that way. The solution is to use a curing motor or to turn the rod more rapidly. Sagging can also be caused by adding too much finish to the wraps or by not smoothing the finish out completely. To solve this problem, use less finish and add several coats if necessary. Also, be sure to smooth out the finish with the brush. If the finish is excessively lumpy, use an emery board to sand down the high lumps and then recoat. Even though the sanded areas appear opaque and are not shiny, they will completely fill in with a new coat and any sanding will not show.

5. Bubbles on the surface or in the finish are another problem. As previously mentioned, this can be caused by not using a color preserver (which expels bubbles), by mixing the epoxy finish too rapidly, or by not expelling the bubbles by breathing on the finish before adding it to the rod. Once the finish is on the rod, a torch can be used, along with breathing, to expel bubbles when the finish is still wet and uncured.

6. Dimples on the surface are caused by large bubbles that escape to the surface and then break open. If this happens when the finish is close to setting up, the resulting dimple will not float out and become smooth. If you have a larger bubble that will not dissipate from your breathing on it, use a toothpick or bodkin to break the bubble; then use a finish-filled brush to flood this area and smooth it. If you notice this problem only after the finish is cured, roughen the area slightly with steel wool and recoat with a new batch of finish.

7. Some two-part epoxy finishes are too thick for light rods such as light fly rods and ultralight spinning rods. For this there are several solutions, although this is best recognized *before* adding the finish, to prevent having to cut off the wraps and rewrap. There is no easy way to remove the finish from a wrap. One possibility is to use some of the lighter finishes available. Flex Coat produces Flex Coat Lite for a thinner two-part epoxy finish on light rods; Gudebrod Speed Coat Rod Finish is a thinner one-part coating, as is U-40 Perma Gloss. Thinning thick finishes with a solvent (acetone for most epoxies, such as Flex Coat) is a possibility.

Although no manufacturer recommends this, try acetone in a ratio of 1 drop to 1 to 5 cubic centimeters of rod epoxy mix, but be sure to test first on a scrap wrap or blank to check for any adverse reactions or problems.

8. An oily or waxy appearance is often caused by high humidity. To prevent this in the first place, do not coat a rod under very high-humidity or low-temperature conditions. The ideal temperature is between 70 and 85 degrees Fahrenheit for most finishes. To solve this problem after it has occurred, you usually must apply a second coat of finish.

   If you notice this oily or waxy look on the finish while it is still wet, one suggested solution is to use a torch to heat the entire area, then wait 30 minutes and torch it again. The oily slick should disappear.

9. If you mixed up too much finish and don't want to waste it, try sealing it and storing it in the refrigerator. Often finish can be stored this way for about a week or more; frozen, it can be stored for a month or more. Obviously the refrigerated finish will require some warming or heating up before use. Some epoxy finishes cannot be frozen, so try a sample amount of thawed-out finish on a simple wrap on a scrap rod blank first.

26
Chopping Blanks and Making Ferrules

Introduction • Tools and Materials • Cutting Blanks: Purposes • Cutting Blanks: Methods • Measuring for Ferrules • Making Sleeve Ferrules • Making Spigot Ferrules • Reinforcing Ferrules • Seating Metal Ferrules • Wrapping Ferrules

Basic Safety Equipment

Safety goggles

Shop apron

Basic Tools

Fine-tooth (32 teeth per inch) hacksaw blade and handle or jeweler's saw

Triangular file

Centering miter box

Helpful Tools

Ruler

Calipers

Marking pen

INTRODUCTION

Most custom rods are built on blanks that are used the way the manufacturer supplies them. That's great, because rod and blank manufacturers try to build blanks that are designed for a specific purpose, fishing method, action, and power. It is to their advantage to have each of their blanks bought by as many anglers as possible.

There are good reasons for chopping blanks, however. In some cases you may want a shorter, heavier rod built from a blank that you have on hand, or you may want to modify a one-piece rod into a two-piece rod or a two-piece rod into a four-piece rod by ferruling, or you may need to remove a damaged or broken tip from an existing rod to rebuild the rod with a slightly shorter tip section.

In this context I am referring to making self-ferrules—ferrules of glass or graphite for glass or graphite rods. However, it is important to understand some of the basics of adding metal ferrules to blanks, even though this is rarely done today. Obviously there is no point in adding ferrules to a rod other than to make it easier to transport. Installing ferrules takes time, something manufacturers understand. Blank manufacturers often offer the same blank in one- and two-piece styles—the two-piece model is always more expensive. This is a reflection of the additional material and labor costs associated with two-piece blanks.

TOOLS AND MATERIALS

Tools for chopping and modifying blanks and making ferrules are relatively simple. The following tools are the only tools you'll really need:

A fine-tooth hacksaw blade or jeweler's saw. The only hacksaws or blades that should be considered for cutting blanks are those with 32 teeth to the inch. If I ever find a hacksaw blade with more teeth to the inch, I'll buy it, because it should be even better. For that reason jeweler's saws are even better, although they are harder to find. Some of the large major tool catalog houses carry jeweler's saws, although they are more expensive than standard hacksaws. The reason for the fine-tooth blade is that you want to cut through delicate material. When cutting any material, the larger the teeth of the saw, the more likely it is that those teeth will tear and splinter the longitudinal graphite material being cut. You obviously don't want to splinter the graphite or glass materials you are cutting. Thus a fine-tooth blade is a must.

Fine-tooth triangular file. This is really a substitute for the above, because blanks can be cut with either a saw or a file. The triangular file should also be fine-toothed so that you avoid tearing the material.

Centering miter box. This is a homemade mitering tool that will aid you if you frequently cut and modify blanks. It is nothing more than a wood miter box with a V shape, instead of a U or square shape, inside in order to center the blank for cutting. The easiest way to make one is to rip a 1-foot-long board in half lengthwise at a 45-degree angle, flip one piece end to end to make a V, and nail this securely to a second board. Then, using a right-angle square, cut through the top part of the miter box (the V part at right angles to the length of the board). The blank can be centered in the V and the hacksaw blade fitted into the slot to cut through the blank.

Masking tape. To prevent splintering, it helps to wrap several layers of masking tape around the blank where the cut is to be made.

Epoxy glue. You will need this for gluing ferrule parts to the rod, whether you use metal ferrules or make ferrules from rod-blank parts.

Sandpaper. A little fine sandpaper is handy for dressing and smoothing cut blanks and also for roughing the blank and ferrule surfaces that are to be glued together.

Scrap blanks. You will need some scrap blanks if you are making sleeve or spigot ferrules. Sources are broken rods that you or a buddy might have accumulated over the years and scraps from dealers, which are often available at no or low cost. These scraps must be about the same diameter as the blank you are planning to chop and ferrule.

CUTTING BLANKS: PURPOSES

You cut blanks for different purposes. In some cases cutting is necessary to finish a rod properly. For example, I have seen blanks that are rough at the tip and butt ends (more often at the butt end), a result of some of the rough blank materials being left on the rod when the mandrel is pulled out of the blank. In most cases this is easily trimmed by removing just a few inches of the rough area. Often this is extra length anyway—not really a part of the measured length of the rod blank—and thus there is no loss to the rod. Although this can happen on any rod, most manufacturers check carefully to prevent blanks with untrimmed ends from getting out of the factory. Although this can happen on any style of rod blank, I have seen it mostly on big surf rods and offshore trolling blanks.

Another reason for cutting blanks is to remove a broken tip if you lose a few inches due to a fishing mishap. By cutting the blank back, it is possible to salvage the rod. As an example, my longtime friend Norm Bartlett built a beautiful split-bamboo fly rod, splitting the culms himself and making the rod from scratch. It had one of the finest actions of any bamboo rod I've ever tried.

Unfortunately he lost a few inches off the tip end in a fishing accident. He cut down the rod, added a new tip-top, and went on to use the rod to take a new IGFA record on a two-pound test tippet for striped bass with a 6-pound, 11-ounce fish. The lost tip might have affected the rod aesthetically but not functionally.

You also would need to cut a rod blank when customizing a rod or blank to make it easier to pack. One-piece rods can be made into two or more pieces, two-piece rods can be made into four-piece pack rods, and so on. If you wish to keep all sections of a two- or three-piece rod the same length, you must end up with double the number of pieces you currently have. (Thus you would make a two-piece rod into a four-piece rod, although you could also make it into a six- or eight-piece rod if desired. A three-piece rod can be cut and made into a six-piece rod.) When starting with a two- or three-piece rod, you can't end up with a three-, five-, or seven-piece rod or some other odd number of pieces unless you plan on one section being longer than the others, which defeats one of the main purposes of ferruling.

An exception to this would be if you are working with a one-piece rod that you can cut into three, five, or seven pieces as easily as into two, four, or six pieces.

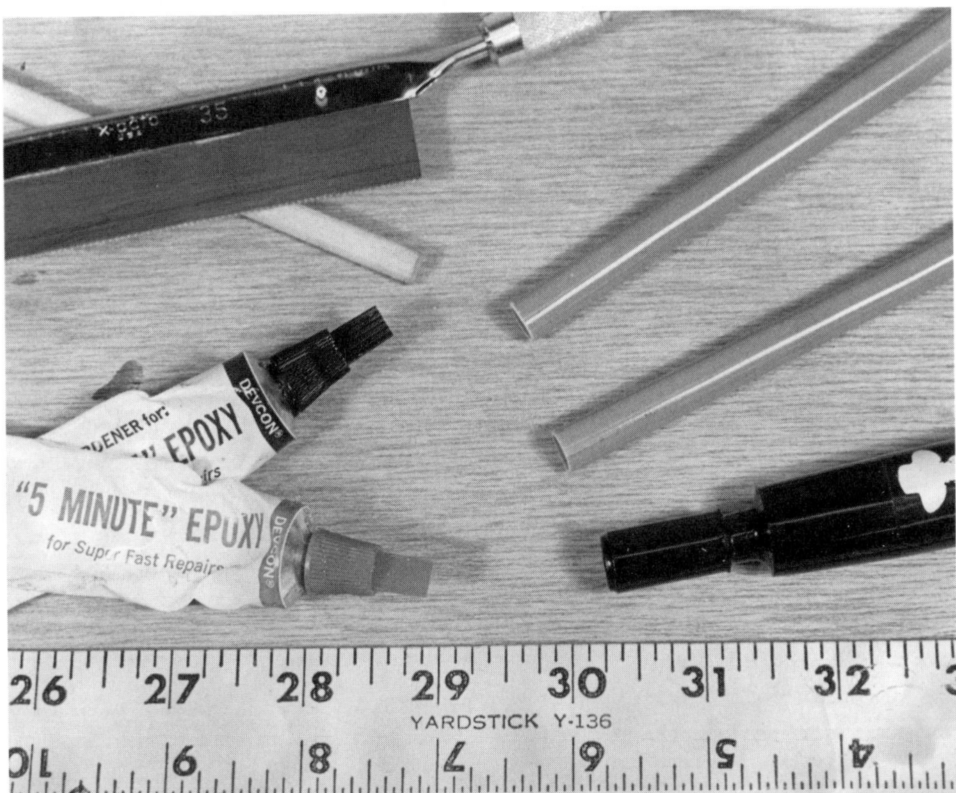

Materials and tools needed for making self-ferrules.

CUTTING BLANKS: METHODS

There are two basic ways to cut a blank. One is with a file; the other is with a fine-tooth hacksaw blade. Most rod blank manufacturers recommend using a triangular file, but I have never had any problem with the hacksaw blade. If there are base guidelines that apply to both methods, they are to measure carefully to be sure you are cutting in the right place, to use care in all steps, and to not force the cut in any way. A gentle touch is required throughout the process.

To cut through a blank using a file, first measure the blank carefully and mark it. Recheck the measurement. Then wrap several layers of masking tape around the blank and mark the measurement on the center of the tape again.

Support the blank on a flat surface and, using a fine-cut triangular file, begin stroking the corner of the file back and forth on the tape mark. Once you've cut through the tape, move the rod blank slightly and continue until you have a groove in the tape all the way around the rod. Continue around a second time, gradually cutting a slight groove into the skin of the blank. Use the lightest possible pressure—bearing down hard will tend to splinter the blank and may even crush it as you come close to cutting through. Continue in this way, working slowly and carefully, until the blank is completely scored and cut through. This method will work on all hollow-glass and graphite rods (and also on the solid thin tip ends of some of the newer rods), but it will not work on thick solid-glass blanks. Solid-glass blanks should be cut with a hacksaw.

To cut through a hollow blank using a hacksaw, first make sure you have a fine-tooth hacksaw blade with 32 teeth per inch. Do not attempt to cut blanks with a coarser blade or you may tear or splinter the blank. It helps if you have a small handle to hold the blade, but do *not* use one of the standard bracket-style frames that stretch the blade between two ends. They are too bulky, heavy, and difficult to control for this purpose. If you don't have a small handle, hold the blade in your hand (wear a glove) or wrap one end of the blade with tape to make a handle. You can arrange the blade in the small handle with the teeth pointing toward or away from you. The secret in using the blade, however, is to begin by dragging the blade backward (pushing or pulling, as the case may be). Note that this is contrary to the way you were taught in high school shop class, but it will protect the blank against splintering. Do not use any appreciable pressure; let the weight of the blade and the dragging of the teeth make the cut.

You may wish to use a miter box, as described earlier. This will help to center the rod blank and position the blade at right angles for an easy cut. For best results place the miter box in a vise to secure it and to hold the rod blank securely in the V-slot.

The technique for cutting is almost the same as for using a file. Measure the blank and mark it, then tape the blank with masking tape and mark the tape. Pull or push the blade so it drags backward over the mark, and rotate the rod so that you work completely around the blank. After cutting through the tape, cut through the skin of the blank and continue on to deepen this groove.

Once part of the blank is cut through, rotate the blank to cut through the rest of it. It is always best to work so that you are cutting from the surface of the blank toward the center and constantly rotating the rod blank, rather than beginning at one spot and cut straight through

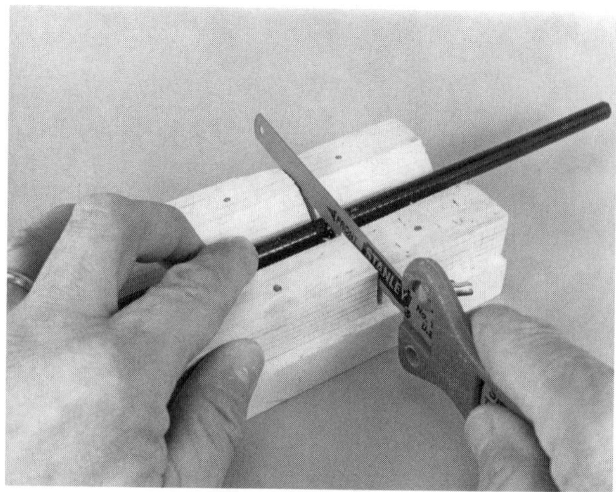

Using a homemade miter tool for cutting rod blanks (see directions in chapter 2). When used with a fine-toothed saw blade, such a box will not damage the rod blank.

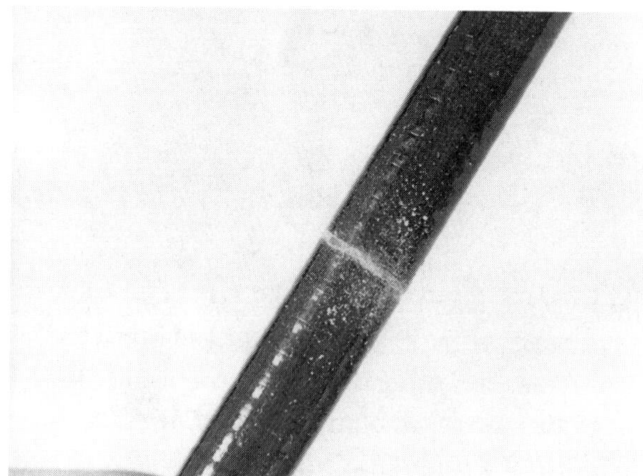

Example of a smooth cut around the rod. The entire perimeter should be scored or cut before cutting through.

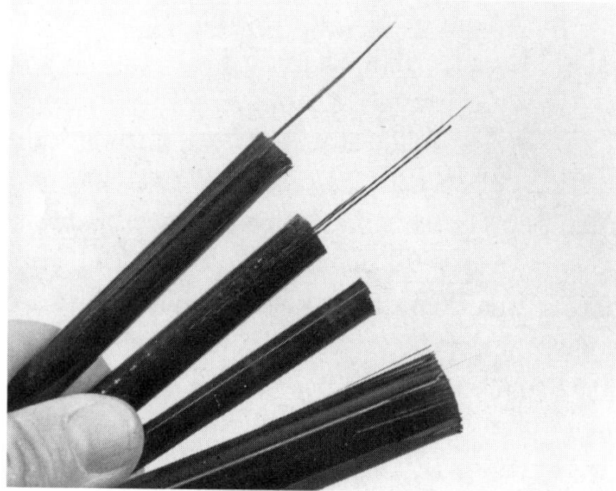

Proper cutting of rod blanks is a must. Failure to do so can result in split or torn ends, as shown here.

Once the blank is scored, the rod can be cut through with a fine-toothed saw.

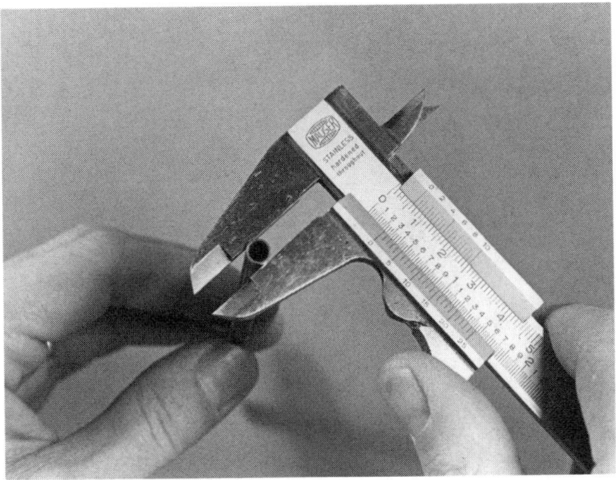

Using a caliper to check the diameter and wall thickness of a blank for choosing an insert spigot ferrule or external sleeve ferrule.

as you would do with a piece of wood. By cutting through the blank skin first, you minimize splitting the material fibers. If you cut straight through, you risk tearing some of these fibers on the sides and bottom of the blank.

You will want to sand the end of the blank after cutting, but sand only from the outside to the center to avoid the possibility of splintering the blank fibers.

MEASURING FOR FERRULES

Blanks must be measured precisely and cut accurately when you make or add ferrules. There are three types of ferrules that can be added to rods. They include the metal ferrule that used to be common before the self-ferruling system was developed by Fenwick; the sleeve-type of slipover ferrule, in which an outer sleeve is glued to the butt end of the tip section to friction-fit with the butt section; and the spigot ferrule, which consists of a plug glued into the upper part of the butt section to friction-fit with the tip section.

Measurements for Metal Ferrules

Metal ferrules don't really require any measurements if the blank is already cut or supplied in sections. In most cases the extension of the female portion of the ferrule matches or closely approximates in length the extension of the main ferrule. Thus, although the ferrules will add perhaps an inch or two of length to the broken-down rod, the measurement of the rod sections before these ferrules are added will not be affected. On some ferrules the butt end of the upper section (the tip section in a two-piece rod) fits all the way down into the end of the main ferrule, so to match lengths of the separate sections, the upper end of the butt section must be cut back the length of the male extension or the butt end of the rod must be cut off. Often the latter suggestion is better, particularly if there is a snug fit of the female ferrule to the blank. Cutting back the upper end of this section may make it impossible to fit the ferrule in place. Cutting back the butt end for 1 or 2 inches does not affect the action.

Measurements for Sleeve Ferrules

With sleeve ferrules you will be using a sleeve that is an identical taper to the blank. This sleeve is slipped over the tip end of the blank and glued in place so that there is a sleeve extension of 1 to 2 or more inches beyond the bottom end of the tip section(s) or the butt end of multisection rods. If a two-piece blank is cut exactly in half and the sleeve extension to the tip end adds 2 inches, then the tip end will be 2 inches longer than the butt section. This isn't a problem functionally but rather aesthetically and makes it more difficult to case and pack the rod with unequal sections.

In order to measure for the point at which to cut the blank, you must first decide on the length of extension of this sleeve. (This is the extension beyond the end of the blank—not the total length of this sleeve. Obviously the sleeve must be longer than these figures to include 1 or 2 inches to be glued to the blank.) For a light rod it might be no more than 1½ inches. For a heavy rod it could be 3 inches. To properly measure the rod for cutting, first mark the rod at the exact halfway point. Then make the cutting mark exactly one-half the length of the ferrule extension to the tip side of the rod. As an example, let's use a 6-foot-long spinning rod to be cut into two pieces with a 2-inch ferrule extension sleeve. For this 72-inch-long blank, the halfway point is at 36 inches from each end. The blank should be cut 1 inch to the tip side of this mark (one-half of the 2-inch extension) so that the tip section is 35 inches long and the butt section is 37 inches long. When the sleeve ferrule is added to the tip section and extends 2 inches from the butt end, the total length of this section becomes 37 inches (35 inches + 2 inches), or the length of the butt section. Both are identical.

Another way to think of this is to add the 72-inch length and the 2-inch extension together to make 74 inches as the total length of the two separate sections (even though they are not cut yet). Divide by 2 to equal 37 inches, or the length of the butt section and the position of the cut. The tip section becomes 37 inches through the addition of the 2-inch extension onto the 35-inch blank section.

This method also helps when you cut a blank into three or more sections, because the more sections, the more additions of ferrule-sleeve extensions that must be added. For cutting a 72-inch spinning blank into three sections, you use a slightly different method of adding the blank length to the length of the two sleeve extensions. Using 2 inches for this again, it becomes 72 inches + 2 inches + 2 inches = 76 inches, or a total of 76 inches for the rod plus the two ferrule extensions. Divide this by 3 and you get 25⅓ inches, or the position of the first mark from the butt of the rod. The next mark will be 23⅓ inches up (25⅓ inches - 2 inches), leaving a final upper section of 23⅓ inches. The 2-inch sleeve additions to these two upper sections brings them back to a 25⅓-inch length, the same as for the butt section. For a four-piece pack rod made from a one-piece 72-inch blank, the formula is 72 inches + 2 inches + 2 inches + 2 inches, or 78 inches total. Thus each of the four sections (with the 2-inch sleeve ferrules added to the upper three sections) will be 19½ inches. This means that the cut on the butt section will be at 19½ inches, the next cut will be at 17½ inches, and the third cut will be at 17½ inches, leaving a 17½-inch upper section, for a total of 72 inches.

The same formulation can be applied to any length or type of rod, any length of ferrule extension, and any number of pieces. Just remember that you must always subtract the extensions from any marks and cuts and that it is extremely important to measure, check, and recheck several times until you're sure of the results—and of your math—when you cut. If you are not sure, or don't understand the formula, don't cut!

You can even use this formula for making ferrules of different lengths for different sections of the rod, such as a four-piece rod that might have a 3-inch sleeve in the butt for strength, a 2-inch sleeve in the center of the rod, and a 1-inch sleeve in the tip end, where less strength is required. Just be sure to add the respective extensions to any total length and to make the marks on the blank relative to and compensating for the different extension lengths. As an example of this, let's assume that same 72-inch-long blank is cut into four sections but with a 3-inch extension sleeve for the butt section, a 2-inch sleeve for the center of the rod, and a 1-inch sleeve for the tip section. The formula would still be 72 inches + 3 inches + 2 inches + 1 inch = 78 inches, divided by 4 = 19½

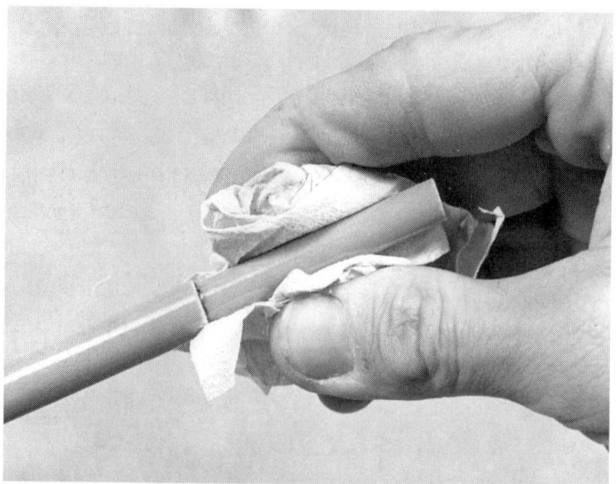

A spigot ferrule uses a short section that is glued into the upper end of the butt section to mate with the lower end of the tip section of the rod. Here a spigot has been pushed and pulled into place and is being cleaned with a rag.

inches for the butt section. The next cut would be at 16½ inches (19½ inches - 3 inches for the extension that will be added to this section), the third cut would be at 17½ inches (19½ inches - 2 inches of sleeve extension), leaving a final 18½-inch section that with the 1-inch extension will measure 19½ inches. Use this formula, and all sections of any multipiece rod will be equal when the rod is finished.

Measurements for Spigot Ferrules

Spigot ferrules are made as self-ferrules to fit on any blank, but unlike the sleeve ferrule, which is glued to the butt end of each section to fit over the tip end of the next section lower, spigot ferrules consist of a plug of blank material glued into the tip end of each section to mate with the inside diameter of the next upper section. Thus the measurements for these will be just the opposite of the sleeve ferrules.

For example, a 72-inch rod cut exactly in half and with a 2-inch plug inserted into the butt section would have a butt 38 inches long and a tip section 36 inches long. To prevent this, measure the exact center for a two-piece rod, and then mark *toward the butt side* exactly one-half the length of the plug ferrule. (As with sleeve ferrules, this is not the total length of the plug, because there must be 1 or 2 inches that will be glued to the inside of the blank. This is just the length of the extension.) Thus for a 2-inch plug extension, a cut 1 inch to the butt side will result in a butt section that will be 35 inches long and a tip section 37 inches long. When the 2-inch plug extends from the butt end, both sections will be 37 inches long.

To expand this to a four-piece rod from a 72-inch blank, the formula would be 72 inches + 2 inches + 2 inches + 2 inches = 78 inches, divided by 4 = 19.5 inches. But in this case the 2-inch plug is *subtracted* from the butt section to make a section of 17½ inches. The next two sections will be the same length. The final, uppermost section will be 19½ inches, which will be the length of the three lower sections when the 2-inch plug ferrules are added to each. The formulas for each of these

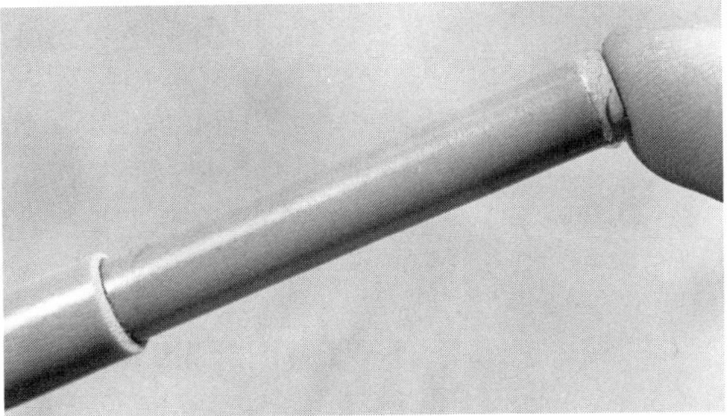

Spigot ferrule with a cork added to the end to seal the rod. Both sleeve and spigot ferrules must be wrapped to give them hoop strength.

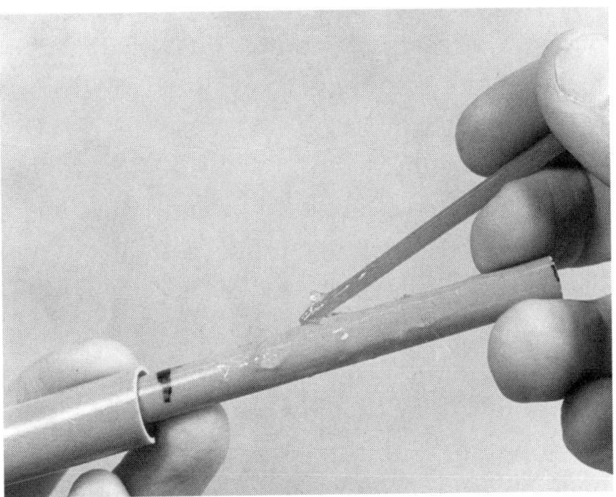

An external sleeve ferrule is made by gluing a sleeve over the tip section of the cut rod so that the sleeve will mate with the upper end of the butt section. Here glue is added to the butt end of the tip section so that the sleeve (to the left) can be slid and glued in place.

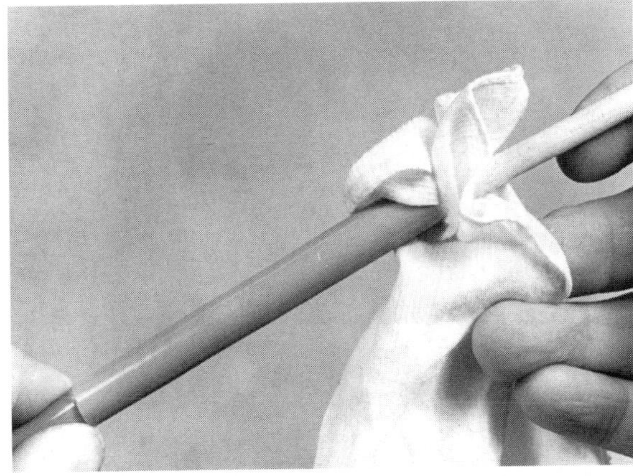

Once the sleeve is in place, glue must be removed from the ferrule. A small dowel or rod blank and rag work well for this. All glue must be removed for proper seating of the sleeve on the rod section.

are simple—just remember in which direction you are cutting, which end gets the extension, and which section remains full length, to be matched by the others when the sleeves or plugs are glued in place.

MAKING SLEEVE FERRULES

To add sleeve ferrules to a rod, you will need a minimal number of tools, but you will need some scrap blank material with an internal diameter approximately the same as the outside diameter of the blank where the ferrule will be placed. The scrap blank must be the same taper as the blank you are fitting, although this can be adjusted slightly.

Begin by measuring and cutting the blank. Once the blank is cut and the ends are sanded, cut a section of the scrap blank to slide down over the upper or tip section of the rod blank. If the taper of the scrap blank is the same as the rod blank, then you can avoid cutting out any sections and simply slide the scrap over the blank. The purpose here is to determine the approximate area where the scrap will fit snugly onto the end of the blank. Because the scrap blank will cover and hide the end of the rod blank, the best way to do this is to measure the rod-blank section, slide the scrap blank in place, and then measure down to determine the approximate position of the end of the external sleeve rod blank. Mark this spot on the scrap blank and remove it. If the taper of the blank and the scrap are the same, you can then cut about 4 inches on each side of this mark on the scrap. If you're unsure of the amount of play between the two sections, or of the tapers, cut about 4 inches below the mark and about 6 inches above the mark. This will allow room for adjustment with a second fitting.

Slide the scrap sleeve onto the blank again to check for fit, remark the position of the end of the blank on the scrap, and trim the scrap to fit. At the same time that the scrap is fitted snugly to the tip end, slide the butt end into place to see if you get a match as to taper and fit. You will probably have to cut about ¼ to ½ inch off the end of the butt section or the lower end of the tip section. This assures a tight fit of the sleeve to the butt section. Failure to do this may result in the two rod sections "bottoming out" against each other, making for a loose fit. Ideally I like to cut about ¼ inch from the butt end of the tip section, glue the ferrule on, and then make any additional cuts and trimming of the butt section if needed.

At this point check to make sure the tapers are compatible. First the scrap sleeve should fit snugly onto the end of the tip section without any play at either end. If there is play, use a rat-tail file or sandpaper wrapped around a dowel to lightly sand the tight end, checking frequently until you get a tight, snug fit with no play. Once this sleeve fits the upper end, check for play, and fit with the butt end lightly fitted into the sleeve.

Cut the sleeve so that there is about 2 to 3 inches of sleeve to be glued onto the blank, the final length depending on the blank's diameter and power. Use longer sections for strength, shorter sections for light rods and tip ends. Mark the blank at the upper end of the sleeve, and remove the sleeve. Use steel wool to lightly roughen the blank for better gluing. Use sandpaper or a fine file to shape a tapered angle on the edge of the sleeve, which will make it easier to wrap thread onto this ferrule section for increased hoop strength.

To glue the sleeve onto the blank, coat the end of the rod section with epoxy rod glue or any good 24-hour epoxy glue (not epoxy rod finish!) and slide the ferrule down the blank. When you reach the glued section, slide the sleeve rapidly over the glue; as it starts to seat, twist several times to assure a good glue bond. Do *not* pull too much, because the glue will serve as a lubricant, and too much tension could split the sleeve at this point.

Once the sleeve is glued on, use a cotton swab, a dowel covered with a paper towel or thin rag, or a similar probe to thoroughly wipe the glue out of the end of what is now the female ferrule. This is most important—any remaining glue residue will prevent the proper seating of the ferrule onto the butt section. Allow the glue to cure overnight. Once the glue is cured, check for a tight, proper fit of the ferrule onto the butt section, but do not force; the ferrule still needs wrapping to provide hoop strength. If the butt end bottoms out, remove and cut it back by ¼ inch and try again. (It is a must to have some small space between the butt end of the tip section and the tip end of the butt section so that the friction of the ferrule maintains the tight joint during the action of fishing.)

At this point the ferrule is ready to wrap to provide hoop strength. This method can be used for any number of ferrules on a rod of any diameter and any material.

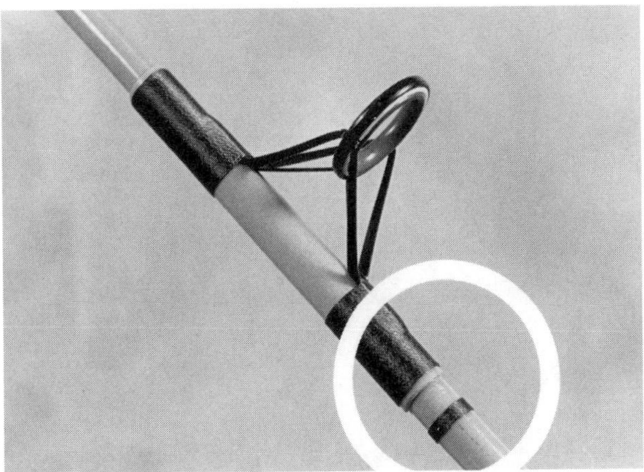

Example of sleeve ferrule with a guide mounted on the ferrule. The wrap thus has two purposes—to hold the guide in place and to provide hoop strength to the ferrule.

MAKING SPIGOT FERRULES

The technique of adding a spigot ferrule to a rod is not unlike that of adding sleeve ferrules—only in this case you are adding a separate plug into the butt section rather than a sleeve over the tip section. For this you will also need sections of scrap blank, in this case scraps that will have an outside diameter and taper that is the same as or similar to the internal diameter and taper of the upper end of the butt section.

Begin by measuring and cutting the rod blank as previously described. Then slide the scrap section up through the butt end in the lower rod section and out the upper end. If you have a short section of scrap blank, you might need a dowel or straightened-coat-hanger pusher to push the scrap out of the end. Pull snug and mark the end of the blank on the scrap. Remove the scrap and cut about 4 inches on each side of this mark. Replace this scrap in the butt end of the blank and check the mark again; check too for any play of the scrap in the blank. If there is play at either end, remove the scrap and sand and file it, rechecking frequently until the play is removed and the scrap fits precisely and snugly. Check for the fit of the tip end over this plug. If the two ends of the rod meet, cut back the butt end about ¼ inch.

Lightly sand the scrap for a better fit on the blank and into the tip section. Use a thin dowel or skewer to spread 24-hour epoxy or rod-building epoxy into the end of the blank. Make sure you use plenty of glue and spread it thoroughly into the blank for about 3 or 4 inches. Using the pusher, push the plug into the butt section and out the end. Pull it snug, but do not pull too tight and risk splitting the blank. Use a rag and solvent to immediately wipe up any glue on the exposed plug ferrule. Allow the glue to cure overnight. Once it's cured, check the fit with the tip end and, if necessary, cut back about ¼ inch so that a firm fit onto the ferrule still leaves a gap of about ¼ to ⅜ inch between the rod-section ends. This is necessary to maintain a firm fit and to allow for some wear.

This type of ferrule can be used for any type of rod and on any diameter of rod blank. At this point the ferrule is ready to wrap.

REINFORCING FERRULES

Sometimes the section of blank used in the above ferrules is not strong enough for the rod. This is more typical of spigot ferrules than of sleeve ferrules, but it can occur in either type. Part of this is because we are all dependent on getting and using scrap-blank sections for these sleeves and plugs, and there is no way to judge beforehand the thickness and strength of these sections.

One way to adjust for this is to reinforce the sleeves and plugs. To do this with a sleeve, use an additional sleeve over the initial sleeve, repeating the steps described above. You can do this after the first sleeve is added to the blank, or you can make up the double-wall sleeve and then glue it onto the blank. In most cases it is easier to add the second sleeve to the first after the first is glued to the blank.

Additional smaller diameter plugs can be glued into the main plug that forms the plug spigot ferrule in rods. I find it easier to make up a thicker, reinforced double- or triple-walled plug and then trim this reinforced plug to length and finally glue it into the blank. This seems to be more important in the spigot ferrules, because the plug is thinner than the rod blank and thus has less strength for this critical area.

In some cases you can find solid plugs for spigot ferrules. Some mail-order companies have sold these in the past, and sections of solid-glass blanks are often used for this. This is ideal, because there is less work involved (no building of double- or triple-wall ferrules) and the strength is unquestioned.

SEATING METAL FERRULES

Metal ferrules are measured in sixty-fourths of an inch internal diameter, sometimes sized slightly larger for the female section that is fitted onto the upper end of the butt section or the upper ends of sections of multipiece rods. To fit them to a rod, first cut the blank. Check to see if the blank fits all the way into the male section or stops where the male section fits into the ferrule. The difference will determine how to cut the blank; otherwise the blank section with the female section will be longer than the other section.

A snug fit is a must. You may have to sand slightly to get a proper fit. For example, a female ferrule that just fits onto the tip end of a butt section but does not seat all the way down (measure to check) might require light sanding of the blank below this area to accommodate the ferrule. If the ferrule just barely fits on, or if the rod is of a steep taper that will require a lot of sanding (and possibly weakening), try going to the next larger size ferrule.

Male ferrules that fit onto the tip section of the rod have the opposite problem because the taper is thickest at the end of the blank. Thus sand lightly only at the tip end, because it is likely that the ferrule will fit fine if the blank sides are made close to parallel.

Once the fit is correct, lightly sand the blanks in this area (protect the rest of the blank here with masking tape), add 24-hour epoxy glue to the blank and also to the inside of the ferrules, and slide the ferrules in place. Rotate slightly to assure a good glue bond, and immediately wipe up any

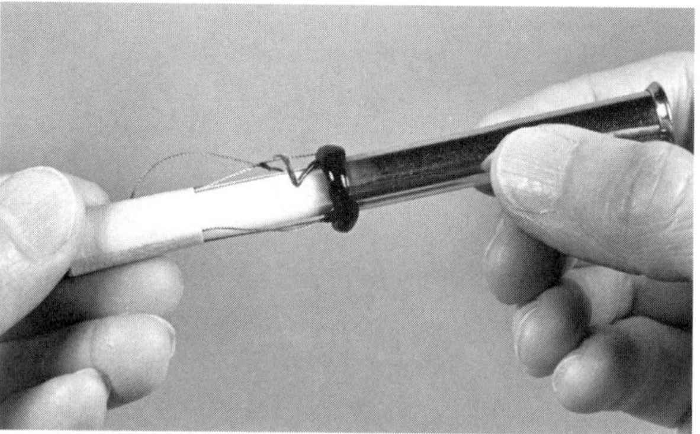

Mounting a metal ferrule using heat-melt ferrule cement. Thread shims have been used here for an accurate mounting.

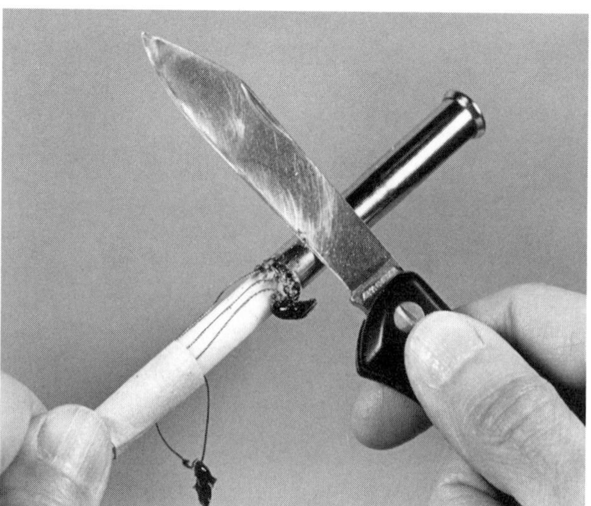

Once the ferrule cement hardens, it can be cracked off with a knife blade, as shown. This is better than trying to remove it while hot.

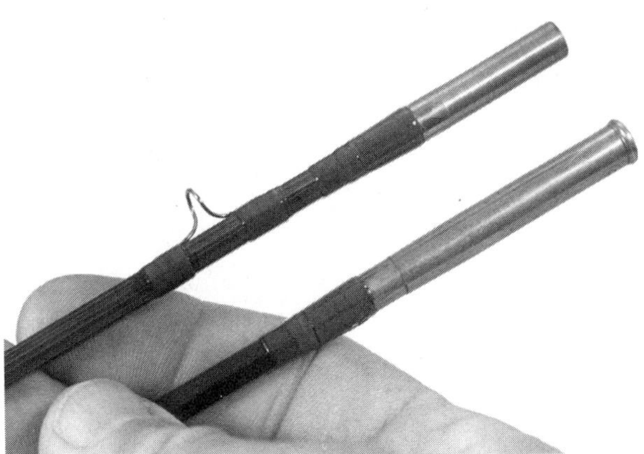

Example of the ferrule set on a bamboo rod. Ferrules must be glued in place and wrapped as shown for both strength and appearance.

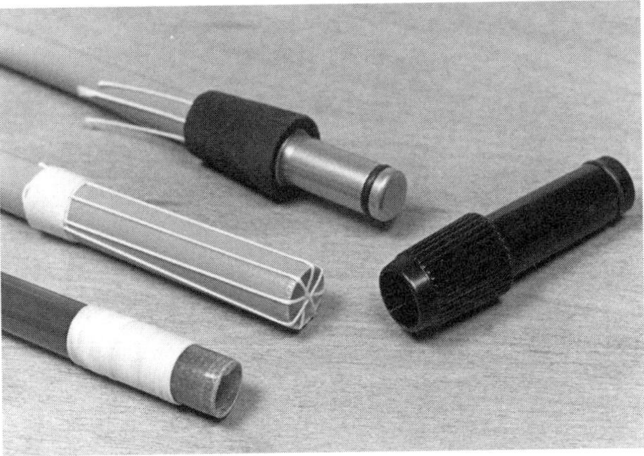

Examples of adapters for rod blanks, showing shims used for accurate sizing to the rod blank. Such adapters usually are designed for casting-rod handles or for boat rods with a separate handle.

excess glue. Allow the glue to cure overnight. At this point the ferrules are ready for wrapping.

WRAPPING FERRULES

Wrapping directions are described completely in chapter 22, but some tips specific to ferrules are included here. Metal ferrules have a shoulder area that should be wrapped. Begin the wrap on the blank, and wrap up and over the end of the ferrule to the end of this shoulder area. It is usually obvious as a slight visible ridge on the ferrule. The wraps are coated with color preserver and rod finish along with the guide wraps.

Self-ferrules that are built into blanks must also be wrapped to provide hoop strength to the female ferrule. Follow the manufacturer's directions. If such directions are not available, wrap manufactured sleeve ferrules completely with a thread wrap, beginning on the blank and running up to finish as close as possible to the ferrule end. Use the same tension as for guide wraps to provide hoop strength.

Plug ferrules that are built in by the manufacturer or installed by you should also be wrapped. In this case wrap not only the female section (the butt end of the tip section) but also the area where the plug is glued into the butt end. This butt end is the equivalent of a female ferrule in construction and does require the wrapping for hoop strength. In both cases begin on the body of the blank and work as close to the end of the blank or ferrule as possible.

Sleeve ferrules do not require a wrap on the butt section, although rod builders often add a slight band here as a decorative addition. They do require a complete wrap of the sleeve, beginning on the blank and wrapping up, over, and onto the sleeve and to the end of the sleeve. This presents some problems, however. Earlier it was suggested that you might want to taper the end of the blank end of the sleeve. The reason is that it will thus be easier to control the thread as you make this step up from the blank to the sleeve.

One tip here is to slightly lessen the tension on the thread during this critical step so that you can run the thread up the steep taper of this area and get it onto the flat sleeve without overwraps or gaps. If the thickness of the sleeve is too much for this, here's another tip: First lay down a separate wrap on the blank that ends at the sleeve. Then begin the regular wrap on the blank; go up over the short band wrap and from that up onto the sleeve. The short band provides an additional step to make this transition easier. An alternative is to begin the wrap right next to the sleeve, wrap back down the blank, and then reverse the wrap as a double wrap to go back up and over the sleeve to the end.

27
Rod Variations

Introduction • Twisted-Guide Rods • Pack Rods • Ice-Fishing Rods • Right-Hand and Left-Hand Fly Rods • Right-Hand and Left-Hand Spinning Rods • Mixed-Material Rods • Rod Butt-Section Reinforcers • Telescoping Rods • Other Possibilities

Basic Safety Requirements

- Safety goggles
- Rubber gloves for epoxy

Basic Tools

- Coat hangers
- Book and cup
- Razor blade
- Burnisher
- Masking tape

Helpful Tools

- Rod-wrapping tool, thread-tension device
- Rod miter box
- Rod-handle seater
- Cork-grip clamp
- Ruler
- Brushes
- Reamers
- Tip-top gauge
- Curing motor
- Diamond wrapping tools

INTRODUCTION

The basics of rod building are covered in chapters 18 and 19. Details on specific parts of rod building are covered in chapters 20, 21, and 22. These chapters should be checked for details on rod-building specifics. This chapter is meant to describe some of the odd rod variations possible. However, basic and standard rod-building methods and procedures, along with basic safety considerations, apply to all the rods listed in this chapter.

Some of these rods have very specific applications. Some are more widely applicable to a wide range of fishing; others are simply unusual variations that can be applied to any type of rod or type of fishing.

For example, pack rods are useful primarily for traveling anglers, especially those traveling by plane or needing a short rod pack for a Western pack trip. These rods would be less useful for anyone traveling by car and of very little use to an angler traveling exclusively by car or living on a lakefront, whose tackle is taken from garage to a boat.

Casting rods with twisted guides—guides that rotate around the blank and end up on the opposite side of the rod from the reel—have their champions, primarily among anglers who want something slightly different and those who fight big fish on light tackle and don't want line rubbing against the rod.

Ice-fishing rods are highly specialized and are made with specific ice-fishing requirements in mind.

TWISTED-GUIDE RODS

These rods go by several names—some "invented" by anglers. In essence they are all casting (revolving-spool) rods where the guides rotate around the rod in progression from butt to tip. The rationale for this evolves from one of the typical problems of light-casting tackle where, even with a normal complement of guides, the stress of fighting a big fish will result in line rubbing against the rod. These rods bend so much under extreme stress that the rod section between each two guides arches enough for the line to hit it. One solution to this of course is to use high-frame guides—more like spinning guides than casting-rod guides—but this can also increase the torque on the rod, twisting the blank.

The solution of "twisting" the guides eliminates the problem of line-to-blank contact completely and also minimizes the torque problem. Building a casting rod with twisted guides is the same as building a normal casting rod until the guides and tip-top are fitted. First the tip-top (usually added to the rod blank before the guides are in order to aid in lining up the guides) is placed on the blank 180 degrees from the normal position. When the tip-top is glued, it must be positioned on the opposite side of the rod from its normal position. The guides are positioned so that when the line comes off the reel, it will run in a spiral around the blank to exit directly under the rod.

There are several ways to position these guides, but the best way is to first calculate the position of each (this will not vary from the guide positions on a normal rod) and then tape the guides in place. Begin with the butt guide at about a 30-degree angle from the normal position; the second guide will be about 120 degrees from the normal position, with the remaining guides directly under the rod. Some rods will require one more guide at an angle, so the first guide might be at 20 degrees from normal, the second guide at 80 degrees from normal (60 degrees from the butt guide), the third guide at 140 degrees from normal (60 degrees from the second guide and 120 degrees from the butt guide), and the rest of the guides at 180 degrees from the normal positions. Occasionally you may have to keep the butt guide in the normal position and vary the other guides. Usually you can get away with only two additional guides traversing around the blank, with the second guide after the butt guide at 45 degrees, the third at 135 degrees, and the rest at 180 degrees.

Naturally you will have to check the rod to be sure you accomplish the goal of not allowing any line-to-blank contact at any time under any circumstances. With the guides only taped in place, you can't run line through the guides and stress the rod to check. So you must attach a line to the tip-top (make sure it is securely glued in place and cures overnight) and at the same time run a line off the attached reel and through the guides and tip-top ring. Attach a light weight (or less than an ounce) to the end of this line. Then slightly stress the rod by bending it, pulling against the line tied to the tip-top. At the same time, reel in the line through the guides until the sinker used is hanging free.

Check the rod at this point for any contact of the line with the rod blank. There will be enough tension from the weight to indicate the path of the line through the guides but not enough to twist the guides away from their taped-on positions. Make any adjustments as necessary to be sure the line clears. Once you are satisfied with the positioning of the guides, remove the line carefully and wrap the guides in place.

Such guides can be used for any type of revolving-spool rod, not just casting rods for bass or walleye or light-tackle saltwater rods. They are ideal for downrigger rods that are bent into a sharp arc as a result of the tension put in the line from downrigger fishing. They are also ideal for casting-style noodle rods and long-handled steelhead and West Coast salmon rods. In all cases it takes only two or three guides to route the line from on top of the rod to completely underneath—the rest of the guides can run straight in line with the tip-top.

Although the guides can route the line around either side of the rod, I prefer to run it to the left as I hold to rod. My slight argument for this is that because I am a right-handed caster and because this means my casting rod

Example of twisted-guide rod; arrows show the guides as they spiral around the rod. This design is used only on casting rods and most often on downrigger rods.

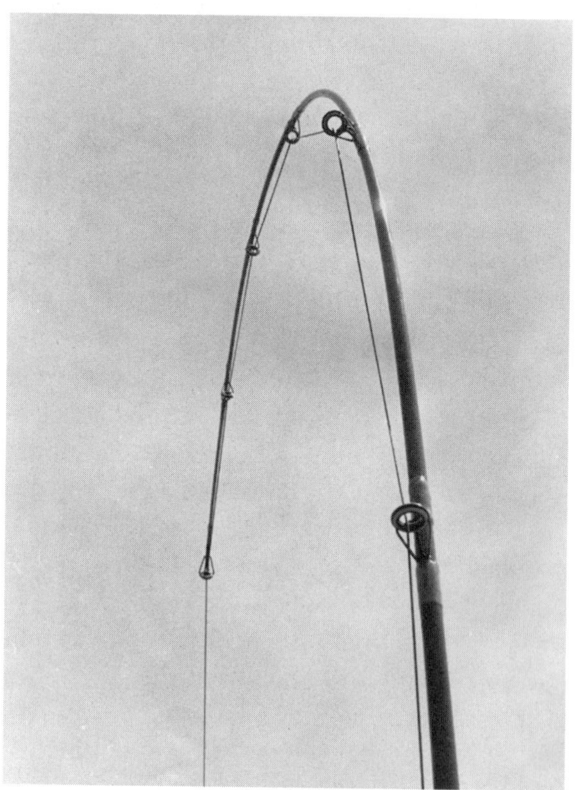

Another view of the above showing how the guides spiral around the rod.

View of casting rod with spiral guides.

is turned 90 degrees to the left (counterclockwise) when I make a cast, any gravity during the cast will pull the line away from the blank, not toward it. Admittedly this effect will be minimal and the force of gravity will only be at the end of the cast, when any such drag of the line on the rod blank would be minimal anyway.

PACK RODS

Pack-rod blanks for fly rods and sometimes light spinning rods are available from a number of manufacturers. Some are three-piece blanks, most are four-piece, and a few have even more pieces. The techniques for building these are no different from building any fly or light spinning rod, except for some new additional thoughts, as follow:

1. With pack rods it helps to pinpoint the spine of each section of the rod if this is not already marked on the individual blank sections by the manufacturer. This is a little more difficult on shorter sections, because the reduced length makes it harder to bend the section enough to determine jumping or stiff and soft sides to find the spine. Bending will be easiest to do on the light tip section and most difficult on the heaviest and stiffest butt section. Thus you can usually determine the spine where it is most helpful—on the tip and upper sections. If possible, mark the spine of every section.

2. The ferrules must be wrapped in accordance with manufacturer's directions. If there are no directions, then the female ferrules must be wrapped. If the blank has spigot ferrules (unlikely today), the blank portion of the male ferrule should also be wrapped.

3. The additional ferrules (three instead of one on a four-piece rod) require additional concern in guide placement. Often you can reduce stiffening in the blank by combining the ferrule wraps with the guide wrappings; by adjusting the position of the guides so that they will fall on the female ferrule, where one wrapping will suffice for the guide wrap; and by wrapping to give the ferrule hoop strength.

In addition to making rods that are supplied in pack-rod versions, you can also make your own by cutting a blank to make it into the pack rod desired. Your choices as to section length and number of pieces are limited by the length of the rod and what you start with. Start with a one-piece rod and you can cut and ferrule it any way you wish—into two, three, four, five, or more sections. If you start with a two-piece rod, you are limited to four or six pieces, depending on whether you cut each of the two sections into two or three pieces. If you start with a three-piece rod, you can only end up with a six-piece pack rod, because each piece must be cut into two pieces.

In working with two- or three-piece rods, it is better if you stick to the same type of ferrule the manufacturer supplied. This will be impossible if the rod has a female ferrule built in as part of the rod blank—as Fenwick does with its Feralite ferrules.

Because this is a slipover type of ferrule, however, you can make the other ferrules sleeve-style, which will most closely imitate the manufacturer's ferrule. Similarly, if the rod has a spigot ferrule, it is easy to make additional spigot ferrules.

Before you begin any of this, make sure you have or can get the appropriate size plugs or sleeves to fit the rod where the ferrules will be required. If you are planning a certain type or length of rod to break down into a certain length to fit a rod case, suitcase, or satchel, the ferrules will add approximately 2 inches to the section length. Thus an 8-foot one-piece blank, when cut and ferruled into a four-piece rod, will have sections measuring about 26 to 27 inches, not 24 inches. The additional 2 or 3 inches will be a result of the plugs or sleeves added to make the ferrules. There are definite formulas to aid in cutting blanks for the type of ferrule used, the number of ferrules, and the length of the rod; check chapter 26 for details and instructions.

Because good fly and light-spinning blanks are often readily available, many rod builders concentrate on other styles for their pack rods. Thus rods for every conceivable type of fishing have been made into pack rods. Casting, popping, heavy spinning, spin-cast, surf, boat, and offshore rods have all been successfully converted into or built as pack rods. One caution with all of these involves the strength of the ferrule. The heavier the rod, the heavier the ferrule required. With the heaviest rods, such as those for offshore or surf fishing, the ferrules must be reinforced hollow sections of blank (as described in chapter 26) or must be of the solid-glass or graphite-plug type, properly tapered and securely glued into place.

The other instructions and guidelines for making manufacturer-ferruled pack rods also apply to those you ferrule on your own.

ICE-FISHING RODS

Ice-fishing rods are very specific rods for very specific fishing. Although you could argue that one can use any type, style, size, or length of rod for ice fishing (and you would be right in one sense), ice-fishing rods are typically short and very light in power. They are designed this way so that an angler can sit in an ice-fishing shanty or on a sled, poised over an ice-fishing hole. This provides more control of the rod and the lure than would be possible if the angler were sitting back 8 feet and trying to work or control a long casting or spinning rod with the line dangling through a small hole in the ice. In addition, the short rod allows for far greater close control and action of the lure or bait, as well as the quickest possible response from the angler on each bite or tap on the line. If a float is used, it also provides the closest view of the float.

Some ice-fishing-rod blanks are available, but most are cut down from damaged or scrap blanks. The tip sections of these damaged standard casting or spinning rods are used. Most ice-fishing rods measure about 24 to 36 inches and thus may be cut from old or discarded freshwater fishing rods.

Ice-fishing rods can be built as casting, spin-cast, or spinning rods, with the appropriate guides added. Because of the shorter length, they require only two or three guides and a tip-top, and because the line is dropped straight down into a hole—not cast—special guides or guide sizes are not needed to funnel the line. Most guides are small—about 10 to 12 millimeters; this is not so small that ice in the guides would be more of a problem than it is for any other type of rod.

The main changes come in the way the handles are made and used, because ice fishing implies severe weather conditions. Thus avoid metal reel seats and spinning-rod rings and other parts, because metal transmits cold. Under extremely cold conditions, your skin can freeze to the metal reel seat—not a happy situation. All-graphite reel seats are ideal, and graphite rings are available for spinning where rings are to be used. (If you can't avoid metal, you can cover the metal parts with several layers of masking, duct, or electrician's tape after the reel is attached. But it is better to build for the cold rather than to try and adjust for it later.) Grips and handles of cork, foam, and graphite (ideal for sensitivity) are best.

If you are building the handle onto the tip-section blank, you will build it just as with any other handle. The only difference is that the thin diameter of the tip section of a thin blank will require handle materials with very small diameter holes. Cork or foam with ¼-inch holes are best, and even this might require shimming in some cases. If necessary, shim with paper tape, a tight thread wrapping, or cord or thick thread. (See chapter 20 for details.)

One additional concern when building casting- or spin-cast-style ice-fishing rods using a standard casting-rod handle is that they require a fixed or removable adapter to fit into the handle; the adapter is glued onto the rod. Even though adapters are made to fit different sizes of blanks, they are sometimes not small enough to fit the thin blanks used for ice fishing. Adapters range from a small size of about 9 millimeters (a little larger than ⅓ inch) to 7 millimeters (a little larger than ¼ inch), depending on the adapter style. Some blanks could be thinner than that. If you will be using an adapter in these cases, it will be necessary to shim the adapter by wrapping the rod blank with cork, thread, paper tape, masking tape, or fiberglass tape, as described in chapter 20.

One final thought on ice-fishing rods is that some anglers eschew standard grips and handles and simply drill the end of a 1-inch or larger dowel, glue the blank tip into the dowel, and drill the side of the dowel to accept two short pegs. The pegs serve as a simple line winder. These anglers don't use a reel at all but simply run the line through the few guides from the line winder and store line by running it back and forth between the two wooden pegs. It is also possible to use a Tennessee handle or to just glue a rod section into a hole in a wood handle and then tape the reel onto the handle (almost like a Tennessee handle) using electricians or masking tape.

RIGHT-HAND AND LEFT-HAND FLY RODS

According to a tip I first learned from Lefty Kreh, fly rods can be right-handed and left-handed. This has more to do with the line as it comes off the deck of a boat when an angler shoots a long cast than it does with the hand that holds the rod. The theory here is that the thick line coming up off the boat deck—or from the water surface—comes up at a high rate of speed, and often a high incidence of tangle. There is a benefit from the line going through a larger guide that is angled to the side. When shooting long casts, most of us will funnel the line through a circle made with our line-hand index finger and thumb. A large guide (16 or 20 millimeters in most cases) canted slightly to the line-hand side will more easily funnel the line from the line hand and up through the rest of the stripper and snake guides. The handle is no different, even though the rod when built must have the guide canted and wrapped to the left for right-hand casters and to the right for left-hand casters.

In making a right- or left-handed fly rod, the wrapping techniques, other guides, grip, and reel seat are no different from those of a standard fly rod. It should be noted, however, that this method of building a fly rod is best primarily on larger rods that will be used with heavy lines and long casts. Largemouth bass rods, saltwater fly rods, and salmon rods are the prime beneficiaries.

RIGHT-HAND AND LEFT-HAND SPINNING RODS

Though it's rarely done, it is possible to build rods with grips specifically for the right or left hand. This is easier for spinning rods than for casting rods, because spinning rods stay in one hand for casting and retrieving. Casting rods are more difficult because they are usually cast with one hand and then switched to the other for retrieving.

The technique of making these grips involves individual finger grooves. Finger grooves are sometimes built into custom-made knives and other outdoor equipment but rarely into rod grips. And such grooves for the fingers are not made straight across but at a slight angle. Thus a rod grip made with grooves on an angle for the right hand would make a good grip with the left hand impossible.

Admittedly, grooves on rod grips will not be pronounced, because on most spinning rods the reel seat will interfere with all but those for the ring and little finger. Using spinning rings on a straight cork grip will allow for more extensive grooves, but it is still best to leave a flat spot on which to seat the reel foot.

The best way to make these grooves on a cork grip is to first leave the grip slightly oversized. You don't have to sand it smooth at this point, but it should be close to a final finish. Because the reel seat or spinning rod rings will already be mounted, placed a rod in the reel seat. Then grab the rod with the preferred hand, holding it in a comfortable position. To mark the ridges between the finger grooves, lift each finger in turn and draw a line against the adjoining finger. Do this with all the fingers, then remove your hand and check the marks. It helps to regrasp the rod several times, lifting one finger at a time to see if the original lines are accurate.

Once you are satisfied with the position of the lines, use a rasp to lightly cut in between them, keeping the finger grooves on a slight angle as indicated by the lines. Use successively finer sandpaper to shape, smooth, and polish the grip, as per the instructions in chapter 20.

MIXED-MATERIAL RODS

"Mixed-material" in this case does not refer to rods or blanks of a mixture of graphite and glass and/or other materials. It refers instead to rods—usually two-piece—that are composed of one material for the butt section and a second material for the tip end. First popularized by rod-builder Russ Peak, these rods have been built by the large rod manufacturers. Rods have been made with graphite butts for power and fiberglass tips for slow flexibility. The theory here is that when fishing crankbaits (for which these spinning and casting rods are usually made), the slow-reacting fiberglass tip allows a bass to inhale the crankbait deeper, thus producing deeper, surer hooking as opposed to fast-reacting graphite, which can pull a lure from the fish's mouth. Not all anglers agree with this theory, but that is the concept behind the slow tip and fast, powerful butt.

Building these rods is no different from building any other two-piece spinning or casting rod. The main concern is to acquire one blank with the combination of materials or to combine two blanks into one rod. For the latter, the only possibility, and admittedly it's an expensive one, is to find a graphite rod or blank with a butt section that will fit the fiberglass tip section of another rod and to buy both. Even if you are willing to pay the price to do this, it is best done at a local store where you can check the accuracy of the fit of the two parts or determine the degree of adjustment by sanding and fitting that will have to take place.

ROD BUTT-SECTION REINFORCERS

At one time Fenwick produced a fly rod that was used extensively for big-game fly fishing. Basically it was a heavy fly rod with a removable butt cap and a separate long, insertable section that fits into the butt section. The rod was used without the insert for casting and during the hookup, but after that the insert was added to increase the rod's butt-section strength. In essence it provided a double-wall butt section to provide more lifting power for big fish on heavy tippets. This was in the days of glass rods, when heavy graphite rods were not available for big-game fishing.

Although some criticized this insert method of strengthening rods, it accomplished its stated purpose well and allowed the landing of big fish that might otherwise have been impossible. Admittedly, then and now, many serious fly anglers are opposed to modifying a rod during the act of fishing. Regardless, such an insert for a fly rod (or for that matter, a spinning or casting rod) is relatively easy to make.

If you wish to try something like this, it can be done by building any big-game fly rod (or any other rod) in the traditional manner, with special attention paid to a removable butt cap and access to the hollow end of the blank at the base of the reel seat. Any rod for which this is being considered must have blank-through-the-handle construction in order for the insert to fit properly. The insert usually has a small butt on the end of a short section of an inch or two, or a couple of cork rings ending in a butt cap. Ideally the insert blank should friction-fit into the base of the rod-blank butt. If it fits too loosely, the insert blank can be shimmed with a layer or two of fiberglass tape about 4 inches wide. The tape should be well soaked with resin and then sanded and shaped to fit the rod blank after complete curing. Naturally any such insert will have to be shorter than the butt section of the rod, since the insert cannot extend beyond the plug used in some spigot ferrules.

You should note that such additions are not allowed in most fly rod fishing tournaments and are not allowed for tournaments or record-keeping purposes by the IGFA. If records are your goal, stay away from this idea!

TELESCOPING RODS

Telescoping rods are one form of pack rod but are built so differently that they deserve a section of their own.

Telescoping rods are just that—rods whose several sections slide out of one another from the butt end just like a telescope or a camera-tripod leg. In all honesty I don't care for them much, but they are sold commercially and can be built by the tackle crafter—although building them is not easy.

You can cut blanks so that each piece fits inside another for as many sections as you want based on the length of the rod. The upper end of each blank section must be wrapped to provide hoop strength. Because usually only one guide is added to each section, often this guide's wrap is incorporated into the hoop-strength wrap, or the wrap for hoop strength is used as an underwrap beneath the rod wrap.

While building a telescoping rod is simple in theory, in practice you often need two blanks to make up the rod, because simply cutting a blank into several pieces and sliding each one into a larger section will result in too much net loss of blank length. It also results in too much extra blank length inside the rod, although this can be reduced with measuring, marking, and trimming.

Unfortunately there is no way to plan all of this out, because there is no easy way to measure the inside diameter of the rod blank at several points on the rod. You just have to cut and hope for the best. For this reason it is best to use this method only if you have a scrap blank that you care little about or wish to experiment just for the sake of experimenting.

To measure and check the rod, you just have to cut—say, a 6-foot rod into four pieces—and then slide each section into the next larger section and see how long a rod you get when the sections are pulled out. Obviously a rod with a shallow gradual taper is better suited for this, because a steep taper will result in too much rod being "lost" inside the previous section.

Once you have pulled the rod sections out so that they are snug inside the previous sections, use a felt-tip marker to mark each blank section at its exit point from the previous section. Then remove the blank sections and check for the mark that will indicate the exit point of that section. If you are satisfied with the result and are confident you will not be losing too much length, cut off any excess butt ends but leave about 4 to 5 inches below the marks on each section.

Then reinsert the sections and check for any looseness or play. If there is some, you might have to sand slightly or remove the section and add some epoxy glue to build up the blank for sanding and precise fitting to the inside of the larger section. If you add glue, use the 5-minute kind or rotate the rod section—just as you would do on a curing motor with rod-wrap finish—to produce an even coat of epoxy that will be easier to sand and size later on.

Once you are ready to build the rod, add the handle components to the butt section first, because you will not be able to do this after the internal rod parts are assembled. You can make any kind of rod you want, using any handle components previously described to make casting, spin-cast, or spinning rods. Once the handle is built on, insert the sections. At the end of each, apply a hoop-wrap underwrap followed by a guide wrap, or just use a guide wrap at the end of the rod, which will also give the rod hoop strength. Glue the tip-top to the end, pull the rod out to full length, and coat it with epoxy rod finish. Rotate the rod while the finish is curing, and the rod is ready to go.

An additional thought is that there is only one guide for each section on a telescoping rod, which is often too few for a good distribution of stress. You can't wrap another guide on each section, because this would prevent the rod from collapsing—the very reason for making it telescope in the first place. You can, however, use scrap sections of blank that were cut away, cut small 2- to 3-inch lengths that will fit onto the rod in the appropriate places, and wrap a guide to these. This then creates sliding friction-fit guides in the middle of the sections; thus these guides can slide free and still allow the rod to telescope after fishing. The guides will take up a little more space, so the resulting collapsed rod will be longer with these sliding guides than without, but the action and stress distribution will be much improved.

Add these short lengths to each rod section, and then slide the rod sections in place (all after building the handle), wrapping the guides in place on the ends of the sections and on the short sliding-guide sections. Finish as previously described.

OTHER POSSIBILITIES

There are some other rod variations. One, which seems to get reinvented every ten years or so, is the idea of avoiding guides completely and running the line off the reel, up through the center of a hollow blank, and out through a special tip-top that is almost like a ceramic tip on a fly tier's bobbin. Several years ago one company even had a rod in which the line flowed off the casting or spin-cast reel normally, but at the upper end of the rod the line went through a short (perhaps 2 feet long) length of blank that was spliced to, but did not make a continuous tunnel with, the lower portion of the blank.

The problem with any of these methods is that basically they will not work well, at least as far as current development in rods is concerned. To make them you have to drill a hole in the blank—which then has to be reinforced—a foot or two up the handle in order for the line to flow from the reel into the hollow rod blank. Then you must figure out how to make a tip-top, since nothing appropriate is commercially available. Assuming you overcome all this, the main problem is that the line running through the blank creates excessive friction, and the inside of the blank rapidly chews up the line. As great as this idea sounds, avoid it and stick to rods with guides.

Another rod variation that is difficult or impossible for the home custom rod builder is to make pack rods with several extra sections that make up a rod of varying lengths and even varying actions, depending on which section is used where. Although manufacturers have done this semi-successfully, the difficulty for the home craftsman is in finding the right length, taper, and fit of short blank sections or in being able to cut and fit sections to achieve these. In essence this rod is like a pack rod with extra sections. One possibility if you ever end up with extra butt sections or with scraps that can be made into extra butt sections is to make one butt section with a spinning grip and reel seat and another with a casting handle. Usually there will have to be a compromise on the guides so that the rod will work with either handle, but this is a good workable variation for a double-duty rod if you have an extra butt section.

Appendix A
Rod and Tackle Care

To cover the basics of tackle care would require a book of its own, and indeed several have been written on the subject. My books *Tackle Care: The Tackle Maintenance Handbook* (Lyons and Burford, 1987) and *The Field & Stream Tackle Care and Repair Handbook* (The Lyons Press, 1999) describe the care and repair of not only tackle you can build but also other types of tackle, including reels, boots and waders, accessory equipment, all types of lures and hooks, field tool kits, and more. Both books contain extensive photos that illustrate various phases of tackle care and repairs. For detailed information on care and repair of all types of tackle, consult one of these books.

This appendix will provide some general information on the types of problems you can encounter when fishing with your home-crafted rods, lures, and miscellaneous equipment. Obviously tackle care is important. Once you build lures or a custom rod, you want them to stay nice—that's where proper care comes into play.

Proper care begins in the home by properly storing rods in cases or racks and avoiding overstressing the rod by standing it in a corner or piling equipment on top of it. Lures should be stored properly, which means that hard baits should be separated from soft-plastic lures to prevent the solvents and plasticizers in the soft plastics from harming the finish of other items.

Similarly, soft-plastic lures should be separated by color, because mixed colors will bleed into one another and ruin the lures. If you store soft plastics you have molded (or purchased), make sure they are stored in "worm-proof" containers. Almost all modern tackle boxes made today are worm-proof.

During travel, keep lures properly separated and stored, and keep your rods cased and protected. When fishing, make sure that lures are hung in racks on a boat or are kept in tackle boxes until they are needed. Rods should be similarly racked or stored so that they will not cause accidents or get stepped on.

Once you're done fishing, tackle should be checked and cleaned. This is necessary to prevent corrosion if the tackle has been used in or around salt water. Clean rods with a good soaking from a garden hose or by rinsing in a shower. Scrub the rod lightly with a brush or washcloth, and allow it to dry thoroughly before casing or racking it. Pay particular attention to the threads and hoods of reel seats and around the frames of guides. Check guides for any chipping, grooving, or cracking of the guide ring, and replace guides if necessary. A new finish coat can be added over the old. Tip-tops often break more frequently than other guides yet are easy to replace. Mark the rod blank to protect it, heat the tip-top tube, slide it off, add more heat-set cement to the rod blank, and fit on a new tip-top.

If desired, smooth and clean the cork grip with fine sandpaper. Butt caps sometimes come off but are easily glued back on.

Rod blanks are often rejuvenated by the use of paraffin, candle wax, or a lubricant (such as U-40 Ferrule Lube) to get a good friction fit of the two sections. Rod wraps on guides should be checked and the finish replaced if it is chipped or scratched.

Reels, although they are not covered in this book, should be rinsed, and the drags should be backed off to preserve the soft drag washers. Once the reel is clean, spray its metal parts with a demoisturizer. Check the line capacity and respool with new premium line if necessary.

It also helps to rinse off lures and allow them to dry before being stored. If the tackle box is noticeably damp from wet lures or a drizzle, open the box to allow it to dry thoroughly before storing lures and closing the box up again. This simple step can prevent rusted hooks, metal lures, and tackle parts.

Check hooks and sharpen them with a good hook sharpener. Lures that have chipped finishes can be repainted following the methods outlined in chapter 15.

Specific lures need specific care. Often it helps to polish spinners, spinnerbait blades, buzzbait blades, and spoons with a metal or silver polish. The life of skirts on jigs and spinnerbaits is often prolonged by cleaning and drying them thoroughly and then coating them with talcum powder, cornmeal, or cornstarch to prevent the rubber from sticking to itself.

Fur skirts, such as are found on some jigs, should be washed gently, combed out, and allowed to dry.

Check the hardware on all lures: Jump rings, split rings, hook harnesses, screw eyes, and so on should all be checked for strength and durability. If there is any sign of weakness or corrosion, remove and replace the part.

Lures can be washed, but do not drop them in hot or boiling water. Hollow-plastic crankbaits in particular can be deformed by the heat. Check wood plugs for any cracks that can lead to warping, and repair them by coating the area with a clear epoxy finish.

Appendix B
Sales of Tackle

This book is meant as a handbook for the tackle and fishing hobbyist—not a business manual for the fledging manufacturer. However, it is likely that some readers will sell or attempt to sell the tackle they've made following the methods outlined here. Several things must be considered before beginning such a venture. First, most manufacturing processes are different from those outlined here. This is not so much in the methods used but in assembly-line procedures and some of the manufacturing equipment. For example, many jig and sinker manufacturers use expensive centrifugal molding machines in which two-part molds are in the shape of a wheel. The wheel is spun at high speed, and the molten lead is poured into a central cavity where the molten lead flows by centrifugal force to the mold cavities in the outer edges. Soft-plastic worms are made in similar two-part aluminum molds that create a number of worms at one time: The molds are fed from 55-gallon drums of liquid plastic.

A more important consideration than any of this is in dealing with the legal aspects of manufacturing tackle. Some of these are the laws requiring payment of excise tax on tackle items, the result of the Wallop-Breaux Act and the previous Dingell-Johnson Act. The original act of 1951 required a tax on most fishing tackle; the 1984 Wallop-Breaux supplemented this and broadened it. Officially the act is known as the Sport Fish Restoration and Boating Trust Fund (SFRBTF).

The Sport Fish Restoration Program was established in 1950 by the Dingell-Johnson Act. Using a 10 percent manufacturers' excise tax on certain fishing equipment, it funds various projects designed to enhance sportfishing in all fifty states. The Recreational Boating Safety Program was established in 1971 to fund boating safety and education programs and amended in 1980 to draw its funding from taxes on motorboat fuels. These programs were combined in 1984 under the Wallop-Breaux Act.

The Wallop-Breaux amendment expanded the 10 percent excise tax to nearly all sportfishing products and captured over half of the federal motorboat fuel taxes that were paid by boaters and anglers. This subsequently increased the funds collected by the federal government to be returned to the states for fishing and boating-related projects.

In 2005 Congress reauthorized the transfer of motorboat and small engine fuel taxes to the SFRBTF. Until then only 13.5 cents of the 18.3 cents in federal fuel taxes on each gallon of gasoline used by recreational boats and small engine was being transferred from the Highway Transportation Fund to the SFRBTF. The 4.8-cent balance was being diverted to the general treasury. However, the 2005 reauthorization authorized the transfer of the entire federal fuel tax to the SFRBTF. Anglers and boaters paying this tax finally received the full benefit of their tax payment investments.

Since its creation, the Sport Fish Restoration Act has been refined and expanded by Congress. It is unquestionably the most valuable federal legislation for anglers and fishery resources, delivering millions each year to state fishing and boating programs. This is the most important program for boating and angler access and fishery management in each state. It is also the core funding for each state's sport fish restoration program.

One final point: There seem to be constant raids or threads of raids on this fund by Congress. It is important to remind our representatives that these taxes are *user fees* creating dedicated funds for fisheries from anglers, boaters, and manufacturers. Such funds should not be appropriated for the general revenue or to reduce our deficit-spending problems!

An additional consideration is the increasing importance of trademark registration by manufacturers of their products. More and more manufacturers are applying for and being granted trademark protection. This protection applies to specific rods, reels, lures, and terminal tackle. Zebco has trademark protection on the shape of the Zebco 33/202/404 reels, Shakespeare has it on the clear-tip Ugly Stik rod, Arbogast has it on its Hula Popper and Jitterbug, Sampo has it on the shape of its swivel, AFTCO has it on the shape of its roller guides, Red Eye Tackle has it on its Red Eye Wiggler and Evil Eye spoons, and Wheatley has it on its sixteen-compartment fly box.

This protection makes it illegal for anyone to manufacture, distribute, or sell (at any level) copy, fake, or counterfeit products that might be confused with the original protected item. These are not patents, and unlike utility patents, which run out in seventeen years, or design patents, which run out in fourteen years, a trademark registration lasts forever.

What this means to budding tackle designer and manufacturers is that you cannot—upon threat of severe penalties—copy for sale a product already in existence and readily identifiable as a product with a particular name and made by a particular company. Technically, some experts tell me, you can't even make one item for your own use, even if you have no plans to make more, sell that one, or give it to a friend. The making of an exact copy *by appearance* (this is how the item is protected) is a violation of the trademark registration law. Other experts indicate that you can make particular items for your own use—you just can't sell any. From a practical standpoint, no manufacturer is likely to go after you for this, but the best rule is to stay away from exact copies of existing tackle. Besides, making exact copies would be somewhat self-defeating, because part of the joy of tackle crafting is in making new tackle of original design.

The brochure *Basic Facts about Trademarks* is also useful. This brochure (document C 21.2:T 67/4/2001) is available from the Superintendent of Documents: Government Printing Office, Washington, DC 20402.

Other helpful brochures include *A Guide to Proper Trademark Use* and *A Trademark Is Not a Patent*, both available from the Publications Office: U.S. Trademark Association, 6 East 45th St., New York, NY 10017; (212) 986-5880. There is a cost for these publications—inquire about current prices.

Naturally, as with any business, you must also become familiar with and conform to the laws affecting your business, including those from local municipalities, counties, states, and the federal government. For more information check with your local tax office or your accountant or business consultant.

Appendix C

Conversion Tables

ENGLISH-METRIC CONVERSION TABLE

INCHES DEC.	MM	INCHES DEC.	MM
0.01	0.2540	0.51	12.9540
0.02	0.5080	0.52	13.2080
0.03	0.7620	0.53	13.4620
0.04	1.0160	0.54	13.7160
0.05	1.2700	0.55	13.9700
0.06	1.5240	0.56	14.2240
0.07	1.7780	0.57	14.4780
0.08	2.0320	0.58	14.7320
0.09	2.2860	0.59	14.9860
0.10	2.5400	0.60	15.2400
0.11	2.7940	0.61	15.4940
0.12	3.0480	0.62	15.7480
0.13	3.3020	0.63	16.0020
0.14	3.5560	0.64	16.2560
0.15	3.8100	0.65	16.5100
0.16	4.0640	0.66	16.7640
0.17	4.3180	0.67	17.0180
0.18	4.5720	0.68	17.2720
0.19	4.8260	0.69	17.5260
0.20	5.0800	0.70	17.7800
0.21	5.3340	0.71	18.0340
0.22	5.5880	0.72	18.2880
0.23	5.8420	0.73	18.5420
0.24	6.0960	0.74	18.7960
0.25	6.3500	0.75	19.0500
0.26	6.6040	0.76	19.3040
0.27	6.8580	0.77	19.5580
0.28	7.1120	0.78	19.8120
0.29	7.3660	0.79	20.0660
0.30	7.6200	0.80	20.3200
0.31	7.8740	0.81	20.5740
0.32	8.1280	0.82	20.8280
0.33	8.3820	0.83	21.0820
0.34	8.6360	0.84	21.3360
0.35	8.8900	0.85	21.5900
0.36	9.1440	0.86	21.8440
0.37	9.3980	0.87	22.0980
0.38	9.6520	0.88	22.3520
0.39	9.9060	0.89	22.6060
0.40	10.1600	0.90	22.8600
0.41	10.4140	0.91	23.1140
0.42	10.6680	0.92	23.3680
0.43	10.9220	0.93	23.6220
0.44	11.1760	0.94	23.8760
0.45	11.4300	0.95	24.1300
0.46	11.6840	0.96	24.3840
0.47	11.9380	0.97	24.6380
0.48	12.1920	0.98	24.8920
0.49	12.4460	0.99	25.1460
0.50	12.7000	1.00	25.4000

INCHES FRAC.	INCHES DEC.	MM	INCHES FRAC.	INCHES DEC.	MM
1/64	0.015625	0.3969	33/64	0.515625	13.0969
1/32	0.031250	0.7938	17/32	0.531250	13.4938
3/64	0.046875	1.1906	35/64	0.546875	13.8906
1/16	0.062500	1.5875	9/16	0.562500	14.2875
5/64	0.078125	1.9844	37/64	0.578125	14.6844
3/32	0.093750	2.3812	19/32	0.593750	15.0812
7/64	0.109375	2.7781	39/64	0.609375	15.4781
1/8	0.125000	3.1750	5/8	0.625000	15.8750
9/64	0.140625	3.5719	41/64	0.640625	16.2719
5/32	0.156250	3.9688	21/32	0.656250	16.6688
11/64	0.171875	4.3656	43/64	0.671875	17.0656
3/16	0.187500	4.7625	11/16	0.687500	17.4625
13/64	0.203125	5.1594	45/64	0.703125	17.8594
7/32	0.218750	5.5562	23/32	0.718750	18.2562
15/64	0.234375	5.9531	47/64	0.734375	18.6531
1/4	0.250000	6.3500	3/4	0.750000	19.0500
17/64	0.265625	6.7469	49/64	0.765625	19.4469
9/32	0.281250	7.1438	25/32	0.781250	19.8437
19/64	0.296875	7.5406	51/64	0.796875	20.2406
5/16	0.312500	7.9375	13/16	0.812500	20.6375
21/64	0.328125	8.3344	53/64	0.828125	21.0344
11/32	0.343750	8.7312	27/32	0.843750	21.4312
23/64	0.359375	9.1281	55/64	0.859375	21.8281
3/8	0.375000	9.5250	7/8	0.875000	22.2250
25/64	0.390625	9.9219	57/64	0.890625	22.6219
13/32	0.406250	10.3188	29/32	0.906250	23.0188
27/64	0.421875	10.7156	59/64	0.921875	23.4156
7/16	0.437500	11.1125	15/16	0.937500	23.8125
29/64	0.453125	11.5094	61/64	0.953125	24.2094
15/32	0.468750	11.9062	31/32	0.968750	24.6062
31/64	0.484375	12.3031	63/64	0.984375	25.0031
1/2	0.500000	12.7000	1	1.000000	25.4000

For converting decimal-inches in "thousandths," move decimal point in both columns to left.

Courtesy: The L.S. Starrett Company

METRIC-ENGLISH CONVERSION TABLE

MM	INCHES	MM	INCHES	MM	INCHES	MM	INCHES	MM	INCHES
0.01	.00039	0.41	.01614	0.81	.03189	21	.82677	61	2.40157
0.02	.00079	0.42	.01654	0.82	.03228	22	.86614	62	2.44094
0.03	.00118	0.43	.01693	0.83	.03268	23	.90551	63	2.48031
0.04	.00157	0.44	.01732	0.84	.03307	24	.94488	64	2.51968
0.05	.00197	0.45	.01772	0.85	.03346	25	.98425	65	2.55905
0.06	.00236	0.46	.01811	0.86	.03386	26	1.02362	66	2.59842
0.07	.00276	0.47	.01850	0.87	.03425	27	1.06299	67	2.63779
0.08	.00315	0.48	.01890	0.88	.03465	28	1.10236	68	2.67716
0.09	.00354	0.49	.01929	0.89	.03504	29	1.14173	69	2.71653
0.10	.00394	0.50	.01969	0.90	.03543	30	1.18110	70	2.75590
0.11	.00433	0.51	.02008	0.91	.03583	31	1.22047	71	2.79527
0.12	.00472	0.52	.02047	0.92	.03622	32	1.25984	72	2.83464
0.13	.00512	0.53	.02087	0.93	.03661	33	1.29921	73	2.87401
0.14	.00551	0.54	.02126	0.94	.03701	34	1.33858	74	2.91338
0.15	.00591	0.55	.02165	0.95	.03740	35	1.37795	75	2.95275
0.16	.00630	0.56	.02205	0.96	.03780	36	1.41732	76	2.99212
0.17	.00669	0.57	.02244	0.97	.03819	37	1.45669	77	3.03149
0.18	.00709	0.58	.02283	0.98	.03858	38	1.49606	78	3.07086
0.19	.00748	0.59	.02323	0.99	.03898	39	1.53543	79	3.11023
0.20	.00787	0.60	.02362	1.00	.03937	40	1.57480	80	3.14960
0.21	.00827	0.61	.02402	1	.03937	41	1.61417	81	3.18897
0.22	.00866	0.62	.02441	2	.07874	42	1.65354	82	3.22834
0.23	.00906	0.63	.02480	3	.11811	43	1.69291	83	3.26771
0.24	.00945	0.64	.02520	4	.15748	44	1.73228	84	3.30708
0.25	.00984	0.65	.02559	5	.19685	45	1.77165	85	3.34645
0.26	.01024	0.66	.02598	6	.23622	46	1.81102	86	3.38582
0.27	.01063	0.67	.02638	7	.27559	47	1.85039	87	3.42519
0.28	.01102	0.68	.02677	8	.31496	48	1.88976	88	3.46456
0.29	.01142	0.69	.02717	9	.35433	49	1.92913	89	3.50393
0.30	.01181	0.70	.02756	10	.39370	50	1.96850	90	3.54330
0.31	.01220	0.71	.02795	11	.43307	51	2.00787	91	3.58267
0.32	.01260	0.72	.02835	12	.47244	52	2.04724	92	3.62204
0.33	.01299	0.73	.02874	13	.51181	53	2.08661	93	3.66141
0.34	.01339	0.74	.02913	14	.55118	54	2.12598	94	3.70078
0.35	.01378	0.75	.02953	15	.59055	55	2.16535	95	3.74015
0.36	.01417	0.76	.02992	16	.62992	56	2.20472	96	3.77952
0.37	.01457	0.77	.03032	17	.66929	57	2.24409	97	3.81889
0.38	.01496	0.78	.03071	18	.70866	58	2.28346	98	3.85826
0.39	.01535	0.79	.03110	19	.74803	59	2.32283	99	3.89763
0.40	.01575	0.80	.03150	20	.78740	60	2.36220	100	3.93700

For converting millimeters in "thousandths," move decimal point in both columns to left.

Appendix D
Size Charts

Size Charts for Connector Sleeves

CATALOG NO.	INSIDE DIAMETER	LENGTH	FITS WIRE MULTISTRAND	FITS WIRE NYLO-STRAND	FITS MONOFILAMENT
11	0.027	0.215	90	30	40
21	0.028	0.215	150, 210	45, 60	60, 80
31	0.048	0.310	275 "49"-STR.	90, 150	100, 130
41	0.063	0.394	480 "49"-STR.	210	150, 200
51	0.075	0.394	600 "49"-STR.		200
61	0.087	0.470	800 "49"-STR.		300
71	0.115	0.550			525

Courtesy: Mason Tackle Co.

CATALOG NO.	INSIDE DIAMETER	OUTSIDE DIAMETER	LENGTH	FITS WIRE MULTISTRAND	FITS WIRE NYLO-STRAND	FITS MONO-FILAMENT
1	0.033	0.062	0.187	30	10	10, 15
2	0.046	0.086	0.250	45, 60	15	20, 30
3	0.055	0.094	0.250	90, 100	20, 30	30, 40
4	0.070	0.125	0.250	125, 150	45, 60	50, 60
6	0.082	0.156	0.375	210	90, 125	80
7	0.106	0.190	0.400	210	150, 210	100, 130
8	0.116	0.190	0.400	275 ("49" Str)	210	150
9	0.125	0.190	0.400	480 ("49" Str)		180
10	0.140	0.215	0.500			200
12	0.159	0.250	0.500	600 ("49" Str)		200
14	0.203	0.312	0.500	800 ("49" Str)		300

Courtesy: Mason Tackle Co.

SLEEVES

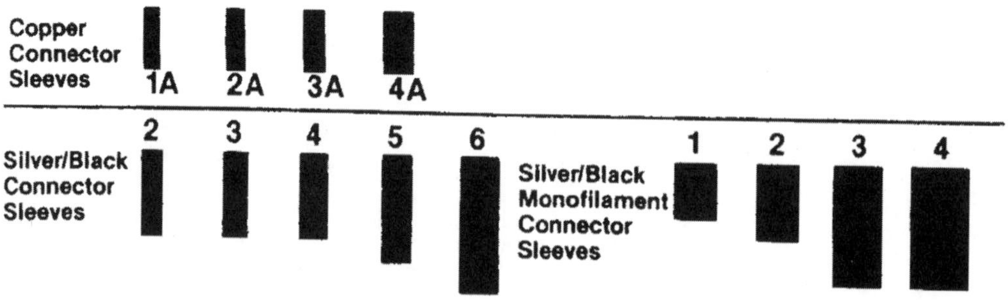

Copper Connector Sleeves: 1A 2A 3A 4A

Silver/Black Connector Sleeves: 2 3 4 5 6

Silver/Black Monofilament Connector Sleeves: 1 2 3 4

Description	Size	Inside Diameter	Length	Steelon® Lb. Test	Steelstrand Lb. Test	Nylon Lb. Test
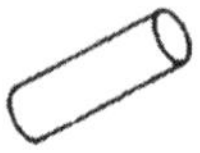 Copper Connector Sleeves	1A	.025	.250		20	4-10
	2A	.033	.250		30	12-15
	3A	.044	.250	10-15	45	17-25
	4A	.058	.250	20-45	60-100	30-40
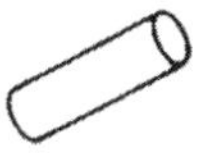 Silver/Black Connector Sleeves	2	.040	.375	10	20-45	12-20
	3	.062	.375	15-45	60-140	25-50
	4	.080	.375	60-80	210	60-80
	5	.098	.500	120		90-125
	6	.137	.625	210		150-225
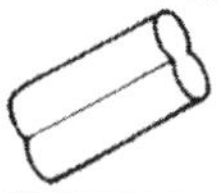 Silver/Black Monofilament Connector Sleeves	1	.055	.250			60-100
	2	.065	.375			125-150
	3	.080	.562			200-250
	4	.095	.562			300-400

Courtesy: Berkley and Co., Inc.

Sleeves

Wire Sleeve Stock No.	Fits Sevenstrand Wire Sizes	Fits Sevalon Wire Sizes	Fits Duratest Wire Sizes	Fits Mono-filament Sizes
A1	8, 12, 18, 27 lbs.			
A2	40, 60	8, 12, 18 27 lbs.		10 lbs.
A3	90	40		15 & 20
A4	135			30 & 40
A5	170	60		50 & 60
A6	250		175 lbs.	80
A7		90	275 lbs.	100 & 125
A8			400	150
A9		135		165
A10		170	480	185
A11		250	600	200
A12			800	220
A14				250

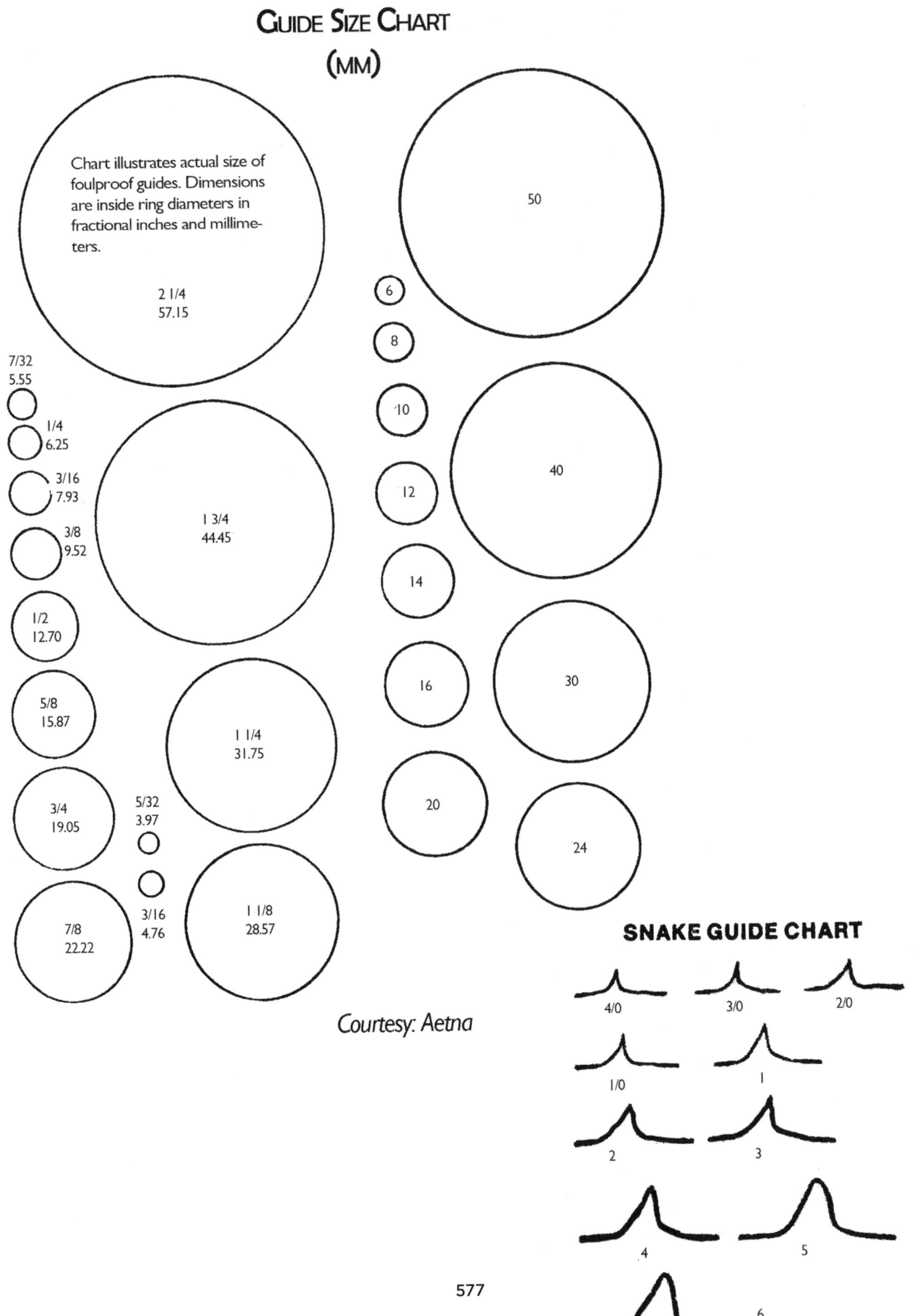

Courtesy: Aetna

Selecting the correct size guide

Determine the Perfection guide size for your rod building requirement by referring to the chart. When sizing a guide needing replacement, simply use the chart to match its outside ring diameter to the corresponding Perfection size.

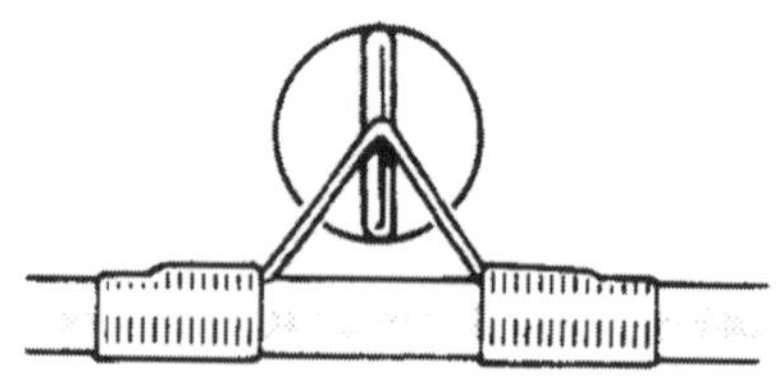

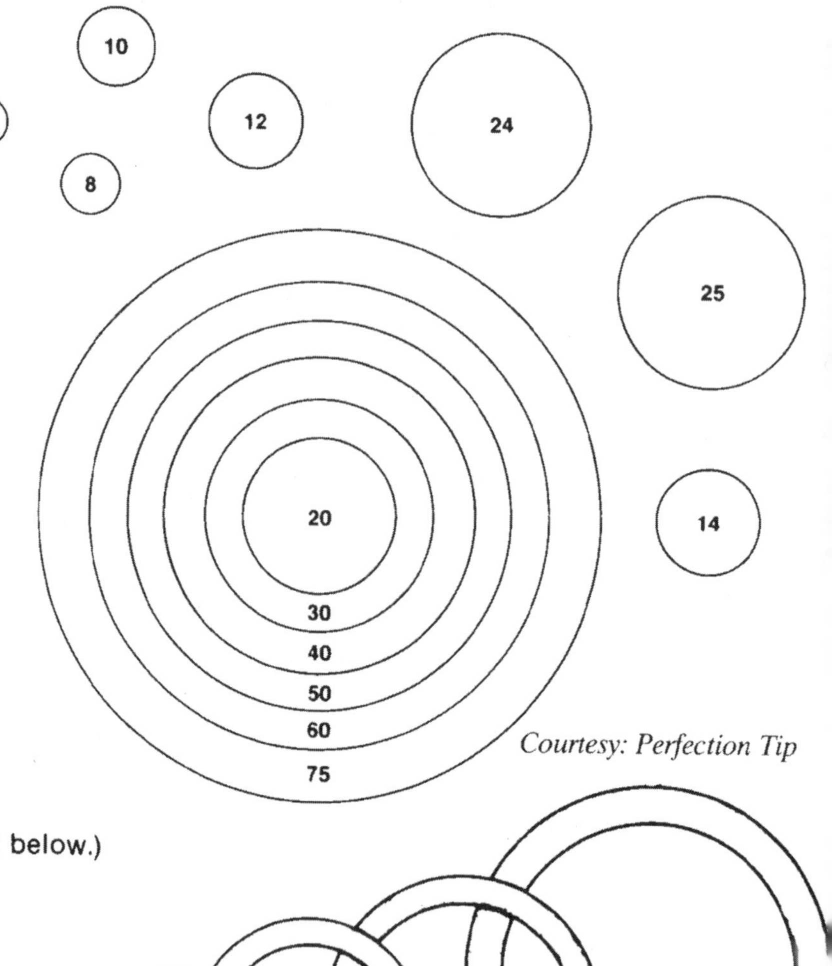

Lay your rod on this page as shown. Look straight down on the guide ring from above and match it with the Perfection Guide closest in size.

Courtesy: Perfection Tip

(Ring sizes and dimensions are shown in chart below.)

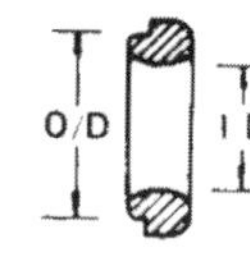

light duty ring | heavy duty ring | flanged ring

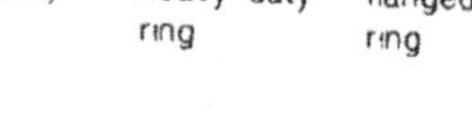
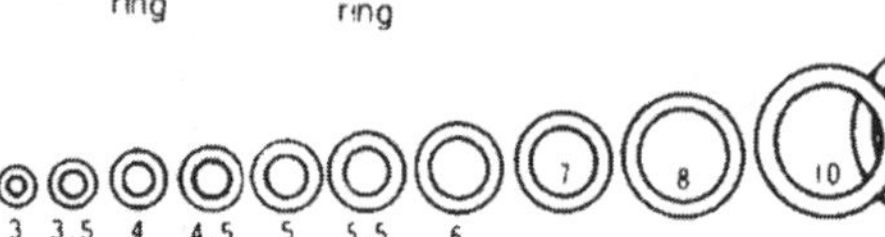

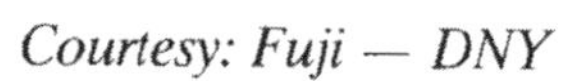

Courtesy: Fuji — DNY

64th OF AN INCH SCALE FOR TOPS

½"

Place your rod tip on this ½" mark.

Courtesy: Perfection Tip

4 5 6 7 8 9 10 12 14 16 18 20 22 24 26 28 30 32

Courtesy: Mildrum

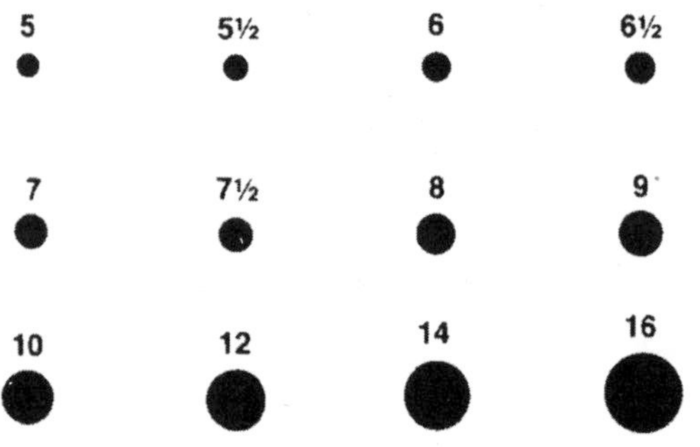

NOTE: When mounting Aftco guides, the "Size No." stamped on the guide frame should face the reel seat or rod butt.

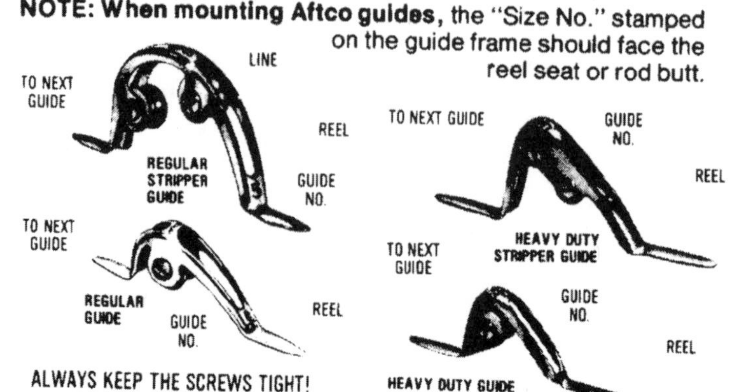

Courtesy: AFTCO

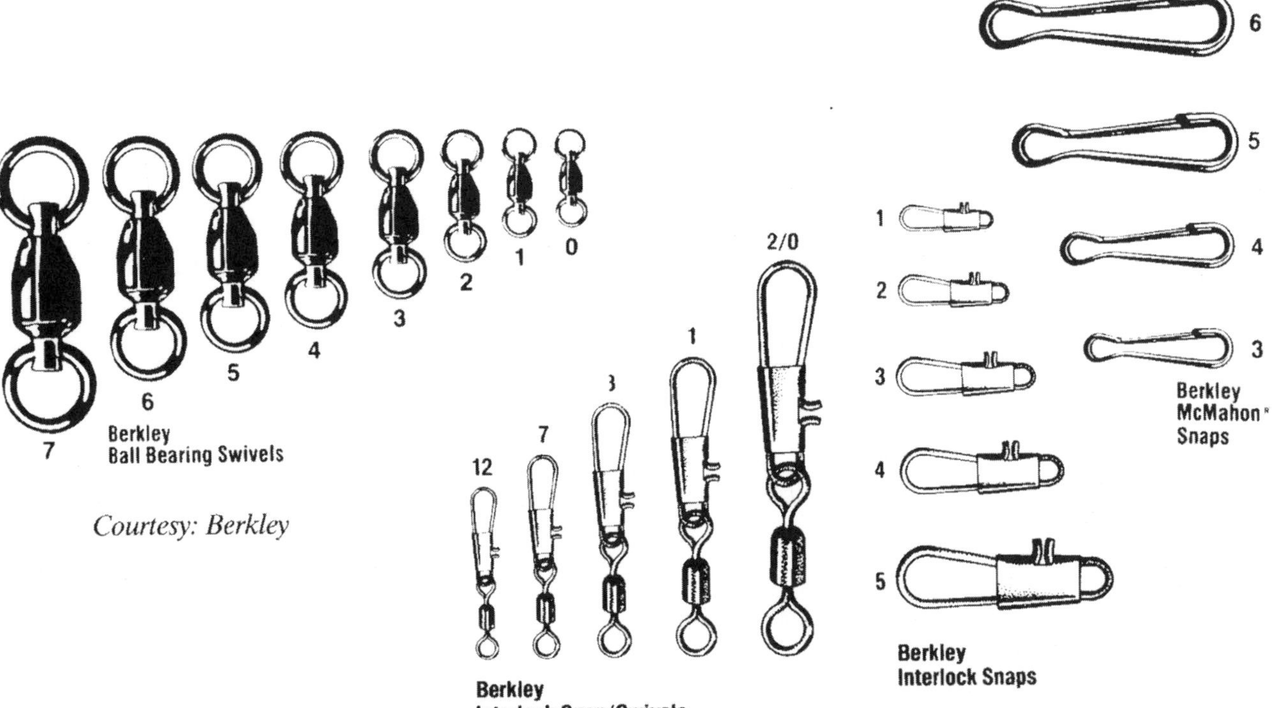

Courtesy: Berkley

BALL BEARING CROSS-LOK® SNAP/SWIVELS

Size	0	2	3	5	6	7
Lb. Test	25	75	125	175	175	275

McMAHON® SNAP/SWIVELS

Size	10	7	3	1	2/0	4/0
Lb. Test	18	40	80	80	110	150

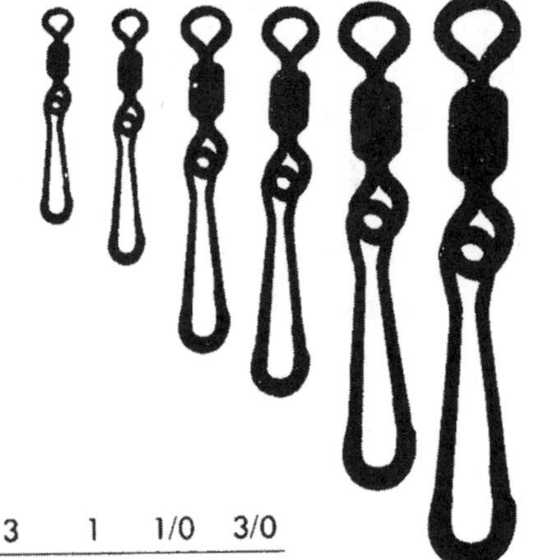

CROSS-LOK® SNAP/SWIVELS

Size	12	7	5	3	1	1/0	3/0
Lb. Test	40	65	100	100	150	175	275

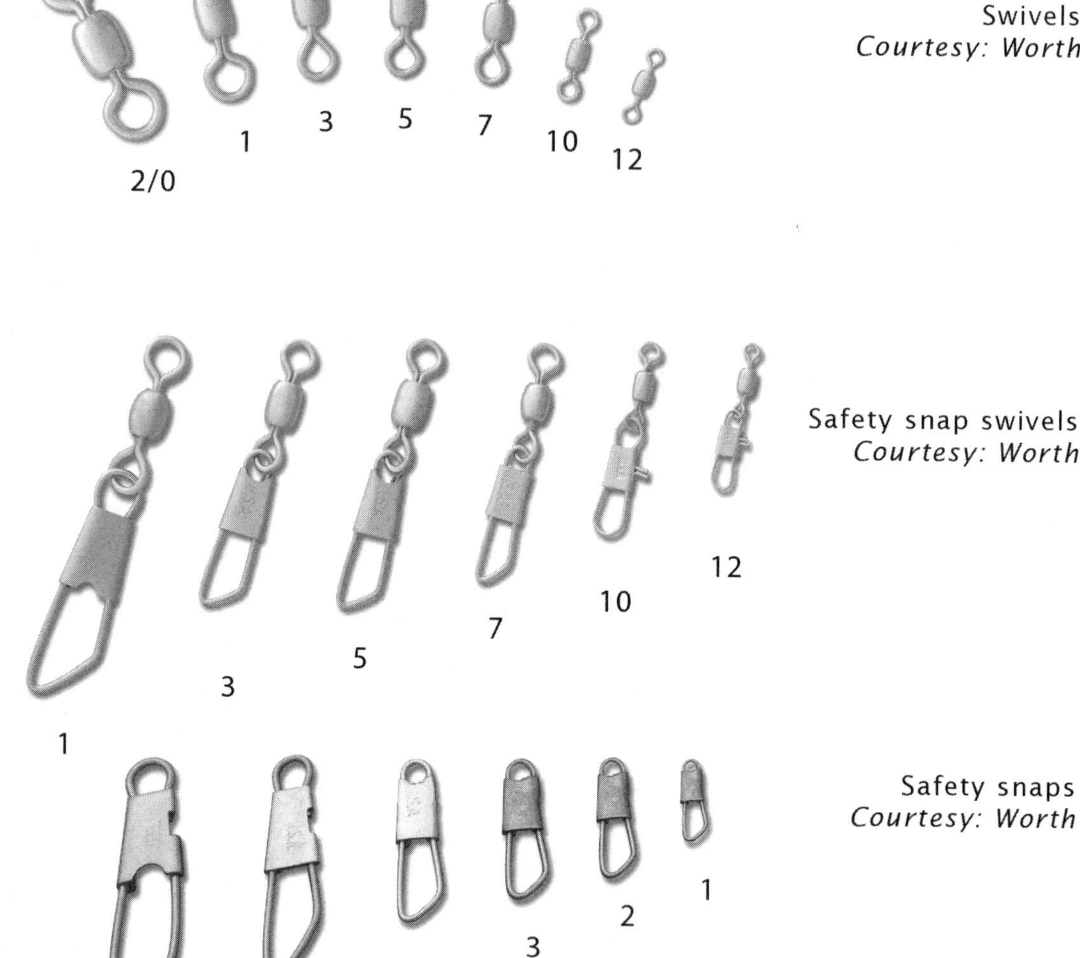

Swivels
Courtesy: Worth

Safety snap swivels
Courtesy: Worth

Safety snaps
Courtesy: Worth

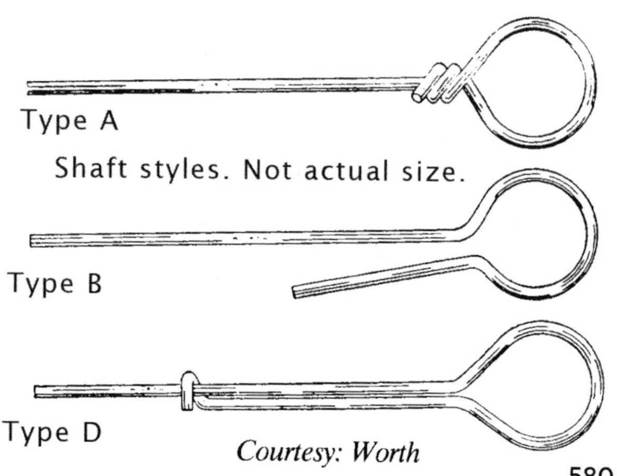

Shaft styles. Not actual size.

Courtesy: Worth

BALL BEARING SWIVELS

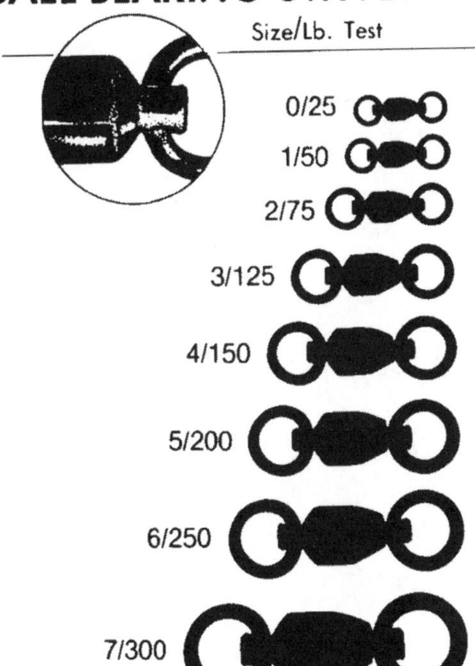

McMAHON® SWIVELS

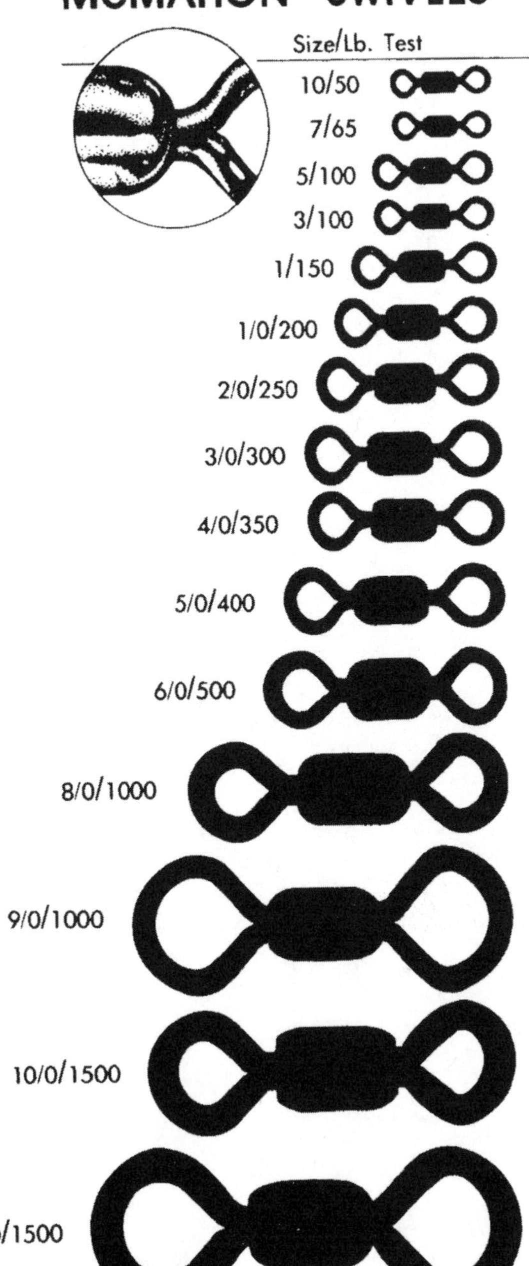

Courtesy: Berkley

CROSS-LOK® SNAPS

Size	1	3	6	9	10
Lb. Test	40	75	125	175	275

McMAHON® SNAPS

Size	3	4	5	6
Lb. Test	80	80	110	150

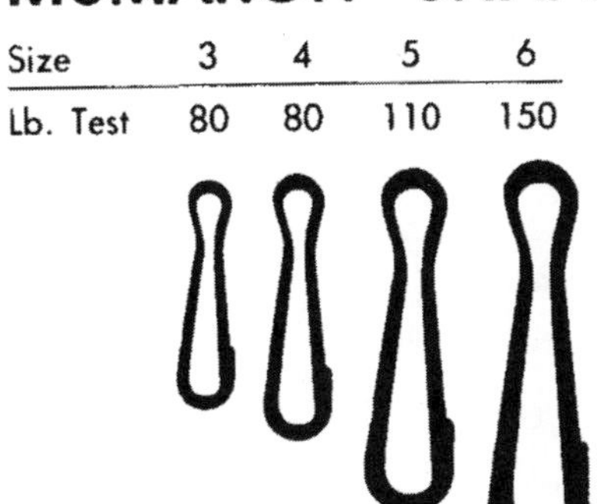

Courtesy: Sampo

FRESH WATER SERIES

General usage: nos. 1 and 2, light spin fishing; no. 2, casting also; no. 3, spinning, casting and trolling; no. 4, casting and trolling; no. 5, heavy casting and trolling; no. 6, extra heavy trolling.

The pound designation figure below each number indicates swivel test.

6R 70 lbs. — 5R 50 lbs. — 4R 30 lbs. — 3R 15 lbs. — 2R 12 lbs.

6L 70 lbs. — 5L 50 lbs. — 4L 30 lbs. — 3L 15 lbs. — 2L 12 lbs. — 1L 10 lbs.

Lock Snap

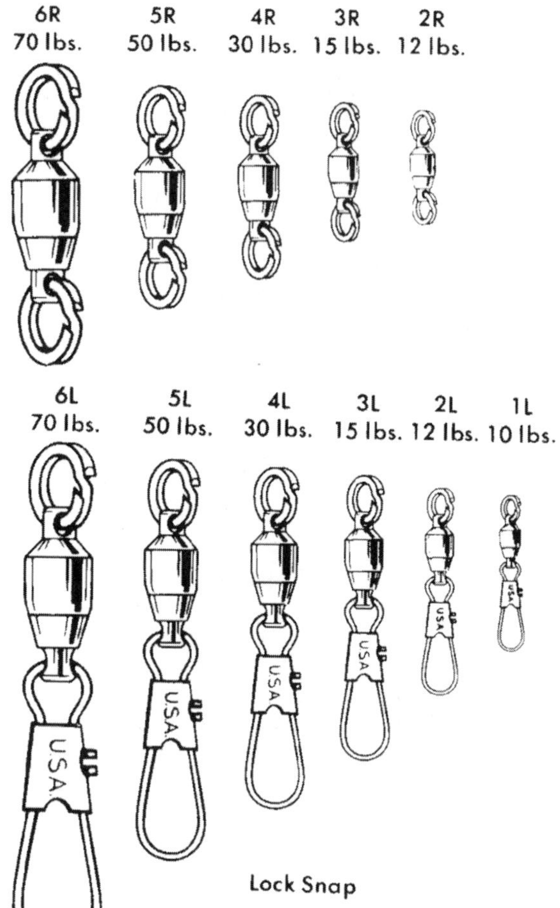

SALT WATER SERIES

Designed for use in all types of salt water fishing. Different riggings are available for local fishing requirements and preferences.

The pound designation figure below each number indicates swivel test.

X8R 600 lbs. — X6R 300 lbs. — X5R 200 lbs. — X4R 100 lbs. — X3R 75 lbs.

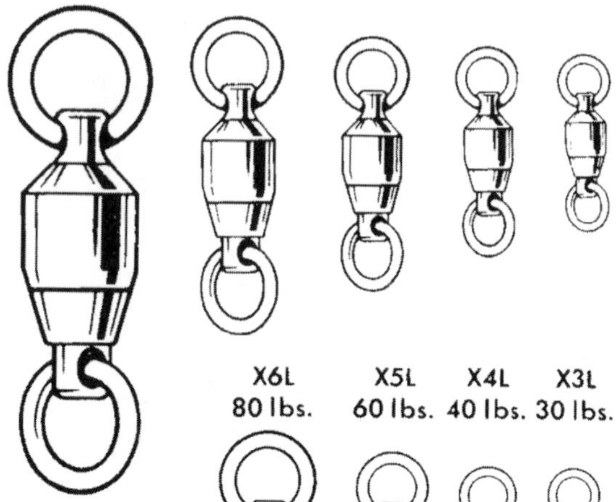

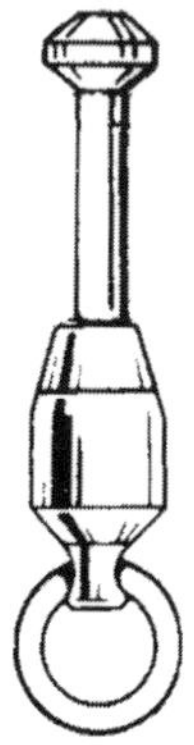

X6SC
300 lbs.
Tubing Connector

X6L 80 lbs. — X5L 60 lbs. — X4L 40 lbs. — X3L 30 lbs.

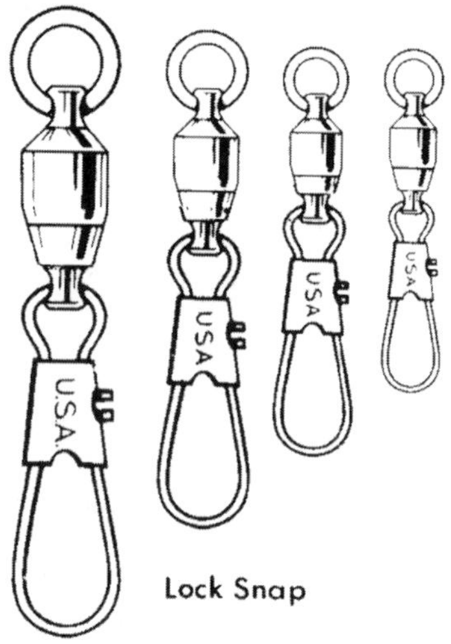

Lock Snap

X6M 150 lbs. — X5M 100 lbs. — X4M 80 lbs.

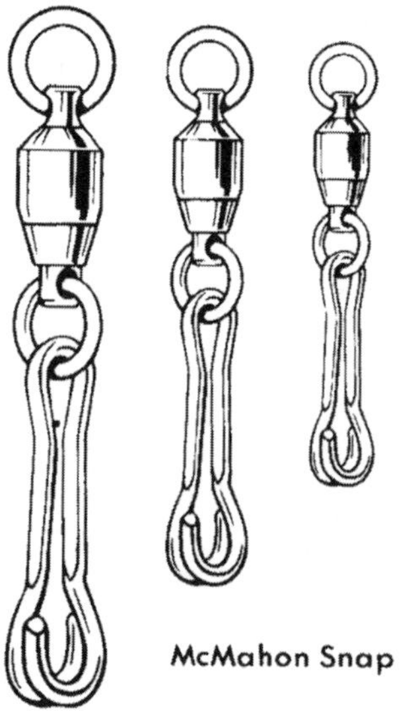

McMahon Snap

X6C 200 lbs. — X5C 165 lbs. — X4C 100 lbs.

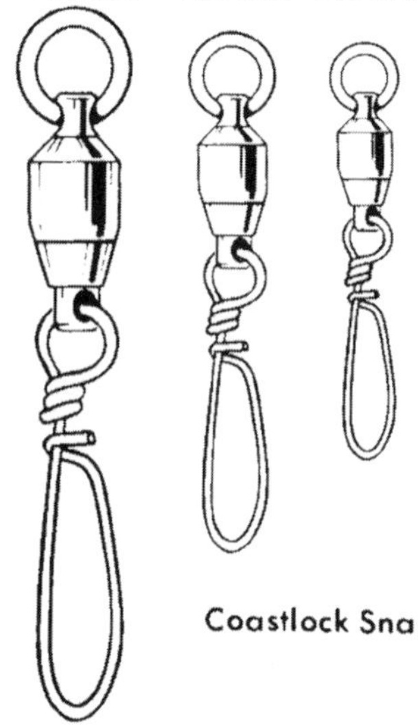

Coastlock Snap

BEAD CHAIN
Deluxe NATURAL ACTION **Flexible Spinners**
"EVERY BEAD A SWIVEL"

Courtesy: Bead Chain

SINGLE SPINNERS

2/00 3/0 6/1 6/2 6/3

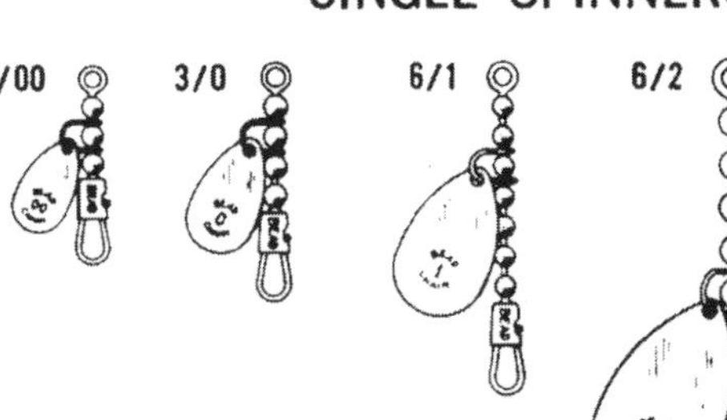

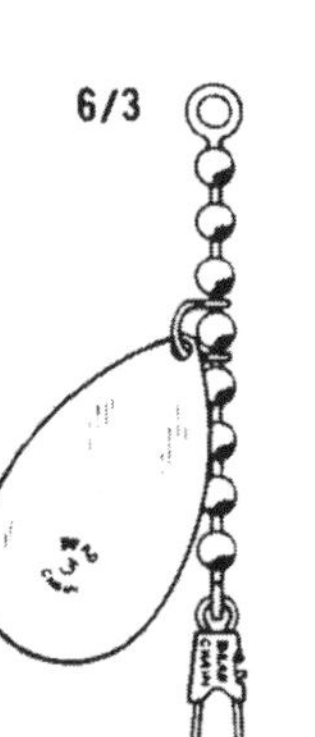

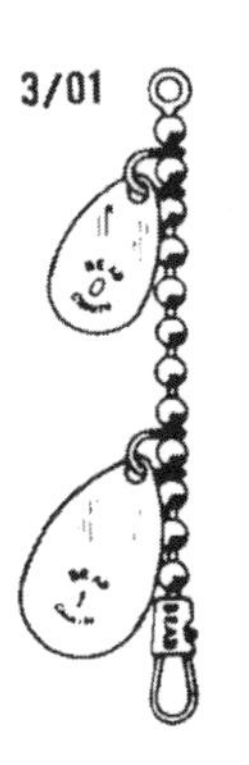

DOUBLE SPINNERS

3/01 6/12 6/23 10/45

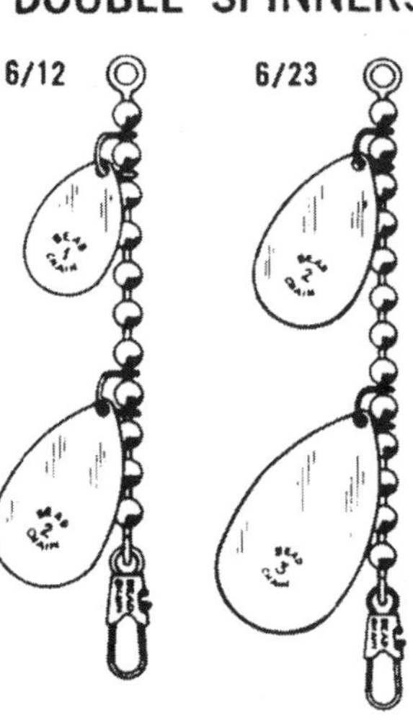

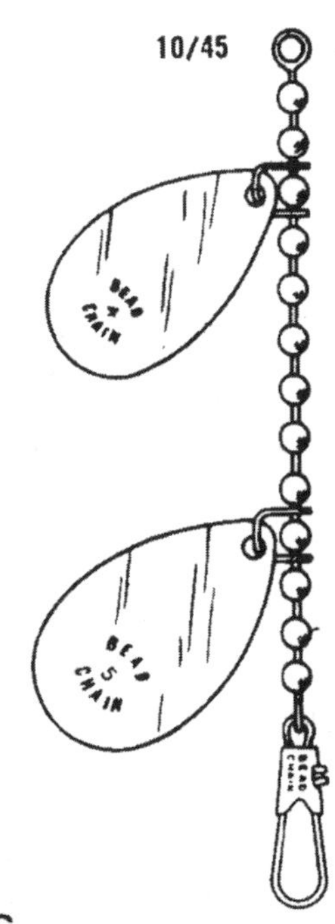

BEAD CHAIN
Monel Swivels
"EVERY BEAD A SWIVEL"

ITEM NO.	LBS. TEST
PLAIN	
21	25
61	35
101	75
131	175
SINGLE SNAP	
22	25
32	30
62	35
645	45
102	75
132	120
LOCK TYPE SNAP	
62L	35
102L	75
132L	150
DOUBLE SNAP	
63	35
103	75
133	120

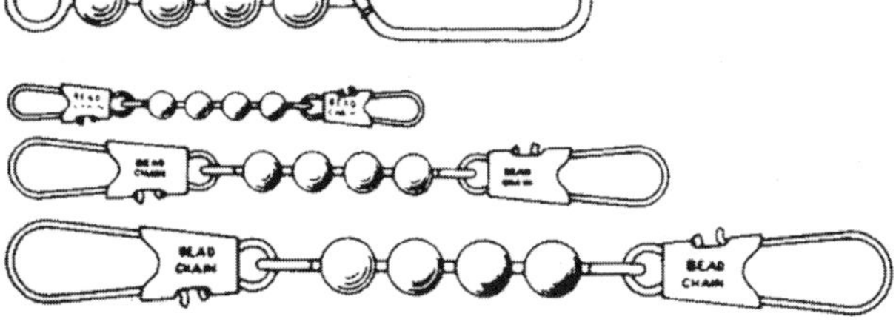

KEEL LEADS

ITEM NO.	LBS. TEST
1/16 oz.	30
1/8 oz.	30
1/4 oz.	35
3/8 oz.	35
5/8 oz.	35
1 1/4 oz.	75
2 1/4 oz.	75
4 oz.	150

CASTING & TROLLING LEADS

ITEM NO.	LBS. TEST
1/4 oz.	35
1/2 oz.	35
3/4 oz.	35
1 oz.	75
1 1/4 oz.	75
1 1/2 oz.	75
1 3/4 oz.	75
2 oz.	75
3 oz.	75
4 oz.	150
6 oz.	150
8 oz.	150
16 oz.	150

Stainless Steel SAFETY SNAPS

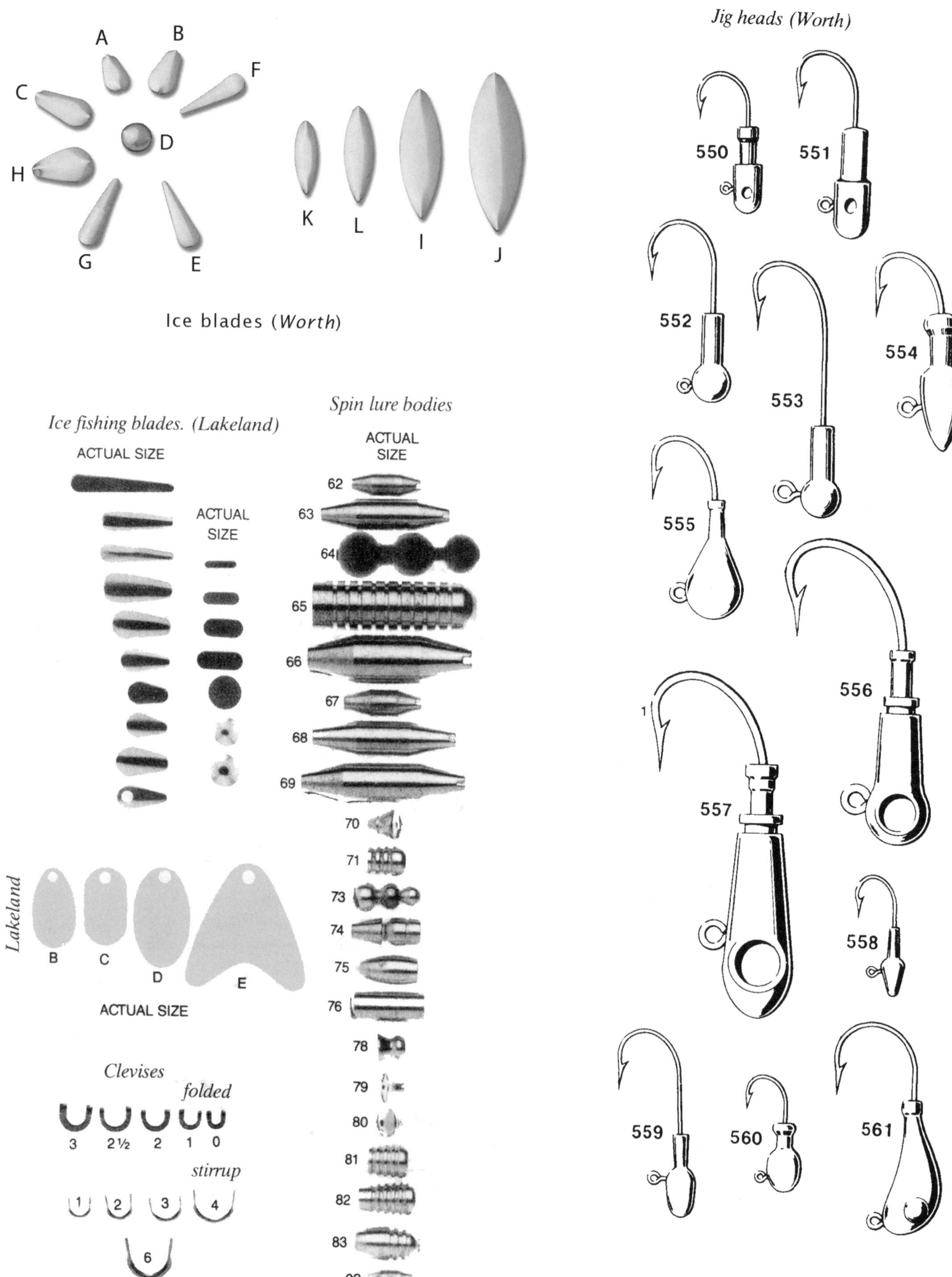
A
B
F
C
D
H
G
E
K
L
I
J
Ice blades (*Worth*)
Jig heads (Worth)
550
551
552
553
554
555
556
557
558
559
560
561
Ice fishing blades. (Lakeland)
ACTUAL SIZE
ACTUAL SIZE
Spin lure bodies
ACTUAL SIZE
62
63
64
65
66
67
68
69
70
71
73
74
75
76
78
79
80
81
82
83
92
Lakeland
B
C
D
E
ACTUAL SIZE
Clevises
folded
3
2½
2
1
0
stirrup
1
2
3
4
6

SIZE CHARTS FOR SPINNER PARTS

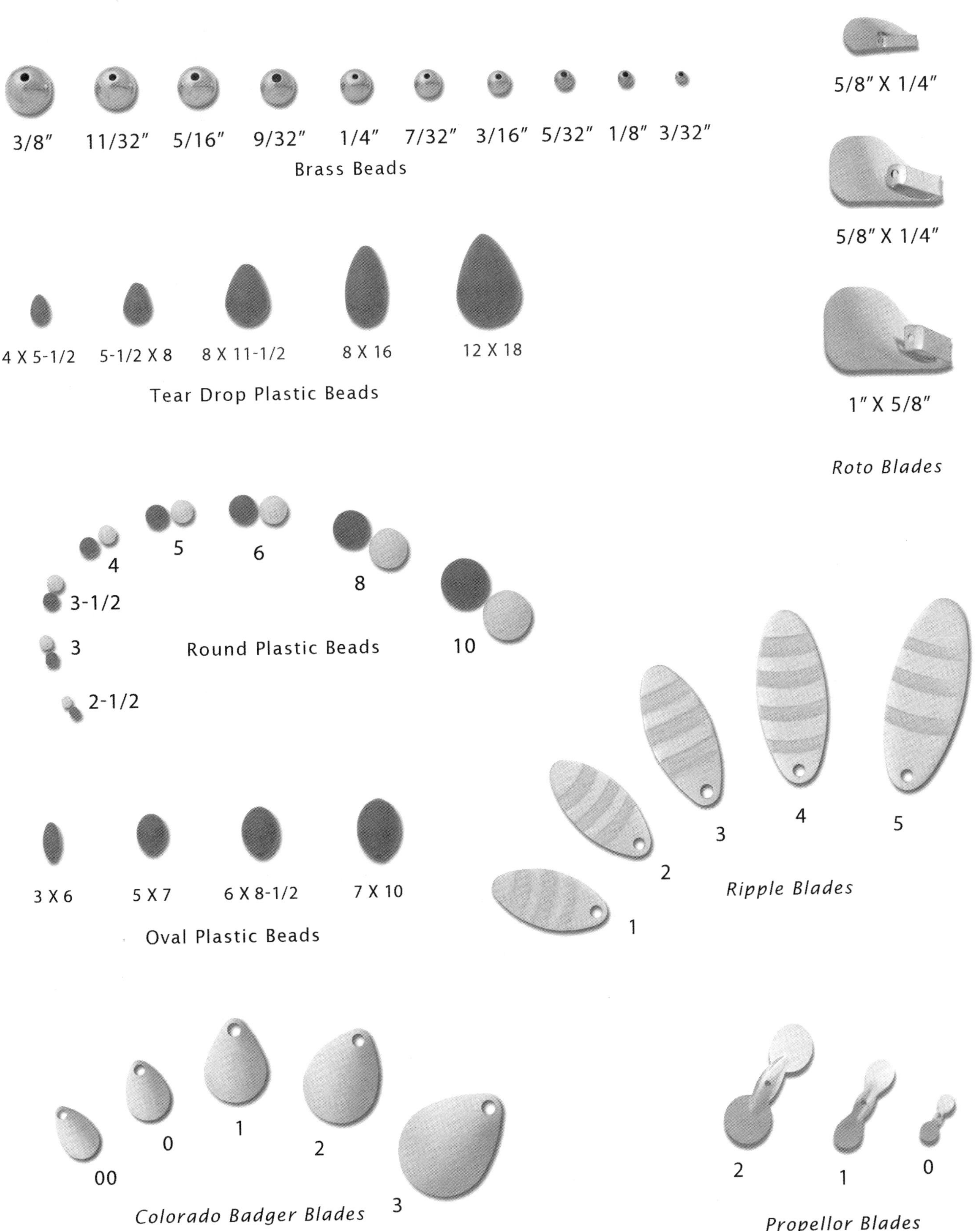

All Courtesy of *Worth*

SIZE CHARTS FOR SPINNER BLADES AND TROLLING BLADES

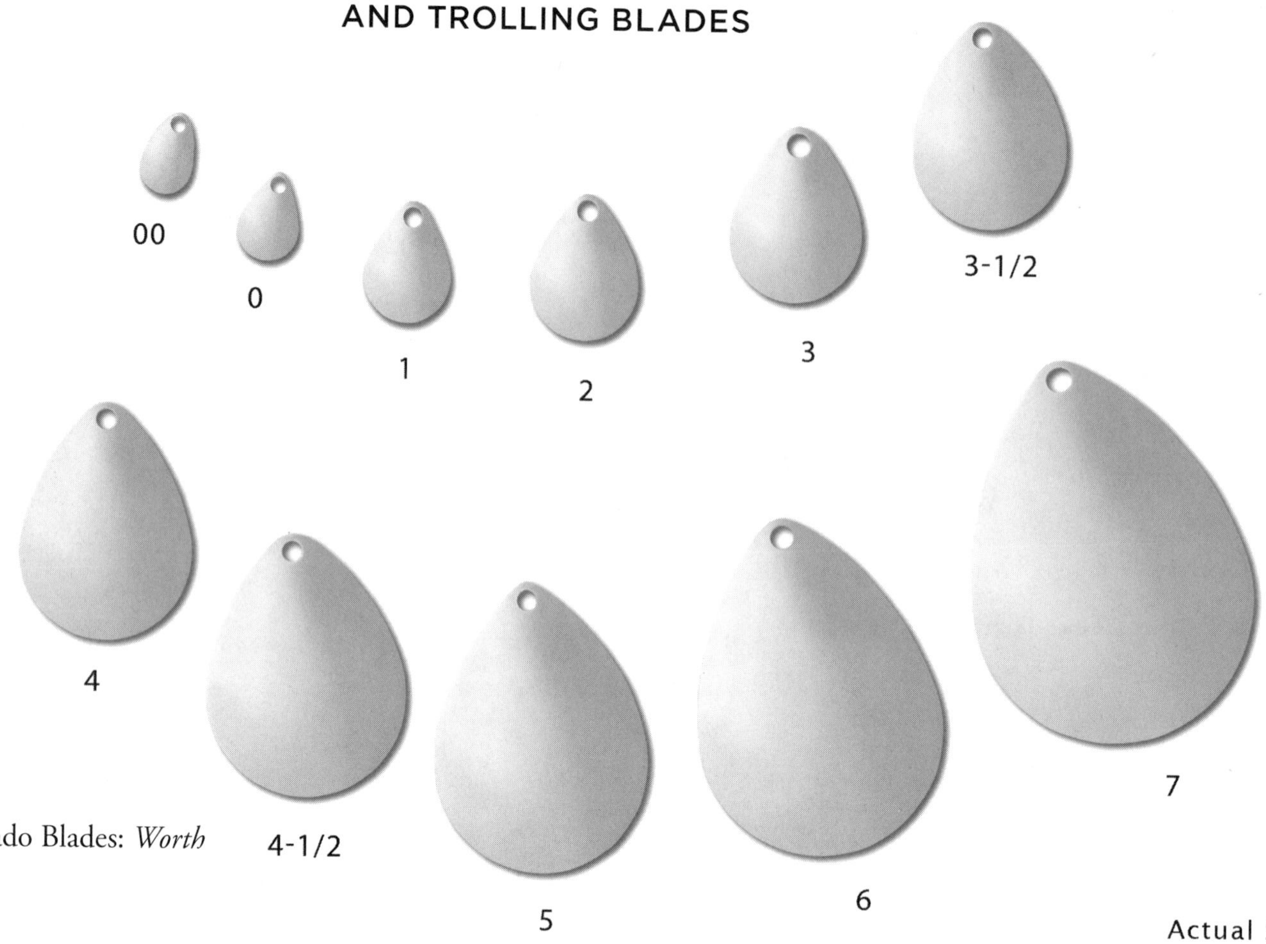

00
0
1
2
3
3-1/2
4
4-1/2
5
6
7

Colorado Blades: *Worth*

Actual Size

3
4
5
6
7
8

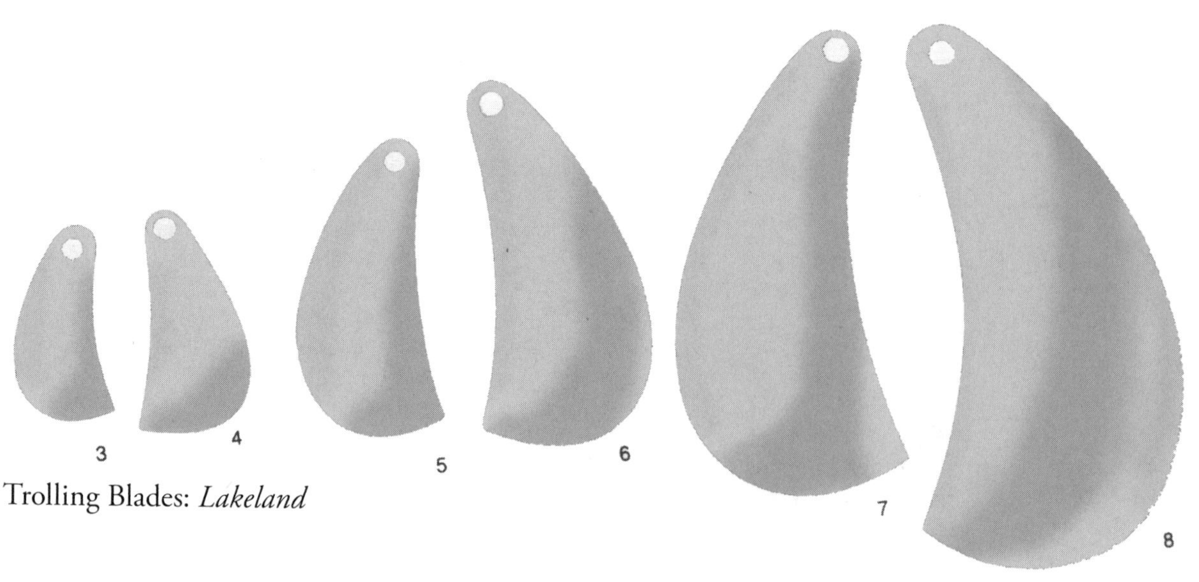

Trolling Blades: *Lakeland*

SIZE CHARTS FOR SPINNER BLADES

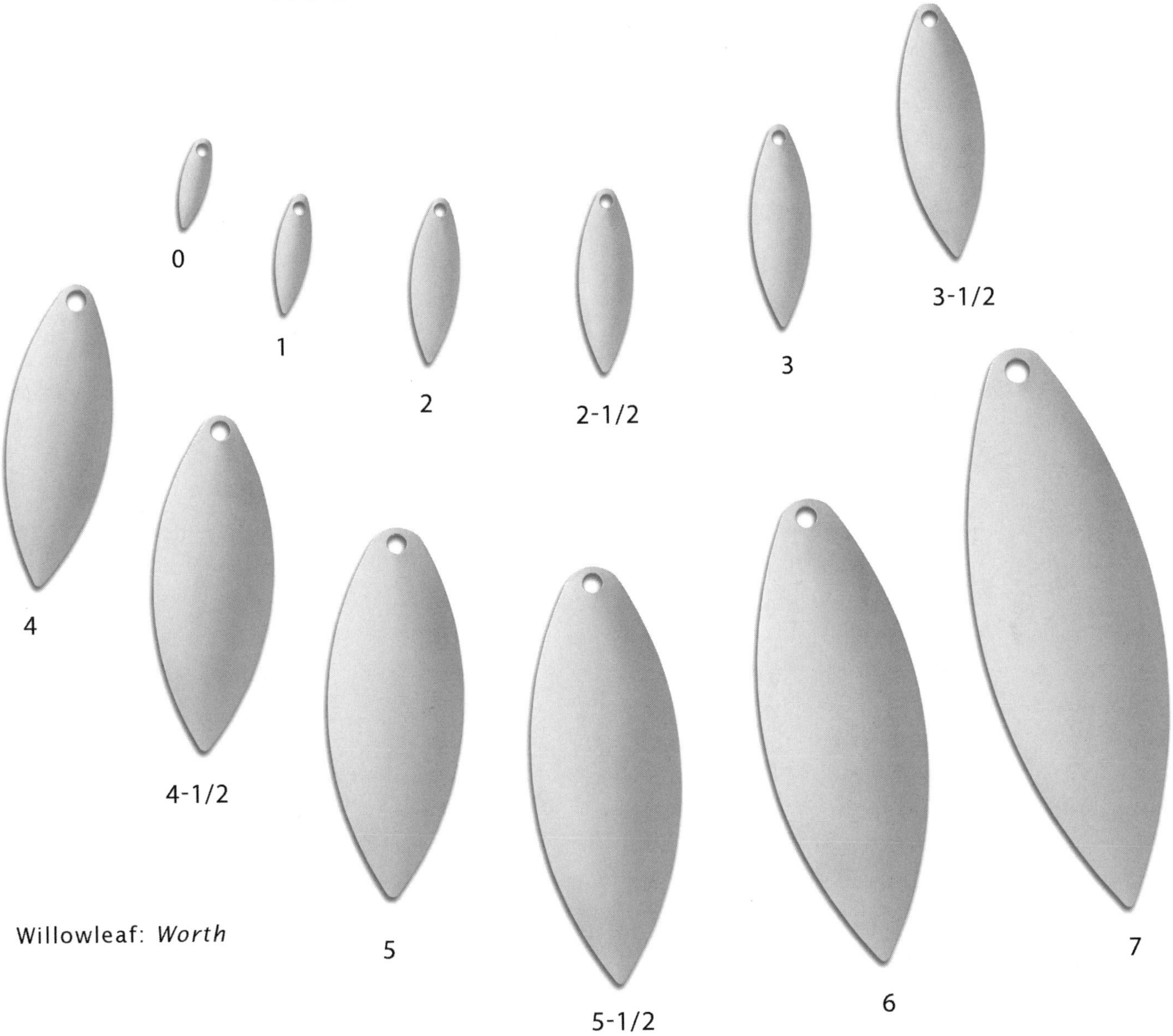

0
1
2
2-1/2
3
3-1/2
4
4-1/2
5
5-1/2
6
7

Willowleaf: *Worth*

4
6
7
8

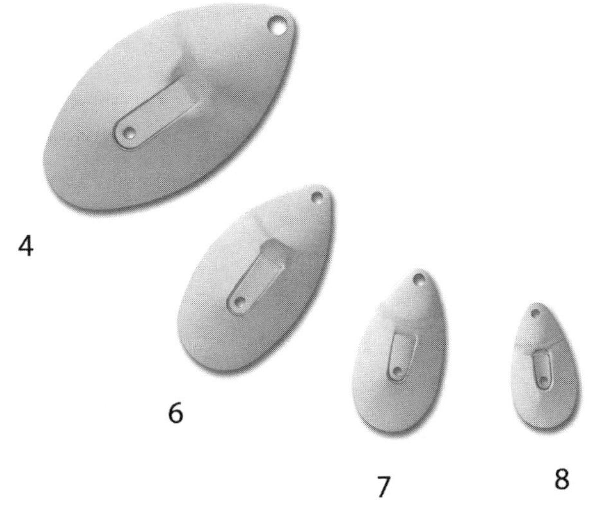

Junebug: *Worth*

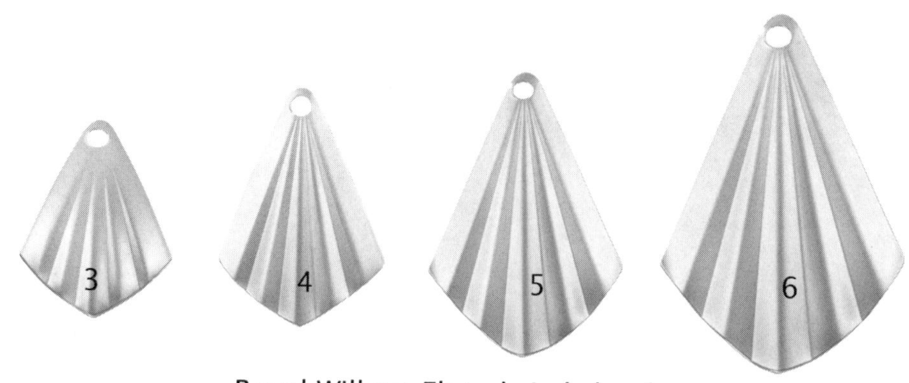

Royal Willow, Fluted: *Lakeland*

Actual Size

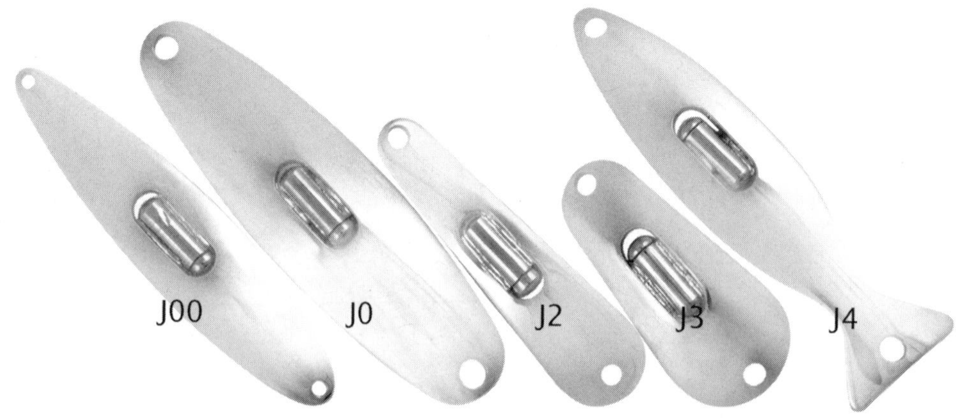

Jigging Spoons, Plain: *Lakeland*

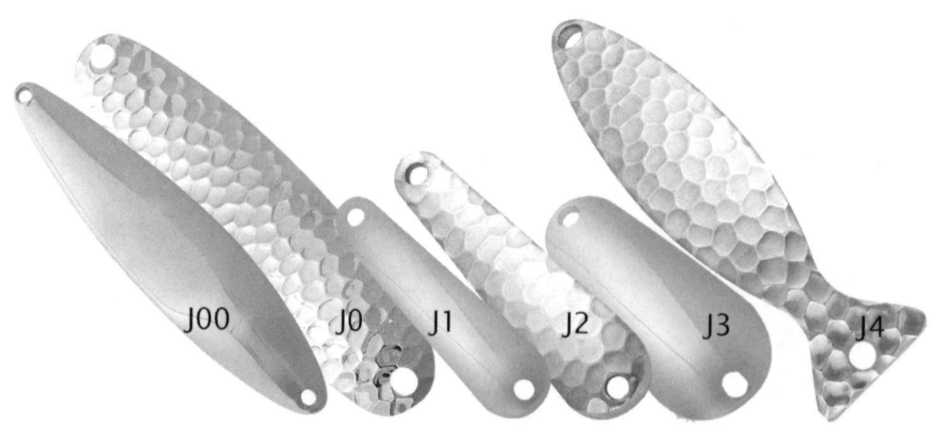

Jigging Spoons, Hammered: *Lakeland*

SIZE CHARTS FOR SPINNER BLADES

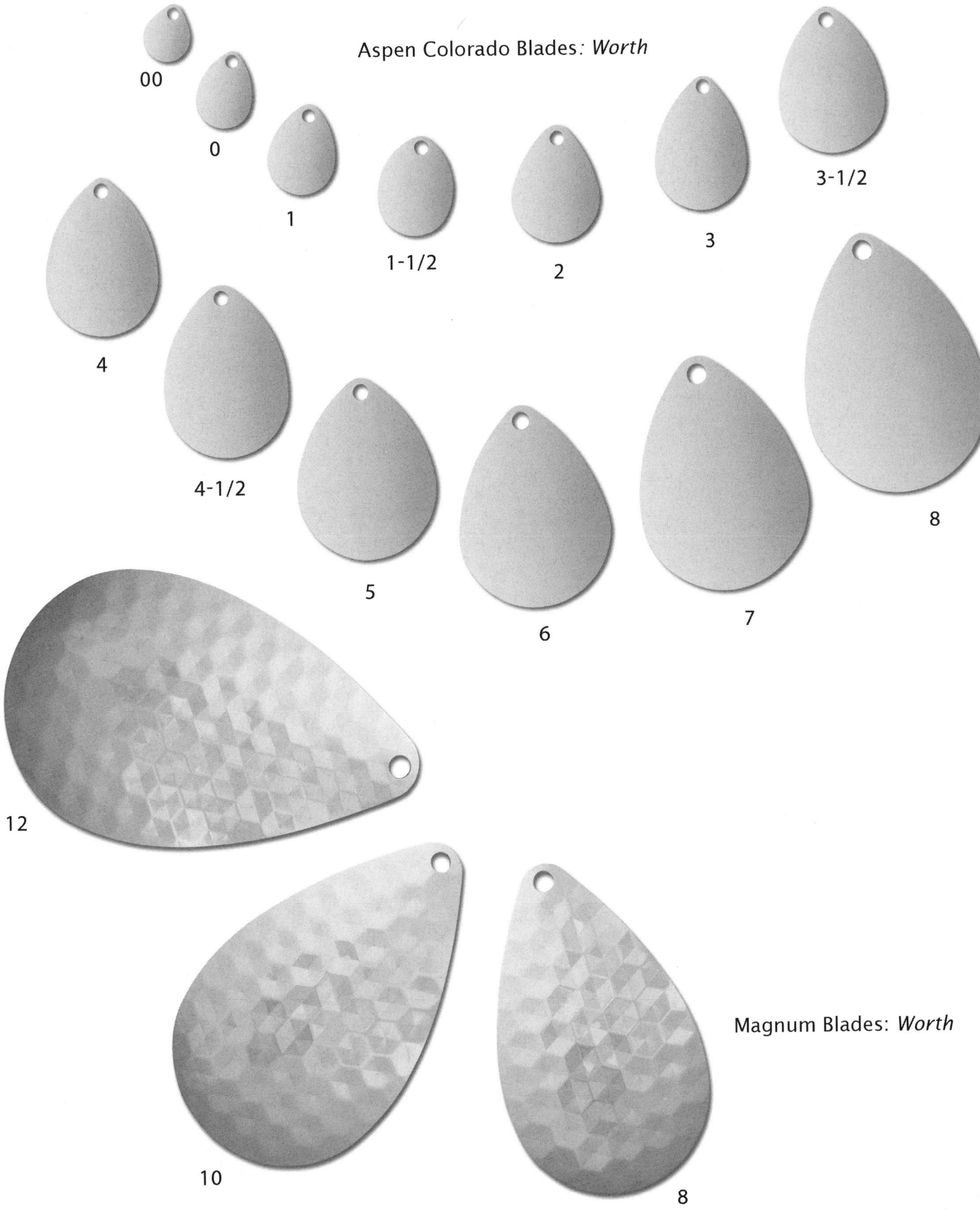

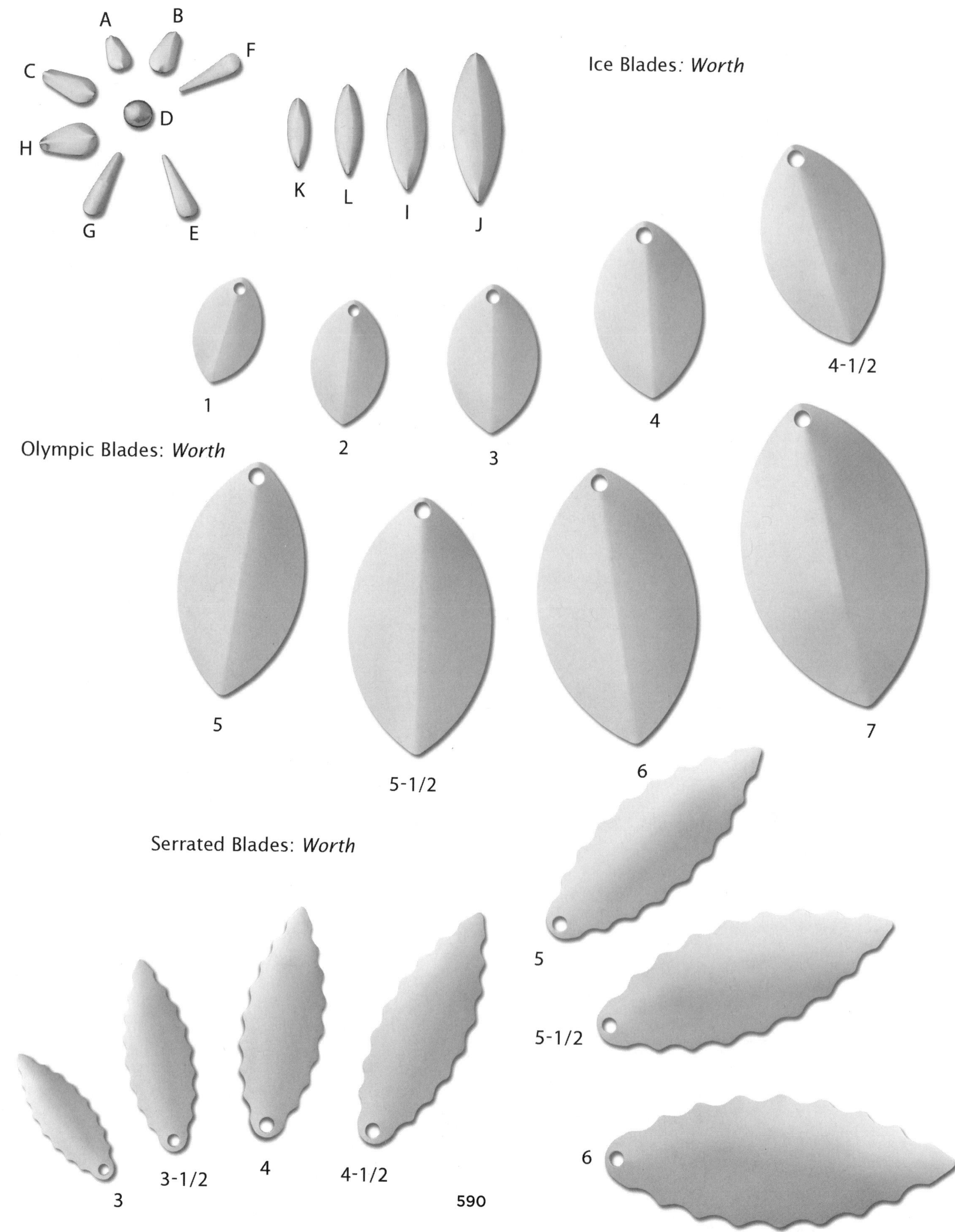
A
B
F
C
D
H
G
E
K
L
I
J
Ice Blades: *Worth*
1
2
3
4
4-1/2
Olympic Blades: *Worth*
5
5-1/2
6
7
Serrated Blades: *Worth*
3
3-1/2
4
4-1/2
5
5-1/2
6

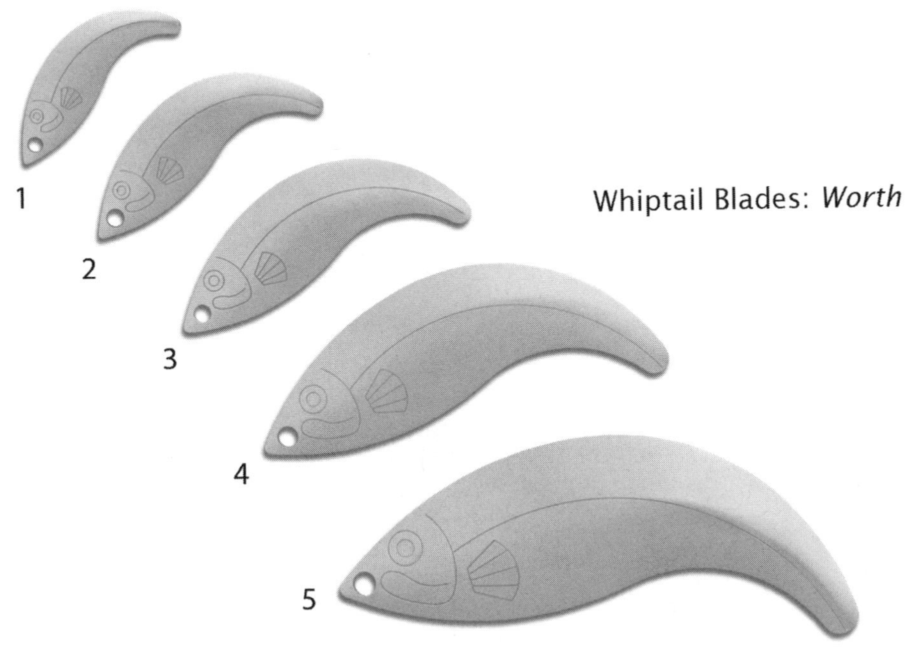

Whiptail Blades: *Worth*

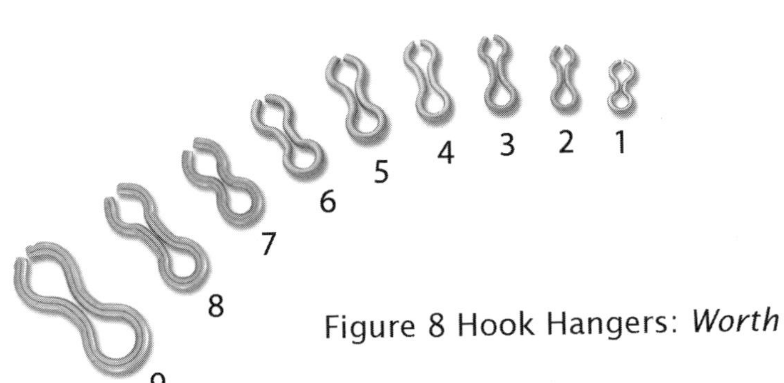

Figure 8 Hook Hangers: *Worth*

X2 Oval Split Rings: *Worth*

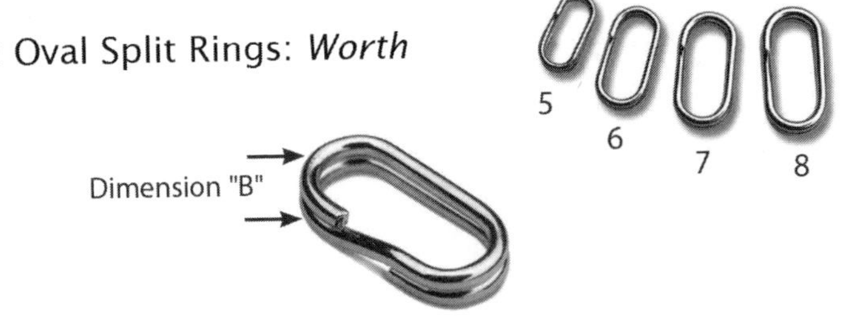

SIZE CHARTS FOR SPINNER BLADES AND TROLLING BLADES

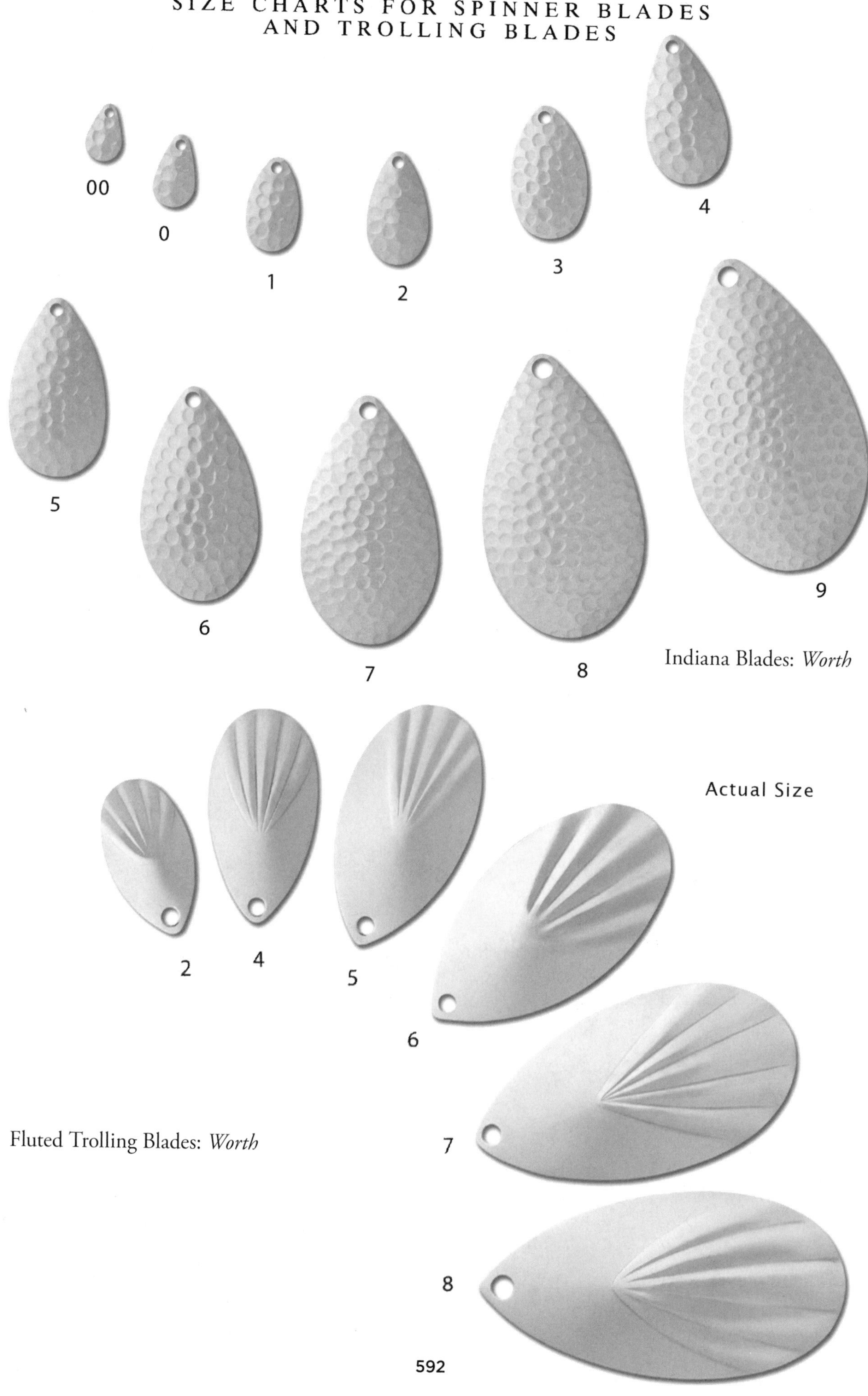

SIZE CHARTS FOR SPINNER PARTS

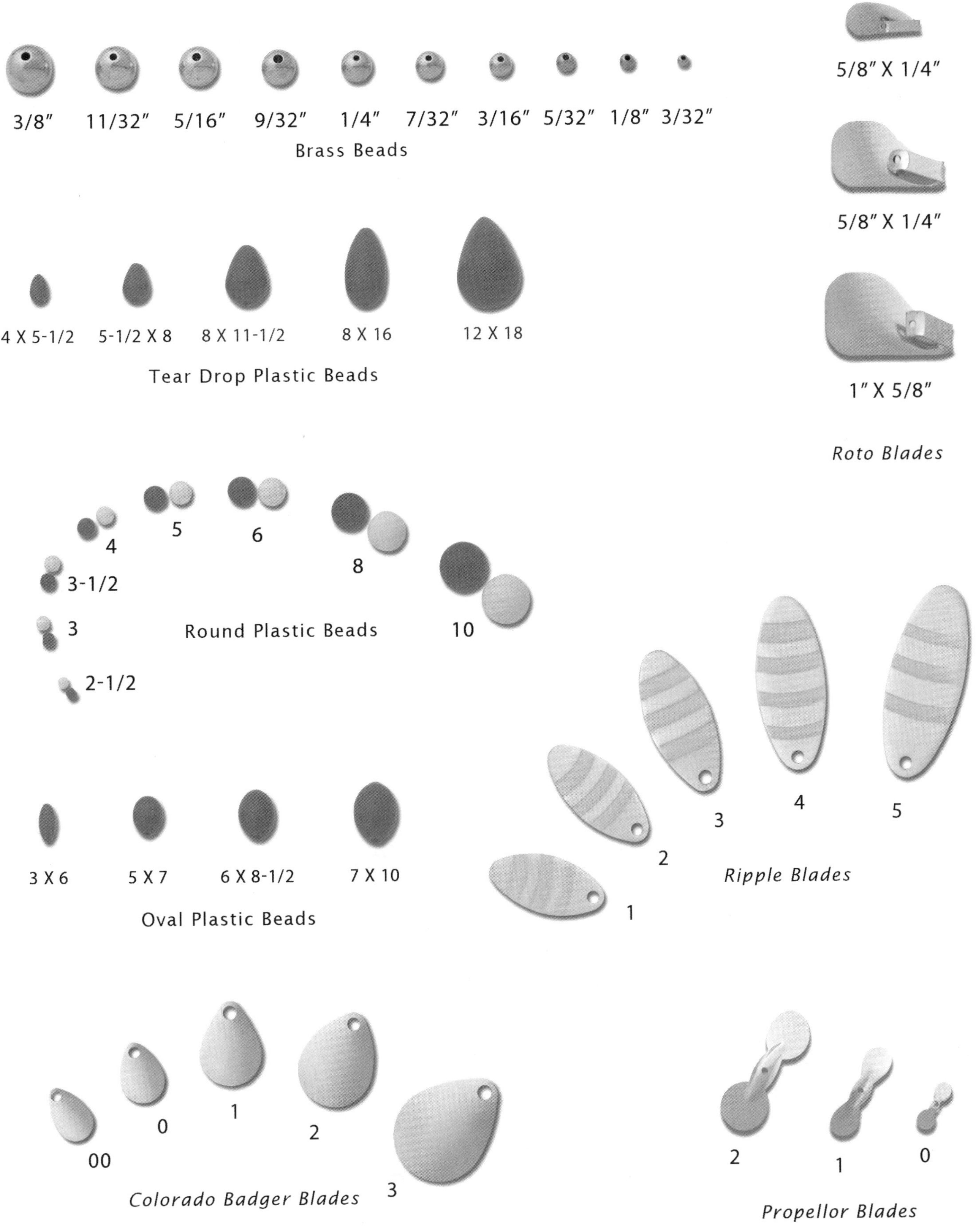

All Courtesy of *Worth*

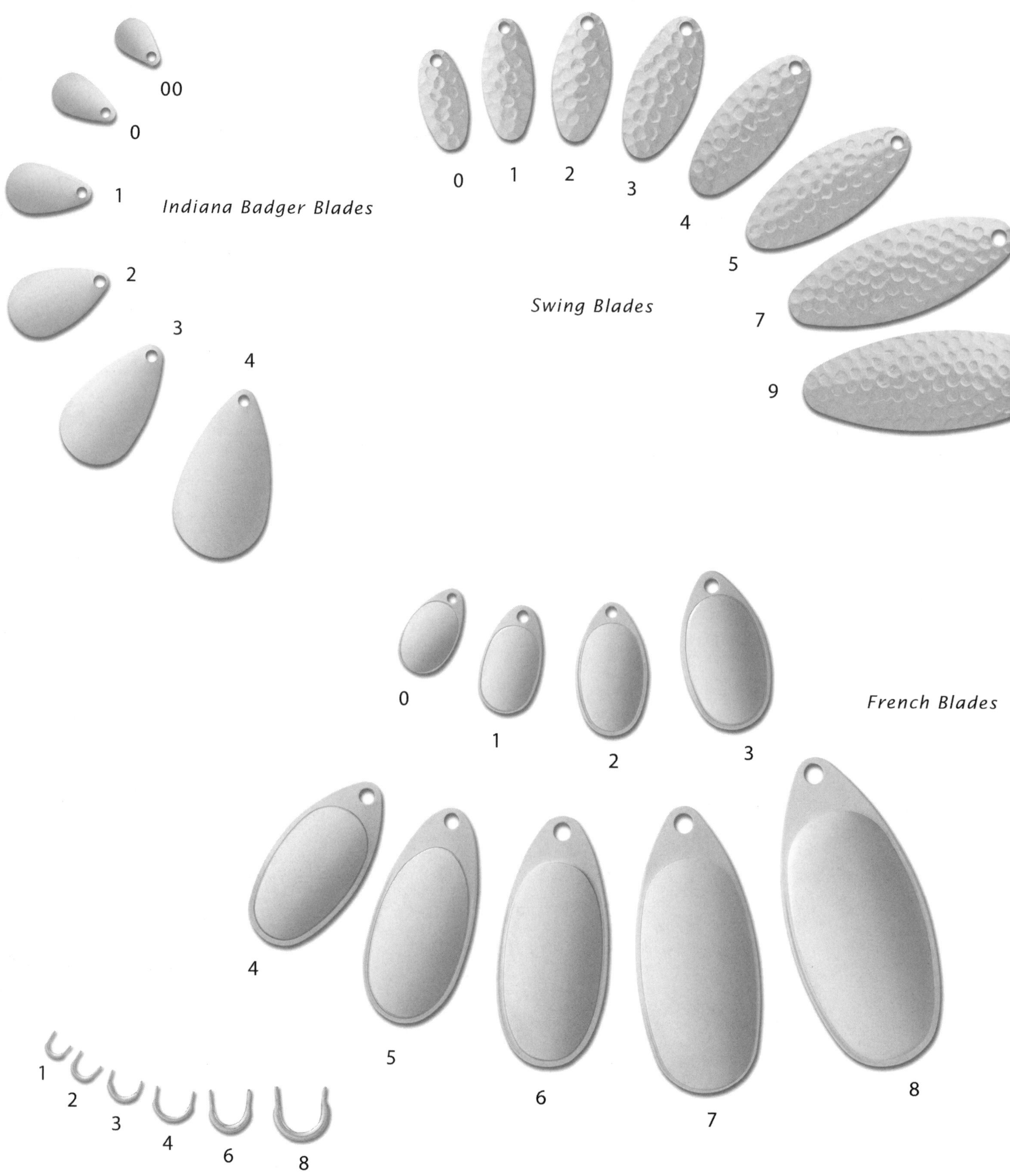
00
0
1
Indiana Badger Blades
2
3
4
0
1
2
3
4
5
Swing Blades
7
9
0
French Blades
1
2
3
4
5
6
7
8
1
2
3
4
6
8
Easy Spin Clevis

SIZE CHARTS FOR SPINNER BAIT, BUZZBAIT, AND JIG SPINNER WIREFORMS

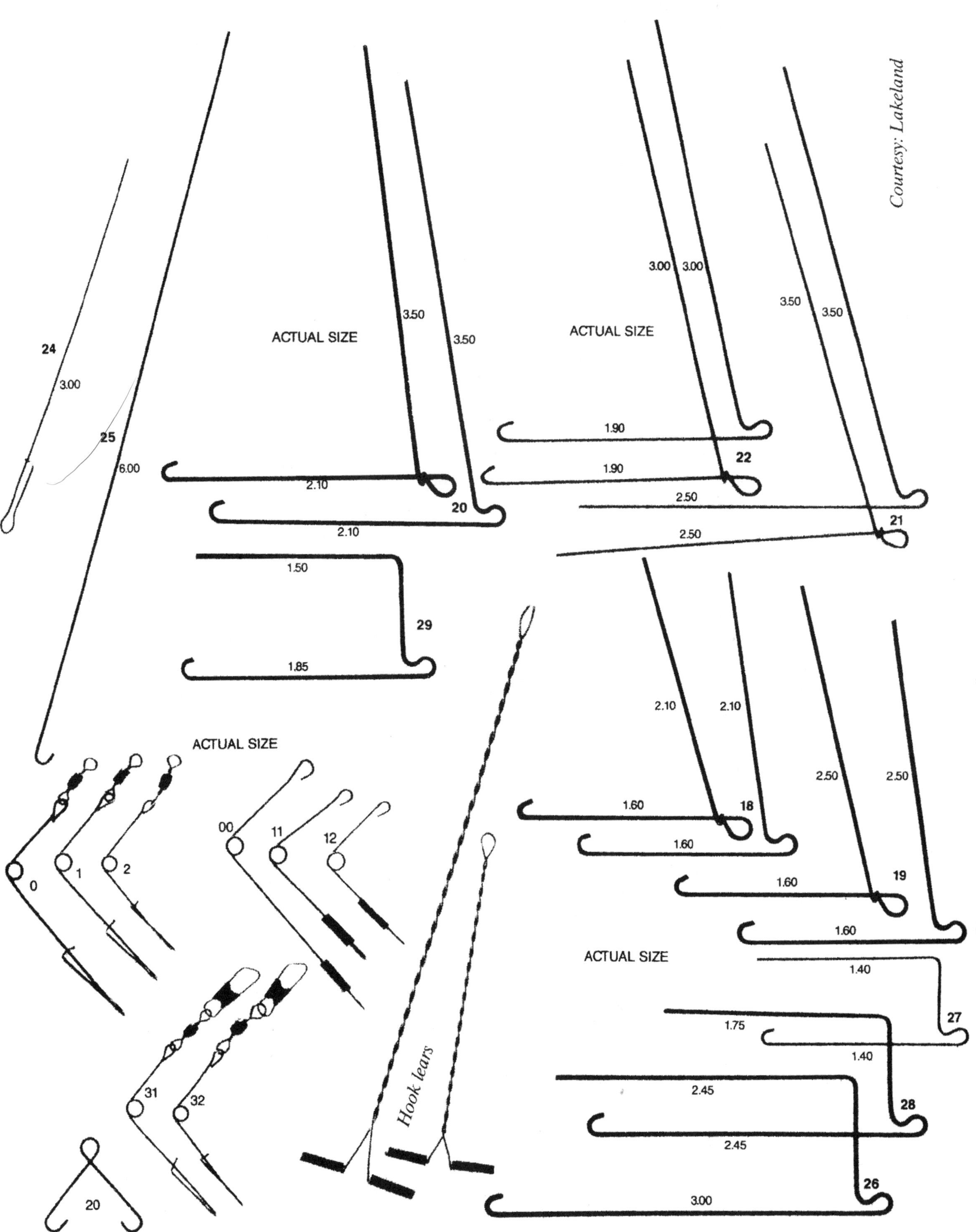

SIZE CHARTS FOR HOOKS

SHANK BENT DOWN SUPERIOR MUSTAD-O'SHAUGHNESSY HOOKS

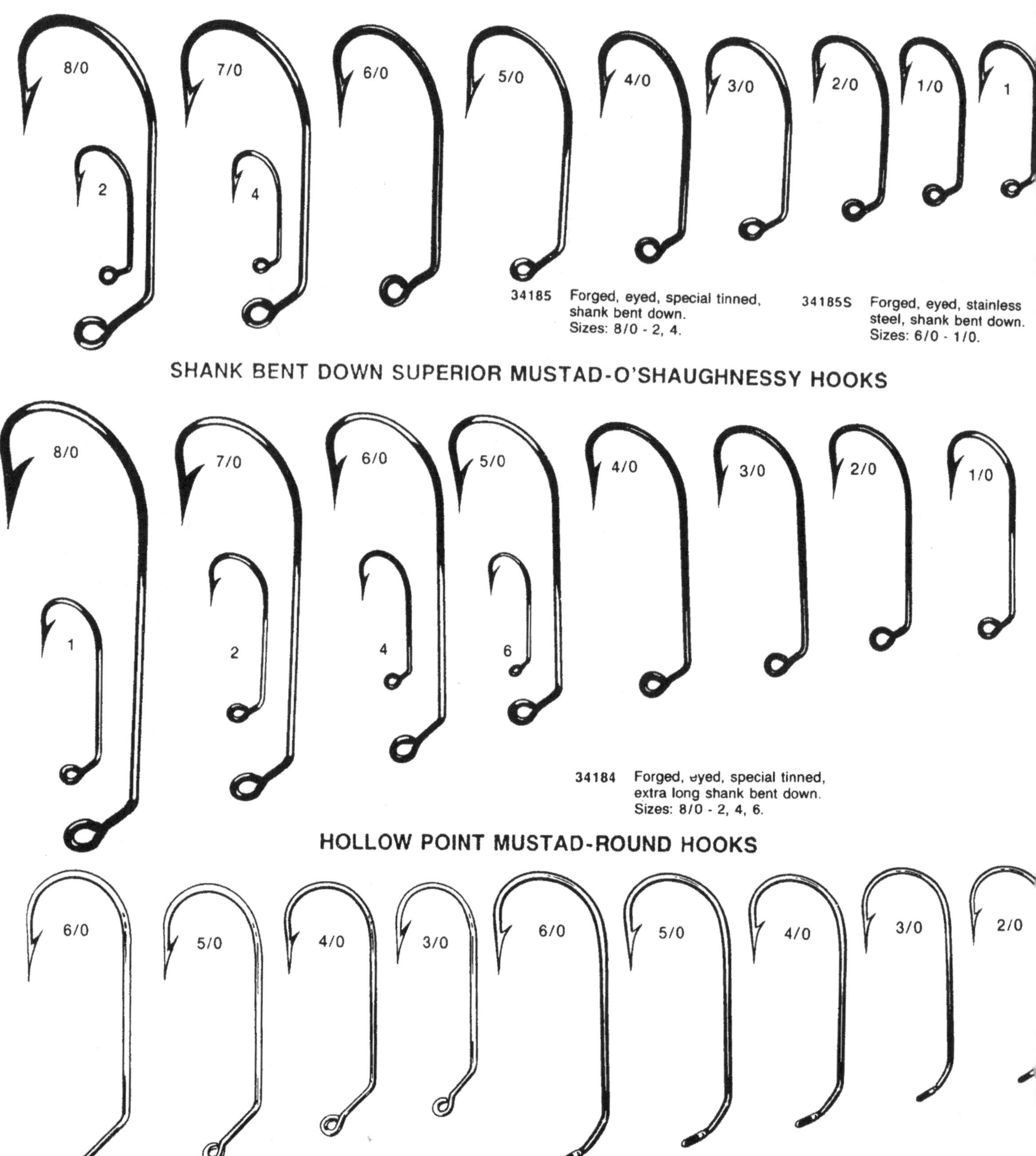

34185 Forged, eyed, special tinned, shank bent down. Sizes: 8/0 - 2, 4.

34185S Forged, eyed, stainless steel, shank bent down. Sizes: 6/0 - 1/0.

SHANK BENT DOWN SUPERIOR MUSTAD-O'SHAUGHNESSY HOOKS

34184 Forged, eyed, special tinned, extra long shank bent down. Sizes: 8/0 - 2, 4, 6.

HOLLOW POINT MUSTAD-ROUND HOOKS

90752BR Forged, eyed, bronzed, shank bent down. Sizes: 6/0 - 3/0.

90752CT Forged, eyed, special tinned, shank bent down, special sizes: 6/0 - 3/0.

90751 Forged, turned down ball eye, bronzed, shank bent down. Sizes: 6/0 - 2/0.

Courtesy: Mustad

SUPERIOR MUSTAD-ABERDEEN HOOKS-EXTRA SHORT SHANK BENT DOWN

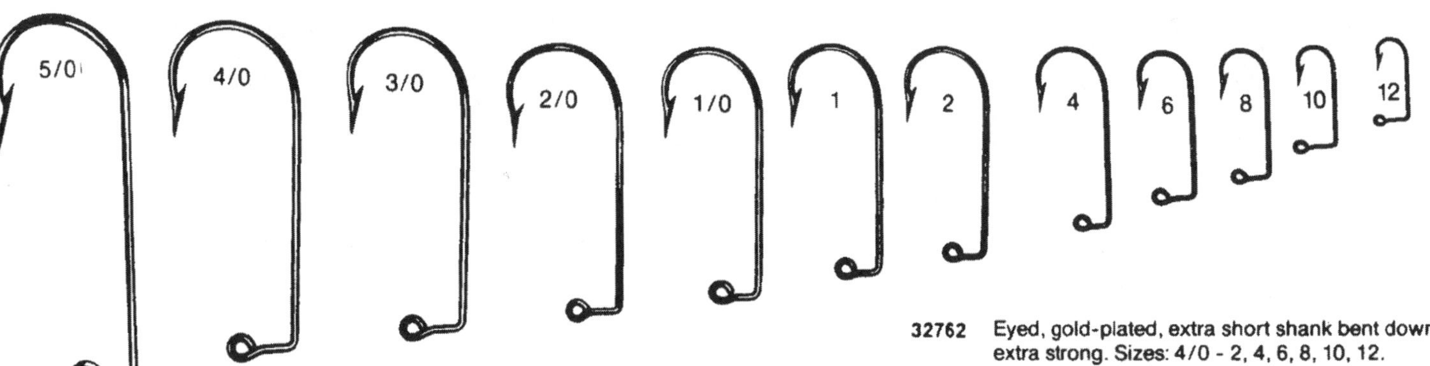

32760 Eyed, bronzed, extra short shank bent down, extra strong. Sizes: 5/0 - 2, 4, 6, 8, 10, 12.

32762 Eyed, gold-plated, extra short shank bent down, extra strong. Sizes: 4/0 - 2, 4, 6, 8, 10, 12.

32763 Eyed, tinned, extra-short shank bent down, extra strong. Sizes: 3/0 - 2, 4, 6, 8, 10.

SUPERIOR MUSTAD-ABERDEEN HOOKS-SHORT SHANK BENT DOWN

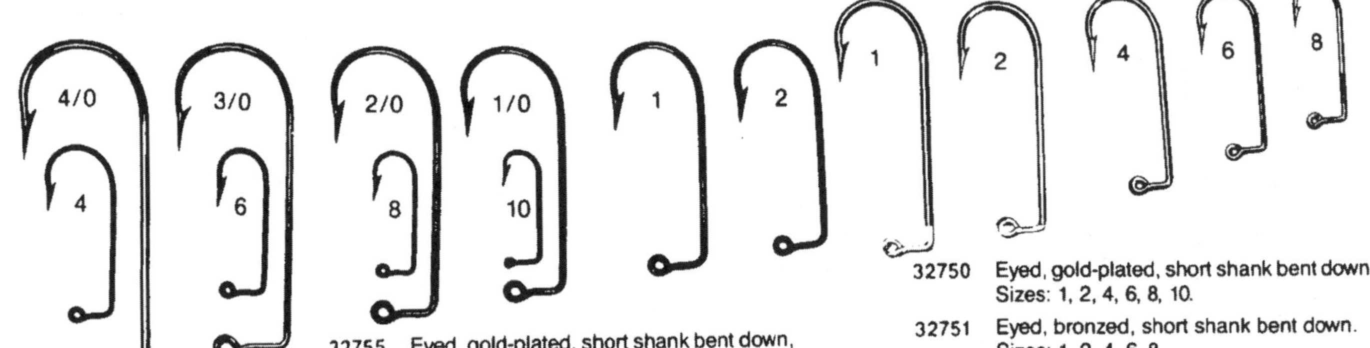

32755 Eyed, gold-plated, short shank bent down, extra strong. Sizes: 4/0 - 2, 4, 6, 8, 10.

32756 Eyed, bronzed, short shank bent down, extra strong. Sizes: 4/0 - 2, 4, 6, 8, 10.

32750 Eyed, gold-plated, short shank bent down. Sizes: 1, 2, 4, 6, 8, 10.

32751 Eyed, bronzed, short shank bent down. Sizes: 1, 2, 4, 6, 8.

SHANK BENT DOWN SUPERIOR MUSTAD-O'SHAUGHNESSY HOOKS

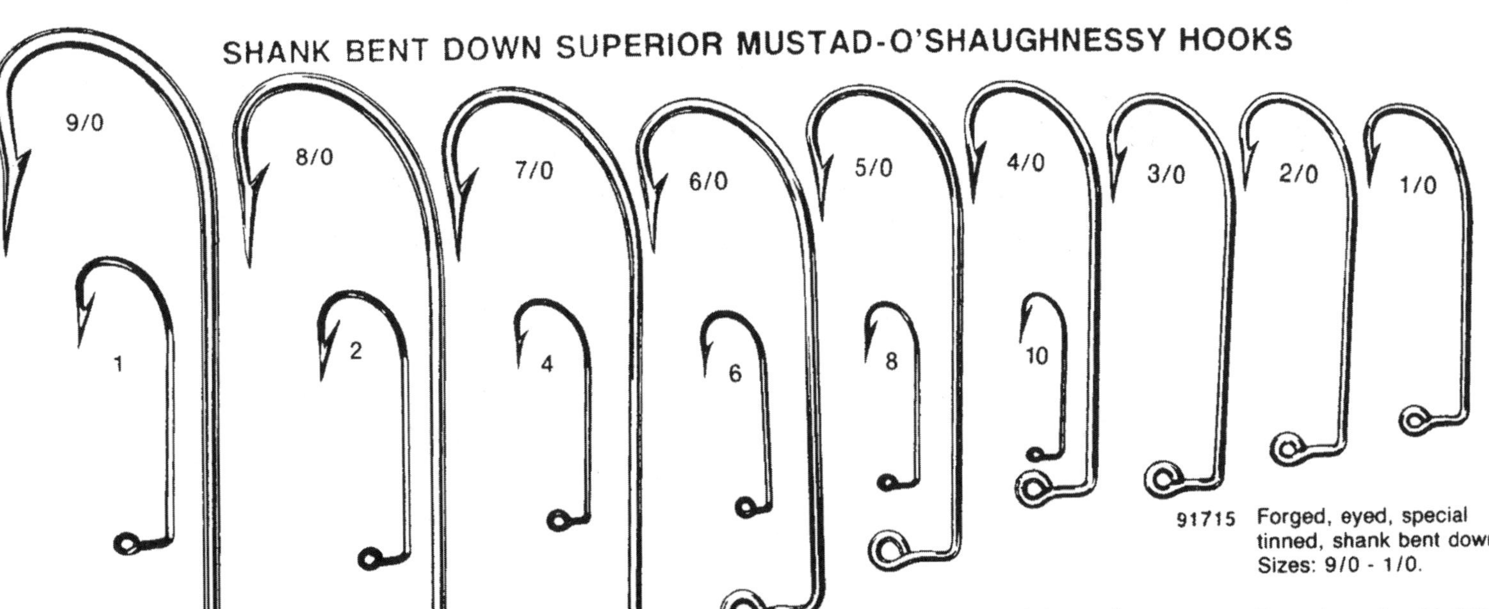

91750ST Not forged, eyed, special tinned, shank bent down. Sizes: 9/0 - 2, 4, 6, 8, 10.

91751 Not forged, eyed, bronzed, shank bent down. Sizes: 4/0 - 2, 4, 6, 8.

91753 Not forged, eyed, gold-plated, shank bent down. Sizes: 5/0 - 2, 4, 6, 8, 10.

91715 Forged, eyed, special tinned, shank bent down. Sizes: 9/0 - 1/0.

91716G Forged, eyed, gold-plated, shank bent down. Sizes: 4/0 - 6.

91718 Forged, eyed, nickel-plated, shank bent down. Sizes: 3/0, 2/0, 1/0.

Courtesy: Mustad

SUPERIOR MUSTAD-TREBLE HOOKS

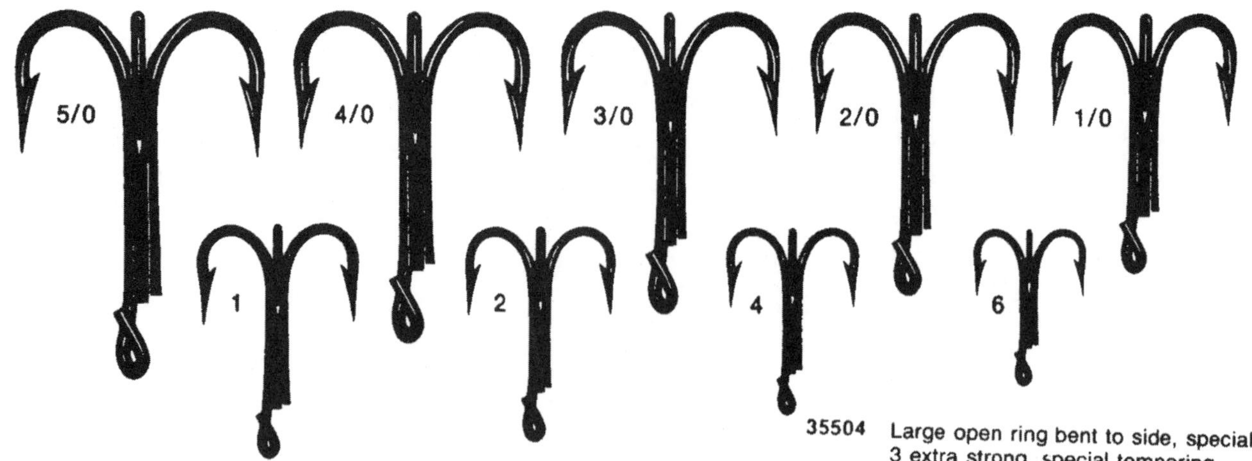

35504 Large open ring bent to side, special tinned, 3 extra strong, special tempering. Sizes: 6/0 - 2, 4, 6, 8.

1/0 4 6

4/0 3/0 2/0 1/0 4 6 8

7790X Open ring and shank, bronzed. Sizes: 2, 4, 6, 8, 10, 12, 14, 16.

35517 Open straight ring, special tinned, 3 extra strong, special tempering. Sizes: 7/0 - 4, 6, 8, 10.

35517B Open, straight ring, bronzed, 3 extra strong, special tempering. Sizes: 4, 6, 8.

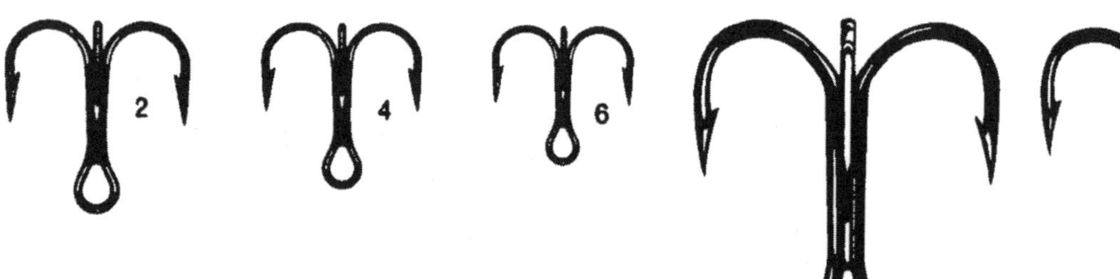

35657 Ringed, round bend, nickel-plated extra short shank, extra strong. Sizes: 1, 2, 4, 6.

35657BR Ringed, round bend, bronzed, extra short shank, extra strong. Sizes: 2, 4, 6, 8, 10, 12, 14.

35657D Ringed, round bend, Duratin, extra short shank, extra strong. Sizes: 2, 4, 6, 8.

35656BR Ringed, round bend, extra strong, bronzed. Sizes: 5/0, 3/0, 1/0 - 14.

Courtesy: Mustad

SUPERIOR MUSTAD-TREBLE HOOKS

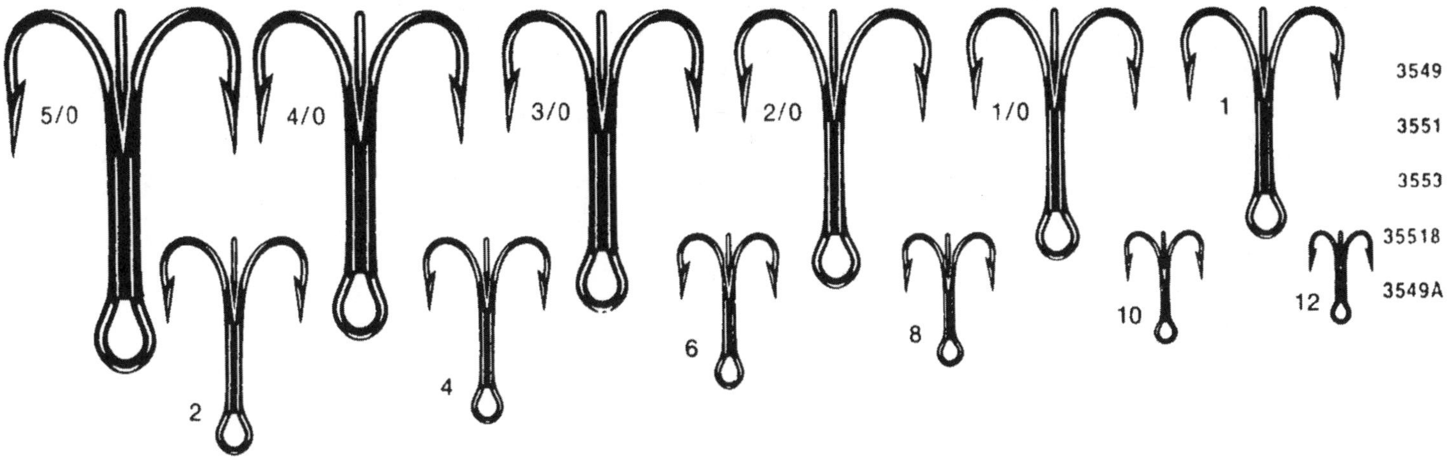

5/0
4/0
3/0
2/0
1/0
1
2
4
6
8
10
12
3549
3551
3553
35518
3549A

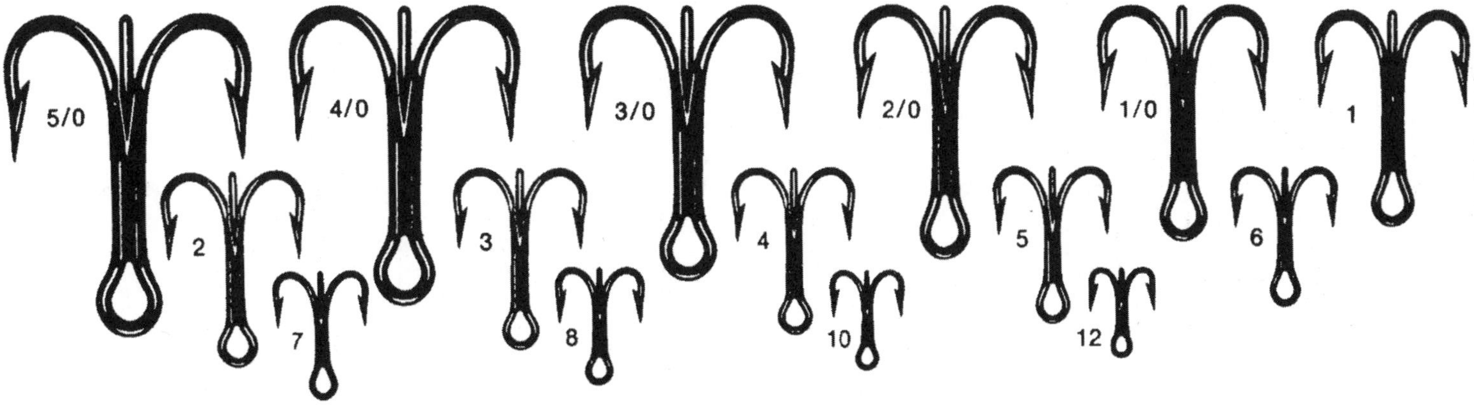

5/0
4/0
3/0
2/0
1/0
1
2
7
3
8
4
10
5
12
6

3565B Ringed, special tinned, short shank, 2 extra strong. Sizes: 3/0, 2, 4, 6, 8, 10, 12.

3566A Ringed, nickel-plated, short shank, 2 extra strong. Sizes: 7/0 - 6, 8, 10, 12, 14.

3567B Ringed, bronzed, short shank, 2 extra strong. Sizes: 6/0 - 2, 4, 6, 8, 10, 12, 14, 16.

7794B Ringed, special tinned, short shank, 3 extra strong. Sizes: 6/0 - 6, 8, 10, 12.

5/0
4/0
3/0
2/0
1/0
1
2
4
6
8
10
12

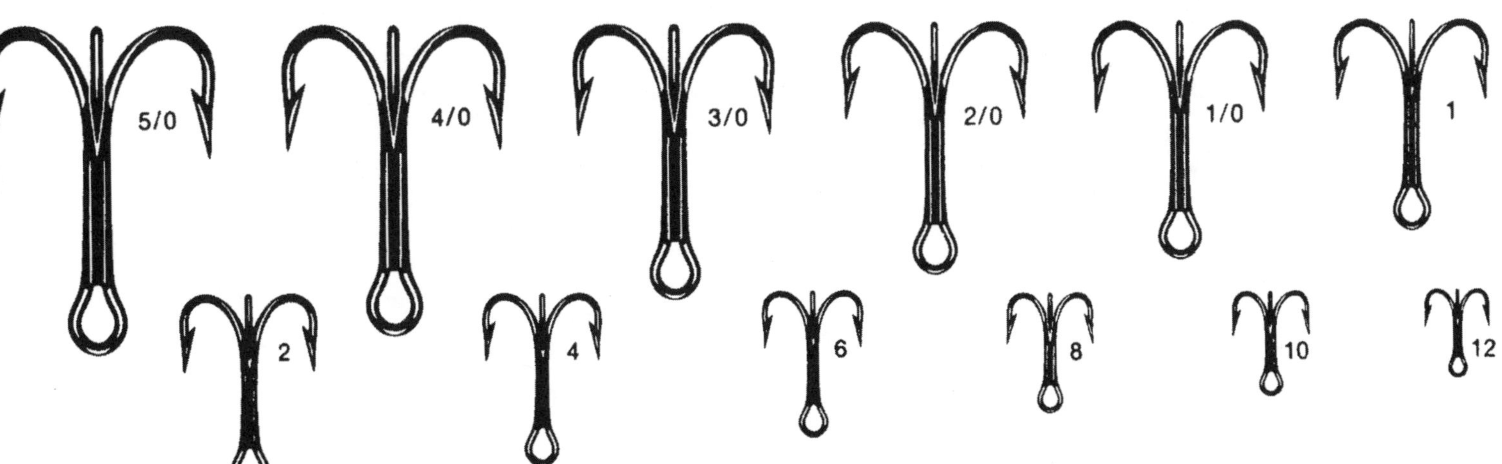

3551A Ringed, bronzed, short shank. Sizes: 3 - 8, 10.

3553A Ringed, nickel-plated, short shank. Sizes: 1/0, 2 - 10.

3553B Ringed, special tinned, short shank. Sizes: 2 - 6, 8, 10.

3562E Ringed, special tinned, short shank, extra strong. Sizes: 2 - 4.

Courtesy: Mustad

SUPERIOR MUSTAD-TREBLE HOOKS

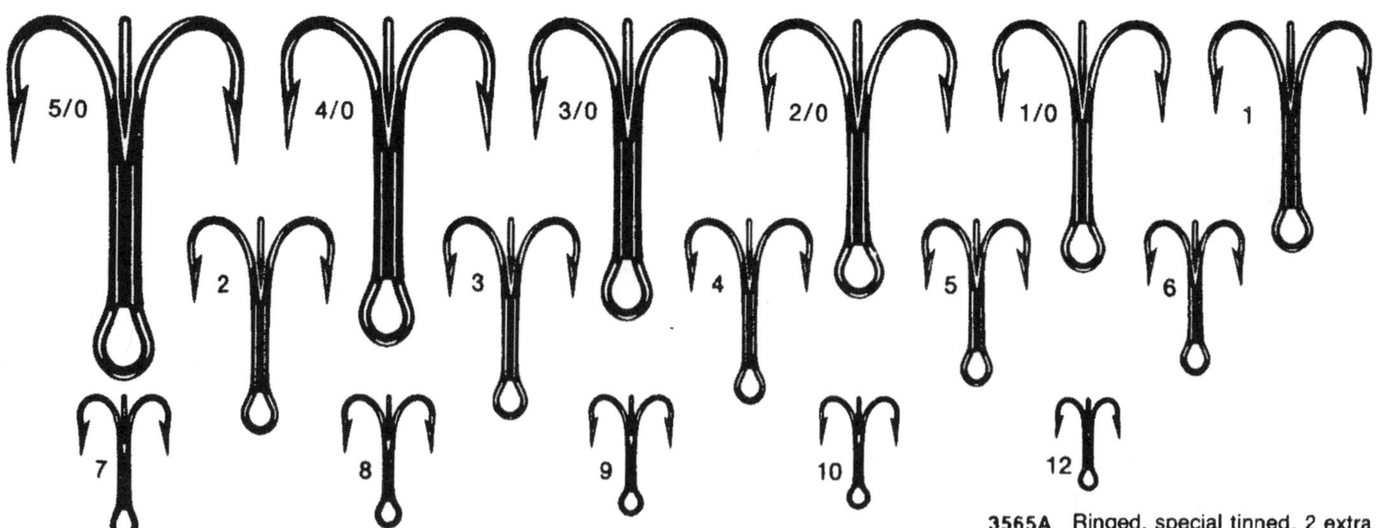

3561C Ringed, nickel-plated, 3 extra strong. Sizes: 6/0 - 2, 4, 6, 8, 10, 12.

3561D Ringed, bronzed, 3 extra strong. Sizes: 2/0 - 2, 4, 6, 8, 10, 12, 14.

3561E Ringed, special tinned, 3 extra strong. Sizes: 11/0 - 4, 6, 8, 10, 12.

3565A Ringed, special tinned, 2 extra strong. Sizes: 8/0 - 2, 4, 6, 8, 10, 12, 14.

3566 Ringed, nickel-plated, 2 extra strong. Sizes: 6/0 - 4, 6, 8, 10, 12, 14.

3567 Ringed, bronzed, 2 extra strong. Sizes: 3/0 - 6, 8, 10, 12.

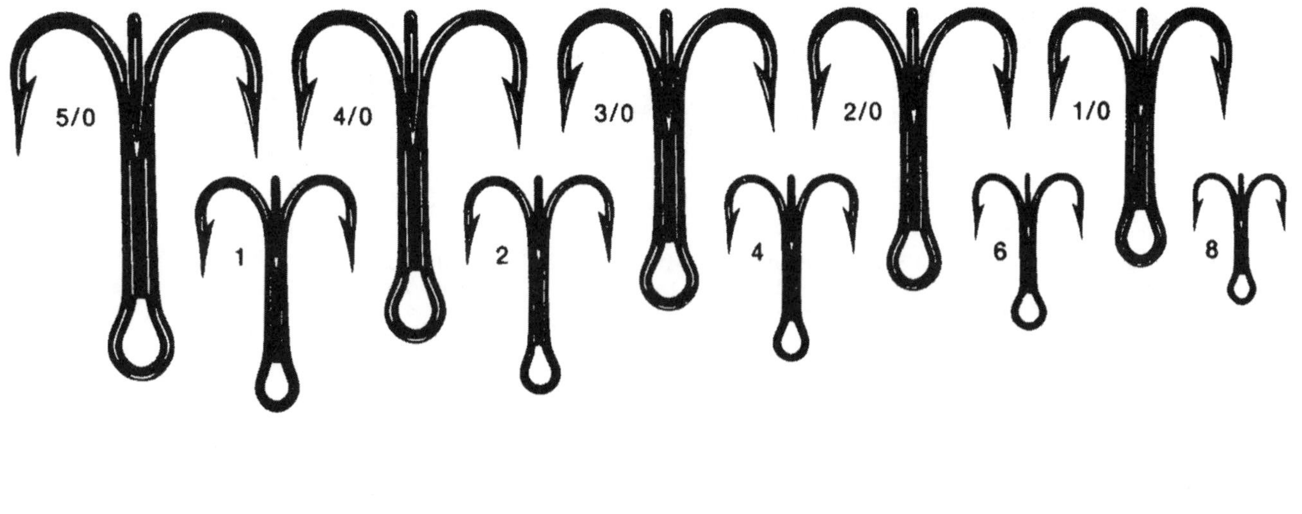

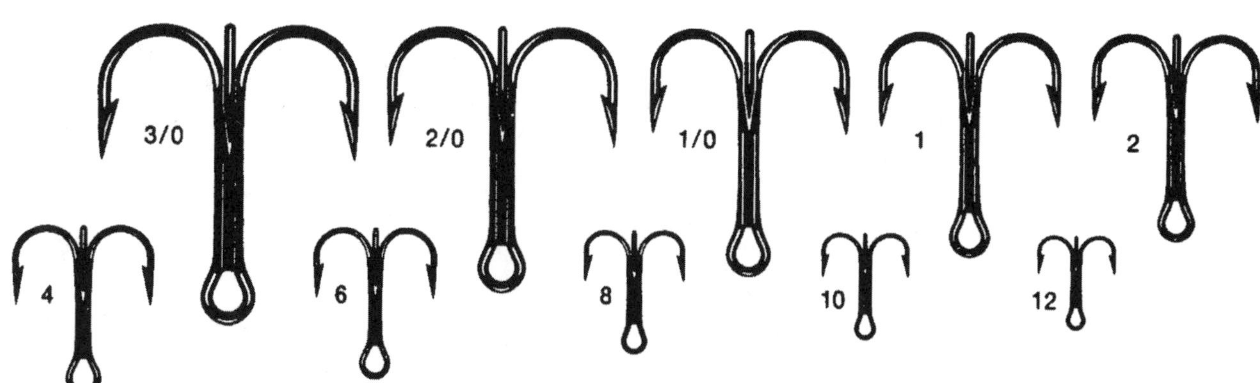

35647 Ringed, round bend, bronzed. Sizes: 3/0 - 4, 6, 8, 9, 10, 12, 14, 16, 18.

35648 Ringed, round bend, nickel-plated. Sizes: 2/0 - 2, 4, 6, 8, 10, 12.

35648A Ringed, round bend, gold-plated. Sizes: 1 - 6, 8, 10, 12, 14, 16, 18.

Courtesy: Mustad

POINT BENT IN MUSTAD-ABERDEEN HOOKS

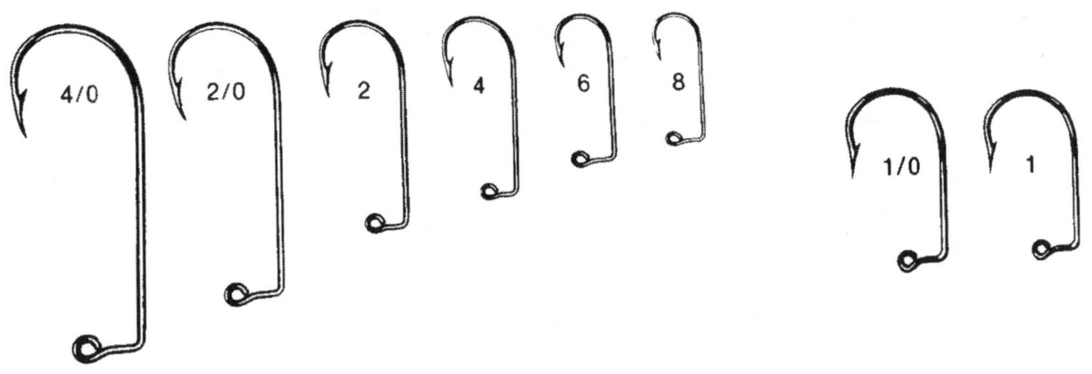

37400 Eyed, bronzed, extra short shank bent down, extra strong. Sizes: 4/0, 2/0 - 2, 4, 6, 8.

37402 Eyed, gold-plated, extra short shank bent down, extra strong. Sizes: 2/0 - 2, 4, 6.

32761BR Eyed, bronzed, 5 extra short shank, bent down, extra strong. Sizes: 1/0 - 1.

ROUND BEND MUSTAD-ABERDEEN HOOKS

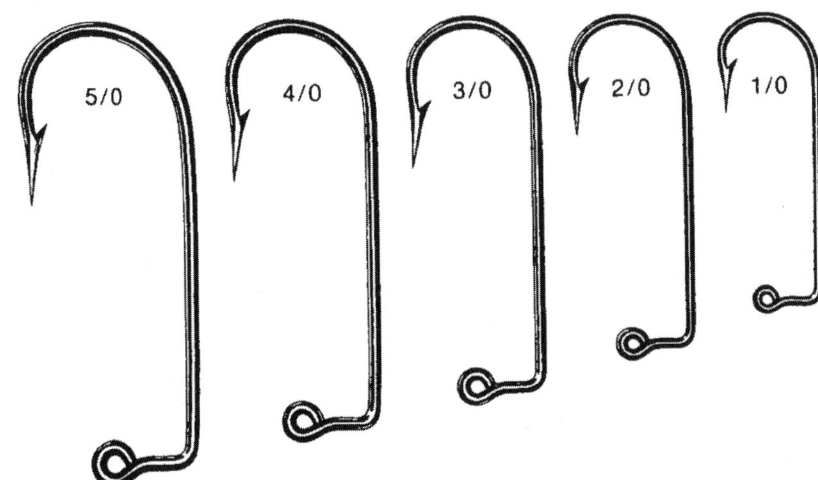

32771BR Eyed, bronzed, short shank, bent down, 4 extra strong, special. Sizes: 5/0 - 1/0.

32771CT Eyed, special tinned, short shank, bent down, 4 extra strong, special. Sizes: 5/0 - 1/0.

SUPERIOR MUSTAD-ABERDEEN HOOKS

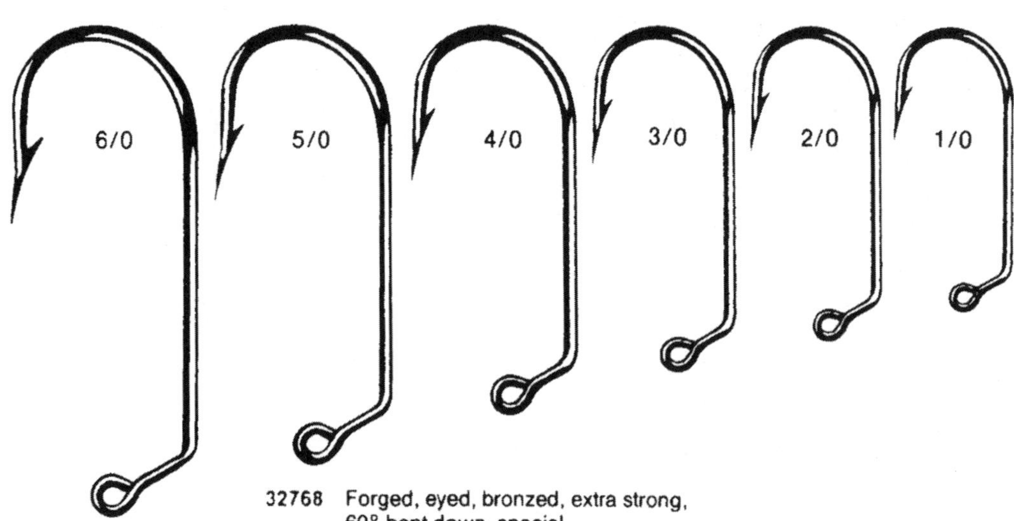

32768 Forged, eyed, bronzed, extra strong, 60° bent down, special. Sizes: 6/0 - 1/0.

Courtesy: Mustad

SIZE CHARTS FOR HOOKS

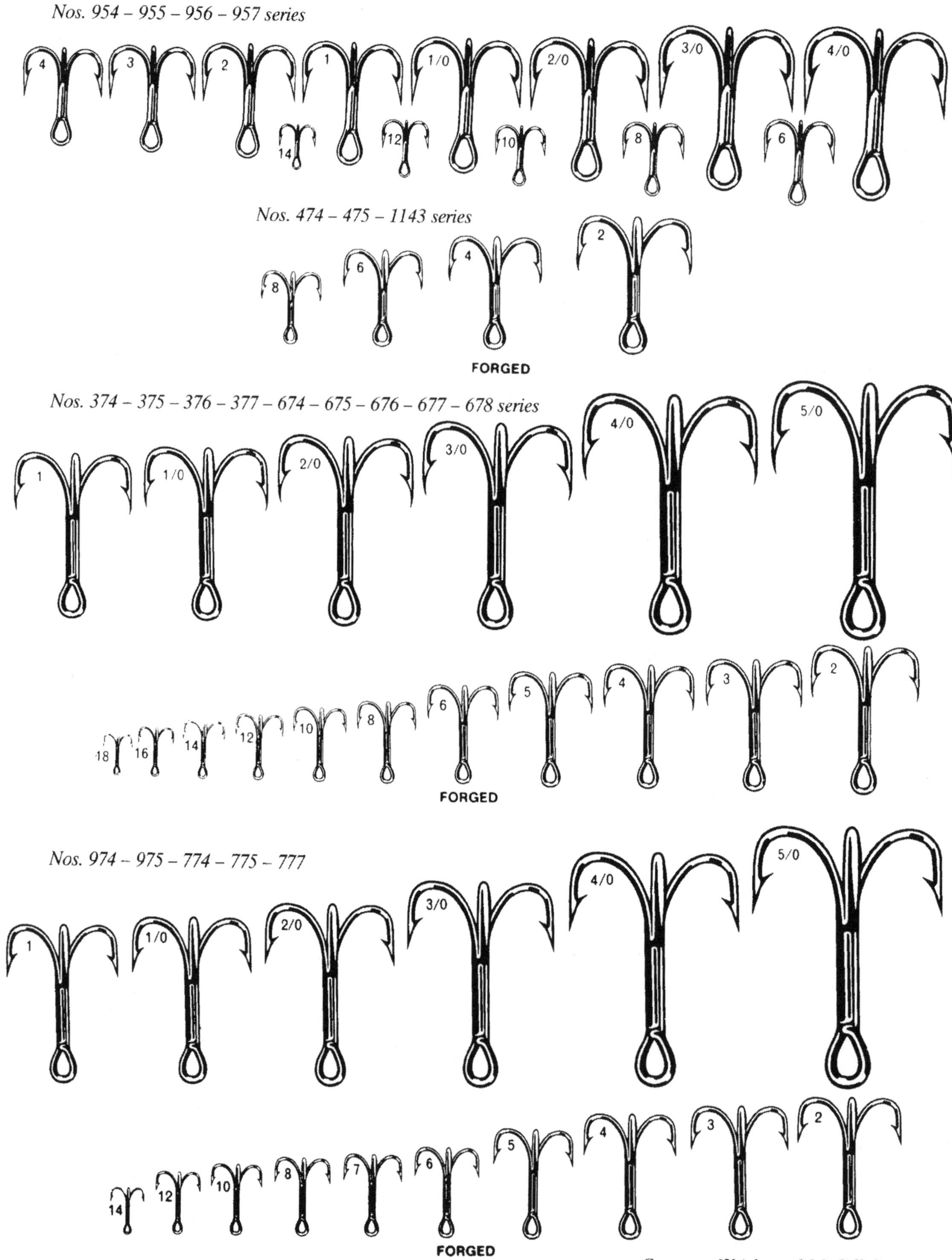

Courtesy: Wright and McGill Co.

SIZE CHARTS FOR WORM HOOKS

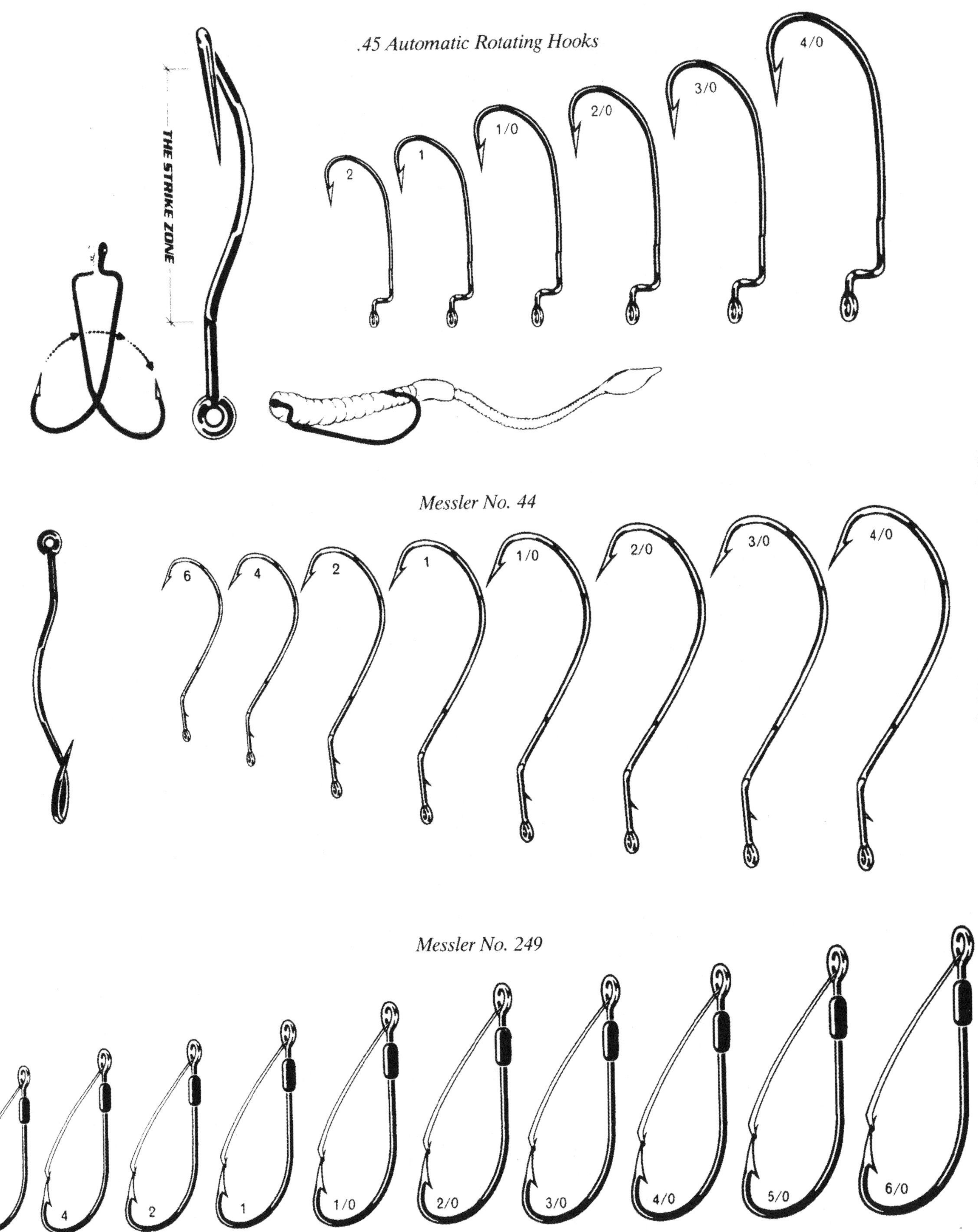

Courtesy: Wright and McGill Co.

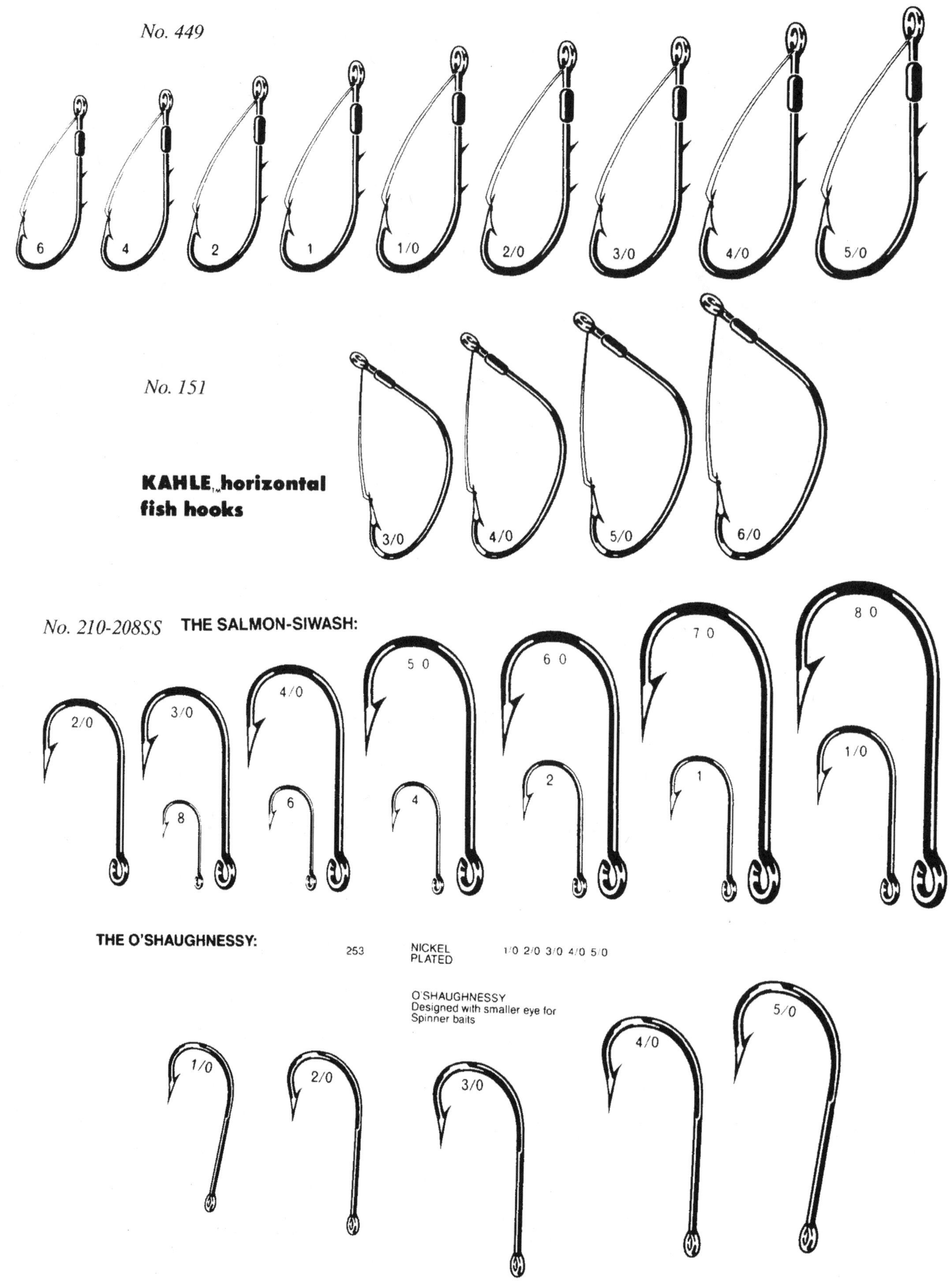

Courtesy: Wright and McGill Co.

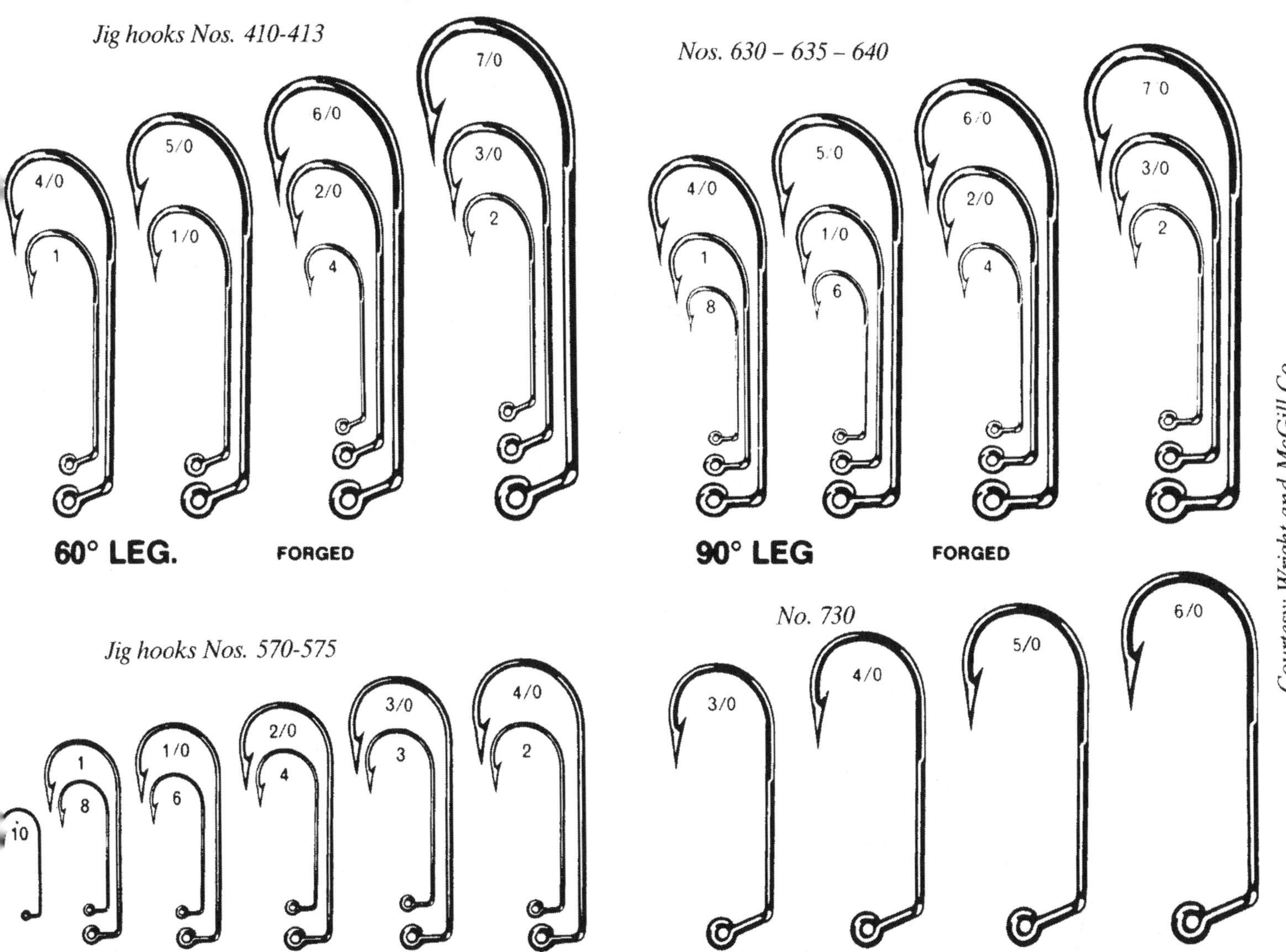

GUDEBROD ROD WRAPPING THREADS

Thread Specification Chart

Size	Diameter	MM	Yards Per Spool 521	524	519	Break Strength (Pounds)
REGULAR NYLON THREAD						
OO	.0045	.113	100	NA	NA	1.8
A	.0070	.175	100	950	4800	2.8
D	.0104	.260	100	450	2300	6.0
E	.0132	.330	100	350	1200	9.0
EE	.0154	.385	100	220	1065	11.8
FF	.0175	.438	50	NA	NA	17.5
N.C.P. NYLON THREAD						
A	.0070	.175	NA	950	4800	2.8
C	.0104	.260	NA	450	2300	6.0
D	.0132	.330	NA	350	1200	9.0
TRIMAR THREAD						
C	.0104	.260	100	450	2300	6.0
METALLIC THREAD						
A	.0070	.150	100	350	4800	0.85
D	.0104	.260	100	300	2300	3.1

Courtesy: Gudebrod, Inc.

7312 BZ

A wide gap 90° offset shank worm hook forged for strength used for Texan style large bait rigging in sizes 5/0 to 1/0.

5/0 4/0 3/0 2/0 1/0

7650 BZ-PS ROUND TREBLE

VMC's round bend design has become very popular with the pros across the country because of its increased hooking capabilities. Made in bronze and perma steel in sizes 3/0 to 8.

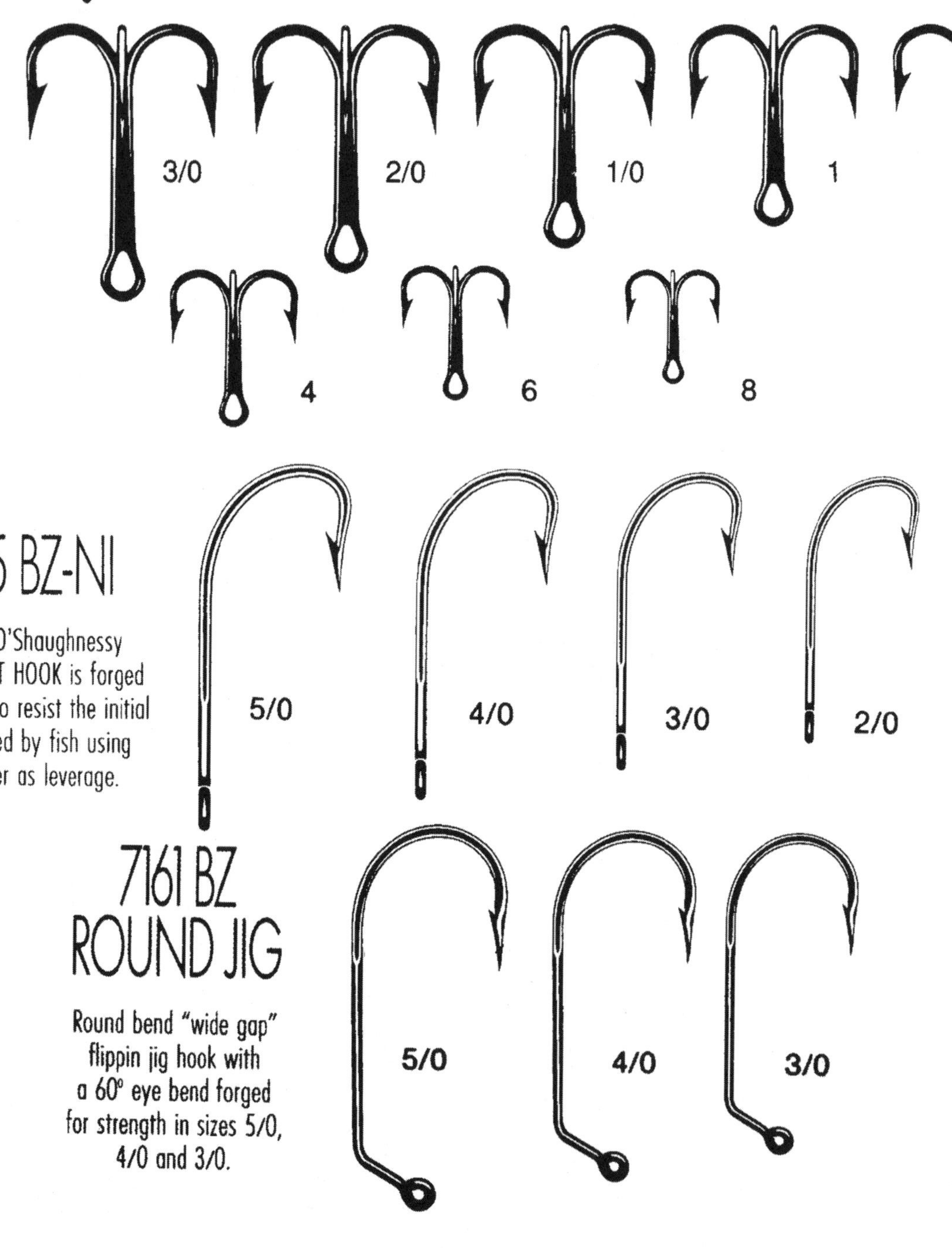

7255 BZ-NI

The VMC O'Shaughnessy SPINNER BAIT HOOK is forged for strength to resist the initial force exerted by fish using the spinner as leverage.

7161 BZ ROUND JIG

Round bend "wide gap" flippin jig hook with a 60° eye bend forged for strength in sizes 5/0, 4/0 and 3/0.

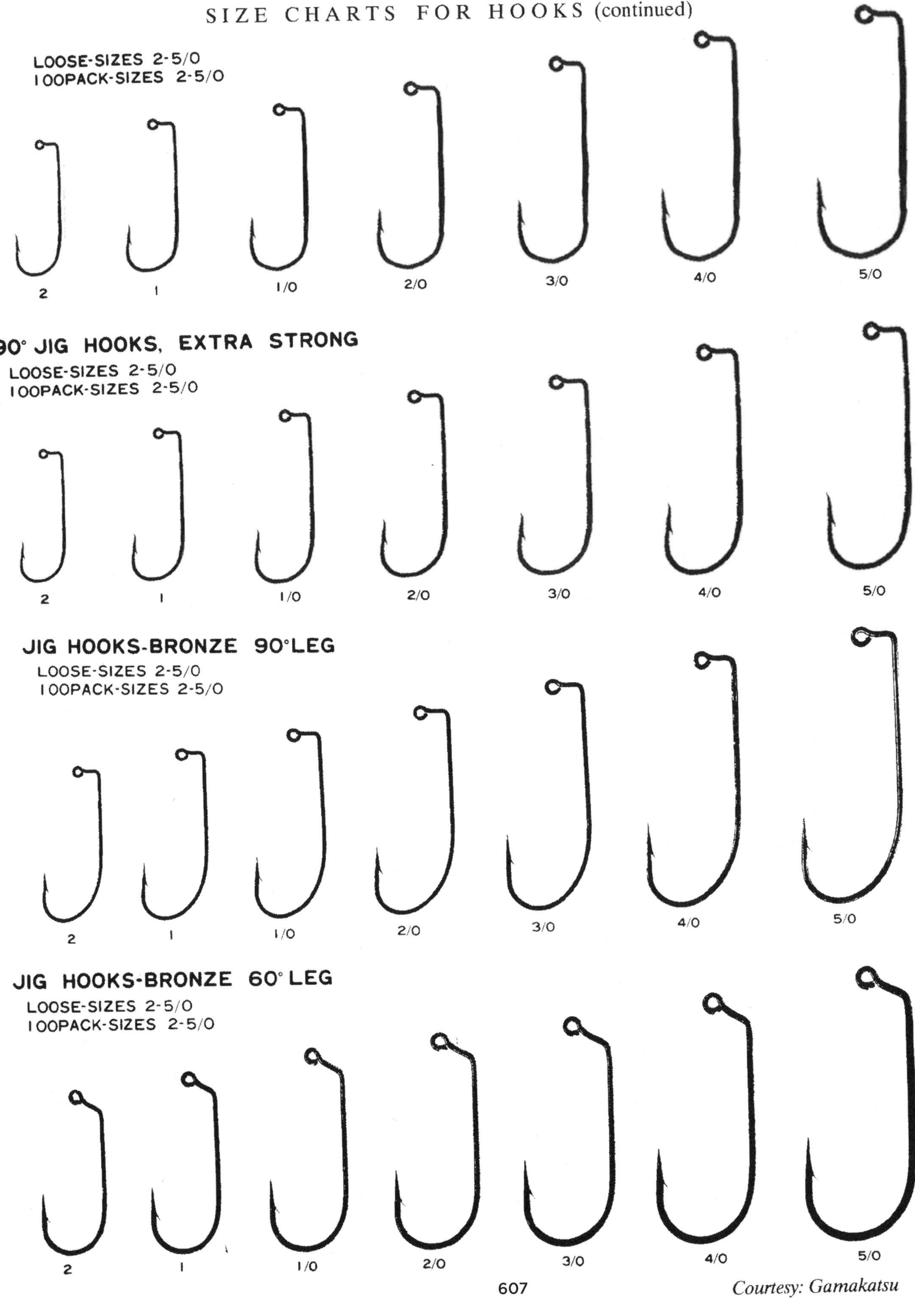

Courtesy: Gamakatsu

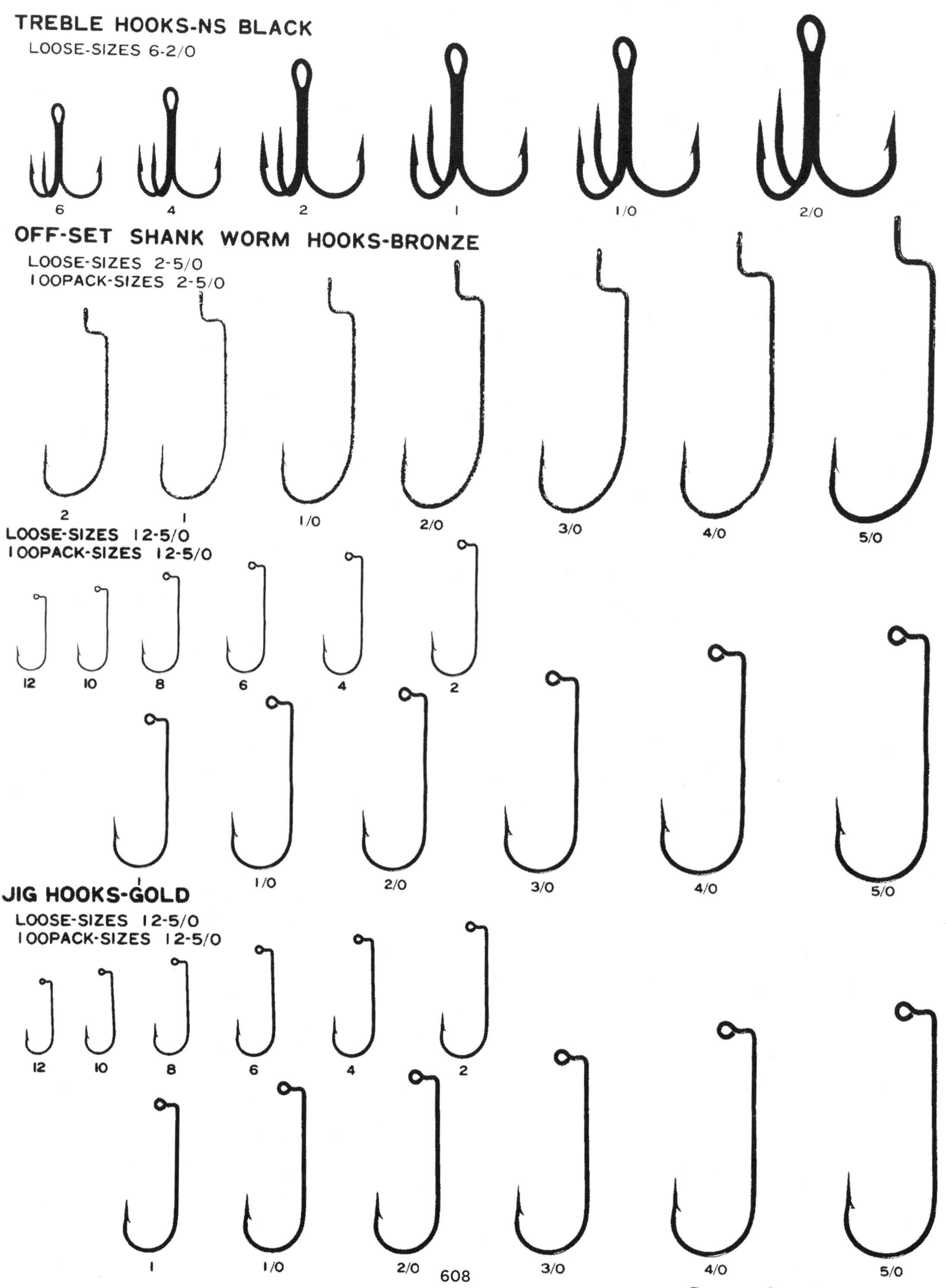

Courtesy: Gamakatsu

HOW TO MAKE A PROPER CRIMP

1 Thread end of leader material through sleeve, forming a loop, do not allow end to protrude. To avoid the possibility of slippage, be certain to use the proper size sleeve.

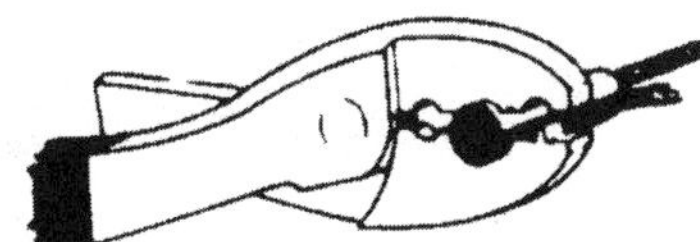

2 Hold the loop in a horizontal position. Be careful not to cross wire inside sleeves. Apply the crimping tool in a horizontal position to the sleeve, and crimp in one or more places, depending on the length of the sleeve.

3 NOTICE HOW FIRMLY AND COMPLETELY The Sleeve Strand Swadges Around All Strands of the Wire! We recommend the use of two sleeves spaced one inch apart on the 90 to 400 lb. test leader material.

TO GAIN A STRONGER LOOP WHEN APPLYING SLEEVES TO SEVALON AND DURATEST

1 Thread Sevalon through sleeve and hook eye.

2 Make overhand knot.

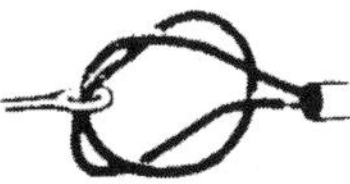

3 Go through hook a second time.

4 Make second overhand knot through sleeve, draw up loop and crimp twice.

Courtesy: Fenwick

Appendix E
Knots, Splices, and Snells

Improved Clinch Knot

1. An old standby. Pass line through eye of the hook, swivel, or lure. Double back and make five turns around the standing line. Holding the coils in place, thread the end of the line through the first loop above the eye, then through the big loop, as shown.

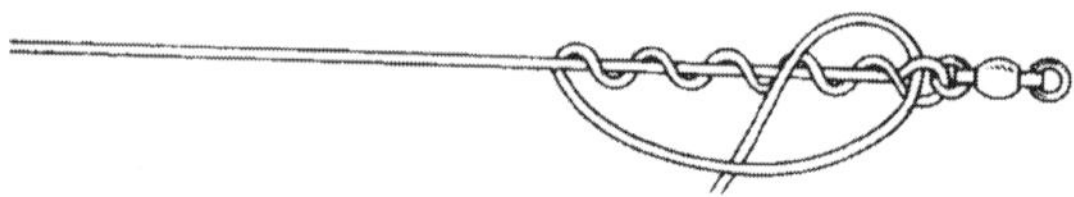

2. Hold tag end and standing line while coils are pulled up. Take care that coils are in a spiral, not overlapping one another. Slide tight against the eye. Clip tag end.

Palomar Knot

1. Easier to tie correctly and consistently the strongest knot for holding terminal tackle. Double about 4 inches of line, and pass the loop through the eye.

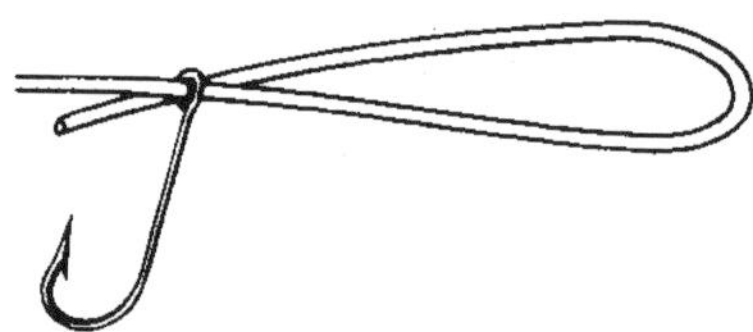

2. Let the hook hang loose, and tie an overhand knot in the doubled line. Avoid twisting the lines, and don't tighten the knot.

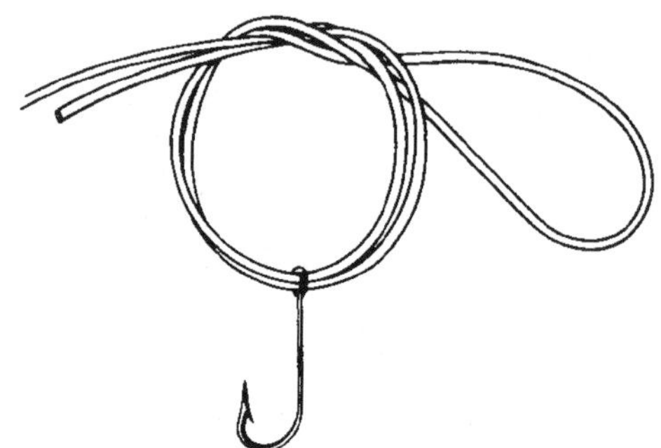

3. Pull loop of line far enough to pass it over the hook, swivel, or lure. Make sure the loop passes completely over this attachment.

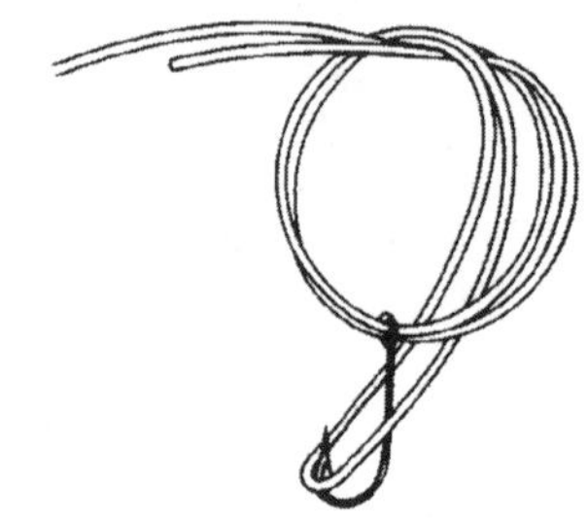

4. Pull both tag end and standing line to tighten. Clip about ⅛ inch.

THE UNI-KNOT SYSTEM

One basic knot that can be varied to meet virtually every knot-tying need in either fresh- or saltwater fishing. That was the objective of Vic Dunaway, author of numerous books on fishing and editor of *Florida Sportsman* magazine. Here is the system that resulted from his efforts.

Tying to Terminal Tackle

1. Run line through eye of the hook, swivel, or lure at least 6 inches, and fold to make two parallel lines. Bring end of line back in a circle toward the hook or lure.

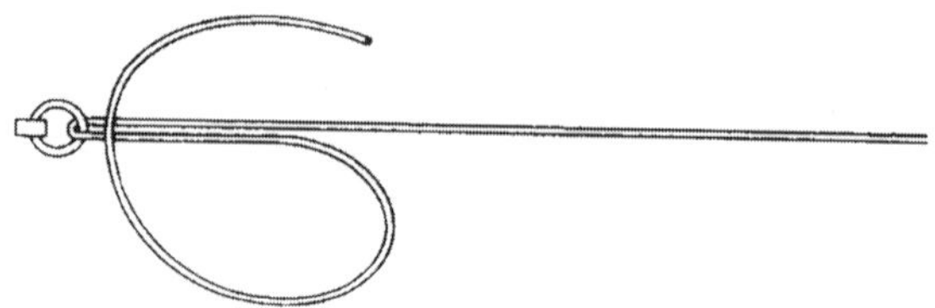

2. Make six turns with the tag end around the double line and through the circle. Hold the

double line at the point where it passes through the eye, and pull tag to snug up turns.

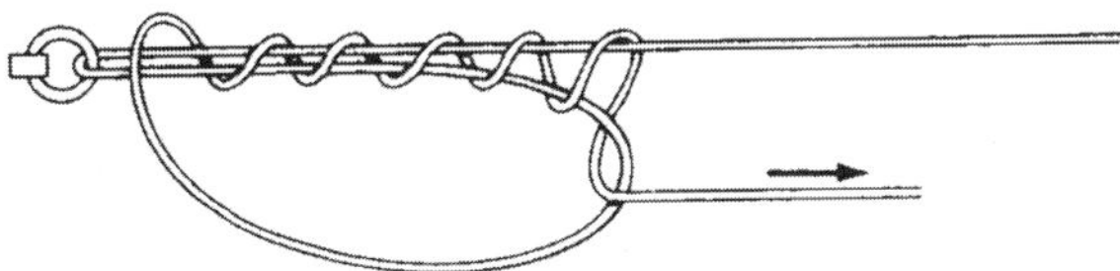

3. Now pull standing line to slide the knot up against the eye.

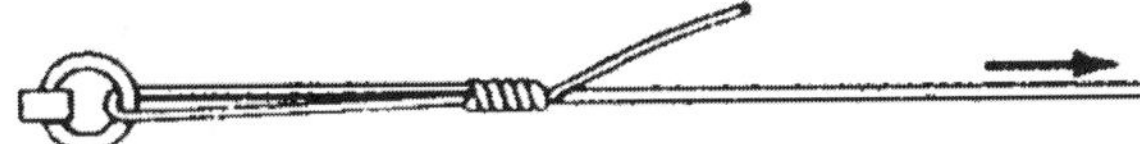

4. Continue pulling until the knot is tight. Trim tag end flush with closest coil of knot; the Uni-Knot will not slip.

Leader to Line

1. Tying on leader of no more than four times the pound/test of the line, double the end of the line and overlap with leader for about 6 inches. Make a Uni-Knot circle with doubled line.

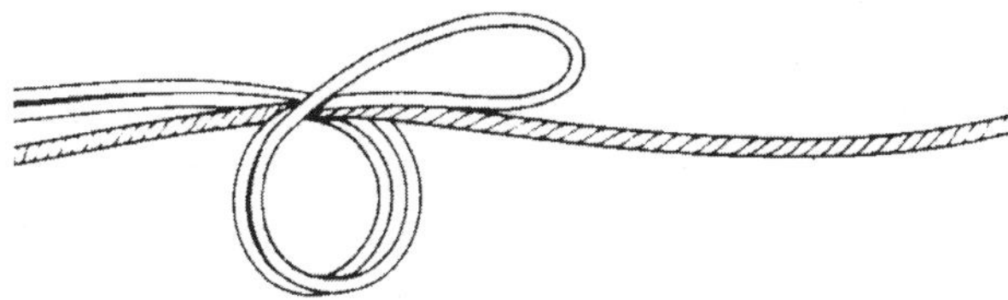

2. Tie a basic Uni-Knot, making three turns around the two lines, and snug up.

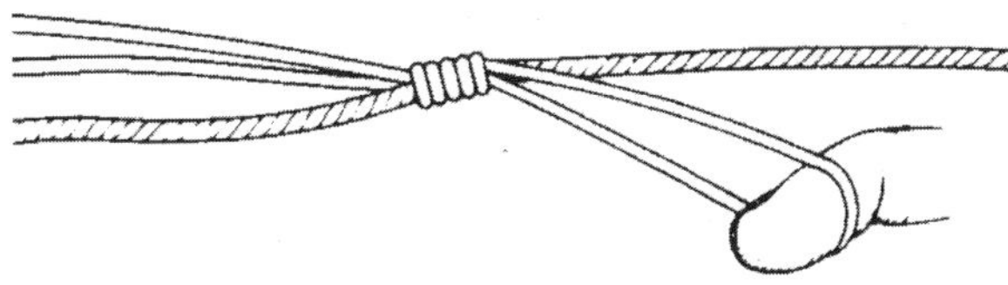

3. Now tie the Uni-Knot with the leader around the double line. Again, use only three turns.

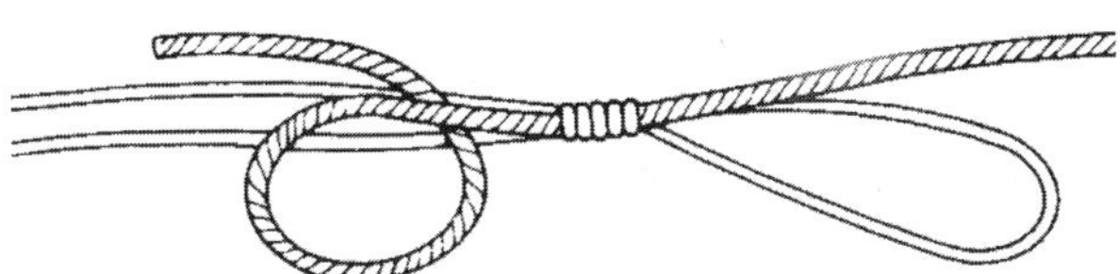

4. Pull knots together as tightly as possible, and trim ends and loop.

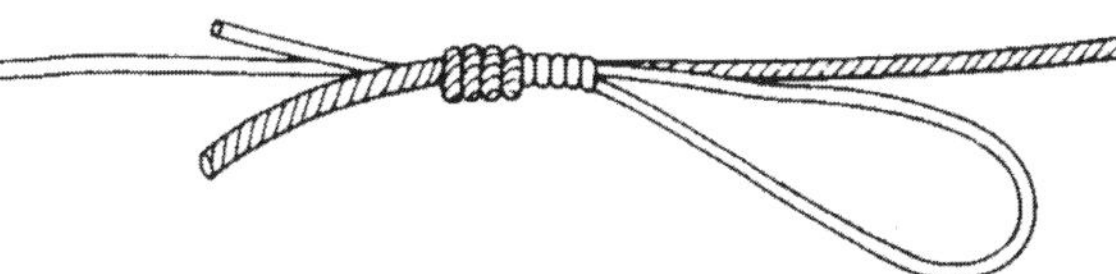

Snell Knot

The snell knot provides a strong connection when fishing with bait and using a separate length of leader. (You can only use a snell knot with a leader.)

1. Insert one end of the leader through the hook's eye, extending 1 to 2 inches past the eye. Insert the other end of the leader through the eye in the opposite direction, pointing toward the barb of the hook. Hold the hook and leader ends between thumb and forefinger on your left hand. The leader will hang below the hook in a large loop.

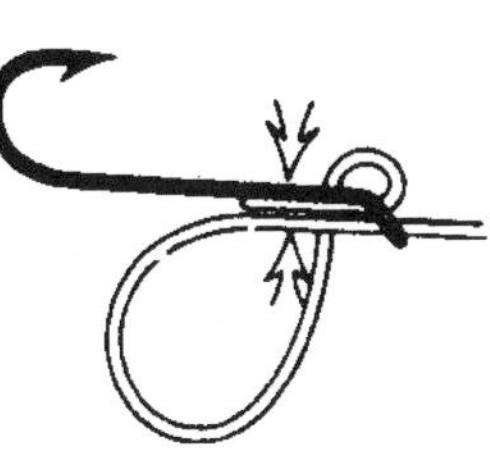

2. Take the part of this loop that is closest to the eye, and wrap it over the hook shank and both ends of the leader toward the hook's barb.

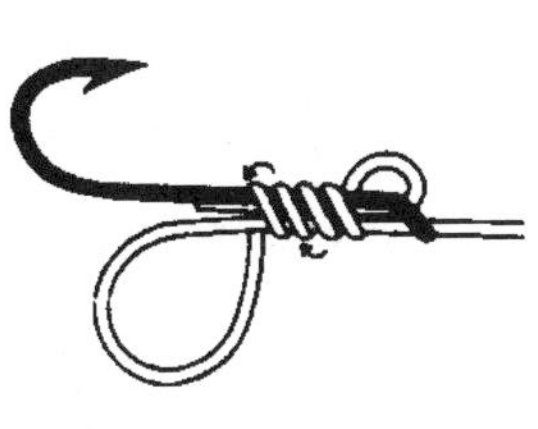

3. Wrap for seven or eight turns, holding the wraps with your left hand. Grip the end of the leader that is through the eyelet with your right hand, and pull it slowly and steadily. Hold the turns with your left hand or the knot will unravel. When the knot is almost tight, slide it up against the eye of the hook. Grip the short end lying along the shank of the hook with a pair of pliers. Pull this end and the standing line at the same time to completely tighten the knot. Trim the tag end.

Loop Connection

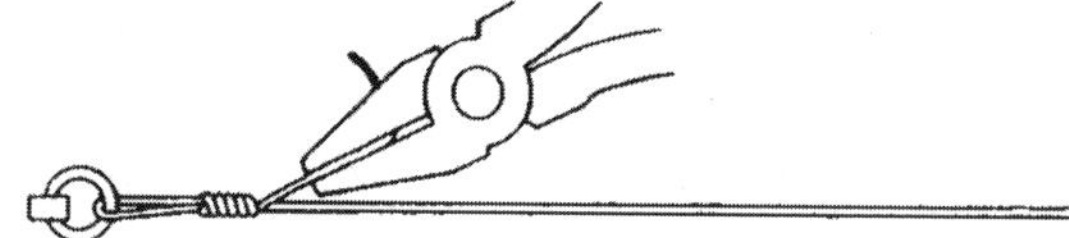

1. Tie the same knot to point where turns are snugged up around the standing line. Slide knot toward the eye until you reach the loop size desired. Pull tag end with pliers to maximum tightness. This gives the lure or fly natural free movement in water. When a fish is hooked, the knot will slide tight against the eye.

The Uni-Knot System

Joining Lines

1. Overlap ends of two lines of about the same diameter for about 6 inches. With one end form a Uni-Knot circle, crossing the two lines about midway of the overlapped distance.

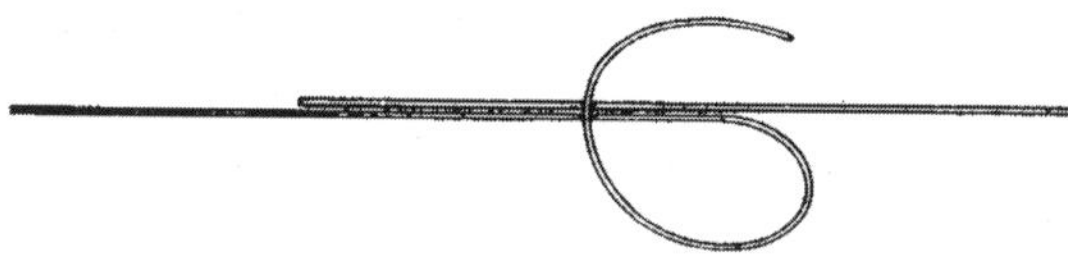

2. Tie a Uni-Knot, making six turns around the two lines.

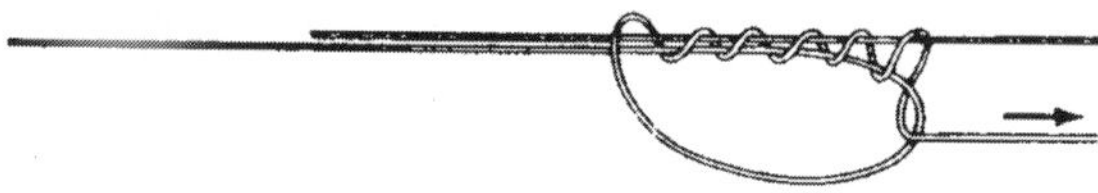

3. Pull tag end to snug knot tight around line.

4. Use loose end of the overlapped line to tie another Uni-Knot, and snug up.

5. Pull the two standing lines in opposite directions to slide knots together. Pull as tight as possible, and snip ends closer to the nearest coil.

Snelling a Hook

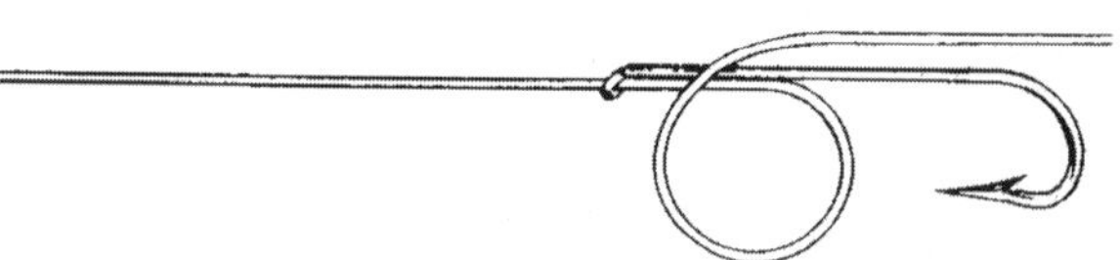

1. Thread line through the hook eye about 6 inches. Hold the line against the hook shank, and form a Uni-Knot circle.

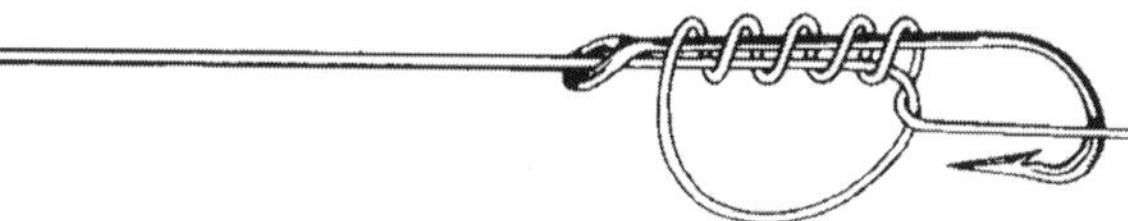

2. Make as many turns through the loop and around the line and shank as desired. Close the knot by pulling on the tag end of the line.

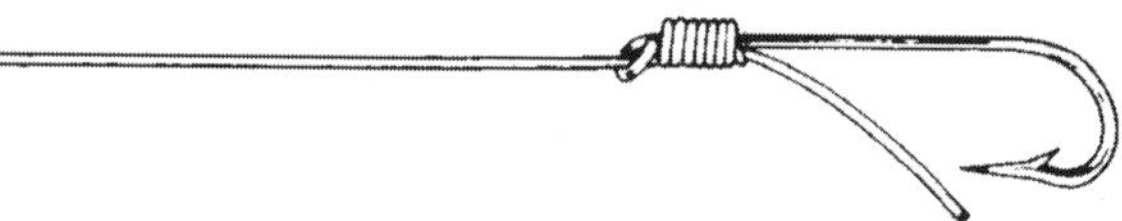

3. Tighten by pulling the standing line in one direction and the hook in the other.

Line to Reel Spool

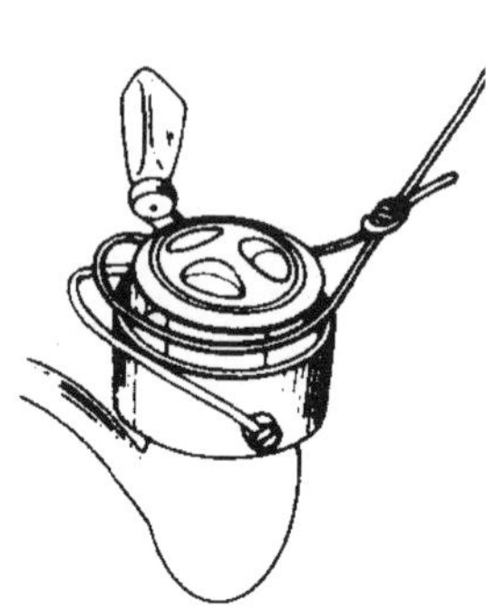

1. Tie loop in the end of the line with a Uni-Knot; only three turns are needed. With the ball of the spinning reel open, slip loop over the spool. (With revolving spool reel, line must be passed around the reel hub before tying the Uni-Knot.)
2. Pull on line to tighten the loop.

KNOTS TO TIE LINE TO LINE—LINE TO LEADER

The two most often used knots to join line: The simplified blood knot is for two lines of about the same diameter. The surgeon's knot is used to join a leader to line where the diameters vary considerably.

Simplified Blood Knot

1. Take the ends of the two lines and tie a simple overhand knot (which will be clipped off later). Then tighten to combine the two lines into one.

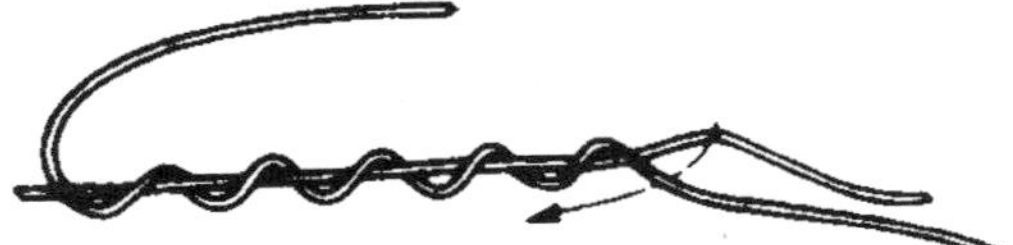

2. Form a loop where the two lines meet, with the overhand knot in the loop. Pull one side of the loop down, and begin taking turns with it around the standing line. Keep the point where turns are made open so that turns gather equally on each side.

3. After eight to ten turns, reach through the center opening and pull remaining loop (and overhand knot) through. Keep finger in the loop so that it will not spring back. Holding loop with your teeth, pull both ends of line, making turns gather on either side of the loop.

4. Set the knot by pulling lines tightly as possible. Tightening coils will make the loop stand out perpendicular to the line. Then clip off the loop and overhand knot close to the newly formed knot.

Surgeon's Knot

1. Lay the line and leader parallel, overlapping 6 to 8 inches.

2. Treating the two lines like a single line, tie an overhand knot, pulling the entire leader through the loop.

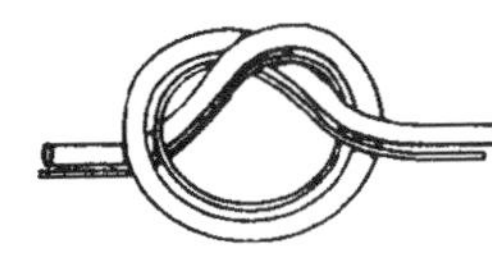

3. Leaving the loop of the overhand open, pull both the tag end of line and the leader through again.

4. Hold both lines and both ends to pull the knot tight. Clip ends close to avoid foul-up in rod guides.

Double Surgeon's Loop

The double surgeon's loop is a quick, easy way to tie a loop in the end of a leader. It is often used as part of a leader system because it is relatively strong.

1. Double the end of the line to form a loop, and tie an overhand knot at base of the double line.

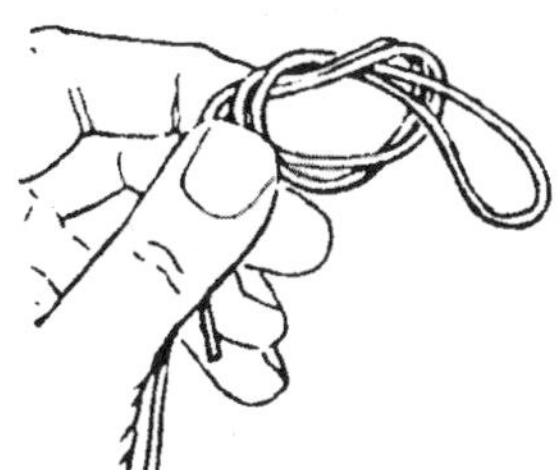

2. Leaving the loop open in the knot, bring the doubled line through once more.

3. Hold the standing line and tag end, and pull the loop to tighten the knot. Loop size can be determined by pulling the loose knot to the desired point and holding it while the knot is tightened. Clip end ⅛ inch from the knot.

KNOTS TO FORM DOUBLE-LINE LEADERS

Used primarily for offshore trolling, double-line leaders create a long loop of line that is stronger than the single strand of the standing line.

Bimini Twist

1. Measure a little more than twice the footage you'll want for the double-line leader. Bring an end back to the standing line, and hold together. Rotate end of the loop twenty times, putting twists in it.

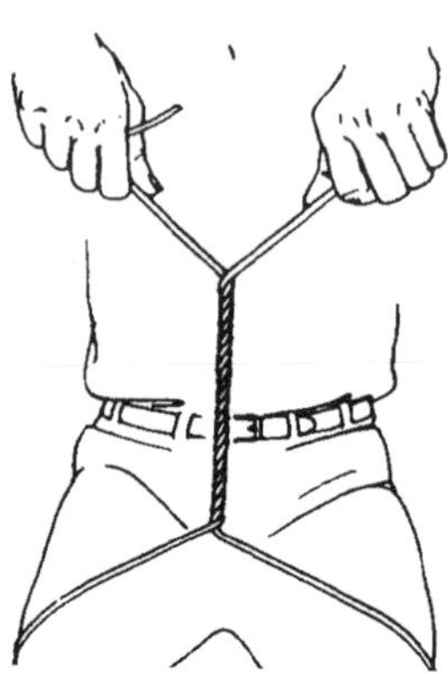

2. Spread loop to force twists together about 10 inches below the tag end. Step both feet through the loop and bring it up around your knees so that pressure can be placed on column of twists by spreading your knees apart.
3. With twists forced tightly together, hold standing line in one hand with tension just slightly off the vertical position. With your other hand move the tag end to position it at a right angle to the twists. Keeping tension on loop with knees, gradually ease tension of tag end so that it will roll over the column of twists, beginning just below the upper twist.

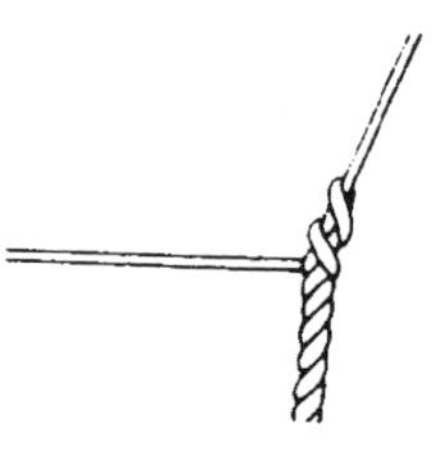

4. Spread your knees apart slowly to maintain pressure on the loop. Steer the tag end into a tight spiral coil as it continues to roll over the twisted line.
5. When spiral of tag end has rolled over the column of twists, continue keeping knee pressure on the loop; move the hand that has held the standing line down to grasp the knot. Place a finger in the crotch of line where the loop joins the knot to prevent slippage of the last turn. Make a half-hitch with the tag end around nearest leg of the loop, and pull up tight.

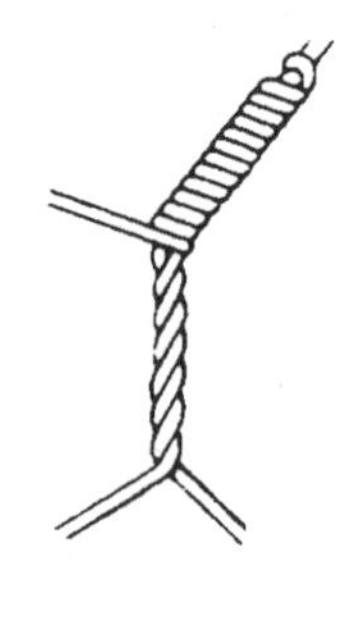

6. With the half-hitch holding the knot, release knee pressure but keep the loop stretched out tight. Using remaining tag end, take a half-hitch around both legs of the loop, but do not pull tight.

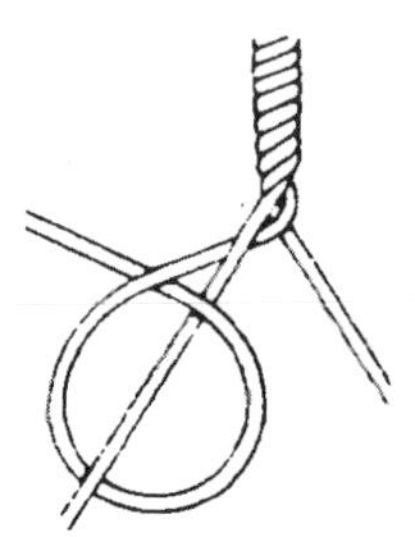

7. Make two more turns with the tag end around both legs of the loop, winding inside the bend of line formed by the loose half-hitch and toward the main knot. Pull the tag end slowly, forcing the three loops to gather in a spiral.

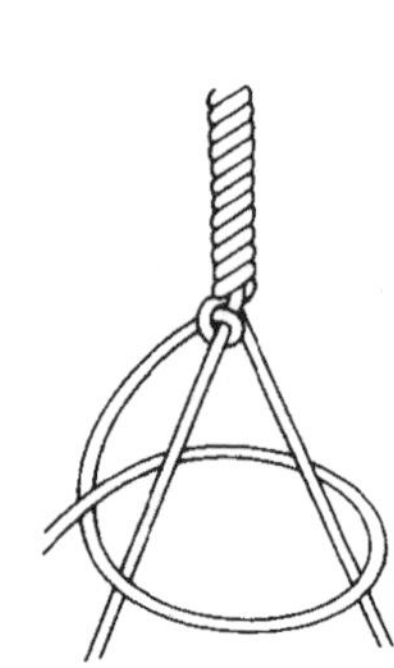

8. When the loops are pulled up neatly against the main knot, tighten to lock the knot in place. Trim tag end about ¼ inch from knot.

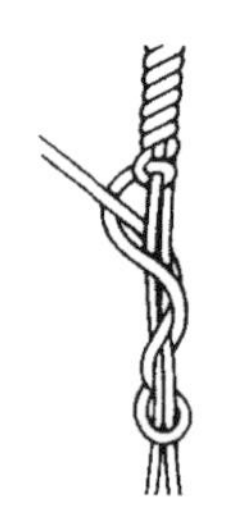

These directions apply to tying double-line leaders of around 5 feet or less. For longer double-line sections, two people may be required to hold the line and make the initial twists.

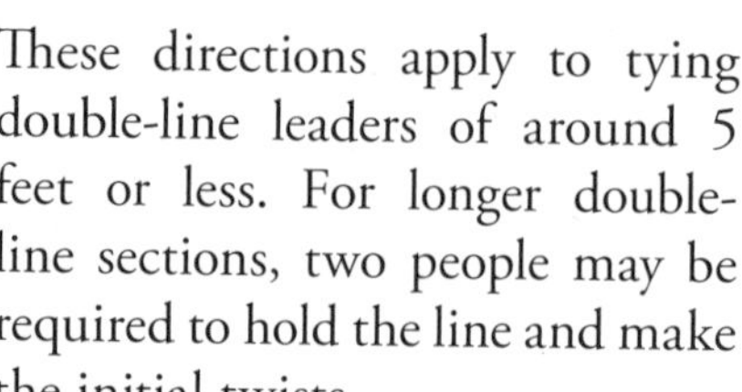

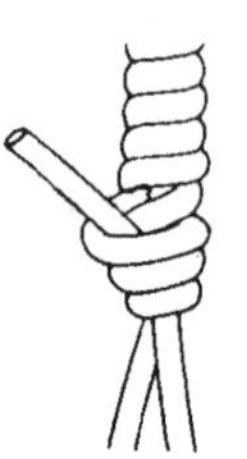

Spider Hitch

This is a faster, easier knot for creating a double-line leader. Under steady pressure it is equally strong but does not have the resilience of the Bimini twist under sharp impact. Not practical with lines above thirty-pound test.

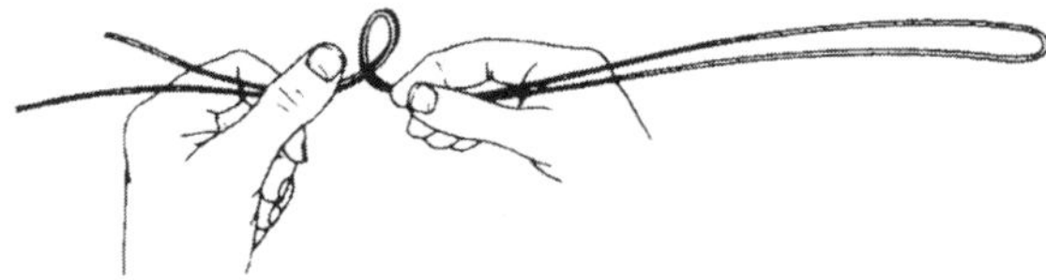

1. Form a loop of the leader length desired. Near the point where it meets the standing line, twist a section into a small reverse loop.

2. Hold the small loop between thumb and fore-finger, with the thumb extended well above the finger and the loop standing out beyond the end of your thumb.

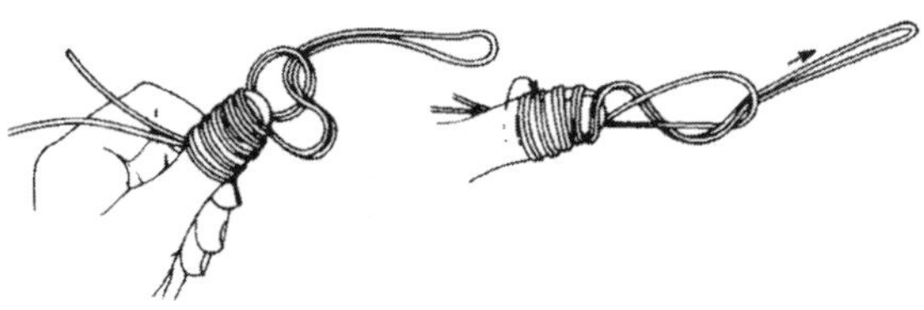

3. Wind the double line around both thumb and loop, taking five turns. Pass remainder of the large loop through the smaller one, and pull to make five turns unwind off the thumb.

4. Pull turns around the base of the loop up tight, and snip off the tag end.

Homer Rhode Loop Knot

For trolling lures or jigs, this is a good knot because it allows the lure to work freely at the end of the line.

1. Tie an overhand knot in the fishing line a few inches above the end, but don't snug it up. After passing the end of the line through the eye of the lure, push the end back through the opening of the overhand knot.

2. Tie another overhand knot above the first, making sure to tie the knot around the line. Finally, snug the overhand knots together.

Arbor Knot

The arbor knot provides the angler with a quick, easy connection for attaching line to the reel spool.

1. Pass line around the reel arbor.
2. Tie an overhand knot around the standing line.

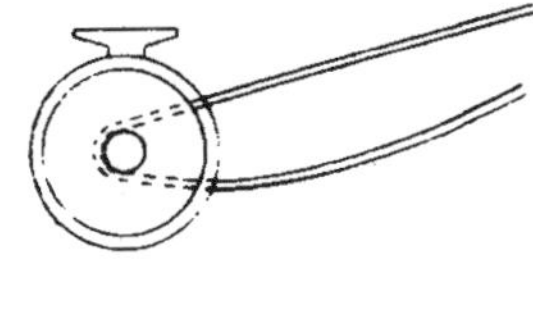

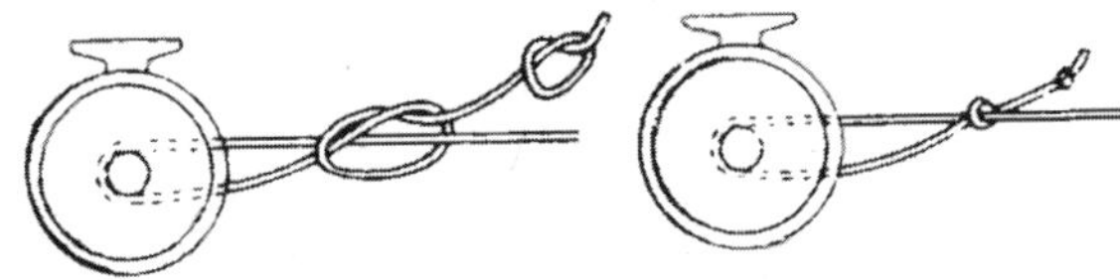

3. Tie a second overhand knot in the tag end.
4. Pull the knot tight, and snip off excess. Snug down the first overhand knot on the reel arbor.

Improved Blood Knot

The improved blood knot is used for tying two pieces of monofilament together of relatively equal diameters.

1. Overlap the ends of the two strands to be joined, and twist them together about ten turns.

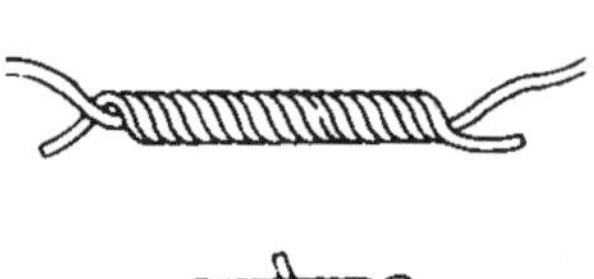

2. Separate one of the center twists, and thrust the two ends through the space as illustrated.

3. Pull the knot together, and trim off the short ends.

Albright Knot

The Albright knot is most commonly used for joining monofilament lines of unequal diameters, for creating shock leaders, and when a Bimini twist is tied in the end of the lighter casting line. It is also used for connecting monofilament to wire.

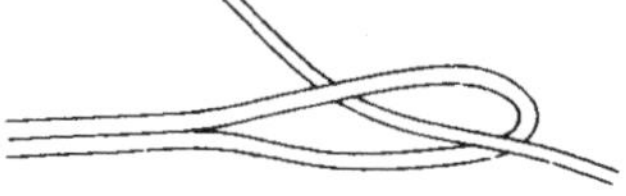

1. Bend a loop in the tag end of the heavier monofilament, and hold the loop between thumb and forefinger of your left hand. Insert the tag end of the lighter monofilament through the loop from the top.
2. Slip the tag end of the lighter monofilament under your left thumb, and pinch it tightly against the heavier strands of the loop. Wrap the first turn of the lighter monofilament over itself, and continue wrapping toward the round end of the loop. Take at least twelve turns with the lighter monofilament around all three strands.

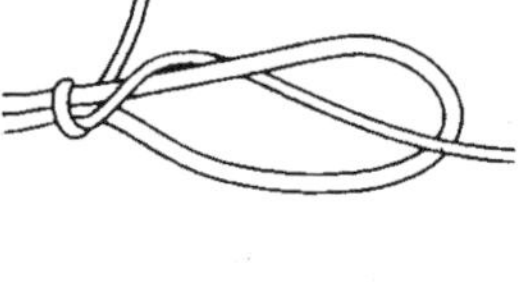

3. Insert tag end of the lighter monofilament through the end of the loop from the bottom. It must enter and leave the loop on the same side.
4. With the thumb and forefinger of your left hand, slide the coils of the lighter monofilament toward the end of the loop, stopping ⅛ inch from end of the loop. Using pliers, pull the tag end of the lighter mono tight to keep the coils from slipping off the loop.
5. With your left hand still holding the heavier mono, pull on the standing part of the lighter mono. Pull the tag end of the lighter mono and the standing part a second time. Pull the standing part of the heavy mono and the standing part of the light mono.
6. Trim both tag ends.

Attaching Swivel or Snap to Double-Line Leader

Offshore Swivel Knot

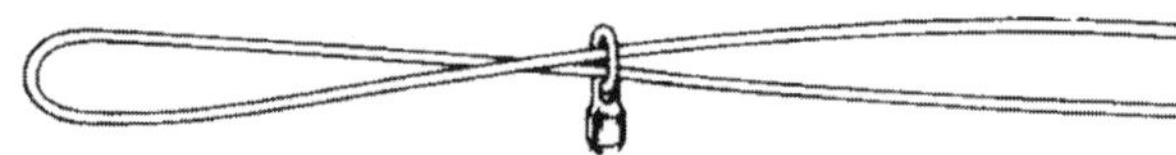

1. Slip loop end of the double-line leader through eye of the swivel. Rotate loop end a half-turn to put a single twist between the loop and swivel eye.
2. Pass the loop with the twist over the swivel. Hold end of the loop plus both legs of the double-line leader with one hand. Let the swivel slide to the other end of the double loops now formed.

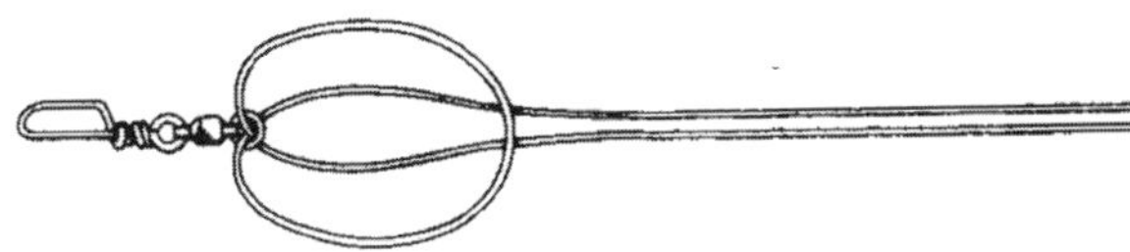

3. Still holding the loop and lines with one hand, use the other to rotate the swivel through center of both loops at least six times.

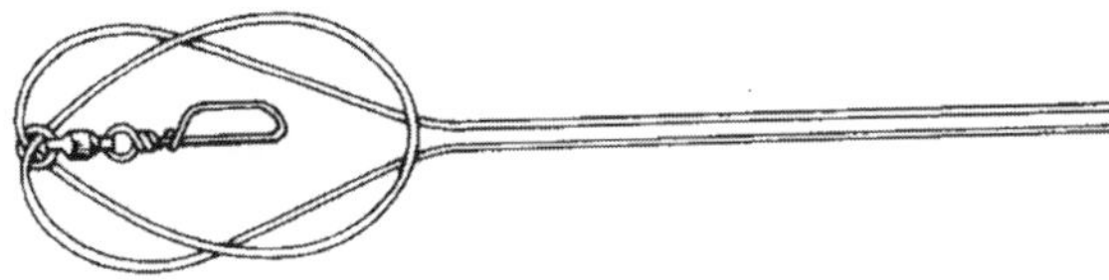

4. Continue holding both legs of double-line leader tightly, but release end of the loop. Pull on the swivel, and loops will begin to gather.

5. To draw the knot tight, grip the swivel with pliers and push loops toward the eye with your fingers while still keeping the standing lines of the leader pulled tight.

Crimping Pointers

Here's how to make a crimp correctly. The procedure works with one sleeve or two.

1. Put the end of the wire through the sleeve and then through the eye.
2. Bring the end back through the sleeve. There shouldn't be any excess sticking through.

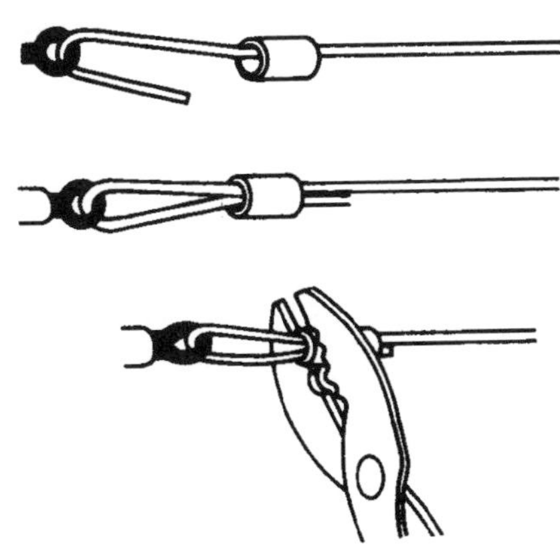

3. Using a crimping tool and matching the correct slot on the tool to the sleeve, crimp down as hard as you can near the bottom end of the sleeve. Then move up near the top of the sleeve and crimp it at a 90-degree angle to the first crimp.

Heavy-Duty Crimping

Big-game anglers often use the rigging technique when they're crimping a wire cable or heavy-duty monofilament leader to a lure hook.

1. Slip two crimping sleeves over the cable or mono, then pass the cable or mono through the hook eye twice.

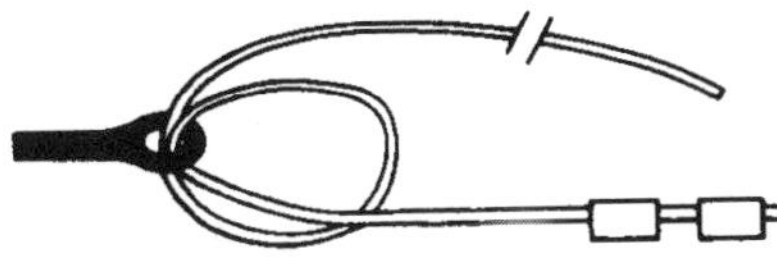

2. After the second loop is made, pass the tag end through the loop in three overhands.

3. Snug up the loop, pass the tag end through the two sleeves, and crimp both close together as shown.

Understanding Hooks

Today's sophisticated sportsman knows there's a lot more to catching fish than just tying any type of hook to the line. Hooks just may be the most important part of your arsenal, and if you skimp in this area, your results may suffer accordingly.

That's why it's important to find the hooks that work best for you—and stick with them. Hook size is determined by its pattern and is given in terms of the gap widths in the hook. The two important dimensions of the hook are

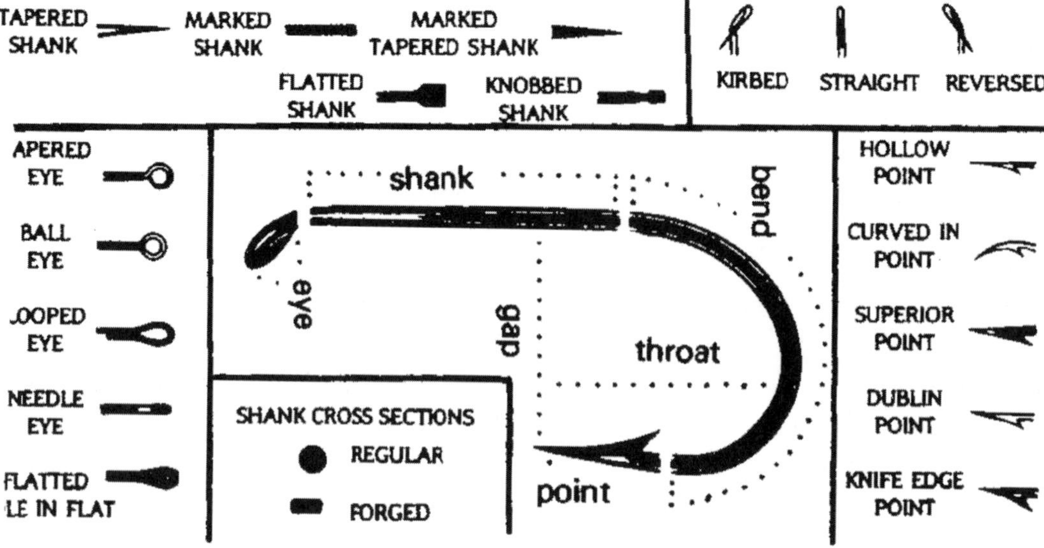

its gap and throat, as illustrated by the Mustad-Viking hook below.

Note the width of the gap, clearance between point and shank, and the depth of its throat. These generous dimensions make for a bigger bite, deeper penetration, and better holding power.

WORLD'S FAIR KNOT

Created by Gary L. Martin of Lafayette, Indiana, this terminal tackle knot was selected by a panel of outdoor writers as the best new, easy-to-tie, all-purpose fishing knot from 498 entries in the Du Pont Great Knot Search. Martin named it the World's Fair Knot because it was first publicly demonstrated by him at the 1982 World's Fair in Knoxville, Tennessee.

1. Double a 6-inch length of line, and pass the loop through the eye.

2. Bring the loop back next to the doubled line, and grasp the doubled line through the loop.

3. Put the tag end through the new loop formed by the double line.

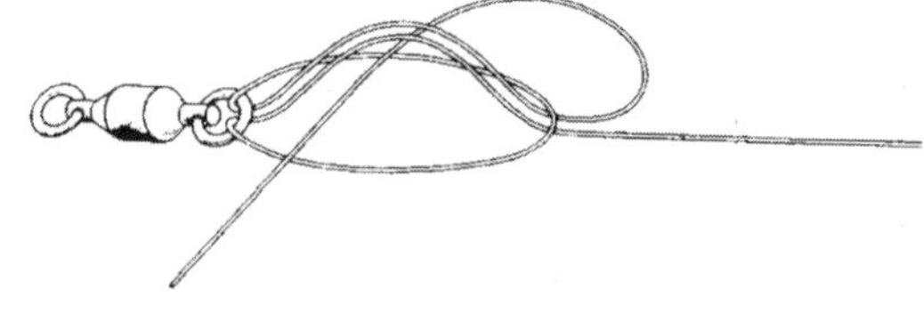

4. Bring the tag end back through the new loop created by step 3.

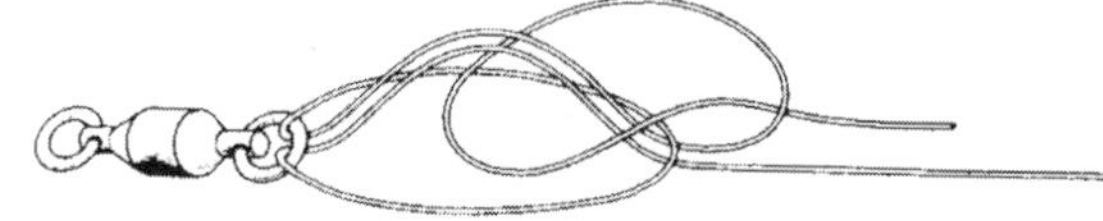

5. Pull the tag end snug, and slide the knot up tight. Clip the tag end.

Appendix F

List of Suppliers, Distributors, and Manufacturers

The following is a partial list of suppliers, distributors, and manufacturers of tackle-crafting supplies. Obviously the first place to look for supplies is your local tackle shop. Often it will have a lot of what you need or will be able to get it on short order for you. Tackle shops exist to help you—it pays to give them your business when possible. Mail-order companies like those listed here often specialize in do-it-yourself items more than most tackle shops can. Some even specialize in certain areas, such as tools and materials for soft-plastic lures, general lures, spinners, rods, and so on.

In addition, it often pays to check out craft stores, art supply stores, hobby shops, and similar outlets. These places often sell items that, while not specifically designed for tackle crafting, can be adapted to it. Examples include various types of glitter for finishing lures, moldable plastic, glue guns, various glues, beads, doll eyes, and plastic parts that can serve as spinner bodies. Hobby shops sell casting plastic, tubing with which spoons and lures can be made, glues, and lots of neat tools. Art supply stores carry airbrushes, paints, and stencils. Fly-tying supply houses are also excellent sources for materials such as furs, feathers, threads, and other soft goods for tying on bucktails and finishing other lures.

Rod builders should subscribe to *RodMaker* magazine, published six times a year. In addition to great articles on the latest cutting-edge techniques and ideas on building rods, it carries ads from suppliers and manufacturers of rod-building supplies and services. For information contact RodMaker Magazine, PO Box 1322, High Point, NC 27261; (336) 882-3226; www.rodmakermagazine.com; e-mail: info@rodmakermagazine.com.

AFTCO
American Fishing Tackle Company
2400 South Garnsey St.
Santa Ana, CA 92707
(877) 489-4278
www.aftco.com
E-mail: customercare@aftco.com
Manufacturer of saltwater guides, reel seats, and handles.

AFW
American Fishing Wire—HI SEAS
440 Highlands Blvd.
Coatesville, PA 19320-5808
(610) 466-6100; (800) 824-9473
www.americanfishingwire.com
www.hiseas.net
E-mail: sales@americanfishingwire.com
E-mail: sales@hiseas.net
Manufacturer of wire, tools for making lures, and fishing rigs.

American Star Cork Co., Inc.
33-53 62nd St.
PO Box 770449
Woodside, NY 11377
(718) 335-3000; (800) 338-3581
www.amstarcork.com
E-mail: info@amstarcork.com
Cork products for rod building.

American Tackle Company, Inc.
Distribution Center
400 Kane Court
Suite 100
Oviedo, FL 32765
(407) 706-0321; (800) 516-1750, ext. 1204
www.americantackle.us
E-mail: sales@americantackle.us
Rod-building supplies and tools, including guides, reel seats, grips, and more.

Angler's Workshop
PO Box 1044
Woodland, WA 98674
(360) 225-9445
www.anglersworkshop.com
E-mail: info@anglersworkshop.com
Sales of rod-building blanks, guides, reel seats, grips, and other parts and tools. Catalog available.

Batson Enterprises
130 Harrison Rd.
Suite 8
Sequim, WA 98382
(877) 875-2381
www.batsonenterprises.com
E-mail: batson@batsonenterprises.com
Manufacturer/distributor of rod-building supplies, including blanks, guides, grips, reel seats, and tools.

Berkley
1900 18th St.
Spirit Lake, IA 51360
(800) 237-5539
www.berkley-fishing.com
Manufacturer of line, wire, terminal snaps and swivels, and rigs.

Bingham Enterprises
12004 Perry St.
Overland Park, KS 66213-1626
(913) 897-6657
www.angelfire.com/ks/bingham
E-mail: binghamenterprises@kc.rr.com
Blanks and components for building rods.

Biscayne Rod Company
425 East Ninth St.
Hialeah, FL 33010
(305) 884-0808; (866) 969-0808
www.biscaynerod.com
E-mail: sales@biscaynerod.com
Rod-building blanks and component parts.

C&D Trading Co.
1650 Fairway Dr.
Columbia Heights, MN 55421
(763) 574-1563
www.cdtradinginc.com
E-mail: ckishish@cpinternet.com
Supplier of cork products for fishing, including rod handles and rings.

C. Palmer Mfg. Co. Inc.
5 Palmer Rd.
West Newton, PA 15089
(724) 872-8200
www.cpalmermfg.com
E-mail: cpalmer@yukonwaltz.com
Manufacturer and sales of electric pots for melting lead and soft metals for making jigs and sinkers.

Caney Creek Molds
Lake Fork
522 Private Road 5986
Yantis, TX 75497
(903) 383-3231
www.caneycreekmolds.com
Molds for making lures.

Cape Cod Tackle
Route 6, 149 Main St.
Wareham, MA 02571-2124
(508) 291-0820
http://capecodtackle.com
Tackle parts and other fishing equipment.

Chesapeake Cork Products
8307 Alston Rd.
Towson, MD 21204
(410) 296-1746
Cork products for fishing, fishing rod grips.

Do-It Corporation
501 North State St.
Denver, IA 50622
(319) 984-6055
www.do-itfishing.com
Manufacturer of molds for lead jigs, lures, sinkers, and parts for making lures.

DonJer Products Corp.
13142 Murphy Rd.
Winnebago, IL 61088
(815) 247-8775; (800) 336-6537
www.donjer.com
www.softflock.com
E-mail: info@donjer.com
Manufacturer of flocking materials and tools for making flocked custom fishing rod grips.

Eagle Claw Fishing Tackle
4245 East 46th Ave.
PO Box 16011
Denver, CO 80216
(303) 321-1481
www.eagleclaw.com
E-mail: info@eagleclaw.com
Manufacturer of tackle and hooks, including hooks for making lures.

Feather-Craft Fly Fishing
8307 Manchester Rd.
PO Box 440128
St. Louis, MO 63144
(800) 659-1707
www.feather-craft.com
Sales of fly-fishing equipment, including rod-building kits. Catalog.

Fishing Tackle Unlimited
12800 Gulf Freeway @ Fuqua
Houston, TX 77034
(281) 481-6838
www.fishingtackleunlimited.com
Rod blanks and component parts.

Flex Coat Company, Inc.
PO Box 190
Driftwood, TX 78619
(512) 858-7742
www.flexcoat.com
E-mail: questions@flexcoat.com
Manufacturer of adhesives, tools, supplies, and instructions.

Grizzly Industrial, Inc.
1203 Lycoming Mall Circle
Muncy, PA 17756
(800) 523-4777
www.grizzly.com
Industrial tools for wood and metalworking.

Hagen's Fishing Components
3150 West Havens
Mitchell, SD 57301
(800) 541-4586
www.hagensfish.com
Sales of components for making all types of lures. Online catalog.

The Hook & Hackle Company
607 Ann St. Rear
Homestead, PA 15120
(412) 476-8620; (800) 552-8342
www.hookhack.com
E-mail: ron@hookhack.com
Blanks and component parts for building fishing rods.

IASCO
Industrial Arts Supply Co.
5724 West 36th St.
Minneapolis, MN 55416-2494
(952) 920-7393; (888) 919-0899
www.iasco-tesco.com
E-mail: info@iasco-tesco.com
Supplier of many types of tools and materials for making small items, including all types of soft- and hard-plastic lures.

J. Kennedy Fisher, Incorporated
33 Brown Drive
Carson City, NV 89702
(702) 246-5220
Manufacturer of rod blanks.

J. Stockard Fly Fishing
14 Flanders Lane
PO Box 800
Kent, CT 06757
(860) 359-8946; (877) 359-8946
www.jsflyfishing.com
E-mail: service@jsflyfishing.com
Supplier of fly-fishing rod-building supplies. Catalog.

Jann's Netcraft
3350 Briarfield Blvd.
Maumee, OH 43537
(419) 868-8288 (technical questions); (800) 638-2723
www.jannsnetcraft.com
E-mail: techhelp@jannsnetcraft.com
Sales of lure-making, rod-building, net-making, and fly-tying parts and supplies. Catalog.

Klondike Rod Company
97 Leesburg Station Rd.
New Wilmington, PA 16142-1901
(724) 674-0481
www.klondikerod.com
E-mail: info@klondikerod.com
Sales of custom inlaid reel seats and grip assemblies.

Lakeland Incorporated
One Lakeland Dr.
250 East Isle St.
PO Box 378
Isle, MN 56342
(320) 676-3666
www.lakelandinc.com
E-mail: lakeland@lakelandinc.com
Manufacturer and distributor of lure and spinner parts.

Li'l Mac Molds
PO Box 319
Lewiston, ID 83501
(208) 743-3858
http://lilmacmolds.com
E-mail: info@alpinearchery.com
Manufacturer of molds for making lead fishing lures and sinkers. Online catalog.

M-F Manufacturing Co., Inc.
4424 McLean Rd.
Fort Worth, TX 76117
(817) 281-9488
www.pouryourownworms.com
E-mail: pouryourownworms@swbell.net
Catalog of supplies and tools for making and pouring soft-plastic lures.

Madison River Fishing Company
109 Main St.
PO Box 627
Ennis, MT 59729
(800) 227-7127
www.mrfc.com
E-mail: mrfc@3rivers.net
Supplier of fly-fishing rod-building supplies. Catalog.

Merrick Tackle Center, Inc.
7349 Route 28
Shandaken, NY 12480
(800) 628-8904
www.merricktackle.com
E-mail: sales@merricktackle.com
Catalog house and retail for blanks, parts, and components for rod building.

Mud Hole Custom Tackle, Inc.
400 Kane Court
Oviedo, FL 32765
(866) 790-7637
www.mudhole.com
E-mail: sales@mudhole.com
Catalog house for parts and components for making rods and lures.

North Fork Composites
PO Box 2223
Woodland, WA 98674
(360) 225-2211
www.northforkcomposites.com
E-mail: info@northforkcomposites.com
Manufacturer of all types of fishing rod blanks.

O. Mustad & Son (USA) Inc.
241 Grant Ave.
PO Box 838
Auburn, NY 13021
(315) 253-2793
www.mustad.no
E-mail: FrontOffice@mustad-usa.com
Manufacturer of hooks, including those for lures of all types.

PacBay
Pacific Bay International, Inc.
PO Box 177
Carlsborg, WA 98324
www.fishpacbay.com
E-mail: info@fishpacbay.com
Manufacturer of tools, guides, reel seats, etc.

Pace Products LLC
2764 North Green Valley Pkwy.
Suite 379
Henderson, NV 89014
(800) 796-2675
www.pacecork.com
E-mail: pacecork@msn.com
Cork products for fishing rod grips and handles.

Penn State Industries
9900 Global Rd.
Philadelphia, PA 19115
(800) 377-7297
www.pennstateind.com
Tools and supplies for small woodworking projects, including wood lures.

REC Components
17 Middle River Dr.
Stafford Springs, CT 06076
(860) 749-3476
http://rec.com
E-mail: info@rec.com
Sales of rod blanks and component parts.

Renzetti, Inc.
8800 Grissom Pkwy.
Titusville, FL 32780
(321) 267-7705
www.truerotary.com
Manufacturer and sales of the Jim Upton Wonder Weaver tool for weaving designs on rods and the Master Rod Lathe. Catalog.

Sage Manufacturing
8500 Northeast Day Rd.
Bainbridge Island, WA 98110
(206) 842-6608; (888) 848-7243
www.sageflyfish.com
E-mail: sage@sageflyfish.com
Manufacturer of fly-rod blanks.

St. Croix of Park Falls, Ltd.
856 Fourth Ave. North
PO Box 279
Park Falls, WI 54552
(715) 762-3226
www.stcroixrods.com
Manufacturer of rod blanks.

SAMPO
119 Remsen Rd.
PO Box 328
Barneveld, NY 13304
(315) 896-2606
www.sampoinc.com
E-mail: info@sampoinc.com
Manufacturer of swivels and terminal tackle for making lures.

Seeker Rods USA
1340 West Cowles St.
Long Beach, CA 90813
(562) 491-0076
www.seekerrods.com
Manufacturer of graphite and glass rod blanks.

Shakespeare Company
7 Science Court
Columbia, SC 29203
(800) 466-5643
www.shakespeare-fishing.com
Manufacturer of glass and graphite rod blanks.

Shoff Tackle
Puyallup, WA 98375
(253) 904-8732; (866) 867-4004
www.shofftackle.com/catalog.pdf
www.shofftackle.com/catalog.html
E-mail: sales@shofftackle.com
Rod parts. Online catalog only.

SPRO Corporation
3900 Kennesaw 75 Pkwy.
Suite 140
Kennesaw, GA 30144
(770) 919-1722
www.spro.com
E-mail: sales@spro.com
Manufacturer of hooks.

The Surfcaster
360 Sniffens Lane
Stratford, CT 06615-7559
(203) 610-6965; (800) 551-7873
www.thesurfcaster.com
Rod-building supplies for surf fishing.

Swampland Tackle
204 Angelle Dr.
Houma, LA 70360
(985) 852-1703
http://swamplandtackle.com
E-mail: swamplandrods@msn.com
Blanks, component parts, guides, and designs for making rods.

Trondak, Inc.
17631 147th St. Southeast #7
Monroe, WA 98272
(360) 794-8250
E-mail: info@aquaseal.net
Manufacturer of rod sealers and adhesives such as Permagloss, DuraGloss, and Rod Bond adhesive.

Tru-Turn Inc.
100 Red Eagle Dr.
PO Box 1177
Wetumpka, AL 36092
(334) 567-2011; (800) 421-5768
Manufacturer of unique bent-shank hooks.

Woodcraft Supply, LLC
1177 Rosemar Rd.
PO Box 1686
Parkersville, WV 26102-1686
(304) 422-5412; (800) 535-4486
www.woodcraft.com
E-mail: custserv@woodcraft.com
Catalog of woodworking tools and supplies for making wood lures.

Worth Manufacturing Company
Box 88
Stevens Point, WI 54481
(715) 344-6081
www.worthco.com
E-mail: sales@worthco.com
Manufacturers of all types of lure, spinner, and spoon parts; wire-forming tools.

Glossary

Many of these terms will be familiar to you while others may be unfamiliar or may have meanings in rod building and lure making that are far different from their usual dictionary definition. In addition, with permission from Tom Kirkman of *RodMaker* magazine, I have also included some terms that Tom included in a glossary of his magazine, edition volume 7, number 2. To give credit where credit is due, these definitions are marked with an asterisk.*

Note: Terms in boldface are also defined.

ABS. A type of plastic used to mold hard-plastic plug bodies. Used extensively by modem manufacturers. Other plastics used include **butyrate** and **Tenite.**

Acceleration. *An increase in speed or velocity. Can be measured by units of ft/sec squared.

Acid wrap. *Another term for the **spiral wrap.** The term originated on the West Coast when one proponent of the wrap was said to have been on "acid" when he wrapped his rod in spiral fashion.

Action. Describes the type of bend a rod makes during casting or fighting. Some manufacturers still refer to action when they mean not only the way in which a rod bends but also the resistance to bending. Resistance to bending is better referred to as **power.** The action is the bend the rod makes as a result of the mandrel and the cut of the graphite or glass fabric used to wrap around the mandrel. The result can be a rod that bends almost evenly from tip to butt **(parabolic)**, one that has more of a tippy action or bend (fast action), or one that is very tippy (extra-fast action). Other terms are sometimes used, and some manufacturers refer to a "worm" action when describing a fast rod or a rod with extra-fast tip action rod. A rod can have a given action and still be light or heavy power.

Adhesive. *Bonding agent made from chemically synthesized materials.

Adhesive failure. *Condition that exists when a bonding agent pull loose from a surface.

Adhesive strength. *Strength of the bond between a bonding agent and the strength of the items being bonded.

Aetna guide. A once-popular guide that is sometimes still found on the market. It is made with a strand of wire that is bent into a complete circle to form a ring for the line flow; the ends form the guide feet. Similar wire guides in different brand names are available.

Airbrush. A special type of painting tool used primarily by artists. Air is sprayed through a nozzle along with paint to create a smooth, feathered effect. Ideal for painting some lures and used by many lure manufacturers.

Aircraft cable. A very-large-diameter twisted wire leader used in big-game fishing. Often consisting of wire made by first twisting seven strands of single-strand wire into one cable, then twisting seven of these cables into one aircraft cable.

Airplane cable. Another name for **aircraft cable.**

Aluminum oxide. A ceramic material used in guide rings. The material is very hard, essentially nongrooving, and is one of several ceramic materials used in guide rings.

Artificial fur. Synthetic fur that is used in fly tying and lure making. It can go by any number of names, perhaps the earliest of which was FishHair. Craft fur, available in large sheets from hobby shops, is similar and is often used by fly tiers and lure builders. Many colors are available.

Attractor tubing. A round hollow tubing, usually composed of vinyl or a similar plastic, that is cut into short lengths and added to the shaft of hooks (usually treble hooks) that are placed on spinners and similar lures. It is used to create an attraction for fish and comes in bright colors, including fluorescent and standard red, yellow, orange, and green.

Back bouncing rods. Stout, medium-action rods designed for use with back bouncing rigs consisting of a heavy sinker which holds a swimming plug near the bottom. Rigs are lowered to the bottom, not cast. Back bouncing rods can be used for other types of fishing as well.

Ball-bearing swivel. A swivel with tiny ball bearings used between the swiveling surfaces. Used primarily in big-game fishing and trolling, where freely moving and rotating lures are a must and line twist must be reduced or eliminated. More expensive than regular swivels.

Ball-head jig. A lead-head jig with a spherical head that is often used for making crappie jigs and lures.

Banjo-eye jig. A large bucktail with bulging eyes. Usually the eyes are molded into the lure, but sometimes they are made of glass or plastic and then added to the finished lure.

Bank sinker. A teardrop-shaped sinker with hexagonal sides; designed to be used in rocky areas. The shape of the sinker resists hanging up on rocks.

Barrel swivel. A simple two-eye swivel in which the central part resembles a small barrel.

Bass-casting sinker. A pear-shaped sinker with a molded-in swivel eye. Also called a dipsy doodle sinker, dipsy sinker, or bell sinker.

Basswood. One of several woods used to carve fishing plugs. This popular fine-grained wood is easy to carve. Other woods used for plugs include **cedar** and fine-grain clear pine.

Beads. Various types of beads are used in spinners and lures, both as attractors and as bearings or swiveling surfaces for spinner-blade clevises. Beads are available in glass, plastic, and metal; in faceted, plain, and patterned surfaces; and in a wide range of opaque and translucent colors.

Bell sinker. Another name for **bass-casting sinker.**

Belmar frame. See **Belmar guide.**

Belmar guide. A rod guide in which the frame that supports the guide ring is much longer and more extended than in a standard guide. Also called a bridge guide, it is found mostly on big-game and trolling rods.

Bent handle. A special type of offshore rod handle that is made of aluminum. The handle is bent below the reel seat to provide greater leverage and fish-fighting ability when the angler is working from a fighting chair.

Beveler. A machine, generally automated to some degree, used for milling cane sections into beveled strips.

Bib. A small, short, wiggling-plate lip, usually attached by small screws to the front of a wood crankbait or plug.

Blade. The flat, rotating part of a spinner or the wobbling part of a spoon, sometimes called a spinner or spoon blade, before hooks are added or before being built into a lure. Sometimes also called a **blank,** although this can be confused with a rod blank.

Blank. The fiberglass, graphite, or bamboo stick or "pole" used as the basis of a fishing rod. The blank is a plain pole without any of the appointments of the finished rod, such as a reel seat, butt cap, grips, guides, and tip-top. The term may also refer to a metal (sometimes plastic) blade for a spinner or spoon.

Blem. Generally refers to a rod blank that has been culled by the manufacturer and not offered as a first quality product due to a cosmetic flaw. Sometimes offered for sale, but rarely comes with any sort of warranty.

Body. The entire part of the female ferrule (separate from the blank) except the cap onto which the thread windings are adjusted. Also the center-drilled solid piece of metal (usually brass or steel), tapered or bullet shaped, that fits onto the shaft of a spinner to provide most of the weight of the lure.

Box swivel. A simple two-eye swivel in which the center swiveling part resembles the sides of a box. Not commonly used today.

Boxing-glove jig. A large bucktail with a head similar in shape to a boxing glove. Used mostly in saltwater fishing.

Brass lure wire. A heavy wire, usually about 0.060 inch in diameter, used for making through-wire riggings for plugs, hook lears, bottom rigs, and the like because it is both strong and easy to form.

Bridge frame. See **Belmar guide.**

Bridge guide. See **Belmar guide.**

Bucktail. The fur from the tail of a deer that is often used for tying flies and jigs; the jigs are often called bucktails for this reason. Also, another name for a jig, but one that has only fur for a tail, usually bucktail from the tail of a deer. Often the term "bucktail" is used in salt water and "jig" is used in fresh water, but this distinction is blurring.

Bullet-head bucktail. A lead bucktail with a head shaped like a bullet.

Bushing. Most frequently used to describe the cork, fiber, wood, or similar material used to fill up the space between the rod blank and the reel seat on a fly, spinning, popping, surf, or similar rod, where the reel seat is placed over the rod blank and where there is a size differential between the two. Special bushings are sometimes available for specific reel seats and to fit certain sizes of rod blank. Also called a reel-seat bushing.

Butt cap. A plastic, metal, or rubber cap that fits onto or over the butt end of a rod handle and is designed to give the rod a finished look while at the same time protecting the rod end from damage. Some lightweight butt plates serve the same purpose for ultralight rods and are glued in place.

Butt-ferruled. A term sometimes used to describe a two-piece rod in which the ferruled sections are of two different lengths, with the tip section the longer. As a result the ferrule is closer to the butt. Seldom seen anymore, the purported advantage of this system was to prevent a deadening of the action at the center of the rod, but the disadvantage was that the rod would not fit easily into a rod case. Also a term used to describe rods, usually spin-cast or casting models, in which the rod blank separates from the handle by means of a butt ferrule or adapter that allows the rod blank to be joined to the handle. The ferrule or adapter fits into a collet in the rod handle.

Butt grip. *The grip installed behind the reel seat on the rear portion of the rod.

Butt guide. A term sometimes used for the first guide, through which line flows as it comes off the reel.

Butt plate. A small, lightweight metal plate screwed or glued onto the end of the handle of a rod. Most often used on light or ultralight tackle.

Butt section. The lower or butt portion of the rod that incorporates the rod handle. In a two-piece rod, it is the lower and heavier of the two sections. In a multipiece rod it is the lowest of the several sections. In some cases the term "butt section" or "end" is used to refer to the lower or butt end of any rod piece. Thus the center section of a three-piece rod might have its two ends referred to as the "butt section" (or end) and the "tip section" (or end).

Butt wrap alignment tool. *Specialty rod-building tool used for laying out and making center points on a rod blank for any decorative cross wrap.

Butyrate. A plastic used by modern manufacturers for molding hard-plastic plugs. Other plastics used for this include **ABS** and **Tenite.**

Buzz blade. This is a blade specifically used on buzzbaits. It is usually available in right- and left-rotating styles in short and larger, triangular delta-wing blades, sometimes called by this name.

Calcutta cane. A type of cane used for rods but not as popular as the **Tonkin cane** used for split-bamboo rods. No longer used, it was once highly thought of for rods, particularly long, stout surf rods. It was never split to make split-bamboo rods.

Cam-action hook. The first of these hooks was from Tru-Turn, although other companies now have similar designs. These hooks, most often used for bass fishing, have a sideways bend in the shank that theoretically causes the hook to turn in the fish's mouth for better, deeper hooking.

Cap. That part of a male or female metal ferrule onto which decorative thread windings are wrapped.

Carboloy guides. Any of a number of types of guides in which the ring is made of **tungsten carbide.** Carboloy is a trademark of General Electric. Mildrum calls the guides it makes of this material Mildarbide.

Cedar. A wood used for carving plugs. Other good woods include **basswood** and fine-grain pine.

Center. The portion of a male metal ferrule that fits into the female ferrule.

Center-ferruled. Applies to two-piece rods in which the ferrule (any type of ferrule) is in the exact center of the rod. Almost all two-piece rods and blanks are built this way.

Center pin reel. Simple, single action reel most often used for float and drift fishing.

Ceramic. Term used somewhat generically to describe any of the various synthetic materials used for guide ring material.

Chemically sharpened hook. A hook made by many manufacturers that is chemically sharpened by a slow, controlled drip of acid. These hooks are very sharp right out of the box.

Chevron. A type of cross-wrap where each additional thread is added to the same side rather than on each side of a pattern as in a **Diamond Wrap.**

Cigar grip. See **Phillippe grip.**

Clamp-type mold. A bucktail, sinker, or jig mold in which the two mold halves are separate and are clamped together in use with built-in pinned clamps.

Class rod. A rod designed for a certain category of fishing line or class line. Such rods are usually offshore rods and designed in the various IGFA line-class categories, typically beginning with about 12-pound class rods and going through 16, 20, 30, 50, 80, and 130.

Clevis. A small U-shaped wire or sheet-stamped device used to attach spinner blades to the spinner shaft. The clevis is run through the eye of the spinner blade, and then the spinner shaft is run through the holes in the ends of the clevis. See also **folded clevis** and **wire clevis.**

Coarse angling. *Name given to bait fishing for "coarse" fish. In most parts of the world this is generally any fish other than a salmonid.

Coastlock snap. A very long snap, designed for maximum strength and used extensively on the East Coast.

Cohesive failure. *Failure of a bonding agent when surface adhesion remains intact and failure occurs within the bonding agent itself.

Cohesive strength. *Strength of the bonding agent itself.

Coil-spring fastener. The tightly coiled spring that is used to close and fasten the loop shaft of a spinner.

Collet The chucklike device at the fore end of a casting or spin-cast rod handle that is tightened on the butt ferrule or adapter of the rod to hold it securely.

Color change weave. *A decorative thread weave in which the color of the thread may change along any particular thread line.

Color preserver. A thin, watery finishing liquid that must be used over thread wraps before any final finish coats are added if the original color of the thread is to be preserved. It is not a must for protecting the wraps (the epoxy of varnish does that) but must be used to preserve thread color. If color preserver is not used, epoxy, acrylic, or varnish coating will turn light thread colors lighter and dark thread colors darker and will make all threads slightly translucent. Color preservers are available in solvent types and with a water base for easy cleanup.

Colorado blade. A slightly tapered spinner blade; rounder than an **Indiana blade.**

Cone of Flight. *Common and traditional method for sizing spinning rod guides. Each guide is slightly smaller than the previous one. Together they frame a cone-shaped area extending from the outer edges of the reel spool to a single point at the tip of the rod.

Connecting link. Looks almost like a very long link of chain with a sliding locking sleeve in the center to keep the ends from springing apart, yet it opens for adding and removing parts. Sometimes used as the line-tie for plugs.

Core pin. See **core rod.**

Core rod. A brass or steel rod placed in a sinker mold to form a hole in egg-sinker molds, plastic worm slip sinkers, and molds for spinner bodies.

Cork grip. The handle used for most fine rods. The grip is formed of round, usually ½-inch thick, center-drilled rings of cork that are glued together on the blank and shaped to form the grip.

Cork ring. A round, drilled, ½-inch-thick ring (a few are ¼ inch thick) used to build up a handle on a rod blank. It comes in either **specie cork** or **mustard cork** based on the way the cork plugs are cut out of the bark. Specie cork is by far the best, although many different grades of specie cork are available. The rings come in several outside diameters and many inside hole sizes.

Crimping pliers. Specially made pliers with jaws for crimping different sizes of leader sleeves. Several sizes and types are available; some have built-in wire cutters.

Cross-line swivel. A swivel with three eyes in which two are in a single plane and the third is at a right angle to them—almost like a T. Used for hanging drop sinkers in trolling.

Cross wrap. *A method of overlaying/wrapping threads to form decorative butt wraps on fishing rods. Generally based on threads crossing each other in such a way as to form an X at each intersection.

Culm. *A stalk of bamboo.

Cup washer. A small cupped washer, about ⅛ inch in diameter, used under a screw eye in a plug for a finished appearance and also to limit the movement of the hooks to prevent tangling. A deeper washer, used principally under screw eyes holding hooks, is often called a **derby washer** because of its resemblance to a derby hat.

Damp/damping/damps. *Any system which, when set in motion, creates a force which exhibits that same motion, is said to exhibit damping. Damping forces are usually created by friction, either aerodynamic (external) or material (internal). (Most true damping with regard to fishing rods is caused by air friction. Some internal material friction does exist, however.) Although most often incorrectly used within the confines of rod building, the term is generally used and understood to describe how long a rod takes to return to straight or stop, after being cast or flexed; i.e., "This rod damps quickly."

Dart jig. A small, tapered jig with a flat face. Also called a **quill-dart jig** or shad-dart jig.

Decal eyes. Fishing-plug eyes that are decals. These eyes are placed on the finished plug and covered with a clear coat of epoxy or varnish.

Decorative winding. See **windings.**

Deep-cup spinner blade. This is exactly what it seems: a spinner blade that has a deeper concavity in the blade than a normal blade does. These are preferred by some anglers for the different wobbling action they have in the water.

Degloss. *To scour or scuff a glossy surface until any shine or gloss has been completely removed.

Delta-wing blade. This is a large triangle-like or delta-shaped blade used on buzzbaits. Sometimes it is called simply "delta blade."

Density. Weight per amount of unit of volume. Can be measured as lbs/in^3.

Derby washer. Similar to a **cup washer** but deeper. Designed to go under the screw eye holding the hook on a plug, these deeper washers limit the movement of a hook to prevent it from scarring the plug finish or tangling with other hooks or the line.

Diamond wrap. *A type of decorative thread wrap where threads are wrapped to each side of the pattern in order to form boxes or to widen the basic X shape. Viewed from any corner (and depending upon the elongation of the pattern), they appear diamond shaped.

Dipsy doodle sinker. See **bass-casting sinker.**

Do. *An instruction used on a weaving "left list" meaning to repeat the previous step.

Doll eyes. Also called "rattle eyes" or "movable eyes" because the pupil is loose in a cuplike clear bubble with an opaque back. Many sizes and colors are available in various styles. Most are round, but oval eyes are available.

Double-snap swivel. A standard snap swivel to which a second snap is attached to the free eye.

Down gate. See **sprue hole.**

Down locking. *Used to describe a reel seat that has been mounted with the fixed hood to the rear (butt) and the movable hood to the front (tip).

Drail. A heavy, large L-shaped sinker used in deep trolling. The shape works as a keel and prevents line twist.

Drop shot rod. *Specialty rod with a very light tip used for fishing a plastic worm or lure just above the sinker. The light tip allows minute movements to be imparted to the lure. Generally these are light power rods.

Drum dryer. *Type of "rod dryer" where large round flats are used to hold a number of rods on the circumference and the entire assembly turns around a center shaft. Resembles a drum mounted and turning on a center axis.

Dry-fly action. A fly-rod action in which the tip does most of the bending. Designed for dry-fly fishing when the fast action of the tip end (in the days of the very slow bamboo rods) was required to dry a fly between casts. (This is the opposite of a wet-fly action, in which the action extends well down into or toward the grip of the rod.) Today rods are seldom characterized by this term, even though there is a recent return to labeling rods by the type of fishing they are designed for. In some cases these labels refer to a type of action or bend.

Drying motor. *A slow rpm motor used to rotate a fishing rod to prevent slow-curing thread finishes/coatings from dripping or sagging until they have set.

Duo-Lock snap. Trademarked name for a simple single-wire snap, the construction of which makes it possible to unhook the snap at either end. The snap has a double-locking arrangement that makes it strong, but it does not swivel. Can be combined with a swivel. Predates the similar Berkley Cross-Lok snap, also a single-wire double open-end snap.

Durometer. *The international standard for measuring hardness of rubber, plastic and other nonmetallic materials. Also, the instrument for taking these measurements is referred to as a Durometer.

Ear-grip sinker. See **pinch-on sinker.**

Egg sinker. A round or torpedo-shaped sinker with a hole running through its long axis. Designed for bottom fishing, the line running through the sinker prevents the fish from detecting the sinker weight while it's mouthing or running with the bait.

Electric lead pot. A pot with a built-in or built-on A/C heating element. Available in small, simple, inexpensive styles as well as large, bottom-feeding, sophisticated styles.

Epoxy glue. Probably the best glue type today for most tackle building. These are two-part glues, usually in a 1:1 mix. They are easy to use, have a high bonding strength, and are completely waterproof.

Epoxy rod finish. Generally less viscous than the epoxy glues, these finishes also often have special additives to release bubbles, prevent ultraviolet-ray damage and yellowing, and keep the finish flexible. Epoxy rod finish can be used as a glue but will take much longer to dry than will regular epoxy glue. Epoxy glue should not be used as a rod finish.

EVA. *Ethylene vinyl acetate synthetic foam material. Available in various grades and hardnesses. The more firm variety makes an excellent and lightweight rod grip material. Not as resilient as Hypalon, but considerably lighter in weight.

Eyed shaft. A spinner shaft that comes with a closed eye formed in one end for line attachment. Available in several lengths, it is the most popular spinner shaft for making spinners.

Faceted bead. A bead that has flat surfaces to reflect light; sometimes used in place of round beads in a spinner body.

Fast tip. A rod action in which the tip bends sharply while the butt remains relatively straight. Also called worm action. See also **action.**

Female ferrule. The half of a ferrule set that has a hollow center into which the male ferrule fits. In a set of metal ferrules, the female is fitted to the butt section of the rod, and the male ferrule is fitted to the tip section. In self-ferrules of the Fenwick style (graphite to graphite or glass to glass), the female ferrule is really an extension of the tip section, and the butt section ends with the male ferrule. This is also true of **spigot** ferrules, although that construction method is different.

Feralite ferrule. *A type of tip-over-butt ferrule designed by Jim Green at Fenwick. The first tip-over-butt ferrule.

Ferrule. The metal built-in or built-on glass or graphite part that allows different sections of rods too be joined. Metal ferrules are glued to the rod; and self-ferrules, such as the Fenwick style, are built into the rod as a part of blank construction. **Spigot** ferrules are added to the rod during manufacture but include a separate plug of glass or graphite in the butt section of the rod—this plug is the male part of the ferrule.

Ferrule cement. A resin- or plastic-based cement in stick form that must be heated to be used. It can be used to glue ferrules and tip-tops to a rod blank and allows for easy replacement of damaged ferrules and tip-tops by the application of heat to the part to be removed, which melts the ferrule cement.

Fighting butt. *Normally used on fly reel seats. A short extension of cork or foam, either fixed or removable on the rear of a fly reel seat.

Fighting chair. *Special chair mounted to a boat's deck to allow an angler to fight a fish from a sitting down position. In use, the rod is placed into a gimbal nock on the chair which then becomes an aid to the angler against large and powerful fish.

Figure-eight attachment. A figure-eight-shaped piece of wire for lure attachments and line-ties. Often attached to the metal wiggle lip of a plug.

First quality. *Generally refers to a rod blank that is offered as a first quality product and comes complete with a manufacturer's warranty.

Five-minute epoxy. *A two-part epoxy adhesive with a very short (five minutes or so) working or pot life.

Fixed hood. *The hood on a reel seat that is fixed and cannot be adjusted or moved.

Flag. *The pattern cut from a prepeg material which is wrapped around a **mandrel** to form a rod blank.

Flash. The excess lead, lead alloy, or tin that leaks out along the joint between two mold halves during the pouring of lead or tin bucktail heads, squids, or sinkers. It forms a line that runs through the center plane of the lure or sinker. Ideally it should not occur in better molds, but when it does it must be removed by cutting or filing. It will not interfere with sinkers but is usually removed from them.

Flat sinker. A sinker that may come in several shapes—all flat—that is designed to be snagless. It is shaped much like a flat spinner blade.

Flipping stick. *Term popularized by tournament bass fishermen for a stout rod used for accurately "flipping" a lure or bait into close quarters. Usually long (7 feet or more) and often telescoping to allow fitting into short rod boxes on bass boats.

Float rod. *Used for a variety of species. Available in both very fast, light tipped models, as well as more moderate action models, these rods are usually quite long (12 feet to 14 feet) and are used for fishing with a variety of float styles. Originated in the U. K. for "coarse fishing."

Folded clevis. A clevis stamped from sheet metal in the shape of an O and folded over to make a U-shaped clevis. See **clevis.**

Football. *Term used to describe the shape of a finished guide wrap when the finish is thicker in the middle than at the edges. Shaped like a football.

Foregrip. The part of a cork or wood handle in front of or above the reel seat. Casting-rod handles come with or without a foregrip; all spinning- and boat-rod handles have a foregrip of some type.

Forhan locking wrap. *Guide wrap developed by rod builder Rich Forhan. Completely encircles and secures single-foot guides.

Foul-proof guide. Still sold in some areas, this is a guide formed of wire that is bent into a circle. The ends of the wire form the guide feet.

French-type blade. Used in popular spinners, this blade has an egg-shaped raised surface on its convex side.

Full Wells grip. Used on fly rods, this is a grip with a cigar-shaped swollen center that narrows before flaring out at both ends. Named for the angling writer of the late 1800s, Henry P. Wells.

Gathering guide. Another term for **stripping guide** or **butt guide.**

Gimbal. A heavy, solid butt cap primarily for big-game rods, in which the bottom of the metal butt cap is slotted (or double-slotted in an X) to fit onto a bar placed in the gimbal socket of a fighting chair or on a belt. Usually made of aluminum or heavy chrome-plated brass. Sometimes called a "gimbal knock" or "knock."

Glass eyes. Glass eyes come paired on a long wire and are used to finish wood fishing plugs. The wire is cut off ½ inch from the eye, and the short wire is inserted with pliers into the wood body. An advantage to these eyes is that they can be painted any desired color around the blank pupil.

Gordon grip. A fly-rod handle similar to the **Phillippe grip** except that the rear grip flares out instead of remaining straight.

Grip check. See **winding check.**

Half Wells grip. A fly-rod grip, almost a reversed **Hardy grip,** in which the front is flared, is followed by a swelled area, and is then tapered at the rear of the grip. Really a grip that is in the shape of a half of a full Wells grip.

Hammered blade. A lure blade that has been hammered or given a hammered finish. Can apply to any type of spinner or spoon blade.

Hammerhead jig. A bucktail or jig with very pronounced protruding eyes on each side of the head, much like a hammerhead shark.

Handle. The part of the rod held in the hand as the rod is cast. Fly rod handles are above the reel seat, spinning rods have fixed or sliding-ring reel seats in the middle of the handle, and casting rods have built-on or separate handles that include a reel seat. Depending upon who is using the term, "handle" can mean only the grip that is held (though "grip" is a more accurate term for this), or it can mean the entire grip, reel seat, and butt cap assembly.

Handled mold. A bucktail, sinker, or lead-head mold that is hinged on one side with handles on the opposite side of each of the two halves. It has the advantage of making lead molding a quick and easy operation.

Hardy grip. A modified **cigar** or **Phillippe grip** used on fly rods in which the rear part of the grip flares out slightly.

Hold-down clamp. The small, flat piece of metal found on the reel seat of some casting or spin-cast handles that holds the foot of the reel.

Hood liners. *Usually made from plastic or nylon and used to line reel seat hoods of steel or aluminum. Prevents marring of the reel foot and provides an elastic cushioning effect.

Hook hanger. A small metal device, shaped like a bent garden trowel, by which hooks are added to a plug or crankbait. Hangers are fastened to the plug with very small round-head screws. The advantage of hangers over screw eyes is that hangers limit the forward movement of the hook to prevent tangling with the line or other hooks.

Hook-hanger spreader. A small wire device, first popularized in early plugs (primarily the Helin Flatfish), by which treble hooks are held away from the body of a lure, presumably to aid in hooking fish that are short strikers.

Hook-keeper. A small device that is wrapped down on the rod blank just in front of the fore-grip and by which hooks and lures are fastened in place.

Hosel. A large, usually plastic, device designed to serve the same purpose as a winding check but usually found only on larger saltwater rods. Center-drilled, hosels fit over the rod blank and up against the rod handle.

Hot Shot rods. *Stout butted yet very light tipped rods designed for use with swimming/diving plugs which are fished stationary or drifting. The river or stream current causes the plug to dive and hold near the river bottom. The angler watches the action of the plug by the movement of the light rod tip, and the heavy butt section usually sets the hook on the fish. May be used for many other fishing applications as well.

Hypalon. *Trademarked name for a chlorsulfonated polyethylene synthetic rubber product. While it is used in a variety of industrial applications, it has long been used with good results in the form of rod grips. Somewhat heavy, but extremely resistant to sunlight, solvents, and detergents.

Ice rod. *Generally a very short rod specifically intended for use in fishing through a small opening in ice-covered lakes and streams.

Ice-tong snap. A special type of terminal rigging snap, the end of which resembles a pair of ice tongs. Often used in attaching sinkers with bottom rigs for saltwater fishing. Preferred mainly on the West Coast. Also called a "McMahon snap."

IGFA. *Abbreviation for the International Game Fish Association.

IGFA class rod. *Rod designed specifically for use with a particular IGFA class rated line. Categories include 12, 20, 30, 50, 80, and 130 pound classes.

Indiana blade. A pear-shaped spinner blade. Not as fat as a **Colorado blade.** Available in many sizes and finishes.

Ingot mold. A mold for making ingots or bars of lead or tin. Most molds make about four bars of approximately 2 pounds each.

Injection mold. A mold into which the molding material is injected with pressure. Used primarily by manufacturers to mold liquid plastic into worms and other soft-plastic lures. This method can be used by the tackle crafter with a Hilts worm mold, which has a special syringe system to inject the liquid plastic.

Inlay. *Can refer to a single thread inlaid in a wider thread wrap or a section of grip material inlaid into another section of grip material.

Jig hook. A special hook designed to be used in molding jigs and bucktails. It has an upward bend (toward the hook point, because the jig rides with the hook up) in the hook shank and an eye that is parallel to the hook bend for easy placement and removal in the mold. The bend in the hook shank is usually at right angles but can be 60 degrees for some hooks and some molds.

Jigging spoon. A heavy-blade spoon used for vertical jigging that is similar to the metal thrown by surf casters. Also called a "structure spoon" by bass anglers to differentiate it from the weedless spoons used in grass and weeds.

Jigs. Another name for a **bucktail** or bucktail lead head. This term is more commonly used for freshwater fishing, while the term "bucktail" is more common in saltwater fishing, but such distinctions are blurring. A jig is also a device used to hold materials or to form materials. Examples in tackle crafting would be special jigs used to hold plug bodies upright for through-wire drilling in a drill press, jigs used to bend wire for making bottom rigs and hook lears, and jigs for bending tubing for making landing nets.

Jointed plug. A plug or crankbait that is jointed. These plugs are usually in two parts, occasionally in three or more.

Jump ring. A small open ring sometimes used to attach hooks or swivels to spoons and spinners. The parts to be attached are placed in the ring, and the ring is closed with pliers and welded or soldered for strength. Not as easy to use as a **split ring.**

June Bug spinner. A trademarked spinner using a blade with a cutout central portion that forms a leg that attaches to the spinner shaft. The leg running from the center of the blade holds the blade at a certain angle from the spinner shaft. June Bug spinners are often used in conjunction with bait.

Keeper ring. A **hook-keeper.** Designed to hold a hook or lure and wrapped onto a rod blank just above the handle.

Kevlar. *An aramid/nylon fiber trademarked by DuPont.

Knock. See **gimbal.**

Latex tubing. A pure-rubber tubing used for making lures fished primarily on the Atlantic coast. The resulting long lure presumably resembles an eel. Shorter lengths of hose are used in some lures. The tubing comes in a variety of colors and sizes for making lures.

Lead-cutting pliers. More a cutter than pliers, this tool is used to cut lead sprue from molded lures and sinkers and to cut lead and other soft wire.

Lead dipper. A small, deeply cupped, specialized pouring ladle.

Leader sleeve. A small metallic cylinder used to fit over leader wire to form loops and eyes and to make leader and riggings. Leader sleeves come in different sizes for use with different wire (there are also specialized leader sleeves used for monofilament) but cannot be used with single-strand wire. Also called a "sleeve fastener."

Lead pot. A large pot for melting lead; often made of cast iron. Lead is not poured into the mold from these large pots but is transferred to smaller, long-handled pouring ladles. The capacity of these pots varies from about 5 to 20 pounds of lead.

Left list. *The pattern for making a decorative thread weave. Instructs which threads are lifted and not wrapped over during each revolution of the process.

Lima bean jig. *A jig or bucktail shaped like a lima bean so that it will drop rapidly and still have a noticeable profile when seen from the side.

Live bait rod. *Rods made for use with live bait. Generally, such rods have extremely soft and flexible tips, allowing the fish to take the bait without pulling the bait off of the hook. These light tips also allow the angler to detect movement of the bait or subtle strikes from fish. Butt sections can range from light to heavy, depending on the application, but the tips are usually always fairly soft.

Loop shaft. A shaft for spinners that comes with a loop eye formed in one end. Used to make some types of spinners (such as the French-style spinner) where the hook is added to the loop shaft and followed by the body and other parts, with the line-tie eye formed last. Also used with coil-spring fasteners to change hooks and parts. Used on June Bug and similar spinners with long-shank hooks for bait fishing.

Mandrel. The tapered steel rod used as a core when making hollow glass or graphite rod blanks. The cloth used to make the rod is wrapped around the mandrel and baked. The mandrel is then pulled out and a tapered, flexible fishing rod blank results.

Mandrel (straight). *Shaft of steel or wood for mounting or turning of grips, reel seat bushings, etc.

Mask. A term used in finishing, when a lure is painted selectively with dots, streaks, stripes, or similar patterns. A "mask" of paper, tape, plastic, or similar material prevents the sprayed-on paint from hitting other parts of the lure. The term can also refer to the materials used for the masking process.

McMahon snap. See **ice-tong snap.**

Mesh gauge. A gauge used to measure the size of the mesh squares in landing and fishing nets. Gauge sizes range from ½ inch to 3 inches, although any long rectangular piece of plastic, metal, wood, or stiff cardboard can serve as a mesh gauge.

Mildarbide. Trademark of the Mildrum company for tungsten-carbide guide-ring material.

Minus one. *Term used to describe the deleting of one thread per pass on a decorative cross wrap.

Modulus. The degree of stiffness with which a rod rebounds from a bent position. This term became important to the rod and blank industry with the introduction of graphite, and various companies strive for high-modulus rods and blanks with increased performance, casting distance, and sensitivity.

Mold furnace. A special furnace used mostly by bullet casters. It is electric and varies widely in cost, capacity, and style. Some models feed from the bottom; others take lead from the top. Most have thermostatic temperature controls for melting lead. Although some are designed for bullet casting, they are also ideal for molding sinkers and jigs.

Multiple-cavity mold. A bucktail, jig, sinker, or worm mold with more than one cavity.

Mustard cork. A low-quality cork (see **cork ring**) seldom used today in cork handles.

NCP thread. *An opaque nylon thread which does not require color preserver in order to keep it from turning translucent when a wrapping finish is applied. Somewhat dull and lacking sparkle in contrast to regular nylon wrapping thread.

Netting knot. A special knot used for making the mesh squares in fishing nets. In essence it is a sheet bend.

New Guide Concept. *A term coined by the Fuji Kogyo Company for a particular system of guide sizing and placement. Normally employs smaller and lighter guides, and employs them in greater number than other guide systems.

Node. The swollen part of a bamboo pole or culm. In making split-bamboo fishing rods, nodes are planed down and usually staggered along the rod blank so that the weaker node points will not all be in the same place. When a rod is shaken, the point where the two curves of the rod intersect is called a "nodal point."

Noodle rod. *Soft, light, and usually long (9 feet to 12 feet) rod designed to be used with very light line. The rod's softness prevents even large fish from being able to break light lines. Deemed as "unsporting" by some, as the time taken to land larger fish can be lengthy and extremely tiring to the fish.

Nylon-coated leader wire. Twisted leader wire coated with nylon for easy handling.

Off-center-ferruled rod. A two-piece rod in which the sections are cut in unequal lengths; the butt section is always the shorter of the two. The theory is that the action and power will be less adversely affected with the ferrule closer to the butt. A disadvantage is that the rod will need a longer rod case to accommodate the longer tip section. Also called **butt-ferruled,** but this is not to be confused with rods (primarily casting and spin-cast) with separate handles that are ferruled at the blank-to-handle joint.

Open-face mold. A one-piece mold for making tin squids, plastic worms, and lures in which the molten metal or liquid plastic is poured into the open mold. Because the mold is in one piece, the lure shape is formed on one side only; the topside is flat. Also called a one-piece mold.

Open screw eye. A screw eye used for lure making in which the eye is open to allow the addition of hooks. In use the screw eye is partially screwed into the lure, then the hook is added and the eye closed with pliers. Finally, the screw eye is completely seated into the plug body.

Pack rod. A rod, usually a spinning, fly, or casting model, which by means of multiple sections and ferrules breaks down easily for packing and travel. Once rare in good blanks, the lightness of the self-ferrule has made the pack rod more popular. Many blanks are now available, although most are in the fly and spinning category. Also called a "travel rod."

Parabolic action. Rod action in which the rod bends evenly and uniformly from the tip to the handle. This is the best type of action for casting accuracy but often lacks the power for fighting big fish.

Payne grip. A fly-rod grip similar to the **cigar** or **Phillippe** style except that the rear of the grip has straight parallel sides. Only the front is tapered like a cigar.

Phillippe grip. A round fly-rod grip that is large in the middle and tapered at both ends, similar to a fat cigar.

Phillippe tapered grip. A tapered fly-rod grip with straight sides. The forward end of the grip is thicker than the rear.

Pinch-on sinker. A long tapered sinker with a slot cut into the long axis for the line and small ears or projections at each end to clamp the sinker to the line.

Pistol grip. A large grip used on casting and spin-cast rods used primarily for bass fishing. It is usually made of wood, cork, or foam and is sometimes called a "comfort grip" or "bass grip."

Pompanette snap. A very long snap usually made in extra-heavy wire and designed primarily for big-game use. Comes in large sizes only, with one-hundred-pound test the usual minimum size.

Popping rod. *Rod used for casting shrimp, under a "popping cork." Generally these rods have fast light tips to prevent tearing the bait off the hook during the cast. Can be used for many other types of fishing as well.

Pot life. *Generally used to describe the working time of an epoxy adhesive or wrapping finish. *Not* the time taken for curing, but the time period when the adhesive remains workable or easy to apply.

Pouring ladle. A long-handled ladle, usually made of cast iron and used for pouring molten lead into jig and sinker molds. It comes in various sizes and styles with capacities from about 1 to 6 pounds.

Power. *Generally used to describe a rod or blank's stiffness or resistance to bending.

Press fit. *Snug-fitting assembly that requires some measure of force to bring the parts into place.

Prismatic tape. A self-adhesive tape embossed with prismatic patterns and added to lures. The tape comes in a variety of prismatic patterns, finishes, and colors and is available in sheets of various patterns, bars, and eyes. All are designed to resemble fish scales and to increase the attractiveness of the lure to which they are added.

Progressive action. *Term used to describe a rod blank that continues to bend farther back towards the butt end as load upon it is increased. As the load is increased, the blank responds by shifting the load onto the larger, more powerful area towards the middle and rear of the blank.

Propeller blades. Blades similar to a plane propeller: The two blades are on a center hub through which the spinner shaft or screw eye runs. Usually used for top-water plugs.

Quill-dart jig. See **dart jig.**

Rattles. Many different types of rattles are available for lure making. Small rattles originally designed for insertion into plastic worms are available in glass, plastic, and aluminum, and each has a slightly different sound. Larger rattles are available for saltwater lures. In addition, medium- and large-sized rattles can be built into some lures using BBs and shot.

Reel bands. See **spinning-rod rings.**

Reel seat. A tubular device fitted with hoods to hold a reel foot and with locking threads to hold a sliding hood in place. It comes in a number of styles, colors, sizes, and finishes for fly, spinning casting, spin-cast, boat, surf, and big-game rods. Some have a trigger (casting rods), some have incorporated ferrules (big-game rods), some are skeletal (ultralight spinning rods), and some have slip-in extension-butt sections (saltwater fly rods).

Reel-seat bushing. See **bushing.**

Resin. *An adhesive which, when combined with fiber material into a prepeg, is used for making a composite rod blank.

Revolver Rod. *Trademarked name for a type of rod developed by rod builder Rich Forhan. Normally utilizes either all, or a combination of, features such as a specific style of spiral wrap, a split rear grip/handle, and no foregrip.

Ripple blade. A spinner blade with a rippled surface almost like the surface of corrugated cardboard.

Robert's wrap. *Another term for the spiral wrap named after rod builder Chuck Roberts, proponent of spiral wrapping for casting rods.

Rod Bond. *Trademarked name for a specialty, gel-type rod-building epoxy.

Rod dryer. *Usually composed of a "drying motor" and some type of enclosure or box to turn a fishing rod while the final wrap coating finish is curing and drying.

Rod hosel. See **hosel.**

Rod tip. The upper section of a two-piece or multipiece rod. Can also refer to the uppermost end of any rod, or the "tip end" of any section.

Rod winding check. See **winding check.**

***RodMaker* magazine.** *Publication for custom rod builders.

Roller guide. A big-game rod guide in which the guide is fitted with a smooth roller or pulley, over which the line runs. The advantage of roller guides is that the roller will prevent wear during the strong fast runs of a large fish and will also prevent line damage when the run stalls and the friction-caused heat buildup in a ring guide could cause line damage and weakening.

Rolling table. *Used in the rod blank manufacturing process. Composed of two larger surfaces or platens above and below and moving in opposite directions. Automates the process of rolling the flag or pattern around the tapered mandrel.

Ruby-lip bucktail. A bucktail or jig with pronounced lips molded into the lure. Usually the lips of the finished lure are painted bright red, thus the name.

Safety snap. A small snap that closes and locks almost like a safety pin. Used for attaching lures to line.

Scale-finish netting. A small-mesh, hexagonal-hole netting designed for use in painting scale finish on lures. Such netting is available from fabric stores. In use the lure is painted a base color and held tightly against the netting, and paint is sprayed over the netting in the finish color. The base color shows through the finish as scales.

Scoop. A term sometimes used for a large type of wiggle plate or lip that causes a lure to dive deeply.

ScotchBrite. *Trademarked name (3M) for an abrasive pad used for sanding, scouring, and deglossing various materials.

Screw eyes. Either open or closed small-wire screw eyes used in plug construction. The closed-eye screws are used for plug heads (where the line is tied on); open-eye screws are used where the hooks are to be added to the lure. Both styles come in several wire thicknesses and lengths.

Scrim. *Lightweight cloth, mat, or fiber added to rod blanks to reinforce structural fibers and resin in a prepeg. Can also be used to contribute to hoop strength.

Second. *Generally refers to a rod blank that has been culled by the manufacturer due to cosmetic or structure flaws. Sometimes offered for sale, but almost never with any sort of warranty. Whereas a **blem** is usually confined to cosmetic flaws, a "second" may involve structural problems.

Security wrap. *Additional short wrap of thread, either separate or integral, on the backside of any single-footed guide. Helps secure the guide during heavy loads or long-term use.

Self-lock snap shaft. A type of spinner shaft in which the open loop end of the eye can be closed in a manner similar to fastening a safety pin. It makes the use of coil-spring fasteners on a loop-eye shaft unnecessary and still allows hook changing.

Shoulder. The part of a male ferrule extending from the center portion (which fits into the female ferrule) to the cap. The cap is the tapered end onto which the thread windings are wrapped. No longer a widely used term.

Shuttle. The plastic device used to hold net-making twine so that it can be passed easily through the net to make rows of net meshes. Shuttles come in different sizes and lengths for use with different net twines and for different sizes of mesh squares.

Single-cavity mold. A bucktail or jig mold that makes only one lure at a time. This type of mold is usually found only in the highly finished professional-type molds that mold lures with little or no flash. This term can also apply to an open-faced worm mold that has only one cavity for making one worm at a time.

Slag. The waste material found in most lead and lead alloys used for molding lead-head lures and sinkers. It floats to the surface of the molten lead and can be skimmed off before the lead is poured into the mold.

Slick butt. *Rod butt made of aluminum or nylon and used in place of a rear cork or foam-type grip. The hard slick surface permits the easy removal of a rod from a rod holder even if the rod is under pressure from a hooked fish.

Sliding bands. *Rings of bands which free-float or slide on a reel seat or grip. These rings are forced onto the reel feet and held in place by friction or pressure.

Slip sinker. A bullet-shaped sinker used with plastic worms. See **egg sinker.**

Slow-cure epoxy. *Generally any two-part epoxy that provides more than just a few minutes of working or pot life. Depending on the brand and type, pot life may be 15 minutes to several hours.

SmoothScuff. *Another material similar to ScotchBrite.

Snake guide. A small guide used on fly rods that is made from a single length of wire and looks almost like a twisted snake. Comes in different sizes and finishes.

Snell. The technique of wrapping line around a hook shank to secure it to the line; a substitute for a knot in the hook's eye. The eye of the hook does not have to be used, but if it is used should be a turned-up or turned-down eye. Also a term sometimes used for a hook with a snell-attached monofilament leader.

Solid brass rings. Small, solid brass rings used in lures and terminal riggings when a high degree of strength for size is needed.

Specie cork. The better of two methods by which cork rings are cut from cork bark. In specie cork the natural pits in the cork run parallel to the central hole drilled in the cork ring. Even specie cork comes in a number of grades, however, from excellent down to lesser grades.

Spey rod. *Name for the type of rods commonly used on the River Spey going back some 150 years. Today, Spey rods are generally regarded as any of the longer (11 feet to 15 feet) two-handed fly rod types that allow long casts without the necessity of making a back cast.

Spigot. *A type of ferrule comprised of a plug or internal sleeve joined internally and permanently to one rod section and fitting inside another section by means of a friction fit.

Spine. The stiffest plane of the rod blank. The spine of a rod blank should be determined for guide placement.

Spinner. A lure in which a blade rotates around a central shaft by means of a clevis; the central shaft holds a body or beads and the lure, ending with the hook.

Spinner bearing. A small bearing used between the clevis and the body of a spinner that allows less friction from the rotating spinner blade. Without a spinner bearing of some sort, the clevis will have a tendency to bind on the spinner body. Also called a "unispin" or "uni." Small plastic and glass beads can substitute for this.

Spinner body. A small, usually tapered, body with a hole through the long axis, used in building spinners. Available in brass and other metals as well as in painted lead. Molds for making these bodies out of lead are available as well.

Spinning guide. A guide with a larger diameter ring (at least in the butt guides used) to be used on spinning rods. The smaller sizes are often used on casting and spin-cast rods. The theory of the large ring for the butt guides is that the rod will cast better because the line is coming off the spinning reel in large loops. One theory asserts that the first butt guide on the rod should be about two-thirds the diameter of the spinning reel-spool lip. The guide rings decrease in size toward the tip-top.

Spinning-rod rings. Rings placed over the spinning-rod cork grip (sometimes over foam grips as well) to hold the reel in place when a fixed reel seat is not used. The two rings fit snugly on the handle and are usually tapered or swaged to hold the foot of the reel.

Spiral wrap. *A method for taking the line to the bottom of the rod on conventional casting-type rods. The result is that the rod blank will favor bending along a particular axis when load is applied.

Split-ring pliers. These small pliers have a tooth at the end of one jaw for use in opening a split ring to make spinners and spoons. Indispensable for the spoon and spinner maker. Both inexpensive and better high-quality models are available.

Split rings. Like miniature key rings, these round rings make possible easy attachment of hooks, swivels, and other fittings to the body of a spoon or spinner. Also used to attach hooks to some plugs and to make other terminal riggings. A half dozen sizes are available.

Sprue hole. The funnel-shaped opening into a two piece mold cavity through which molten lead or liquid plastic is poured to make sinkers, lead-head jigs, and soft-plastic lures. Also called a "gate" or "down gate."

Stainless steel leader wire. Single-strand leader wire made from stainless steel. Used in salt water.

Stand-up rod. *Generally used to describe shorter high-leverage-type trolling and boat rods. Shorter length allows them to be used by an angler in a "stand up" position rather than in a fighting chair.

Straddle mounting. A special type of guide that uses four feet—two at each end of the frame. These feet straddle the rod blank. Used mainly on big-game rods, these guides are wrapped in the same way as other guides.

Stripping guide. The lowest or butt guide on a fly rod, this guide is not a snake guide or single-foot fly-rod ceramic guide (such as are commonly used on the rest of the rod) but is instead a lightweight small-ring spinning or spin-cast guide. It is also called a **butt guide.** Light fly rods will have only one stripper guide; larger fly rods will have two or three. Larger stripper guides are more common today than in years past.

Swing blade. A narrow elliptical spinner blade used in popular spinners.

Swivel shaft. A spinner shaft in which half a swivel is built into the end used for line attachment. It helps prevent line twist.

Tack free. *Term used to describe the point at which a thread wrap finish is no longer tacky to the touch. The point at which foreign objects or dust-making incidental contact will not adhere.

Tag. *Trim wrap. Can be narrow or wide, but is generally narrower than any main wrap used in conjunction with it.

Tail tags. Small bright pieces of plastic drilled with a hole at one end and attached to the eye of a spinner shaft along with the hook. Used to make a spinner more attractive to fish and to provide a visual "strike point."

Template. A paper, cardboard, steel, or plastic sheet cut into the outline shape of a plug, spoon, spinner blade, rod handle, or similar item. The template makes it easy to duplicate tackle parts.

Tenite. Trademarked name for a tough plastic sometimes used for injection-molding or plastic fishing lures. Most plastics used today are of this material, **butyrate,** or **ABS.**

Test casting. *Trial and error process of casting a rod while adjusting guide spacing or sizing to determine the optimal location and size for the guides.

Three-way swivel. A swivel with three eyes for tying line. All three are equidistant around the central ring that holds them.

Through-butt. *Rod construction method where the rod blank is inserted into and extends completely though any sort of handle or butt.

Through-wire construction. A method by which all the hooks of a plug, as well as the eye to which the line is tied, are connected through the center of the plug by a heavy wire. Used primarily on saltwater plugs where the chances are far greater that a fish may shatter the plug on a strike or during a fight, there are several construction methods that use wire and also metal plates.

Tip action. Rod action in which most of the bending is in the tip of the rod. Also called fast action or extra-fast action (depending upon degree); used to be called **dry-fly action** on fly rods.

Tip guide. *The guide located closest to the tip of the rod.

Tip-top. The correct term, although this is sometimes called the "top guide" or "top eye." It is the topmost line guide on the rod and is attached to the rod by means of a small metal tube sized to fit onto the end of the blank. There are specific tip-tops for spinning, casting, surf, big-game, and other rods.

Tonkin cane. One of the 2,000 species of bamboo, a member of the grass family, and the only one used seriously for split-bamboo rods. (**Calcutta cane** was once used intact for rods, often for cane poles or surf rods.) Comes from the Tonkin area of Viet Nam.

Top guide. See **tip-top.**

Transition guides. *Term normally used to describe those guides on a **spiral wrap** which take the line from the top of the rod at the reel seat to the bottom of the rod. Located between the 0 and 180 degree axis guides.

Travel rod. See **pack rod.**

Trim windings. See **windings.**

Trolling sinker. A sinker made specifically for trolling. These can be crescent-shaped, L-shaped (this is often called a **drail),** keeled to prevent twisting, or a simple torpedo shape. Those intended to minimize twist are most often used in trolling.

Tube heads. Special lead heads used with tube lures. Molds in these shapes are available to tackle crafters. A tube head has a smooth rounded shape that will easily fit into and conform to the shape of a tube lure.

Tungsten carbide guide. A guide in which the ring is made of tungsten carbide, a very hard and tough—though slightly brittle—material. The tungsten carbide called Carboloy is a trademark of General Electric. Mildarbide is a trademarked tungsten carbide of the Mildrum company.

Twisted leader wire. Leader wire made from a number of smaller strands. Often these are twisted around one another, and several strands make up one wire. Cable is composed of these twisted strands to make up heavier leaders.

Two-part plug. A plug with a front half and a rear half that are joined in the middle with two screw eyes or a plate-and-pin coupling. These plugs wiggle more in the water as a result of the jointed sections. They are also called **jointed plugs.** The term also refers to plastic-plug blanks that come in two halves and must be glued or welded together (usually with acetone) before finishing or use.

Two-piece mold. A mold for making sinkers, bucktails, or plastic lures in which the two mold halves are joined by hinges, locked by clamps, or pinned together to assure proper registration. Molten metal or plastic is poured into the mold cavities through a gate or **sprue hole.**

U-frame guide. A spinning, casting, or spin-cast guide in which the frame holding the guide ring looks like a U when viewed from the end of the guide. See **V-frame guide.**

Underwrapping. A thread wrapping placed on the rod before a guide is seated and wrapped in place. Not often used on light or ultralight rods. On heavier rods the underwrapping helps protect the finish of the rod blank, cushions the blank from the metal guide feet, and provides a more secure base for the guide foot.

Uni. See **spinner bearing.**

Unibutt. *Trademarked name (AFTCO), although often used generically to describe any aluminum butt section with an integral reel seat for use on heavy-duty saltwater rods. Normally, it can be detached from the rod by means of a threaded ferrule just forward of the reel seat area.

Unispin. See **spinner bearing.**

Uplocking. *Used to describe a reel seat that has been mounted with the fixed hood to the front (tip) and the movable hood to the rear (butt).

Varnish. A clear protective finish for rods and rod wrappings. At one time the standard for finishing wraps, today it has been replaced by various epoxy rod finishes. It is still used on bamboo rods, where tradition is important.

V-frame guide. A spinning, casting, or spin-cast guide in which the frame holding the guide ring looks like a V when viewed from the end. See **U-frame guide.**

Vinyl skirt. A soft, flexible skirt of plastic strands that can be attached to a plug, spinner, bucktail, or other lure either as a primary skirt or as an additional attraction. Skirts may be molded and made in large sizes for saltwater lures and offshore trolling lures.

Water break free. *Optimal surface condition for bonding. Surfaces that exhibit a "water break free" condition will not repel or bead water.

Weaving. *A decorative thread wrap employing the technique of wrapping either over or under threads running lengthwise along a rod blank to form a pattern or design.

Weed guard. A wire, plastic, or nylon device that extends over the hook to prevent it from catching weeds while being retrieved. Many styles are available for single, double, and even treble hooks and for a variety of baits and lures.

Welt. The thicker outer lip of a female metal ferrule (separate from and added to the rod blank) that is designed to protect the lip from expanding or splitting under the strain of the flexing rod.

Wet-fly action. A slow or **parabolic** type of action in a fly rod. This is an almost obsolete term and is applicable primarily to older bamboo fly rods. Years ago this action was desired for wet-fly fishing.

Wiggle eye. A small plastic bubble with a flat back (to be glued to a plug or lure) and a loose, dark central pupil. Because the pupil is loose in the plastic bubble eye, it rolls around as the lure moves through the water. Sometimes called **doll eyes.** Available in many sizes and several colors.

Wiggle lips. Metal or plastic lips (the latter primarily of Lexan) that are glued or screwed into a plug to make it dive under water. Available in several shapes and sizes.

Willowleaf blade. A spinner blade that is long and slender with pointed ends, like a willow leaf.

Winding check. A small, round, dish-shaped piece of plastic, metal, or rubber with a hole in the center that is designed to fit snugly over a rod blank and up against the foregrip. Primarily decorative. Sometimes also called a **grip check.** Larger plastic fittings like this for saltwater rods are sometimes called rod hosels. See **hosel.**

Windings. The wraps of thread that are used to hold guides in place on a rod or to reinforce the ferrules. Also, any decorative wraps in front of the foregrip or at the tip-top. There are a number of types of windings, such as the single wrap, double wrap, underwrap, trim wrapping, spiral wrap, spiral wrap over Mylar, and decorative wraps such as diamonds and chevrons. Winding are usually made with nylon thread, which is available in several sizes and many colors.

Wire clevis. A clevis formed from round wire. The ends are flattened and drilled with holes to fit onto the spinner shaft.

Wire former. A tool used for bending and forming wire for spinners and riggings. Some are simple tools, and there are also large bench tools for making complex wraps and rigs that are designed for near-production work. The simple tools are best for simple wraps, eyes, and loops.

Selected Bibliography and More Information

Some of the following books are out of print; however, they are listed for those who, like me, browse used book stores and college book sales for books on fishing. Some of these old books have unique tips for and approaches to building tackle. Some of the older books are available in libraries or from used-book mail-order lists.

Barnes, George W. *How to Make Bamboo Fly Rods* (New York: Winchester Press, 1977). Out of print. Good book on the subject of making bamboo rods from raw culms of bamboo. Recommended for those interested in this aspect of rod making.

Bates, L. Vernon. *Tackle Making for Anglers* (London: Herbert Jenkins, 1958). Out of print.

Breining, Greg, and Dick Sternberg. *Fishing Tips and Tricks (*Minnetonka, MN: Cy DeCosse, Inc.). Mostly fishing tricks and tips, modifications of lures, etc., but some material on tackle care and repair.

Burch, Monte. *The Outdoorsman's Workshop* (New York: Winchester Press, 1977). General book on making outdoor equipment; some fishing.

Clark, Nancy, Thomas Cutter, and Jean-Ann McGrane. *Ventilation* (New York: Lyons & Burford, 1984). An excellent book on all aspects of ventilation for craftsmen and the subject of dealing with working materials and their potential fumes.

Clemens, Dale P. *Custom Rod Thread Art* (Wescosville, PA: RodCrafters Press, 1982). A book of detailed instructions on complex thread wraps and weaving.

———. *Fiberglass Rod Making* (New York: Winchester Press, 1974).

———. *The New Advanced Custom Rod Building* (New York: Winchester Press, 1987).

Emery, John. *How to Build Custom-made Handcrafted Fishing Rods* (Miami, FL: Windward Publishing, 1977).

Evanoff, Vlad. *Basic Bottom Rigs* (Patterson, NJ: Athletic Activities Publishing Co., 1968). Out of print.

———. *Fishing Rigs for Fresh & Salt Water* (New York: Harper and Row, 1977). An excellent book on the many possible riggings for fish and the various terminal tackle parts needed for this.

———. *Fresh Water Fishing Rigs* (Coral Springs, FL: Catchmore, 1984).

———. *How to Make Fishing Lures* (New York: Ronald Press Company, 1959). Out of print.

———. *Make Your Own Fishing Lures* (New York: A. S. Barnes, 1975).

Finnysports. *Bait Makers Bible: Here's How to Make Your Own Lures* (Toledo, OH: Finnysports Fishing Specialties, 1957). Out of print.

Frazer, Perry D. *Amateur Rodmaking* (New York: The Macmillan Co., 1949). Out of print.

Garcia-Vela, Luis Agustin. *Handcrafting a Graphite Fly Rod* (Lakewood, CO: The Rodcrafter, 1978).

Garrison, Everett (with Hoagy B. Carmichael). *A Masters Guide to Building a Bamboo Fly*

Rod (Katonah, NY: Martha's Glen Publishing, 1977). An excellent book on the subject of making the blanks for split-bamboo rods from the raw culms of Tonkin cane. Recommended for those interested in this aspect of rod making.

Graumot, Raoul, and Elmer Wenstrom. *Fisherman's Knots and Nets* (Cambridge, MD: Cornell Maritime Press).

Jones, Robert H. *Make Your Own Fishing Tackle, vol. 1—Lures* (Vancouver, BC: Special Interest Publications, Maclean Hunter Ltd., 1984).

Herter, George Leonard. *Professional Fly Tying, Spinning, and Tackle Making Manual and Manufacturing Guide* (Waseca, MN: Herter's Inc., 1961). Out of print, but a fascinating book on the subject and far underrated considering its time. Mostly on fly tying, however.

———. *Professional Glass and Split-Bamboo Rod Building Manual and Manufacturer's Guide* (Waseca, MN: Herter's, 1953). Out of print, but interesting on the varieties of early bamboo rods made.

Kirkfield, Stuart. *The Fine Bamboo Fly Rod* (Harrisburg, PA: Stackpole Books, 1986). Primarily on restoration and repair.

Kirkman, Tom. *Rod-Building Guide* (Portland, OR: Frank Amato Publications, 2001). Excellent basic book on rod building.

Kreh, Lefty, and Mark Sosin. *Practical Fishing Knots* (New York: Lyons Burford). Out of print. Excellent books on fishing knots.

Kreider, Claude M. *The Bamboo Rod and How to Build It* (New York: The Macmillan Company, 1951). Out of print.

Lambuth, Letcher. *The Angler's Workshop* (Portland, OR: Champoeg Press, 1979). General book on making fishing equipment; some material on tackle, rods.

Ludgate, H. T. *Make Nets—Here's How* (Toledo, OH: The Netcraft Co., 1976). Currently available from Netcraft.

———. *Popular Netcraft* (Toledo, OH: Netcraft Co., 1948). Details on all types of nets and how to make them.

———. *Tackle Tricks with Wire* (Toledo, OH: The Netcraft Co., 1969). Details on wire formers, fishing, tackle, and rigs made with wire. Currently available from Netcraft.

Major, Harlan. *Salt Water Fishing Tackle* (New York: Funk & Wagnalls Company, 1955). Out of print, but good information on early tackle design.

Marshall, Mel. *How to Make Your Own Fishing Rods* (Harrisburg, PA: Stackpole Books, 1978).

———. *How to Make Your Own Lures and Flies* (New York: Outdoor Life Books, 1976).

Mayes, Jim. *How to Make and Repair Your Own Fishing Tackle* (New York: Dodd, Mead & Company, 1986).

Mohney, Russ. *The Complete Book of Lurecraft* (New York, 1987).

Morris, Skip. *The Custom Graphite Fly Rod—Design and Construction* (New York: Lyons & Burford, 1989).

Pfeiffer, C. Boyd. *Tackle Care* (New York: Lyons & Burford, 1987). Completely covers all aspects of tackle care, maintenance, and repair.

———. *Tackle Craft* (New York: Crown Publishers, 1974). Out of print; the original of this completely rewritten book.

———. *Modern Tackle Craft* (New York: Lyons & Burford Press, 1993). Greatly expanded version (about three times larger) of *Tackle Craft* with 552 pages and 800 photos.

———. *The Complete Book of Tackle Making* (New York: The Lyons Press, 1999). The same book as above, except in paperback instead of the hardback of the above volume.

Saindon, Gary L. *The Off-Season Angler* (Whitefish, MT: Gary Saindon, 1985). General book on making some fishing equipment, some tackle.

Scheck, Art. *Fly Rod Building Made Easy* (Woodstock, VT: The Countryman Press, 2002). Complete, excellent, and just on fly rods.

Stinson, Bill. *Do It Yourself Rod Building* (Portland, OR: Frank Amato Publications, 1983).

Sosin, Mark, and Lefty Kreh. *Practical Fishing Knots II* (New York: Lyons & Burford, 1991). A current update of the above book and also excellent.

Soucie, Gary. *Hook, Line, and Sinker—The Complete Angler's Guide to Terminal Tackle* (New York: Holt Rinehart and Winston, 1982). Excellent book on the subject of terminal tackle.

———. *Soucie's Fishing Databook* (New York: Lyons & Burford, 1985). An excellent small handbook on all types of terminal tackle, tests and specs on same, etc. Highly recommended.

Tapply, H. G. *Tackle Tinkering* (New York: A. S. Barnes and Company). Out of print.

Upton, James. *A Guide to Thread Weaving For The Custom Rod Builder* (n.p., n.d.).

Vare, Alan, and Ken Whitehead. *Rod Building* (London: Rod and Gun Publishing, Ltd., 1975).

Vivona, Billy. *Decorative Wraps* (n.p., n.d.). Decorative wraps including diamonds, chevrons, crosses, spiders, etc.

Walker, J. B. *Rods—How to Make Them* (London: Herbert Jenkins, Ltd., 1959). Not readily available.

Watson, Bill. *Floatmaker's Manual* (London: Ernest Benn Ltd.). A small but definitive book; all ninety-six pages on the making of floats.

Wilson, Loring D. *The Handy Sportsman* (New York: Winchester Press, 1976). General book on outdoor equipment; some fishing.

In addition, several booklets are available from tackle component manufacturers. Most of the following are available from tackle shops or mail-order supply catalogs.

Carson, Wally. *Rod Building by Lamiglas* (Woodland, WA: Lamiglas, Inc.).

Flex Coat Co. *Decorative Rod Wrapping, Step By Step, Book I* (Driftwood, TX: Flex Coat Co.). Fold-out instruction guide including fish, boxes, American flag, and diamonds.

———. *Decorative Rod Wrapping, Step by Step, Book II* (Driftwood, TX: Flex Coat Co.). Fold-out instruction guide including tuna, cross, maze, and thunderbird.

Gudebrod, Inc. *How to Build and Wrap a Rod with Gudebrod, Inc.* (Pottstown, PA: Gudebrod).

Seiders, Roger. *Flex Coat Step-by-Step Rod Building* (Driftwood, TX: Flex Coat Company).

Several videos have also been produced covering tackle building. Those available include:

Clark, Cam. *Fundamentals of Weaving* (Wescoville, PA: Rodcrafters Press, 1990).

Clemens, Dale P. *Build Your Own Rod* (St. Paul, MN: 3M/Scientific Anglers, 1985).

———. *Creative Rod Crafting* (St. Paul, MN: 3M/Scientific Anglers, 1985).

———. *Creativity of Custom Rod Design* (Anglers Video, 1985).

Foxen, Sean. *Hilts Molds How-To Video* (Santa Ana, CA, 1984).

———. *Fundamentals of Custom Rod Building* (Anglers Video, 1985).

———. *Make Your Own Bass Lures* (Fish Tale Productions, 1989).

Index

H

About the Author

C. Boyd Pfeiffer is an award-winning outdoor journalist known for his expertise in fresh- and saltwater fishing, tackle, fly tying, fly fishing, and outdoor photography. He has authored twenty-three books, served as outdoor editor of the *Washington Post,* and served as a consultant to the fishing tackle industry. He lives in Phoenix, Maryland.